AN INTRODUCTION TO PHILOSOPHY

AN INTRODUCTION TO PHILOSOPHY
IN BLACK AND WHITE AND COLOR

Edited by
Jeff McLaughlin
Thompson Rivers University

Prentice Hall

Boston   Columbus   Indianapolis   New York   San Francisco   Upper Saddle River
Amsterdam   Cape Town   Dubai   London   Madrid   Milan   Munich   Paris   Montreal   Toronto
Delhi   Mexico City   São Paulo   Sydney   Hong Kong   Seoul   Singapore   Taipei   Tokyo

Editorial Director: Craig Campanella
Editor in Chief: Dickson Musslewhite
Publisher: Nancy Roberts
Editorial Project Manager: Kate Fernandes
Editorial Assistant: Nart Varoqua
Director of Marketing: Brandy Dawson
Senior Marketing Manager: Laura Lee Manley
Marketing Assistant: Pat Walsh
Production Project Manager: Clara Bartunek
Copy Editor: Maggie Sears

Printer/Binder: Edwards Brother
Art Director: Jayne Conte
Manager, Visual Research: Beth Brenzel
Manager, Rights and Permissions: Zina Arabia
Manager, Cover Visual Research & Permissions: Karen Sanatar
Cover Art: Getty Images, Inc.
Composition: PreMediaGlobal
Cover Printer: Lehigh-Phoenix Color/Hagerstown
Text Font: Garamond

Credits and acknowledgments borrowed from other sources and reproduced, with permission, in this textbook appear on page 546.

Chapter Opener Credits: Page 19, Total Recall, Photofest; page 84, Back To The Future, Universal Studios Copyright © by Universal City Studios, Inc. Courtesy of Universal Studios Publishing Rights, a division of Universal Studios Licensing, Inc. All Rights Reserved; page 166, Contact, Warner Brothers; page 240, Sense and Sensibility, Sony Pictures Entertainment; page 332, Saving Private Ryan, Photofest; page 424 Andromeda Strain. Universal Studios Copyright © by Universal City Studios, Inc. Courtesy of Universal Studios Publishing Rights, a division of Universal Studios Licensing, Inc. All Rights Reserved; page 463, Polluck, Sony Pictures Entertainment.

Microsoft® and Windows® are registered trademarks of the Microsoft Corporation in the U.S.A. and other countries. Screen shots and icons reprinted with permission from the Microsoft Corporation. This book is not sponsored or endorsed by or affiliated with the Microsoft Corporation.

Copyright © 2011 Pearson Education, Inc., publishing as Prentice Hall, 1 Lake St., Upper Saddle River, NJ 07458. All rights reserved. Manufactured in the United States of America. This publication is protected by Copyright, and permission should be obtained from the publisher prior to any prohibited reproduction, storage in a retrieval system, or transmission in any form or by any means, electronic, mechanical, photocopying, recording, or likewise. To obtain permission(s) to use material from this work, please submit a written request to Pearson Education, Inc., Permissions Department, 1 Lake St., Upper Saddle River, NJ 07458.

Many of the designations by manufacturers and seller to distinguish their products are claimed as trademarks. Where those designations appear in this book, and the publisher was aware of a trademark claim, the designations have been printed in initial caps or all caps.

Library of Congress Cataloging-in-Publication Data

An introduction to philosophy in black and white and color / edited by Jeff McLaughlin.
    p. cm.
Includes bibliographical references and index.
ISBN-13: 978-0-205-60743-3 (alk. paper)
ISBN-10: 0-205-60743-8 (alk. paper)
 1. Philosophy.   I. McLaughlin, Jeff,
BD41.I58 2011
  100—dc22

                                                              2010005110

10 9 8 7 6 5 4 3 2 1

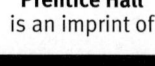

www.pearsonhighered.com

ISBN-10:   0-205-60743-8
ISBN-13: 978-0-205-60743-3

DEDICATION

Great teachers introduce us not only to the world but also to our world and our place in it. At first we might be blinded by the light (to paraphrase Plato and Bruce Springsteen), but with care and concern they lead us ever on.

I dedicate this book to those who have helped me see, including:

Al Wiebe, who introduced me to architecture

Reevan Cramer, who introduced me to art

George Toles, who introduced me to film

Michael Stack, who introduced me to philosophy

Glenn Greiner, who introduced me to the practical importance of philosophy

Tom Boyd and John King-Farlow, who introduced me to teaching philosophy

Jeff McLaughlin

CONTENTS

Preface for Instructors ix
Preface for Students xiii
Acknowledgements xv

Introduction What Value does Philosophy Have? 1
    1 *Bertrand Russell:* The Value of Philosophy 2
    2 *Plato:* The Apology of Socrates 4

Chapter 1 Epistemology 19
    3 *Sextus Empiricus:* Pyrrhonic Sketches, Book I, Chapters I–XVI, XVIII–XXVII 27
    4 *René Descartes:* Meditations I & II 35
    5 *John Locke:* An Essay Concerning Human Understanding—Book I, Chapter II 42
    6 *Immanuel Kant:* Critique of Pure Reason 49
    7 *John Hospers:* An Argument against Skepticism 58
    8 *Russell Bertrand:* Truth and Falsehood, from Problems of Philosophy 64
    9 *William James:* Pragmatism 68
    10 *David Hume:* An Enquiry Concerning Human Understanding (1777 edition) 73
    11 *W.T. Stace:* Science and the Physical World 79

Chapter 2 Metaphysics 84
    12 *Peter van Inwagen:* The Nature of Metaphysics 94
    13 *Plato:* Allegory of the Cave 101
    14 *Plato:* Parmenides 105
    16 *Aristotle:* Categories 110
    17 *Aristotle:* De Interpretatione 114
    18 *David Hume:* Of Liberty and Necessity 119
    19 *Richard Taylor:* Freedom and Determinism 126
    20 *John R. Searle:* Minds, Brains, and Programs 138
    21 *Paul Churchland:* Reductive and Eliminative Materialism 150
    22 *Thomas Nagel:* What Is It like to Be a Bat? 156
    23 *Bertrand Russell:* Other Minds Are Known by Analogy from One's Own Case 163

Chapter 3 Religion 166
    24 *St. Anselm:* Ontological Argument 175
    25 *Aquinas:* The Five Ways 177
    26 *William Paley:* The Watch and the Watchmaker 178
    27 *Blaise Pascal:* Of the Necessity of the Wager 183
    28 *Richard Swinburne:* Some Major Strands of Theodicy 187

29 *David Hume:* Section X of Miracles 200
30 *Alvin Plantinga:* Religious Belief Without Evidence 209
31 *William James:* The Will to Believe and other Essays in Popular Philosophy 218
32 *Soren Kierkegaard:* Fear and Trembling: A Dialectical Lyric 229
33 *JohnHick:* Problems of Religious Pluralism 233

Chapter 4 Socio-Political Philosophy 240
34 *Thomas Hobbes:* Leviathan 247
35 *John Locke:* Second Treatise of Government 259
36 *Karl Marx:* Estranged Labour 270
37 *John Rawls:* A Theory of Justice 277
38 *R. Nozick:* Anarchy, State and Utopia 281
39 *Jean-Jacques Rousseau:* Discourse on Inequality 291
40 *Mary Wollstonecraft:* A Vindication of the Rights of Woman 306
41 *John Stuart Mill:* The Subjection of Women 316
42 *Simone de Beauvoir:* The Second Sex 327

Chapter 5 Ethics 332
43 *Aristotle:* Nicomachean Ethics 341
44 *Plato:* Republic, Book II 358
45 *Jeremy Bentham:* An Introduction to the Principles of Morals and Legislation 374
46 *John Stuart Mill:* Utilitarianism 382
47 *James Rachels:* The Challenge of Cultural Relativism 394
48 *Immanuel Kant:* Foundations of the Metaphysics of Morals 400
49 *David Hume:* An Enquiry Concerning the Principles of Morals 410

Chapter 6 Science 424
50 *Michael Ruse:* Creation Science Is Not Science 432
51 *Karl Popper:* Science, Conjecture and Refutation 438
52 *Thomas Kuhn:* The Structure of Scientific Revolutions 448
53 *Paul K. Feyerabend:* How To Defend Society Against Science 456

Chapter 7 Aesthetics 463
54 *David Hume:* Of the Standard of Taste 476
55 *Plato:* Republic, Book X 485
56 *Aristotle:* Poetics 494
57 *W. K. Wimsatt, Jr., and M. C. Beardsley:* The Intentional Fallacy 499
58 *E. D. Hirsch Jr.,:* In Defense of the Author 508
59 *Nelson Goodman:* Art and Authenticity 515

Appendix Films for further philosophical consideration 524
Credits 546
Index 548

PREFACE FOR INSTRUCTORS

"If it can be written, or thought, it can be filmed."—Stanley Kubrick

It is embarrassingly obvious to point out that an Introduction to Philosophy course introduces students to important questions and answers. Such a course enables students to get a sense of what they can expect to study in other philosophy courses and as we know, almost any philosophy course will provide students with the opportunity to develop essential reasoning skills by means of understanding, interpretation, analysis, and reflection. By combining a sufficiently broad spectrum of topics, articles, and philosophers with helpful examples from film, it is hoped that this anthology will assist in bringing new philosophy students into the fold.

Professors should be reassured that the readings and additional editorial features were chosen by an exhaustive selection process, drawing on the best from other potential readers. The selection process included:

1. An examination and comparison of twenty of the most popular introductory texts.
2. A compilation of the most often used articles in these introductory texts.
3. A refinement of these articles based on such criteria as topic, authorship, time period, point of view, gender, etc.
4. An anonymous review of the preliminary table of contents by six professors of philosophy who rated each reading on a scale of 1 (not essential) to 5 (very essential). Only those that received a total score of 24 or more (out of 30) were kept.
5. Professors on the widely used discussion list PHILOSOP were invited to submit suggestions for what they considered to be "recent must-reads" in their respective fields.
6. The penultimate version of the text was anonymously reviewed by philosophy professors to ensure its broad appeal. These reviewers also suggested including or excluding certain readings.
7. A survey was then developed for professors to anonymously select various editorial features that they most appreciated in anthologies.
8. The same survey was then given to first, second, and fourth-year philosophy students at my university.
9. Based on the results of the two surveys, the editorial features which students selected as most desirable *and* that professors also considered to be pedagogically sound were chosen for inclusion.
10. The final package was tweaked to include pieces that I found informative and helpful for this level of course.
11. An instructor's manual was developed to assist both the instructor and the student with regards to doing philosophy and which also provides an extensive film list with comments.

EDITORIAL FEATURES

It may be surprising to learn that the surveyed students and the instructors had very different opinions regarding what they perceived to be useful in an introductory anthology. By "useful" I mean "would help the student learn the material better." While the survey was small (only a hundred participants), it did show some clear trends. For example, although the instructors believed book introductions essential, they were readily dismissed by the students. Students placed more importance on being able to identify more closely with the material through examples that they would already be familiar with. The students also seemed to want features that would help them understand the material rather than having additional resources such as discussion questions or further readings. Perhaps this simply reflected the view that students would not have time to do anything more than what was required of them.

As the students are the ones for whom the book should be primarily designed (since the instructors already know the material), I focused on what they *reasonably* believed would help them the most. Accordingly, instead of a lengthy book introduction, chapter introductions are included to provide the students a rough context with which to understand the readings. Although students were attracted to the idea of having a bulleted list of key points for each article, I was concerned that they would use this information as an excuse to skip the articles. It is also for this reason that lengthy summaries or overviews of the articles are not included. It is one thing to assist the student in developing his or her ability to understand and evaluate a reading; it is another to give a reason to ignore it.

All major areas of philosophy are covered in this text including Ethics, Epistemology, Metaphysics, Philosophy of Religion, Philosophy of Science, Philosophy of Mind, Socio-Political Philosophy, and Aesthetics. Care is taken to ensure that a large number of philosophers are represented, which allows for a full spectrum of ideas to be presented from different schools of thought and from different historical periods. Most articles are presented in their entirety or with minor excisions to ensure that the overall argument and "voice" of the original author is maintained.

In order to facilitate the understanding and appreciation of the significant philosophical writings herein, short thematic summaries and examples of film dialogue are woven into the chapter introductions. These excerpts from screenplays are used to bridge the gap between what students may already be exposed to and what they need to know about potentially intimidating subjects. Simply put, the writing styles and subject matter of philosophers and philosophy can present large hurdles to students not accustomed to the field. However, students have watched movies all their lives, and so this book capitalizes on their experiences and visual literacy skills in order to reach out and make the material more accessible for them. Students will not only get to see the point being made but by being comfortable with movies, their level of apprehension when approaching the new and unknown may be reduced. Indeed, the students will find that the philosophical articles allow them to revisit films that they have already seen and gain a greater appreciation of both.

ABOUT THE FILMS

When quoting from a screenplay, I have tried to use contemporary works as much as possible since students may already be familiar with the movie cited and they should be easier to locate for further use in and out of the classroom. When I have incorporated older films, I have selected only classics that should be readily available either at the library, local store, or online. I leave how best to make use of these snippets up to the desire and ingenuity of the instructors. For example, one may wish to show the whole film, or just the excerpts from the text or have the students incorporate certain films into an assignment. At the end of each chapter, I have chosen ten films from the past decade or so as additional examples of some of the points raised. These are not necessarily the 'best films of all time', but they serve their purpose nicely. For example, skepticism is a plot point in the film *Total Recall* as we learn that people's memories can be artificially created; and in the films *Blow-Up, The Conversation,* and *Rear Window,* appearance is contrasted with reality as people make leaps in logic and draw conclusions about what is true on the basis of what their senses tell them. Films such as *Blade Runner, Ghost in the Shell, I Robot,* and *AI* raise issues such as the mind/body problem, the nature of consciousness, and the problem of other minds. The problem of evil takes on a visible form in *The Exorcist* and it remains palpable in the Holocaust films *Schindler's List* and *The Grey Zone.* Indeed, in these latter two films, not only are ethical questions raised but one can also see the need to ask "Is there a God?" and perhaps even the more troubling question (for theists), "Has God forsaken us?" *Rosencrantz and Guildenstern are Dead* and *A Beautiful Mind* demonstrate how natural observations can lead to scientific theories; and in the last chapter, *Lust for Life, Amadeus, Gilbert and Sullivan, Crumb, Pollock,* and *Frida* each offer a glimpse into the creative process and the artist.

While a few hundred films are referenced in one form or another in the text, there are hundreds more that you'll find in the instructor's manual. For each of those films I have provided the title, year released, director, a one-sentence plot summary, the relevant philosophical concepts, and the appropriate philosophical topic or field. Please use this concise information as the starting point for further investigation!

The instructor manual also includes a "How to Do Philosophy" guide for students. This is an expanded version of something that has been on my website for more than a decade and which has been copied or linked to by many philosophy departments over the years. It aims to help the novice with some of the particularities of reading and writing philosophy as compared with other academic fields.

PREFACE FOR STUDENTS

Movies are primarily a visual medium. Their images may be accompanied by sound (e.g., dialogue, sound effects, musical score) or text (e.g., subtitles for silent films or chapter titles such as "A long time ago in a galaxy far, far away.") and as such movies do not literally tell the viewer anything. They can hint, suggest, impose ideas or give examples but they do not argue or explain anything like the printed word does. Even if a character on the screen were to turn to the camera and directly speak to the audience (as in *Ferris Bueller's Day Off*), we would still wonder about the veracity of the moment. Is it the *character* saying this? Is it the *actor*? What is the motive or intent? What is the dramatic purpose? Is this what the screenwriter is personally thinking? Is he or she being honest with us? Even if we are told specifically what the film is truly about by having a character state "You. There in the third row. Let me explain what's going on . . . " This act of telling presents us with another layer of meaning and therefore another layer of complexity. However in an argumentative essay such as those that are included in this book we can safely assume that what the author writes is what he or she believes and what he or she actually intends for us to understand.

With the study of film the viewer needs to do more work because there are so many different creative elements. But this is the beauty of film, as you have at your disposal all the different components to work with in order to draw a personal interpretation. What components? Well, let's start with color.

The color palette or lack thereof in a film is not a random choice. Care is taken to select colors that will represent themes, characters, and moods throughout the movie. Blues are cool; reds are hot. Watch *The Matrix* and notice how blue is used to represent being in one world and green is used for another. Imagine the climax of the films *2001: A Space Odyssey* or *Close Encounters of the Third Kind in black and white.* Indeed, even if we had color, the sheer spectacle and otherness of the alien landscapes that Dave witnesses would be lost to us if they were shot in the blue-greens that we are familiar with on Earth rather than the shimmering purples and golds that director Stanley Kubrick gives us in 2001. The majesty and delight of the color-coded musical communications of the mothership in *Close Encounters* would appear less joyous if filmed in muted pastels rather than in vibrant neons.

The shock of color or its absence can also be dramatic. Imagine if *Schindler's List* was filmed in glorious Technicolor. For one thing, the little girl in the red coat would not stand out in the sea of black-and-white figures running in the Warsaw Ghetto.[1] The fact that she is the only color in the film brings her to our attention. Director Steven Spielberg uses this device to show that people, *individuals,* were being tormented and exterminated; and that here was one such girl. This point is sometimes lost when we hear the numbers 100,000, 1.1 million, 11 million killed.

Later in *Schindler's List* when the train arrives at the extermination camp Auschwitz-Berkenau, the sharp black-and-white cinematography plays one of its most important roles as the environment almost becomes another character. The sky is black and the ground is stark white; it is covered in snow as smoke from the train belches forth as it enters the camp. Snow flakes fall on the shoulders of the victims as does the ash from the crematoriums. It might be more realistic since the events were obviously in color in the real world if the scene were in color, but the horror would be lessened. This is not to say that it was less horrible in reality—far from it. Rather, since the average moviegoer could never truly comphrend or appreciate the historical experience the viewer's emotional center has to be reached by other means.

---

[1] If you haven't seen the film, you won't understand the significance of Oskar Schindler seeing this girl twice—first running away from the Nazis and then lying dead in a pile of corpses about to be thrown onto a pyre.

Camera angles may also be used to convey meaning. Cinematographers do not merely place a camera and let the scene unfold; if they did, the result would be akin to a home movie. For more realism, the camera is usually placed at eye level; for less, the camera might be above the action or below or tilted on its axis. When above looking down, the characters seem less important, small, almost as if we looking down on them from God's perspective. From below looking up, the characters appear more powerful; like a child's view of an adult. If the camera is tilted or skewed, the world or the characters appear off kilter; out of sorts.

The placement of actors to other actors or to objects within the frame also has significance. What kind of relationship would you say existed between two people if you saw them eating very close together at a restaurant? Probably one of intimacy. And if the two were sitting at the far ends of a large formal dining table? Probably one where their relationship is as figuratively distant as they are literally distant from each other. Where one character stands and the other sits looking upsuggests an imbalance of power in favor of the person standing. A figure in the lower foreground of the frame and one in the upper background projects the feeling that the person in the foreground has more control or significance than the person in the background. This is simply because of their relative size and proximity to the audience. However, if the person in the background was out of focus and then slowly came into focus either by moving toward the first person or by the camera becoming more focused, then the balance of power would be seen as shifting to this individual. Of course, these are just some rudimentary possibilities and you probably already are aware of most of them

Reading a film requires a different skill set than reading a philosophy paper. Sometimes a movie will have an implicit message presented either by words or symbolic uses of motifs, sometimes not. Sometimes a movie might just be intended as pure mindless entertainment, and there's absolutely nothing wrong with that at all. At other times we might come out of the theatre shaken and stirred by the movie's emotional impact on us. The ineffable quality that makes movies great is what gives them their power over us. And since we are beings with many senses, movies can reach us in many ways and on many levels. Students are highly encouraged to use the provided bits and pieces as an opportunity to seek out the original. Still, since this text is not a book about movies but rather a philosophical book with "movie moments," our use of them will be primarily driven by plot and dialogue rather than the visuals or sounds. They are provided to give you another means to 'see' and understand some of the topics that you will be reading about.

ACKNOWLEDGEMENTS

The groundwork for this book has taken a goodly amount of time. A few years have passed since the idea of using film to help explain philosophy started to gel in my head (which sounds a bit like one of the horror movies listed herein) and as such there are number of people who have directly contributed to this project and many, many more that have indirectly done so. All those associated with the publishing house deserve my thanks for guiding me through this long process. Likewise, I am indebted to those instructors and students who responded to my survey questions, which helped shape the overall project. Furthermore, the constructive suggestions made by reviewers of the manuscript gave me the impetus to push on . . .

I completed most of this book in the lovely city of Graz, Austria, where I was on sabbatical in 2008. Dr. Walter Hoeflechner and Dr. Hubert Sigler were kind enough to offer a couple courses for me to teach at Karl-Franzens University. Another good friend, Dr. Gerhard Apfelthaler at the Fachhochschule Joanneum, gave me a ethics class filled with an incredibly intelligent group of international business students. With thanks to my German language teacher Nicki Donau and Christoph Hofrichter, I had the opportunity to be a student too.

Gratitude must also be extended to Emilio Gonzalez Villanueva from the Tecnológico de Monterrey and Jessica Bowen from Thompson Rivers University for helping out on some of the more tedious but crucial and important work.

Finally to all of my dear, dear friends in Austria, *Prost!*

Jeff McLaughlin

List of Reviewers for Philosophy in Black & White and Color

Christopher Blakley
Louisiana State University Baton Rouge, LA

Sharon Kaye
John Carroll University University Heights, OH

Warren Shrader
Indiana University South Bend, IN

Craig Duncan
Ithaca College Ithaca, NY

Pedro Amaral
California State University Fresno, CA

Lisa Watkins
Florida State University Tallahassee, FL

Phillip Spivey
University of Central Arkansas Conway, AR

Introduction

What Value does Philosophy Have?

About $8.50. Does that answer make you happy? Probably not.

Should it be more? The cost of this book? The cost of your course tuition? These clearly are facetious comments for the value of philosophy cannot have a price tag put on it. What you get out of philosophy is not just what you put into it. Anyone being introduced to the study of philosophy will spend the vast majority of their time just trying to figure out what it is, what the questions mean, and what the different answers entail. So your own contributions may be limited at the beginning. But this is not a bad thing. For while you might not change the world today, you will change yourself—not necessarily change your views—but you will change by learning more about what you yourself think about things. And perhaps by learning new things about yourself, you will have indirectly transformed the world.

Among the variety of essays in this book there are some very old readings and for some reason some students will find that puzzling as if what they read needs to be current in order for it to be valuable. This might be appropriate for a few other subjects (for example, medicine) but we cannot understand the current debates without knowing the context and the background. But these so called "old readings" are not just presented here as historical footnotes; it is the other way around . . . for the modern readings directly or indirectly continue the discussions started centuries ago. Classic philosophical essays and arguments are as relevant today as when they were first presented. They ask questions that we still ask and they often provide answers that we still accept. Thus, philosophical works are for the most part timeless just as the pursuit of knowledge, the quest to understand the world, and the desire to learn our place within it remain timeless. We have always sought out the truth be it profound or mundane. For the truth, or at least what we perceive to be the truth, shapes who we are and shapes how we see the world around us. And so before jumping into discussions about the big philosophical questions, we start off by presenting two pieces written two thousand years apart that discuss the nature and value of philosophy.

The Value of Philosophy
Bertrand Russell

Having now come to the end of our brief and very incomplete review of the problems of philosophy, it will be well to consider, in conclusion, what is the value of philosophy and why it ought to be studied. It is the more necessary to consider this question, in view of the fact that many men, under the influence of science or of practical affairs, are inclined to doubt whether philosophy is anything better than innocent but useless trifling, hair-splitting distinctions, and controversies on matters concerning which knowledge is impossible.

This view of philosophy appears to result, partly from a wrong conception of the ends of life, partly from a wrong conception of the kind of goods which philosophy strives to achieve. Physical science, through the medium of inventions, is useful to innumerable people who are wholly ignorant of it; thus the study of physical science is to be recommended, not only, or primarily, because of the effect on the student, but rather because of the effect on mankind in general. Thus utility does not belong to philosophy. If the study of philosophy has any value at all for others than students of philosophy, it must be only indirectly, through its effects upon the lives of those who study it. It is in these effects, therefore, if anywhere, that the value of philosophy must be primarily sought.

But further, if we are not to fail in our endeavour to determine the value of philosophy, we must first free our minds from the prejudices of what are wrongly called 'practical' men. The 'practical' man, as this word is often used, is one who recognizes only material needs, who realizes that men must have food for the body, but is oblivious of the necessity of providing food for the mind. If all men were well off, if poverty and disease had been reduced to their lowest possible point, there would still remain much to be done to produce a valuable society; and even in the existing world the goods of the mind are at least as important as the goods of the body. It is exclusively among the goods of the mind that the value of philosophy is to be found; and only those who are not indifferent to these goods can be persuaded that the study of philosophy is not a waste of time.

Philosophy, like all other studies, aims primarily at knowledge. The knowledge it aims at is the kind of knowledge which gives unity and system to the body of the sciences, and the kind which results from a critical examination of the grounds of our convictions, prejudices, and beliefs. But it cannot be maintained that philosophy has had any very great measure of success in its attempts to provide definite answers to its questions. If you ask a mathematician, a mineralogist, a historian, or any other man of learning, what definite body of truths has been ascertained by his science, his answer will last as long as you are willing to listen. But if you put the same question to a philosopher, he will, if he is candid, have to confess that his study has not achieved positive results such as have been achieved by other sciences. It is true that this is partly accounted for by the fact that, as soon as definite knowledge concerning any subject becomes possible, this subject ceases to be called philosophy, and becomes a separate science. The whole study of the heavens, which now belongs to astronomy, was once included in philosophy; Newton's great work was called 'the mathematical principles of natural philosophy.' Similarly, the study of the human mind, which was a part of philosophy, has now been separated from philosophy and has become the science of psychology. Thus, to a great extent, the uncertainty of philosophy is more apparent than real: those questions which are already capable of definite answers are placed in the sciences, while those only to which, at present, no definite answer can be given, remain to form the residue which is called philosophy.

This is, however, only a part of the truth concerning the uncertainty of philosophy. There are many questions—and among them those that are of the profoundest interest to our spiritual life—which, so far as we can see, must remain insoluble to the human intellect unless its powers become of quite a different order from what they are now. Has the universe any unity of plan or purpose, or is it a fortuitous concourse of atoms? Is consciousness a permanent part of the universe, giving hope of indefinite growth in wisdom, or is it a transitory accident on a small planet on which life must ultimately become impossible? Are good and evil of importance to the universe or only to man? Such questions are asked by philosophy, and variously answered by various philosophers. But it would seem that, whether answers be otherwise discoverable or not, the answers suggested by philosophy are none of them demonstrably true. Yet, however slight may be the hope of discovering an answer, it is part of the business of philosophy to continue the consideration of such questions, to make us aware of their importance, to examine all the approaches to them, and to keep alive that speculative interest in the universe which is apt to be killed by confining ourselves to definitely ascertainable knowledge.

Many philosophers, it is true, have held that philosophy could establish the truth of certain answers to such fundamental questions. They have supposed that what is of most importance in religious beliefs could be proved by strict demonstration to be true. In order to judge of such attempts, it is necessary to take a survey of human knowledge, and to form an opinion as to its methods and its limitations. On such a subject it would be unwise to pronounce dogmatically; but if the investigations of our previous chapters have not led us astray, we shall be compelled to renounce the hope of finding philosophical proofs of religious beliefs. We cannot, therefore, include as part of the value of philosophy any definite set of answers to such questions. Hence, once more, the value of philosophy must not depend upon any supposed body of definitely ascertainable knowledge to be acquired by those who study it.

The value of philosophy is, in fact, to be sought largely in its very uncertainty. The man who has no tincture of philosophy goes through life imprisoned in the prejudices derived from common sense, from the habitual beliefs of his age or his nation, and from convictions which have grown up in his mind without the co-operation or consent of his deliberate reason. To such a man the world tends to become definite, finite, obvious; common objects rouse no questions, and unfamiliar possibilities are contemptuously rejected. As soon as we begin to philosophize, on the contrary, we find, as we saw in our opening chapters, that even the most everyday things lead to problems to which only very incomplete answers can be given. Philosophy, though unable to tell us with certainty what is the true answer to the doubts which it raises, is able to suggest many possibilities which enlarge our thoughts and free them from the tyranny of custom. Thus, while diminishing our feeling of certainty as to what things are, it greatly increases our knowledge as to what they may be; it removes the somewhat arrogant dogmatism of those who have never travelled into the region of liberating doubt, and it keeps alive our sense of wonder by showing familiar things in an unfamiliar aspect.

Apart from its utility in showing unsuspected possibilities, philosophy has a value—perhaps its chief value—through the greatness of the objects which it contemplates, and the freedom from narrow and personal aims resulting from this contemplation. The life of the instinctive man is shut up within the circle of his private interests: family and friends may be included, but the outer world is not regarded except as it may help or hinder what comes within the circle of instinctive wishes. In such a life there is something feverish and confined, in comparison with which the philosophic life is calm and free. The private world of instinctive interests is a small one, set in the midst of a great and powerful world which must, sooner or later, lay our private world in ruins. Unless we can so enlarge our interests as to include the whole outer world, we remain like a garrison in a beleaguered fortress, knowing that the enemy prevents escape and that ultimate surrender is inevitable. In such a life there is no peace, but a constant strife between the insistence of desire and the powerlessness of will. In one way or another, if our life is to be great and free, we must escape this prison and this strife.

One way of escape is by philosophic contemplation. Philosophic contemplation does not, in its widest survey, divide the universe into two hostile camps—friends and foes, helpful and hostile, good and bad—it views the whole impartially. Philosophic contemplation, when it is unalloyed, does not aim at proving that the rest of the universe is akin to man. All acquisition of knowledge is an enlargement of the Self, but this enlargement is best attained when it is not directly sought. It is obtained when the desire for knowledge is alone operative, by a study which does not wish in advance that its objects should have this or that character, but adapts the Self to the characters which it finds in its objects. This enlargement of Self is not obtained when, taking the Self as it is, we try to show that the world is so similar to this Self that knowledge of it is possible without any admission of what seems alien. The desire to prove this is a form of self-assertion and, like all self-assertion, it is an obstacle to the growth of Self which it desires, and of which the Self knows that it is capable. Self-assertion, in philosophic speculation as elsewhere, views the world as a means to its own ends; thus it makes the world of less account than Self, and the Self sets bounds to the greatness of its goods. In contemplation, on the contrary, we start from the not-Self, and through its greatness the boundaries of Self are enlarged; through the infinity of the universe the mind which contemplates it achieves some share in infinity.

(continued)

The Value of Philosophy (*continued*)

For this reason greatness of soul is not fostered by those philosophies which assimilate the universe to Man. Knowledge is a form of union of Self and not-Self; like all union, it is impaired by dominion, and therefore by any attempt to force the universe into conformity with what we find in ourselves. There is a widespread philosophical tendency towards the view which tells us that Man is the measure of all things, that truth is man-made, that space and time and the world of universals are properties of the mind, and that, if there be anything not created by the mind, it is unknowable and of no account for us. This view, if our previous discussions were correct, is untrue; but in addition to being untrue, it has the effect of robbing philosophic contemplation of all that gives it value, since it fetters contemplation to Self. What it calls knowledge is not a union with the not-Self, but a set of prejudices, habits, and desires, making an impenetrable veil between us and the world beyond. The man who finds pleasure in such a theory of knowledge is like the man who never leaves the domestic circle for fear his word might not be law.

The true philosophic contemplation, on the contrary, finds its satisfaction in every enlargement of the not-Self, in everything that magnifies the objects contemplated, and thereby the subject contemplating. Everything, in contemplation, that is personal or private, everything that depends upon habit, self-interest, or desire, distorts the object, and hence impairs the union which the intellect seeks. By thus making a barrier between subject and object, such personal and private things become a prison to the intellect. The free intellect will see as God might see, without a *here* and *now*, without hopes and fears, without the trammels of customary beliefs and traditional prejudices, calmly, dispassionately, in the sole and exclusive desire of knowledge—knowledge as impersonal, as purely contemplative, as it is possible for man to attain. Hence also the free intellect will value more the abstract and universal knowledge into which the accidents of private history do not enter, than the knowledge brought by the senses, and dependent, as such knowledge must be, upon an exclusive and personal point of view and a body whose sense-organs distort as much as they reveal.

The mind which has become accustomed to the freedom and impartiality of philosophic contemplation will preserve something of the same freedom and impartiality in the world of action and emotion. It will view its purposes and desires as parts of the whole, with the absence of insistence that results from seeing them as infinitesimal fragments in a world of which all the rest is unaffected by any one man's deeds. The impartiality which, in contemplation, is the unalloyed desire for truth, is the very same quality of mind which, in action, is justice, and in emotion is that universal love which can be given to all, and not only to those who are judged useful or admirable. Thus contemplation enlarges not only the objects of our thoughts, but also the objects of our actions and our affections: it makes us citizens of the universe, not only of one walled city at war with all the rest. In this citizenship of the universe consists man's true freedom, and his liberation from the thraldom of narrow hopes and fears.

Thus, to sum up our discussion of the value of philosophy: Philosophy is to be studied, not for the sake of any definite answers to its questions, since no definite answers can, as a rule, be known to be true, but rather for the sake of the questions themselves; because these questions enlarge our conception of what is possible, enrich our intellectual imagination, and diminish the dogmatic assurance which closes the mind against speculation; out above all because, through the greatness of the universe which philosophy contemplates, the mind also is rendered great, and becomes capable of that union with the universe which constitutes its highest good.

The Apology of Socrates
Plato

I Know not, O Athenians, how far you have been influenced by my accusers: for my part, in listening to them I almost forgot myself, so plausible were their arguments: however, so to speak, they have said nothing true. But of the many falsehoods which they uttered I wondered at one of them especially, that in which they said that you ought to be on your guard lest you should be deceived by me, as being eloquent in speech. For that they are not ashamed of being forthwith convicted by me in fact, when I shall shew that I am not by any means eloquent, this seemed to me the most shameless thing in them, unless indeed they call him eloquent who speaks the truth. For, if they mean this, then I would allow that I am an orator, but not after their fashion: for they, as I affirm, have said nothing true; but from me you shall hear the whole truth. Not indeed, Athenians, arguments highly wrought, as theirs were, with choice phrases and expressions, nor adorned, but you shall hear a speech uttered without premeditation, in such words as first present themselves. For I am confident that what I say will be just, and let none of you expect otherwise: for surely it would not become my time of life to come before you like a youth with a got up speech. Above all things therefore I beg and implore this of you, O Athenians, if you hear me defending myself in the same language as that in which I am accustomed to speak both in the forum at the counters, where many of you have heard me, and elsewhere, not to be surprised or disturbed on this account. For the case is this: I now for the first time come before a court of justice, though more than seventy years old; I am therefore utterly a stranger to the language here. As, then, if I were really a stranger, you would have pardoned me if I spoke in the language and the manner in which I had been educated, so now I ask this of you as an act of justice, as it appears to me, to disregard the manner of my speech, for perhaps it may be somewhat worse, and perhaps better, and to consider this only, and to give your attention to this, whether I speak what is just or not; for this is the virtue of a judge, but of an orator to speak the truth.

2. First then, O Athenians, I am right in defending myself against the first false accusations alleged against me, and my first accusers, and then against the latest accusations, and the latest accusers. For many have been accusers of me to you, and for many years, who have asserted nothing true, of whom I am more afraid than of Anytus and his party, although they too are formidable; but those are still more formidable, Athenians, who laying hold of many of you from childhood, have persuaded you, and accused me of what is not true:—"that there is one Socrates, a wise man, who occupies himself about celestial matters, and has explored every thing under the earth, and makes the worse appear the better reason." Those, O Athenians, who have spread abroad this report are my formidable accusers: for they who hear them think that such as search into these things do not believe that there are gods. In the next place, these accusers are numerous, and have accused me now for a long time; moreover they said these things to you at that time of life in which you were most credulous, when you were boys and some of you youths, and they accused me altogether in my absence, when there was no one to defend me. But the most unreasonable thing of all is, that it is not possible to learn and mention their names, except that one of them happens to be a comic poet[1]. Such, however, as influenced by envy and calumny have persuaded you, and those who, being themselves persuaded, have persuaded others, all these are most difficult to deal with; for it is not possible to bring any of them forward here, nor to confute any; but it is altogether necessary, to fight as it were with a shadow, in making my defence, and to convict when there is no one to answer. Consider, therefore, as I have said, that my accusers are twofold, some who have lately accused me, and others long since, whom I have made mention of; and believe that I ought to defend myself against these first; for you heard them accusing me first, and much more than these last.

Well. I must make my defence then, O Athenians, and endeavour in this so short a space of time to remove from your minds the calumny which you have long entertained. I wish, indeed, it might be so, if it were at all better both for you and me, and that in making my defence I could effect something more advantageous still: I think however that it will be difficult, and I am not entirely ignorant what the difficulty is. Nevertheless let this turn out as may be pleasing to God, I must obey the law, and make my defence.

3. Let us then repeat from the beginning what the accusation is from which the calumny against me has arisen, and relying on which Melitus has preferred this indictment against me. Well. What then do they who charge me say in their charge? For it is necessary to read their deposition as of public accusers. "Socrates acts wickedly, and is criminally curious in searching into things under the earth, and in the heavens, and in making the worse appear the better cause, and in teaching these same things to others." Such is the accusation: for such things you have yourselves seen in the comedy of Aristophanes, one Socrates there carried about, saying that he walks in the

(continued)

The Apology of Socrates   (continued)

air, and acting many other buffooneries, of which I understand nothing whatever. Nor do I say this as disparaging such a science, if there be any one skilled in such things, only let me not be prosecuted by Melitus on a charge of this kind; but I say it, O Athenians, because I have nothing to do with such matters. And I call upon most of you as witnesses of this, and require you to inform and tell each other, as many of you as have ever heard me conversing; and there are many such among you. Therefore tell each other, if any one of you has ever heard me conversing little or much on such subjects. And from this you will know that other things also, which the multitude assert of me, are of a similar nature.

4. However not one of these things is true; nor, if you have heard from any one that I attempt to teach men, and require payment, is this true. Though this indeed appears to me to be an honourable thing, if one should be able to instruct men, like Gorgias the Leontine, Prodicus the Cean, and Hippias the Elean. For each of these, O Athenians, is able, by going through the several cities, to persuade the young men, who can attach themselves gratuitously to such of their own fellow citizens as they please, to abandon their fellow citizens and associate with them, giving them money and thanks besides. There is also another wise man here, a Parian, who I hear is staying in the city. For I happened to visit a person who spends more money on the sophists than all others together, I mean Callias, son of Hipponicus. I therefore asked him, for he has two sons, "Callias," I said, "if your two sons were colts or calves, we should have had to choose a master for them and hire a person who would make them excel in such qualities as belong to their nature: and he would have been a groom or an agricultural labourer. But now, since your sons are men, what master do you intend to choose for them? Who is there skilled in the qualities that become a man and a citizen? For I suppose you must have considered this, since you have sons. Is there any one," I said, "or not?" "Certainly," he answered. "Who is he?" said I, "and whence does he come? and on what terms does he teach?" He replied, "Evenus the Parian, Socrates, for five mine." And I deemed Evenus happy, if he really possesses this art, and teaches so admirably. And I too should think highly of myself and be very proud, if I possessed this knowledge; but I possess it not, O Athenians.

5. Perhaps, one of you may now object: "But, Socrates, what have you done then? Whence have these calumnies against you arisen? For surely if you had not busied yourself more than others, such a report and story would never have got abroad, unless you had done something different from what most men do. Tell us, therefore, what it is, that we may not pass, a hasty judgment on you." He who speaks thus appears to me to speak justly, and I will endeavour to shew you what it is that has occasioned me this character and imputation. Listen then: to some of you perhaps I shall appear to jest, yet be assured that I shall tell you the whole truth. For I, O Athenians, have acquired this character through nothing else than a certain wisdom. Of what kind, then, is this wisdom? Perhaps it is merely human wisdom. For in this, in truth I appear to be wise. They probably, whom I just now mentioned, possessed a wisdom more than human, otherwise I know not what to say about it; for I am not acquainted with it, and whosoever says I am, speaks falsely and for the purpose of calumniating me. But, O Athenians, do not cry out against me, even though I should seem to you to speak somewhat arrogantly. For the account which I am going to give you, is not my own, but I shall refer to an authority whom you will deem worthy of credit. For I shall adduce to you the god at Delphi as a witness of my wisdom, if I have any, and of what it is. You doubtless know Chærepho: he was my associate from youth, and the associate of most of you; he accompanied you in your late exile and returned with you. You know, then, what kind of a man Chærepho was, how earnest in whatever he undertook. Having once gone to Delphi, he ventured to make the following inquiry of the oracle, (and, as I said, O Athenians, do not cry out,) for he asked if there was any one wiser than me. The Pythian thereupon answered that there was not one wiser: and of this, his brother here will give you proofs, since he himself is dead.

6. Consider then why I mention these things: it is because I am going to shew you whence the calumny against me arose. For when I heard this, I reasoned thus with myself, What does the god mean? What enigma is this? For I am not conscious to myself that I am wise, either much or little. What then does he mean by saying that I am the wisest? For assuredly he does not speak falsely: that he cannot do. And for a long time, I was in doubt what he meant; afterwards with considerable difficulty I had recourse to the following method of searching cut his meaning. I went to one

of those who have the character of being wise, thinking that there, if any where, I should confute the oracle, and shew in answer to the response that This man is wiser than I, though you affirmed that I was the wisest. Having then examined this man, (for there is no occasion to mention his name, he was however one of our great politicians, in examining whom I felt as I proceed to describe, O Athenians,) having fallen into conversation with him, this man appeared to me to be wise in the opinion of most other men, and especially in his own opinion, though in fact he was not so. I thereupon endeavoured to shew him that he fancied himself to be wise, but really was not. Hence I became odious both to him, and to many others who were present. When I left him, I reasoned thus with myself, I am wiser than this man, for neither of us appear to know any thing great and good: but he fancies he knows something, although he knows nothing, whereas I, as I do not know any thing, so I do not fancy I do. In this trifling particular, then, I appear to be wiser than him, because I do not fancy I know what I do not know. After that I went to another who was thought to be wiser than the former, and formed the very same opinion. Hence I became odious to him and to many others.

7. After this I went to others in turn, perceiving indeed and grieving and alarmed that I was making myself odious; however it appeared necessary to regard the oracle of the god as of the greatest moment, and that in order to discover its meaning, I must go to all who had the reputation of possessing any knowledge. And by the dog, O Athenians, for I must tell you the truth, I came to some such conclusion as this: those who bore the highest reputation appeared to me to be most deficient, in my researches in obedience to the god, and others who were considered inferior, more nearly approaching to the possession of understanding. But I must relate to you my wandering, and the labours which I underwent, in order that the oracle might prove incontrovertible. For after the politicians I went to the poets as well the tragic as the dithyrambic and others, expecting that here I should in very fact find myself more ignorant than them. Taking up, therefore, some of their poems, which appeared to me most elaborately finished, I questioned them as to their meaning, that at the same time I might learn something from them. I am ashamed, O Athenians, to tell you the truth; however it must be told. For, in a word, almost all who were present could have given a better account of them than those by whom they had been composed. I soon discovered this, therefore, with regard to the poets, that they do not effect their object by wisdom, but by a certain natural inspiration and under the influence of enthusiasm like prophets and seers; for these also say many fine things, but they understand nothing that they say. The poets appeared to me to be affected in a similar manner: and at the same time I perceived that they considered themselves, on account of their poetry, to be the wisest of men in other things, in which they were not. I left them, therefore, under the persuasion that I was superior to them, in the same way that I was to the politicians.

8. At last, therefore, I went to the artizans. For I was conscious to myself that I knew scarcely any thing, but I was sure that I should find them possessed of much beautiful knowledge. And in this I was not deceived; for they knew things which I did not, and in this respect they were wiser than me. But, O Athenians, even the best workmen appeared to me to have fallen into the same error as the poets: for each, because he excelled in the practice of his art, thought that he was very wise in other most important matters, and this mistake of theirs obscured the wisdom that they really possessed. I therefore asked myself in behalf of the oracle, whether I should prefer to continue as I am, possessing none either of their wisdom or their ignorance, or to have both as they have. I answered, therefore, to myself and to the oracle, that it was better for me to continue as I am.

9. From this investigation, then, O Athenians, many enmities have arisen against me, and those the most grievous and severe, so that many calumnies have sprung from them and amongst them this appellation of being wise. For those who are from time to time present think that I am wise in those things, with respect to which I expose the ignorance of others. The god however, O Athenians, appears to be really wise, and to mean this by his oracle, that human wisdom is worth little or nothing; and it is clear that he did not say this of Socrates, but made use of my name, putting me forward as an example, as if he had said, that man is the wisest among you, who, like Socrates, knows that he is in reality worth nothing with respect to wisdom. Still therefore I go about and search and inquire into these things, in obedience to the god, both among citizens and strangers, if I think any one of them is wise; and when he appears to me not to be so, I take the part of the god, and shew

(continued)

The Apology of Socrates (continued)

that he is not wise. And in consequence of this occupation I have no leisure to attend in any considerable degree to the affairs of the state or my own; but I am in the greatest poverty through my devotion to the service of the god.

10. In addition to this, young men, who have much leisure and belong to the wealthiest families, following me of their own accord, take great delight in hearing men put to the test, and often imitate me, and themselves attempt to put others to the test: and then, I think, they find a great abundance of men who fancy they know something, although they know little or nothing. Hence those who are put to the test by them are angry with me, and not with them, and say that "there is one Socrates, a most pestilent fellow, who corrupts the youth." And when any one asks them by doing or teaching what, they have nothing to say, for they do not know: but that they may not seem to be at a loss, they say such things as are ready at hand against all philosophers; "that he searches into things in heaven and things under the earth, that he does not believe there are gods, and that he makes the worse appear the better reason." For they would not, I think, be willing to tell the truth, that they have been detected in pretending to possess knowledge, whereas they know nothing. Therefore, I think, being ambitious and vehement and numerous, and speaking systematically and persuasively about me, they have filled your ears, for a long time and diligently calumniating me. From amongst these, Melitus, Anytus, and Lycon, have attacked me; Melitus being angry on account of the poets, Anytus on account of the artizans and politicians, and Lycon on account of the rhetoricians. So that as I said in the beginning, I should wonder if I were able in so short a time to remove from your minds a calumny that has prevailed so long. This, O Athenians, is the truth; and I speak it without concealing or disguising any thing from you, much or little; though I very well know that by so doing I shall expose myself to odium. This however is a proof that I speak the truth, and that this is the nature of the calumny against me, and that these are its causes. And if you will investigate the matter, either now or hereafter, you will find it to be so.

11. With respect then to the charges which my first accusers have alleged against me, let this be a sufficient apology to you. To Melitus, that good and patriotic man, as he says, and to my later accusers, I will next endeavour to give an answer; and here again, as there are different accusers let us take up their deposition. It is pretty much as follows: "Socrates," it says, "acts unjustly in corrupting the youth, and in not believing in those gods in whom the city believes, but in other strange divinities." Such is the accusation; let us examine each particular of it. It says that I act unjustly in corrupting the youth. But I, O Athenians, say that Melitus acts unjustly, because he jests on serious subjects, rashly putting men upon trial, under pretence of being zealous and solicitous about things in which he never at any time took any concern. But that this is the case I will endeavour to prove to you.

12. Come then, Melitus, tell me; do you not consider it of the greatest importance that the youth should be made as virtuous as possible?

MEL. I do.

SOCR. Well now, tell the judges who it is that makes them better, for it is evident that you know, since it concerns you so much: for, having detected me in corrupting them, as you say, you have cited me here and accused me; come then, say, and inform the judges who it is that makes them better. Do you see, Melitus, that you are silent, and have nothing to say? But does it not appear to you to be disgraceful and a sufficient proof of what I say, that you never took any concern about the matter? But tell me, friend, who makes them better?

MEL. The laws.

SOCR. I do not ask this, most excellent sir, but what man, who surely must first know this very thing, the laws?

MEL. These, Socrates, the judges.

SOCR. How say you, Melitus? Are these able to instruct the youth, and make them better?

MEL. Certainly.

SOCR. Whether all, or some of them, and others not?

MEL. All.

SOCR. You say well, by Juno, and have found a great abundance of those that confer benefit. But what further? Can these hearers make them better, or not?

MEL. They too can.

SOCR. And what of the senators?

MEL. The senators also.

SOCR. But, Melitus, do those who attend the public assemblies corrupt the younger men? or do they all make them better?

MEL. They too.

SOCR. All the Athenians therefore, as it seems, make them honourable and good, except me, but I alone corrupt them. Do you say so?

MEL. I do assert this very thing.

SOCR. You charge me with great ill-fortune. But answer me: does it appear to you to be the same with respect to horses? do all men make them better, and is there only some one that spoils them? or does quite the contrary of this take place? is there some one person who can make them better, or very few, that is the trainers? but if the generality of men should meddle with and make use of horses, do they spoil them? Is not this the case, Melitus, both with respect to horses and all other animals? It certainly is so, whether you and Anytus deny it or not. For it would be a great good-fortune for the youth if only one person corrupted, and the rest benefited them. However, Melitus, you have sufficiently shewn that you never bestowed any care upon youth; and you clearly evince your own negligence, in that you have never paid any attention to the things with respect to which you accuse me.

13. Tell us further, Melitus, in the name of Jupiter, whether is it better to dwell with good or bad citizens? Answer, my friend: for I ask you nothing difficult. Do not the bad work some evil to those that are continually near them, but the good some good?

MEL. Certainly.

SOCR. Is there any one that wishes to be injured rather than benefited by his associates? Answer, good man: for the law requires you to answer. Is there any one who wishes to be injured?

MEL. No, surely.

SOCR. Come then, whether do you accuse me here, as one that corrupts the youth, and makes them more depraved, designedly or undesignedly?

MEL. Designedly, I say.

SOCR. What then, Melitus, are you at your time of life so much wiser than me at my time of life, as to know that the evil are always working some evil to those that are most near to them, and the good some good; but I have arrived at such a pitch of ignorance as not to know, that if I make any one of my associates depraved, I shall be in danger of receiving some evil from him, and yet I designedly bring about this so great evil, as you say? In this I cannot believe you, Melitus, nor do I think would any other man in the world: but either I do not corrupt the youth, or if I do corrupt them, I do it undesignedly: so that in both cases you speak falsely. But if I corrupt them undesignedly, for such involuntary offences it is not usual to accuse one here, but to take one apart and teach and admonish one. For it is evident that if I am taught, I shall cease doing what I do undesignedly. But you shunned me, and were not willing to associate with and instruct me, but you accuse me here, where it is usual to accuse those who need punishment, and not instruction.

14. Thus, then, O Athenians, this now is clear that I have said, that Melitus never paid any attention to these matters, much or little. However tell us, Melitus, how you say I corrupt

(continued)

The Apology of Socrates   (continued)

the youth? Is it not evidently, according to the indictment which you have preferred, by teaching them not to believe in the gods in whom the city believes, but in other strange deities? Do you not say that by teaching these things, I corrupt the youth?

MEL. Certainly I do say so.

SOCR. By those very gods, therefore, Melitus, of whom the discussion now is, speak still more clearly both to me and to these men. For I cannot understand whether you say that I teach them to believe that there are certain gods, (and in that case I do believe that there are gods, and am not altogether an atheist, nor in this respect to blame,) not however those which the city believes in, but others, and this it is that you accuse me of, that I introduce others; or do you say outright that I do not myself believe that there are gods, and that I teach others the same?

MEL. I say this, that you do not believe in any gods at all.

SOCR. O wonderful Melitus, how come you to say this? Do I not then like the rest of mankind, believe that the sun and moon are gods?

MEL. No, by Jupiter, O judges: for he says that the sun is a stone, and the moon an earth.

SOCR. You fancy that you are accusing Anaxagoras, my dear Melitus, and thus you put a slight on these men, and suppose them to be so illiterate, as not to know that the books of Anaxagoras of Clazomene are full of such assertions. And the young, moreover, learn these things from me, which they might purchase for a drachma, at most, in the orchestra, and so ridicule Socrates, if he pretended they were his own, especially since they are so absurd? I ask then, by Jupiter, do I appear to you to believe that there is no god?

MEL. No, by Jupiter, none whatever.

SOCR. You say what is incredible, Melitus, and that, as appears to me, even to yourself. For this man, O Athenians, appears to me to be very insolent and intemperate, and to have preferred this indictment through downright insolence, intemperance and wantonness. For he seems, as it were, to have composed an enigma for the purpose of making an experiment. "Whether will Socrates the wise know that I am jesting, and contradict myself, or shall I deceive him and all who hear me? For in my opinion he clearly contradicts himself in the indictment, as if he should say, Socrates is guilty of wrong in not believing that there are gods, and in believing that there are gods. And this, surely, is the act of one who is trifling.

15. Consider with me now, Athenians, in what respect he appears to me to say so. And do you, Melitus, answer me; and do ye, as I besought you at the outset, remember not to make an uproar if I speak after my usual manner.

Is there any man, Melitus, who believes that there are human affairs, but does not believe that there are men? Let him answer, judges, and not make so much noise. Is there any one who does not believe that there are horses, but that there are things pertaining to horses? or who does not believe that there are pipers, but that there are things pertaining to pipes ? There is not, O best of men: for since you are not willing to answer, I say it to you and to all here present. But answer to this at least: is there any one who believes that there are things relating to demons, but does not believe that there are demons?

MEL. There is not.

SOCR. How obliging you are in having hardly answered, though compelled by these judges. You assert then that I do believe and teach things relating to demons, whether they be new or old; therefore, according to your admission, I do believe in things relating to demons, and this you have sworn in the bill of indictment. If then I believe in things relating to demons, there is surely an absolute necessity that I should believe that there are demons. Is it not so? It is. For I suppose you to assent, since you do not answer. But with respect to demons, do we not allow that they are gods, or the children of gods? Do you admit this or not?

MEL. Certainly.

SOCR. Since then I allow that there are demons as you admit, if demons are a kind of gods, this is the point in which I say you speak enigmatically and divert yourself in saying that I do not allow there are gods, and again that I do allow there are, since I allow that there are demons? But if demons are the children of gods, spurious ones, either from nymphs or any others, of whom they are reported to be, what man can think that there are sons of gods, and yet that there are not gods? For it would be just as absurd, as if any one should think that there are mules the offspring of horses and asses, but should not think there are horses and asses. However, Melitus, it cannot be otherwise than that you have preferred this indictment for the purpose of trying me, or because you were at a loss what real crime to allege against me: for that you should persuade any man who has the smallest degree of sense, that the same person can think that there are things relating to demons and to gods, and yet that there are neither demons, nor gods, nor heroes, is utterly impossible.

16. That I am not guilty then, O Athenians, according to the indictment of Melitus, appears to me not to require a lengthened defence; but what I have said is sufficient. And as to what I said at the beginning, that there is a great enmity towards me among the multitude, be assured it is true. And this it is which will condemn me, if I am condemned, not Melitus, nor Anytus, but the calumny and envy of the multitude, which have already condemned many others, and those good men, and will I think condemn others also; for there is no danger that it will stop with me.

Perhaps, however, some one may say, "Are yon not ashamed, Socrates, to have pursued a study, from which you are now in danger of dying?" To such a person I should answer with good reason, You do not say well, friend, if you think that a man, who is even of the least value, ought to take into the account the risk of life or death, and ought not to consider that alone when he performs any action, whether he is acting justly or unjustly, and the part of a good man or bad man. For according to your reasoning, all those demi-gods that died at Troy would be vile characters, as well all the rest as the son of Thetis, who so far despised danger in comparison of submitting to disgrace, that when his mother, who was a goddess, spoke to him, in his impatience to kill Hector, something to this effect, as I think,[2] "My son, if you revenge the death of your friend Patroclus, and slay Hector, you will yourself die, for," she said, "death awaits you immediately after Hector." But he, on hearing this, despised death and danger, and dreading much more to live as a coward, and not avenge his friends said; "May I die immediately, when I have inflicted punishment on the guilty, that I may not stay here an object of ridicule, by the curved ships, a burden to the ground?" Do you think that he cared for death and danger? For thus it is, O Athenians, in truth; wherever any one has posted himself, either thinking it to be better, or has been posted by his chief, there, as it appears to me, he ought to remain and meet danger taking no account either of death or any thing else in comparison with disgrace.

17. I then should be acting strangely, O Athenians, if, when the generals whom you chose to command me assigned me my post at Potidæa, at Amphipolis, and at Delium, I then remained where they posted me, like any other person, and encountered the danger of death, but when the deity as I thought and believed, assigned it as my duty to pass my life in the study of philosophy, and in examining myself and others, I should on that occasion, through fear of death or any thing else whatsoever, desert my post. Strange indeed would it be, and then in truth any one might justly bring me to trial, and accuse me of not believing in the gods, from disobeying the oracle, fearing death, and thinking myself to be wise when I am not. For to fear death, O Athenians, is nothing else than to appear to be wise, without being so; for it is to appear to know what one does not know. For no one knows but that death is the greatest of all goods to man; but men fear it, as if they well knew that it is the greatest of evils. And how is not this the most reprehensible ignorance, to think that one knows what one does not know? But I, O Athenians, in this perhaps differ from most men; and if I should say that I am in any thing wiser than another, it would be in this, that not having a competent knowledge of the things in Hades, I also think that I have not such knowledge. But to act unjustly, and to disobey my superior, whether God or man, I know is evil and base. I shall never, therefore, fear or shun things which, for aught I know, may be good, before evils which I know to be evils. So that even if you should now dismiss me, not yielding to the instances of Anytus, who said that either I should

(continued)

The Apology of Socrates   (*continued*)

not[3] appear here at all, or that, if I did appear, it was impossible not to put me to death, telling you that if I escaped, your sons, studying what Socrates teaches, would all be utterly corrupted; if you should address me thus, "Socrates, we shall not now yield to Anytus, but dismiss you, on this condition however, that you no longer persevere in your researches nor study philosophy, and if hereafter you are detected in so doing, you shall die,"—if, as I said, you should dismiss me on these terms, I should say to you; "O Athenians, I honour and love you: but I shall obey God rather than you; and as long as I breathe and am able, I shall not cease studying philosophy, and exhorting you and warning any one of you I may happen to meet, saying as I have been accustomed to do: 'O best of men, seeing you are an Athenian, of a city the most powerful and most renowned for wisdom and strength, are you not ashamed of being careful for riches, how you may acquire them in greatest abundance, and for glory and honour, but care not nor take any thought for wisdom and truth, and for your soul, how it may be made most perfect?'" And if any one of you should question my assertion, and affirm that he does care for these things, I shall not at once let him go, nor depart, but I shall question him, sift and prove him. And if he should appear to me not to possess virtue, but to pretend that he does, I shall reproach him for that he sets the least value on things of the greatest worth, but the highest on things that are worthless. Thus I shall act to all whom I meet, both young and old, stranger and citizen, but rather to you my fellow citizens, because ye are more nearly allied to me. For be well assured, this the deity commands. And I think that no greater good has ever befallen you in the city, than my zeal for the service of the god. For I go about doing nothing else than persuading you, both young and old, to take no care either for the body, or for riches, prior to or so much as for the soul, how it may be made most perfect, telling yon that virtue does not spring from riches, but riches and all other human blessings, both private and public, from virtue. If, then, by saying these things, I corrupt the youth, these things must be mischievous; but if any one says that I speak other things than these, he misleads you.[4] Therefore I must say, O Athenians, either yield to Anytus or do not, either dismiss me or not, since I shall not act otherwise, even though I must die many deaths.

  18. Murmur not, O Athenians, but continue to attend to my request, not to murmur at what I say, but to listen, for as I think, you will derive benefit from listening. For I am going to say other things to you, at which perhaps you will raise a clamour; but on no account do so. Be well assured, then, if you put me to death, being such a man as I say I am, you will not injure me more than yourselves. For neither will Melitus nor Anytus harm me; nor have they the power: for I do not think that it is possible for a better man to be injured by a worse. He may perhaps have me condemned to death, or banished or deprived of civil rights; and he or others may perhaps consider these as mighty evils: I however do not consider them so, but that it is much more so to do what he is now doing, to endeavour to put a man to death unjustly. Now, therefore, O Athenians, I am far from making a defence on my own behalf, as any one might think, but I do so on your behalf, lest by condemning me you should offend at all with respect to the gift of the deity to you. For, if you should put me to death, you will not easily find such another, though it may be ridiculous to say so, altogether attached by the deity to this city as to a powerful and generous horse, somewhat sluggish from his size, and requiring to be roused by a gad-fly; so the deity appears to have united me, being such a person as I am, to the city, that I may louse you, and persuade and reprove every one of you, nor ever cease besetting you throughout the whole day. Such another man, O Athenians, will not easily be found, therefore, if you will take my advice, you will spare me. But you, perhaps, being irritated, like drowsy persons who are roused from sleep, will strike me, and, yielding to Anytus, will unthinkingly condemn me to death; and then you will pass the rest of your life in sleep, unless the deity, caring for you, should send some one else to you. But that I am a person who has been given by the deity to this city, you may discern from hence; for it is not like the ordinary conduct of men, that I should have neglected all my own affairs and suffered my private interest to be neglected for so many years, and that I should constantly attend to your concerns, addressing myself to each of you separately, like a father, or elder brother, persuading you to the pursuit of virtue. And if I had derived any profit from this course, and had received pay for my exhortations, there would have been some reason for my conduct; but now you see yourselves, that my accusers, who have so shamelessly calumniated me in every thing else, have not had the impudence to charge me with this, and to bring witnesses to prove that I ever either exacted or demanded any reward. And I think I produce a sufficient proof that I speak the truth, *namely*, my poverty.

19. Perhaps, however, it may appear absurd, that I, going about, thus advise you in private and make myself busy, but never venture to present myself in public before your assemblies and give advice to the city. The cause of this is that which you have often and in many places heard me mention: because I am moved by a certain divine and spiritual influence, which also Melitus, through mockery, has set out in the indictment. This began with me from childhood, being a kind of voice which, when present, always diverts me from what I am about to do, but never urges me on. This it is which opposed my meddling in public politics; and it appears to me to have opposed me very properly. For be well assured, O Athenians, if I had long since attempted to intermeddle with politics, I should have perished long ago, and should not have at all benefited you or myself. And be not angry with me for speaking the truth. For it is not possible that any man should be safe, who sincerely opposes either you, or any other multitude, and who prevents many unjust and illegal actions from being committed in a city; but it is necessary that he who in earnest contends for justice, if he will be safe for but a short time, should live privately, and take no part in public affairs.

20. I will give you strong proofs of this, not words, but, what you value, facts. Hear then what has happened to me, that you may know that I would not yield to any one contrary to what is just, through fear of death, at the same time that, by not yielding, I must perish. I shall tell you what will be displeasing and wearisome,[5] yet true. For I, O Athenians, never bore any other magisterial office in the city, but have been a senator: and our Antiochean tribe happened to supply the Prytanes when you chose to condemn in a body the ten generals, who had not taken off those that perished in the sea-fight, in violation of the law, as you afterwards all thought. At that time I alone of the Prytanes opposed your doing any thing contrary to the laws, and I voted against you; and when the orators were ready to denounce me, and to carry me before a magistrate, and you urged and cheered them on, I thought I ought rather to meet the danger with law and justice on my side, than through fear of imprisonment or death to take part with you in your unjust designs. And this happened while the city was governed by a democracy. But when it became an oligarchy the Thirty, having sent for me with four others to the Tholus, ordered us to bring Leon the Salaminian from Salamis, that he might be put to death; and they gave many similar orders to many others, wishing to involve as many as they could in guilt. Then however I shewed, not in word but in deed, that I did not care for death, if the expression be not too rude, in the smallest degree, but that all my care was to do nothing unjust or unholy. For that government, strong as it was, did not so overawe me as to make me commit an unjust action; but when we came out from the Tholus, the four went to Salamis, and brought back Leon; but I went away home. And perhaps for this I should have been put to death, if that government had not been, speedily broken up. And of this you can have many witnesses.

21. Do you think, then, that I should have survived so many years, if I had engaged in public affairs, and, acting as becomes a good man, had aided the cause of justice, and, as I ought, had deemed this of the highest importance? Far from it, O Athenians: nor would any other man have done so. But I, through the whole of my life, if have done any thing in public, shall be found to be a man, and the very same in private, who has never made a concession to any one contrary to justice, neither to any other, nor to any one of these whom my calumniators say are my disciples. I however was never the preceptor of any one; but if any one desired to hear me speaking and to see me busied about my own mission, whether he were young or old, I never refused him. Nor do I discourse when I receive money, and not when I do not receive any, but I allow both rich and poor alike to question me, and, if any one wishes it, to answer me and hear what I have to say. And for these, whether any one proves to be a good man or not, I cannot justly be responsible, because I never either promised them any instruction or taught them at all. But if any one says that he has ever learnt or heard any thing from me in private, which all others have not, be well assured that he does not speak the truth.

22. But why do some delight to spend so long a time with me? Ye have heard, O Athenians. I have told you the whole truth, that they delight to hear those closely questioned who think that they are wise but are not: for this is by no means disagreeable. But this duty, as I say, has been enjoined me by the deity, by oracles, by dreams, and by every mode by which any other divine decree has ever enjoined any thing to man to do. These things, O Athenians, are both true, and easily confuted if not true. For if I am now corrupting some of the youths, and have already corrupted others, it were fitting, surely, that if any of them, having become advanced in life, had discovered that

(continued)

> **The Apology of Socrates** *(continued)*
>
> I gave them bad advice when they were young, they should now rise up against me, accuse me, and have me punished; or if they were themselves unwilling to do this, some of their kindred, their fathers, or brothers, or other relatives, if their kinsmen have ever sustained any damage from me, should now call it to mind. Many of them however are here present, whom I see: first, Crito, my contemporary and fellow-burgher, father of this Critobulus; then, Lysanias of Sphettus, father of this Æschines; again, Antiphon of Cephisus, father of Epigenes; there are those others too, whose brothers maintained the same intimacy with me, namely, Nicostratus, son of Theosdotidus, brother of Theodotus—Theodotus indeed is dead, so that he could not deprecate his brother's proceedings, and Paralus here, son of Demodocus, whose brother was Theages; and Adimantus son of Ariston, whose brother is this Plato; and Æantodorus, whose brother is this Apollodorus. I could also mention many others to you, some one of whom certainly Melitus ought to have adduced in his speech as a witness. If however he then forgot to do so, let him now adduce them, I give him leave to do so, and let him say it, if he has any thing of the kind to allege. But quite contrary to this, you will find, O Athenians, all ready to assist me, who have corrupted and injured their relatives, as Melitus and Anytus say. For those who have been themselves corrupted might perhaps have some reason for assisting me; but those who have not been corrupted, men now advanced in life, their relatives, what other reason can they have for assisting me, except that right and just one, that they know that Melitus speaks falsely, and that I speak the truth.
>
> 23. Well then, Athenians; these are pretty much the things I have to say in my defence, and others perhaps of the same kind. Perhaps, however, some among you will be indignant on recollecting his own case, if he, when engaged in a cause far less than this, implored and besought the judges with many tears, bringing forward his children in order that he might excite their utmost compassion, and many others of his relatives and friends, whereas I do none of these things, although I may appear to be incurring the extremity of danger. Perhaps, therefore, some one, taking notice of this, may become more determined against me, and, being enraged at this very conduct of mine, may give his vote under the influence of anger. If then any one of you is thus affected,—I do not however suppose that there is,—but if there should be, I think I may reasonably say to him; "I too, O best of men, have relatives; for to make use of that saying of Homer, I am not sprung from an oak, nor from a rock, but from men, so that I too, O Athenians, have relatives, and three sons, one now grown up, and two boys: I shall not however bring any one of them forward and implore you to acquit me. Why then shall I not do this? Not from contumacy, O Athenians, nor disrespect towards you. Whether or not I am undaunted at the prospect of death, is another question, but out of regard to my own character, and yours, and that of the whole city, it does not appear to me to be honourable that I should do any thing of this kind at my age, and with the reputation I have, whether true or false. For it is commonly agreed that Socrates in some respects excels the generality of men. If, then, those among you who appear to excel either in wisdom, or fortitude, or any other virtue whatsoever, should act in such a manner as I have often seen some when they have been brought to trial, it would be shameful, who appearing indeed to be something, have conducted themselves in a surprising manner, as thinking they should suffer something dreadful by dying, and as if they would be immortal if you did not put them to death. Such men appear to me to bring disgrace on the city, so that any stranger might suppose that such of the Athenians as excel in virtue, and whom they themselves choose in preference to themselves for magistracies and other honours, are in no respect superior to women. For these things, O Athenians, neither ought we to do who have attained to any height of reputation, nor, should we do them, ought you to suffer us; but you should make this manifest, that you will much rather condemn him who introduces these piteous dramas, and makes the city ridiculous, than him who quietly awaits your decision.
>
> 24. But reputation apart, O Athenians, it does not appear to me to be right to entreat a judge, or to escape by entreaty, but one ought to inform and persuade him. For a judge does not sit for the purpose of administering justice out of favour, but that he may judge rightly, and he is sworn not to shew favour to whom he pleases, but that he will decide according to the laws. It is therefore right that neither should we accustom you, nor should you accustom yourselves to violate your oaths; for in so doing neither of us would act righteously. Think not then, O Athenians, that I ought to adopt such a course towards you as I neither consider honourable, nor just, nor holy, as well, by Jupiter, on any other occasion, and now especially when I am accused of impiety by this Melitus. For clearly, if

I should persuade you, and by my entreaties should put a constraint on you who are bound by an oath, I should teach you to think that there are no gods, and in reality, while making my defence, should accuse myself of not believing in the gods. This, however, is far from being the case: for I believe, O Athenians, as none of my accusers do, and I leave it to you and to the deity to judge concerning me in such way as will be best both for me and for you.

[Socrates here concludes his defence, and the votes being taken, he is declared guilty by a majority of voices. He thereupon resumes his address.]

25. That I should not be grieved, O Athenians, at what has happened, namely, that you have condemned me, as well many other circumstances concur in bringing to pass, and moreover this, that what has happened has not happened contrary to my expectation; but I much rather wonder at the number of votes on either side. For I did not expect that I should be condemned by so small a number, but by a large majority; but now, as it seems, if only three more votes had changed sides, I should have been acquitted. As far as Melitus is concerned, as it appears to me, I have been already acquitted, and not only have I been acquitted, but it is clear to every one that had not Anytus and Lycon come forward to accuse me, he would have been fined a thousand drachmas, for not having obtained a fifth part of the votes.

26. The man then awards me the penalty of death. Well. But what shall I, on my part, O Athenians, award myself? Is it not clear that it will be such as I deserve? What then is that? do I deserve to suffer or to pay a fine, for that I have purposely during my life not remained quiet, but neglecting what most men seek after, money-making, domestic concerns, military command, popular oratory, and moreover all the magistracies, conspiracies and cabals that are met with in the city, thinking that I was in reality too upright a man to be safe if I took part in such things, I therefore did not apply myself to those pursuits, by attending to which I should have been of no service either to you or to myself; but in order to confer the greatest benefit on each of you privately, as I affirm, I thereupon applied myself to that object, endeavouring to persuade every one of you, not to take any care of his own affairs, before he had taken care of himself, in what way he may become the best and wisest, nor of the affairs of the city before he took care of the city itself; and that he should attend to other things in the same manner. What treatment then do I deserve, seeing I am such a man? Some reward, O Athenians, if at least I am to be estimated according to my real deserts; and moreover such a reward as would be suitable to me. What then is suitable to a poor man, a benefactor, and who has need of leisure in order to give you good advice? There is nothing so suitable, O Athenians, as that such a man should be maintained in the Prytaneum, and this much more than if one of you had been victorious at the Olympic games in a horse race, or in the two or four-horsed chariot race: for such a one makes you appear to be happy, but I, to be so: and he does not need support, but I do. If, therefore, I must award a sentence according to my just deserts, I award this, maintenance in the Prytaneum.

27. Perhaps, however, in speaking to you thus, I appear to you to speak in the same presumptuous manner as I did respecting commiseration and entreaties: but such is not the case, O Athenians, it is rather this. I am persuaded that I never designedly injured any man, though I cannot persuade you of this, for we have conversed with each other but for a short time. For if there was the same law with you as with other men, that in capital cases the trial should last not only one day but many, I think you would be persuaded; but it is not easy in a short time to do away with great calumnies. Being persuaded then that I have injured no one, I am far from intending to injure myself, and of pronouncing against myself that I am deserving of punishment, and from awarding myself any thing of the kind. Through fear of what? lest I should suffer that which Melitus awards me, of which I say I know not whether it be good or evil? instead of this, shall I choose what I well know to be evil, and award that? Shall I choose imprisonment? And why should I live in prison, a slave to the established magistracy, the Eleven? Shall I choose a fine, and to be imprisoned until I have paid it? But this is the same as that which I just now mentioned, for I have not money to pay it. Shall I then award myself exile? For perhaps you would consent to this award. I should indeed be very fond of life, O Athenians, if I were so devoid of reason as not to be able to reflect that you, who are my fellow citizens, have been unable to endure my manner of life and discourses, but they have become so burdensome and odious to you, that you now seek to be rid of them: others however will easily bear them: far from it, O Athenians. A fine life it would be for me at my age to go out

(continued)

The Apology of Socrates   (continued)

'wandering and driven from city to city, and so to live. For I well know that, wherever I may go, the youth will listen to me when I speak, as they do here. And if I repulse them, they will themselves drive me out, persuading the elders; and if I do not repulse them, their fathers and kindred will banish me on their account.

28. Perhaps however some one will say, Can you not, Socrates, when you have gone from us, live a silent and quiet life? This is the most difficult thing of all to persuade some of you. For if I say that that would be to disobey the deity, and that therefore it is impossible for me to live quietly, you would not believe me, thinking I spoke ironically. If, on the other hand, I say that this is the greatest good to man, to discourse daily on virtue, and other things which you have heard me discussing, examining both myself and others, but that a life without investigation is not worth living for, still less would you believe me if I said this. Such however is the case, as I affirm, O Athenians, though it is not easy to persuade you. And at the same time I am not accustomed to think myself deserving of any ill. If indeed I were rich, I would amerce myself in such a sum as I should be able to pay; for then I should have suffered no harm, but now—for I cannot, unless you are willing to amerce me in such a sum as I am able to pay. But perhaps I could pay you a mina of silver: in that sum then I amerce myself. But Plato here, O Athenians, and Crito Critobulus, and Apollodorus bid me amerce myself in thirty minæ, and they offer to be sureties. I amerce myself then to you in that sum; and they will be sufficient sureties for the money.

[The judges now proceeded to pass the sentence, and condemned Socrates to death; whereupon he continued:]

29. For the sake of no long space of time, O Athenians, you will incur the character and reproach at the hands of those who wish to defame the city, of having put that wise man, Socrates, to death. For those who wish to defame you will assert that I am wise, though I am not. If, then, you had waited for a short time, this would have happened of its own accord; for observe my age, that it is far advanced in life, and near death. But I say this not to you all, but to those only who have condemned me to die. And I say this too to the same persons. Perhaps you think, O Athenians, that I have been convicted through the want of arguments, by which I might have persuaded you, had I thought it right to do and say any thing, so that I might escape punishment. Far otherwise: I have been convicted through want indeed, yet not of arguments, but of audacity and impudence, and of the inclination to say such things to you as would have been most agreeable for you to hear, had I lamented and bewailed and done and said many other things unworthy of me, as I affirm, but such as you are accustomed to hear from others. But neither did I then think that I ought, for the sake of avoiding danger, to do any thing unworthy of a freeman, nor do I now repent of having so defended myself; but I should much rather choose to die, having so defended myself, than to live in that way. For neither in a trial nor in battle, is it right that I or any one else should employ every possible means whereby he may avoid death; for in battle it is frequently evident that a man might escape death by laying down his arms, and throwing himself on the mercy of his pursuers. And there are many other devices in every danger, by which to avoid death, if a man dares to do and say every thing. But this is not difficult, O Athenians, to escape death, but it is much more difficult to avoid depravity, for it runs swifter than death. And now I, being slow and aged, am overtaken by the slower of the two; but my accusers, being strong and active, have been overtaken by the swifter, wickedness. And now I depart, condemned by you to death; but they condemned by truth, as guilty of iniquity and injustice: and I abide my sentence and so do they. These things, perhaps, ought so to be, and I think that they are for the best.

30. In the next place, I desire to predict to you who have condemned me, what will be your fate: for I am now in that condition in which men most frequently prophecy, namely, when they are about to die. I say then to you, O Athenians, who have condemned me to death, that immediately after my death a punishment will overtake you, far more severe, by Jupiter, than that which you have inflicted on me. For you have done this, thinking you should be freed from the necessity of giving an account of your life. The very contrary however, as I affirm, will happen to you. Your accusers will be more numerous, whom I have now restrained, though you did not perceive it; and they will be more severe, inasmuch as they are younger, and you will be more indignant. For, if you think that by putting men to death you will restrain any one from upbraiding you because you do not live well, you are much mistaken; for this method of escape is neither possible nor honourable,

but that other is most honourable and most easy, not to put a check upon others, but for a man to take heed to himself, how he may be most perfect. Having predicted thus much to those of you who have condemned me, I take my leave of you.

31. But with you who have voted for my acquittal, I would gladly hold converse on what has now taken place, while the magistrates are busy and I am not yet carried to the place where I must die. Stay with me then, so long, O Athenians, for nothing hinders our conversing with each other, whilst we are permitted to do so; for I wish to make known to you, as being my friends, the meaning of that which has just now befallen me. To me then, O my judges,—and in calling you judges I call you rightly,—a strange thing has happened. For the wonted prophetic voice of my guardian deity, on every former occasion even in the most trifling affairs opposed me, if I was about to do any thing wrong; but now, that has befallen me which ye yourselves behold, and which any one would think and which is supposed to be the extremity of evil, yet neither when I departed from home in the morning did the warning of the god oppose me, nor when I came up here to the place of trial, nor in my address when I was about to say any thing; yet on other occasions it has frequently restrained me in the midst of speaking. But now, it has never throughout this proceeding opposed me, either in what I did or said. What then do I suppose to be the cause of this? I will tell you: what has befallen me appears to be a blessing; and it is impossible that we think rightly who suppose that death is an evil. A great proof of this to me is the fact that it is impossible but that the accustomed signal should have opposed me, unless I had been about to meet with some good.

32. Moreover we may hence conclude that there is great hope that death is a blessing. For to die is one of two things: for either the dead may be annihilated and have no sensation of any thing whatever; or, as it is said, there is a certain change and passage of the soul from one place to another. And if it is a privation of all sensation, as it were a sleep in which the sleeper has no dream, death would be a wonderful gain. For I think that if any one, having selected a night, in which he slept so soundly as not to have had a dream, and having compared this night with all the other nights and days of his life, should be required on consideration to say how many days and nights he had passed better and more pleasantly than this night throughout his life, I think that not only a private person, but even the great king himself would find them easy to number in comparison with other days and nights. If, therefore, death is a thing of this kind, I say it is a gain; for thus all futurity appears to be nothing more than one night. But if, on the other hand, death is a removal from hence to another place, and what is said be true, that all the dead are there, what greater blessing can there be than this, my judges? For if, on arriving at Hades, released from these who pretend to be judges, one shall find those who are true judges, and who are said to judge there, Minos and Rhadamanthus, Æacus and Triptolemus, and such others of the demigods as were just during their own life, would this be a sad removal? At what price would you not estimate a conference with Orpheus and Musæus, Hesiod and Homer? I indeed should be willing to die often, if this be true. For to me the sojourn there would be admirable, when I should meet with Palamedes, and Ajax son of Telamon, and any other of the ancients who has died by an unjust sentence. The comparing my sufferings with theirs would, I think, be no unpleasing occupation. But the greatest pleasure would be to spend my time in questioning and examining the people there as I have done those here, and discovering who among them is wise, and who fancies himself to be so but is not. At what price, my judges, would not any one estimate the opportunity of questioning him who led that mighty army against Troy, or Ulysses, or Sisyphus, or ten thousand others, whom one might mention, both men and women? with whom to converse and associate, and to question them, would be an inconceivable happiness. Surely for that the judges there do not condemn to death; for in other respects those who live there are more happy than those that are here, and are henceforth immortal, if at least what is said be true.

33. You, therefore, O my judges, ought to entertain good hopes with respect to death, and to meditate on this one truth, that to a good man nothing is evil, neither while living nor when dead, nor are his concerns neglected by the gods. And what has befallen me is not the effect of chance; but this is clear to me, that now to die, and be freed from my cares, is better for me. On this account the warning in no way turned me aside; and I bear no resentment towards those who condemned me, or against my accusers, although they did not condemn and accuse me with this intention, but thinking to injure me: in this they deserve to be blamed.

(continued)

The Apology of Socrates   (continued)

Thus much however I beg of them. Punish my sons, when they grow up, O judges, paining them as I have pained you, if they appear to you to care for riches or any thing else before virtue, and if they think themselves to be something when they are nothing, reproach them as I have done you, for not attending to what they ought, and for conceiving themselves to be something when they are worth nothing. If ye do this, both I and my sons shall have met with just treatment at your hands.

But it is now time to depart,—for me to die, for you to live. But which of us is going to a better state is unknown to every one but God.

NOTES

1. Aristophanes.
2. Iliad, lib. xviii. ver 94, &c.
3. See the Crito- s. 5.
4. $Οὐδὲν\ λεγει$, literally "he says nothing:" on se trompe, ou l'on vous impose, *Cousin*.
5. But for the authority of Stallbaum, I should have translated $δκIαvIκα$ "forensic;" that is, such arguments as an advocate would use in a court of justice.

Chapter 1
Epistemology

All areas of serious human inquiry make one philosophical assumption: that knowledge is possible. The field of philosophy that is concerned with the nature of knowledge is called epistemology from the Greek word "*epistēmē*" meaning "knowledge" and "*logos*" meaning "theory of," "account," or "story." Epistemologists are interested in such issues as determining what knowledge is, what the limits of knowledge are, the nature of truth, and what counts as a justified belief.

$2 \times 7 = 14$

Cats and dogs can sometimes get along with each other.

Exercise is good for you.

There are more than five planets in our solar system.

All mammals are warm blooded.

Today is the first day of the rest of your life.

You are reading a sentence in a book right now.

We claim to know all of these things but knowledge is not something that we can establish by simply taking a vote.[1] So how exactly do we go about acquiring it?

Skeptics maintain that knowledge is impossible. They claim that we ultimately cannot know whether what we believe is true or not. They are not suggesting that what we believe to be true *is* false but rather that we cannot draw any conclusions about what is true or false. It is important not to be confused about this point. For if the skeptic merely stated that for every claim "X," the truth is really "not X," then this would commit them to knowing something—which is contrary to their very views.

Considered by many as the father of modern philosophy, French philosopher René Descartes (1596–1650) was determined to meet the serious threat of the skeptic head on. The skeptic's challenge had the potential to be devastating to the surging interest in science and to traditional religious beliefs. In his writings, Descartes begins what will amount to an intellectual journey by writing a series of meditations in which he reflects on what he knows or rather what he thinks he knows—and by extrapolation what we the readers know or think we know, as well.

In his first *Meditation,* Descartes begins by realizing that he (like all of us) has believed many things to be true that turned out later to be false. For example, as children we might have believed in Santa Claus or the Tooth Fairy but learned later that these were not real. Science is always discovering new things and in doing so it revises or replaces old theories. How often have we been frustrated by scientific advances that tell us one week that red wine is good for us and then in the following week that it is detrimental? Indeed, in the 1950s there were television commercials that told the audience that cigarettes were actually good for your health![2]

It is a good policy to revisit and re-evaluate our beliefs. Perhaps we thought a friend was trustworthy but then new evidence suggests otherwise. Perhaps we were certain that we knew our neighbor's name but we were mistaken. Even our own memories are notoriously unreliable. Can you remember every detail of what you did last year, or last week? Perhaps keeping a journal of our experiences would help. But then how do we know *now* that what we wrote down *then* was accurate? The film *Memento* presents us with one extreme example of how our memories can fail us and how we need to be more skeptical about them.

> **. . . Int. Discount Inn Office—day**
> *Leonard enters, confident, smiling at the man behind the desk, BURT (fat, sweaty, 40's). Burt smiles back.*
>
> BURT   Hiya.
>
> LEONARD   I'm Mr. Shelby from 304.
>
> BURT   What can I do for you, Leonard?
>
> LEONARD   I'm sorry . . . um . . . ?
>
> BURT   Burt.
>
> LEONARD   Burt, I'm not sure, but I may have asked you to hold my calls -
>
> BURT   You don't know?
>
> LEONARD   I think I may have. I'm not good on the phone.
>
> BURT   (nods) You said you like to look people in the eye when you talk to them. Don't you remember?
>
> LEONARD   That's the thing. I have this condition.
>
> BURT   Condition?
>
> LEONARD   I have no memory.
>
> BURT   Amnesia?

---

[1] If this were the case, then Harrison Ford's characters in *The Fugitive* and *Presumed Innocent* would still be on the run. This is because the characters in the films seemed to have all agreed that the Harrison character is guilty even though he isn't.

[2] One now infamous commercial in the 1960s had the popular family friendly Flintstone cartoon characters enjoying a good smoke.

LEONARD   No. It's different. I have no short-term memory. I know who I am and all about myself, but since my injury I can't make any new memories. Everything fades. If we talk for too long, I'll forget how we started. I don't know if we've ever met before, and the next time I see you I won't remember this conversation. So if I seem strange or rude, that's probably . . .

He notices that Burt is staring at him as if he were an exotic insect.

LEONARD   (cont'd) I've told you this before, haven't I?

BURT   (nods) I don't mean to mess with you. It's just so weird. You don't remember me at all, and we talked a bunch of times.

Leonard shrugs.

Like Leonard we often depend on clues and assumptions and memories that we have no trustworthy means of verifying. These beliefs can range from the mundane, such as the sun will rise tomorrow, to the profound, such as someone telling you they are truly evil but always do good things to cover it up. Indeed, unlike Leonard, we may not even consider the logical possibility that everything we do, we have already done before but have forgotten it.

Int. Motel Room 21 — Day

Leonard sits on the bed applying SHAVING FOAM to his thigh. The ICE BUCKET sits on the bedside table, steaming.

Leonard starts awkwardly SHAVING his right thigh. The PHONE RINGS and Leonard FLINCHES, NICKING his leg. He looks at the phone, then reaches for the receiver.

INT. A RESTAURANT RESTROOM - DAY   Leonard, in BEIGE SUIT and BLUE SHIRT flushes the urinal, then moves to the sink and starts washing his hands. He notices a MESSAGE written on the back of his hand.

"REMEMBER SAMMY JANKIS"   He stares at the message for a second, thoughtful, then tries to scrub the writing off his skin. To his surprise, it is INDELIBLE. Leonard looks at it, quizzical, then notices some markings on his wrist, pulling his sleeve back to get a better look. He can read the start of a message:

"THE FACTS:"

Since Leonard suffers from short-term memory loss, how can Leonard assume that he both interpreted "the facts" correctly and wrote them down correctly? The issue is not that he always failed to do either one of these but that he *may* have. Since he may have, doubt is created.

In the film *Total Recall,* false memories of the protagonist Doug Quaid (played by Arnold Schwarzenegger) are literally implanted into his mind. The impetus for the story is that when a person has been on a trip he or she forms memories of it, so why not instead just give people just those memories and save them the trouble and expense of going on the trip in the first place? If the memories are strong enough, real enough, the result will be just as if one had actually had the genuine experience. A person would not be able to tell the difference between the false memories and what he or she really did during that time in their past.

Int. McClane's Office at Recall — Day

McClane ushers Quaid into a stylishly decorated room.

McCLANE   Have a seat, sit down, make yourself comfortable.

Quaid lowers himself into a sleek, futuristic chair. McClane sits behind his desk.

McCLANE   (cont'd) Now help me out here, Doug. You were interested in a memory of . . .

QUAID   Mars.

McCLANE   (unenthusiastic) Right. Mars.

QUAID   That a problem?

McCLANE   To be perfectly honest with you, Doug, if outer space is your thing, I think you'd be much happier with one of our Saturn cruises. Everybody raves about 'em.

QUAID   (irritated) I'm not interested in Saturn. I said Mars.

McCLANE   Okay, you're the boss—Mars it is.

McClane types on his computer keyboard, and figures come up on his screen.

McCLANE   (cont'd) Let's see . . . the basic Mars package will run you just eight hundred and ninety-nine credits. That's for two full weeks of memories, complete in every detail. —A longer trip'll run you a little more, cause you need a deeper implant.

QUAID   What's in the two week package?

MCCLANE   First of all, Doug, when you go Rekall, you get nothing but first class memories: private cabin on the shuttle; deluxe suite at the Hilton; plus all the major sights: Mount Pyramid, the Grand Canals, and of course . . .

(leers)

Venusville.

QUAID   How real does it seem?

MCCLANE   As real as any memory in your head.

QUAID   Come on, don't bullsh*t me.

MCCLANE   I'm telling you, Doug, your brain won't know the difference. Guaranteed, or your money back.

MCCLANE   Now while you fill out the questionnaire, I'll familiarize you with some of our options.

QUAID   No options.

MCCLANE   Whatever you say . . . Just answer one question. What is it that is exactly the same about every vacation you've ever taken?

Quaid fills out the questionnaire on his video screen.

QUAID   I give up.

MCCLANE   You. You're the same.

(pauses for effect) No matter where you go, there you are. Always the same old you.

(grins enigmatically) Let me suggest that you take a vacation from yourself. I know it sounds wild, but it's the latest thing in travel. We call it an "Ego Trip".

QUAID   I'm not interested in that.

MCCLANE   You're gonna love this. —We offer you a choice of alternate identities during your trip.

McClane pre-empts Quaid's questionnaire on the video monitor with CLOSE UP: the following list.

A-14 MILLIONAIRE PLAYBOY
A-15 SPORTS HERO
A-16 INDUSTRIAL TYCOON
A-17 SECRET AGENT

MCCLANE (O.S.)

Face it . . . Why go to Mars as a tourist when you can go as a playboy, or a famous jock, or a . . .

Total Recall is based on a short story by science-fiction writer Philip K. Dick.[3] Screenwriters Shusett, O'Bannon, and Goldman take the concept of false memories one step further in the film. What if not only your memories of your experiences are false but also the memories of who you really are, are false? Can you prove that you are who you think you are? For some of you, such a question is outlandish and not deserving of a serious reply; however, it is raised to force you to accept that some of the beliefs that you have held on to dearly may not be as accurate as you insist. Raising such questions as we shall see should awaken the objective thinker from his or her "dogmatic slumber."[4]

In the *Meditations,* Descartes begins to examine all the ways in which he appears to have gained knowledge, and he is going to reject all of them as unacceptable. Descartes does not need to show that everything he believes is really false in order to be concerned. Instead he decides he should simply doubt everything that is not known with certainty. He is going to withhold acceptance of his beliefs[5] until he knows for sure. He recognizes that once he accepted as true things he received from his senses yet his senses sometimes deceived him. For example, if you pour water into a red glass pitcher, the water appears to turn red as well. Place a straw in the pitcher and the straw seems to bend. Yet there is no good evidence beyond just what one sees to suggest that a red glass container will somehow alter the color of a clear liquid, or that a straw will meet some sort of resistance in water that will cause its shape to alter. Descartes reasons that if he has been deceived once he should no longer be confident in that sense or in the conclusions that he draws from that sense. While this is a pretty severe step to take, Descartes is being very cautious because he is not just concerned about having *sufficient justification* to believe something; he wants a *guarantee* that he knows it.

Even if he can be fooled by his senses, surely it is impossible for Descartes to doubt what is happening to him right now. Can he seriously believe that there is a good reason to doubt that he is sitting there beside the fire and that he is clothed in night garments and that he has a body that is wearing these garments?

---

[3] Philip K. Dick, "We Can Remember It for You Wholesale" *The Magazine of Fantasy & Science Fiction,* April 1966.
[4] To quote Immanuel Kant (*Immanuel Kant: Philosophical Correspondence 1759–99,* tr. A. Zweig [Chicago: The University of Chicago Press, 1986], p. 252).
[5] When one believes X, one believes that X is true.

Well, Descartes has had dreams where he has been sitting next to a fire when he is actually asleep in bed. Maybe he is dreaming that very same thing right now. We all are probably familiar with this sort of event. Sometimes we are disappointed that what we experienced in our dreams was just that, a dream, and other times we are thankful! How can we tell if we are awake or dreaming? Their nature, like implanted memories, is so convincingly real at times that dreams have become a cliché in horror movies. We have all seen the one where something terrifying happens and the protagonist is startled out of his or her sleep only to remark: "Whew! It was only a dream!"[6]

Another Frenchman, this time the fictional captain of the Star Trek Enterprise, Jean-Luc Picard, provides us with another example of how hard it is to distinguish between dreams and reality.

In the opening scene of *Star Trek: First Contact*, Jean-Luc Picard is surrounded by an expanse of machinery and the dead faces of millions of humanoid species who have been assimilated to cyborgs. Next we see him strapped to an examination table as parts of his body are replaced with alien technology. His captors are the deadly Borg, an unfeeling collective of alien beings with whom he has done battle before. A needle-like instrument descends from above toward the Captain. The probe extends and pushes into his eye . . .

Fortunately, it is only a nightmare; a replaying of a past event.

Picard awakens with a start, finding himself in familiar surroundings aboard the Enterprise. Somewhat shaken he moves to the lavatory and splashes water onto his face. Staring into the mirror, Picard runs a hand along his cheek where the alien implants once were. But something is not quite right. Picard's skin stretches and pulsates and suddenly a small metallic starburst-shaped device erupts through his cheek. He opens his mouth to scream and then . . .

The captain pitches himself forward from his couch. This too was but a dream!

Just as Captain Picard's dream and his subsequent dream-within-a-dream have some basis in his reality (in the context of the Star Trek universe), Descartes realizes that what he is dreaming about has to exist in reality; otherwise he would have no conception of it. That is, if he did not know what hands and feet were, he would not be able to dream about them. But one might argue we all have had dreams when we have done things that we have never done before (such as flying or falling off a cliff), or that were set in lands that we have never visited. Descartes notes that we do not have to have experienced these things; we just have to be familiar with them. He notes that even mythical creatures that are painted by artists have to have some connection with general objects in the real world. For example, a unicorn is just the combination of a horse with a Narwhal whale horn growing out of its forehead. Yet the existence of real horses and strange-looking whales are not a given since our perception of these things does not mean they really are there. Even if what is created by talented artists is completely original and incomparable to things in the universe then at a minimum the colors that they used must be real. At the most basic level there has to exist some objects that have shape, color, and size. And, continues Descartes, whether we are asleep or awake, 2 + 3 still equals 5.

However, suppose that there existed an all-powerful being but instead of being a praiseworthy deity (i.e., God), it is a demon. This demon seeks to deceive human beings in all ways. So when Descartes adds 2 + 3 together, he only thinks it equals 5 but it really does not. "So", says Descartes, "let me assume that I am being deceived, that I am without body, or senses, and that what I perceive all around me is nothing but illusion." If this is the case, then all can be doubted. And if all things can be doubted then it is not possible to arrive at knowledge. We cannot know anything about anything. Descartes has—for the time being at least—followed the skeptic's path and rejected the possibility of knowledge.

In *The Game*, Nicholas Van Orton has been forced to the same level of doubt that Descartes has at the end of the *First Meditation*. Since the game is so intertwined with his real life, Nicholas cannot know what is real and what is not, so he doubts everything. The game is a complex real life puzzle that is inserted into the player's life. The player does not know which part of his or her daily routine is normal and which part has been purposely created by the game makers C.R.S. The person who serves you coffee and says "Hello" could just be a friendly waitress or she could be part of the game's storyline as is the case with Christine who tells Nicholas some distressing news about his bank account.

CHRISTINE   They did the same to him as they did to you.

NICHOLAS   What are you talking about . . . ?

She gives him a pitying look.

CHRISTINE   They've already got it, Nicholas. They got everything.

---

[6] A now classic use of dreams in horror movies is the *Nightmare on Elm Street* series.

Nicholas shoots her a glance; this is absurd.

CHRISTINE   Check your accounts. That night in your office, when we were there . . .

FLASHBACK—NICHOLAS' OFFICE— THAT NIGHT

Christine runs her finger down Nicholas' TELEPHONE. She looks to see Nicholas is preoccupied, lifts the receiver . . .

Reads the PHONE NUMBER underneath. She turns, looks down . . .

There's a NUMBER written on the PHONE JACK on the wall: #C4.

CHRISTINE   I got the number to your private line and modem. I gave C.R.S. remote access to your computer . . .

FLASHBACK—VARIOUS INSERTS

NICHOLAS' C.R.S. TESTING   Nicholas' hand scribbles his SIGNATURE . . . fills out a FINANCIAL QUESTIONNAIRE. A TAPE RECORDER'S REEL SPINS . . . a PENCIL blackens TEST BLOCKS . . .

CHRISTINE   You already gave them everything else. Handwriting, voice samples, psych-info. They used it all to figure out your passwords.

FLASHBACK   ON A MONITOR, combinations of LETTERS and NUMBERS SCROLL BY, multiplying, too quickly for the eye to see . . .

CHRISTINE   From there, they only had to keep you distracted while they broke into the network and transferred your holdings to dummy accounts.

FLASHBACK   FIGURES appear on a COMPUTER SCREEN; HIGH NUMBERS flying down to 000,000,000's. More NUMBERS, falling.

CHRISTINE   Remember Jim Feingold, the guy who signed you up? He did five years for hacking Citibank in eighty-four . . .

FLASHBACK   PAN UP from deft fingers at a keyboard to JIM FEINGOLD, lit by cold COMPUTER SCREEN GLOW.

BACK TO SCENE IN BENTLEY   Nicholas sweats. He checks his watch, takes out his cellular, dialing with his thumb. Christine smokes.

CHRISTINE   Why else would they be willing to put you under . . . ?

NICHOLAS   (into cellular) Overseas operator? Please dial Allgemeine Bank, Zurich.

CHRISTINE   They don't care about you anymore. Alive or dead is the same, as long as they bury you deep enough.

Nicholas discovers that his $600 million bank account has been emptied. Doubting that this is truly happening, or at least hoping that it isn't real, he calls his lawyer to independently confirm what may have happened. Is money still there? Is the apparent theft just part of the game?

The CELLULAR CHIRPS.

Nicholas goes to pick it up off a table.

NICHOLAS   (into cellular) Yes.

SUTHERLAND (V.O.)   (from cellular) I got your message. I was disturbed, to say the least . . .

Christine stands.

CHRISTINE   Who is it?

NICHOLAS   (into cellular) What do we do?

SUTHERLAND (V.O.) (from cellular)   I've been on the phone for an hour already. Nicholas, your funds are intact. Nothing's been touched.

CHRISTINE (worried, insistent)   Who is it?

NICHOLAS   (still into cellular) What do you mean? I checked them myself. I made the calls . . .

SUTHERLAND (V.O.)   Nothing's changed. I'm telling you, not a cent is unaccounted for . . .

NICHOLAS   (cups phone, to Christine) My lawyer . . . says nothing's missing.
She shakes her head ominously.

CHRISTINE   (fear, whisper) He's in on it . . .

Nicholas stares at Christine, trying to comprehend . . .

Nicholas Van Orton is playing in a modern-day version of Descartes's demon hypothesis. He is told that he is a pawn in a game and he is unable to separate what is real from what is not. As such any of his beliefs that are true and any that are false are presently indistinguishable. He witnessed the emptying of his bank account, yet his lawyer tells him that the account is not empty. Is his lawyer being honest, or is he part of the game too? It is difficult to separate truth from fiction when you cannot trust anything. Descartes states that you would not build a house on silt and sand, and so you ought not to build your beliefs on anything less than certainty, otherwise you risk it all coming crashing down around you. Accordingly, Descartes has to continue to dig until he is able to reach a solid foundation on which to build knowledge. It is in the *Second Meditation,* Descartes will try to rescue some fact, some *thing,* from this philosophically and psychologically disturbing position. What he arrives at is one of the landmarks of intellectual history.

In his writings Descartes alluded to the fact that this cognitive exercise is something that only insane individuals or philosophers would think of. However, if all we claim to know and if all that we rely on rests on a lie or an illusion that cannot be disproven, then what basis do we have to claim anything? Not only do we not have knowledge, but just imagine the psychological impact of learning that everything you once held to be true may be false.[7] In *The Wizard of Oz,* Oz was more real to Dorothy than the terrible times that she was born into (i.e., the Depression era in the United States of America). At the end of the film, Dorothy awakens to find that what she thought was real was not. She did not kill the Wicked Witch of the West; she did not follow the yellow brick road; she did not engage in lively discourse with the Tin Man, the Lion, and the Scarecrow. Instead, she simply got hit on the head by flying debris and dreamt of these colorful events. The realization that she was back in the miserable "real world" during the American Depression leads Dorothy to long for "Somewhere over the Rainbow." Depressing indeed!

In order to know whether you or I or Descartes has acquired knowledge, we need to know what is meant by the term *knowledge.* You cannot claim to have found something until you know what it is that you found. Obviously our belief must be true, but we can have true beliefs that are *not* justified. I am thinking of a number between one and ten. Do you know what it is?[8] If you got the answer right, would we say that you *knew* it? No. It was just a lucky guess. A person who purchases a lottery ticket usually believes that he or she will win. Given the odds, most of the buyers of lottery tickets will lose, so their individual beliefs that they will win the lottery are false. The winner's claim of "I will win the lottery," while true, is an unjustified belief.

One can have beliefs that are justified but that are also false. You might be told by your professor that there is going to be a test tomorrow. Given that every other time your professor has mentioned that there will be a test, there has been a test, you are justified in believing it to be true. However, there is a freak snow storm overnight and the university is forced to close for the remainder of the week. All classes are cancelled. So although you were justified in your belief that there would be a test, it is not true.

In one of the remaining readings in this chapter, David Hume (1711–1776) examines the application of a commonly relied on form of justification, namely making inductive predictions about the future based on seemingly justified claims from the past. For example, if it is early winter in Canada, I can safely predict that it will be colder tomorrow than it was today. But I might be wrong—there might be a warming trend moving in from the coast. More significantly, argues Hume, just because some event has been regularly caused in the past, it does not mean that such a connection will occur again.

Next, Bertrand Russell (1872–1970) and William James (1842–1910) present us with differing positions concerning the nature of truth. For Russell, "truth consists in some form of correspondence between belief and fact." In other words, if the belief is true, then what you believe copies, or agrees with, or corresponds to, what is actually the case. So, if I have the true belief that "the horse is white," it is true because there exists a horse that is white. But how can this be confirmed?

Michael Antonioni's film *Blow Up* reveals the difficulties of connecting our beliefs with reality. In this film, the main character is a professional photographer who takes a series of photos of a nearly empty park. When he blows up the images to larger and larger sizes the resolution becomes grainier and grainer, but with each increase in size what appears to be a man with a gun comes more and more into focus. Arranging the photographs into a meaningful order, the photographer sees what appears to be a murder taking place. Does his belief that there was a murder correspond to the reality, or does he make reality out of his perceptions of what is real? This theme of piecing bits of our beliefs and perceptions together to form reality re-occurs in Francis Ford Coppola's equally masterful film *The Conversation.*[9] Here, the protagonist is a sound engineer, and by selectively focusing

---

[7] Even dead people are traumatized by this sort of event—at least they are in the movies. Witness the reactions of Bruce Willis in *The Sixth Sense* and Nicole Kidman in *The Others* after they both learn that they are actually dead. The ghosts in *Poltergeist* are downright hostile when they find out that they are not among the living anymore.
[8] 7

---

[9] A film that many argue is more significant than the other movie he released that same year: *The Godfather.*

on bits of taped dialogue he overhears a murder plot. Again, like in *Blow Up* we question whether we are uncovering the truth or just seeing and hearing something that we want to see and hear.

The fact that we are *participating* in the process of discovery leads critics of the correspondence theory to charge that it leads us back to skepticism. We cannot step outside our world and compare what we believe with how the world actually is. There is no way to independently verify that an accurate assessment of a certain state of affairs has ever been achieved. So we can never know. This theme is also hinted at in *Blow Up* because we never do find out if the murder actually occurred.

For William James, truth is just a means of achieving something worthwhile. In other words "the truth works." I might not be able to prove that dinosaurs once lived on the earth, but the evidence that this is the case fits with the claim. Critics of this pragmatic view argue that it really does not amount to anything more than utility. My version of events could equally explain how the world is just as your version does, and so both would be equally useful. In my version, I posit that a demon (or a deity) planted dinosaur bones here and there a few thousand years ago and in your version you claim there were actually living breathing beasts roaming the land millions of years ago.[10] Clearly both versions cannot be true, can they? So there seems to be something more required. If we think back to the apparent murders in *Blow Up* and *The Conversation,* the evidence suggests that there were murders, but it also suggests that there were not. The evidence works both ways. So how is one to decide? For William James, one would seek out further evidence—a dead body would work better with the supposition that a murder took place rather than not. Likewise if positing that dinosaurs lived millions of years ago instead of thousands fits better within our commonly shared world view then this works better too. However, is simply 'working better' enough to quiet the skeptic?

---

[10] You might further argue that Carbon dating confirms your view but this is just an assumption that Carbon dating works. Need I mention Descartes again?

Films Cited

The Fugitive. Dir. Andrew Davis. Perfs. Harrison Ford, Tommy Lee Jones. Film. Warner Bros. Pictures. 1993.

Presumed Innocent. Dir. Alan J. Pakula. Perfs. Harrison Ford, Brian Dennehy. Film. Mirage. Pictures. 1990.

Memento. Dir. Christopher Nolan. Perfs. Guy Pearce and Carrie-Anne Moss. Film. New Market Capital Group. 2000.

Total Recall. Dir. Paul Verhoeven. Perfs. Arnold Schwarzenegger, Sharon Stone. Film. Carolco International N.V. 1990.

Nightmare on Elm Street. Dir. Wes Craven. Perfs. John Saxon, Ronee Blakley. Film. New Line Cinema, 1984.

Star Trek: First Contact. Dir. Jonathan Frakes. Perfs. Patrick Stewart, Jonathan Frakes. Film. Paramount Pictures. 1996.

The Game. Dir. David Fincher. Perfs. Michael Douglas, Sean Penn. Film. A&B Producers, Lda. 1997.

The Sixth Sense. Dir. M. Night Shyamalan. Perfs. Bruce Willis, Haley Joel Osment. Film. Barry Mendel Productions. 1999.

The Others. Dir. Alejandro Amenábar. Perfs. Nicole Kidman, Fionnula Flanagan. Film. Canal España. 2001.

Poltergeist. Dir. Tobe Hooper. Perfs. Craig T. Nelson, JoBeth Williams. Film. Metro-Goldwyn-Mayer (MGM). 1982.

Blow Up. Dir. Michelangelo Antonioni. Perfs. Vanessa Redgrave, Sarah Miles. Film. Bridge Films. 1966.

The Conversation. Dir. Francis Ford Coppola. Perfs. Gene Hackman, John Cazale. Film. American Zoetrope. 1974.

The Godfather. Dir. Francis Ford Coppola. Perfs. Marlon Brando, Al Pacino, James Caan. Film. Paramount Pictures. 1972.

The Wizard of Oz. Dir. Victor Fleming. Perfs. Judy Garland, Ray Bolger, Jack Haley. Film. MGM. 1939.

ADDITIONAL MOVIES FOR FURTHER VIEWING

(For a comprehensive listing of movies and themes, please consult the online appendix.)

1. *Dark City*—Cartesian Demon Hypothesis
2. *Eternal Sunshine of the Spotless Mind, The*—Nature of memory and knowledge
3. *Fahrenheit 9/11*—Seeking the truth
4. *Fight Club*—Appearance and reality
5. *Goodbye, Lenin!*—Appearance and reality
6. *JFK*—Theories of truth
7. *The Matrix*—Theories of truth
8. *The Sixth Sense*—Appearance and reality
9. *The Truman Show*—Cartesian Demon Hypothesis
10. *The Usual Suspects*—Theories of truth

Pyrrhonic Sketches, Book I, Chapters I–XVI, XVIII–XXVII
Sextus Empiricus

Chapter I
The Principal Differences between Philosophers
It is probable that those who seek after anything whatever, will either find it as they continue the search, will deny that it can be found and confess it to be out of reach, or will go on seeking it. Some have said, accordingly, in regard to the things sought in philosophy, that they have found the truth, while others have declared it impossible to find, and still others continue to seek it. Those who think that they have found it are those who are especially called Dogmatics, as for example, the Schools of Aristotle and Epicurus, the Stoics, and some others. Those who have declared it impossible to find are Clitomachus, Carneades, with their respective followers, and other Academicians. Those who still seek it are the Sceptics. It appears therefore, reasonable to conclude that the three principal kinds of philosophy are the Dogmatic, the Academic, and the Sceptic. Others may suitably treat of the other Schools, but as for the Sceptical School, we shall now give an outline of it, remarking in advance that in respect to nothing that will be said do we speak positively, that it must be absolutely so, but we shall state each thing historically as it now appears to us.

Chapter II
Ways of Treating Scepticism
One way of treating the Sceptical philosophy is called 'general,' and the other 'special.' The general method is that by which we set forth the character of Scepticism, declaring what its idea is, what its principles are, its mode of reasoning, its criterion, and its aim. It presents also, the aspects of doubt, *hoi tropoi tes epoches,* and the way in which we should understand the Sceptical formulae, and the distinction between Scepticism and the related Schools of philosophy. The special method, on the contrary, is that by which we speak against each part of so-called philosophy. Let us then treat Scepticism at first in the general way, beginning our delineation with the nomenclature of the Sceptical School.

Chapter III
The Nomenclature of Scepticism
The Sceptical School is also called the "Seeking School," from its spirit of research and examination; the "Suspending School," from the condition of mind in which one is left after the search, in regard to the things that he has examined; and the "Doubting School," either because, as some say, the Sceptics doubt and are seeking in regard to everything, or because they never know whether to deny or affirm. It is also called the Pyrrhonean School, because Pyrrho appears to us the best representative of Scepticism, and is more prominent than all who before him occupied themselves with it.

Chapter IV
What is Scepticism?
The *dynamis* of the Sceptical School is to place the phenomenal in opposition to the intellectual "in any way whatever," and thus through the equilibrium of the reasons and things *(isostheneia ton logon)* opposed to each other, to reach, first the state of suspension of judgment, *epoche* and afterwards that of imperturbability, *ataraxia*. We do not use the word *dynamis* in any unusual sense, but simply, meaning the force of the system. By the phenomenal, we understand the sensible, hence we place the intellectual in opposition to it. The phrase "in any way whatever," may refer to the word *dynamis* in order that we may understand that word in a simple sense as we said, or it may refer to the placing the phenomenal and intellectual in opposition. For we place these in opposition to each other in a variety of ways, the phenomenal to the phenomenal, and the intellectual to the intellectual, or reciprocally, and we say "in any way whatever," in order that all methods of opposition may be

(continued)

> **Pyrrhonic Sketches, Book I, Chapters I–XVI, XVIII–XXVII**   *(continued)*
>
> included. Or "in any way whatever" may refer to the phenomenal and the intellectual, so that we need not ask how does the phenomenal appear, or how are the thoughts conceived, but that we may understand these things in a simple sense. By "reasons opposed to each other," we do not by any means understand that they deny or affirm anything, but simply that they offset each other. By equilibrium, we mean equality in regard to trustworthiness and untrustworthiness, so that of the reasons that are placed in opposition to each other, one should not excel another in trustworthiness. *Epoche* is a holding back of the opinion, in consequence of which we neither deny nor affirm anything. *Ataraxia* is repose and tranquillity of soul. We shall explain how *Ataraxia* accompanies *epoche* when we speak of the aim.
>
> ### Chapter V
> ***The Sceptic***
>
> What is meant by a Pyrrhonean philosopher can be understood from the idea of the Sceptical School. He is a Pyrrhonean, namely, who identifies himself with this system.
>
> ### Chapter VI
> ***The Origin of Scepticism***
>
> Scepticism arose in the beginning from the hope of attaining *ataraxia*; for men of the greatest talent were perplexed by the contradiction of things, and being at a loss what to believe, began to question what things are true, and what false, hoping to attain *ataraxia* as a result of the decision. The fundamental principle of the Sceptical system is especially this, namely, to oppose every argument by one of equal weight, for it seems to us that in this way we finally reach the position where we have no dogmas.
>
> ### Chapter VII
> ***Does the Sceptic Dogmatise?***
>
> We say that the Sceptic does not dogmatise. We do not say this, meaning by the word dogma the popular assent to certain things rather than others (for the Sceptic does assent to feelings that are a necessary result of sensation, as for example, when he is warm or cold, he cannot say that he thinks he is not warm or cold), but we say this, meaning by dogma the acceptance of any opinion in regard to the unknown things investigated by science. For the Pyrrhonean assents to nothing that is unknown. Furthermore, he does not dogmatise even when he utters the Sceptical formulae in regard to things that are unknown, such as "Nothing more," or "I decide nothing," or any of the others about which we shall speak later. For the one who dogmatises regards the thing about which he is said to dogmatise, as existing in itself; the Sceptic does not however regard these formulae as having an absolute existence, for he assumes that the saying "All is false," includes itself with other things as false, and likewise the saying "Nothing is true"; in the same way "Nothing more," states that together with other things it itself is nothing more, and cancels itself therefore, as well as other things. We say the same also in regard to the other Sceptical expressions. In short, if he who dogmatises, assumes as existing in itself that about which he dogmatises, the Sceptic, on the contrary, expresses his sayings in such a way that they are understood to be themselves included, and it cannot be said that he dogmatises in saying these things. The principal thing in uttering these formulae is that he says what appears to him, and communicates his own feelings in an unprejudiced way, without asserting anything in regard to external objects.
>
> ### CHAPTER VIII
> ***Is Scepticism a Sect?***
>
> We respond in a similar way if we are asked whether Scepticism is a sect or not. If the word sect is defined as meaning a body of persons who hold dogmas which are in conformity with each other, and also with phenomena, and dogma means an assent to anything that is unknown, then we

reply that we have no sect. If, however, one means by sect, a school which follows a certain line of reasoning based on phenomena, and that reasoning shows how it is possible to apparently live rightly, not understanding "rightly" as referring to virtue only, but in a broader sense; if, also, it leads one to be able to suspend the judgment, then we reply that we have a sect. For we follow a certain kind of reasoning which is based upon phenomena, and which shows us how to live according to the habits, laws, and teachings of the fatherland, and our own feelings.

Chapter IX
Does the Sceptic Study Natural Science?

We reply similarly also to the question whether the Sceptic should study natural science. For we do not study natural science in order to express ourselves with confidence regarding any of the dogmas that it teaches, but we take it up in order to be able to meet every argument by one of equal weight, and also for the sake of *ataraxia*. In the same way we study the logical and ethical part of so-called philosophy.

Chapter X
Do the Sceptics deny Phenomena?

Those who say that the Sceptics deny phenomena appear to me to be in ignorance of our teachings. For as we said before, we do not deny the sensations which we think we have, and which lead us to assent involuntarily to them, and these are the phenomena. When, however, we ask whether the object is such as it appears to be, while we concede that it appears so and so, we question, not the phenomenon, but in regard to that which is asserted of the phenomenon, and that is different from doubting the phenomenon itself. For example, it appears to us that honey is sweet. This we concede, for we experience sweetness through sensation. We doubt, however, whether it is sweet by reason of its essence, which is not a question of the phenomenon, but of that which is asserted of the phenomenon. Should we, however, argue directly against the phenomena, it is not with the intention of denying their existence, but to show the rashness of the Dogmatics. For if reasoning is such a deceiver that it well nigh snatches away the phenomena from before your eyes, how should we not distrust it in regard to things that are unknown, so as not to rashly follow it?

Chapter XI
The Criterion of Scepticism

It is evident that we pay careful attention to phenomena from what we say about the criterion of the Sceptical School. The word criterion is used in two ways. First, it is understood as a proof of existence or non-existence, in regard to which we shall speak in the opposing argument. Secondly, when it refers to action, meaning the criterion to which we give heed in life, in doing some things and refraining from doing others, and it is about this that we shall now speak. We say, consequently, that the criterion of the Sceptical School is the phenomenon, and in calling it so, we mean the idea of it. It cannot be doubted, as it is based upon susceptibility and involuntary feeling. Hence no one doubts, perhaps, that an object appears so and so, but one questions if it is as it appears. Therefore, as we cannot be entirely inactive as regards the observances of daily life, we live by giving heed to phenomena, and in an unprejudiced way. But this observance of what pertains to the daily life, appears to be of four different kinds. Sometimes it is directed by the guidance of nature, sometimes by the necessity of the feelings, sometimes by the tradition of laws and of customs, and sometimes by the teaching of the arts. It is directed by the guidance of nature, for by nature we are capable of sensation and thought; by the necessity of the feelings, for hunger leads us to food, and thirst to drink; by the traditions of laws and customs, for according to them we consider piety a good in daily life, and impiety an evil; by the teaching of the arts, for we are not inactive in the arts we undertake. We say all these things, however, without expressing a decided opinion.

(continued)

Pyrrhonic Sketches, Book I, Chapters I–XVI, XVIII–XXVII (*continued*)

Chapter XII

What is the aim of Scepticism?

It follows naturally in order to treat of the aim of the Sceptical School. An aim is that for which as an end all things are done or thought, itself depending on nothing, or in other words, it is the ultimatum of things to be desired. We say, then, that the aim of the Sceptic is *ataraxia* in those things which pertain to the opinion, and moderation in the things that life imposes. For as soon as he began to philosophise he wished to discriminate between ideas, and to understand which are true and which are false, in order to attain *ataraxia*. He met, however, with contradictions of equal weight, and, being unable to judge, he withheld his opinion; and while his judgment was in suspension *ataraxia* followed, as if by chance, in regard to matters of opinion. For he who is of the opinion that anything is either good or bad by nature is always troubled, and when he does not possess those things that seem to him good he thinks that he is tortured by the things which are by nature bad, and pursues those that he thinks to be good. Having acquired them, however, he falls into greater perturbation, because he is excited beyond reason and without measure from fear of a change, and he does everything in his power to retain the things that seem to him good. But he who is undecided, on the contrary, regarding things that are good and bad by nature, neither seeks nor avoids anything eagerly, and is therefore in a state of *ataraxia*. For that which is related of Apelles the painter happened to the Sceptic. It is said that as he was once painting a horse he wished to represent the foam of his mouth in the picture, but he could not succeed in doing so, and he gave it up and threw the sponge at the picture with which he had wiped the colors from the painting. As soon, however, as it touched the picture it produced a good copy of the foam. The Sceptics likewise hoped to gain *ataraxia* by forming judgments in regard to the anomaly between phenomena and the things of thought, but they were unable to do this, and so they suspended their judgment; and while their judgment was in suspension *ataraxia* followed, as if by chance, as the shadow follows a body. Nevertheless, we do not consider the Sceptic wholly undisturbed, but he is disturbed by some things that are inevitable. We confess that sometimes he is cold and thirsty, and that he suffers in such ways. But in these things even the ignorant are beset in two ways, from the feelings themselves, and not less also from the fact that they think these conditions are bad by nature. The Sceptic, however, escapes more easily, as he rejects the opinion that anything is in itself bad by nature. Therefore we say that the aim of the Sceptic is *ataraxia* in matters of opinion, and moderation of feeling in those things that are inevitable. Some notable Sceptics have added also suspension of judgment in investigation.

Chapter XIII

The General Method of Scepticism

Since we have said that *ataraxia* follows the suspension of judgment in regard to everything, it behooves us to explain how the suspension of judgment takes place. Speaking in general it takes place through placing things in opposition to each other. We either place phenomena in opposition to phenomena, or the intellectual in opposition to the intellectual, or reciprocally. For example, we place phenomena in opposition to phenomena when we say that this tower appears round from a distance but square near by; the intellectual in opposition to the intellectual, when to the one who from the order of the heavens builds a tower of reasoning to prove that a providence exists, we oppose the fact that adversity often falls to the good and prosperity to the evil, and that therefore we draw the conclusion that there is no providence. The intellectual is placed in opposition to phenomena, as when Anaxagoras opposed the fact that snow is white, by saying that snow is frozen water, and, as water is black, snow must also be black. Likewise we sometimes place the present in opposition to the present, similarly to the above-mentioned cases, and sometimes also the present in opposition to the past or the future. As for example, when someone proposes an argument to us that we cannot refute, we say to him, "Before the founder of the sect to which you belong was born, the argument which you propose in accordance with it had not appeared as a valid argument, but was dormant in nature, so in the same way it is possible that its refutation also exists in nature, but has not yet appeared to us, so that it is not at all necessary for us to agree with an argument that now seems to be strong." In order to make it clearer to us what we mean by these oppositions, I will proceed to give the Tropes (*tropoi*), through which the suspension of judgment is produced, without asserting anything about their meaning or their number, because they may be unsound, or there may be more than I shall enumerate.

Chapter XIV
The Ten Tropes

Certain Tropes were commonly handed down by the older Sceptics, by means of which *epoche* seems to take place. They are ten in number, and are called synonymously *logoi* and *tropoi*. They are these: The first is based upon the differences in animals; the second upon the differences in men; the third upon the difference in the constitution of the organs of sense; the fourth upon circumstances; the fifth upon position, distance, and place; the sixth upon mixtures; the seventh upon the quantity and constitution of objects; the eighth upon relation; the ninth upon frequency or rarity of occurences; the tenth upon systems, customs, laws, mythical beliefs, and dogmatic opinions. We make this order ourselves. These Tropes come under three general heads: the standpoint of the judge, the standpoint of the thing judged, and the standpoint of both together. Under the standpoint of the judge come the first four, for the judge is either an animal, or a man, or a sense, and exists under certain circumstances. Under the standpoint of that which is judged, come the seventh and the tenth. Under the one composed of both together, come the fifth and the sixth, the eighth and the ninth. Again, these three divisions are included under the Trope of relation, because that is the most general one; it includes the three special divisions, and these in turn include the ten. We say these things in regard to their probable number, and we proceed in the following chapter to speak of their meaning . . .

Chapter XV
The Five Tropes

The later Sceptics, however, teach the following five Tropes of *epoche:* first, the one based upon contradiction; second, the 'regressus in infinitum;' third, relation; fourth, the hypothetical; and fifth, the 'circulus in probando.' The one based upon contradiction is the one from which we find, that in reference to the thing put before us for investigation, a position has been developed which is impossible to be judged, either practically, or theoretically, and therefore, as we are not able to either accept or reject anything, we end in suspending the judgment. The one based upon the 'regressus in infinitum' is that in which we say that the proof brought forward for the thing set before us calls for another proof, and that one another, and so on to infinity, so that, not having anything from which to begin the reasoning, the suspension of judgment follows. The one based upon relation, as we have said before, is that one in which the object appears of this kind or that kind, as related to the judge and to the things regarded together with it, but we suspend our judgment as to what it is in reality. The one based upon hypothesis is illustrated by the Dogmatics, when in the 'regressus in infinitum' they begin from something that they do not found on reason, but which they simply take for granted without proof. The Trope, 'circulus in probando,' arises when the thing which ought to prove the thing sought for, needs to be sustained by the thing sought for, and as we are unable to take the one for the proof of the other, we suspend our judgment in regard to both. Now we shall briefly show that it is possible to refer every thing under investigation to one or another of these Tropes, as follows: the thing before us is either sensible or intellectual; difference of opinion exists, however, as to what it is in itself, for some say that only the things of sense are true, others, only those belonging to the understanding, and others say that some things of sense, and some of thought, are true. Now, will it be said that this difference of opinion can be judged or cannot be judged? If it cannot be judged, then we have the result necessarily of suspension of judgment, because it is impossible to express opinion in regard to things about which a difference of opinion exists which cannot be judged. If it can be judged, then we ask how it is to be judged? For example, the sensible, for we shall limit the argument first to this — Is it to be judged by sensible or by intellectual standards? For if it is to be judged by

(continued)

Pyrrhonic Sketches, Book I, Chapters I–XVI, XVIII–XXVII (continued)

a sensible one, since we are in doubt about the sensible, that will also need something else to sustain it; and if that proof is also something sensible, something else will again be necessary to prove it, and so on in infinitum. If, on the contrary, the sensible must be judged by something intellectual, as there is disagreement in regard to the intellectual, this intellectual thing will require also judgment and proof. Now, how is it to be proved? If by something intellectual, it will likewise be thrown into infinitum; if by something sensible, as the intellectual has been taken for the proof of the sensible, and the sensible has been taken for that of the intellectual, the 'circulus in probando' is introduced. If, however, in order to escape from this, the one who is speaking to us expects us to take something for granted which has not been proved, in order to prove what follows, the hypothetical Trope is introduced, which provides no way of escape. For if the one who makes the hypothesis is worthy of confidence, we should in every case be no less worthy of confidence in making a contrary hypothesis. If the one who makes the assumption assumes something true, he makes it suspicious by using it as a hypothesis, and not as an established fact; if it is false, the foundation of the reasoning is unsound. If a hypothesis is any help towards a trustworthy result, let the thing in question itself be assumed, and not something else, by which, forsooth, one would establish the thing under discussion. If it is absurd to assume the thing questioned, it is also absurd to assume that upon which it rests. That all things belonging to the senses are also in relation to something else is evident, because they are in relation to those who perceive them. It is clear then, that whatever thing of sense is brought before us, it may be easily referred to one of the five Tropes. And we come to a similar conclusion in regard to intellectual things. For if it should be said that there is a difference of opinion regarding them which cannot be judged, it will be granted that we must suspend the judgment concerning it. In case the difference of opinion can be judged, if it is judged through anything intellectual, we fall into the 'regressus in infinitum,' and if through anything sensible into the 'circulus in probando;' for, as the sensible is again subject to difference of opinion, and cannot be judged by the sensible on account of the 'regressus in infinitum,' it will have need of the intellectual, just as the intellectual has need of the sensible. But he who accepts anything which is hypothetical again is absurd. Intellectual things stand also in relation, because the form in which they are expressed depends on the mind of the thinker, and, if they were in reality exactly as they are described, there would not have been any difference of opinion about them. Therefore the intellectual also is brought under the five Tropes, and consequently it is necessary to suspend the judgment altogether with regard to every thing that is brought before us. Such are the five Tropes taught by the later Sceptics. They set them forth, not to throw out the ten Tropes, but in order to put to shame the audacity of the Dogmatics in a variety of ways, by these Tropes as well as by those.

Chapter XVI
The Two Tropes

Two other Tropes of *epoche* are also taught. For as it appears that everything that is comprehended is either comprehended through itself or through something else, it is thought that this fact introduces doubt in regard to all things. And that nothing can be understood through itself is evident, it is said, from the disagreement which exists altogether among the physicists in regard to sensible and intellectual things. I mean, of course, a disagreement which cannot be judged, as we are not able to use a sensible or an intellectual criterion in judging it, for everything that we would take has a part in the disagreement, and is untrustworthy. Nor is it conceded that anything can be comprehended through something else; for if a thing is comprehended through something, that must always in turn be comprehended through something else, and the 'regressus in infinitum' or the 'circulus in probando' follow. If, on the contrary, a thing is comprehended through something that one wishes to use as if it had been comprehended through itself, this is opposed to the fact that nothing can be comprehended through itself, according to what we have said. We do not know how that which contradicts itself can be comprehended, either through itself or through something else, as no criterion of the truth or of comprehension appears, and signs without proof would be rejected, as we shall see in the next book. So much will suffice for the present about suspension of judgment.

Chapter XVIII
The Sceptical Formulae

When we use any one of these Tropes, or the Tropes of *epoche,* we employ with them certain formulae which show the Sceptical method and our own feeling, as for instance, the sayings, "No more," "One must determine nothing," and certain others. It is fitting therefore to treat of these in this place. Let us begin with "No more."

Chapter XIX
The Formula "No more"

We sometimes express this as I have given it, and sometimes thus, "Nothing more." For we do not accept the "No more," as some understand it, for the examination of the special, and "Nothing more" for that of the general, but we use "No more" and "Nothing more" without any difference, and we shall at present treat of them as one and the same expression. Now this formula is defective, for as when we say a double one we really mean a double garment, and when we say a broad one we really mean a broad road; so when we say "No more" we mean really no more than this, or in every way the same. But some of the Sceptics use instead of the interrogation "No?" the interrogation "What, this rather than this?" using the word "what" in the sense of "what is the reason," so that the formula means, "What is the reason for this rather than for this?" It is a customary thing, however, to use an interrogation instead of a statement, as "Who of the mortals does not know the wife of Jupiter?" and also to use a statement instead of an interrogation, as "I seek where Dion dwells," and "I ask why one should admire a poet." The word "what" is also used instead of "what for" by Menander—"(For) what did I remain behind?" The formula "Not more this than this" expresses our own condition of mind, and signifies that because of the equality of the things that are opposed to each other we finally attain to a state of equilibrium of soul. We mean by equality that equality which appears to us as probable, by things placed in opposition to each other we mean simply things which conflict with each other, and by a state of equilibrium we mean a state in which we do not assent to one thing more than to another. Even if the formula "Nothing more" seems to express assent or denial, we do not use it so, but we use it loosely, and not with accuracy, either instead of an interrogation or instead of saying, "I do not know to which of these I would assent, and to which I would not." What lies before us is to express what appears to us, but we are indifferent to the words by which we express it. This must be understood, however, that we use the formula "Nothing more" without affirming in regard to it that it is wholly sure and true, but we present it as it appears to us.

Chapter XX
Aphasia

We explain *Aphasia* as follows: The word *phasis* is used in two ways, having a general and a special signification. According to the general signification, it expresses affirmation or negation, as "It is day" or "It is not day"; according to the special signification, it expresses an affirmation only, and negations are not called *phaseis*. Now *Aphasia* is the opposite of *phasis* in its general signification, which, as we said, comprises both affirmation and negation. It follows that *Aphasia* is a condition of mind, according to which we say that we neither affirm nor deny anything. It is evident from this that we do not understand by *Aphasia* something that inevitably results from the nature of things, but we mean that we now find ourselves in the condition of mind expressed by it in regard to the things that are under investigation. It is necessary to remember that we do not say that we affirm or deny any of those things that are dogmatically stated in regard to the unknown, for we yield assent only to those things which affect our feelings and oblige us to assent to them.

Chapter XXI
"Perhaps," and "It is possible," and "It may be"

The formulae "Perhaps," and "Perhaps not," and "It is possible," and "It is not possible," and "It may be," and "It may not be," we use instead of "Perhaps it is," and "Perhaps it is not," and "It is possible that it is," and "It is possible that it is not," and "It may be that it is," and "It may be that

(continued)

Pyrrhonic Sketches, Book I, Chapters I–XVI, XVIII–XXVII   (*continued*)

it is not." That is, we use the formula "It is not possible" for the sake of brevity, instead of saying "It is not possible to be," and "It may not be" instead of "It may not be that it is," and "Perhaps not" instead of "Perhaps it is not." Again, we do not here dispute about words, neither do we question if the formulae mean these things absolutely, but we use them loosely, as I said before. Yet I think it is evident that these formulae express *Aphasia*. For certainly the formula "Perhaps it is" really includes that which seems to contradict it, i.e. the formula "Perhaps it is not," because it does not affirm in regard to anything that it is really so. It is the same also in regard to the others.

Chapter XXII

Epoche, or the Suspension of Judgment

When I say that I suspend my judgment, I mean that I cannot say which of those things presented should be believed, and which should not be believed, showing that things appear equal to me in respect to trustworthiness and untrustworthiness. Now we do not affirm that they are equal, but we state what appears to us in regard to them at the time when they present themselves to us. *Epoche* means the holding back of the opinion, so as neither to affirm nor deny anything because of the equality of the things in question.

Chapter XXIII

The Formula "I determine Nothing"

In regard to the formula "I determine nothing," we say the following: By "determine" we mean, not simply to speak, but to give assent to an affirmation with regard to some unknown thing. For it will soon be found that the Sceptic determines nothing, not even the formula "I determine nothing," for this formula is not a dogmatic opinion, that is an assent to something unknown, but an expression declaring what our condition of mind is. When, for example, the Sceptic says, "I determine nothing," he means this: "According to my present feeling I can assert or deny nothing dogmatically regarding the things under investigation," and in saying this he expresses what appears to him in reference to the things under discussion. He does not express himself positively, but he states what he feels.

Chapter XXIV

The Formula "Every thing is Undetermined"

The expression "Indetermination" furthermore shows a state of mind in which we neither deny nor affirm positively anything regarding things that are investigated in a dogmatic way, that is the things that are unknown. When then the Sceptic says "Every thing is undetermined," he uses "is undetermined," in the sense of "it appears undetermined to him." The words "every thing" do not mean all existences, but those that he has examined of the unknown things that are investigated by the Dogmatists. By "undetermined," he means that there is no preference in the things that are placed in opposition to each other, or that they simply conflict with each other in respect to trustworthiness or untrustworthiness. And as the one who says "I am walking" really means "It is I that am walking," so he who says "Every thing is undetermined" means at the same time, according to our teachings, "as far as I am concerned," or "as it appears to me," as if he were saying "As far as I have examined the things that are under investigation in a dogmatic manner, it appears to me that no one of them excels the one which conflicts with it in trustworthiness or untrustworthiness."

Chapter XXV

The Formula "Every thing is Incomprehensible"

We treat the formula "Every thing is incomprehensible" in the same way. For "every thing" we interpret in the same way as above, and we supply the words "to me" so that what we say is this: "As far as I have inspected the unknown things which are dogmatically examined, it appears to me that every thing is incomprehensible." This is not, however, to affirm that the things which are examined by the Dogmatists are of such a nature as to be necessarily incomprehensible, but one expresses his own feeling in saying "I see that I have not thus far comprehended any of those things because of the equilibrium of the things that are placed in opposition to each other." Whence it seems to me that every thing that has been brought forward to dispute our formulae has fallen wide of the mark.

Chapter XXVI
The Formulae "I do not comprehend" and "I do not Understand"

The formulae "I do not comprehend" and "I do not understand" show a condition of mind in which the Sceptic stands aloof for the present from asserting or denying anything in regard to the unknown things under investigation, as is evident from what we said before about the other formulae.

Chapter XXVII
The Formula "To place an equal Statement in opposition to every Statement"

Furthermore, when we say "Every statement may have an equal statement placed in opposition to it," by "every," we mean all the statements that we have examined; we do not use the word "statement" simply, but for a statement which seeks to prove something dogmatically about things that are unknown, and not at all one that shows a process of reasoning from premises and conclusions, but something which is put together in any sort of way. We use the word "equal" in reference to trustworthiness or untrustworthiness. "Is placed in opposition" we use instead of the common expression "to conflict with," and we supply "as it appears to me." When therefore one says, "It seems to me that every statement which I have examined, which proves something dogmatically, may have another statement placed in opposition to it which also proves something dogmatically, and which is equal to it in trustworthiness and untrustworthiness," this is not asserted dogmatically, but is an expression of human feeling as it appears to the one who feels it. Some Sceptics express the formula as follows: "Every statement should have an equal one placed in opposition to it," demanding it authoritatively thus: "Let us place in opposition to every statement that proves something dogmatically another conflicting statement which also seeks to prove something dogmatically, and is equal to it in trustworthiness and untrustworthiness." Naturally this is directed to the Sceptics, but the infinitive should be used instead of the imperative, that is, "to oppose" instead of "let us oppose." This formula is recommended to the Sceptic, lest he should be deceived by the Dogmatists and give up his investigations, and rashly fail of the *ataraxia* which is thought to accompany *epoche* in regard to everything, as we have explained above.

Meditations I & II
René Descartes

Meditation I
Of the Things of Which We May Doubt

1. SEVERAL years have now elapsed since I first became aware that I had accepted, even from my youth, many false opinions for true, and that consequently what I afterward based on such principles was highly doubtful; and from that time I was convinced of the necessity of undertaking once in my life to rid myself of all the opinions I had adopted, and of commencing anew the work of building from the foundation, if I desired to establish a firm and abiding superstructure in the sciences. But as this enterprise appeared to me to be one of great magnitude, I waited until I had attained an age so mature as to leave me no hope that at any stage of life more advanced I should be better able to execute my design. On this account, I have delayed so long that I should henceforth consider I was doing wrong were I still to consume in deliberation any of the time that now remains for action. To-day, then, since I have opportunely freed my mind from all cares [and am happily disturbed by no passions], and since I am in the secure possession of leisure in a

(continued)

Meditations I & II *(continued)*

peaceable retirement, I will at length apply myself earnestly and freely to the general overthrow of all my former opinions.

2. But, to this end, it will not be necessary for me to show that the whole of these are false—a point, perhaps, which I shall never reach; but as even now my reason convinces me that I ought not the less carefully to withhold belief from what is not entirely certain and indubitable, than from what is manifestly false, it will be sufficient to justify the rejection of the whole if I shall find in each some ground for doubt. Nor for this purpose will it be necessary even to deal with each belief individually, which would be truly an endless labor; but, as the removal from below of the foundation necessarily involves the downfall of the whole edifice, I will at once approach the criticism of the principles on which all my former beliefs rested.

3. All that I have, up to this moment, accepted as possessed of the highest truth and certainty, I received either from or through the senses. I observed, however, that these sometimes misled us; and it is the part of prudence not to place absolute confidence in that by which we have even once been deceived.

4. But it may be said, perhaps, that, although the senses occasionally mislead us respecting minute objects, and such as are so far removed from us as to be beyond the reach of close observation, there are yet many other of their informations (presentations), of the truth of which it is manifestly impossible to doubt; as for example, that I am in this place, seated by the fire, clothed in a winter dressing gown, that I hold in my hands this piece of paper, with other intimations of the same nature. But how could I deny that I possess these hands and this body, and withal escape being classed with persons in a state of insanity, whose brains are so disordered and clouded by dark bilious vapors as to cause them pertinaciously to assert that they are monarchs when they are in the greatest poverty; or clothed [in gold] and purple when destitute of any covering; or that their head is made of clay, their body of glass, or that they are gourds? I should certainly be not less insane than they, were I to regulate my procedure according to examples so extravagant.

5. Though this be true, I must nevertheless here consider that I am a man, and that, consequently, I am in the habit of sleeping, and representing to myself in dreams those same things, or even sometimes others less probable, which the insane think are presented to them in their waking moments. How often have I dreamt that I was in these familiar circumstances, that I was dressed, and occupied this place by the fire, when I was lying undressed in bed? At the present moment, however, I certainly look upon this paper with eyes wide awake; the head which I now move is not asleep; I extend this hand consciously and with express purpose, and I perceive it; the occurrences in sleep are not so distinct as all this. But I cannot forget that, at other times I have been deceived in sleep by similar illusions; and, attentively considering those cases, I perceive so clearly that there exist no certain marks by which the state of waking can ever be distinguished from sleep, that I feel greatly astonished; and in amazement I almost persuade myself that I am now dreaming.

6. Let us suppose, then, that we are dreaming, and that all these particulars—namely, the opening of the eyes, the motion of the head, the forth-putting of the hands—are merely illusions; and even that we really possess neither an entire body nor hands such as we see. Nevertheless it must be admitted at least that the objects which appear to us in sleep are, as it were, painted representations which could not have been formed unless in the likeness of realities; and, therefore, that those general objects, at all events, namely, eyes, a head, hands, and an entire body, are not simply imaginary, but really existent. For, in truth, painters themselves, even when they study to represent sirens and satyrs by forms the most fantastic and extraordinary, cannot bestow upon them natures absolutely new, but can only make a certain medley of the members of different animals; or if they chance to imagine something so novel that nothing at all similar has ever been seen before, and such as is, therefore, purely fictitious and absolutely false, it is at least certain that the colors of which this is composed are real. And on the same principle, although these general objects, viz. [a body], eyes, a head, hands, and the like, be imaginary, we are nevertheless absolutely necessitated to admit the reality at least of some other objects still more simple and universal than these, of which, just as of certain real colors, all those images of things, whether true and real, or false and fantastic, that are found in our consciousness *(cogitatio)*, are formed.

7. To this class of objects seem to belong corporeal nature in general and its extension; the figure of extended things, their quantity or magnitude, and their number, as also the place in, and the time during, which they exist, and other things of the same sort.

8. We will not, therefore, perhaps reason illegitimately if we conclude from this that Physics, Astronomy, Medicine, and all the other sciences that have for their end the consideration of composite objects, are indeed of a doubtful character; but that Arithmetic, Geometry, and the other sciences of the same class, which regard merely the simplest and most general objects, and scarcely inquire whether or not these are really existent, contain somewhat that is certain and indubitable: for whether I am awake or dreaming, it remains true that two and three make five, and that a square has but four sides; nor does it seem possible that truths so apparent can ever fall under a suspicion of falsity [or incertitude].

9. Nevertheless, the belief that there is a God who is all powerful, and who created me, such as I am, has, for a long time, obtained steady possession of my mind. How, then, do I know that he has not arranged that there should be neither earth, nor sky, nor any extended thing, nor figure, nor magnitude, nor place, providing at the same time, however, for [the rise in me of the perceptions of all these objects, and] the persuasion that these do not exist otherwise than as I perceive them? And further, as I sometimes think that others are in error respecting matters of which they believe themselves to possess a perfect knowledge, how do I know that I am not also deceived each time I add together two and three, or number the sides of a square, or form some judgment still more simple, if more simple indeed can be imagined? But perhaps Deity has not been willing that I should be thus deceived, for he is said to be supremely good. If, however, it were repugnant to the goodness of Deity to have created me subject to constant deception, it would seem likewise to be contrary to his goodness to allow me to be occasionally deceived; and yet it is clear that this is permitted.

10. Some, indeed, might perhaps be found who would be disposed rather to deny the existence of a Being so powerful than to believe that there is nothing certain. But let us for the present refrain from opposing this opinion, and grant that all which is here said of a Deity is fabulous: nevertheless, in whatever way it be supposed that I reach the state in which I exist, whether by fate, or chance, or by an endless series of antecedents and consequents, or by any other means, it is clear (since to be deceived and to err is a certain defect) that the probability of my being so imperfect as to be the constant victim of deception, will be increased exactly in proportion as the power possessed by the cause, to which they assign my origin, is lessened. To these reasonings I have assuredly nothing to reply, but am constrained at last to avow that there is nothing of all that I formerly believed to be true of which it is impossible to doubt, and that not through thoughtlessness or levity, but from cogent and maturely considered reasons; so that henceforward, if I desire to discover anything certain, I ought not the less carefully to refrain from assenting to those same opinions than to what might be shown to be manifestly false.

11. But it is not sufficient to have made these observations; care must be taken likewise to keep them in remembrance. For those old and customary opinions perpetually recur—long and familiar usage giving them the right of occupying my mind, even almost against my will, and subduing my belief; nor will I lose the habit of deferring to them and confiding in them so long as I shall consider them to be what in truth they are, viz, opinions to some extent doubtful, as I have already shown, but still highly probable, and such as it is much more reasonable to believe than deny. It is for this reason I am persuaded that I shall not be doing wrong, if, taking an opposite judgment of deliberate design, I become my own deceiver, by supposing, for a time, that all those opinions are entirely false and imaginary, until at length, having thus balanced my old by my new prejudices, my judgment shall no longer be turned aside by perverted usage from the path that may conduct to the perception of truth. For I am assured that, meanwhile, there will arise neither peril nor error from this course, and that I cannot for the present yield too much to distrust, since the end I now seek is not action but knowledge.

12. I will suppose, then, not that Deity, who is sovereignly good and the fountain of truth, but that some malignant demon, who is at once exceedingly potent and deceitful, has employed all his artifice to deceive me; I will suppose that the sky, the air, the earth, colors, figures, sounds, and all external things, are nothing better than the illusions of dreams, by means of which this being has

(continued)

Meditations I & II   (*continued*)

laid snares for my credulity; I will consider myself as without hands, eyes, flesh, blood, or any of the senses, and as falsely believing that I am possessed of these; I will continue resolutely fixed in this belief, and if indeed by this means it be not in my power to arrive at the knowledge of truth, I shall at least do what is in my power, viz, [suspend my judgment], and guard with settled purpose against giving my assent to what is false, and being imposed upon by this deceiver, whatever be his power and artifice. But this undertaking is arduous, and a certain indolence insensibly leads me back to my ordinary course of life; and just as the captive, who, perchance, was enjoying in his dreams an imaginary liberty, when he begins to suspect that it is but a vision, dreads awakening, and conspires with the agreeable illusions that the deception may be prolonged; so I, of my own accord, fall back into the train of my former beliefs, and fear to arouse myself from my slumber, lest the time of laborious wakefulness that would succeed this quiet rest, in place of bringing any light of day, should prove inadequate to dispel the darkness that will arise from the difficulties that have now been raised.

Meditation II
Of the Nature of the Human Mind; and that it is More Easily Known Than the Body

1. The Meditation of yesterday has filled my mind with so many doubts, that it is no longer in my power to forget them. Nor do I see, meanwhile, any principle on which they can be resolved; and, just as if I had fallen all of a sudden into very deep water, I am so greatly disconcerted as to be unable either to plant my feet firmly on the bottom or sustain myself by swimming on the surface. I will, nevertheless, make an effort, and try anew the same path on which I had entered yesterday, that is, proceed by casting aside all that admits of the slightest doubt, not less than if I had discovered it to be absolutely false; and I will continue always in this track until I shall find something that is certain, or at least, if I can do nothing more, until I shall know with certainty that there is nothing certain. Archimedes, that he might transport the entire globe from the place it occupied to another, demanded only a point that was firm and immovable; so, also, I shall be entitled to entertain the highest expectations, if I am fortunate enough to discover only one thing that is certain and indubitable.

2. I suppose, accordingly, that all the things which I see are false (fictitious); I believe that none of those objects which my fallacious memory represents ever existed; I suppose that I possess no senses; I believe that body, figure, extension, motion, and place are merely fictions of my mind. What is there, then, that can be esteemed true? Perhaps this only, that there is absolutely nothing certain.

3. But how do I know that there is not something different altogether from the objects I have now enumerated, of which it is impossible to entertain the slightest doubt? Is there not a God, or some being, by whatever name I may designate him, who causes these thoughts to arise in my mind? But why suppose such a being, for it may be I myself am capable of producing them? Am I, then, at least not something? But I before denied that I possessed senses or a body; I hesitate, however, for what follows from that? Am I so dependent on the body and the senses that without these I cannot exist? But I had the persuasion that there was absolutely nothing in the world, that there was no sky and no earth, neither minds nor bodies; was I not, therefore, at the same time, persuaded that I did not exist? Far from it; I assuredly existed, since I was persuaded. But there is I know not what being, who is possessed at once of the highest power and the deepest cunning, who is constantly employing all his ingenuity in deceiving me. Doubtless, then, I exist, since I am deceived; and, let him deceive me as he may, he can never bring it about that I am nothing, so long as I shall be conscious that I am something. So that it must, in fine, be maintained, all things being maturely and carefully considered, that this proposition (pronunciatum) *I am, I exist,* is necessarily true each time it is expressed by me, or conceived in my mind.

4. But I do not yet know with sufficient clearness what I am, though assured that I am; and hence, in the next place, I must take care, lest perchance I inconsiderately substitute some other object in room of what is properly myself, and thus wander from truth, even in that knowledge (cognition) which I hold to be of all others the most certain and evident. For this reason, I will now consider anew what I formerly believed myself to be, before I entered on the present train of thought; and of my previous opinion I will retrench all that can in the least be invalidated by the

grounds of doubt I have adduced, in order that there may at length remain nothing but what is certain and indubitable.

5. What then did I formerly think I was? Undoubtedly I judged that I was a man. But what is a man? Shall I say a rational animal? Assuredly not; for it would be necessary forthwith to inquire into what is meant by animal, and what by rational, and thus, from a single question, I should insensibly glide into others, and these more difficult than the first; nor do I now possess enough of leisure to warrant me in wasting my time amid subtleties of this sort. I prefer here to attend to the thoughts that sprung up of themselves in my mind, and were inspired by my own nature alone, when I applied myself to the consideration of what I was. In the first place, then, I thought that I possessed a countenance, hands, arms, and all the fabric of members that appears in a corpse, and which I called by the name of body. It further occurred to me that I was nourished, that I walked, perceived, and thought, and all those actions I referred to the soul; but what the soul itself was I either did not stay to consider, or, if I did, I imagined that it was something extremely rare and subtile, like wind, or flame, or ether, spread through my grosser parts. As regarded the body, I did not even doubt of its nature, but thought I distinctly knew it, and if I had wished to describe it according to the notions I then entertained, I should have explained myself in this manner: By body I understand all that can be terminated by a certain figure; that can be comprised in a certain place, and so fill a certain space as therefrom to exclude every other body; that can be perceived either by touch, sight, hearing, taste, or smell; that can be moved in different ways, not indeed of itself, but by something foreign to it by which it is touched [and from which it receives the impression]; for the power of self-motion, as likewise that of perceiving and thinking, I held as by no means pertaining to the nature of body; on the contrary, I was somewhat astonished to find such faculties existing in some bodies.

6. But [as to myself, what can I now say that I am], since I suppose there exists an extremely powerful, and, if I may so speak, malignant being, whose whole endeavors are directed toward deceiving me? Can I affirm that I possess any one of all those attributes of which I have lately spoken as belonging to the nature of body? After attentively considering them in my own mind, I find none of them that can properly be said to belong to myself. To recount them were idle and tedious. Let us pass, then, to the attributes of the soul. The first mentioned were the powers of nutrition and walking; but, if it be true that I have no body, it is true likewise that I am capable neither of walking nor of being nourished. Perception is another attribute of the soul; but perception too is impossible without the body; besides, I have frequently, during sleep, believed that I perceived objects which I afterward observed I did not in reality perceive. Thinking is another attribute of the soul; and here I discover what properly belongs to myself. This alone is inseparable from me. I am—I exist: this is certain; but how often? As often as I think; for perhaps it would even happen, if I should wholly cease to think, that I should at the same time altogether cease to be. I now admit nothing that is not necessarily true. I am therefore, precisely speaking, only a thinking thing, that is, a mind *(mens sive animus)*, understanding, or reason, terms whose signification was before unknown to me. I am, however, a real thing, and really existent; but what thing? The answer was, a thinking thing.

7. The question now arises, am I aught besides? I will stimulate my imagination with a view to discover whether I am not still something more than a thinking being. Now it is plain I am not the assemblage of members called the human body; I am not a thin and—air diffused through all these members, or wind, or flame, or vapor, or breath, or any of all the things I can imagine; for I supposed that all these were not, and, without changing the supposition, I find that I still feel assured of my existence. But it is true, perhaps, that those very things which I suppose to be nonexistent, because they are unknown to me, are not in truth different from myself whom I know. This is a point I cannot determine, and do not now enter into any dispute regarding it. I can only judge of things that are known to me: I am conscious that I exist, and I who know that I exist inquire into what I am. It is, however, perfectly certain that the knowledge of my existence, thus precisely taken, is not dependent on things, the existence of which is as yet unknown to me: and consequently it is not dependent on any of the things I can feign in imagination. Moreover, the phrase itself, I frame an image *(efffingo)*, reminds me of my error; for I should in truth frame one if I were to imagine myself to be anything, since to imagine is nothing more than to contemplate the figure or image of a corporeal thing; but I already know that I exist, and that it is possible at the same time that all those images, and in general all that relates to the nature of body, are merely

(continued)

Meditations I & II (continued)

dreams [or chimeras]. From this I discover that it is not more reasonable to say, I will excite my imagination that I may know more distinctly what I am, than to express myself as follows: I am now awake, and perceive something real; but because my perception is not sufficiently clear, I will of express purpose go to sleep that my dreams may represent to me the object of my perception with more truth and clearness. And, therefore, I know that nothing of all that I can embrace in imagination belongs to the knowledge which I have of myself, and that there is need to recall with the utmost care the mind from this mode of thinking, that it may be able to know its own nature with perfect distinctness.

8. But what, then, am I? A thinking thing, it has been said. But what is a thinking thing? It is a thing that doubts, understands, [conceives], affirms, denies, wills, refuses; that imagines also, and perceives.

9. Assuredly it is not little, if all these properties belong to my nature. But why should they not belong to it? Am I not that very being who now doubts of almost everything; who, for all that, understands and conceives certain things; who affirms one alone as true, and denies the others; who desires to know more of them, and does not wish to be deceived; who imagines many things, sometimes even despite his will; and is likewise percipient of many, as if through the medium of the senses. Is there nothing of all this as true as that I am, even although I should be always dreaming, and although he who gave me being employed all his ingenuity to deceive me? Is there also any one of these attributes that can be properly distinguished from my thought, or that can be said to be separate from myself? For it is of itself so evident that it is I who doubt, I who understand, and I who desire, that it is here unnecessary to add anything by way of rendering it more clear. And I am as certainly the same being who imagines; for although it may be (as I before supposed) that nothing I imagine is true, still the power of imagination does not cease really to exist in me and to form part of my thought. In fine, I am the same being who perceives, that is, who apprehends certain objects as by the organs of sense, since, in truth, I see light, hear a noise, and feel heat. But it will be said that these presentations are false, and that I am dreaming. Let it be so. At all events it is certain that I seem to see light, hear a noise, and feel heat; this cannot be false, and this is what in me is properly called perceiving *(sentire),* which is nothing else than thinking.

10. From this I begin to know what I am with somewhat greater clearness and distinctness than heretofore. But, nevertheless, it still seems to me, and I cannot help believing, that corporeal things, whose images are formed by thought [which fall under the senses], and are examined by the same, are known with much greater distinctness than that I know not what part of myself which is not imaginable; although, in truth, it may seem strange to say that I know and comprehend with greater distinctness things whose existence appears to me doubtful, that are unknown, and do not belong to me, than others of whose reality I am persuaded, that are known to me, and appertain to my proper nature; in a word, than myself. But I see clearly what is the state of the case. My mind is apt to wander, and will not yet submit to be restrained within the limits of truth. Let us therefore leave the mind to itself once more, and, according to it every kind of liberty [permit it to consider the objects that appear to it from without], in order that, having afterward withdrawn it from these gently and opportunely [and fixed it on the consideration of its being and the properties it finds in itself], it may then be the more easily controlled.

11. Let us now accordingly consider the objects that are commonly thought to be [the most easily, and likewise] the most distinctly known, viz, the bodies we touch and see; not, indeed, bodies in general, for these general notions are usually somewhat more confused, but one body in particular. Take, for example, this piece of wax; it is quite fresh, having been but recently taken from the beehive; it has not yet lost the sweetness of the honey it contained; it still retains somewhat of the odor of the flowers from which it was gathered; its color, figure, size, are apparent (to the sight); it is hard, cold, easily handled; and sounds when struck upon with the finger. In fine, all that contributes to make a body as distinctly known as possible, is found in the one before us. But, while I am speaking, let it be placed near the fire—what remained of the taste exhales, the smell evaporates, the color changes, its figure is destroyed, its size increases, it becomes liquid, it grows hot, it can hardly be handled, and, although struck upon, it emits no sound. Does the same wax still remain after this change? It must be admitted that it does remain; no one doubts it, or judges otherwise. What, then, was it I knew with so much distinctness in the piece of wax? Assuredly, it could be nothing of all that I observed by means of

the senses, since all the things that fell under taste, smell, sight, touch, and hearing are changed, and yet the same wax remains.

12. It was perhaps what I now think, viz, that this wax was neither the sweetness of honey, the pleasant odor of flowers, the whiteness, the figure, nor the sound, but only a body that a little before appeared to me conspicuous under these forms, and which is now perceived under others. But, to speak precisely, what is it that I imagine when I think of it in this way? Let it be attentively considered, and, retrenching all that does not belong to the wax, let us see what remains. There certainly remains nothing, except something extended, flexible, and movable. But what is meant by flexible and movable? Is it not that I imagine that the piece of wax, being round, is capable of becoming square, or of passing from a square into a triangular figure? Assuredly such is not the case, because I conceive that it admits of an infinity of similar changes; and I am, moreover, unable to compass this infinity by imagination, and consequently this conception which I have of the wax is not the product of the faculty of imagination. But what now is this extension? Is it not also unknown? for it becomes greater when the wax is melted, greater when it is boiled, and greater still when the heat increases; and I should not conceive [clearly and] according to truth, the wax as it is, if I did not suppose that the piece we are considering admitted even of a wider variety of extension than I ever imagined, I must, therefore, admit that I cannot even comprehend by imagination what the piece of wax is, and that it is the mind alone (*mens*, Lat., *entendement*, F.) which perceives it. I speak of one piece in particular; for as to wax in general, this is still more evident. But what is the piece of wax that can be perceived only by the [understanding or] mind? It is certainly the same which I see, touch, imagine; and, in fine, it is the same which, from the beginning, I believed it to be. But (and this it is of moment to observe) the perception of it is neither an act of sight, of touch, nor of imagination, and never was either of these, though it might formerly seem so, but is simply an intuition *(inspectio)* of the mind, which may be imperfect and confused, as it formerly was, or very clear and distinct, as it is at present, according as the attention is more or less directed to the elements which it contains, and of which it is composed.

13. But, meanwhile, I feel greatly astonished when I observe [the weakness of my mind, and] its proneness to error. For although, without at all giving expression to what I think, I consider all this in my own mind, words yet occasionally impede my progress, and I am almost led into error by the terms of ordinary language. We say, for example, that we see the same wax when it is before us, and not that we judge it to be the same from its retaining the same color and figure: whence I should forthwith be disposed to conclude that the wax is known by the act of sight, and not by the intuition of the mind alone, were it not for the analogous instance of human beings passing on in the street below, as observed from a window. In this case I do not fail to say that I see the men themselves, just as I say that I see the wax; and yet what do I see from the window beyond hats and cloaks that might cover artificial machines, whose motions might be determined by springs? But I judge that there are human beings from these appearances, and thus I comprehend, by the faculty of judgment alone which is in the mind, what I believed I saw with my eyes.

14. The man who makes it his aim to rise to knowledge superior to the common, ought to be ashamed to seek occasions of doubting from the vulgar forms of speech: instead, therefore, of doing this, I shall proceed with the matter in hand, and inquire whether I had a clearer and more perfect perception of the piece of wax when I first saw it, and when I thought I knew it by means of the external sense itself, or, at all events, by the common sense *(sensus communis)*, as it is called, that is, by the imaginative faculty; or whether I rather apprehend it more clearly at present, after having examined with greater care, both what it is, and in what way it can be known. It would certainly be ridiculous to entertain any doubt on this point. For what, in that first perception, was there distinct? What did I perceive which any animal might not have perceived? But when I distinguish the wax from its exterior forms, and when, as if I had stripped it of its vestments, I consider it quite naked, it is certain, although some error may still be found in my judgment, that I cannot, nevertheless, thus apprehend it without possessing a human mind.

15. But finally, what shall I say of the mind itself, that is, of myself? for as yet I do not admit that I am anything but mind. What, then! I who seem to possess so distinct an apprehension of the piece of wax, do I not know myself, both with greater truth and certitude, and also much more distinctly and clearly? For if I judge that the wax exists because I see it, it assuredly follows, much more evidently, that I myself am or exist, for the same reason: for it is possible that what I see may not in

(continued)

Meditations I & II (*continued*)

truth be wax, and that I do not even possess eyes with which to see anything; but it cannot be that when I see, or, which comes to the same thing, when I think I see, I myself who think am nothing. So likewise, if I judge that the wax exists because I touch it, it will still also follow that I am; and if I determine that my imagination, or any other cause, whatever it be, persuades me of the existence of the wax, I will still draw the same conclusion. And what is here remarked of the piece of wax, is applicable to all the other things that are external to me. And further, if the [notion or] perception of wax appeared to me more precise and distinct, after that not only sight and touch, but many other causes besides, rendered it manifest to my apprehension, with how much greater distinctness must I now know myself, since all the reasons that contribute to the knowledge of the nature of wax, or of any body whatever, manifest still better the nature of my mind? And there are besides so many other things in the mind itself that contribute to the illustration of its nature, that those dependent on the body, to which I have here referred, scarcely merit to be taken into account.

16. But, in conclusion, I find I have insensibly reverted to the point I desired; for, since it is now manifest to me that bodies themselves are not properly perceived by the senses nor by the faculty of imagination, but by the intellect alone; and since they are not perceived because they are seen and touched, but only because they are understood [or rightly comprehended by thought], I readily discover that there is nothing more easily or clearly apprehended than my own mind. But because it is difficult to rid one's self so promptly of an opinion to which one has been long accustomed, it will be desirable to tarry for some time at this stage, that, by long continued meditation, I may more deeply impress upon my memory this new knowledge.

An Essay Concerning Human Understanding: Book I, Chapter II
John Locke

No Innate Principles in the Mind

1. *The way shown how we come by any knowledge, sufficient to prove it not innate.*—It is an established opinion amongst some men, that there are in the understanding certain innate principles; some primary notions, *koιvaì Ėvvoιaι*, characters, as it were, stamped upon the mind of man, which the soul receives in its very first being, and brings into the world with it. It would be sufficient to convince unprejudiced readers of the falseness of this supposition, if I should only show (as I hope I shall in the following parts *of* this discourse) how men, barely by the use of their natural faculties, may attain to all the knowledge they have, without the help of any innate impressions, and may arrive at certainty without any such original notions or principles. For I imagine any one will easily grant, that it would be impertinent to suppose, the ideas of colours innate in a creature to whom God hath given sight and a power to receive them by the eyes from external objects: and no less unreasonable would it be to attribute several truths to the impressions of nature, and innate characters, when we may observe in ourselves faculties fit to attain as easy and certain knowledge of them, as if they were originally imprinted on the mind.

   But because a man is not permitted without censure to follow his own thoughts in the search of truth, when they lead him ever so little out of the common road, I shall set down the reasons that made me doubt *of* the truth of that opinion as an excuse for my mistake, if I be in one; which I leave to be considered by those who, with me, dispose-themselves to embrace truth wherever they find it.

2. *General assent, the great argument.*—There is nothing more commonly taken for granted, than that there are certain principles, both speculative and practical, (for they speak of both,) universally agreed upon by all mankind; which, therefore, they argue, must needs be constant impressions which the souls of men receive in their first beings, and which they bring into the world with them, as necessarily and really as they do any of their inherent faculties.

3. *Universal consent proves nothing innate.*—This argument drawn from universal consent, has the misfortune in it, that if it were true in matter of fact, that there were certain truths, wherein all mankind agreed, it would not prove them innate, if there can be any other way shown, how men may come to that universal agreement in the things they do consent in; which I presume may be done.
4. *"What is, is;" and "it is impossible for the same thing to be, and not to be," not universally assented to.*—But, which is worse, this argument of universal consent, which is made use of to prove innate principles, seems to me a demonstration that there are none such; because there are none to which all mankind give an universal assent. I shall begin with the speculative, and instance in those magnified principles and demonstration, "whatsoever is, is," and "it is impossible for the same thing to be, and not to be," which, of all others, I think, have the most hallowed title to innate. These have so settled a reputation of maxims universally received, that it will, no doubt, be thought strange if any one should seem to question it. But yet I take liberty to say, that these propositions are so far from having an universal assent, that there are a great part of mankind to whom they are not so much as known.
5. *Not on the mind naturally imprinted, because not known to children, idiots.*—For, first, it is evident that all children and idiots have not the least apprehension or thought of them; and the want of that is enough to destroy that universal assent which must needs be the necessary concomitant of all innate truths: it seeming to me near a contradiction to say, that there are truths imprinted on the soul, which it perceives or understands not; imprinting, if it signify any thing, being nothing else but the making certain truths to be perceived. For to imprint any thing on the mind, without the mind's perceiving it, seems to me hardly intelligible. If, therefore, children and idiots have souls, have minds, with those impressions upon them, they must unavoidably perceive them, and necessarily know and assent to these truths; which, since they do not, it is evident that there are no such impressions. For if they are not notions naturally imprinted, how can they be innate? and if they are notions imprinted, how can they be unknown? To say a notion is imprinted on the mind, and yet at the same time to say that the mind is ignorant of it, and never yet took notice of it, is to make this impression nothing. No proposition can be said to be in the mind which it never yet knew, which it was never yet conscious of. For if any one may, then, by the same reason, all propositions that are true, and the mind is capable of ever assenting to, may be said to be in the mind, and to be imprinted; since, if any one can be said to be in the mind, which it never yet knew, it must be only because it is capable of knowing it, and so the mind is of all truths it ever shall know. Nay, thus truths may be imprinted on the mind, which it never did, nor never shall know: for a man may live long, and die at last in ignorance of many truths which his mind was capable of knowing, and that with certainty. So that if the capacity of knowing be the natural impression contended for, all the truths a man ever comes to know, will, by this account, be every one of them innate: and this great point will amount to no more, but only to a very improper way of speaking; which, whilst it pretends to assert the contrary, says nothing different from those who deny innate principles. For nobody, I think, ever denied that the mind was capable of knowing several truths. The capacity, they say, is innate; the knowledge acquired. But then, to what end such contest for certain innate maxims? If truths can be imprinted on the understanding without being perceived, I can see no difference there can be between any truths the mind is capable of knowing in respect of their original; they must all be innate or all adventitious; in vain shall a man go about to distinguish them. He, therefore, that talks of innate notions in the understanding, cannot (if he intend thereby any distinct sort of truths) mean such truths to be in the understanding, as it never perceived, and is yet wholly ignorant of. For if these words (to be in the understanding) have any propriety, they signify to be understood; so that, to be in the understanding, and not to be understood; to be in the mind, and never to be perceived, is all one, as to say, any thing is, and is not, in the mind or understanding. If, therefore, these two propositions, "whatsoever is, is;" and, "it is impossible for the same thing to be, and not to be," are by nature imprinted, children cannot be ignorant of them; infants and all that have souls, must necessarily have them in their understandings, know the truth of them, and assent to it.

(continued)

An Essay Concerning Human Understanding: Book I, Chapter II (*continued*)

6. *That men know them when they come to the use of reason, answered.*—To avoid this, it is usually answered, that all men know and assent to them, when they come to the use of reason, and this is enough to prove them innate. I answer,

7. Doubtful expressions, that have scarce any signification, go for clear reasons to those who, being prepossessed, take not the pains to examine even what they themselves say. For to apply this answer with any tolerable sense to our present purpose, it must signify one of these two things: either, that as soon as men come to the use of reason, these supposed native inscriptions come to be known and observed by them; or else, that the use and exercise of men's reason assists them in the discovery of these principles, and certainly makes them known to them.

8. *If reason discovered them, that would not prove them innate.*—If they mean that, by the use of reason, men may discover these principles, and that this is sufficient to prove them innate, their way of arguing will stand thus, viz.: That whatever truths reason can certainly discover to us, and make us firmly assent to, those are all naturally imprinted on the mind; since that universal assent which is made the mark of them, amounts to no more but this: that by the use of reason we are capable to come to a certain knowledge of, and assent to, them; and by this means there will be no difference between the maxims of the mathematicians, and theorems they deduce from them; all must be equally allowed innate; they being all discoveries made by the use of reason, and truths that a rational creature may certainly come to know, if he apply his thoughts rightly that way.

9. *It is false that reason discovers them.*—But how can these men think the use of reason necessary to discover principles that are supposed innate, when reason (if we may believe them) is nothing else but the faculty of deducing unknown truths from principles or propositions that are already known? That certainly can never be thought innate which we have need of reason to discover, unless, as I have said, we will have all the certain truths that reason ever teaches us, to be innate. We may as well think the use of reason necessary to make our eyes discover visible objects, as that there should be need of reason, or the exercise thereof, to make the understanding see what is originally engraven on it, and cannot be in the understanding, before it be perceived by it. So that to make reason discover those truths thus imprinted, is to say that the use of reason discovers to a man what he knew before; and if men have those innate impressed truths originally, and before the use of reason, and yet are always ignorant of them, till they come to the use of reason, it is in effect to say, that men know, and know them not, at the same time.

10. It will here perhaps be said, that mathematical demonstrations, and other truths, that are not innate, are not assented to, as soon as proposed, wherein they are distinguished from these maxims, and other innate truths. I shall have occasion to speak of assent, upon the first proposing, more particularly, by-and-by. I shall here only, and that very readily, allow, that these maxims, and mathematical demonstrations, are in this different; that the one have need of reason, using of proofs, to make them out and to gain our assent: but the other, as soon as understood, are, without any the least reasoning, embraced and assented to. But I withal beg leave to observe, that it lays open the weakness of this subterfuge, which requires the use of reason for the discovery of these general truths: since it must be confessed, that in their discovery, there is no use made of reasoning at all. And I think those who give this answer will not be forward to affirm, that the knowledge of this maxim, that "it is impossible for the same thing to be, and not to be" is a deduction of our reason. For this would be to destroy that bounty of nature they seem so fond of, whilst they make the knowledge of those principles to depend on the labour of our thoughts. For all reasoning is search, and casting about, and requires pains and application. And how can it with any tolerable sense be supposed, that, what was imprinted by nature, as the foundation and guide of our reason, should need the use of reason to discover it?

11. Those who will take the pains to reflect with a little attention on the operations of the understanding, will find that this ready assent of the mind to some truths, depends not either on native inscription, or the use of reason: but on a faculty of the mind quite distinct from both of them, as we shall see hereafter. Reason, therefore, having nothing to do in procuring our

assent to these maxims, if by saying, that men know and assent to them, when they come to the use of reason, be meant, that the use of reason assists us in the knowledge of these maxims, it is utterly false; and, were it true, would prove them not to be innate.

12. *The coming to the use of reason, not the time we come to know these maxims.*—If by knowing and assenting to them when we come to the use of reason, be meant, that this is the time when they come to be taken notice of by the mind; and that as soon as children come to the use of reason, they come also to know and assent to these maxims; this also is false and frivolous. *First,* It is false, because it is evident these maxims are not in the mind so early as the use of reason; and, therefore, the coming to the use of reason, is falsely assigned as the time of their discovery. How many instances of the use of reason may we observe in children, a long time before they have any knowledge of this maxim, that "it is impossible for the same thing to be, and not to be?" And a great part of illiterate people, and savages, pass many years, even of their rational age, without ever thinking on this and the like general propositions. I grant, men come not to the knowledge of these general and more abstract truths, which are thought innate, till they come to the use of reason; and I add, nor then neither. Which is so, because till after they come to the use of reason, those general abstract ideas are not framed in the mind, about which those general maxims are, which are mistaken for innate principles, but are indeed discoveries made, and verities introduced, and brought into the mind by the same way, and discovered by the same steps, as several other propositions, which nobody was ever so extravagant as to suppose innate. This I hope to make plain in the sequel of this discourse. I allow, therefore, a necessity that men should come to the use of reason, before they get the knowledge of those general truths; but deny that men's coming to the use of reason is the time of their discovery.

13. *By this they are not distinguished from other knowable truths.*—In the meantime it is observable, that this saying, That men know and assent to these maxims, when they come to the use of reason, amounts, in reality of fact, to no more but this, that they are never known or taken notice of, before the use of reason, but may possibly be assented to some time after, during a man's life; but when, is uncertain: and so may all other knowable truths, as well as these; which, therefore, have no advantage nor distinction from others, by this note of being known when we come to the use of reason; nor are thereby proved to be innate, but quite the contrary.

14. *If coming to the use of reason were the time of their discovery, it would not prove them innate.*—But, secondly, were it true, that the precise time of their being known, and assented to were, when men come to the use of reason, neither would that prove them innate. This way of arguing is as frivolous, as the supposition of itself is false. For by what kind of logic will it appear, that any notion is originally by nature imprinted in the mind in its first constitution, because it comes first to be observed and assented to, when a faculty of the mind, which has quite a distinct province, begins to exert itself? and, therefore, the coming to the use of speech, if it were supposed the time that these maxims are first assented to (which it may be with as much truth, as the time when men come to the use of reason) would be as good a proof that they were innate, as to say, they are innate, because men assent to them when they come to the use of reason. I agree then with these men of innate principles, that there is no knowledge of these general and self-evident maxims in the mind, till it comes to the exercise of reason; but I deny that the coming to the use of reason, is the precise time when they are first taken notice of; and if that were the precise time, I deny that it would prove them innate. All that can with any truth be meant by this proposition, that men assent to them when they come to the use of reason, is no more but this, that the making of general abstract ideas, and the understanding of general names, being a concomitant of the rational faculty, and growing up with it, children commonly get not those general ideas, nor learn the names that stand for them, till, having for a good while exercised their reason about familiar and more particular ideas, they are, by their ordinary discourse and actions with others, acknowledged to be capable of rational conversation. If assenting to these maxims, when men come to the use of reason, can be true in any other sense, I desire it may be shown; or, at least, how in this, or any other sense, it proves them innate.

(continued)

An Essay Concerning Human Understanding: Book I, Chapter II *(continued)*

15. *The steps by which the mind attains several truths.*—The senses at first let in particular ideas, and furnish the yet empty cabinet: and the mind by degrees growing familiar with some of them, they are lodged in the memory, and names got to them. Afterwards the mind, proceeding farther, abstracts them, and by degrees learns the use of general names. In this manner the mind comes to be furnished with ideas and language, the materials about which to exercise the discursive faculty; and the use of reason becomes daily more visible, as these materials that give it employment, increase. But though the having of general ideas, and the use of general words and reason, usually grow together, yet I see not how this any way proves them innate. The knowledge of some truths, I confess, is very early in the mind, but in a way that shows them not to be innate; for if we will observe, we shall find it still to be about ideas not innate, but acquired; it being about those first which are imprinted by external things, with which infants have earliest to do, which make the most frequent impressions on their senses. In ideas thus got, the mind discovers, that some agree, and others differ, probably as soon as it has any use of memory, as soon as it is able to retain and perceive distinct ideas. But whether it be then or no, this is certain, it does so long before it has the use of words, or comes to that which we commonly call "the use of reason;" for a child knows as certainly, before it can speak, the difference between the ideas of sweet and bitter (*i.e.* that sweet is not bitter) as it knows afterwards, when it comes to speak, that wormwood and sugar-plums are not the same thing.

16. A child knows not that three and four are equal to seven, until he comes to be able to count seven, and has got the name and idea of equality; and then, upon explaining those words, he presently assents to, or rather perceives the truth of that proposition. But neither does he then readily assent, because it is an innate truth, nor was his assent wanting till then, because he wanted the use of reason; but the truth of it appears to him, as soon as he has settled in his mind the clear and distinct ideas that these names stand for; and then he knows the truth of that proposition, upon the same grounds, and by the same means, that he knew before, that a rod and a cherry are not the same thing; and upon the same grounds also, that he may come to know afterwards, that "it is impossible for the same thing to be, and not to be," as shall be more fully shown hereafter; so that the later it is before any one comes to have those general ideas about which those maxims are; or to know the signification of those general terms that stand for them; or to put together in his mind the ideas they stand for; the later also will it be before he comes to assent to those maxims, whose terms, with the ideas they stand for, being no more innate than those of a cat or a weasel, he must stay till time and observation have acquainted him with them; and then he will be in a capacity to know the truth of these maxims, upon the first occasion that shall make him put together those ideas in his mind, and observe whether they agree or disagree, according as is expressed in those propositions. And therefore it is, that a man knows that eighteen and nineteen are equal to thirty-seven, by the same self-evidence that he knows one and two to be equal to three; yet a child knows this not so soon as the other, not for want of the use of reason; but because the ideas the words eighteen, nineteen, and thirty-seven stand for, are not so soon got, as those which are signified by one, two, and three.

17. *Assenting, as soon as proposed and understood, proves them not innate.*—This evasion, therefore, of general assent when men come to the use of reason, failing as it does, and leaving no difference between those supposed innate, and other truths, that are afterwards acquired and learned, men have endeavoured to secure an universal assent to those they call maxims, by saying, they are generally assented to as soon as proposed, and the terms they are proposed in understood: seeing all men, even children, as soon as they hear and understand the terms, assent to these propositions, they think it is sufficient to prove them innate. For since men never fail, after they have once understood the words, to acknowledge them for undoubted truths, they would infer that certainly these propositions were first lodged in the understanding, which, without any teaching, the mind, at the very first proposal, immediately closes with and assents to, and after that never doubts again.

18. *If such as assent be a mark of innate, then, "that one and two are equal to three,—that sweetness is not bitterness," and a thousand the like, must be innate.*—In answer to this,

I demand whether "ready assent given to a proposition upon first hearing and understanding the terms, be a certain mark of an innate principle?" If it be not, such a general assent is in vain urged as a proof of them. If it be said that it is a mark of innate, they must then allow all such' propositions to be innate which are generally assented to as soon as heard, whereby they will find themselves plentifully stored with innate principles. For upon the same ground, viz. of assent at first hearing and understanding the terms, that men would have those maxims pass for innate, they must also admit several propositions about numbers to be innate; and thus, that one and two are equal to three, that two and two are equal to four, and a multitude of other the like propositions in numbers, that every body assents to at first hearing and understanding the terms, must have a place amongst these innate axioms. Nor is this the prerogative of numbers alone, and propositions made about several of them; but even natural philosophy, and all the other sciences, afford propositions which are sure to meet with assent as soon as they are understood. That two bodies cannot be in the same place, is a truth that nobody any more sticks at than at these maxims: "That it is impossible for the same thing to be, and not to be; that white is not black; that a square is not a circle, and that bitterness is not sweetness;" these, and a million of such other propositions, as many, at least, as we have distinct ideas of, every man in his wits, at first hearing and knowing what the names stand for, must necessarily assent to. If these men will be true to their own rule, and have assent at first hearing and understanding the terms to be a mark of innate, they must allow not only as many innate propositions as men have distinct ideas, but as many as men can make propositions wherein different ideas are denied one of another. Since every proposition wherein one different idea is denied of another will as certainly find assent at first hearing and understanding the terms, as this general one, " it is impossible for the same thing to be, and not to be," or that which is the foundation of it, and is the easier understood of the two, " the same is not different;" by which account they will have legions of innate propositions of this one sort, without mentioning any other. But since no proposition can be innate, unless the ideas about which it is, be innate, this will be to suppose all our ideas of colours, sounds, tastes, figure, &c., innate; than which there cannot be any thing more opposite to reason and experience. Universal and ready assent upon hearing and understanding the terms, is, I grant, a mark of self-evidence; but self-evidence depending not on innate impressions, but on something else, (as we shall show hereafter,) belongs to several propositions which nobody was yet so extravagant as to pretend to be innate.

19. *Such less general propositions known before these universal maxims.*—Nor let it be said, that those more particular self-evident propositions, which are assented to at first hearing, as, that one and two are equal to three, that green is not red, &c., are received as the consequences of those more universal propositions, which are looked on as innate principles; since any one, who will but take the pains to observe what passes in the understanding, will certainly find that these, and the like less general propositions, are certainly known, and firmly assented to, by those who are utterly ignorant of those more general maxims; and so, being earlier in the mind than those (as they are called) first principles, cannot owe to them the assent wherewith they are received at first hearing.

20. *One and one equal to two, &c., not general nor useful, answered.*—If it be said, that "these propositions, viz. two and two are equal to four, red is not blue, &c., are not general maxims, nor of any great use;" I answer, that makes nothing to the argument of universal assent, upon hearing and understanding. For if that be the certain mark of innate, whatever proposition can be found that receives general assent as soon as heard and understood, that must be admitted for an innate proposition, as well as this maxim, "that it is impossible for the same thing to be, and not to be," they being upon this ground equal. And as to the difference of being more general, that makes this maxim more remote from being innate; those general and abstract ideas being more strangers to our first apprehensions, than those of more particular self-evident propositions; and, therefore, it is longer before they are admitted and assented to by the growing understanding. And as to the usefulness of these magnified maxims, that perhaps will not be found so great as is generally conceived, when it comes in its due place to be more fully considered.

(continued)

An Essay Concerning Human Understanding: Book I, Chapter II   (*continued*)

21. *These maxims not being known sometimes until proposed, proves them not innate.*—But we have not yet done with assenting to propositions at first hearing and understanding their terms: it is fit we first take notice that this, instead of being a mark that they are innate, is a proof of the contrary, since it supposes that several who understand and know other things, are ignorant of these principles, until they are proposed to them; and that one may be unacquainted with these truths, until he hears them from others. For if they were innate, what need they be proposed, in order to gain assent; when, by being in the understanding, by a natural and original impression, (if there were any such,) they could not but be known before? Or, doth the proposing them print them clearer in the mind than nature did? If so, then the consequence will be that a man knows them better after he has been thus taught them than he did before. Whence it will follow that these principles may be made more evident to us by others' teaching, than nature has made them by impression; which will ill agree with the opinion of innate principles, and give but little authority to them; but, on the contrary, makes them unfit to be the foundations of all our other knowledge, as they are pretended to be. This cannot be denied, that men grow first acquainted with many of these self-evident truths, upon their being proposed; but it is clear that whosoever does so, finds in himself that he then begins to know a proposition which he knew not before; and which from thenceforth he never questions; not because it was innate, but because the consideration of the nature of the things contained in those words, would not suffer him to think otherwise, how, or whensoever, he is brought to reflect on them. And if whatever is assented to at first hearing and understanding the terms, must pass for an innate principle, every well-grounded observation, drawn from particulars into a general rule, must be innate. When yet it is certain, that not all, but only sagacious heads, light at first on these observations, and reduce them into general propositions, not innate, but collected from a preceding acquaintance and reflection on particular instances. These, when observing men have made them, unobserving men, when they are proposed to them, cannot refuse their assent to.

22. *Implicitly known before proposing, signifies that the mind is capable of understanding them, or else signifies nothing.*—If it be said, "the understanding hath an implicit knowledge of these principles, but not an explicit, before this first hearing," (as they must, who will say, "that they are in the understanding before they are known,") it will be hard to conceive what is meant by a principle imprinted on the understanding implicitly; unless it be this, that the mind is capable of understanding and assenting firmly to such propositions. And thus all mathematical demonstrations, as well as first principles, must be received as native impressions on the mind; which, I fear, they will scarce allow them to be, who find it harder to demonstrate a proposition, than assent to it when demonstrated. And few mathematicians will be forward to believe that all the diagrams they have drawn were but copies of those innate characters which nature had engraven upon their minds.

23. *The argument of assenting on first hearing, is upon a false supposition of no precedent teaching.*—There is, I fear, this further weakness in the foregoing argument, which would persuade us, that, therefore those maxims are to be thought innate, which men admit at first hearing, because they assent to propositions which they are not taught, nor do receive from the force of any argument or demonstration, but a bare explication or understanding of the terms. Under which, there seems to me to lie this fallacy: that men are supposed not to be taught nor to learn any thing *de novo;* when, in truth, they are taught and do learn something they were ignorant of before. For, *first,* it is evident that they have learned the terms and their signification; neither of which was born with them. But this is not all the acquired knowledge in the case; the ideas themselves, about which the proposition is, are not born with them, no more than their names, but got afterwards. So that in all propositions that are assented to at first hearing, the terms of the proposition, their standing for such ideas, and the ideas themselves that they stand for, being neither of them innate, I would fain know what there is remaining in such propositions that is innate. For I would gladly have any one name that proposition whose terms or ideas were either of them innate. We, by degrees, get ideas and names, and learn their appropriated connexion one with another; and then to propositions made in such terms, whose signification we have learned, and wherein the agreement or

disagreement we can perceive in our ideas, when put together, is expressed, we at first hearing assent; though to other propositions, in themselves as certain and evident, but which are concerning ideas not so soon or so easily got, we are at the same time no way capable of assenting. For though a child quickly assents to this proposition, "that an apple is not fire," when, by familiar acquaintance, he has got the ideas of those two different things distinctly imprinted on his mind, and has learned that the names apple and fire stand for them, yet it will be some years after, perhaps, before the same child will assent to this proposition, "that it is impossible for the same thing to be and not to be;" because, that though, perhaps, the words are as easy to be learned, yet the signification of them being more large, comprehensive, and abstract, than of the names annexed to those sensible things the child hath to do with, it is longer before he learns their precise meaning, and it requires more time plainly to form in his mind those general ideas they stand for. Until that be done, you will in vain endeavour to make any child assent to a proposition made up of such general terms; but as soon as ever he has got those ideas, and learned their names, he forwardly closes with the one as well as the other, of the fore-mentioned propositions, and with both for the same reason, viz.: because he finds the ideas he has in his mind to agree or disagree, according as the words standing for them are affirmed or denied one of another in the proposition. But if propositions be brought to him in words, which stand for ideas he has not yet in his mind, to such propositions, however evidently true or false in themselves, he affords neither assent nor dissent, but is ignorant. For words being but empty sounds, any farther than they are signs of our ideas, we cannot but assent to them as they correspond to those ideas we have, but no farther than that. But the showing by what steps and ways knowledge comes into our minds, and the grounds of several degrees of assent, being the business of the following discourse, it may suffice to have only touched on it here, as one reason that made me doubt of those innate principles.

24. *Not innate, because not universally assented to.*—To conclude this argument of universal consent, I agree with these defenders of innate principles, that if they are innate, they must needs have universal assent. For that a truth should be innate, and yet not assented to, is to me as unintelligible, as for a man to know a truth and be ignorant of it at the same time. But then, by these men's own confession, they cannot be innate; since they are not assented to by those who understand not the terms, nor by a great part of those who do understand them, but have yet never heard nor thought of those propositions, which, I think, is at least one half of mankind. But were the number far less, it would be enough to destroy universal assent, and thereby show these propositions not to be innate, if children alone were ignorant of them.

Critique of Pure Reason
Immanuel Kant

Introduction

I. —OF THE DIFFERENCE BETWEEN PURE AND EMPIRICAL KNOWLEDGE

That all our knowledge begins with experience there can be no doubt. For how is it possible that the faculty of cognition should be awakened into exercise otherwise than by means of objects which affect our senses, and partly of themselves produce representations, partly rouse our powers of understanding into activity, to compare, to connect, or to separate these, and so to convert the raw material of our sensuous impressions into a knowledge of objects, which is called experience? In respect of time, therefore, no knowledge of ours is antecedent to experience, but begins with it.

But, though all our knowledge begins with experience, it by no means follows that all arises out of experience. For, on the contrary, it is quite possible that our empirical knowledge

(continued)

Critique of Pure Reason (*continued*)

is a compound of that which we receive through impressions, and that which the faculty of cognition supplies from itself (sensuous impressions giving merely the *occasion*), an addition which we cannot distinguish from the original element given by sense, till long practice has made us attentive to, and skilful in separating it. It is, therefore, a question which requires close investigation, and is not to be answered at first sight—whether there exists a knowledge altogether independent of experience, and even of all sensuous impressions? Knowledge of this kind is called *à priori,* in contradistinction to empirical knowledge, which has its sources *à posteriori,* that is, in experience.

But the expression, "*à priori,*" is not as yet definite enough adequately to indicate the whole meaning of the question above started. For, in speaking of knowledge which has its sources in experience, we are wont to say, that this or that may be known *à priori,* because we do not derive this knowledge immediately from experience, but from a general rule, which, however, we have itself borrowed from experience. Thus, if a man undermined his house, we say, "he might know *à priori* that it would have fallen"; that is, he needed not to have waited for the experience that it did actually fall. But still, *à priori,* he could not know even this much. For, that bodies are heavy, and, consequently, that they fall when their supports are taken away, must have been known to him previously, by means of experience.

By the term "knowledge *à priori,*" therefore, we shall in the sequel understand, not such as is independent of this or that kind of experience, but such as is absolutely so of *all* experience. Opposed to this is empirical knowledge, or that which is possible only *à posteriori,* that is, through experience. Knowledge *à priori* is either pure or impure. Pure knowledge *à priori* is that with which no empirical element is mixed up. For example, the proposition, "Every change has a cause," is a proposition *à priori,* but impure, because change is a conception which can only be derived from experience.

II. —The Human Intellect, Even in an Unphilosophical State, is in Possession of Certain Cognitions À Priori

The question now is as to a *criterion,* by which we may securely distinguish a pure from an empirical cognition. Experience no doubt teaches us that this or that object is constituted in such and such a manner, but not that it could not possibly exist otherwise. Now, in the first place, if we have a proposition which contains the idea of necessity in its very conception, it is a judgment *à priori;* if, moreover, it is not derived from any other proposition, unless from one equally involving the idea of necessity, it is absolutely *à priori.* Secondly, an empirical judgment never exhibits strict and absolute, but only assumed and comparative universality (by induction); therefore, the most we can say is—so far as we have hitherto observed, there is no exception to this or that rule. If, on the other hand, a judgment carries with it strict and absolute universality, that is, admits of no possible exception, it is not derived from experience, but is valid absolutely *à priori.*

Empirical universality is, therefore, only an arbitrary extension of validity, from that which may be predicated of a proposition valid in most cases, to that which is asserted of a proposition which holds good in all; as, for example, in the affirmation, "all bodies are heavy." When, on the contrary, strict universality characterizes a judgment, it necessarily indicates another peculiar source of knowledge, namely, a faculty of cognition *à priori.* Necessity and strict universality, therefore, are infallible tests for distinguishing pure from empirical knowledge, and are inseparably connected with each other. But as in the use of these criteria the empirical limitation is sometimes more easily detected than the contingency of the judgment, or the unlimited universality which we attach to a judgment is often a more convincing proof than its necessity, it may be advisable to use the criteria separately, each being by itself infallible.

Now, that in the sphere of human cognition, we have judgments which are necessary, and in the strictest sense universal, consequently pure *à priori,* it will be an easy matter to snow. If we desire an example from the sciences, we need only take any proposition in mathematics. If we cast our eyes upon the commonest operations of the understanding, the proposition, "every change must have a cause," will amply serve our purpose. In the latter case, indeed, the conception of a cause so plainly involves the conception of a necessity of connection with an effect, and of a strict universality of the law, that the very notion of a cause would entirely disappear, were we to derive it, like Hume, from a frequent association of what happens with that which precedes, and the habit thence originating of connecting representations—the necessity inherent in the judgment being therefore merely subjective. Besides, without seeking for such examples of principles existing *à priori* in cognition, we might easily show that such principles are the indispensable basis of the possibility of experience itself, and consequently prove their existence *à priori*. For whence could our experience itself acquire certainty, if all the rules on which it depends were themselves empirical, and consequently fortuitous? No one, therefore, can admit the validity of the use of such rules as first principles. But, for the present, we may content ourselves with having established the fact, that we do possess and exercise a faculty of pure *à priori* cognition; and, secondly, with having pointed out the proper tests of such cognition, namely, universality and necessity.

Not only in judgments, however, but even in conceptions, is an *à priori* origin manifest. For example, if we take away by degrees from our conceptions of a body all that can be referred to mere sensuous experience—color, hardness or softness, weight, even impenetrability—the body will then vanish; but the space which it occupied still remains, and this it is utterly impossible to annihilate in thought. Again, if we take away, in like manner, from our empirical conception of any object, corporeal or incorporeal, all properties which mere experience has taught us to connect with it, still we cannot think away those through which we cogitate it as substance, or adhering to substance, although our conception of substance is more determined than that of an object. Compelled, therefore, by that necessity with which the conception of substance forces itself upon us, we must confess that it has its seat in our faculty of cognition *à priori*.

III. —Philosophy Stands in Need of a Science which Shall Determine the Possibility, Principles, and Extent of Human Knowledge *À Priori*

Of far more importance than all that has been above said, is the consideration that certain of our cognitions rise completely above the sphere of all possible experience, and by means of conceptions, to which there exists in the whole extent of experience no corresponding object, seem to extend the range of our judgments beyond its bounds. And just in this transcendental or supersensible sphere, where experience affords us neither instruction nor guidance, lie the investigations of *Reason,* which, on account of their importance, we consider far preferable to, and as having a far more elevated aim than, all that the understanding can achieve within the sphere of sensuous phenomena. So high a value do we set upon these investigations, that even at the risk of error, we persist in following them out, and permit neither doubt nor disregard nor indifference to restrain us from the pursuit. These unavoidable problems of mere pure reason are God, Freedom (of will) and Immortality. The science which, with all its preliminaries, has for its especial object the solution of these problems is named metaphysics—a science which is at the very outset dogmatical, that is, it confidently takes upon itself the execution of this task without any previous investigation of the ability or inability of reason for such an understanding.

Now the safe ground of experience being thus abandoned, it seems nevertheless natural that we should hesitate to erect a building with the cognitions we possess, without knowing whence they come, and on the strength of principles, the origin of which is undiscovered. Instead of thus trying to build without a foundation, it is rather to be expected that we should long ago have put the question, how the understanding can arrive at these *à priori* cognitions, and what is the extent, validity, and worth which they may possess? We say, this is natural enough, meaning by the word natural that which is consistent with a just and reasonable way of thinking; but if we understand by the term, that which usually happens, nothing indeed could be more natural and more comprehensible than that this investigation should be left long unattempted. For one part of our pure knowledge, the science of mathematics, has been long firmly established, and thus leads us to form flattering expectations with regard to others, though these may be of quite a different nature. Besides, when we get beyond the bounds of experience, we are of course safe from opposition in that quarter; and the charm of

(continued)

Critique of Pure Reason (*continued*)

widening the range of our knowledge is so great, that unless we are brought to a standstill by some evident contradiction, we hurry on undoubtingly in our course. This, however, may be avoided, if we are sufficiently cautious in the construction of our fictions, which are not the less fictions on that account.

Mathematical science affords us a brilliant example, how far, independently of all experience, we may carry our *à priori* knowledge. It is true that the mathematician occupies himself with objects and cognitions only in so far as they can be represented by means of intuition. But this circumstance is easily overlooked, because the said intuition can itself be given *à priori,* and therefore is hardly to be distinguished from a mere pure conception. Deceived by such a proof of the power of reason, we can perceive no limits to the extension of our knowledge. The light dove cleaving in free flight the thin air, whose resistance it feels, might imagine that her movements would be far more free and rapid in airless space. Just in the same way did Plato, abandoning the world of sense because of the narrow limits it sets to the understanding, venture upon the wings of ideas beyond it, into the void space of pure intellect. He did not reflect that he made no real progress by all his efforts; for he met with no resistance which might serve him for a support, as it were, whereon to rest, and on which he might apply his powers, in order to let the intellect acquire momentum for its progress. It is, indeed, the common fate of human reason in speculation, to finish the imposing edifice of thought as rapidly as possible, and then for the first time to begin to examine whether the foundation is a solid one or no. Arrived at this point, all sorts of excuses are sought after, in order to console us for its want of stability, or rather indeed, to enable us to dispense altogether with so late and dangerous an investigation. But what frees us during the process of building from all apprehension or suspicion, and flatters us into the belief of its solidity, is this. A great part, perhaps the greatest part, of the business of our reason consists in the analyzation of the conceptions which we already possess of objects. By this means we gain a multitude of cognitions, which, although really nothing more than elucidations or explanations of that which (though in a confused manner) was already thought in our conceptions, are, at least in respect of their form, prized as new introspections; while, so far as regards their matter or content, we have really made no addition to our conceptions, but only disinvolved them. But as this process does furnish real *à priori* knowledge, which has a sure progress and useful results, reason, deceived by this, slips in, without being itself aware of it, assertions of a quite different kind; in which, to given conceptions it adds others, *à priori* indeed, but entirely foreign to them, without our knowing how it arrives at these, and, indeed, without such a question ever suggesting itself. I shall therefore at once proceed to examine the difference between these two modes of knowledge.

IV. —OF THE DIFFERENCE BETWEEN ANALYTICAL AND SYNTHETICAL JUDGMENTS

In all judgments wherein the relation of a subject to the predicate is cogitated (I mention affirmative judgments only here; the application to negative will be very easy), this relation is possible in two different ways. Either the predicate B belongs to the subject A, as somewhat which is contained (though covertly) in the conception A; or the predicate B lies completely out of the conception A, although it stands in connection with it. In the first instance, I term the judgment analytical, in the second, synthetical. Analytical judgments (affirmative) are therefore those in which the connection of the predicate with the subject is cogitated through identity; those in which this connection is cogitated without identity, are called synthetical judgments. The former may be called *explicative,* the latter *augmentative*[1] judgments; because the former add in the predicate nothing to the conception of the subject, but only analyze it into its constituent conceptions, which were thought already in the subject, although in a confused manner; the latter add to our conceptions of the subject a predicate which was not contained in it, and which no analysis could ever have discovered therein. For example, when I say, "all bodies are extended," this is an analytical judgment. For I need not go beyond the conception of *body* in order to find extension connected with it, but merely analyze the conception, that is, become conscious of the manifold properties which I think in that conception, in order to discover this predicate in it: it is therefore an analytical judgment. On the other hand, when I say, "all bodies are heavy," the predicate is something totally different from that which I think in the mere conception of a body. But the addition of such a predicate therefore, it becomes a synthetical judgment.

Judgments of experience, as such, are always synthetical. For it would be absurd to think of grounding an analytical judgment on experience, because in forming such a judgment, I need not go out of the sphere of my conceptions, and therefore recourse to the testimony of experience is quite unnecessary. That "bodies are extended" is not an empirical judgment, but a proposition which stands firm *à priori*. For before addressing myself to experience, I already have in my conception all the requisite conditions for the judgment, and I have only to extract the predicate from the conception, according to the principle of contradiction, and thereby at the same time become conscious of the necessity of the judgment, a necessity which I could never learn from experience. On the other hand, though at first I do not at all include the predicate of weight in my conception of body in general, that conception still indicates an object of experience, a part of the totality of experience, to which I can still add other parts; and this I do when I recognize by observation that bodies are heavy. I can cognize beforehand by analysis the conception of body through the characteristics of extension, impenetrability, shape, etc., all which are cogitated in this conception. But now I extend my knowledge, and looking back on experience from which I had derived this conception of body, I find weight at all times connected with the above characteristics, and therefore I synthetically add to my conceptions this as a predicate, and say, "all bodies are heavy." Thus it is experience upon which rests the possibility of the synthesis of the predicate of weight with the conception of body, because both conceptions, although the one is not contained in the other, still belong to one another (only contingently, however), as parts of a whole, namely, of experience, which is itself a synthesis of intuitions.

But to synthetical judgments *à priori,* such aid is entirely wanting. If I go out of and beyond the conception A, in order to recognize another B as connected with it, what foundation have I to rest on, whereby to render the synthesis possible? I have here no longer the advantage of looking out in the sphere of experience for what I want. Let us take, for example, the proposition, "everything that happens has a cause." In the conception of *something that happens,* I indeed think an existence which a certain time antecedes, and from this I can derive analytical judgments. But the conception of a cause lies quite out of the above conception, and indicates something entirely different from "that which happens," and is consequently not contained in that conception. How then am I able to assert concerning the general conception—"that which happens"—something entirely different from that conception, and to recognize the conception of cause although not contained in it, yet as belonging to it, and even necessarily? what is here the unknown = X, upon which the understanding rests when it believes it has found, out of the conception A a foreign predicate B, which it nevertheless considers to be connected with it? It cannot be experience, because the principle adduced annexes the two representations, cause and effect, to the representation existence, not only with universality, which experience cannot give, but also with the expression of necessity, therefore completely *à priori* and from pure conceptions. Upon such synthetical, that is augmentative propositions, depends the whole aim of our speculative knowledge *à priori;* for although analytical judgments are indeed highly important and necessary, they are so, only to arrive at that clearness of conceptions which is requisite for a sure and extended synthesis, and this alone is a real acquisition.

V. In all Theoretical Sciences of Reason, Synthetical Judgments *À Priori* are Contained as Principles

I. Mathematical judgments are always synthetical. Hitherto this fact, though incontestably true and very important in its consequences, seems to have escaped the analysts of the human mind, nay, to be in complete opposition to all their conjectures. For as it was found that mathematical conclusions all proceed according to the principle of contradiction (which the nature of every apodictic certainty requires), people became persuaded that the fundamental principles of the science also were recognized and admitted in the same way. But the notion is fallacious; for although a synthetical proposition can certainly be discerned by means of the

(continued)

Critique of Pure Reason   (*continued*)

principle of contradiction, this is possible only when another synthetical proposition precedes, from which the latter is deduced, but never of itself.

Before all, be it observed, that proper mathematical propositions are always judgments *à priori*, and not empirical, because they carry along with them the conception of necessity, which cannot be given by experience. If this be demurred to, it matters not; I will then limit my assertion to *pure* mathematics, the very conception of which implies, that it consists of knowledge altogether non-empirical and *à priori*.

We might, indeed, at first suppose that the proposition $7 + 5 = 12$, is a merely analytical proposition, following (according to the principle of contradiction), from the conception of the sum of seven and five. But if we regard it more narrowly, we find that our conception of the sum of seven and five contains nothing more than the uniting of both sums into one, whereby it cannot at all be cogitated what this single number is which embraces both. The conception of twelve is by no means obtained by merely cogitating the union of seven and five; and we may analyze our conception of such a possible sum as long as we will, still we shall never discover in it the notion of twelve. We must go beyond these conceptions, and have recourse to an intuition which corresponds to one of the two—our five fingers, for example, or like Segner in his "Arithmetic," five points, and so by degrees, add the units contained in the five given in the intuition, to the conception of seven. For I first take the number 7, and, for the conception of 5 calling in the aid of the fingers of my hand as objects of intuition, I add the units, which I before took together to make up the number 5, gradually now by means of the material image my hand, to the number 7, and by this process, I at length see the number 12 arise. That 7 should be added to 5, I have certainly cogitated in my conception of a sum $= 7 + 5$, but not that this sum was equal to 12. Arithmetical propositions are therefore always synthetical, of which we may become more clearly convinced by trying large numbers. For it will thus become quite evident, that, turn and twist our conceptions as we may, it is impossible, without having recourse to intuition, to arrive at the sum total or product by means of the mere analysis of our conceptions. Just as little is any principle of pure geometry analytical. "A straight line between two points is the shortest," is a synthetical proposition. For my conception of *straight*, contains no notion of *quantity*, but is merely *qualitative*. The conception of the *shortest* is therefore wholly an addition, and by no analysis can it be extracted from our conception of a straight line. Intuition must therefore here lend its aid, by means of which and thus only, our synthesis is possible.

Some few principles preposited by geometricians are, indeed, really analytical, and depend on the principle of contradiction. They serve, however, like identical propositions, as links in the chain of method, not as principles—for example, $a = a$, the whole is equal to itself, or $(a + b) > a$, the whole is greater than its part. And yet even these principles themselves, though they derive their validity from pure conceptions, are only admitted in mathematics because they can be presented in intuition. What causes us here commonly to believe that the predicate of such apodictic judgments is already contained in our conception, and that the judgment is therefore analytical, is merely the equivocal nature of the expression. We must join in thought a certain predicate to a given conception, and this necessity cleaves already to the conception. But the question is, not what we must join in thought to the given conception, but what we really think therein, though only obscurely, and then it becomes manifest, that the predicate pertains to these conceptions, necessarily indeed, yet not as thought in the conception itself, but by virtue of an intuition, which must be added to the conception.

2. The science of Natural Philosophy (Physics) contains in itself synthetical judgments *à priori*, as principles. I shall adduce two propositions. For instance, the proposition, "in all changes of the material world, the quantity of matter remains unchanged"; or, that, "in all communication of motion, action and reaction must always be equal." In both of these, not only is the necessity, and therefore their origin, *à priori* clear, but also that they are synthetical propositions. For in the conception of matter, I do not cogitate its permanency, but merely its presence in space, which it fills. I therefore really go out of and beyond the conception of matter, in order to think on to it something *à priori*, which I did not think in it. The proposition is therefore not analytical, but synthetical, and nevertheless conceived *à priori*; and so it is with regard to the other propositions of the pure part of natural philosophy.

3. As to Metaphysics, even if we look upon it merely as an attempted science, yet, from the nature of human reason, an indispensable one, we find that it must contain synthetical propositions *à priori*. It is not merely the duty of metaphysics to dissect, and thereby analytically to illustrate the conceptions which we form *à priori* of things; but we seek to widen the range of our *à priori* knowledge. For this purpose, we must avail ourselves of such principles as add something to the original conception—something not identical with, nor contained in it, and by means of synthetical judgments *à priori*, leave far behind us the limits of experience; for example, in the proposition, "the world must have a beginning," and such like. Thus metaphysics, according to the proper aim of the science, consists merely of synthetical propositions *à priori*.

VI. —The Universal Problem of Pure Reason

It is extremely advantageous to be able to bring a number of investigations under the formula of a single problem. For in this manner, we not only facilitate our own labor, inasmuch as we define it clearly to ourselves, but also render it more easy for others to decide whether we have done justice to our undertaking. The proper problem of pure reason, then, is contained in the question, "How are synthetical judgments *à priori* possible?"

That metaphysical science has hitherto remained in so vacillating a state of uncertainty and contradiction, is only to be attributed to the fact that this great problem, and perhaps even the difference between analytical and synthetical judgments, did not sooner suggest itself to philosophers. Upon the solution of this problem, or upon sufficient proof of the impossibility of synthetical knowledge *à priori*, depends the existence or downfall of the science of metaphysics. Among philosophers, David Hume came the nearest of all to this problem; yet it never acquired in his mind sufficient precision, nor did he regard the question in its universality. On the contrary, he stopped short at the synthetical proposition of the connection of an effect with its cause *(principium causalitatis)*, insisting that such proposition *à priori* was impossible. According to his conclusions, then, all that we term metaphysical science is a mere delusion, arising from the fancied insight of reason into that which is in truth borrowed from experience, and to which habit has given the appearance of necessity. Against this assertion, destructive to all pure philosophy, he would have been guarded, had he had our problem before his eyes in its universality. For he would then have perceived that, according to his own argument, there likewise could not be any pure mathematical science, which assuredly cannot exist without synthetical propositions *à priori*—an absurdity from which his good understanding must have saved him.

In the solution of the above problem is at the same time comprehended the possibility of the use of pure reason in the foundation and construction of all sciences which contain theoretical knowledge *à priori* of objects, that is to say, the answer to the following questions:

How is pure mathematical science possible?

How is pure natural science possible?

Respecting these sciences, as they do certainly exist, it may with propriety be asked, *how* they are possible?—for that they must be possible, is shown by the fact of their really existing.[2] But as to metaphysics, the miserable progress it has hitherto made, and the fact that of no one system yet brought forward, as far as regard its true aim, can it be said that this science really exists, leaves anyone at liberty to doubt with reason the very possibility of its existence.

Yet, in a certain sense, this kind of knowledge must unquestionably be looked upon as *given;* in other words, metaphysics must be considered as really existing, if not as a science, nevertheless as a natural disposition of the human mind (*metaphysica naturalis*). For human reason, without any instigations imputable to the mere vanity of great knowledge, unceasingly progresses, urged on by its own feeling of need, towards such questions as cannot be answered by any empirical application of reason, or principles derived therefrom; and so there has ever really existed in every man some system of metaphysics. It will always exist, so soon as reason awakes to the exercise of its power of speculation. And now the question arises—How is metaphysics, as a natural disposition, possible? In other words, how, from the nature of universal human reason, do those questions arise which pure reason proposes to itself, and which it is impelled by its own feeling of need to answer as well as it can?

(continued)

Critique of Pure Reason (*continued*)

But as in all the attempts hitherto made to answer the questions which reason is prompted by its very nature to propose to itself, for example, whether the world had a beginning, or has existed from eternity, it has always met with unavoidable contradictions, we must not rest satisfied with the mere natural disposition of the mind to metaphysics, that is, with the existence of the faculty of pure reason, whence, indeed, some sort of metaphysical system always arises; but it must be possible to arrive at certainty in regard to the question whether we know or do not know the things of which metaphysics treats. We must be able to arrive at a decision on the subjects of its questions, or on the ability or inability of reason to form any judgment respecting them; and therefore either to extend with confidence the bounds of our pure reason, or to set strictly defined and safe limits to its action. This last question, which arises out of the above universal problem, would properly run thus: How is metaphysics possible as a science?

Thus, the critique of reason leads at last, naturally and necessarily, to science; and, on the other hand, the dogmatical use of reason without criticism leads to groundless assertions, against which others equally specious can always be set, thus ending unavoidably in scepticism.

Besides, this science, cannot be of great and formidable prolixity, because it has not to do with objects of reason, the variety of which is inexhaustible, but merely with reason herself and her problems; problems which arise out of her own bosom, and are not proposed to her by the nature of outward things, but by her own nature. And when once reason has previously become able completely to understand her own power in regard to objects which she meets with in experience, it will be easy to determine securely the extent and limits of her attempted application to objects beyond the confines of experience.

We may and must, therefore, regard the attempts hitherto made to establish metaphysical science dogmatically as nonexistent. For what of analysis, that is, mere dissection of conceptions, is contained in one or other, is not the aim of, but only a preparation for metaphysics proper, which has for its object the extension, by means of synthesis, of our *à priori* knowledge. And for this purpose, mere analysis is of course useless, because it only shows what is contained in these conceptions, but not how we arrive, *à priori,* at them; and this it is her duty to show, in order to be able afterwards to determine their valid use in regard to all objects of experience, to all knowledge in general. But little self-denial, indeed, is needed to give up these pretensions, seeing the undeniable, and in the dogmatic mode of procedure, inevitable contradictions of Reason with herself, have long since ruined the reputation of every system of metaphysics that has appeared up to this time. It will require more firmness to remain undeterred by difficulty from within, and opposition from without, from endeavoring, by a method quite opposed to all those hitherto followed, to further the growth and fruitfulness of a science indispensable to human reason—a science from which every branch it has borne may be cut away, but whose roots remain indestructible.

VII. IDEA AND DIVISION OF A PARTICULAR SCIENCE, UNDER THE NAME OF A CRITIQUE OF PURE REASON

From all that has been said, there results the idea of a particular science, which may be called the *Critique of Pure Reason*. For reason is the faculty which furnishes us with the principles of knowledge *à priori*. Hence, pure reason is the faculty which contains the principles of cognizing anything absolutely *à priori*. An Organon of pure reason would be a compendium of those principles according to which alone all pure cognitions *à priori* can be obtained. The completely extended application of such an organon would afford us a system of pure reason. As this, however, is demanding a great deal, and it is yet doubtful whether any extension of our knowledge be here possible, or if so, in what cases; we can regard a science of the mere criticism of pure reason, its sources and limits, as the *propædeutic* to a system of pure reason. Such a science must not be called a Doctrine, but only a Critique of pure Reason; and its use, in regard to speculation, would be only negative, not to enlarge the bounds of, but to purify our reason, and to shield it against error—which alone is no little gain. I apply the term *transcendental* to all knowledge which is not so much occupied with objects as with the mode of our cognition of these objects, so far as this mode of cognition is possible *à priori*. A system of such conceptions would be called *Transcendental Philosophy*. But this, again, is still beyond the bounds of our present essay. For as such a science must contain a complete exposition not only of our synthetical *à priori*, but of our analytical *à priori* knowledge, it is of too wide a range for our present purpose, because we do not require to carry our analysis any farther than is necessary to understand, in their full extent, the principles of synthesis *à priori*, with which alone we have to do. This investigation, which we cannot properly call a doctrine, but only a transcendental critique, because it aims not at the enlargement, but at the correction and guidance of our knowledge, and is to serve as a touchstone of the worth or worthlessness of all knowledge *à priori*, is the sole object of our present essay. Such a critique is consequently, as far as possible, a preparation for an organon; and if this new organon should be found to fail, at least for a canon of pure reason, according to which the complete system of the philosophy of pure reason, whether it extend or limit the bounds of that reason, might one day be set forth both analytically and synthetically. For that this is possible, nay, that such a system is not of so great extent as to preclude the hope of its ever being completed, is evident. For we have not here to do with the nature of outward objects, which is infinite, but solely with the mind, which judges of the nature of objects, and, again, with the mind only in respect of its cognition *à priori*. And the object of our investigations, as it is not to be sought without, but altogether within ourselves, cannot remain concealed, and in all probability is limited enough to be completely surveyed and fairly estimated, according to its worth or worth-lessness. Still less let the reader here expect a critique of books and systems of pure reason; our present object is exclusively a critique of the faculty of pure reason itself. Only when we make this critique our foundation, do we possess a pure touchstone for estimating the philosophical value of ancient and modern writings on this subject; and without this criterion, the incompetent historian or judge decides upon and corrects the groundless assertions of others with his own, which have themselves just as little foundation.

Transcendental philosophy is the idea of a science, for which the Critique of Pure Reason must sketch the whole plan architectonically, that is, from principles, with a full guarantee for the validity and stability of all the parts which enter into the building. It is the system of all the principles of pure reason. If this Critique itself does not assume the title of transcendental philosophy, it is only because, to be a complete system, it ought to contain a full analysis of all human knowledge *à priori*. Our critique must, indeed, lay before us a complete enumeration of all the radical conceptions which constitute the said pure knowledge. But from the complete analysis of these conceptions themselves, as also from a complete investigation of those derived from them, it abstains with reason; partly because it would be deviating from the end in view to occupy itself with this analysis, since this process is not attended with the difficulty and insecurity to be found in the synthesis, to which our critique is entirely devoted, and partly because it would be inconsistent with the unity of our plan to burden this essay with the vindication of the completeness of such an analysis and deduction, with which, after all, we have at present nothing to do. This completeness of the analysis of these radical conceptions, as well as of the deduction from the conceptions *à priori* which may be given by the analysis, we can, however, easily attain, provided only that we are in possession of all these radical conceptions, which are to serve as principles of the synthesis, and that in respect of this main purpose nothing is wanting.

To the Critique of Pure Reason, therefore, belongs all that constitutes transcendental philosophy; and it is the complete idea of transcendental philosophy, but still not the science itself; because it only proceeds so far with the analysis as is necessary to the power of judging completely of our synthetical knowledge *à priori*.

The principal thing we must attend to, in the division of the parts of a science like this, is: that no conceptions must enter it which contain aught empirical; in other words, that the knowledge *à priori* must be completely pure. Hence, although the highest principles and fundamental conceptions of morality are certainly cognitions *à priori*, yet they do not belong to transcendental philosophy; because, though they certainly do not lay the conceptions of pain, pleasure, desires, inclinations, etc. (which are all of empirical origin), at the foundation of its

(continued)

Critique of Pure Reason (*continued*)

precepts, yet still into the conception of duty—as an obstacle to be overcome, or as an incitement which should not be made into a motive—these empirical conceptions must necessarily enter, in the construction of a system of pure morality. Transcendental philosophy is consequently a philosophy of the pure and merely speculative reason. For all that is practical, so far as it contains motives, relates to feelings, and these belong to empirical sources of cognition.

If we wish to divide this science from the universal point of view of a science in general, it ought to comprehend, first, a *Doctrine of the Elements,* and, secondly, a *Doctrine of the Method* of pure reason. Each of these main divisions will have its subdivisions, the separate reasons for which we cannot here particularize. Only so much seems necessary, by way of introduction or premonition, that there are two sources of human knowledge (which probably spring from a common, but to us unknown root), namely, sense and understanding. By the former, objects are *given* to us; by the latter, *thought.* So far as the faculty of sense may contain representations *à priori,* which form the conditions under which objects are given, in so far it belongs to transcendental philosophy. The transcendental doctrine of sense must form the first part of our science of elements, because the conditions under which alone the objects of human knowledge are given, must precede those under which they are thought.

NOTES

1. That is, judgments which really add to, and do not merely analyze or explain the conceptions which make up the sum of our knowledge.
2. As to the existence of pure natural science, or physics, perhaps many may still express doubts. But we have only to look at the different propositions which are commonly treated of at the commencement of proper (empirical) physical science—those, for example, relating to the permanence of the same quantity of matter, the *vis inertia,* the equality of action and reaction, etc.—to be soon convinced that they form a science of pure physics (*physica pura,* or *rationalis*), which well deserves to be separately exposed as a special science, in its whole extent, whether that be great or confined.

An Argument against Skepticism
John Hospers

I. Requirements for Knowing

THE WORD "KNOW" IS SLIPPERY. It is not always used in the same way. Here are some of its principal uses:

[*Senses of "know"*] 1. Sometimes when we talk about knowing, we are referring to *acquaintance* of some kind. For example, "Do you know Richard Smith?" means approximately the same as "Are you acquainted with Richard Smith? (have you met him? etc.) . . ."

2. Sometimes we speak of knowing *how:* Do you know how to ride a horse, do you know how to use a soldering iron? We even use a colloquial noun, "know-how," in talking about this. Knowing how is an *ability*—we know how to ride a horse if we have the ability to ride a horse, and the test of whether we have the ability is whether in the appropriate situation we can perform the activity in question. . . .

3. But by far the most frequent use of the word "know"—and the one with which we shall be primarily concerned—is the *propositional* sense: "I know that . . ." where the word "that" is followed by a proposition: "I know that I am now reading a book," "I know that I am an American citizen," and so on. There is some relation between this last sense of "know" and the earlier ones. We cannot be acquainted with Smith without knowing some things about him (without knowing *that* certain propositions about him are true), and it is difficult to see how one can know *how* to swim without knowing some true propositions about swimming, concerning what you must do with your arms and legs when in the water. (But the dog knows how to swim, though presumably he knows no propositions about swimming.) . . .

[*Conditions for knowing that*] Now, what is required for us to know in this third and most important sense? Taking the letter *p* to stand for any proposition, what requirements must be met in order for one to assert truly that he knows *p*? There are, after all, many people who claim to know something when they don't; so how can one separate the rightful claims to know from the mistaken ones?

a. *p must be true.* The moment you have some reason to believe that a proposition is not true, this immediately negates a person's claim to know it: You can't know *p* if *p* isn't true. If I say, "I know *p*, but *p* is not true," my statement is self-contradictory, for part of what is involved in knowing *p* is that *p* is true. Similarly, if I say, "He knows *p*, but *p* is not true," this too is self-contradictory. It may be that I *thought* I knew *p;* but if *p* is false, I didn't really know it. I only thought I did. If I nevertheless claim to know *p,* while admitting that *p* is false, my hearers may rightly conclude that I have not yet learned how to use the word "know." This is already implicit in our previous discussion, for what is it that you know about *p* when you know *p*? You know that *p* is true, of course; the very formulation gives away the case: Knowing *p* is knowing that *p* is true . . .

But the truth-requirement, though necessary, is not sufficient. There are plenty of true propositions, for example in nuclear physics, that you and I do not know to be true unless we happen to be specialists in that area. But the fact that they are true does not imply that we know them to be true . . .

b. *Not only must p be true: We must believe that p is true.* This may be called the "subjective requirement": We must have a certain attitude toward *p*—not merely that of wondering or speculation about *p*, but positively *believing* that *p* is true. "I know that *p* is true, but I don't believe that it is" would not only be a very peculiar thing to say, it would entitle our hearers to conclude that we had not learned is what circumstances to use the word "know." There may be numerous statements that zou believe but do not know to be true, but there can be none which you know to be true but don't believe, since believing is a part (a defining characteristic) of knowing.

'I know *p*" implies "I believe *p*," and "He knows *p*." implies "He believes *p*." for believing is a defining characteristic of knowing. But believing *p* is *not* a defining characteristic of *p*'s *being true: p* can be true even though neither he nor I nor anyone else believes it (the earth was round even before anyone believed that it was.) There is no contradiction whatever in saying, "He believed *p* (that is, believed it to be true), but *p* is not true." Indeed, we say things of this kind all the time: "He believes that people are persecuting him, but of course it isn't true." . . .

We have now discussed two requirements for knowing, an "objective" one *(p* must be true) and a "subjective " one (one must believe *p*). Are these sufficient? Can you be said to know something if you believe it and if what you believe is true? If so, you can simply define knowledge as true belief, and that will be the end of the matter.

Unfortunately, however, the situation is not so simple. True belief is not yet knowledge. A proposition may be true, and you may believe it to be true, and yet you may not *know* it to be true. Suppose you believe that there are sentient beings on Mars, and suppose that in the course of time, after space-travelers from the earth have landed there, your belief turns out to be true. The statement was true at the time you uttered it, and you also believed it at the time you uttered it—but did you *know* it to be true at the time you uttered it? Certainly not, we would be inclined to say; you were not in a position to know. It was a lucky guess. Even if you had *some* evidence that it was true, you didn't *know* that it was true at the time you said it. Some further condition, therefore, is required to prevent a lucky guess from passing as knowledge . . . .

c. *You must have evidence for p (reason to believe p).* When you guessed which tosses of the coin would be heads, you had no reason to believe that your guesses would be correct, so you did not *know.* But after you watched all the tosses and carefully observed which way the coin tossed each time, then you knew. You had the evidence of your senses—as well as of people around you, and photographs if you wished to take them—that this throw was heads, that one tails, and so on. Similarly, when you predict on the basis of tonight's red sunset that tomorrow's weather will be fair, you don't yet *know* that your prediction will be borne out by the facts; you have some reason (perhaps) to believe it, but you cannot be sure. But tomorrow when you go outdoors and see for yourself what the weather is like, you do know for sure; when tomorrow comes you have the full evidence before you, which you do not yet have tonight. Tomorrow "the evidence is in"; tonight, it is not knowledge but only an "educated guess."

(continued)

An Argument against Skepticism   (*continued*)

[*Problem*] This, then, is our third requirement—evidence. But at this point our troubles begin. How much evidence must there be? "Some evidence" won't suffice as an answer: there may be *some* evidence that tomorrow will be sunny, but you don't yet know it. How about "all the evidence that is available"? But this won't do either; all the evidence that is now available may not be enough. All the evidence that is now available is far from sufficient to enable us to know whether there are conscious beings on other planets. We just don't know, even after we have examined all the evidence at our disposal.

How about "enough evidence to give *us good reason* to believe it"? But how much evidence is this? I may have known someone for years and found him to be scrupulously honest during all that time; by virtually any criterion, this would constitute good evidence that he will be honest the next time—and yet he may not be; suppose that the next time he steals someone's wallet. I had good reason to believe that he would remain honest, but nevertheless I didn't *know* that he would remain honest, for it was not true. We are all familiar with cases in which someone had good reason to believe a proposition that nevertheless turned out to be false.

What then *is* sufficient? We are now tempted to say, "Complete evidence—all the evidence there could ever be—the works, everything." But if we say this, let us notice at once that there are very few propositions whose truth we can claim to know. Most of those propositions that in daily life we claim to know without the slightest hesitation we would *not* know according to this criterion. For example, we say, "I know that if I were to let go of this pencil, it would fall," and we don't have the slightest hesitation about it; but although we may have excellent evidence (pencils and other objects have always fallen when let go), we don't have *complete* evidence, for we have not yet observed the outcome of letting go of it *this* time. To take an even more obvious case, we say, "I know that there is a book before me now," but we have not engaged in every possible observation that would be relevant to determining the truth of this statement: We have not examined the object (the one we take to be a book) from *all* angles (and since there are an infinite number of angles, who could?), and even if we have looked at it steadily for half an hour, we have not done so for a hundred hours, or a million; and yet it would *seem* (though some have disputed this, as we shall see) that if one observation provides evidence, a thousand observations should provide more evidence—and when could the accumulation of evidence end? . . .

We might, nevertheless, stick to our definition and say that we really do *not* know most of the propositions that in daily life we claim to know: Perhaps I don't *know* that this is a book before me, that I am now indoors and not outdoors, that I am now reading sentences written in the English language, or that there are any other people in the world. But this is a rather astounding claim and needs to be justified. We are all convinced that we know these things: We act on them every day of our lives, and if we were asked outside a philosophy classroom whether we knew them, we would say "yes" without hesitation. Surely we cannot accept a definition of "know" that would practically define knowledge out of existence? But if not, what alternative have we?

"Perhaps we don't have to go so far as to say '*all* the evidence,' '*complete* evidence,' and so on. All we have to say is that we must have "*adequate* evidence." But when is the evidence adequate? Is anything less than "all the evidence there could ever be" adequate? "Well, adequate for enabling us to know." But this little addition to our definition lands us in a circle. We are trying to define "know," and we cannot in doing so employ the convenient phrase "enough to enable us to know"—for the last word in this definition is the "very one we are trying to define. But once we have dropped the phrase "to know," we are left with our problem once more: How much evidence is adequate evidence? Is it adequate when anything less than *all* the evidence is in? If not all the evidence is in, but only 99.99 percent of it, couldn't that .01 percent go contrary to the rest of it and require us to conclude that the proposition might not be true after all, and that therefore we didn't know it? Surely it has happened often enough that a statement that we thought we knew, perhaps even would have staked our lives on, turned out in the end to be false, or just doubtful. But in that case we didn't really *know it* after all: The evidence was good, even overwhelming, but yet not good enough, not really adequate, for it was not enough to guarantee the truth of the proposition. Can we know *p* with anything less than *all* the evidence there ever could be for *p?*

II. Strong and Weak Senses of "Know"

[*Disputes About Knowing*] In daily life we say we know—not just believe or surmise, but *know*—that heavier-than-air objects fall, that snow is white, that we can read and write, and countless other things. If someone denies this, and no fact cited by the one disputant suffices to convince the other, we may well suspect that there is a verbal issue involved: In this case, that they are operating on two different meanings of "know," because they construe the third requirement—the evidence requirement—differently.

[*Case 1*] Suppose I say, "There is a bookcase in my office," and someone challenges this assertion. I reply, "I *know* that there is a bookcase in my office. I put it there myself, and I've seen it there for years. In fact, I saw it there just two minutes ago when I took a book out of it and left the office to go into the classroom." Now suppose we both go to my office, take a look, and there is the bookcase, exactly as before. "See, I *knew* it was here," I say. "Oh no," he replies, "you *believed with good reason* that it was still there, because you had seen it there often before and you didn't see or hear anyone removing it. But you didn't *know* it was there when you said it, for at that moment you were in the classroom and not in your office."

At this point, I may reply, "But I did know it was there, even when I said it. I knew it because *(1) I believed it, (2) I had good grounds on which to base the belief, and (3) the belief was true*. And I would call it knowledge whenever these three conditions are fulfilled. This is the way we use the word 'know' every day of our lives. One knows those true propositions that one believes with good reason. And when I said the bookcase was still in my office, I was uttering one of those propositions."

But now my opponent may reply, "But you still didn't know it. You had good reason to say it, I admit, for you had not seen or heard anyone removing it. You had good reason, but not *sufficient* reason. The evidence you gave was still compatible with your statement being false—and if it was false, you of course did not *know* that it was true. [*Case 2*] Suppose that you had made your claim to knowledge, and I had denied your claim, and we had both gone into your office, and to your great surprise (and mine too) the bookcase was no longer there. Could you *then* have claimed to know that it was still there?"

"Of course not. The falsity of a statement always invalidates the claim to know it. If the bookcase had not been there, I would not have been entitled to say that I knew it was there; my claim would have been mistaken."

"Right—it would have been mistaken. But now please note that the only difference between the two cases is that in the first case the bookcase was there and in the second case it wasn't. *The evidence in the two cases was exactly the same*. You had exactly the same reason for saying that the bookcase was still there in the *second* case (when we found it missing) that you did in the *first* case (when we found it still there). And since you—as you yourself admit—didn't know it in the second case, you couldn't have known it in the first case either. You believed it with good reason, but you didn't *know* it."

[*Solution*] Here my opponent may have scored an important point; he may have convinced me that since I admittedly didn't know in the second case I couldn't have known in the first case either. But here I may make an important point in return: "My belief was the same in the two cases; the evidence was the same in the two cases (I had seen the bookcase two minutes before, had heard or seen no one removing it). The only difference was that in the first case the bookcase was there and in the second case it wasn't (*p* was true in the first case, false in the second). But *this doesn't show that I didn't know* in the first case. What it does show is that *although I might have been mistaken, I wasn't mistaken*. Had the bookcase not been there, I couldn't have claimed to know that it was; but since the bookcase in fact *was* still there, I *did* know, although (on the basis of the evidence I had) I *might* have been mistaken."

"Yes, it turned out to be true—you were lucky. But as we both agree, a lucky guess isn't the same as knowledge."

"But this wasn't just a lucky guess. I had excellent reasons for believing that the bookcase was still there. So the evidence requirement was fulfilled."

"No, it wasn't. You had good reason, excellent reason, but not *sufficient* reason—both times—for believing that the bookcase was still there. But in the second case it wasn't there, so you

(*continued*)

An Argument against Skepticism   (*continued*)

didn't know; therefore, in the first case where your evidence was *exactly the same*, you didn't know either; you just believed it with good reason, but that wasn't enough: Your reason wasn't sufficient, and so you didn't *know.*"

Now the difference in the criterion of knowing between the two disputants begins to emerge. According to me, I did know *p* in the first case because my belief was based on excellent evidence and was also true. According to my opponent, I did not know *p* in the first case because my evidence was still less than complete—I wasn't in the room seeing or touching the bookcase when I made the statement. It seems, then, that I am operating with a less demanding definition of "know" than he is. I am using "know" in the *weak* sense, in which I know a proposition when I believe it, have good reason for believing it, and it is true. But he is using "know" in a more demanding sense: He is using it in the *strong* sense, which requires that in order to know a proposition, it must be true, I must believe it, and I must have absolutely *conclusive* evidence in favor of it.

[*Examples*] Let us contrast these two cases:

Suppose that after a routine medical examination the excited doctor reports to me that the X-ray photographs show that I have no heart. I should tell him to get a new machine. I should be inclined to say that the fact that I have a heart is one of the few things that I can count on as absolutely certain. I can feel it beat. I know it's there. Furthermore, how could my blood circulate if I didn't have one? Suppose that later on I suffer a chest injury and undergo a surgical operation. Afterwards the astonished surgeons solemnly declare that they searched my chest cavity and found no heart, and that they made incisions and looked about in other likely places but found it not. They are convinced that I am without a heart. They are unable to understand how circulation can occur or what accounts for the thumping in my chest. But they are in agreement and obviously sincere, and they have clear photographs of my interior spaces. What would be my attitude? Would it be to insist that they were all mistaken? I think not. I believe that I should eventually accept their testimony and the evidence of the photographs. I should consider to be false what I now regard as an absolute certainty. [When I say I know I have a heart, I know it in the weak sense.]

Suppose that as I write this paper someone in the next room were to call out to me, "I can't find an ink-bottle; is there one in the house?" I should reply, "Here is an ink-bottle." If he said in a doubtful tone, "Are you sure? I looked there before," I should reply, "Yes, I know there is; come and get it."

Now could it turn out to be false that there is an ink-bottle directly in front of me on this desk? Many philosophers have thought so. They would say that many things could happen of such a nature that if they did happen it would be proved that I am deceived. I agree that many extraordinary things could happen, in the sense that there is no logical absurdity in the supposition. It could happen that when I next reach for this ink-bottle my hand should seem to pass *through* it and I should not feel the contact of any object. It could happen that in the next moment the ink-bottle will suddenly vanish from sight; or that I should find myself under a tree in the garden with no ink-bottle about; or that one or more persons should enter this room and declare with apparent sincerity that they see no ink-bottle on this desk; or that a photograph taken now of the top of the desk should clearly show all of the objects on it except the ink-bottle. Having admitted that these things *could happen*, am I compelled to admit that if they did happen, then it would be proved that there is no ink-bottle here *now*? Not at all. I could say that when my hand seemed to pass through the ink-bottle I should *then* be suffering from hallucination; that if the ink-bottle suddenly vanished, it would have miraculously ceased to exist; that the other persons were conspiring to drive me mad, or were themselves victims of remarkable concurrent hallucinations; that the camera possessed some strange flaw or that there was trickery in developing the negative: . . . Not only do I not *have* to admit that those extraordinary occurrences would be evidence that there is no ink-bottle here; the fact is that I *do not* admit it. There is nothing whatever that could happen in the next moment or the next year that would by me be called *evidence* that there is not an ink-bottle here now.

No future experience or investigation could prove to me that I am mistaken. Therefore, if I were to say, "I know that there is an ink-bottle here," I should be using "know" in the strong sense.[1]

It is in the weak sense that we use the word "know" in daily life, as when I say I know that I have a heart, that if I let go of this piece of chalk it will fall, that the sun will rise tomorrow, and so on. I have excellent reason (evidence) to believe all these things, evidence so strong that (so we say) it amounts to certainty. And yet there are events that could conceivably occur which, if they did occur, would cast doubt on the beliefs or even show them to be false. . . .

III. Argument Against Skepticism

[*Skepticism*] But the philosopher is apt to be more concerned with "know" in the strong sense. He wants to inquire whether there are any propositions that we know without the shadow of a doubt will never be proved false, or even rendered dubious to the smallest degree. "You can say," he will argue, "and I admit that it would be good English usage to say, that you know that you have a heart and that the sun is more than 90 million miles from the earth. But you don't know it until you have absolutely conclusive evidence, and you must admit that the evidence you have, while very strong, is not conclusive. So I shall say, using 'know' in the strong sense, that you do not know these propositions. I want then to ask what propositions can be known in the strong sense, the sense that puts the proposition forever past the possibility of doubt."

And on this point many philosophers have been quite skeptical; they have granted few if any propositions whose truth we could know in the strong sense . . . . Such a person is a *skeptic*. We claim (he says) to know many things about the world, but in fact none of these propositions can be known for certain. What are we to say of the skeptic's position?

[*Criticism*] Let us first note that in the phrase "know for certain" the "for certain" is redundant—how can we know except for certain? If it is less than certain, how can it be knowledge? We do, however, use the word "certain" ambiguously: (1) Sometimes we say "I am certain," which just means that I have a feeling of certainty about it—"I feel certain that I locked the door of the apartment"— and of course the feeling of certainty is no guarantee that the statement is true. People have very strong feelings of certainty about many propositions that they have no evidence for at all, particularly if they want to believe them or are consoled by believing them. The phrase "feeling certain," then, refers simply to a psychological state, whose existence in no way guarantees that what the person feels certain about is true. But (2) sometimes when we say "I am certain" we mean that it *is* certain—in other words, that we *do* know the proposition in question to be true. This, of course, is the sense of "certain" that is of interest to philosophers (the first sense is of more interest to psychiatrists in dealing with patients). Thus we could reformulate our question, "Is anything certain?" or "Are any propositions certain?"

"I can well understand," one might argue, "how you could question some statements, even most statements. But if you carry on this merry game until you have covered *all* statements, you are simply mistaken, and I think I can show you why. You may see someone in a fog or in a bad light and not know (not be certain) whether he has a right hand. But don't you know that *you* have a right hand? There it is! Suppose I now raise my hand and say, 'Here is a hand.' Now you say to me, 'I doubt that there's a hand.' But what evidence do you want? What does your doubt consist of? You don't believe your eyes, perhaps? Very well, then come up and touch the hand. You still aren't satisfied? Then keep on looking at it steadily and touching it, photograph it, call in other people for testimony if you like. If after all this you still say it isn't certain, what more do you want? Under what conditions would you admit that it *is* certain, that you *do* know it? I can understand your doubt when there is some condition left unfulfilled, some test left uncompleted. At the beginning, perhaps you doubted that *if* you tried to touch my hand you would find anything there to touch; but then you did touch, and so you resolved *that* doubt. You resolved further doubts by calling in other people and so on. You performed all the relevant tests, and they turned out favorably. So now, at the end of the process, what is it that you doubt? Oh, I know what you *say*: 'I still doubt that that's a hand.' But isn't this saying 'I doubt' now an empty formula? I can no longer attach any content to that so-called doubt, for there is nothing left to doubt; you yourself *cannot*

(continued)

An Argument against Skepticism   (*continued*)

specify any further test that, if performed, would resolve your doubt. 'Doubt' now becomes an empty word. You're not doubting now that *if* you raised your hand to touch mine, you would touch it, or that *if* Smith and others were brought in, they would also testify that this is a hand—we've already gone through all that. So what is it specifically that you doubt? What possible test is there the negative result of which you fear? I submit that there isn't any. You are confusing a situation in which doubt is understandable *(before* you made the tests) with the later situation in which it isn't, for it has all been dispelled. . . .

"But your so-called doubt becomes meaningless when there is nothing left to doubt—when the tests have been carried out and their results are all favorable. Suppose a physician examines a patient and says, 'It's probable that you have an inflamed appendix.' Here one can still doubt, for the signs may be misleading. So the physician operates on the patient, finds an inflamed appendix and removes it, and the patient recovers. *Now* what would be the sense of the physician's saying, 'It's *probable* that he had an inflamed appendix'? If seeing it and removing it made it only *probable*, what would make it certain? Or you are driving along and you hear a rapid regular thumping sound and you say, 'It's probable that I have a flat tire.' So far you're right; it's only probable—the thumping might be caused by something else. So you go out and have a look, and there is the tire, flat. You find a nail embedded in it, change the tire, and then resume your ride with no more thumping. Are you *now* going to say, 'It's merely *probable* that the car had a flat tire'? But if given all those conditions it would be merely probable, what in the world would make it certain? Can you describe to me the circumstances in which you would say it's certain? If you can't, then the phrase 'being certain' has no meaning as you are using it. You are simply using it in such a special: way that it has no application at all, and there is no reason at all why anyone else should follow your usage. In daily life we have a very convenient and useful distinction between the application of the words 'probable' and 'certain.' We say appendicitis is probable *before* the operation, but when the physician has the patient's appendix visible before him on the operating table, now it's certain—that's just the kind of situation in which we apply the word 'certain,' as opposed to 'probable.' Now you, for some reason, are so fond of the word 'probable' that you want to use it for everything—you use it to describe *both* the preoperative and postoperative situations, and the word 'certain' is left without any application at all. But this is nothing but a *verbal manipulation* on your part. You have changed nothing; you have only taken, as it were, two bottles with different contents, and instead of labeling them differently ('probable' and 'certain'), as the rest of us do, you put the same label ('probable') on both of them! What possible advantage is there in this? It's just verbal contrariness. And since you have preempted the word 'probable' to cover *both the* situations, we now have to devise a *different* pair of words to mark the perfectly obvious distinction between the situation *before* the surgery and the situation *during* the surgery—the same difference are previously marked by the words 'probable' and 'certain' until you used the word 'probable' to apply to both of them. What gain is there in this *verbal manipulation* of yours?" . . .

NOTE

1. Norman Malcolm, "Knowledge and Belief," in *Knowledge and Certainty,* pp. 66–68.

Truth and Falsehood from Problems of Philosophy
Russell Bertrand

OUR KNOWLEDGE OF TRUTHS, unlike our knowledge of things, has an opposite, namely *error.* So far as things are concerned, we may know them or not know them, but there is no positive state of mind which can be described as erroneous knowledge of things, so long, at any rate, as we confine ourselves to knowledge by acquaintance. Whatever we are acquainted with must be something; we may draw wrong inferences from our acquaintance, but the acquaintance itself cannot be deceptive. Thus there is no dualism as regards acquaintance. But as regards knowledge of truths, there is a dualism. We may believe what is false as well as what is true. We know that on very many subjects different people hold different and incompatible opinions: hence some beliefs must be erroneous. Since erroneous beliefs are often held just as strongly as true beliefs, it becomes a difficult question how they are to be distinguished from true beliefs. How are we to know, in a given case, that our belief is not erroneous? This is a question of the very greatest difficulty, to which no completely satisfactory answer is possible. There is, however, a preliminary question which is rather less difficult, and that is: What do we *mean* by truth and falsehood? It is this preliminary question which is to be considered in this chapter.

In this chapter we are not asking how we can know whether a belief is true or false: we are asking what is meant by the question whether a belief is true or false. It is to be hoped that a clear answer to this question may help us to obtain an answer to the question what beliefs are true, but for the present we ask only 'What is truth?' and 'What is falsehood?', not 'What beliefs are true?' and 'What beliefs are false?' It is very important to keep these different questions entirely separate, since any confusion between them is sure to produce an answer which is not really applicable to either.

There are three points to observe in the attempt to discover the nature of truth, three requisites which any theory must fulfil.

1. Our theory of truth must be such as to admit of its opposite, falsehood. A good many philosophers have failed adequately to satisfy this condition. they have constructed theories according to which all our thinking ought to have been true, and have then had the greatest difficulty in finding a place for falsehood. In this respect our theory of belief must differ from our theory of acquaintance, since in the case of acquaintance it was not necessary to take account of any opposite.
2. It seems fairly evident that if there were no beliefs there could be no falsehood, and no truth either, in the sense in which truth is correlative to falsehood. If we imagine a world of mere matter, there would be no room for falsehood in such a world, and although it would contain what may be called 'facts', it would not contain any truths, in the sense in which truths are things of the same kind as falsehoods. In fact, truth and falsehood are properties of beliefs and statements: hence a world of mere matter, since it would contain no beliefs or statements, would also contain no truth or falsehood.
3. But, as against what we have just said, it is to be observed that the truth or falsehood of a belief always depends upon something which lies outside the belief itself. If I believe that Charles I died on the scaffold, I believe truly, not because of any intrinsic quality of my belief, which could be discovered by merely examining the belief, but because of an historical event which happened two and a half centuries ago. If I believe that Charles I died in his bed, I believe falsely: no degree of vividness in my belief, or of care in arriving at it, prevents it from being false, again because of what happened long ago, and not because of any intrinsic property of my belief. Hence, although truth and falsehood are properties of beliefs, they are properties dependent upon the relations of the beliefs to other things, not upon any internal quality of the beliefs.

The third of the above requisites leads us to adopt the view—which has on the whole been commonest among philosophers—that truth consists in some form of correspondence between belief and fact. It is, however, by no means an easy matter to discover a form of correspondence to which there are no irrefutable objections. By this partly—and partly by the feeling that, if truth consists in a correspondence of thought with something outside thought, thought can never know when truth has been attained—many philosophers have been led to try to find some definition of truth which shall not consist in relation to something wholly outside belief. The most important attempt at a definition of this sort is the theory that truth consists in *coherence*. It is said that the mark of falsehood is failure to cohere in the body of our beliefs, and that it is the essence of a truth to form part of the completely rounded system which is The Truth.

There is, however, a great difficulty in this view, or rather two great difficulties. The first is that there is no reason to suppose that only *one* coherent body of beliefs is possible. It may be that, with sufficient imagination, a novelist might invent a past for the world that would perfectly fit on to

(continued)

Truth and Falsehood from Problems of Philosophy (*continued*)

what we know, and yet be quite different from the real past. In more scientific matters, it is certain that there are often two or more hypotheses which account for all the known facts on some subject, and although, in such cases, men of science endeavour to find facts which will rule out all the hypotheses except one, there, is no reason why they should always succeed.

In philosophy, again, it seems not uncommon for two rival hypotheses to be both able to account for all the facts. Thus, for example, it is possible that life is one long dream, and that the outer world has only that degree of reality that the objects of dreams have; but although such a view does not seem inconsistent with known facts, there is no reason to prefer it to the common-sense view, according to which other people and things do really exist. Thus coherence as the definition of truth fails because there is no proof that here can be only one, coherent system.

The other objection to this definition of truth is that it assumes the meaning of 'coherence' known, whereas, in fact, 'coherence' presupposes the truth of the laws of logic. Two propositions are coherent when both may be true, and are incoherent when one at least must be false. Now in order to know whether two propositions can both be true, we must know such truths as the law of contradiction. For example, the two propositions, 'this tree is a beech' and 'this tree is not a beech', are not coherent, because of the law of contradiction. But if the law of contradiction itself were subjected to the test of coherence, we should find that, if we choose to suppose it false, nothing will any longer be incoherent with anything else. Thus the laws of logic supply the skeleton or framework within which the test of coherence applies, and they themselves cannot be established by this test.

For the above two reasons, coherence cannot be accepted as giving the *meaning* of truth, though it is often a most important *test* of truth after a certain amount of truth has become known.

Hence we are driven back to *correspondence with fact* as constituting the nature of truth. It remains to define precisely what we mean by 'fact', and what is the nature of the correspondence which must subsist between belief and fact, in order that belief may be true.

In accordance with our three requisites, we have to seek a theory of truth which (1) allows truth to have an opposite, namely falsehood, (2) makes truth a property of beliefs, but (3) makes it a property wholly dependent upon the relation of the beliefs to outside things.

The necessity of allowing for falsehood makes it impossible to regard belief as a relation of the mind to a single object, which could be said to be what is believed. If belief were so regarded, we should find that, like acquaintance, it would not admit of the opposition of truth and falsehood, but would have to be always true. This may be made clear by examples. Othello believes falsely that Desdemona loves Cassio. We cannot say that this belief consists in a relation to a single object, 'Desdemona's love for Cassio', for if there were such an object, the belief would be true. There is in fact no such object, and therefore Othello cannot have any relation to such an object. Hence his belief cannot possibly consist in a relation to this object.

It might be said that his belief is a relation to a different object, namely 'that Desdemona loves Cassio'; but it is almost as difficult to suppose that there is such an object as this, when Desdemona does not love Cassio, as it was to suppose that there is 'Desdemona's love for Cassio'. Hence it will be better to seek for a theory of belief which does not make it consist in a relation of the mind to a single object.

It is common to think of relations as though they always held between *two* terms, but in fact this is not always the case. Some relations demand three terms, some four, and so on. Take, for instance, the relation 'between'. So long as only two terms come in, the relation 'between' is impossible: three terms are the smallest number that render it possible. York is between London and Edinburgh; but if London and Edinburgh were the only places in the world, there could be nothing which was between one place and another. Similarly *jealousy* requires three people: there can be no such relation that does not involve three at least. Such a proposition as 'A wishes B to promote C's marriage with D' involves a relation of four terms; that is to say, A and B and C and D all come in, and the relation involved cannot be expressed otherwise than in a form involving all four. Instances might be multiplied indefinitely, but enough has been said to show that there are relations which require more than two terms before they can occur.

The relation involved *in judging* or *believing* must, if falsehood is to be duly allowed for, be taken to be a relation between several terms, not between two. When Othello believes that

Desdemona loves Cassio, he must not have before his mind a single object, 'Desdemona's love for Cassio', or 'that Desdemona loves Cassio', for that would require that there should be objective falsehoods, which subsist independently of any minds' and this, though not logically refutable, is a theory to be avoided if possible. Thus it is easier to account for falsehood if we take judgement to be a relation in which the mind and the various objects concerned all occur severally; that is to say, Desdemona and loving and Cassio must all be terms in the relation which subsists when Othello believes that Desdemona loves Cassio. This relation, therefore, is a relation of four terms, since Othello also is one of the terms of the relation. When we say that it is a relation of four terms, we do not mean that Othello has a certain relation to Desdemona, and has the same relation to loving and also to Cassio. This may be true of some other relation than believing; but believing, plainly, is not a relation which Othello has to *each* of the three terms concerned, but to *all* of them together: there is only one example of the relation of believing involved, but this one example knits together four terms. Thus the actual occurrence, at the moment when Othello is entertaining his belief, is that the relation called 'believing' is knitting together into one complex whole the four terms Othello, Desdemona, loving, and Cassio. What is called belief or judgement is nothing but this relation of believing or judging, which relates a mind to several things other than itself. An *act* of belief or of judgement is the occurrence between certain terms at some particular time, of the relation of believing or judging.

We are now in a position to understand what it is that distinguishes a true judgement from a false one. For this purpose we will adopt certain definitions. In every act of judgement there is a mind which judges, and there are terms concerning which it judges. We will call the mind the *subject* in the judgement, and the remaining terms the *objects*. Thus, when Othello judges that Desdemona loves Cassio, Othello is the subject, while the objects are Desdemona and loving and Cassio. The subject and the objects together are called the *constituents* of the judgement. It will be observed that the relation of judging has what is called a 'sense' or 'direction'. We may say, metaphorically, that it puts its objects in a certain *order,* which we may indicate by means of the order of the words in the sentence. (In an inflected language, the same thing will be indicated by inflections, e.g. by the difference between nominative and accusative.) Othello's judgement that Cassio loves Desdemona differs from his judgement that Desdemona loves Cassio, in spite of the fact that it consists of the same constituents, because the relation of judging places the constituents in a different order in the two cases. Similarly, if Cassio judges that Desdemona loves Othello, the constituents of the judgement are still the same, but their order is different. This property of having a 'sense' or 'direction' is one which the relation of judging shares with all other relations. The 'sense' of relations is the ultimate source of order and series and a host of mathematical concepts; but we need not concern ourselves further with this aspect.

We spoke of the relation called 'judging' or 'believing' as knitting together into one complex whole the subject and the objects. In this respect, judging is exactly like every other relation. Whenever a relation holds between two or more terms, it unites the terms into a complex whole. If Othello loves Desdemona, there is such a complex whole as 'Othello's love for Desdemona'. The terms united by the relation may be themselves complex, or may be simple, but the whole which results from their being united must be complex. Wherever there is a relation which relates certain terms, there is a complex object formed of the union of those terms; and conversely, wherever there is a complex object, there is a relation which relates its constituents. When an act of believing occurs, there is a complex, in which 'believing' is the uniting relation, and subject and objects are arranged in a certain order by the 'sense' of the relation of believing. Among the objects, as we saw in considering 'Othello believes that Desdemona loves Cassio', one must be a relation—in this instance, the relation 'loving'. But this relation, as it occurs in the act of believing, is not the relation which creates the unity of the complex whole consisting of the subject and the objects. The relation 'loving', as it occurs in the act of believing, is one of the objects—it is a brick in the structure, not the cement. The cement is the relation 'believing'. When the belief is *true,* there is another complex unity, in which the relation which was one of the objects of the belief relates the other objects. Thus, e.g., if Othello believes *truly* that Desdemona loves Cassio, then there is a complex unity, 'Desdemona's love for Cassio', which is composed exclusively of the *objects* of the belief, in the same order as they had in the belief, with the relation which was one of the objects

(continued)

Truth and Falsehood from Problems of Philosophy   (*continued*)

occurring now as the cement that binds together the other objects of the belief. On the other hand, when a belief is *false,* there is no such complex unity composed only of the objects of the belief If Othello believes *falsely* that Desdemona loves Cassio, then there is no such complex unity as 'Desdemona's love for Cassio'.

Thus a belief is *true* when it *corresponds to a certain* associated complex *and false* when it does not. Assuming, for the sake of definiteness, that the objects of the belief are two terms and a relation, the terms being put in a certain order by the 'sense' of the believing, then if the two terms in that order are united by the relation into a complex, the belief is true; if not, it is false. This constitutes the definition of truth and falsehood that we were in search of. Judging or believing is a certain complex unity of which a mind is a constituent; if the remaining constituents, taken in the order which they have in the belief, form a complex unity, then the belief is true; if not, it is false.

Thus although truth and falsehood are properties of beliefs, yet they are in a sense extrinsic properties, for the condition of the truth of a belief is something not involving beliefs, or (in general) any mind at all, but only the *objects* of the belief. A mind, which believes, believes truly when there is a *corresponding* complex not involving the mind, but only its objects. This correspondence ensures truth, and its absence entails falsehood. Hence we account simultaneously for the two facts that beliefs *(a)* depend on minds for their *existence, (b)* do not depend on minds for their *truth.*

We may restate our theory as follows: If we take such a belief as 'Othello believes that Desdemona loves Cassio', we will call Desdemona and Cassio the *object-terms,* and loving the *object-relation.* If there is a complex unity 'Desdemona's love for Cassio', consisting of the object-terms related by the object-relation in the same order as they have in the belief, then this complex unity is called the *fact corresponding to the belief.* Thus a belief is true when there is a corresponding fact, and is false when there is no corresponding fact.

It will be seen that minds do not *create* truth or falsehood. They create beliefs, but when once the beliefs are created, the mind cannot make them true or false, except in the special case where they concern future things which are within the power of the person believing, such as catching trains. What makes a belief true is a *fact,* and this fact does not (except in exceptional cases) in any way involve the mind of the person who has the belief.

Having now decided what we *mean* by truth and falsehood, we have next to consider what ways there are of knowing whether this or that belief is true or false. This consideration will occupy the next chapter.

Pragmatism
William James

From Lecture VI (pp. 198–209)

. . . I fully expect to see the pragmatist view of truth run through the classic stages of a theory's career. First, you know, a new theory is attacked as absurd; then it is admitted to be true, but obvious and insignificant; finally it is seen to be so important that its adversaries claim that they themselves discovered it. Our doctrine of truth is at present in the first of these three stages, with symptoms of the second stage having begun in certain quarters. I wish that this lecture might help it beyond the first stage in the eyes of many of you.

Truth, as any dictionary will tell you, is a property of certain of our ideas. It means their 'agreement,' as falsity means their disagreement, with 'reality.' Pragmatists and intellectualists both accept this definition as a matter of course. They begin to quarrel only after the question is raised as to what may precisely be meant by the term 'agreement,' and what by the term 'reality,' when reality is taken as something for our ideas to agree with.

In answering these questions the pragmatists are more analytic and painstaking, the intellectualists more offhand and irreflective. The popular notion is that a true idea must copy its reality. Like other popular views, this one follows the analogy of the most usual experience. Our true ideas of sensible things do indeed copy them. Shut your eyes and think of yonder clock on the wall, and you get just such a true picture or copy of its dial. But your idea of its 'works' (unless you are a clockmaker) is much less of a copy, yet it passes muster, for it in no way clashes with the reality. Even tho it should shrink to the mere word 'works,' that word still serves you truly; and when you speak of the 'time-keeping function' of the clock, or of its spring's 'elasticity, ' it is hard to see exactly what your ideas can copy.

You perceive that there is a problem here. Where our ideas cannot copy definitely their object, what does agreement with that object mean? Some idealists seem to say that they are true whenever they are what God means that we ought to think about that object. Others hold the copy-view all through, and speak as if our ideas possessed truth just in proportion as they approach to being copies of the Absolute's eternal way of thinking.

These views, you see, invite pragmatistic discussion. But the great assumption of the intellectualists is that truth means essentially an inert static relation. When you've got your true idea of anything, there's an end of the matter. You're in possession; you KNOW; you have fulfilled your thinking destiny. You are where you ought to be mentally; you have obeyed your categorical imperative; and nothing more need follow on that climax of your rational destiny. Epistemologically you are in stable equilibrium.

Pragmatism, on the other hand, asks its usual question. "Grant an idea or belief to be true," it says, "what concrete difference will its being true make in anyone's actual life? How will the truth be realized? What experiences will be different from those which would obtain if the belief were false? What, in short, is the truth's cash-value in experiential terms?"

The moment pragmatism asks this question, it sees the answer: TRUE IDEAS ARE THOSE THAT WE CAN ASSIMILATE, VALIDATE, CORROBORATE AND VERIFY. FALSE IDEAS ARE THOSE THAT WE CANNOT. That is the practical difference it makes to us to have true ideas; that, therefore, is the meaning of truth, for it is all that truth is known-as.

This thesis is what I have to defend. The truth of an idea is not a stagnant property inherent in it. Truth HAPPENS to an idea. It BECOMES true, is MADE true by events. Its verity is in fact an event, a process: the process namely of its verifying itself, its veri-FICATION. Its validity is the process of its valid-ATION.

But what do the words verification and validation themselves pragmatically mean? They again signify certain practical consequences of the verified and validated idea. It is hard to find any one phrase that characterizes these consequences better than the ordinary agreement-formula—just such consequences being what we have in mind whenever we say that our ideas 'agree' with reality. They lead us, namely, through the acts and other ideas which they instigate, into or up to, or towards, other parts of experience with which we feel all the while-such feeling being among our potentialities—that the original ideas remain in agreement. The connexions and transitions come to us from point to point as being progressive, harmonious, satisfactory. This function of agreeable leading is what we mean by an idea's verification . . .

. . . Let me begin by reminding you of the fact that the possession of true thoughts means everywhere the possession of invaluable instruments of action; and that our duty to gain truth, so far from being a blank command from out of the blue, or a 'stunt' self-imposed by our intellect, can account for itself by excellent practical reasons.

The importance to human life of having true beliefs about matters of fact is a thing too notorious. We live in a world of realities that can be infinitely useful or infinitely harmful. Ideas that tell us which of them to expect count as the true ideas in all this primary sphere of verification, and the pursuit of such ideas is a primary human duty. The possession of truth, so far from being here an end in itself, is only a preliminary means towards other vital satisfactions. If I am lost in the woods and starved, and find what looks like a cow-path, it is of the utmost importance that I should think of a human habitation at the end of it, for if I do so and follow it, I save myself. The true thought is useful here because the house which is its object is useful. The practical value of true ideas is thus primarily derived from the practical importance of their objects to us. Their objects are, indeed, not important at all times. I may on another occasion have no use for the house; and then my idea of it, however verifiable, will be practically irrelevant, and had better remain latent. Yet since almost any object may some day become temporarily important, the advantage of having a general stock of

(continued)

Pragmatism (*continued*)

extra truths, of ideas that shall be true of merely possible situations, is obvious. We store such extra truths away in our memories, and with the overflow we fill our books of reference. Whenever such an extra truth becomes practically relevant to one of our emergencies, it passes from cold-storage to do work in the world, and our belief in it grows active. You can say of it then either that 'it is useful because it is true' or that 'it is true because it is useful.' Both these phrases mean exactly the same thing, namely that here is an idea that gets fulfilled and can be verified. True is the name for whatever idea starts the verification-process, useful is the name for its completed function in experience. True ideas would never have been singled out as such, would never have acquired a class-name, least of all a name suggesting value, unless they had been useful from the outset in this way.

From this simple cue pragmatism gets her general notion of truth as something essentially bound up with the way in which one moment in our experience may lead us towards other moments which it will be worth while to have been led to. Primarily, and on the common-sense level, the truth of a state of mind means this function of A LEADING THAT IS WORTH WHILE. When a moment in our experience, of any kind whatever, inspires us with a thought that is true, that means that sooner or later we dip by that thought's guidance into the particulars of experience again and make advantageous connexion with them. This is a vague enough statement, but I beg you to retain it, for it is essential.

Our experience meanwhile is all shot through with regularities. One bit of it can warn us to get ready for another bit, can 'intend' or be 'significant of' that remoter object. The object's advent is the significance's verification. Truth, in these cases, meaning nothing but eventual verification, is manifestly incompatible with waywardness on our part. Woe to him whose beliefs play fast and loose with the order which realities follow in his experience: they will lead him nowhere or else make false connexions.

By 'realities' or 'objects' here, we mean either things of common sense, sensibly present, or else common-sense relations, such as dates, places, distances, kinds, activities. Following our mental image of a house along the cow-path, we actually come to see the house; we get the image's full verification. SUCH SIMPLY AND FULLY VERIFIED LEADINGS ARE CERTAINLY THE ORIGINALS AND PROTOTYPES OF THE TRUTH-PROCESS. Experience offers indeed other forms of truth-process, but they are all conceivable as being primary verifications arrested, multiplied or substituted one for another.

Take, for instance, yonder object on the wall. You and I consider it to be a 'clock,' altho no one of us has seen the hidden works that make it one. We let our notion pass for true without attempting to verify. If truths mean verification-process essentially, ought we then to call such unverified truths as this abortive? No, for they form the overwhelmingly large number of the truths we live by. Indirect as well as direct verifications pass muster. Where circumstantial evidence is sufficient, we can go without eye-witnessing. Just as we here assume Japan to exist without ever having been there, because it WORKS to do so, everything we know conspiring with the belief, and nothing interfering, so we assume that thing to be a clock. We USE it as a clock, regulating the length of our lecture by it. The verification of the assumption here means its leading to no frustration or contradiction. VerifiABILITY of wheels and weights and pendulum is as good as verification. For one truth-process completed there are a million in our lives that function in this state of nascency. They turn us TOWARDS direct verification; lead us into the SURROUNDINGS of the objects they envisage; and then, if everything runs on harmoniously, we are so sure that verification is possible that we omit it, and are usually justified by all that happens.

Truth lives, in fact, for the most part on a credit system. Our thoughts and beliefs 'pass,' so long as nothing challenges them, just as bank-notes pass so long as nobody refuses them. But this all points to direct face-to-face verifications somewhere, without which the fabric of truth collapses like a financial system with no cash- basis whatever. You accept my verification of one thing, I yours of another. We trade on each other's truth. But beliefs verified concretely by SOMEBODY are the posts of the whole superstructure.

Another great reason—beside economy of time—for waiving complete verification in the usual business of life is that all things exist in kinds and not singly. Our world is found once for all to have that peculiarity. So that when we have once directly verified our ideas about one specimen of a kind, we consider ourselves free to apply them to other specimens without verification. A mind that habitually discerns the kind of thing before it, and acts by the law of the kind immediately, without pausing to verify, will be a 'true' mind in ninety-nine out of a hundred emergencies, proved so by its conduct fitting everything it meets, and getting no refutation.

INDIRECTLY OR ONLY POTENTIALLY VERIFYING PROCESSES MAY THUS BE TRUE AS WELL AS FULL VERIFICATION-PROCESSES. They work as true processes would work, give us the same advantages, and claim our recognition for the same reasons . . .

From Lecture VI (pp. 218–223)

Our account of truth is an account of truths in the plural, of processes of leading, realized in rebus, and having only this quality in common, that they PAY. They pay by guiding us into or towards some part of a system that dips at numerous points into sense-percepts, which we may copy mentally or not, but with which at any rate we are now in the kind of commerce vaguely designated as verification. Truth for us is simply a collective name for verification-processes, just as health, wealth, strength, etc., are names for other processes connected with life, and also pursued because it pays to pursue them. Truth is MADE, just as health, wealth and strength are made, in the course of experience.

Here rationalism is instantaneously up in arms against us. I can imagine a rationalist to talk as follows:

"Truth is not made," he will say; "it absolutely obtains, being a unique relation that does not wait upon any process, but shoots straight over the head of experience, and hits its reality every time. Our belief that yon thing on the wall is a clock is true already, altho no one in the whole history of the world should verify it. The bare quality of standing in that transcendent relation is what makes any thought true that possesses it, whether or not there be verification. You pragmatists put the cart before the horse in making truth's being reside in verification-processes. These are merely signs of its being, merely our lame ways of ascertaining after the fact, which of our ideas already has possessed the wondrous quality. The quality itself is timeless, like all essences and natures. Thoughts partake of it directly, as they partake of falsity or of irrelevancy. It can't be analyzed away into pragmatic consequences."

The whole plausibility of this rationalist tirade is due to the fact to which we have already paid so much attention. In our world, namely, abounding as it does in things of similar kinds and similarly associated, one verification serves for others of its kind, and one great use of knowing things is to be led not so much to them as to their associates, especially to human talk about them. The quality of truth, obtaining ante rem, pragmatically means, then, the fact that in such a world innumerable ideas work better by their indirect or possible than by their direct and actual verification. Truth ante rem means only verifiability, then; or else it is a case of the stock rationalist trick of treating the NAME of a concrete phenomenal reality as an independent prior entity, and placing it behind the reality as its explanation . . .

In the case of 'wealth' we all see the fallacy. We know that wealth is but a name for concrete processes that certain men's lives play a part in, and not a natural excellence found in Messrs. Rockefeller and Carnegie, but not in the rest of us.

Like wealth, health also lives in rebus. It is a name for processes, as digestion, circulation, sleep, etc., that go on happily, tho in this instance we are more inclined to think of it as a principle and to say the man digests and sleeps so well BECAUSE he is so healthy.

With 'strength' we are, I think, more rationalistic still, and decidedly inclined to treat it as an excellence pre-existing in the man and explanatory of the herculean performances of his muscles.

With 'truth' most people go over the border entirely, and treat the rationalistic account as self-evident. But really all these words in TH are exactly similar. Truth exists ante rem just as much and as little as the other things do.

The scholastics, following Aristotle, made much of the distinction between habit and act. Health in actu means, among other things, good sleeping and digesting. But a healthy man need not always be sleeping, or always digesting, any more than a wealthy man need be always handling money, or a strong man always lifting weights. All such qualities sink to the status of 'habits' between their times of exercise; and similarly truth becomes a habit of certain of our ideas and beliefs in their intervals of rest from their verifying activities. But those activities are the root of the whole matter, and the condition of there being any habit to exist in the intervals.

(continued)

Pragmatism (*continued*)

'The true,' to put it very briefly, is only the expedient in the way of our thinking, just as 'the right' is only the expedient in the way of our behaving. Expedient in almost any fashion; and expedient in the long run and on the whole of course; for what meets expediently all the experience in sight won't necessarily meet all farther experiences equally satisfactorily. Experience, as we know, has ways of BOILING OVER, and making us correct our present formulas.

The 'absolutely' true, meaning what no farther experience will ever alter, is that ideal vanishing-point towards which we imagine that all our temporary truths will some day converge. It runs on all fours with the perfectly wise man, and with the absolutely complete experience; and, if these ideals are ever realized, they will all be realized together. Meanwhile we have to live today by what truth we can get to-day, and be ready to-morrow to call it falsehood. Ptolemaic astronomy, euclidean space, aristotelian logic, scholastic metaphysics, were expedient for centuries, but human experience has boiled over those limits, and we now call these things only relatively true, or true within those borders of experience. 'Absolutely' they are false; for we know that those limits were casual, and might have been transcended by past theorists just as they are by present thinkers . . .

From Lecture II (pp. 75–79)

. . . Truth is ONE SPECIES OF GOOD, and not, as is usually supposed, a category distinct from good, and co-ordinate with it.

THE TRUE IS THE NAME OF WHATEVER PROVES ITSELF TO BE GOOD IN THE WAY OF BELIEF, AND GOOD, TOO, FOR DEFINITE, ASSIGNABLE REASONS. Surely you must admit this, that if there were NO good for life in true ideas, or if the knowledge of them were positively disadvantageous and false ideas the only useful ones, then the current notion that truth is divine and precious, and its pursuit a duty, could never have grown up or become a dogma. In a world like that, our duty would be to SHUN truth, rather. But in this world, just as certain foods are not only agreeable to our taste, but good for our teeth, our stomach and our tissues; so certain ideas are not only agreeable to think about, or agreeable as supporting other ideas that we are fond of, but they are also helpful in life's practical struggles. If there be any life that it is really better we should lead, and if there be any idea which, if believed in, would help us to lead that life, then it would be really BETTER FOR US to believe in that idea, UNLESS, INDEED, BELIEF IN IT INCIDENTALLY CLASHED WITH OTHER GREATER VITAL BENEFITS.

'What would be better for us to believe'! This sounds very like a definition of truth. It comes very near to saying 'what we OUGHT to believe': and in THAT definition none of you would find any oddity. Ought we ever not to believe what it is BETTER FOR US to believe? And can we then keep the notion of what is better for us, and what is true for us, permanently apart?

Pragmatism says no, and I fully agree with her. Probably you also agree, so far as the abstract statement goes, but with a suspicion that if we practically did believe everything that made for good in our own personal lives, we should be found indulging all kinds of fancies about this world's affairs, and all kinds of sentimental superstitions about a world hereafter. Your suspicion here is undoubtedly well founded, and it is evident that something happens when you pass from the abstract to the concrete, that complicates the situation.

I said just now that what is better for us to believe is true UNLESS THE BELIEF INCIDENTALLY CLASHES WITH SOME OTHER VITAL BENEFIT. Now in real life what vital benefits is any particular belief of ours most liable to clash with? What indeed except the vital benefits yielded by OTHER BELIEFS when these prove incompatible with the first ones? In other words, the greatest enemy of any one of our truths may be the rest of our truths. Truths have once for all this desperate instinct of self-preservation and of desire to extinguish whatever contradicts them. My belief in the Absolute, based on the good it does me, must run the gauntlet of all my other beliefs. Grant that it may be true in giving me a moral holiday. Nevertheless, as I conceive it,—and let me speak now confidentially, as it were, and merely in my own private person,—it clashes with other truths of mine whose benefits I hate to give up on its account. It happens to be associated with a kind of logic of which I am the enemy, I find that it entangles me in metaphysical paradoxes that are inacceptable, etc., etc. But as I have enough trouble in life already without adding the trouble of carrying these intellectual inconsistencies, I personally just give up the Absolute.

I just TAKE my moral holidays; or else as a professional philosopher, I try to justify them by some other principle.

If I could restrict my notion of the Absolute to its bare holiday-giving value, it wouldn't clash with my other truths. But we cannot easily thus restrict our hypotheses. They carry supernumerary features, and these it is that clash so. My disbelief in the Absolute means then disbelief in those other supernumerary features, for I fully believe in the legitimacy of taking moral holidays.

You see by this what I meant when I called pragmatism a mediator and reconciler and said, borrowing the word from Papini, that he unstiffens our theories. She has in fact no prejudices whatever, no obstructive dogmas, no rigid canons of what shall count as proof. She is completely genial. She will entertain any hypothesis, she will consider any evidence. It follows that in the religious field she is at a great advantage both over positivistic empiricism, with its anti-theological bias, and over religious rationalism, with its exclusive interest in the remote, the noble, the simple, and the abstract in the way of conception.

In short, she widens the field of search for God. Rationalism sticks to logic and the empyrean. Empiricism sticks to the external senses. Pragmatism is willing to take anything, to follow either logic or the senses, and to count the humblest and most personal experiences. She will count mystical experiences if they have practical consequences. She will take a God who lives in the very dirt of private fact-if that should seem a likely place to find him.

Her only test of probable truth is what works best in the way of leading us, what fits every part of life best and combines with the collectivity of experience's demands, nothing being omitted. If theological ideas should do this, if the notion of God, in particular, should prove to do it, how could pragmatism possibly deny God's existence? She could see no meaning in treating as 'not true' a notion that was pragmatically so successful. What other kind of truth could there be, for her, than all this agreement with concrete reality?

In my last lecture I shall return again to the relations of pragmatism with religion. But you see already how democratic she is. Her manners are as various and flexible, her resources as rich and endless, and her conclusions as friendly as those of mother nature.

An Enquiry Concerning Human Understanding (1777 edition)
David Hume

Section IV. Sceptical Doubts concerning the Operations of the Understanding

Part I

ALL the objects of human reason or enquiry may naturally be divided into two kinds, to wit, *Relations of Ideas,* and *Matters of Fact.* Of the first kind are the sciences of Geometry, Algebra, and Arithmetic; and in short, every affirmation, which is either intuitively or demonstratively certain. *That the square of the hypothenuse is equal to the square of the two sides,* is a proposition, which expresses a relation between these figures. *That three times five is equal to the half of thirty,* expresses a relation between these numbers. Propositions of this kind are discoverable by the mere operation of thought, without dependence on what is any where existent in the universe. Though there never were a circle or triangle in nature, the truths, demonstrated by Euclid, would for ever retain their certainty and evidence.

Matters of fact, which are the second objects of human reason, are not ascertained in the same manner; nor is our evidence of their truth, however great, of a like nature with the foregoing. The contrary of every matter of fact is still possible; because it can never imply a contradiction, and is conceived by the mind with the same facility and distinctness, as if ever so conformable to reality. *That the sun will not rise to-morrow* is no less intelligible a proposition, and implies no more contradiction, than the affirmation, *that it will rise.* We should in vain, therefore, attempt to demonstrate

(continued)

An Enquiry Concerning Human Understanding (1777 edition)   (*continued*)

its falsehood. Were it demonstratively false, it would imply a contradiction, and could never be distinctly conceived by the mind.

It may, therefore, be a subject worthy of curiosity, to enquire what is the nature of that evidence, which assures us of any real existence and matter of fact, beyond the present testimony of our senses, or the records of our memory. This part of philosophy, it is observable, has been little cultivated, either by the ancients or moderns; and therefore our doubts and errors, in the prosecution of so important an enquiry, may be the more excusable; while we march through such difficult paths, without any guide or direction. They may even prove useful, by exciting curiosity, and destroying that implicit faith and security, which is the bane of all reasoning and free enquiry. The discovery of defects in the common philosophy, if any such there be, will not, I presume, be a discouragement, but rather an incitement, as is usual, to attempt something more full and satisfactory, than has yet been proposed to the public.

All reasonings concerning matter of fact seem to be founded on the relation of *Cause and Effect*. By means of that relation alone we can go beyond the evidence of our memory and senses. If you were to ask a man, why he believes any matter of fact, which is absent; for instance, that his friend is in the country, or in FRANCE; he would give you a reason; and this reason would be some other fact; as a letter received from him, or the knowledge of his former resolutions and promises. A man, finding a watch or any other machine in a desert island, would conclude, that there had once been men in that island. All our reasonings concerning fact are of the same nature. And here it is constantly supposed, that there is a connexion between the present fact and that which is inferred from it. Were there nothing to bind them together, the inference would be entirely precarious. The hearing of an articulate voice and rational discourse in the dark assures us of the presence of some person: Why? because these are the effects of the human make and fabric, and closely connected with it. If we anatomize all the other reasonings of this nature, we shall find, that they are founded on the relation of cause and effect, and that this relation is either near or remote, direct or collateral. Heat and light are collateral effects of fire, and the one effect may justly be inferred from the other.

If we would satisfy ourselves, therefore, concerning the nature of that evidence, which assures us of matters of fact, we must enquire how we arrive at the knowledge of cause and effect.

I shall venture to affirm, as a general proposition, which admits of no exception, that the knowledge of this relation is not, in any instance, attained by reasonings *à priori;* but arises entirely from experience, when we find, that any particular objects are constantly conjoined with each other. Let an object be presented to a man of ever so strong natural reason and abilities; if that object be entirely new to him, he will not be able, by the most accurate examination of its sensible qualities, to discover any of its causes or effects. ADAM, though his rational faculties be supposed, at the very first, entirely perfect, could not have inferred from the fluidity, and transparency of water, that it would suffocate him, or from the light and warmth of fire, that it would consume him. No object ever discovers, by the qualities which appear to the senses, either the causes which produced it, or the effects which will arise from it; nor can our reason, unassisted by experience, ever draw any inference concerning real existence and matter of fact.

This proposition, *that causes and effects are discoverable, not by reason, but by experience*, will readily be admitted with regard to such objects, as we remember to have once been altogether unknown to us; since we must be conscious of the utter inability, which we then lay under, of foretelling, what would arise from them. Present two smooth pieces of marble to a man, who has no tincture of natural philosophy; he will never discover, that they will adhere together, in such a manner as to require great force to separate them in a direct line, while they make so small a resistance to a lateral pressure. Such events, as bear little analogy to the common course of nature, are also readily confessed to be known only by experience; nor does any man imagine that the explosion of gunpowder, or the attraction of a loadstone, could ever be discovered by arguments *à priori*. In like manner, when an effect is supposed to depend upon an intricate machinery or secret structure of parts, we make no difficulty in attributing all our knowledge of it to experience. Who will assert, that he can give the ultimate reason, why milk or bread is proper nourishment for a man, not for a lion or a tyger?

But the same truth may not appear, at first sight, to have the same evidence with regard to events, which have become familiar to us from our first appearance in the world, which bear a close analogy to the whole course of nature, and which are supposed to depend on the simple qualities of objects, without any secret structure of parts. We are apt to imagine, that we could discover these effects by the mere operation of our reason, without experience. We fancy, that were we brought, on a sudden, into this world, we could at first have inferred, that one Billiard-ball would communicate motion to another upon impulse; and that we needed not to have waited for the event, in order to pronounce with certainty concerning it. Such is the influence of custom, that, where it is strongest, it not only covers our natural ignorance, but even conceals itself, and seems not to take place, merely because it is found in the highest degree.

But to convince us, that all the laws of nature, and all the operations of bodies without exception, are known only by experience, the following reflections may, perhaps, suffice. Were any object presented to us, and were we required to pronounce concerning the effect, which will result from it, without consulting past observation; after what manner, I beseech you, must the mind proceed in this operation? It must invent or imagine some event, which it ascribes to the object as its effect; and it is plain that this invention must be entirely arbitrary. The mind can never possibly find the effect in the supposed cause, by the most accurate scrutiny and examination. For the effect is totally different from the cause, and consequently can never be discovered in it. Motion in the second Billiard-ball is a quite distinct event from motion in the first; nor is there any thing in the one to suggest the smallest hint of the other. A stone or piece of metal raised into the air, and left without any support, immediately falls: But to consider the matter *à priori,* is there any thing we discover in this situation, which can beget the idea of a downward, rather than an upward, or any other motion, in the stone or metal?

And as the first imagination or invention of a particular effect, in all natural operations, is arbitrary, where we consult not experience; so must we also esteem the supposed tye or connexion between the cause and effect, which binds them together, and renders it impossible, that any other effect could result from the operation of that cause. When I see, for instance, a Billiard-ball moving in a straight line towards another; even suppose motion in the second ball should by accident be suggested to me, as the result of their contact or impulse; may I not conceive, that a hundred different events might as well follow from that cause? May not both these balls remain at absolute rest? May not the first ball return in a straight line, or leap off from the second in any line or direction? All these suppositions are consistent and conceivable. Why then should we give the preference to one, which is no more consistent or conceivable than the rest? All our reasonings *à priori* will never be able to shew us any foundation for this preference.

In a word, then, every effect is a distinct event from its cause. It could not, therefore, be discovered in the cause, and the first invention or conception of it, *à priori,* must be entirely arbitrary. And even after it is suggested, the conjunction of it with the cause must appear equally arbitrary; since there are always many other effects, which, to reason, must seem fully as consistent and natural. In vain, therefore, should we pretend to determine any single event, or infer any cause or effect, without the assistance of observation and experience.

Hence we may discover the reason, why no philosopher, who is rational and modest, has ever pretended to assign the ultimate cause of any natural operation, or to show distinctly the action of that power, which produces any single effect in the universe. It is confessed, that the utmost effort of human reason is, to reduce the principles, productive of natural phaenomena, to a greater simplicity, and to resolve the many particular effects into a few general causes, by means of reasonings from analogy, experience, and observation. But as to the causes of these general causes, we should in vain attempt their discovery; nor shall we ever be able to satisfy ourselves, by any particular explication of them. These ultimate springs and principles are totally shut up from human curiosity and enquiry. Elasticity, gravity, cohesion of parts, communication of motion by impulse; these are probably the ultimate causes and principles which we shall ever discover in nature; and we may esteem ourselves sufficiently happy, if, by accurate enquiry and reasoning, we can trace up the particular phenomena to, or near to, these general principles. The most perfect philosophy of the natural kind only staves off our ignorance a little longer: As perhaps the most perfect philosophy of the moral or

(continued)

An Enquiry Concerning Human Understanding (1777 edition)   (*continued*)

metaphysical kind serves only to discover larger portions of it. Thus the observation of human blindness and weakness is the result of all philosophy, and meets us, at every turn, in spite of our endeavours to elude or avoid it.

Nor is geometry, when taken into the assistance of natural philosophy, ever able to remedy this defect, or lead us into the knowledge of ultimate causes, by all that accuracy of reasoning, for which it is so justly celebrated. Every part of mixed mathematics proceeds upon the supposition, that certain laws are established by nature in her operations; and abstract reasonings are employed, either to assist experience in the discovery of these laws, or to determine their influence in particular instances, where it depends upon any precise degree of distance and quantity. Thus, it is a law of motion, discovered by experience, that the moment or force of any body in motion is in the compound ratio or proportion of its solid contents and its velocity; and consequently, that a small force may remove the greatest obstacle or raise the greatest weight, if, by any contrivance or machinery, we can encrease the velocity of that force, so as to make it an overmatch for its antagonist. Geometry assists us in the application of this law, by giving us the just dimensions of all the parts and figures, which can enter into any species of machine; but still the discovery of the law itself is owing merely to experience, and all the abstract reasonings in the world could never lead us one step towards the knowledge of it. When we reason *à priori*, and consider merely any object or cause, as it appears to the mind, independent of all observation, it never could suggest to us the notion of any distinct object, such as its effect; much less, shew us the inseparable and inviolable connexion between them. A man must be very sagacious, who could discover by reasoning, that crystal is the effect of heat, and ice of cold, without being previously acquainted with the operation of these qualities.

Part II

But we have not, yet, attained any tolerable satisfaction with regard to the question first proposed. Each solution still gives rise to a new question as difficult as the foregoing, and leads us on to farther enquiries. When it is asked, *What is the nature of all our reasonings concerning matter of fact?* the proper answer seems to be, that they are founded on the relation of cause and effect. When again it is asked, *What is the foundation of all our reasonings and conclusions concerning that relation?* it may be replied in one word, EXPERIENCE. But if we still carry on our sifting humour, and ask, *What is the foundation of all conclusions from experience?* this implies a new question, which may be of more difficult solution and explication. Philosophers, that give themselves airs of superior wisdom and sufficiency, have a hard task, when they encounter persons of inquisitive dispositions, who push them from every corner, to which they retreat, and who are sure at last to bring them to some dangerous dilemma. The best expedient to prevent this confusion, is to be modest in our pretensions; and even to discover the difficulty ourselves before it is objected to us. By this means, we may make a kind of merit of our very ignorance.

I shall content myself, in this section, with an easy task, and shall pretend only to give a negative answer to the question here proposed. I say then, that, even after we have experience of the operations of cause and effect, our conclusions from that experience are *not* founded on reasoning, or any process of the understanding. This answer we must endeavour, both to explain and to defend.

It must certainly be allowed, that nature has kept us at a great distance from all her secrets, and has afforded us only the knowledge of a few superficial qualities of objects; while she conceals from us those powers and principles, on which the influence of these objects entirely depends. Our senses inform us of the colour, weight, and consistence of bread; but neither sense nor reason can ever inform us of those qualities, which fit it for the nourishment and support of a human body. Sight or feeling conveys an idea of the actual motion of bodies; but as to that wonderful force or power, which would carry on a moving body for ever in a continued change of place, and which bodies never lose but by communicating it to others; of this we cannot form the most distant conception. But notwithstanding this ignorance of natural powers[1] and principles, we always presume, when we see like sensible qualities, that they have like secret powers, and expect, that effects, similar to those which we have experienced, will follow from them. If a body of like colour and consistence with that bread, which we have formerly eat, be presented to us, we make no scruple of repeating the experiment, and foresee, with certainty, like nourishment and support. Now this is a process of the mind or thought, of which I would willingly know the foundation. It is allowed on all hands, that there is no known connexion between the sensible qualities and the secret powers; and consequently, that the mind is not led to form such a conclusion concerning their constant and regular conjunction, by any thing which it knows of their nature. As to past *Experience*, it can be allowed to give *direct* and *certain* information of those precise objects only, and that precise period of time, which fell under its cognizance: But why this experience should be extended to future times, and to other objects, which for aught we know, may be only in appearance similar; this is the main question on which I would insist. The bread, which I formerly eat, nourished me; that is, a body of such sensible qualities, was, at that time, endued with such secret powers: But does it follow, that other bread must also nourish me at another time, and that like sensible qualities must always be attended with like secret powers? The consequence seems nowise necessary. At least, it must be acknowledged, that there is here a consequence drawn by the mind; that there is a certain step taken; a process of thought, and an inference, which wants to be explained. These two propositions are far from being the same, *I have found that such an object has always been attended with such an effect,* and *I foresee, that other objects, which are, in appearance, similar, will be attended with similar effects*. I shall allow, if you please, that the one proposition may justly be inferred from the other: I know in fact, that it always is inferred. But if you insist, that the inference is made by a chain of reasoning, I desire you to produce that reasoning. The connexion between these propositions is not intuitive. There is required a medium, which may enable the mind to draw such an inference, if indeed it be drawn by reasoning and argument. What that medium is, I must confess, passes my comprehension; and it is incumbent on those to produce it, who assert, that it really exists, and is the origin of all our conclusions concerning matter of fact.

This negative argument must certainly, in process of time, become altogether convincing, if many penetrating and able philosophers shall turn their enquiries this way; and no one be ever able to discover any connecting proposition or intermediate step, which supports the understanding in this conclusion. But as the question is yet new, every reader may not trust so far to his own penetration, as to conclude, because an argument escapes his enquiry, that therefore it does not really exist. For this reason it may be requisite to venture upon a more difficult task; and enumerating all the branches of human knowledge, endeavour to shew, that none of them can afford such an argument.

All reasonings may be divided into two kinds, namely demonstrative reasoning, or that concerning relations of ideas, and moral reasoning, or that concerning matter of fact and existence. That there are no demonstrative arguments in the case, seems evident; since it implies no contradiction, that the course of nature may change, and that an object, seemingly like those which we have experienced, may be attended with different or contrary effects. May I not clearly and distinctly conceive, that a body, falling from the clouds, and which, in all other respects, resembles snow, has yet the taste of salt or feeling of fire? Is there any more intelligible proposition than to affirm, that all the trees will flourish in DECEMBER and JANUARY, and decay in MAY and JUNE? Now whatever is intelligible, and can be distinctly conceived, implies no contradiction, and can never be proved false by any demonstrative argument or abstract reasoning *à priori*.

If we be, therefore, engaged by arguments to put trust in past experience, and make it the standard of our future judgment, these arguments must be probable only, or such as regard matter of fact and real existence, according to the division above mentioned. But that there is no argument of this kind, must appear, if our explication of that species of reasoning be admitted as solid and satisfactory. We have said, that all arguments concerning existence are founded on the relation of cause and effect; that our knowledge of that relation is derived entirely from experience; and that all our experimental conclusions proceed upon the supposition, that the future will be conformable to the past. To endeavour, therefore, the proof of this last supposition by probable arguments, or arguments regarding existence, must be evidently going in a circle, and taking that for granted, which is the very point in question.

(continued)

An Enquiry Concerning Human Understanding (1777 edition)   (continued)

In reality, all arguments from experience are founded on the similarity, which we discover among natural objects, and by which we are induced to expect effects similar to those, which we have found to follow from such objects. And though none but a fool or madman will ever pretend to dispute the authority of experience, or to reject that great guide of human life; it may surely be allowed a philosopher to have so much curiosity at least, as to examine the principle of human nature, which gives this mighty authority to experience, and makes us draw advantage from that similarity, which nature has placed among different objects. From causes, which appear *similar*, we expect similar effects. This is the sum of all our experimental conclusions. Now it seems evident, that, if this conclusion were formed by reason, it would be as perfect at first, and upon one instance, as after ever so long a course of experience. But the case is far otherwise. Nothing so like as eggs; yet no one, on account of this appearing similarity, expects the same taste and relish in all of them. It is only after a long course of uniform experiments in any kind, that we attain a firm reliance and security with regard to a particular event. Now where is that process of reasoning, which, from one instance, draws a conclusion, so different from that which it infers from a hundred instances, that are nowise different from that single one? This question I propose as much for the sake of information, as with an intention of raising difficulties. I cannot find, I cannot imagine any such reasoning. But I keep my mind still open to instruction, if any one will vouchsafe to bestow it on me.

Should it be said, that, from a number of uniform experiments, we *infer a* connexion between the sensible qualities and the secret powers; this, I must confess, seems the same difficulty, couched in different terms. The questions still recurs, on what process of argument this *inference* is founded? Where is the medium, the interposing ideas, which join propositions so very wide of each other? It is confessed, that the colour, consistence, and other sensible qualities of bread appear not, of themselves, to have any connexion with the secret powers of nourishment and support. For otherwise we could infer these secret powers from the first appearance of these sensible qualities, without the aid of experience; contrary to the sentiment of all philosophers, and contrary to plain matter of fact. Here then is our natural state of ignorance with regard to the powers and influence of all objects. How is this remedied by experience? It only shews us a number of uniform effects, resulting from certain objects, and teaches us, that those particular time, were endowed with such powers and forces. When a new object, endowed with similar sensible qualities, is produced, we expect similar powers and forces, and look for a like effect. From a body of like colour and consistence with bread, we expect like nourishment and support. But this surely is a step or progress of the mind, which wants to be explained. When a man says, *I have found, in all past instances, such sensible qualities conjoined with such secret powers:* And when he says, *similar sensible qualities will always be conjoined with similar secret powers;* he is not guilty of a tautology, nor are these propositions in any respect the same. You say that the one proposition is an inference from the other. But you must confess that the inference is not intuitive; neither is it demonstrative: Of what nature is it then? To say it is experimental, is begging the question. For all inferences from experience suppose, as their foundation, that the future will resemble the past, and that similar powers will be conjoined with similar sensible qualities. If there be any suspicion, that the course of nature may change, and that the past may be no rule for the future, all experience becomes useless, and can give rise to no inference or conclusion. It is impossible, therefore, that any arguments from experience can prove this resemblance of the past to the future; since all these arguments are founded on the supposition of that resemblance. Let the course of things be allowed hitherto ever so regular; that alone, without some new argument or inference, proves not, that, for the future, it will continue so. In vain do you pretend to have learned the nature of bodies from your past experience. Their secret nature, and consequently, all their effects and influence, may change, without any change in their sensible qualities. This happens sometimes, and with regard to some objects: Why may it not happen always, and with regard to all objects? What logic, what process of argument secures you against this supposition? My practice, you say, refutes my doubts. But you mistake the purport of my question. As an agent, I am quite satisfied in the point; but as a philosopher, who has some share of curiosity, I will not say scepticism, I want to learn the foundation of this inference. No reading, no enquiry has yet been able to remove my difficulty, or give me satisfaction in a matter of such importance. Can I do better than propose the difficulty to the public, even though, perhaps, I have small hopes of obtaining a solution? We shall at least, by this means, be sensible of our ignorance, if we do not augment our knowledge.

I must confess, that a man is guilty of unpardonable arrogance, who concludes, because an argument has escaped his own investigation, that therefore it does not really exist. I must also confess, that, though all the learned, for several ages, should have employed themselves in fruitless search upon any subject, it may still, perhaps, be rash to conclude positively, that the subject must, therefore, pass all human comprehension. Even though we examine all the sources of our knowledge, and conclude them unfit for such a subject, there may still remain a suspicion, that the enumeration is not complete, or the examination not accurate. But with regard to the present subject, there are some considerations, which seem to remove all this accusation of arrogance or suspicion of mistake.

It is certain, that the most ignorant and stupid peasants, nay infants nay even brute beasts, improve by experience, and learn the qualities of natural objects, by observing the effects, which result from them. When a child has felt the sensation of pain from touching the flame of a candle, he will be careful not to put his hand near any candle; but will expect a similar effect from a cause, which is similar in its sensible qualities and appearance. If you assert, therefore, that the understanding of the child is led into this conclusion by any process of argument or ratiocination, I may justly require you to produce that argument; nor have you any pretence to refuse so equitable a demand. You cannot say, that the argument is abstruse, and may possibly escape your enquiry; since you confess, that it is obvious to the capacity of a mere infant. If you hesitate, therefore, a moment, or if, after reflection, you produce any intricate or profound argument, you, in a manner, give up the question, and confess, that it is not reasoning which engages us to suppose the past resembling the future, and to expect similar effects from causes, which are, to appearance, similar. This is the proposition which I intended to enforce in the present section. If I be right, I pretend not to have made any mighty discovery. And if I be wrong, I must acknowledge myself to be indeed a very backward scholar; since I cannot now discover an argument, which, it seems, was perfectly familiar to me, long before I was out of my cradle.

NOTE

1. The word, Power, is here used in a loose and popular sense. The more accurate explication of it would give additional evidence to this argument.

Science and the Physical World
W. T. Stace

So far as I know scientists still talk about electrons, protons, neutrons, and so on. We never directly perceive these, hence if we ask how we know of their existence the only possible answer seems to be that they are an inference from what we do directly perceive. What sort of an inference? Apparently a causal inference. The atomic entities in some way impinge upon the sense of the animal organism and cause that organism to perceive the familiar world of tables, chairs, and the rest.

But is it not clear that such a concept of causation, however interpreted, is invalid? The only reason we have for believing in the law of causation is that we *observe* certain regularities or sequences. We observe that, in certain conditions, A is always followed by B. We call A the cause, B the effect. And the sequence A-B becomes a causal law. It follows that all *observed* causal sequences are between sensed objects in the familiar world of perception, and that all known causal laws apply solely to the world of sense and not to anything beyond or behind it. And this in turn means that we

(continued)

Science and the Physical World (*continued*)

have not got, and never could have, one jot of evidence for believing that the law of causation can be applied *outside* the realm of perception, or that that realm can have any causes (such as the supposed physical objects) which are not themselves perceived.

Put the same thing in another way. Suppose there is an observed sequence *A-B-C,* represented by the vertical lines in the diagram below.

The observer X sees, and can see, nothing except things in the familiar world of perception. What *right* has he, and what *reason* has he, to assert causes of A, B, and C, such as *a', b', c',* which he can never observe, behind the perceived world? He has no *right,* because the law of causation on which he is relying has never been observed to operate outside the series of perceptions, and he can have, therefore, no evidence that it does so. And he has no *reason* because the phenomenon C is *sufficiently* accounted for by the cause B, B by A, and so on. It is unnecessary and superfluous to introduce a *second* cause *b'* for B, *c'* for C, and so forth. To give two causes for each phenomenon, one in one world and one in another, is unnecessary, and perhaps even self-contradictory.

Is it denied, then, it will be asked, that the star causes light waves, that the waves cause retinal changes, that these cause changes in the optic nerve, which in turn causes movements in the brain cells, and so on? No, it is not denied. But the observed causes and effects are all in the world of perception. And no sequences of sense-data can possibly justify going outside that world. If you admit that we never observe anything except sensed objects and their relations, regularities, and sequences, then it is obvious that we are completely shut in by our sensations and can never get outside them. Not only causal relations, but all other observed relations, upon which *any* kind of inferences might be founded, will lead only to further sensible objects and their relations. No inference, therefore, can pass from what is sensible to what is not sensible.

The fact is that atoms are *not* inferences from sensations. No one denies, of course, that a vast amount of perfectly valid inferential reasoning takes place in the physical theory of the atom. But it will not be found to be in any strict logical sense inference *from sense-data to atoms.* An *hypothesis* is set up, and the inferential processes are concerned with the application of the hypothesis, that is, with the prediction by its aid of further possible sensations and with its own internal consistency.

That atoms are not inferences from sensations means, of course, that from existence of sensations we cannot validly infer the existence of atoms. And this means that we cannot have any reason at all to believe that they exist. And that is why I propose to argue that they do not exist—or at any rate that no one could know it if they did, and that we have absolutely no evidence of their existence.

What status have they, then? Is it meant that they are false and worthless, merely untrue? Certainly not. No one supposes that the entries in the nautical almanac "exist" anywhere except on the pages of that book and in the brains of its compilers and readers. Yet they are "true," inasmuch as they enable us to predict certain sensations, namely, the positions and times of certain perceived objects which we call the stars. And so the formulae of the atomic theory are true in the same sense, and perform a similar function.

I suggest that they are nothing but shorthand formulae, ingeniously worked out by the human mind, to enable it to predict its experience, i.e. to predict what sensations will be given to it. By "predict" here I do not mean to refer solely to the future. To calculate that there was an eclipse of the sun visible in Asia Minor in the year 585 S.C. is, in the sense in which I am using the term, to predict.

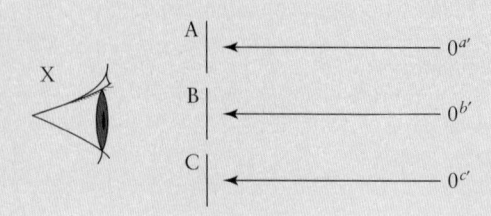

In order to see more clearly what is meant, let us apply the same idea to another case, that of gravitation. Newton formulated a law of gravitation in terms of "forces." It was supposed that this law—which was nothing but a mathematical formula—governed the operation of these existent forces. Nowadays it is no longer believed that these forces exist at all. And yet the law can be applied just as well without them to the prediction of astronomical phenomena. It is a matter of no importance to the scientific man whether the forces exist or not. That may be said to be a purely philosophical question. And I think the philosopher should pronounce them fictions. But that would not make the law useless or untrue. If it could still be used to predict phenomena, it would be just as true as it was.

It is true that fault is now found with Newton's law, and that another law, that of Einstein, has been substituted for it. And it is sometimes supposed that the reason for this is that forces are no longer believed in. But this is not the case. Whether forces exist or not simply does not matter. What matters is the discovery that Newton's law does *not* enable us accurately to predict certain astronomical facts such as the exact position of the planet Mercury. Therefore another formula, that of Einstein, has been substituted for it which permits correct predictions. This new law, as it happens, is a formula in terms of geometry. It is pure mathematics and nothing else. It does not contain anything about forces. In its pure form it does not even contain, so I am informed, anything about "humps and hills in space-time." And it does not matter whether any such humps and hills exist. It is truer than Newton's law, not because it substitutes humps and hills for forces, but solely because it is a more accurate formula of prediction.

Not only may it be said that forces do not exist. It may with equal truth be said that "gravitation" does not exist. Gravitation is not a "thing," but a mathematical formula, which exists only in the heads of mathematicians. And as a mathematical formula cannot cause a body to fall, so gravitation cannot cause a body to fall. Ordinary language misleads us here. We speak of the law "of" gravitation, and suppose that this law "applies to" the heavenly bodies. We are thereby misled into supposing that there are *two* things, namely, the gravitation and the heavenly bodies, and that one of these things, the gravitation, causes changes in the other. In reality nothing exists except the moving bodies. And neither Newton's law nor Einstein's law is, strictly speaking, a law of gravitation. They are both laws of moving bodies, that is to say, formulae which tell us how these bodies will move.

Now, just as in the past "forces" were foisted into Newton's law (by himself, be it said), so now certain popularizers of relativity foisted "humps and hills in space-time" into Einstein's law. We hear that the reason why the planets move in curved courses is that they cannot go through these humps and hills, but have to go round them! The planets just get "shoved about," not by forces, but by the humps and hills! But these humps and hills are pure metaphors. And anyone who takes them for "existences" gets asked awkward questions as to what "curved space" is curved "in."

It is not irrelevant to our topic to consider *why* human beings invent these metaphysical monsters of forces and bumps in space-time. The reason is that they have never emancipated themselves from the absurd idea that science "explains" things. They were not content to have laws which merely told them *that* the planets will, as a matter of fact, move in such and such ways. They wanted to know "why" the planets move in those ways. So Newton replied, "Forces." "Oh," said humanity, "that explains it. We understand forces. We feel them every time someone pushes or pulls us." Thus the movements were supposed to be "explained" by entities familiar because analogous to the muscular sensations which human beings feel. The humps and hills were introduced for exactly the same reason. They seem so familiar. If there is a bump in the billiard table, the rolling billiard ball is diverted from a straight to a curved course. Just the same with the planets. "Oh, I see!" says humanity, "that's quite simple. That *explains* everything."

But scientific laws, properly formulated, never "explain" anything. They simply state, in an abbreviated and generalized form, *what happens*. No scientist, and in my opinion no philosopher, knows *why* anything happens, or can "explain" anything. Scientific laws do nothing except state the brute fact that "when *A* happens, *B* always happens too." And laws of this kind obviously enable us to predict. If certain scientists substituted humps and hills for forces, then they have just substituted one superstition for another. For my part I do not believe that *science* has done this, though some *scientists* may have. For scientists, after all, are human beings with the same craving for "explanations" as other people.

I think that atoms are in exactly the same position as forces and the humps and hills of space-time. In reality the mathematical formulae which are the scientific ways of stating the atomic theory are simply formulae for calculating what sensations will appear in given conditions. But just as the weakness of the human mind demanded that there should correspond to the formula of gravitation a real

(continued)

Science and the Physical World   (*continued*)

"thing" which could be called "gravitation itself" or "force," so the same weakness demands that there should be a real thing corresponding to the atomic formulae, and this real thing is called the atom. In reality the atoms no more cause sensations than gravitation causes apples to fall. The only causes of sensations are other sensations. And the relation of atoms to sensations to be felt is not the relation of cause to effect, but the relation of a mathematical formula to the facts and happenings which it enables the mathematician to calculate.

Some writers have said that the physical world has no color, no sound, no taste, no smell. It has no spatiality. Probably it has not even number. We must not suppose that it is in any way like our world, or that we can understand it by attributing to it the characters of our world, Why not carry this progress to its logical conclusion? Why not give up the idea that it has even the character of "existence" which our familiar world has? We have given up smell, color, taste. We have given up even space and shape. We have given up number. Surely, after all that, mere existence is but a little thing to give up. No? Then is it that the idea of existence conveys "a sort of halo"? I suspect so. The "existence" of atoms is but the expiring ghost of the pellet and billiard-ball atoms of our forefathers. They, of course, had size, shape, weight, hardness. These have gone. But thinkers still cling to their existence, just as their fathers clung to the existence of forces, and for the same reason. Their reason is not in the slightest that science has any use for the existent atom. But the *imagination* has. It seems somehow to explain things, to make them homely and familiar.

It will not be out of place to give one more example to show how common fictitious existences are in science, and how little it matters whether they really exist or not. This example has no strange and annoying talk of "bent spaces" about it. One of the foundations of physics is, or used to be, the law of the conservation of energy. I do not know how far, if at all, this has been affected by the theory that matter sometimes turns into energy. But that does not affect the lesson it has for us. The law states, or used to state, that the amount of energy in the universe is always constant, that energy is never either created or destroyed. This was highly convenient, but it seemed to have obvious exceptions. If you throw a stone up into the air, you are told that it exerts in its fall the same amount of energy which it took to throw it up. But suppose it does not fall. Suppose it lodges on the roof of your house and stays there. What has happened to the energy which you can nowhere perceive as being exerted? It seems to have disappeared out of the universe. No, says the scientist, it still exists as *potential* energy. Now what does this blessed word "potential"—which is thus brought in to save the situation—mean as applied to energy? It means, of course, that the energy does not exist in any of its regular "forms," heat, light, electricity, etc. But this is merely negative. What positive meaning has the term? Strictly speaking, none whatever. Either the energy exists or it does not exist. There is no realm of the "potential" half-way between existence and non existence. And the existence of energy can only consist in its being exerted. If the energy is not being exerted, then it is not energy and does not exist. Energy can no more exist without energizing than heat can exist without being hot. The "potential" existence of the energy is, then, a fiction. The actual empirically verifiable facts are that if a certain quantity of energy *e* exists in the universe and then disappears out the universe (as happens when the stone lodges on the roof) the same amount of energy *e* will always reappear, begin to exist again, in certain known conditions. That is the fact which the law of the conservation of energy actually expresses. And the fiction of potential energy is introduced simply because it is convenient and makes the equations easier to work. They could be worked quite well without it, but would be slightly more complicated. In either case the function of the law is the same. Its object is to apprise us that if in certain conditions we have certain perceptions (throwing up the stone), then in certain other conditions we shall get certain other perceptions (heat, light, stone hitting skull, or other such). But there will always be a temptation to hypostatize the potential energy as an "existence," and to believe that it is a "cause" which "explains" the phenomena.

If the views which I have been expressing are followed out, they will lead to the conclusion that, strictly speaking, *nothing exists except sensations* (and the minds which perceive them). The rest is mental construction or fiction. But this does not mean that the conception of a star or the conception of an electron are worthless or untrue. Their truth and value consist in their capacity for helping us to organize our experience and predict our sensations.

BRIAN SKYRMS, "The Pragmatic Justification of Induction," *Choice and Chance,* 1966, 37–42. Reprinted with permission from Wadsworth Publishing Company.

ERNEST SOSA, "Knowledge and Intellectual Virtue," *The Monist,* 1985. Copyright ©1985 *The Monist,* La Salle, IL 61301. Reprinted by permission.

WILLIAM STACE, "Science and the Physical World" from *Man Against Darkness* by W. T. Stace. Copyright ©1967 by University of Pittsburgh Press. Reprinted by permission of the University of Pittsburgh Press.

P.F. STRAWSON, "Hume, Wittgenstein and Induction," from *Skepticism and Naturalism* by P. F. Strawson. Copyright ©1985 Columbia University Press. Reprinted with the permission of the publisher. BARRY STROUD, "Understanding Human Knowledge in General," *Knowledge and Skepticism,* edited by Marjorie Clay and Keith Lehrer, Westview Press, 1989, 31–49. Reprinted with permission.

Chapter 2
Metaphysics

The man is released from his bonds and struggles toward the bright light. He suffers greatly during this extraction and finds it difficult to open his eyes because of the intense luminosity that surrounds him. Only after determining that where he is is the real world and what he is learning is the truth does he attempt to return to free his enslaved companions.

For those of you who are familiar with science-fiction movies from the 1990s, the previous passage might remind you of the plot from *The Matrix*. However, it is not. It is a summary of Plato's Allegory of the Cave. This allegory is used to explain the nature of reality. Plato (427–347 BCE) suggests that what we perceive is not the real world but rather a shadow of its true nature. It is the difficult but necessary role of the philosopher to escape his or her chains and discover truth and once it is known, bring that knowledge back to the rest of humanity.

Metaphysics is the field of philosophical inquiry that examines the nature of reality. It comes from the Greek words *meta,* which can mean "with", "beyond", "beside", "after", "during", and *physis,* which means "nature". Since Aristotle (384–322 BCE) did not give his books titles, one interpretation of the word "metaphysics" is that it is simply the book that came after the book he wrote on nature that we now call his *Physics*. One other interpretation, which is closer to how we use the term, is that metaphysics refers to works (or ideas) that go beyond physics in terms of content or subject matter.

The proposition "You have read the previous chapter" must be either true or false. It is a purported event in the past and so must have either occurred or not. But what about the future? The proposition "You will read the next chapter" must be either true or false as well. But is its truth value (i.e., its truth or falsity) already determined even though we do not know what it is? Perhaps it is not true until you read the chapter and in reading it you will prove the proposition to be true but only in the future. So if it is not true now and only will be true when you read it, it has to be false *now*. But that seems a bit odd to say that "You will read the next chapter" is false until you read it since the claim is that you *will* read it, not *will have* read it (i.e., read it in the past). Should we argue instead that the proposition "You will read the next paragraph" is neither true nor false?

Consider the proposition "July 15, 2045, is a sunny Saturday." Since this is a meaningful statement about a purported fact, it must be either true or false. Do we have to wait until that date for it to become true or false, or is it true or false right now? When, to end your confusion, is something true or false? We are not stating that we *know* it to be true or false, but rather we are stating that it *is* true or false right now and it is this information we may *know* in the future. Are propositions always true or false and we simply discover or learn their truth value? Here is another example that does not involve the passage of time which may help you better understand this concept.

Consider the proposition "There is life on other planets." Undoubtedly, we currently do not know the truth value of the proposition; that is, we do not possess the knowledge of whether there is life on other planets. Yet surely the truth or falsity of the claim is independent of whether we happen to know it. Just because no one knew the earth was round five thousand years ago does not mean that once they figured it out the roundness of the earth suddenly became true *then*. The proposition that "There is life on other planets is either true or false" must be a true proposition regardless of which truth valuation is correct regardless of when we learn which valuation is correct.

If truth is timeless and positive statements about every thing and event irrespective of when it actually occurs are true, then every thing and every event has, is, and will be already determined. If so, then it would seem that we are unable to alter the truth value of these events since they are true when they occur(ed) and are true now. If this also applies to our own actions, then what happens, happens, and what does not happen, does not happen. It cannot have been any other way in spite of what we would wish (for even our wishing it so would already be determined). If we do what we said we would do, it is determined to be the case, and if we quickly change our minds and do the opposite then that too is determined to be the case.

In *Run Lola Run* we witness a series of possible actions, causes, and effects, repeated over and over with slight variations. Lola needs to get $100,000 to her boyfriend because of a drug deal that went wrong, and a variety of scenarios are played out over the course of the movie. It is as if she is saying to the viewer: "I could do this and this, or this and this. And which one would achieve my goal?" Her choices cause a series of acts to occur, and she becomes part of a larger chain of events. According to the determinist, whether she achieves her goal or not is already set in stone. So, can she really change the ultimate outcome?

In *Sliding Doors* Helen runs to catch a subway train. She hurries down a flight of stairs and a woman moves her child out of the way but Helen is too late and the train leaves without her. The camera pulls back and the same scene replays itself but this time Helen is able to put her arm in between the sliding doors of the subway car and she makes her connection. Both individuals are Helen and we see her life (lives) unfold in two different ways. Some of the events are the same, others are radically different. But in neither film do we see the character making the decision to do something differently from what she actually does. For how could she? One cannot do something "differently" from what one actually does. Lola's and Helen's destinies do not change even though it may seem like they are able to manipulate them.

Manipulation suggests control, and having control suggests that one can make a voluntary choice. But if our statements about everything are true or false and we are unable to change this valuation, then how we will act has already been cast. So if we are unable to change our destiny because what is, is, and what will be, will be, then control is an illusion. And if having control over one's life is an illusion, then we have some serious difficulties with assigning moral blame and praise.

If someone pushes you and you knock another person down, we would explain this in terms of causal responsibility and not moral responsibility. You were not in control. You were acting involuntarily. You have to be able to freely choose to act in a certain way in order to justify being held morally culpable. If every event has a cause, and every event can be explained, then there is a long series of causes and events that occurred before you fell and that will occur afterward. To word it stronger, we would not say it was your fault if you were forced to do something, and this is exactly what cause and effect is about. For example, there had to be a person there for you to knock down and another person had to push you. That person who pushed you also had to see the taxi coming in your direction, and that taxi had to be coming in your direction because it was late for the airport . . . Because the taxi driver stopped to help the person that you knocked down, the passenger in the taxi will miss her flight. Because she will miss the flight, she will miss her job interview; and because she misses the job interview she will go back to Wisconsin where she will start a successful Internet company. So because you knocked someone down on that day, she will be a billionaire . . . So who made her rich?

Philosophers have debated whether we can act voluntarily while also maintaining some form of determinism. One attempt to rescue morality is to argue that nothing is determined. However, if nothing is determined then you cannot be held culpable. Why? Because if nothing caused the event then you could not have caused it either. Can we freely choose? Can we affect our future? Some claim that you can no more alter your future than you can modify your past. Or wait; perhaps you *can* change the past. At least, that is what many people in the movies try to do.

In the film *Terminator*, Arnold Schwarzenegger plays the role of a single-minded cyborg from the future. He has been sent back in time to kill Sarah Connor, who is the mother of John Connor. In the future, John will lead the battle against the machines so by killing Sarah, the Terminator will stop John from being born and if John is not born then he cannot lead the battle against the machines. A soldier named Reese who is also from the future comes back to stop the Terminator. In the following early scene, Reese has managed to save Sarah from her first encounter with the cyborg, and Reese explains how the future has already been determined.

Int. Grey Sedan—Night
Sarah is slumped way down in the seat, turned away from the window, trying not to see the landscape reeling outside.

SARAH (hoarse whisper) This is a mistake. I haven't done anything.

REESE No. But you will. It's very important that you live.

Sarah closes her eyes, as if to shut it all out.

REESE (cutting her off) Pay attention. The 600 series had rubber skin. We spotted them easy. But these are new. They look human. Sweat, bad breath, everything. Very hard to spot. I had to wait 'til he moved on you before I could zero him.

SARAH Hey, I'm not stupid, y'know. They can't build anything like that yet.

REESE No. Not yet. Not for about forty years.

Later . . .

Int. Division HQ/Interrogation Room—Night
The room is small, furnished with only a table and two chairs. Reese, his arms handcuffed behind him, sits opposite Dr. Silberman. Behind Silberman is a large mirror. A DETECTIVE leans against the wall.

SILBERMAN So. You're a soldier. Fighting for whom?

REESE With the One Thirty Second under Perry, from '21 to '27—

SILBERMAN (interrupting) The year 2027?

Int. Interrogation Room

REESE   Then I was assigned Recon/ Security, last two years, under John Connor.

SILBERMAN   And who was the enemy?

REESE   SKYNET. A computer defense system built for SAC-NORAD by Cyber Dynamics. A modified Series 4800.

SILBERMAN   (gravely) I see. And this . . . computer, thinks it can win by killing the mother of its enemy, killing him, in effect, before he is even conceived? A sort of retroactive abortion?

REESE   Yes.

REESE   John gave me a message for you. Made me memorize it. "Sarah" . . . this is the message . . . 'Sarah, thank you. For your courage through the dark years. I can't help you with what you must soon face, except to tell you that the future is not set . . . there is no such thing as Fate, but what we make for ourselves by our own will. You must be stronger than you imagine you can be. You must survive, or I will never exist.' That's all.

The practical difficulty is that if John is "retroactively aborted" he will not lead the battle against the machines. If he does not lead the battle then the machines will not need to send the Terminator back to kill him. But if they do not send him back, John lives to lead the battle of the machines. Since the Terminator is sent back in time, then they must have failed in killing John in the past, otherwise they would not need to try to kill him. Thus the mission is doomed to failure. The past establishes the future and the future tells us what happens in the past. This paradox of time-travel seems to show how events in the future cannot be changed because we cannot change the past. It also shows how determinism appears to be a substantial claim.

Instead of going from the future to the present, in *Back to the Future,* Marty and Doc attempt to go from the present to the past.[1] In this scene, Doc shows Marty his time-travelling car.

MARTY   Doc!

DOC   Marty, you made it! Welcome to my latest experiment, this is the big one, the one I've been waiting for all my life.

MARTY   Uh, well, It's a Delorian?

DOC   Stay with me MARTY, all your questions will be answered. Roll tape. We'll proceed.

MARTY   OK, hey Doc, is that a de . . .

DOC   Never mind that, never mind that now. Not now, not now.

MARTY   OK, I'm ready.

DOC   Good evening, I'm Doctor Emmit Brown, and I'm standing on the parking lot of Twin pines mall. It is Saturday morning, October 26th, 1985, 1:18 a.m., and this is temporal displacement experiment number 1. C'mon Einey, here boy, get in there, good boy, sit down, put your seat belt on. That's it. Please note . . . that Einstein's clock is in precise synchronization with my control watch. In you go, have a good trip Einstein. Watch your head.

MARTY   You got that thing hooked up to the . . . car.

DOC   Watch this.

MARTY   k

(Car starts and gets into position)

DOC   Not me, the car, the car!

If my calculations are correct, when this baby hits 88 mph. You're gonna see some serious stuff! Watch this, watch this . . .

(Car goes 1 minute into the future) What did I tell you, 88 miles per hour! The temporal displacement occurred at exactly 1:20 AM and 0 seconds.

MARTY   Hot, Jesus Christ. Jeez Louise Doc, you disintegrated Einstein.

DOC   Calm down Marty, I didn't disintegrate anything. The molecular structure of both Einstein and the car are completely intact.

MARTY   Then where in the hell are they?

DOC   The appropriate question is . . .When in the hell are they. You see, Einstein has just become the world's first time traveler. I sent him . . . Into the future. One minute into the future to be exact. At precisely 1:21 AM and 0 seconds, we will catch up with him and the time machine.

---

[1] In the first of two sequels, DOC and MARTY go from the present to the future, then after altering it, they go back to the newly changed present and then forward again to a future based on that newly changed present, and then back into the present-past of the Wild West, or is that the past-present? Time travel gets confusing!

MARTY   Wait a minute, wait a minute, DOC, uh, are you telling me that you built a time machine out of a Delorian?

DOC   The way I see it . . . if you're going to build a time machine into a car, Why not do it with some style? Besides the stainless steel construction made the flux dispersal . . . look out. (car returns)

MARTY   What, what is it hot . . .

DOC   It's cold . . . air cold, ah ha ha. Einstein, you little devil. Einstein's watch is exactly one minute behind mine and still ticking.

MARTY   He's all right!

DOC   He's fine, and he's completely unaware that anything happened. As far as he's concerned, the trip was instantaneous. That's why his watch is exactly one minute behind mine. He skipped over that minute to instantly arrive at this moment in time. Come here, lemme show you how it works.

After successfully going into the past and completing his mission, Marty runs into a problem where he cannot get "back to the future," which is in fact his present (but which is the future from the perspective of the past):

MARTY   Whoa, whoa Doc, stuck here, I can't be stuck here, I got a life in 1985. I got a girl.

DOC   Is she pretty?

MARTY   Doc, she's beautiful. She's crazy about me. Look at this, look what she wrote me, Doc. That says it all. Doc, you're my only hope.

DOC   Marty, you interacted with anybody else today, besides me?

MARTY   Um, yeah well I might have sort of ran into my parents.

DOC   Great Scott. Let me see that photograph again of your brother. Just as I thought, this proves my theory, look at your brother.

MARTY   His head's gone, it's like it's been erased.

DOC   Erased from existence.

MARTY   Whoa, they really cleaned this place up, looks brand new.

DOC   Now remember, according to my theory you interfered with your parent's first meeting. They don't meet, they don't fall in love, they won't get married and they won't have kids. That's why your older brother's disappeared from that photograph. Your sister will follow and unless you repair the damages, you will be next.

Just like with the *Terminator*, the problem here is that if Marty disappears then he will not exist in the future and if he does not exist in the future, then he cannot go back in time to damage his future and erase himself. So it would seem that if he does not exist in the future, his future is secure because he cannot go back and mess with it! And if he does exist and he damages his future in the past, then he will not exist. So we are left with the realization that at some time, Marty could potentially exist and not exist at different times, which is fine if we are talking about people living (existing) and dying (not existing) but Marty's mortality is not linked to our notion of time. Like his disappearing brother, Marty's fate is to exist and non-exist at the same time.

Circles upon circles, dreams within dreams; Movies help us witness the difficulties of talking about the future or the past being malleable. But if we cannot change what was, is, or will be, we are faced with the nagging problem of determinism. To paraphrase Yoda, when it comes to time-travel or to our actions, we can only "do or do not, there is no try."[2]

Another reason why philosophers seem set on trying to come up with an answer that will satisfy us regarding cause and effect (be it in the context of determinism or time-travel) is that human beings are mortal. That we are here for some period of time then gone never to return (depending on your religious views of course) means that we lose opportunities for further experiences. Add to this the deterministic belief that we cannot change bad things into good, or have a second chance to do things differently, and we get the result that many people fear death and see it as a harm.

Thomas Nagel (1937–) questions whether it makes sense to speak of harm and suffering when one is dead. Can the dearly departed be harmed if we speak ill of them or do not fulfill our promises to them? Why do we insist on adhering to their last requests when they cannot be affected by our following or not following them? Nagel discusses why so many

---

[2] *Star Wars: The Return of the Jedi.*

people dread their own demise and whether these beliefs are well reasoned or whether they are, for example, attempts to imagine what is unimaginable. What is unimaginable is of course what it would be like to be dead. As far as we know, a dead person does not lie there and think, "Oh, so this is what it is like! It's not that bad. A bit cramped for space but . . ." The dead, once dead, are simply no more (at least for those who do not believe in a soul or reincarnation). To wonder what the experience of death is like is about as productive an exercise as wondering what your nonexistent children would like for breakfast tomorrow. One does not experience death. You simply cease to be. The process of dying may cause suffering, but death itself does not.

Death is the great unknown, and for that reason alone moviemakers love to play on our uncertainties and fears about it. Although they might succeed in their attempts to entertain and/or scare us, most movie fictions about death are logically self-defeating and serve as good examples of how we need to think critically about what is truly possible. We have learned this lesson already in our discussions concerning time-travel and determinism, but let us examine another metaphysical issue: The Mind / Body problem.

If you have read Descartes's *Meditations*, you will recall that the foundation on which he builds knowledge is that he is "a thinking thing." That is, Descartes can doubt that he is awake, or that he has hands, or that 2 + 3 = 5, however regardless of what he doubts, in order to doubt he must be doubting. That he can also conceive of his mind (or soul) without his body he argues that the mind is a non-extended thing, different from the physical body. And so the question that follows is whether he is right. Is there a mind? If so, what is its nature? How is it connected and how *can* it be connected to our physical body, assuming that we do in fact have a physical body?

Descartes's view is called the Interactionist Substance Dualist theory of mind. That is, he believes that the mind and the body are two (hence 'Dual') separate substances—one substance is extended in space (the body) and one substance thinks (the mind). Sometimes these two substances interact with each other. If I cut myself (a physical event), I feel pain (a non-physical event). If I am scared (a non-physical event), my heart rate increases (a physical event). This view captures our commonsense beliefs about the mind and body: The mind affects the body and the body affects the mind. This interconnectiveness between the mind and body is shown and discussed in the film *The Cell*. By means of some pretty fancy drug cocktails (i.e., the physical cause) psychotherapist Dr. Miriam Kent is able to create certain experiences (i.e., the non-physical effect) that allow Catherine to enter the dreams of her patients. There, Catherine attempts to help them work out their psychological problems. In the following sequences, the dialogue moves from explaining the physical cause and its non-physical effect to the opposite: the non-physical cause resulting in a physical effect.

> *Dr. Miriam Kent prepares a series of CHEMICAL CARTRIDGES and loads them into a container connected to the IV-like tubes linked to the suspension device.*

RAMSEY   What is it—are they—exactly?

MIRIAM   Psychostimulants, serotonin, stabilizers, meprobamate, Neurontin, lithium carbonate. And my baby. It duplicates and expands upon the effects of a chemical called oxytocin, forcing a break in the neuron connections that hold experience. So new experience can form.

> *IN THE PROCEDURE ROOM, Catherine takes a deep breath and as the drugs take effect, feels herself losing consciousness. She glances at Stargher, a man who tortures and kills women, then looks up as the CLOTH MASK descends from the ceiling.*

MIRIAM (O.S.) (CONT'D)   Intravenous administration complete.

HENRY (O.S.)   Initiating connection.

We follow fibrous wires running from Catherine's mask to Stargher's. Their blood mixing with chemicals in the IV-like containers. The computer system humming.

HENRY (O.S.) (CONT'D)   Transfer begins 1100 hours, 34 minutes, 12 seconds.

Catherine's eye focuses on the mask. As it comes closer, we see the lining is laced with thread-like wires and microchips forming hyper-miniature circuit boards. Catherine's eye blinks. The mask covers her face. Catherine's eye shuts.

HENRY (V.O.)   Gentlemen?

> *Novak looks at an INTERCOM SPEAKER.*

HENRY (V.O.) (CONT'D)   She's back, [from the dream world]

RAMSEY   What happens here?

HENRY   We don't talk about that.

NOVAK   What happens?

HENRY   Well, theoretically, while she's inside if she came to believe that Stargher's world is her world, her mind has the power to convince the body that anything done to it is, um, actually done.

To justify the claim that there is a physical and non-physical component to what or who we are, dualists will rely on a number of arguments. These arguments will in turn result in some proponents adopting different types of dualist theories.[3] Two such subtheories that tend to be quickly dismissed are Parallelism (the mind and body work in parallel with each other but do not interact) and Epiphenomenology (mental events are caused by physical events, but not the other way around). Few philosophers hold either theory because the former suggests that every appearance of a causal connection is sheer coincidence while the latter suggests that only half are.

Some of the evidence to support the dualist position includes intentionality, direct introspection, and private experiences. These concepts do not all of seem to be appropriate concepts that can be applied to purely physical brain states. Our desires and intentions seem to involve a state of being that only the individual can know. I might make a face and grimace, which suggests that I am in pain, however, only I know what that pain feels like to me. If I see spots in front of my eyes, only I know what color they appear to me as. We both might agree as to when something is "red" but our experience of the redness is private.

That you see me running to the store and buying ice cream allows you to infer that I had a craving for ice cream. You drew this conclusion from observing my behavior. You saw me run, buy, and then eat ice cream. Yet it would be silly of *me* to infer from my actions (running into the store and buying ice cream) that I desired ice cream. Instead, I would know immediately from direct introspection what my personal desire was and then (presumably) act according.

I desire ice cream. I want to take a walk. I plan on taking a holiday next week. These elements of intentionality also do not seem to fit with what we know about the brain. How can a complex chemical transaction between neurons really be "my love for my country"? Using an MRI machine you might scan my brain while I am eating a red apple. You might be able to see where my neurons are firing as I am having this apple-eating experience, however you cannot know what it is like for me to see the apple's redness, feel its texture, smell its sweetness, and taste its flavor.

When a movie has ghosts[4] or spirits in it, it is implicitly relying on the dualist notion of human beings. Being a dualist does not necessarily entail you also believe in ghosts, but if you believe in ghosts you are probably a dualist. Some people believe in ghosts because they believe that human beings have a non-corporeal component—a mind or a soul—and that this part survives our physical death. For some reason however, even though our physical body is supposedly just a vessel that contains our essential or true "self", movie ghosts often appear to physically resemble the people they were while alive. They will also tend to exhibit the same personality traits.[5] If they were nice in life, they are typically nice in the afterworld, and if they were not so nice in life, then they are not nice at all in the after world.[6] These attributes further support religious claims that who the person really is is to be identified with their soul rather then their physical body. Indeed, Some religions claim that non-human animals do not think or possess a soul.[7] Perhaps this explains why in the rare occurrence when animals do come back to life in movies they tend to be things like hellhounds![8]

If you think about ghosts (either in the actual world or in movies), there are a few logical concerns

---

[3] Accordingly, the student must realize that there can be many philosophical variations and differences even within particular schools of thought.

[4] A few typical ghost movies include *Candyman, Ghost Story, Ghostbusters, Jug-on: The Grudge, Ring, The Amityville Horror, The Changeling, The Haunting, The Legend of Hell House,* and *The Shining.*

[5] Rarely are the dead brought back to life in order to learn some personal lesson about how they should have lived. Indeed, if determinism is true then these "second chances" (such as those depicted in *Heaven Can Wait* and *Here Comes Mr. Jordan*) are a waste of supernatural energies.

[6] *Beetlejuice* has examples of both types of personality traits: the kind but dead newlyweds and the sneaky Beetle juice.

[7] A view that is alluded to in the animated film *All Dogs go to Heaven*.

[8] In *Pet Semetary,* people's pet cats and dogs come back to life after being buried in a certain graveyard, and in *Resident Evil,* the testing animals are clearly animated dead tissue. I say "tend to be" for in *The Nightmare Before Christmas,* the main character Jack is a skeleton and yet his pet dog Zero is a ghost. However it still fits with the view that ghosts' personalities tend to be similar to what the person was like when he or she was alive since Jack's dog is quite friendly, barking playfully, fetching bones, and so on.

regarding the possibility, let alone the plausibility, of their existence. If the soul survives, should not all ghosts be disembodied spirits (as in *The Haunting*) rather than their original physical form (as in *The Frighteners*)? If ghosts are non-physical, why are they only sometimes affected by physical objects? That is, why are they capable of walking through walls yet they do not sink through floors? And how do ghosts vocalize if they do not have physical bodies, and in particular, larynxes? These are not facile questions. By analogy, if the mind is non-physical, where is it located? Does it even make sense to speak of it having a location? If the mind is like a ghost and both are so radically different in kind than bodies, how is it possible for such things to affect physical bodies? If the mind can move a body (i.e., the owner's), why can it not move other bodies as well? Why must it be necessarily and solely linked to only one person?

According to the movies if the mind survives the death of the body, we get ghosts. And in a reversal of fortune, if the mind dies along with the body but somehow the whole body is re-animated, we get zombies.[9] Zombies do for materialists what ghosts do for dualists. That is, a zombie does not need a mind to exhibit behavior that suggests intentionality. Remember, no one can access another person's mind directly, so we can only infer what is going on between their ears by what they say and do. I desire ice cream, so I eat ice cream, and since I eat ice cream, (you infer) I must desire ice cream. Zombies desire brains, so they eat brains; Zombies eat brains so (we infer) they must desire brains. No dualist position is needed!

Unfortunately, while an extremely open-minded philosopher[10] might point to zombies[11] as representations of the materialistic view of the mind/body problem, zombies can also point toward dualism. Both the materialist and the dualist would agree that zombies are mindless. The materialist would reach this conclusion because they maintain zombies never had minds, only brains. However, the dualist would say the zombies are clearly unable to think for themselves as they once did so perhaps they once had minds to direct their behavior but no longer. This latter view will become clearer in the following excerpt from *Day of the Dead*.

---

[9] A few typical zombie movies include *Plan 9 from Outer Space, Planet Terror, 28 Days Later, Resident Evil, Dead Alive, Night of the Living Dead, Dawn of the Dead, I Walked with a Zombie,* and *The Incredibly Strange Creatures Who Stopped Living and Became Mixed-Up Zombies.*
[10] I say this because we are talking about zombies after all!
[11] For the scientific explanation of zombies, see *The Serpent and the Rainbow* (loosely based on a true story).

On the monitors, we see the rescue stations blink off over shots of the two men who still argue on the air.

TV MAN 1   Well I don't believe in ghosts, Doctor

TV MAN 2   These are not ghosts. Nor are these humans! These are dead corpses. Any unburied human corpse with its brain intact will in fact re-activate. And it's precisely because of incitement by irresponsible public figures like yourself that this situation is being dealt with irresponsibly by the public at large!

Another outraged cry goes up from the stagehands and observers. Doctor Foster tries to out-scream the cries . . .

TV MAN 2   You have not listened . . . You have not listened. For the last three weeks . . . What does it take . . . What does it take to make people see?

Fran moves into the large studio area where the broadcasters argue. The commotion is maddening. Fran stares for a moment.

TV MAN 2   (now distraught . . . almost pleading) This situation is controllable. People must come to grips with this concept. It's extremely difficult . . . with friends . . . with family . . . but a dead body must be de-activated by either destroying the brain or severing the brain from the rest of the body.

Another outburst in the studio.

TV MAN 2   The situation must be controlled . . . before it's too late . . . They are multiplying too rapidly . . .

In the hall, the male Zombie appears, and the crowd panics. The Troopers try to keep things calm.

S.W.A.T. 3   It's one of them . . . My God . . . It's one of them.

S.W.A.T. 4   Shoot for the head.

FRAN   (still staring down through a bubble [at the zombies gathering around the local shopping mall])

What are they doing? Why do they come here?

STEVE (also looking down)

   Some kind of instinct. Memory . . . of what they used to do. This was an important place in their lives.

VOICE . . . not actually cannibalism . . . Cannibalism in the true sense of the word implies an intraspecies activity . . . These creatures cannot be considered human. They prey on humans . . . They do not prey on each other.

   We see the mall balcony now. Zombies wander past the stores. Some move down the stationary stairs onto the main concourse below.

VOICE They attack and . . . and feed . . . only on warm human flesh . . .

   At the mall entrances, some creatures drift out into the night. Others still enter the enormous building. There are not as many as there were in the afternoon, but there are certainly enough to be threatening.

VOICE Intelligence? Seemingly little or no reasoning power. What basic skills remain are more remembered behaviors from . . . normal life.

   Several creatures are clawing at the roll gate to the department store. It is a strange and eerie sight. The staring, painted eyes of the mannequins within the store seem to watch the Zombies. The gate rattles but does not budge.

VOICE There are reports of the creatures using tools, but even these actions are the most primitive . . . The use of external articles as bludgeons etc., even animals will adopt the basic use of tools in this manner.

   Fran's eyes pop open, the voice has awakened her. She has been asleep on the blanket.

VOICE These creatures are nothing but pure, motorized instinct . . .

In these scenes, zombies, although mindless, are still able to act. In order to stop them, one does not disconnect them like one might a robot, or drive a stake through their heart like a vampire; instead one must shoot them in the head. The materialist symbolism is obvious. It is brain matter that governs their behavior. Kill the brain and you stop the rest of the body as well. Yet the dualist can point to the fact that the zombie does not seem to be self-aware or conscious of what it is doing as evidence of something missing. In other words, any sense of intentionality or sentient desire comes from what observers project onto these individuals. Without a mind, zombies merely go through the motions of life driven by "pure, motorized instinct." With a mind, they could be capable of learning and remembering and would be even more dangerous![12]

In horror movies such as *Dawn of the Dead,* the characteristics of zombies are contrasted with the living. The undead are mindless, we are not. Yet is this an acceptable assumption? We can only have immediate access to our own inner states (what we are seeing, feeling, thinking, etc.) We cannot know what it is like to have the mental experiences of someone else for it is impossible for us to have direct intimate knowledge of other minds. As already mentioned, we may surmise from others' behavior what they are experiencing but we cannot know for certain what those experiences are truly like or whether they even exist. We cannot even tell whether others have a mind. I might know I have a mind, but can I conclude on that basis alone that everyone else does as well? Just because I have a dollar in my pocket does not mean that everyone else does!

That you tell me you have a mind is not sufficient evidence. A robot might be programmed to respond to certain stimuli in a way that mimics human intent. The robot may be programmed to respond in the affirmative to queries regarding personal awareness yet never be truly aware of their response. In other words, Data,[13] or Hal,[14] or Robbie[15] might all agree with Descartes and state "I think, therefore I am," but saying it and knowing it are not the same thing. These robots (or "artificial life-forms" as Data preferred to call himself), remain non-sentient until proven otherwise. Furthermore, to conclude that any or all other human beings have a mind on the basis of one example—your own—is to draw a weak inductive analogy. Would you conclude all people are friendly on the basis of just your own personality or

---

[12] In a remake of the *Day of the Dead,* one of the zombies exhibits learning behavior and ultimately becomes one of the leaders of the zombie nation.
[13] The android Commander Data from the *Star Trek* movies 7–10.
[14] The computer Hal 9000 from *2001: A Space Odyssey.*
[15] The robot from the original *Forbidden Planet* film. The film spawned a television series called *Lost in Space* and a movie remake of the TV series.

that all dogs love to play ball just because yours does? Of course not. Critics charge that not only is dualism fraught with internal explanatory difficulties but it also leads us to skepticism about the existence of other minds. We might know individually that we are not a zombie or a robot, but we cannot know for sure that others are not zombies or robots. They might be very nice and very articulate zombies and robots, but they remain zombies and robots nonetheless.[16]

Given the progress of neuroscience, reductive materialists have argued that mental states reduce to brain states. That is, the mind just is the brain. This view has been supplanted by those who argue for a functional definition of the mind. A thought or a belief is to be explained by the function or role that it plays. For humans, it might be the stimulation of certain nerve fibers; for computers or aliens, it might be something else entirely. Eliminative materialists argue that there only is the brain and so in a sense we are mindless creatures, but not in the sense of having lost something. For materialists, to speak of there being a "mind" is just mistaken for a non-physical mind is not needed to explain what needs to be explained. These theories all have strong proponents as you will read in the selections in this chapter. But as to be expected, you'll need to be mindful of many arguments and counterarguments.

---

[16] Granted one might be upset to define other people as zombies or robots on the basis that we cannot prove that they have minds, so we are open to other terms. Perhaps zombie-like or robot-like is a kinder and more accurate description since we are not claiming that other people are undead or artificial.

Films Cited

2001: A Space Odyssey. Dir. Stanley Kubrick. Perfs. Keir Dullea, Gary Lockwood. Film. Metro-Goldwyn-Mayer (MGM). 1968.

28 Days Later. Dir. Danny Boyle. Perfs. Alex Palmer, Bindu De Stoppani. Film. British Film Council. 2002.

All Dogs go to Heaven. Dirs. Don Bluth, Gary Goldman. Perfs. Burt Reynolds, Dom Delusive. Film. Goldcrest Films International. 1989.

Amityville Horror. Dir. Stuart Rosenberg. Perfs. James Brolin, Margot Kidder. Film. American International Pictures. 1979.

Back to the Future. Dir. Robert Zemeckis. Perfs. Michael J. Fox, Christopher Lloyd. Film. Amblin Entertainment. 1985.

Beetlejuice. Dir. Tim Burton. Perfs. Alec Baldwin, Geena Davis. Film. Geffen Pictures. 1988.

Candyman. Dir. Bernard Rose. Perfs. Virginia Madsen, Tony Todd. Film. PolyGram Filmed Entertainment. 1992.

Cell, The. Dir. Tarsem Singh. Perfs. Jennifer Lopez, Vince Vaughn. Film. Avery Pix. 2000.

Changeling, The. Dir. Peter Medak. Perfs. George C. Scott, Trish Van Devere. Film. Chessman Park Productions. 1980.

Children Shouldn't Play with Dead Things. Dir. Bob Clark. Perfs. Alan Ormsby, Valerie Mamches. Film. Geneni Film Distributors. 1972.

Dawn of the Dead. Dir. Zack Snyder. Perfs. Sarah Polley, Ving Rhames. Film. Strike Entertainment. 2004.

Dawn of the Dead. Dir. George A. Romero. Perfs. David Emge, Ken Foree. Film. Laurel Group. 1978.

Day of the Dead. Dir. George A. Romero. Perfs. Lori Cardille, Terry Alexander. Dead Films Inc. 1985.

Forbidden Planet. Dir. Fred M. Wilcox. Perfs. Walter Pidgeon, Anne Francis. Film. Metro-Goldwyn-Mayer (MGM). 1956.

Frighteners, The. Dir. Peter Jackson. Perfs. Michael J. Fox, Trini Alvarado. Film. Universal Pictures. 1996.

Ghost Story. Dir. John Irvin. Perfs. Fred Astaire, Melvyn Douglas. Film. Universal Pictures. 1981.

Ghostbusters. Dir. Ivan Reitman. Perfs. Bill Murray, Dan Ackroyd. Film. Black Rhino Productions. 1984.

Haunting, The. Dir. Jan de Bont. Perfs. Lili Taylor, Liam Neeson. Film. Dreamworks SKG. 1999.

Haunting, The. Dir. Robert Wise. Perfs. Julie Harris, Claire Bloom. Film. Argyle Enterprises. 1963.

Heaven Can Wait. Dir. Warren Beatty, Buck Henry. Perfs. Warren Beatty, Julie Christie. Film. Paramount Pictures. 1978.

Here Comes Mr. Jordan. Dir. Alexander Hall. Perfs. Robert Montgomery, Evelyn Keyes. Film. Columbia Pictures Corporation. 1941.

I Walked with a Zombie. Dir. Jacques Tourneur. Perfs. James Ellison, Frances Dee. Film. RKO Radio Pictures. 1943.

Incredibly Strange Creatures Who Stopped Living and Became Mixed-Up Zombies, The. Dir. Ray Dennis Steckler. Perfs. Ray Dennis Steckler, Carolyn Brandt. Film. Morgan-Steckler Productions. 1964.

Ju-on: The Grudge. Dir. Takashi Shimizu. Perfs. Megumi Okina, Misaki Ito. Film. Oz Company. 2003.

Legend of Hell House, The. Dir. John Hough. Perfs. Pamela Franklin, Roddy McDowall. Film. Academy Pictures Corporation. 1973.

Lost in Space. Dir. Stephen Hopkins. Perfs. William Hurt, Mimi Rogers. Film. Irwin Allen Productions. 1998.

Night of the Living Dead. Dir. Tom Savini. Perfs. Tony Todd, Patricia Tallman. Film. 21st Century Film Corporation. 1990.

Night of the Living Dead. Dir. George A. Romero. Perfs. Duane Jones, Judith O'Dea. Film. Image Ten. 1968.

94 Chapter 2 • Metaphysics

Nightmare Before Christmas, The. Dir. Henry Selick. Perfs. Danny Elfman, Chris Sarandon. Film. Skellington Productions Inc. 1993.

Pet Sematary. Dir. Mary Lambert. Perfs. Dale Midkiff, Fred Gwynne. Film. Laurel Productions. 1989.

Plan 9 from Outer Space, Planet Terror. Dir. Edward D. Wood Jr. Perfs. Gregory Walcott, Mona McKinnon, Film. Reynolds Pictures. 1959.

Resident Evil. Dir. Paul W.S. Anderson. Perfs. Milla Jovovich, Michelle Rodriguez. Film. Constantine Film Produktion. 2002.

Ringu. Dir. Hideo Nakata. Perfs. Nanako Matsushima, Miki Nakatani. Film. Kadokawa Shoten Publishing Co. Ltd. 1998.

Run Lola Run. Dir. Tom Tykwer. Perfs. Franka Potente, Moritz Bleibtreu. Film. X-Filme Creative Pool. 1998.

Serpent and the Rainbow, The. Dir. Wes Craven. Perfs. Bill Pullman, Cathy Tyson. Film. Serpent and the Rainbow. 1988.

Shining, The. Dir. Stanley Kubrick. Perfs. Jack Nicholson, Shelley Duvall. Film. Hawk Films Ltd. 1980.

Sliding Doors. Dir. Peter Howitt. Perfs. Gwyneth Paltrow, John Hannah. Film. Intermedia Films. 1998.

Star Trek: First Contact. Dir. Jonathan Frakes. Perfs. Patrick Stewart, Jonathan Frakes. Film. Paramount Pictures. 1996.

Star Trek: Generations. Dir. David Carson. Perfs. Patrick Stewart, Jonathan Frakes. Film. Paramount Pictures. 1994.

Star Trek: Nemesis. Dir. Stuart Baird. Perfs. Patrick Stewart, Jonathan Frakes. Film. Paramount Pictures. 2002.

Star Wars: The Return of the Jedi. Dir. Richard Marquand. Perfs. Mark Hamill, Harrison Ford. Film. Lucasfilm.1983.

Terminator, The. Dir. James Cameron. Perfs. Arnold Schwarzenegger, Michael Biehn. Film. Hemdale Film. 1984.

ADDITIONAL MOVIES FOR FURTHER VIEWING

(For a comprehensive listing of movies and themes, please consult the online appendix.)

1. *A.I.: Artificial Intelligence*—Artificial intelligence and nature of minds
2. *Babel*—Cause and effect
3. *Being John Melodic*—Mind-body problem; personal identity
4. *Groundhog Day*—Determinism
5. *Minority Report*—Determinism
6. *Solaris*—Personal identity
7. *The Butterfly Effect*—Cause and effect
8. *Twelve Monkeys*—Determinism
9. *Waking Life*—Meaning and purpose of life
10. *What Dreams May Come*—Life after death

The Nature of Metaphysics
Peter van Inwagen

1 What is Metaphysics?

The best approach to an understanding of what is meant by 'metaphysics' is by way of the concepts of appearance and reality. It is a commonplace that the way things seem to be is often not the way they are, that the way things *apparently* are is often not the way they *really* are. The sun apparently moves across the sky—but not *really*. The moon seems larger when it is near the horizon—but its size never *really* changes. We might say that one is engaged in 'metaphysics' if one is attempting to get behind all appearances and to describe things as they really are. This statement points in the right direction, but it is certainly rather vague. What would it *be* to 'get behind all appearances and describe things as they really are'? How could one determine whether someone was engaged in this activity? What does 'engaging in metaphysics' look like?

We can say this: if one is attempting to 'get behind all appearances and describe things as they really are', if one is 'engaging in metaphysics', one is attempting to determine certain things with respect to certain statements (or assertions or propositions or theses), those statements that, if true, would be descriptions of the reality that lies behind all appearances, descriptions of things as they really are. (Primarily to determine which of them are true and which of them are false. But also, perhaps, to determine various other things about them, such as which ones are reasonable to believe, and which ones are logically consistent with one another.)

Let us call this 'reality that lies behind all appearances' simply Reality (with a capital). And let us call statements that, if true, would be descriptions of this Reality *metaphysical statements.* Which statements are, if true, descriptions of Reality? This is a difficult question, because it cannot be determined simply from examining a speaker's words whether the speaker has made a metaphysical statement: one must also examine the context in which those words were spoken. It is necessary to do this because different 'restrictions of intended reference' may be in force in different contexts, and this has the consequence that the same words can express different things in different contexts. If, for example, you look into your refrigerator and say sadly 'There is no beer', you are asserting that the existence of that beverage is a myth or an illusion. And this is because, in the context in which you are speaking, you and your audience know that your statement is intended to describe only the state of things inside your refrigerator. Let us see how this point might apply in a case in which we want to know whether a speaker has made a metaphysical statement. The late Carl Sagan, in his television series *Cosmos*, made the following much-quoted statement: 'The cosmos [i.e. the physical universe] is all there is or was or ever will be'. Was this a metaphysical statement? Well, that depends. In the context in which Sagan made his statement, were there any restrictions of intended reference in force? Did Sagan, perhaps, intend his statement to apply only to physical things? Was he perhaps saying only that the cosmos was the totality of physical things, past, present and future? In that case, his statement was not a metaphysical statement, but simply an explanation of the meaning of the word 'cosmos'. Or did Sagan perhaps make his statement in a context in which there were *no* restrictions of intended reference in force? Did he mean to say that *everything*—everything without qualification—was a part of the cosmos? (Notice that, on the 'unrestricted' interpretation of his statement, the statement implies that there is no God or anything else that is not physical; on the 'restricted' interpretation, the statement has no such implication.) In that case, his statement can plausibly be described as a metaphysical statement—for if we learned that there was no God or anything else non-physical, would we not learn something about the reality that lay behind all appearances?

One requirement on a metaphysical statement, then, is that it be made with no restrictions of intended reference in force. A second, and closely related requirement, is that the statement represents a serious attempt by the speaker to state the strict and literal truth. We often express ourselves carelessly or loosely or metaphorically. (Restriction of intended reference might be seen as a special case of not speaking 'strictly'.) We say things like 'The sun is trying to come out', 'The car doesn't want to start', 'Time passes slowly when one is bored' and 'Dark, angry clouds filled the sky'. Since metaphysics is an attempt to get at how things really are, this requirement is not hard to understand. Those who say things like these do not mean to assert that the sun, the car or the clouds are conscious beings, or that time can pass at different rates, and, therefore, at least some of the features of these statements do not represent an attempt to say how things really are. Our second requirement can also be expressed this way; the speaker must be willing to take responsibility for the strict and literal consequences of the words he or she has used to make the statement.

May we then understand a metaphysical statement as one that (1) is made in a context in which no restrictions of intended reference are in force and (2) is such that the speaker who makes it has made a serious effort to speak the strict and literal truth? This would not be satisfactory, for to call a statement 'metaphysical' is to imply that it is a very general statement, and these two conditions include nothing that implies generality. An example may help us to understand the kind of generality that a statement must have to be a metaphysical statement. Suppose Alice Says, 'All Greeks are mortal'. Let us assume that when she makes this statement, no restrictions of intended reference are in force: she means her statement to apply to *all* Greeks, and not only to the members of some 'understood' special class of Greeks. And let us assume that this statement represents a serious effort on her part to speak the strict and literal truth. (Since the statement contains no figurative language and no 'well, I hope you see what I mean' linguistic shortcuts, this assumption is reasonable enough.) Perhaps these two assumptions imply that her statement, if true, describes Reality, but it certainly does not describe very *much* of Reality. After all, it tells us only about Greeks; it tells us nothing about elephants or neutron stars or even non-Greek human beings. It is therefore not sufficiently general to count as a metaphysical statement.

What sort of statement would be 'sufficiently general'? Might we say that to be sufficiently general to be a metaphysical statement, a statement must be about *everything*? This will not do, and for two reasons. First, *any* 'all' statement is in one sense 'about everything'. For example, the statement 'All Greeks are mortal' is logically equivalent to 'Everything is mortal if it is a Greek'. (Every elephant and every neutron star and every non-Greek immortal is mortal if it is Greek.) It is therefore not easy to say in any precise and useful way what it is for a statement to be 'about everything'. Second, even if we ignore this difficulty and decide to rely on our intuitive sense of which statements are 'about everything', we shall run up against the fact that most philosophers would want to classify as 'metaphysical' many statements that we would, speaking intuitively, say were

(*continued*)

The Nature of Metaphysics (*continued*)

not 'about everything'. For example: 'Every event has a cause' (this statement is, intuitively, not about everything, but only about events); 'Every physical thing is such that it might not have existed' (. . . only about physical things); 'Any two objects that occupy space are spatially related to each other' (. . . only about objects that occupy space). And there is a further problem: most philosophers would want to classify as metaphysical certain statements that are not 'all' statements, not even ones that pertain to some special class: of things like events -or- physical things: 'There is a God'; 'Some things have no parts'; 'There could be two things that had all the same properties'.[1]

Perhaps in the end, all we can say is this: some 'categories' or 'concepts' are sufficiently 'general' that a statement will count as a 'metaphysical statement' if—given that it is made in a context in which no restrictions of intended reference are in force, and given that the person who makes it is making a serious effort to say what is strictly and literally true—it employs only these categories. Among these categories are many that we have already used in our examples: 'physical thing', 'spatial object', 'cause', 'event', 'part', 'property'. If we so define 'metaphysical statement', then the concept of a metaphysical statement will be open-ended and vague. It will be open-ended in that no final list of the categories that can occur in a 'metaphysical statement' will be possible: we could try to make a complete list (we might go through all the historical texts that were uncontroversially 'metaphysical' and mark all the categories we came across that seemed to us to be 'sufficiently general'), but, even if we had a list that satisfied us for the moment, we should have to admit that we might have to enlarge the list tomorrow. It is vague in that there will be borderline cases of 'sufficiently general' categories: 'impenetrable', 'pain', 'straight' and 'surface' are possible examples of such borderline cases. But there will also be perfectly clear cases of categories that are not 'sufficiently general': 'Greek', 'chair', 'elephant', 'neutron star', 'diminished seventh chord', 'non-linear partial differential equation' . . . . (Words like 'chair' and 'elephant' can occur in a work on metaphysics, but only in examples meant to illustrate—or in counterexamples meant to refute—theses whose statement requires only very general concepts.)

Where does this leave us? Let us suppose that Charles has made a certain statement. Let us suppose that when he made this statement, no restrictions of intended reference were in force. Let us suppose that Charles was willing to take responsibility for the strict and literal consequences of the words he has used to make the statement. And let us suppose that all the concepts or categories that Charles employed in making this statement were 'sufficiently general'. (And let us suppose that his statement was not some logical truism like 'Everything is either material or not material'.) Then, or so I would suggest, Charles has made a statement that, if true, describes Reality. That is, he has made a metaphysical statement. And if we try to decide whether his statement is true or false, reasonable or unreasonable, probable or improbable, consistent or inconsistent with various other metaphysical or non-metaphysical statements, then we are engaged in metaphysics.

2 Is Metaphysics Possible?

Is metaphysics, so conceived, possible?—that is, is it possible to 'engage in metaphysics' in the above sense and to reach any interesting or important conclusions? Various philosophers have argued that metaphysics is impossible. The thesis that metaphysics is impossible comes in what might be called strong and weak forms. The strong form of the thesis is this: the goal is not there, since there is no Reality to be described; all the statements we have called metaphysical are false or meaningless. (And it is hard to see how all metaphysical statements could be simply false. If one metaphysician says that everything is material and another says that it is false that everything is material, then, if their statements are meaningful, one or the other of them must be true.) The weak form of the thesis is this: the goal is there, but we human beings are unable to reach it, since the task of describing Reality is beyond our powers; metaphysical statements are meaningful, but we can never discover whether any metaphysical statement is true or false (or discover anything else interesting or important about the class of metaphysical statements).

Let us briefly examine an example of the strong form of the thesis that metaphysics is impossible. In the years between the world wars, the 'logical positivists' argued that the meaning of a statement consisted entirely in the predictions it made about possible experience. And they argued that metaphysical statements, statements that purported to describe Reality, made no predictions about experience. (The metaphysician asks, 'Is time real, or are temporal phenomena mere appearances?' But our experiences would be the same—they would be just as they are—whether or not time was real. The metaphysician asks, 'Are there universals, or is the appearance of there being attributes and relations a mere appearance, an illusion created by the way we think and speak?' But our experiences would be the same—like *this*—whether or not there were universals. And so, the logical positivists argued, for every metaphysical question. Metaphysical theses, being essentially attempts to *get behind* the way things appear to us, can make no predictions about the way things will appear to us.) Therefore, they argued, metaphysical statements are meaningless. Or, since 'meaningless statement' is a contradiction in terms, the 'statements' we classify as metaphysical are not really statements at all: they are things that look like statements but aren't, rather as mannequins are things that look like human beings but aren't.

But how does the logical positivist's thesis fare by its own standards? Consider the statement,

The meaning of a statement consists entirely in the predictions it makes about possible experience.

Does this statement make any predictions about possible experiences? Could some observation show that this statement was true? Could some laboratory experiment show that it was false? It would seem not. It would seem that everything in the world would look the same—like *this*—whether or not this statement was true. And, therefore, if the statement is true it is meaningless; or, what is the same thing, if it is meaningful, it is false. Logical positivism would therefore seem to say of itself that it is false or meaningless; it would seem to be, as some philosophers say, 'self-referentially incoherent'.

We have not the space to consider all the attempts that have been made to show that the idea of a reality that lies behind all appearances is in some sense defective. (Current exponents of 'anti-realism' are only the latest example of such philosophers.) I must record, without further argument, my conviction that all such attempts are victims of self-referential incoherency. The general case goes like this. Alfred the anti-metaphysician argues that any proposition that does not pass some test he specifies is in some sense defective (it is, say, self-contradictory or meaningless). And he argues that any metaphysical proposition must fail this test. But it invariably turns out that some proposition that is essential to Alfred's anti-metaphysical argument itself fails to pass his test. Or so it seems to me that it invariably turns out. The reader is warned, however, that most anti-metaphysicians will say that I am mistaken, and that their own anti-metaphysical arguments are not self-referentially incoherent. (The remainder will say that everyone who is anyone in philosophy knows that 'the self-referential incoherency ploy' is invalid. This response has all the merits of a certain famous, if apocryphal, solicitor's brief: 'No case. Abuse plaintiff's counsel.')

What about the 'weak form' of the thesis that metaphysics is impossible? In my view, the weak form of the thesis can be usefully discussed only in the context of a comprehensive and detailed examination of some actual and serious attempts at metaphysics. And we are not, in the present essay, in a position to do this in sufficient detail for the effort to have any value.[2]

Let us tentatively conclude that no decisive case has been made for the impossibility of metaphysics. In the remainder of this essay, I will attempt to give some content to the very abstract remarks I have made about the nature of metaphysics by examining a particular metaphysical problem.

3 A Metaphysical Problem: The Existence and Nature of Universals

One very important part of metaphysics has to do with what there is, with what exists. This part of metaphysics is called ontology. Ontology, that is, is that part of metaphysics that deals with metaphysical statements having general forms like 'An X exists' and 'There are Y's'. (In this essay, it will be assumed that 'there is (are)' and 'exist(s)' mean essentially the same thing—that there is no important difference in meaning between 'Horses exist' and 'There are horses'. There are philosophers who deny this thesis: such philosophers exist.) In ontology, the second of our three requirements on a metaphysical statement is especially important—the requirement that the philosopher who makes a metaphysical statement be willing to take responsibility for the strict and literal consequences of the words used to make the statement. This is because we very frequently say things of the forms 'An X exists' and 'There are Y's' when we do not think there are *really* any X's or Y's. An example will help to make what is meant by this clear.

(continued)

The Nature of Metaphysics   (continued)

Our friend Jan is an adherent of the metaphysical position known as materialism, the thesis that everything—everything without qualification—is material. We notice, however, that, despite her allegiance to materialism, Jan frequently says things that, when taken strictly and literally, are inconsistent with materialism. For example, just this morning we heard her say, 'There's a big hole in my favourite blouse that wasn't there yesterday'.[3] But no material object is a hole: material things are made of atoms, and nothing made of atoms is a hole; holes, so to speak, result from the *absence* of atoms. And yet Jan has said that there was one of them in her blouse. We point out to her that she has made a statement that is on the face of it inconsistent with materialism, and she replies:

> It's true that I said there was a hole in my blouse, and that this statement, taken strictly and literally, implies that there is a hole; and it's true that a hole, if there really were such *things* as holes, wouldn't be a material thing. But I was speaking the language of everyday life; by the standards of metaphysics, I was speaking loosely. What I *could* have said, and what I would have said if I'd known that you were going to hold me responsible for the strict and literal consequences of my words, is that my blouse is *perforate*. The predicate 'is perforate', when it is applied to a material object like my blouse, simply says something about the object's *shape*. If you perforate a coin, the resulting object will have a shape different from that of an imperforate, but otherwise identical, coin. When I say that a given material thing is perforate, this obviously does not imply that there is *another* thing, a thing not made of atoms, a thing called a 'hole', that is 'in' the material thing. The words 'there's a hole in this thing' are just an idiomatic way of saying 'this thing is perforate'.

This speech provides an example of a philosophical tool, extremely important in ontology, called 'paraphrase'. Various idioms and expressions that are perfectly serviceable for everyday, practical purposes have metaphysically unwanted implications when they are interpreted strictly and literally—which is the way we are supposed to interpret a metaphysician's idioms and expressions. To find a *paraphrase* of a statement involving such 'misleading' forms of words is to find a way of conveying what the statement is intended to convey that does not have the unwanted implications. (This is what we imagined Jan doing with the statement 'There's a hole in my blouse'.)

Metaphysicians have not spent a lot of time disputing about whether there really are holes. But they have spent a lot of time disputing about whether there really are so-called abstract things (such as properties, relations, propositions and numbers). The medieval dispute about the reality of 'universals' is an especially important example of this. This ancient dispute, or something very much like it, goes on today in several different forms. One of these 'forms' is due to the work of the American philosopher W. V. O. Quine.[4] We shall examine it. It will be our example of a way to approach a metaphysical problem.

A universal is, near enough, a property—such as humanity (the property that is 'universal' to the members of the class of human beings and to the members of no more inclusive class), wisdom, the colour blue and widowhood. There are *apparently* properties. There is, for example, apparently such a thing as humanity. The members of the class of human beings, as the idiom has it, 'have something in common', and what could this 'something' be but the property 'humanity'? It could certainly not be anything physical, for—Siamese twins excepted—no two human beings have any physical thing in common. And, of course, what goes for the class of human beings goes for the class of birds, the class of white things and the class of intermediate vector bosons: the members of each of these classes have something in common with one another, and what the members of a class have in common is a property—or so it appears. But there are metaphysicians who contend that this appearance is mere appearance and that *in reality* there are no properties. Other metaphysicians argue that in this case, at least, appearances are not misleading and that there really *are* properties. The metaphysicians who deny the real existence of properties are called nominalists and the metaphysicians who affirm the real existence of properties are called platonists.[5] (Each of these terms could be objected to on historical grounds. But let us pass over these objections.)

How can the dispute between the nominalists and the platonists be resolved? Quine has proposed an answer to this question.[6] Nominalists and platonists have different beliefs about what there is. How should one go about deciding what to believe about what there is? According to

Quine, the problem of deciding what to believe about what there is a very straightforward special case of the problem of deciding what to believe, (The problem of deciding what to believe is no trivial problem, to be sure, but it is a problem everyone is going to have somehow to come to terms with.) Let us look at the problem that is our present concern, the problem of what to believe about the existence of properties. If we want to decide whether to believe that there are properties—Quine tells us—we should examine the beliefs that we already have, and see whether any of them commits us to the existence of properties. If any does, then we have a reason to believe in the existence of properties: it is whatever reason we had for accepting the belief that commits us to the existence of properties—plus the general intellectual requirement that if one becomes aware that one's belief that p commits one to the further belief that q, then one should either believe that q or cease to believe that p.[7] But let us consider an example. Suppose we find the following proposition among our beliefs:

Spiders share some of the anatomical features of insects.

A plausible case can be made for the thesis that this belief commits us to the existence of properties. We may observe, first, that it is very hard to see what an 'anatomical feature' (such as 'having an exoskeleton') could be if it were not a property: property', 'quality', 'characteristic', 'attribute' and 'feature' are all more or less synonyms. Does our belief that spiders share some of the anatomical features of insects therefore commit us to the existence of 'anatomical features'? If we carefully examine the meaning of the sentence 'Spiders share some of the anatomical features of insects', we find that what it says is this:

There are anatomical features that insects have and spiders also have.

And it is a straightforward logical consequence of this proposition that there are anatomical features: if there are anatomical features that insects have and spiders also have, then there are anatomical features that insects have; if there are anatomical features that insects have, then there are anatomical features—full stop.

Does this little argument show that anyone who believes that spiders share some of the anatomical features of insects is committed to platonism, to a belief in the existence of properties? How might a nominalist respond? Suppose we present this argument to Ned, a convinced nominalist (who believes, as most people do, that spiders share some of the anatomical features of insects). Assuming that Ned is unwilling simply to have inconsistent beliefs, there would seem to be four possible ways for him to respond to this argument:

1. He might become a platonist.
2. He might abandon his belief that spiders share some of the anatomical features of insects.
3. He might attempt to show that it does not after all follow from this belief that there are anatomical features.
4. He might admit that his beliefs (his belief in nominalism and his belief that spiders share some of the anatomical features of insects) are apparently inconsistent, affirm his nominalistic faith that this inconsistency is apparent, not real, and confess that, although he is confident that there is some fault in our alleged demonstration that his belief about spiders and insects commits him to the existence of properties, he is at present unable to discover it.

Possibility (2) is not really very attractive. It is unattractive for at least two reasons. First, it seems to be a simple fact of biology that spiders share some of the anatomical features of insects. Second, there are many, many 'simple facts' that could have been used as the premise of an essentially identical argument for the conclusion that there are properties. (For example: elements in the same column in the Periodic Table tend to have many of the same chemical properties; some of the most important characteristics of the nineteenth-century novel are rarely present in the twentieth-century novel.) Possibility (4) is always an option, but no philosopher is likely to embrace it except as a last resort. What Ned is likely to do is to try to avail himself of possibility (3). He is likely to try to show that his belief about spiders and insects does not in fact commit him to platonism. What he will attempt to do in respect of this belief (and of all the others among his beliefs

(continued)

The Nature of Metaphysics (*continued*)

that apparently commit him to a belief in properties) is just what Jan did in respect of the belief that apparently committed her to a belief in holes: he will try to find a *paraphrase,* a sentence that (1) he could use in place of 'Spiders share some of the anatomical features of insects' and (2) does not even seem to have 'There are anatomical features' as one of its logical consequences. If he can do this, then he will be in a position to argue that the commitment to the existence of properties that is apparently 'carried by' his belief about spiders and insects is only apparent.[8] And he will be in a position to argue—no doubt further argument would be required to establish this—that the apparent existence of properties is mere appearance (an appearance that is due to the forms of words we use).

Is it possible to find such a paraphrase? (And to find paraphrases of all the other apparently true statements that seem to commit those who make them to the reality of properties?) This is a difficult and technical question. I record my conviction that it is at least very hard to do so.[9] If Quine is right about 'ontological commitment', therefore, there is no easy way for anyone to be a consistent nominalist.

It must be emphasized that we have said almost nothing about the *nature* of 'properties'. If what we have said so far is correct, some of the sentences we use to express certain very ordinary and non-metaphysical beliefs, sentences like 'Spiders share some of the anatomical features of insects' and 'Elements in the same column in the Periodic Table tend to have many of the same chemical properties' define what we may call the 'property role'; a property is whatever it is (beyond ordinary things like spiders and chemical elements) that using these sentences to express our beliefs carries prima facie commitment to. And if what we have said so far is correct, it is very hard to avoid the conclusion that objects of *some* sort play the property role. But philosophers who accepted *this* conclusion could differ fundamentally about the nature of the objects that play this role. Some philosophers think that the property role is played by things that are in some sense constituents of objects, that properties are in some very subtle and abstract sense of the word *parts* of the objects whose properties they are.[10] Other philosophers (including the present author) think that this conception of properties is not so much false as meaningless and that the things that play the property role are in no sense parts or constituents of objects, but simply things that can be 'said of' objects. According to this view of the nature of properties, the property 'being white' is simply something that can be said truly of table salt and the Taj Mahal and cannot be said truly of copper sulphate or the Eiffel Tower. (But what kind of thing would *that* be? You may well ask.) There has perhaps been little progress since the Middle Ages in the attempt to say anything both informative and meaningful about the *nature* of universals, the nature of the things that play the property role. But it can be plausibly argued that even if we do not understand universals much better than the medieval philosophers, we now have a better understanding *of the problem* of universals. We now see that the best way to look at the debate between the nominalist and the platonist is as follows: the task of the nominalist is to establish the conclusion that our beliefs about ordinary things do not commit us to the thesis that anything plays the property role. The task of the platonist is to attempt to establish the conclusion that our beliefs about ordinary things do commit us to the existence of things that play the property role, and to attempt to give a plausible account of the nature of these things.

NOTES

1. These statements are in effect the denials or negations of 'all' statements—the denial or negation of a statement being the result of prefixing 'it is false that' or 'it is not the case that' to that statement. For example, 'Some things have no parts' is logically equivalent to 'It is false that everything has no parts'. (This logical point depends for its validity on the assumption that there is at least one thing. This assumption is made in standard systems of logic.)
2. For an extremely interesting and sophisticated defence of the weak form of the sis, see Colin McGinn, *Problems in Philosophy: The Limits of Inquiry* (Oxford: Blackwell, 1993).
3. This example is based on David and Stephanie Lewis, 'Holes', *Australasian Journal of Philosophy* 48 (1970), pp. 206–12.
4. For another, very different form, see David Armstrong, *Universals: An Opinionated Introduction* (Boulder, Col.: Westview Press, 1988).

5. The philosophers we are calling platonists are often called realists. I will avoid the terms 'realist' and 'realism', since they have several other meanings in metaphysics.
6. The issues that we are about to discuss are generally said to pertain to 'ontological commitment', a term that is due to Quine. For Quine's views on ontological commitment, see his classic essay, 'On What There Is' (chapter 3, this volume) and chapter 7, 'Ontic Decision', of his *Word and Object* (Cambridge, Mass." MIT Press, 1960).

    Discussions of ontological commitment are generally rather technical—see, for example, chapter 5 in the present volume, by Susan Haack. They are technical because they represent issues of ontological commitment as essentially related to 'the existential quantifier', the symbol used in formal logic (it is most often a backwards 'E') to express 'there is' or 'there exists'. The tendency of philosophers to connect issues of ontological commitment with the existential quantifier is (in one way) entirely justified, and (in another) somewhat misleading. It is justified because any *technically fully adequate* formulation of Quine's theses on ontological commitment must involve the existential quantifier and the related device of 'bound variables'. It is misleading because it suggests that it is impossible to present an account of the essential philosophical points contained in these theses without at some point introducing the existential quantifier—and not simply the symbol, but the technical apparatus that governs its use in formal logic and the various philosophical disputes that have arisen concerning its 'interpretation'. And this is false: it is possible to give a useful introductory account of the philosophical points contained in Quine's various discussions of ontological commitment that contains no 'existential apparatus' but the ordinary words and phrases—'there is', 'exists'—for which the existential quantifier is the formal replacement. The discussion of 'there is' and paraphrase in the present essay is an attempt at such an introductory account of these points.
7. Suppose we were to discover that some belief of ours—that Mars has two moons, let us say—committed us to the existence of properties. Should that discovery move us to question, or perhaps even to abandon, our belief that Mars had two moons? That would depend on whether we had, or thought we had, some reason to believe that the there were no properties. If we did dunk we had some reason to believe that there were no properties, we should have to try to decide whether our reason for thinking that Mars had two moons (presumably we have one) was more or less compelling than our reason for thinking that there were no properties.
8. Paraphrase is thus, as I have said, extremely important in ontology. But see chapter 4 of this volume by William Alston for an attempt to show that paraphrase cannot play an important role in ontology. The reader may find it instructive to try to identify the premise of Alston's argument that is rejected in the present essay.
9. In one sense, Quine himself believes that the required paraphrase is possible. He believes that statements like our 'spider-insect' statement can be understood in such a way that they commit those who make them to nothing other, than *sets*—besides, of course, spiders and insects or whatever other 'ordinary' objects the statements may mention. But these sets, it must be emphasized, are very far from being ordinary objects. The set of all spiders, for example, is not a spider or any other sort of physical object, and reference to 'the set of spiders' cannot be dismissed as a mere linguistic device for referring to all spiders collectively: sets are *objects*. Sets are, in fact, from the point of view of those who call themselves nominalists, hardly more acceptable than properties, and, in present-day discussions of ontology, 'nominalism' is generally taken to imply that there are no such objects as sets.
10. See chapter 4, 'Particulars as Bundles of Universals', of Armstrong's *Universals: An Opinionated Introduction*.

Allegory of the Cave
Plato

Book VII

Next, said I, compare our nature in respect of education and its lack to such an experience as this. Picture men dwelling in a sort of subterranean cavern with a long entrance open to the light on its entire width. Conceive them as having their legs and necks fettered from childhood, so that they remain in the same spot, able to look forward only, and prevented by the fetters from turning their heads. Picture further the light from a fire burning higher up and at a distance behind them, and between the fire and the prisoners and above them a road along which a low wall has been built, as the exhibitors of puppet shows have partitions before the men themselves, above which they show the puppets.

(continued)

Allegory of the Cave (continued)

All that I see, he said.

See also, then, men carrying past the wall implements of all kinds that rise above the wall, and human images and shapes of animals as well, wrought in stone and wood and every material, some of these bearers presumably speaking and others silent.

A strange image you speak of, he said, and strange prisoners.

Like to us, I said. For, to begin with, tell me do you think that these men would have seen anything of themselves or of one another except the shadows cast from the fire on the wall of the cave that fronted them?

How could they, he said, if they were compelled to hold their heads unmoved through life?

And again, would not the same be true of the objects carried past them?

Surely.

If then they were able to talk to one another, do you not think that they would suppose that in naming the things that they saw they were naming the passing objects?

Necessarily.

And if their prison had an echo from the wall opposite them, when one of the passers-by uttered a sound, do you think that they would suppose anything else than the passing shadow to be the speaker?

By Zeus, I do not, said he.

Then in every way such prisoners would deem reality to be nothing else than the shadows of the artificial objects.

Quite inevitably, he said.

Consider, then, what would be the manner of the release and healing from these bonds and this folly if in the course of nature something of this sort should happen to them. When one was freed from his fetters and compelled to stand up suddenly and turn his head around and walk and to lift up his eyes to the light, and in dong all this felt pain and, because of the dazzle and glitter of the light, was unable to discern the objects whose shadows he formerly saw, what do you suppose would be his answer if someone told him that what he had seen before was all a cheat and an illusion, but that now, being nearer to reality and turned toward more real things, he saw more truly? And if also one should point out to him each of the passing objects and constrain him by questions to say what it is, do you not think that he would be at a loss and that he would regard what he formerly saw as more real than the things now pointed out to him?

Far more real, he said.

And if he were compelled to look at the light itself, would not that pain his eyes, and would he not turn away and flee to those things which he is able to discern and regard them as in very deed more clear and exact then the objects pointed out?

It is so, he said.

And if, said I, someone should drag him thence by force up the ascent which is rough and steep, and not let him go before he had drawn him out into the light of the sun, do you not think that he would find it painful to be so haled along, and would chafe at it, and when he came out into the light, that his eyes would be filled with its beams so that he would not be able to see even one of the things that we call real?

Why, no, not immediately, he said.

Then there would be need of habituation, I take it, to enable him to see the things higher up. And at first he would most easily discern the shadows and, after that, the likenesses or reflections in water of men and other things, and later, the things themselves, and from these he would go on to contemplate the appearances in the heavens and heaven itself, more easily by night, looking at the light of the stars and the moon, than by day the sun and the sun's light.

Of course.

And so, finally, I suppose, he would be able to look upon the sun itself and see its true nature, not by reflections in water or phantasms of it in an alien setting, but in and by itself in its own place.

Necessarily, he said.

And at this point he would infer and conclude that this it is that provides the seasons and the courses of the year and presides over all things in the visible region, and is in some sort the cause of all these things that they had seen.

Obviously, he said, that would be the next step.

Well then, if he recalled to mind his first habitation and what passed for wisdom there, and his fellow bondsmen, do you not think that he would count himself happy in the change and pity them?

He would indeed.

And if there had been honors and commendations among them which they bestowed on one another and prizes for the man who is quickest to make out the shadows as they pass and best able to remember their customary precedences, sequences, and coexistences, and so most successful in guessing at what was to come, do you think he would be very keen about such rewards, and that he would envy and emulate those who were honored by these prisoners and lorded it among them, or that he would feel with Homer and greatly prefer while living on earth to be serf of another, a landless man, and endure anything rather than opine with them and live that life?

Yes, he said, I think that he would choose to endure anything rather than such a life.

And consider this also, said I. If such a one should go down again and take his old place would he not get his eyes full of darkness, thus suddenly coming out of the sunlight?

He would indeed.

Now if he should be required to contend with these perpetual prisoners in 'evaluating' these shadows while his vision was still dim and before his eyes were accustomed to the dark— and this time required for habituation would not be very short—would he not provoke laughter, and would it not be said of him that he had returned from his journey aloft with his eyes ruined and that it was not worth while even to attempt the ascent? And if it were possible to lay hands on and to kill the man who tried to release them and lead them up, would they not kill him?

They certainly would, he said.

This image then, dear Glaucon, we must apply as a whole to all that has been said, likening the region revealed through sight to the habitation of the prison, and the light of the fire in it to the power of the sun. And if you assume that the ascent and the contemplation of the things above is the soul's ascension to the intelligible region, you will not miss my surmise, since that is what you desire to hear. But God knows whether it is true. But, at any rate, my dream as it appears to me is that in the region of the known the last thing to be seen and hardly seen is the idea of good, and that when seen it must needs point us to the conclusion that this is indeed the cause for all things of all that is right and beautiful, giving birth in the visible world to light, and the author of light and itself in the intelligible world being the authentic source of truth and reason, and that anyone who is to act wisely in private or public must have caught sight of this.

I concur, he said, so far as I am able.

Come then, I said, and join me in this further thought, and do not be surprised that those who have attained to this height are not willing to occupy themselves with the affairs of men, but their souls ever feel the upward urge and the yearning for that sojourn above. For this, I take it, is likely if in this point too the likeness of our image holds.

Yes, it is likely.

And again, do you think it at all strange, said I, if a man returning from divine contemplations to the petty miseries of men cuts a sorry figure and appears most ridiculous, if, while still blinking though the gloom, and before he has become sufficiently accustomed to the environing darkness, he is compelled in courtrooms or elsewhere to contend about the shadows of justice or the images that cast the shadows and to wrangle in debate about the notions of these things in the minds of those who have never seen justice itself?

It would be by no means strange, he said.

But a sensible man, I said, would remember that there are two distinct disturbances of the eyes arising from two causes, according as the shift is from light to darkness or from darkness to light, and, believing that the same thing happens to the soul too, whenever he saw a soul perturbed and unable to discern something, he would not laugh unthinkingly, but would observe whether coming from a brighter life its vision was obscured by the unfamiliar darkness, or whether the passage from the deeper dark of ignorance into a more luminous world and the greater brightness had dazzled its vision. And so he would deem the one happy in its experience and way of life and pity the other, and if it pleased him to laugh at it, his laughter would be less laughable than that at the expense of the soul that had come down from the light above.

That is a very fair statement, he said.

(continued)

Allegory of the Cave (*continued*)

Then, if this is true, our view of these matters must be this, that education is not in reality what some people proclaim it to be in their professions. What they aver is that they can put true knowledge into a soul that does not possess it, as if they were inserting vision into blind eyes.

They do indeed, he said.

But our present argument indicates, said I, that the true analogy for this indwelling power in the soul and the instrument whereby each of us apprehends is that of an eye that could not be converted to the light from the darkness except by turning the whole body. Even so this organ of knowledge must be turned around from the world of becoming together with the entire soul, like the scene-shifting periactus in the theater, until the soul is able to endure the contemplation of essence and the brightest region of being. And this, we say, is the good, do we not?

Yes.

Of this very thing, then, I said, there might be an art, an art of the speediest and most effective shifting or conversion of the soul, not an art of producing vision in it, but on the assumption that it possesses vision but does not rightly direct it and does not look where it should, an art of bringing this about.

Yes, that seems likely, he said.

Then the other so-called virtues of the soul do seem akin to those of the body. For it is true that where they do not pre-exist, they are afterward created by habit and practice. But the excellence of thought, it seems, is certainly of a more divine quality, a thing that never loses its potency, but, according to the direction of its conversion, becomes useful and beneficent, or, again, useless and harmful. Have you never observed in those who are popularly spoken of as bad, but smart men how keen is the vision of the little soul, how quick it is to discern the things that interest it, a proof that it is not a poor vision which it has, but one forcibly enlisted in the service of evil, so that the sharper its sight the more mischief it accomplishes?

I certainly have, he said.

Observe then, said I, that this part of such a soul, if it had been hammered from childhood, and had thus been struck free of the leaden weights, so to speak, of our birth and becoming, which attaching themselves to it by food and similar pleasures and gluttonies turn downward the vision of the soul—if, I say, freed from these, it had suffered a conversion toward the things that are real and true, that same faculty of the same men would have been most keen in its vision of the higher things, just as it is for the things toward which it is now turned.

It is likely, he said.

Well, then, said I, is not this also likely and a necessary consequence of what has been said, that neither could men who are uneducated and inexperienced in truth ever adequately preside over a state, nor could those who had been permitted to linger on to the end in the pursuit of culture—the one because they have no single aim and purpose in life to which all their actions, public and private, must be directed, and the others, because they will not voluntarily engage in action, believing that while still living they have been transported to the Islands of the Blessed?

True, he said.

It is the duty of us, the founders, then, said I, to compel the best natures to attain the knowledge which we pronounced the greatest, and to win to the vision of the good, to scale that ascent, and when they have reached the heights and taken and adequate view, we must not allow what is now permitted.

What is that?

That they should linger there, I said, and refuse to go down again among those bondsmen and share their labors and honors, whether they are of less or of greater worth.

Do you mean to say that we must do them this wrong, and compel them to live an inferior life when the better is in their power?

You have again forgotten, my friend, said I, that the law is not concerned with the special happiness of any class in the state, but is trying to produce this condition in the city as a whole, harmonizing and adapting the citizens to one another by persuasion and compulsion, and requiring them to impart to one another any benefit which they are severally able to bestow upon the community, and that it itself creates such men in the state, not that it may allow each to take what course pleases him, but with a view to using them for the binding together of the commonwealth.

Parmenides
Plato

(The dialogue is supposed to be narrated by Antiphon, the half-brother of Adeimantus and Glaucon, to certain Clazomenians.)

We went from our home at Clazomenae to Athens, and met Adeimantus and Glaucon in the Agora. Welcome, said Adeimantus, taking me by the hand; is there anything which we can do for you in Athens?

Why, yes, I said, I am come to ask a favor of you.

What is that? he said.

I want you to tell me the name of your half-brother, which I have forgotten; he was a mere child when I last came hither from Clazomenae, but that was a long time ago; your father's name, if I remember rightly, is Pyrilampes?

Yes, he said, and the name of our brother, Antiphon; but why do you ask?

Let me introduce some countrymen of mine, I said; they are lovers of philosophy, and have heard that Antiphon was in the habit of meeting Pythodorus, the friend of Zeno, and remembers certain arguments which Socrates and Zeno and Parmenides had together, and which Pythodorus had often repeated to him.

That is true.

And could we hear them? I asked.

Nothing easier, he replied; when he was a youth he made a careful study of the pieces; at present his thoughts run in another direction; like his grandfather, Antiphon, he is devoted to horses. But, if that is what you want, let us go and look for him; he dwells at Melita, which is quite near, and he has only just left us to go home.

Accordingly we went to look for him; he was at home, and in the act of giving a bridle to a blacksmith to be fitted. When he had done with the blacksmith, his brothers told him the purpose of our visit; and he saluted me as an acquaintance whom he remembered from my former visit, and we asked him to repeat the dialogue. At first he was not very willing, and complained of the trouble, but at length he consented. He told us that Pythodorus had described to him the appearance of Parmenides and Zeno; they came to Athens, he said, at the great Panathenaea; the former was, at the time of his visit, about sixty-five years old, very white with age, but well favored. Zeno was nearly forty years of age, of a noble figure and fair aspect; and in the days of his youth he was reported to have been beloved of Parmenides. He said that they lodged with Pythodorus in the Ceramicus, outside the wall, whither Socrates and others came to see them; they wanted to hear some writings of Zeno, which had been brought to Athens by them for the first time. He said that Socrates was then very young, and that Zeno read them to him in the absence of Parmenides, and had nearly finished when Pythodorus entered, and with him Parmenides and Aristoteles who was afterward one of the Thirty; there was not much more to hear, and Pythodorus had heard Zeno repeat them before.

When the recitation was completed, Socrates requested that the first hypothesis of the first discourse might be read over again, and this having been done, he said: What do you mean, Zeno? Is your argument that the existence of many necessarily involves like and unlike, and that this is impossible, for neither can the like be unlike, nor the unlike like; is that your position? Just that, said Zeno. And if the unlike cannot be like, or the like unlike, then neither can the many exist, for that would involve an impossibility. Is the design of your argument throughout to disprove the existence of the many? and is each of your treatises intended to furnish a separate proof of this, there being as many proofs in all as you have composed arguments, of the non-existence of the many? Is that your meaning, or have I misunderstood you?

No, said Zeno; you have quite understood the general drift of the treatise. I see, Parmenides, said Socrates, that Zeno is your second self in his writings too; he puts what you say in another way, and half deceives us into believing that he is saying what is new. For you, in your compositions, say that the all is one, and of this you adduce excellent proofs; and he, on the other hand, says that the many is naught, and gives many great and convincing evidences of this. To deceive the world, as you have done, by saying the same thing in different ways, one of you affirming and the other denying the many, is a strain of art beyond the reach of most of us.

(continued)

Parmenides (*continued*)

    Yes, Socrates, said Zeno. But although you are as keen as a Spartan hound in pursuing the track, you do not quite apprehend the true motive of the performance, which is not really such an artificial piece of work as you imagine; there was no intention of concealment effecting any grand result—that was a mere accident. For the truth is, that these writings of mine were meant to protect the arguments of Parmenides against those who ridicule him, and urge the many ridiculous and contradictory results which were supposed to follow from the assertion of the one. My answer is addressed to the partisans of the many, and intended to show that greater or more ridiculous consequences follow from their hypothesis of the existence of the many if carried out, than from the hypothesis of the existence of the one. A love of controversy led me to write the book in the days of my youth, and some one stole the writings, and I had therefore no choice about the publication of them; the motive, however, of writing, was not the ambition of an old man, but the pugnacity of a young one. This you do not seem to see, Socrates; though in other respects, as I was saying, your notion is a very just one.

    That I understand, said Socrates, and quite accept your account. But tell me, Zeno, do you not further think that there is an idea of likeness in the abstract, and another idea of unlikeness, which is the opposite of likeness, and that in these two, you and I and all other things to which we apply the term many, participate; and that the things which participate in likeness are in that degree and manner like; and that those which participate in unlikeness are in that degree unlike, or both like and unlike in the degree in which they participate in both? And all things may partake of both opposites, and be like and unlike to themselves, by reason of this participation. Even in that there is nothing wonderful. But if a person could prove the absolute like to become unlike, or the absolute unlike to become like, that, in my opinion, would be a real wonder; not, however, if the things which partake of the ideas experience likeness and unlikeness—there is nothing extraordinary in this. Nor, again, if a person were to show that all is one by partaking of one, and that the same is many by partaking of many, would that be very wonderful? But if he were to show me that the absolute many was one, or the absolute one many, I should be truly amazed. And I should say the same of other things. I should be surprised to hear that the genera and species had opposite qualities in themselves; but if a person wanted to prove of me that I was many and also one, there would be no marvel in that. When he wanted to show that I was many he would say that I have a right and a left side, and a front and a back, and an upper and a lower half, for I cannot deny that I partake of multitude; when, on the other hand, he wants to prove that I am one, he will say, that we who are here assembled are seven, and that I am one and partake of the one, and in saying both he speaks truly. Or if a person shows that the same wood and stones and the like, being many are also one, we admit that he shows the existence of the one and many, but he does not show that the many are one or the one many; he is uttering not a wonder but a truism. If, however, as I was suggesting just now, we were to make an abstraction, I mean of like, unlike, one, many, rest, motion, and similar ideas, and then to show that these in their abstract form admit of admixture and separation, I should greatly wonder at that. This part of the argument appears to be treated by you, Zeno, in a very spirited manner; nevertheless, as I was saying, I should be far more amazed if any one found in the ideas themselves which are conceptions, the same puzzle and entanglement which you have shown to exist in visible objects.

    While Socrates was saying this, Pythodorus thought that Parmenides and Zeno were not altogether pleased at the successive steps of the argument; but still they gave the closest attention, and often looked at one another, and smiled as if in admiration of him. When he had finished, Parmenides expressed these feelings in the following words:—

    Socrates, he said, I admire the bent of your mind towards philosophy; tell me now, was this your own distinction between abstract ideas and the things which partake of them? and do you think that there is an idea of likeness apart from the likeness which we possess, or of the one and many, or of the other notions of which Zeno has been speaking?

    I think that there are such abstract ideas, said Socrates.

    Parmenides proceeded. And would you also make abstract ideas of the just and the beautiful and the good, and of all that class of notions?

Yes, he said, I should.

And would you make an abstract idea of man distinct from us and from all other human creatures, or of fire and water?

I am often undecided, Parmenides, as to whether I ought to include them or not.

And would you feel equally undecided, Socrates, about things the mention of which may provoke a smile?—I mean such things as hair, mud, dirt, or anything else that is foul and base; would you suppose that each of these has an idea distinct from the phenomena with which we come into contact, or not?

Certainly not, said Socrates; visible things like these are such as they appear to us, and I am afraid that there would be an absurdity in assuming any idea of them, although I sometimes get disturbed, and begin to think that there is nothing without an idea; but then again, when I have taken up this position, I run away, because I am afraid that I may fall into a bottomless pit of nonsense, and perish; and I return to the ideas of which I was just now speaking, and busy myself with them.

Yes, Socrates, said Parmenides; that is because you are still young; the time will come when philosophy will have a firmer grasp of you, if I am not mistaken, and then you will not despise even the meanest things; at your age, you are too much disposed to look to the opinions of men. But I should like to know whether you mean that there are certain forms or ideas of which all other things partake, and from which they are named; that similars, for example, become similar, because they partake of similarity; and great things become great, because they partake of greatness; and that just and beautiful things become just and beautiful, because they partake of justice and beauty?

Yes, certainly, said Socrates, that is my meaning.

And does not each individual partake either of the whole of the idea or of a part of the idea? Is any third way possible?

Impossible, he said.

Then do you think that the whole idea is one, and yet being one, exists in each one of many?

Why not, Parmenides? said Socrates.

Because one and the same existing as a whole in many separate individuals, will thus be in a state of separation from itself.

Nay, replied the other; the idea may be like the day, which is one and the same in many places, and yet continuous with itself; in this way each idea may be one and the same in all.

I like your way, Socrates, of dividing one into many; and if I were to spread out a sail and cover a number of men, that, as I suppose, in your way of speaking, would be one and a whole in or on many—that will be the sort of thing which you mean?

I am not sure.

And would you say that the whole sail is over each man, or a part only?

A part only.

Then, Socrates, the ideas themselves will be divisible, and the individuals will have a part only and not the whole existing in them?

That seems to be true.

Then would you like to say, Socrates, that the one idea is really divisible and yet remains one?

Certainly not, he said.

Suppose that you divide greatness, and that of many great things each one is great by having a portion of greatness less than absolute greatness—is that conceivable?

No.

Or will each equal part, by taking some portion of equality less than absolute equality, be equal to some other?

Impossible.

Or suppose one of us to have a portion of smallness; this is but a part of the small, and therefore the small is greater; and while the absolute small is greater, that to which the part of the small is added, will be smaller and not greater than before.

That is impossible, he said.

Then in what way, Socrates, will all things participate in the ideas, if they are unable to participate in them either as parts or wholes?

Indeed, he said, that is a question which is not easily determined.

(continued)

Parmenides (*continued*)

Well, said Parmenides, and what do you say of another question?

What is that?

I imagine that the way in which you are led to assume the existence of ideas is as follows: You see a number of great objects, and there seems to you to be one and the same idea of greatness pervading them all; and hence you conceive of a single greatness.

That is true, said Socrates.

And if you go on and allow your mind in like manner to contemplate the idea of greatness and these other greatnesses, and to compare them, will not another idea of greatness arise, which will appear to be the source of them all?

That is true.

Then another abstraction of greatness will appear over and above absolute greatness, and the individuals which partake of it; and then another, which will be the source of that, and then others, and so on; and there will be no longer a single idea of each kind, but an infinite number of them.

But may not the ideas, asked Socrates, be cognitions only, and have no proper existence except in our minds, Parmenides? For in that case there may be single ideas, which do not involve the consequences which were just now mentioned.

And can there be individual cognitions which are cognitions of nothing?

That is impossible, he said.

The cognition must be of something?

Yes.

Of something that is or is not?

Of something that is.

Must it not be of the unity, or single nature, which the cognition recognizes as attaching to all?

Yes.

And will not this unity, which is always the same in all, be the idea?

From that, again, there is no escape.

Then, said Parmenides, if you say that other things participate in the ideas, must you not say that everything is made up of thoughts or cognitions, and that all things think; or will you say that being thoughts they are without thought?

But that, said Socrates, is irrational. The more probable view, Parmenides, of these ideas is, that they are patterns fixed in nature, and that other things are like them, and resemblances of them; and that what is meant by the participation of other things in the ideas, is really assimilation to them.

But if, said he, the individual is like the idea, must not the idea also be like the individual, in as far as the individual is a resemblance of the idea? That which is like, cannot be conceived of as other than the like of like.

Impossible.

And when two things are alike, must they not partake of the same idea?

They must.

And will not that of which the two partake, and which makes them alike, be the absolute idea [of likeness]?

Certainly.

Then the idea cannot be like the individual, or the individual like the idea; for if they are alike, some further idea of likeness will always arise, and if that be like anything else, another and another; and new ideas will never cease being created, if the idea resembles that which partakes of it?

Quite true.

The theory, then, that other things participate in the ideas by resemblance, has to be given up, and some other mode of participation devised?

That is true.

Do you see then, Socrates, how great is the difficulty of affirming self-existent ideas?

Yes, indeed.

And, further, let me say that as yet you only understand a small part of the difficulty which is involved in your assumption, that there are ideas of all things, which are distinct from them.

What difficulty? he said.

There are many, but the greatest of all is this: If an opponent argues that these self-existent ideas, as we term them, cannot be known, no one can prove to him that he is wrong, unless he who is disputing their existence be a man of great genius and cultivation, and is willing to follow a long and laborious demonstration—he will remain unconvinced, and still insist that they cannot be known.

How is that, Parmenides? said Socrates.

In the first place, I think, Socrates, that you, or any one who maintains the existence of absolute ideas, will admit that they cannot exist in us.

Why, then they would be no longer absolute, said Socrates.

That is true, he said; and any relation in the absolute ideas, is a relation which is among themselves only, and has nothing to do with the resemblances, or whatever they are to be termed, which are in our sphere, and the participation in which gives us this or that name. And the subjective notions in our mind, which have the same name with them, are likewise only relative to one another, and not to the ideas which have the same name with them, and belong to themselves and not to the ideas.

How do you mean? said Socrates.

I may illustrate my meaning in this way, said Parmenides: A master has a slave; now there is nothing absolute in the relation between them; they are both relations of some man to another man; but there is also an idea of mastership in the abstract, which is relative to the idea of slavery in the abstract; and this abstract nature has nothing to do with us, nor we with the abstract nature; abstract natures have to do with themselves alone, and we with ourselves. Do you see my meaning?

Yes, said Socrates, I quite see your meaning.

And does not knowledge, I mean absolute knowledge, he said, answer to very and absolute truth?

Certainly.

And each kind of absolute knowledge answers to each kind of absolute being?

Yes.

And the knowledge which we have, will answer to the truth which we have; and again, each kind of knowledge which we have, will be a knowledge of each kind of being which we have?

Certainly.

But the ideas themselves, as you admit, we have not, and cannot have?

No, we cannot.

And the absolute ideas or species, are known by the absolute idea of knowledge?

Yes.

And that is an idea which we have not got?

No.

Then none of the ideas are known to us, because we have no share in absolute knowledge?

They are not.

Then the ideas of the beautiful, and of the good, and the like, which we imagine to be absolute ideas, are unknown to us?

That appears to be the case.

I think that there is a worse consequence still.

What is that?

Would you, or would you not, say, that if there is such a thing as absolute knowledge, that must be a far more accurate knowledge than our knowledge, and the same of beauty and other things?

Yes.

And if there be anything that has absolute knowledge, there nothing more likely than God to have this most exact knowledge?

Certainly.

But then, will God, having this absolute knowledge, have a knowledge of human things?

And why not?

Because, Socrates, said Parmenides, we have admitted that the ideas have no relation to human notions, nor human notions to them; the relations of either are in their respective spheres.

(continued)

> **Parmenides** (*continued*)
>
> Yes, that has been admitted.
>
> And if God has this truest authority, and this most exact knowledge, that authority cannot rule us, nor that knowledge know us, or any human thing; and in like manner, as our authority does not extend to the gods, nor our knowledge know anything which is divine, so by parity of reason they, being gods, are not our masters; neither do they know the things of men.
>
> Yet, surely, said Socrates, to deprive God of knowledge is monstrous.
>
> These, Socrates, said Parmenides, are a few, and only a few, of the difficulties which are necessarily involved in the hypothesis of the existence of ideas, and the attempt to prove the absoluteness of each of them; he who hears of them will doubt or deny their existence, and will maintain that even if they do exist, they must necessarily be unknown to man, and he will think that there is reason in what he says, and as we were remarking just now, will be wonderfully hard of being convinced; a man must be a man of real ability before he can understand that everything has a class and an absolute essence; and still more remarkable will he be who makes out all these things for himself, and can teach another to analyze them satisfactorily.
>
> I agree with you, Parmenides, said Socrates; and what you say is very much to my mind.
>
> And yet, Socrates, said Parmenides, if a man, fixing his mind on these and the like difficulties, refuses to acknowledge ideas or species of existences, and will not define particular species, he will be at his wit's end; in this way he will utterly destroy the power of reasoning; and that is what you seem to me to have particularly noted.
>
> Very true, he said.
>
> But, then, what is to become of philosophy? What resource is there, if the ideas are unknown? I certainly do not see my way at present.

> **Categories**
> *Aristotle*
>
> **I**
>
> Things are called *homonymous* that are the same in name only and differ in definition. For example the animal man and the picture of an animal have only the name "animal" in common, and the definition of animal will be different in each case. For if someone were to make clear what it is to be an animal in each case, they would explain animal differently in each case.
>
> Things are called *synonymous* that have the same name and the same definition. For example the animal man and the animal ox are animals in the same way, both in name and in definition. If someone were to explain "animal" in each case, the same explanation of the word would be given in each case.
>
> Things are called *paronymous* that derive their name from the same root, but differ in ending. For example grammarian is paronymous with grammar and brave with bravery.
>
> **II**
>
> Things are said either in combination or without combination. Examples of things said in combination are "man runs," "man wins". Without combination–"man," "ox," "runs," "wins." Of the things that are:
>
> 1. Some are said of a subject and never in a subject. For example, man is said of a subject, of a certain man, but man is not in any subject.
> 2. Some are in a subject but never said of any subject (I call "in a subject" that which is in something not as a part, and which cannot exist apart from that which it is in). For example a piece of grammar is in a subject–the soul–but it is never said of any subject; a patch of white is in a subject the body (for all color is in some body) but it is never said of a subject.

3. Some are both in a subject and said of a subject. For example, knowledge is in a subject–knowledge in the soul–and said of a subject–knowledge of grammar.
4. Some are never said of a subject nor in a subject, such as "this man" or "this horse". Nothing like this is ever in a subject nor is it ever said of a subject. Put simply, things that are individual or one in number are never said of a subject, but nothing stops them from being in a subject. For an individual piece of grammar is in a subject.

III

When one thing is predicated of another such as of a subject, all things that are said of what is predicated will also apply to the subject. For example if man is predicated of a certain man, and animal is predicated of man, it follows that animal is predicated of a certain man as well, and that a certain man is both a man and an animal.

Differentiae of different genera, genera that are different and not subordinate to each other are different in kind, such as in the case of differentiae of the genera animal and knowledge. The differentiae of animals are footed, two-footed, winged, aquatic, whereas knowledge has none of these differentiae. We never differentiate knowledge on the basis of being two-footed. However if one genus is subordinate to another, nothing stops their differentiae from being the same. For we predicate the higher of the lower such that the differentiae of what is predicated will also apply to the subject.

IV

Everything that is said without combination signifies substance, quantity, quality, relation, place, time, position, having, acting, or being acted upon. A rough sketch is as follows:

Substance—man, horse

Quantity—two units, three units

Quality—white, grammatical

Relation—double, half, larger

Place—in the Lyceum, in the marketplace

Time—yesterday, last year

Position—lying, sitting

Having—wearing shoes, being armed

Acting—cutting, burning

Being acted upon—being cut, being burned.

Each of these by itself makes no affirmation. Affirmation or denial comes about when they are combined with each other. For it seems that every affirmation or denial is either true or false, but that un-combined words like man, white, runs, wins, are neither true nor false.

V

Substance in the first, primary and truest sense of the term is that which is never said of any subject and never in any subject, like "a man" or "a horse". Species that include primary substances as well as the genera of these species are called secondary substances. For example, "a certain man" belongs to the species "man" and the genus of the species "man" is "animal". We say that "animal" and "man" are secondary substances.

It is clear from what has been said that both the name and the definition of a subject are necessarily predicated of a subject. Man is said of the subject "a certain man" and the name is predicated of the certain man. Man is predicated of a certain man, and the definition of man will be predicated of a certain man as well. For both man and a certain man are animals. In this way the name and the definition will be predicated of the subject.

For the most part, neither the name nor the definition of things *in* a subject are predicated of the subject. Sometimes, nothing stops the *name* from being predicated of the subject, but it is impossible to predicate the definition. For example, the white in a subject is predicated of it (for white is said of the body) but the definition of white is never predicated of the body.

(continued)

Categories (*continued*)

All things that are not primary substances are said to be subjects of primary substances or in them. This is evident when we look at particular cases. Animal is predicated of man. Thus animal is predicated of a certain man. For if animal were not predicated of certain men it would not be predicated of man at all. Again, colour is in body. Thus it is in certain bodies. If it were not in certain bodies it would not be in body at all. In short all things except primary substances are said of or in primary substances. If there were no primary substances nothing else could exist.

Of secondary substances, species is more like substance than genus, since species is closer to primary substance. If someone asks of a certain primary substance "what is it?" to offer the species as an answer is more informative and appropriate than if we reply with the genus. For example, to answer "man" about a certain man is more informative than to answer "animal". The former is more specific, the latter too general. It is more informative to answer "tree" than "plant" concerning a certain tree.

Since the primary substances are the subjects of all other things and all other things are in them or predicated of them, primary substances are most properly called substances. Primary substances stand to all other existent things as species stands to genus. The species is the subject of its genus. We predicate the genus of the species, but not conversely, the species of the genus. And because of this species is more properly substance than is genus.

As for species themselves, no one of these is more substance than any other, unless it is also a genus. Man is not a more appropriate answer about a certain man than horse is about a certain horse. The same applies to primary substances. No one primary substance is more substance than any other. A certain man is no more primary substance than is a certain ox.

It is reasonable that beyond primary substance, only genera and species are called secondary substances; only these predicates reveal primary substance. If we say what a certain man is, we should state the species or the genus, and it is more informative to say man than animal. Other possible things we could say such as "white" or "runs" or other things of that nature would miss the mark. Thus only these [genera and species] are called substance.

Since primary substances are the subjects for all other things, it is they that are chiefly called substances. As primary substances hold other substances, so genera and species of primary substances hold everything else, since their relationship to everything else is like that of primary substances to them. Call a certain man grammatical. You will be calling man and animal grammatical. The same goes for everything like this.

What all substance has in common is that it is never in a subject. Primary substance can neither be in a subject nor said of a subject. Clearly secondary substances are not in a subject either. Man is said of the subject a certain man, but man is not in the subject. For man is not in a certain man. Similarly, animal is said of the subject a certain man, but animal is not in a certain man. The definition of man can be predicated of a certain man, just as the definition of animal can be.

Again nothing stops things in a substance from being predicated of the subject, but this is impossible in the case of the definition. However, of secondary substances, both the name and the definition may be predicated of the subject. For the definition of man can be predicated of a certain man just as the definition of animal can be. Thus no substance will be in a subject.

It is true not only of substance, but also of differentiae that they cannot be in a subject. Footed and two-footed are said of the subject man, but they are not in the subject. Neither footed nor two-footed is in man. The definition of the differentia will be predicated when the differentia is said of something, so that if footed is said of man, the definition of footed will also be predicated of man. For man is footed.

It should not worry us if parts of substances are in the subject as in wholes, nor make us say that they are not substances. For things in a substance was not meant to mean things belonging to something as parts.

Substances and differentiae are always said of something synonymously. For all such predicates are predicated of individuals or of the species. Now primary substance is never said of anything, never said of a subject, but secondary substances are predicated of individuals or species, and the genus is predicated of the species and of the individual. Similarly, differentiae are predicated of species and of individuals. The definition of the species and genus of a primary substance also applies to the primary substance, and the definition of the genus applies to the species of the genus. For whatever is said of a predicate is also said of its subject. The same goes for the definition of the differentiae applying to the species and the individual. As we have seen, synonyms are such that the name and the definition are the same, and as such the substance and the differentiae are said of everything synonymously.

Every substance seems to indicate a certain this. It is indisputable and true that primary substance does so, for it is shown to be individual and one in number. It may seem that secondary substances follow the same pattern of indicating a certain this, when man or animal is said, but this is not true—what is really indicated is a type. The subject is not one as in the case of primary substance, but rather it is said of many men and many animals. This does not simply indicate a quality like white does. White indicates nothing other than a quality. Genus and species mark off a type of substance, they indicate what kind of substance it is. The genus marks a wider boundary than the species, since animal marks off more than man.

Another characteristic of substances is that they do not have contraries. How could a primary substance such as this man or this animal have a contrary? There is no contrary. Nor is there a contrary of man or animal. This is not peculiar to substance but applies to many things. Take for example quantity. Two units or three units has no opposite, nor does ten nor anything like it. Although one could say that many and few or large and small are contraries, definite quantities have no opposites.

It seems like more or less do not apply to substance. I don't say that one substance is not more properly substance than another (this has already been said). Rather each substance is not said to be more or less of what it is. For example the same substance man cannot be more or less man than himself or another man. He cannot be said to be more or less man in the way that one white is more or less white than another white, or one beauty is more or less beautiful than another beautiful. It *is* said that a thing is more or less "something" than itself, as when a pale body is said to be paler now than it was before, or when a warm body is said to be more or less warm. But substance is never more or less substance than itself.

What is most unique to substance seems to be that while remaining itself and one in number, it can receive contraries. We cannot put forth anything that is not a substance that is one in number and capable of receiving contraries. For example, colour, which is one and the same in number, cannot be both white and black; and action, one and the same in number, cannot be both good and bad. The same goes for anything except substance. Substance remains one and the same in number but admits of contraries. A certain man can remain himself but become darker or lighter, hot or cold, good or bad. This never appears to be the case with anything else, although one might say that opinions and statements admit of contraries. For example, the same statement can be both true and false. "He sits" may be true while someone sits but it will be false if the person stands. The same goes for opinions. Someone might have a true belief that a person is sitting, if he holds the same belief once the person has stood up, the belief will be false.

Even if we allow this exception, there is still a difference in the way it comes about. It is by a change in substance itself that contraries are admitted. When something hot becomes cold, it changes (is altered) as is the case when something becomes darker from being lighter, or bad from good. Similarly in other cases, the thing that receives the contraries is what changes. A statement or opinion, however, remains completely unmoved. It is the facts that change and make the contrary come about. The statement "he sits" remains unmoved but the changing of the facts is what makes what is said true or false. The same goes for beliefs. Thus the unique manner in which substance admits of contraries is by a change in itself. If someone makes the exception that statements and beliefs receive contraries, this will not be true. For statements and beliefs are not said to receive contraries in themselves, but rather because something else undergoes change. It is when the facts are or are not a certain way that we say a statement is true or false, not because the statement admits of contraries. Nothing at all in statements or beliefs changes allowing them to receive contraries; nothing comes to be in them. Substance receives contraries in itself, and that is why it is said to receive contraries. It receives sickness and health, paleness and darkness, and it is said to receive contraries because it receives things of this sort. Thus substance is the only thing that is numerically one and receives contraries through a change in itself. Let this be enough about substance.

De Interpretatione
Aristotle

1

First we must define the terms 'noun' and 'verb', then the terms 'denial' and 'affirmation', then 'proposition' and 'sentence.'

Spoken words are the symbols of mental experience and written words are the symbols of spoken words. Just as all men have not the same writing, so all men have not the same speech sounds, but the mental experiences, which these directly symbolize, are the same for all, as also are those things of which our experiences are the images. This matter has, however, been discussed in my treatise about the soul, for it belongs to an investigation distinct from that which lies before us.

As there are in the mind thoughts which do not involve truth or falsity, and also those which must be either true or false, so it is in speech. For truth and falsity imply combination and separation. Nouns and verbs, provided nothing is added, are like thoughts without combination or separation; 'man' and 'white', as isolated terms, are not yet either true or false. In proof of this, consider the word 'goat-stag.' It has significance, but there is no truth or falsity about it, unless 'is' or 'is not' is added, either in the present or in some other tense.

2

By a noun we mean a sound significant by convention, which has no reference to time, and of which no part is significant apart from the rest. In the noun 'Fairsteed,' the part 'steed' has no significance in and by itself, as in the phrase 'fair steed.' Yet there is a difference between simple and composite nouns; for in the former the part is in no way significant, in the latter it contributes to the meaning of the whole, although it has not an independent meaning. Thus in the word 'pirate-boat' the word 'boat' has no meaning except as part of the whole word.

The limitation 'by convention' was introduced because nothing is by nature a noun or name-it is only so when it becomes a symbol; inarticulate sounds, such as those which brutes produce, are significant, yet none of these constitutes a noun.

The expression 'not-man' is not a noun. There is indeed no recognized term by which we may denote such an expression, for it is not a sentence or a denial. Let it then be called an indefinite noun.

The expressions 'of Philo', 'to Philo', and so on, constitute not nouns, but cases of a noun. The definition of these cases of a noun is in other respects the same as that of the noun proper, but, when coupled with 'is', 'was', or will be', they do not, as they are, form a proposition either true or false, and this the noun proper always does, under these conditions. Take the words 'of Philo is' or 'of or 'of Philo is not'; these words do not, as they stand, form either a true or a false proposition.

3

A verb is that which, in addition to its proper meaning, carries with it the notion of time. No part of it has any independent meaning, and it is a sign of something said of something else.

I will explain what I mean by saying that it carries with it the notion of time. 'Health' is a noun, but 'is healthy' is a verb; for besides its proper meaning it indicates the present existence of the state in question.

Moreover, a verb is always a sign of something said of something else, i.e. of something either predicable of or present in some other thing.

Such expressions as 'is not-healthy', 'is not, ill', I do not describe as verbs; for though they carry the additional note of time, and always form a predicate, there is no specified name for this variety; but let them be called indefinite verbs, since they apply equally well to that which exists and to that which does not.

Similarly 'he was healthy', 'he will be healthy', are not verbs, but tenses of a verb; the difference lies in the fact that the verb indicates present time, while the tenses of the verb indicate those times which lie outside the present.

Verbs in and by themselves are substantival and have significance, for he who uses such expressions arrests the hearer's mind, and fixes his attention; but they do not, as they stand, express any judgement, either positive or negative. For neither are 'to be' and 'not to be' the participle 'being' significant of any fact, unless something is added; for they do not themselves indicate anything, but imply a copulation, of which we cannot form a conception apart from the things coupled.

4

A sentence is a significant portion of speech, some parts of which have an independent meaning, that is to say, as an utterance, though not as the expression of any positive judgement. Let me explain. The word 'human' has meaning, but does not constitute a proposition, either positive or negative. It is only when other words are added that the whole will form an affirmation or denial. But if we separate one syllable of the word 'human' from the other, it has no meaning; similarly in the word 'mouse', the part 'ouse' has no meaning in itself, but is merely a sound. In composite words, indeed, the parts contribute to the meaning of the whole; yet, as has been pointed out, they have not an independent meaning.

Every sentence has meaning, not as being the natural means by which a physical faculty is realized, but, as we have said, by convention. Yet every sentence is not a proposition; only such are propositions as have in them either truth or falsity. Thus a prayer is a sentence, but is neither true nor false.

Let us therefore dismiss all other types of sentence but the proposition, for this last concerns our present inquiry, whereas the investigation of the others belongs rather to the study of rhetoric or of poetry.

5

The first class of simple propositions is the simple affirmation, the next, the simple denial; all others are only one by conjunction.

Every proposition must contain a verb or the tense of a verb. The phrase which defines the species 'man', if no verb in present, past, or future time be added, is not a proposition. It may be asked how the expression 'a footed animal with two feet' can be called single; for it is not the circumstance that the words follow in unbroken succession that effects the unity. This inquiry, however, finds its place in an investigation foreign to that before us.

We call those propositions single which indicate a single fact, or the conjunction of the parts of which results in unity: those propositions, on the other hand, are separate and many in number, which indicate many facts, or whose parts have no conjunction.

Let us, moreover, consent to call a noun or a verb an expression only, and not a proposition, since it is not possible for a man to speak in this way when he is expressing something, in such a way as to make a statement, whether his utterance is an answer to a question or an act of his own initiation.

To return: of propositions one kind is simple, i.e. that which asserts or denies something of something, the other composite, i.e. that which is compounded of simple propositions. A simple proposition is a statement, with meaning, as to the presence of something in a subject or its absence, in the present, past, or future, according to the divisions of time.

6

An affirmation is a positive assertion of something about something, a denial a negative assertion.

Now it is possible both to affirm and to deny the presence of something which is present or of something which is not, and since these same affirmations and denials are possible with reference to those times which lie outside the present, it would be possible to contradict any affirmation or denial. Thus it is plain that every affirmation has an opposite denial, and similarly every denial an opposite affirmation.

We will call such a pair of propositions a pair of contradictories. Those positive and negative propositions are said to be contradictory which have the same subject and predicate. The identity of subject and of predicate must not be 'equivocal'. Indeed there are definitive qualifications besides this, which we make to meet the casuistries of sophists.

(continued)

De Interpretatione (*continued*)

7

Some things are universal, others individual. By the term 'universal' I mean that which is of such a nature as to be predicated of many subjects, by 'individual' that which is not thus predicated. Thus 'man' is a universal, 'Callias' an individual.

Our propositions necessarily sometimes concern a universal subject, sometimes an individual.

If, then, a man states a positive and a negative proposition of universal character with regard to a universal, these two propositions are 'contrary'. By the expression 'a proposition of universal character with regard to a universal', such propositions as 'every man is white', 'no man is white' are meant. When, on the other hand, the positive and negative propositions, though they have regard to a universal, are yet not of universal character, they will not be contrary, albeit the meaning intended is sometimes contrary. As instances of propositions made with regard to a universal, but not of universal character, we may take the 'propositions 'man is white', 'man is not white'. 'Man' is a universal, but the proposition is not made as of universal character; for the word 'every' does not make the subject a universal, but rather gives the proposition a universal character. If, however, both predicate and subject are distributed, the proposition thus constituted is contrary to truth; no affirmation will, under such circumstances, be true. The proposition 'every man is every animal' is an example of this type.

An affirmation is opposed to a denial in the sense which I denote by the term 'contradictory', when, while the subject remains the same, the affirmation is of universal character and the denial is not. The affirmation 'every man is white' is the contradictory of the denial 'not every man is white', or again, the proposition 'no man is white' is the contradictory of the proposition 'some men are white'. But propositions are opposed as contraries when both the affirmation and the denial are universal, as in the sentences 'every man is white', 'no man is white', 'every man is just', 'no man is just'.

We see that in a pair of this sort both propositions cannot be true, but the contradictories of a pair of contraries can sometimes both be true with reference to the same subject; for instance 'not every man is white' and 'some men are white' are both true. Of such corresponding positive and negative propositions as refer to universals and have a universal character, one must be true and the other false. This is the case also when the reference is to individuals, as in the propositions 'Socrates is white', 'Socrates is not white'.

When, on the other hand, the reference is to universals, but the propositions are not universal, it is not always the case that one is true and the other false, for it is possible to state truly that man is white and that man is not white and that man is beautiful and that man is not beautiful; for if a man is deformed he is the reverse of beautiful, also if he is progressing towards beauty he is not yet beautiful.

This statement might seem at first sight to carry with it a contradiction, owing to the fact that the proposition 'man is not white' appears to be equivalent to the proposition 'no man is white'. This, however, is not the case, nor are they necessarily at the same time true or false.

It is evident also that the denial corresponding to a single affirmation is itself single; for the denial must deny just that which the affirmation affirms concerning the same subject, and must correspond with the affirmation both in the universal or particular character of the subject and in the distributed or undistributed sense in which it is understood.

For instance, the affirmation 'Socrates is white' has its proper denial in the proposition 'Socrates is not white'. If anything else be negatively predicated of the subject or if anything else be the subject though the predicate remain the same, the denial will not be the denial proper to that affirmation, but on that is distinct.

The denial proper to the affirmation 'every man is white' is 'not every man is white'; that proper to the affirmation 'some men are white' is 'no man is white', while that proper to the affirmation 'man is white' is 'man is not white'.

We have shown further that a single denial is contradictorily opposite to a single affirmation and we have explained which these are; we have also stated that contrary are distinct from contradictory propositions and which the contrary are; also that with regard to a pair of opposite propositions it is not always the case that one is true and the other false. We have pointed out, moreover, what the reason of this is and under what circumstances the truth of the one involves the falsity of the other.

<h2 style="text-align:center">8</h2>

An affirmation or denial is single, if it indicates some one fact about some one subject; it matters not whether the subject is universal and whether the statement has a universal character, or whether this is not so. Such single propositions are: 'every man is white', 'not every man is white'; 'man is white', 'man is not white'; 'no man is white', 'some men are white'; provided the word 'white' has one meaning. If, on the other hand, one word has two meanings which do not combine to form one, the affirmation is not single. For instance, if a man should establish the symbol 'garment' as significant both of a horse and of a man, the proposition 'garment is white' would not be a single affirmation, nor its opposite a single denial. For it is equivalent to the proposition 'horse and man are white', which, again, is equivalent to the two propositions 'horse is white', 'man is white'. If, then, these two propositions have more than a single significance, and do not form a single proposition, it is plain that the first proposition either has more than one significance or else has none; for a particular man is not a horse.

This, then, is another instance of those propositions of which both the positive and the negative forms may be true or false simultaneously.

<h2 style="text-align:center">9</h2>

In the case of that which is or which has taken place, propositions, whether positive or negative, must be true or false. Again, in the case of a pair of contradictories, either when the subject is universal and the propositions are of a universal character, or when it is individual, as has been said,' one of the two must be true and the other false; whereas when the subject is universal, but the propositions are not of a universal character, there is no such necessity. We have discussed this type also in a previous chapter.

When the subject, however, is individual, and that which is predicated of it relates to the future, the case is altered. For if all propositions whether positive or negative are either true or false, then any given predicate must either belong to the subject or not, so that if one man affirms that an event of a given character will take place and another denies it, it is plain that the statement of the one will correspond with reality and that of the other will not. For the predicate cannot both belong and not belong to the subject at one and the same time with regard to the future.

Thus, if it is true to say that a thing is white, it must necessarily be white; if the reverse proposition is true, it will of necessity not be white. Again, if it is white, the proposition stating that it is white was true; if it is not white, the proposition to the opposite effect was true. And if it is not white, the man who states that it is making a false statement; and if the man who states that it is white is making a false statement, it follows that it is not white. It may therefore be argued that it is necessary that affirmations or denials must be either true or false.

Now if this be so, nothing is or takes place fortuitously, either in the present or in the future, and there are no real alternatives; everything takes place of necessity and is fixed. For either he that affirms that it will take place or he that denies this is in correspondence with fact, whereas if things did not take place of necessity, an event might just as easily not happen as happen; for the meaning of the word 'fortuitous' with regard to present or future events is that reality is so constituted that it may issue in either of two opposite directions. Again, if a thing is white now, it was true before to say that it would be white, so that of anything that has taken place it was always true to say 'it is' or 'it will be'. But if it was always true to say that a thing is or will be, it is not possible that it should not be or not be about to be, and when a thing cannot not come to be, it is impossible that it should not come to be, and when it is impossible that it should not come to be, it must come to be. All, then, that is about to be must of necessity take place. It results from this that nothing is uncertain or fortuitous, for if it were fortuitous it would not be necessary.

Again, to say that neither the affirmation nor the denial is true, maintaining, let us say, that an event neither will take place nor will not take place, is to take up a position impossible to defend. In the first place, though facts should prove the one proposition false, the opposite would still be untrue.

(continued)

De Interpretatione   (*continued*)

Secondly, if it was true to say that a thing was both white and large, both these qualities must necessarily belong to it; and if they will belong to it the next day, they must necessarily belong to it the next day. But if an event is neither to take place nor not to take place the next day, the element of chance will be eliminated. For example, it would be necessary that a sea-fight should neither take place nor fail to take place on the next day.

These awkward results and others of the same kind follow, if it is an irrefragable law that of every pair of contradictory propositions, whether they have regard to universals and are stated as universally applicable, or whether they have regard to individuals, one must be true and the other false, and that there are no real alternatives, but that all that is or takes place is the outcome of necessity. There would be no need to deliberate or to take trouble, on the supposition that if we should adopt a certain course, a certain result would follow, while, if we did not, the result would not follow. For a man may predict an event ten thousand years beforehand, and another may predict the reverse; that which was truly predicted at the moment in the past will of necessity take place in the fullness of time.

Further, it makes no difference whether people have or have not actually made the contradictory statements. For it is manifest that the circumstances are not influenced by the fact of an affirmation or denial on the part of anyone. For events will not take place or fail to take place because it was stated that they would or would not take place, nor is this any more the case if the prediction dates back ten thousand years or any other space of time. Wherefore, if through all time the nature of things was so constituted that a prediction about an event was true, then through all time it was necessary that that should find fulfillment; and with regard to all events, circumstances have always been such that their occurrence is a matter of necessity. For that of which someone has said truly that it will be, cannot fail to take place; and of that which takes place, it was always true to say that it would be.

Yet this view leads to an impossible conclusion; for we see that both deliberation and action are causative with regard to the future, and that, to speak more generally, in those things which are not continuously actual there is potentiality in either direction. Such things may either be or not be; events also therefore may either take place or not take place. There are many obvious instances of this. It is possible that this coat may be cut in half, and yet it may not be cut in half, but wear out first. In the same way, it is possible that it should not be cut in half; unless this were so, it would not be possible that it should wear out first. So it is therefore with all other events which possess this kind of potentiality. It is therefore plain that it is not of necessity that everything is or takes place; but in some instances there are real alternatives, in which case the affirmation is no more true and no more false than the denial; while some exhibit a predisposition and general tendency in one direction or the other, and yet can issue in the opposite direction by exception.

Now that which is must needs be when it is, and that which is not must needs not be when it is not. Yet it cannot be said without qualification that all existence and non-existence is the outcome of necessity. For there is a difference between saying that that which is, when it is, must needs be, and simply saying that all that is must needs be, and similarly in the case of that which is not. In the case, also, of two contradictory propositions this holds good. Everything must either be or not be, whether in the present or in the future, but it is not always possible to distinguish and state determinately which of these alternatives must necessarily come about.

Let me illustrate. A sea-fight must either take place to-morrow or not, but it is not necessary that it should take place to-morrow, neither is it necessary that it should not take place, yet it is necessary that it either should or should not take place to-morrow. Since propositions correspond with facts, it is evident that when in future events there is a real alternative, and a potentiality in contrary directions, the corresponding affirmation and denial have the same character.

This is the case with regard to that which is not always existent or not always nonexistent. One of the two propositions in such instances must be true and the other false, but we cannot say determinately that this or that is false, but must leave the alternative undecided. One may indeed be more likely to be true than the other, but it cannot be either actually true or actually false. It is therefore plain that it is not necessary that of an affirmation and a denial one should be true and the other false. For in the case of that which exists potentially, but not actually, the rule which applies to that which exists actually does not hold good. The case is rather as we have indicated.

Of Liberty and Necessity
David Hume

Part I

IT might reasonably be expected in questions which have been canvassed and disputed with great eagerness, since the first origin of science, and philosophy, that the meaning of all the terms, at least, should have been agreed upon among the disputants; and our enquiries, in the course of two thousand years, been able to pass from words to the true and real subject of the controversy. For how easy may it seem to give exact definitions of the terms employed in reasoning, and make these definitions, not the mere sound of words, the object of future scrutiny and examination? But if we consider the matter more narrowly, we shall be apt to draw a quite opposite conclusion. From this circumstance alone, that a controversy has been long kept on foot, and remains still undecided, we may presume that there is some ambiguity in the expression, and that the disputants affix different ideas to the terms employed in the controversy. For as the faculties of the mind are supposed to be naturally alike in every individual; otherwise nothing could be more fruitless than to reason or dispute together; it were impossible, if men affix the same ideas to their terms, that they could so long form different opinions of the same subject; especially when they communicate their views, and each party turn themselves on all sides, in search of arguments which may give them the victory over their antagonists. It is true, if men attempt the discussion of questions which lie entirely beyond the reach of human capacity, such as those concerning the origin of worlds, or the economy of the intellectual system or region of spirits, they may long beat the air in their fruitless contests, and never arrive at any determinate conclusion. But if the question regard any subject of common life and experience, nothing, one would think, could preserve the dispute so long undecided but some ambiguous expressions, which keep the antagonists still at a distance, and hinder them from grappling with each other.

1

This has been the case in the long disputed question concerning liberty and necessity; and to so remarkable a degree that, if I be not much mistaken, we shall find, that all mankind, both learned and ignorant, have always been of the same opinion with regard to this subject, and that a few intelligible definitions would immediately have put an end to the whole controversy. I own that this dispute has been so much canvassed on all hands, and has led philosophers into such a labyrinth of obscure sophistry, that it is no wonder, if a sensible reader indulge his ease so far as to turn a deaf ear to the proposal of such a question, from which he can expect neither instruction or entertainment. But the state of the argument here proposed may, perhaps, serve to renew his attention; as it has more novelty, promises at least some decision of the controversy, and will not much disturb his ease by any intricate or obscure reasoning.

2

I hope, therefore, to make it appear that all men have ever agreed in the doctrine both of necessity and of liberty, according to any reasonable sense, which can be put on these terms; and that the whole controversy, has hitherto turned merely upon words. We shall begin with examining the doctrine of necessity.

3

It is universally allowed that matter, in all its operations, is actuated by a necessary force, and that every natural effect is so precisely determined by the energy of its cause that no other effect, in such particular circumstances, could possibly have resulted from it. The degree and direction of every motion is, by the laws of nature, prescribed with such exactness that a living creature may as soon arise from the shock of two bodies as motion in any other degree or direction than what is actually produced by it. Would we, therefore, form a just and precise idea of *necessity,* we must consider whence that idea arises when we apply it to the operation of bodies.

(continued)

Of Liberty and Necessity   (continued)

4

It seems evident that, if all the scenes of nature were continually shifted in such a manner that no two events bore any resemblance to each other, but every object was entirely new, without any similitude to whatever had been seen before, we should never, in that case, have attained the least idea of necessity, or of a connexion among these objects. We might say, upon such a supposition, that one object or event has followed another; not that one was produced by the other. The relation of cause and effect must be utterly unknown to mankind. Inference and reasoning concerning the operations of nature would, from that moment, be at an end; and the memory and senses remain the only canals, by which the knowledge of any real existence could possibly have access to the mind. Our idea, therefore, of necessity and causation arises entirely from the uniformity observable in the operations of nature, where similar objects are constantly conjoined together, and the mind is determined by custom to infer the one from the appearance of the other. These two circumstances form the whole of that necessity, which we ascribe to matter. Beyond the constant *conjunction* of similar objects, and the consequent *inference* from one to the other, we have no notion of any necessity or connexion.

5

If it appear, therefore, that all mankind have ever allowed, without any doubt or hesitation, that these two circumstances take place in the voluntary actions of men, and in the operations of mind; it must follow, that all mankind have ever agreed in the doctrine of necessity, and that they have hitherto disputed, merely for not understanding each other.

6

As to the first circumstance, the constant and regular conjunction of similar events, we may possibly satisfy ourselves by the following considerations: It is universally acknowledged that there is a great uniformity among the actions of men, in all nations and ages, and that human nature remains still the same, in its principles and operations. The same motives always produce the same actions: the same events follow from the same causes. Ambition, avarice, self-love, vanity, friendship, generosity, public spirit: these passions, mixed in various degrees, and distributed through society, have been, from the beginning of the world, and still are, the source of all the actions and enterprises, which have ever been observed among mankind. Would you know the sentiments, inclinations, and course of life of the Greeks and Romans? Study well the temper and actions of the French and English: You cannot be much mistaken in transferring to the former *most* of the observations which you have made with regard to the latter. Mankind are so much the same, in all times and places, that history informs us of nothing new or strange in this particular. Its chief use is only to discover the constant and universal principles of human nature, by showing men in all varieties of circumstances and situations, and furnishing us with materials from which we may form our observations and become acquainted with the regular springs of human action and behaviour. These records of wars, intrigues, factions, and revolutions, are so many collections of experiments, by which the politician or moral philosopher fixes the principles of his science, in the same manner as the physician or natural philosopher becomes acquainted with the nature of plants, minerals, and other external objects, by the experiments which he forms concerning them. Nor are the earth, water, and other elements, examined by Aristotle, and Hippocrates, more like to those which at present lie under our observation than the men described by Polybius and Tacitus are to those who now govern the world.

7

Should a traveller, returning from a far country, bring us an account of men, wholly different from any with whom we were ever acquainted; men, who were entirely divested of avarice, ambition, or revenge; who knew no pleasure but friendship, generosity, and public spirit; we should immediately, from these circumstances, detect the falsehood, and prove him a liar, with the same certainty as if he had stuffed his narration with stories of centaurs and dragons, miracles and prodigies. And if we would explode any forgery in history, we cannot make use of a more convincing argument, than to prove, that the actions ascribed to any person are directly contrary to the course of nature, and that no human motives, in such circumstances, could ever induce him to such a conduct. The veracity of Quintus Curtius is as much to be suspected, when he describes the supernatural courage of Alexander, by which he was hurried on singly to attack multitudes, as when he describes his supernatural force and activity, by which he was able to resist them. So readily and universally do we acknowledge a uniformity in human motives and actions as well as in the operations of body.

8

Hence likewise the benefit of that experience, acquired by long life and a variety of business and company, in order to instruct us in the principles of human nature, and regulate our future conduct, as well as speculation. By means of this guide, we mount up to the knowledge of men's inclinations and motives, from their actions, expressions, and even gestures; and again descend to the interpretation of their actions from our knowledge of their motives and inclinations. The general observations treasured up by a course of experience, give us the clue of human nature, and teach us to unravel all its intricacies. Pretexts and appearances no longer deceive us. Public declarations pass for the specious colouring of a cause. And though virtue and honour be allowed their proper weight and authority, that perfect disinterestedness, so often pretended to, is never expected in multitudes and parties; seldom in their leaders; and scarcely even in individuals of any rank or station. But were there no uniformity in human actions, and were every experiment which we could form of this kind irregular and anomalous, it were impossible to collect any general observations concerning mankind; and no experience, however accurately digested by reflection, would ever serve to any purpose. Why is the aged husbandman more skilful in his calling than the young beginner but because there is a certain uniformity in the operation of the sun, rain, and earth towards the production of vegetables; and experience teaches the old practitioner the rules by which this operation is governed and directed.

9

We must not, however, expect that this uniformity of human actions should be carried to such a length as that all men, in the same circumstances, will always act precisely in the same manner, without making any allowance for the diversity of characters, prejudices, and opinions. Such a uniformity in every particular, is found in no part of nature. On the contrary, from observing the variety of conduct in different men, we are enabled to form a greater variety of maxims, which still suppose a degree of uniformity and regularity.

10

Are the manners of men different in different ages and countries? We learn thence the great force of custom and education, which mould the human mind from its infancy and form it into a fixed and established character. Is the behaviour and conduct of the one sex very unlike that of the other? Is it thence we become acquainted with the different characters which nature has impressed upon the sexes, and which she preserves with constancy and regularity? Are the actions of the same person much diversified in the different periods of his life, from infancy to old age? This affords room for many general observations concerning the gradual change of our sentiments and inclinations, and the different maxims which prevail in the different ages of human creatures. Even the characters, which are peculiar to each individual, have a uniformity in their influence; otherwise our acquaintance with the persons and our observation of their conduct could never teach us their dispositions, or serve to direct our behaviour with regard to them.

11

I grant it possible to find some actions, which seem to have no regular connexion with any known motives, and are exceptions to all the measures of conduct which have ever been established for the government of men. But if we would willingly know what judgment should be formed of such irregular and extraordinary actions, we may consider the sentiments commonly entertained with regard to those irregular events which appear in the course of nature, and the operations of

(continued)

Of Liberty and Necessity (*continued*)

external objects. All causes are not conjoined to their usual effects with like uniformity. An artificer, who handles only dead matter, may be disappointed of his aim, as well as the politician, who directs the conduct of sensible and intelligent agents.

12

The vulgar, who take things according to their first appearance, attribute the uncertainty of events to such an uncertainty in the causes as makes the latter often fail of their usual influence; though they meet with no impediment in their operation. But philosophers, observing that, almost in every part of nature, there is contained a vast variety of springs and principles, which are hid, by reason of their minuteness or remoteness, find, that it is at least possible the contrariety of events may not proceed from any contingency in the cause, but from the secret operation of contrary causes. This possibility is converted into certainty by farther observation, when they remark that, upon an exact scrutiny, a contrariety of effects always betrays a contrariety of causes, and proceeds from their mutual opposition. A peasant can give no better reason for the stopping of any clock or watch than to say that it does not commonly go right: But an artist easily perceives that the same force in the spring or pendulum has always the same influence on the wheels; but fails of its usual effects, perhaps by reason of a grain of dust, which puts a stop to the whole movement. From the observation of several parallel instances, philosophers form a maxim that the connexion between all causes and effects is equally necessary, and that its seeming uncertainty in some instances proceeds from the secret opposition of contrary causes.

13

Thus, for instance, in the human body, when the usual symptoms of health or sickness disappoint our expectation; when medicines operate not with their wonted powers; when irregular events follow from any particular cause; the philosopher and physician are not surprised at the matter, nor are ever tempted to deny, in general, the necessity and uniformity of those principles by which the animal economy is conducted. They know that a human body is a mighty complicated machine: That many secret powers lurk in it, which are altogether beyond our comprehension: That to us it must often appear very uncertain in its operations: And that therefore the irregular events, which outwardly discover themselves, can be no proof that the laws of nature are not observed with the greatest regularity in its internal operations: And that therefore the irregular events, which outwardly discover themselves, can be no proof that the laws of nature are not observed with the greatest regularity in its internal operations and government.

14

The philosopher, if he be consistent, must apply the same reasoning to the actions and volitions of intelligent agents. The most irregular and unexpected resolutions of men may frequently be accounted for by those who know every particular circumstance of their character and situation. A person of an obliging disposition gives a peevish answer: But he has the toothache, or has not dined. A stupid fellow discovers an uncommon alacrity in his carriage: But he has met with a sudden piece of good fortune. Or even when an action, as sometimes happens, cannot be particularly accounted for, either by the person himself or by others; we know, in general, that the characters of men are, to a certain degree, inconstant and irregular. This is, in a manner, the constant character of human nature; though it be applicable, in a more particular manner, to some persons who have no fixed rule for their conduct, but proceed in a continued course of caprice and inconstancy. The internal principles and motives may operate in a uniform manner, notwithstanding these seeming irregularities; in the same manner as the winds, rain, cloud, and other variations of the weather are supposed to be governed by steady principles; though not easily discoverable by human sagacity and enquiry.

15

Thus it appears, not only that the conjunction between motives and voluntary actions is as regular and uniform as that between the cause and effect in any part of nature; but also that this regular conjunction has been universally acknowledged among mankind, and has never been the subject of dispute, either in philosophy or common life. Now, as it is from past experience that we draw all inferences concerning the future, and as we conclude that objects will always be conjoined together which we find to have always been conjoined; it may seem superfluous to prove that this experienced uniformity in human actions is a source whence we draw *inferences* concerning them. But in order to throw the argument into a greater variety of lights we shall also insist, though briefly, on this latter topic.

16

The mutual dependence of men is so great in all societies that scarce any human action is entirely complete in itself, or is performed without some reference to the actions of others, which are requisite to make it answer fully the intention of the agent. The poorest artificer, who labours alone, expects at least the protection of the magistrate, to ensure him the enjoyment of the fruits of his labour. He also expects that, when he carries his goods to market, and offers them at a reasonable price, he shall find purchasers, and shall be able, by the money he acquires, to engage others to supply him with those commodities which are requisite for his subsistence. In proportion as men extend their dealings, and render their intercourse with others more complicated, they always comprehend, in their schemes of life, a greater variety of voluntary actions, which they expect, from the proper motives, to co-operate with their own. In all these conclusions they take their measures from past experience, in the same manner as in their reasonings concerning external objects; and firmly believe that men, as well as all the elements, are to continue, in their operations, the same that they have ever found them. A manufacturer reckons upon the labour of his servants for the execution of any work as much as upon the tools which he employs, and would be equally surprised were his expectations disappointed. In short, this experimental inference and reasoning concerning the actions of others enters so much into human life that no man, while awake, is ever a moment without employing it. Have we not reason, therefore, to affirm that all mankind have always agreed in the doctrine of necessity according to the foregoing definition and explication of it?

17

Nor have philosophers even entertained a different opinion from the people in this particular. For, not to mention that almost every action of their life supposes that opinion, there are even few of the speculative parts of learning to which it is not essential. What would become of *history*, had we not a dependence on the veracity of the historian according to the experience which we have had of mankind? How could *politics* be a science, if laws and forms of government had not a uniform influence upon society? Where would be the foundation of *morals,* if particular characters had no certain or determinate power to produce particular sentiments, and if these sentiments had no constant operation on actions? And with what pretence could we employ our *criticism* upon any poet or polite author, if we could not pronounce the conduct and sentiments of his actors either natural or unnatural to such characters, and in such circumstances? It seems almost impossible, therefore, to engage either in science or action of any kind without acknowledging the doctrine of necessity, and this *inference* from motive to voluntary actions, from characters to conduct.

18

And indeed, when we consider how aptly *natural* and *moral* evidence link together, and form only one chain of argument, we shall make no scruple to allow that they are of the same nature, and derived from the same principles. A prisoner who has neither money nor interest, discovers the impossibility of his escape, as well when he considers the obstinacy of the gaoler, as the walls and bars with which he is surrounded; and, in all attempts for his freedom, chooses rather to work upon the stone and iron of the one, than upon the inflexible nature of the other. The same prisoner, when conducted to the scaffold, foresees his death as certainly from the constancy and fidelity of his guards, as from the operation of the axe or wheel. His mind runs along a certain train of ideas: the refusal of the soldiers to consent to his escape; the action of the executioner; the separation of the head and body; bleeding, convulsive motions, and death. Here is a connected chain of natural causes

(continued)

Of Liberty and Necessity   (continued)

and voluntary actions; but the mind feels no difference between them in passing from one link to another: Nor is it less certain of the future event than if it were connected with the objects present to the memory or senses, by a train of causes, cemented together by what we are pleased to call a *physical* necessity. The same experienced union has the same effect on the mind, whether the united objects be motives, volition, and actions; or figure and motion. We may change the name of things; but their nature and their operation on the understanding never change.

19

Were a man, whom I know to be honest and opulent, and with whom I live in intimate friendship, to come into my house, where I am surrounded with my servants, I rest assured that he is not to stab me before he leaves it in order to rob me of my silver standish; and I no more suspect this event than the falling of the house itself, which is new, and solidly built and founded.—*But he may have been seized with a sudden and unknown frenzy.*—So may a sudden earthquake arise, and shake and tumble my house about my ears. I shall therefore change the suppositions. I shall say that I know with certainty that he is not to put his hand into the fire and hold it there till it be consumed: and this event, I think I can foretell with the same assurance, as that, if he throw himself out at the window, and meet with no obstruction, he will not remain a moment suspended in the air. No suspicion of an unknown frenzy can give the least possibility to the former event, which is so contrary to all the known principles of human nature. A man who at noon leaves his purse full of gold on the pavement at Charing-Cross, may as well expect that it will fly away like a feather, as that he will find it untouched an hour after. Above one half of human reasonings contain inferences of a similar nature, attended with more or less degrees of certainty proportioned to our experience of the usual conduct of mankind in such particular situations.

20

I have frequently considered, what could possibly be the reason why all mankind, though they have ever, without hesitation, acknowledged the doctrine of necessity in their whole practice and reasoning, have yet discovered such a reluctance to acknowledge it in words, and have rather shown a propensity, in all ages, to profess the contrary opinion. The matter, I think, may be accounted for after the following manner. If we examine the operations of body, and the production of effects from their causes, we shall find that all our faculties can never carry us farther in our knowledge of this relation than barely to observe that particular object are *constantly conjoined* together, and that the mind is carried, by a *customary transition*, from the appearance of one to the belief of the other. But though this conclusion concerning human ignorance be the result of the strictest scrutiny of this subject, men still entertain a strong propensity to believe that they penetrate farther into the powers of nature, and perceive something like a necessary connexion between the cause and the effect. When again they turn their reflections towards the operations of their own minds, and *feel* no such connexion of the motive and the action; they are thence apt to suppose, that there is a difference between the effects which result from material force, and those which arise from thought and intelligence. But being once convinced that we know nothing farther of causation of any kind than merely the *constant conjunction* of objects, and the consequent *inference* of the mind from one to another, and finding that these two circumstances are universally allowed to have place in voluntary actions; we may be more easily led to own the same necessity common to all causes. And though this reasoning may contradict the systems of many philosophers, in ascribing necessity to the determinations of the will, we shall find, upon reflection, that they dissent from it in words only, not in their real sentiment. Necessity, according to the sense in which it is here taken, has never yet been rejected, nor can ever, I think, be rejected by any philosopher. It may only, perhaps, be pretended that the mind can perceive, in the operations of matter, some farther connexion between the cause and effect; and connexion that has not place in voluntary actions of intelligent beings. Now whether it be so or not, can only appear upon examination; and it is incumbent on these philosophers to make good their assertion, by defining or describing that necessity, and pointing it out to us in the operations of material causes.

21

It would seem, indeed, that men begin at the wrong end of this question concerning liberty and necessity, when they enter upon it by examining the faculties of the soul, the influence of the understanding, and the operations of the will. Let them first discuss a more simple question, namely, the operations of body and of brute unintelligent matter; and try whether they can there form any idea of causation and necessity, except that of a constant conjunction of objects, and subsequent inference of the mind from one to another. If these circumstances form, in reality, the whole of that necessity, which we conceive in matter, and if these circumstances be also universally acknowledged to take place in the operations of the mind, the dispute is at an end; at least, must be owned to be thenceforth merely verbal. But as long as we will rashly suppose, that we have some farther idea of necessity and causation in the operations of external objects; at the same time, that we can find nothing farther in the voluntary actions of the mind; there is no possibility of bringing the question to any determinate issue, while we proceed upon so erroneous a supposition. The only method of undeceiving us is to mount up higher; to examine the narrow extent of science when applied to material causes; and to convince ourselves that all we know of them is the constant conjunction and inference above mentioned. We may, perhaps, find that it is with difficulty we are induced to fix such narrow limits to human understanding: but we can afterwards find no difficulty when we come to apply this doctrine to the actions of the will. For as it is evident that these have a regular conjunction with motives and circumstances and characters, and as we always draw inferences from one to the other, we must be obliged to acknowledge in words that necessity, which we have already avowed, in every deliberation of our lives, and in every step of our conduct and behaviour.[1]

22

But to proceed in this reconciling project with regard to the question of liberty and necessity; the most contentious question of metaphysics, the most contentious science; it will not require many words to prove, that all mankind have ever agreed in the doctrine of liberty as well as in that of necessity, and that the whole dispute, in this respect also, has been hitherto merely verbal. For what is meant by liberty, when applied to voluntary actions? We cannot surely mean that actions have so little connexion with motives, inclinations and circumstances, that one does not follow with a certain degree of uniformity from the other, and that one affords no inference by which we can conclude the existence of the other. For these are plain and acknowledged matters of fact. By liberty, then, we can only mean *a power of acting or not acting, according to the determinations of the will;* this is, if we choose to remain at rest, we may; if we choose to move, we also may. Now this hypothetical liberty is universally allowed to belong to every one who is not a prisoner and in chains. Here, then, is no subject of dispute.

23

Whatever definition we may give of liberty, we should be careful to observe two requisite circumstances; *First,* that it be consistent with plain matter of fact; *secondly*, that it be consistent with itself. If we observe these circumstances, and render our definition intelligible, I am persuaded that all mankind will be found of one opinion with regard to it.

24

It is universally allowed that nothing exists without a cause of its existence, and that chance, when strictly examined, is a mere negative word, and means not any real power which has anywhere a being in nature. But it is pretended that some causes are necessary, some not necessary. Here then is the advantage of definitions. Let any one *define* a cause, without comprehending, as a part of the definition, a *necessary connexion* with its effect; and let him show distinctly the origin of the idea, expressed by the definition; and I shall readily give up the whole controversy. But if the foregoing explication of the matter be received, this must be absolutely impracticable. Had not objects a regular conjunction with each other, we should never have entertained any notion of cause and effect; and

(continued)

Of Liberty and Necessity (*continued*)

this regular conjunction produces that inference of the understanding, which is the only connexion, that we can have any comprehension of. Whoever attempts a definition of cause, exclusive of these circumstances, will be obliged either to employ unintelligible terms or such as are synonymous to the term which he endeavours to define.[2] And if the definition above mentioned be admitted; liberty, when opposed to necessity, not to constraint, is the same thing with chance; which is universally allowed to have no existence.

NOTES

1. The prevalence of the doctrine of liberty may be accounted for, from another cause, viz. a false sensation or seeming experience which we have, or may have, of liberty or indifference, in many of our actions. The necessity of any action, whether of matter or of mind, is not, properly speaking, a quality in the agent, but in any thinking or intelligent being, who may consider the action; and it consists chiefly in the determination of his thoughts to infer the existence of that action from some preceding objects; as liberty, when opposed to necessity, is nothing but the want of that determination, and a certain looseness or indifference, which we feel, in passing, or not passing, from the idea of one object to that of any succeeding one. Now we may observe, that, though, in *reflecting* on human actions, we seldom feel such a looseness, or indifference, but are commonly able to infer them with considerable certainty from their motives, and from the dispositions of the agent; yet it frequently happens, that, in *performing* the actions themselves, we are sensible of something like it: And as all resembling objects are readily taken for each other, this has been employed as a demonstrative and even intuitive proof of human liberty. We feel, that our actions are subject to our will, on most occasions; and imagine we feel, that the will itself is subject to nothing, because, when by a denial of it we are provoked to try, we feel, that it moves easily every way, and produces an image of itself (or a *Velleïty*, as it is called in the schools) even on that side, on which it did not settle. This image, or faint motion, we persuade ourselves, could, at that time, have been compleated into the thing itself; because, should that be denied, we find, upon a second trial, that, at present, it can. We consider not, that the fantastical desire of shewing liberty, is here the motive of our actions. And it seems certain, that, however we may imagine we feel a liberty within ourselves, a spectator can commonly infer our actions from our motives and character; and even where he cannot, he concludes in general, that he might, were he perfectly acquainted with every circumstance of our situation and temper, and the most secret springs of our complexion and disposition. Now this is the very essence of necessity, according to the foregoing doctrine
2. Thus, if a cause be defined, *that which produces any thing,* it is easy to observe, that *producing* is synonymous to *causing.* In like manner, if a cause be defined, *that by which any thing exists,* this is liable to the same objection. For what is meant by these words, *by which?* Had it been said, that a cause is *that* after which *any thing constantly exists;* we should have understood the terms. For this is, indeed, all we know of the matter. And this constantly forms the very essence of necessity, nor have we any other idea of it.

Freedom and Determinism
Richard Taylor

If I consider the world or any part of it at any particular moment, it seems certain that it is perfectly determinate in every detail. There is no vagueness, looseness, or ambiguity. There is, indeed, vagueness, and even error, in my conceptions of reality, but not in reality itself. A lilac bush, which surely has a certain exact number of blossoms, appears to me only to have many blossoms, and I do not know how many. Things seen in the distance appear of indefinite form, and often of a color and size that in fact they are not. Things near the border of my visual field seem to me vague and amorphous, and I can never even say exactly where that border itself is, it is so indefinite and vague. But all such indeterminateness resides solely in my conceptions and ideas; the world itself shares none of it. The sea, at any exact time and place, has exactly a certain salinity and temperature, and every grain of sand on its shore is exactly disposed with respect to all the others. The wind at any point in space has at any moment a certain direction and force, not more nor less. It matters not whether these properties and relations are known to anyone. A field of wheat at any moment contains just an exact number of ripening grains, each having reached just the ripeness it exhibits, each presenting a determinate color and shade, an exact shape and mass. A person, too, at any given point in his life, is perfectly determinate to the minutest cells of his body. My own brain, nerves—even my thoughts, intentions, and feelings—are at any moment just what they then specifically are. These thoughts might, to be sure, be vague and even false as representations, but as thoughts they are not, and even a false idea is no less an exact and determinate idea than a true one.

Nothing seems more obvious. But if I now ask *why* the world and all its larger or smaller parts are this moment just what they are, the answer comes to mind: because the world, the moment before, was precisely what it then was. Given exactly what went before, the world, it seems, could now be none other than it is. And what it was a moment before, in all its large and minuter parts, was the consequence of the what had gone just before then, and so on, back to the very beginning of the world, if it had a beginning, or through an infinite past time, in case it had not. In any case, the world as it now is, and every part of it, and every detail of every part, would seem to be the only world that now could be, given just what it has been.

Determinism

Reflections such as this suggest that, in the case of everything that exists, there are antecedent conditions, known or unknown, which, because they are given, mean that things could not be other than they are. That is an exact statement of the metaphysical thesis of determinism. More loosely, it says that everything, including every cause, is the effect of some cause or causes; or that everything is not only determinate but causally determined. The statement, moreover, makes no allowance for time, for past, or for future. Hence, if true, it holds not only for all things that have existed but for all things that do or ever will exist.

Of course people rarely think of such a principle, and hardly one in a thousand will ever formulate it to himself in words. Yet all do seem to assume it in their daily affairs, so much so that some philosophers have declared it an *a priori* principle of the understanding, that is, something that is known independently of experience, while others have deemed it to be at least a part of the common sense of mankind. Thus, when I hear a noise I look up to see where it came from. I never suppose that it was just a noise that came from nowhere and had no cause. Everyone does the same—even animals, though they have never once thought about metaphysics or the principle of universal determinism. People believe, or at least act as though they believed, that things have causes, without exception. When a child or animal touches a hot stove for the first time, it unhesitatingly believes that the pain then felt was caused by that stove, and so firm and immediate is that belief that hot stoves are avoided ever after. We all use our metaphysical principles, whether we think of them or not, or are even capable of thinking of them. If I have a bodily or other disorder—a rash, for instance, or a fever or a phobia—I consult a physician for a diagnosis and explanation in the hope that the cause of it might be found and removed or moderated. I am never tempted to suppose that such things just have no causes, arising from nowhere, else I would take no steps to remove the causes. The principle of determinism is here, as in everything else, simply assumed, without being thought about.

Determinism and Human Behavior

I am a part of the world. So is each of the cells and minute parts of which I am composed. The principle of determinism, then, in case it is true, applies to me and to each of those minute parts, no less than to the sand, wheat, winds, and waters of which we have spoken. There is no particular difficulty in thinking so, as long as I consider only what are sometimes called the 'purely physiological" changes of my body, like growth, the pulse, glandular secretions, and the like. But what of my thoughts and ideas? And what of my behavior that is supposed to be deliberate, purposeful, and perhaps morally significant? These are all changes of my own being, changes that I undergo, and if these are all but the consequences of the conditions under which they occur, and these conditions are the only ones that could have obtained, given the state of the world just before and when they arose, what now becomes of my responsibility for my behavior and of the control over my conduct that I fancy myself to possess? What am I but a helpless product of nature, destined by her to do whatever I do and to become whatever I become?

(continued)

Freedom and Determinism (*continued*)

There is no moral blame nor merit in anyone who cannot help what he does. It matters not whether the explanation for his behavior is found within him or without, whether it is expressed in terms of ordinary physical causes or allegedly "mental" ones, or whether the causes be proximate or remote. I am not responsible for being a man rather than a woman, nor for having the temperament and desires characteristic of that sex. I was never asked whether these should be given to me. The kleptomaniac, similarly, steals from compulsion, the alcoholic drinks from compulsion, and sometimes even the hero dies from compulsive courage. Though these causes are within them, they compel no less for that, and their victims never chose to have them inflicted upon themselves. To say they are compulsions is to say only that they compel. But to say that they compel is only to say that they cause; for the cause of a thing being given, the effect cannot fail to follow. By the thesis of determinism, however, everything whatever is caused, and not one single thing could ever be other than exactly what it is. Perhaps one thinks that the kleptomaniac and the drunkard did not have to become what they are, that they could have done better at another time and thereby ended up better than they are now, or that the hero could have done worse and then ended up a coward. But this shows only an unwillingness to understand what made them become as they are. Having found that their behavior is caused from within them, we can hardly avoid asking what caused these inner springs of action, and then asking what were the causes of these causes, and so on through the infinite past. We shall not, certainly, with our small understanding and our fragmentary knowledge of the past ever know why the world should at just this time and place have produced just this thief, this drunkard, and this hero, but the vagueness and smattered nature of our knowledge should not tempt us to imagine a similar vagueness in nature herself. Everything in nature is and always has been determinate, with no loose edges at all, and she was forever destined to bring forth just what she has produced, however slight may be our understanding of the origins of these works. Ultimate responsibility for anything that exists, and hence for any person and his deeds, can thus rest only with the first cause of all things, if there is such a cause, or nowhere at all, in case-here is not. Such, at least, seems to be the unavoidable implication of determinism.

Determinism and Morals

Some philosophers, faced with all this, which seems quite clear to the ordinary understanding, have tried to cling to determinism while modifying traditional conceptions of morals. They continue to *use* such words as *merit, blame, praise,* and *desert,* but they so divest them of their meanings as to finish by talking about things entirely different, sometimes, without themselves realizing that they are no longer on the subject. An ordinary person will hardly understand that anyone can possess merit or vice and be deserving of moral praise or blame, as a result of traits that he has or of behavior arising from those traits, once it is well understood that he could never have avoided being just what he is and doing just what he does.

We are happily spared going into all this, however, for the question whether determinism is true of human nature is not a question of ethics at all but of metaphysics. There is accordingly no hope of answering it within the context of ethics. One can, to be sure, simply *assume* an answer to it—assume that determinism is true, for instance—and then see what are the implications of this answer for ethics; but that does not answer the question. Or one can *assume* some theory or other of ethics—assume some version of 'the greatest happiness' principle, for instance—and then see whether that theory is consistent with determinism. But such confrontations of theories with theories likewise make us no wiser, so far as any fundamental question is concerned. We can suppose at once that determinism is consistent with some conceptions of morals, and inconsistent with others, and that the same holds for indeterminism. We shall still not know what theories are true; we shall only know which are consistent with another.

We shall, then, eschew all considerations of ethics as having no real bearing on our problem. We want to learn, if we can, whether determinism is true, and this is a question of metaphysics. It can, like all good questions of philosophy, be answered only on the basis of certain data; that is, by seeing whether or not it squares with certain things that everyone knows, or believes himself to know, or with things everyone is at least more sure about than the answer to the question at issue.

Now I could, of course, simply affirm that I am a morally responsible being, in the sense in which my responsibility for my behavior implies that I could have avoided that behavior. But this would take us into the nebulous realm of ethics, and it is, in fact, far from obvious that I am responsible in that sense. Many have doubted that they are responsible in that sense, and it is in any case not difficult to doubt it, however strongly one might feel about it.

There are, however, two things about myself of which I feel quite certain and that have no necessary connection with morals. The first is that I sometimes deliberate, with the view to making a decision; a decision, namely, to do this thing or that. And the second is that whether or not I deliberate about what to do, it is sometimes up to me what I do. This might all be an illusion, of course; but so also might any philosophical theory, such as the theory of determinism, be false. The point remains that it is far more difficult for me to doubt that I sometimes deliberate, and that it is sometimes up to me what to do, than to doubt any philosophical theory whatever, including the theory of determinism. We must, accordingly, if we ever hope to be wiser, adjust our theories to our data and not try to adjust our data to our theories.

Let us, then, get these two data quite clearly before us so we can see what they are, what they presuppose, and what they do and do not entail.

Deliberation

Deliberation is an activity, or at least a kind of experience, that cannot be defined, or even described, without metaphors. We speak of weighing this and that in our minds, of trying to anticipate consequences of various possible courses of action, and so on, but such descriptions do not convey to us what deliberation is unless we already know.

Whenever I deliberate, however, I find that I make certain presuppositions, whether I actually think of them or not. That is, I assume that certain things are true, certain things which are such that, if I thought they were not true, it would be impossible for me to deliberate at all. Some of these can be listed as follows:

First, I find that I can deliberate only about my own behavior and never about the behavior of another. I can try to guess, speculate, or figure out what another person is going to do; I can read certain signs and sometimes infer what he will do; but I cannot deliberate about it. When I deliberate I try to decide something, to make up my mind, and this is as remote as anything could be from speculating, trying to guess, or inferring from signs. Sometimes one *does* speculate on what he is going to do, by trying to draw conclusions from certain signs or omens—he might infer that he is going to sneeze, for instance, or speculate that he is going to become a grandfather—but he is not then deliberating whether to do things or not. One does, to be sure, sometimes deliberate about whether another person will do a certain act, when that other person is subject to his command or otherwise under his control; but then he is not really deliberating about another person's acts at all, but about his own—namely, whether or not to have that other person carry out the order.

Second, I find that I can deliberate only about future things, never things past or present. I may not know what I did at a certain time in the past, in case I have forgotten, but I can no longer deliberate whether to do it then or not. I can, again, only speculate, guess, try to infer, or perhaps try in remember. Similarly I cannot deliberate whether or not to be doing something now; I can only ascertain whether or not I am in fact doing it. If I am sitting I cannot deliberate about whether or not to be sitting. I can only deliberate about whether to remain sitting—and this has to do with the future.

Third, I cannot deliberate about what I shall do if I already know what I am going to do. If I were to say, for example, "I know that I am going to be married tomorrow and in the meantime I am going to deliberate about whether to get married," I would contradict myself. There are only two ways that I could know now what I am going to do tomorrow; namely, either by inferring this from certain signs and omens or by having already decided what I am going to do. But if I have inferred from signs and omens what I am going to do, I cannot deliberate about it—there is just nothing for me to decide; and similarly if I have already decided. If, on the other hand, I can still deliberate about what I am going to do, to that extent I must regard the signs and omens as unreliable, and the inference uncertain, and I therefore do not know what I am going to do after all.

(continued)

Freedom and Determinism (*continued*)

And finally, I cannot deliberate about what to do, even though I may not know what I am going to do, unless I believe that it is up to me what I am going to do. If I am within the power of another person, or at the mercy of circumstances over which I have no control, then, although I may have no idea what I am going to do, I cannot deliberate about it. I can only wait and see. If, for instance, I am a serviceman, and regulations regarding uniforms are posted each day by my commanding officer and are strictly enforced by him, then I shall not know what uniforms I shall be wearing from time to time, but I cannot deliberate about it. I can only wait and see what regulations are posted; it is not up to me. Similarly, a woman who is about to give birth to a child cannot deliberate whether to have a boy or a girl, even though she may not know. She can only wait and see; it is not up to her. Such examples can be generalized to cover any case wherein one does not know what he is going to do but believes that it is not up to him, and hence no matter for his decision and hence none for his deliberation.

"It Is Up to Me"

I sometimes feel certain that it is, at least to some extent, up to me what I am going to do; indeed, I must believe this if I am to deliberate about what to do. But what does this mean? It is, again, hard to say, but the idea can be illustrated, and we can fairly easily see what it does *not* mean.

Let us consider the simplest possible sort of situation in which this belief might be involved. At this moment for instance, it seems quite certain to me that holding my finger before me, I can move it either to the left or to the right, that each of these motions is possible for me. This does not mean merely that my finger can move either way, although it entails that, for this would be true in case nothing obstructed it, even if I had no control over it at all. I can say of a distant, fluttering leaf that it can move either way, but not that I can move it, since I have no control over it. How it moves is not up to me. Nor does it mean merely that my finger can be moved either way, although it entails this too. If the motions of my finger are under the control of some other person or of some machine, then it might be true that the finger can be moved either way, by that person or machine, though false that I can move it at all.

If I say, then, that it is up to me how I move my finger, I mean that I can move it in this way and I can move it in that way, and not merely that it can move or be moved in this way and that. I mean that the motion of my finger is within my direct control. If someone were to ask me to move it to the right, I could do that, and if he were to ask me to move it to the left, I could do that too. Further, I could do these simple acts without being asked at all, and having been asked, I could move it in a manner the exact opposite of what was requested, since I can ignore the request. There are, to be sure, some motions of my finger that I cannot make, so it is not *entirely* up to me how it moves. I cannot bend it backward, for instance, or bend it into a knot, for these motions are obstructed by the very anatomical construction of the finger itself; and to say that I can move my finger at all means at least that nothing obstructs such a motion, though it does not mean merely this. There is, however, at this moment, no obstruction, anatomical or otherwise, to my moving it to the right, and none to my moving it to the left.

This datum, it should be noted, is properly expressed as a conjunction and not as a disjunction. That is, my belief is that I can move my finger in one way *and* that I can also move it another way; and it does not do justice to this belief to say that I can move it one way *or* the other. It is fairly easy to see the truth of this, for the latter claim, that I can move it one way *or* the other, would be satisfied in case there were only one way I could move it, and *that* is not what I believe. Suppose, for instance, that my hand were strapped to a device in such a fashion that I could move my finger to the right but not to the left. Then it would still be entirely true that I could move it either to the left *or* to the right—since it would be true that I could move it to the right. But that is not what I now believe. My finger is not strapped to anything, and nothing obstructs its motion in either direction. And what I believe, in this situation, is that I can move it to the right *and* I can move it to the left.

We must note further that the belief expressed in our datum is not a belief in what is logically impossible. It is the belief that I now *can* move my finger in different ways but not that I can move it in different ways at once. What I believe is that I am now able to move my finger one way and that I am now equally able to move it another way, but I do not claim to be able now or at any other time to move it both ways simultaneously. The situation here is analogous to one in which I might, for instance, be offered a choice of either of two apples but forbidden to take both. Each apple is such that I may select it, but neither is such that I may select it together with the other.

Now, are these two data—the belief that I do sometimes deliberate, and the belief that it is sometimes up to me what I do—consistent with the metaphysical theory of determinism? We do not know yet. We intend to find out. It is fairly clear, however, that they are going to present difficulties to that theory. But let us not, in any case, try to avoid those difficulties by just denying the data themselves. If we eventually deny the data, we shall do so for better reasons than this. Virtually everyone is convinced that beliefs such as are expressed in our data are sometimes true. They cannot be simply dismissed as false just because they might appear to conflict with a metaphysical theory that hardly anyone has ever really thought much about at all. Almost anyone, unless his fingers are paralyzed, bound, or otherwise incapable of movement, believes sometimes that the motions of his fingers are within his control, in exactly the sense expressed by our data. If consequences of considerable importance to him depend on how he moves his fingers, he sometimes deliberates before moving them, or at least he is convinced that he does or that he can. Philosophers might have different notions of just what things are implied by such data, but there is in any case no more, and in fact considerably less, reason for denying the data than for denying some philosophical theory.

Causal Versus Logical Necessity

Philosophers have long since pointed out that causal connections involve no logical necessity, that the denial of a particular causal connection is never self-contradictory, and this is undoubtedly true. But neither does the assertion or the denial of determinism involve any concept of what is and what is not logically necessary. If determinism is true, then anything that happens is, given the conditions under which it occurs, the only thing possible, the thing that is necessitated by those conditions. But it is not the only thing that is logically possible, nor do those conditions logically necessitate it. Similarly, if one denies the thesis of determinism by asserting, for instance, that each of two bodily motions is possible for him under identical conditions, he is asserting much more than that each is logically possible, for that would be a trivial claim.

This distinction, between logical necessity and the sort of necessity involved in determinism, can be illustrated with examples. If, for instance, a man is beheaded, we can surely say that it is impossible for him to go on living, that his being beheaded necessitates his death, and so on; but there are no logical necessities or impossibilities involved here. It is not logically impossible for a man to live without his head. Yet no one will deny that a man cannot live under conditions that include his being headless, that such a state of affairs is in a perfectly clear sense impossible. Similarly, if my finger is in a tight and fairly strong cast, then it is impossible for me to move it in any way at all, though this is not logically impossible. It is logically possible that I should be vastly stronger than I am, and that I should move my finger and, in doing so, break the cast, though this would ordinarily not be possible in the sense that concerns us. Again, it is not logically impossible that I should bend my finger backward, or into a knot, though it is, in fact, impossible for me to do either or, what means the same thing, necessary that I should do neither. Certain conditions prohibit my doing such things, though they impose no logical barrier. And finally, if someone—a physician, for example—should ask me whether I can move my finger, and I should reply truthfully that I can, I would not merely be telling her that it is logically possible for me to move it, for this she already knows. I would be telling her that I am able to move it, that it is within my power to do so, that there are no conditions, such as paralysis or whatnot, that prevent my moving it.

It follows that not all necessity is logical necessity, nor all impossibility logical impossibility, and that to say that something is possible is sometimes to say much more than that it is logically possible. The kind of necessity involved in the thesis of determinism is quite obviously the nonlogical kind, as is also the kind of possibility involved in its denial. If we needed a *name* for these nonlogical modalities, we could call them *causal* necessity, impossibility, and possibility, but the concepts are clear enough without making a great deal of the name.

(continued)

Freedom and Determinism   (continued)

Freedom

To say that it is in a given instance, up to me what I do is to say that I am in that instance *free* with respect to what I then do. Thus, I am sometimes free to move my finger this way and that, but not, certainly, to bend it backward or into a knot. But what does this mean?

It means, first that there is no *obstacle* or *impediment* to my activity. Thus, there is sometimes no obstacle to my moving my finger this way and that, though there are obvious obstacles to my moving it backward or into a knot. Those things, accordingly, that pose obstacles to my motions limit my freedom. If my hand were strapped in such a way as to permit only a leftward motion of my finger, I would not then be free to move it to the right. If it were encased in a tight cast that permitted no motion, I would not be free to move it at all. Freedom of motion, then, is limited by obstacles.

Further, to say that it is, in a given instance, up to me what I do, means that nothing *constrains* or *forces* me to do one thing rather than another. Constraints are like obstacles, except that while the latter prevent, the former enforce. Thus, if my finger is being forcibly bent to the left—by a machine, for instance, or by another person, or by any force that I cannot overcome—then I am not free to move it this way and that. I cannot, in fact, move it at all; I can only watch to see how it is moved, and perhaps vainly resist: Its motions are not up to me, or within my control, but in the control of some other thing or person.

Obstacles and constraints, then, both obviously limit my freedom. To say that I am free to perform some action thus means at least that there is no obstacle to my doing it, and that nothing constrains me to do otherwise.

Now if we rest content with this observation, as many have, and construe free activity simply as activity that is unimpeded and unconstrained, there is evidently no inconsistency between affirming both the thesis of determinism and the claim that I am sometimes free. For to say that some action of mine is neither impeded nor constrained does not by itself imply that it is not causally determined. The absence of obstacles and constraints is a mere negative condition, and does not by itself rule out the presence of positive causes. It might seem, then, that we can say of some of my actions that there are conditions antecedent to their performance so that no other actions were possible, and also that these actions were unobstructed and unconstrained. And to say that would logically entail that such actions were both causally determined, and free.

Soft Determinism

It is this kind of consideration that has led many philosophers to embrace what is sometimes called "soft determinism." All versions of this theory have in common three claims, by means of which, it is naively supposed, a reconciliation is achieved between determinism and freedom. Freedom being, furthermore, a condition of moral responsibility and the only condition that metaphysics seriously questions, it is supposed by the partisans of this view that determinism is perfectly compatible with such responsibility. This, no doubt, accounts for its great appeal and wide acceptance, even by some people of considerable learning.

The three claims of soft determinism are (1) that the thesis of determinism is true, and that accordingly all human behavior, voluntary or other, like the behavior of all other things, arises from antecedent conditions, given which no other behavior is possible—in short, that all human behavior is caused and determined; (2) that voluntary behavior is nonetheless free to the extent that it is not externally constrained or impeded; and (3) that, in the absence of such obstacles and constraints, the causes of voluntary behavior are certain states, events, or conditions within the agent himself; namely, his own acts of will or volitions, choices, decisions, desires, and so on.

Thus, on this view, I am free, and therefore sometimes responsible for what I do, provided nothing prevents me from acting according to my own choice, desire, or volition, or constrains me to act otherwise. There may, to be sure, be other conditions for my responsibility—such as, for example, an understanding of the probable consequences of my behavior, and that sort of thing—but absence of constraint or impediment is, at least, one such condition. And, it is claimed, it is a condition that is compatible with the supposition that my behavior is caused—for it is, by hypothesis, caused by my own inner choices, desires, and volitions.

The Refutation of This

The theory of soft determinism looks good at first—so good that it has for generations been solemnly taught from innumerable philosophical chairs and implanted in the minds of students as sound philosophy—but no great acumen is needed to discover that far from solving any problem, it only camouflages it.

My free actions are those unimpeded and unconstrained motions that arise from my own inner desires, choices, and volitions; let us grant this provisionally. But now, whence arise those inner states that determine what my body shall do? Are they within my control or not? Having made my choice or decision and acted upon it, could I have chosen otherwise or not?

Here the determinist, hoping to surrender nothing and yet to avoid the problem implied in that question, bids us not to ask it; the question itself, he announces, is without meaning. For to say that I could have done otherwise, he says, means only that I *would* have done otherwise, *if* those inner states that determined my action had been different; if, that is, I had decided or chosen differently. To ask, accordingly, whether I could have chosen or decided differently is only to ask whether, had I decided to decide differently or chosen to choose differently, or willed to will differently, I *would* have decided or chosen or willed differently. And this, of course, *is* unintelligible nonsense.

But it is not nonsense to ask whether the causes of my actions—my own inner choices, decisions, and desires—are themselves caused. And of course they are, if determinism is true, for on that thesis everything is caused and determined. And if they are, then we cannot avoid concluding that, given the causal conditions of those inner states, I could not have decided, willed, chosen, or desired other than I, in fact, did, for this is a logical consequence of the very definition of determinism. Of course we can still say that, *if the* causes of those inner states, whatever they were, had been different, then their effects, those inner states themselves, would have been different, and that in this hypothetical sense I could have decided, chosen, willed, or desired differently—but that only pushes our problem back still another step. For we will then want to know whether the causes of those inner states were within my control, and so on *ad infinitum*. We are, at each step, permitted to say "could have been otherwise" only in a provisional sense—provided, that is, that something else had been different—but must then retract it and replace it with "could not have been otherwise" as soon as we discover, as we must at each step, that whatever would have to have been different could not have been different.

Examples

Such is the dialectic of the problem. The easiest way to see the shadowy quality of soft determinism, however, is by means of examples.

Let us suppose that my body is moving in various ways, that these motions are not externally constrained or impeded, and that they are all exactly in accordance with my own desires, choices, or acts of will and whatnot. When I will that my arm should move in a certain way, I find it moving in that way, unobstructed and unconstrained. When I will to speak, my lips and tongue move, unobstructed and unconstrained, in a manner suitable to the formation of the words I choose to utter. Now, given that this is a correct description of my behavior, namely, that it consists of the unconstrained and unimpeded motions of my body in response to my own volitions, then it follows that my behavior is free, on the soft determinist's definition of "free." It follows further that I am responsible for that behavior; or at least, that if I am not, it is not from any lack of freedom on my part.

But if the fulfillment of these conditions renders my behavior free—that is to say, if my behavior satisfies the conditions of free action set forth in the theory of soft determinism—then my behavior will be no less free if we assume further conditions that are perfectly consistent with those already satisfied.

We suppose further, accordingly, that while my behavior is entirely in accordance with my own volitions, and thus "free" in terms of the conception of freedom we are examining, my volitions themselves are caused. To make this graphic, we can suppose that an ingenious physiologist can induce in me any volition he pleases, simply by pushing various buttons on an instrument to which, let us suppose, I am attached by numerous wires. All the volitions I have in that situation are, accordingly, precisely the ones he gives me. By pushing one button, he evokes in me the volition to raise my hand; and my hand, being unimpeded, rises in response to that volition. By pushing another, he induces the volition in me to kick, and my foot, being unimpeded, kicks in response to that volition. We can even

(continued)

Freedom and Determinism (*continued*)

suppose that the physiologist puts a rifle in my hands, aims it at some passerby, and then, by pushing the proper button, evokes in me the volition to squeeze my finger against the trigger, whereupon the passerby falls dead of a bullet wound.

This is the description of a man who is acting in accordance with his inner volitions, a man whose body is unimpeded and unconstrained in its motions, these motions being the effects of those inner states. It is hardly the description of a free and responsible agent. It is the perfect description of a puppet. To render someone your puppet, it is not necessary forcibly to constrain the motions of his limbs, after the fashion that real puppets are moved. A subtler but no less effective means of making a person your puppet would be to gain complete control of his inner states, and ensuring, as the theory of soft determinism does ensure, that his body will move in accordance with them.

The example is somewhat unusual, but it is no worse for that. It is perfectly intelligible, and it does appear to refute the soft determinist's conception of freedom. One might think that, in such a case, the agent should not have allowed himself to be so rigged in the first place, but this is irrelevant; we can suppose that he was not aware that he was and was hence unaware of the source of those inner states that prompted his bodily motions. The example can, moreover, be modified in perfectly realistic ways, so as to coincide with actual and familiar cases. One can, for instance, be given a compulsive desire for certain drugs, simply by having them administered over a course of time. Suppose, then, that I do, with neither my knowledge nor consent, thus become a victim of such a desire and act upon it. Do I act freely, merely by virtue of the fact that I am unimpeded in my quest for drugs? In a sense I do, surely, but I am hardly free with respect to whether or not I shall use drugs. I never chose to have the desire for them inflicted upon me.

Nor does it, of course, matter whether the inner states that allegedly prompt all my "free" activity are evoked in me by another agent or by perfectly impersonal forces. Whether a desire that causes my body to behave in a certain way is inflicted upon me by another person, for instance, or derived from hereditary factors, or indeed from anything at all, matters not the least. In any case, if it is in fact the cause of my bodily behavior, I cannot help but act in accordance with it. Wherever it came from, whether from personal or impersonal origins, it was entirely caused or determined, and not within my control. Indeed, if determinism is true, as the theory of soft determinism holds it to be, all those inner states that cause my body to behave in whatever ways it behaves must arise from circumstances that existed before I was born; for the chain of causes and effects is infinite, and none could have been the least different, given those that preceded.

Simple Indeterminism

We might at first now seem warranted in simply denying determinism, and saying that, insofar as they are free, my actions are not caused; or that, if they are caused by my own inner states—my own desires, impulses, choices, volitions, and whatnot—then these, in any case, are not caused. This is a perfectly clear sense in which a person's action, assuming that it was free, could have been otherwise. If it was uncaused, then, even given the conditions under which it occurred and all that preceded, some other act was nonetheless possible, and he did not have to do what he did. Or if his action was the inevitable consequence of his own inner states, and could not have been otherwise, given these, we can nevertheless say that these inner states, being uncaused, could have been otherwise, and could thereby have produced different actions.

Only the slightest consideration will show, however, that this simple denial of determinism has not the slightest plausibility. For let us suppose it is true, and that some of my bodily motions—namely, those that I regard as my free acts—are not caused at all or, if caused by my own inner states, that these are not caused. We shall thereby avoid picturing a puppet, to be sure—but only by substituting something even less like a human being; for the conception that now emerges is not that of a free person, but of an erratic and jerking phantom, without any rhyme or reason at all.

Suppose that my right arm is free, according to this conception; that is, that its motions are uncaused. It moves this way and that from time to time, but nothing causes these motions. Sometimes it moves forth vigorously, sometimes up, sometimes down, sometimes it just drifts vaguely about—these motions all being wholly free and uncaused. Manifestly I have nothing to do with them at all; they just happen, and neither I nor anyone can ever tell what this arm will be doing next. It might seize a club and lay it on the head of the nearest bystander, no less to my astonishment than his. There will never be any point in asking why these motions occur, or in seeking any explanation of them, for under the conditions assumed there is no explanation. They just happen, from no causes at all.

This is no description of free, voluntary, or responsible behavior. Indeed, so far as the motions of my body or its parts are entirely uncaused, such motions cannot even be ascribed to me as my behavior in the first place, since I have nothing to do with them. The behavior of my arm is just the random motion of a foreign object. Behavior that is mine must be behavior that is within my control but motions that occur from no causes are beyond the control of anyone. I can have no more to do with, and no more control over, the uncaused motions of my limbs than a gambler has over the motions of an honest roulette wheel. I can only, like him, idly wait to see what happens.

Nor does it improve things to suppose that my bodily motions are caused by my own inner states, so long as we suppose these to be wholly uncaused. The result will be the same as before. My arm, for example, will move this way and that, sometimes up and sometimes down, sometimes vigorously and sometimes just drifting about, always in response to certain inner states, to be sure. But since these are supposed to be wholly uncaused, it follows that I have no control over them and hence none over their effects. If my hand lays a club forcefully on the nearest bystander, we can indeed say that this motion resulted from an inner club-wielding desire of mine; but we must add that I had nothing to do with that desire, and that it arose, to be followed by its inevitable effect, no less to my astonishment than to his. Things like this do, alas, sometimes happen. We are all sometimes seized by compulsive impulses that arise we know not whence, and we do sometimes act upon these. But because they are far from being examples of free, voluntary, and responsible behavior, we need only to learn that the behavior was of this sort to conclude that it was not free, voluntary, or responsible. It was erratic, impulsive, and irresponsible.

Determinism and Simple Indeterminism as Theories

Both determinism and simple indeterminism are loaded with difficulties, and no one who has thought much on them can affirm either of them without some embarrassment. Simple indeterminism has nothing whatever to be said for it, except that it appears to remove the grossest difficulties of determinism, only, however, to imply perfect absurdities of its own. Determinism, on the other hand, is at least initially plausible. People seem to have a natural inclination to believe in it; it is, indeed, almost required for the very exercise of practical intelligence. And beyond this, our experience appears always to confirm it, so long as we are dealing with everyday facts of common experience, as distinguished from the esoteric researches of theoretical physics. But determinism, as applied to human behavior, has implications that few can casually accept, and they appear to be implications that no modification of the theory can efface.

Both theories, moreover, appear logically irreconcilable to the two items of data that we set forth at the outset; namely, (1) that my behavior is sometimes the outcome of my deliberation, and (2) that in these and other cases it is sometimes up to me what I do. Because these were our data, it is important to see, as must already be quite clear, that these theories cannot be reconciled to them.

I can deliberate only about my own future actions, and then only if I do not already know what I am going to do. If a certain nasal tickle warns me that I am about to sneeze, for instance, then I cannot deliberate whether to sneeze or not; I can only prepare for the impending convulsion. But if determinism is true, then there are always conditions existing antecedently to everything I do, sufficient for my doing just that, and such as to render it inevitable. If I can know what those conditions are and what behavior they are sufficient to produce, then I can in every such case know what I am going to do and cannot then deliberate about it.

By itself this only shows, of course, that I can deliberate only in ignorance of the causal conditions of my behavior; it does not show that such conditions cannot exist. It is odd, however, to suppose that deliberation should be a mere substitute for clear knowledge. Ignorance is a condition of speculation, inference, and guesswork, which have nothing whatever to do with deliberation. A prisoner awaiting execution may not know when he is going to die, and he may even entertain the hope of reprieve, but he cannot deliberate about this. He can only speculate, guess—and wait.

(continued)

Freedom and Determinism   (*continued*)

Worse yet, however, it now becomes clear that I cannot deliberate about what I am going to do, if it is even *possible* for me to find out in advance, whether I do in fact find out in advance or not. I can deliberate only with the view to deciding what to do, to making up my mind; and this is impossible if I relieve that it could be inferred what I am going to do from conditions already existing, even though I have not made that inference myself. If I believe that what I am going to do has been rendered inevitable by conditions already existing, and could be inferred by anyone having the requisite sagacity, then I cannot try to decide whether to do it or not, for there is simply nothing left to decide. I can at best only guess or try to figure it out myself or, all prognostics failing, I can wait and see; but I cannot deliberate. I deliberate in order to *decide* what *to* do, not to *discover* what it is that I am *going* to do. But if determinism is true, then there are always antecedent conditions sufficient for everything that I do, and this can always be inferred by anyone having the requisite sagacity; that is, by anyone having a knowledge of what those conditions are and what behavior they are sufficient to produce.

This suggests what in fact seems quite clear, that determinism cannot be reconciled with our second datum either, to the effect that it is sometimes up to me what I am going to do. For if it is ever really up to me whether to do this thing or that then, as we have seen, each alternative course of action must be such that I can do it; not that I can do it in some abstruse or hypothetical sense of "can"; not that I could do it if only something were true that is not true; but in the sense that it is then and there within my power to do it. But this is never so, if determinism is true, for on the very formulation of that theory whatever happens at any time is the only thing that can then happen, given all that precedes it. It is simply a logical consequence of this that whatever I do at any time is the only thing I can then do, given the conditions that precede my doing it. Nor does it help in the least to interpose, among the causal antecedents of my behavior, my own inner states, such as my desires, choices, acts of will, and so on. For even supposing these to be always involved in voluntary behavior—which is highly doubtful in itself—it is a consequence of determinism that these, whatever they are at any time, can never be other than what they then are. Every chain of causes and effects, if determinism is true, is infinite. This is why it is not now up to me whether I shall a moment hence be male or female. The conditions determining my sex have existed through my whole life, and even prior to my life. But if determinism is true, the same holds of anything that I ever am, ever become, or ever do. It matters not whether we are speaking of the most patent facts of my being, such as my sex; or the most subtle, such as my feelings, thoughts, desires, or choices. Nothing could be other than it is, given what was; and while we may indeed say, quite idly, that something—some inner state of mind, for instance—*could* have been different, had only something *else* been different, any consolation of this thought evaporates as soon as we add that whatever would have to have been different could not have been different.

It is even more obvious that our data cannot be reconciled to the theory of simple indeterminism. I can deliberate only about my own actions; this is obvious. But the random, uncaused motion of any body whatever, whether it be a part of my body or not, is no action of mine and nothing that is within my power. I might try to guess what these motions will be, just as I might try to guess how a roulette wheel will behave, but I cannot deliberate about them or try to decide what they shall be, simply because these things are not up to me. Whatever is not caused by anything is not caused by me, and nothing could be more plainly inconsistent with saying that it is nevertheless up to me what it shall be.

The Theory of Agency

The only conception of action that accords with our data is one according to which people—and perhaps some other things too—are sometimes, but of course not always, self-determining beings; that is, beings that are sometimes the causes of their own behavior. In the case of an action that is free, it must not only be such that it is caused by the agent who performs it, but also such that no antecedent conditions were sufficient for his performing just that action. In the case of an action that is both free and rational, it must be such that the agent who performed it did so for some reason, but this reason cannot have been the cause of it.

Now, this conception fits what people take themselves to be; namely, beings who act, or who are agents, rather than beings that are merely acted upon, and whose behavior is simply the causal consequence of conditions that they have not wrought. When I believe that I have done something, I do believe that it was I who caused it to be done, I who made something happen, and not merely something within me, such as one of my own subjective states, which is not identical with myself. If I believe that something not identical with myself was the cause of my behavior—some event wholly external to myself, for instance, or even one internal to myself, such as a nerve impulse, volition, or whatnot—then I cannot regard that behavior as being an act of mine, unless I further believe that I was the cause of that external or internal event. My pulse, for example, is caused and regulated by certain conditions existing within me, and not by myself. I do not, accordingly, regard this activity of my body as my action, and would be no more tempted to do so if I became suddenly conscious within myself of those conditions or impulses that produce it. This is behavior with which I have nothing to do, behavior that is not within my immediate control, behavior that is not only not free activity, but not even the activity of an agent to begin with; it is nothing but a mechanical reflex. Had I never learned that my very life depends on this pulse beat, I would regard it with complete indifference, as something foreign to me, like the oscillations of a clock pendulum that I idly contemplate.

Now this conception of activity, and of an agent who is the cause of it, involves two rather strange metaphysical notions that are never applied elsewhere in nature. The first is that of a *self* or *person*—for example, a man—who is not merely a collection of things or events, but a self-moving being. For on this view it is a person, and not merely some part of him or something within him, that is the cause of his own activity. Now, we certainly do not know that a human being is anything more than an assemblage of physical things and processes that act in accordance with those laws that describe the behavior of all other physical things and processes. Even though he is a living being, of enormous complexity, there is nothing, apart from the requirements of this theory, to suggest that his behavior is so radically different in its origin from that of other physical objects, or that an understanding of it must be sought in some metaphysical realm wholly different from that appropriate to the understanding of nonliving things.

Second, this conception of activity involves an extraordinary conception of causation according to which an agent, which is a substance and not an event, can nevertheless be the cause of an event. Indeed, if he is a free agent then he can, on this conception, cause an event to occur—namely, some act of his own—without anything else causing him to do so. This means that an agent is sometimes a cause, without being an antecedent sufficient condition; for if I affirm that I am the cause of some act of mine, then I am plainly not saying that my very existence is sufficient for its occurrence, which would be absurd. If I say that my hand causes my pencil to move, then I am saying that the motion of my hand is, under the other conditions then prevailing, sufficient for the motion of the pencil. But if I then say that I cause my hand to move, I am not saying anything remotely like this, and surely not that the motion of myself is sufficient for the motion of my arm and hand, since these are the only things about me that are moving.

This conception of the causation of events by things that are not events is, in fact, so different from the usual philosophical conception of a cause that it should not even bear the same name, for "being a cause" ordinarily just means "being an antecedent sufficient condition or set of conditions." Instead, then, of speaking of agents as *causing* their own acts, it would perhaps be better to use another word entirely, and say, for instance, that they *originate* them, *initiate* them, or simply that they *perform* them.

Now this is, on the face of it, a dubious conception of what a person is. Yet it is consistent with our data, reflecting the presuppositions of deliberation, and appears to be the only conception that is consistent with them, as determinism and simple indeterminism are not. The theory of agency avoids the absurdities of simple indeterminism by conceding that human behavior is caused, while at the same time avoiding the difficulties of determinism by denying that every chain of causes and effects is infinite. Some such causal chains, on this view, have beginnings, and they begin with agents themselves. Moreover, if we are to suppose that it is sometimes up to me what I do, and understand this in a sense that is not consistent with determinism, we must suppose that I am an agent or a being who initiates his own actions, sometimes under conditions that do not determine

(continued)

Freedom and Determinism   (continued)

what action I shall perform. Deliberation becomes, on this view, something that is not only possible but quite rational, for it does make sense to deliberate about activity that is truly my own and that depends in its outcome upon me as its author, and not merely upon something more or less esoteric that is supposed to be intimately associated with me, such as my thoughts, volitions, choices or whatnot.

One can hardly affirm such a theory of agency with complete comfort, however, and not wholly without embarrassment, for the conception of agents and their powers which is involved in it is strange indeed, if not positively mysterious. In fact, one can hardly be blamed here for simply denying our data outright, rather than embracing this theory to which they do most certainly point. Our data—to the effect that we do sometimes deliberate before acting, and that, when we do, we presuppose among other things that it is up to us what we are going to do—rest upon nothing more than fairly common consent. These data might simply be illusions. It might, in fact, be that no one ever deliberates but only imagines that he does, that from pure conceit he supposes himself to be the master of his behavior and the author of his acts. Spinoza has suggested that if a stone, having been thrown into the air, were suddenly to become conscious, it would suppose itself to be the source of its own motion, being then conscious of what it was doing but not aware of the real cause of its behavior. Certainly we are *sometimes* mistaken in believing that we are behaving as a result of choice deliberately arrived at. A man might, for example, easily imagine that his embarking upon matrimony is the result of the most careful and rational deliberation, when in fact the causes, perfectly sufficient for that behavior, might be of an entirely physiological, unconscious origin. If it is sometimes false that we deliberate and then act as the result of a decision deliberately arrived at, even when we suppose it to be true, it might always be false. No one seems able, as we have noted, to describe deliberation without metaphors, and the conception of a thing's being "within one's power" or "up to him" seems to defy analysis or definition altogether, if taken in a sense that the theory of agency appears to require.

These are, then, dubitable conceptions, despite their being so well implanted in common sense. Indeed, when we turn to the theory of fatalism, we shall find formidable metaphysical considerations that appear to rule them out altogether. Perhaps here, as elsewhere in metaphysics, we should be content with discovering difficulties, with seeing what is and what is not consistent with such convictions as we happen to have, and then drawing such satisfaction as we can from the realization that, no matter where we begin, the world is mysterious and that we who try to understand it are even more so. This realization can, with some justification, make one feel wise, even in the full realization of his ignorance.

Minds, Brains, and Programs
John R. Searle

What psychological and philosophical significance should we attach to recent efforts at computer simulations of human cognitive capacities? In answering this question, I find it useful to distinguish what I will call "strong" AI from "weak" or "cautious" AI (artificial intelligence). According to weak AI, the principal value of the computer in the study of the mind is that it gives us a very powerful tool. For example, it enables us to formulate and test hypotheses in a more rigorous and precise fashion. But according to strong AI, the computer is not merely a tool in the study of the mind; rather, the appropriately programmed computer really is a mind, in the sense that computers given the right programs can be literally said to *understand* and have other cognitive states. In strong AI, because the programmed computer has cognitive states, the programs are not mere tools that enable us to test psychological explanations; rather, the programs are themselves the explanations.

I have no objection to the claims of weak AI, at least as far as this article is concerned. My discussion here will be directed at the claims I have defined as those of strong AI, specifically the claim that the appropriately programmed computer literally has cognitive states and that the programs thereby explain human cognition. When I hereafter refer to AI, I have in mind the strong version, as expressed by these two claims.

I will consider the work of Roger Schank and his colleagues at Yale (Schank and Abelson 1977), because I am more familiar with it than I am with any other similar claims, and because it provides a very clear example of the sort of work I wish to examine. But nothing that follows depends upon the details of Schank's programs. The same arguments would apply to Winograd's SHRDLU (Winograd 1973), Weizenbaum's ELIZA (Weizenbaum 1965), and indeed any Turing machine simulation of human mental phenomena. [See "Further Reading" for Searle's references.]

Very briefly, and leaving out the various details, one can describe Schank's program as follows: The aim of the program is to simulate the human ability to understand stories. It is characteristic of human beings' story-understanding capacity that they can answer questions about the story even though the information that they give was never explicitly stated in the story. Thus, for example, suppose you are given the following story: "A man went into a restaurant and ordered a hamburger. When the hamburger arrived it was burned to a crisp, and the man stormed out of the restaurant angrily, without paying for the hamburger or leaving a tip." Now, if you are asked "Did the man eat the hamburger?" you will presumably answer, "No, he did not." Similarly, if you are given the following story: "A man went into a restaurant and ordered a hamburger; when the hamburger came he was very pleased with it; and as he left the restaurant he gave the waitress a large tip before paying his bill," and you are asked the question, "Did the man eat the hamburger?" you will presumably answer, "Yes, he ate the hamburger." Now Schank's machines call similarly answer, questions about restaurants in this fashion. To do this, they have a "representation" of the sort of information that human beings have about restaurants, which enables them to answer such questions as those above, given these sorts of stories. When the machine is given the story and then asked the question, the machine will print out answers of the sort that we would expect human beings to give if told similar stories. Partisans of strong AI claim that in this question and answer sequence the machine is not only simulating a human ability but also (1) that the machine can literally be said to *understand* the story and provide the answers to questions, and (2) that what the machine and its program do *explains* the human ability to understand the story and answer questions about it.

Both claims seem to me to be totally unsupported by Schank's work, as I will attempt to show in what follows. I am not, of course, saying that Schank himself is to these claims.

One way to test any theory of the mind is to ask oneself what it would be like if my mind actually worked on the principles that the theory says all minds work on. Let us apply this test to the Schank program with the following *Gedankenexperiment*. Suppose that I'm locked in a room and given a large batch of Chinese writing. Suppose furthermore (as is indeed the case) that I know no Chinese, either written or spoken, and that I'm not even confident that I could recognize Chinese writing as Chinese writing distinct from, say, Japanese writing or meaningless squiggles. To me, Chinese writing is just so many meaningless squiggles. Now suppose further that after this first batch of Chinese writing I am given a second batch of Chinese script together with a set of rules for correlating the second batch with the first batch. The rules are in English, and I understand these rules as well as any other native speaker of English. They enable me to correlate one set of formal symbols with another set of formal symbols, and all that "formal" means here is that I can identify the symbols entirely by their shapes. Now suppose also that I am given a third batch of Chinese symbols together with some instructions, again in English, that enable me to correlate elements of this third batch with the first two batches, and these rules instruct me how to give back certain Chinese symbols with certain sorts of shapes in response to certain sorts of shapes given me in the third batch. Unknown to me, the people who are giving me all of these symbols call the first batch a "script," they call the second batch a "story," and they call the third batch "questions." Furthermore, they call the symbols I give them back in response to the third batch "answers to the questions," and the set of rules in English that they gave me, they call the "program." Now just to complicate the story a little, imagine that these people also give me stories in English, which I understand, and they then ask me questions in English about these stories, and I give them back answers in English. Suppose also that after a while I get so good at following the instructions

(continued)

Minds, Brains, and Programs *(continued)*

for manipulating the Chinese symbols and the programmers get so good at writing the programs that from the external point of view—that is, from tile point of view of somebody outside the room in which I am locked—my answers to the questions are absolutely indistinguishable from those of native Chinese speakers. Nobody just looking at my answers can tell that I don't speak a word of Chinese. Let us also suppose that my answers to the English questions are, as they no doubt would be, indistinguishable from those of other native English speakers, for the simple reason that I am a native English speaker. From the external point of view—from the point of view of someone reading my "answers"—the answers to the Chinese questions and the English questions are equally good. But in the Chinese case, unlike the English case, I produce the answers by manipulating uninterpreted formal symbols. As far as the Chinese is concerned, I simply behave like a computer; I perform computational operations on formally specified elements. For the purposes of the Chinese, I am simply an instantiation of the computer program.

Now the claims made by strong AI are that the programmed computer understands the stories and that the program in some sense explains human understanding. But we are now in a position to examine these claims in light of our thought experiment.

1. As regards the first claim, it seems to me quite obvious in the example that I do not understand a word of the Chinese stories. I have inputs and outputs that are indistinguishable from those of the native Chinese speaker, and I can have any formal program you like, but I still understand nothing. For the same reasons, Schank's computer understands nothing of any stories, whether in Chinese, English, or whatever, since in the Chinese case the computer is me, and in cases where the computer is not me, the computer has nothing more than I have in the case where I understand nothing.

2. As regards the second claim, that the program explains human understanding, we can see that the computer and its program do not provide sufficient conditions of understanding since the computer and the program are functioning, and there is no understanding. But does it even provide a necessary condition or a significant contribution to understanding? One of the claims made by the supporters of strong AI is that when I understand a story in English, what I am doing is exactly the same—or perhaps more of the same—as what I was doing in manipulating the Chinese symbols. It is simply more formal symbol manipulation that distinguishes the case in English, where I do understand, from the case in Chinese, where I don't. I have not demonstrated that this claim is false, but it would certainly appear an incredible claim in the example. Such plausibility as the claim has derives from the supposition that we can construct a program that will have the same inputs and outputs as native speakers, and in addition we assume that speakers have some level of description where they are also instantiations of a program. On the basis of these two assumptions we assume that even if Schank's program isn't the whole story about understanding, it may be part of the story. Well, I suppose that is an empirical possibility, but not the slightest reason has so far been given to believe that it is true, since what is suggested—though certainly not demonstrated—by the example is that the computer program is simply irrelevant to my understanding of the story. In the Chinese case I have everything that artificial intelligence can put into me by way of a program, and I understand nothing; in the English case I understand everything, and there is so far no reason at all to suppose that my understanding has anything to do with computer programs, that is, with computational operations on purely formally specified elements. As long as the program is defined in terms of computational operations on purely formally defined elements, what the example suggests is that these by themselves have no interesting connection with understanding. They are certainly not sufficient conditions, and not the slightest reason has been given to suppose that they are necessary conditions or even that they make a significant contribution to understanding. Notice that the force of the argument is not simply that different machines can have the same input and output while operating on different formal principles—that is not the point at all. Rather, whatever purely formal principles you put into the computer, they will not be sufficient for understanding, since a human will be able to follow the formal principles without understanding anything. No reason whatever has been

offered to suppose that such principles are necessary or even contributory, since no reason has been given to suppose that when I understand English I am operating with any formal program at all.

Well, then, what is it that I have in the case of the English sentences that I do not have in the case of the Chinese sentences? The obvious answer is that I know what the former mean, while I haven't the faintest idea what the latter mean. But in what does this consist and why couldn't we give it to a machine, whatever it is? I will return to this question later, but first I want to continue with the example.

I have had the occasions to present this example to several workers in artificial intelligence, and, interestingly, they do not seem to agree on what the proper reply to it is. I get a surprising variety of replies, and in what follows I will consider the most common of these (specified along with their geographic origins).

But first I want to block some common misunderstandings about "understanding": In many of these discussions one finds a lot of fancy footwork about the word "understanding." My critics point out that there are many different degrees of understanding; that "understanding" is not a simple two-place predicate; that there are even different kinds and levels of understanding, and often the law of excluded middle doesn't even apply in a straightforward way to statements of the form "*x* understands *y*"; that in many cases it is a matter for decision and not a simple matter of fact whether *x* understands *y*; and so on. To all of these points I want to say: of course, of course. But they have nothing to do with the points at issue. There are clear cases in which "understanding" literally applies and clear cases in which it does not apply; and these two sorts of cases are all I need for this argument.[1] I understand stories in English; to a lesser degree I can understand stories in French; to a still lesser degree, stories in German; and in Chinese, not at all. My car and my adding machine, on the other hand, understand nothing: they are not in that line of business. We often attribute "understanding" and other cognitive predicates by metaphor and analogy to cars, adding machines, and other artifacts, but nothing is proved by such attributions. We say, "The door *knows* when to open because of its photoelectric cell," "The adding machine *knows how (understands how,* is *able)* to do addition and subtraction but not division," and "The thermostat *perceives* changes in the temperature." The reason we make these attributions is quite interesting, and it has to do with the fact that in artifacts we extend our own intentionality;[2] our tools are extensions of our purposes, and so we find it natural to make metaphorical attributions of intentionality to them; but I take it no philosophical ice is cut by such examples. The sense in which an automatic door "understands instructions" from its photoelectric cell is not at all the sense in which I understand English. If the sense in which Schank's programmed computers understand stories is supposed to be the metaphorical sense in which the door understands, and not the sense in which I understand English, the issue would not be worth discussing. But Newell and Simon (1963) write that the kind of cognition they claim for computers is exactly the same as for human beings. I like the straightforwardness of this claim, and it is the sort of claim I will be considering. I will argue that in the literal sense the programmed computer understands what the car and the adding machine understand, namely, exactly nothing. The computer understanding is not just (like my understanding of German) partial or incomplete; it is zero.

Now to the replies:

1. THE SYSTEMS REPLY (BERKELEY). "While it is true that the individual person who is locked in the room does not understand the story, the fact is that he is merely a part of a whole system, and the system does understand the story. The person has a large ledger in front of him in which are written the rules, he has a lot of scratch paper and pencils for doing calculations, he has 'data banks' of sets of Chinese symbols. Now, understanding is not being ascribed to the mere individual; rather it is being ascribed to this whole system of which he is a part."

My response to the systems theory is quite simple: Let the individual internalize all of these elements of the system. He memorizes the rules in the ledger and the data banks of Chinese symbols, and he does all the calculations in his head. The individual then incorporates the entire system. There isn't anything at all to the system that he does not encompass. We can even get rid of the room and suppose he works outdoors. All the same, he understands nothing of the Chinese, and a fortiori neither does the system, because there isn't anything in the system that isn't in him. If he

(continued)

Minds, Brains, and Programs (*continued*)

doesn't understand, then there is no way the system could understand because the system is just a part of him.

Actually I feel somewhat embarrassed to give even this answer to the systems theory because the theory seems to me so implausible to start with. The idea is that while a person doesn't understand Chinese, somehow the *conjunction* of that person and bits of paper might understand Chinese. It is not easy for me to imagine how someone who was not in the grip of an ideology would find the idea at all plausible. Still, I think many people who are committed to the ideology of strong AI will in the end be inclined to say something very much like this; so let us pursue it a bit further. According to one version of this view, while the man in the internalized systems example doesn't understand Chinese in the sense that a native Chinese speaker does (because, for example, he doesn't know that the story refers to restaurants and hamburgers, etc.), still "the man as a formal symbol manipulation system" *really does understand Chinese*. The subsystem of the man that is the formal symbol manipulation system for Chinese should not be confused with the subsystem for English.

So there are really two subsystems in the man; one understands English, the other Chinese, and "it's just that the two systems have little to do with each other." But, I want to reply, not only do they have little to do with each other, they are not even remotely alike. The subsystem that understands English (assuming we allow ourselves to talk in this jargon of "subsystems" for a moment) knows that the stories are about restaurants and eating hamburgers, he knows that he is being asked questions about restaurants and that he is answering questions as best he can by making various inferences from the content of the story, and so on. But the Chinese system knows none of this. Whereas the English subsystem knows that "hamburgers" refers to hamburgers, the Chinese subsystem knows only that "squiggle squiggle" is followed by "squoggle squoggle." All he knows is that various formal symbols are being introduced at one end and manipulated according to rules written in English, and other symbols are going out at the other end. The whole point of the original example was to argue that such symbol manipulation by itself couldn't be sufficient for understanding Chinese in any literal sense because the man could write "squoggle squoggle" after "squiggle squiggle" without understanding anything in Chinese. And it doesn't meet that argument to postulate subsystems within the man, because the subsystems are no better off than the man was in the first place; they still don't have anything even remotely like what the English-speaking man (or subsystem) has. Indeed, in the case as described, the Chinese subsystem is simply a part of the English subsystem, a part that engages in meaningless symbol manipulation according to rules in English.

Let us ask ourselves what is supposed to motivate the systems reply in the first place; that is, what *independent* grounds are there supposed to be for saying that the agent must have a subsystem within him that literally understands stories in Chinese? As far as I can tell the only grounds are that in the example I have the same input and output as native Chinese speakers and a program that goes from one to the other. But the whole point or the examples has been to try to show that that couldn't be sufficient for understanding, in the sense in which I understand stories in English, because a person, and hence the set of systems that go to make up a person, could have the right combination of input, output, and program and still not understand anything in the relevant literal sense in which I understand English. The only motivation for saying there *must* be a subsystem in me that understands Chinese is that I have a program and I can pass the Turing test; I can foot native Chinese speakers. But precisely one of the points at issue is the adequacy of the Turing test. The example shows that there could be two "systems," both of which pass the Turing test, but only one of which understands; and it is no argument against this point to say that since they both pass the Turing test they must both understand, since this claim fails to meet the argument that the system in me that understands English has a great deal more than the system that merely processes Chinese. In short, the systems reply simply begs the question by insisting without argument that the system must understand Chinese.

Furthermore, the systems reply would appear to lead to consequences that are independently absurd. If we are to conclude that there must be cognition in me on the grounds that I have a certain sort of input and output and a program in between, then it looks like all sorts of noncognitive subsystems are going to turn out to be cognitive. For example, there is a level of description at which my stomach does information processing, and it instantiates any number of computer programs, but I take it we do not want to say that it has any understanding (cf. Pylyshyn 1980). But if we accept the systems reply, then it is hard to see how we avoid saying that stomach, heart, liver, and so on are all understanding subsystems, since there is no principle way to distinguish the motivation for saying the Chinese subsystem understands from saying that the stomach understands. It is, by the way, not an answer to this point to say that the Chinese system has information as input and output and the stomach has food and food products as input and output, since from the point of view of the agent, from my point of view, there is no information in either the food or the Chinese—the Chinese is just so many meaningless squiggles. The information in the Chinese case is solely in the eyes of the programmers and the interpreters, and there is nothing to prevent them from treating the input and output of my digestive organs as information if they so desire.

This last point bears on some independent problems in strong AI, and it is worth digressing for a moment to explain it. If strong AI is to be a branch of psychology, then it must be able to distinguish those systems that are genuinely mental from those that are not. It must be able to distinguish the principles on which the mind works from those on which nonmental systems work; otherwise it will offer us no explanations of what is specifically mental about the mental. And the mental-nonmental distinction cannot be just in the eye of the beholder but it must be intrinsic to the systems; otherwise it would be up to any beholder to treat people as nonmental and, for example, hurricanes as mental if he likes. But quite often in the AI literature the distinction is blurred in ways that would in the long run prove disastrous to the claim that AI is a cognitive inquiry. McCarthy, for example, writes. "Machines as simple as thermostats can be said to have beliefs, and having beliefs seems to be a characteristic of most machines capable of problem solving performance" (McCarthy 1979). Anyone who thinks strong AI has a chance as a theory of the mind ought to ponder the implications of that remark. We are asked to accept it as a discovery of strong AI that the hunk of metal on the wall that we use to regulate the temperature has beliefs in exactly the same sense that we, our spouses, and our children have beliefs, and furthermore that "most" of the other machines in the room—telephone, tape recorder, adding machine, electric fight switch—also have beliefs in this literal sense. It is not the aim of this article to argue against McCarthy's point, so I will simply assert the following without argument. The study of the mind starts with such facts as that humans have beliefs, while thermostats, telephones, and adding machines don't. If you get a theory that denies this point you have produced a counterexample to the theory and the theory is false. One gets the impression that people in AI who write this sort of thing think they can get away with it because they don't really take it seriously, and they don't think anyone else will either. I propose, for a moment at least, to take it seriously. Think hard for one minute about what would be necessary to establish that that hunk of metal on the wall over there had real beliefs, beliefs with direction of fit, propositional content, and conditions of satisfaction; beliefs that had the possibility of being strong beliefs or weak beliefs; nervous, anxious, or secure beliefs; dogmatic, rational, or superstitious beliefs; blind faiths or hesitant cogitations; any kind of beliefs. The thermostat is not a candidate. Neither is stomach, liver, adding machine, or telephone. However, since we are taking the idea seriously, notice that its truth would be fatal to strong AI's claim to be a science of the mind. For now the mind is everywhere. What we wanted to know is what distinguishes the mind from thermostats and livers. And if McCarthy were right, strong AI wouldn't have a hope of telling us that.

2. THE ROBOT REPLY (YALE). "Suppose we wrote a different kind of program from Schank's program. Suppose we put a computer inside a robot, and this computer would not just take in formal symbols as input and give out formal symbols as output, but rather would actually operate the robot in such a way that the robot does something very much like perceiving, walking, moving about, hammering nails, eating, drinking—anything you like. The robot would, for example, have a television camera attached to it that enabled it to see, it would have arms and legs that enabled it to 'act,' and all of this would be controlled by its computer 'brain.' Such a robot would, unlike Schank's computer, have genuine understanding and other mental states."

The first thing to notice about the robot reply is that it tacitly concedes that cognition is not solely a matter of formal symbol manipulation, since this reply adds a set of causal relations with the outside world (cf. Fodor 1980). But the answer to the robot reply is that the addition of such "perceptual" and "motor" capacities adds nothing by way of understanding, in particular, or intentionality, in general, to Schank's original program. To see this, notice that the same thought

(continued)

Minds, Brains, and Programs (*continued*)

experiment applies to the robot case. Suppose that instead of the computer inside the robot, you put me inside the room and, as in the original Chinese case, you give me more Chinese symbols with more instructions in English for matching Chinese symbols to Chinese symbols and feeding back Chinese symbols to the outside. Suppose, unknown to me, some of the Chinese symbols that come to me come from a television camera attached to the robot and other Chinese symbols that I am giving out serve to make the motors inside the robot move the robot's legs or arms. It is important to emphasize that all I am doing is manipulating formal symbols: I know none of these other facts. I am receiving "information" from the robot's perceptual" apparatus and I am giving out "instructions" to its motor apparatus without knowing either of these facts. I am the robot's homunculus, but unlike the traditional homunculus, I don't know what's going on. I don't understand anything except the rules for symbol manipulation. Now in this case I want to say that the robot has no intentional states at all; it is simply moving about as a result of its electrical wiring and its program. And furthermore, by instantiating the program I have no intentional states of the relevant type. All I do is follow formal instructions about manipulating formal symbols.

3. THE BRAIN SIMULATOR REPLY (BERKELEY AND M.I.T.). "Suppose we design a program that doesn't represent information that we have about the world, such as the information in Schank's scripts, but simulates the actual sequence of neuron firings at the synapses of the brain of a native Chinese speaker when he understands stories in Chinese and gives answers to them. The machine takes in Chinese stories and questions about them as input, it simulates the formal structure of actual Chinese brains in processing these stories, and it gives out Chinese answers as outputs. We can even imagine that the machine operates, not with a single serial program, but with a whole set of programs operating in parallel, in the manner that actual human brains presumably operate when they process natural language. Now surely in such a case we would have to say that the machine understood the stories; and if we refuse to say that, wouldn't we also have to deny that native Chinese speakers understood the stories? At the level of the synapses, what would or could be different about the program of the computer and the program of the Chinese brain?"

Before countering this reply I want to digress to note that it is an odd reply for any partisan of artificial intelligence (or functionalism, etc.) to make: I thought the whole idea of strong AI is that we don't need to know how the brain works to know how the mind works. The basic hypothesis, or so I had supposed, was that there is a level of mental operations consisting of computational processes over formal elements that constitute the essence of the mental and can be realized in all sorts of different brain processes, in the same way that any computer program can be realized in different computer hardwares: On the assumptions of strong AI, the mind is to the brain as the program is to the hardware, and thus we can understand the mind without doing neurophysiology. If we had to know how the brain worked to do AI, we wouldn't bother with AI. However, even getting this close to the operation of the brain is still not sufficient to produce understanding. To see this, imagine that instead of a monolingual man in a room shuffling symbols we have the man operate an elaborate set of water pipes with valves connecting them. When the man receives the Chinese symbols, he looks up in the program, written in English, which valves he has to turn on and off. Each water connection corresponds to a synapse in the Chinese brain, and the whole system is rigged up so that after doing all the right firings, that is after turning on all the right faucets, the Chinese answers pop out at the output end of the series of pipes.

Now where is the understanding in this system? It takes Chinese as input, it simulates the formal structure of the synapses of the Chinese brain, and it gives Chinese as output. But the man certainly doesn't understand Chinese, and neither do the water pipes, and if we are tempted to adopt what I think is the absurd view that somehow the *conjunction* of man *and* water pipes understands, remember that in principle the man can internalize the formal structure of the water pipes and do all the "neuron firings" in his imagination. The problem with the brain simulator is that it is simulating the wrong things about the brain. As long as it simulates only the formal structure of the sequence of neuron firings at the synapses, it won't have simulated what matters about the brain, namely its causal properties, its ability to produce intentional states. And that the formal properties are not sufficient for the causal properties is shown by the water pipe example: we can have all the formal properties carved off from the relevant neurobiological causal properties.

4. THE COMBINATION REPLY (BERKELEY AND STANFORD). "While each of the previous three replies might not be completely convincing by itself as a refutation of the Chinese room counterexample, if you take all three together they are collectively much more convincing and even decisive. Imagine a robot with a brain-shaped computer lodged in its cranial cavity, imagine the computer programmed with all the synapses of a human brain, imagine the whole behavior of the robot is indistinguishable from human behavior, and now think of the whole thing as a unified system and not just as a computer with inputs and outputs. Surely in such a case we would have to ascribe intentionality to the system."

I entirely agree that in such a case we would find it rational and indeed irresistible to accept the hypothesis that the robot had intentionally, as long as we know nothing more about it. Indeed, besides appearance and behavior, the other elements of the combination are really irrelevant. If we could build a robot whose behavior was indistinguishable over a large range from human behavior, we would attribute intentionality to it, pending some reason not to. We wouldn't need to know in advance that its computer brain was a formal analogue of the human brain.

But I really don't see that this is any help to the claims of strong AI, and here's why: According to strong AI, instatitiating a formal program with the right input and output is a sufficient condition of, indeed is constitutive of, intentionality. As Newell (1979) puts it, the essence of the mental is the operation of a physical symbol system. But the attributions of intentionality that we make to the robot in this example have nothing to do with formal programs. They are simply based on the assumption that if the robot looks and behaves sufficiently like us, then we would suppose, until proven otherwise, that it must have mental states like ours that cause and are expressed by its behavior and it must have an inner mechanism capable of producing such mental states. If we knew independently how to account for its behavior without such assumptions we would not attribute intentionality to it, especially if we knew it had a formal program. And this is precisely the point of my earlier reply to objection II.

Suppose we knew that the robot's behavior was entirely accounted for by the fact that a man inside it was receiving uninterpreted formal symbols from the robot's sensory receptors and sending out uninterpreted formal symbols to its motor mechanisms, and the man was doing this symbol manipulation in accordance with a bunch of rules. Furthermore, suppose the man knows none of these facts about the robot, all he knows is which operations to perform on which meaningless symbols. In such a case we would regard the robot as an ingenious mechanical dummy. The hypothesis that the dummy has a mind would now be unwarranted and unnecessary, for there is now no longer any reason to ascribe intentionality to the robot or to the system of which it is a part (except of course for the man's intentionality in manipulating the symbols). The formal symbol manipulations go on, the input and output are correctly matched, but the only real locus of intentionality is the man, and he doesn't know any of the relevant intentional states; he doesn't, for example, *see* what comes into the robot's eyes, he doesn't *intend* to move the robot's arm, and he doesn't *understand* any of the remarks made to or by the robot. Nor, for the reasons stated earlier, does the system of which man and robot are a part.

To see this point, contrast this case with cases in which we find it completely natural to ascribe intentionality to members of certain other primate species such as apes and monkeys and to domestic animals such as dogs. The reasons we find it natural are, roughly, two: We can't make sense of the animal's behavior without the ascription of intentionality and we can see that the beasts are made of similar stuff to ourselves—that is an eye, that a nose, this is its skin, and so on. Given the coherence of the animal's behavior and the assumption of the same causal stuff underlying it, we assume both that the animal must have mental states underlying its behavior, and that the mental states intent be produced by mechanisms made out of the stuff that is like our stuff. We would certainly make similar assumptions about the robot unless we had some reasons not to, but as soon as we knew that the behavior was the result of a formal program, and that the actual causal properties of the physical substance were irrelevant we would abandon the assumption of intentionality.

There are two other responses to my example that come up frequently (and so are worth discussing) but really miss the point.

5. THE OTHER MINDS REPLY (YALE). "How do you know that other people understand Chinese or anything else? Only by their behavior. Now the computer can pass the behavioral tests as well as they can (in principle), so if you are going to attribute cognition to other people you must in principle also attribute it to computers."

(continued)

Minds, Brains, and Programs   (*continued*)

This objection really is only worth a short reply. The problem in this discussion is not about how I know that other people have cognitive states, but rather what it is that I am attributing to them when I attribute cognitive states to them. The thrust of the argument is that it couldn't be just computational processes and their output because the computational processes and their output can exist without the cognitive state. It is no answer to this argument to feign anesthesia. In "cognitive sciences" one presupposes the reality and knowability of the mental in the same way that in physical sciences one has to presuppose the reality and knowability of physical objects.

6. THE MANY MANSIONS REPLY (BERKELEY).   "Your whole argument presupposes that AI is only about analog and digital computers. But that just happens to be the present state of technology. Whatever these causal processes are that you say are essential for intentionality (assuming you are right), eventually we will be able to build devices that have these causal processes, and that will be artificial intelligence. So your arguments are in no way directed at the ability of artificial intelligence to produce and explain cognition."

I really have no objection to this reply save to say that it in effect trivializes the project of strong AI by redefining it as whatever artificially produces and explains cognition. The interest of the original claim made on behalf of artificial intelligence is that it was a precise, well defined thesis: mental processes are computational processes over formally defined elements. I have been concerned to challenge that thesis. If the claim is redefined so that it is no longer that thesis, my objections no longer apply because there is no longer a testable hypothesis for them to apply to.

Let us now return to the question I promised I would try to answer: Granted that in my original example I understand the English and I do not understand the Chinese, and granted therefore that the machine doesn't understand either English or Chinese, still there must be something about me that makes it the case that I understand English and a corresponding something lacking in me that makes it the case that I fail to understand Chinese. Now why couldn't we give those somethings, whatever they are, to a machine?

I see no reason in principle why we couldn't give a machine the capacity to understand English or Chinese, since in an important sense our bodies with our brains are precisely such machines. But I do see very strong arguments for saying that we could not give such a thing to a machine where the operation of the machine is defined solely in terms of computational processes over formally defined elements; that is, where the operation of the machine is defined as an instantiation of a computer program. It is not because I am the instantiation of a computer program that I am able to understand English and have other forms of intentionality (I am, I suppose, the instantiation of any number of computer programs), but as far as we know it is because I am a certain sort of organism with a certain biological (i.e., chemical and physical) structure, and this structure, under certain conditions, is causally capable of producing perception, action, understanding, learning, and other intentional phenomena. And part of the point of the present argument is that only something that had those causal powers could have that intentionality. Perhaps other physical and chemical processes could produce exactly these effects; perhaps, for example, Martians also have intentionality but their brains are made of different stuff. That is an empirical question, rather like the question whether photosynthesis can be done by something with a chemistry different from that of chlorophyll.

But the main point of the present argument is that no purely formal model will ever be sufficient by itself for intentionality because the formal properties are not by themselves constitutive of intentionality, and they have by themselves no causal powers except the power, when instantiated, to produce the next stage of the formalism when the machine is running. And any other causal properties that particular realizations of the formal model have, are irrelevant to the formal model because we can always put the same formal model in a different realization where those causal properties are obviously absent. Even if, by some miracle, Chinese speakers exactly realize Schank's program, we can put the same program in English speakers, water pipes, or computers, none of which understand Chinese, the program notwithstanding.

What matters about brain operations is not the formal shadow cast by the sequence of synapses but rather the actual properties of the sequences. All the arguments for the strong version of artificial intelligence that I have seen insist on drawing an outline around the shadows cast by cognition and then claiming that the shadows are the real thing.

By way of concluding I want to try to state some of the general philosophical points implicit in the argument. For clarity I will try to do it in a question-and-answer fashion, and I begin with that old chestnut of a question:

"Could a machine think?" The answer is, obviously, yes. We are precisely such machines.

"Yes, but could an artifact, a man-made machine, think?"

Assuming it is possible to produce artificially a machine with a nervous system, neurons with axons and dendrites, and all the rest of it, sufficiently like ours, again the answer to the question seems to be obviously, yes. If you can exactly duplicate the causes, you could duplicate the effects. And indeed it might be possible to produce consciousness, intentionality, and all the rest of it using some other sorts of chemical principles than those that human beings use. It is, as I said, an empirical question.

"OK, but could a digital computer think?"

If by "digital computer" we mean anything at all that has a level of description where it can correctly be described as the instantiation of a computer program, then again the answer is, of course, yes, since we are the instantiations of any number of computer programs, and we can think.

"But could something think, understand, and so on *solely* in virtue of being a computer with the right sort of program? Could instantiating a program, the right program of course, by itself be a sufficient condition of understanding?"

This I think is the right question to ask, though it is usually confused with one or more of the earlier questions, and the answer to it is no.

"Why not?"

Because the formal symbol manipulations by themselves don't have any intentionality; they are quite meaningless; they aren't even *symbol* manipulations, since the symbols don't symbolize anything. In the linguistic jargon, they have only a syntax but no semantics. Such intentionality as computers appear to have is solely in the minds of those who program them and those who use them, those who send in the input and those who interpret the output.

The aim of the Chinese room example was to try to show this by showing that as soon as we put something into the system that really does have intentionality (a man), and we program him with the formal program, you can see that the formal program carries no additional intentionality. It adds nothing, for example, to a man's ability to understand Chinese.

Precisely that feature of AI that seemed so appealing—the distinction between the program and the realization—proves fatal to the claim that simulation could be duplication. The distinction between the program and its realization in the hardware seems to be parallel to the distinction between the level of mental operations and the level of brain operations. And if we could describe the level of mental operations as a formal program, then it seems we could describe what was essential about the mind without doing either introspective psychology or neurophysiology of the brain. But the equation "mind is to brain as program is to hardware" breaks down at several points, among them the following three:

First, the distinction between program and realization has the consequence that the same program could have all sorts of crazy realizations that had no form of intentionality. Weizenbaum (1976, Ch. 2), for example, shows in detail how to construct a computer using a roll of toilet paper and a pile of small stones. Similarly, the Chinese story understanding program can be programmed into a sequence of water pipes, a set of wind machines, or a monolingual English speaker, none of which thereby acquires an understanding of Chinese. Stones, toilet paper, wind, and water pipes are the wrong kind of stuff to have intentionality in the first place—only something that has the same causal powers as brains can have intentionality—and though the English speaker has the right kind of stuff for intentionality you can easily see that he doesn't get any extra intentionality by memorizing the program, since memorizing it won't teach him Chinese.

Second, the program is purely formal, but the intentional states are not in that way formal. They are defined in terms of their content, not their form. The belief that it is raining, for example, is not defined as a certain formal shape, but as a certain mental content with conditions of satisfaction, a direction of fit (see Searle 1979), and the like. Indeed the belief as such hasn't even got a formal shape in this syntactic sense, since one and the same belief can be given an indefinite number of different syntactic expressions in different linguistic systems.

Third, as I mentioned before, mental states and events are literally a product of the operation of the brain, but the program is not in that way a product of the computer.

(continued)

Minds, Brains, and Programs (*continued*)

"Well if programs are in no way constitutive of mental processes, why have so many people believed the converse? That at least needs some explanation."

I don't really know the answer to that one. The idea that computer simulations could be the real thing ought to have seemed suspicious in the first place because the computer isn't confined to simulating mental operations, by any means. No one supposes that computer simulations of a five-alarm fire will burn the neighborhood down or that a computer simulation of a rainstorm will leave us all drenched. Why on earth would anyone suppose that a computer simulation of understanding actually understood anything? It is sometimes said that it would be frightfully hard to get computers to feel pain or fall in love, but love and pain are neither harder nor easier than cognition or anything else. For simulation, all you need is the right input and output and a program in the middle that transforms the former into the latter. That is all the computer has for anything it does. To confuse simulation with duplication is the same mistake, whether it is pain, love, cognition, fires, or rainstorms.

Still, there are several reasons why AI must have seemed—and to many people perhaps still does seem—in some way to reproduce and thereby explain mental phenomena, and I believe we will not succeed in removing these illusions until we have fully exposed the reasons that give rise to them.

First, and perhaps most important, is a confusion about the notion of "information processing": many people in cognitive science believe that the human brain, with its mind, does something called "information processing," and analogously the computer with its program does information processing; but fires and rainstorms, on the other hand, don't do information processing at all. Thus, though the computer can simulate the formal features of any process whatever, it stands in a special relation to the mind and brain because when the computer is properly programmed, ideally with the same program as the brain, the information processing is identical in the two cases, and this information processing is really the essence of the mental. But the trouble with this argument is that it rests on an ambiguity in the notion of "information." In the sense in which people "process information" when they reflect, say, on problems in arithmetic or when they read and answer questions about stories, the programmed computer does not do "information processing." Rather, what it does is manipulate formal symbols. The fact that the programmer and the interpreter of the computer output use the symbols to stand for objects in the world is totally beyond the scope of the computer. The computer, to repeat, has a syntax but no semantics. Thus, if you type into the computer "2 plus 2 equals?" it will type out "4." But it has no idea that "4" means 4 or that it means anything at all. And the point is not that it lacks some second-order information about the interpretation of its first-order symbols, but rather that its first-order symbols don't have any interpretations as far as the computer is concerned. All the computer has is more symbols. The introduction of the notion of "information processing" therefore produces a dilemma: either we construe the notion of "information processing" in such a way that it implies intentionality as part of the process or we don't. If the former, then the programmed computer does not do information processing, it only manipulates formal symbols. If the latter, then, though the computer does information processing, it is only doing so in the sense in which adding machines, typewriters, stomachs, thermostats, rainstorms, and hurricanes do information processing; namely, they have a level of description at which we can describe them as taking information in at one end, transforming it, and producing information as output. But in this case it is up to outside observers to interpret the input and output as information in the ordinary sense. And no similarity is established between the computer and the brain in terms of any similarity of information processing.

Second, in much of AI there is a residual behaviorism or operationalism. Since appropriately programmed computers can have input-output patterns similar to those of human beings, we are tempted to postulate mental states in the computer similar to human mental states. But once we see that it is both conceptually and empirically possible for a system to have human capacities in some realm without having any intentionality at all, we should be able to overcome this impulse. My desk adding machine has calculating capacities, but no intentionality, and in this paper I have tried to show that a system could have input and output capabilities that duplicated those of a native Chinese speaker and still not understand Chinese, regardless of how it was programmed.

The Turing test is typical of the tradition in being unashamedly behaviorism and operationalistic, and I believe that if AI workers totally repudiated behaviorism and operatiotialism much of the confusion between simulation and duplication would be eliminated.

Third, this residual operationalism is joined to a residual form of dualism; indeed strong AI only makes sense given the dualistic assumption that, where the mind is concerned, the brain doesn't matter. In strong AI (and in functionalism, as well) what matters are programs, and programs are independent of their realization in machines; indeed, as far as AI is concerned, the same program could be realized by an electronic machine, a Cartesian mental substance, or a Hegelian world spirit. The single most surprising discovery that I have made in discussing these issues is that many AI workers are quite shocked by my idea that actual human mental phenomena might be dependent on actual physical-chemical properties of actual human brains. But if you think about it a minute you can see that I should not have been surprised; for unless you accept some form of dualism, the strong AI project hasn't got a chance. The project is to reproduce and explain the mental by designing programs, but unless the mind is not only conceptually but empirically independent of the brain you couldn't carry out the project, for the program is completely independent of any realization. Unless you believe that the mind is separable from the brain both conceptually and empirically—dualism in a strong form—you cannot hope to reproduce the mental by writing and running programs since programs must be independent of brains or any other particular forms of instantiation. If mental operations consist in computational operations on formal symbols, then it follows that they have no interesting connection with the brain; the only connection would be that the brain just happens to be one of the indefinitely many types of machines capable of instantiating the program. This form of dualism is not the traditional Cartesian variety that claims there are two sorts of *substances,* but it is Cartesian in the sense that it insists that what is specifically mental about the mind has no intrinsic connection with the actual properties of the brain. This underlying dualism is masked from us by the fact that AI literature contains frequent fulminations against "dualism"; what the authors seem to be unaware of is that their position presupposes a strong version of dualism. "Could a machine think?" My own view is that *only* a machine could think, and indeed only very special kinds of machines, namely brains and machines that had the same causal powers as brains. And that is the main reason strong AI has had little to tell us about thinking, since it has nothing to tell us about machines. By its own definition, it is about programs, and programs are not machines. Whatever else intentionality is, it is a biological phenomenon, and it is as likely to be as causally dependent on the specific biochemistry of its origins as lactation, photosynthesis, or any other biological phenomena. No one would suppose that we could produce milk and sugar by running a computer simulation of the formal sequences in lactation and photosynthesis, but where the mind is concerned many people are willing to believe in such a miracle because of a deep and abiding dualism: the mind they suppose is a matter of formal processes and is independent of quite specific material causes in the way that milk and sugar are not. In defense of this dualism the hope is often expressed that the brain is a digital computer (early computers, by the way, were often called "electronic brains"). But that is no help. Of course the brain is a digital computer. Since everything is a digital computer, brains are too. The point is that the brain's causal capacity to produce intentionality cannot consist in its instantiating a computer program, since for any program you like it is possible for something to instantiate that program and still not have any mental states. Whatever it is that the brain does to produce intentionality, it cannot consist in instantiating a program since no program, by itself, is sufficient for intentionality.[3]

NOTES

1. Also, "understanding" implies both the possession of mental (intentional) states and the truth (validity, success) of these states. For the purposes of this discussion we are concerned only with the possession of the states.
2. "Intenionality is by definition that feature of certain mental states by which they are directed at or about objects and states of affairs in the world. Thus, beliefs, desires, and intentions are intentional states; undirected forms of anxiety and depression are not.
3. I am indebted to a rather large number of people for discussion of these matters and for their patient attempts to overcome my ignorance of artificial intelligence. I would especially like to thank Ned Block, Hubert Dreyfus, John Haugeland, Roger Schank. Robert Wilensky, and Terry Winograd.

Reductive and Eliminative Materialism
Paul Churchland

3. Reductive Materialism (the Identity Theory)

Reductive materialism, more commonly known as *the identity theory,* is the most straightforward of the several materialist theories of mind. Its central claim is simplicity itself: Mental states *are* physical states of the brain. That is, each type of mental state or process is *numerically identical with* (is one and the very same thing as) some type of physical state or process within the brain or central nervous system. At present we do not know enough about the intricate functionings of the brain actually to state the relevant identities, but the identity theory is committed to the idea that brain research will eventually reveal them. (Partly to help us evaluate that claim, we shall examine current brain research in chapter 7.)

HISTORICAL PARALLELS   As the identity theorist sees it, the result here predicted has familiar parallels elsewhere in our scientific history. Consider sound. We now know that sound is just a train of compression waves traveling through the air, and that the property of being high pitched is identical with the property of having a high oscillatory frequency. We have learned that light is just electromagnetic waves, and our best current theory says that the color of an object is identical with a triplet of reflectance efficiencies the object has, rather like a musical chord that it strikes, though the 'notes' are struck in electromagnetic waves instead of in sound waves. We now appreciate that the warmth or coolness of a body is just the energy of motion of the molecules that make it up: warmth is identical with high average molecular kinetic energy, and coolness is identical with low average molecular kinetic energy. We know that lightning is identical with a sudden large-scale discharge of electrons between clouds, or between the atmosphere and the ground. What we now think of as 'mental states,' argues the identity theorist, are identical with brain states in exactly the same way.

INTERTHEORETIC REDUCTION   These illustrative parallels are all cases of successful *intertheoretic reduction*. That is, they are all cases where a new and very powerful theory turns out to entail a set of propositions and principles that mirror perfectly (or almost perfectly) the propositions and principles of some older theory or conceptual framework. The relevant principles entailed by the new theory have the same structure as the corresponding principles of the old framework, and they apply in exactly the same cases. The only difference is that where the old principles contained (for example) the notions of "heat", "is hot", and "is cold", the new principles contain instead the notions of "total molecular kinetic energy", "has a high mean molecular kinetic energy", and "has a low mean molecular kinetic energy".

If the new framework is far better than the old at explaining and predicting phenomena, then we have excellent reason for believing that the theoretical terms of the *new* framework are the terms that describe reality correctly. But if the old framework worked adequately, so far as it went, and if it parallels a portion of the new theory in the systematic way described, then we may properly conclude that the old terms and the new terms refer to the very same things, or express the very same properties. We conclude that we have apprehended the very same reality that is incompletely described by the old framework, but with a new and more penetrating conceptual framework. And we announce what philosophers of science call "intertheoretic identities": light *is* electromagnetic waves, temperature *is* mean molecular kinetic energy, and so forth.

The examples of the preceding two paragraphs share one more important feature in common. They are all cases where the things or properties on the receiving end of the reduction are *observable* things and properties within our *common-sense* conceptual framework. They show that intertheoretic reduction occurs not only between conceptual frameworks in the theoretical stratosphere: common-sense observables can also be reduced. There would therefore be nothing particularly surprising about a reduction of our familiar introspectible mental states to physical states of the brain. All that would be required would be that an explanatorily successful neuroscience develop to the point where it entails a suitable 'mirror image' of the assumptions and principles that constitute our common-sense conceptual framework for mental states, an image where brain-state terms occupy the positions held by mental-state terms in the assumptions and principles of common sense. If this (rather demanding) condition were indeed met, then, as in the historical cases cited, we would be justified in announcing a reduction, and in asserting the identity of mental states with brain states.

4. Functionalism

According to *functionalism,* the essential or defining feature of any type of mental state is the set of causal relations it bears to (1) environmental effects on the body, (2) other types of mental states, and (3) bodily behavior. Pain, for example, characteristically results from some bodily damage or trauma; it causes distress, annoyance, and practical reasoning aimed at relief; and it causes wincing, blanching, and nursing of the traumatized area. Any state that plays exactly that functional role is a pain, according to functionalism. Similarly, other types of mental states (sensations, fears, beliefs, and so on) are also defined by their unique causal roles in a complex economy of internal states mediating sensory inputs and behavioral outputs.

This view may remind the reader of behaviorism, and indeed it is the heir to behaviorism, but there is one fundamental difference between the two theories. Where the behaviorist hoped to define each type of mental state solely in terms of environmental input and behavioral output, the functionalist denies that this is possible. As he sees it, the adequate characterization of almost any mental state involves an in-eliminable reference to a variety of other mental states with which it is causally connected, and so a reductive definition solely in terms of publicly observable inputs and outputs is quite impossible. Functionalism is therefore immune to one of the main objections against behaviorism.

Thus the difference between functionalism and behaviorism. The difference between functionalism and the identity theory will emerge from the following argument raised against the identity theory.

Imagine a being from another planet, says the functionalist, a being with an alien physiological constitution, a constitution based on the chemical element silicon, for example, instead of on the element carbon, as ours is. The chemistry and even the physical structure of the alien's brain would have to be systematically different from ours. But even so, that alien brain could well sustain a functional economy of internal states whose mutual *relations* parallel perfectly the mutual relations that define our own mental states. The alien may have an internal state that meets all the conditions for being a pain state, as outlined earlier. That state, considered from a purely physical point of view, would have a very different makeup from a human pain state, but it could nevertheless be identical to a human pain state from a purely functional point of view. And so for all of his functional states.

If the alien's functional economy of internal states were indeed *functionally isomorphic* with our own internal economy—if those states were causally connected to inputs, to one another, and to behavior in ways that parallel our own internal connections—then the alien would have pains, and desires, and hopes, and fears just as fully as we, despite the differences in the physical system that sustains or realizes those functional states. What is important for mentality is not the matter of which the creature is made, but the structure of the internal activities which that matter sustains.

If we can think of one alien constitution, we can think of many, and the point just made can also be made with an artificial system. Were we to create an electronic system—a computer of some kind—whose internal economy were functionally isomorphic with our own in all the relevant ways, then it too would be the subject of mental states.

What this illustrates is that there are almost certainly many more ways than one for nature, and perhaps even for man, to put together a thinking, feeling, perceiving creature. And this raises a problem for the identity theory, for it seems that there is no single type of physical state to which a given type of mental state must always correspond. Ironically, there are *too many* different kinds of physical systems that can realize the functional economy characteristic of conscious intelligence. If we consider the universe at large, therefore, and the future as well as the present, it seems quite unlikely that the identity theorist is going to find the one-to-one match-ups between the concepts of our common-sense mental taxonomy and the concepts of an overarching theory that encompasses all of the relevant physical systems. But that is what intertheoretic reduction is standardly said to require. The prospects for universal identities, between types of mental states and types of brain states, are therefore slim.

(continued)

Reductive and Eliminative Materialism   (*continued*)

If the functionalists reject the traditional 'mental-type = physical type' identity theory, virtually all of them remain committed to a weaker 'mental token = physical token' identity theory, for they still maintain that each *instance* of a given type of mental state is numerically identical with some specific physical state in some physical system or other. It is only universal (type/type) identities that are rejected. Even so, this rejection is typically taken to support the claim that the science of psychology is or should be *methodologically autonomous* from the various physical sciences such as physics, biology, and even neurophysiology. Psychology, it is claimed, has its own irreducible laws and its own abstract subject matter.

As this book is written, functionalism is probably the most widely held theory of mind among philosophers, cognitive psychologists, and artificial intelligence researchers. Some of the reasons are apparent from the preceding discussion, and there are further reasons as well. In characterizing mental states as essentially functional states, functionalism places the concerns of psychology at a level that abstracts from the teeming detail of a brain's neurophysiological (or crystallographic or microelectronic) structure. The science of psychology, it is occasionally said, is methodologically autonomous from those other sciences (biology, neuroscience, circuit theory) whose concerns are with what amount to engineering details. This provides a rationale for a great deal of work in cognitive psychology and artificial intelligence, where researchers postulate a system of abstract functional states and then test the postulated system, often by way of its computer simulation, against human behavior in similar circumstances. The aim of such work is to discover in detail the functional organization that makes us what we are. (Partly in order to evaluate the prospects for a functionalist philosophy of mind, we shall examine some of the recent research in artificial intelligence in chapter 6.)

5. Eliminative Materialism

The identity theory was called into doubt not because the prospects for a materialist account of our mental capacities were thought to be poor, but because it seemed unlikely that the arrival of an adequate materialist theory would bring with it the nice one-to-one match-ups, between the concepts of folk psychology and the concepts of theoretical neuroscience, that intertheoretic reduction requires. The reason for that doubt was the great variety of quite different physical systems that could instantiate the required functional organization. *Eliminative materialism* also doubts that the correct neuroscientific account of human capacities will produce a neat reduction of our common-sense framework, but here the doubts arise from a quite different source.

As the eliminative materialists see it, the one-to-one match-ups will not be found, and our common-sense psychological framework will not enjoy an intertheoretic reduction, *because our common-sense psychological framework is a false and radically misleading conception of the causes of human behavior and the nature of cognitive activity.* On this view, folk psychology is not just an incomplete representation of our inner natures; it is an outright *mis*representation of our internal states and activities. Consequently, we cannot expect a truly adequate neuroscientific account of our inner lives to provide theoretical categories that match up nicely with the categories of our common-sense framework. Accordingly, we must expect that the older framework will simply be eliminated, rather than be reduced, by a matured neuroscience.

HISTORICAL PARALLELS   As the identity theorist can point to historical cases of successful intertheoretic reduction, so the eliminative materialist can point to historical cases of the outright elimination of the ontology of an older theory in favor of the ontology of a new and superior theory. For most of the eighteenth and nineteenth centuries, learned people believed that heat was a subtle *fluid* held in bodies, much in the way water is held in a sponge. A fair body of moderately successful theory described the way this fluid substance—called "caloric"—flowed within a body, or from one body to another, and how it produced thermal expansion, melting, boiling, and so forth. But by the end of the last century it had become abundantly clear that heat was not a substance at all, but just the energy of motion of the trillions of jostling molecules that make up the heated body itself. The new theory—the "corpuscular/kinetic theory of matter and heat"—was much more successful than the old in explaining and predicting the thermal behavior of bodies. And since we were unable to *identify* caloric fluid with kinetic energy (according to the old theory, caloric is a material *substance;* according to the new theory, kinetic energy is a form of *motion),* it was finally agreed that there is *no such thing* as caloric. Caloric was simply eliminated from our accepted ontology.

A second example. It used to be thought that when a piece of wood burns, or a piece of metal rusts, a spiritlike substance called "phlogiston" was being released: briskly, in the former case, slowly in the latter. Once gone, that 'noble' substance left only a base pile of ash or rust. It later came to be appreciated that both processes involve, not the loss of something, but the *gaining* of a substance taken from the atmosphere: oxygen. Phlogiston emerged, not as an incomplete description of what was going on, but as a radical misdescription. Phlogiston was therefore not suitable for reduction to or identification with some notion from within the new oxygen chemistry, and it was simply eliminated from science.

Admittedly, both of these examples concern the elimination of something nonobservable, but our history also includes the elimination of certain widely accepted 'observables'. Before Copernicus' views became available, almost any human who ventured out at night could look up at *the starry sphere of the heavens,* and if he stayed for more than a few minutes he could also see that it *turned,* around an axis through Polaris. What the sphere was made of (crystal?) and what made it turn (the gods?) were theoretical questions that exercised us for over two millennia. But hardly anyone doubted the existence of what everyone could observe with their own eyes. In the end, however, we learned to reinterpret our visual experience of the night sky within a very different conceptual framework, and the turning sphere evaporated.

Witches provide another example. Psychosis is a fairly common affliction among humans, and in earlier centuries its victims were standardly seen as cases of demonic possession, as instances of Satan's spirit itself, glaring malevolently out at us from behind the victims' eyes. That witches exist was not a matter of any controversy. One would occasionally see them, in any city or hamlet, engaged in incoherent, paranoid, or even murderous behavior. But observable or not, we eventually decided that witches simply do not exist. We concluded that the concept of a witch is an element in a conceptual framework that misrepresents so badly the phenomena to which it was standardly applied that literal application of the notion should be permanently withdrawn. Modern theories of mental dysfunction led to the elimination of witches from our serious ontology.

The concepts of folk psychology—belief, desire, fear, sensation, pain, joy, and so on—await a similar fate, according to the view at issue. And when neuroscience has matured to the point where the poverty of our current conceptions is apparent to everyone, and the superiority of the new framework is established, we shall then be able to set about *re*conceiving our internal states and activities, within a truly adequate conceptual framework at last. Our explanations of one another's behavior will appeal to such things as our neuropharmacological states, the neural activity in specialized anatomical areas, and whatever other states are deemed relevant by the new theory. Our private introspection will also be transformed, and may be profoundly enhanced by reason of the more accurate and penetrating framework it will have to work with—just as the astronomer's perception of the night sky is much enhanced by the detailed knowledge of modern astronomical theory that he or she possesses.

The magnitude of the conceptual revolution here suggested should not be minimized: it would be enormous. And the benefits to humanity might be equally great. If each of us possessed an accurate neuroscientific understanding of (what we now conceive dimly as) the varieties and causes of mental illness, the factors involved in learning, the neural basis of emotions, intelligence, and socialization, then the sum total of human misery might be much reduced. The simple increase in mutual understanding that the new framework made possible could contribute substantially toward a more peaceful and humane society. Of course, there would be dangers as well: increased knowledge means increased power, and power can always be misused.

ARGUMENTS FOR ELIMINATIVE MATERIALISM   The arguments for eliminative materialism are diffuse and less than decisive, but they are stronger than is widely supposed. The distinguishing feature of this position is its denial that a smooth intertheoretic reduction is to be expected—even a species-specific reduction—of the framework of folk psychology to the framework of a matured neuroscience. The reason for this denial is the eliminative materialist's conviction that folk psychology is a hopelessly primitive and deeply confused conception of our internal activities. But why this low opinion of our common-sense conceptions?

(continued)

Reductive and Eliminative Materialism *(continued)*

There are at least three reasons. First, the eliminative materialist will point to the widespread explanatory, predictive, and manipulative failures of folk psychology. So much of what is central and familiar to us remains a complete mystery from within folk psychology. We do not know what *sleep* is, or why we have to have it, despite spending a full third of our lives in that condition. (The answer, "For rest," is mistaken. Even if people are allowed to rest continuously, their need for sleep is undiminished. Apparently, sleep serves some deeper functions, but we do not yet know what they are.) We do not understand how *learning* transforms each of us from a gaping infant to a cunning adult, or how differences in *intelligence* are grounded. We have not the slightest idea how *memory* works, or how we manage to retrieve relevant bits of information instantly from the awesome mass we have stored. We do not know what *mental illness* is, nor how to cure it.

In sum, the most central things about us remain almost entirely mysterious from within folk psychology. And the defects noted cannot be blamed on inadequate time allowed for their correction, for folk psychology has enjoyed no significant changes or advances in well over 2,000 years, despite its manifest failures. Truly successful theories may be expected to reduce, but significantly unsuccessful theories merit no such expectation.

This argument from explanatory poverty has a further aspect. So long as one sticks to normal brains, the poverty of folk psychology is perhaps not strikingly evident. But as soon as one examines the many perplexing behavioral and cognitive deficits suffered by people with *damaged* brains, one's descriptive and explanatory resources start to claw the air (see, for example chapter 7.3, p. 143). As with other humble theories asked to operate successfully in unexplored extensions of their old domain (for example, Newtonian mechanics in the domain of velocities close to the velocity of light, and the classical gas law in the domain of high pressures or temperatures), the descriptive and explanatory inadequacies of folk psychology become starkly evident.

The second argument tries to draw an inductive lesson from our conceptual history. Our early folk theories of motion were profoundly confused, and were eventually displaced entirely by more sophisticated theories. Our early folk theories of the structure and activity of the heavens were wildly off the mark, and survive only as historical lessons in how wrong we can be. Our folk theories of the nature of fire, and the nature of life, were similarly cockeyed. And one could go on, since the vast majority of our past folk conceptions have been similarly exploded. All except folk psychology, which survives to this day and has only recently begun to feel pressure. But the phenomenon of conscious intelligence is surely a more complex and difficult phenomenon than any of those just listed. So far as accurate understanding is concerned, it would be a *miracle* if we had got *that* one right the very first time, when we fell down so badly on all the others. Folk psychology has survived for so very long, presumably, not because it is basically correct in its representations, but because the phenomena addressed are so surpassingly difficult that any useful handle on them, no matter how feeble, is unlikely to be displaced in a hurry.

A third argument attempts to find an a priori advantage for eliminative materialism over the identity theory and functionalism. It attempts to counter the common intuition that eliminative materialism is distantly possible, perhaps, but is much less probable than either the identity theory or functionalism. The focus again is on whether the concepts of folk psychology will find vindicating match-ups in a matured neuroscience. The eliminativist bets no; the other two bet yes. (Even the functionalist bets yes, but expects the match-ups to be only species-specific, or only person-specific. Functionalism, recall, denies the existence only of *universal* type/type identities.)

The eliminativist will point out that the requirements on a reduction are rather demanding. The new theory must entail a set of principles and embedded concepts that mirrors very closely the specific conceptual structure to be reduced. And the fact is, there are vastly many more ways of being an explanatorily successful neuroscience while *not* mirroring the structure of folk psychology, than there are ways of being an explanatorily successful neuroscience while also *mirroring* the very specific structure of folk psychology. Accordingly, the a priori probability of eliminative materialism is not lower, but substantially *higher* than that of either of its competitors. One's initial intuitions here are simply mistaken.

Granted, this initial a priori advantage could be reduced if there were a very strong presumption in favor of the truth of folk psychology— true theories are better bets to win reduction.

But according to the first two arguments, the presumptions on this point should run in precisely the opposite direction.

ARGUMENTS AGAINST ELIMINATIVE MATERIALISM The initial plausibility of this rather radical view is low for almost everyone, since it denies deeply entrenched assumptions. That is at best a question-begging complaint, of course, since those assumptions are precisely what is at issue. But the following line of thought does attempt to mount a real argument.

Eliminative materialism is false, runs the argument, because one's introspection reveals directly the existence of pains, beliefs, desires, fears, and so forth. Their existence is as obvious as anything could be.

The eliminative materialist will reply that this argument makes the same mistake that an ancient or medieval person would be making if he insisted that he could just see with his own eyes that the heavens form a turning sphere, or that witches exist. The fact is, all observation occurs within some system of concepts, and our observation judgments are only as good as the conceptual framework in which they are expressed. In all three cases—the starry sphere, witches, and the familiar mental states—precisely what is challenged is the integrity of the background conceptual frameworks in which the observation judgments are expressed. To insist on the validity of one's experiences, *traditionally interpreted,* is therefore to beg the very question at issue. For in all three cases, the question is whether we should reconceive the nature of some familiar observational domain.

A second criticism attempts to find an incoherence in the eliminative materialist's position. The bald statement of eliminative materialism is that the familiar mental states do not really exist. But that statement is meaningful, runs the argument, only if it is the expression of a certain *belief,* and an *intention* to communicate, and a *knowledge* of the language, and so forth. But if the statement is true, then no such mental states exist, and the statement is therefore a meaningless string of marks or noises, and cannot be true. Evidently, the assumption that eliminative materialism is true entails that it cannot be true.

The hole in this argument is the premise concerning the conditions necessary for a statement to be meaningful. It begs the question. If eliminative materialism is true, then meaningfulness must have some different source. To insist on the 'old' source is to insist on the validity of the very framework at issue. Again, an historical parallel may be helpful here. Consider the medieval theory that being biologically *alive* is a matter of being ensouled by an immaterial *vital spirit*. And consider the following response to someone who has expressed disbelief in that theory.

> My learned friend has stated that there is no such thing as vital spirit. But this statement is incoherent. For if it is true, then my friend does not have vital spirit, and must therefore be *dead*. But if he is dead, then his statement is just a string of noises, devoid of meaning or truth. Evidently, the assumption that antivitalism is true entails that it cannot be true!   Q.E.D.

This second argument is now a joke, but the first argument begs the question in exactly the same way.

A final criticism draws a much weaker conclusion, but makes a rather stronger case. Eliminative materialism, it has been said, is making mountains out of molehills. It exaggerates the defects in folk psychology, and underplays its real successes. Perhaps the arrival of a matured neuroscience will require the elimination of the occasional folk-psychological concept, continues the criticism, and a minor adjustment in certain folk-psychological principles may have to be endured. But the large-scale elimination forecast by the eliminative materialist is just an alarmist worry or a romantic enthusiasm.

Perhaps this complaint is correct. And perhaps it is merely complacent. Whichever, it does bring out the important point that we do not confront two simple and mutually exclusive possibilities here: pure reduction versus pure elimination. Rather, these are the end points of a smooth spectrum of possible outcomes, between which there are mixed cases of partial elimination and partial reduction. Only empirical research (see chapter 7) can tell us where on that spectrum our own case will fall. Perhaps we should speak here, more liberally, of "revisionary materialism", instead of concentrating on the more radical possibility of an across-the-board elimination. Perhaps we should. But it has been my aim in this section to make it at least intelligible to you that our collective conceptual destiny lies substantially toward the revolutionary end of the spectrum.

What Is It Like to Be a Bat?
Thomas Nagel

Consciousness is what makes the mind-body problem really intractable. Perhaps that is why current discussions of the problem give it little attention or get it obviously wrong. The recent wave of reductionist euphoria has produced several analyses of mental phenomena and mental concepts designed to explain the possibility of some variety of materialism, psychophysical identification, or reduction.[1] But the problems dealt with are those common to this type of reduction and other types; and what makes the mind-body problem unique, and unlike the water-H_2O problem or the Turing machine-IBM machine problem or the lightning-electrical discharge problem or the gene-DNA problem or the oak tree-hydrocarbon problem, is ignored.

Every reductionist has his favorite analogy from modern science. It is most unlikely that any of these unrelated examples of successful reduction will shed light on the relation of mind to brain. But philosophers share the general human weakness for explanations of what is incomprehensible in terms suited for what is familiar and well understood, though entirely different. This has led to the acceptance of implausible accounts of the mental largely because they would permit familiar kinds of reduction. I shall try to explain why the usual examples do not help us to understand the relation between mind and body—why, indeed, we have at present no conception of what an explanation of the physical nature of a mental phenomenon would be. Without consciousness the mind-body problem would be much less interesting. With consciousness it seems hopeless. The most important and characteristic feature of conscious mental phenomena is very poorly understood. Most reductionist theories do not even try to explain it. And careful examination will show that no currently available concept of reduction is applicable to it. Perhaps a new theoretical form can be devised for the purpose, but such a solution, if it exists, lies in the distant intellectual future.

Conscious experience is a widespread phenomenon. It occurs at many levels of animal life, though we cannot be sure of its presence in the simpler organisms, and it is very difficult to say in general what provides evidence of it. (Some extremists have been prepared to deny it even of mammals other than man.) No doubt it occurs in countless forms totally unimaginable to us, on other planets in other solar systems throughout the universe. But no matter how the form may vary, the fact that an organism has conscious experience *at all* means, basically, that there is something it is like to *be* that organism. There may be further implications about the form of the experience; there may even (though I doubt it) be implications about the behavior of the organism. But fundamentally an organism has conscious mental states if and only if there is something that it is like to *be* that organism—something it is like *for* the organism.

We may call this the subjective character of experience. It is not captured by any of the familiar, recently devised reductive analyses of the mental, for all of them are logically compatible with its absence. It is not analyzable in terms of any explanatory system of functional states, or intentional states, since these could be ascribed to robots or automata that behaved like people though they experienced nothing.[2] It is not analyzable in terms of the causal role of experiences in relation to typical human behavior—for similar reasons.[3] I do not deny that conscious mental states and events cause behavior, nor that they may be given functional characterizations. I deny only that this kind of thing exhausts their analysis. Any reductionist program has to be based on an analysis of what is to be reduced. If the analysis leaves something out, the problem will be falsely posed. It is useless to base the defense of materialism on any analysis of mental phenomena that fails to deal explicitly with their subjective character. For there is no reason to suppose that a reduction which seems plausible when no attempt is made to account for consciousness can be extended to include consciousness. Without some idea, therefore, of what the subjective character of experience is, we cannot know what is required of a physicalist theory.

While an account of the physical basis of mind must explain many things, this appears to be the most difficult. It is impossible to exclude the phenomenological features of experience from a reduction in the same way that one excludes the phenomenal features of an ordinary substance from a physical or chemical reduction of it—namely, by explaining them as effects on the minds of human observers.[4] If physicalism is to be defended, the phenomenological features must themselves be given a physical account. But when we examine their subjective character it seems that such a result is impossible. The reason is that every subjective phenomenon is essentially connected with a single point of view, and it seems inevitable that an objective, physical theory will abandon that point of view.

Let me first try to state the issue somewhat more fully than by referring to the relation between the subjective and the objective, or between the *pour-soi* and the *en-soi*. This is far from easy. Facts about what it is like to be an *X* are very peculiar, so peculiar that some may be inclined to doubt their reality, or the significance of claims about them. To illustrate the connection between subjectivity and a point of view, and to make evident the importance of subjective features, it will help to explore the matter in relation to an example that brings out clearly the divergence between the two types of conception, subjective and objective.

I assume we all believe that bats have experience. After all, they are mammals, and there is no more doubt that they have experience than that mice or pigeons or whales have experience. I have chosen bats instead of wasps or flounders because if one travels too far down the phylogenetic tree, people gradually shed their faith that there is experience there at all. Bats, although more closely related to us than those other species, nevertheless present a range of activity and a sensory apparatus so different from ours that the problem I want to pose is exceptionally vivid (though it certainly could be raised with other species). Even without the benefit of philosophical reflection, anyone who has spent some time in an enclosed space with an excited bat knows what it is to encounter a fundamentally *alien* form of life.

I have said that the essence of the belief that bats have experience is that there is something that it is like to be a bat. Now we know that most bats (the Microchiroptera, to be precise) perceive the external world primarily by sonar, or echolocation, detecting the reflections, from objects within range, of their own rapid, subtly modulated, high-frequency shrieks. Their brains are designed to correlate the outgoing impulses with the subsequent echoes, and the information thus acquired enables bats to make precise discriminations of distance, size, shape, motion, and texture comparable to those we make by vision. But bat sonar, though clearly a form of perception, is not similar in its operation to any sense that we possess, and there is no reason to suppose that it is subjectively like anything we can experience or imagine. This appears to create difficulties for the notion of what it is like to be a bat. We must consider whether any method will permit us to extrapolate to the inner life of the bat from our own case,[5] and if not, what alternative methods there may be for understanding the notion.

Our own experience provides the basic material for our imagination, whose range is therefore limited. It will not help to try to imagine that one has webbing on one's arms, which enables one to fly around at dusk and dawn catching insects in one's mouth; that one has very poor vision, and perceives the surrounding world by a system of reflected high-frequency sound signals; and that one spends the day hanging upside down by one's feet in an attic. Insofar as I can imagine this (which is not very far), it tells me only what it would be like for *me* to behave as a bat behaves. But that is not the question. I want to know what it is like for a *bat* to be a bat. Yet if I try to imagine this, I am restricted to the resources of my own mind, and those resources are inadequate to the task. I cannot perform it either by imagining additions to my present experience, or by imagining segments gradually subtracted from it, or by imagining some combination of additions, subtractions, and modifications.

To the extent that I could look and behave like a wasp or a bat without changing my fundamental structure, my experiences would not be anything like the experiences of those animals. On the other hand, it is doubtful that any meaning can be attached to the supposition that I should possess the internal neurophysiological constitution of a bat. Even if I could by gradual degrees be transformed into a bat, nothing in my present constitution enables me to imagine what the experiences of such a future stage of myself thus metamorphosed would be like. The best evidence would come from the experiences of bats, if we only knew what they were like.

So if extrapolation from our own case is involved in the idea of what it is like to be a bat, the extrapolation must be incompletable. We cannot form more than a schematic conception of what it *is* like. For example, we may ascribe general *types* of experience on the basis of the animal's structure and behavior. Thus we describe bat sonar as a form of three-dimensional forward perception; we believe that bats feel some versions of pain, fear, hunger, and lust, and that they have other, more familiar types of perception besides sonar. But we believe that these experiences also have in

(continued)

What Is It Like to Be a Bat? (*continued*)

each case a specific subjective character, which it is beyond our ability to conceive. And if there is conscious life elsewhere in the universe, it is likely that some of it will not be describable even in the most general experiential terms available to us.[6] (The problem is not confined to exotic cases, however, for it exists between one person and another. The subjective character of the experience of a person deaf and blind from birth is not accessible to me, for example, nor presumably is mine to him. This does not prevent us each from believing that the other's experience has such a subjective character.)

If anyone is inclined to deny that we can believe in the existence of facts like this whose exact nature we cannot possibly conceive, he should reflect that in contemplating the bats we are in much the same position that intelligent bats or Martians[7] would occupy if they tried to form a conception of what it was like to be us. The structure of their own minds might make it impossible for them to succeed, but we know they would be wrong to conclude that there is not anything precise that it is like to be us: that only certain general types of mental state could be ascribed to us (perhaps perception and appetite would be concepts common to us both; perhaps not). We know they would be wrong to draw such a skeptical conclusion because we know what it is like to be us. And we know that while it includes an enormous amount of variation and complexity, and while we do not possess the vocabulary to describe it adequately, its subjective character is highly specific, and in some respects describable in terms that can be understood only by creatures like us. The fact that we cannot expect ever to accommodate in our language a detailed description of Martian or bat phenomenology should not lead us to dismiss as meaningless the claim that bats and Martians have experiences fully comparable in richness of detail to our own. It would be fine if someone were to develop concepts and a theory that enabled us to think about those things; but such an understanding may be permanently denied to us by the limits of our nature. And to deny the reality or logical significance of what we can never describe or understand is the crudest form of cognitive dissonance.

This brings us to the edge of a topic that requires much more discussion than I can give it here: namely, the relation between facts on the one hand and conceptual schemes or systems of representation on the other. My realism about the subjective domain in all its forms implies a belief in the existence of facts beyond the reach of human concepts. Certainly it is possible for a human being to believe that there are facts which humans never *will* possess the requisite concepts to represent or comprehend. Indeed, it would be foolish to doubt this, given the finiteness of humanity's expectations. After all, there would have been transfinite numbers even if everyone had been wiped out by the Black Death before Cantor discovered them. But one might also believe that there are facts which *could* not ever be represented or comprehended by human beings, even if the species lasted forever—simply because our structure does not permit us to operate with concepts of the requisite type. This impossibility might even be observed by other beings, but it is not clear that the existence of such beings, or the possibility of their existence, is a precondition of the significance of the hypothesis that there are humanly inaccessible facts. (After all, the nature of beings with access to humanly inaccessible facts is presumably itself a humanly inaccessible fact.) Reflection on what it is like to be a bat seems to lead us, therefore, to the conclusion that there are facts that do not consist in the truth of propositions expressible in a human language. We can be compelled to recognize the existence of such facts without being able to state or comprehend them.

I shall not pursue this subject, however. Its bearing on the topic before us (namely, the mind-body problem) is that it enables us to make a general observation about the subjective character of experience. Whatever may be the status of facts about what it is like to be a human being, or a bat, or a Martian, these appear to be facts that embody a particular point of view.

I am not adverting here to the alleged privacy of experience to its possessor. The point of view in question is not one accessible only to a single individual. Rather it is a *type*. It is often possible to take up a point of view other than one's own, so the comprehension of such facts is not limited to one's own case. There is a sense in which phenomenological facts are perfectly objective: one person can know or say of another what the quality of the other's experience is. They are subjective, however, in the sense that even this objective ascription of experience is possible only for someone sufficiently similar to the object of ascription to be able to adopt his point of view—to understand the ascription in the first person as well as in the third, so to speak. The more different from oneself the other experiencer is, the less success one can expect with this enterprise. In our own case we occupy the relevant point of view, but we will have as much difficulty understanding our own experience properly if we approach it from another point of view as we would if we tried to understand the experience of another species without taking up *its* point of view.[8]

This bears directly on the mind-body problem. For if the facts of experience—facts about what it is like *for* the experiencing organism—are accessible only from one point of view, then it is a mystery how the true character of experiences could be revealed in the physical operation of that organism. The latter is a domain of objective facts *par excellence*—the kind that can be observed and understood from many points of view and by individuals with differing perceptual systems. There are no comparable imaginative obstacles to the acquisition of knowledge about bat neurophysiology by human scientists, and intelligent bats or Martians might learn more about the human brain than we ever will.

This is not by itself an argument against reduction. A Martian scientist with no understanding of visual perception could understand the rainbow, or lightning, or clouds as physical phenomena, though he would never be able to understand the human concepts of rainbow, lightning, or cloud, or the place these things occupy in our phenomenal world. The objective nature of the things picked out by these concepts could be apprehended by him because, although the concepts themselves are connected with a particular point of view and a particular visual phenomenology, the things apprehended from that point of view are not: they are observable from the point of view but external to it; hence they can be comprehended from other points of view also, either by the same organisms or by others. Lightning has an objective character that is not exhausted by its visual appearance, and this can be investigated by a Martian without vision. To be precise, it has a *more* objective character than is revealed in its visual appearance. In speaking of the move from subjective to objective characterization, I wish to remain noncommittal about the existence of an end point, the completely objective intrinsic nature of the thing, which one might or might not be able to reach. It may be more accurate to think of objectivity as a direction in which the understanding can travel. And in understanding a phenomenon like lightning, it is legitimate to go as far away as one can from a strictly human viewpoint.[9]

In the case of experience, on the other hand, the connection with a particular point of view seems much closer. It is difficult to understand what could be meant by the *objective* character of an experience, apart from the particular point of view from which its subject apprehends it. After all, what would be left of what it was like to be a bat if one removed the viewpoint of the bat? But if experience does not have, in addition to its subjective character, an objective nature that can be apprehended from many different points of view, then how can it be supposed that a Martian investigating my brain might be observing physical processes which were my mental processes (as he might observe physical processes which were bolts of lightning), only from a different point of view? How, for that matter, could a human physiologist observe them from another point of view?[10]

We appear to be faced with a general difficulty about psychophysical reduction. In other areas the process of reduction is a move in the direction of greater objectivity, toward a more accurate view of the real nature of things. This is accomplished by reducing our dependence on individual or species-specific points of view toward the object of investigation. We describe it not in terms of the impressions it makes on our senses, but in terms of its more general effects and of properties detectable by means other than the human senses. The less it depends on a specifically human viewpoint, the more objective is our description. It is possible to follow this path because although the concepts and ideas we employ in thinking about the external world are initially applied from a point of view that involves our perceptual apparatus, they are used by us to refer to things beyond themselves—toward which we *have* the phenomenal point of view. Therefore we can abandon it in favor of another, and still be thinking about the same things.

Experience itself, however, does not seem to fit the pattern. The idea of moving from appearance to reality seems to make no sense here. What is the analogue in this case to pursuing a more objective understanding of the same phenomena by abandoning the initial subjective viewpoint toward them in favor of another that is more objective but concerns the same thing?

(continued)

What Is It Like to Be a Bat? (*continued*)

Certainly it *appears* unlikely that we will get closer to the real nature of human experience by leaving behind the particularity of our human point of view and striving for a description in terms accessible to beings that could not imagine what it was like to be us. If the subjective character of experience is fully comprehensible only from one point of view, then any shift to greater objectivity—that is, less attachment to a specific viewpoint—does not take us nearer to the real nature of the phenomenon: it takes us farther away from it.

In a sense, the seeds of this objection to the reducibility of experience are already detectable in successful cases of reduction; for in discovering sound to be, in reality, a wave phenomenon in air or other media, we leave behind one viewpoint to take up another, and the auditory, human, or animal viewpoint that we leave behind remains unreduced. Members of radically different species may both understand the same physical events in objective terms, and this does not require that they understand the phenomenal forms in which those events appear to the senses of members of the other species. Thus it is a condition of their referring to a common reality that their more particular viewpoints are not part of the common reality that they both apprehend. The reduction can succeed only if the species-specific viewpoint is omitted from what is to be reduced.

But while we are right to leave this point of view aside in seeking a fuller understanding of the external world, we cannot ignore it permanently, since it is the essence of the internal world, and not merely a point of view on it. Most of the neobehaviorism of recent philosophical psychology results from the effort to substitute an objective concept of mind for the real thing, in order to have nothing left over which cannot be reduced. If we acknowledge that a physical theory of mind must account for the subjective character of experience, we must admit that no presently available conception gives us a clue how this could be done. The problem is unique. If mental processes are indeed physical processes, then there is something it is like, intrinsically,[11] to undergo certain physical processes. What it is for such a thing to be the case remains a mystery.

What moral should be drawn from these reflections, and what should be done next? It would be a mistake to conclude that physicalism must be false. Nothing is proved by the inadequacy of physicalist hypotheses that assume a faulty objective analysis of mind. It would be truer to say that physicalism is a position we cannot understand because we do not at present have any conception of how it might be true. Perhaps it will be thought unreasonable to require such a conception as a condition of understanding. After all, it might be said, the meaning of physicalism is clear enough: mental states are states of the body; mental events are physical events. We do not know *which* physical states and events they are, but that should not prevent us from understanding the hypothesis. What could be clearer than the words "is" and "are"?

But I believe it is precisely this apparent clarity of the word "is" that is deceptive. Usually, when we are told that X is Y we know *how* it is supposed to be true, but that depends on a conceptual or theoretical background and is not conveyed by the "is" alone. We know how both "X" and "Y" refer, and the kinds of things to which they refer, and we have a rough idea how the two referential paths might converge on a single thing, be it an object, a person, a process, an event, or whatever. But when the two terms of the identification are very disparate it may not be so clear how it could be true. We may not have even a rough idea of how the two referential paths could converge, or what kind of things they might converge on, and a theoretical framework may have to be supplied to enable us to understand this. Without the framework, an air of mysticism surrounds the identification.

This explains the magical flavor of popular presentations of fundamental scientific discoveries, given out as propositions to which one must subscribe without really understanding them. For example, people are now told at an early age that all matter is really energy. But despite the fact that they know what "is" means, most of them never form a conception of what makes this claim true, because they lack the theoretical background.

At the present time the status of physicalism is similar to that which the hypothesis that matter is energy would have had if uttered by a pre-Socratic philosopher. We do not have the beginnings of a conception of how it might be true. In order to understand the hypothesis that a mental event is a physical event, we require more than an understanding of the word "is." The idea of how a mental and a physical term might refer to the same thing is lacking, and the usual analogies with theoretical identification in other fields fail to supply it. They fail because if we construe the reference of mental terms to physical events on the usual model, we either get a reappearance of separate subjective events as the effects through which mental reference to physical events is secured, or else we get a false account of how mental terms refer (for example, a causal behaviorist one).

Strangely enough, we may have evidence for the truth of something we cannot really understand. Suppose a caterpillar is locked in a sterile safe by someone unfamiliar with insect metamorphosis, and weeks later the safe is reopened, revealing a butterfly. If the person knows that the safe has been shut the whole time, he has reason to believe that the butterfly is or was once the caterpillar, without having any idea in what sense this might be so. (One possibility is that the caterpillar contained a tiny winged parasite that devoured it and grew into the butterfly.)

It is conceivable that we are in such a position with regard to physicalism. Donald Davidson has argued that if mental events have physical causes and effects, they must have physical descriptions. He holds that we have reason to believe this even though we do not—and in fact *could* nor—have a general psychophysical theory.[12] His argument applies to intentional mental events, but I think we also have some reason to believe that sensations are physical processes, without being in a position to understand how. Davidson's position is that certain physical events have irreducibly mental properties, and perhaps some view describable in this way is correct. But nothing of which we can now form a conception corresponds to it; nor have we any idea what a theory would be like that enabled us to conceive of it.[13]

Very little work has been done on the basic question (from which mention of the brain can be entirely omitted) whether any sense can be made of experiences' having an objective character at all. Does it make sense, in other words, to ask what my experiences are *really* like, as opposed to how they appear to me? We cannot genuinely understand the hypothesis that their nature is captured in a physical description unless we understand the more fundamental idea that they *have* an objective nature (or that objective processes can have a subjective nature).[14]

I should like to close with a speculative proposal. It may be possible to approach the gap between subjective and objective from another direction. Setting aside temporarily the relation between the mind and the brain, we can pursue a more objective understanding of the mental in its own right. At present we are completely unequipped to think about the subjective character of experience without relying on the imagination—without taking up the point of view of the experiential subject. This should be regarded as a challenge to form new concepts and devise a new method—an objective phenomenology not dependent on empathy or the imagination. Though presumably it would not capture everything, its goal would be to describe, at least in part, the subjective character of experiences in a form comprehensible to beings incapable of having those experiences.

We would have to develop such a phenomenology to describe the sonar experiences of bats; but it would also be possible to begin with humans. One might try, for example, to develop concepts that could be used to explain to a person blind from birth what it was like to see. One would reach a blank wall eventually, but it should be possible to devise a method of expressing in objective terms much more than we can at present, and with much greater precision. The loose intermodal analogies—for example, "Red is like the sound of a trumpet"—which crop up in discussions of this subject are of little use. That should be clear to anyone who has both heard a trumpet and seen red. But structural features of perception might be more accessible to objective description, even though something would be left out. And concepts alternative to those we learn in the first person may enable us to arrive at a kind of understanding even of our own experience which is denied us by the very ease of description and lack of distance that subjective concepts afford.

Apart from its own interest, a phenomenology that is in this sense objective may permit questions about the physical[15] basis of experience to assume a more intelligible form. Aspects of subjective experience that admitted this kind of objective description might be better candidates for objective explanations of a more familiar sort. But whether or not this guess is correct, it seems unlikely that any physical theory of mind can be contemplated until more thought has been given to the general problem of subjective and objective. Otherwise we cannot even pose the mind-body problem without sidestepping it.[16]

(continued)

What Is It Like to Be a Bat? (*continued*)

NOTES

1. Examples are J. J. C. Smart, *Philosophy and Scientific Realism* (London, 1963); David K. Lewis, "An Argument for the Identity Theory," *Journal of Philosophy,* LXIII (1966), reprinted with addenda in David M. Rosenthal, *Materialism & the Mind-Body Problem* (Englewood Cliffs, N.J., 1971); Hilary Putnam, "Psychological Predicates" in Capitan and Merrill, *Art, Mind, & Religion* (Pittsburgh, 1967), reprinted in Rosenthal, *op. cit.,* as "The Nature of Mental States"; D. M. Armstrong, *A Materialist Theory of the Mind* (London, 1968); D. C. Dennett, *Content and Consciousness* (London, 1969). I have expressed earlier doubt in "Armstrong on the Mind," *Philosophical Review,* LXXIX (1970), 394-403; "Brain Bisection and the Unity of Consciousness," *Synthèse,* 22 (1971); and a review of Dennett, *Journal of Philosophy,* LXIX (1972). See also Saul Kripke, "Naming and Necessity" in Davidson and Harman, *Semantics of Natural Language* (Dordrecht, 1972), esp. pp. 334–342; and M. T. Thornton, "Ostensive Terms and Materialism," *The Monist,* 56(1972).
2. Perhaps there could not actually be such robots. Perhaps anything complex enough to behave like a person would have experiences. But that, if true, is a fact which cannot be discovered merely by analyzing the concept of experience.
3. It is not equivalent to that about which we are incorrigible, both because we are not incorrigible about experience and because experience is present in animals lacking language and thought, who have no beliefs at all about their experiences.
4. Cf. Richard Rorty, "Mind-Body Identity, Privacy, and Categories," *The Review of Metaphysics,* XIX (1965), esp. 37–38.
5. By "our own case" I do not mean just "my own case," but rather the mentalistic ideas that we apply unproblematically to ourselves and other human beings.
6. Therefore the analogical form of the English expression "what it is *like*" is misleading. It does not mean "what (in our experience) it *resembles,*" but rather "how it is for the subject himself."
7. Any intelligent extraterrestrial beings totally different from us.
8. It may be easier than I suppose to transcend interspecies barriers with the aid of the imagination. For example, blind people are able to detect objects near them by a form of sonar, using vocal clicks or taps of a cane. Perhaps if one knew what that was like, one could by extension imagine roughly what it was like to possess the much more refined sonar of a bat. The distance between oneself and other persons and other species can fall anywhere on a continuum. Even for other persons the understanding of what it is like to be them is only partial, and when one moves to species very different from oneself, a lesser degree of partial understanding may still be available. The imagination is remarkably flexible. My point, however, is not that we cannot *know* what it is like to be a bat. I am not raising that epistemological problem. My point is rather that even to form a *conception* of what it is like to be a bat (and a fortiori to know what it is like to be a bat) one must take up the bat's point of view. If one can take it up roughly, or partially, then one's conception will also be rough or partial. Or so it seems in our present state of understanding.
9. The problem I am going to raise can therefore be posed even if the distinction between more subjective and more objective descriptions or viewpoints can itself be made only within a larger human point of view. I do not accept this kind of conceptual relativism, but it need not be refuted to make the point that psychophysical reduction cannot be accommodated by the subjective-to-objective model familiar from other cases.
10. The problem is not just that when I look at the 'Mona Lisa,' my visual experience has a certain quality, no trace of which is to be found by someone looking into my brain. For even if he did observe there a tiny image of the 'Mona Lisa,' he would have no reason to identify it with the experience.
11. The relation would therefore not be a contingent one, like that of a cause and its distinct effect. It would be necessarily true that a certain physical state felt a certain way. Saul Kripke *(op cit.)* argues that causal behaviorist and related analyses of the mental fail because they construe, e.g., "pain" as a merely contingent name of pains. The subjective character of an experience ("its immediate phenomenological quality" Kripke calls it [p. 340]) is the essential property left out by such analyses, and the one in virtue of which it is, necessarily, the experience it is. My view is closely related to his. Like Kripke, I find the hypothesis that a certain brain state should *necessarily* have a certain subjective character incomprehensible without further explanation. No such explanation emerges from theories which view the mind-brain relation as contingent, but perhaps there are other alternatives, not yet discovered.

    A theory that explained how the mind-brain relation was necessary would still leave us with Kripke's problem of explaining why it nevertheless appears contingent. That difficulty seems to me surmountable, in the following way. We may imagine something by representing it to ourselves either perceptually, sympathetically, or symbolically. I shall not try to say how symbolic imagination works, but part of what happens in the other two cases is this. To imagine something perceptually, we put ourselves in a conscious state resembling the state we would be in if we perceived it. To imagine something sympathetically, we put ourselves in a conscious state resembling the thing itself. (This method can be used only to imagine mental events and states—our own or another's.) When we try to imagine a mental state occurring without its associated brain state, we first sympathetically imagine the occurrence of the mental state: that is, we put ourselves into a state that resembles it mentally. At the same time, we attempt to perceptually imagine the non-occurrence of the associated physical state, by putting ourselves into another state unconnected with the first: one resembling that which we would be in if we perceived the non-occurrence of the physical state. Where the imagination of physical features is perceptual and the imagination of mental features is sympathetic, it appears, to us that we can imagine any experience occurring without its associated brain state, and vice versa. The relation between them will appear contingent even if it is necessary, because of the independence of the disparate types of imagination.

(Solipsism, incidentally, results if one misinterprets sympathetic imagination as if it worked like perceptual imagination: it then seems impossible to imagine any experience that is not one's own.)

12. See "Mental Events" in Foster and Swanson, *Experience and Theory* (Amherst, 1970); though I don't understand the argument against psychophysical laws.
13. Similar remarks apply to my paper "Physicalism," *Philosophical Review*, LXXIV (1965), 339–356, reprinted with postscript in John O'Connor, *Modern Materialism* (New York, 1969).
14. This question also lies at the heart of the problem of other minds, whose close connection with the mind-body problem is often overlooked. If one understood how subjective experience could have an objective nature, one would understand the existence of subjects other than oneself.
15. I have not defined the term "physical." Obviously it does not apply just to what can be described by the concepts of contemporary physics, since we expect further developments. Some may think there is nothing to prevent mental phenomena from eventually being recognized as physical in their own right. But whatever else may be said of the physical, it has to be objective. So if our idea of the physical ever expands to include mental phenomena, it will have to assign them an objective character—whether or not this is done by analyzing them in terms of other phenomena already regarded as physical. It seems to me more likely, however, that mental-physical relations will eventually be expressed in a theory whose fundamental terms cannot be placed clearly in either category.
16. I have read versions of this paper to a number of audiences, and am indebted to many people for their comments.

Other Minds Are Known by Analogy from One's Own Case
Bertrand Russell

The problem with which we are concerned is the following. We observe in ourselves such occurrences as remembering, reasoning, feeling pleasure, and feeling pain. We think that sticks and stones do not have these experiences, but that other people do. Most of us have no doubt that the higher animals feel pleasure and pain, though I was once assured by a fisherman that "Fish have no sense nor feeling." I failed to find out how he had acquired this knowledge. Most people would disagree with him, but would be doubtful about oysters and starfish. However this may be, common sense admits an increasing doubtfulness as we descend in the animal kingdom, but as regards human beings it admits no doubt.

It is clear that belief in the minds of others requires some postulate that is not required in physics, since physics can be content with a knowledge of structure. My present purpose is to suggest what this further postulate may be.

It is clear that we must appeal to something that may be vaguely called "analogy". The behavior of other people is in many ways analogous in our own, and we suppose that it must have analogous causes. What people say is what we should say if we had certain thoughts, and so we infer that they probably have these thoughts. They give us information which we can sometimes subsequently verify. They behave in ways in which we behave when we are pleased (or displeased) in circumstances in which we should be pleased (or displeased). We may talk over with a friend some incident which we have both experienced, and find that his reminiscences dovetail with our own; this is particularly convincing when he remembers something that we have forgotten but that he recalls to our thoughts. Or again: you set your boy a problem in arithmetic, and with luck

(continued)

Other Minds Are Known by Analogy from One's Own Case (*continued*)

he gets the right answer; this persuades you that he is capable of arithmetical reasoning. There are, in short, very many ways in which my responses to stimuli differ from those of "dead" matter, and in all these ways other people resemble me. As it is clear to me that the causal laws governing my behavior have to do with "thoughts," it is natural to infer that the same is true of the analogous behavior of my friends.

The inference with which we are at present concerned is not merely that which takes us beyond solipsism, by maintaining that sensations have causes about which *something* can be known. This kind of inference . . . suffices for physics. . . . We are concerned now with a much more specific kind of inference, the kind that is involved in our knowledge of the thoughts and feelings of others—assuming that we have such knowledge. It is of course obvious that such knowledge is more or less doubtful. There is not only the general argument that we may be dreaming; there is also the possibility of ingenious automata. There are calculating machines that do sums much better than our schoolboy sons; there are gramophone records that remember impeccably what So-and-so said on such-and-such an occasion; there are people in the cinema who, though copies of real people, are not themselves alive. There is no theoretical limit to what ingenuity could achieve in the ways of producing the illusion of life where in fact life is absent.

But, you will say, in all such cases it was the thoughts of human beings that produced the ingenious mechanism. Yes, but how do you know this? And how do you know that the gramophone does *not* "think"?

There is, in the first place, a difference in the causal laws of observable behavior. If I say to a student, "Write me a paper on Descartes's reasons for believing in the existence of matter," I shall, if he is industrious, cause a certain response. A gramophone record might be so constructed as to respond to this stimulus perhaps better than the student, but if so it would be incapable of telling me anything about any other philosopher, even if I threatened to refuse to give it a degree. One of the most notable peculiarities of human behavior is change of response to a given stimulus. An ingenious person could construct an automaton which would always laugh at his jokes, however often it heard them; but a human being, after laughing a few times, will yawn, and end by saying, "How I laughed the first time I heard that joke."

But the differences in observable behavior between living, and dead matter do not suffice to prove that there are "thoughts" connected with living bodies other than my own. It is probably possible theoretically to account for the behavior of living bodies by purely physical causal laws, and it is probably impossible to refute materialism by external observation alone. If we are to believe that there are thoughts and feelings other than our own, that must be in virtue of some inference in which our own thoughts and feelings are relevant, and such an inference must go beyond what is needed in physics.

I am, of course, not discussing the history of how we come to believe in other minds. We find ourselves believing in them when we first begin to reflect; the thought that Mother may be angry or pleased is one which arises in early infancy. What I am discussing is the possibility of a postulate which shall establish a rational connection between this belief and data, e.g., between the belief "Mother is angry" and the hearing of a loud voice.

The abstract schema seems to be as follows. We know, from observation of ourselves, a causal law of the form "A causes B," where A is a "thought" and B a physical occurrence. We sometimes observe a B when we cannot observe any A; we then infer an unobserved A. For example: I know when I say, "I'm thirsty," I say so, usually, because I am thirsty, and therefore, when I hear the sentence "I'm thirsty" at a time when I am not thirsty, I assume that someone else is thirsty. I assume this more readily if I see before me a hot, drooping body which goes on to say, "I have walked twenty desert miles in this heat with never a drop to drink." It is evident that my confidence in the "inference" is increased by increased complexity in the datum and also by increased certainty of the causal law derived from subjective observation, provided the causal law is such as to account for the complexities of the datum.

It is clear that insofar as plurality of causes is to be suspected, the kind of inference we have been considering is not valid. We are supposed to know "A causes B," and also to know that B has occurred; if this is to justify us in inferring A, we must know that *only* A causes B. Or, if we are content to infer that A is probable, it will suffice if we can know that in most cases it is A that causes B. If you hear thunder without having seen lightning, you confidently infer that there was lightning, because you are convinced that the sort of noise you heard is seldom caused by anything except lightning. As this example shows, our principle is not only employed to establish the existence of other minds but is habitually assumed, though in a less concrete form, in physics. I say "a less concrete form" because unseen lightning is only abstractly similar to seen lightning, whereas we suppose the similarity of other minds to our own to be by no means purely abstract.

Complexity in the observed behavior of another person, when this can all be accounted for by a simple cause such as thirst, increases the probability of the inference by diminishing the probability of some other cause. I think that in ideally favorable circumstances the argument would be formally as follows:

From subjective observation I know that A, which is a thought or feeling, causes B, which is a bodily act, e.g., a statement. I know also that, whenever B is an act of my own body, A is its cause. I now observe an act of the kind B in a body not my own, and I am having no thought or feeling of the kind A. But I still believe, on the basis of self-observation, that only A can cause B; I therefore infer that there was an A. which caused B, though it was not an A that I could observe. On this ground I infer that other people's bodies are associated with minds, which resemble main in proportion as then bodily behavior resembles my own.

In practice the exactness and certainty of the above statement must be softened. We cannot be sure that in our subjective experience, A is the only cause of B. And even if A is the only cause of B in our experience, how can we know that this holds outside our experience? It is not necessary that we should know this with any certainty; it is enough it is highly probable. It is the assumption of probability in such cases is our postulate. The postulate may therefore be stated as follows:

> If, whenever we can observe whether A and B are present or absent, we find that every case of B has an A as a causal antecedent, then it is probable that most B's have A as causal antecedents, even in cases where observation does not enable us to know whether A is present or not.

This postulate, if accepted, justifies the inference to other minds, as well as many other inferences that are made unreflectingly by common sense.

Chapter 3
Religion

How shall we begin to answer the important question "Is there a God?" Do we assume that there is one and then try to prove it? Do we assume that there is no God and argue that we are right? Do we start by being noncommittal and seek out the truth whatever it might be? While this last approach sounds the most objective, religion and objectivity have not always been the best companions. Many people, if not most, are born into a family or a culture that already assigns the particular faith that they will follow. Some individuals (though not many in relation to the sheer numbers of believers) may convert from one religion to another on the basis of some personal dissatisfaction or because of a desire to marry outside their own faith. Others may reject the concept that there is, was, or could be a supernatural being (or beings) that play some role in the affairs of humankind. Still others might shrug and say, "If there is such a being, there is no way to know anything more about what He or She or It or They are like so their existence is irrelevant to me." Finally, if there is no evidence to support one's position—whatever one's position is—is one willing to admit that the argument is false, or does one accept without reason and instead rely on faith?

While working on this book, I was sitting in a café in Austria having an espresso with a friend. When asked what I was working on, I said "I'm studying the proofs of God's existence." Taken aback with surprise, my friend remarked: "There are proofs?!" to which I replied: "Merely saying that it is a proof does not make it one." Infact there are at least three famous "proofs" of a Judeo-Christian God's existence. St. Anselm's (1033–1109) Ontological Argument maintains that God must exist by His very nature. St. Aquinas's (1224–1274) Five Ways tells us (among other things) that we must avoid an infinite regress of causation so there must be a first cause and that first cause is God. Then there is William Paley's (1743–1805) proof, which offers what is probably the most popular argument called the Teleological Argument for God's existence. *Teleos* means "design" and thus this argument is also known as "The Argument from Design." Paley argued that if there is design in the world, then there must be a designer and since there is design in the world, it follows that there must be a God.

The first flaw in the Teleological Argument concerns the difficulty of trying to move from a conclusion of there being a supernatural designer to identifying this particular designer as the Judeo-Christian God. Even if there is a divine designer, one would also have to show that it is not one of the many other possible candidates. Why not have a whole collection of deities responsible for different parts of the world as the ancient Greeks and Romans did? Maybe it was an alien architect who moved on to other universes to do other designs? In other words, the Teleological Argument does not justify accepting one organized religion over another.

Another flaw is that although we may perceive design in the world, this does not necessarily entail that it is really there. In *Cast Away*, Chuck Noland survives a horrific plane crash and washes up on a deserted island. There are no signs of anyone else on the island, so he lives as a modern day Robinson Crusoe. One day, flotsam from the downed plane comes ashore. Included in the assortment is a soccer ball. After cutting himself, Chuck accidentally places his bloodied palm on the ball. His bloodied print looks somewhat like a face and so Chuck names his new "companion" Wilson (after the brand name of the ball). The fact that Chuck sees a face in his palm print and that we also recognize it as one is something that seems to be a human trait. We see patterns and designs everywhere, even when there are none. A painter paints an abstract image and people see it as a portrait. People see elephants in cloud formations and they see the face of Virgin Mary in burned grilled cheese sandwiches. While I can safely claim "the hat *appears* red to me," I cannot just assume that the hat *is* red. The former statement can be used as justification for the latter, but it may simply be the case that I am looking at a white hat in a red lit room. In other words, I could be wrong and there could be a different explanation. After satellite photographs of Mars were taken in 1976, many people saw what they described as a human face on the planet. Some went further and suggested that since it looks like a face, then there must have been someone who put it there. Of course, the fact that it looked *human* should have been our first reason for being skeptical; the second reason was that on another satellite flyby the face was shown to be a series of hills. Indeed, what would be the reason for aliens to carve a human face that could only be recognized when looked at from a vast distance and angle? So strong was the public fascination with this Martian image that it formed the basis for the movie *Mission to Mars*.

Design does not entail intentionality. We know from past experience that soccer balls are objects that people make and soccer balls have a specific design that serves a special function or purpose. By definition, to find a soccer ball (and not just something that can be *used* as a soccer ball) growing in nature is impossible. While as moviegoers we might have been surprised that *Cast Away's* Chuck finds a soccer ball on the island, we would be even more surprised if he found a palm tree that grew soccer balls instead of coconuts. Still, things in nature appear to have functions or purposes as well. Hands allow us to pick up things such as fruits and vegetables. Fruits and vegetables provide us with nutrition. Rain makes these plants grow and so on.

168 Chapter 3 • Religion

Some people would claim that all these things have purposes. But just because we *give* an item a purpose does not mean it was created by someone for that purpose. If Chuck found a coconut and started to kick it around like a soccer ball, *he* would have given it its purpose. *He* would have found a use for it. That we find design and function in some natural object does not mean that it has a purposeful design built into it.

If we are to identify Paley's designer as the God of Judeo-Christianity, then there seems to be strong evidence to suggest that either God is not omnipotent (all-powerful) or if He is omnipotent, then He is not omni-benevolent (all good). The reason for this is simple. When we looks at things in the universe, we note that some of them suffer from serious design flaws. Just examining our own bodies we see numerous weaknesses and have had to use our own intellectual powers and abilities to compensate for flaws such as poor eyesight, failing joints, and natural diseases. According to this particular criticism, either God could not make His designs perfect, or He did not want to. If He *could* not then He is flawed and if He *would* not them perfect then he is equally flawed. One might reply that He gave us other means such as our intellect to combat these shortcomings. But while our intellect has allowed us to make eyeglasses, our intellect has not solved all of the problems we face in the world that He created. Thus, theists continue to struggle with the religious doctrine of an all-perfect God existing harmoniously with the apparent imperfections in the world.

Nowhere does the struggle for resolution become more disconcerting than with what is known as *Theodicy*, or the problem of evil. The Judeo-Christian God is defined as being omniscient, omnipresent, omnipotent, and morally perfect. Yet innocent children die—sometimes at the hands of other people yes, but also by disease, famine, and other natural (i.e., not human caused) disasters. There are regular reports of the faithful who are trampled to death by crowds of fellow pilgrims or who are swept away by mudslides as they make their way to church. Their mourners rightfully question whether their God is truly all good, truly all powerful, or truly *is*. Accordingly, a theist and an atheist might be engaged in the following spirited discussion about the role of evil in the world.

There is no evil in the world. There are only events. And we, in our limited capacity, make judgments about them. We say "this is good" and "that is bad," but things just are.

But if there is truly no evil in the world, then why would a good and loving God deceive us into thinking there is?

Perhaps he wants us to learn which things we should do. In order for there to be good, there must be evil or the appearance of evil. For how else can we tell what a thing is unless we also know that thing's opposite?

Not all things have opposites. I know what a horse is but not because I know its opposite. What would be the opposite of a horse?

Horses do not have opposites, things like colors or emotions do.

I understand that black is the opposite of white because black is the absence of color and white is all colors combined. But instead of creating black, why could He not just give us white and every other color: yellow, blue, green and so on? In other words, if God was all powerful, could He not just give us one without requiring the other? Could He give us the good without the evil? Or if He must provide contrast, then how about just providing us with an option between doing something that is really, really good and something that is less good but not evil? For example, giving $1,000 to charity as compared with only giving $100.

But in order for people to be good and be held responsible for it, they must be tempted by or have the possibility of doing evil.

Yet this only accounts for a small portion of the evil in the world. Earthquakes are not caused by people.

But earthquakes give people an opportunity to do good, to show their love and care for their neighbor.

But then this means that God is trying to teach us a lesson—but for what reason? Why do we need to learn a lesson? Surely events like tsunamis, floods, and human-created events like the Holocaust that result in thousands if not millions of lives lost is far too high a price to pay for the rest of us just to learn a lesson. With the Holocaust, that is a lesson that continues to be ignored.

That is our fault, not His.

But He made us!

And so it goes . . .

There are numerous fiction and non-fiction films that one could cite for examples of the problem of evil—all one has to do is think of movies that do not have neat and tidy happy endings. Films can represent evil in different ways. Take for example the 1970s thriller *The Odessa File*. It is based on the novel of the same name that intertwines fictional accounts with real people and events. The main character Eduard Roschmann is based on the actual Austrian SS officer. The protagonist, Peter Miller, is a twenty-nine-year old German who is given the diary of a Jewish man who survived the Riga concentration camp. Miller reads:

> *Roschmann had a hobby.*
> *He liked to destroy human beings.*
> *First their soul, then their body.*
> *Sometimes Roschmann amused himself . . .*
> *by kicking those about to die*
> *as they huddled together naked . . .*
> *stripped of dignity and of all hope.*
> *He liked watching the dogs feed on them*
> *while they were still breathing . . .*
> *I saw him go and I was determined*
> *one day to bring him to justice.*
> *But now I know I never will.*
> *I bear no hatred nor bitterness*
> *towards the German people.*
> *Peoples are not evil.*
> *Only individuals are evil.*
> *If, after my death,*
> *this diary should be found and read . . .*
> *will some kind friend*
> *please say Kaddish for me?*

After reading this document, Miller decides bring Commandant Roschmann to justice. Miller finds the notorious "Butcher of Riga" at the end of the movie, yet two startling things occur. First, the audience discovers that the reason Miller went after Roschmann was not because of the thousands of people he murdered but because of just one selfish one: Miller's own father was a German soldier whom Roschmann had killed during an argument. Second, the real Roschmann escaped justice and fled to South America. In the real world, thousands died under this one man and yet he, like thousands of other members of the SS, lived out his life in freedom after the war.

Although we can easily point to movies about serial killers[1] or major disasters,[2] evil can also be quiet, subtle, and even polite.[3] Evil need not be something spectacular. It is those personal instances in life that can make even the most devout question their relationship with their God. Consider this exchange between Martin Luther, founder of Protestantism, and his spiritual father in the film *Luther*:

LUTHER   I live in terror of judgment.
        And you think self-hatred will save you?
LUTHER   Have you ever dared to think that God is not just?
        He has us born tainted by sin, then He's angry with us all our lives for our faults, this righteous Judge . . . who damns us . . . threatening us with the fires of hell. I know. I know I'm evil to think it.
MENTOR   You're not evil. You're just not honest. God isn't angry with you.
        You are angry with God.
LUTHER   I wish there were no God.
MENTOR   Martin, what is it you seek?
LUTHER   A merciful God. A God whom I can love. A God who loves me.

It is relatively easy for a theist to believe in the goodness of God when there are obvious examples of goodness, but when life becomes difficult and matters seem contradictory to one's understanding of God, then it becomes a challenge to remain faithful. In the selection by Søren Kierkegaard, he argues that faith is not easy. He complains about those individuals who assume faith can be created in a matter of days as opposed to a lifetime. From the outside a person of faith looks just like you and me, but on the inside they have given themselves over to faith. Religious doubt seeps in when life does not seem to be going well, but it is at this time that a person who has surrendered to God *knows* the truth. It is this leap of faith that allows that person to continue on in hope and in trust in his or her God.

For many, the question of whether there is a God is the most important question of all. Indeed, it gives some meaning to their lives. Should we ignore our ability to use reason when faced with such an important area of inquiry? Should we step out of the

---

[1] For example, there is the seemingly infinite number of killers who attack teenagers in such films as *Halloween* or *Friday the 13th*. But for films based on or inspired by real "evil," see: *From Hell, Summer of Sam, The Boston Strangler, Henry: Portrait of a Serial Killer, Texas Chain Saw Massacre, Psycho, Silence of the Lambs, Helter Skelter, In Cold Blood, Badlands, Monster,* or *Zodiac*.
[2] For example, there are the classic disaster films of the 1970s such as *The Towering Inferno* and *The Poseidon Adventure*, to the localized natural disasters such as *Twister* and *Volcano* to the planet-wide disaster movies of *Deep Impact, Armageddon,* and *The Day After Tomorrow*.

[3] Consider the Nazi dentist in *The Marathon Man*, or Professor Umbridge in *Harry Potter and the Order of the Phoenix* both of whom are excruciatingly well-mannered while inflicting pain onto others.

darkness and into the light without first trying to see where the different paths may lead? Should we deny or be denied the opportunity to find our own way and our own reasons for saying "yes" or "no"? In *The Name of the Rose,* Father William of Baskerville is struck by this tragedy when he learns that all sorts of books that raise troubling questions about faith have been hidden or even denied to exist.

> BROTHER WILLIAM How many more rooms? How many more books?
>
> No one should be forbidden to consult these books.
>
> ADSO Perhaps they're thought to be too precious, too fragile.
>
> BROTHER WILLIAM No, it's not that, Adso. It's because they often contain a wisdom that's different from ours . . . and ideas that could encourage us to doubt . . . the infallibility of the word of God.
>
> ADSO Master?
>
> BROTHER WILLIAM And doubt, Adso, is the enemy of faith.

Doubt may be the enemy of faith, but should we ignore it or embrace it? In *Contact,* one of the smartest science fiction films to come along in recent memory, aliens have sent plans to earth for building a machine that is capable of bringing the two species together. Ellie, who lost her father while young, is the hard scientist, while her potential love interest Joss is a religious leader. In the following excerpt, the issue of reason versus faith moves from grand talk of science versus religion to more personal and intimate realizations about what one believes.

> **Int. Another Part of Museum—Night**
> *Their voices and FOOTSTEPS ECHO as they walk past old spacecraft. They sip their champagne.*
>
> JOSS . . . What I'm curious about are the wilderness years. You're out there all alone, no money, mocked by the skeptics. It must have taken tremendous faith.
>
> ELLIE I'd say logic more than faith. The odds were on my side.
>
> JOSS And what would you have done if the odds had gone against you?
>
> ELLIE I guess I would've felt sorry for the universe.
>
> JOSS Spoken like a true believer.
>
> ELLIE What about you? Doesn't all of this shake your faith at all?
>
> JOSS How do you mean?
>
> ELLIE Well it's been a while, but I don't recall the Bible saying too much about alien civilizations.
>
> JOSS (thinks, then) "My father's house has many mansions."
>
> ELLIE Very smooth. It's Palmer, right? Where I came from a palmer was a person who cheated at cards. (as Joss laughs) Really though . . . the Bible describes a God who watches over one tiny world a few thousand years old. I look out there and see a universe of hundreds of billions of galaxies, each with hundreds of billions of stars . . . I mean burn me for a heretic, but your God seems awfully small.
>
> *Joss looks at her—challenged, intrigued. Slowly:*
>
> JOSS Who was it who said—it was a scientist I think—that one's sophistication is determined by the ability to tolerate paradox—to hold contradictory ideas at the same time . . .
>
> *They approach a circular brass railing surrounding a circular mosaic below; at its center is a Foucault pendulum; a basketball-sized iron sphere suspended from the ceiling. They lean on the railing.*
>
> JOSS . . . which I suppose is as good a definition of faith as any. (getting an idea; he smiles) Care to test yours?
>
> *He takes her champagne glass, sets it down on the floor alongside his, then climbs under the rail. At her surprise—*
>
> JOSS It's okay. I'm a preacher.
>
> *He offers her his hand. She takes it, climbs under the railing. Joss helps her down into the circular space below.*
>
> JOSS Your "faith" tells you that the distance a pendulum swings from the vertical can never get bigger, only smaller.
>
> ELLIE That's not faith, it's physics. The second law of thermodynamics.

Joss places his arms around the metal ball and walks it over to the outer rim of the circle, right in front of Ellie's nose.

JOSS   And you believe this law with all your heart and soul.

ELLIE   And mind, yes. What are you—

JOSS   So if I let the pendulum go, when it swings back you wouldn't flinch.

Ellie pauses. Then, almost curiously.

ELLIE   No.

Joss lets go. We see the ball fall away and reach the opposite railing. As it slows and then reverses direction it appears to approach much faster than we expected.

JOSS   Don't lean forward. Not even a hair.

As it careens towards her, the ball grows alarmingly in size. We understand completely when the pendulum almost reaches her and she instinctively moves. But Ellie can't believe it.

ELLIE   I flinched.

JOSS   Only a tiny bit. Even the most devout believer is allowed a little doubt.

ELLIE   That's not doubt. That's four hundred years of science fighting a billion years of instinct.

(studying him)

I always wondered what you religious types did with your free time.

JOSS   Now you know.

Joss has just shown Ellie (and us) that even though she might claim to be comfortable with certain scientific truths, doubt remains. Furthermore, doubt is not a bad thing to hold on to since it allows us to explore our own beliefs with greater objectivity. But what about the "truth of science" versus the "faith of religion"? Consider Joss and Ellie's next exchange:

Ext. National Science Museum—Night

Stars shine down as Ellie and Joss walk along the portico. The party continues inside. The mood is subdued, intimate.

JOSS   . . . It's an old story. I grew up in South Boston, more or less on the streets. By the time I was thirteen I'd tried my first hit of heroin, by fifteen I'd stopped using but I was dealing full-time. By the time I was nineteen I decided I didn't want to live any more, at least not in a world like that. One day I got on a bus; I got as far as Ohio before my money ran out, and after that I just kept walking. Didn't eat, didn't sleep . . . just walked. I ended up collapsing in a wheat field. There was a storm . . . I woke up . . . (beat) And that's about as far as words'll go.

ELLIE   Can you try?

JOSS   I had . . . an experience. Of belonging. Of unconditional love. And for the first time in my life I wasn't terrified, and I wasn't alone.

ELLIE   (delicately) And there's no chance you had this experience simply because some part of you needed to have it?

JOSS   Look, I'm a reasonable person, and reasonably intelligent. But this experience went beyond both. For the first time I had to consider the possibility that intellect, as wonderful as it is, is not the only way of comprehending the universe. That it was too small and inadequate a tool to deal with what it was faced with.

ELLIE   (a beat, then softly) You may not believe this . . . but there's a part of me that wants more than anything to believe in your God. To believe that we're all here for a purpose, that all this . . . means something. But it's because that part of me wants it so badly that I'm so stubborn about making sure it isn't just self-delusion. Of course I want to know God if there is one . . . but it has to be real. Unless I have proof how can I be sure?

JOSS   Do you love your parents?

ELLIE   (startled) I never knew my mother. My father died when I was nine.

JOSS   Did you love him?

ELLIE   (softly) Yes. Very much.

JOSS   Prove it.

Ellie stops and looks at him, truly disarmed.

Joss's point is simple: Being a scientist does not mean one does not have faith in some things that cannot be proven, nor does it mean that one always trusts what one takes for granted.

Still, faith and trust will take us only so far. Imagine someone tells you that she saw a man come back to life. While there have been stories of people awakening from years of being in a coma, or being revived shortly after drowning in cold water, this man came back to life after been dead and buried. What are you more likely to believe, that the sincere and honest eyewitness is somehow mistaken or that even though there has never been a single verified account of this ever happening in the history of humankind, the eyewitness report is true? In one of the readings in this chapter, philosopher David Hume poses a similar query concerning miracles. Who is telling us the miraculous story may influence our judgment, but one must still objectively consider the probability and possibility of the situation. For example, we would not be justified in believing the story if it came from the mouth of the always exaggerating Chunk in *The Goonies*.

> CHUNK   (Outside, in background) Hey guys, I just got the best . . . you're not gonna believe. (shouting) Hey you guys, you gotta let me in.
>
> CHUNK   I just saw the most amazing thing in my entire life.
>
> CHUNK   Listen, okay. You guys will never believe me. There was two cop cars, okay. And they were chasing this four wheel deal, it was this real neat ORV, and there were bullets flying all over the place. It was the most amazing thing I ever saw!
>
> MIKEY   More amazing than the time Michael Jackson came over to your house to use the bathroom?
>
> BRAND   More amazing than the time you saved those old people from that nursing home fire, right?
>
> MOUTH   Yeah, and I bet it was even more amazing than the time you ate your weight in Godfather's Pizza, right?
>
> CHUNK   Okay Brand, Michael Jackson didn't come over to my house, to use the bathroom. But his sister did!

But what if the report of something miraculous came from Ellie the hard-nosed scientist in *Contact*?

> *Every corner of the cavernous Senate Chamber is jammed with media, politicians, onlookers. The world stage. The big show.*
>
> *The International Committee is composed of eight men and two women, including Kitz. Occupying the center seat is the COMMITTEE CHAIRMAN, An Asian American Senator in his sixties.*
>
> *Sitting all by herself at a long table opposite them, Ellie looks very small and alone.*
>
> SENATOR   You were in the machine for seven minutes, thirty-five seconds, is that correct, Doctor?
>
> ELLIE   Earth time, yes.
>
> SENATOR   (pausing) Earth time.
>
> ELLIE   (a deep breath) Senator . . . I believe I traveled through a series of wormholes. Wormholes are a phenomenon deduced by Einstein; they're essentially tears in the fabric of space/time. Because of the effects of relativity what I experienced as a period of approximately eighteen hours passed almost instantaneously on Earth. To you I seemed to depart and arrive back at the same moment.
>
> KITZ   Doctor, isn't it true that wormholes are merely predictions of relativity theory? That there's no evidence they actually exist?
>
> *Ellie hesitates. Looks up at Joss in the gallery. Then:*
>
> ELLIE   There is no direct evidence, no.
>
> KITZ   And current theory holds that to sustain the sort of wormholes you're talking about, even for a fraction of a second, would require more energy than our sun produces in a year, is that correct?
>
> ELLIE   I don't have the figures in front of me, but yes, that sounds about right.
>
> KITZ   In fact, by all the laws of physics we know what you claim to have experienced is simply impossible.
>
> ELLIE   (beat, then, softly) By our standards . . . yes.
>
> *Palmer Joss, sitting in the gallery, closes his eyes.*
>
> SAME SCENE—LATER
>
> *The Chairman flips slowly through a file as he questions Ellie.*
>
> CHAIRMAN   . . . And this is how the extraterrestrial presented himself to you? As your father?

ELLIE   Yes, sir.

CHAIRMAN   He died . . . (looks at file) . . . in 1972.

ELLIE   Yes, sir.

CHAIRMAN   (pausing) Dr. Arroway, do you think it's possible you had some kind of . . . delusional episode.

Joss leans forward in his chair.

ELLIE   Is it possible . . .?

CHAIRMAN   All the elements are there. A woman, orphaned young, under a great deal of stress. The failure of a project she's staked her self-worth and very sense of identity on—induces a fantasy of reuniting with her "father in heaven" as it were. Is it possible?

Ellie is silent.

KITZ   Please answer the question, Doctor.

ELLIE   (a long silence) Is it possible. Yes. But—

KITZ   Thank you, Doctor. Now—

ELLIE   (overriding him) —but I don't believe it to be the truth.

CHAIRMAN   (peering at her; intrigued) You don't believe it to be . . . tell me something, Doctor. Why do you think they would go to all this trouble . . . bring you tens of thousands of light years, and then send you home without a shred of proof? Sort of bad form, wouldn't you say? What was their intent?

ELLIE   (hesitates) I don't know. Ultimately their motives may be as incomprehensible as their technology.

The crowd murmurs. Committee members exchange glances.

CHAIRMAN   (sigh) Dr. Arroway, you come before us with no evidence. No records, no artifacts—only a story that—to put it mildly—strains credibility. Over two trillion dollars was spent, hundreds of lives were lost, many more may be in jeopardy due to the almost incalculable worldwide psychological impact . . . Are you going to sit there and tell us that we should simply take this all on faith?

The word rings out like a shot. Silence.

KITZ   Answer the question, Doctor. As a scientist—can you prove any of this?

JOSS   Holding his breath.

ELLIE   (closes her eyes. Finally, almost inaudibly):

The room is silent. Almost gently:

KITZ   So why don't you admit what by your own standards must be the truth: that this experience simply didn't happen.

ELLIE   (pauses, then, simply) Because I can't.

The crowd reacts.

Ellie looks up to the gallery . . . and finds Joss.

As she speaks with great emotion and restraint, she seems to be talking directly to him.

ELLIE   I had . . . an experience. I can't prove it. I can't even explain it. All I can tell you is that everything I know as a human being, everything I am—tells me that it was real.

The room grows quiet.

ELLIE   (softly) I was given something wonderful. Something that changed me. A vision of the universe that made it overwhelmingly clear just how tiny and insignificant—and at the same time how rare and precious we all are. A vision . . . that tells us we belong to something greater than ourselves . . . that we're not—that none of us—is alone.

Joss is moved beyond words.

Ellie looks lovingly at Palmer . . . then shifts her gaze to Michael Kitz. (Softly)

ELLIE   I wish I could share it. I wish everyone, if only for a moment—could feel that sense of awe, and humility . . . and hope. That continues to be my wish.

Although Ellie is clearly more trustworthy than Chunk, she is still unable to convince others of the truth because she has no proof other than her singular experience. But on a personal level how important is it that others accept a person's most intimate beliefs? Should the doubt of others in the absence of objective verification shake one's deeply held conviction? Reason tells us that what is more probable is more justified but even so, that something is highly improbable does not mean it is impossible.

Ellie has a choice to make. She can either believe or not believe. As William James notes in his article included here, if you are stranded in a snow storm and you come across two paths—one leads to safety and the other leads to doom—you must still choose. For if you stay put you will certainly freeze to death. So too it is with theists who are put in situations where their faith is challenged by argument or by evidence. They must choose.

One reason to choose to believe is on account of personal salvation. If you believe that God will save you if you believe in Him, then it would seem to follow that you should believe. For if you believe in God and He does not exist, then what has this cost you in comparison with the alternative? This argument is known as Pascal's Wager. Blaise Pascal (1623–1662) argues that it is in a person's best interests to believe in God rather than not believe. If you believe and there is no God, you might lose a bit of extra sleep on the holy days, but this is nothing of real significance when there is the possibility of everlasting life. If there is a God, you "win"; if not, then your losses are minimal if at all.

Critics charge that accepting the wager is selfish and is not in keeping with the whole point of religious belief. Moreover, what if God gets annoyed at you for believing in Him because you think you'll be better off in the end? Does that sound like someone who is worthy of salvation? Besides if a non-believer is a morally good person, why would a morally praiseworthy God deny him or her salvation?

Still it remains a huge step to go from believing in the existence of a deity to following a specific religion. Is there only one right religion and all the others are wrong? Are some religions closer to the truth than others? Should we should adopt John Hick's position and argue for religious pluralism? In simple terms, religious pluralism is the view that while there may be different and diverse religions, they all refer to the same ultimate reality. Thus in this interpretation, there are many different paths that lead to the same destination. For example, many major religions share a common moral teaching akin to The Golden Rule.

Judaism: "What is hateful to you, do not to your fellow man. This is the law: all the rest is commentary."[4]

Islam: "None of you [truly] believes until he wishes for his brother what he wishes for himself."[5]

Hinduism: "This is the sum of duty: do not do to others what would cause pain if done to you.[6]

Confucianism: "Do not do to others what you do not want them to do to you"[7]

Christianity: "And as ye would that men should do to you, do ye also to them likewise."[8]

Buddhism: "Hurt not others in ways that you yourself would find hurtful."[9]

The pluralist approach sounds promising and encourages tolerance; however critics will point out that the major religions are incompatible or inconsistent with each other in terms of their basic epistemological, social, political, ethical, and metaphysical leanings. Perhaps then the different faiths are all justified in their quarrels and disagreements as they seek to discover the truth, or perhaps we are justified in rejecting them all completely.

---

[4] Talmud, Shabbat 31a.
[5] Number 13 of Imam "Al-Nawawi's Forty Hadiths."
[6] Mahabharata 5:1517.
[7] Analects 15:23.
[8] Luke 6:31 (King James Version).
[9] Udana-Varga 5:1.

Films Cited

Armageddon. Dir. Michael Bay. Perfs. Bruce Willis, Billy Bob Thorton. Film. Touchstone Pictures. 1998.

Badlands. Dir. Terrence Malick. Perfs. Martin Sheen, Sissy Spacek. Film. Badlands Company. 1973.

Boston Strangler, The. Dir. Richard Fleischer. Perfs. Tony Curtis, Henry Fonda. Film. Twentieth Century–Fox Film Corporation. 1968.

Cast Away. Dir. Robert Zemekis. Perfs. Tom Hanks, Paul Sanchez, Lari White. Film. DreamWorks SKG. 2000.

Contact. Dir. Robert Zemeckis. Perfs. Jena Malone, David Morse, Jodie Foster. Film. Warner Bros. Pictures. 1997.

Day After Tomorrow, The. Dir. Roland Emmerich. Perfs. Dennis Quaid, Jake Gyllenhaal. Film. Twentieth Century Fox Film Corporation. 2004.

Deep Impact. Dir. Mimi Leder. Perfs. Robert Duvall, Téa Leoni. Film. Paramount Pictures. 1998.

Friday the 13th. Dir. Sean S. Cunningham. Perfs. Betsy Palmer, Adrienne King. Film. Georgetown Productions. 1980.

From Hell. Dir. Albert Hughes and Allen Hughes. Perfs. Johnny Depp, Heather Graham. Film. Twentieth Century Fox Film Corporation. 2001.

Goonies, The. Dir. Richard Dormer. Perfs. Sean Astin, Josh Brolin. Film. Amblin Entertainment. 1985.

Halloween. Dir. John Carpenter. Perfs. Donald Pleasence, Jamie Lee Curtis. Film. Compass International Pictures. 1978.

Harry Potter and the Order of the Phoenix. Dir. David Yates. Perfs. Daniel Radcliffe, Emma Watson. Film. Warner Bros. Pictures. 2007.

Helter Skelter. Dir. Tom Gries. Perfs. George DiCenzo, Steve Railsback. Film. Lorimar Productions. 1976.

Henry: Portrait of a Serial Killer. Dir. John McNaughton. Perfs. Mary Demas, Michael Rooker. Film. Malijack Productions. 1986.

In Cold Blood. Dir. Richard Brooks. Perfs. Robert Blake, Scott Wilson. Film. Columbia Pictures Corporation. 1967.

Luther. Dir. Eric Till. Perfs. Joseph Fiennes, Jonathan Firth. Film. Eikon Film. 2003.

Marathon Man, The. Dir. John Schiesinger. Perfs. Dustin Hoffman, Laurence Olivier. Film. Gelderse Maatschappij N.V. 1976.

Monster. Dir. Patty Jenkins. Perfs. Charlize Theron, Christina Ricci. Media 8 Entertainment. 2003.

Name of the Rose, The. Dir. Jean-Jacques Annaud. Perfs. Sean Connery, Christian Slater. Film. Cristaldifilm. 1986.

Odessa File, The. Dir. Ronald Neame. Perfs. Jon Voight, Maximilian Schell. Film. John Woolf Productions. 1974.

Poseidon Adventure, The. Dir. Ronald Neame. Perfs. Gene Hackman, Ernest Borgnine. Film. Irwin Allen Production. 1972.

Psycho. Dir. Alfred Hitchcock. Perfs. Anthony Perkins, Janet Leigh. Film. Shamley Productions. 1960.

Silence of the Lambs. Dir. Jonathan Demme. Perfs. Jodie Foster, Anthony Hopkins. Film. Orion Pictures Corporation. 1991.

Summer of Sam. Dir. Spike Lee. Perfs. John Leguizamo, Adrien Brody. Film. 40 Acres & A Mule Filmworks. 1999.

Texas Chain Saw Massacre. Dir. Tobe Hooper. Perfs. Marilyn Burns, Allen Danziger. Film. Vortex. 1974.

Towering Inferno, The. Dir. John Guillermin, Irwin Allen. Perfs. Steve McQueen, Paul Newman. Film. Irwin Allen Productions. 1974.

Twister. Dir. Jan de Bont. Perfs. Helen Hunt, Bill Paxton. Film. Warner Bros. Pictures. 1996.

Volcano. Dir. Mick Jackson. Perfs. Tommy Lee Jones, Anne Heche. Film. Donner/Shuler-Donner Productions. 1997.

Zodiac. Dir. David Fincher. Perfs. Jake Gyllenhaal, Mark Ruffalo. Film. Warner Bros. Pictures. 2007.

ADDITIONAL MOVIES FOR FURTHER VIEWING

(For a comprehensive listing of movies and themes, please consult the online appendix.)

1. *Book of Life, The*—Good versus Evil
2. *Devil's Playground, The*—Choosing one's religion
3. *Dogma*—Doubt
4. *Dogville*—Religion and morality
5. *Kadosh*—Ultra Orthodox Judaism
6. *Kingdom of Heaven*—Clash of religions
7. *Life is Beautiful*—Problem of Evil
8. *Mission, The*—Socio-politics and religion
9. *Passion of the Christ, The*—Sacrifice and suffering of Jesus
10. *Third Miracle, The*—Miracles

Ontological Argument
St. Anselm

Chapter II
Truly there is a God, although the fool hath said in his heart, There is no God.

AND So, Lord, do thou, who dost give understanding to faith, give me, so far as thou knowest it to be profitable, to understand that thou art as we believe; and that thou art that which we believe. And, indeed, we believe that thou art a being than which nothing greater can be conceived. Or is there no such, nature, since the fool hath said in his heart, there is no God? (Psalms xiv. I). But, at any rate, this very fool, when he hears of this being of which I speak—a being than which nothing greater can be conceived—understands what he hears, and what he understands is in his understanding; although he does not understand it to exist.

For, it is one thing for an object to be in the understanding, and another to understand that the object exists. When a painter first conceives of what he will afterwards perform, he has it in his understanding, but he does not yet understand it to be, because he has not yet performed it. But after he has made the painting, he both has it in his understanding, and he understands that it exists, because he has made it.

Hence, even the fool is convinced that something exists in the understanding, at least, than which nothing greater can be conceived. For, when he hears of this, he understands it. And whatever is understood, exists in the understanding. And assuredly that, than which nothing greater can be

(continued)

Ontological Argument (*continued*)

conceived, cannot exist in the understanding alone. For, suppose it exists in the understanding alone: then it can be conceived to exist in reality; which is greater.

Therefore, if that, than which nothing greater can be conceived, exists in the understanding alone, the very being, than which nothing greater can be conceived, is one, than which a greater can be conceived. But obviously this is impossible. Hence, there is no doubt that there exists a being, than which nothing greater can be conceived, and it exists both in the understanding and in reality.

Chapter III

God cannot be conceived not to exist.—God is that, than which nothing greater can be conceived.—That which can be conceived not to exist is not God.

AND it assuredly exists so truly that it cannot be conceived not to exist. For, it is possible to conceive of a being which cannot be conceived not to exist; and this is greater than one which can be conceived not to exist. Hence, if that, than which nothing greater can be conceived, can be conceived not to exist, it is not that, than which nothing greater can be conceived. But this is an irreconcilable contradiction. There is, then, so truly a being than which nothing greater can be conceived to exist, that it cannot even be conceived not to exist; and this being thou art, O Lord, our God.

So truly, therefore, dost thou exist, O Lord, my God, that thou canst not be conceived not to exist; and rightly. For, if a mind could conceive of a being better than thee, the creature would rise above the Creator; and this is most absurd. And, indeed, whatever else there is, except thee alone, can be conceived not to exist. To thee alone, therefore, it belongs to exist more truly than all other beings, and hence in a higher degree than all others. For, whatever else exists does not exist so truly, and hence in a less degree it belongs to it to exist. Why, then, has the fool said in his heart, there is no God (Psalms xiv. I), since it is so evident, to a rational mind, that thou dost exist in the highest degree of all? Why, except that he is dull and a fool?

Chapter IV

How the fool has said in his heart what cannot be conceived.—A thing may be conceived in two ways: (1) when the word signifying it is conceived; (2) when the thing itself is understood. As far as the word goes, God can be conceived not to exist; in reality he cannot.

BUT how has the fool said in his heart what he could not conceive; or how is it that he could not conceive what he said in his heart? since it is the same to say in the heart, and to conceive.

But, if really, nay, since really, he both conceived, because he said in his heart; and did not say in his heart, because he could not conceive; there is more than one way in which a thing is said in the heart or conceived. For, in one sense, an object is conceived, when the word signifying it is conceived; and in another, when the very entity, which the object is, is understood.

In the former sense, then, God can be conceived not to exist; but in the latter, not at all. For no one who understands what fire and water are can conceive fire to be water, in accordance with the nature of the facts themselves, although this is possible according to the words. So, then, no one who understands what God is can conceive that God does not exist; although he says these words in his heart, either without any, or with some foreign, signification. For, God is that than which a greater cannot be conceived. And he who thoroughly understands this, assuredly understands that this being so truly exists, that not even in concept can it be non-existent. Therefore, he who understands that God so exists, cannot conceive that he does not exist.

I thank thee, gracious Lord, I thank thee; because what I formerly believed by thy bounty, I now so understand by thine illumination, that if I were unwilling to believe that thou dost exist, I should not be able not to understand this to be true.

Chapter V

God is whatever it is better to be than not to be; and he, as the only self-existent being, creates all things from nothing.

WHAT art thou, then, Lord God, than whom nothing greater can be conceived? But what art thou, except that which, as the highest of all beings, alone exists through itself, and creates all other things from nothing? For, whatever is not this is less than a thing which can be conceived of. But this cannot be conceived of thee. What good, therefore, does the supreme Good lack, through which every good is? Therefore, thou are just, truthful, blessed, and whatever it is better to be than not to be. For it is better to be just than not just; better to be blessed than not blessed.

The Five Ways
Aquinas

. . . The existence of God can be proved in five ways.

The first and more manifest way is the argument from motion. It is certain, and evident to our senses, that in the world some things are in motion. Now whatever is in motion is put in motion by another, for nothing can be in motion except it is in potentiality to that towards which it is in motion; whereas a thing moves inasmuch as it is in act. For motion is nothing else than the reduction of something from potentiality to actuality. But nothing can be reduced from potentiality to actuality, except by something in a state of actuality. Thus that which is actually hot, as fire, makes wood, which is potentially hot, to be actually hot, and thereby moves and changes it. Now it is not possible that the same thing should be at once in actuality and potentiality in the same respect, but only in different respects. For what is actually hot cannot simultaneously be potentially hot; but it is simultaneously potentially cold. It is therefore impossible that in the same respect and in the same way a thing should be both mover and moved, i.e., that it should move itself. Therefore, whatever is in motion must be put in motion by another. If that by which it is put in motion be itself put in motion, then this also must needs be put in motion by another, and that by another again. But this cannot go on to infinity, because then there would be no first mover, and, consequently, no other mover; seeing that subsequent movers move only inasmuch as they are put in motion by the first mover; as the staff moves only because it is put in motion by the hand. Therefore it is necessary to arrive at a first mover, put in motion by no other; and this everyone understands to be God.

The second way is from the nature of the efficient cause. In the world of sense we find there is an order of efficient causes. There is no case known (neither is it, indeed, possible) in which a thing is found to be the efficient cause of itself; for so it would be prior to itself, which is impossible. Now in efficient causes it is not possible to go on to infinity, because in all efficient causes following in order, the first is the cause of the intermediate cause, and the intermediate is the cause of the ultimate cause, whether the intermediate cause be several, or only one. Now to take away the cause is to take away the effect. Therefore, if there be no first cause among efficient causes, there will be no ultimate, nor any intermediate cause. But if in efficient causes it is possible to go on to infinity, there will be no first efficient cause, neither will there be an ultimate effect, nor any intermediate efficient causes; all of which is plainly false. Therefore it is necessary to admit a first efficient cause, to which everyone gives the name of God.

The third way is taken from possibility and necessity, and runs thus. We find in nature things that are possible to be and not to be, since they are found to be generated, and to corrupt, and consequently, they are possible to be and not to be. But it is impossible for these always to exist, for that which is possible not to be at some time is not. Therefore, if everything is possible not to be, then at one time there could have been nothing in existence. Now if this were true, even now there would be nothing in existence, because that which does not exist only begins to exist by something already existing. Therefore, if at one time nothing was in existence, it would have been impossible for anything to have begun to exist; and thus even now nothing would be in existence—which is absurd.

(continued)

The Five Ways (*continued*)

Therefore, not all beings are merely possible, but there must exist something the existence of which is necessary. But every necessary thing either has its necessity caused by another, or not. Now it is impossible to go on to infinity in necessary things which have their necessity caused by another, as has been already proved in regard to efficient causes. Therefore we cannot but postulate the existence of some being having of itself its own necessity, and not receiving it from another, but rather causing in others their necessity. This all men speak of as God.

The fourth way is taken from the gradation to be found in things. Among beings there are some more and some less good, true, noble and the like. But "more" and "less" are predicated of different things, according as they resemble in their different ways something which is the maximum, as a thing is said to be hotter according as it more nearly resembles that which is hottest; so that there is something which is truest, something best, something noblest and, consequently, something which is uttermost being; for those things that are greatest in truth are greatest in being, as it is written in Metaph. ii. Now the maximum in any genus is the cause of all in that genus; as fire, which is the maximum heat, is the cause of all hot things. Therefore there must also be something which is to all beings the cause of their being, goodness, and every other perfection; and this we call God.

The fifth way is taken from the governance of the world. We see that things which lack intelligence, such as natural bodies, act for an end, and this is evident from their acting always, or nearly always, in the same way, so as to obtain the best result. Hence it is plain that not fortuitously, but designedly, do they achieve their end. Now whatever lacks intelligence cannot move towards an end, unless it be directed by some being endowed with knowledge and intelligence; as the arrow is shot to its mark by the archer. Therefore some intelligent being exists by whom all natural things are directed to their end; and this being we call God.

The Watch and the Watchmaker
William Paley

Chapter One: State of the Argument

IN CROSSING A HEATH, suppose I pitched my foot against a *stone* and were asked how the stone came to be there, I might possibly answer that for anything I knew to the contrary it had lain there forever; nor would it, perhaps, be very easy to show the absurdity of this answer. But suppose I had found a *watch* upon the ground, and it should be inquired how the watch happened to be in that place, I should hardly think of the answer which I had before given, that for anything I knew the watch might have always been there. Yet why should not this answer serve for the watch as well as for the stone? Why is it not as admissible in the second case as in the first? For this reason, and for no other, namely, that when we come to inspect the watch, we perceive—what we could not discover in the stone—that its several parts are framed and put together for a purpose, e.g., that they are so formed and adjusted as to produce motion, and that motion so regulated as to point out the hour of the day; that if the different parts had been differently shaped from what they are, of a different size from what they are, or placed after any other manner or in any other order than that in which they are placed, either no motion at all would have been carried on in the machine, or none which would have answered the use that is now served by it. To reckon up a few of the plainest of these parts and of their offices, all tending to one result; we see a cylindrical box containing a coiled elastic spring, which, by its endeavor to relax itself, turns round the box. We next observe a flexible chain—artificially wrought for the sake of flexure—communicating the action of the spring from the box to the fusee. We then find a series of wheels, the teeth of which catch in and apply to each other, conducting the motion from the fusee to the balance and from the balance to the pointer, and at the same time, by the size and shape of those wheels, so regulating that motion as to terminate in causing an index, by an equable and measured progression, to pass over a given space in a given time. We take notice that the wheels are made of brass, in order to keep them from rust; the springs of steel, no other metal being so elastic; that over the face of the watch there is placed a glass, a material employed in no other part of the work, but in the room of which, if there had been any other than a transparent substance, the hour could not be seen without opening the case. This mechanism being observed—it requires indeed an examination of the instrument, and perhaps some previous knowledge of the subject, to perceive and understand it; but being once, as we have said, observed and understood—the inference we think is inevitable, that the watch must have had a maker—that there must have existed, at some time and at some place or other, an artificer or artificers who formed it for the purpose which we find it actually to answer, who comprehended its construction and designed its use.

I. Nor would it, I apprehend, weaken the conclusion, that we had never seen a watch made—that we had never known an artist capable of making one—that we were altogether incapable of executing such a piece of workmanship ourselves, or of understanding in what manner it was performed; all this being no more than what is true of some exquisite remains of ancient art, of some lost arts, and, to the generality of mankind, of the more curious productions of modern manufacture. Does one man in a million know how oval frames are turned? Ignorance of this kind exalts our opinion of the unseen and unknown artist's skill, if he be unseen and unknown, but raises no doubt in our minds of the existence and agency of such an artist, at some former time and in some place or other. Nor can I perceive that it varies at all the inference, whether the question arise concerning a human agent or concerning an agent of a different species, or an agent possessing in some respects of different nature.

II. Neither, secondly, would it invalidate our conclusion, that the watch sometimes went wrong or that it seldom went exactly right. The purpose of the machinery, the design, and the designer might be evident, and in the case supposed, would be evident, in whatever way we accounted for the irregularity of the movement, or whether we could account for it or not. It is not necessary that a machine be perfect in order to show with what design it was made: still less necessary, where the only question is whether it were made with any design at all.

III. Nor, thirdly, would it bring any uncertainty into the argument, if there were a few parts of the watch, concerning which we could not discover or had not yet discovered in what manner they conduced to the general effect; or even some parts, concerning which we could not ascertain whether they conduced to that effect in any manner whatever. For, as to the first branch of the case, if by the loss, or disorder, or decay of the parts in question, the movement of the watch were found in fact to be stopped, or disturbed, or retarded, no doubt would remain in our minds as to the utility or intention of these parts, although we should be unable to investigate the manner according to which, or the connection by which, the ultimate effect depended upon their action or assistance; and the more complex is the machine, the more likely is this obscurity to arise. Then, as to the second thing supposed, namely, that there were parts which might be spared without prejudice to the movement of the watch, and that we had proved this by experiment, these superfluous parts, even if we were completely assured that they were such, would not vacate the reasoning which we had instituted concerning other parts. The indication of contrivance remained, with respect to them, nearly as it was before.

IV. Nor, fourthly, would any man in his senses think the existence of the watch with its various machinery accounted for, by being told that it was one out of possible combinations of material forms; that whatever he had found in the place where he found the watch, must have contained some internal configuration or other; and that this configuration might be the structure now exhibited, namely, of the works of a watch, as well as a different structure.

V. Nor, fifthly, would it yield his inquiry more satisfaction, to be answered that there existed in things a principle of order, which had disposed the parts of the watch into their present form and situation. He never knew a watch made by the principle of order; nor can he even form to himself an idea of what is meant by a principle of order distinct from the intelligence of the watchmaker.

VI. Sixthly, he would be surprised to hear that the mechanism of the watch was no proof of contrivance, only a motive to induce the mind to think so:

VII. And not less surprised to be informed that the watch in his hand was nothing more than the result of the laws of *metallic* nature. It is a perversion of language to assign any law as the efficient, operative cause of any thing. A law presupposes an agent, for it is only the mode according

(continued)

The Watch and the Watchmaker (*continued*)

to which an agent proceeds: it implies a power, for it is the order according to which that power acts. Without this agent, without this power, which are both distinct from itself, the *law* does nothing, is nothing. The expression, "the law of metallic nature," may sound strange and harsh to a philosophic ear; but it seems quite as justifiable as some others which are more familiar to him, such as "the law of vegetable nature," "the law of animal nature," or, indeed, as "the law of nature" in general, when assigned as the cause of phenomena, in exclusion of agency and power, or when it is substituted into the place of these.

VIII. Neither, lastly, would our observer be driven out of his conclusion or from his confidence in its truth by being told that he knew nothing at all about the matter. He knows enough for his argument; he knows the utility of the end; he knows the subserviency and adaptation of the means to the end. These points being known, his ignorance of other points, his doubts concerning other points affect not the certainty of his reasoning. The consciousness of knowing little need not beget a distrust of that which he does know.

Chapter two: State of the Argument Continued

Suppose, in the next place, that the person who found the watch should after some time discover that, in addition to all the properties which he had hitherto observed in it, it possessed the unexpected property of producing in the course of its movement another watch like itself—the thing is conceivable; that it contained within it a mechanism, a system of parts—a mold, for instance, or a complex adjustment of lathes, files, and other tools—evidently and separately calculated for this purpose, let us inquire what effect ought such a discovery to have upon his former conclusion.

I. The first effect would be to increase his admiration of the contrivance, and his conviction of the consummate skill of the contriver. Whether he regarded the object of the contrivance, the distinct apparatus, the intricate, yet in many parts intelligible mechanism by which it was carried on, he would perceive in this new observation nothing but an additional reason for doing what he had already done—for referring the construction of the watch to design and to supreme art. If that construction *without* this property, or, which is the same thing, before this property had been noticed, proved intention and art to have been employed about it, still more strong would the proof appear when he came to the knowledge of this further property, the crown and perfection of all the rest.

II. He would reflect, that though the watch before him were, *in some sense*, the maker of the watch, which, was fabricated in the course of its movements, yet it was in a very different sense from that in which a carpenter, for instance, is the maker of a chair—the author of its contrivance, the cause of the relation of its parts to their use. With respect to these, the first watch was no cause at all to the second; in no such sense as this was it the author of the constitution and order, either of the parts which the new watch contained, or of the parts by the aid and instrumentality of which it was produced. We might possibly say, but with great latitude of expression, that a stream of water ground corn; but no latitude of expression could lead us to think that the stream of water built the mill, though it were too ancient for us to know who the builder was. What the stream of water does in the affair is neither more nor less than this by the application of an unintelligent impulse to a mechanism previously arranged, arranged independently of it and arranged by intelligence, an effect is produced, namely, the corn is ground. But the effect results from the arrangement. The force of the stream cannot be said to be the cause of author of the effect, still less of the arrangement. Understanding and plan in the formation of the mill were not the less necessary for any share which the water has in grinding the corn; yet is this share the same as that which the watch would have contributed to the production of the new watch, upon the supposition assumed in the last section. Therefore.

III. Though it be now no longer probable that the individual watch which our observer had found was made immediately by the hand of an artificer, yet does not this alteration in anyway affect the inference that an artificer had been originally employed and concerned in the production. The argument from design remains as it was. Marks of design and contrivance are no more accounted for now than they were before. In the same thing, we may ask for the cause of different properties. We may ask for the cause of the color of a body, of its hardness, of its heat; and these causes may be all different. We are now asking for the cause of that subserviency to a use, that relation to an end, which we have remarked in the watch before us. No answer is given to this question by telling us that a preceding watch produced it. There cannot be design without a designer, contrivance without a contriver; order without choice; arrangement without anything capable of arranging; subserviency and relation to a purpose without that which could intend a purpose; means suitable to an end, and executing their office in accomplishing that end, without the end ever having been contemplated or the means accommodated to it. Arrangement, disposition of parts, subserviency of means to an end, relation of instruments to a use imply the presence of intelligence and mind. No one, therefore, can rationally believe that the insensible, intimate watch, from which the watch before us issued, was the proper cause of the mechanism we so much admire in it—could be truly said to have constructed the instrument, disposed its parts, assigned their office, determined their order, action, and mutual dependency, combined their several motions into one result, and that also a result connected with the utilities of other beings. All these properties, therefore, are as much unaccounted for as they were before.

IV. Nor is anything gained by running the difficulty farther back, that is, by supposing the watch before us to have been produced from another watch, that from a former, and so on indefinitely. Our going back ever so far brings us no nearer to the least degree of satisfaction upon the subject. Contrivance is still unaccounted for. We still want a contriver. A designing mind is neither supplied by this supposition nor dispensed with. If the difficulty were diminished the farther we went back, by going back indefinitely we might exhaust it. And this is the only case to which this sort of reasoning applies. Where there is a tendency, or, as we increase the number of terms, a continual approach toward a limit, *there*, by supposing the number of terms to be what is called infinite, we may conceive the limit to be attained; but where there is no such tendency or approach, nothing is effected by lengthening the series. There is no difference as to the point in question, whatever there may be as to many points, between one series and another—between a series which is finite and a series which is infinite. A chain composed of an infinite number of links, can no more support itself, than a chain composed of a finite number of links. And of this we are assured, though we never *can* have tried the experiment; because, by increasing the number of links, from ten, for instance, to a hundred, from a hundred to a thousand, etc., we make not the smallest approach, we observe not the smallest tendency toward self-support. There is no difference in this respect—yet there may be a great difference in several respects—between a chain of a greater or less length, between one chain and another, between one that is finite and one that is infinite. This very much resembles the case before us. The machine which we are inspecting demonstrates, by its construction, contrivance and design. Contrivance must have had a contriver, design a designer, whether the machine immediately proceeded from another machine or not. That circumstance alters not the case. That other machine may, in like manner, have proceeded from a former machine; nor does that alter the case; contrivance must have had a contriver. That former one from one preceding it: no alteration still; a contriver is still necessary. No tendency is perceived, no approach toward a diminution of this necessity. It is the same with any and every succession of these machines—a succession of ten, of a hundred, of a thousand; with one series, as with another—a series which is finite, as with a series which is infinite. In whatever other respects they may differ, in this they do not. In all equally, contrivance and design are unaccounted for.

The question is not simply, How came the first watch into existence? which question, it may be pretended, is done away by supposing the series of watches thus produced from one another to have been infinite, and consequently to have had no such *first* for which it was necessary to provide a cause. This, perhaps, would have been nearly the state of the question, if nothing had been before us but an unorganized, unmechanized substance, without mark or indication of contrivance. It might be difficult to show that such substance could not have existed from eternity, either in succession—if it were possible, which I think it is not, for unorganized bodies to spring from one another—or by individual perpetuity. But that is not the question now. To suppose it to be so is to suppose that it made no difference whether he had found a watch or a stone. As it is, the metaphysics of that question have no place; for, in the watch which we are examining are seen contrivance, design, and end, a purpose means for the end, adaptation to the purpose. And the question which irresistibly

(continued)

The Watch and the Watchmaker (*continued*)

presses upon our thoughts is, whence this contrivance and design? The thing required is the intending mind, the adapting hand, the intelligence by which that hand was directed. This question, this demand is not shaken off by increasing a number or succession of substances destitute of these properties; nor the more, by increasing that number to infinity. If it be said that, upon the supposition of one watch being produced from another in the course of that other's movements and by means of the mechanism within it, we have a cause for the watch in my hand, namely, the watch from which it proceeded; I deny that for the design, the contrivance, the suitableness of means to an end, the adaptation of instruments to a use, all of which we discover in the watch, we have any cause whatever. It is in vain, therefore, to assign a series of such causes or to allege that a series may be carried back to infinity; for I do not admit that we have yet any cause at all for the phenomena, still less any series of causes either finite or infinite. Here is contrivance but no contriver; proofs of design, but no designer.

V. Our observer would further also reflect that the maker of the watch before him was in truth and reality the maker of every watch produced from it: there being no difference, except that the latter manifests a more exquisite skill, between the making of another watch with his own hands, by the mediation of files, lathes, chisels, etc., and the disposing, fixing, and inserting of these instruments, or of others equivalent to them, in the body of the watch already made, in such a manner as to form a new watch in the course of the movements which he had given to the old one. It is only working by one set of tools instead of another.

The conclusion which the *first* examination of the watch, of its works, construction, and movement, suggested, was that it must have had, for cause and author of that construction, an artificer who understood its mechanism and designed its use. This conclusion is invincible. A *second* examination presents us with a new discovery. The watch is found, in the course of its movement, to produce another watch similar to itself; and not only so, but we perceive in it a system of organization separately calculated for that purpose. What effect would this discovery have or ought it to have upon our former inference? What, as has already been said, but to increase beyond measure our admiration of the skill which had been employed in the formation of such a machine? Or shall it, instead of this, all at once turn us round to an apposite conclusion, namely, that no art or skill whatever has been concerned in the business, although all other evidences of art and skill remain as they were, and this last and supreme piece of art be now added to the rest? Can this be maintained without absurdity? Yet this is atheism. . . .

Chapter Five Application of The Argument Continued

Every observation which was made in our first chapter concerning the watch may be repeated with strict propriety concerning the eye, concerning animals, concerning plants, concerning, indeed, all the organized parts of the works of nature. As,

I. When we are inquiring simply after the *existence* of an intelligent Creator, imperfection, inaccuracy, liability to disorder, occasional irregularities may subsist in a considerable degree without inducing any doubt into the question; just as a watch may frequently go wrong, seldom perhaps exactly right, may be faulty in some parts, defective in some, without the smallest ground of suspicion from thence arising that it was not a watch, not made, or not made for the purpose ascribed to it. When faults are pointed out, and when a question is started concerning the skill of the artist or dexterity with which the work is executed, then, indeed, in order to defend these qualities from accusation, we must be able either to expose some intractableness and imperfection in the materials or point out some invincible difficulty in the execution, into which imperfection and difficulty the matter of complaint may be resolved; or, if we cannot do this, we must adduce such specimens of consummate art and contrivance proceeding from the same hand as may convince the inquirer of the existence, in the case before him, of impediments like those which we have mentioned, although, what form the nature of the case is very likely to happen, they be unknown and unperceived by him. This we must do in order to vindicate the artist's skill, or at least the perfection of it; as we must also judge of his intention and of the provisions employed in fulfilling that intention, not from an instance in which they fail but from the great plurality of instances in which they succeed. But, after all, these are different questions from the question of the artist's existence;

or, which is the same, whether the thing before us be a work of art or not; and the questions ought always to be kept separate in the mind. So likewise it is in the works of nature. Irregularities and imperfections are of little or no weight in the consideration when that consideration relates simply to the existence of a Creator. When the argument respects His attributes, they are of weight; but are then to be taken in conjunction—the attention is not to rest upon them, but they are to be taken in conjunction with the unexceptionable evidence which we possess of skill, power, and benevolence displayed in other instances; which evidences may, in strength, number, and variety, be such and may so overpower apparent blemishes as to induce us, upon the most reasonable ground, to believe that these last ought to be referred to some cause, though we be ignorant of it, other than defect of knowledge or of benevolence in the author. . . .

Of the Necessity of the Wager
Blaise Pascal

233

Infinite—nothing.—Our soul is cast into a body, where it finds number, time, dimension. Thereupon it reasons, and calls this nature, necessity, and can believe nothing else.

Unity joined to infinity adds nothing to it, no more than one foot to an infinite measure, The finite is annihilated in the presence of the infinite, and becomes a pure nothing, So our spirit before God, so our justice before divine justice. There is not so great a disproportion between our justice and that of God, as between unity and infinity.

The justice of God must be vast like His compassion. Now justice to the outcast is less vast, and ought less to offend our feelings than mercy towards the elect.

We know that there is an infinite, and are ignorant of its nature. As we know it to be false that numbers are finite, it is therefore true that there is an infinity in number, But we do not know what it is. It is false that it is even, it is false that it is odd; for the addition of a unit can make no change in its nature. Yet it is a number, and every number is odd or even (this is certainly true of every finite number). So we may well know that there is a God without knowing what He is. Is there not one substantial truth, seeing there are so many things which are not the truth itself?

We know then the existence and nature of the finite, because we also are finite and have extension. We know the existence of the infinite, and are ignorant of its nature, because it has extension like us, but not limits like us. But we know neither the existence nor the nature of God, because He has neither extension nor limits.

But by faith we know His existence; in glory we shall know His nature. Now, I have already shown that we may well know the existence of a thing, without knowing its nature.

Let us now speak according to natural lights.

If there is a God, He is infinitely incomprehensible, since, having neither parts nor limits, He has no affinity to us. We are then incapable of knowing either what He is or if He is. This being so, who will dare to undertake the decision of the question? Not we, who have no affinity to Him.

Who then will blame Christians for not being able to give a reason for their belief, since they profess a religion for which they cannot give a reason? They declare, in expounding it to the world, that it is a foolishness, *stultitiam;* and then you complain that they do not prove it! If they proved it, they would not keep their word; it is in lacking proofs, that they are not lacking in sense. "Yes, but although this excuses those who offer it as such, and takes away from them the blame of putting it forward without reason, it does not excuse those who receive it." Let us then examine this point, and say, "God is, or He is not." But to which side shall we incline? Reason can decide nothing here. There is an infinite chaos which separates us. A game is being played at the extremity of this infinite distance where heads or tails will turn up. What will you wager? According to reason, you can do neither the one thing nor the other; according to reason, you can defend neither of the propositions.

(continued)

Of the Necessity of the Wager (*continued*)

Do not then reprove for error those who have made a choice; for you know nothing about it "No, but I blame them for having made, not this choice, but a choice; for again both he who chooses heads and he who chooses tails are equally at fault, they are both in the wrong. The true course is not to wager at all."

—Yes; but you must wager. It is not optional. You are embarked. Which will you choose then? Let us see. Since you must choose, let us see which interests you least. You have two things to lose, the true and the good; and two things to stake, your reason and your will, your knowledge and your happiness; and your nature has two things to shun, error and misery. Your reason is no more shocked in choosing one rather than the other, since you must of necessity choose. This is one point settled. But your happiness? Let us weigh the gain and the loss in wagering that God is. Let us estimate these two chances. If you gain, you gain all; if you lose, you lose nothing. Wager then without hesitation that He is.—"That is very fine. Yes, I must wager; but I may perhaps wager too much."—Let us see. Since there is an equal risk of gain and of loss, if you had only to gain two lives, instead of one, you might still wager. But if there were three lives to gain, you would have to play (since you are under the necessity of playing), and you would be imprudent, when you are forced to play, not to chance your life to gain three at a game where there is an equal risk of loss and gain. But there is an eternity of life and happiness. And this being so, if there were an infinity of chances, of which one only would be for you, you would still be right in wagering one to win two, and you would act stupidly, being obliged to play, by refusing to stake one life against three at a game in which out of an infinity of chances there is one for you, if there were an infinity of an infinitely happy life to gain. But there is here an infinity of an infinitely happy life to gain, a chance of gain against a finite number of chances of loss, and what you stake is finite. It is all divided; wherever the infinite is and there is not an infinity of chances of loss against that of gain, there is no time to hesitate, you must give all. And thus, when one is forced to play, he must renounce reason to preserve his life, rather than risk it for infinite gain, as likely to happen as the loss of nothingness.

For it is no use to say it is uncertain if we will gain, and it is certain that we risk, and that the infinite distance between the *certainty* of what is staked and the *uncertainty* of what will be gained, equals the finite good which is certainly staked against the uncertain infinite. It is not so, as every player stakes a certainty to gain an uncertainty, and yet he stakes a finite certainty to gain a finite uncertainty, without transgressing against reason. There is not an infinite distance between the certainty staked and the uncertainty of the gain; that is untrue. In truth, there is an infinity between the certainty of gain and the certainty of loss. But the uncertainty of the gain is proportioned to the certainty of the stake according to the proportion of the chances of gain and loss. Hence it comes that, if there are as many risks on one side as on the other, the course is to play even; and then the certainty of the stake is equal to the uncertainty of the gain, so far is it from fact that there is an Infinite distance between them. And so our proposition is of infinite force, when there is the finite to stake in a game where there are equal risks of gain and of loss, and the infinite to gain. This is demonstrable; and if men are capable of any truths, this is one.

"I confess it, I admit it. But still is there no means of seeing the faces of the cards?"—Yes, Scripture and the rest, & c.—"Yes, but I have my hands tied and my mouth closed; I am forced to wager, and am not free. I am not released, and am so made that I cannot believe. What then would you have me do?"

True. But at least learn your inability to believe, since reason brings you to this, and yet you cannot believe. Endeavour then to convince yourself, not by increase of proofs of God, but by the abatement of your passions. You would like to attain faith, and do not know the way; you would like to cure yourself of unbelief, and ask the remedy for it. Learn of those who have been bound like you, and who now stake all their possessions. These are people who know the way which you would follow, and who are cured of an ill of which you would be cured. Follow the way by which they began; by acting as if they believe, taking the holy water, having masses said, & c. Even this will naturally make you believe, and deaden your acuteness.— "But this is what I am afraid of."—And why? What have you to lose?

But to show you that this leads you there, it is this which will lessen the passions, which are your stumbling-blocks.

The end of this discourse.—Now what harm will befall you in taking this side? You will be faithful, honest, humble; grateful, generous, a sincere friend, truthful. Certainly you will not have those poisonous pleasures, glory and luxury; but will you not have others? I will tell you that you will thereby gain in this life, and that, at each step you take on this road, you will see so great certainty of gain, so much nothingness in what you risk, that you will at last recognize that you have wagered for something certain and infinite, for which you have given nothing.

"Ah! This discourse transports me, charms me," & c.

If this discourse pleases you and seems impressive, know that it is made by a man who has knelt, both before and after it, in prayer to that Being, infinite and without parts, before whom he lays all he has, for you also to lay before Him all you have for your own good and for His glory, that so strength may be given to lowliness.

And it was manifested unto me, that those things be good which yet are corrupted; which neither were they sovereignly good, nor unless they were good could be corrupted: for if sovereignly good, they were incorruptible, if not good at all, there were nothing in them to be corrupted. For corruption injures, but unless it diminished goodness, it could not injure. Either then corruption injures not, which cannot be; or which is most certain, all which is corrupted is deprived of good. But if they be deprived of all good, they shall cease to be. For if they shall be, and can now no longer be corrupted, they shall be better than before, because they shall abide incorruptibly. And what more monstrous than to affirm things to become better by losing all their good? Therefore, if they shall be deprived of all good, they shall no longer be. So long therefore as they are, they are good: therefore whatsoever is, is good. That evil then which I sought, whence it is, is not my substance: for were it a substance, it should be good. For either it should be an incorruptible substance, and so a chief good: or a corruptible substance; which unless it were good, could not be corrupted. I perceived therefore, and it was manifested to me that Thou madest all things good, nor is there any substance at all, which Thou madest not; and for that Thou madest not all things equal, therefore are all things; because each is good, and altogether very good, because our God *made all things very good.*

And to Thee is nothing whatsoever evil: yea, not only to Thee, but also to Thy creation as a whole, because there is nothing without, which may break in, and corrupt that order which Thou hast appointed it. But in the parts thereof some things, because unharmonising with other some, are accounted evil: whereas those very things harmonise with others, and are good; and in themselves are good. And all these things which harmonise not altogether, do yet with the inferior part, which we call Earth, having its own cloudy and windy sky harmonising with it. Far be it then that I should say, "These things should not be:" for should I see nought but these, I should indeed long for the better; but still must even for these alone praise Thee; for that Thou art to be *praised,* do show *from the earth, dragons, and all deeps, fire, hail, snow, ice, and stormy wind which fulfil Thy word; mountains and all hills, fruitful trees, and all cedars; beasts, and all cattle, creeping things, and flying fowls; kings of the earth, and all people, princes, and all judges of the earth; young men and maidens, old men and young, praise Thy Name.* But when, from heaven, these *praise Thee, praise Thee, our God, in the heights, all Thy angels, all Thy hosts, sun and moon, all the stars and light, the Heaven of heavens, and the waters that be above the heavens, praise Thy Name;* I did not now long for things better because I conceived of all: and with a sounder judgment I apprehended that the things above were better than these below, but all together better than those above by themselves. . . .

. . . It is enough for the Christian to believe, that the cause of created things, whether heavenly or earthly, whether visible or invisible, is none other than the goodness of his Creator, Who is God, One and True; and that there is no nature which is not either Himself or from Himself: and that He Himself is a Trinity; the Father, that is, and the Son begotten by the Father, and the Holy Spirit proceeding from the same Father, but one and the same Spirit of the Father and of the Son. By this Trinity, supremely and equally and unchangeably good, all things were created, and that neither supremely, nor equally, nor unchangeably good, but yet good even each one: but the whole together *very good;* in that out of all these is made an admirable beauty, of the whole. In which even that which is called evil, being rightly set and put in its own place, commends more strikingly things that are good, so as that they are more pleasing and more praiseworthy through comparison

(continued)

Of the Necessity of the Wager (*continued*)

with things that are evil. For neither would Almighty God, as even heathens confess, 'Ruler supreme of things,' being, as He is, supremely good, in any way suffer any evil to be in His works, were He not Almighty and good even to this, out of any evil to work what is good. But what else is that which is called evil, but a privation of good? For like as in the bodies of animals, to be affected by diseases and wounds is nothing else than to be deprived of health, (for the object is not, when a remedial system is applied, that those evils which were in the body, that is, diseases and wounds, may depart hence and be in some other place; but that they may not be at all. For wound or disease is not any substance, but the fault of a carnal substance; the substance itself being the flesh, certainly some good thing, to which those evils are accidents, that is, the privations of that good which is called health,) so also, whatsoever are the faults of minds, are privations of natural good things; which when they are healed are not transferred to any place, but those things which were there, will be no where, seeing that in that health they will not be.

Therefore all natures, in that the Author of all natures whatsoever is supremely good, are good: but because they are not, as their Author, supremely and unchangeably good, therefore in them good may be both increased and diminished. But for good to be diminished is evil; although however much it be diminished, there must necessarily remain something (if it is still nature) whence it may be nature. For neither, if it be nature of what kind and how little soever, can the good be destroyed, by which it is nature, unless the nature also itself be destroyed. Deservedly indeed is an uncorrupted nature praised: still further if it be uncorruptible also, such as cannot altogether be corrupted, without doubt it is much more deserving of praise. When, however, it is corrupted, its corruption is therefore an evil, in that it deprives it of good of some kind or other; for if it deprive it of no good, it harms it not: but it does harm it, therefore it takes away a good. As long therefore as a nature is undergoing corruption, there exists in it a good of which it may be deprived: and on this account if any thing of the nature shall remain such as cannot be any further corrupted, certainly the nature will be uncorruptible, and to this so great good it will arrive through corruption. But if it shall not cease to be corrupted, neither will it assuredly cease to possess good, such as corruption may be able to deprive it of. Which (nature) if it shall have consumed utterly and altogether, there will therefore be no good in it, because there will be no nature in it. Wherefore corruption cannot destroy what is good, except by destroying the nature. Every nature therefore is a good; a great, if it cannot be corrupted; a small, if it can: yet can it in no sense be denied to be a good, except foolishly and ignorantly. Which if it be destroyed by corruption, neither will the corruption itself remain, there existing no nature in which it may be.

And for this reason that which is called evil is not, if good be not. But good free from all evil is perfect good; that however in which evil is, is good marred or faulty[1]. Nor can evil ever be where good is not. Whence a wonderful thing is brought to pass, that, whereas every nature, as far as it is nature, is a good, nothing else would seem to be said, when a faulty nature is called an evil nature, but this, that that is an evil which is a good; and that neither is there any evil, but what is a good; since every nature is a good, nor would any thing be evil, if the thing itself that is evil were not a nature. There cannot therefore be evil, except it be some good. Which however it appear an absurd thing to say, yet the connection of this reasoning, as it were unavoidably, compels us to say it. And care is to be taken that we fall not under that saying of the Prophet, wherein we read, *Woe unto them who call that which is good evil, and that which is evil good; who call darkness light, and light darkness; who call sweet bitter, and bitter sweet.* And yet the Lord says, *An evil man out of the evil treasure of his heart, bringeth forth evil things.* But what is *an evil man*, but an evil nature; because man is a nature? Further, if a man is some good, because he is a nature, what is a bad man, but an evil good? Yet when we distinguish between these two things, we find that neither is he therefore an evil because a man, nor therefore a good because unrighteous; but a good, because a man; an evil, because unrighteous. Whosoever therefore says, it is evil to be a man; or, it is good to be unrighteous; falls himself under that sentence of the Prophet, *Woe unto them who call that which is good evil, and that which is evil good*. For he blames the work of God, which is man, and praises the fault of man, which is unrighteousness. Every nature therefore, although it be faulty, so far as it is nature, is good; so far as it is faulty, is evil. Wherefore in those contraries which are called evils and goods, that rule of logicians ceases to hold, by which they say that nothing has in it two contraries at the same time. For no air is at the same time both dark and bright; no meat or drink at the same time sweet and bitter; no body at the same time, in parts where it is white, is there black also; none at the same time, in parts where it is deformed, is there beautiful also. And this property is found in many, and nearly in all, contraries, that they cannot be at the same time in one thing. Yet, no one doubting that goods and evils are contraries, not only can they be at the same time, but evils cannot absolutely be without goods, and except in goods: although goods can without evils. For it is possible that a man or an angel may not be unjust; but except a man or an angel there cannot be that is unjust. And that he is a man is a good, that he is an angel is a good, that he is unjust is an evil. And these two contraries are so at the same time, that, were there not the good in which the evil might be, neither would the evil at all be, in that not only would the corruption not have where to exist, but not even whence to arise, were there not something that should be corrupted, and neither could this be corrupted, unless it were a good; since corruption is nothing else than the banishing a good. Out of goods therefore have evils arisen, and except in certain goods they are not. Nor was there any other source whence any nature of evil could arise. For if it were, so far as it was nature, it would assuredly be good: and either an incorruptible nature would be a great good, or even a corruptible nature could no way be otherwise than somewhat good, by corrupting which very good corruption might be able to injure it. But in asserting that evils have their origin from goods, let us not be thought to oppose the saying of the Lord, wherein He said, *A good tree cannot produce evil fruit*. For, as the Truth saith, 'the grape cannot be gathered of thorns,' because the grape cannot grow of thorns; but we see that both vines and thorns can grow of the good ground. And in the same manner, as it were, an evil tree cannot produce good fruit, that is, an evil will good works; but out of the good nature of man, will, both good and evil, can arise; nor was there absolutely any source whence originally evil will should arise, except from the good nature of Angel and Man. Which the Lord Himself most clearly shews in the same place, where He was speaking of the tree and its fruits: for He says, *Either make the tree good, and its fruit good, or make the tree evil, and its fruit evil:* sufficiently admonishing us, that indeed of a good tree evil fruits cannot grow, nor good of an evil tree; yet that from the earth itself, to which He was speaking, either tree may.

Some Major Strands of Theodicy
Richard Swinburne

God is by definition omnipotent and perfectly good. Yet manifestly there is evil of many diverse kinds. It would appear that an omnipotent being can prevent evil if he tries to do so, and that a perfectly good being will try. The existence of such evil appears, therefore, to be inconsistent with the existence of God, or at least to render it improbable.[1] Theodicy is the enterprise of showing that appearances are misleading: that evils of the kind and quantity we find on Earth are neither incompatible with nor render improbable the existence of God.[2] Even if the evils around us do render improbable the existence of God, we may still have stronger evidence to show that there is a God which outweighs the counterevidence, which suffices to make it rational for us to believe that there is a God. My own view, however, is that theodicy is a viable enterprise, that we do not need to rely on stronger evidence for the existence of God to outweigh counterevidence from evil. This paper is a contribution to theodicy. I accept that an omnipotent being can prevent any evil he chooses, but I deny that a perfectly good being will always try to do so. If a perfectly good being is to allow evil to occur, he must have the right to do so, and there must be some good which is brought about by allowing the evil to occur and could not be brought about by him in any better way, and so great that it is worth allowing the evil to occur. If the perfectly good being is also omnipotent (i.e., can do anything logically possible), then it must be logically impossible for him to bring about the greater good in any better way. The condition about the right is important: even if my allowing you to

(continued)

Some Major Strands of Theodicy (*continued*)

suffer will do you great good, unless I am in some special position in regard to you (e.g., I am your parent), I do not have the right to allow you to suffer. I believe that God does have the right to allow humans (and animals) to suffer for the sake of greater good—to a limited extent and for a limited period (e.g., 100 years per human)—but I shall not argue for that here for reason of space.[3] My concern will be rather with contributing toward showing that evils of the kind and quantity we find on Earth serve greater goods.

I believe that theodicy seems to many people an impossible task because they have a very narrow conception of good and evil—e.g., in extremis, that the only goods are sensory pleasures and the only evils sensory pains. If that conception were correct, then obviously God could create sensory pleasures without creating sensory pains. But that conception is not merely too narrow, it is absurdly too narrow—someone whose conception of the good was thus limited would be a moral pygmy. But when you start having a wider conception good and evil, theodicy does not seem so impossible a task; it just seems difficult. The difficulty arises because of the variety of the goods and evils and the complexity of the logical relations between them.

My approach in this paper will be to list various good states of affairs (understood in a wide sense, which includes events and actions), which a good God might well seek to bring about and which do in fact occur on Earth, and show how so many of them could not be realized without the occurrence (or possible occurrence) of corresponding evils. (By the "possible occurrence" of some evil I mean some agent, animate or inanimate, having the power to bring about the evil which nothing inside or outside the agent causes the agent either to exercise or not to exercise.) In the course of running through the good states, I shall mention the major evils we find on Earth—both those involving humans and those involving animals—and show that they contribute to goods, in that the goods could not be realized without their actual or possible occurrence or the actual or possible occurrence of evils equally bad. That I hope I shall show fairly conclusively. What I shall also begin to show but could not within the compass of a philosophical paper of normal length possibly show conclusively to those without considerable sympathies toward certain general moral views is that the good states of affairs are so good that it is worth allowing the evils to occur in order to make possible the good states. There are two main reasons why I cannot show the latter conclusively within the stated space. The first of these reasons is that, I believe, there are so many different kinds of good states and so many different ways in which evil is required for their occurrence. For example, I believe that the occurrence of natural evils (i.e., evils such as disease and accidents unpredictable by humans) is required for humans to have the power to choose between doing significant good or evil to their fellows, for the reason that the observation of the processes which produce natural evil is required for humans to have the knowledge of how to do significant evil to their fellows. Without that knowledge the choice between good and evil will not be available. We learn how to poison by observing someone accidentally eating a berry and being poisoned by it; that then puts us in a position deliberately to poison others (by giving them similar berries), or through negligence to allow others to be poisoned, or alternatively to prevent their being poisoned. I believe that what goes for this schematically simple example goes generally, and that evils of the kind and quantity we find around us are required if humans are to have the power to choose between doing good or evil of varied significant kinds to their fellows. It is good that they have this latter choice, as I shall be arguing in due course. But the demonstration that natural evil is required to give us the requisite knowledge is a complicated one which I have expounded elsewhere,[4] and a fuller defense of it would require at least an article of its own. I therefore deprive myself of the strand of theodicy provided by "the argument from the need for knowledge," and rely on other strands.

The second and major reason, however, why I cannot show conclusively within the allotted space that the goods are so great that it is worth allowing the evils which they require to occur is that my assessment of the relative worth of the goods depends on more general moral views which are not fashionable today. Now, people only come to see the strength of a moral position rather different from their initial one as a result of reflection upon their experiences of life or description at some considerable length of real or fictional incidents. The philosopher can assist in the process of reflection or description; but convincing conclusions will not be reached solely by a few pages of rigorous deductive argument, aided by numbered propositions. For those of my readers who have considerable initial sympathy with the general moral views which I shall be expounding, I hope that I shall say enough to clarify and to strengthen those views in such a way as to enable the readers to see that they lead to a viable theodicy. But for the readers without much initial sympathy with the views in question, I hope that I shall say enough to make the readers more sympathetic, and so enable them to see that there are prospects for a theodicy of the kind I shall expound, that theodicy could well be a viable enterprise.[5]

So let's begin to list some goods. I have no general formula for picking out good states of affairs—I believe them to be too diverse to fall under any formula—but I list quite a number of them relevant to theodicy. Perhaps the most basic good of all is the good of the satisfaction of desire, basic in the sense that its goodness makes for the greater goodness of many other states of affairs. A desire, as I understand it, is an involuntary inclination with which an agent finds himself to do some action or to have something happen.[6] Desires may be for almost anything—for mental states, including sensory states, for bodily states, for states of the world far distant from the agent. I may desire to have a certain tingling sensation, or for a piece of poetry to run through my mind, to waggle my ears, to be president of the United States. Or my desires may be focused on others—that my children be happy or successful or inherit my wealth when I am dead.

Enjoyment or pleasure consists in the known satisfaction of present desire. It consists in doing what you are inclined to do, or letting happen what you are inclined to let happen, when you know that you are doing the action or letting the state occur. I enjoy eating cake or playing golf if I'm inclined to do so, do so while inclined, and know that I am doing so. I get pleasure out of sitting in the sun if I let myself continue to sit in the sun when inclined so to do (do not struggle against sitting there) and know that is what I am doing. I get pleasure out of being president if I am inclined to be president, and am, and know that I am president. The most primitive kind of pleasure is sensory pleasure, pleasure in the having of certain sensations, the occurrence of which I cannot be mistaken. But the more remote from my immediate environment is the state of affairs on which my inclinations are focused, the more serious is the possibility that I may believe some inclination to be satisfied when it is not. I may believe that I am president when I am not; in that case what I get pleasure from is not being president but believing that I am. I am in one state in which I desire to be—believing that I am. I am in one state in which I desire to be—believing that I am president but not in another such one—being president. When I am disabused of my false belief, there is nothing left out of which I can get pleasure.

Pleasure is the known satisfaction of present desire. Is there good in the present satisfaction of past desire? I suggest so, if it is uncanceled desire (i.e., the agent hasn't given it up). If, aged five, I long to be an engine driver but I give up this desire when I am aged ten, when I desire to be a naval captain instead; I am then declared medically unfit for the navy when conscription arrives and drafted to become an engine driver instead, there would seem little (if any) good in this. But this is because my earlier desire has been replaced by a different desire. Yet contrast this with the desire of a man for being buried here rather than there when he is dead. Surely it is good that his relatives should bury him here rather than there, even if but for the dead man's known past desire, there would be nothing particularly good about burial here rather than there.

As such, the satisfaction of desire, and above all pleasure, is a good thing. But the satisfaction of certain desires is not a good thing. The satisfaction of desires for things bad in themselves is not good. The satisfaction of a desire that others, or even one's later self, suffer pain, lose their reputation, fortune, or family is a bad thing; and any pleasure derived from these things is not merely not a good, but very much an evil. Only the pervert rejoices at the sufferings of others. Also, I suggest, pleasure is not a good where the belief needed to sustain it is false. The pleasure which a man gets from believing his son to be a successful businessman when in fact he is unemployed is not a good thing. We can see this when we consider that if we had the opportunity to plug into an "experience machine" which would inculcate in us the false beliefs that our desires were currently being satisfied, we would—almost all of us—refrain, under normal circumstances (i.e., unless life without the machine was so intolerable that "plugging in" was the lesser of two evils).

(continued)

Some Major Strands of Theodicy (*continued*)

The satisfaction of a strong desire is as such a greater good than the satisfaction of a weak desire. Further, the satisfaction of a desire is the better if it is a desire for a state of affairs good for other reasons. Desires to drink good wine rather than Coca-Cola, to read great novels rather than pornography, to understand quantum physics, or to develop a correct theodicy rather than know Wisden's Almanac by heart are like this, because of the subtlety of the sensitivity we desire to indulge in the former cases, and width and depth of the knowledge we desire to attain in the latter cases. The satisfaction of joint desires—e.g., the desires of two creatures for the common end of their nest being built—is very good because of the goodness of sharing and cooperation. It is better to have a desire for the satisfaction of desire as such—viz., the desire for pleasure in whatever way it can be achieved rather than the desire for a particular sensation—for it shows sensitivity to what is good in the satisfaction of desire. And it is yet better that the desire of one for the satisfaction of the desire of another—e.g., my desire that your desire to eat cream cake be satisfied; or more generally that the desire of a mother for the satisfaction of her offspring's desire be satisfied—than that the desire of each of us to eat cream cake be satisfied. This is because of the goodness of mutual concern and involvement. Much better that my desire that your desire to eat cream cake-be satisfied than that the desire of each of us to eat cream cake be satisfied. It follows, because of the goodness of mutual concern, that even better is the satisfaction of joint desires for the satisfaction of the desire of a third creature, e.g., the satisfaction of the desire of both parents for the desired success in examinations of their child. Even better still is the satisfaction of desires to perform actions of certain sorts benefiting oneself and others, to the goodness of which actions (desired or not) I shall come in due course.

In cases such as those just described, where one person, A, desires the satisfaction of the desire of a second person, B, and the desire is satisfied, there is a triple good. There is the primitive good of the satisfaction of B's desire. There is the greater good of the satisfaction of A's desire, greater because A's desire focused on the fulfillment of another's desire (as such, quite apart from what it is) is a desire for a better good than B's desire. And there is the further good for B that A desired his (B's) desire to be satisfied. It is a good for us when other people mind about us. We are fortunate if our happiness gives happiness to others—even if we don't know that it does. We can see this by the fact that we regard ourselves as fortunate when we discover that another was made happy by our being happy; but although the discovery causes us so to regard ourselves, what we regard ourselves as fortunate in respect of is what we discover (not the fact of our discovering it)—and that is something which could occur without our having discovered it.

Just as the satisfaction of desire is good, so is its frustration (i.e., the desire continuing when it is for a present state of affairs but is not known to be satisfied)[7] an evil. Pains are evils because they involve desires for the nonoccurrence of a sensation, which are not satisfied. And an unfulfilled longing to be president is an evil for the same reason.

God has reason to bring about the existence of creatures with desires for good states of affairs which are satisfied. He can do so without any evil occurring so long as the satisfaction is known and immediate. But if the creature continues to exist with his desire unsatisfied or not known to be satisfied, we have immediately the evil of frustrated desire. Yet there is special good in the satisfaction of persisting desire. For a desire which persists through varied experiences and new desires is a thought-through and committed desire. Hence the special good of the satisfaction of an animal's desire for the return of its offspring lost for hours or days, of the satisfaction of the desire for a mate the longing for which has deterred the animal from the search for other goods such as food, and of the satisfaction of the desire for food by those hungry for some hours. The greater good of the satisfaction of persisting desire is greater when what is desired is the success of some action of some kind. It is good that someone persists in attempting to search for food and doesn't just grab it off the table; to stick at trying to learn to type or drive or swim and finally succeed. But the eventual satisfaction of persisting desires involves on the way the evil of temporary frustrations: pangs of hunger on the way to getting food' feelings of exhaustion in the course of the long search for a mate, etc. And note of course that in these as in other cases, the good of the satisfaction of desire does not lie solely in its known satisfaction. It follows that there is significant good in the satisfaction of a persisting desire after the desirer's death. The greater good of the satisfaction of persisting desires is yet greater, the better their object; and so there is special good in the satisfaction of shared persisting desires for the satisfaction of the persisting desire of a third individual, a good which involves more evil on the way. The goodness of the satisfaction of persisting desire is the first aspect of that logical straightjacket which means that good cannot be achieved save through evil and which provides the key to theodicy. God has reason to give to creatures the good of persistent desires, despite the agony of their temporary frustration.

It is not just the satisfaction of desire which is in general a good, and especially when it is of a desire for a state of affairs good for other reasons. The mere having of desire is good, especially when it is desire for a state of affairs good for other reasons. It is good that I want things, long for things, am inclined to try to bring about things. It is better that I be someone to whom things matter rather than a "cold fish" who acts under the guidance of reason alone. Desires in themselves are good, except when they are desires for what is bad; but they are better, the better the states desired. And if my desires are focused on your well-being, that is a good not merely for me but also for you—how lucky we are if people care about us. But there are some desires for what is good which can never be satisfied. The desire to be monogamously married to beautiful Jane for all her adult life is a desire for what is good, and so it is good that both John and George have it. But of course both of their desires cannot be satisfied. Likewise, it is good to desire to be president of the United States for the next four years, to hold a great office of public service; but we can't all occupy the office. A world in which all our desires were satisfied at some time would be a world in which we were deprived of desires for certain great goods, just because we couldn't get them. If God wants to make creatures sensitive to all that is good, He will allow them to have desires which are permanently frustrated. So we are rightly sentenced to ambitions that we cannot achieve, and to the consequent deprivation, and (because of the goodness of true beliefs about these matters) to feelings of failure.

There is also great good in certain emotional states, including desire as well as other elements. It is good that I love all creatures, but especially those with whom I have contact and in particular those greatly dependent on me or on whom I am greatly dependent. It is good that I love these latter more than others—otherwise I do not pay proper tribute to their connection with myself; I trivialize our personal relations. And again, the love that persists despite inadequate response or is evoked by bad states has its own special greatness. It is good that I feel compassion for the sufferer, sadness at failure, and grief at the loss of the departed.[8] Again, these attitudes are good both for him who has these right attitudes and good for him on whom they are focused—very good if the latter knows about them and that gives him some pleasure, but good even if he doesn't—for the reason given earlier. What gives him pleasure is the knowledge of the existence of a good state (e.g., someone else's compassion for him), and that state can exist without his knowing about it. We are fortunate if others mourn for us when we are dead; we can see this by the fact that we regard people as unfortunate if no one is sorry when they die. So too it lessens the evil of the suffering of a fawn caught in a forest fire if others know about this and respond with compassion—both other deer at the time and humans centuries later. Our compassion for sentient creatures is often far too narrow; it needs to extend far over space and time.

A natural reaction to examples such as these is to urge that while compassion may be a good state, which mitigates the evil of suffering, a world would be much better without either of them; and likewise for the other two examples. That reaction seems to me overgeneral—a world without any suffering or in consequence any compassion would not be better than a world with a little suffering and its proper response (other things being equal), and likewise for the other two examples. For compassion is an involvement in the inner life of another in a deep kind of way, which simply cannot be provided by a sharing of their joy. This is because the sufferer is one whose desires are frustrated. He is at his most naked. He has little to cling to by way of a structure of desire being fulfilled or which he may hope can be fulfilled. Our involvement with him is therefore an involvement with him as he is in himself, not as someone who has as it were exteriorized himself in the fulfillment of plans for himself or others, but someone with a unique opportunity to cope with his nakedness. "Sorrow shared is sorrow halved," says the proverb, and it is only doing the sums insofar as they affect the original sufferer who knows of the compassion. If we add the benefit (not altogether an enjoyed benefit) to the sympathizer, the sums may well sometimes come out level. God will not give us endless pain, failure, and felt loss of dear ones in order to allow us to show proper compassion,

(continued)

Some Major Strands of Theodicy (continued)

sadness, and grief; but he may well give us some pain, failure, and felt loss in order to allow us to be involved with each other in ways and at levels we could not otherwise have.

So far I've been concerned largely with the goodness of passive states. But doing is more important than having happen. Causing matters, and above all, intentional actions matter, in particular actions of promoting the goods so far described, and certainly not just because it is good that those goods come about. A good (intentional) action is good to the extent to which it is done intentionally (under the description under which it is good), efficaciously, freely, spontaneously, or contrary to temptation. An action can have all of the first three characteristics, and a free intentional action will be either spontaneous or contrary to temptation, but to the extent to which it has one of the latter characteristics it will lack the other. Performing some intentional action (e.g., I buy your house), I may unintentionally do something else good (e.g., I save you from bankruptcy). Such a good action will derive its goodness not from its intention but from its effect (so long as the effect is closely connected to the intentional action and not a remote effect dependent also on many other and very different causes). What is achieved is a good, and it is also a good for the agent who effected it, even if unintentionally; he is lucky to be a vehicle of benefit. Conversely, an unsuccessful action which aimed at something good is also a good for the agent.[9] It is good that people try to help the starving, even if they don't succeed. We can see the good of unintended success better than in my earlier example by bringing in this latter point, and considering an action which is aimed at a good but fails and is better for having an unintended good result than it would be otherwise. I toil to save a life and fail, but the record of my efforts makes possible the development of a technique for saving other lives in the future. Is that better than if I failed and by chance someone else hit on the new technique? Yes, because my efforts are crowned, and therefore it is a good for me, not merely for those whose lives were ultimately saved. But clearly things are better if the good which I achieve is intended. While it is good that I try to feed the starving, even if I don't succeed, it is better if I do succeed—but not just because it is good that the starving have enough to eat; it is a good for me that I am privileged to help them, that I am of use.

An intended good action is the better if done freely in the sense of not being fully caused.[10] An agent's freely bringing about the good is indeed a good for the agent. It is a good for any agent to have a free choice, for that makes him an ultimate source of the way things happen in the universe. He is no longer totally at the mercy of forces from without, but himself an autonomous minicreator. And if he exercises that choice in forwarding the good, that is a further good for him. But the good of forwarding the good is a lot better if the agent has a free choice between good and evil, not just between alternative goods, for then his choice is deeply significant for the way the world goes. Yet if he is to have a choice between good and evil, he must be subject to temptation, i.e., desires for the evil. An action would not be intentional unless it was done for a reason, i.e., seen as in some way a good tiling (either in itself or because of its consequences). And if reasons alone influence actions, that regarded by the subject as most important will determine what is done; an agent under the influence of reason alone will inevitably do the action which he regards as overall the best (or one of the actions, if there are such, which he regards as overall equal best). If an agent is to have a free choice of whether to do an action which he regards as over- all best, factors other than reason must exert an influence on him. In other words, desires for what he regards as good only in a certain respect, but not overall and so on balance evil, must be influencing him. Then he has a choice of whether to yield to desire or to pursue the best, despite contrary desire, i.e., temptation. Just as if reasons alone influence action, an agent inevitably does what he believes to be the best; so if desires alone influence action, an agent will inevitably follow his strongest desire. Free choice of action only comes in when there is a choice between two actions which the agent regards as equally good, or between two actions which he desires to do equally, or—the serious free choice—between two actions, one of which he desires to do more, and the other of which he believes it is better to do.[11] An agent's free choice of good despite contrary temptation is indeed a good—for the agent. For he has determined the flow of events in favor of the good rather than the bad. And he will have exerted more influence on that flow, the greater the temptation to the bad.

But while the pursuit of the good, despite serious contrary temptation, is a good, so too is the spontaneous pursuit of the good, the pursuit of the good which the agent fully desires to pursue.

We value the willingly generous action, the naturally honest, spontaneously loving action. The spontaneous ready pursuit of the good has its own special kind of goodness, which—given the risk that, if he is tempted, the subject will yield to temptation, and a bad act be done and bad consequences follow—I cannot rank as either better or worse than the pursuit of the good, despite contrary temptation. (The spontaneous pursuit of the good may or may not involve a free choice. There may be a free choice between two actions seen as equally good and equally desired; or desire and reason may combine to make one choice inevitable.)

A good action is better, the greater the goals sought and attained. Especially good are supererogatory acts of helping people in great need. And just as it is good that there be a crisscrossing of desires and their satisfaction, so it is good that we seek each other's good and cooperate in seeking the good of others.

Just as having the desire and not merely its fulfillment is a good, so is having the opportunity to pursue the good, even if the opportunity is not taken. As I wrote earlier, having the opportunity to pursue the good intentionally, efficaciously, and freely is indeed a good for the agent; and if he has a free choice between good and evil, that makes him an ultimate source of how things go in the world in a very significant way. That, as we have seen, will involve his being subject to temptation to pursue the evil. The greater the choice of goods and evils we have, and (up to a limit) the greater the genuine freedom provided by serious temptation to pursue the bad instead, the more how the world goes is up to us and so the greater the privilege of our position. It is this which leads to the "free-will" defense of theodicy in respect of moral evil, the evil knowingly caused or constituted by the actions or negligence of human beings. God cannot give us the great good of the possibility of intentional, efficacious, free action, involving a choice between good and evil without at the same time providing the natural possibility (i.e., possibility allowed by natural laws) of evil which he will not prevent (not "cannot prevent" but "will not prevent," in order that the freedom he gives us may be efficacious freedom). The "free-will defense," carefully spelled out, must be a central core of theodicy, as it has been for the last two or three thousand years. But one point of this paper is to stress that the incompatibility of significant efficacious freedom and the absence of a natural possibility of evil is but one aspect of the logical straightjacket of goods which cannot be realized without actual or possible evils.

It is good that the free choices of humans between good and evil should include choices which make a difference to other humans for good or ill. A world where agents can benefit but not harm each other is a world where they have only very limited responsibility for each other. But the good of responsibility for each other is a very great good. We recognize this when we recognize. it as a good gift to our own children to give them the responsibility for things, animals, and even other humans, and do not pressure them too much as to how they are to act. But if my responsibility for you is limited to whether or not to give you some quite unexpected new piece of photographic equipment, but I cannot make you unhappy, stunt your growth, or limit your education, then I do not have a great deal of responsibility for you. If God gave agents only such limited responsibility for their fellows, He would not have given much. He would be like a father asking his elder son to look after the younger son, and adding that he would be watching the elder son's every move and would intervene the moment the elder son did a thing wrong. The elder son might justly retort that while he would be happy to share his father's work, he could only really do so if he was left to make his own judgments as to what to do within a significant range of the options available to the father. God, like a good father, has reason to delegate responsibility. In order to allow creatures a share in creation, he has reason to allow them the choice of hurting and maiming, of frustrating the divine plan. Given that human choices are free ones (and I believe that there are reasons for supposing so),[12] then our world is one where humans have deep responsibility for each other.

This responsibility is not limited to the short term. By choices now I can affect the welfare of my own children in years to come; and I and others can make great differences for good or ill to life on this earth in decades to come. And by our choices now—to pursue certain kinds of scientific research and invest our wealth in certain sorts of technology we may be able in centuries to come to influence for how long the human race lives and on which planet. My claim is that so good a thing is that deep responsibility that there is justification for God's allowing the evils caused by humans to each other (and themselves) to occur.

(continued)

Some Major Strands of Theodicy (continued)

If an agent is to choose freely between good and evil, he needs, we have seen, to have contrary desires, evil inclinations; and these are themselves evils. I cannot choose freely to give money to the starving rather than hoard it unless I have some inherent miserly inclination, and my having that is itself an evil. For that reason, as well as for the reason of the evil which will be brought about if the agent yields to temptation, there is, as I noted earlier, a special kind of goodness in the good act done naturally and spontaneously without contrary temptation. God has reason to create creatures simpler than ourselves who naturally pursue the good. God has reason to make higher animals who often act spontaneously (without, I assume, free will) to benefit themselves (not just by acquiring food, but by playing and exploring) and others of their kind (mates and offspring whom they feed, clean, protect, etc.) and indeed often other kinds too (e.g., humans). And it is good too that humans often spontaneously pursue the good of their fellows.

What is known as the "higher-order goods defense" draws to our attention the good of performing certain sorts of good action, viz., those done in the face of evils, and of having the opportunity freely to choose to do such actions. There are certain actions which cannot be done unless there is pain and suffering (which I suggest centrally involve frustration of desire) to which they react. Showing sympathy (as opposed to the passive state of feeling compassion), helping the suffering, and showing courage of a certain sort are like this. I cannot show you sympathy unless you are suffering, nor help the suffering unless there is suffering nor bravely bear my pain unless I have pain to bear. The evil of pain is the grit which makes possible the growth of the pearl. Of course, no benevolent creator would multiply pains without limit in order to give creatures the opportunity to show courage, sympathy, and help of this sort. But he might well give us some pain in order to give us the opportunity to perform some actions good in the special way that these actions are good.

In these cases, as with feeling compassion, we are involved with the sufferer (ourself or another) at his lowest. But here we can do something about the situation, not merely have the appropriate feelings. It is good that an agent do good actions, and he expresses his most substantial commitment to the good when he does such actions when it is hardest, when he gets no encouragement from the success of other plans and things are happening to him which he does not desire. He does so when he shows courage of a certain sort. And it is good that others should be involved with people at their most naked making the hard choices, when the sufferer can see the others as concerned for him and not anything slightly exterior to him (aspects of his appearance of success which make him attractive), doing what they can for him and helping him to make the right choices. Help is most significant when it is most needed, and it is most needed when its recipient is suffering and deprived. Whatever it is good that we do, it is good that others help us to do—even if sometimes it is also good that we have available the ever harder choice of showing courage on our own.

Showing sympathy and showing courage are good actions which may be done in the face of the simple natural evil of frustration of desire involved in pain and suffering. But there are good actions of other kinds which can only be done in the face of evil actions of various kinds. I can only make reparation if I have wronged you, or forgive you if you have wronged me. In these cases, while of course it is not overall a good that wrong be done, reparation made and it be forgiven, still these actions do in part compensate for the wrong done. And while the possibility of its misuse provides a reason for God not to create creatures with significant freedom, the possibility of such compensation for misuse reduces the force of that reason. There is some truth, though not as much as the writer of the Exultet supposed, in "O Felix Culpa, quae talem ac tantum meruit habere redemptorem."[13] There are good actions of certain kinds which can only be done in the face of good actions of various kinds—such as showing gratitude, recognition of achievement, and reward; and the possibility of these responses to actions which may themselves be responses to pain and suffering (e.g., showing gratitude to doctors who have worked hard to relieve pain) provides further reason for permitting the pain and suffering.[14]

It is good that some actions, including the actions of animals lacking free will, should be serious actions which involve benefiting despite loss or foreseen risk of loss to themselves and so actions of looking for a mate, despite failure to find; or decoying predators or exploring despite risk of loss of life. But again an action good in this kind of way cannot be done without evil. You cannot intentionally avoid forest fires, or take trouble to rescue your offspring from forest fires, unless there exists a serious danger of getting caught in a forest fire. The action of rescuing despite danger simply cannot be done unless the danger exists—and the danger will not exist unless there is a significant natural probability of being caught in the fire. To the extent that the world is deterministic, that involves creatures actually being caught in the fire;[15] and to the extent that the world is indeterministic, that involves an inclination of nature to produce that effect unprevented by God. Fawns are bound to get caught in forest fires sometimes if other fawns are to have the opportunity of intentionally avoiding fires and if deer are to have the opportunities of rescuing other fawns from fires.[16]

Not all evil actions are actions of agents with free will and so to be justified by the free-will defense. Animals sometimes reject their offspring or hurt other animals.[17] Yet these actions, like physical pain, provide opportunities for good actions to be done in response to them, e.g., make possible adoption of the rejected offspring by other animals, or rescue of the injured by other animals, or the animal courageously coping with his injury or rejection.

I have argued so far for the great good of the having and satisfaction of desire, and shown how the satisfaction of persisting desires and the having of compassionate desires involves the occurrence of various evils. I then went on to show how the great good of having significant free choice involves actual bad desires and the possible occurrence of further significant harm to ourselves and others; and how having the opportunity to show courage or compassion involves the actual occurrence of pain and suffering. I also brought out the lesser value of serious beneficiary action by animals lacking free will.

As with desire, so with action, I have stressed the good for the subject of desire and action of having and satisfying good desires and performing or trying to perform good actions, especially ones whose object is someone else. It is a great good for me to bring the goods of life to others. Helping, contributing, being of use to others, even more than to ourselves, is a great good, a blessing, a privilege—especially if it is by free action, but also if it is by a spontaneous action, a significantly greater good than are the goods (which are indeed goods) of having tingles of sensory pleasure. And, as we have seen, there is special value in helping those who most need help. That helping is an immense good for the helper has always been difficult for humans to see, but it is especially hard for twentieth-century secularized Western people to see. It is however, something quite often near the surface of New Testament writings; and it was aptly summarized by Saint Paul in his farewell sermon to the church at Ephesus when he urged them "to remember the words of the Ford Jesus, how he himself said, It is more blessed to give than to receive" (Acts 20:35).

We don't, most of us, think that most of the time. We think that our well-being consists in the things that we possess or the experiences we enjoy. Sometimes, true, all men find themselves in circumstances in which they ought to give—alas, the starving appear on our doorstep and we ought to give them some of our wealth, perhaps something large which will deprive us of future enjoyments. But that, the common thinking goes, is our misfortune, good for the starving but bad for us. Life would have been better for us if they hadn't turned up on the doorstep. But what the words of Christ say, taken literally, is "not so." We are lucky that they turned up on the doorstep. It would have been our misfortune if there had been no starving to whom to give; life would have been worse for us.

And even twentieth-century people can begin to see that—sometimes—when they seek to help prisoners not by providing more comfortable quarters but by letting prisoners help the handicapped; or when they pity rather than envy the "poor little rich girl" who has everything and does nothing for anyone else. And one phenomenon prevalent in end-of-century Britain draws this especially to our attention—the evil of unemployment. Because of our system of social security the unemployed on the whole have enough money to live without too much discomfort; certainly they are a lot better off than are many employed in Africa or Asia or Victorian Britain. What is evil about unemployment is not so much any resulting poverty but the uselessness of the unemployed. They often report feeling unvalued by society, of no use, "on the scrap heap." They rightly think it would be a good for them to contribute, but they can't.

It is not only intentional actions freely chosen, but also ones performed involuntarily, which have good consequences which constitute a good for the person who does them. If the unemployed were compelled to work for some useful purpose, they would still—most of them—regard that as a good for them in comparison with being useless. Or consider the conscript killed in a just

(continued)

Some Major Strands of Theodicy (*continued*)

and ultimately successful war in defense of his country against a tyrannous aggressor. Almost all peoples, apart from those of the Western world in our generation, have recognized that dying for one's country is a great good for him who dies, even if he was conscripted.[18] And it is not only intentional actions but experiences undergone involuntarily (or involuntary curtailment of good experiences, as by death) which have good consequences—so long as those experienced are closely connected with their consequences—which constitute a good for him who has them (even if a lesser good than that of a free intentional action causing those consequences, and a good often outweighed by the evil of the experience in question). Consider someone hurt or killed in an accident, where the accident leads to some reform which prevents the occurrence of similar accidents in the future (e.g., someone killed in a rail crash which leads to the installation of a new system of railway signaling which avoids similar accidents in the future). He and his relatives may comment in such a situation that at any rate the victim did not suffer or die in vain. They would have regarded it as a greater misfortune even for the victim if his suffering or death served no useful purpose. It is a good for us if our experiences are not wasted but are used for the good of others, if they are the means of a benefit which would not have come to others without them, which will at least in part compensate for those experiences. It follows from this insight that it is a blessing for a person if the possibility of his suffering makes possible the good for others of having the free choice of hurting or harming him; and if his actual suffering makes possible the good for others of feeling compassion for him, and of choosing to show or not show sympathy or provides knowledge for others. Thus it is a good for the fawn caught in the thicket in the forest fire that its suffering provides knowledge for the deer and other animals who see it to avoid the fire and deter their other offspring from being caught in it. The supreme good of being of use is worth paying a lot to get. It is much better if the being of-use is chosen voluntarily, but it is good even if it isn't. Blessed is the man or woman whose life is of use.

If A desires the satisfaction of B's desire, the satisfaction of this desire is, I argued, a good for B in having his desire satisfied, a good for A in that his especially good desire is satisfied, and also an additional good for B in that the satisfaction of his desire was something that A cared about. Similarly, and much more so, with intentional actions. If A secures the fulfillment of some desire of B, not merely is it a good for B that his desire is fulfilled, and a good for A that he is the instrument of this, but it is a further good for B that the fulfillment of desire did not come by chance but by A actively seeking his well-being. We are lucky if people mind about us, and the natural expression of minding is seeking well-being. Some times those who "don't like to be beholden to others" don't see this. "I wish that I were not so dependent on my parents for money," says the undergraduate. But "so" is the crucial word—dependence can come in irksome forms or be too complete; but how awful it would be if nobody ever cared for us enough to give us anything. Fortunately, if God exists, no human or animal is ever in that position.

In the course of this paper I have run through many good states which we find on Earth and which God might seek to bring about. I have shown how often various evils (or their possibility) are (logically) necessary for their attainment. The evils include moral evils—the harm we humans do to each other or negligently allow to occur—the natural evils of various kinds, both animal and human suffering. The same goods could exist in a world different from ours in which there was less natural evil and more moral evil—e.g., there was so much moral evil in virtue of stronger human desires for evil—that there was no need for so much natural evil if humans were to have the same opportunity for courage in face of pain. But it is far from obvious that such a world would be a better world than ours. In general we need a similar amount of evil if we are to have the similar amount of good by way of the having and satisfaction of desire, and of significant choice and serious beneficiary action. There are also, I believe, other goods and other ways in which evil is necessary for good which I have not described.

None of the goods which I have listed are such that their production would justify God in causing endless suffering, but he does not do that. There is a limit of intensity and above all time (the length of a human life) to the suffering caused to any individual. In the perspective of eternity, the evils of this world are very limited in number and duration; and the issue concerns only whether God would allow such narrowly limited evils to occur for the sake of the great goods they make possible. A central theme of this paper is to draw attention to goods of two kinds which the modern world tends not to notice. It is when you take them into serious account, I suggest, that you begin to realize that not merely are certain evils necessary for certain goods, hut they are necessary for goods at least as great as the evils are evil. There is first the good of being of use, or helping, and secondly the good of being helped. God will seek to bestow generously these great blessings.

I have almost always found in discussion of these matters that my opponents are usually happy to grant me, when I bring the suggestion to their attention, that the states which I describe as "goods" cannot be had without the corresponding evils, and quite often happy to grant that the former states are indeed good states and even that a world is not on balance worse for containing a few of these goods in the mildest of forms with the corresponding evils than it would otherwise be. But my opponents usually object to the scale—there are, they claim, too many, too various, and too serious evils to justify bringing about the goods which they make possible. Yet it must be stressed that each evil or possible evil removed takes away one more actual good.

If the fawn does not suffer in the thicket, other deer will not so readily have the opportunity of intentionally avoiding fires; he will not through his suffering be able to show courage or have the privilege of providing knowledge for other deer of how to avoid such tragedies; other deer and humans centuries later will not be able to show compassion for his suffering, etc. The sort of world where so many such evils are removed and which in effect my opponents think that God's goodness requires him to make, turns out—as regards the kinds of good to which I have drawn attention—to be a toy world. Things matter in the kinds of respect which I mention, but they don't matter very much. I cannot see that God would be less than perfectly good if he gave us a world where things matter a lot more than that.

I suggest that the reluctance of my opponents to see that arises primarily from overestimating the goodness of mere pleasure and the evil of mere pain, and grossly underestimating the value of being of use and being helped. Our culture has dulled our moral sensitivities in these respects. Yet even if an opponent allows the formal point that there is great value for the subject in being of use and being helped, he may fail to see that that has the consequence for theodicy which I commend because of two characteristic human vices—short-term and short-distance thinking. He tends to think of the worth of a sentient life as dependent on things that happen during that life and fairly close in space to the life. But once you grant the formal point that things outside a life, e.g., its causes and effects, make a great difference to the value of that life, it seems totally arbitrary to confine those things to ones near to the life in space and time. The sufferings of the Jewish victims of the Nazi concentration camps were the result of a web of choices that stretched back over centuries and continents and caused or made possible a whole web of actions and reactions that will stretch forward over centuries and continents (and the same goes to a lesser extent for the suffering of the fawn). Such sufferings made heroic choices possible for people normally too timid to make them (e.g., to harbor the prospective victims) and for people normally too hardhearted (as a result of previous bad choices) to make them (e.g., for a concentration camp guard not to obey orders). And they make possible reactions of courage (e.g., by the victims), of compassion, sympathy, penitence, forgiveness, reform, avoidance of repetition, etc., stretching down time and space. In saying this, I am not of course saying that those Nazi officials who sent Jews to the concentration camps were justified in doing so. For they had no right whatever to do that to others. But I am saying that God, who has rights over us that we do not have over others, is not less than perfectly good if he allowed the Jews for a short period to be subjected to these terrible evils through the evil free choice of others—in virtue of the hard heroic value of their lives of suffering.

There is no other way to get the evils of this world into the right perspective, except to reflect at length on innumerable very detailed thought experiments (in addition to actual experiences of life) in which we postulate very different sorts of worlds from our own, then ask ourselves whether the perfect goodness of God would require him to create one of these (or no world at all) rather than our, own.[19] But I conclude with a very small thought experiment, which may help my opponents to begin this process. Suppose that you exist in another world before your birth in this one and are given a choice as to the sort of life you are to lead. You are told that you are to have only a short life, maybe of only a few minutes, although it will be an adult life in the sense that you will have the richness of sensation and belief characteristic of adults. You have a choice as to the sort of

(continued)

Some Major Strands of Theodicy   (*continued*)

life you will have. You can have either a few minutes of very considerable pleasure of the kind produced by some drug such as heroin, which you will experience by yourself and will have no effects at all in the world (e.g., no one else will know about it); or you can have a few minutes of considerable pain, such as the pain of childbirth, which will have (unknown to you at the time of pain) consider- able good effects on others over a few years. You are told that if you do not make the second choice, those others will never exist—and so you are under no moral obligation to make the second choice. But you seek to make the choice which will make your own life the best life for you to have led. How will you choose? The choice is, I hope, obvious. You must choose the second alternative. And it would of course make no difference to your choice if the good effects are to be very distant in time and space from your life.[20]

If we go on to meditate on how we should choose between other alternatives with longer lives or different lives—incarnation as a fawn or a suffering child[21] maybe—against a background of many centuries of effect and cause and place in the web of human and animal society, we may begin to look at things a little more sub specie aeternitatis. If God is generously to give to creatures the privilege of forming other creatures, developing their desires and freedom of choice and informing them about the possible choices open to them, he cannot (for logical reasons) ask the latter before they are born what sort of life they would like to live. He has to make the choice on their behalf, and he will therefore seek to make a choice which, if rational, we might make for ourselves. He sometimes pays us the compliment of supposing that we would choose to be heroes.

For someone who remains unconvinced by my claims about the relative strengths of the goods and evils involved, holding that great though the goods are they do not justify the evils which they involve, there is a fall-back position. My arguments may have convinced the reader of the greatness of the goods involved sufficiently for him to allow that God would be justified in bringing about the evils for the sake of the goods which they make possible, if and only if God also provides compensation in the form of happiness after death to the victims whose sufferings make possible the goods. Someone whose, theodicy requires buttressing in this way will need independent reason for believing that God does provide such life after death if he is to be justified in holding his theodicy, and he may well have such reason.[22] While believing that God does provide at any rate (for many humans such life after death, I have expounded a theodicy without relying on this assumption. But I can understand someone thinking that the assumption is needed. If for example, the goods making possible free choice for the Nazi concentration camp guards (in choosing whether to disobey orders), for the Jewish victims (in deciding how to bear their suffering), and for many others involved are not goods great enough to justify God's allowing the Nazis to choose to exterminate Jews, maybe they would be if the evil is compensated by some years of happy afterlife for the Jews involved.

It remains the case, however, that evil is evil, and there is a substantial price to pay for the goods of our world. God would not be less than perfectly good if he created instead a world without pain and suffering, and so without the particular goods which they make possible. Christian tradition claims that God has created worlds of both kinds—our world, and the heaven of the blessed. The latter is a marvelous world with a vast range of possible deep goods, but it lacks a few goods which our world contains, including the good of being able to reject the good. Out of generosity, God might well choose to give some of us the choice of rejecting the good in a world like ours, before giving to those who accept it a wonderful world in which that possibility no longer exists.[23]

NOTES

1. Given that an omnipotent being can prevent and that a perfectly good being will always try to prevent evils of the kind and quantity we find on Earth, the argument from such evils is a conclusive deductive argument against the existence of God. But insofar as it is only probable that an omnipotent being can prevent or that a perfectly good being will try to prevent evils of the kind and quantity we find on Earth, then the conclusion that there is no God will only be probable.
2. Some writers have used "theodicy" as the name of the enterprise of showing God's actual reasons for allowing evil to occur and have contrasted it with a "defense" to the argument from evil to the nonexistence of God which merely shows that the argument doesn't work. See, e.g., Alvin Plantinga, *The Nature of Necessity* (Oxford: Clarendon Press, 1974), 192. Given this contrast, what I am seeking to do is provide a "defense"

rather than a "theodicy," but I do so by showing what reasons God could have for allowing evil to occur; I am not, however, claiming that the reasons which I give are God's actual reasons. I believe, however, that my use of "theodicy" is that normal to the tradition of discussion of these issues.

3. For argument on this, see my book *The Existence of God* (Oxford: Clarendon Press, 1979), 216–18.
4. See *The Existence of God*. 202–14. I present the argument at greater length and defend it against objections in "Knowledge from Experience, and the Problem of Evil" in Win. Abraham and S. Holtzer, eds. *The Rationality Religious Belief* (Oxford: Clarendon Press, 1987). While I accept the need for yet further tightening of the argument, to do so would require at least an article devoted entirely to that topic.
5. I plan to write a full-length book on Providence, in which I shall defend the moral views in question at much greater length than I do in this paper.
6. For a fuller account of desire, see my book *The Evolution of the Soul* (Oxford: Clarendon Press, 1986), chap. 6.
7. I stress that the desire is only "frustrated" when it is a (believedly) unfulfilled desire for something to happen now. A desire to go to London tomorrow is today neither satisfied nor frustrated. Of course, some frustrations are so mild that we might hesitate to call them that in ordinary speech—but my unfulfilled mild desire for cream cake is on a continuum with my strong desire that a certain sensation go away, or that peace come to the Middle East; and hence it is appropriate in philosophical discussion to call the former also a case of frustration of desire.
8. The evil is not the death of the loved ones but our being deprived of intercourse with them. Death is simply in itself the point at which the finite good of life comes to an end. Death is only an evil for the dead one if it occurs under certain circumstances (e.g., prematurely, when life's ambitions are suddenly frustrated). That death is not as such an evil (i.e., for the dead one under normal circumstances) but that in many respects it is good that the world contain death, see *The Existence of God,* 193–96.
9. In discussing intentional actions, I am assuming that the agent's moral beliefs are correct. It would complicate the discussion too much to bring in the goodness of actions aimed at some end falsely believed to be good. But I do not believe that this simplification in any way affects the main points of the argument.
10. That is, the agent has libertarian free will—his choices are not fully determined; not just compatibilist free will—no one puts psychological or physical pressure on him to act as he does. Of course, libertarian free will only belongs to an agent choosing intentionally between alternatives; it doesn't belong to any nonmental events, such as the random swervings of atoms, which are not fully caused.
11. There is a further circumstance under which free choice is possible. That is where an agent has a choice between an infinite number of good actions, each of which is, he believes, worse than some other such action; there is, he believes, no best or equal best action. However, since only a being whose power is unlimited in some respect will be in such a situation, humans or animals are never in such a situation; and so for the sake of simplicity of exposition, I ignore this possibility.
12. I have given my reasons for my belief, that they do have such free will else where—see my *Evolution of the Soul,* chap. 13. Insofar as there is reason to suppose that they do not have such free will, the free-will defense will fail.
13. This is the comment of the Exultet, the hymn of the traditional Easter Eve Liturgy, on the sin of Adam: "O happy fault which merited a redeemer so great and of such a kind."
14. For analysis of such notions as reparation, forgiveness, gratitude, and reward, see my *Responsibility and Atonement* (Oxford: Clarendon Press, 1989), chaps. 4 and 5.
15. If the behavior of tossed coins is deterministic, talk about a natural probability or a coin landing heads can only be intelligibly construed as talk about proportions of construed in typical setups which result in heads. ("Natural probability" or "physical probability" is probability in nature in contrast to "epistemic probability," which is probability relative to our knowledge.) See my *Introduction to Confirmation Theory* (Oxford: Methuen, 1973), chaps. 1 and 2.
16. Those familiar with recent philosophical writing on the problem of evil will realize that I choose the example of a lawn caught in a forest fire because of its prevalence in that literature. It was put forward by William Rowe (see chapter I in this volume) as an example of apparently pointless evil.
17. It is a mistake, in my view, to regard the killing of one animal by another for food as in itself an evil. To be killed and eaten by another animal is as natural an end to life as would be death by other natural causes at the same age. For, given that animals lack free will and moral concepts, the killing of one by another is as much part of the natural order as is accident or disease not involving its transmission by other animals. And if death by such natural causes is not as such an evil, as I have urged (see note 8), but simply the end of a good, so too with death by predator. Evil comes insofar as there is pain involved in the killing, or offspring are knowingly deprived of a parent. I do not see any very good reason to suppose that invertebrates who do not have a central nervous system similar to that of humans suffer pain, let alone have knowledge. The evil of suffering arises, I suspect, only with the vertebrates and possibly only with mammals. Plausibly, too, since the central nervous systems of other vertebrates and mammals are less developed than ours, their sufferings are less than ours.

(continued)

Some Major Strands of Theodicy *(continued)*

18. This good, others have recognized, exists as a this-worldly good, quite apart from any reward for patriotic behavior which might accrue in the afterlife. The hope of such reward was not a major motive among Romans and Greeks who died for their country: "The doctrine of a future life was far too vague among the pagans to exercise any powerful general influence," writes W. E. H. Lecky in his *History of European Morals from Augustus to* Charlemagne, vol. 2 (1899), 3. And he states that "the Spartan and the Roman died for his country because he loved it. The martyr's ecstasy of hope had no place in his dying hour. He gave up all he had, he closed his eyes, as he believed for ever, and he asked for no reward in this world or in the next" (vol. 1, 178). The lines of Horace, "dulce et decorum propatria mori" (it is sweet and proper to die for one's country) in his *Odes* (3.2.13), were written by a man whose belief in personal immortality was negligible—see 3.30, in which Horace sees his "immortality" as consisting in his subsequent reputation and seems to convey the view that dying for one's country was a good for the one who died. It was of course a Socratic view that doing just acts was a good for the one who does them; see Plato, *Gorgias* 479.
19. Note that the issue is not whether this world is the best of all possible worlds. There cannot, I suggest, be a best of all possible worlds, because any world could always be bettered in some respect—see *The Existence of God,* 113–14. The issue is whether there is too much evil in this world, despite the goods it makes possible, for God to create it at all. He may of course create other worlds as well.
20. The thought experiment is only meant to bring out the value of such a life for the sufferer. It is not put forward as a case when God could not produce the good effect in any other way. But it is meant to begin to help us to assess correctly cases of the latter kind.
21. See Ivan's speech in Dostoyevsky's *Brothers Karamazov,* bk. 5, chap. 4.
22. This may, for example, be provided by revelation. On the evidence for revealed truth, see my *Revelation* (Oxford: Clarendon Press, 1992).
23. For comments on earlier drafts of this paper, I thank C. Stephen Layman, Bruce Russell, Eleonore Stump, and Mark O. Webb.

Section X of Miracles
David Hume

Part I

There is, in Dr. Tillotson's writings, an argument against the *real presence,* which is as concise, and elegant, and strong as any argument can possibly be supposed against a doctrine, so little worthy of a serious refutation. It is acknowledged on all hands, says that learned prelate, that the authority, either of the scripture or of tradition, is founded merely in the testimony of the apostles, who were eye-witnesses to those miracles of our Saviour, by which he proved his divine mission. Our evidence, then, for the truth of the *Christian* religion is less than the evidence for the truth of our senses; because, even in the first authors of our religion, it was no greater; and it is evident it must diminish in passing from them to their disciples; nor can any one rest such confidence in their testimony, as in the immediate object of his senses. But a weaker evidence can never destroy a stronger; and therefore, were the doctrine of the real presence ever so clearly revealed in scripture, it were directly contrary to the rules of just reasoning to give our assent to it. It contradicts sense, though both the scripture and tradition, on which it is supposed to be built, carry not such evidence with them as sense; when they are considered merely as external evidences, and are not brought home to every one's breast, by the immediate operation of the Holy Spirit.

Nothing is so convenient as a decisive argument of this kind, which must at least *silence* the most arrogant bigotry and superstition, and free us from their impertinent solicitations. I flatter myself, that I have discovered an argument of a like nature, which, if just, will, with the wise and learned, be an everlasting check to all kinds of superstitious delusion, and consequently, will be useful as long as the world endures. For so long, I presume, will the accounts of miracles and prodigies be found in all history, sacred and profane.

Though experience be our only guide in reasoning concerning matters of fact; it must be acknowledged, that this guide is not altogether infallible, but in some cases is apt to lead us into errors. One, who in our climate, should expect better weather in any week of June than in one of

December, would reason justly, and conformably to experience; but it is certain, that he may happen, in the event, to find himself mistaken. However, we may observe, that, in such a case, he would have no cause to complain of experience; because it commonly informs us beforehand of the uncertainty, by that contrariety of events, which we may learn from a diligent observation. All effects follow not with like certainty from their supposed causes. Some events are found, in all countries and all ages, to have been constantly conjoined together: Others are found to have been more variable, and sometimes to disappoint our expectations; so that, in our reasonings concerning matter of fact, there are all imaginable degrees of assurance, from the highest certainty to the lowest species of moral evidence.

A wise man, therefore, proportions his belief to the evidence. In such conclusions as are founded on an infallible experience, he expects the event with the last degree of assurance, and regards his past experience as a full *proof* of the future existence of that event. In other cases, he proceeds with more caution: He weighs the opposite experiments: He considers which side is supported by the greater number of experiments: to that side he inclines, with doubt and hesitation; and when at last he fixes his judgement, the evidence exceeds not what we properly call *probability*. All probability, then, supposes an opposition of experiments and observations, where the one side is found to overbalance the other, and to produce a degree of evidence, proportioned to the superiority. A hundred instances or experiments on one side, and fifty on another, afford a doubtful expectation of any event; though a hundred uniform experiments, with only one that is contradictory, reasonably beget a pretty strong degree of assurance. In all cases, we must balance the opposite experiments, where they are opposite, and deduct the smaller number from the greater, in order to know the exact force of the superior evidence.

To apply these principles to a particular instance; we may observe, that there is no species of reasoning more common, more useful, and even necessary to human life, than that which is derived from the testimony of men, and the reports of eye-witnesses and spectators. This species of reasoning, perhaps, one may deny to be founded on the relation of cause and effect. I shall not dispute about a word. It will be sufficient to observe that our assurance in any argument of this kind is derived from no other principle than our observation of the veracity of human testimony, and of the usual conformity of facts to the reports of witnesses. It being a general maxim, that no objects have any discoverable connexion together, and that all the inferences, which we can draw from one to another, are founded merely on our experience of their constant and regular conjunction; it is evident, that we ought not to make an exception to this maxim in favour of human testimony, whose connexion with any event seems, in itself, as little necessary as any other. Were not the memory tenacious to a certain degree, had not men commonly an inclination to truth and a principle of probity; were they not sensible to shame, when detected in a falsehood: Were not these, I say, discovered by experience to be qualities, inherent in human nature, we should never repose the least confidence in human testimony. A man delirious, or noted for falsehood and villany, has no manner of authority with us.

And as the evidence, derived from witnesses and human testimony, is founded on past experience, so it varies with the experience, and is regarded either as a *proof* or a *probability*, according as the conjunction between any particular kind of report and any kind of object has been found to be constant or variable. There are a number of circumstances to be taken into consideration in all judgements of this kind; and the ultimate standard, by which we determine all disputes, that may arise concerning them, is always derived from experience and observation. Where this experience is not entirely uniform on any side, it is attended with an unavoidable contrariety in our judgements, and with the same opposition and mutual destruction of argument as in every other kind of evidence. We frequently hesitate concerning the reports of others. We balance the opposite circumstances, which cause any doubt or uncertainty; and when we discover a superiority on any side, we incline to it; but still with a diminution of assurance, in proportion to the force of its antagonist.

This contrariety of evidence, in the present case, may be derived from several different causes; from the opposition of contrary testimony; from the character or number of the witnesses; from the manner of their delivering their testimony; or from the union of all these circumstances. We entertain a suspicion concerning any matter of fact, when the witnesses contradict each other; when

(continued)

Section X of Miracles (*continued*)

they are but few, or of a doubtful character; when they have an interest in what they affirm; when they deliver their testimony with hesitation, or on the contrary, with too violent asseverations. There are many other particulars of the same kind, which may diminish or destroy the force of any argument, derived from human testimony.

Suppose, for instance, that the fact, which the testimony endeavours to establish, partakes of the extraordinary and the marvellous; in that case, the evidence, resulting from the testimony, admits of a diminution, greater or less, in proportion as the fact is more or less unusual. The reason why we place any credit in witnesses and historians, is not derived from any *connexion,* which we perceive *a priori,* between testimony and reality, but because we are accustomed to find a conformity between them. But when the fact attested is such a one as has seldom fallen under our observation, here is a contest of two opposite experiences; of which the one destroys the other, as far as its force goes, and the superior can only operate on the mind by the force, which remains. The very same principle of experience, which gives us a certain degree of assurance in the testimony of witnesses, gives us also, in this case, another degree of assurance against the fact, which they endeavour to establish; from which contradiction there necessarily arises a counterpoize, and mutual destruction of belief and authority.

I should not believe such a story were it told me by Cato, was a proverbial saying in Rome, even during the lifetime of that philosophical patriot. The incredibility of a fact, it was allowed, might invalidate so great an authority.

The Indian prince, who refused to believe the first relations concerning the effects of frost, reasoned justly; and it naturally required very strong testimony to engage his assent to facts, that arose from a state of nature, with which he was unacquainted, and which bore so little analogy to those events, of which he had had constant and uniform experience. Though they were not contrary to his experience, they were not conformable to it.

But in order to encrease the probability against the testimony of witnesses, let us suppose, that the fact, which they affirm, instead of being only marvellous, is really miraculous; and suppose also, that the testimony considered apart and in itself, amounts to an entire proof; in that case, there is proof against proof, of which the strongest must prevail, but still with a diminution of its force, in proportion to that of its antagonist.

A miracle is a violation of the laws of nature; and as a firm and unalterable experience has established these laws, the proof against a miracle, from the very nature of the fact, is as entire as any argument from experience can possibly be imagined. Why is it more than probable, that all men must die; that lead cannot, of itself, remain suspended in the air; that fire consumes wood, and is extinguished by water; unless it be, that these events are found agreeable to the laws of nature, and there is required a violation of these laws, or in other words, a miracle to prevent them? Nothing is esteemed a miracle, if it ever happen in the common course of nature. It is no miracle that a man, seemingly in good health, should die on a sudden: because such a kind of death, though more unusual than any other, has yet been frequently observed to happen. But it is a miracle, that a dead man should come to life; because that has never been observed in any age or country. There must, therefore, be a uniform experience against every miraculous event, otherwise the event would not merit that appellation. And as a uniform experience amounts to a proof, there is here a direct and full *proof,* from the nature of the fact, against the existence of any miracle; nor can such a proof be destroyed, or the miracle rendered credible, but by an opposite proof, which is superior.[22]

The plain consequence is (and it is a general maxim worthy of our attention), 'That no testimony is sufficient to establish a miracle, unless the testimony be of such a kind, that its falsehood would be more miraculous, than the fact, which it endeavours to establish; and even in that case there is a mutual destruction of arguments, and the superior only gives us an assurance suitable to that degree of force, which remains, after deducting the inferior.' When anyone tells me, that he saw a dead man restored to life, I immediately consider with myself, whether it be more probable, that this person should either deceive or be deceived, or that the fact, which he relates, should really have happened. I weigh the one miracle against the other; and according to the superiority, which I discover, I pronounce my decision, and always reject the greater miracle. If the falsehood of his testimony would be more miraculous, than the event which he relates; then, and not till then, can he pretend to command my belief or opinion.

Part II

In the foregoing reasoning we have supposed, that the testimony, upon which a miracle is founded, may possibly amount to an entire proof, and that the falsehood of that testimony would be a real prodigy: But it is easy to shew, that we have been a great deal too liberal in our concession, and that there never was a miraculous event established on so full an evidence.

For *first,* there is not to be found, in all history, any miracle attested by a sufficient number of men, of such unquestioned good-sense, education, and learning, as to secure us against all delusion in themselves; of such undoubted integrity, as to place them beyond all suspicion of any design to deceive others; of such credit and reputation in the eyes of mankind, as to have a great deal to lose in case of their being detected in any falsehood; and at the same time, attesting facts performed in such a public manner and in so celebrated a part of the world, as to render the detection unavoidable: All which circumstances are requisite to give us a full assurance in the testimony of men.

Secondly. We may observe in human nature a principle which, if strictly examined, will be found to diminish extremely the assurance, which we might, from human testimony, have, in any kind of prodigy. The maxim, by which we commonly conduct ourselves in our reasonings, is, that the objects, of which we have no experience, resembles those, of which we have; that what we have found to be most usual is always most probable; and that where there is an opposition of arguments, we ought to give the preference to such as are founded on the greatest number of past observations. But though, in proceeding by this rule, we readily reject any fact which is unusual and incredible in an ordinary degree; yet in advancing farther, the mind observes not always the same rule; but when anything is affirmed utterly absurd and miraculous, it rather the more readily admits of such a fact, upon account of that very circumstance, which ought to destroy all its authority. The passion of *surprise* and *wonder,* arising from miracles, being an agreeable emotion, gives a sensible tendency towards the belief of those events, from which it is derived. And this goes so far, that even those who cannot enjoy this pleasure immediately, nor can believe those miraculous events, of which they are informed, yet love to partake of the satisfaction at second-hand or by rebound, and place a pride and delight in exciting the admiration of others.

With what greediness are the miraculous accounts of travellers received, their descriptions of sea and land monsters, their relations of wonderful adventures, strange men, and uncouth manners? But if the spirit of religion join itself to the love of wonder, there is an end of common sense; and human testimony, in these circumstances, loses all pretensions to authority. A religionist may be an enthusiast, and imagine he sees what has no reality: he may know his narrative to be false, and yet persevere in it, with the best intentions in the world, for the sake of promoting so holy a cause: or even where this delusion has not place, vanity, excited by so strong a temptation, operates on him more powerfully than on the rest of mankind in any other circumstances; and self-interest with equal force. His auditors may not have, and commonly have not, sufficient judgement to canvass his evidence: what judgement they have, they renounce by principle, in these sublime and mysterious subjects: or if they were ever so willing to employ it, passion and a heated imagination disturb the regularity of its operations. Their credulity increases his impudence: and his impudence overpowers their credulity.

Eloquence, when at its highest pitch, leaves little room for reason or reflection; but addressing itself entirely to the fancy or the affections, captivates the willing hearers, and subdues their understanding. Happily, this pitch it seldom attains. But what a Tully or a Demosthenes could scarcely effect over a Roman or Athenian audience, every *Capuchin,* every itinerant or stationary teacher can perform over the generality of mankind, and in a higher degree, by touching such gross and vulgar passions.

The many instances of forged miracles, and prophecies, and supernatural events, which, in all ages, have either been detected by contrary evidence, or which detect themselves by their absurdity, prove sufficiently the strong propensity of mankind to the extraordinary and the marvellous, and ought reasonably to beget a suspicion against all relations of this kind. This is our natural way of

(continued)

Section X of Miracles (*continued*)

thinking, even with regard to the most common and most credible events. For instance: There is no kind of report which rises so easily, and spreads so quickly, especially in country places and provincial towns, as those concerning marriages; insomuch that two young persons of equal condition never see each other twice, but the whole neighbourhood immediately join them together. The pleasure of telling a piece of news so interesting, of propagating it, and of being the first reporters of it, spreads the intelligence. And this is so well known, that no man of sense gives attention to these reports, till he find them confirmed by some greater evidence. Do not the same passions, and others still stronger, incline the generality of mankind to believe and report, with the greatest vehemence and assurance, all religious miracles?

Thirdly. It forms a strong presumption against all supernatural and miraculous relations, that they are observed chiefly to abound among ignorant and barbarous nations; or if a civilized people has ever given admission to any of them, that people will be found to have received them from ignorant and barbarous ancestors, who transmitted them with that inviolable sanction and authority, which always attend received opinions. When we peruse the first histories of all nations, we are apt to imagine ourselves transported into some new world; where the whole frame of nature is disjointed, and every element performs its operations in a different manner, from what it does at present. Battles, revolutions, pestilence, famine and death, are never the effect of those natural causes, which we experience. Prodigies, omens, oracles, judgements, quite obscure the few natural events, that are intermingled with them. But as the former grow thinner every page, in proportion as we advance nearer the enlightened ages, we soon learn, that there is nothing mysterious or supernatural in the case, but that all proceeds from the usual propensity of mankind towards the marvellous, and that, though this inclination may at intervals receive a check from sense and learning, it can never be thoroughly extirpated from human nature.

It is strange, a judicious reader is apt to say, upon the perusal of these wonderful historians, *that such prodigious events never happen in our days.* But it is nothing strange, I hope, that men should lie in all ages. You must surely have seen instances enough of that frailty. You have yourself heard many such marvellous relations started, which, being treated with scorn by all the wise and judicious, have at last been abandoned even by the vulgar. Be assured, that those renowned lies, which have spread and flourished to such a monstrous height, arose from like beginnings; but being sown in a more proper soil, shot up at last into prodigies almost equal to those which they relate.

It was a wise policy in that false prophet, Alexander, who though now forgotten, was once so famous, to lay the first scene of his impostures in Paphlagonia, where, as Lucian tells us, the people were extremely ignorant and stupid, and ready to swallow even the grossest delusion. People at a distance, who are weak enough to think the matter at all worth enquiry, have no opportunity of receiving better information. The stories come magnified to them by a hundred circumstances. Fools are industrious in propagating the imposture; while the wise and learned are contented, in general, to deride its absurdity, without informing themselves of the particular facts, by which it may be distinctly refuted. And thus the impostor above mentioned was enabled to proceed, from his ignorant Paphlagonians, to the enlisting of votaries, even among the Grecian philosophers, and men of the most eminent rank and distinction in Rome: nay, could engage the attention of that sage emperor Marcus Aurelius; so far as to make him trust the success of a military expedition to his delusive prophecies.

The advantages are so great, of starting an imposture among an ignorant people, that, even though the delusion should be too gross to impose on the generality of them *(which, though seldom, is sometimes the case)* it has a much better chance for succeeding in remote countries, than if the first scene had been laid in a city renowned for arts and knowledge. The most ignorant and barbarous of these barbarians carry the report abroad. None of their countrymen have a large correspondence, or sufficient credit and authority to contradict and beat down the delusion. Men's inclination to the marvellous has full opportunity to display itself. And thus a story, which is universally exploded in the place where it was first started, shall pass for certain at a thousand miles distance. But had Alexander fixed his residence at Athens, the philosophers of that renowned mart of learning had immediately spread, throughout the whole Roman empire, their sense of the matter; which, being supported by so great authority, and displayed by all the force of reason and eloquence, had entirely opened the eyes of mankind. It is true; Lucian, passing by chance through Paphlagonia, had an opportunity of performing this good office. But, though much to be wished, it does not always happen, that every Alexander meets with a Lucian, ready to expose and detect his impostures.

I may add as a *fourth* reason, which diminishes the authority of prodigies, that there is no testimony for any, even those which have not been expressly detected, that is not opposed by an infinite number of witnesses; so that not only the miracle destroys the credit of testimony, but the testimony destroys itself. To make this the better understood, let us consider, that, in matters of religion, whatever is different is contrary; and that it is impossible the religions of ancient Rome, of Turkey, of Siam, and of China should, all of them, be established on any solid foundation. Every miracle, therefore, pretended to have been wrought in any of these religions (and all of them abound in miracles), as its direct scope is to establish the particular system to which it is attributed; so has it the same force, though more indirectly, to overthrow every other system. In destroying a rival system, it likewise destroys the credit of those miracles, on which that system was established; so that all the prodigies of different religions are to be regarded as contrary facts, and the evidences of these prodigies, whether weak or strong, as opposite to each other. According to this method of reasoning, when we believe any miracle of Mahomet or his successors, we have for our warrant the testimony of a few barbarous Arabians: And on the other hand, we are to regard the authority of Titus Livius, Plutarch, Tacitus, and, in short, of all the authors and witnesses, Grecian, Chinese, and Roman Catholic, who have related any miracle in their particular religion; I say, we are to regard their testimony in the same light as if they had mentioned that Mahometan miracle, and had in express terms contradicted it, with the same certainty as they have for the miracle they relate. This argument may appear over subtile and refined; but is not in reality different from the reasoning of a judge, who supposes, that the credit of two witnesses, maintaining a crime against any one, is destroyed by the testimony of two others, who affirm him to have been two hundred leagues distant, at the same instant when the crime is said to have been committed.

One of the best attested miracles in all profane history, is that which Tacitus reports of Vespasian, who cured a blind man in Alexandria, by means of his spittle, and a lame man by the mere touch of his foot; in obedience to a vision of the god Serapis, who had enjoined them to have recourse to the Emperor, for these miraculous cures. The story may be seen in that fine historian; where every circumstance seems to add weight to the testimony, and might be displayed at large with all the force of argument and eloquence, if any one were now concerned to enforce the evidence of that exploded and idolatrous superstition. The gravity, solidity, age, and probity of so great an emperor, who, through the whole course of his life, conversed in a familiar manner with his friends and courtiers, and never affected those extraordinary airs of divinity assumed by Alexander and Demetrius. The historian, a cotemporary writer, noted for candour and veracity, and withal, the greatest and most penetrating genius, perhaps, of all antiquity; and so free from any tendency to credulity, that he even lies under the contrary imputation, of atheism and profaneness: The persons, from whose authority he related the miracle, of established character for judgement and veracity, as we may well presume; eye-witnesses of the fact, and confirming their testimony, after the Flavian family was despoiled of the empire, and could no longer give any reward, as the price of a lie. *Utrumque, qui interfuere, nunc quoque memorant, postquam nullum mendacio pretium.* To which if we add the public nature of the facts, as related, it will appear, that no evidence can well be supposed stronger for so gross and so palpable a falsehood.

There is also a memorable story related by Cardinal de Retz, which may well deserve our consideration. When that intriguing politician fled into Spain, to avoid the persecution of his enemies, he passed through Saragossa, the capital of Arragon, where he was shewn, in the cathedral, a man, who had served seven years as a door-keeper, and was well known to every body in town, that had ever paid his devotions at that church. He had been seen, for so long a time, wanting a leg; but recovered that limb by the rubbing of holy oil upon the stump; and the cardinal assures us that he saw him with two legs. This miracle was vouched by all the canons of the church; and the

(continued)

Section X of Miracles (*continued*)

whole company in town were appealed to for a confirmation of the fact; whom the cardinal found, by their zealous devotion, to be thorough believers of the miracle. Here the relater was also cotemporary to the supposed prodigy, of an incredulous and libertine character, as well as of great genius; the miracle of so *singular* a nature as could scarcely admit of a counterfeit, and the witnesses very numerous, and all of them, in a manner, spectators of the fact, to which they gave their testimony. And what adds mightily to the force of the evidence, and may double our surprise on this occasion, is, that the cardinal himself, who relates the story, seems not to give any credit to it, and consequently cannot be suspected of any concurrence in the holy fraud. He considered justly, that it was not requisite, in order to reject a fact of this nature, to be able accurately to disprove the testimony, and to trace its falsehood, through all the circumstances of knavery and credulity which produced it. He knew, that, as this was commonly altogether impossible at any small distance of time and place; so was it extremely difficult, even where one was immediately present, by reason of the bigotry, ignorance, cunning, and roguery of a great part of mankind. He therefore concluded, like a just reasoner, that such an evidence carried falsehood upon the very face of it, and that a miracle, supported by any human testimony, was more properly a subject of derision than of argument.

There surely never was a greater number of miracles ascribed to one person, than those, which were lately said to have been wrought in France upon the tomb of Abb(c) Paris, the famous Jansenist, with whose sanctity the people were so long deluded. The curing of the sick, giving hearing to the deaf, and sight to the blind, were every where talked of as the usual effects of that holy sepulchre. But what is more extraordinary; many of the miracles were immediately proved upon the spot, before judges of unquestioned integrity, attested by witnesses of credit and distinction, in a learned age, and on the most eminent theatre that is now in the world. Nor is this all: a relation of them was published and dispersed every where; nor were the *Jesuits,* though a learned body, supported by the civil magistrate, and determined enemies to those opinions, in whose favour the miracles were said to have been wrought, ever able distinctly to refute or detect them.[24] Where shall we find such a number of circumstances, agreeing to the corroboration of one fact? And what have we to oppose to such a cloud of witnesses, but the absolute impossibility or miraculous nature of the events, which they relate? And this surely, in the eyes of all reasonable people, will alone be regarded as a sufficient refutation.

Is the consequence just, because some human testimony has the utmost force and authority in some cases, when it relates the battle of Philippi or Pharsalia for instance; that therefore all kinds of testimony must, in all cases, have equal force and authority? Suppose that the Caesarean and Pompeian factions had, each of them, claimed the victory in these battles, and that the historians of each party had uniformly ascribed the advantage to their own side; how could mankind, at this distance, have been able to determine between them? The contrariety is equally strong between the miracles related by Herodotus or Plutarch, and those delivered by Mariana, Bede, or any monkish historian.

The wise lend a very academic faith to every report which favours the passion of the reporter; whether it magnifies his country, his family, or himself, or in any other way strikes in with his natural inclinations and propensities. But what greater temptation than to appear a missionary, a prophet, an ambassador from heaven? Who would not encounter many dangers and difficulties, in order to attain so sublime a character? Or if, by the help of vanity and a heated imagination, a man has first made a convert of himself, and entered seriously into the delusion; who ever scruples to make use of pious frauds, in support of so holy and meritorious a cause?

The smallest spark may here kindle into the greatest flame; because the materials are always prepared for it. The *avidum genus auricularum,*[25] the gazing populace, receive greedily, without examination, whatever sooths superstition, and promotes wonder.

How many stories of this nature have, in all ages, been detected and exploded in their infancy? How many more have been celebrated for a time, and have afterwards sunk into neglect and oblivion? Where such reports, therefore, fly about, the solution of the phenomenon is obvious; and we judge in conformity to regular experience and observation, when we account for it by the known and natural principles of credulity and delusion. And shall we, rather than have a recourse to so natural a solution, allow of a miraculous violation of the most established laws of nature?

I need not mention the difficulty of detecting a falsehood in any private or even public history, at the place, where it is said to happen; much more when the scene is removed to ever so small a distance. Even a court of judicature, with all the authority, accuracy, and judgement, which they can employ, find themselves often at a loss to distinguish between truth and falsehood in the most recent actions. But the matter never comes to any issue, if trusted to the common method of altercations and debate and flying rumours; especially when men's passions have taken part on either side.

In the infancy of new religions, the wise and learned commonly esteem the matter too inconsiderable to deserve their attention or regard. And when afterwards they would willingly detect the cheat, in order to undeceive the deluded multitude, the season is now past, and the records and witnesses, which might clear up the matter, have perished beyond recovery.

No means of detection remain, but those which must be drawn from the very testimony itself of the reporters: and these, though always sufficient with the judicious and knowing, are commonly too fine to fall under the comprehension of the vulgar.

Upon the whole, then, it appears, that no testimony for any kind of miracle has ever amounted to a probability, much less to a proof; and that, even supposing it amounted to a proof, it would be opposed by another proof; derived from the very nature of the fact, which it would endeavour to establish. It is experience only, which gives authority to human testimony; and it is the same experience, which assures us of the laws of nature. When, therefore, these two kinds of experience are contrary, we have nothing to do but substract the one from the other, and embrace an opinion, either on one side or the other, with that assurance which arises from the remainder. But according to the principle here explained, this substraction, with regard to all popular religions, amounts to an entire annihilation; and therefore we may establish it as a maxim, that no human testimony can have such force as to prove a miracle, and make it a just foundation for any such system of religion.

I beg the limitations here made may be remarked, when I say, that a miracle can never be proved, so as to be the foundation of a system of religion. For I own, that otherwise, there may possibly be miracles, or violations of the usual course of nature, of such a kind as to admit of proof from human testimony; though, perhaps, it will be impossible to find any such in all the records of history. Thus, suppose, all authors, in all languages, agree, that, from the first of January 1600, there was a total darkness over the whole earth for eight days: suppose that the tradition of this extraordinary event is still strong and lively among the people: that all travellers, who return from foreign countries, bring us accounts of the same tradition, without the least variation or contradiction: it is evident, that our present philosophers, instead of doubting the fact, ought to receive it as certain, and ought to search for the causes whence it might be derived. The decay, corruption, and dissolution of nature, is an event rendered probable by so many analogies, that any phenomenon, which seems to have a tendency towards that catastrophe, comes within the reach of human testimony, if that testimony be very extensive and uniform.

But suppose, that all the historians who treat of England, should agree, that, on the first of January 1600, Queen Elizabeth died; that both before and after her death she was seen by her physicians and the whole court, as is usual with persons of her rank; that her successor was acknowledged and proclaimed by the parliament; and that, after being interred a month, she again appeared, resumed the throne, and governed England for three years: I must confess that I should be surprised at the concurrence of so many odd circumstances, but should not have the least inclination to believe so miraculous an event. I should not doubt of her pretended death, and of those other public circumstances that followed it: I should only assert it to have been pretended, and that it neither was, nor possibly could be real. You would in vain object to me the difficulty, and almost impossibility of deceiving the world in an affair of such consequence; the wisdom and solid judgement of that renowned queen; with the little or no advantage which she could reap from so poor an artifice: All this might astonish me; but I would still reply, that the knavery and folly of men are such common phenomena, that I should rather believe the most extraordinary events to arise from their concurrence, than admit of so signal a violation of the laws of nature.

(continued)

Section X of Miracles (*continued*)

But should this miracle be ascribed to any new system of religion; men, in all ages, have been so much imposed on by ridiculous stories of that kind, that this very circumstance would be a full proof of a cheat, and sufficient, with all men of sense, not only to make them reject the fact, but even reject it without farther examination. Though the Being to whom the miracle is ascribed, be, in this case, Almighty, it does not, upon that account, become a whit more probable; since it is impossible for us to know the attributes or actions of such a Being, otherwise than from the experience which we have of his productions, in the usual course of nature. This still reduces us to past observation, and obliges us to compare the instances of the violation of truth in the testimony of men, with those of the violation of the laws of nature by miracles, in order to judge which of them is most likely and probable. As the violations of truth are more common in the testimony concerning religious miracles, than in that concerning any other matter of fact; this must diminish very much the authority of the former testimony, and make us form a general resolution, never to lend any attention to it, with whatever specious pretence it may be covered.

Lord Bacon seems to have embraced the same principles of reasoning. 'We ought,' says he, 'to make a collection or particular history of all monsters and prodigious births or productions, and in a word of every thing new, rare, and extraordinary in nature. But this must be done with the most severe scrutiny, lest we depart from truth. Above all, every relation must be considered as suspicious, which depends in any degree upon religion, as the prodigies of Livy: And no less so, every thing that is to be found in the writers of natural magic or alchimy, or such authors, who seem, all of them, to have an unconquerable appetite for falsehood and fable.'

I am the better pleased with the method of reasoning here delivered, as I think it may serve to confound those dangerous friends or disguised enemies to the *Christian Religion,* who have undertaken to defend it by the principles of human reason. Our most holy religion is founded on *Faith,* not on reason; and it is a sure method of exposing it to put it to such a trial as it is, by no means, fitted to endure. To make this more evident, let us examine those miracles, related in scripture; and not to lose ourselves in too wide a field, let us confine ourselves to such as we find in the *Pentateuch,* which we shall examine, according to the principles of these pretended Christians, not as the word or testimony of God himself, but as the production of a mere human writer and historian. Here then we are first to consider a book, presented to us by a barbarous and ignorant people, written in an age when they were still more barbarous, and in all probability long after the facts which it relates, corroborated by no concurring testimony, and resembling those fabulous accounts, which every nation gives of its origin. Upon reading this book, we find it full of prodigies and miracles. It gives an account of a state of the world and of human nature entirely different from the present: Of our fall from that state: Of the age of man, extended to near a thousand years: Of the destruction of the world by a deluge: Of the arbitrary choice of one people, as the favourites of heaven; and that people the countrymen of the author: Of their deliverance from bondage by prodigies the most astonishing imaginable: I desire any one to lay his hand upon his heart, and after a serious consideration declare, whether he thinks that the falsehood of such a book, supported by such a testimony, would be more extraordinary and miraculous than all the miracles it relates; which is, however, necessary to make it be received, according to the measures of probability above established.

What we have said of miracles may be applied, without any variation, to prophecies; and indeed, all prophecies are real miracles, and as such only, can be admitted as proofs of any revelation. If it did not exceed the capacity of human nature to foretell future events, it would be absurd to employ any prophecy as an argument for a divine mission or authority from heaven. So that, upon the whole, we may conclude, that the *Christian Religion* not only was at first attended with miracles, but even at this day cannot be believed by any reasonable person without one. Mere reason is insufficient to convince us of its veracity: And whoever is moved by *Faith* to assent to it, is conscious of a continued miracle in his own person, which subverts all the principles of his understanding, and gives him a determination to believe what is most contrary to custom and experience.

Religious Belief Without Evidence
Alvin Plantinga

The Evidentialist Objection to Theistic Belief

MANY PHILOSOPHERS—Clifford, Blanshard, Russell, Scriven, and Flew, to name a few—have argued that belief in God is irrational, or unreasonable, or not rationally acceptable, or intellectually irresponsible, or somehow noetically below par because, as they say, there is *insufficient evidence* for it.[1] Bertrand Russell was once asked what he would say if, after dying, he were brought into the presence of God and asked why he hadn't been a believer. Russell's reply: "I'd say, 'Not enough evidence, God! Not enough evidence!'"[2] I don't know just how such a response would be received, but Russell, like many others, held that theistic belief is unreasonable because there is insufficient evidence for it. We all remember W. K. Clifford, that delicious *enfant terrible,* as William James called him, and his insistence that it is immoral, wicked, and monstrous, and maybe even impolite to accept a belief for which you don't have sufficient evidence:

> Who so would deserve well of his fellows in this matter will guard the purity of his belief with a very fanaticism of jealous care, lest at any time it should rest on an unworthy object, and catch a stain which can never be wiped away.

He adds that if a

> belief has been accepted on insufficient evidence, the pleasure is a stolen one. Not only does it deceive ourselves by giving us a sense of power which we do not really possess, but it is sinful, because it is stolen in defiance of our duty to mankind. That duty is to guard ourselves from such beliefs as from a pestilence which may shortly master our body and spread to the rest of the town.

and finally:

> To sum up: it is wrong always, everywhere, and for anyone to believe anything upon insufficient evidence.

(It is not hard to detect, in these quotations, the "tone of robustious pathos" with which James credits him.) Clifford, of course, held that one who accepts belief in God *does* accept that belief on insufficient evidence, and has indeed defied his duty to mankind. More recently, Bertrand Russell has endorsed the evidentialist injunction "Give to any hypothesis which is worth your while to consider, just that degree or credence which the evidence warrants."

More recently, Antony Flew[3] has commended what he calls Clifford's "luminous and compulsive essay" (perhaps "compulsive" here is a misprint for "compelling"), and Flew goes on to claim that there is, in his words a "presumption of atheism." What is a presumption of atheism, and why should we think there is one? Flew puts it as follows:

> The debate about the existence of God should properly begin from the presumption of atheism . . . the onus of proof must lie upon the theist. The word "atheism," however, has in this contention to be construed unusually. Whereas nowadays the usual meaning of "atheist" in English is "someone who asserts there is no such being as God," I want the word to be understood not positively but negatively. I want the original Greek prefix "a" to be read in the same way in "atheist" as it is customarily read in such other Greco-English words as "amoral," "atypical," and "asymmetrical." In his interpretation an atheist becomes not someone who positively asserts the non-existence of God, but someone who is simply not a theist.
>
> What the protagonist of my presumption of atheism wants to show is that the debate about the existence of God ought to be conducted in a particular way, and that the issue should be seen in a certain perspective. His thesis about the onus of proof involves that it is up to the theist: first to introduce and to defend his proposed concept of God, and second, to provide sufficient reason for believing that this concept of his does in fact have an application.

(continued)

Religious Belief Without Evidence   (continued)

How shall we understand this? What does it mean, for example, to say that the debate "should properly begin from the presumption of atheism"? What sorts of things do debates begin from, and what is it for one to begin from such a thing? Perhaps Flew means something like this: to speak of where a debate should begin is to speak of the sorts of premises to which the affirmative and negative sides can properly appeal in arguing their cases. Suppose you and I are debating the question whether, say, the United States has a right to seize Mideast oil fields if the OPEC countries refuse to sell us oil at what we think is a fair price. I take the affirmative, and produce for my conclusion an argument one premise of which is the proposition that the United States has indeed a right to seize these oil fields under those conditions. Doubtless that maneuver would earn me very few points. Similarly, a debate about the existence of God cannot sensibly start from the assumption that God does indeed exist. That is to say, the affirmative can't properly appeal, in its arguments, to such premises as that there is such a person as God; if it could, it'd have much too easy a time of it. So in this sense of "start," Flew is quite right: the debate can't start from the assumption that God exists.

Of course, it is also true that the debate can't start from the assumption that God does *not* exist; using "atheism" in its ordinary sense, there is equally a presumption of aatheism (which, by a familiar principle of logic, reduces to theism). So it looks as if there is in Flew's sense a presumption of atheism, all right, but in that same sense an equal presumption of atheism. If this is what Flew means, then what he says is entirely correct, if something of a truism.

In another passage, however, Flew seems to understand the presumption of atheism in quite another different fashion:

> It is by reference to this inescapable demand for grounds that the presumption of atheism is justified. If it is to be established that there is a God, then we have to have good grounds for believing that this is indeed so. Until or unless some such grounds are produced we have literally no reason at all for believing; and in that situation the only reasonable posture must be that of either the negative atheist or the agnostic.

Here we have the much more substantial suggestion that it is unreasonable or irrational to accept theistic belief in the absence of sufficient grounds or reasons. And of course Flew, along with Russell, Clifford, and many others, holds that in fact there aren't sufficient grounds or evidence for belief in God. The evidentialist objection, therefore, appeals to the following two premises:

a. It is irrational or unreasonable to accept theistic belief in the absence of sufficient evidence or reasons.

and

b. There is no evidence, or at any rate not sufficient evidence, for the proposition that God exists.

(B), I think, is at best dubious. At present, however, I'm interested in the objector's other premise—the claim that it is irrational or unreasonable to accept theistic belief in the absence of evidence or reasons. Why suppose *that's* true? Why suppose a theist must have evidence or reason to think there *is* evidence for this belief, if he is not to be irrational? This isn't just *obvious,* after all.

Now many Reformed thinkers and theologians[4] have rejected *natural theology* (thought of as the attempt to provide proofs or arguments for the existence of God). They have held not merely that the proffered arguments are unsuccessful, but that the whole enterprise is in some way radically misguided. I have argued (1980) that the Reformed rejection of natural theology is best construed as an inchoate and unfocused rejection of (A). What these Reformed thinkers really mean to hold, I think, is that belief in God is properly basic: it need not be based on argument or evidence from other propositions at all. They mean to hold that the believer is entirely within his intellectual right in believing as he does, even if he doesn't know of any good theistic argument (deductive or inductive), even if he doesn't believe that there is any such argument, and even if in fact no such argument exists. They hold that it is perfectly rational to accept belief in God without accepting it on the basis of any other beliefs or propositions at all. Why suppose that the believer must have evidence if he is not to be irrational? Why should anyone accept (A)? What is to be said in its favor?

Suppose we begin by asking what the objector means by describing a belief as *irrational*. What is the force of his claim that the theistic belief is irrational and how is it to be understood? The first thing to see is that this claim is rooted in a *normative* contention. It lays down conditions that must be met by anyone whose system of beliefs is *rational;* and here "rational" is to be taken as a normative or evaluative term. According to the objector, there is a right way and a wrong way with respect to belief. People have responsibilities, duties and obligations with respect to their believings just as they do with respect to their actions—or if we think believings are a kind of action, their *other* actions. Professor Brand Blanshard puts this clearly:

> everywhere and always belief has an ethical aspect. There is such a thing as a general ethics of the intellect. The main principle of that ethic I hold to be the same inside and outside religion. This principle is simple and sweeping: Equate your assent to the evidence. *(Reason and Belief,* p. 401)

and according to Michael Scriven:

> Now even belief in something for which there is no evidence, i.e., a belief which goes beyond the evidence, although a lesser sin than a belief in something which is contrary to well-established laws, is plainly irrational in that it simply amounts to attaching belief where it is not justified. So the proper alternative, when there is no evidence, is not mere suspension of belief, e.g., about Santa Claus, it is disbelief. It most certainly is not faith. *(Primary Philosophy,* p.103)

Perhaps this sort of obligation is really a special case of a more general moral obligation; or perhaps, on the other hand, it is *sui generis*. In any event, says the objector, there are such obligations: to conform to them is to be rational and to go against them is to be irrational.

Now here the objector seems right; there are duties and obligations with respect to beliefs. One's own welfare and that of others sometimes depends on what one believes. If we're descending the Grand Teton and I'm setting the anchor for the 120-foot rappel into the Upper Saddle, I have an obligation to form such beliefs as *this anchor point is solid* only on the basis of careful scrutiny and testing. One commissioned to gather intelligence—the spies Joshua sent into Canaan, for example—has an obligation to get it right. I have an obligation with respect to the belief that Justin Martyr was a Latin apologist—an obligation arising from the fact that I teach medieval philosophy, must make a declaration on this issue, and am obliged not to mislead my students here. The precise *form* of these obligations may be hard to specify: Am I obliged to believe that J. M. was a Latin apologist if and only if J. M. *was* a Latin apologist? Or to form a belief on this topic only after the appropriate amount of checking and investigating? Or maybe just to tell the students the truth about it, whatever I myself believe in the privacy of my own study? Or to tell them what's generally thought by those who should know? In the rappel case: Do I have a duty to believe that the anchor point is solid if and only if it is? Or just to check carefully before forming the belief? Or perhaps there's no obligation to believe at all, but only to *act on* a certain belief only after appropriate investigation. In any event, it seems plausible to hold that there are obligations and norms with respect to belief, and I do not intend to contest this assumption.

The objector begins, therefore, from the plausible contention that there are duties or obligations with respect to belief: call them *intellectual duties*. These duties can be understood in several ways. First, we could construe them teleologically, we could adopt an intellectual utilitarianism. Here the rough idea is that our intellectual obligations arise out of a connection between our beliefs and what is intrinsically good and intrinsically bad, and our intellectual obligations are just a special case of the general obligation so to act to maximize good and minimize evil. Perhaps this is how W. K. Clifford thinks of the matter. If people accepted such propositions as *this DC-10 is airworthy* when the evidence is insufficient, the consequences could be disastrous; so perhaps some of us, at any rate, have an obligation to believe that proposition only in the presence of adequate evidence. The intellectual utilitarian could be an ideal utilitarian; he could hold that certain epistemic states are intrinsically valuable—knowledge, perhaps, or believing the truth, or a skeptical and judicial temper that is not blown about by every wind of doctrine. Among our duties, then, is a duty to try

(continued)

Religious Belief Without Evidence   (*continued*)

to bring about these valuable states of affairs. Perhaps this is how Professor Roderick Chisholm is to be understood when he says

> Let us consider the concept of what might be called an "intellectual requirement." We may assume that every person is subject to a purely intellectual requirement: that of trying his best to bring it about that, for every proposition that he considers, he accepts it if and only if it is true. (*Theory of Knowledge*, 2nd ed., p. 9)

Secondly, we could construe intellectual obligations *aretetically;* we could adopt what Professor Frankena calls a "mixed ethics of virtue" with respect to the intellect. There are valuable noetic or intellectual states (whether intrinsically or intrinsically valuable); there are also the corresponding intellectual virtues, the habits of acting so as to produce or promote or enhance those valuable states. One's intellectual obligations, then, are to try to produce and enhance these intellectual virtues in oneself and others.

Thirdly, we could construe intellectual obligations *deontologically*; we could adopt a *pure* ethics of obligation with respect to the intellect. Perhaps there are intellectual obligations that do not arise from any connection with good or evil, but attach to us just by virtue of our having the sorts of noetic powers human beings do in fact display. The quotation from Chisholm could also be understood along these lines.

Intellectual obligations, therefore, can be understood teleologically or aretetically or deontologically. And perhaps there are purely intellectual obligations of the following sorts. Perhaps I have a duty not to take as basic a proposition whose denial seems self-evident. Perhaps I have a duty to take as basic the proposition *I seem to see a tree* under certain conditions. With respect to certain kinds of propositions, perhaps I have a duty to believe them only if I have evidence for them, and a duty to proportion the strength of my belief to the strength of my evidence.

Of course, these would be *prima facie* obligations. One presumably has an obligation not to take bread from the grocery store without permission and another to tell the truth. Both can be overridden, in specific circumstances, by other obligations—in the first case, perhaps, an obligation to feed my starving children and in the second, an obligation to protect a human life. So we must distinguish *prima facie* duties or obligations from *all-things-considered* or *on-balance (ultima facie?)* obligations. I have a *prima facie* obligation to tell the truth; in a given situation, however, that obligation may be overridden by others, so that my duty, all things considered, is to tell a lie. This is the grain of truth contained in situation ethics and the ill-named "new morality."

And *prima facie* intellectual obligations can conflict, just as obligations of other sorts. Perhaps I have a *prima facie* obligation to believe what seems to me self-evident, and what seems to me to follow self-evidently from what seems to me self-evident. But what if, as in the Russell paradoxes, something that seems self-evidently false apparently follows, self-evidently, from what seems self-evidently true? Here *prima facie* intellectual obligations conflict, and no matter what I do I will violate a *prima facie* obligation. Another example: in reporting the Grand Teton rappel, I neglected to mention the violent electrical storm coming in from the southwest; to escape it we must get off in a hurry, so that I have a *prima facie* obligation to inspect the anchor point carefully, but anchor to set up the rappel rapidly, which means I can't spend a lot of time inspecting the anchor point.

Thus lightly armed, suppose we return to the evidential objector. Does he mean to hold that the theist without evidence is violating some intellectual obligation? If so, which one? Does he claim, for example, that the theist is violating his *ultima facie* intellectual obligation in thus believing? Perhaps he thinks anyone who believes in God without evidence is violating his all-things-considered intellectual duty. This, however, seems unduly harsh. What about the fourteen-year-old theist brought up to believe in God in a community where everyone believes? This fourteen-year-old theist, we may suppose, doesn't believe on the basis of evidence. He doesn't argue thus: everyone around here says God loves us and cares for us; most of what everyone around here says is true; so probably *that's* true. Instead, he simply believes what he's taught. Is he violating an all-things-considered intellectual duty? Surely not. And what about the mature theist—Thomas Aquinas, let's say—who thinks he *does* have adequate evidence? Let's suppose he's wrong; let's suppose all of his arguments are failures. Nevertheless, he has reflected long, hard, and conscientiously on the matter and thinks he *does* have adequate evidence. Shall we suppose he's violating an all-things-considered intellectual duty here? I should think not. So construed, the objector's contention is totally implausible.

Perhaps, then, he is to be understood as claiming that there is a *prima facie* intellectual duty not to believe in God without evidence. This duty can be overridden by circumstances, of course, but there is a *prima facie* obligation to believe propositions of this sort only on the basis of evidence. But here too there are problems. The suggestion is that I now have the *prima facie* obligation to believe propositions of this sort only on the basis of evidence. I have a *prima facie* duty to comply with the following command: either have evidence or don't believe. But this may be command I can't comply with. The objector thinks there *isn't* adequate evidence for this belief, so presumably I can't *have* adequate evidence for it, unless we suppose I could create some. And it is also not within my power to refrain from believing this proposition. My beliefs aren't for the most part directly within my control. If you order me now, for example, to cease believing that the earth is very old, there's no way I can comply with your order. But in the same way it isn't within my power to cease believing in God now. So this alleged *prima facie* duty is one it isn't within my power to comply with. But how can I have a *prima facie* duty to do what isn't within my power to do?

Presumably, then, the objector means to be understood in still another fashion. Although it is not within my power now to cease believing now, there may be a series of actions now, such that I can now take the first, and after taking the first, will be able to take the second, and so on, and after taking the whole series of actions, I will no longer believe in God. Perhaps the objector thinks it is my *prima facie* duty to undertake whatever sort of regimen will at some time in the future result in my not believing without evidence. Perhaps I should attend a Universalist Unitarian Church, for example, and consort with members of the Rationalist Society of America. Perhaps I should read a lot of Voltaire and Bertrand Russell. Even if I can't now stop believing without evidence, perhaps there are other actions I can now take, such that if I do take them, then at some time in the future I won't be in this deplorable condition.

There is still another option available to the objector. He need not hold that the theist without evidence is violating some duty, *prima facie, ultima facie* or otherwise. Consider someone who believes that Venus is smaller than Mercury, not because he has evidence, but because he finds it amusing to believe what everyone disbelieves—or consider someone who holds this belief on the basis of an outrageously bad argument. Perhaps there is no obligation he has failed to meet; nevertheless his intellectual condition is defective in some way; or perhaps alternatively there is a commonly achieved excellence he fails to display. Perhaps he is like someone who is easily gulled, or walks with a limp, or has a serious astigmatism, or is unduly clumsy. And perhaps the evidentialist objection is to be understood, not as the claim that the theist without evidence has failed to meet some obligation, but that he suffers from a certain sort of intellectual deficiency. If this is the objector's view, then his proper attitude towards the theist would be one of sympathy rather than censure.

These are some of the ways, then, in which the evidentialist objection could be developed, and of course there are still other possibilities. For ease of exposition, let us take the claim deontologically; what I shall say will apply *mutatis mutandis* if we take it one of the other ways. The evidentialist objector, then, holds that it is irrational to believe in God without evidence. He doesn't typically hold, however, that the same goes for *every* proposition; for given certain plausible conditions on the evidence relation it would follow that if we believe anything, then we are under obligation to believe infinitely many propositions. Let's say that proposition p is *basic* for a person S if S believes p but does not have evidence for p; and let's say that p is *properly basic* for S if S is within his epistemic rights in taking p as basic. The evidentialist objection, therefore, presupposes some view about what sorts of propositions are correctly or rightly or justifiably taken as basic; it presupposes a view about what is properly basic. And the minimally relevant claim for the evidentialist objector is that belief in God is *not* properly basic. Typically this objection has been rooted in some form of *classical foundationalism*, an enormously popular picture or total way of looking at faith, knowledge, justified belief, rationality and allied topics. This picture has been widely accepted ever since the days of Plato and Aristotle; its near relatives, perhaps, remain the dominant ways of thinking about these topics. According to the classical foundationalist, some propositions are *properly* or *rightly* basic for a person and some are not. Those that are not are rationally accepted

(continued)

Religious Belief Without Evidence (*continued*)

only on the basis of *evidence* where the evidence must trace back, ultimately, to what is properly basic. Now there are two varieties of classical foundationalism. According to the ancient and medieval variety, a proposition is properly basic for a person S if and only if it is either self-evident to S or "evident to the senses," to use Aquinas' term, for S; according to the modern variety, a proposition is properly basic for S if and only if it is either self-evident to S or incorrigible for him. For ease of exposition, let's say that classical foundationalism is the disjunction of ancient and medieval with modern foundationalism; according to the classical foundationalist, then, a proposition is properly basic for a person S if and only if it is either self-evident to S or incorrigible for S or evident to the senses for S.

Now I said that the evidentialist objection to theistic belief is typically rooted in classical foundationalism. Insofar as it is so rooted, it is *poorly* rooted. For classical foundationalism is self-referentially incoherent. Consider the main tenet of classical foundationalism:

(C) *p* is properly basic for S if and only if *p* is self-evident, incorrigible, or evident to the senses for S.

Now of course the classical foundationalist accepts (C) and proposes that we do so as well. And either he takes (C) as basic or he doesn't. If he doesn't, then if he is rational in accepting it, he must by his own claims have an argument for it from propositions that are properly basic, by argument forms whose corresponding conditionals are properly basic. Classical foundationalists do not, so far as I know, offer such arguments for (C). I suspect the reason is that they don't know of any arguments of that sort for (C). It is certainly hard to see what such an argument would be. Accordingly, classical foundationalists probably take (C) as basic. But then according to (C) itself, if (C) is properly taken as basic, it must be either self-evident, incorrigible, or evident to the senses for the foundationalist, and clearly it isn't any of those. If the foundationalist takes (C) as basic, therefore, he is self-referentially inconsistent. We must conclude, I think, that the classical foundationalist is in self-referential hot water—his own acceptance of the central tenet of his view is irrational by his own standards.

Objections to Taking Belief in God as Basic

Insofar as the evidentialist objection is rooted in classical foundationalism, it is poorly rooted indeed; and so far as I know, no one has developed and articulated any other reason for supporting that belief in God is not properly basic. Of course it doesn't follow that it *is* properly basic; perhaps the class of properly basic propositions is broader than classical foundationalists think, but still not broad enough to admit belief in God. But why think so? What might be the objections to the Reformed view that belief in God is properly basic?

I've heard it argued that if I have no evidence for the existence of God, then if I accept that proposition, my belief will *be groundless,* or *gratuitous,* or *arbitrary.* I think this is an error; let me explain.

Suppose we consider perceptual beliefs, memory beliefs, and beliefs ascribing mental states to other persons; such beliefs as

1. I see a tree.
2. I had breakfast this morning.
3. That person is angry.

Although beliefs of this sort are typically and properly taken as basic, it would be a mistake to describe them as *groundless.* Upon having experience of a certain sort, I believe that I am perceiving a tree. In the typical case I do not hold this belief on the basis of other beliefs; it is nonetheless not groundless. My having that characteristic sort of experience—to use Professor Chisholm's language, my being appeared treely to—plays a crucial role in the formation and justification of that belief. We might say this experience, together, perhaps, with other circumstances, is what *justifies* me in holding it; this is the *ground* of my justification, and, by extension, the ground of the belief itself.

If I see someone displaying typical pain behavior, I take it that he or she is in pain. Again, I don't take the displayed behavior as *evidence* for that belief; I don't infer that belief from others I hold; I don't accept it on the basis of other beliefs. Still, my perceiving the pain behavior plays a unique role in the formation and justification of that belief; as in the previous case, it forms the ground of my justification for the belief in question. The same holds for memory beliefs. I seem to remember having breakfast this morning; that is, I have an inclination to believe the proposition that I had breakfast, along with a certain past-tinged experience that is familiar to all but hard to describe. Perhaps we should say that I am appeared to pastly, but perhaps that insufficiently distinguishes the experience in question from that accompanying beliefs about the past not grounded in my own memory. The phenomenology of memory is a rich and unexplored realm; here I have no time to explore it. In this case as in the others, however, there is a justifying circumstance present, a condition that forms the ground of my justification for accepting the memory belief in question.

In each of these cases, a belief is taken as basic, and in each case properly taken as basic. In each case there is some circumstance or condition that confers justification; there is a circumstance that serves as the *ground* of justification. So in each case there will be some true proposition of the sort:

4. In condition C, S is justified in taking p as basic. Of course C will vary with p.

For a perceptual judgment such as

5. I see a rose-colored wall before me,

C will include my being appeared to in a certain fashion. No doubt C will include more. If I'm appeared to in the familiar fashion but know that I am wearing rose-colored glasses, or that I am suffering from a disease that causes me to be thus appeared to, no matter what the color of the nearby objects, then I am not justified in taking (5) as basic. Similarly for memory. Suppose I know that my memory is unreliable; it often plays me tricks. In particular, when I seem to remember having breakfast, then, more often than not, I *haven't* had breakfast. Under these conditions I am not justified in taking it as basic that I had breakfast, even though I seem to remember that I did.

So being appropriately appeared to, in the perceptual case, is not sufficient for justification; some further condition—a condition hard to state in detail—is clearly necessary. The central point, here, however, is that a belief is properly basic only in certain conditions; these conditions are, we might say, the ground of its justification and, by extension, the ground of the belief itself. In this sense, basic beliefs are not, or are not necessarily, *groundless* beliefs.

Now similar things may be said about belief in God. When the Reformers claim that this belief is properly basic, they do not mean to say, of course, that there are no justifying circumstances for it, or that it is in that sense groundless or gratuitous. Quite the contrary. Calvin holds that God "reveals and daily discloses himself in the whole workmanship of the universe," and the divine art "reveals itself in the innumerable and yet distinct and well-ordered variety of the heavenly host." God has so created us that we have a tendency or disposition to see his hand in the world about us. More precisely, there is in us a disposition to believe propositions of the sort *this flower was created by God* or *this vast and intricate universe was created by God* when we contemplate the flower or behold the starry heavens or think about the vast reaches of the universe.

Calvin recognizes, at least implicitly, that other sorts of conditions may trigger this disposition. Upon reading the Bible, one may be impressed with a deep sense that God is speaking to one. Upon having done what I know is cheap, or wrong, or wicked, I may feel guilty in God's sight and form the belief *God disapproves of what I've done.* Upon confession and repentance, I may feel forgiven, forming the belief *God forgives me for what I've done.* A person in grave danger may turn to God, asking for His protection and help, and of course he or she then forms the belief that God is indeed able to hear and help if He sees fit. When life is sweet and satisfying, a spontaneous sense of gratitude may well up within the soul; someone in this condition may thank and praise the Lord for His goodness, and will of course form the accompanying belief that indeed the Lord is to be thanked and praised.

There are therefore many conditions and circumstances that call forth belief in God: guilt, gratitude, danger, a sense of God's presence, a sense that He speaks, perception of various parts

(continued)

Religious Belief Without Evidence (*continued*)

of the universe. A complete job would explore the phenomenology of all these conditions and of more besides. This is a large and important topic, but here I can only point to the existence of these conditions.

Of course, none of the beliefs I mentioned a moment ago is the simple belief that God exists. What we have instead are such beliefs as

6. God is speaking to me.
7. God has created all this.
8. God disapproves of what I have done.
9. God forgives me.
10. God is to be thanked and praised.

These propositions are properly basic in the right circumstances. But it is quite consistent with this to suppose that the proposition *there is such a person as God* is neither properly basic nor taken as basic by those who believe in God. Perhaps what they take as basic are such propositions as (6)–(10), believing in the existence of God on the basis of such propositions. From this point of view, it isn't exactly right to say that belief in God is properly basic; more exactly, what are properly basic are such propositions (6)–(10), each of which self-evidently entails that God exists. It isn't the relatively high level and general proposition *God exists* that is properly basic, but instead propositions detailing some of His attributes or actions.

Suppose we return to the analogy between belief in God and belief in the existence of perceptual objects, other persons, and the past. Here too it is relatively specific and concrete propositions rather than their more general and abstract colleagues that are properly basic. Perhaps such items as

11. There are trees.
12. There are other persons.
13. The world has existed for more than 5 minutes

are not properly basic; it is instead such propositions as

14. I see a tree.
15. That person is pleased.
16. I had breakfast more than an hour ago

that deserve the accolade. Of course, propositions of the latter sort immediately and self-evidently entail propositions of the former sort, and perhaps there is thus no harm in speaking of the former as properly basic, even though so to speak is to speak a bit loosely.

The same must be said about belief in God. We may say, speaking loosely, that belief in God is properly basic; strictly speaking, however, it is probably not that proposition but such propositions as (6)–(10) that enjoy that status. But the main point, here, is this: belief in God or (6)–(10) are properly basic; to say so, however, is not to deny that there are justifying conditions for these beliefs, or conditions that confer justification on one who accepts them as basic. They are therefore not groundless or gratuitous.

A second objection I've often heard: If belief in God is properly basic, why can't *just any* belief be properly basic? What about voodoo or astrology? What about the belief that the Great Pumpkin returns every Halloween? Could I properly take *that* as basic? And if I can't, why can I properly take belief in God as basic? Suppose I believe that if I flap my arms with sufficient vigor, I can take off and fly about the room; could I defend myself against the charge of irrationality by claiming this belief is basic? If we say that belief in God is properly basic, won't we be committed to holding that just anything, or nearly anything, can properly be taken as basic, thus throwing wide the gates to irrationalism and superstition?

Certainly not. What might lead one to think the Reformed epistemologist is in this kind of trouble? The fact that he rejects the criteria for proper basicality purveyed by classical foundationalism? But why should *that* be thought to commit him to such tolerance or irrationality? Consider an analogy. In the palmy days of positivism, the positivists went about confidently wielding their verifiability criterion and declaring meaningless much that was obviously meaningful. Now suppose someone rejected a formulation of that criterion—the one to be found in the second edition of A. J. Ayer's *Language, Truth and Logic,* for example. Would that mean she was committed to holding that

17. 'Twas brillig; and the slithy toves did gyre and gimble in the wabe

contrary to appearances, makes good sense? Of course not. But then the same goes for the Reformed epistemologist; the fact that he rejects the Classical Foundationalist's criterion of proper basicality does not mean that he is committed to supposing just anything is properly basic.

But what then is the problem? Is it that the Reformed epistemologist not only rejects those criteria for proper basicality, but seems in no hurry to produce what he takes to be a better substitute? If he has no such criterion, how can he fairly reject belief in the Great Pumpkin as properly basic?

This objection betrays an important misconception. How do we rightly arrive at or develop criteria for meaningfulness, or justified belief, or proper basicality? Where do they come from? Must one have such a criterion before one can sensibly make any judgments—positive or negative—about proper basicality? Surely not. Suppose I don't know of a satisfactory substitute for the criteria proposed by Classical Foundationalism; I am nevertheless entirely within my rights in holding that certain propositions are not properly basic in certain conditions. Some propositions seem self-evident when in fact they are not; that is the lesson of some of the Russell paradoxes. Nevertheless it would be irrational to take as basic the denial of a proposition that seems self-evident to you. Similarly, suppose it seems to you that you see a tree; you would then be irrational in taking as basic the proposition that you don't see a tree, or that there aren't any trees. In the same way, even if I don't know of some illuminating criterion of meaning, I can quite properly declare (17) meaningless.

And this raises an important question—one Roderick Chisholm has taught us to ask. What is the status of the criteria for knowledge, or proper basicality, or justified belief? Typically, these are universal statements. The modern foundationalist's criterion for proper basicality, for example, is doubly universal:

18. For any proposition *A* and person *S*, *A* is properly basic for *S* if and only if *A* is incorrigible for *S* or self-evident to *S*.

But how could one know a thing like that? What are its credentials? Clearly enough, (18) isn't self-evident or just obviously true. But if it isn't, how does one arrive at it? What sorts of arguments would be appropriate? Of course, a foundationalist might find (18) so appealing, he simply takes it to be true, neither offering argument for it, nor accepting it on the basis of other things he believes. If he does so, however, his noetic structure will be self-referentially incoherent. (18) itself is neither self-evident nor incorrigible; hence in accepting (18) as basic, the modern foundationalist violates the condition of proper basicality he himself lays down in accepting it. On the other hand, perhaps the foundationalist will try to produce some argument for it from premises that are self-evident or incorrigible: it is exceedingly hard to see, however, what such an argument might be like. And until he has produced such arguments, what shall the rest of us do—we who do not find (18) at all obvious or compelling? How could he use (18) to show us that belief in God, for example, is not properly basic? Why should we believe (18), or pay it any attention?

The fact is, I think, that neither (18) nor any other revealing necessary and sufficient condition for proper basicality follows from clearly self-evident premises by clearly acceptable arguments. And hence the proper way to arrive at such a criterion is, broadly speaking, *inductive.* We must assemble examples of beliefs and conditions such that the former are obviously properly basic in the latter, and examples of beliefs and conditions such that the former are obviously *not* properly basic in the latter. We must then frame hypotheses on the necessary and sufficient conditions of proper basicality and test these hypotheses by reference to those examples. Under the right conditions, for example, it is clearly rational to believe that you see a human person before you: a being who has thoughts and feelings, who knows and believes things, who makes decisions and acts. It is clear, furthermore, that you are under no obligation to reason to this belief from others you hold; under those conditions that belief is properly basic for you. But then (18) must be mistaken; the belief in

(continued)

Religious Belief Without Evidence (*continued*)

question, under those circumstances, is properly basic, though neither self-evident nor incorrigible for you. Similarly, you may seem to remember that you had breakfast this morning, and perhaps you know of no reason to suppose your memory is playing you tricks. If so, you are entirely justified in taking that belief as basic. Of course it isn't properly basic on the criteria offered by classical foundationalists, but that fact counts not against you but against those criteria.

Accordingly, criteria for proper basicality must be reached from below rather than above; they should not be presented as *obiter dicta,* but argued to and tested by a relevant set of examples. But there is no reason to assume, in advance, that everyone will agree on the examples. The Christian will of course suppose that belief in God is entirely proper and rational; if he doesn't accept this belief on the basis of other propositions, he will conclude that it is basic for him and quite properly so. Followers of Bertrand Russell and Madelyn Murray O'Hare may disagree, but how is that relevant? Must my criteria, or those of the Christian community, conform to their examples? Surely not. The Christian community is responsible to *its* set of examples, not to theirs.

Accordingly, the Reformed epistemologist can properly hold that belief in the Great Pumpkin is not properly basic, even though he holds that belief in God *is* properly basic and even if he has no full-fledged criterion of proper basicality. Of course he is committed to supposing that there is a relevant *difference* between belief in God and belief in the Great Pumpkin, if he holds that the former, but not the latter, is properly basic. But this should prove no great embarrassment; there are plenty of candidates. These candidates are to be found in the neighborhood of the conditions I mentioned in the last section that justify and ground belief in God. Thus, for example, the Reformed epistemologist may concur with Calvin in holding that God has implanted in us a natural tendency to see his hand in the world around us; the same cannot be said for the Great Pumpkin, there being no Great Pumpkin and no natural tendency to accept beliefs about the Great Pumpkin.

By way of conclusion, then: being self-evident, or incorrigible, or evident to the senses is not a necessary condition of proper basicality. Furthermore, one who holds that belief in God *is* properly basic is not thereby committed to the idea that belief in God is groundless or gratuitous or without justifying circumstances. And even if he lacks a general criterion of proper basicality, he is not obliged to suppose that just any, or nearly any, belief—belief in the Great Pumpkin, for example—is properly basic. Like everyone should, he begins with examples, and he may take belief in the Great Pumpkin, in certain circumstances, as a paradigm of irrational basic belief.

NOTES

1. See, for example, Blanshard, *Reason and Belief,* pp. 400ff; Clifford, "The Ethics of Belief," pp. 345ff; Flew, *The Presumption of Atheism,* p. 22; Russell, "Why I Am Not a Christian," pp. 3ff; and Scriven, *Primary Philosophy,* pp. 87ff. In Plantinga, "Is Belief in God Rational?"
2. W. Salmon, "Religion and Science: A New Look at Hume's Dialogues," *Philosophical Studies* 33 (1978), p. 176.
3. A. G. N. Flew, *The Presumption of Atheism* (London: Pemberton Publishing Co., 1976).
4. A Reformed thinker or theologian is one whose intellectual sympathies lie with the Protestant tradition going back to John Calvin (not someone who was formerly a theologian and has since seen the light).

The Will to Believe and other Essays in Popular Philosophy
William James

The Will to Believe.

In the recently published Life by Leslie Stephen of his brother, Fitz-James, there is an account of a school to which the latter went when he was a boy. The teacher, a certain Mr. Guest, used to converse with his pupils in this wise: "Gurney, what is the difference between justification and sanctification?—Stephen, prove the omnipotence of God!" etc. In the midst of our Harvard freethinking and indifference we are prone to imagine that here at your good old orthodox

College conversation continues to be somewhat upon this order; and to show you that we at Harvard have not lost all interest in these vital subjects, I have brought with me to-night something like a sermon on justification by faith to read to you, —I mean an essay in justification *of* faith, a defence of our right to adopt a believing attitude in religious matters, in spite of the fact that our merely logical intellect may not have been coerced. 'The Will to Believe,' accordingly, is the title of my paper.

I have long defended to my own students the lawfulness of voluntarily adopted faith; but as soon as they have got well imbued with the logical spirit, they have as a rule refused to admit my contention to be lawful philosophically, even though in point of fact they were personally all the time chock-full of some faith or other themselves. I am all the while, however, so profoundly convinced that my own position is correct, that your invitation has seemed to me a good occasion to make my statements more clear. Perhaps your minds will be more open than those with which I have hitherto had to deal. I will be as little technical as I can, though I must begin by setting up some technical distinctions that will help us in the end.

I

Let us give the name of *hypothesis* to anything that may be proposed to our belief; and just as the electricians speak of live and dead wires, let us speak of any hypothesis as either *live* or *dead*. A live hypothesis is one which appeals as a real possibility to him to whom it is proposed. If I ask you to believe in the Mahdi, the notion makes no electric connection with your nature, it refuses to scintillate with any credibility at all. As an hypothesis it is completely dead. To an Arab, however (even if he be not one of the Mahdi's followers), the hypothesis is among the mind's possibilities: it is alive. This shows that deadness and liveness in an hypothesis are not intrinsic properties, but relations to the individual thinker. They are measured by his willingness to act. The maximum of liveness in an hypothesis means willingness to act irrevocably. Practically, that means belief; but there is some believing tendency wherever there is willingness to act at all.

Next, let us call the decision between two hypotheses an *option*. Options may be of several kinds. They may be—1, *living* or *dead;* 2, *forced* or *avoidable;* 3, *momentous* or *trivial;* and for our purposes we may call an option a *genuine* option when it is of the forced, living, and momentous kind.

1. A living option is one in which both hypotheses are live ones. If I say to you: "Be a theosophist or be a Mohammedan," it is probably a dead option, because for you neither hypothesis is likely to be alive. But if I say: "Be an agnostic or be a Christian," it is otherwise: trained as you are, each hypothesis makes some appeal, however small, to your belief.
2. Next, if I say to you: "Choose between going out with your umbrella or without it," I do not offer you a genuine option, for it is not forced. You can easily avoid it by not going out at all. Similarly, if I say, "Either love me or hate me," "Either call my theory true or call it false," your option is avoidable. You may remain indifferent to me, neither loving nor hating, and you may decline to offer any judgment as to my theory. But if I say, "Either accept this truth or go without it," I put on you a forced option, for there is no standing place outside of the alternative. Every dilemma based on a complete logical disjunction, with no possibility of not choosing, is an option of this forced kind.
3. Finally, if I were Dr. Nansen and proposed to you to join my North Pole expedition, your option would be momentous; for this would probably be your only similar opportunity, and your choice now would either exclude you from the North Pole sort of immortality altogether or put at least the chance of it into your hands. He who refuses to embrace a unique opportunity loses the prize as surely as if he tried and failed. *Per contra*, the option is trivial when the opportunity is not unique, when the stake is insignificant, or when the decision is reversible if it later prove unwise. Such trivial options abound in the scientific life. A chemist finds an hypothesis live enough to spend a year in its verification: he believes in it to that extent. But if his experiments prove inconclusive either way, he is quit for his loss of time, no vital harm being done.

It will facilitate our discussion if we keep all these distinctions well in mind.

(continued)

The Will to Believe and other Essays in Popular Philosophy   (*continued*)

II

The next matter to consider is the actual psychology of human opinion. When we look at certain facts, it seems as if our passional and volitional nature lay at the root of all our convictions. When we look at others, it seems as if they could do nothing when the intellect had once said its say. Let us take the latter facts up first.

Does it not seem preposterous on the very face of it to talk of our opinions being modifiable at will? Can our will either help or hinder our intellect in its perceptions of truth? Can we, by just willing it, believe that Abraham Lincoln's existence is a myth, and that the portraits of him in McClure's Magazine are all of some one else? Can we, by any effort of our will, or by any strength of wish that it were true, believe ourselves well and about when we are roaring with rheumatism in bed, or feel certain that the sum of the two one-dollar bills in our pocket must be a hundred dollars? We can *say* any of these things, but we are absolutely impotent to believe them; and of just such things is the whole fabric of the truths that we do believe in made up,—matters of fact, immediate or remote, as Hume said, and relations between ideas, which are either there or not there for us if we see them so, and which if not there cannot be put there by any action of our own.

In Pascal's Thoughts there is a celebrated passage known in literature as Pascal's wager. In it he tries to force us into Christianity by reasoning as if our concern with truth resembled our concern with the stakes in a game of chance. Translated freely his words are these: You must either believe or not believe that God is—which will you do? Your human reason cannot say. A game is going on between you and the nature of things which at the day of judgment will bring out either heads or tails. Weigh what your gains and your losses would be if you should stake all you have on heads, or God's existence: if you win in such case, you gain eternal beatitude; if you lose, you lose nothing at all. If there were an infinity of chances, and only one for God in this wager, still you ought to stake your all on God; for though you surely risk a finite loss by this procedure, any finite loss is reasonable, even a certain one is reasonable, if there is but the possibility of infinite gain. Go, then, and take holy water, and have masses said; belief will come and stupefy your scruples,—*Cela vous fera croire et vous abêtira*. Why should you not? At bottom, what have you to lose?

You probably feel that when religious faith expresses itself thus, in the language of the gaming-table, it is put to its last trumps. Surely Pascal's own personal belief in masses and holy water had far other springs; and this celebrated page of his is but an argument for others, a last desperate snatch at a weapon against the hardness of the unbelieving heart. We feel that a faith in masses and holy water adopted wilfully after such a mechanical calculation would lack the inner soul of faith's reality; and if we were ourselves in the place of the Deity, we should probably take particular pleasure in cutting off believers of this pattern from their infinite reward. It is evident that unless there be some pre-existing tendency to believe in masses and holy water, the option offered to the will by Pascal is not a living option. Certainly no Turk ever took to masses and holy water on its account; and even to us Protestants these means of salvation seem such foregone impossibilities that Pascal's logic, invoked for them specifically, leaves us unmoved. As well might the Mahdi write to us, saying, "I am the Expected One whom God has created in his effulgence. You shall be infinitely happy if you confess me; otherwise you shall be cut off from the light of the sun. Weigh, then, your infinite gain if I am genuine against your finite sacrifice if I am not!" His logic would be that of Pascal; but he would vainly use it on us, for the hypothesis he offers us is dead. No tendency to act on it exists in us to any degree.

The talk of believing by our volition seems, then, from one point of view, simply silly. From another point of view it is worse than silly, it is vile. When one turns to the magnificent edifice of the physical sciences, and sees how it was reared; what thousands of disinterested moral lives of men lie buried in its mere foundations; what patience and postponement, what choking down of preference, what submission to the icy laws of outer fact are wrought into its very stones and mortar; how absolutely impersonal it stands in its vast augustness,—then how besotted and contemptible seems every little sentimentalist who comes blowing his voluntary smoke-wreaths, and pretending to decide things from out of his private dream! Can we wonder if those bred in the rugged and manly school of science should feel like spewing such subjectivism out of their mouths? The whole system of loyalties which grow up in the schools of science go dead against its toleration; so that it is only natural that those who have caught the scientific fever should pass over to the opposite extreme, and write sometimes as if the incorruptibly truthful intellect ought positively to prefer bitterness and unacceptableness to the heart in its cup.

> It fortifies my soul to know
> That, though I perish, Truth is so—

sings Clough, while Huxley exclaims: "My only consolation lies in the reflection that, however bad our posterity may become, so far as they hold by the plain rule of not pretending to believe what they have no reason to believe, because it may be to their advantage so to pretend [the word 'pretend' is surely here redundant], they will not have reached the lowest depth of immorality." And that delicious *enfant terrible* Clifford writes: "Belief is desecrated when given to unproved and unquestioned statements for the solace and private pleasure of the believer.... Whoso would deserve well of his fellows in this matter will guard the purity of his belief with a very fanaticism of jealous care, lest at any time it should rest on an unworthy object, and catch a stain which can never be wiped away.... If [a] belief has been accepted on insufficient evidence [even though the belief be true, as Clifford on the same page explains] the pleasure is a stolen one.... It is sinful because it is stolen in defiance of our duty to mankind. That duty is to guard ourselves from such beliefs as from a pestilence which may shortly master our own body and then spread to the rest of the town.... It is wrong always, everywhere, and for every one, to believe anything upon insufficient evidence."

III

All this strikes one as healthy, even when expressed, as by Clifford, with somewhat too much of robustious pathos in the voice. Free-will and simple wishing do seem, in the matter of our credences, to be only fifth wheels to the coach. Yet if any one should thereupon assume that intellectual insight is what remains after wish and will and sentimental preference have taken wing, or that pure reason is what then settles our opinions, he would fly quite as directly in the teeth of the facts.

It is only our already dead hypotheses that our willing nature is unable to bring to life again. But what has made them dead for us is for the most part a previous action of our willing nature of an antagonistic kind. When I say 'willing nature,' I do not mean only such deliberate volitions as may have set up habits of belief that we cannot now escape from,—I mean all such factors of belief as fear and hope, prejudice and passion, imitation and partisanship, the circumpressure of our caste and set. As a matter of fact we find ourselves believing, we hardly know how or why. Mr. Balfour gives the name of 'authority' to all those influences, born of the intellectual climate, that make hypotheses possible or impossible for us, alive or dead. Here in this room, we all of us believe in molecules and the conservation of energy, in democracy and necessary progress, in Protestant Christianity and the duty of fighting for 'the doctrine of the immortal Monroe,' all for no reasons worthy of the name. We see into these matters with no more inner clearness, and probably with much less, than any disbeliever in them might possess. His unconventionality would probably have some grounds to show for its conclusions; but for us, not insight, but the *prestige* of the opinions, is what makes the spark shoot from them and light up our sleeping magazines of faith. Our reason is quite satisfied, in nine hundred and ninety-nine cases out of every thousand of us, if it can find a few arguments that will do to recite in case our credulity is criticised by some one else. Our faith is faith in some one else's faith, and in the greatest matters this is most the case. Our belief in truth itself, for instance, that there is a truth, and that our minds and it are made for each other,—what is it but a passionate affirmation of desire, in which our social system backs us up? We want to have a truth; we want to believe that our experiments and studies and discussions must put us in a continually better and better position towards it; and on this line we agree to fight out our thinking lives. But if a pyrrhonistic sceptic asks us *how we know* all this, can our logic find a reply? No! certainly it cannot. It is just one volition against another,—we willing to go in for life upon a trust or assumption which he, for his part, does not care to make.[1]

As a rule we disbelieve all facts and theories for which we have no use. Clifford's cosmic emotions find no use. Clifford's cosmic emotions find no use for Christian feelings. Huxley belabors the bishops because there is no use for sacerdotalism in his scheme of life. Newman, on the

(continued)

The Will to Believe and other Essays in Popular Philosophy (*continued*)

contrary, goes over to Romanism, and finds all sorts of reasons good for staying there, because a priestly system is for him an organic need and delight. Why do so few 'scientists' even look at the evidence for telepathy, so called? Because they think, as a leading biologist, now dead, once said to me, that even if such a thing were true, scientists ought to band together to keep it suppressed and concealed. It would undo the uniformity of Nature and all sorts of other things without which scientists cannot carry on their pursuits. But if this very man had been shown something which as a scientist he might *do* with telepathy, he might not only have examined the evidence, but even have found it good enough. This very law which the logicians would impose upon us—if I may give the name of logicians to those who would rule out our willing nature here—is based on nothing but their own natural wish to exclude all elements for which they, in their professional quality of logicians, can find no use.

Evidently, then, our non-intellectual nature does influence our convictions. There are passional tendencies and volitions which run before and others which come after belief, and it is only the latter that are too late for the fair; and they are not too late when the previous passional work has been already in their own direction. Pascal's argument, instead of being powerless, then seems a regular clincher, and is the last stroke needed to make our faith in masses and holy water complete. The state of things is evidently far from simple; and pure insight and logic, whatever they might do ideally, are not the only things that really do produce our creeds.

IV

Our next duty, having recognized this mixed-up state of affairs, is to ask whether it be simply reprehensible and pathological, or whether, on the contrary, we must treat it as a normal element in making up our minds. The thesis I defend is, briefly stated, this: *Our passional nature not only lawfully may, but must, decide an option between propositions, whenever it is a genuine option that cannot by its nature be decided on intellectual grounds; for to say, under such circumstances, "Do not decide, but leave the question open" is itself a passional decision,—just like deciding yes or no,—and is attended with the same risk of losing the truth*. The thesis thus abstractly expressed will, I trust, soon become quite clear. But I must first indulge in a bit more of preliminary work.

V

It will be observed that for the purposes of this discussion we are on 'dogmatic' ground,—ground, I mean, which leaves systematic philosophical scepticism altogether out of account. The postulate that there is truth, and that it is the destiny of our minds to attain it, we are deliberately resolving to make, though the sceptic will not make it. We part company with him, therefore, absolutely, at this point. But the faith that truth exists, and that our minds can find it, may be held in two ways. We may talk of the *empiricist* way and of the *absolutist* way of believing in truth. The absolutists in this matter say that we not only can attain to knowing truth, but we can *know when* we have attained to knowing it; while the empiricists think that although we may attain it, we cannot infallibly know when. To *know* is one thing, and to know for certain *that* we know is another. One may hold to the first being possible without the second; hence, the empiricists and the absolutists, although neither of them is a sceptic in the usual philosophic sense of the term, show very different degrees of dogmatism in their lives.

If we look at the history of opinions, we see that the empiricist tendency has largely prevailed in science, while in philosophy the absolutist tendency has had everything its own way. The characteristic sort of happiness, indeed, which philosophies yield has mainly consisted in the conviction felt by each successive school or system that by it bottom-certitude had been attained. "Other philosophies are collections of opinions, mostly false; *my* philosophy gives standing-ground forever,"—who does not recognize in this the key-note of every system worthy of the name? A system, to be a system at all, must come as a *closed* system, reversible in this or that detail, perchance, but in its essential features never!

Scholastic orthodoxy, to which one must always go when one wishes to find perfectly clear statement, has beautifully elaborated this absolutist conviction in a doctrine which it calls that of 'objective evidence.' If, for example, I am unable to doubt that I now exist before you, that two is less than three, or that if all men are mortal then I am mortal too, it is because these things illumine my intellect irresistibly. The final ground of this objective evidence possessed by certain propositions is the *adequatio intellectûs nostri cum rê*. The certitude it brings involves an *aptitudinem ad extorquendum certum assensum* on the part of the truth envisaged, and on the side of the subject a *quietem in cognitione,* when once the object is mentally received, that leaves no possibility of doubt behind; and in the whole transaction nothing operates but the *entitas ipsa* of the object and the *entitas ipsa* of the mind. We slouchy modern thinkers dislike to talk in Latin,—indeed, we dislike to talk in set terms at all; but at bottom our own state of mind is very much like this whenever we uncritically abandon ourselves: You believe in objective evidence, and I do. Of some things we feel that we are certain: we know, and we know that we do know. There is something that gives a click inside of us, a bell that strikes twelve, when the hands of our mental clock have swept the dial and meet over the meridian hour. The greatest empiricists among us are only empiricists on reflection: when left to their instincts, they dogmatize like infallible popes. When the Cliffords tell us how sinful it is to be Christians on such 'insufficient evidence,' insufficiency is really the last thing they have in mind. For them the evidence is absolutely sufficient, only it makes the other way. They believe so completely in an anti-christian order of the universe that there is no living option: Christianity is a dead hypothesis from the start.

VI

But now, since we are all such absolutists by instinct, what in our quality of students of philosophy ought we to do about the fact? Shall we espouse and indorse it? Or shall we treat it as a weakness of our nature from which we must free ourselves, if we can?

I sincerely believe that the latter course is the only one we can follow as reflective men. Objective evidence and certitude are doubtless very fine ideals to play with, but where on this moonlit and dream-visited planet are they found? I am, therefore, myself a complete empiricist so far as my theory of human knowledge goes. I live, to be sure, by the practical faith that we must go on experiencing and thinking over our experience, for only thus can our opinions grow more true; but to hold any one of them—I absolutely do not care which—as if it never could be reinterpretable or corrigible, I believe to be a tremendously mistaken attitude, and I think that the whole history of philosophy will bear me out. There is but one indefectibly certain truth, and that is the truth that pyrrhonistic scepticism itself leaves standing,—the truth that the present phenomenon of consciousness exists. That, however, is the bare starting-point of knowledge, the mere admission of a stuff to be philosophized about. The various philosophies are but so many attempts at expressing what this stuff really is. And if we repair to our libraries what disagreement do we discover! Where is a certainly true answer found? Apart from abstract propositions of comparison (such as two and two are the same as four), propositions which tell us nothing by themselves about concrete reality, we find no proposition ever regarded by any one as evidently certain that has not either been called a falsehood, or at least had its truth sincerely questioned by some one else. The transcending of the axioms of geometry, not in play but in earnest, by certain of our contemporaries (as Zöllner and Charles H. Hinton), and the rejection of the whole Aristotelian logic by the Hegelians, are striking instances in point.

No concrete test of what is really true has ever been agreed upon. Some make the criterion external to the moment of perception, putting it either in revelation, the *consensus gentium,* the instincts of the heart, or the systematized experience of the race. Others make the perceptive moment its own test,—Descartes, for instance, with his clear and distinct ideas guaranteed by the veracity of God; Reid with his 'common-sense;' and Kant with his forms of synthetic judgment *a priori*. The inconceivability of the opposite; the capacity to be verified by sense; the possession of complete organic unity or self-relation, realized when a thing is its own other,—are standards which, in turn, have been used. The much lauded objective evidence is never triumphantly there; it is a mere aspiration or *Grenzbegriff,* marking the infinitely remote ideal of our thinking life. To claim that certain truths now possess it, is simply to say that when you think them true and they *are* true, then their evidence is objective, otherwise it is not. But practically one's conviction that the evidence one goes by is of the real objective brand, is only one more subjective opinion added to the lot. For what a contradictory array of opinions have objective evidence and absolute certitude been claimed! The

(continued)

The Will to Believe and other Essays in Popular Philosophy (*continued*)

world is rational through and through,—its existence is an ultimate brute fact; there is a personal God,—a personal God is inconceivable; there is an extra-mental physical world immediately known,—the mind can only know its own ideas; a moral imperative exists,—obligation is only the resultant of desires; a permanent spiritual principle is in every one,—there are only shifting states of mind; there is an endless chain of causes,—there is an absolute first cause; an eternal necessity,—a freedom; a purpose,—no purpose; a primal One,—a primal Many; a universal continuity,—an essential discontinuity in things; an infinity,—no infinity. There is this,—there is that; there is indeed nothing which some one has not thought absolutely true, while his neighbor deemed it absolutely false; and not an absolutist among them seems ever to have considered that the trouble may all the time be essential, and that the intellect, even with truth directly in its grasp, may have no infallible signal for knowing whether it be truth or no. When, indeed, one remembers that the most striking practical application to life of the doctrine of objective certitude has been the conscientious labors of the Holy Office of the Inquisition, one feels less tempted than ever to lend the doctrine a respectful ear.

But please observe, now, that when as empiricists we give up the doctrine of objective certitude, we do not thereby give up the quest or hope of truth itself. We still pin our faith on its existence, and still believe that we gain an ever better position towards it by systematically continuing to roll up experiences and think. Our great difference from the scholastic lies in the way we face. The strength of his system lies in the principles, the origin, the *terminus a quo* of his thought; for us the strength is in the outcome, the upshot, the *terminus ad quem.* Not where it comes from but what it leads to is to decide. It matters not to an empiricist from what quarter an hypothesis may come to him: he may have acquired it by fair means or by foul; passion may have whispered or accident suggested it; but if the total drift of thinking continues to confirm it, that is what he means by its being true.

VII

One more point, small but important, and our preliminaries are done. There are two ways of looking at our duty in the matter of opinion,—ways entirely different, and yet ways about whose difference the theory of knowledge seems hitherto to have shown very little concern. *We must know the truth;* and *we must avoid error,*—these are our first and great commandments as would-be knowers; but they are not two ways of stating an identical commandment, they are two separable laws. Although it may indeed happen that when we believe the truth *A*, we escape as an incidental consequence from believing the falsehood *B*, it hardly ever happens that by merely disbelieving *B* we necessarily believe *A*. We may in escaping *B* fall into believing other falsehoods, *C* or *D*, just as bad as *B*; or we may escape *B* by not believing anything at all, not even *A*.

Believe truth! Shun error!—these, we see, are two materially different laws; and by choosing between them we may end, coloring differently our whole intellectual life. We may regard the chase for truth as paramount, and the avoidance of error as secondary; or we may, on the other hand, treat the avoidance of error as more imperative, and let truth take its chance. Clifford, in the instructive passage which I have quoted, exhorts us to the latter course. Believe nothing, he tells us, keep your mind in suspense forever, rather than by closing it on insufficient evidence incur the awful risk of believing lies. You, on the other hand, may think that the risk of being in error is a very small matter when compared with the blessings of real knowledge, and be ready to be duped many times in your investigation rather than postpone indefinitely the chance of guessing true. I myself find it impossible to go with Clifford. We must remember that these feelings of our duty about either truth or error are in any case only expressions of our passional life. Biologically considered, our minds are as ready to grind out falsehood as veracity, and he who says, "Better go without belief forever than believe a lie!" merely shows his own preponderant private horror of becoming a dupe. He may be critical of many of his desires and fears, but this fear he slavishly obeys. He cannot imagine any one questioning its binding force. For my own part, I have also a horror of being duped; but I can believe that worse things than being duped may happen to a man in this world: so Clifford's exhortation has to my ears a thoroughly fantastic sound. It is like a general informing his soldiers that it is better to keep out of battle forever than to risk a single wound. Not so are victories either over enemies or over nature gained. Our errors are surely not such awfully solemn things. In a world where we are so certain to incur them in spite of all our caution, a certain lightness of heart seems healthier than this excessive nervousness on their behalf. At any rate, it seems the fittest thing for the empiricist philosopher.

VIII

And now, after all this introduction, let us go straight at our question. I have said, and now repeat it, that not only as a matter of fact do we find our passional nature influencing us in our opinions, but that there are some options between opinions in which this influence must be regarded both as an inevitable and as a lawful determinant of our choice.

I fear here that some of you my hearers will begin to scent danger, and lend an inhospitable ear. Two first steps of passion you have indeed had to admit as necessary,—we must think so as to avoid dupery, and we must think so as to gain truth; but the surest path to those ideal consummations, you will probably consider, is from now onwards to take no further passional step.

Well, of course, I agree as far as the facts will allow. Wherever the option between losing truth and gaining it is not momentous, we can throw the chance of *gaining truth* away, and at any rate save ourselves from any chance of *believing falsehood,* by not making up our minds at all till objective evidence has come. In scientific questions, this is almost always the case; and even in human affairs in general, the need of acting is seldom so urgent that a false belief to act on is better than no belief at all. Law courts, indeed, have to decide on the best evidence attainable for the moment, because a judge's duty is to make law as well as to ascertain it, and (as a learned judge once said to me) few cases are worth spending much time over: the great thing is to have them decided on *any* acceptable principle, and got out of the way. But in our dealings with objective nature we obviously are recorders, not makers, of the truth; and decisions for the mere sake of deciding promptly and getting on to the next business would be wholly out of place. Throughout the breadth of physical nature facts are what they are quite independently of us, and seldom is there any such hurry about them that the risks of being duped by believing a premature theory need be faced. The questions here are always trivial options, the hypotheses are hardly living (at any rate not living for us spectators), the choice between believing truth or falsehood is seldom forced. The attitude of sceptical balance is therefore the absolutely wise one if we would escape mistakes. What difference, indeed, does it make to most of us whether we have or have not a theory of the Röntgen rays, whether we believe or not in mind-stuff, or have a conviction about the causality of conscious states? It makes no difference. Such options are not forced on us. On every account it is better not to make them, but still keep weighing reasons *pro et contra* with an indifferent hand.

I speak, of course, here of the purely judging mind. For purposes of discovery such indifference is to be less highly recommended, and science would be far less advanced than she is if the passionate desires of individuals to get their own faiths confirmed had been kept out of the game. See for example the sagacity which Spencer and Weismann now display. On the other hand, if you want an absolute duffer in an investigation, you must, after all, take the man who has no interest whatever in its results: he is the warranted incapable, the positive fool. The most useful investigator, because the most sensitive observer, is always he whose eager interest in one side of the question is balanced by an equally keen nervousness lest he become deceived.[2] Science has organized this nervousness into a regular *technique,* her so-called method of verification; and she has fallen so deeply in love with the method that one may even say she has ceased to care for truth by itself at all. It is only truth as technically verified that interests her. The truth of truths might come in merely affirmative form, and she would decline to touch it. Such truth as that, she might repeat with Clifford, would be stolen in defiance of her duty to mankind. Human passions, however, are stronger than technical rules. "Le cœur a ses raisons," as Pascal says, "que lá raison ne connaît pas;" and however indifferent to all but the bare rules of the game the umpire, the abstract intellect, may be, the concrete players who furnish him the materials to judge of are usually, each one of them, in love with some pet 'live hypothesis' of his own. Let us agree, however, that wherever there is no forced option, the dispassionately judicial intellect with no pet hypothesis, saving us, as it does, from dupery at any rate, ought to be our ideal.

(continued)

The Will to Believe and other Essays in Popular Philosophy   (*continued*)

The question next arises: Are there not somewhere forced options in our speculative questions, and can we (as men who may be interested at least as much in positively gaining truth as in merely escaping dupery) always wait with impunity till the coercive evidence shall have arrived? It seems *a priori* improbable that the truth should be so nicely adjusted to our needs and powers as that. In the great boarding-house of nature, the cakes and the butter and the syrup seldom come out so even and leave the plates so clean. Indeed, we should view them with scientific suspicion if they did.

IX

Moral questions immediately present themselves as questions whose solution cannot wait for sensible proof. A moral question is a question not of what sensibly exists, but of what is good, or would be good if it did exist. "Science" can tell us what exists; but to compare the *worths,* both of what exists and of what does not exist, we must consult not science, but what Pascal calls our heart. Science herself consults her heart when she lays it down that the infinite ascertainment of fact and correction of false belief are the supreme goods for man. Challenge the statement, and science can only repeat it oracularly, or else prove it by showing that such ascertainment and correction bring man all sorts of other goods which man's heart in turn declares. The question of having moral beliefs at all or not having them is decided by our will. Are our moral preferences true or false, or are they only odd biological phenomena, making things good or bad for *us,* but in themselves indifferent? How can your pure intellect decide? If your heart does not *want* a world of moral reality, your head will assuredly never make you believe in one. Mephistophelian scepticism, indeed, will satisfy the head's play-instincts much better than any rigorous idealism can. Some men (why at the student age) are so naturally cool-hearted that the moralistic hypothesis never has for them any pungent life, and in their supercilious presence the hot young moralist always feels strangely ill at ease. The appearance of knowingness is on their side, of *naïveté* and gullibility on his. Yet, in the inarticulate heart of him, he clings to it that he is not a dupe, and that there is a realm in which (as Emerson says) all their wit and intellectual superiority is no better than the cunning of a fox. Moral scepticism can no more be refuted or proved by logic than intellectual scepticism can. When we stick to it that there *is* truth (be it of either kind), we do so with our whole nature, and resolve to stand or fall by the results. The sceptic with his whole nature adopts the doubting attitude; but which of us is the wiser, Omniscience only knows.

Turn now from these wide questions of good to a certain class of questions of fact, questions concerning personal relations, states of mind between one man and another. *Do you like me or not?*— for example. Whether you do or not depends, in countless instances, on whether I meet you half-way, am willing to assume that you must like me, and show you trust and expectation. The previous faith on my part in your liking's existence is in such cases what makes your liking come. But if I stand aloof, and refuse to budge an inch until I have objective evidence, until you shall have done something apt, as the absolutists say, *ad extorquendum assensum meum,* ten to one your liking never comes. How many women's hearts are few vanquished by the mere sanguine insistence of some man that they *must* love him! he will not consent to the hypothesis that they cannot. The desire for a certain kind of truth here brings about that special truth's existence; and so it is in innumerable cases of other sorts. Who gains promotions, boons, appointments, but the man in whose life they are seen to play the part of live hypotheses, who discounts them, sacrifices other things for their sake before they have come, and takes risks for them in advance? His faith acts on the powers above him as a claim, and creates its own verification.

A social organism of any sort whatever, large or small, is what it is because each member proceeds to his own duty with a trust that the other members will simultaneously do theirs. Wherever a desired result is achieved by the co-operation of many independent persons, its existence as a fact is a pure consequence of the precursive faith in one another of those immediately concerned. A government, an army, a commercial system, a ship, a college, an athletic team, all exist on this condition, without which not only is nothing achieved, but nothing is even attempted. A whole train of passengers (individually brave enough) will be looted by a few highwaymen, simply because the latter can count on one another, while each passenger fears that if he makes a movement of resistance, he will be shot before any one else backs him up. If we believed that the whole car-full would rise at once with us, we should each severally rise, and train-robbing would never even be attempted. There are, then, cases where a fact cannot come at all unless a preliminary faith exists in its coming. *And where faith in a fact can help create the fact,* that would be an insane logic which should say that faith running ahead of scientific evidence is the 'lowest kind of immorality' into which a thinking being can fall. Yet such is the logic by which our scientific absolutists pretend to regulate our lives!

X

In truths dependent on our personal action, then, faith based on desire is certainly a lawful and possibly an indispensable thing.

But now, it will be said, these are all childish human cases, and have nothing to do with great cosmical matters, like the question of religious faith. Let us then pass on to that. Religions differ so much in their accidents that in discussing the religious question we must make it very generic and broad. What then do we now mean by the religious hypothesis? Science says things are; morality says some things are better than other things; and religion says essentially two things.

First, she says that the best things are the more eternal things, the overlapping things, the things in the universe that throw the last stone, so to speak, and say the final word. "Perfection is eternal,"—this phrase of Charles Secrétan seems a good way of putting this first affirmation of religion, an affirmation which obviously cannot yet be verified scientifically at all.

The second affirmation of religion is that we are better off even now if we believe her first affirmation to be true.

Now, let us consider what the logical elements of this situation are *in case the religious hypothesis in both its branches be really true.* (Of course, we must admit that possibility at the outset. If we are to discuss the question at all, it must involve a living option. If for any of you religion be a hypothesis that cannot, by any living possibility be true, then you need go no farther. I speak to the 'saving remnant' alone.) So proceeding, we see, first, that religion offers itself as a *momentous* option. We are supposed to gain, even now, by our belief, and to lose by our non-belief, a certain vital good. Secondly, religion is a *forced* option, so far as that good goes. We cannot escape the issue by remaining sceptical and waiting for more light, because, although we do avoid error in that way *if religion be untrue,* we lose the good, *if it be true,* just as certainly as if we positively chose to disbelieve. It is as if a man should hesitate indefinitely to ask a certain woman to marry him because he was not perfectly sure that she would prove an angel after he brought her home. Would he not cut himself off from that particular angel-possibility as decisively as if he went and married some one else? Scepticism, then, is not avoidance of option; it is option of a certain particular kind of risk. *Better risk loss of truth than chance of error,*—that is your faith-vetoer's exact position. He is actively playing his stake as much as the believer is; he is backing the field against the religious hypothesis, just as the believer is backing the religious hypothesis against the field. To preach scepticism to us as a duty until 'sufficient evidence' for religion be found, is tantamount therefore to telling us, when in presence of the religious hypothesis, that to yield to our fear of its being error is wiser and better than to yield to our hope that it may be true. It is not intellect against all passions, then; it is only intellect with one passion laying down its law. And by what, forsooth, is the supreme wisdom of this passion warranted? Dupery for dupery, what proof is there that dupery through hope is so much worse than dupery through fear? I, for one, can see no proof; and I simply refuse obedience to the scientist's command to imitate his kind of option, in a case where my own stake is important enough to give me the right to choose my own form of risk. If religion be true and the evidence for it be still insufficient, I do not wish, by putting your extinguisher upon my nature (which feels to me as if it had after all some business in this matter), to forfeit my sole chance in life of getting upon the winning side,—that chance depending, of course, on my willingness to run the risk of acting as if my passional need of taking the world religiously might be prophetic and right.

All this is on the supposition that it really may be prophetic and right, and that, even to us who are discussing the matter, religion is a live hypothesis which may be true. Now, to most of us religion comes in a still further way that makes a veto on our active faith even more illogical. The more perfect and more eternal aspect of the universe is represented in our religions as having personal form.

(continued)

The Will to Believe and other Essays in Popular Philosophy   (*continued*)

The universe is no longer a mere *It* to us, but a *Thou*, if we are religious; and any relation that may be possible from person to person might be possible here. For instance, although in one sense we are passive portions of the universe, in another we show a curious autonomy, as if we were small active centres on our own account. We feel, too, as if the appeal of religion to us were made to our own active good-will, as if evidence might be forever withheld from us unless we met the hypothesis halfway. To take a trivial illustration: just as a man who in a company of gentlemen made no advances, asked a warrant for every concession, and believed no one's word without proof, would cut himself off by such churlishness from all the social rewards that a more trusting spirit would earn,—so here, one who should shut himself up in snarling logicality and try to make the gods extort his recognition willy-nilly, or not get it at all, might cut himself off forever from his only opportunity of making the gods' acquaintance. This feeling, forced on us we know not whence, that by obstinately believing that there are gods (although not to do so would be so easy both for our logic and our life) we are doing the universe the deepest service we can, seems part of the living essence of the religious hypothesis. If the hypothesis *were* true in all its parts, including this one, then pure intellectualism, with its veto on our making willing advances, would be an absurdity; and some participation of our sympathetic nature would be logically required. I, therefore, for one, cannot see my way to accepting the agnostic rules for truth-seeking, or wilfully agree to keep my willing nature out of the game. I cannot do so for this plain reason, that *a rule of thinking which would absolutely prevent me from acknowledging certain kinds of truth if those kinds of truth were really there, would be an irrational rule.* That for me is the long and short of the formal logic of the situation, no matter what the kinds of truth might materially be.

   I confess I do not see how this logic can be escaped. But sad experience makes me fear that some of you may still shrink from radically saying with me, *in abstracto,* that we have the right to believe at our own risk any hypothesis that is live enough to tempt our will. I suspect, however, that if this is so, it is because you have got away from the abstract logical point of view altogether, and are thinking (perhaps without realizing it) of some particular religious hypothesis which for you is dead. The freedom to 'believe what we will' you apply to the case of some patent superstition; and the faith you think of is the faith defined by the schoolboy when he said, "Faith is when you believe something that you know ain't true." I can only repeat that this is misapprehension. *In concreto,* the freedom to believe can only cover living options which the intellect of the individual cannot by itself resolve; and living options never seem absurdities to him who has them to consider. When I look at the religious question as it really puts itself to concrete men, and when I think of all the possibilities which both practically and theoretically it involves, then this command that we shall put a stopper on our heart, instincts, and courage, and *wait*—acting of course meanwhile more or less as if religion were *not* true[3]—till doomsday, or till such time as our intellect and senses working together may have raked in evidence enough,—this command, I say, seems to me the queerest idol ever manufactured in the philosophic cave. Were we scholastic absolutists, there might be more excuse. If we had an infallible intellect with its objective certitudes, we might feel ourselves disloyal to such a perfect organ of knowledge in not trusting to it exclusively, in not waiting for its releasing word. But if we are empiricists, if we believe that no bell in us tolls to let us know for certain when truth is in our grasp, then it seems a piece of idle fantasticality to preach so solemnly our duty of waiting for the bell. Indeed we *may* wait if we will,—I hope you do not think that I am denying that,—but if we do so, we do so at our peril as much as if we believed. In either case we *act,* taking our life in our hands. No one of us ought to issue vetoes to the other, nor should we bandy words of abuse. We ought, on the contrary, delicately and profoundly to respect one another's mental freedom: then only shall we bring about the intellectual republic; then only shall we have that spirit of inner tolerance without which all our outer tolerance is soulless, and which is empiricism's glory; then only shall we live and let live, in speculative as well as in practical things.

   I began by a reference to Fitz James Stephen; let me end by a quotation from him. "What do you think of yourself? What do you think of the world? . . . These are questions with which all must deal as it seems good to them. They are riddles of the Sphinx, and in some way or other we must deal with them. . . . In all important transactions of life we have to take a leap in the dark. . . . If we decide to leave the riddles unanswered, that is a choice; if we waver in our answer, that, too, is a choice: but whatever choice we make, we make it at our peril. If a man chooses to turn his back altogether on God and the future, no one can prevent him; no one can show beyond reasonable doubt that he is mistaken. If a man thinks otherwise and acts as he thinks, I do not see that any one can prove that *he* is mistaken. Each must act as he thinks best; and if he is wrong, so much the worse for him. We stand on a mountain pass in the midst of whirling snow and blinding mist, through which we get glimpses now and then of paths which may be deceptive. If we stand still we shall be frozen to death. If we take the wrong road we shall be dashed to pieces. We do not certainly know whether there is any right one. What must we do? 'Be strong and of a good courage.' Act for the best, hope for the best, and take what comes. . . . If death ends all, we cannot meet death better."[4]

NOTES

1. Compare the admirable page 310 in S. H. Hodgson's "Time and Space," London, 1865.
2. Compare Wilfrid Ward's Essay, "The Wish to Believe," in his *Witnesses to the Unseen*, Macmillan & Co., 1893.
3. Since belief is measured by action, he who forbids us to believe religion to be true, necessarily also forbids us to act as we should if we did believe it to be true. The whole defence of religious faith hinges upon action. If the action required or inspired by the religious hypothesis is in no way different from that dictated by the naturalistic hypothesis, then religious faith is a pure superfluity, better pruned away, and controversy about its legitimacy is a piece of idle trifling, unworthy of serious minds. I myself believe, of course, that the religious hypothesis gives to the world an expression which specifically determines our reactions, and makes them in a large part unlike what they might be on a purely naturalistic scheme of belief.
4. Liberty, Equality, Fraternity, p. 353, 2d edition. London, 1874.

Fear and Trembling: A Dialectical Lyric
Soren Kierkegaard

Preface

Not only in the business world but also in the world of ideas, our age stages *ein wirklicher Ausverkauf* [a real sale]. Everything can be had at such a bargain price that it becomes a question whether there is finally anyone who will make a bid. Every speculative monitor who conscientiously signals the important trends in modern philosophy, every assistant professor, tutor, and student, every rural outsider and tenant incumbent in philosophy is unwilling to stop with doubting everything but goes further. Perhaps it would be premature and untimely to ask them where they really are going, but in all politeness and modesty it can probably be taken for granted that they have doubted everything, since otherwise it certainly would be odd to speak of their having gone further. They have all made this preliminary movement and presumably so easily that they find it unnecessary to say a word about how, for not even the person who in apprehension and concern sought a little enlightenment found any, not one suggestive hint or one little dietetic prescription with respect to how a person is to act in carrying out this enormous task.

What those ancient Greeks, who after all did know a little about philosophy, assumed to be a task for a whole lifetime, because proficiency in doubting is not acquired in days and weeks, what the old veteran disputant attained, he who had maintained the equilibrium of doubt throughout all the specious arguments, who had intrepidly denied the certainty of the senses and the certainty of thought, who, uncompromising, had defied the anxiety of self-love and the insinuations of fellow feeling—with that everyone begins in our age.

In our age, everyone is unwilling to stop with faith but goes further. It perhaps would be rash to ask where they are going, whereas it is a sign of urbanity and culture for me to assume that everyone has faith, since otherwise it certainly would be odd to speak of going further. It was different in those ancient days. Faith was then a task for a whole lifetime, because it was assumed

(continued)

Fear and Trembling: A Dialectical Lyric (*continued*)

that proficiency in believing is not acquired either in days or in weeks. When the tried and tested oldster approached his end, had fought the good fight and kept the faith, his heart was still young enough not to have forgotten the anxiety and trembling that disciplined the youth, that the adult learned to control, but that no man outgrows—except to the extent that he succeeds in going further as early as possible. The point attained by those venerable personages is in our age the point where everyone begins in order to go further.

It is commonly supposed that what faith produces is no work of art, that it is a coarse and boorish piece of work, only for the more uncouth natures, but it is far from being that. The dialectic of faith is the finest and the most extraordinary of all; it has an elevation of which I can certainly form a conception, but no more than that. I can make the mighty trampoline leap whereby I cross over into infinity; my back is like a tightrope dancer's, twisted in my childhood, and therefore it is easy for me. One, two, three—I can walk upside down in existence, but I cannot make the next movement, for the marvelous I cannot do—I can only be amazed at it. Indeed, if Abraham,[1] the moment he swung his leg over the ass's back, had said to himself: Now Isaac is lost, I could just as well sacrifice him here at home as ride the long way to Moriah—then I do not need Abraham, whereas now I bow seven times to his name and seventy times to his deed. This he did not do, as I can prove by his really fervent joy on receiving Isaac and by his needing no preparation and no time to rally to finitude and its joy. If it had been otherwise with Abraham, he perhaps would have loved God but would not have had faith, for he who loves God without faith reflects upon himself; he who loves God in faith reflects upon God.

This is the peak on which Abraham stands. The last stage to pass from his view is the stage of infinite resignation. He actually goes further and comes to faith. All those travesties of faith—the wretched, lukewarm lethargy that thinks: There's no urgency, there's no use in grieving beforehand; the despicable hope that says: One just can't know what will happen, it could just possibly be—those travesties are native to the paltriness of life, and infinite resignation has already infinitely disdained them.

Abraham I cannot understand; in a certain sense I can learn nothing from him except to be amazed. If someone deludes himself into thinking he may be moved to have faith by pondering the outcome of that story, he cheats himself and cheats God out of the first movement of faith—he wants to suck worldly wisdom out of the paradox. Someone might succeed, for our generation does not stop with faith, does not stop with the miracle of faith, turning water into wine[2]—it goes further and turns wine into water.

Would it not be best to stop with faith, and is it not shocking that everyone wants to go further? Where will it all end when in our age, as declared in so many ways, one does not want to stop with love? In worldly shrewdness, in petty calculation, in paltriness and meanness, in everything that can make man's divine origin doubtful. Would it not be best to remain standing at faith and for him who stands to see to it that he does not fall, for the movement of faith must continually be made by virtue of the absurd, but yet in such a way, please note, that one does not lose the finite but gains it whole and intact. For my part, I presumably can describe the movements of faith, but I cannot make them. In learning to go through the motions of swimming, one can be suspended from the ceiling in a harness and then presumably describe the movements, but one is not swimming. In the same way I can describe the movements of faith. If I am thrown out into the water, I presumably do swim (for I do not belong to the waders), but I make different movements, the movements of infinity, whereas faith makes the opposite movements: after having made the movements of infinity, it makes the movements of finitude. Fortunate is the person who can make these movements! He does the marvelous, and I shall never weary of admiring him; it makes no difference to me whether it is Abraham or a slave in Abraham's house, whether it is a professor of philosophy or a poor servant girl—I pay attention only to the movements. But I do pay attention to them, and I do not let myself be fooled, either by myself or by anyone else. The knights of the infinite resignation are easily recognizable—their walk is light and bold. But they who carry the treasure of faith are likely to disappoint, for externally they have a striking resemblance to bourgeois philistinism, which infinite resignation, like faith, deeply disdains.

I honestly confess that in my experience I have not found a single authentic instance, although I do not therefore deny that every second person may be such an instance. Meanwhile, I have been looking for it for many years, but in vain. Generally, people travel around the world to see rivers and mountains, new stars, colorful birds, freakish fish, preposterous races of mankind; they indulge in the brutish stupor that gawks at life and thinks it has seen something. That does not occupy me. But if I knew where a knight of faith lived, I would travel on foot to him, for this marvel occupies me absolutely. I would not leave him for a second, I would watch him every minute to see how he made the movements; I would consider myself taken care of for life and would divide my time between watching him and practicing myself, and thus spend all my time in admiring him. As I said before, I have not found anyone like that; meanwhile, I may very well imagine him. Here he is. The acquaintance is made, I am introduced to him. The instant I first lay eyes on him, I set him apart at once; I jump back, clap my hands, and say half aloud, "Good Lord, is this the man, is this really the one—he looks just like a tax collector!" But this is indeed the one. I move a little closer to him, watch his slightest movement to see if it reveals a bit of heterogeneous optical telegraphy from the infinite, a glance, a facial expression, a gesture, a sadness, a smile that would betray the infinite in its heterogeneity with the finite. No! I examine his figure from top to toe to see if there may not be a crack through which the infinite would peek. No! He is solid all the way through. His stance? It is vigorous, belongs entirely to finitude; no spruced-up burgher walking out to Fresberg on a Sunday afternoon treads the earth more solidly. He belongs entirely to the world; no bourgeois philistine could belong to it more. Nothing is detectable of that distant and aristocratic nature by which the knight of the infinite is recognized. He finds pleasure in everything, takes part in everything, and every time one sees him participating in something particular, he does it with an assiduousness that marks the worldly man who is attached to such things. He attends to his job. To see him makes one think of him as a pen-pusher who has lost his soul to Italian bookkeeping, so punctilious is he. Sunday is for him a holiday. He goes to church. No heavenly gaze or any sign of the incommensurable betrays him; if one did not know him, it would be impossible to distinguish him from the rest of the crowd, for at most his hearty and powerful singing of the hymns proves that he has good lungs. In the afternoon, he takes a walk to the woods. He enjoys everything he sees, the swarms of people, the new omnibuses, the Sound. Encountering him on Strandveien, one would take him for a mercantile soul enjoying himself. He finds pleasure in this way, for he is not a poet, and I have tried in vain to lure the poetic incommensurability out of him. Toward evening, he goes home, and his gait is as steady as a postman's. On the way, he thinks that his wife surely will have a special hot meal for him when he comes home—for example, roast lamb's head with vegetables. If he meets a kindred soul, he would go on talking all the way to Østerport about this delicacy with a passion befitting a restaurant operator. It so happens that he does not have four shillings to his name, and yet he firmly believes that his wife has this delectable meal waiting for him. If she has, to see him eat would be the envy of the elite and an inspiration to the common man, for his appetite is keener than Esau's. His wife does not have it—curiously enough, he is just the same. On the way he passes a building site and meets another man. They converse for a moment; in an instant he erects a building, and he himself has at his disposition everything required. The stranger leaves him thinking that he surely is a capitalist, while my admired knight thinks: Well, if it came right down to it, I could easily get it. He sits at an open window and surveys the neighborhood where he lives: everything that happens—a rat scurrying under a plank across the gutter, children playing—engages him with an equanimity akin to that of a sixteen-year-old girl. And yet he is no genius, for I have sought in vain to spy out the incommensurability of genius in him. In the evening, he smokes his pipe; seeing him, one would swear it was the butcher across the way vegetating in the gloaming. With the freedom from care of a reckless good-for-nothing, he lets things take care of themselves, and yet every moment of his life he buys the opportune time at the highest price, for he does not do even the slightest thing except by virtue of the absurd. And yet, yet—yes, I could be infuriated over it if for no other reason than envy—and yet this man has made and at every moment is making the movement of infinity. He drains the deep sadness of life in infinite resignation, he knows the blessedness of infinity, he has felt the pain of renouncing everything, the most precious thing in the world, and yet the finite tastes just as good to him as to one who never knew anything higher, because his remaining in finitude would have no trace of a timorous, anxious routine, and yet he has this security that makes him delight in it as if finitude were the surest thing of all. And yet, yet the whole earthly figure he presents is a new creation by virtue of the absurd. He resigned everything infinitely, and then he grasped everything again by virtue of the absurd. He is continually making the movement of infinity, but he does it with such precision and assurance that he continually gets

(continued)

Fear and Trembling: A Dialectical Lyric   (*continued*)

finitude out of it, and no one ever suspects anything else. It is supposed to be the most difficult feat for a ballet dancer to leap into a specific posture in such a way that he never once strains for the posture but in the very leap assumes the posture. Perhaps there is no ballet dancer who can do it—but this knight does it. Most people live completely absorbed in worldly joys and sorrows; they are benchwarmers who do not take part in the dance. The knights of infinity are ballet dancers and have elevation. They make the upward movement and come down again, and this, too, is not an unhappy diversion and is not unlovely to see. But every time they come down, they are unable to assume the posture immediately, they waver for a moment, and this wavering shows that they are aliens in the world. It is more or less conspicuous according to their skill, but even the most skillful of these knights cannot hide this wavering. One does not need to see them in the air; one needs only to see them the instant they touch and have touched the earth—and then one recognizes them. But to be able to come down in such a way that instantaneously one seems to stand and to walk, to change the leap into life into walking, absolutely to express the sublime in the pedestrian—only that knight can do it, and this is the one and only marvel.

The act of resignation does not require faith, for what I gain in resignation is my eternal consciousness. This is a purely philosophical movement that I venture to make when it is demanded and can discipline myself to make, because every time some finitude will take power over me, I starve myself into submission until I make the movement, for my eternal consciousness is my love for God, and for me that is the highest of all. The act of resignation does not require faith, but to get the least little bit more than my eternal consciousness requires faith, for this is the paradox. The movements are often confused. It is said that faith is needed in order to renounce everything. Indeed, one hears what is even more curious: a person laments that he has lost his faith, and when a check is made to see where he is on the scale, curiously enough, he has only reached the point where he is to make the infinite movement of resignation. Through resignation I renounce everything. I make this movement all by myself, and if I do not make it, it is because I am too cowardly and soft and devoid of enthusiasm and do not feel the significance of the high dignity assigned to every human being, to be his own censor, which is far more exalted than to be the censor general of the whole Roman republic. This movement I make all by myself, and what I gain thereby is my eternal consciousness in blessed harmony with my love for the eternal being. By faith I do not renounce anything; on the contrary, by faith I receive everything exactly in the sense in which it is said that one who has faith like a mustard seed can move mountains. It takes a purely human courage to renounce the whole temporal realm in order to gain eternity, but this I do gain and in all eternity can never renounce—it is a self-contradiction. But it takes a paradoxical and humble courage to grasp the whole temporal realm now by virtue of the absurd, and this is the courage of faith. By faith Abraham did not renounce Isaac, but by faith Abraham received Isaac. By virtue of resignation, that rich young man[3] should have given away everything, but if he had done so, then the knight of faith would have said to him: By virtue of the absurd, you will get every penny back again—believe it! And the formerly rich young man should by no means treat these words lightly, for if he were to give away his possessions because he is bored with them, then his resignation would not amount to much.

Be it a duty or whatever, I cannot make the final movement, the paradoxical movement of faith, although there is nothing I wish more. Whether a person has the right to say this must be his own decision; whether he can come to an amicable agreement in this respect is a matter between himself and the eternal being, who is the object of faith. Every person can make the movement of infinite resignation, and for my part I would not hesitate to call a coward anyone who imagines that he cannot do it. Faith is another matter, but no one has the right to lead others to believe that faith is something inferior or that it is an easy matter, since on the contrary it is the greatest and most difficult of all.

The story of Abraham is understood in another way. We praise God's mercy, that he gave him Isaac again and that the whole thing was only an ordeal *[Prøvelse]*.

NOTES

1. See Genesis 22.
2. See John 2:1–10.
3. See Luke 18:18–23.

Problems of Religious Pluralism
John Hick

Wilfred Cantwell Smith in his work on the concepts of religion and of religions has been responsible, more than any other one individual, for the change which has taken place within a single generation in the way in which many of us perceive the religious life of mankind.

Seen through pre-Cantwell Smith eyes there are a number of vast, long-lived historical entities or organisms known as Christianity, Hinduism, Islam, Buddhism, and so on. Each has an inner skeletal framework of beliefs, giving shape to a distinctive form of religious life, wrapped in a thick institutional skin which divides it from other religions and from the secular world within which they exist. Thus Buddhism, Islam, Christianity, and the rest, are seen as contraposed socio-religious entities which are the bearers of distinctive creeds; and every religious individual is a member of one or other of these mutually exclusive groups.

This way of seeing the religious life of humanity, as organised in a number of communities based upon rival sets of religious beliefs, leads to the posing of questions about religion in a certain way. For the beliefs which a religion professes are beliefs about God, or the Ultimate, and as such they define a way of human salvation or liberation and are accordingly a matter of spiritual life and death. Looking at the religions of the world, then, in the plural we are presented with competing claims to possess the saving truth. For each community believes that its own gospel is true and that other gospels are false in so far as they differ from it. Each believes that the way of salvation to which it witnesses is the authentic way, the only sure path to eternal blessedness. And so the proper question in face of this plurality of claims is, which is the true religion?

In practice, those who are concerned to raise this question are normally fully convinced that theirs is the true religion; so that for them the task is to show the spiritual superiority of their own creed and the consequent moral superiority of the community which embodies it. A great deal of the mutual criticism of religions, and of the derogatory assessment of one by another, has been in fulfilment of this task.

This view of mankind's religious life as divided into great contraposed entities, each claiming to be the true religion, is not however the only possible way of seeing the religious situation. Cantwell Smith has offered an alternative vision.

He shows first that the presently dominant conceptually has a history that can be traced back to the European Renaissance. It was then that the different streams of religious life began to be reified in Western thought as solid structures called Christianity, Judaism, and so forth. And having reified their own faith in this way Westerners have then exported the notion of 'a religion' to the rest of the world, causing others to think of themselves as belonging to the Hindu, or the Confucian, or the Buddhist religion, and so on, over against others. But an alternative perception can divide the scene differently. It sees something of vital religious significance taking different forms all over the world within the contexts of the different historical traditions. This 'something of vital religious significance' Cantwell Smith calls faith. I would agree with some of his critics that this is not the ideal word for it; for 'faith' is a term that is more at home in the Semitic than in the Indian family of traditions and which has, as his own historical researches have shown, become badly overintellectualised. But I take it that he uses the term to refer to the spiritual state, or existential condition, constituted by a person's present response to the ultimate divine Reality. This ranges from the negative response of a self-enclosed consciousness which is blind to the divine presence, whether beyond us or in the depths of our own being, to a positive openness to the Divine which gradually transforms us and which is called salvation or liberation or enlightenment. This transformation is essentially the same within the different religious contexts within which it occurs: I would define it formally as the transformation of human existence from self-centredness to Reality-centredness. This is the event or process of vital significance which one can see to be occurring in individuals all over the world, taking different forms within the contexts of the different perceptions of the Ultimate made available by the various religious traditions.

These cumulative traditions themselves are the other thing that one sees with the aid of the new conceptuality suggested by Cantwell Smith. They are distinguishable strands of human history in each of which a multitude of religious and cultural elements interact to form a distinctive pattern,

(continued)

Problems of Religious Pluralism   (continued)

constituting, say, the Hindu, Buddhist, Confucian, Jewish, Christian or Muslim tradition. These traditions are not static entities but living movements; and they are not tightly homogeneous but have each become in the course of time internally highly various. Thus there are large differences between, for example, Buddhism in the time of Gautama and Buddhism after the development of the Mahāyāna and its expansion northwards into China; or between the Christian movement in Roman Palestine and that in medieval Europe. And there are large differences today between, say, Zen and Amida Buddhism in Japan, or between Southern Baptist and Northern Episcopalian Christianity in the United States. Indeed, since we cannot always avoid using the substantives, we might do well to speak of Buddhisms, Christianities, and so on, in the plural. A usage consonant with Cantwell Smith's analysis has however already become widespread, and many of us now often prefer to speak not of Christianity but of the Christian tradition, the Hindu tradition, and so on, when referring to these historically identifiable strands of history.

These cumulative traditions are composed of a rich complex of inner and outer elements cohering in a distinctive living pattern which includes structures of belief, life-styles, scriptures and their interpretations, liturgies, cultic celebrations, myths, music, poetry, architecture, literature, remembered history and its heroes. Thus the traditions constitute religious cultures, each with its own unique history and ethos. And each such tradition creates human beings in its own image. For we are not human in general, participating in an eternal Platonic essence of humanity. We are human in one or other of the various concrete ways of being human which constitute the cultures of the earth. There is a Chinese way of being human, an African way, an Arab way, a European way, or ways, and so on. These are not fixed moulds but living organisms which develop and interact over the centuries, so that the patterns of human life change, usually very slowly but sometimes with startling rapidity. But we are all formed in a hundred ways of which we are not normally aware by the culture into which we were born, by which we are fed, and with which we interact.

Let us then enter, with Cantwell Smith, into the experiment of thinking, on the one hand, of 'faith,' or human response to the divine, which in its positive and negative forms is salvation and non-salvation and, on the other hand, of the cumulative religious traditions within which this occurs; and let us ask what the relation is between these two realities—on the one hand salvation/liberation and on the other the cumulative traditions. . . .

However, we may now turn to a second Christian answer to our question, which can be labelled 'inclusivism.' This can be expressed in terms either of a juridical or of a transformation-of-human-existence conception of salvation. In the former terms it is the view that God's forgiveness and acceptance of humanity have been made possible by Christ's death, but that the benefits of this sacrifice are not confined to those who respond to it with an explicit act of faith. The juridical transaction of Christ's atonement covered *all* human sin, so that all human beings are now open to God's mercy, even though they may never have heard of Jesus Christ and why he died on the cross of Calvary. . . . [We omit Hick's discussion of the first answer to the relation between the realities, exclusivism.]

Rahner's is a brave attempt to attain an inclusivist position which is in principle universal but which does not thereby renounce the old exclusivist dogma. But the question is whether in this new context the old dogma has not been so emptied of content as no longer to be worth affirming. When salvation is acknowledged to be taking place without any connection with the Christian Church or Gospel, in people who are living on the basis of quite other faiths, is it not a somewhat empty gesture to insist upon affixing a Christian label to them? Further, having thus labelled them, why persist in the aim of gathering all humankind into the Christian Church? Once it is accepted that salvation does not depend upon this, the conversion of the people of the other great world faiths to Christianity hardly seems the best way of spending one's energies.

The third possible answer to the question of the relation between salvation/liberation and the cumulative religious traditions can best be called pluralism. As a Christian position this can be seen as an acceptance of the further conclusion to which inclusivism points. If we accept that salvation/liberation is taking place within all the great religious traditions, why not frankly acknowledge that there is a plurality of saving human responses to the ultimate divine Reality?

Pluralism, then, is the view that the transformation of human existence from self-centredness to Reality-centredness is taking place in different ways within the contexts of all the great religious traditions. There is not merely one way but a plurality of ways of salvation or liberation. In Christian theological terms, there is a plurality of divine revelations, making possible a plurality of forms of saving human response.

What however makes it difficult for Christians to move from inclusivism to pluralism, holding the majority of Christian theologians today in the inclusivist position despite its evident logical instability, is of course the traditional doctrine of the Incarnation, together with its protective envelope, the doctrine of the Trinity. For in its orthodox form, as classically expressed at the Councils of Nicaea and Chalcedon, the incarnational doctrine claims that Jesus was God incarnate, the Second Person of the Triune God living a human life, it is integral to this faith that there has been (and will be) no other divine incarnation. This makes Christianity unique in that it, alone among the religions of the world, was founded by God in person. Such a uniqueness would seem to demand Christian exclusivism—for must God not want all human beings to enter the way of salvation which he has provided for them? However, since such exclusivism seems so unrealistic in the light of our knowledge of the wider religious life of mankind, many theologians have moved to some form of inclusivism, but now feel unable to go further and follow the argument to its conclusion in the frank acceptance of pluralism. The break with traditional missionary attitudes and long-established ecclesiastical and liturgical language would, for many, be so great as to be prohibitive.

There is however the possibility of an acceptable Christian route to religious pluralism in work which has already been done, and which is being done, in the field of Christology with motivations quite other than to facilitate pluralism, and on grounds which are internal to the intellectual development of Christianity. For there is a decisive watershed between what might be called all-or-nothing Christologies and degree Christologies. The all-or-nothing principle is classically expressed in the Chalcedonian Definition, according to which Christ is 'to be acknowledged in Two Natures,' 'Consubstantial with the Father according to his Deity, Consubstantial with us according to his Humanity.' Substance is an all-or-nothing notion, in that A either is or is not composed of the same substance, either has or does not have the same essential nature, as B. Using this all-or-nothing conceptuality Chalcedon attributed to Christ two complete natures, one divine and the other human, being in his divine nature of one substance with God the Father. Degree Christologies, on the other hand, apply the term 'incarnation' to the activity of God's Spirit or of God's grace in human lives, so that the divine will is done on earth. This kind of reinterpretation has been represented in recent years by, for example, the 'paradox of grace' Christology of Donald Baillie (in *God Was in Christ*, 1948) and the 'inspiration Christology' of Geoffrey Lampe (in *God as Spirit, 1977*). In so far as a human being is open and responsive to God, so that God is able to act in and through that individual, we can speak of the embodiment in human life of God's redemptive activity. And in Jesus this 'paradox of grace'—the paradox expressed by St Paul when he wrote 'it was not I, but the grace of God which is in me' (I Corinthians 15:10)—or the inspiration of God's Spirit, occurred to a startling extent. The paradox, or the inspiration, are not however confined to the life of Jesus; they are found, in varying degrees, in all free human response to God. Christologies of the same broad family occur in the work of Norman Pittenger *(The Word Incarnate,* 1957), John Knox *(The Humanity and Divinity of Christ,* 1967), and earlier in John Baillie *(The Place of Jesus Christ in Modern Christianity,* 1929), and more recently in the authors of *The Myth of God Incarnate* (1977).

These modern degree Christologies were not in fact for the most part developed in order to facilitate a Christian acceptance of religious pluralism. They were developed as alternatives to the old substance Christology, in which so many difficulties, both historical and philosophical, had become apparent. They claim to be compatible with the teachings of Jesus and of the very early Church, and to avoid the intractable problem, generated by a substance Christology, of the relation between Jesus's two natures. But, as an unintended consequence, degree Christologies open up the possibility of seeing God's activity in Jesus as being of the same kind as God's activity in other great human mediators of the divine. The traditional Christian claim to the unique superiority of Christ and of the Christian tradition is not of course precluded by a degree Christology; for it may be argued (as it was, for example, by both Baillie and Lampe) that Christ was the *supreme* instance of the paradox of grace or of the inspiration of the Spirit, so that Christianity is still

(continued)

Problems of Religious Pluralism (*continued*)

assumed to be the *best* context of salvation/liberation. But, whereas, starting from the substance Christology, the unique superiority of Christ and the Christian Church are guaranteed *a priori*, starting from a degree Christology they have to be established by historical evidence. Whether this can in fact be done is, clearly, an open question. It would indeed be an uphill task today to establish that we know enough about the inner and outer life of the historical Jesus, and of the other founders of great religious traditions, to be able to make any such claim; and perhaps an even more uphill task to establish from the morally ambiguous histories of each of the great traditions, complex mixtures of good and evil as each has been, that one's own tradition stands out as manifestly superior to all others.

I think, then, that a path exists along which Christians can, if they feel so drawn, move to an acceptance of religious pluralism. Stated philosophically such a pluralism is the view that the great world faiths embody different perceptions and conceptions of, and correspondingly different responses to, the Real or the Ultimate from within the major variant cultural ways of being human; and that within each of them the transformation of human existence from self-centredness to Reality-centredness is manifestly taking place—and taking place, so far as human observation can tell, to much the same extent. Thus the great religious traditions are to be regarded as alternative soteriological 'spaces' within which, or 'ways' along which, men and women can find salvation/liberation/enlightenment/fulfilment.

But how can such a view be arrived at? Are we not proposing a picture reminiscent of the ancient allegory of the blind men and the elephant, in which each runs his hands over a different part of the animal, and identifies it differently, a leg as a tree, the trunk as a snake, the tail as a rope, and so on? Clearly, in the story the situation is being described from the point of view of someone who can observe both elephant and blind men. But where is the vantage-point from which one can observe both the divine Reality and the different limited human standpoints from which that Reality is being variously perceived? The advocate of the pluralist understanding cannot pretend to any such cosmic vision. How then does he profess to know that the situation is indeed as he depicts it? The answer is that he does not profess to *know* this, if by knowledge we mean infallible cognition. Nor indeed can anyone else properly claim to have knowledge, in this sense, of either the exclusivist or the inclusivist picture. All of them are, strictly speaking, hypotheses. The pluralist hypothesis is arrived at inductively. One starts from the fact that many human beings experience life in relation to a limitlessly greater transcendent Reality—whether the direction of transcendence be beyond our present existence or within its hidden depths. In theory such religious experience is capable of a purely naturalistic analysis which does not involve reference to any reality other than the human and the natural. But to participate by faith in one of the actual streams of religious experience—in my case, the Christian stream—is to participate in it as an experience of transcendent Reality. I think that there is in fact a good argument for the rationality of trusting one's own religious experience, together with that of the larger tradition within which it occurs, so as both to believe and to live on the basis of it; but I cannot develop that argument here. Treating one's own form of religious experience, then, as veridical—as an experience (however dim, like 'seeing through a glass, darkly') of transcendent divine Reality—one then has to take account of the fact that there are other great streams of religious experience which take different forms, are shaped by different conceptualities, and embodied in different institutions, art forms, and lifestyles. In other words, besides one's own religion, sustained by its distinctive form of religious experience, there are also other religions, through each of which flows the life blood of a different form of religious experience. What account is one to give of this plurality? . . .

But if we look for the transcendence of egoism and a recentring in God or in the transcendent Real, then I venture the proposition that, so far as human observation and historical memory can tell, this occurs to about the same extent within each of the great world traditions.

If this is so, it prompts us to go beyond inclusivism to a pluralism which recognises a variety of human religious contexts within which salvation/liberation takes place.

But such a pluralistic hypothesis raises many questions. What is this divine Reality to which all the great traditions are said to be oriented? Can we really equate the personal Yahweh with the non-personal Brahman, Shiva with the Tao, the Holy Trinity with the Buddhist Trikāya, and all with one another? Indeed, do not the Eastern and Western faiths deal incommensurably with different problems?

As these questions indicate, we need a pluralistic theory which enables us to recognise and be fascinated by the manifold differences between the religious traditions, with their different conceptualisations, their different modes of religious experience, and their different forms of individual and social response to the divine. I should like in these final pages to suggest the ground plan of such a theory—a theory which is, I venture to think, fully compatible with the central themes of Cantwell Smith's thought.

Each of the great religious traditions affirms that in addition to the social and natural world of our ordinary human experience there is a limitlessly greater and higher Reality beyond or within us, in relation to which or to whom is our highest good. The ultimately real and the ultimately valuable are one, and to give oneself freely and totally to this One is our final salvation/liberation/enlightenment/fulfilment. Further, each tradition is conscious that the divine Reality exceeds the reach of our earthly speech and thought. It cannot be encompassed in human concepts. It is infinite, eternal, limitlessly rich beyond the scope of our finite conceiving or experiencing. Let us then both avoid the particular names used within the particular traditions and yet use a term which is consonant with the faith of each of them—Ultimate Reality, or the Real.

Let us next adopt a distinction that is to be found in different forms and with different emphases within each of the great traditions, the distinction between the Real *an sich* (in him/her/itself) and the Real as humanly experienced and thought. In Christian terms this is the distinction between God in God's infinite and eternal self-existent being, 'prior' to and independent of creation, and God as related to and known by us as creator, redeemer and sanctifier. In Hindu thought it is the distinction between *nirguṇa* Brahman, the Ultimate in itself, beyond all human categories, and *saguna* Brahman, the Ultimate as known to finite consciousness as a personal deity, Iśvara. In Taoist thought, 'The Tao that can be expressed is not the eternal Tao' *(Tao-Te Ching,* 1). There are also analogous distinctions in Jewish and Muslim mystical thought in which the Real *an sich* is called *en Soph* and *al Haqq*. In Mahāyāna Buddhism there is the distinction between the *dharmakāya,* the eternal cosmic Buddha-nature, which is also the infinite Void *(śūnyatā),* and on the other hand the realm of heavenly Buddha figures *(sambhogakāya)* and their incarnations in the earthly Buddhas *(nirmāṇakāya).* This varied family of distinctions suggests the perhaps daring thought that the Real *an sich* is one but is nevertheless capable of being humanly experienced in a variety of ways. This thought lies at the heart of the pluralistic hypothesis which I am suggesting.

The next point of which we need to take account is the creative part that thought, and the range of concepts in terms of which it functions, plays in the formation of conscious experience. It was above all Immanuel Kant who brought this realisation into the stream of modern reflection, and it has since been confirmed and amplified by innumerable studies, not only in general epistemology but also in cognitive psychology, in the sociology of knowledge, and in the philosophy of science. The central fact, of which the epistemology of religion also has to take account, is that our environment is not reflected in our consciousness in a simple and straightforward way, just as it is, independently of our perceiving it. At the physical level, out of the immense richness of structure and detail around us, only that minute selection that is relevant to our biological survival and flourishing affects our senses; and these inputs are interpreted in the mind/brain to produce our conscious experience of the familiar world in which we live. Its character as an environment within which we can learn to behave appropriately can be called its *meaning* for us. This all-important dimension of meaning, which begins at the physical level as the habitability of the material world, continues at the personal, or social, level of awareness as the moral significance of the situations of our life, and at the religious level as a consciousness of the ultimate meaning of each situation and of our situation as a whole in relation to the divine Reality. This latter consciousness is not however a general consciousness of the divine, but always takes specific forms; and, as in the case of the awareness of the physical and of the ethical meaning of our environment, such consciousness has an essential dispositional aspect. To experience in this way rather than in that involves being in a state of readiness to behave in a particular range of ways, namely that which is appropriate to our environment having the particular character that we perceive (or of course misperceive) it to have. Thus to be aware of the divine as 'the God and Father of our Lord Jesus Christ,' in so far as this is

(continued)

Problems of Religious Pluralism   (*continued*)

the operative awareness which determines our dispositional state, is to live in the kind of way described by Jesus in his religious and moral teaching—in trust towards God and in love towards our neighbours.

How are these various specific forms of religious awareness formed? Our hypothesis is that they are formed by the presence of the divine Reality, this presence coming to consciousness in terms of the different sets of religious concepts and structures of religious meaning that operate within the different religious traditions of the world. If we look at the range of actual human religious experience and ask ourselves what basic concepts and what concrete images have operated in its genesis, I would suggest that we arrive at something like the following answer. There are, first, the two basic religious concepts which between them dominate the entire range of the forms of religious experience. One is the concept of Deity, or God, i.e. the Real as personal; and the other is the concept of the Absolute, i.e. the Real as non-personal. (The term 'Absolute' is by no means ideal for the purpose, but is perhaps the nearest that we have.) We do not however, in actual religious experience, encounter either Deity in general or the Absolute in general, but always in specific forms. In Kantian language, each general concept is schematised, or made concrete. In Kant's own analysis of sense-experience the schematisation of the basic categories is in terms of time; but religious experience occurs at a much higher level of meaning, presupposing and going beyond physical meaning and involving much more complex and variable modes of dispositional response. Schematisation or concretisation here is in terms of 'filled' human time, or history, as diversified into the different cultures and civilisations of the earth. For there are different concrete ways of being human and of participating in human history, and within these different ways the presence of the divine Reality is experienced in characteristically different ways.

To take the concept of God first, this becomes concrete as the range of specific deities to which the history of religion bears witness. Thus the Real as personal is known in the Christian tradition as God the Father; in Judaism as Adonai; in Islam as Allah, the Qur'ānic Revealer; in the Indian traditions as Shiva, or Vishnu, or Paramātmā, and under the many other lesser images of deity which in different regions of India concretise different aspects of the divine nature. This range of personal deities who are the foci of worship within the theistic traditions constitutes the range of the divine *personae* in relation to mankind. Each *persona*, in his or her historical concreteness, lives within the corporate experience of a particular faith-community. Thus the Yahweh *persona* exists and has developed in interaction with the Jewish people. He is a part of their history, and they are a part of his; and he cannot be extracted from this historical context. Shiva, on the other hand, is a quite different divine *persona*, existing in the experience of hundreds of millions of people in the Shaivite stream of Indian religious life. These two *personae*, Yahweh and Shiva, live within different worlds of faith, partly creating and partly created by the features of different human cultures, being responded to in different patterns of life, and being integral to different strands of historical experience. Within each of these worlds of faith great numbers of people find the ultimate meaning of their existence, and are carried through the crises of life and death; and within this process many are, in varying degrees, challenged and empowered to move forward on the way of salvation/liberation from self-centredness to Reality-centredness. From the pluralist point of view Yahweh and Shiva are not rival gods, or rival claimants to be the one and only God, but rather two different concrete historical *personae* in terms of which the ultimate divine Reality is present and responded to by different large historical communities within different strands of the human story.

This conception of divine *personae*, constituting (in Kantian language) different divine phenomena in terms of which the one divine noumenon is humanly experienced, enables us to acknowledge the degree of truth within the various projection theories of religion from Feuerbach through Freud to the present day. An element of human projection colours our mental images of God, accounting for their anthropomorphic features—for example, as male or female. But human projection does not—on this view—bring God into existence; rather it affects the ways in which the independently existing divine Reality is experienced.

Does this epistemological pattern of the schematisation of a basic religious concept into a range of particular correlates of religious experience apply also to the non-theistic traditions? I suggest that it does. Here the general concept, the Absolute, is schematised in actual religious experience to form the range of divine *impersonae*—Brahman, the Dharma, the Tao, *nirvāna*, *śūnyatā*, and so on—which are experienced within the Eastern traditions. The structure of these *impersonae* is however importantly different from that of the *personae*. A divine *persona* is concrete, implicitly finite, sometimes visualisable and even capable of being pictured. A divine *impersona*, on the other hand, is not a 'thing' in contrast to a person. It is the infinite being—consciousness—bliss *(saccidānanda)* of Brahman; or the beginningless and endless process of cosmic change *(pratītya samutpāda)* of Buddhist teaching; or again the ineffable 'further shore' of *nirvāna*, or the eternal Buddha-nature *(dharmakāya)*; or the ultimate Emptiness *(śūnyatā)* which is also the fullness or suchness of the world; or the eternal principle of the Tao. It is thus not so much an entity as a field of spiritual force, or the ultimate reality of everything, that which gives final meaning and joy. These non-personal conceptions of the Ultimate inform modes of consciousness varying from the advaitic experience of becoming one with the Infinite, to the Zen experience of finding a total reality in the present concrete moment of existence in the ordinary world. And according to the pluralistic hypothesis these different modes of experience constitute different experiences of the Real as non- or transpersonal. As in the case of the divine *personae*, they are formed by different religious conceptualities which have developed in interaction with different spiritual disciplines and methods of mediation. The evidence that a range of *impersonae* of the one Ultimate Reality are involved in the nontheistic forms of religious experience, rather than the direct unmediated awareness of Reality itself, consists precisely in the differences between the experiences reported within the different traditions. How is it that a 'direct experience' of the Real can take such different forms? One could of course at this point revert to the exclusivism of the inclusivism whose limitations we have already noted. But the pluralist answer will be that even the most advanced form of mystical experience, as an experience undergone by an embodied consciousness whose mind/brain has been conditioned by a particular religious tradition, must be affected by the conceptual framework and spiritual training provided by that tradition, and accordingly takes these different forms. In other words the Real is experienced not *an sich*, but in terms of the various non-personal images or concepts that have been generated at the interface between the Real and different patterns of human consciousness.

These many different perceptions of the Real, both theistic and nontheistic, can only establish themselves as authentic by their soteriological efficacy. The great world traditions have in fact all proved to be realms within which or routes along which people are enabled to advance in the transition from self-centredness to Reality-centredness. And, since they reveal the Real in such different lights, we must conclude that they are independently valid. Accordingly, by attending to other traditions than one's own one may become aware of other aspects or dimensions of the Real, and of other possibilities of response to the Real, which had not been made effectively available by one's own tradition. Thus a mutual mission of the sharing of experiences and insights can proceed through the growing network of inter-faith dialogue and the interactions of the faith-communities. Such mutual mission does not aim at conversion—although occasionally individual conversions, in all directions, will continue to occur—but at mutual enrichment and at co-operation in face of the urgent problems of human survival in a just and sustainable world society.

Chapter 4
Socio-Political Philosophy

What good comes from a politically stable society if its members do not have freedom? What good comes from a free society if its members do not have security from potential internal or external threats? What good is security or freedom if you have no food on your table or roof over your head? Few people will say that they live in a utopian or perfect society, but unfortunately many citizens live in a society where their government and/or their social institutions are far from ideal. But what is the ideal form of government? Ask ten different people and you may get ten different answers. We speak of having certain common interests such as freedom, security, equality, justice, and privacy. Many philosophers have argued that some, if not all, of these interests should be considered basic human rights. In order to comprehend what interests we should consider as rights and what sort of society is important to us, let us imagine a situation where there is no government, no society, no rules or restrictions or responsibilities; in other words let us imagine we are starting over from the beginning. By doing so, we may discover that there is truth in the sayings "You never know what you truly had until you lose it" and "Be careful for what you wish for because you may get it."

When we are asked to imagine a world with no institutional order, we might envision either a paradise or a post-apocalyptic world. In the movies, when we are presented with a paradise we know that at some point things are going to go seriously wrong, and when we are presented with a post-apocalyptic world, there is usually some glimmer of hope that offers a chance for things to get better. For our purposes, let us use the setting of a film such as *Mad Max II: The Road Runner* as the background for our thought experiment. Mel Gibson plays an ex-police officer in a world that has destroyed itself.[1] His only goal is to survive long enough to get from point A to B, and in order to do so he has to make sure he has enough gasoline for his car and can avoid becoming another victim of roving highway marauders.

When you consider what sort of life one would have in such a place where there are no rules or restrictions on your behavior and no social safety nets to rely on, the principle of "only the strongest survive" comes to mind. This is because if you are on your own, you will have to take care of all your needs (not to mention trying to satisfy any wants or desires). You will need food, water, shelter, clothing, as well as some form of protection from others who might want to forcibly take these things from you. As Thomas Hobbes (1588–1679) argues in *Leviathan*, trying to meet your needs by yourself will truly be a daunting task.

We all have various skills and abilities and our aptitude in each area will also vary by degrees. Some of us may be better at building shelter; others, at growing food. Regardless of our strengths, we will have weaknesses, and one of the weaknesses that we will all face is that we do not have enough time in the day to do all the things that need to be done. Even Mad Max must at some point rely on strangers to assist him.

Without external sanctions such as laws or moral condemnation by our peers, some people will seek to take short cuts in acquiring what they need. They will take from those who are weaker than them. If the strong survive, this does not necessarily entail that the "strong" refers to a single individual.[2] For reasons of self-interest, the weak might come together and cooperate. In the most primal way, a handful of physically weak people can overpower the one strong person. However and more importantly, those who have weaknesses in differing areas might share the burden that separately none of them could overcome. They do this, argues Hobbes, not because they care about other people's interests but because they care about their own. They cooperate with others because such an act helps them achieve their own personal goals in the long run. So, if I cannot build a shelter but you can, I will farm and exchange my goods or labor with yours so that we both benefit.

Regardless of which socio-political tale we adopt concerning the nature and origin of society, there will always be limited resources and competing claims over them.[3] Hence there will be a need for basic rules of entitlement and behavior. So which burdens and benefits should be put in place, and how are we to distribute them? By burdens we mean to include such things as restrictions on freedom of thought and act, taxation, punishment, and obligatory military service. By benefits we mean to include such things as education, wages, profit, private property, health care, and security. Karl Marx stated that we should "Take from each according to his ability, to each according to his needs."[4] Is this an appropriate motto for a utopian society?

---

[1] It's not really clear if the entire world has been affected or just various parts of it.

[2] The statement "only the strong survive" could be interpreted as a truism because if the weak survive, this would by definition make them the strong. For a hilarious view of a world where the weak do survive (because they breed more), see *Idiocracy*.

[3] There are a number of films dealing with post-apocalyptic societies or attempts at creating them ranging from *Planet of the Apes* to *Waterworld* to *Mad Max III Beyond Thunderdome*, and the cult favorite *A Boy and His Dog*.

[4] Karl Marx, *Critique of the Gotha Programme*.

"To each according to his or her need"? Assuming health care and education are universal needs, how much do we provide? Should everyone get the same access to health care? If I am healthy, why should I be forced to pay (through my labor or taxation) for your medical care? Should high school or university education be free? Who should pay for these things? If I am childless, why should I pay for schools to be built for your children? Let us consider some other possible distributions.

"To each according to his or her want"? Should people be given whatever they desire? More roads, more sports stadiums, more expensive technologies or drugs or amusements? Some people prefer the simple life while others want luxuries. How are scarce resources going to be justly divided when we cannot give everything to everyone?

"To each according to his or her merit"? Why should someone who inherits money be allowed to keep it? Perhaps the smarter deserve to get more; or the stronger, or the morally wise?

"To each according to his or her labor"? We often hear that people who work hard deserve to be paid more. Do professional athletes deserve to be paid millions of dollars a year while teachers live at the poverty level? Why should a lawyer receive five or ten times the salary as a janitor who works the same number of hours at minimum wage? What about people who are unable to contribute to society through work such as the infirm? Sure, the elderly contributed to society at one time, but they no longer do—should they be rewarded or penalized for their age?

"To each according to what would be best for society"? Might we base our decisions on just distribution not on what the people *qua* individuals want or need or deserve or do, but what would be best for society in general? For example, on the islands of Hawai'i the beaches are public property and there must be guaranteed public access to them. Even though there are individuals who would willingly pay enormous sums for the land, privatization is deemed not in the public interest. State monopolies on various services including oil and gas, health, and telecommunications may serve the interests of the populace better than privatization. Should governments control everything or nothing?

Whether you agreed with any of the previous socio-political mottos or not, would you change your mind if you knew what your own position in this society was? If you knew you were a highly skilled athlete or worked at a minimum wage job or had two disabled children, would your views on what just distribution entailed be different? What if you were ignorant to all of the characteristics of the original populace in this newly formed society? That is, what if you did not know anything about your own or anyone else's age, sex, income, intelligence, strength, and so forth? Would you be a risk-taker and hope to be one of the few fortunate ones who got a greater share than others, or would you play it safe? Again, not knowing who you were, would your pattern of just distribution be one of giving everyone an equal share or giving all the wealth and power to just a few? These questions and suggested answers to them are put forward by John Rawls (1921–2002) in a selection included here from his classic work *A Theory of Justice*.

Many women have personally experienced the unjust distribution of society's benefits and burdens. Accordingly, many films have attempted to deal with this issue but instead sometimes just perpetuate stereotypes. In Disney's cartoon classic *Cinderella*, Cinderella is rescued from her life of abject poverty by a Prince who sweeps her off her feet and turns her into a beautiful princess. In 1990, this fairy tale was modernized in the film *Pretty Woman*. Julia Roberts, who plays a cheap street prostitute, is rescued from her life of turning tricks by a wealthy business man who sweeps her off her feet and turns her into a *high*-priced prostitute. The title characters in *Thelma and Louise* become empowered only after an attempted sexual assault. Jodie Foster stands as *The Accused* and has her sexual history, not the men who gang raped her, take the center stage in the courtroom.

Why is it that in the famous shower scene in *Psycho* we are witness to a prolonged knife slashing of a naked woman while the other killings in the film are quite quick? Might it have to do with the notion that somehow Marian deserved to die given her loose morals? We cannot put the reason down to just the director's and screenwriter's intent: director Adrian Lyne had to re-shoot the ending of the film *Fatal Attraction* because test audiences thought that the female villain was not punished enough for breaking up a marriage. There are many similar examples that we can cite. Sarah Connor's motherly role was far less defined than her rippling muscles in *Terminator II*. And in another missed opportunity, the key reason for Lieutenant Ripley's attempt to save a young girl from becoming a host for a stomach-bursting alien was left on the cutting room floor of *Aliens*. In the extended version of the film we discover that Ripley never got a chance to see her own daughter grow up because Ripley was lost in space for seven decades. Saving the life of the young girl named Newt represented her chance to make amends and fulfill her responsibilities. It is not because Ripley is a strong fighter that she is able to rescue Newt, it is because she is a good mother.

Still, in at least one movie of note there can be good role models for women, even within the cliché-ridden realm of daytime television! In the following scene, Dorothy Michaels is applying for a job as an actress on a popular soap opera:

PRODUCER   Dorothy Michaels?

DOROTHY   Yes.

PRODUCER   George Fields is your agent?

DOROTHY   Yes.

PRODUCER   Okay, ladies. Please bring your pages and follow me.

DOROTHY   I hate this line, "You have every right to happiness."

PRODUCER   This is Dorothy Michaels. Our director, Ron Carlysle.

DIRECTOR   I'm afraid you're not right for this role. Thanks for coming by.

DOROTHY   Why am I not right?

DIRECTOR   I'm trying to make a certain statement . . . and I'm looking for a specific physical type.

DOROTHY   Mr. Carlysle, I'm a character actress. I can play it any way you want.

DIRECTOR   I'm sure you're a very good actress. It's just that you're not threatening enough.

DOROTHY   Not threatening enough? Take your hands off me or I'll knee you in the balls!—Is that enough of a threat?

DIRECTOR   It's a start.

DOROTHY   I think I know what you want. You want a caricature of a woman. To prove some point like power makes a woman masculine . . . or masculine women are ugly. Well, shame on any woman that lets you do that. And that means you, Miss Marshall. Shame on you, you macho shithead.

After she successfully lands the job, Dorothy starts ad-libbing her lines to make her character more self-assured and less of a caricature. While dealing with the unwelcome attentions of various men, she slowly realizes that it is her responsibility to become a role model for all women. The twist is that these attentions are unwelcome not because the character is objectified (she is not) but because Dorothy is actually an out-of-work male actor named Michael. The film is *Tootsie*, and the irony is that it takes a man dressed in drag to show women (both Michael's colleagues and the soap opera viewers) that they are men's equals and they should not tolerate sexual discrimination.

These few examples support the view that women have been portrayed in less than ideal ways in many mainstream movies, even when they are sympathetic and heroic. For example, Sigourney Weaver plays a very powerful role in *Gorillas in the Mist*, which is based on the true story of Diane Fossey's fatal attempts to save the mountain gorilla. Here an admirable woman is murdered just because she is a very capable one. The view that women have been historically unjustly oppressed in patriarchal societies is the one common thread that runs throughout different types of feminist theories. It is a mistake to assume that "a feminist is a feminist is a feminist" as there are a number of different and contrasting feminist schools of thought, including the four major schools of Cultural Feminism, Radical Feminism, Liberal Feminism, and Social Feminism.

Cultural feminists argue that there are essential differences between men and women that are not limited to their biological features but also include their different perspectives about the world. It is claimed that women are generally more nurturing and more inclusive whereas men are independent and competitive. If women's values were adopted, then the world would be a better, less violent, less confrontational place. However, cultural feminists believe that what makes women different from men is not respected in most societies.

Radical feminists argue that the differences between men and women should be celebrated. Moreover, women should seek to separate themselves philosophically and physically from men. The ability of women to reproduce and its subsequent complexities in terms of restricting women's behavior is seen as the excuse that men use in order to have power over women.

Liberal feminists argue that men and women are equals. They argue that the differences between men and women that have been used as grounds for discrimination are neither relevant nor essential to the genders. Women are "just as good as" men and should be treated equally. Just because a woman may not be able to lift as much as a man does not mean that no women can. Just because one particular woman is not as smart as one particular man does not mean that most women are not as smart or smarter. Equal opportunities should be provided and arbitrary distinctions should be eliminated. As a question of implementation, one area of continued discussion is how to provide a level playing field when many women are not able to move up the corporate ladder because they are unable to spend the same amount of time at the office without sacrificing their right to motherhood (and all the accompanying commitments). Does providing equal opportunity also mean enacting affirmative action programs to make up for deficiencies elsewhere that have hindered women's progress?

Social feminists argue that the way to put an end to male oppression is to address economic and class discrepancies. Women are often in lower-paying jobs and tend to be the primary caregiver within the family. This latter role is not well supported by social institutions and is often dismissed merely as "women's work." Whereas the positive roles are those that men occupy. The capitalist society is one that oppresses women and thus must be challenged. Social feminists argue that the liberal feminist concerns tend to fit with the trials and tribulations of white, well-educated women while the reality is that far more women around the world are of different races, religions, cultural backgrounds, and classes.

Jane Austin's novels and the films based on them reveal that in Georgian times the existence of different classes in society was considered as natural as one's hair color. One might be able to alter appearances of class briefly for strangers, but the truth was always known to one's family and friends. People struggled to move up in the world, which was no easy feat since those on the higher rungs would be lowered if they married for love married out of love and that spouse a spouse who was economically, professionally, or ancestrally of inferior status. The Academy Award–winning screenplay *Sense and Sensibility* shows that being a woman during this period was to be automatically marginalized—by men, by the law, and even by other women.

Ext. Norland Park—Margaret's Tree-House—Day

> *ELINOR comes to the foot of a large tree from which a small staircase issues.*

ELINOR   Margaret, are you there? Please come down. John and Fanny will be here soon.

> *A pause. ELINOR is about to leave when a disembodied and truculent young voice stops her.*

MARGARET (V.O.)   Why are they coming to live at Norland? They already have a house in London.

ELINOR   Because houses go from father to son, dearest not from father to daughter. It is the law.

> *Silence. ELINOR tries another tack.*

ELINOR   If you come inside, we could play with your atlas.

MARGARET (V.O.)   It's not my atlas any more. It's their atlas.

> *CLOSE on ELINOR as she ponders the truth of this statement.*

While both men and women were discriminated against on account of their positions in society during this time, women were also perceived as having an inherent natural failing on account of their biological sex. No matter what your fortune or family circle, you could not change this fact of nature. Notice the difference of opportunities available to the two sexes in the following dialogue from *Sense and Sensibility*:

> *EDWARD and ELINOR are still talking as they walk arm in arm in the late afternoon sun.*

EDWARD   All I want—all I have ever wanted is the quiet of a private life but my mother is determined to see me distinguished.

ELINOR   As?

EDWARD   She hardly knows. Any fine figure will suit a great orator, a leading politician, even a barrister would serve, but only on the condition that I drive my own barouche and dine in the first circles.

> *His tone is light but there is an underlying bitterness to it.*

ELINOR   And what do you wish for?

EDWARD   I always preferred the church, but that is not smart enough for my mother she prefers the army, but that is a great deal too smart for me.

ELINOR   Would you stay in London?

EDWARD   I hate London. No peace. A country living is my ideal a small parish where I might do some good, keep chickens and give very short sermons.

Ext. Fields Near Norland—Day

> *EDWARD and ELINOR are on horseback. The atmosphere is intimate, the quality of the conversation rooted now in their affections.*

ELINOR   You talk of feeling idle and useless imagine how that is compounded when one has no choice and no hope whatsoever of any occupation.

> *EDWARD nods and smiles at the irony of it.*

EDWARD   Our circumstances are therefore precisely the same.

ELINOR   Except that you will inherit your fortune.

> *He looks at her slightly shocked but enjoying her boldness.*

ELINOR   We cannot even earn ours.

Men were discriminated against because of their class, but women had no easy means to improve themselves and rise above theirs. As Wollstonecraft points out later in this chapter, even the stupidest man could still marry well above himself whereas the smartest woman could not. One hopes such inequities have diminished over time.

In *Norma Rae* we get the all too common blending of sexual discrimination with worker discrimination. Sally Field plays the title character who earns minimum wage as a textile worker. After hearing a speech by a union leader, she tries to organize her fellow laborers. She tells them her reasons:

NORMA   If the union is what everybody believes it is, I'll follow all the way. Excuse me for sayin' this with menfolks in the room, but, when I get my menstrual cramps, which come pretty hard, they don't let me sit down on my job. They say you gotta keep to your feet unless you bring a note from the doctor. We wouldn't say we was sick if we wasn't.

You know, I look at a brick wall all day. There used to be a window there, but they come and brick it up to give us the feelin' that we shut in.

My husband Averil died of brown lung two months ago. His children are gonna grow up not even . . . knowin' him. I got all his clothes if someone could use 'em.

> *Later on Norma Rae speaks openly with her children; telling them to be wary of the things that anti-unionists will tell them about her past.*

NORMA   I want life to be better for you than it is for me. That's why I joined up with the union, and that's why I got fired for it.

In 1936, Charlie Chaplin released yet another one of his masterpieces, *Modern Times*. As an attack on the industrial dehumanization of the individual, this film still resonates today. Set during the Depression, the film's use of imagery and sparing use of sound helps the viewer connect with the theme of worker alienation. The long periods of silence are only broken up by the strange clanking and clunking of the machines or by the factory boss who speaks just to get the workers working harder. "Section 5—speed 'er up -41." or "Hey, quit stalling. Get back to work. Go on."

The opening shot of a flock of sheep rushing into a pen and then into a chute dissolves into a shot of industrial workers rushing out of a subway getting to their places of work. The point is obvious. Because they do not seem to have any other option, the sheep accept being turned into things for consumption, and the city workers willingly doing the same. They do so willingly because the only alternatives are unemployment, poverty, and crime. However, the machines give them work; the machines give them life. The machines turn these very same people into machines themselves.

In this film, Charlie Chaplin in his last role as the Tramp finds himself on an assembly line as a nut-tightener. He must tighten the nuts as they come along with clockwork precision. There is no change or variety in his movements; there is no thinking required as he mechanically and without change jerks his arms in precise timing with the machine. If he sneezes or tries to brush away an annoying fly he disrupts the entire assembly line. He is but another cog in the engine that drives the Industrial Revolution. Even when he takes his short coffee break his hands continue to twitch. He tightens nonexistent nuts and goes so far as to attempt to tighten the buttons on a lady's blouse. He is treated as and has become a machine.

In order to increase production by reducing the time that employees take for lunch, the president of the company evaluates a feeding machine. The Tramp is strapped into a chair and force-fed by a tiny metallic sweeper that pushes food from a plate into his mouth. So now even the process of eating is taken over by the machines. The Tramp cannot even relax and enjoy a moment away from the production line. He must eat from the machine, and he must eat what and when it tells him to eat. All sense of freedom and all sense of humanity are stripped from the worker.

The Tramp, now driven to mental exhaustion, lies down on the assembly line conveyor belt and is carried into the machine's interior. In an iconic sequence we see him moving through gears and curved passageways just as food would move through our own digestion system. He truly has become nothing more than food for the machine. Now driven insane (a "nut"), he is dismissed from his workplace. He is no longer of any use.

This theme of sexual and worker commodification, that is, of turning men and women into products or parts of processes that are used up and discarded by society, is presented in a number of films. Be it the famous "Soylent Green is people!" line from the movie of the same name, or the more recent documentary *Roger and Me,* where entire automotive factories are shut down while the rich play croquet, or *The Island,* where people are grown for body parts, there are many films that explore the issue of social and political injustice. Perhaps this is because so many in the movie theater audience can personally relate to it.

Films Cited

A Boy and His Dog. Dir. L. Q. Jones. Perfs. Don Johnson, Susanne Benton. Film. LQ/JAF. 1975.
Accused, The. Dir. Jonathan Kaplan. Perfs. Kelly McGillis, Jodie Foster. Film. Paramount Pictures Corporation (Canada). 1988.
Aliens. Dir. James Cameron. Perfs. Sigourney Weaver, Carrie Henn. Film. Twentieth Century Fox Film Corporation. 1986.
Cinderella. Dir. Clyde Geronimi, Wilfred Jackson. Perfs. Ilene Woods, Eleanor Audley. Film. Walt Disney Pictures. 1950.
Fatal Attraction. Dir. Adrian Lyne. Perfs. Michael Douglas, Glenn Close. Film. Paramount Pictures. 1987.
Gorillas in the Mist. Dir. Michael Apted. Perfs. Sigourney Weaver, Bryan Brown. Film. Guber-Peters Company. 1988.
Idiocracy. Dir. Mike Judge. Perfs. Luke Wilson, Maya Rudolph. Film. Twentieth Century Fox Film Corporation. 2007.
Island, The. Dir. Michael Bay. Perfs. Ewan McGregor, Scarlett Johansson. Film. DreamWorks SKG. 2005.
Mad Max II: The Road Runner. Dir. George Miller. Perfs. Mel Gibson, Bruce Spence. Film. Kennedy Miller Productions. 1981.
Mad Max III Beyond Thunderdome. Dir. George Miller, George Ogilvie. Perfs. Mel Gibson, Tina Turner. Film. Kennedy Miller Productions. 1985.
Modern Times. Dir. Charles Chaplin. Perfs. Charles Chaplin, Paulette Goddard. Film. Charles Chaplin Productions. 1936.
Planet of the Apes. Dir. Franklin J. Schaffner. Perfs. Charlton Heston, Roddy McDowall. Film. APJAC Productions. 1968.
Planet of the Apes. Dir. Tim Burton. Perfs. Mark Wahlberg, Tim Roth. Film. Twentieth Century Fox Film Corporation. 2001.

Pretty Woman. Dir. Garry Marshall. Perfs. Richard Gere, Julia Roberts. Film. Silver Screen Productions IV. 1990.
Roger and Me. Dir. Michael Moore. Perfs. Michael Moore, James Blanchard. Film. Dog Eat Dog Films. 1989.
Sense and Sensibility. Dir. Ang Lee. Perfs. James Fleet, Tom Wilkinson. Film. Columbia Pictures Corporation. 1995.
Soylent Green. Dir. Richard Fleischer. Perfs. Charlton Heston, Leigh Taylor-Young. Film. Metro-Goldwyn-Mayer. 1973.
Terminator II. Dir. James Cameron. Perfs. Arnold Schwarzenegger, Linda Hamilton. Film. Canal+. 1991.
Thelma and Louise. Dir. Ridley Scott. Perfs. Susan Sarandon, Geena Davis. Film. Metro-Goldwyn Mayer. 1991.
Tootsie. Dir. Sydney Pollack. Perfs. Dustin Hoffman, Jessica Lange. Film. Columbia Pictures Corporation. 1982.
Waterworld. Dir. Kevin Reynolds. Perfs. Kevin Costner, Chaim Girafi. Film. Davis Entertainment. 1995.

ADDITIONAL MOVIES FOR FURTHER VIEWING

(For a comprehensive listing of movies and themes, please consult the online appendix.)

1. *American History X*—Racism
2. *Bowling for Columbine*—Violence in society
3. *Crash*—Equality, racism, and class struggle
4. *Elizabeth*—Feminism
5. *Glory*—Racism
6. *Good Night, and Good Luck*—Political witch hunt
7. *Letters from Iwo Jima*—Effect of war on combatants
8. *People Vs. Larry Flynt, The*—Freedom of speech and censorship
9. *Persepolis*—Women in society
10. *V for Vendetta*—Liberty, political violence, and authoritarianism

Leviathan
Thomas Hobbes

Chapter XIII
Of the Natural Condition of Mankind as Concerning Their Felicity and Misery

NATURE HAS MADE MEN so equal in the faculties of the body and mind as that, though there be found one man sometimes manifestly strong in body or of quicker mind than another, yet, when all is reckoned together, the difference between man and man is not so considerable as that one man can thereupon claim to himself any benefit to which another may not pretend as well as he. For as to the strength of body, the weakest has strength enough to kill the strongest, either by secret machination or by confederacy with others that are in the same danger with himself.

And as to the faculties of the mind, setting aside the arts grounded upon words, and especially that skill of proceeding upon general and infallible rules called science—which very few have and but in few things, as being not a native faculty born with us, nor attained, as prudence, while we look after somewhat else—I find yet a greater equality among men than that of strength. For prudence is but experience, which equal time equally bestows on all men in those things they equally apply themselves unto. That which may perhaps make such equality incredible is but a vain conceit of one's own wisdom, which almost all men think they have in a greater degree than the vulgar—that is, than all men but themselves and a few others whom, by fame or for concurring with themselves, they approve. For such is the nature of men that howsoever they may acknowledge many others to be more witty or more eloquent or more learned, yet they will hardly believe there be many so wise as themselves; for they see their own wit at hand and other men's at a distance. But this proves rather that men are in that point equal than unequal. For there is not ordinarily a greater sign of the equal distribution of anything than that every man in contented with his share.

From this equality of ability arises equality of hope in the attaining of our ends. And therefore if any two men desire the same thing, which nevertheless they cannot both enjoy, they become enemies; and in the way to their end, which is principally their own conservation, and sometimes their delectation only, endeavor to destroy or subdue one another. And from hence it comes to pass that where an invader has no more to fear than another man's single power, if one plant, sow, build, or possess a convenient seat, others may probably be expected to come prepared with forces united to dispossess and deprive him, not only of the fruit of his labor, but also of his life or liberty. And the invader again is in the like danger of another.

And from this diffidence of one another there is no way for any man to secure himself so reasonable as anticipation—that is, by force or wiles to master the persons of all men he can, so long till he see no other power great enough to endanger him; and this is no more than his own conservation requires, and is generally allowed. Also, because there be some that take pleasure in contemplating their own power in the acts of conquest, which they pursue farther than their security requires, if others that otherwise would be glad to be at ease within modest bounds should not by invasion increase their power, they would not be able, long time, by standing only on their defense, to subsist. And by consequence, such augmentation of dominion over men being necessary to a man's conservation, it ought to be allowed him.

Again, men have no pleasure, but on the contrary a great deal of grief, in keeping company where there is no power able to overawe them all. For every man looks that his companion should value him at the same rate he sets upon himself; and upon all signs of contempt or undervaluing naturally endeavors, as far as he dares (which among them that have no common power to keep them in quiet is far enough to make them destroy each other), to extort a greater value from his contemners by damage and from others by the example.

So that in the nature of man we find three principal causes of quarrel: first, competition; secondly, diffidence; thirdly, glory.

The first makes men invade for gain, the second for safety, and the third for reputation. The first use violence to make themselves masters of other men's persons, wives, children, and cattle;

(continued)

Leviathan (continued)

the second, to defend them; the third, for trifles, as a word, a smile, a different opinion, and any other sign of undervalue, either direct in their persons or by reflection in their kindred, their friends, their nation, their profession, or their name.

Hereby it is manifest that, during the time men live without a common power to keep them all in awe, they are in that condition which is called war, and such a war as is of every man against every man. For WAR consists not in battle only, or the act of fighting, but in a tract of time wherein the will to contend by battle is sufficiently known; and therefore the notion of *time* is to be considered in the nature of war as it is in the nature of weather. For as the nature of foul weather lies not in a shower or two of rain but in an inclination thereto of many days together, so the nature of war consists not in actual fighting but in the known disposition thereto during all the time there is no assurance to the contrary. All other time is PEACE.

Whatsoever, therefore, is consequent to a time of war where every man is enemy to every man, the same is consequent to the time wherein men live without other security than what their own strength and their own invention shall furnish them withal. In such condition there is no place for industry, because the fruit thereof is uncertain: and consequently no culture of the earth; no navigation nor use of the commodities that may be imported by sea; no commodious building; no instruments of moving and removing such things as require much force; no knowledge of the face of the earth; no account of time; no arts; no letters; no society; and, which is worst of all, continual fear and danger of violent death; and the life of man solitary, poor, nasty, brutish, and short.

It may seem strange to some man that has not well weighed these things that nature should thus dissociate and render men apt to invade and destroy one another; and he may therefore, not trusting to this inference made from the passions, desire perhaps to have the same confirmed by experience. Let him therefore consider with himself—when taking a journey he arms himself and seeks to go well accompanied, when going to sleep he locks his doors, when even in his house he locks his chests, and this when he knows there be laws and public officers, armed, to revenge all injuries shall be done him—what opinion he has of his fellow subjects when he rides armed, of his fellow citizens when he locks his doors, and of his children and servants when he locks his chests. Does he not there as much accuse mankind by his actions as I do by my words? But neither of us accuse man's nature in it. The desires and other passions of man are in themselves no sin. No more are the actions that proceed from those passions till they know a law that forbids them, which, till laws be made, they cannot know, nor can any law be made till they have agreed upon the person that shall make it.

It may peradventure be thought there was never such a time nor condition of war as this, and I believe it was never generally so over all the world; but there are many places where they live so now. For the savage people in many places of America, except the government of small families, the concord whereof depends on natural lust, have no government at all and live at this day in that brutish manner as I said before. Howsoever, it may be perceived what manner of life there would be where there were no common power to fear by the manner of life which men that have formerly lived under a peaceful government use to degenerate into in a civil war.

But though there had never been any time wherein particular men were in a condition of war one against another, yet in all times kings and persons of sovereign authority, because of their independency, are in continual jealousies and in the state and posture of gladiators, having their weapons pointing and their eyes fixed on one another—that is, their forts, garrisons, and guns upon the frontiers of their kingdoms, and continual spies upon their neighbors—which is a posture of war. But because they uphold thereby the industry of their subjects, there does not follow from it that misery which accompanies the liberty of particular men.

To this war of every man against every man, this also is consequent: that nothing can be unjust. The notions of right and wrong, justice and injustice, have there no place. Where there is no common power, there is no law; where no law, no injustice. Force and fraud are in war the two cardinal virtues. Justice and injustice are none of the faculties neither of the body nor mind. If they were, they might be in a man that were alone in the world, as well as his senses and passions. They are qualities that relate to men in society, not in solitude. It is consequent also to the same condition that there be no propriety, no dominion, no *mine* and *thine* distinct; but only that to be every man's that he can get, and for so long as he can keep it. And thus much for the ill condition which man by mere nature is actually placed in though with a possibility to come out of it consisting partly in the passions, partly in his reason.

The passions that incline men to peace are fear of death, desire of such things as are necessary to commodious living, and a hope by their industry to obtain them. And reason suggests convenient articles of peace, upon which men may be drawn to agreement. These articles are they which otherwise are called the Laws of Nature, whereof I shall speak more particularly in the two following chapters.

Chapter XIV
Of the First and Second Natural Laws, and of Contracts

THE RIGHT OF NATURE, which writers commonly call *jus naturale*, is the liberty each man has to use his own power, as he will himself, for the preservation of his own nature—that is to say, of his own life—and consequently of doing anything which, in his own judgment and reason, he shall conceive to be the aptest means thereunto.

BY LIBERTY is understood, according to the proper signification of the word, the absence of external impediments; which impediments may oft take away part of a man's power to do what he would, but cannot hinder him from using the power left him according as his judgment and reason shall dictate to him.

A LAW OF NATURE, *lex naturalis,* is a percept or general rule, found out by reason, by which a man is forbidden to do that which is destructive of his life or takes away the means of preserving the same and to omit that by which he thinks it may be best preserved. For though they that speak of this subject use to confound *jus* and *lex, right* and *law,* yet they ought to be distinguished; because RIGHT consists in liberty to do or to forbear, whereas LAW determines and binds to one of them; so that law and right differ as much as obligation and liberty, which in one and the same matter are inconsistent.

And because the condition of man, as has been declared in the precedent chapter, is a condition of war of every one against every one—in which case everyone is governed by his own reason and there is nothing he can make use of that may not be a help unto him in preserving his life against his enemies—it follows that in such a condition every man has a right to everything, even to one another's body. And therefore, as long as this natural right of every man to everything endures, there can be no security to any man, how strong or wise soever he be, of living out the time which nature ordinarily allows men to live. And consequently it is a precept or general rule of reason *that every man ought to endeavor peace, as far as he has hope of obtaining it; and when he cannot obtain it, that he may seek and use all helps and advantages of war.* The first branch of which rule contains the first and fundamental law of nature, which is *to seek peace and follow it.* The second, the sum of the right of nature, which is, *by all means we can to defend ourselves.*

From this fundamental law of nature, by which men are commanded to endeavor peace, is derived this second law: *that a man be willing, when others are so too, as far forth as for peace and defense of himself he shall think it necessary, to lay down this right to all things, and be contented with so much liberty against other men as he would allow other men against himself.* For as long as every man holds this right of doing anything he likes, so long are all men in the condition of war. But if other men will not lay down their right as well as he, then there is no reason for anyone to divest himself of his, for that were to expose himself to prey, which no man is bound to, rather than to dispose himself to peace. This is that law of the gospel: *whatsoever you require that others should do to you, that do ye to them.* And that law of all men, *quod tibi fieri non vis, alteri ne feceris.*[1]

To *lay down* a man's *right* to anything is to *divest* himself of the *liberty* of hindering another of the benefit of his own right to the same. For he that renounces or passes away his right gives not to any other man a right which he had not before—because there is nothing to which every man had not right by nature—but only stands out of his way, that he may enjoy his own original right without hindrance from him, not without hindrance from another. So that the effect which redounds to one man by another man's defect of right is but so much diminution of impediments to the use of his own right original. Right is laid aside either by simply renouncing it or by transferring it to another.

(continued)

Leviathan (continued)

By *simply* RENOUNCING, when he cares not to whom the benefit thereof redounds. By TRANSFERRING, when he intends the benefit thereof to some certain person or persons. And when a man has in either manner abandoned or granted away his right, then he is said to be OBLIGED or BOUND not to hinder those to whom such right is granted or abandoned from the benefit of it; and that he *ought*, and it is his DUTY, not to make void that voluntary act of his own; and that such hindrance is INJUSTICE and INJURY as being *sine jure*,[2] the right being before renounced or transferred. So that *injury* or *injustice* in the controversies of the world is somewhat like to that which in the disputations of scholars is called *absurdity*. For as it is there called an absurdity to contradict what one maintained in the beginning, so in the world it is called injustice and injury voluntarily to undo that which from the beginning he had voluntarily done. The way by which a man either simply renounces or transfers his right is a declaration or signification by some voluntary and sufficient sign or signs that he does so renounce or transfer, or has so renounced or transferred, the same to him that accepts it. And these signs are either words only or actions only; or as it happens most often, both words and actions. And the same are the BONDS by which men are bound and obliged—bonds that have their strength, not from their own nature, for nothing is more easily broken than a man's word, but from fear of some evil consequence upon the rupture.

Whensoever a man transfers his right or renounces it, it is either in consideration of some right reciprocally transferred to himself or for some other good he hopes for thereby. For it is a voluntary act; and of the voluntary acts of every man, the object is some *good to himself*. And therefore there be some rights which no man can be understood by any words or other-signs to have abandoned or transferred. As, first, a man cannot lay down the right of resisting them that assault him by force to take away his life, because he cannot be understood to aim thereby at any good to himself. The same may be said of wounds and chains and imprisonment, both because there is no benefit consequent to such patience as there is to the patience of suffering another to be wounded or imprisoned, as also because a man cannot tell, when he sees men proceed against him by violence, whether they intend his death or not. And, lastly, the motive and end for which this renouncing and transferring of right is introduced is nothing else but the security of a man's person in his life and in the means of so preserving life as not to be weary of it. And therefore if a man by words or other signs seem to despoil himself of the end for which those signs were intended, he is not to be understood as if he meant it or that it was his will, but that he was ignorant of how such words and actions were to be interpreted.

The mutual transferring of right is that which men call CONTRACT.

There is difference between transferring of right to the thing and transferring, or tradition—that is, delivery—of the thing itself. For the thing may be delivery—of the thing itself. For the thing may be delivered together with the translation of the right, as in buying and selling with ready money or exchange of goods or lands, and it may be delivered some time after.

Again, one of the contractors may deliver the thing contracted for on his part and leave the other to perform his part at some determinate time after and in the meantime be trusted, and then the contract on his part is called PACT or COVENANT; or both parts may contract now to perform hereafter, in which cases he that is to perform in time to come, being trusted, his performance is called *keeping of promise* or faith, and the failing of performance, if it be voluntary, *violation of faith*.

When the transferring of right is not mutual, but one of the parties transfers in hope to gain thereby friendship or service from another or from his friends, or in hope to gain the reputation of charity or magnanimity, or to deliver his mind from the pain of compassion, or in hope of reward in heaven—this is not contract but GIFT, FREE GIFT, GRACE, which words signify one and the same thing.

Signs of contract are either *express* or *by inference*. Express are words spoken with understanding of what they signify, and such words are either of the time *present* or *past*—as *I give, I grant, I have given, I have granted, I will that this be yours*—or of the future— as *I will give, I will grant*—which words of the future are called PROMISE.

Signs by inference are sometimes the consequence of works, sometimes the consequence of silence, sometimes the consequence of actions, sometimes the consequence of forbearing an action; and generally a sign by inference of any contract is whatsoever sufficiently argues the will of the contractor.

Words alone, if they be of the time to come and contain a bare promise, are an insufficient sign of a free gift and therefore not obligatory. For if they be of the time to come, as *tomorrow I will give*, they are a sign I have not given yet and consequently that my right is not transferred but remains till I transfer it by some other act. But if the words be of the time present or past, as *I have given* or *do give* to be delivered tomorrow, then is my tomorrow's right given away today, and that by the virtue of the words though there were no other argument of my will. And there is a great difference in the signification of these words: *volo hoc tuum esse cras and cras dabo*—that is, between *I will that this be* yours *tomorrow* and *I will* give *it you tomorrow*—for the word *I will*, in the former manner of speech, signifies an act of the will present, but in the latter it signifies a promise of an act of the will to come; and therefore the former words, being of the present, transfer a future right; the latter, that be of the future, transfer nothing. But if there be other signs of the will to transfer a right besides words, then, though the gift be free, yet may the right be understood to pass by words of the future as if a man propound a prize to him that comes first to the end of a race, the gift is free; and though the words be of the future, yet the right passes; for if he would not have his words so be understood, he should not have let them run.

In contracts, the right passes not only where the words are of the time present or past but also where they are of the future, because all contract is mutual translation or change of right, and therefore he that promises only because he has already received the benefit for which he promises is to be understood as if he intended the right should pass; for unless he had been content to have his words so understood, the other would not have performed his part first. And for that cause, in buying and selling and other acts of contract a promise is equivalent to a covenant and therefore obligatory.

He that performs first in the case of a contract is said to MERIT that which he is to receive by the performance of the other; and he has it as *due*. Also when a prize is propounded to many which is to be given to him only that wins, or money is thrown among many to be enjoyed by them that catch it, though this be a free gift, yet so to win or so to catch is to *merit* and to have it as DUE. For the right is transferred in the propounding of the prize and in throwing down the money, though it be not determined to whom but by the event of the contention. But there is between these two sorts of merit this difference: that in contract I merit by virtue of my own power and the contractor's need, but in this case of free gift I am enabled to merit only by the benignity of the giver; in contract I merit at the contractor's hand that he should depart with his right, in this case of gift I merit not that the giver should part with his right but that when he has parted with it, it should be mine rather than another's. And this I think to be the meaning of that distinction of the Schools between *meritum congrui* and *meritum condigni*.[3] For God Almighty having promised Paradise to those men, hoodwinked with carnal desires, that can walk through this world according to the precepts and limits prescribed by him, they say he that shall so walk shall merit Paradise *ex congruo*. But because no man can demand a right to it, by his own righteousness or any other power in himself, but by the free grace of God only, they say no man can merit Paradise *ex condigno*. This, I say, I think is the meaning of that distinction; but because disputers do not agree upon the signification of their own terms of art longer than it serves their turn, I will not affirm anything of their meaning; only this I say: when a gift is given indefinitely, as a prize to be contended for, he that wins merits and may claim the prize as due.

If a covenant be made wherein neither of the parties perform presently but trust one another, in the condition of mere nature, which is a condition of war of every man against every man, upon any reasonable suspicion, it is void; but if there be a common power set over them both, with right and force sufficient to compel performance, it is not void. For he that performs first has no assurance the other will perform after, because the bonds of words are too weak to bridle men's ambition, avarice, anger, and other passions without the fear of some coercive power which in the condition of mere nature, where all men are equal and judges of the justness of their own fears, cannot possibly be supposed. And therefore he which performs first does but betray himself to his enemy, contrary to the right he can never abandon of defending his life and means of living.

But in a civil estate, where there is a power set up to constrain those that would otherwise violate their faith, that fear is no more reasonable; and for that cause, he which by the covenant is to perform first is obliged so to do.

The cause of fear which makes such a covenant invalid must be always something arising after the covenant made, as some new fact or other sign of the will not to perform; else it cannot

(continued)

Leviathan (continued)

make the covenant void. For that which could not hinder a man from promising ought not to be admitted as a hindrance of performing.

He that transfers any right transfers the means of enjoying it, as far as lies in his power. As he that sells land is understood to transfer the herbage and whatsoever grows upon it; nor can he that sells a mill turn away the stream that drives it. And they that give to a man the right of government in sovereignty are understood to give him the right of levying money to maintain soldiers and of appointing magistrates for the administration of justice.

To make covenants with brute beasts is impossible because, not understanding our speech, they understand not nor accept of any translation of right, nor can translate any right to another; and without mutual acceptation there is no covenant.

To make covenant with God is impossible but by mediation of such as God speaks to, either by revelation supernatural or by his lieutenants that govern under him and in his name; for otherwise we know not whether our covenants be accepted or not. And therefore they that vow anything contrary to any law of nature vow in vain, as being a thing unjust to pay such vow. And if it be a thing commanded by the law of nature, it is not the vow but the law that binds them.

The matter or subject of a covenant is always something that falls under deliberation, for to covenant is an act of the will—that is to say, an act, and the last act, of deliberation—and is therefore always understood to be something to come, and which is judged possible for him that covenants to perform.

And therefore to promise that which is known to be impossible is no covenant. But if that prove impossible afterwards which before was thought possible, the covenant is valid, and binds, though not to the thing itself, yet to the value, or, if that also be impossible, to the unfeigned endeavor of performing as much as is possible, for to more no man can be obliged.

Men are freed of their covenants two ways: by performing or by being forgiven. For performance is the natural end of obligation, and forgiveness the restitution of liberty, as being a retransferring of that right in which the obligation consisted.

Covenants entered into by fear, in the condition of mere nature, are obligatory. For example, if I covenant to pay a ransom or service for my life to an enemy, I am bound by it; for it is a contract, wherein one receives the benefit of life, the other is to receive money or service for it; and consequently, where no other law, as in the condition of mere nature, forbids the performance, the covenant is valid. Therefore prisoners of war, if trusted with the payment of their ransom, are obliged to pay it; and if a weaker prince make a disadvantageous peace with a stronger, for fear, he is bound to keep it; unless, as has been said before, there arises some new and just cause of fear to renew the war. And even in commonwealths, if I be forced to redeem myself from a thief by promising him money, I am bound to pay it till the civil law discharge me. For whatsoever I may lawfully do without obligation, the same I may lawfully covenant to do through fear; and what I lawfully covenant, I cannot lawfully break. A former covenant makes void a later. For a man that has passed away his right to one man today has it not to pass tomorrow to another; and therefore the later promise passes no right, but is null.

A covenant not to defend myself from force by force is always void. For, as I have showed before, no man can transfer or lay down his right to save himself from death, wounds, and imprisonment, the avoiding whereof is the only end of laying down any right; and therefore the promise of not resisting force in no covenant transfers any right, nor is obliging. For though a man may covenant thus: *unless I do so or so, kill me*, he cannot covenant thus: *unless I do so or so, I will not resist you when you come to kill me*. For man by nature chooses the lesser evil, which is danger of death in resisting, rather than the greater, which is certain and present death in not resisting. And this is granted to be true by all men, in that they lead criminals to execution and prison with armed men, notwithstanding that such criminals have consented to the law by which they are condemned.

A covenant to accuse oneself, without assurance of pardon, is likewise invalid. For in the condition of nature, where every man is judge, there is no place for accusation; and in the civil state, the accusation is followed with punishment, which, being force, a man is not obliged not to resist. The same is also true of the accusation of those by whose condemnation a man falls into misery, as of a father, wife, or benefactor. For the testimony of such an accuser, if it be not willingly given, is presumed to be corrupted by nature, and therefore not to be received; and where a man's testimony is not to be credited, he is not bound to give it. Also accusations upon torture are not to be reputed as testimonies. For torture is to be used but as means of conjecture and light in the further examination and search of truth; and what is in that case confessed tends to the ease of him that is tortured, not to the informing of the torturers, and therefore ought not to have the credit of a sufficient testimony; for whether he deliver himself by true or false accusation, he does it by the right of preserving his own life.

The force of words being, as I have formerly noted, too weak to hold men to the performance of their covenants, there are in man's nature but two imaginable helps to strengthen it. And those are either a fear of the consequence of breaking their word, or a glory or pride in appearing not to need to break it. This latter is a generosity too rarely found to be presumed on, especially in the pursuers of wealth, command, or sensual pleasure—which are the greatest part of mankind. The passion to be reckoned upon is fear, whereof there be two very general objects: one, the power of spirits invisible; the other, the power of those men they shall therein offend. Of these two, though the former be the greater power, yet the fear of the latter is commonly the greater fear. The fear of the former is in every man his own religion, which has place in the nature of man before civil society. The latter has not so, at least not place enough to keep men to their promises, because in the condition of mere nature the inequality of power is not discerned but by the event of battle. So that before the time of civil society, or in the interruption thereof by war, there is nothing can strengthen a covenant of peace agreed on against the temptations of avarice, ambition, lust, or other strong desire but the fear of that invisible power, which they everyone worship as God and fear as a revenger of their perfidy. All therefore that can be done between two men not subject to civil power is to put one another to swear by the God he fears, which *swearing or* OATH *is a form of speech, added to a promise, by which he that promises signifies that, unless he perform, he renounces the mercy of his God, or calls to him for vengeance on himself*. Such was the heathen form, *Let Jupiter kill me else, as I kill this beast*. So is our form, *I shall do thus and thus, so help me God*. And this, with the rites and ceremonies which everyone uses in his own religion, that the fear of breaking faith might be the greater.

By this it appears that an oath taken according to any other form or rite than his that swears is in vain and no oath, and that there is no swearing by anything which the swearer thinks not God. For though men have sometimes used to swear by their kings, for fear or flattery, yet they would have it thereby understood they attributed to them divine honor. And that swearing unnecessarily by God is but profaning of his name; and swearing by other things, as men do in common discourse, is not swearing but an impious custom gotten by too much vehemence of talking.

It appears also that the oath adds nothing to the obligation. For a covenant, if lawful, binds in the sight of God without the oath as much as with it; if unlawful, binds not at all, though it be confirmed with an oath.

Chapter XV
Of other Laws of Nature

From that law of nature by which we are obliged to transfer to another such rights as, being retained, hinder the peace of mankind, there follows a third, which is this: *that men perform their covenants made;* without which covenants are in vain and but empty words, and, the right of all men to all things remaining, we are still in the condition of war.

And in this law of nature consists the fountain and original of JUSTICE. For where no covenant has preceded there has no right been transferred, and every man has right to every thing; and consequently no action can be unjust. But when a covenant is made, then to break it is *unjust;* and the definition of INJUSTICE is no other than *the not performance of covenant.* And whatsoever is not unjust is *just.*

But because covenants of mutual trust, where there is a fear of not performance on either part, as has been said in the former chapter, are invalid, though the original of justice be the making of covenants, yet injustice actually there can be none till the cause of such fear be taken away, which, while men are in the natural condition of war, cannot be done. Therefore, before the names of just and unjust can have place, there must be some coercive power to compel men equally to the

(continued)

Leviathan (*continued*)

performance of their covenants by the terror of some punishment greater than the benefit they expect by the breach of their covenant, and to make good that propriety which by mutual contract men acquire in recompense of the universal right they abandon; and such power there is none before the erection of a commonwealth. And this is also to be gathered out of the ordinary definition of justice in the Schools, for they say that *justice is the constant will of giving to every man his own*. And therefore where there is no *own*—that is, no propriety—there is no injustice; and where there is no coercive power erected—that is, where there is no commonwealth—there is no propriety, all men having right to all things; therefore, where there is no commonwealth, there nothing is unjust. So that the nature of justice consists in keeping of valid covenants; but the validity of covenants begins not but with the constitution of a civil power sufficient to compel men to keep them; and then it is also that propriety begins.

The fool hath said in his heart, there is no such thing as justice;[4] and sometimes also with his tongue, seriously alleging that, every man's conservation and contentment being committed to his own care, there could be no reason why every man might not do what he thought conduced thereunto; and therefore also to make or not make, keep or not keep covenants was not against reason when it conduced to one's benefit. He does not therein deny that there be covenants and that they are sometimes broken, sometimes kept, and that such breach of them may be called injustice and the observance of them justice; but he questions whether injustice, taking away the fear of God—for the same fool hath said in his heart there is no God—may not sometimes stand with that reason which dictates to every man his own good, and particularly then when it conduces to such a benefit as shall put a man in a condition to neglect not only the dispraise and revilings, but also the power of other men. The kingdom of God is gotten by violence; but what if it could be gotten by unjust violence? Were it against reason so to get it, when it is impossible to receive hurt by it? And if it be not against reason, it is not against justice, or else justice is not to be approved for good. From such reasoning as this, successful wickedness has obtained the name of virtue; and some that in all other things have disallowed the violation of faith yet have allowed it when it is for the getting of a kingdom. And the heathen that believed that Saturn was deposed by his son Jupiter believed nevertheless the same Jupiter to be the avenger of injustice—somewhat like to a piece of law in Coke's *Commentaries on Littleton*[5] where he says: if the right heir of the crown be at tainted of treason, yet the crown shall descend to him and *eo instante* the attainder be void; from which instances a man will be very prone to infer that when the heir apparent of a kingdom shall kill him that is in possession, though his father, you may call it injustice or by what other name you will, yet it can never be against reason, seeing all the voluntary actions of men tend to the benefit of themselves, and those actions are most reasonable that conduce most to their ends. This specious reasoning is nevertheless false.

For the question is not of promises mutual where there is no security of performance on either side—as when there is no civil power erected over the parties promising—for such promises are no covenants; but either where one of the parties has performed already or where there is a power to make him perform, there is the question whether it be against reason—that is, against the benefit of the other—to perform or not. And I say it is not against reason. For the manifestation whereof we are to consider, first, that when a man does a thing which, notwithstanding anything can be foreseen and reckoned on, tends to his own destruction, howsoever some accident which he could not expect, arriving, may turn it to his benefit, yet such events do not make it reasonably or wisely done. Secondly, that in a condition of war, wherein every man to every man, for want of a common power to keep them all in awe, is an enemy, there is no man who can hope by his own strength or wit to defend himself from destruction without the help of confederates, where everyone expects the same defense by the confederation that anyone else does; and therefore he which declares he thinks, it reason to deceive those that help him can in reason expect no other means of safety than what can be had from his own single power. He, therefore, that breaks his covenant, and consequently declares that he thinks he may with reason do so, cannot be received into any society that unite themselves for peace and defense, but by the error of them that receive him; nor, when he is received, be retained in it without seeing the danger of their error, which errors a man cannot reasonably reckon upon at the means of his security; and therefore if he be left or cast out of society he perishes, and if he live in society, it is by the error of other men, which he could not foresee nor reckon upon, and consequently against the reason of his preservation; and so, as all men that contribute not to his destruction, forbear him only out of ignorance of what is good for themselves.

As for the instance of gaining the secure and perpetual felicity of heaven by any way, it is frivolous, there being but one way imaginable, and that is not breaking but keeping of covenant.

And for the other instance of attaining sovereignty by rebellion, it is manifest that, though the event follow, yet because it cannot reasonably be expected, but rather the contrary, and because by gaining it so others are taught to gain the same in like manner, the attempt thereof is against reason. Justice, therefore—that is to say, keeping of covenant—is a rule of reason by which we are forbidden to do anything destructive to our life, and consequently a law of nature.

There be some that proceed further and will not have the law of nature to be those rules which conduce to the preservation of man's life on earth but to the attaining of an eternal felicity after death, to which they think the breach of covenant may conduce and consequently be just and reasonable; such are they that think it a work of merit to kill or depose or rebel against the sovereign power constituted over them by their own consent. But because there is no natural knowledge of man's estate after death—much less of the reward that is then to be given to breach of faith—but only a belief grounded upon other men's saying that they know it super-naturally, or that they know those that knew them that knew others that knew it supernaturally, breach of faith cannot be called a precept of reason or nature.

Others that allow for a law of nature the keeping of faith do nevertheless make exception of certain persons, as heretics and such as use not to perform their covenant to others; and this also is against reason. For if any fault of a man be sufficient to discharge our covenant made, the same ought in reason to have been sufficient to have hindered the making of it.

The names of just and unjust, when they are attributed to men, signify one thing, and when they are attributed to actions, another. When they are attributed to men, they signify conformity or inconformity of manners to reason. But when they are attributed to actions, they signify the conformity or inconformity to reason, not of manners or manner of life, but of particular actions. A just man, therefore, is he that takes all the care he can that his actions may be all just; and an unjust man is he that neglects it. And such men are more often in our language styled by the names of righteous and unrighteous than just and unjust, though the meaning be the same. Therefore a righteous man does not lose that title by one or a few unjust actions that proceed from sudden passion or mistake of things or persons; nor does an unrighteous man lose his character for such actions as he does or forbears to do for fear, because his will is not framed by the justice but by the apparent benefit of what he is to do. That which gives to human actions the relish of justice is a certain nobleness or gallantness of courage, rarely found, by which a man scorns to be beholden for the contentment of his life to fraud or breach of promise. This justice of the manners is that which is meant where justice is called a virtue and injustice a vice.

But the justice of actions denominates men, not just, but *guiltless*; and the injustice of the same, which is also called injury, gives them but the name of *guilty*.

Again, the injustice of manners is the disposition or aptitude to do injury, and is injustice before it proceeds to act and without supposing any individual person injured. But the injustice of an action—that is to say, injury—supposes an individual person injured—namely, him to whom the covenant was made—and therefore many times the injury is received by one man when the damage redounds to another. As when the master commands his servant to give money to a stranger: if it be not done, the injury is done to the master, whom he had before covenanted to obey; but the damage redounds to the stranger, to whom he had no obligation and therefore could not injure him. And so also in commonwealths private men may remit to one another their debts but not robberies or other violences whereby they are endamaged; because the detaining of debt is an injury to themselves, but robbery and violence are injuries to the person of the commonwealth.

Whatsoever is done to a man, conformable to his own will signified to the doer, is no injury to him. For if he that does it has not passed away his original right to do what he pleases by some antecedent covenant, there is no breach of covenant and therefore no injury done him. And if he have, then his will to have it done, being signified, is release of that covenant, and so again there is no injury done him.

(continued)

Leviathan (continued)

Justice of actions is by writers divided into *commutative* and *distributive;* and the former they say consists in proportion arithmetical, the latter in proportion geometrical. Commutative, therefore, they place in the equality of value of the things contracted for, and distributive in the distribution of equal benefit to men of equal merit. As if it were injustice to sell dearer than we buy, or to give more to a man than he merits. The value of all things contracted for is measured by the appetite of the contractors, and therefore the just value is that which they be contented to give. And merit (besides that which is by covenant, where the performance on one part merits the performance of the other part, and falls under justice commutative, not distributive) is not due by justice, but is rewarded of grace only. And therefore this distinction, in the sense wherein it uses to be expounded, is not right. To speak properly, commutative justice is the justice of a contractor—that is, a performance of covenant in buying and selling, hiring and letting to hire, lending and borrowing, exchanging, bartering, and other acts of contract.

And distributive justice, the justice of an arbitrator—that is to say, the act of defining what is just. Wherein, being trusted by them that make him arbitrator, if he performs his trust, he is said to distribute to every man his own; and this is indeed just distribution, and may be called, though improperly, distributive justice, but more properly equity, which also is a law of nature, as shall be shown in due place. [P. 128.]

As justice depends on antecedent covenant, so does GRATITUDE depend on antecedent grace—that is to say, antecedent free gift—and is the fourth law of nature, which may be conceived in this form: *that a man which receives benefit from another of mere grace endeavor that* he *which gives it have no reasonable cause to repent him of his good will.* For no man gives but with intention of good to himself, because gift is voluntary, and of all voluntary acts the object is to every man his own good; of which if men see they shall be frustrated, there will be no beginning of benevolence or trust nor consequently of mutual help nor of reconciliation of one man to another; and therefore they are to remain still in the condition of *war*, which is contrary to the first and fundamental law of nature, which commands men to *seek peace*. The breach of this law is called *ingratitude,* and has the same relation to grace that injustice has to obligation by covenant.

A fifth law of nature is COMPLAISANCE—that is to say, *that every man strive to accommodate himself to the rest*. For the understanding whereof we may consider that there is in men's aptness to society a diversity of nature rising from their diversity of affections not unlike to that we see in stones brought together for building of an edifice. For as that stone which by the asperity and irregularity of figure takes more room from others than itself fills, and for the hardness cannot be easily made plain and thereby hinders the building, is by the builders cast away as unprofitable and troublesome, so also a man that by asperity of nature will strive to retain those things which to himself are superfluous and to others necessary, and for the stubbornness of his passions cannot be corrected, is to be left or cast out of society as cumbersome thereunto. For seeing every man, not only by right but also by necessity of nature, is supposed to endeavor all he can to obtain that which is necessary for his conservation, he that shall oppose himself against it for things superfluous is guilty of the war that thereupon is to follow, and therefore does that which is contrary to the fundamental law of nature, which commands *to seek peace*. The observers of this law may be called SOCIABLE (the Latins call them *commodi*), the contrary *stubborn, insociable, forward, intractable*.

A sixth law of nature is this: *that upon caution of the future time, a man ought to pardon the offenses past of them that, repenting, desire it.* For PARDON is nothing but granting of peace, which, though granted to them that persevere in their hostility, be not peace but fear, yet, not granted to them that give caution of the future time, is sign of an aversion to peace, and therefore contrary to the law of nature.

A seventh is *that in revenges*—that is, retribution of evil for evil—*men look not at the greatness of the evil past, but the greatness of the good to follow.* Whereby we are forbidden to inflict punishment with any other design than for correction of the offender or direction of others. For this law is consequent to the next before it that commands pardon upon security of the future time. Besides, revenge without respect to the example and profit to come is a triumph or glorying in the hurt of another, tending to no end; for the end is always somewhat to come, and glorying to no end is vain-glory and contrary to reason; and to hurt without reason tends to the introduction of war, which is against the law of nature and is commonly styled by the name of *cruelty*.

And because all signs of hatred or contempt provoke to fight, insomuch as most men choose rather to hazard their life than not to be revenged, we may in the eighth place for a law of nature set down this precept: *that no man by deed, word, countenance, or gesture declare hatred or contempt of another.* The breach of which law is commonly called *contumely.*

The question who is the better man has no place in the condition of mere nature, where, as has been shown before, all men are equal. The inequality that now has been introduced by the laws civil. I know that Aristotle in the first book of his *Politics,* for a foundation of his doctrine, makes men by nature some more worthy to command, meaning the wiser sort such as he thought himself to be for his philosophy, others to serve, meaning those that had strong bodies but were not philosophers as he; as if master and servant were not introduced by consent of men but by difference of wit, which is not only against reason but also against experience. For there are very few so foolish that had not rather govern themselves than be governed by others; nor when the wise in their own conceit contend by force with them who distrust their own wisdom, do they always, or often, or almost at any time, get the victory. If nature therefore have made men equal, that equality is to be acknowledged; or if nature have made men unequal, yet because men that think themselves equal will not enter into conditions of peace but upon equal terms, such equality must be admitted. And therefore for the ninth law of nature, I put this: *that every man acknowledge another for his equal by nature.* The breach of this precept is *pride.*

On this law depends another: *that at the entrance into conditions of peace, no man require to reserve to himself any right which he is not content should be reserved to every one of the rest.* As it is necessary for all men that seek peace to lay down certain rights of nature—that is to say, not to have liberty to do all they list—so is it necessary for man's life to retain some, as right to govern their own bodies, enjoy air, water, motion, ways to go from place to place, and all things else without which a man cannot live or not live well. If in this case, at the making of peace, men require for themselves that which they would not have to be granted to others, they do contrary to the precedent law that commands the acknowledgment of natural equality and therefore also against the law of nature. The observers of this law are those we call *modest,* and the breakers *arrogant* men. The Greeks call the violation of this law πλεονεξία—that is, a desire of more than their share.

Also if *a man be trusted to judge between man and man,* it is a precept of the law of nature *that he deal equally between them.* For without that, the controversies of men cannot be determined but by war. He, therefore, that is partial in judgment does what in him lies to deter men from the use of judges and arbitrators, and consequently, against the fundamental law of nature, is the cause of war.

The observance of this law, from the equal distribution to each man of that which in reason belongs to him, is called EQUITY and, as I have said before, distributive justice; the violation, *acception of persons,* προσωποληψία.

And from this follows another law: *that such things as cannot be divided be enjoyed in common, if it can be; and if the quantity of the thing permit, without stint; otherwise proportionably to the number of them that have right.* For otherwise the distribution is unequal and contrary to equity.

But some things there be that can neither be divided nor enjoyed in common. Then the law of nature, which prescribes equity, requires *that the entire right, or else—making the use alternate—the first possession, be determined by lot.* For equal distribution is of the law of nature; and other means of equal distribution cannot be imagined.

Of *lots* there be two sorts: *arbitrary* and *natural.* Arbitrary is that which is agreed on by the competitors; natural is either *primogeniture* (which the Greek calls κληρονομία, which signifies *given by lot*) or *first seizure.*

And therefore those things which cannot be enjoyed in common, nor divided, ought to be adjudged to the first possessor; and in some cases to the first-born, as acquired by lot.

It is also a law of nature *that all men that mediate peace be allowed safe conduct.* For the law that commands peace, as the *end,* commands intercession, as the *means;* and to intercession the means is safe conduct.

And because, though men be never so willing to observe these laws, there may nevertheless arise questions concerning a man's action—first, whether it were done or not done; secondly, if done, whether against the law or not against the law; the former whereof is called a question *of*

(continued)

Leviathan (continued)

fact, the latter a question *of right*—therefore, unless the parties to the question covenant mutually to stand to the sentence of another, they are as far from peace as ever. This other to whose sentence they submit is called an ARBITRATOR. And therefore it is of the law of nature *that they that are at controversy submit their right to the judgment of an arbitrator.*

And seeing every man is presumed to do all things in order to his own benefit, no man is a fit arbitrator in his own cause; and if he were never so fit, yet, equity allowing to each party equal benefit, if one be admitted to be judge the other is to be admitted also; and so the controversy—that is, the cause of war—remains against the law of nature.

For the same reason no man in any cause ought to be received for arbitrator to whom greater profit or honor or pleasure apparently arises out of the victory of one party that of the other; for he has taken, though an unavoidable bribe, yet a bribe, and no man can be obliged to trust him. And thus also the controversy and the condition of war remains, contrary to the law of nature.

And in a controversy of *fact,* the judge being to give no more credit to one than to the other, if there be no other arguments, must give credit to a third, or to a third and fourth, no more; for else the question is undecided and left to force, contrary to the law of nature.

These are the laws of nature dictating peace for a means of the conservation of men in multitudes, and which only concern the doctrine of civil society. There be other things tending to the destruction of particular men—as drunkenness and all other parts of intemperance—which may therefore also be reckoned among those things which the law of nature has forbidden, but are not necessary to be mentioned nor are pertinent enough to this place.

And though this may seem too subtle a deduction of the laws of nature to be taken notice of by all men—whereof the most part are too busy in getting food and the rest too negligent to understand—yet to leave all men inexcusable they have been contracted into one easy sum, intelligible even to the meanest capacity, and that is *Do not that to another which you would not have done to yourself;* which shows him that he has no more to do in learning the laws of nature but, when weighing the actions of other men with his own they seem too heavy, to put them into the other part of the balance and his own into their place, that his own passions and self-love may add nothing to the weight, and then there is none of these laws of nature that will not appear unto him very reasonable.

The laws of nature oblige *in foro interno*[6]—that is to say, they bind to a desire they should take place—but in *foro externo*[7]—that is, to the putting them in act—not always. For he that should be modest and tractable and perform all he promises in such time and place where no man else should do so should but make himself a prey to others and procure his own certain ruin, contrary to the ground of all laws of nature, which tend to nature's preservation. And again, he that, having sufficient security that others shall observe the same laws toward him, observes them not himself, seeks not peace but war and consequently the destruction of his nature by violence.

And whatsoever laws bind in *foro interno* may be broken, not only by a fact contrary to the law, but also by a fact according to it, in case a man think it contrary. For though his action in this case be according to the law, yet his purpose was against the law; which, where the obligation is in *foro interno*, is a breach.

The laws of nature are immutable and eternal; for injustice, ingratitude, arrogance, pride, iniquity, acception of persons, and the rest can never be made lawful. For it can never be that war shall preserve life, and peace destroy it.

The same laws, because they oblige only to a desire and endeavour, mean an unfeigned and constant endeavour, are easy to be observed. For in that they require nothing but endeavour, he that endeavoureth their performance fulfilleth them; and he that fulfilleth the law is just.

And the science of them is the true and only moral philosophy. For moral philosophy is nothing else but the science of what is good and evil in the conversation and society of mankind. Good and evil are names that signify our appetites and aversions, which in different tempers, customs, and doctrines of men are different: and diverse men differ not only in their judgement on the senses of what is pleasant and unpleasant to the taste, smell, hearing, touch, and sight; but also of what is conformable or disagreeable to reason in the actions of common life. Nay, the same man, in diverse times, differs from himself; and one time praiseth, that is, calleth good, what another time he dispraiseth, and calleth evil: from whence arise disputes, controversies, and at last war. And therefore so long as a man is in the condition of mere nature, which is a condition of war, private appetite is the measure of good and evil: and consequently all men agree on this, that peace is good, and therefore also the way or means of peace, which (as I have shown before) are justice, gratitude, modesty, equity, mercy, and the rest of the laws of nature, are good; that is to say, moral virtues; and their contrary vices, evil. Now the science of virtue and vice is moral philosophy; and therefore the true doctrine of the laws of nature is the true moral philosophy. But the writers of moral philosophy, though they acknowledge the same virtues and vices; yet, not seeing wherein consisted their goodness, nor that they come to be praised as the means of peaceable, sociable, and comfortable living, place them in a mediocrity of passions: as if not the cause, but the degree of daring, made fortitude; or not the cause, but the quantity of a gift, made liberality.

These dictates of reason men used to call by the name of laws, but improperly: for they are but conclusions or theorems concerning what conduceth to the conservation and defence of themselves; whereas law, properly, is the word of him that by right hath command over others. But yet if we consider the same theorems as delivered in the word of God that by right commandeth all things, then are they properly called laws.

NOTES

1. Matt. 7:12; Luke 6:31. The Latin expresses the same rule negatively: "What you would not have done to you, do not do to others."
2. Without legal basis.
3. Merit based on conformity and merit based on worthiness.
4. 1.Pss. 14, 53.
5. Sir Edward Coke (1552–1634), English jurist, the first Lord Chief Justice of England. The first volume of his *Institution* was a translation of, and commentary on, the *Treatise on Tenures* of Sir Thomas de Littleton (c. 1407–1481). It is commonly called on *Coke on* Littleton.
6. In conscience.
7. In civil law.

Second Treatise of Government
John Locke

Chapter II
Of the State of Nature

4. To understand political power right, and derive it from its original, we must consider what state all men are naturally in, and that is, a state of perfect freedom to order their actions, and dispose of their possession, and persons as they think fit, within the bounds of the law of Nature, without asking leave, or depending upon the will of any other man.

A state also of equality, wherein all the power and jurisdiction is reciprocal, no one having more than another: there being nothing more evident, than that creatures of the same species and rank promiscuously born to all the same advantages of Nature, and the use of the same faculties, should also be equal one amongst another without subordination or subjection, unless the Lord and Master of them all, should by any manifest declaration of his will set one above another, and confer on him by an evident and clear appointment an undoubted right to dominion and sovereignty.

6. But though this be a state of liberty, yet it is not a state of licence, though man in that state have an uncontrollable liberty, to dispose of his person or possessions, yet he has not liberty to destroy himself, or so much as any creature in his possession, but where some nobler use, than its bare preservation calls for it. The state of Nature has a law of Nature to govern it, which obliges every one: and reason, which is that law, teaches all mankind, who will but consult it, that being all equal and independent, no one ought to harm another in his life, health, liberty, or possessions. For men being all the workmanship

(continued)

Second Treatise of Government (*continued*)

of one Omnipotent, and infinitely wise Maker; all the servants of one Sovereign Master, sent into the world by his order and about his business; they are his property, whose workmanship they are, made to last during his, not one another's pleasure. And being furnished with like faculties, sharing all in one community of Nature, there cannot be supposed any such subordination among us, that may authorize us to destroy one another, as if we were made for one another's uses, as the inferior ranks of creatures are for ours. Every one as he is bound to preserve himself, and not to quit his station willfully; so by the like reason when his own preservation comes not in competition, ought he, as much as he can, to preserve the rest of mankind, and may not unless it be to do justice on an offender, take away, or impair the life, or what tends to the preservation of the life, liberty, health, limb or goods of another.

7. And that all men may be restrained from invading others' rights, and from doing hurt to one another, and the law of Nature be observed, which wills the peace and preservation of all mankind, the execution of the law of Nature is in that state, put into every man's hands, whereby every one has a right to punish the transgressors of that law to such a degree, as may hinder its violation. For the law of Nature would, as all other laws that concern men in this world, be in vain, if there were no body that in the state of Nature, had a power to execute that law, and thereby preserve the innocent and restrain offenders, and if any one in the state of Nature may punish another, for any evil he has done, every one may do so. For in that state of perfect equality, where naturally there is no superiority or jurisdiction of one, over another, what any may do in prosecution of that law, every one must needs have a right to do.

8. And thus in the state of Nature, one man comes by a power over another; but yet no absolute or arbitrary power, to use a criminal when he has got him in his hands, according to the passionate heats, or boundless extravagancy of his own will, but only to retribute to him, so far as calm reason and conscience dictates, what is proportionate to his transgression, which is so much as may serve for reparation and restraint. For these two are the only reasons, why one man may lawfully do harm to another, which is that we call punishment. In transgressing the law of Nature, the offender declares himself to live by another rule, than that of reason and common equity, which is that measure God has set to the actions of men, for their mutual security: and so he becomes dangerous to mankind, the tie, which is to secure them from injury and violence, being slighted and broken by him. Which being a trespass against the whole species, and the peace and safety of it, provided for by the law of Nature, every man upon this score, by the right he has to preserve mankind in general, may restrain, or where it is necessary, destroy things noxious to them, and so may bring such evil on any one, who has transgressed that law, as may make him repent the doing of it, and thereby deter him, and by his example others, from doing the like mischief. And in this case, and upon this ground, every man has a right to punish the offender, and be executioner of the law of Nature.

14. It is often asked as a mighty objection, Where are, or ever were, there any men in such a state of Nature? To which it may suffice as an answer at present; that since all princes and rulers of independent governments all through the world, are in a state of Nature, it is plain the world never was, nor ever will be, without numbers of men in that state. I have named all governors of independent communities, whether they are, or are not, in league with others: for it is not every compact that puts an end to the state of Nature between men, but only this one of agreeing together mutually to enter into one community, and make one body politic; other promises and compacts, men may make one with another, and yet still be in the state of Nature. The promises and bargains for truck, & c. between the two men in the desert island, mentioned by Garcilasso de la Vega, in his history of Peru, or between a Swiss and an Indian, in the woods of America, are binding to them, though they are perfectly in a state of Nature, in reference to one another. For truth and keeping of faith belongs to men, as men, and not as members of society.

Chapter V
Of Property

25. Whether we consider natural reason, which tells us, that men, being once born, have a right to their preservation, and consequently to meat and drink, and such other things, as Nature affords for their subsistence: or revelation, which gives us an account of those grants God made of the world to Adam, and to Noah, and his sons, it is very clear, that God, as King David says, *Psal.* CXV, xvi. has given the Earth to the children of men, given it to mankind in common. But this being supposed, it seems to some a very great difficulty, how any one should ever come to have a property in anything: I will not content myself to answer, that if it be difficult to make out property, upon a supposition, that God gave the world to Adam and his posterity in common; it is impossible that any man, but one universal monarch, should have any property, upon an supposition, that God gave the world to Adam, and his heirs in succession, exclusive of all the rest of his posterity. But I shall endeavour to show how men might come to have a property in several parts of that which God gave to mankind in common, and that without any express compact of all the commoners.

26. God, who has given the world to men in common, has also given them reason to make use of it, to the best advantage of life, and convenience. The Earth, and all that is therein, is given to men for the support and comfort of their being. And though all the fruits it naturally produces, and beasts it feeds, belong to mankind in common, as they are produced by the spontaneous hand of Nature; and nobody has originally a private dominion, exclusive of the rest of mankind, in any of them, as they are thus in their natural state: yet being given for the use of men, there must of necessity be a means to appropriate them some way or other before they can be of any use, or at all beneficial to any particular man. The fruit, or venison, which nourishes the wild Indian, who knows no inclosure, and is still a tenant in common, must be his, and so his, i.e. a part of him, that another can no longer have any right to it, before it can do him any good for the support of his life.

27. Though the Earth, and all inferior creatures be common to all men, yet every man has a property in his own person. This nobody has any right to but himself. The labour of his body, and the work of his hands, we may say, are properly his. Whatsoever then he removes out of the state that Nature has provided, and left it in, he has mixed his labour with, and joined to it something that is his own, and thereby makes it his property. It being by him removed from the common state Nature placed it in, has by his labour something annexed to it, that excludes the common right of other men. For this labour being the unquestionable property of the labourer, no man but he can have a right to what that is once joined to, at least where there is enough, and as good left in common for others.

28. He that is nourished by the acorns he picked up under an oak, or the apples he gathered from the trees in the wood, has certainly appropriated them to himself. Nobody can deny but the nourishment is his. I ask then, When did they begin to be his? When he digested? Or when he eat? Or when he boiled? Or when he brought them home? Or when he picked them up? And it is plain, if the first gathering made them not his, nothing else could. That labour put a distinction between them and common. That added something to them more than Nature, the common mother of all, had done; and so they became his private right. And will any one say he had no right to those acorns or apples he thus appropriated, because he had not the consent of all mankind to make them his? Was it a robbery thus to assume to himself what belonged to all in common? If such a consent as that was necessary, man had starved, notwithstanding the plenty God had given him. We see in commons, which remain so by compact, that it is the taking any part of what is common, and removing it out of the state Nature leaves it in, which begins the property; without which the common is of no use. And the taking of this or that part does not depend on the express consent of all the commoners. Thus the grass my horse has bit; the turfs my servant has cut; and the ore I have dug in any place where I have a right to them in common with others, become my property, without the assignation or consent of any body. The labour that was mine, removing them out of the common state they were in, has fixed my property in them.

31. It will perhaps be objected to this, that if gathering the acorns, or other fruits of the earth, & c. makes a right to them, then any one may ingross as much as he will. To which I answer, not so. The same law of Nature, that does by this means give us property, does also bound that property too. "God has given us all things richly" (*I Tim.* vi. 17) is the voice of reason confirmed by inspiration. But how far has he given it to us? To enjoy. As much as any one can make use of to any advantage of life before it spoils; so much he may by his labour fix a property in. Whatever is beyond this, is more than his share, and belongs to others. Nothing was made by God for man to spoil or destroy. And thus considering the plenty of natural provisions there was a long time in the world, and the few spenders, and to how small a part of that provision the industry of one man could extend itself, and ingross it to the prejudice of others; especially keeping within the bounds, set by reason of what

(continued)

Second Treatise of Government   (continued)

might serve for his use; there could be then little room for quarrels or contentions about property so established.

32. But the chief matter of property being now not the fruits of the Earth, and the beasts that subsist on it, but the Earth itself; as that which takes in and carries with it all the rest: I think it is plain, that property in that too is acquired as the former. As much land as a man tills, plants, improves, cultivates, and can use the product of, so much is his property. He by his labour does, as it were, inclose it from the common. Nor will it invalidate his right to say, everybody else has an equal title to it; and therefore he cannot appropriate, he cannot inclose, without the consent of all his fellow commoners, all mankind. God, when he gave the world in common to all mankind, commanded man also to labour, and the penury of his condition required it of him. God and his reason commanded him to subdue the Earth, i.e. improve it for the benefit of life, and therein lay out something upon it that was his own, his labour. He that, in obedience to this command of God, subdued, tilled and sowed any part of it. thereby annexed to it something that was his property, which another had no title to, nor could without injury take from him.

33. Nor was this appropriation of any parcel of land, by improving it, any prejudice to any other man, since there was still enough, and as good left; and more than the yet unprovided could use. So that in effect, there was never the less left for others because of his enclosure for himself. For he that leaves as much as another can make use of, does as good as take nothing at all. Nobody could think himself injured by the drinking of another man, though he took a good draught, who had a whole river of the same water left him to quench his thirst. And the case of land and water, where there is enough of both, is perfectly the same.

Chapter VI
Of Paternal Power

52. It may perhaps be censured as an impertinent criticism, in a discourse of this nature, to find fault with words and names that have obtained in the world; and yet possibly it may not be amiss to offer new ones when the old are apt to lead men into mistakes, as this of "paternal power" probably has done, which seems so to place the power of parents over their children wholly in the father, as if the mother had no share in it; whereas, if we consult reason or revelation, we shall find she has an equal title. This may give one reason to ask whether this might not be more properly called "parental power," for whatever obligation nature and the right of generation lays on children, it must certainly bind them equally to both concurrent causes of it. And accordingly we see the positive law of God everywhere joins them together without distinction when it commands the obedience of children: "Honour thy father and thy mother" (Exod. xx. 12); "Whosoever curseth his father or his mother" (Lev. xx. 9); "Ye shall fear every man his mother and his father" (Lev. xix. 5); "Children, obey your parents," etc. (Eph. vi. I), is the style of the Old and New Testament.

53. Had but this one thing been well considered, without looking any deeper into the matter, it might perhaps have kept men from running into those gross mistakes they have made about this power of parents, which, however it might without any great harshness bear the name of absolute dominion and regal authority, when under the tide of "paternal power" it seemed appropriated to the father, would yet have sounded but oddly and in the very name shown the absurdity if this supposed absolute power over children had been called "parental," and thereby have discovered that it belonged to the mother, too; for it will but very ill serve the turn of those men who contend so much for the absolute power and authority of the fatherhood, as they call it, that the mother should have any share in it; and it would have but ill supported the monarchy they contend for, when by the very name it appeared that that fundamental authority from whence they would derive their government of a single person only was not placed in one but two persons jointly. But to let this of names pass.

54. Though I have said above (Chap. II) that all men by nature are equal, I cannot be supposed to understand all sorts of equality. Age or virtue may give men a just precedence; excellence of parts and merit may place others above the common level; birth may subject some, and alliance or benefits others, to pay an observance to those whom nature, gratitude, or other respects may have made it due; and yet all this consists with the equality which all men are in, in respect of jurisdiction or dominion one over another, which was the equality I there spoke of as proper to the business in hand, being that equal right that every man has to his natural freedom, without being subjected to the will or authority of any other man.

55. Children, I confess, are not born in this state of equality, though they are born to it. Their parents have a sort of rule and jurisdiction over them when they come into the world, and for some time after, but it is but a temporary one. The bonds of this subjection are like the swaddling clothes they are wrapped up in and supported by in the weakness of their infancy; age and reason, as they grow up, loosen them, till at length they drop quite off and leave a man at his own free disposal.

57. The law that was to govern Adam was the same that was to govern all his posterity—the law of reason. But his offspring having another way of entrance into the world, different from him, by a natural birth that produced them ignorant and without the use of reason, they were not presently under the law; for nobody can be under a law which is not promulgated to him; and this law being promulgated or made known by reason only, he that is not come to the use of his reason cannot be said to be under this law; and Adam's children, being not presently as soon as born under this law of reason, were not presently free; for law, in its true notion, is not so much the limitation as the direction of a free and intelligent agent to his proper interest, and prescribes no further than is for the general good of those under that law. Could they be happier without it, the law, as a useless thing, would of itself vanish; and that ill deserves the name of confinement which hedges us in only from bogs and precipices. So that, however it may be mistaken, the end of law is not to abolish or restrain but to preserve and enlarge freedom; for in all the states of created beings capable of laws, where there is no law, there is no freedom. For liberty is to be free from restraint and violence from others, which cannot be where there is not law; but freedom is not, as we are told: a liberty for every man to do what he lists—for who could be free, when every other man's humor might domineer over him?—but a liberty to dispose and order as he lists his person, actions, possessions, and his whole property, within the allowance of those laws under which he is, and therein not to be subject to the arbitrary will of another, but freely follow his own.

58. The power, then, that parents have over their children arises from that duty which is incumbent on them—to take care of their offspring during the imperfect state of childhood. To inform the mind and govern the actions of their yet ignorant nonage till reason shall take its place and ease them of that trouble is what the children want and the parents are bound to; for God, having given man an understanding to direct his actions, has allowed him a freedom of will and liberty of acting as properly belonging thereunto, within the bounds of that law he is under. But while he is in an estate wherein he has not understanding of his own to direct his will, he is not to have any will of his own to follow; he that understands for him must will for him, too; he must prescribe to his will and regulate his actions; but when he comes to the estate that made his father a freeman, the son is a freeman, too.

Chapter VII
Of Political or Civil Society

77. God, having made man such a creature that in his own judgment it was not good for him to be alone, put him under strong obligations of necessity, convenience, and inclination to drive him into society, as well as fitted him with understanding and language to continue and enjoy it. The first society was between man and wife, which gave beginning to that between parents and children; to which, in time, that between master and servant came to be added; and though all these might, and commonly did, meet together and make up but one family wherein the master or mistress of it had some sort of rule proper to a family—each of these, or all together, came short of political society, as well shall see if we consider the different ends, ties, and bounds of each of these.

78. Conjugal society is made by a voluntary compact between man and woman; and though it consist chiefly in such a communion and right in one another's bodies as is necessary to its chief end, procreation, yet it draws with it mutual support and assistance, and a communion of interests, too, as necessary not only to unite their care and affection, but also necessary to their common offspring, who have a right to be nourished and maintained by them till they are able to provide for themselves.

(continued)

Second Treatise of Government (*continued*)

79. For the end of conjunction between male and female being not barely procreation but the continuation of the species, this conjunction betwixt male and female ought to last, even after procreation, so long as is necessary to the nourishment and support of the young ones who are to be sustained by those that got them till they are able to shift and provide for themselves. This rule, which the infinite wise Maker has set to the works of his hands, we find the inferior creatures steadily obey. In those viviparous animals which feed on grass, the conjunction between male and female lasts no longer than the very act of copulation, because the teat of the dam being sufficient to nourish the young till it be able to feed on grass, the male only begets, but concerns not himself for the female or young to whose sustenance he can contribute nothing. But in beasts of prey the conjunction lasts longer because, the dam not being able well to subsist herself and nourish her numerous offspring by her own prey alone, a more laborious as well as more dangerous way of living than by feeding on grass, the assistance of the male is necessary to the maintenance of their common family, which cannot subsist till they are able to prey for themselves but by the joint care of male and female. The same is to be observed in all birds—except some domestic ones, where plenty of food excuses the cock from feeding and taking care of the young brood—whose young needing food in the nest, the cock and hen continue mates till the young are able to use their wing and provide for themselves.

80. And herein, I think, lies the chief, if not the only, reason why the male and female in mankind are tied to a longer conjunction than other creatures, viz., because the female is capable of conceiving, and *de facto* is commonly with child again and brings forth, too, a new birth long before the former is out of a dependency for support on his parents' help and able to shift for himself and has all the assistance that is due to him from his parents; whereby the father, who is bound to take care for those he has begot, is under an obligation to continue in conjugal society with the same woman longer than other creatures whose young being able to subsist of themselves before the time of procreation returns again, the conjugal bond dissolves of itself, and they are at liberty, till Hymen at his usual anniversary season summons them again to choose new mates. Wherein one cannot but admire the wisdom of the great Creator, who, having given to man foresight and an ability to lay up for the future as well as to supply the present necessity, has made it necessary that society of man and wife should be more lasting than of male and female amongst other creatures, that so their industry might be encouraged and their interest better united to make provision and lay up goods for their common issue, which uncertain mixture or easy and frequent solutions of conjugal society would mightily disturb.

81. But though these are ties upon mankind which make the conjugal bonds more firm and lasting in man than the other species of animals, yet it would give one reason to inquire why this compact, where procreation and education are secured and inheritance taken care for, may not be made determinable, either by consent, or at a certain time, or upon certain conditions, as well as any other voluntary compacts, there being no necessity in the nature of the thing nor to the ends of it that it should always be for life; I mean, to such as are under no restraint of any positive law which ordains all such contracts to be perpetual.

82. But the husband and wife, though they have but one common concern, yet having different understandings, will unavoidably sometimes have different wills, too; it therefore being necessary that the last determination—i.e., the rule—should be placed somewhere, it naturally falls to the man's share, as the abler and the stronger. But this, reaching but to the things of their common interest and property, leaves the wife in the full and free possession of what by contract is her peculiar right, and gives the husband no more power over her life than she has over his; the power of the husband being so far from that of an absolute monarch that the wife has in many cases a liberty to separate from him where natural right or their contract allows it, whether that contract be made by themselves in the state of nature, or by the customs or laws of the country they live in; and the children upon such separation fall to the father's or mother's lot, as such contract does determine.

83. For all the ends of marriage being to be obtained under politic government as well as in the state of nature, the civil magistrate does not abridge the right or power of either naturally necessary to those ends, viz., procreation and mutual support and assistance while they are together, but only decides any controversy that may arise between man and wife about them. If it were otherwise, and that absolute sovereignty and power of life and death naturally belonged to the husband and were necessary to the society between man and wife, there could be no matrimony in any of those countries where the husband is allowed no such absolute authority. But the ends of matrimony requiring no such power in the husband, the condition of conjugal society put it not in him, it being not at all necessary to that state. Conjugal society could subsist and attain its ends without it; nay, community of goods and the power over them, mutual assistance and maintenance, and other things belonging to conjugal society, might be varied and regulated by that contract which unites man and wife in that society as far as may consist with procreation and the bringing up of children till they could shift for themselves, nothing being necessary to any society that is not necessary to the ends for which it is made.

86. Let us therefore consider a master of a family with all these subordinate relations of wife, children, servants, and slaves, united under the domestic rule of a family; which, what resemblance soever it may have in its order, offices, and number, too, with a little commonwealth, yet is very far from it, both in its constitution, power, and end; or, if it must be thought a monarchy, and the paterfamilias the absolute monarch in it, absolute monarchy will have but a very shattered and short power when it is plain, by what has been said before, that the master of the family has a very distinct and differently limited power both as to time and extent over those several persons that are in it; for excepting the slave—and the family is as much a family, and his power as paterfamilias as great, whether there be any slaves in his family or no—he has no legislative power of life and death over any of them, and none, too, but what a mistress of a family may have as well as he. And he certainly can have no absolute power over the whole family who has but a very limited one over every individual in it. But how a family or any other society of men differ from that which is properly political society, we shall best see by considering wherein political society itself consists.

87. Man being born, as has been proved, with a title to perfect freedom, and an uncontrolled enjoyment of all the rights and privileges of the law of Nature, equally with any other man, or number of men in the world, has by nature a power, not only to preserve his property, that is, his life, liberty and estate, against the injuries and attempts of other men; but to judge of, and punish the breaches of that law in others, as he is persuaded the offence deserves, even with death itself, in crimes where the heinousness of the fact, in his opinion, requires it. But because no political society can be, nor subsist without having in itself the power to preserve the property, and in order thereunto punish the offences of all those of that society; there, and there only is political society, where every one of the members has quitted this natural power, resigned it up into the hands of the community in all cases that exclude him not from appealing for protection to the law established by it. And thus all private judgment of every particular member being excluded, the community comes to be umpire, by settled standing rules, indifferent, and the same to all parties; and by men having authority from the community, for the execution of those rules, decides all the differences that may happen between any members of that society, concerning any matter of right; and punishes those offences, which any member has committed against the society, with such penalties as the law has established: whereby it is easier to discern who are, and who are not, in political society together. Those who are united into one body, and have a common established law and judicature to appeal to, with authority to decide controversies between them, and punish offenders, are in civil society one with another: but those who have no such common appeal, I mean on Earth, are still in the state of Nature, each being, where there is no other, judge for himself, and executioner; which is, as I have before shown it, the perfect state of Nature.

88. And thus the commonwealth comes by a power to set down, what punishment shall belong to the several transgressions which they think worthy of it, committed amongst the members of that society—which is the power of making laws—as well as it has the power to punish any injury done unto any of its members, by any one that is not of it—which is the power of war and peace—and all this for the preservation of the property of all the members of that society, as far as is possible. But though every man who has entered into civil society, and is become a member of any commonwealth, has thereby quitted his power to punish offences against the law of Nature, in prosecution of his own private judgment; yet with the judgment of offences which he has given up to the legislative in all cases, where he can appeal to the magistrate, he has given a right to the commonwealth to employ his force, for the execution of the judgments of the commonwealth, whenever he shall be called to it; which indeed are his own judgments, they being made by himself, or his representative. And herein we

(continued)

Second Treatise of Government   (*continued*)

have the original of the legislative and executive power of civil society, which is to judge by standing laws how far offences are to be punished, when committed within the commonwealth; and also to determine by occasional judgments founded on the present circumstances of the fact, how far injuries from without are to be vindicated, and in both these to employ all the force of all the members when there shall be need.

89. Wherever therefore any number of men are so united into one society, as to quit everyone his executive power of the law of Nature, and to resign it to the public, there and there only is a political, or civil society. And this is done wherever any number of men, in the state of Nature, enter into society to make one people, one body politic under one supreme government, or else when anyone joins himself to, and incorporates with any government already made. For hereby he authorizes the society, or which is all one, the legislative thereof to make laws for him as the public good of the society shall require; to the execution whereof, his own assistance (as to his own decrees) is due. And this puts men out of a state of Nature into that of a commonwealth, by setting up a judge on Earth, with authority to determine all the controversies, and redress the injuries, that may happen to any member of the commonwealth; which judge is the legislative, or magistrates appointed by it. And wherever there are any number of men, however associated, that have no such decisive power to appeal to, there they are still in the state of Nature.

90. Hence it is evident, that absolute monarchy, which by some men is counted the only government in the world, is indeed inconsistent with civil society, and so can be no form of civil government at all. For the end of civil society, being to avoid, and remedy those inconveniencies of the state of Nature, which necessarily follow from every man's being judge in his own case, by setting up a known authority, to which everyone of that society may appeal upon any injury received, or controversy that may arise, and which everyone of the society ought to obey; wherever any persons are, who have not such an authority to appeal to, for the decision of any difference between them, there those persons are still in the state of Nature. And so is every absolute prince in respect of those who are under his dominion.

Chapter VIII
Of the Beginning of Political Societies

95. Men being, as has been said, by Nature, all free, equal and independent, no one can be put out of this estate, and subjected to the political power of another, without his own consent. The only way whereby any one divests himself of his natural liberty, and puts on the bonds of civil society is by agreeing with other men to join and unite into a community, for their comfortable, safe, and peaceable living one amongst another, in a secure enjoyment of their properties, and a greater security against any that are not of it. This any number of men may do, because it injures not the freedom of the rest; they are left as they were in the liberty of the state of Nature. When any number of men have so consented to make one community or government, they are thereby presently incorporated, and make one body politic, wherein the majority have a right to act and conclude the rest.

96. For when any number of men have, by the consent of every individual, made a community, they have thereby made that community one body, with a power to act as one body, which is only by the will and determination of the majority. For that which acts any community, being only the consent of the individuals of it, and it being necessary to that which is one body to move one way; it is necessary the body should move that way whither the greater force carries it, which is the consent of the majority: or else it is impossible it should act or continue one body, one community, which the consent of every individual that united into it, agreed that it should; and so every one is bound by that consent to be concluded by the majority. And therefore we see that in assemblies empowered to act by positive laws where no number is set by that positive law which empowers them, the act of the majority passes for the act of the whole, and of course determines, as having by the law of Nature and reason, the power of the whole.

97. And thus every man, by consenting with others to make one body politic under one government, puts himself under an obligation to every one of that society, to submit to the determination of the majority, and to be concluded by it; or else this original compact, whereby he with others incorporates into one society, would signify nothing, and be no compact, if he be left free, and under no other ties, than he was in before in the state of Nature. For what appearance would there be of any compact? What new engagement if he were no farther tied by any decrees of the society, than he himself thought fit, and did actually consent to? This would be still as great a liberty, as he himself had before his compact, or any one else in the state of Nature has, who may submit himself and consent to any acts of it if he thinks fit.

98. For if the consent of the majority shall not in reason, be received, as the act of the whole, and conclude every individual; nothing but the consent of every individual can make any thing to be the act of the whole: but such a consent is next impossible ever to be had, if we consider the infirmities of health, and avocations of business, which in a number, though much less than that of a commonwealth, will necessarily keep many away from the public assembly. To which if we add the variety of opinions, and contrariety of interests, which unavoidably happen in all collections of men, the coming into society upon such terms, would be only like Cato's coming into the theatre, only to go out again. Such a constitution as this would make the mighty *Leviathan* of a shorter duration, than the feeblest creatures; and not let it outlast the day it was born in: which cannot be supposed till we can think, that rational creatures should desire and constitute societies only to be dissolved. For where the majority cannot conclude the rest, there they cannot act as one body, and consequently will be immediately dissolved again.

99. Whosoever therefore out of a state of Nature unite into a community, must be understood to give up all the power, necessary to the ends for which they unite into society, to the majority of the community, unless they expressly agreed in any number greater than the majority. And this is done by barely agreeing to unite into one political society, which is all the compact that is, or needs be, between the individuals, that enter into, or make up a commonwealth. And thus that, which begins and actually constitutes any political society, is nothing but the consent of any number of freemen capable of a majority to unite and incorporate into such a society. And this is that, and that only, which did, or could give beginning to any lawful government in the world.

119. Every man being, as has been shown, naturally free, and nothing being able to put him into subjection to any earthly power, but only his own consent; it is to be considered, what shall be understood to be a sufficient declaration of a man's consent, to make him subject to the laws of any government. There is a common distinction of an express and a tacit consent, which will concern our present case. Nobody doubts that an express consent, of any man, entering into any society, makes him a perfect member of that society, a subject of that government. The difficulty is, what ought to be looked upon as a tacit consent, and how far it binds, i.e. how far anyone shall be looked on to have consented, and thereby submitted to any government, where he has made no expressions of it at all. And to this I say, that every Man, that has any possession, or enjoyment, of any part of the dominions of any government, does thereby give his tacit consent, and is as far forth obliged to obedience to the laws of that government, during such enjoyment, as any one under it; whether this his possession be of land, to him and his heirs for ever, or a lodging only for a week; or whether it be barely traveling freely on the highway; and in effect; it reaches as far as the very being, of any one within the territories of that government.

Chapter IX
Of the Ends of Political Society and Government

123. If man in the state of Nature be so free, as has been said; if he be absolute lord of his own person and possessions, equal to the greatest and subject to nobody, why will he part with his freedom? Why will be give up this empire, and subject himself to the dominion and control of any other power? To which it is obvious to answer, that though in the state of Nature he has such a right, yet the enjoyment of it is very uncertain, and constantly exposed to the invasion of others. For all being kings as much as he, every man his equal, and the greater part no strict observers of equity and justice, the enjoyment of the property he has in this state is very unsafe, very insecure. This makes him willing to quit a condition, which however free, is full of fears and continual dangers: and it is not without reason, that he seeks out, and is willing to join in society with others who are already united, or have a mind to unite for the mutual preservation of their lives, liberties and estates, which I call by the general name, property.

124. The great and chief end therefore, of men's uniting into commonwealths, and putting themselves under government, is the preservation of their property. To which in the state of Nature there are many things wanting.

(continued)

Second Treatise of Government (*continued*)

First, there wants an established, settled, known law, received and allowed by common consent to be the standard of right and wrong, and the common measure to decide all controversies between them. For though the law of Nature be plain and intelligible to all rational creatures: yet men being biassed by their interest, as well as ignorant for want of study of it, are not apt to allow it as a law binding to them in the application of it to their particular cases.

125. Secondly, in the state of Nature there wants a known and indifferent judge, with authority to determine all differences according to the established law. For everyone in that state being both judge and executioner of the law of Nature, men being partial to themselves, passion and revenge is very apt to carry them too far, and with too much heat, in their own cases; as well as negligence, and unconcernedness, to make them too remiss, in other men's.

126. Thirdly, in the state of Nature there often wants power to back and support the sentence when right, and to give it due execution. They who by any injustice offended, will seldom fail, where they are able, by force to make good their injustice: such resistance many times makes the punishment dangerous, and frequently destructive, to those who attempt it.

127. Thus mankind, notwithstanding all the privileges of the state of Nature, being but in an ill condition, while they remain in it, are quickly driven into society. Hence it comes to pass, that we seldom find any number of men live any time together in this state. The inconveniences, that they are therein exposed to, by the irregular and uncertain exercise of the power every man has of punishing the transgressions of others, make them take sanctuary, under the established law of government, and therein seek the preservation of their property. It is this makes them so willingly give up every one his single power of punishing to be exercised by such alone as shall be appointed to it amongst them; and by such rules as the community, or those authorised by them to that purpose, shall agree on. And in this we have the original right and rise of both the legislative and executive power, as well as of the governments and societies themselves.

131. But though men when they enter into society, give up the equality, liberty and executive power they had in the state of Nature, into the hands of the society, to be so far disposed of by the legislative, as the good of the society shall require; yet it being only with an intention in every one the better to preserve himself his liberty and property; (for no rational creature can be supposed to change his condition with an intention to be worse) the power of the society, or legislative constituted by them, can never be supposed to extend farther than the common good; but is obliged to secure every one's property by providing against those three defects above-mentioned, that made the state of Nature so unsafe and uneasy. And so whoever has the legislative or supreme power of any commonwealth, is bound to govern by established standing laws, promulgated and known to the people, and not by extemporary decrees; by indifferent and upright judges, who are to decide controversies by those laws; and to employ the force of the community at home, only in the execution of such laws, or abroad to prevent or redress foreign injuries, and secure the community from inroads and invasion. And all this to be directed to no other end, but the peace, safety, and public good of the people.

Chapter XI
Of the Extent of Legislative Power

137. Absolute arbitrary power, or governing without settled standing laws, can neither of them consist with the ends of society and government, which men would not quit the freedom of the state of Nature for, and tie themselves up under, were it not to preserve their lives, liberties and fortunes, and by stated rules of right and property to secure their peace and quiet. It cannot be supposed that they should intend, had they a power so to do, to give to any one, or more, an absolute arbitrary power over their persons and estates, and put a force into the magistrate's hand to execute his unlimited will arbitrarily upon them. This were to put themselves into a worse condition than the state of Nature, wherein they had a liberty to defend their right against the injuries of others, and were upon equal terms of force to maintain it, whether invaded by a single man, or many in combination.

139. But government, into whatsoever hands it is put, being, as I have before shewed, intrusted with this condition, and for this end, that men might have and secure their properties; the prince, or senate, however it may have power to make laws, for the regulating of property between the subjects one amongst another, yet can never have a power to take to themselves the whole, or any part of the subjects, property, without their own consent: for this would be in effect to leave them no property at all.

140. It is true, governments cannot be supported without great charge, and it is fit every one who enjoys his share of the protection, should pay out of his estate his proportion for the maintenance of it. But still it must be with his own consent, i.e. the consent of the majority, giving it either by themselves, or their representatives chosen by them: for if any one shall claim a power to lay and levy taxes on the people, by his own authority, and without such consent of the people, he thereby invades the fundamental law of property, and subverts the end of government: for what property have I in that, which another may by right take, when he pleases, to himself?

142. These are the bounds which the trust, that is put in them by the society, and the law of God and nature, have set to the legislative power of every commonwealth, in all forms of government.

First, They are to govern by promulgated established laws, not to be varied in particular cases, but to have one rule for rich and poor, for the favourite at court, and the country man at plough.

Secondly, These laws also ought to be designed for no other end ultimately, but the good of the people.

Thirdly, They must not raise taxes on the property of the people, without the consent of the people, given by themselves, or their deputies. And this properly concerns only such governments where the legislative is always in being, or at least where the people have not reserved any part of the legislative to deputies, to be from time to time chosen by themselves.

Fourthly, The legislative neither must nor can transfer the power of making laws to any body else, or place it any where, but where the people have.

Chapter XIX
Of the Dissolution of Government

222. The reason why men enter into society, is the preservation of their property; and the end why they choose and authorize a legislative, is, that there may be laws made, and rules set as guards and fences to the properties of all the members of the society, to limit the power, and moderate the dominion of every part and member of the society. For since it can never be supposed to be the will of the society, that the legislative should have a power to destroy that, which every one designs to secure, by entering into society, and for which the people submitted themselves to the legislators of their own making; whenever the legislators endeavour to take away, and destroy the property of the people, or to reduce them to slavery under arbitrary power, they put themselves into a state of war with the people, who are thereupon absolved from any further obedience, and are left to the common refuge, which God has provided for all men, against force and violence. Whensoever therefore the legislative shall transgress this fundamental rule of society; and either by ambition, fear, folly or corruption, endeavour to grasp themselves, or put into the hands of any other an absolute power over the lives, liberties, and estates of the people; by this breach of trust they forfeit the power, the people had put into their hands, for quite contrary ends, and it devolves to the people, who have a right to resume their original liberty, and, by the establishment of a new legislative (such as they shall think fit) provide for their own safety and security, which is the end for which they are in society.

240. Here, it is like, the common question will be made, who shall be judge whether the prince or legislative act contrary to their trust? This, perhaps, ill affected and factious men may spread amongst the people, when the prince only makes use of his due prerogative. To this I reply, the people shall be judge; for who shall be judge whether his trustee or deputy acts well, and according to the trust reposed in him, but he who deputes him, and must, by having deputed him have still a power to discard him, when he fails in his trust? If this be reasonable in particular cases of private men, why should it be otherwise in that of the greatest moment; where the welfare of millions is concerned, and also where the evil, if not prevented, is greater, and the redress very difficult, dear, and dangerous?

(continued)

Second Treatise of Government (*continued*)

243. To conclude, the power that every individual gave the society, when he entered into it, can never revert to the individuals again, as long as the society lasts, but will always remain in the community; because without this, there can be no community, no commonwealth, which is contrary to the original agreement: so also when the society has placed the legislative in any assembly of men, to continue in them and their successors, with direction and authority for providing such successors, the legislative can never revert to the people whilst that government lasts: because having provided a legislative with power to continue forever, they have given up their political power to the legislative, and cannot resume it. But if they have set limits to the duration of their legislative, and made this supreme power in any person, or assembly, only temporary; or else when by the miscarriages of those in authority, it is forfeited; upon the forfeiture of their rulers, or at the determination of the time set, it reverts to the society, and the people have a right to act as supreme, and continue the legislative in themselves, or erect a new form, or under the old form place it in new hands, as they think good.

Estranged Labour
Karl Marx

We have started out from the premises of political economy. We have accepted its language and its laws. We presupposed private property; the separation of labour, capital, and land, and likewise of wages, profit, and capital; the division of labour; competition; the conception of exchange value, etc. From political economy itself, using its own words, we have shown that the worker sinks to the level of a commodity, and moreover the most wretched commodity of all; that the misery of the worker is in inverse proportion to the power and volume of his production; that the necessary consequence of competition is the accumulation of capital in a few hands and hence the restoration of monopoly in a more terrible form; and that, finally, the distinction between capitalist and landlord, between agricultural worker and industrial worker, disappears and the whole of society must split into the two classes *of property owners* and propertyless *workers*.

Political economy proceeds from the fact of private property. It does not explain it. It grasps the *material* process of private property, the process through which it actually passes, in general and abstract formulae which it then takes as *laws*. It does not *comprehend* these laws—i.e., it does not show how they arise from the nature of private property. Political economy fails to explain the reason for the division between labour and capital. For example, when it defines the relation of wages to profit, it takes the interests of the capitalists as the basis of its analysis—i.e., it assumes what it is supposed to explain. Similarly, competition is frequently brought into the argument and explained in terms of external circumstances. Political economy teaches us nothing about the extent to which these external and apparently accidental circumstances are only the expression of a necessary development. We have seen how exchange itself appears to political economy as an accidental fact. The only wheels which political economy sets in motion are *greed,* and the *war of the avaricious—Competition*.

Precisely because political economy fails to grasp the interconnections within the movement, it was possible to oppose, for example, the doctrine of competition to the doctrine of monopoly, the doctrine of craft freedom to the doctrine of the guild, and the doctrine of the division of landed property to the doctrine of the great estate; for competition, craft freedom, and division of landed property were developed and conceived only as accidental, deliberate, violent consequences of monopoly, of the guilds, and of feudal property, and not as their necessary, inevitable, and natural consequences.

We now have to grasp the essential connection between private property, greed, the separation of labour, capital and landed property, exchange and competition, value and the devaluation of man, monopoly, and competition, etc.—the connection between this entire system of estrangement and the *money* system.

We must avoid repeating the mistake of the political economist, who bases his explanations on some imaginary primordial condition. Such a primordial condition explains nothing. It simply pushes the question into the grey and nebulous distance. It assumes as facts and events what it is supposed to deduce—namely, the necessary relationships between two things, between, for example, the division of labour and exchange. Similarly, theology explains the origin of evil by the fall of Man—i.e., it assumes as a fact in the form of history what it should explain.

We shall start out from a *actual* economic fact.

The worker becomes poorer the more wealth he produces, the more his production increases in power and extent. The worker becomes an ever cheaper commodity the more commodities he produces. The *devaluation* of the human world grows in direct proportion to the *increase in value* of the world of things. Labour not only produces commodities; it also produces itself and the workers as a *commodity* and it does so in the same proportion in which it produces commodities in general.

This fact simply means that the object that labour produces, its product, stands opposed to it as *something alien,* as a power independent of the producer. The product of labour is labour embodied and made material in an object, it is the *objectification* of labour. The realization of labour is its objectification. In the sphere of political economy, this realization of labour appears as a *loss of reality* for the worker objectification as loss of and bondage to the object, and appropriation as estrangement, as *alienation*.

So much does the realization of labour appear as loss of reality that the worker loses his reality to the point of dying of starvation. So much does objectification appear as loss of the object that the worker is robbed of the objects he needs most not only for life but also for work. Work itself becomes an object which he can only obtain through an enormous effort and with spasmodic interruptions. So much does the appropriation of the object appear as estrangement that the more objects the worker produces the fewer can he possess and the more he falls under the domination of his product, of capital.

All these consequences are contained in this characteristic, that the worker is related to the *product of labour* as to an *alien* object. For it is clear that, according to this premise, the more the worker exerts himself in his work, the more powerful the alien, objective world becomes which he brings into being over against himself, the poorer he and his inner world become, and the less they belong to him. It is the same in religion. The more man puts into God, the less he retains within himself. The worker places his life in the object; but now it no longer belongs to him, but to the object. The greater his activity, therefore, the fewer objects the worker possesses. What the product of his labour is, he is not. Therefore, the greater this product, the less is he himself. The externalisation of the worker in his product means not only that his labour becomes an object, an *external* existence, but that it exists *outside him,* independently of him and alien to him, and begins to confront him as an autonomous power; that the life which he has bestowed on the object confronts him as hostile and alien.

Let us now take a closer look at objectification, at the production of the worker, and the estrangement, the loss of the object, of his product, that this entails.

The workers can create nothing without nature, without the sensuous external world. It is the material in which his labour realizes itself, in which it is active and from which, and by means of which, it produces.

But just as nature provides labour with the means of life, in the sense of labour cannot live without objects on which to exercise itself, so also it provides the means of life in the narrower sense, namely the means of physical subsistence of the worker.

The more the worker appropriates the external world, sensuous nature, through his labour, the more he deprives himself of the means of life in two respects: firstly, the sensuous external world becomes less and less an object belonging to his labour, a means of life of his labour; and, secondly, it becomes less and less a means of life in the immediate sense, a means for the physical subsistence of the worker.

In these two respects, then, the worker becomes a slave of his object; firstly, in that he receives an object of labour, i.e., he receives work, and, secondly, in that he receives means of subsistence. Firstly, then, so that he can exist as a worker, and secondly as a physical subject. The culmination of this slavery is that it is only as a worker that he can maintain himself as a physical subject and only as a physical subject that he is a worker.

(continued)

Estranged Labour (continued)

(The estrangement of the worker in his object is expressed according to the laws of political economy in the following way:

1. the more the worker produces, the less he has to consume;
2. the more value he creates, the more worthless he becomes;
3. the more his product is shaped, the more misshapen the worker;
4. the more civilized his object, the more barbarous the worker;
5. the more powerful the work, the more powerless the worker;
6. the more intelligent the work, the duller the worker and the more he becomes a slave of nature.)

Political economy conceals the estrangement in the nature of labour by ignoring the direct relationship between the worker (labour) **and production**. It is true that labour produces marvels for the rich, but it produces privation for the worker. It produces palaces, but hovels for the worker. It produces beauty, but deformity for the worker. It replaces labour by machines, but it casts some of the workers back into barbarous forms of labour and turns others into machines. It produces intelligence, but it produces idiocy and cretinism for the worker.

The direct relationship of labour to its products is the relationship of the worker to the objects of his production. The relationship of the rich man to the objects of production and to production itself is only a *consequence* of this first relationship, and confirms it. Later, we shall consider this second aspect. Therefore, when we ask what is the essential relationship of labour, we are asking about the relationship of the worker to production.

Up to now, we have considered the estrangement, the alienation of the worker, only from one aspect—i.e., **the worker's relationship to the products of his labour**. But estrangement manifests itself not only in the result, but also in the *act of production,* within the *activity of production* itself. How could the product of the worker's activity confront him as something alien if it were not for the fact that in the act of production he was estranging himself from himself? After all, the product is simply the resumé of the activity, of the production. So if the product of labour is alienation, production itself must be active alienation, the alienation of activity, the activity of alienation. The estrangement of the object of labour merely summarizes the estrangement, the alienation in the activity of labour itself.

What constitutes the alienation of labour?

Firstly, the fact that labour is *external* to the worker—i.e., does not belong to his essential being; that he, therefore, does not confirm himself in his work, but denies himself, feels miserable and not happy, does not develop free mental and physical energy, but mortifies his flesh and ruins his mind. Hence, the worker feels himself only when he is not working; when he is working, he does not feel himself. He is at home when he is not working, and not at home when he is working. His labour is, therefore, not voluntary but forced, it is *forced labour.* It is, therefore, not the satisfaction of a need but a mere *means* to satisfy needs outside itself. Its alien character is clearly demonstrated by the fact that as soon as no physical or other compulsion exists, it is shunned like the plague. External labour, labour in which man alienates himself, is a labour of self-sacrifice, of mortification. Finally, the external character of labour for the worker is demonstrated by the fact that it belongs not to him but to another, and that in it he belongs not to himself but to another. Just as in religion the spontaneous activity of the human imagination, the human brain, and the human heart, detaches itself from the individual and reappears as the alien activity of a god or of a devil, so the activity of the worker is not his own spontaneous activity. It belongs to another, it is a loss of his self.

The result is that man (the worker) feels that he is acting freely only in his animal functions—eating, drinking, and procreating, or at most in his dwelling and adornment—while in his human functions, he is nothing more than animal.

It is true that eating, drinking, and procreating, etc., are also genuine human functions. However, when abstracted from other aspects of human activity, and turned into final and exclusive ends, they are animal.

We have considered the act of estrangement of practical human activity, of labour, from two aspects:

1. The relationship of the worker to the product of labour as an alien object that has power over him. The relationship is, at the same time, the relationship to the sensuous external world, to natural objects, as an alien world confronting him, in hostile opposition.
2. The relationship of labour to the *act of production* within labour. This relationship is the relationship of the worker to his own activity as something which is alien and does not belong to him, activity as passivity, power as impotence, procreation as emasculation, the worker's own physical and mental energy, his personal life—for what is life but activity?—as an activity directed against himself, which is independent of him and does not belong to him. Self-estrangement, as compared with the estrangement of the object mentioned above.

We now have to derive a third feature of estranged labour from the two we have already examined.

Man is a species-being, not only because he practically and theoretically makes the species—both his own and those of other things—his object, but also—and this is simply another way of saying the same thing—because he looks upon himself as the present, living species, because he looks upon himself as a universal and therefore free being.

Species-life, both for man and for animals, consists physically in the fact that man, like animals, lives from inorganic nature; and because man is more universal than animals, so too is the area of inorganic nature from which he lives more universal. Just as plants, animals, stones, air, light, etc., theoretically form a part of human consciousness, partly as objects of science and partly as objects of art—his spiritual inorganic nature, his spiritual means of life, which he must first prepare before he can enjoy and digest them—so, too, in practice they form a part of human life and human activity. In a physical sense, man lives only from these natural products, whether in the form of nourishment, heating, clothing, shelter, etc. The universality of man manifests itself in practice in that universality which makes the whole of nature his inorganic body, (1) as a direct means of life and (2) as the matter, the object, and the tool of his life activity. Nature is man's inorganic body—that is to say, nature insofar as it is not the human body. Man lives from nature—i.e., nature is his body—and he must maintain a continuing dialogue with it is he is not to die. To say that man's physical and mental life is linked to nature simply means that nature is linked to itself, for man is a part of nature.

Estranged labour not only (1) estranges nature from man and (2) estranges man from himself, from his own function, from his vital activity; because of this, it also estranges man from his species. It turns his species-life into a means for his individual life. Firstly, it estranges species-life and individual life, and, secondly, it turns the latter, in its abstract form, into the purpose of the former, also in its abstract and estranged form.

For in the first place labour, life activity, productive life itself, appears to man only as a means for the satisfaction of a need, the need to preserve physical existence. But productive life is species-life. It is life-producing life. The whole character of a species, its species-character, resides in the nature of its life activity, and free conscious activity constitutes the species-character of man. Life appears only as a means of life.

The animal is immediately one with its life activity. It is not distinct from that activity; it is that activity. Man makes his life activity itself an object of his will and consciousness. He has conscious life activity. It is not a determination with which he directly merges. Conscious life activity directly distinguishes man from animal life activity. Only because of that is he a species-being. Or, rather, he is a conscious being—i.e., his own life is an object for him, only because he is a species-being. Only because of that is his activity free activity. Estranged labour reverses the relationship so that man, just because he is a conscious being, makes his life activity, his *essential being*, a mere means for his *existence.*

The practical creation of an *objective world,* the fashioning of inorganic nature, is proof that man is a conscious species-being—i.e., a being which treats the species as its own essential being or itself as a species-being. It is true that animals also produce. They build nests and dwellings, like the bee, the beaver, the ant, etc. But they produce only their own immediate needs or those of their young;

(continued)

Estranged Labour (*continued*)

they produce only when immediate physical need compels them to do so, while man produces even when he is free from physical need and truly produces only in freedom from such need; they produce only themselves, while man reproduces the whole of nature; their products belong immediately to their physical bodies, while man freely confronts his own product. Animals produce only according to the standards and needs of the species to which they belong, while man is capable of producing according to the standards of every species and of applying to each object its inherent standard; hence, man also produces in accordance with the laws of beauty.

It is, therefore, in his fashioning of the objective that man really proves himself to be a species-being. Such production is his active species-life. Through it, nature appears as *his* work and his reality. The object of labour is, therefore, the objectification of the species-life of man: for man produces himself not only intellectually, in his consciousness, but actively and actually, and he can therefore contemplate himself in a world he himself has created. In tearing away the object of his production from man, estranged labour therefore tears away from him his species-life, his true species-objectivity, and transforms his advantage over animals into the disadvantage that his inorganic body, nature, is taken from him.

In the same way as estranged labour reduces spontaneous and free activity to a means, it makes man's species-life a means of his physical existence.

Consciousness, which man has from his species, is transformed through estrangement so that species-life becomes a means for him.

3. Estranged labour, therefore, turns man's species-being—both nature and his intellectual species-power—into a being alien to him and a means of his individual existence. It estranges man from his own body, from nature as it exists outside him, from his spiritual essence, his human existence.
4. An immediate consequence of man's estrangement from the product of his labour, his life activity, his species-being, is the estrangement of man from man. When man confronts himself, he also confronts other men. What is true of man's relationship to his labour, to the product of his labour, and to himself, is also true of his relationship to other men, and to the labour and the object of the labour of other men.

In general, the proposition that man is estranged from his species-being means that each man is estranged from the others and that all are estranged from man's essence.

Man's estrangement, like all relationships of man to himself, is realized and expressed only in man's relationship to other men.

In the relationship of estranged labour, each man therefore regards the other in accordance with the standard and the situation in which he as a worker finds himself.

We started out from an economic fact, the estrangement of the worker and of his production. We gave this fact conceptual form: estranged, alienated labour. We have analyzed this concept, and in so doing merely analyzed an economic fact.

Let us now go on to see how the concept of estranged, alienated labour must express and present itself in reality.

If the product of labour is alien to me, and confronts me as an alien power, to whom does it then belong?

To a being *other* than me.

Who is this being?

The gods? It is true that in early times most production—e.g., temple building, etc., in Egypt, India, and Mexico—was in the service of the gods, just as the product belonged to the gods. But the gods alone were never the masters of labour. The same is true of nature. And what a paradox it would be if the more man subjugates nature through his labour and the more divine miracles are made superfluous by the miracles of industry, the more he is forced to forgo the joy or production and the enjoyment of the product out of deference to these powers.

The alien being to whom labour and the product of labour belong, in whose service labour is performed, and for whose enjoyment the product of labour is created, can be none other than man himself.

If the product of labour does not belong to the worker, and if it confronts him as an alien power, this is only possible because it belongs to a man other than the worker. If his activity is a torment for him, it must provide pleasure and enjoyment for someone else. Not the gods, not nature, but only man himself can be this alien power over men.

Consider the above proposition that the relationship of man to himself becomes objective and real for him only through his relationship to other men. If, therefore, he regards the product of his labour, his objectified labour, as an alien, hostile, and powerful object which is independent of him, then his relationship to that object is such that another man—alien, hostile, powerful, and independent of him—is its master. If he relates to his own activity as unfree activity, then he relates to it as activity in the service, under the rule, coercion, and yoke of another man.

Every self-estrangement of man from himself and nature is manifested in the relationship he sets up between other men and himself and nature. Thus, religious self-estrangement is necessarily manifested in the relationship between layman and priest, or, since we are dealing here with the spiritual world, between layman and mediator, etc. In the practical, real world, self-estrangement can manifest itself only in the practical, real relationship to other men. The medium through which estrangement progresses is itself a practical one. So through estranged labour man not only produces his relationship to the object and to the act of production as to alien and hostile powers; he also produces the relationship in which other men stand to his production and product, and the relationship in which he stands to these other men. Just as he creates his own production as a loss of reality, a punishment, and his own product as a loss, a product which does not belong to him, so he creates the domination of the non-producer over production and its product. Just as he estranges from himself his own activity, so he confers upon the stranger and activity which does not belong to him.

Up to now, we have considered the relationship only from the side of the worker. Later on, we shall consider it from the side of the non-worker.

Thus, through estranged, alienated labour, the worker creates the relationship of another man, who is alien to labour and stands outside it, to that labour. The relation of the worker to labour creates the relation of the capitalist—or whatever other word one chooses for the master of labour—to that labour. Private property is therefore the product, result, and necessary consequence of alienated labour, of the external relation of the worker to nature and to himself.

Private property thus derives from an analysis of the concept of alienated labour—i.e., alienated man, estranged labour, estranged life, estranged man.

It is true that we took the concept of alienated labour (alienated life) from political economy as a result of the movement of private property. But it is clear from an analysis of this concept that, although private property appears as the basis and cause of alienated labour, it is in fact its consequence, just as the gods were originally not the cause but the effect of the confusion in men's minds. Later, however, this relationship becomes reciprocal.

It is only when the development of private property reaches its ultimate point of culmination that this, its secret, re-emerges; namely, that is

a. the product of alienated labour, and
b. the means through which labour is alienated, the realization of this alienation.

This development throws light upon a number of hitherto unresolved controversies.

1. Political economy starts out from labour as the real soul of production and yet gives nothing to labour and everything to private property. Proudhon has dealt with this contradiction by deciding for labour and against private property. But we have seen that this apparent contradiction is the contradiction of *estranged labour* with itself and that political economy has merely formulated laws of estranged labour.

    It, therefore, follows for us that wages and private property are identical: for there the product, the object of labour, pays for the labour itself, wages are only a necessary consequence of the estrangement of labour; similarly, where wages are concerned, labour appears not as an end in itself but as the servant of wages. We intend to deal with this point in more detail later on: for the present we shall merely draw a few conclusions.

(continued)

Estranged Labour *(continued)*

    An enforced rise in wages (disregarding all other difficulties, including the fact that such an anomalous situation could only be prolonged by force) would therefore be nothing more than better pay for slaves and would not mean an increase in human significance or dignity for either the worker or the labour.

    Even the equality of wages, which Proudhon demands, would merely transform the relation of the present-day worker to his work into the relation of all men to work. Society would then be conceived as an abstract capitalist.

    Wages are an immediate consequence of estranged labour, and estranged labour is the immediate cause of private property. If the one falls, then the other must fall too.

2. It further follows from the relation of estranged labour to private property that the emancipation of society from private property, etc., from servitude, is expressed in the *political* form of the *emancipation of the workers*. This is not because it is only a question of *their* emancipation, but because in their emancipation is contained universal human emancipation. The reason for this universality is that the whole of human servitude is involved in the relation of the worker to production, and all relations of servitude are nothing but modifications and consequences of this relation.

Just as we have arrived at the concept of *private property* through an analysis of the concept of *estranged, alienated labour,* so with the help of these two factors it is possible to evolve all economic categories, and in each of these categories—e.g., trade, competition, capital, money—we shall identify only a particular and developed expression of these basic constituents.

But, before we go on to consider this configuration, let us try to solve two further problems.

1. We have to determine the general nature of private property, as it has arisen out of estranged labour, in its relation to truly human and social property.
2. We have taken the *estrangement of labour,* its *alienation,* as a fact and we have analyzed that fact. How, we now ask, does *man* come to *alienate* his labour, to estrange it? How is this estrangement founded in the nature of human development? We have already gone a long way towards solving this problem by *transforming* the question of the *origin of private property* into the question of the relationship of alienated labour to the course of human development. For, in speaking of private property, one imagines that one is dealing with something external to man. In speaking of labour, one is dealing immediately with man himself. This new way of formulating the problem already contains its solution.

    ad (1): *The general nature of private property and its relationship to truly human property.*

Alienated labour has resolved itself for us into two component parts, which mutually condition one another, or which are merely different expressions of one and the same relationship. Appropriation appears as *estrangement,* as *alienation;* and *alienation* appears as *appropriation,* estrangement as true *admission to citizenship.*

We have considered the one aspect—alienated labour in relation to the worker himself—i.e., *the relation of alienated labour to itself.* And as product, as necessary consequence of this relationship, we have found the property relation of the non-worker to the worker and to labour. Private property as the material, summarized expression of alienated labour embraces both relations—the relation of the worker to labour and to the product of his labour and the non-workers, and the relation of the non-worker to the worker and to the product of his labour.

We have already seen that, in relation to the worker who appropriates nature through his labour, appropriation appears as estrangement, self-activity as activity for another and of another, vitality as a sacrifice of life, production of an object as loss of that object to an alien power, to an *alien* man. Let us now consider the relation between this man, who is *alien* to labour and to the worker, and the worker, labour, and the object of labour.

The first thing to point out is that everything which appears for the worker as an activity of alienation, of estrangement, appears for the non-worker as a situation of alienation, of estrangement.

> Secondly, the real, practical attitude of the worker in production and to the product (as a state of mind) appears for the non-worker who confronts him as a theoretical attitude.
>
> Thirdly, the non-worker does everything against the worker which the worker does against himself, but he does not do against himself what he does against the worker.
>
> Let us take a closer look at these three relationships.

A Theory of Justice
John Rawls

Chapter I. Justice as Fairness

1. The Role of Justice

Justice is the first virtue of social institutions, as truth is of systems of thought. A theory however elegant and economical must be rejected or revised if it is untrue; likewise laws and institutions no matter how efficient and well-arranged must be reformed or abolished if they are unjust. Each person possesses an inviolability founded on justice that even the welfare of society as a whole cannot override. For this reason justice denies that the loss of freedom for some is made right by a greater good shared by others. It does not allow that the sacrifices imposed on a few are outweighed by the larger sum of advantages enjoyed by many. Therefore in a just society the liberties of equal citizenship are taken as settled; the rights secured by justice are not subject to political bargaining or to the calculus of social interests. The only thing that permits us to acquiesce in an erroneous theory is the lack of a better one; analogously, an injustice is tolerable only when it is necessary to avoid an even greater injustice. Being first virtues of human activities, truth and justice are uncompromising.

These propositions seem to express our intuitive conviction of the primacy of justice. No doubt they are expressed too strongly. In any event I wish to inquire whether these contentions or others similar to them are sound, and if so how they can be accounted for. To this end it is necessary to work out a theory of justice in the light of which these assertions can be interpreted and assessed. I shall begin by considering the role of the principles of justice. Let us assume, to fix ideas, that a society is a more or less self-sufficient association of persons who in their relations to one another recognize certain rules of conduct as binding and who for the most part act in accordance with them. Suppose further that these rules specify a system of cooperation designed to advance the good of those taking part in it. Then, although a society is a cooperative venture for mutual advantage, it is typically marked by a conflict as well as by an identity of interests. There is an identity of interests since social cooperation makes possible a better life for all than any would have if each were to live solely by his own efforts. There is a conflict of interests since persons are not indifferent as to how the greater benefits produced by their collaboration are distributed, for in order to pursue their ends they each prefer a larger to a lesser share. A set of principles is required for choosing among the various social arrangements which determine this division of advantages and for underwriting an agreement on the proper distributive shares. These principles are the principles of social justice: they provide a way of assigning rights and duties in the basic institutions of society and they define the appropriate distribution of the benefits and burdens of social cooperation.

Now let us say that a society is well-ordered when it is not only designed to advance the good of its members but when it is also effectively regulated by a public conception of justice, That is, it is a society in which (1) everyone accepts and knows that the others accept the same principles of justice, and (2) the basic social institutions generally satisfy and are generally known to satisfy these principles. In this case while men may put forth excessive demands on one another, they nevertheless acknowledge a common point of view from which their claims may be adjudicated. If men's inclination to self-interest makes their vigilance against one another necessary, their public sense of justice makes their secure association together possible. Among individuals with disparate aims and

(continued)

A Theory of Justice *(continued)*

purposes a shared conception of justice establishes the bonds of civic friendship; the general desire for justice limits the pursuit of other ends. One may think of a public conception of justice as constituting the fundamental charter of a well-ordered human association.

3. The Main Idea of The Theory of Justice

My aim is to present a conception of justice which generalizes and carries to a higher level of abstraction the familiar theory of the social contract as found, say, in Locke, Rousseau, and Kant.[1] In order to do this we are not to think of the original contract as one to enter a particular society or to set up a particular form of government. Rather, the guiding idea is that the principles of justice for the basic structure of society are the object of the original agreement. They are the principles that free and rational persons concerned to further their own interests would accept in an initial position of equality as defining the fundamental terms of their association. These principles are to regulate all further agreements; they specify the kinds of social cooperation that can be entered into and the forms of government that can be established. This way of regarding the principles of justice I shall call justice as fairness.

Thus we are to imagine that those who engage in social cooperation choose together, in one joint act, the principles which are to assign basic rights and duties and to determine the division of social benefits. Men are to decide in advance how they are to regulate their claims against one another and what is to be the foundation charter of their society. Just as each person must decide by rational reflection what constitutes his good, that is, the system of ends which is rational for him to pursue, so a group of persons must decide once and for all what is to count among them as just and unjust. The choice which rational men would make in this hypothetical situation of equal liberty, assuming for the present that this choice problem has a solution, determines the principles of justice.

In justice as fairness the original position of equality corresponds to the state of nature in the traditional theory of the social contract. This original position is not, of course, thought of as an actual historical state of affairs, much less as a primitive condition of culture. It is understood as a purely hypothetical situation characterized so as to lead to a certain conception of justice.[2] Among the essential features of this situation is that no one knows his place in society, his class position or social status, nor does any one know his fortune in the distribution of natural assets and abilities, his intelligence, strength, and the like. I shall even assume that the parties do not know their conceptions of the good or their special psychological propensities. The principles of justice are chosen behind a veil of ignorance. This ensures that no one is advantaged or disadvantaged in the choice of principles by the outcome of natural chance or the contingency of social circumstances. Since all are similarly situated and no one is able to design principles to favor his particular condition, the principles of justice are the result of a fair agreement or bargain. For given the circumstances of the original position, the symmetry of everyone's relations to each other, this initial situation is fair between individuals as moral persons, that is, as rational beings with their own ends and capable, I shall assume, of a sense of justice. The original position is, one might say, the appropriate initial status quo, and thus the fundamental agreements reached in it are fair. This explains the propriety of the name "justice as fairness": it conveys the idea that the principles of justice are agreed to in an initial situation that is fair. The name does not mean that the concepts of justice and fairness are the same, any more than the phrase "poetry as metaphor" means that the concepts of poetry and metaphor are the same.

Justice as fairness begins, as I have said, with one of the most general of all choices which persons might make together, namely, with the choice of the first principles of a conception of justice which is to regulate all subsequent criticism and reform of institutions. Then, having chosen a conception of justice, we can suppose that they are to choose a constitution and a legislature to enact laws, and so on, all in accordance with the principles of justice initially agreed upon. Our social situation is just if it is such that by this sequence of hypothetical agreements we would have contracted into the general system of rules which defines it.

11. Two Principles of Justice

I shall now state in a provisional form the two principles of justice that I believe would be chosen in the original position. In this section I wish to make only the most general comments, and therefore the first formulation of these principles is tentative. As we go on I shall run through several formulations and approximate step by step the final statement to be given much later. I believe that doing this allows the exposition to proceed in a natural way.

The first statement of the two principles reads as follows:

> First: each person is to have an equal right to the most extensive basic liberty compatible with a similar liberty for others.
>
> Second: social and economic inequalities are to be arranged so that they are both (a) reasonably expected to be to everyone's advantage, and (b) attached to positions and offices open to all.

There are two ambiguous phrases in the second principle, namely "everyone's advantage" and "equally open to all." Determining their sense more exactly will lead to a second formulation of the principle in § 13, The final version of the two principles is given in §45; §39 considers the rendering of the first principle.

By way of general comment, these principles primarily apply, as I have said, to the basic structure of society. They are to govern the assignment of rights and duties and to regulate the distribution of social and economic advantages. As their formulation suggests, these principles presuppose that the social structure can be divided into two more or less distinct parts, the first principle applying to the one, the second to the other. They distinguish between those aspects of the social system that define and secure the equal liberties of citizenship and those that specify and establish social and economic inequalities. The basic liberties of citizens are, roughly speaking, political liberty (the right to vote and to be eligible for public office) together with freedom of speech and assembly; liberty of conscience and freedom of thought; freedom of the person along with the right to hold (personal) property; and freedom from arbitrary arrest and seizure as defined by the concept of the rule of law. These liberties are all required to be equal by the first principle, since citizens of a just society are to have the same basic rights.

The second principle applies, in the first approximation, to the distribution of income and wealth and to the design of organizations that make use of differences in authority and responsibility, or chains of command. While the distribution of wealth and income need not be equal, it must be to everyone's advantage, and at the same time, positions of authority and offices of command must be accessible to all. One applies the second principle by holding positions open, and then, subject to this constraint, arranges social and economic inequalities so that everyone benefits.

These principles are to be arranged in a serial order with the first principle prior to the second. This ordering means that a departure from the institutions of equal liberty required by the first principle cannot be justified by, or compensated for, by greater social and economic advantages. The distribution of wealth and income, and the hierarchies of authority, must be consistent with both the liberties of equal citizenship and equality of opportunity.

It is clear that these principles are rather specific in their content, and their acceptance rests on certain assumptions that I must eventually try to explain and justify. A theory of justice depends upon a theory of society in ways that will become evident as we proceed. For the present, it should be observed that the two principles (and this holds for all formulations) are a special case of a more general conception of justice that can be expressed as follows.

> All social values—liberty and opportunity, income and wealth, and the bases of self-respect—are to be distributed equally unless an unequal distribution of any, or all, of these values is to everyone's advantage.

Injustice, then, is simply inequalities that are not to the benefit of all. Of course, this conception is extremely vague and requires interpretation.

As a first step, suppose that the basic structure of society distributes certain primary goods, that is, things that every rational man is presumed to want. These goods normally have a use whatever a person's rational plan of life. For simplicity, assume that the chief primary goods at the disposition of society are rights and liberties, powers and opportunities, income and wealth. (Later on in Part Three the primary good of self-respect has a central place.) These are the social primary goods. Other primary

(continued)

A Theory of Justice (*continued*)

goods such as health and vigor, intelligence and imagination, are natural goods; although their possession is influenced by the basic structure, they are not so directly under its control. Imagine, then, a hypothetical initial arrangement in which all the social primary goods are equally distributed: everyone has similar rights and duties, and income and wealth are evenly shared. This state of affairs provides a benchmark for judging improvements. If certain inequalities of wealth and organizational powers would make everyone better off than in this hypothetical starting situation, then they accord with the general conception.

Now it is possible, at least theoretically, that by giving up some of their fundamental liberties men are sufficiently compensated by the resulting social and economic gains. The general conception of justice imposes no restrictions on what sort of inequalities are permissible; it only requires that everyone's position be improved. We need not suppose anything so drastic as consenting to a condition of slavery. Imagine instead that men forego certain political rights when the economic returns are significant and their capacity to influence the course of policy by the exercise of these rights would be marginal in any case. It is this kind of exchange which the two principles as stated rule out; being arranged in serial order they do not permit exchanges between basic liberties and economic and social gains. The serial ordering of principles expresses an underlying preference among primary social goods. When this preference is rational so likewise is the choice of these principles in this order.

In developing justice as fairness I shall, for the most part, leave aside the general conception of justice and examine instead the special case of the two principles in serial order. The advantage of this procedure is that from the first the matter of priorities is recognized and an effort made to find principles to deal with it. One is led to attend throughout to the conditions under which the acknowledgment of the absolute weight of liberty with respect to social and economic advantages, as defined by the lexical order of the two principles, would be reasonable. Offhand, this ranking appears extreme and too special a case to be of much interest; but there is more justification for it than would appear at first sight. Or at any rate, so I shall maintain (§82). Furthermore, the distinction between fundamental rights and liberties and economic and social benefits marks a difference among primary social goods that one should try to exploit. It suggests an important division in the social system. Of course, the distinctions drawn and the ordering proposed are bound to be at best only approximations. There are surely circumstances in which they fail. But it is essential to depict clearly the main lines of a reasonable conception of justice; and under many conditions anyway, the two principles in serial order may serve well enough. When necessary we can fall back on the more general conception.

The fact that the two principles apply to institutions has certain consequences. Several points illustrate this. First of all, the rights and liberties referred to by these principles are those which are defined by the public rules of the basic structure. Whether men are free is determined by the rights and duties established by the major institutions of society. Liberty is a certain pattern of social forms. The first principle simply requires that certain sorts of rules, those defining basic liberties, apply to everyone equally and that they allow the most extensive liberty compatible with a like liberty for all. The only reason for circumscribing the rights defining liberty and making men's freedom less extensive than it might otherwise be is that these equal rights as institutionally defined would interfere with one another.

Another thing to bear in mind is that when principles mention persons, or require that everyone gain from an inequality, the reference is to representative persons holding the various social positions, or offices, or whatever, established by the basic structure, Thus in applying the second principle I assume that it is possible to assign an expectation of well-being to representative individuals holding these positions. This expectation indicates their life prospects as viewed from their social station. In general, the expectations of representative persons depend upon the distribution of rights and duties throughout the basic structure. When this changes, expectations change. I assume, then, that expectations are connected: by raising the prospects of the representative man in one position we presumably increase or decrease the prospects of representative men in other positions. Since it applies to institutional forms, the second principle (or rather the first part of it) refers to the expectations of representative individuals. As I shall discuss below, neither principle applies to distributions of particular goods to particular individuals who may be identified by their proper names. The situation where someone is considering how to allocate certain commodities to needy persons who are known to him is not within the scope of the principles. They are meant to regulate basic institutional arrangements. We must not assume that there is much similarity from the standpoint of justice between an administrative allotment of goods to specific persons and the appropriate design of society. Our common sense intuitions for the former may be a poor guide to the latter.

Now the second principle insists that each person benefit from permissible inequalities in the basic structure. This means that it must be reasonable for each relevant representative man defined by this structure, when he views it as a going concern, to prefer his prospects with the inequality to his prospects without it. One is not allowed to justify differences in income or organizational powers on the ground that the disadvantages of those in one position are outweighed by the greater advantages of those in another. Much less can infringements of liberty be counterbalanced in this way. Applied to the basic structure, the principle of utility would have us maximize the sum of expectations of representative men (weighted by the number of persons they represent, on the classical view); and this would permit us to compensate for the losses of some by the gains of others. Instead, the two principles require that everyone benefit from economic and social inequalities. It is obvious, however, that there are indefinitely many ways in which all may be advantaged when the initial arrangement of equality is taken as a benchmark. How then are we to choose among these possibilities? The principles must be specified so that they yield a determinate conclusion. I now turn to this problem.

NOTES

1. As the text suggests, I shall regard Locke's *Second Treatise of Government,* Rousseau's *The Social Contract,* and Kant's ethical works beginning with *The Foundations of the Metaphysics of Morals* as definitive of the contract tradition. For all of its greatness, Hobbes's *Leviathan* raises special problems. A general historical survey is provided by J. W. Gough, *The Social Contract,* 2nd ed. (Oxford, The Clarendon Press, 1957), and Otto Gierke, *Natural Law and the Theory of Society,* trans. with an introduction by Ernest Barker (Cambridge, The University Press, 1934). A presentation of the contract view as primarily an ethical theory is to be found in G. R, Grice, *The Grounds of Moral Judgment* (Cambridge, The University Press, 1967). See also §19, note 30.
2. Kant is clear that the original agreement is hypothetical. See *The Metaphysics of Morals,* pt. I (*Rechtslehre*), especially §§ 47, 52; and pt. II of the essay "Concerning the Common Saying: This May Be True in Theory but It Does Not Apply in Practice," in *Kant's Political Writings,* ed. Hans Reiss and trans. by H. B. Nisbet (Cambridge, The University Press, 1970), pp. 73–87. See Georges Vlachos, *La Pensée politique de Kant* (Paris, Presses Universitaires de France, 1962), pp. 326–335; and J. G. Murphy, *Kant; The Philosophy of Right* (London, Macmillan, 1970), pp. 109–112, 133–136, for a further discussion.

Anarchy, State, and Utopia
R. Nozick

Rights and the Entitlement Theory

Individuals have rights, and there are things no person or group may do to them (without violating their rights). So strong and far-reaching are these rights that they raise the question of what, if anything, the state and its officials may do. How much room do individual rights leave for the state? The nature of the state, its legitimate functions and its justifications, if any, is the central concern of this book; a wide and diverse variety of topics intertwine in the course of our investigation.

Our main conclusions about the state are that a minimal state, limited to the narrow functions of protection against force, theft, fraud, enforcement of contracts, and so on, is justified; that any more extensive state will violate persons' rights not to be forced to do certain things, and is unjustified, and that the minimal state is inspiring as well as right. Two noteworthy implications are that the state may not use its coercive apparatus for the purpose of getting some citizens to aid others, or in order to prohibit activities to people for their *own* good or protection. . . .

(continued)

Anarchy, State, and Utopia (*continued*)

Why Side Constraints?

. . . What is the rationale for placing the nonviolation of rights as a side constraint upon action?

Side constraints upon action reflect the underlying Kantian principle that individuals are ends and not merely means; they may not be sacrificed or used for the achieving of other ends without their consent. Individuals are inviolable. More should be said to illuminate this talk of ends and means. . . . In getting pleasure from seeing an attractive person go by, does one use the other solely as a means? Does someone so use an object of sexual fantasies? These and related questions raise very interesting issues for moral philosophy; but not, I think, for political philosophy.

Political philosophy is concerned only with *certain* ways that persons may not use others; primarily, physically aggressing against them. A specific side constraint upon action toward others expresses the fact that others may not be used in the specific ways the side constraint excludes. Side constraints express the inviolability of others, in the ways they specify. These modes of inviolability are expressed by the following injunction: "Don't use people in specified ways." An end-state view, on the other hand, would express the view that people are ends and not merely means (if it chooses to express this view at all), by a different injunction: "Minimize the use in specified ways of persons as means." Following this percept itself may involve using someone as a means in one of the ways specified. Had Kant held this view, he would have given the second formula of the categorical imperative as, "So act as to minimize the use of humanity simply as a means," rather than the one he actually used: "Act in such a way that you always treat humanity, whether in your own person or in the person of any other, never simply as a means, but always at the same time as an end."

Side constraints express the inviolability of other persons. But why may not one violate persons for the greater social good? Individually, we each sometimes choose to undergo some pain or sacrifice for a greater benefit or to avoid a greater harm: we go to the dentist to avoid worse suffering later; we do some unpleasant work for its results; some persons diet to improve their health or looks; some save money to support themselves when they are older. In each case, some cost is borne for the sake of the greater overall good. Why not, *similarly* hold that some persons have to bear some costs that benefit other persons more, for the sake of the overall social good? But there is no *social entity* with a good that undergoes some sacrifice for its own good. There are only individual people, different individual people, with their own individual lives. Using one of these people for the benefit of others, uses him and benefits the others. Nothing more. What happens is that something is done to him for the sake of others. Talk of an overall social good covers this up. (Intentionally?) To use a person in this way does not sufficiently respect and take account of the fact that he is a separate person, that his is the only life he has. *He* does not get some overbalancing good from his sacrifice, and no one is entitled to force this upon him—least of all a state or government that claims his allegiance (as other individuals do not) and that therefore scrupulously must be *neutral* between its citizens. . . .

Distributive Justice

The term "distributive justice" is not a neutral one. Hearing the term "distribution," most people presume that some thing or mechanism uses some principle or criterion to give out a supply of things. Into this process of distributing shares some error may have crept. So it is an open question, at least, whether *re*distribution should take place; whether we should do again what has already been done once, though poorly. However, we are not in the position of children who have been given portions of pie by someone who now makes last minute adjustments to rectify careless cutting. There is no *central* distribution, no person or group entitled to control all the resources, (jointly) deciding how they are to be doled out. What each person gets, he gets from others who give to him in exchange for something, or as a gift. In a free society, diverse persons control different resources, and new holdings arise out of the voluntary exchanges and actions of persons. There is no more a distributing or distribution of shares than there is a distributing of mates in a society in which persons choose whom they shall marry. The total result is the product of many individual decisions which the different individuals involved are entitled to make. Some uses of the term "distribution," it is true, do not imply a previous distributing appropriately judged by some criterion (e.g., "probability distribution"); nevertheless, despite the title of this essay, it would be best to use a terminology that clearly is neutral. We shall speak of people's holdings; a principle of justice in holdings describes (part of) what justice tells us (requires) about holdings. I shall state first what I take to be the correct view about justice in holdings, and then turn to the discussion of alternative views.

The Entitlement Theory

The subject of justice in holdings consists of three major topics. The first is the *original acquisition of holdings*, the appropriation of unheld things. This includes the issues of how unheld things may come to be held, the process(es) by which unheld things may come to be held, the things that may come to be held by these processes, the extent of what comes to be held by a particular process, and so on. We shall refer to the complicated truth about this topic, which we shall not formulate here, as the principle of justice in acquisition. The second topic concerns the *transfer of holdings* from one person to another. By what processes may a person transfer holdings to another? How may a person acquire a holding from another who holds it? Under this topic come general descriptions of voluntary exchange, and gift, and (on the other hand) fraud, as well as reference to particular conventional details fixed upon a given society. The complicated truth about this subject (with placeholders for conventional details) we shall call the principle of justice in transfer. (And we shall suppose it also includes principles governing how a person may divest himself of a holding, passing it into an unheld state.)

If the world were wholly just, the following inductive definition would exhaustively cover the subject of justice in holdings.

1. A person who acquires a holding in accordance with the principle of justice in acquisition is entitled to that holding.
2. A person who acquires a holding in accordance with the principle of justice in transfer. From someone else entitled to the holding, is entitled to the holding.
3. No one is entitled to a holding except by (repeated) applications of 1 and 2.

The complete principle of distributive justice would say simply that a distribution is just if everyone is entitled to the holdings they possess under the distribution.

A distribution is just if it arises from another (just) distribution by legitimate means. The legitimate means of moving from one distribution to another are specified by the principle of justice in transfer. The legitimate first "moves" are specified by the principle of justice in acquisition.[1] Whatever arises from a just situation by just steps is itself just. The means of change specified by the principle of justice in transfer, preserve justice. As correct rules of inference are truth preserving, and any conclusion deduced via repeated application of such rules from only true premisses is itself true, so the means of transition from one situation to another specified by the principle of justice in transfer are justice preserving, and any situation actually arising from repeated transitions in accordance with the principle from a just situation is itself just. The parallel between justice-preserving transformations and truth-preserving transformations illuminates where it fails as well as where it holds. That a conclusion could have been deduced by truth-preserving means from premisses that are true suffices to show its truth. That from a just situation a situation *could* have arisen via justice-preserving means does *not* suffice to show its justice. The fact that a thief's victims voluntarily *could* have presented him with gifts does not entitle the thief to his ill-gotten gains. Justice in holdings is historical; it depends upon what actually has happened. We shall return to this point later.

Not all actual situations are generated in accordance with the two principles of justice in holdings: the principle of justice in acquisition and the principle of justice in transfer. Some people steal from others, or defraud them, or enslave them seizing their product and preventing them from living as they choose, or forcibly exclude others from competing in exchanges. None of these are permissible modes of transition from one situation to another. And some persons acquire holdings by means not sanctioned by the principle of justice in acquisition. The existence of past injustice (previous violations of the first two principles of justice in holdings) raises the third major topic under justice in holdings: the rectification of injustice in holdings. If past injustice has shaped present holdings in various ways, some identifiable and some not, what now, if anything, ought to be done to rectify these injustices? What obligations are the performers of injustice under to their victims? What obligations do the beneficiaries of injustice have to those whose position is worse than

(continued)

Anarchy, State, and Utopia (continued)

it would have been had the injustice not been done? Or, than it would have been had compensation been paid promptly? How, if at all, do things change if the beneficiaries and those made worse off are not the direct parties in the act of injustice, but, for example, their descendants? Is an injustice done to someone whose holding was itself based upon an unrectified injustice? How far back must one go in wiping clean the historical slate of injustices? What may victims of injustice permissibly do in order to rectify the injustices being done to them, including the many injustices done by persons acting through their government? I do not know of a thorough or theoretically sophisticated treatment of such issues. Idealizing greatly, let us suppose theoretical investigation will produce a principle of rectification. This principle uses historical information about previous situations and injustices done in them (as defined by the first two principles of justice, and rights against interference), and information about the actual course of events that flowed from these injustices, up until the present, and it yields a description (or descriptions) of holdings in the society. The principle of rectification presumably will make use of (its best estimate of) subjunctive information about what would have occurred (or a probability distribution over what might have occurred, using the expected value) if the injustice had not taken place. If the actual description of holdings turns out not to be one of the descriptions yielded by the principle, then one of the descriptions yielded must be realized.[2]

The general outlines of the theory of justice in holding are that the holdings of a person are just if he is entitled to them by the principles of justice in acquisition and transfer, or by the principle of rectification of injustice (as specified by the first two principles). If each person's holdings are just then the total set (distribution) of holdings is just. To turn these general outlines into a specific theory we would have to specify the details of each of the three principles of justice in holdings; the principle of acquisition of holdings, the principle of transfer of holdings, and the first two principles. I shall not attempt that task here . . . .

Historical Principles and End-Result Principles

The general outlines of the entitlement theory illuminate the nature and defects of other conceptions of distributive justice. The entitlement theory of justice in distribution is *historical*; whether a distribution is just depends upon how it came about. In contrast, *current time-slice principles* of justice hold that the justice of a distribution is determined by how things are distributed (who has what) as judged by some *structural* principle(s) of just distribution. A utilitarian who judges between any two distributions by seeing which has the greater sum of utility and, if these tie, who applies some fixed equality criterion to choose the more equal distribution, would hold a current time-slice principle of justice. As would someone who had a fixed schedule of trade-offs between the sum of happiness and equality. All that needs to be looked at, in judging the justice of a distribution, according to a current time-slice principle, is who ends up with what; in comparing any two distributions one need took, only at the matrix presenting the distributions. No further information need be fed into a principle of justice. It is a consequence of such principles of justice that any two structurally identical distributions are equally just. (Two distributions are structurally identical if they present the same profile, but (perhaps) have different persons occupying the particular slots. My having ten and your having five, and my having five and your having ten are structurally identical distributions.) Welfare economics is the theory of current time-slice principles of justice. The subject is conceived as operating on matrices representing only current information about distribution. This, as well as some of the usual conditions (e.g., the choice of distribution is invariant under relabeling of columns), guarantees that welfare economics will be a current time-slice theory, with all of its inadequacies.

Most persons do not accept current time-slice principles as constituting the whole story about distributive shares. They think it relevant in assessing the justice of a situation to consider not only the distribution it embodies, but also how that distribution came about. If some persons are in prison for murder or war crimes, we do not say that to assess the justice of the distribution in the society we must look only at what this person has, and that person has, and that person has . . . , at the current time. We think it relevant to ask whether someone did something so that he *deserved* to be punished, deserved to have a lower share. Most will agree to the relevance of further information with regard to punishments and penalties. Consider also desired things. One traditional socialist view is that workers are entitled to the product and full fruits of their labor; they have earned it; a distribution is unjust if it does not give the workers what they are entitled to. Such entitlements are based upon some past history. No socialist holding this view would find it comforting to be told that because the actual distribution *A* happens to coincide structurally with the one he desires *D*, *A* therefore is no less just than *D*; it differs only in that the "parasitic" owners of capital receive under, *A* what the workers are entitled to under *D*, and the workers receive under *A* what the owners are entitled to (under *D*), namely very little. Rightly in my view, this socialist holds onto the notions of earning, producing, entitlement, desert, etc. and he rejects (current time-slice) principles that look only to the structure of the resulting set of holdings. (The set of holdings resulting from what? Isn't it implausible that how holdings are produced and come to exist has no effect at all on who should hold what?) His mistake lies in his view of what entitlements arise out of what sorts of productive processes.

We construe the position we discuss too narrowly by speaking of *current* time-slice principles. Nothing is changed if structural principles operate upon a tune sequence of current time-slice profiles and, for example, give someone more now to counterbalance the less he has had earlier. A utilitarian or an egalitarian or any mixture of the two over time will inherit the difficulties of his more myopic comrades. He is not helped by the fact that *some* of the information others consider relevant in assessing a distribution is reflected, unrecoverably, in past matrices Henceforth, we shall refer to such unhistorical principles of distributive justice, including the current time-slice principles, as *end-result principles* or *end-state principles*.

In contrast to end-result principles of justice, *historical principles* of justice hold that past circumstances or actions of people can create differential entitlements or differential deserts to things. An injustice can be worked by moving from one distribution to another structurally identical one, for the second, in profile the same, may violate people's entitlements or deserts; it may not fit the actual history.

Patterning

The entitlement principles of justice in holdings that we have sketched are historical principles of justice. To better understand their precise character, we shall distinguish them from another subclass of the historical principles. Consider, as an example, the principle of distribution according to moral merit. This principle requires total distributive shares to vary directly with moral merit; no person should have a greater share than anyone whose moral merit is greater. (If moral merit could be not merely ordered but measured on an interval or ratio scale, stronger principles could be formulated.) Or consider the principle that results by substituting "usefulness to society" for "moral merit" in the previous principle. Or instead of "distribute according to moral merit," or "distribute according to moral merit," or "distribute according to usefulness to society," we might consider "distribute according to the weighted sum of moral merit, usefulness to society, and need," with the weights of the different dimensions equal. Let us call a principle of distribution *patterned* if it specifies that a distribution is to vary along with some natural dimension, weighted sum of natural dimensions, or lexicographic ordering of natural dimensions. And let us say a distribution is patterned if it accords with some patterned principle. (I speak of natural dimensions, admittedly without a general criterion for them, because for any set of holdings some artificial dimensions can be gimmicked up to vary along with the distribution of the set.) The principle of distribution in accordance with moral merit is a patterned historical principle, which specifies a patterned distribution. "Distribute according to I.Q." is a patterned principle that looks to information not contained in distributional matrices. It is not historical, however, in that it does not look to any past actions creating differential entitlements to evaluate a distribution; it requires only distributional matrices whose columns are labeled by I.Q. scores. The distribution in a society, however, may be composed of such simple patterned distributions, without itself being simply patterned. Different sectors may operate different patterns, or some combination of patterns may operate in different proportions across a society. A distribution composed in this manner, from a small number of patterned distributions, we also shall term patterned. And we extend the use of "pattern" to include the overall designs put forth by combinations of end-state principles.

(continued)

Anarchy, State, and Utopia   (*continued*)

Almost every suggested principle of distributive justice is patterned: to each according to his moral merit, or needs, or marginal product, or how hard he tries, on the weighted sum of the foregoing, and son on. The principle of entitlement we have sketched is *not* patterned.[3] There is no one natural dimension or weighted sum or combination of (a small number of) natural dimensions that yields the distributions generated in accordance with the principle of entitlement. The set of holdings that results when some persons receive their marginal products, others win at gambling, others receive a share of their mate's income, others receive gifts from foundations, others receive interest on loans, others receive gifts from admirers, others receive returns on investment, others make for themselves much of what they have, others find things, and so on, will not be patterned. Heavy strands of patterns will run through it; significant portions of the variance in holdings will be accounted for by pattern variables. If most people most of the time choose to transfer some of their entitlements to others only in exchange for something from them, then a large part of what many people hold will vary with what they held that others wanted. More details are provided by the theory of marginal productivity. But gifts to relatives, charitable donations, bequests to children, and the like, are not best conceived, in the first instance, in this manner. Ignoring the strands of pattern, let us suppose for the moment that a distribution actually gotten by the operation of the principle of entitlement is random with respect to any pattern. Though the resulting set of holdings will be unpatterned, it will not be incomprehensible, for it can be seen as arising from the operation of a small number of principles. These principles specify how an initial distribution may arise (the principle of acquisition of holdings) and how distributions may be transformed into others (the principle of transfer of holdings). The process whereby the set of holdings is generated will be intelligible, though the set of holdings itself that results from this process will be unpatterned. . . .

How Liberty Upsets Patterns

It is not clear how those holding alternative conceptions of distributive justice can reject the entitlement conception of justice in holdings. For suppose a distribution favored by one of these nonentitlement conceptions is realized. Let us suppose it is your favorite one and call this distribution D_1; perhaps everyone has an equal share, perhaps shares vary in accordance with some dimension you treasure. Now suppose that Wilt Chamberlain is greatly in demand by basketball teams, being a great gate-attraction. (Also suppose contracts run only for a year, with players being free agents. He signs the following sort of contract with a team: In each home game, twenty-five cents from the price of each ticket of admission goes to him. (We ignore the question of whether he is "gouging" the owners, letting them look out for themselves.) The season starts, and people cheerfully attend his team's games; they buy their tickets, each time dropping a separate twenty-five cents of their admission price into a special box with Chamberlain's name on it. They are excited about seeing him play; it is worth the total admission price to them. Let us suppose that in one season one million persons attend his home games, and Wilt Chamberlain winds up with $250,000, a much larger sum than the average income and larger even than anyone else has. Is he entitled to this income? Is this new distribution D_2, unjust? If so, why? There is *no* question about whether each of the people was entitled to the control over the resources they held, in D_1, because that was the distribution (your favorite) that (for the purposes of argument) we assumed was acceptable. Each of these persons *chose* to give twenty-five cents of their money to Chamberlain. They could have spent it on going to the movies, or on candy bars, or on copies of *Dissent* magazine, or of *Monthly Review*. But they all, at least one million of them, converged on giving it to Wilt Chamberlain in exchange for watching him play basketball. If D_1 was a just distribution, and people voluntarily moved from it to D_2, transferring parts of their shares they were given under D_1 (what was it for if not to do something with?), isn't D_2 also just? If the people were entitled to dispose of the resources to which they were entitled (under D_1), didn't this include their being entitled to give it to, or exchange it with, Will Chamberlain? Can anyone else complain on grounds of justice? Each other person already has his legitimate share under D_1. Under D_1 there is nothing that anyone has that anyone else has a claim of justice against. After someone transfers something to Wilt Chamberlain, third parties *still* have their legitimate shares; *their* shares are not changed. By what process could such a transfer among two persons give rise to a legitimate claim of distributive justice on a portion of what was transferred, by a third party who had no claim of justice on any holding of the others *before* the transfer?[4] To cut off objections irrelevant here, we might imagine the exchanges occurring in a socialist society, after hours. After playing whatever basketball he does in his daily work, or doing whatever other daily work he does, Wilt Chamberlain decides to put in *overtime* to earn additional money. (First his work quota is set; he works time over than.) Or imagine it is a skilled juggler people like to see, who puts on shows after hours.

Why might some people work overtime in a society in which it is assumed their needs are satisfied? Perhaps because they care about things other than needs. I like to write in books that I read, and to have easy access to books for browsing at odd hours. It would be very pleasant and convenient to have the resources of Widener Library in my back yard. No society, I assume, will provide such resources close to each person who would like them as part of his regular allotment (under D_1). Thus, persons either must do without some extra things that they want, or be allowed to do something extra to get (some of) these things. On what basis could the inequalities that would eventuate be forbidden? Notice also that small factories would spring up in a socialist society, unless forbidden. I melt down some of my personal possessions (under D_1) and build a machine out of the material. I offer you, and others, a philosophy lecture once a week in exchange for your cranking the handle on my machine, whose products I exchange for yet other things, and so on. (The raw materials used by the machine are given to me by others who possess them under D_1, in exchange for hearing lectures.) Each person might participate to gain things over and above their allotment under D_1. Some persons even might want to leave their job in socialist industry, and work full time in this private sector. I say something more about these issues elsewhere. Here I wish merely to note how private property, even in means of production, would occur in a socialist society that did not forbid people to use as they wished some of the resources they are given under the socialist distribution D_1. The socialist society would have to forbid capitalist acts between consenting adults.[5]

The general point illustrated by the Wilt Chamberlain example and the example of the entrepreneur in a socialist society is that no end-state principle or distributional pattern principle of justice can be continuously realized without continuous interference into people's lives. Any favored pattern would be transformed into one unfavored by the principle, by people choosing to act in various ways; e.g., by people exchanging goods and services with other people, or giving things to other people, things the transferrers are entitled to under the favored distributional pattern. To maintain a pattern one must either continuously interfere to stop people from transferring resources as they wish to, or continually (or periodically) interfere to take from some persons resources that others for some reason chose to transfer to them. (But if some time limit is to be set on how long people may keep resources others voluntarily transfer to them, why let them keep these resources for *any* period of time? Why not have immediate confiscation?) It might be objected that all persons voluntarily will choose to refrain from actions which would upset the pattern. This presupposes unrealistically (a) that all will most want to maintain the pattern (are those who don't, to be "reeducated" or forced to undergo "self-criticism"?); (b) that each can gather enough information about his own actions and the ongoing activities of others to discover which of his actions will upset the pattern; and (c) that diverse and farflung persons can coordinate their actions to dovetail into the pattern. Compare the manner in which the market is neutral among persons' desires, as it reflects and transmits widely scattered information via prices, and coordinates persons' activities. . . .

Redistribution and Property Rights

Apparently patterned principles allow people to choose to expend upon themselves, but not upon others, those resource they are entitled to (or rather, receive) under some favored distributional pattern D_1. For if each of several persons chooses to expend some of his D_1 resources upon one other person, then that other person will receive more than his D_1 share, disturbing the favored distributional pattern. Maintaining a distributional pattern is individualism with a vengeance! Patterned distributional principles do not give people what entitlement principles do, only better distributed. For they do not give the right to choose what to do with what one has; they do not give the right to choose to pursue an end involving (intrinsically, or as a means) the enhancement of another's position. To such

(continued)

Anarchy, State, and Utopia   (continued)

views, families are distributing; for within a family occur transfers that upset the favored distributional pattern. Either families themselves become units to which distribution takes place, the column occupiers (on what rationale?), or loving behavior is forbidden. We should note in passing the ambivalent position of radicals towards the family. Its loving relationships are seen as a model to be emulated and extended across the whole society, while it is denounced as a suffocating institution to be broken, and condemned as a focus of parochial concerns that interfere with achieving radical goals. Need we say that it is not appropriate to enforce across the wider society the relationship of love and care appropriate within family, relationships which are voluntarily undertaken? Incidentally, love is an interesting instance of another relationship that is historical, in that (like justice) it depends upon what actually occurred. An adult may come to love another because of the other's characteristics, but it is the other person, and not the characteristics, that is loved. The love is not transferable to someone else with the same characteristics, even to one who "scores" higher for these characteristics. And the love endures through changes of the characteristics that gave rise to it. One loves the particular person one actually encountered. Why love is historical, attaching to persons in this way and not to characteristics, is an interesting and puzzling question.

Proponents of patterned principles of distributive justice focus upon criteria for determining who is to receive holdings; they consider the reasons for which someone should have something, and also the total picture of holdings. Whether or not it is better to give than to receive, proponents of patterned principles ignore giving altogether. In considering the distribution of goods, income, etc., their theories are theories of recipient-justice; they completely ignore any right a person might have to give something to someone. Even in exchanges where each party is simultaneously giver and recipient, patterned principles of justice focus only upon the recipient role and its supposed rights. Thus discussions tend to focus on whether people (should) have a right to inherit, rather than on whether people (should) have a right to bequeath or on whether persons who have a right to hold also have a right to choose that others hold in their place. I lack a good explanation of why the usual theories of distributive justice are so recipient-oriented; ignoring givers and transferrers and their rights is of a piece with ignoring producers and their entitlements. But why is it *all* ignored?

Patterned principles of distributive justice necessitate *re*distributive activities. The likelihood is small that any actual freely arrived at set of holdings fits a given pattern; and the likelihood is nil that it will continue to fit the pattern as people exchange and give. From the point of view of an entitlement theory, redistribution is a serious mater indeed, involving, as it does the violation of people's rights. (An exception is those takings that fall under the principle of the rectification of injustices.) From other points of view, also, it is serious.

Taxation of earnings from labor is on a par with forced labor.[6] Some persons find this claim obviously true: taking the earnings of *n* hours labor is like taking n hours from the person; it is like forcing the person to work *n* hours for another's purpose. Others find the claim absurd. But even these, *if* they object to forced labour, would oppose forcing unemployed hippies to work for the benefit of the needy. And they also would object to forcing each person to work five extra hours each week for the benefit of the needy. But a system that takes five hours, wages in taxes does not seem to them like one that forces someone to work five hours, since it offers the person forced a wider range of choice in activities than does taxation in kind with the particular labor specified. (But we can imagine a gradation of systems of forced labor, from one that specifies a particular activity, to one that gives a choice among two activities, to . . .; and so on up.) Furthermore, people envisage a system with something like a proportional tax on everything above the amount necessary for basic needs. Some think this does not force someone to work extra hours, since there is no fixed number of extra hours he is forced to work, and since he can avoid the tax entirely by earning only enough to cover his basic needs. This is a very uncharacteristic view of forcing for those who *also* think people are forced to do something *whenever* the alternatives they face are considerably worse. However, *neither* view is correct. The fact that others intentionally intervene, in violation of a side-constraint against aggression to threaten force to limit the alternatives, in this case to paying taxes or (presumably the worse alternative) bare subsistence, makes the taxation system one of forced labor, and distinguishes it from other cases of limited choices which are not forcings.[7]

The man who chooses to work longer to gain an income more than sufficient for his basic needs prefers some extra goods or services to the leisure and activities he could perform during the possible non-working hours; whereas the man who chooses not to work the extra time prefers the leisure activities to the extra goods or services he could acquire by working more. Given this, if it would be illegitimate for a tax system to seize some of a man's leisure (forced labor) for the purpose of serving the needy, how can it be legitimate for a tax system to seize some of a man's goods for that purpose? Why should we treat the man whose happiness requires certain material goods or services differently from the man whose preferences and desires make such goods unnecessary for his happiness? Why should the man who prefers seeing a movie (and who has to earn money for a ticket) be open to the required call to aid the needy, while the person who prefers looking at a sunset (and hence need earn no extra money) is not? Indeed, isn't it surprising that redistributionists choose to ignore the man whose pleasures are so easily attainable without extra labor, while adding yet another burden to the poor unfortunate who must work for his pleasures? If anything, one would have expected the reverse. Why is the person with the nonmaterial or nonconsumption desire allowed to proceed unimpeded to his most favored feasible alternative, whereas the man whose pleasures or desires involve material things and who must work for extra money (thereby serving whoever considers his activities valuable enough to pay him) is constrained in what he can realize? Perhaps there is no difference in principle. And perhaps some think the answer concerns merely administrative convenience. (These questions and issues will not disturb those who think forced labor to serve the needy or realize some favored end-state pattern acceptable.) In a fuller discussion we would have (and want) to extend our argument to include interest, entrepreneurial profits, etc. Those who doubt that this extension can be carried through, and who draw the line here at taxation of income from labor, will have to state rather complicated patterned *historical* principles of distributive justice, since end-state principles would not distinguish *sources* of income in any way. It is enough for now to get away from end-state principles and to make clear how various patterned principles are dependent upon particular views about the sources or the illegitimacy or the lesser legitimacy of profits, interest, etc.; which particular views may well be mistaken.

What sort of right over others does a legally institutionalized end-state pattern give one? The central core of the notion of a property right in *X*, relative to which other parts of the notion are to be explained, is the right to determine what shall be done with *X*; the right to choose which of the constrained set of options concerning *X* shall be realized or attempted.[8] The constraints are set by other principles or laws operating in the society; in our theory by the Lockean rights people possess (under the minimal state). My property rights in my knife allow me to leave it where I will, but not in your chest. I may choose which of the acceptable options involving the knife is to be realized. This notion of property helps us to understand why earlier theorists spoke of people as having property in themselves and their labor. They viewed each person as having a right to decide what would become of himself and what he would do, and as having a right to reap the benefits of what he did.

This right of selecting the alternative to be realized from the constrained set of alternatives may be held by an *individual* or by a *group* with some procedure for reaching a joint decision; or the right may be passed back and forth, so that one year I decide what's to become of *X*, and the next year you do (with the alternative of destruction, perhaps, being excluded). Or, during the same time period, some types of decisions about *X* may be made by me, and others by you. And so on. We lack an adequate, fruitful, analytical apparatus for classifying the *types* of constraints on the set of options among which choices are to be made, and the *types* of ways decision powers can be held, divided, and amalgamated. A *theory* of property would, among other things, contain such a classification of constraints and decision modes, and from a small number of principles would follow a host of interesting statements about the *consequences* and effects of certain combinations of constraints and modes of decision.

When end-result principles of distributive justice are built into the legal structure of a society, they (as do most patterned principles) give each citizen an enforceable claim to some portion of the total social product; that is, to some portion of the sum total of the individually and jointly made products. This total product is produced by individuals laboring, using means of production others have saved to

(continued)

Anarchy, State, and Utopia   (continued)

bring into existence, by people organizing production or creating means to produce new things or things in a new way. It is on this batch of individual activities that patterned distributional principles give each individual an enforceable claim. Each person has a claim to the activities and the products of other persons, independently of whether the other persons enter into particular relationships that give rise to these claims, and independently of whether they voluntarily take these claims upon themselves, in charity or in exchange for something.

Whether it is done trough taxation on wages or on wages over a certain amount, or through seizure of profits, or through there being a big *social pot* so that it's not clear what's coming from where and what's going where, patterned principles of distributive justice involve appropriating the actions of other persons. Seizing the results of some one's labor is equivalent to seizing hours from him and directing him to carry on various activities. If people force you to do certain work, or unrewarded work, for a certain period of time, they decide what you are to do and what purposes your work is to serve apart from your decisions. This process whereby they take this decision from you makes them a *part owner* of you; it gives them a property right in you. Just as having such partial control and power of decision, by right, over an animal or inanimate object would be to have a property right in it.

End-state and most patterned principles of distributive justice institute (partial) ownership by others of people and their actions and labor. These principles involve a shift from the classical liberals, notion of self-ownership to a notion of (partial) property rights in *other* people.

Considerations such as these confront end-state and other patterned conceptions of justice with the question of whether the actions necessary to achieve he selected pattern don't themselves violate moral side-constraints. Any view holding that there are moral side-constraints on actions, that not all moral considerations can be built into end-states that are to be achieved,[9] must face the possibility that some of its goals are not achievable by any morally permissible available means. An entitlement theorist will face such conflicts in a society that deviates from the principles of justice for the generation of holdings, if and only if the only actions available to realize the principles themselves violate some moral constraints. Since deviation from the first two principles of justice (in acquisition and transfer) will involve other persons direct and aggressive intervention to violate rights, and since moral constraints will not exclude defensive or retributive action in such cases, the entitlement theorist's problem rarely will be pressing. And whatever difficulties he has in applying the principle of rectification to persons who did not themselves violate the first two principles, are difficulties in balancing the conflicting considerations so as correctly to formulate the complex principle of rectification itself; he will not violate moral side-constraints by applying the principle. Proponents of patterned conceptions of justice, however, often will face head-on clashes (and poignant ones if they cherish each party to the clash) between moral side constraints on how individuals may be treated on the one hand and, on the other, their patterned conception of justice that presents an end-state or other pattern that *must* be realized.

NOTES

1. Applications of the principle of justice in acquisition may also occur as part of the move from one distribution to another. You may find an unheld thing now, and appropriate it. Acquisitions also are to be understood as included when, to simplify, I speak only of transitions by transfers.
2. If the principle of rectification of violations of the first two principles yields more than one description of holdings, then some choice must be made as to which of these is to be realized. Perhaps the sort of considerations about distributive justice and equality I argue against play a legitimate role in this subsidiary choice. Similarly, there may be room for such considerations in deciding which otherwise arbitrary features a statute will embody, when such features are unavoidable because other considerations do not specify a precise line, yet one must be drawn.
3. One might try to squeeze a patterned conception of distributive justice into the framework of the entitlement conception, by formulating a gimmicky obligatory 'principle of transfer' that would lead to the pattern. For example, the principle that it one has more than the mean income, one must transfer everything one holds above the mean to persons below the mean so as to bring them up (but not over) the mean. We can formulate a criterion for a 'principle of transfer' to rule out such obligatory transfers, or we can say

that no correct principle of transfer, no principle of transfer in a free society will be like this. The former is probably the better course, though the latter also is true. Alternatively, one might think to make the entitlement conception instantiate a pattern, by using matrix entries that express the relative strength of a person's entitlements as measured by some real-valued function. But even if the limitation to natural dimensions failed to exclude this function, the resulting edifice would *not* capture our system of entitlements to *particular* things.
4. Might not a transfer have instrumental effects on a third party, changing his feasible options? (But what if the two parties to the transfer independently had used their holdings in this fashion?) I discuss this question elsewhere, but note here that this question concedes the point for distributions of ultimate intrinsic non-instrumental goods (pure utility experiences, so to speak) that are transferrable. It also might be objected that the transfer might make a third party more envious because it worsens his position relative to someone else. I find it incomprehensible how it can be thought that this involves a claim of justice. On envy, see *Anarchy, State, and Utopia,* chap 8.

Here and elsewhere in this essay, a theory which incorporates elements of pure procedural justice might find what I say acceptable, *if* kept in its proper place; that is, if background institutions exist to ensure the satisfaction of certain conditions on distributive shares. But if these institutions are not themselves the sum of invisible-hand result of people's voluntary (nonaggresive) actions, the constraints they impose require justification. At no point does *our* argument assume any background institutions more extensive than those of the minimal night-watchman state, limited to protecting persons against murder, assault, theft, fraud, etc.
5. See the selection from John Henry Mackay's novel, *The Anarchists,* reprinted in Leonard Krimmerman and Lewis Perry, eds, *Patterns of Anarchy* (New York, 1966), pp 16-33, in which an individualist anarchist presses upon a communist anarchist the question: "Would you, in the system of society which you call 'free Communism' prevent individuals from exchanging their labor among themselves by means of their own medium of exchange? And further: Would you prevent them form occupying land for the purpose of personal use?" The novel continues: "[the] question was not to be escaped. If he answered 'Yes!' he admitted that society had the right of control over the individual and threw overboard the autonomy of the individual which he had always zealously defended; if on the other hand, he answered 'No!' he admitted the right of private property which he had just denied so emphatically. Then he answered 'In Anarchy any number of men must have the right of forming a voluntary association, and so realizing their ideas in practice. Not can I understand how any one could justly be driven from the land and house which he uses and occupies every serious man must declare himself; for Socialism, and thereby for force and against liberty, or for Anarchism, and thereby for liberty and against force.'" In contrast, we find Noam Chomsky writing. "Any consistent anarchist must oppose private ownership of the means of production," and "the consistent anarchist then will be a socialist of a particular sort" (Introduction to Daniel Guerin, *Anarchism From Theory to Practice* [New York, 1970], pp. xiii, xv)
6. I am unsure's to whether the arguments I present below show that such taxation just is forced labor; so that "is on a par with" means "is one kind of". Or alternatively, whether the arguments emphasize the great similarities between such taxation and forced labor, to show it is plausible and illuminating to view such taxation in the light of forced labor. This latter approach would remind one of how John Wisdom conceives of the claims us of metaphysicians.
7. Further details that this statement should include are contained in my essay. "Coercion," in *Philosophy, Science, and Method*, ed S Motgenbesser, P Suppes, and M White (New York, 1969)
8. On the themes in this and the next paragraph, see the writings of Armen Alchian
9. See *Anarchy, State, and Utopia,* chap 3

Discourse on Inequality
Jean-Jacques Rousseau

The Origin of Inequality

The Second Part

THE first man who, having enclosed a piece of ground, bethought himself of saying *This is mine,* and found people simple enough to believe him, was the real founder of *civil* society. From how many crimes, wars and murders, from how many horrors and misfortunes might not any one have saved

(continued)

Discourse on Inequality (*continued*)

mankind, by pulling up the stakes, or filling up the ditch, and crying to his fellows, "Beware of listening to this impostor; you are undone if you once forget that the fruits of the earth belong to us all, and the earth itself to nobody."

But there is great probability that things had then already come to such a pitch, that they could no longer continue as they were; for the idea of property depends on many prior ideas, which could only be acquired successively, and cannot have been formed all at once in the human mind. Mankind must have made very considerable progress, land acquired considerable knowledge and industry which they must also have transmitted and increased from age to age, before they arrived at this last point of the state of nature.

Let us then go farther back and endeavour to unify under a single point of view that slow succession of events and discoveries in the most natural order.

Man's first feeling was that of his own existence, and his first care that of self-preservation. The produce of the earth furnished him with all he needed, and instinct told him how to use it. Hunger and other appetites made him at various times experience various modes of existence; and among these was one which urged him to propagate his species—a blind propensity that, having nothing to do with the heart, produced a merely animal act. The want once gratified, the two sexes knew each other no more; and even the offspring was nothing to its mother, as soon as it could do without her.

Such was the condition of infant man; the life of an animal limited at first to mere sensations, and hardly profiting by the gifts nature bestowed on him, much less capable of entertaining a thought of forcing anything from her. But difficulties soon presented themselves, and it became necessary to learn how to surmount them: the height of the trees, which prevented him from gathering their fruits, the competition of other animals desirous of the same fruits, and the ferocity of those who needed them for their own preservation, all obliged him to apply himself to bodily exercises. He had to be active, swift of foot, and vigorous in fight. Natural weapons, stones and sticks, were easily found: he learnt to surmount the obstacles of nature, to contend in case of necessity with other animals, and to dispute for the means of subsistence even with other men, or to indemnify himself for what he was forced to give up to a stronger.

In proportion as the human race grew more numerous, men's cares increased. The difference of soils, climates and seasons, must have introduced some differences into their manner of living. Barren years, long and sharp winters, scorching summers which parched the fruits of the earth, must have demanded a new industry. On the seashore and the banks of rivers, they invented the hook and line, and became fishermen and eaters of fish. In the forests they made bows and arrows, and became huntsmen and warriors. In cold countries they clothed themselves with the skins of the beasts they had slain. The lightning, a volcano, or some lucky chance acquainted them with fire, a new resource against the rigours of winter: they next learned how to preserve this element, then how to reproduce it, and finally how to prepare with it the flesh of animals which before they had eaten raw.

This repeated relevance of various beings to himself, and one to another, would naturally give rise in the human mind to the perceptions of certain relations between them. Thus the relations which we denote by the terms, great, small, strong, weak, swift, slow, fearful, bold, and the like, almost insensibly compared at need, must have at length produced in him a kind of reflection, or rather a mechanical prudence, which would indicate to him the precautions most necessary to his security.

The new intelligence which resulted from this development increased his superiority over other animals, by making him sensible of it. He would now endeavour, therefore, to ensnare them, would play them a thousand tricks, and though many of them might surpass him in swiftness or in strength, would in time become the master of some and the scourge of others. Thus, the first time he looked into himself, he felt the first emotion of pride; and, at a time when he scarce knew how to distinguish the different orders of beings, by looking upon his species as of the highest order, he prepared the way for assuming pre-eminence as an individual.

Other men, it is true, were not then to him what they now are to us, and he had no greater intercourse with them than with other animals; yet they were not neglected in his observations. The conformities, which he would in time discover between them, and between himself and his female, led him to judge of others which were not then perceptible; and finding that they all behaved as he himself would have done in like circumstances, he naturally inferred that their manner of thinking and acting was altogether in conformity with his own. This important truth, once deeply impressed on his mind, must have induced him, from an intuitive feeling more certain and much more rapid than any kind of reasoning, to pursue the rules of conduct, which he had best observe towards them, for his own security and advantage.

Taught by experience that the love of well-being is the sole motive of human actions, he found himself in a position to distinguish the few cases, in which mutual interest might justify him in relying upon the assistance of his fellows; and also the still fewer cases in which a conflict of interests might give cause to suspect them. In the former case, he joined in the same herd with them, or at most in some kind of loose association, that laid no restraint on its members, and lasted no longer than the transitory occasion that formed it. In the latter case, every one sought his own private advantage, either by open force, if he thought himself strong enough, or by address and cunning, if he felt himself the weaker.

In this manner, men may have insensibly acquired some gross ideas of mutual undertakings, and of the advantages of fulfilling them: that is, just so far as their present and apparent interest was concerned: for they were perfect strangers to foresight, and were so far from troubling themselves about the distant future, that they hardly thought of the morrow. If a deer was to be taken, every one saw that, in order to succeed, he must abide faithfully by his post: but if a hare happened to come within the reach of any one of them, it is not to be doubted that he pursued it without scruple, and, having seized his prey, cared very little, if by so doing he caused his companions to miss theirs.

It is easy to understand that such intercourse would not require a language much more refined than that of rooks or monkeys, who associate together for much the same purpose. Inarticulate cries, plenty of gestures and some imitative sounds, must have been for a long time the universal language; and by the addition, in every country, of some conventional articulate sounds (of which, as I have already intimated, the first institution is not too easy to explain) particular languages were produced; but these were rude and imperfect, and nearly such as are now to be found among some savage nations.

Hurried on by the rapidity of time, by the abundance of things I have to say, and by the almost insensible progress of things in their beginnings, I pass over in an instant a multitude of ages; for the slower the events were in their succession, the more rapidly may they be described.

These first advances enabled men to make others with greater rapidity. In proportion as they grew enlightened, they grew industrious. They ceased to fall asleep under the first tree, or in the first cave that afforded them shelter; they invented several kinds of implements of hard and sharp stones, which they used to dig up the earth, and to cut wood; they then made huts out of branches, and afterwards learnt to plaster them over with mud and clay. This was the epoch of a first revolution, which established and distinguished families, and introduced a kind of property, in itself the source of a thousand quarrels and conflicts. As, however, the strongest were probably the first to build themselves huts which they felt themselves able to defend, it may be concluded that the weak found it much easier and safer to imitate, than to attempt to dislodge them: and of those who were once provided with huts, none could have any inducement to appropriate that of his neighbour; not indeed so much because it did not belong to him, as because it could be of no use, and he could not make himself master of it without exposing himself to a desperate battle with the family which occupied it.

The first expansions of the human heart were the effects of a novel situation, which united husbands and wives, fathers and children, under one roof. The habit of living together soon gave rise to the finest feelings known to humanity, conjugal love and paternal affection. Every family became a little society, the more united because liberty and reciprocal attachment were the only bonds of its union. The sexes, whose manner of life had been hitherto the same, began now to adopt different ways of living. The women became more sedentary, and accustomed themselves to mind the hut and their children, while the men went abroad in search of their common subsistence. From living a softer life, both sexes also began to lose something of their strength and ferocity: but, if individuals became to some extent less able to encounter wild beasts separately, they found it, on the other hand, easier to assemble and resist in common.

The simplicity and solitude of man's life in this new condition, the paucity of his wants, and the implements he had invented to satisfy them, left him a great deal of leisure, which he employed to

(continued)

Discourse on Inequality   (*continued*)

furnish himself with many conveniences unknown to his fathers: and this was the first yoke he inadvertently imposed on himself, and the first source of the evils he prepared for his descendants. For, besides continuing thus to enervate both body and mind, these conveniences lost with use almost all their power to please, and even degenerated into real needs, till the want of them became far more disagreeable than the possession of them had been pleasant. Men would have been unhappy at the loss of them, though the possession did not make them happy.

We can here see a little better how the use of speech became established, and insensibly improved in each family, and we may form a conjecture also concerning the manner in which various causes may have extended and accelerated the progress of language, by making it more and more necessary. Floods or earthquakes surrounded inhabited districts with precipices or waters: revolutions of the globe tore off portions from the continent, and made them islands. It is readily seen that among men thus collected and compelled to live together, a common idiom must have arisen much more easily than among those who still wandered through the forests of the continent. Thus it is very possible that after their first essays in navigation the islanders brought over the use of speech to the continent: and it is at least very probable that communities and languages were first established in islands, and even came to perfection there before they were known on the mainland.

Everything now begins to change its aspect. Men, who have up to now been roving in the woods, by taking to a more settled manner of life, come gradually together, form separate bodies, and at length in every country arises a distinct nation, united in character and manners, not by regulations or laws, but by uniformity of life and food, and the common influence of climate. Permanent neighbourhood could not fail to produce, in time, some connection between different families. Among young people of opposite sexes, living in neighbouring huts, the transient commerce required by nature soon led, through mutual intercourse, to another kind not less agreeable, and more permanent. Men began now to take the difference between objects into account, and to make comparisons; they acquired imperceptibly the ideas of beauty and merit, which soon gave rise to feelings of preference. In consequence of seeing each other often, they could not do without seeing each other constantly. A tender and pleasant feeling insinuated itself into their souls, and the least opposition turned it into an impetuous fury: with love arose jealousy; discord triumphed, and human blood was sacrificed to the gentlest of all passions.

As ideas and feelings succeeded one another, and heart and head were brought into play, men continued to lay aside their original wildness; their private connections became every day more intimate as their limits extended. They accustomed themselves to assemble before their huts round a large tree; singing and dancing, the true offspring of love and leisure, became the amusement, or rather the occupation, of men and women thus assembled together with nothing else to do. Each one began to consider the rest, and to wish to be considered in turn; and thus a value came to be attached to public esteem. Whoever sang or danced best, whoever was the handsomest, the strongest, the most dexterous, or the most eloquent, came to be of most consideration; and this was the first step towards inequality, and at the same time towards vice. From these first distinctions arose on the one side vanity and contempt and on the other shame and envy: and the fermentation caused by these new leavens ended by producing combinations fatal to innocence and happiness.

As soon as men began to value one another, and the idea of consideration had got a footing in the mind, every one put in his claim to it, and it became impossible to refuse it to any with impunity. Hence arose the first obligations of civility even among savages; and every intended injury became an affront; because, besides the hurt which might result from it, the party injured was certain to find in it a contempt for his person, which was often more insupportable than the hurt itself.

Thus, as every man punished the contempt shown him by others, in proportion to his opinion of himself, revenge became terrible, and men bloody and cruel. This is precisely the state reached by most of the savage nations known to us: and it is for want of having made a proper distinction in our ideas, and seen how very far they already are from the state of nature, that so many writers have hastily concluded that man is naturally cruel, and requires civil institutions to make him more mild; whereas nothing is more gentle than man in his primitive state, as he is placed by nature at an equal distance from the stupidity of brutes, and the fatal ingenuity of civilised man. Equally confined by instinct and reason to the sole care of guarding himself against the mischiefs which threaten him, he is restrained by natural compassion from doing any injury to others, and is not led to do such a thing even in return for injuries received. For, according to the axiom of the wise Locke, *There can be no injury, where there is no property.*

But it must be remarked that the society thus formed, and the relations thus established among men, required of them qualities different from those which they possessed from their primitive constitution. Morality began to appear in human actions, and every one, before the institution of law, was the only judge and avenger of the injuries done him, so that the goodness which was suitable in the pure state of nature was no longer proper in the new-born state of society. Punishments had to be made more severe, as opportunities of offending became more frequent, and the dread of vengeance had to take the place of the rigour of the law. Thus, though men had become less patient, and their natural compassion had already suffered some diminution, this period of expansion of the human faculties, keeping a just mean between the indolence of the primitive state and the petulant activity of our egoism, must have been the happiest and most stable of epochs. The more we reflect on it, the more we shall find that this state was the least subject to revolutions, and altogether the very best man could experience; so that he can have departed from it only through some fatal accident, which, for the public good, should never have happened. The example of savages, most of whom have been found in this state, seems to prove that men were meant to remain in it, that it is the real youth of the world, and that all subsequent advances have been apparently so many steps towards the perfection of the individual, but in reality towards the decrepitude of the species.

So long as men remained content with their rustic huts, so long as they were satisfied with clothes made of the skins of animals and sewn together with thorns and fishbones, adorned themselves only with feathers and shells, and continued to paint their bodies different colours, to improve and beautify their bows and arrows and to make with sharp-edged stones fishing boats or clumsy musical instruments; in a word, so long as they undertook only what a single person could accomplish, and confined themselves to such arts as did not require the joint labour of several hands, they lived free, healthy, honest and happy lives, so long as their nature allowed, and as they continued to enjoy the pleasures of mutual and independent intercourse. But from the moment one man began to stand in need of the help of another; from the moment it appeared advantageous to any one man to have enough provisions for two, equality disappeared, property was introduced, work became indispensable, and vast forests became smiling fields, which man had to water with the sweat of his brow, and where slavery and misery were soon seen to germinate and grow up with the crops.

Metallurgy and agriculture were the two arts which produced this great revolution. The poets tell us it was gold and silver, but, for the philosophers, it was iron and corn, which first civilised men, and ruined humanity. *Thus both were unknown to the savages of America, who for that reason are still* savage: the other nations also seem to have continued in a state of barbarism while they practised only one of these arts. One of the best reasons, perhaps, why Europe has been, if not longer, at least more constantly and highly civilised than the rest of the world, is that it is at once the most abundant in iron and the most fertile in corn.

It is difficult to conjecture how men first came to know and use iron; for it is impossible to suppose they would of themselves think of digging the ore out of the mine, and preparing it for smelting, before they knew what would be the result. On the other hand, we have the less reason to suppose this discovery the effect of any accidental fire, as mines are only formed in barren places, bare of trees and plants; so that it looks as if nature had taken pains to keep the fatal secret from us. There remains, therefore, only the extraordinary accident of some volcano which, by ejecting metallic substances already in fusion, suggested to the spectators the idea of imitating the natural operation. And we must further conceive them as possessed of uncommon courage and foresight, to undertake so laborious a work, with so distant a prospect of drawing advantage from it; yet these qualities are united only in minds more advanced than we can suppose those of these first discoverers to have been.

With regard to agriculture, the principles of it were known long before they were put in practice; and it is indeed hardly possible that men, constantly employed in drawing their subsistence from plants and trees, should not readily acquire a knowledge of the means made use of by nature for the propagation of vegetables. It was in all probability very long, however, before their industry took that turn, either because trees, which together with hunting and fishing afforded them food,

(continued)

Discourse on Inequality   (*continued*)

did not require their attention; or because they were ignorant of the use of corn, or without instruments to cultivate it; or because they lacked foresight to future needs; or lastly, because they were without means of preventing others from robbing them of the fruit of their labour.

When they grew more industrious, it is natural to believe that they began, with the help of sharp stones and pointed sticks, to cultivate a few vegetables or roots around their huts; though it was long before they knew how to prepare corn, or were provided with the implements necessary for raising it in any large quantity; not to mention how essential it is, for husbandry, to consent to immediate loss, in order to reap a future gain—a precaution very foreign to the turn of a savage's mind; for, as I have said, he hardly foresees in the morning what he will need at night.

The invention of the other arts must therefore have been necessary to compel mankind to apply themselves to agriculture. No sooner were artificers wanted to smelt and forge iron, than others were required to maintain them; the more hands that were employed in manufactures, the fewer were left to provide for the common subsistence, though the number of mouths to be furnished with food remained the same: and as some required commodities in exchange for their iron, the rest at length discovered the method of making iron serve for the multiplication of commodities. By this means the arts of husbandry and agriculture were established on the one hand, and the art of working metals and multiplying their uses on the other.

The cultivation of the earth necessarily brought about its distribution; and property, once recognised, gave rise to the first rules of justice; for, to secure each man his own, it had to be possible for each to have something. Besides, as men began to look forward to the future, and all had something to lose, every one had reason to apprehend that reprisals would follow any injury he might do to another. This origin is so much the more natural, as it is impossible to conceive how property can come from anything but manual labour: for what else can a man add to things which he does not originally create, so as to make them his own property? It is the husbandman's labour alone that, giving him a title to the produce of the ground he has tilled, gives him a claim also to the land itself, at least till harvest; and so, from year to year, a constant possession which is easily transformed into property. When the ancients, says Grotius, gave to Ceres the title of Legislatrix, and to a festival celebrated in her honour the name of Thesmophoria, they meant by that that the distribution of lands had produced a new kind of right: that is to say, the right of property, which is different from the right deducible from the law of nature.

In this state of affairs, equality might have been sustained, had the talents of individuals been equal, and had, for example, the use of iron and the consumption of commodities always exactly balanced each other; but, as there was nothing to preserve this balance, it was soon disturbed; the strongest did most work; the most skilful turned his labour to best account; the most ingenious devised methods of diminishing his labour: the husbandman wanted more iron, or the smith more corn, and, while both laboured equally, the one gained a great deal by his work, while the other could hardly support himself. Thus natural inequality unfolds itself insensibly with that of combination, and the difference between men, developed by their different circumstances, becomes more sensible and permanent in its effects, and begins to have an influence, in the same proportion, over the lot of individuals.

Matters once at this pitch, it is easy to imagine the rest. I shall not detain the reader with a description of the successive invention of other arts, the development of language, the trial and utilisation of talents, the inequality of fortunes, the use and abuse of riches, and all the details connected with them which the reader can easily supply for himself. I shall confine myself to a glance at mankind in this new situation.

Behold then all human faculties developed, memory and imagination in full play, egoism interested, reason active, and the mind almost at the highest point of its perfection. Behold all the natural qualities in action, the rank and condition of every man assigned him; not merely his share of property and his power to serve or injure others, but also his wit, beauty, strength or skill, merit or talents: and these being the only qualities capable of commanding respect, it soon became necessary to possess or to affect them.

It now became the interest of men to appear what they really were not. To be and to seem became two totally different things; and from this distinction sprang insolent pomp and cheating trickery, with all the numerous vices that go in their train. On the other hand, free and independent as men were before, they were now, in consequence of a multiplicity of new wants, brought into subjection, as it were, to all nature, and particularly to one another; and each became in some degree a slave even in becoming the master of other men: if rich, they stood in need of the services of others; if poor, of their assistance; and even a middle condition did not enable them to do without one another. Man must now, therefore, have been perpetually employed in getting others to interest themselves in his lot, and in making them, apparently at least, if not really, find their advantage in promoting his own. Thus he must have been sly and artful in his behaviour to some, and imperious and cruel to others; being under a kind of necessity to ill-use all the persons of whom he stood in need, when he could not frighten them into compliance, and did not judge it his interest to be useful to them. Insatiable ambition, the thirst of raising their respective fortunes, not so much from real want as from the desire to surpass others, inspired all men with a vile propensity to injure one another, and with a secret jealousy, which is the more dangerous, as it puts on the mask of benevolence, to carry its point with greater security. In a word, there arose rivalry and competition on the one hand, and conflicting interests on the other, together with a secret desire on both of profiting at the expense of others. All these evils were the first effects of property, and the inseparable attendants of growing inequality.

Before the invention of signs to represent riches, wealth could hardly consist in anything but lands and cattle, the only real possessions men can have. But, when inheritances so increased in number and extent as to occupy the whole of the land, and to border on one another, one man could aggrandise himself only at the expense of another; at the same time the supernumeraries, who had been too weak or too indolent to make such acquisitions, and had grown poor without sustaining any loss, because, while they saw everything change around them, they remained still the same, were obliged to receive their subsistence, or steal it, from the rich; and this soon bred, according to their different characters, dominion and slavery, or violence and rapine. The wealthy, on their part, had no sooner begun to taste the pleasure of command, than they disdained all others, and, using their old slaves to acquire new, thought of nothing but subduing and enslaving their neighbours; like ravenous wolves, which, having once tasted human flesh, despise every other food and thenceforth seek only men to devour.

Thus, as the most powerful or the most miserable considered their might or misery as a kind of right to the possessions of others, equivalent, in their opinion, to that of property, the destruction of equality was attended by the most terrible disorders. Usurpations by the rich robbery by the poor, and the unbridled passions of both, suppressed the cries of natural compassion and the still feeble voice of justice, and filled men with avarice, ambition and vice. Between the title of the strongest and that of the first occupier, there arose perpetual conflicts, which never ended but in battles and bloodshed. The new-born state of society thus gave rise to a horrible state of war; men thus harassed and depraved were no longer capable of retracing their steps or renouncing the fatal acquisitions they had made, but, labouring by the abuse of the faculties which do them honour, merely to their own confusion, brought themselves to the brink of ruin.

>Attonitus novitate mali, divesque miserque,
>Effugere optat opes; et quœ voverat odit.[1]

It is impossible that men should not at length have reflected on so wretched a situation, and on the calamities that overwhelmed them. The rich, in particular, must have felt how much they suffered by a constant state of war, of which they bore all the expense; and in which, though all risked their lives, they alone risked their property. Besides, however speciously they might disguise their usurpations, they knew that they were founded on precarious and false titles; so that, if others took from them by force what they themselves had gained by force, they would have no reason to complain. Even those who had been enriched by their own industry, could hardly base their proprietorship on better claims. It was in vain to repeat, "I built this well; I gained this spot by my industry." Who gave you your standing, it might be answered, and what right have you to demand payment of us for doing what we never asked you to do? Do you not know that numbers of your fellow-creatures are starving, for want of what you have too much of? You ought to have had the express and universal consent of mankind, before appropriating more of the common subsistence than you needed for your own maintenance. Destitute of valid reasons to justify and sufficient strength to

(continued)

Discourse on Inequality (*continued*)

defend himself, able to crush individuals with ease, but easily crushed himself by a troop of bandits, one against all, and incapable, on account of mutual jealousy, of joining with his equals against numerous enemies united by the common hope of plunder, the rich man, thus urged by necessity, conceived at length the profoundest plan that ever entered the mind of man: this was to employ in his favour the forces of those who attacked him, to make allies of his adversaries, to inspire them with different maxims, and to give them other institutions as favourable to himself as the law of nature was unfavourable.

With this view, after having represented to his neighbours the horror of a situation which armed every man against the rest, and made their possessions as burdensome to them as their wants, and in which no safety could be expected either in riches or in poverty, he readily devised plausible arguments to make them close with his design. "Let us join," said he, "to guard the weak from oppression, to restrain the ambitious, and secure to every man the possession of what belongs to him: let us institute rules of justice and peace, to which all without exception may be obliged to conform; rules that may in some measure make amends for the caprices of fortune, by subjecting equally the powerful and the weak to the observance of reciprocal obligations. Let us, in a word, instead of turning our forces against ourselves, collect them in a supreme power which may govern us by wise laws, protect and defend all the members of the association, repulse their common enemies, and maintain eternal harmony among us."

Far fewer words to this purpose would have been enough to impose on men so barbarous and easily seduced; especially as they had too many disputes among themselves to do without arbitrators, and too much ambition and avarice to go long without masters. All ran headlong to their chains, in hopes of securing their liberty; for they had just wit enough to perceive the advantages of political institutions, without experience enough to enable them to foresee the dangers. The most capable of foreseeing the dangers were the very persons who expected to benefit by them; and even the most prudent judged it not inexpedient to sacrifice one part of their freedom to ensure the rest; as a wounded man has his arm cut off to save the rest of his body.

Such was, or may well have been, the origin of society and law, which bound new fetters on the poor, and gave new powers to the rich; which irretrievably destroyed natural liberty, eternally fixed the law of property and inequality, converted clever usurpation into unalterable right, and, for the advantage of a few ambitious individuals, subjected all mankind to perpetual labour, slavery and wretchedness. It is easy to see how the establishment of one community made that of all the rest necessary, and how, in order to make head against united forces, the rest of mankind had to unite in turn. Societies soon multiplied and spread over the face of the earth, till hardly a corner of the world was left in which a man could escape the yoke, and withdraw his head from beneath the sword which he saw perpetually hanging over him by a thread. Civil right having thus become the common rule among the members of each community, the law of nature maintained its place only between different communities, where, under the name of the right of nations, it was qualified by certain tacit conventions, in order to make commerce practicable, and serve as a substitute for natural compassion, which lost, when applied to societies, almost all the influence it had over individuals, and survived no longer except in some great cosmopolitan spirits, who, breaking down the imaginary barriers that separate different peoples, follow the example of our Sovereign Creator, and include the whole human race in their benevolence.

But bodies politic, remaining thus in a state of nature among themselves, presently experienced the inconveniences which had obliged individuals to forsake it; for this state became still more fatal to these great bodies than it had been to the individuals of whom they were composed. Hence arose national wars, battles, murders, and reprisals, which shock nature and outrage reason; together with all those horrible prejudices which class among the virtues the honour of shedding human blood. The most distinguished men hence learned to consider cutting each other's throats a duty; at length men massacred their fellow-creatures by thousands without so much as knowing why, and committed more murders in a single day's fighting, and more violent outrages in the sack of a single town, than were committed in the state of nature during whole ages over the whole earth. Such were the first effects which we can see to have followed the division of mankind into different communities. But let us return to their institutions.

I know that some writers have given other explanations of the origin of political societies, such as the conquest of the powerful, or the association of the weak. It is, indeed, indifferent to my argument which of these causes we choose. That which I have just laid down, however, appears to me the most natural for the following reasons. First: because, in the first case, the right of conquest, being no right, in itself, could not serve as a foundation on which to build any other; the victor and the vanquished people still remained with respect to each other in the state of war, unless the vanquished, restored to the full possession of their liberty, voluntarily made choice of the victor for their chief. For till then, whatever capitulation may have been made being founded on violence, and therefore *ipso facto* void, there could not have been on this hypothesis either a real society or body politic, or any law other than that of the strongest. Secondly: because the words *strong* and *weak* are, in the second case, ambiguous; for during the interval between the establishment of a right of property, or prior occupancy, and that of political government, the meaning of these words is better expressed by the terms *rich* and *poor:* because, in fact, before the institution of laws, men had no other way of reducing their equals to submission, than by attacking their goods, or making some of their own over to them. Thirdly: because, as the poor had nothing but their freedom to lose, it would have been in the highest degree absurd for them to resign voluntarily the only good they still enjoyed, without getting anything in exchange: whereas the rich having feelings, if I may so express myself, in every part of their possessions, it was much easier to harm them, and therefore more necessary for them to take precautions against it; and, in short, because it is more reasonable to suppose a thing to have been invented by those to whom it would be of service, than by those whom it must have harmed.

Government had, in its infancy, no regular and constant form. The want of experience and philosophy prevented men from seeing any but present inconveniences, and they thought of providing against others only as they presented themselves. In spite of the endeavours of the wisest legislators, the political state remained imperfect, because it was little more than the work of chance; and, as it had begun ill, though time revealed its defects and suggested remedies, the original faults were never repaired. It was continually being patched up, when the first task should have been to get the site cleared and all the old materials removed, as was done by Lycurgus at Sparta, if a stable and lasting edifice was to be erected. Society consisted at first merely of a few general conventions, which every member bound himself to observe; and for the performance of covenants the whole body went security to each individual. Experience only could show the weakness of such a constitution, and how easily it might be infringed with impunity, from the difficulty of convicting men of faults, where the public alone was to be witness and judge: the laws could not but be eluded in many ways; disorders and inconveniences could not but multiply continually, till it became necessary to commit the dangerous trust of public authority to private persons, and the care of enforcing obedience to the deliberations of the people to the magistrate. For to say that chiefs were chosen before the confederacy was formed, and that the administrators of the laws were there before the laws themselves, is too absurd a supposition to consider seriously.

It would be as unreasonable to suppose that men at first threw themselves irretrievably and unconditionally into the arms of an absolute master, and that the first expedient which proud and unsubdued men hit upon for their common security was to run headlong into slavery. For what reason, in fact, did they take to themselves superiors, if it was not in order that they might be defended from oppression, and have protection for their lives, liberties and properties, which are, so to speak, the constituent elements of their being? Now, in the relations between man and man, the worst that can happen is for one to find himself at the mercy of another, and it would have been inconsistent with common-sense to begin by bestowing on a chief the only things they wanted his help to preserve. What equivalent could he offer them for so great a right? And if he had presumed to exact it under pretext of defending them, would he not have received the answer recorded in the fable: "What more can the enemy do to us?" It is therefore beyond dispute, and indeed the fundamental maxim of all political right, that people have set up chiefs to protect their liberty, and not to enslave them. *If we have a prince,* said Pliny to Trajan, *it is to save ourselves from having a master.*

Politicians indulge in the same sophistry about the love of liberty as philosophers about the state of nature. They judge, by what they see, of very different things, which they have not seen; and attribute to man a natural propensity to servitude, because the slaves within their

(continued)

Discourse on Inequality (*continued*)

observation are seen to bear the yoke with patience; they fail to reflect that it is with liberty as with innocence and virtue; the value is known only to those who possess them, and the taste for them is forfeited when they are forfeited themselves. "I know the charms of your country," said Brasidas to a Satrap, who was comparing the life at Sparta with that at Persepolis, "but you cannot know the pleasures of mine."

An unbroken horse erects his mane, paws the ground and starts back impetuously at the sight of the bridle; while one which is properly trained suffers patiently even whip and spur: so savage man will not bend his neck to the yoke to which civilised man submits without a murmur, but prefers the most turbulent state of liberty to the most peaceful slavery. We cannot therefore, from the servility of nations already enslaved, judge of the natural disposition of mankind for or against slavery; we should go by the prodigious efforts of every free people to save itself from oppression. I know that the former are for ever holding forth in praise of the tranquillity they enjoy in their chains, and that they call a state of wretched servitude a state of peace: *miserrimam servitutem pacem appellant.*[1] But when I observe the latter sacrificing pleasure, peace, wealth, power and life itself to the preservation of that one treasure, which is so disdained by those who have lost it; when I see free-born animals dash their brains out against the bars of their cage, from an innate impatience of captivity; when I behold numbers of naked savages, that despise European pleasures, braving hunger, fire, the sword and death, to preserve nothing but their independence, I feel that it is not for slaves to argue about liberty.

With regard to paternal authority, from which some writers have derived absolute government and all society, it is enough, without going back to the contrary arguments of Locke and Sidney, to remark that nothing on earth can be further from the ferocious spirit of despotism than the mildness of that authority which looks more to the advantage of him who obeys than to that of him who commands; that, by the law of nature, the father is the child's master no longer than his help is necessary; that from that time they are both equal, the son being perfectly independent of the father, and owing him only respect and not obedience. For gratitude is a duty which ought to be paid, but not a right to be exacted: instead of saying that civil society is derived from paternal authority, we ought to say rather that the latter derives its principal force from the former. No individual was ever acknowledged as the father of many, till his sons and daughters remained settled around him. The goods of the father, of which he is really the master, are the ties which keep his children in dependence, and he may bestow on them, if he pleases, no share of his property, unless they merit it by constant deference to his will. But the subjects of an arbitrary despot are so far from having the like favour to expect from their chief, that they themselves and everything they possess are his property, or at least are considered by him as such; so that they are forced to receive, as a favour, the little of their own he is pleased to leave them. When he despoils them, he does but justice, and mercy in that he permits them to live.

By proceeding thus to test fact by right, we should discover as little reason as truth in the voluntary establishment of tyranny. It would also be no easy matter to prove the validity of a contract binding on only one of the parties, where all the risk is on one side, and none on the other; so that no one could suffer but he who bound himself. This hateful system is indeed, even in modern times, very far from being that of wise and good monarchs, and especially of the kings of France; as may be seen from several passages in their edicts; particularly from the following passage in a celebrated edict published in 1667 in the name and by order of Louis XIV.

"Let it not, therefore, be said that the Sovereign is not subject to the laws of his State; since the contrary is a true proposition of the right of nations, which flattery has sometimes attacked but good princes have always defended as the tutelary divinity of their dominions. How much more legitimate is it to say with the wise Plato, that the perfect felicity of a kingdom consists in the obedience of subjects to their prince, and of the prince to the laws, and in the laws being just and constantly directed to the public good!"[2]

I shall not stay here to inquire whether, as liberty is the noblest faculty of man, it is not degrading our very nature, reducing ourselves to the level of the brutes, which are mere slaves of instinct, and even an affront to the Author of our being, to renounce without reserve the most precious of all His gifts, and to bow to the necessity of committing all the crimes He has forbidden, merely to gratify a mad or a cruel master; or if this sublime craftsman ought not to be less angered at seeing His workmanship entirely destroyed than thus dishonoured. I will waive (if my opponents please) the authority of Barbeyrac, who, following Locke, roundly declares that no man can so far sell his liberty as to submit to an arbitrary power which may use him as it likes. *For,* he adds, *this would be to sell his own life, of which he is not master.* I shall ask only what right those who were not afraid thus to debase themselves could have to subject their posterity to the same ignominy, and to renounce for them those blessings which they do not owe to the liberality of their progenitors, and without which life itself must be a burden to all who are worthy of it.

Puffendorf says that we may divest ourselves of our liberty in favour of other men, just as we transfer our property from one to another by contracts and agreements. But this seems a very weak argument. For in the first place, the property I alienate becomes quite foreign to me, nor can I suffer from the abuse of it; but it very nearly concerns me that my liberty should not be abused, and I cannot without incurring the guilt of the crimes I may be compelled to commit, expose myself to become an instrument of crime. Besides, the right of property being only a convention of human institution, men may dispose of what they possess as they please: but this is not the case with the essential gifts of nature, such as life and liberty, which every man is permitted to enjoy, and of which it is at least doubtful whether any have a right to divest themselves. By giving up the one, we degrade our being; by giving up the other, we do our best to annul it; and, as no temporal good can indemnify us for the loss of either, it would be an offence against both reason and nature to renounce them at any price whatsoever. But, even if we could transfer our liberty, as we do our property, there would be a great difference with regard to the children, who enjoy the father's substance only by the transmission of his right; whereas, liberty being a gift which they hold from nature as being men, their parents have no right whatever to deprive them of it. As then, to establish slavery, it was necessary to do violence to nature, so, in order to perpetuate such a right, nature would have to be changed. Jurists, who have gravely determined that the child of a slave comes into the world a slave, have decided, in other words, that a man shall come into the world not a man.

I regard it then as certain, that government did not begin with arbitrary power, but that this is the depravation, the extreme term, of government, and brings it back, finally, to just the law of the strongest, which it was originally designed to remedy. Supposing, however, it had begun in this manner, such power, being in itself illegitimate, could not have served as a basis for the laws of society, nor, consequently, for the inequality they instituted.

Without entering at present upon the investigations which still remain to be made into the nature of the fundamental compact underlying all government, I content myself with adopting the common opinion concerning it, and regard the establishment of the political body as a real contract between the people and the chiefs chosen by them: a contract by which both parties bind themselves to observe the laws therein expressed, which form the ties of their union. The people having in respect of their social relations concentrated all their wills in one, the several articles, concerning which this will is explained, become so many fundamental laws, obligatory on all the members of the State without exception, and one of these articles regulates the choice and power of the magistrates appointed to watch over the execution of the rest. This power extends to everything which may maintain the constitution, without going so far as to alter it. It is accompanied by honours, in order to bring the laws and their administrators into respect. The ministers are also distinguished by personal prerogatives, in order to recompense them for the cares and labour which good administration involves. The magistrate, on his side, binds himself to use the power he is entrusted with only in conformity with the intention of his constituents, to maintain them all in the peaceable possession of what belongs to them, and to prefer on every occasion the public interest to his own.

Before experience had shown, or knowledge of the human heart enabled men to foresee, the unavoidable abuses of such a constitution, it must have appeared so much the more excellent, as those who were charged with the care of its preservation had themselves most interest in it; for magistracy and the rights attaching to it being based solely on the fundamental laws, the magistrates would cease to be legitimate as soon as these ceased to exist; the people would no longer owe them obedience; and as not the magistrates, but the laws, are essential to the being of a State, the members of it would regain the right to their natural liberty.

If we reflect with ever so little attention on this subject, we shall find new arguments to confirm this truth, and be convinced from the very nature of the contract that it cannot be irrevocable:

(continued)

Discourse on Inequality (*continued*)

for, if there were no superior power capable of ensuring the fidelity of the contracting parties, or compelling them to perform their reciprocal engagements, the parties would be sole judges in their own cause, and each would always have a right to renounce the contract, as soon as he found that the other had violated its terms, or that they no longer suited his convenience. It is upon this principle that the right of abdication may possibly be founded. Now, if, as here, we consider only what is human in this institution, it is certain that, if the magistrate, who has all the power in his own hands, and appropriates to himself all the advantages of the contract, has none the less a right to renounce his authority, the people, who suffer for all the faults of their chief, must have a much better right to I renounce their dependence. But the terrible and innumerable quarrels and disorders that would necessarily arise from so dangerous a privilege, show, more than anything else, how much human governments stood in need of a more solid basis than mere reason, and how expedient it was for the public tranquillity that the divine will should interpose to invest the sovereign authority with a sacred and inviolable character, which might deprive subjects of the fatal right of disposing of it. If the world had received no other advantages from religion, this would be enough to impose on men the duty of adopting and cultivating it, abuses and all, since it has been the means of saving more blood than fanaticism has ever spilt. But let us follow the thread of our hypothesis.

The different forms of government owe their origin to the differing degrees of inequality which existed between individuals at the time of their institution. If there happened to be any one man among them pre-eminent in power, virtue, riches or personal influence, he became sole magistrate, and the State assumed the form of monarchy. If several, nearly equal in point of eminence, stood above the rest, they were elected jointly, and formed an aristocracy. Again, among a people who had deviated less from a state of nature, and between whose fortune or talents there was less disproportion, the supreme administration was retained in common, and a democracy was formed. It was discovered in process of time which of these forms suited men the best. Some peoples remained altogether subject to the laws; others soon came to obey their magistrates. The citizens laboured to preserve their liberty; the subjects, irritated at seeing others enjoying a blessing they had lost, thought only of making slaves of their neighbours. In a word, on the one side arose riches and conquests, and on the other happiness and virtue.

In these different governments, all the offices were at first elective; and when the influence of wealth was out of the question, the preference was given to merit, which gives a natural ascendancy, and to age, which is experienced in business and deliberate in council. The Elders of the Hebrews, the Gerontes at Sparta, the Senate at Rome, and the very etymology of our word Seigneur, show how old age was once held in veneration. But the more often the choice fell upon old men, the more often elections had to be repeated, and the more they became a nuisance; intrigues set in, factions were formed, party feeling grew bitter, civil wars broke out; the lives of individuals were sacrificed to the pretended happiness of the State; and at length men were on the point of relapsing into their primitive anarchy. Ambitious chiefs profited by these circumstances to perpetuate their offices in their own families: at the same time the people, already used to dependence, ease, and the conveniences of life, and already incapable of breaking its fetters, agreed to an increase of its slavery, in order to secure its tranquillity. Thus magistrates, having become hereditary, contracted the habit of considering their offices as a family estate, and themselves as proprietors of the communities of which they were at first only the officers, of regarding their fellow-citizens as their slaves, and numbering them, like cattle, among their belongings, and of calling themselves the equals of the gods and kings of kings.

If we follow the progress of inequality in these various revolutions, we shall find that the establishment of laws and of the right of property was its first term, the institution of magistracy the second, and the conversion of legitimate into arbitrary power the third and last; so that the condition of rich and poor was authorised by the first period; that of powerful and weak by the second; and only by the third that of master and slave, which is the last degree of inequality, and the term at which all the rest remain, when they have got so far, till the government is either entirely dissolved by new revolutions, or brought back again to legitimacy.

To understand this progress as necessary we must consider not so much the motives for the establishment of the body politic, as the forms it assumes in actuality, and the faults that necessarily attend it: for the flaws which make social institutions necessary are the same as make the abuse of them unavoidable. If we except Sparta, where the laws were mainly concerned with the education of children, and where Lycurgus established such morality as practically made laws needless—for laws as a rule, being weaker than the passions, restrain men without altering them—it would not be difficult to prove that every government, which scrupulously complied with the ends for which it was instituted, and guarded carefully against change and corruption, was set up unnecessarily. For a country, in which no one either evaded the laws or made a bad use of magisterial power, could require neither laws nor magistrates.

Political distinctions necessarily produce civil distinctions. The growing equality between the chiefs and the people is soon felt by individuals, and modified in a thousand ways according to passions, talents and circumstances. The magistrate could not usurp any illegitimate power, without giving distinction to the creatures with whom he must share it. Besides, individuals only allow themselves to be oppressed so far as they are hurried on by blind ambition, and, looking rather below than above them, come to love authority more than independence, and submit to slavery, that they may in turn enslave others. It is no easy matter to reduce to obedience a man who has no ambition to command; nor would the most adroit politician find it possible to enslave a people whose only desire was to be independent. But inequality easily makes its way among cowardly and ambitious minds, which are ever ready to run the risks of fortune, and almost indifferent whether they command or obey, as it is favourable or adverse. Thus, there must have been a time, when the eyes of the people were so fascinated, that their rulers had only to say to the least of men, "Be great, you and all your posterity," to make him immediately appear great in the eyes of every one as well as in his own. His descendants took still more upon them, in proportion to their distance from him; the more obscure and uncertain the cause, the greater the effect: the greater the number of idlers one could count in a family, the more illustrious it was held to be.

If this were the place to go into details, I could readily explain how, even without the intervention of government, inequality of credit and authority became unavoidable among private persons, as soon as their union in a single society made them compare themselves one with another, and take into account the differences which they found out from the continual intercourse every man had to have with his neighbours. These differences are of several kinds; but riches, nobility or rank, power and personal merit being the principal distinctions by which men form an estimate of each other in society, I could prove that the harmony or conflict of these different forces is the surest indication of the good or bad constitution of a State. I could show that among these four kinds of inequality, personal qualities being the origin of all the others, wealth is the one to which they are all reduced in the end; for, as riches tend most immediately to the prosperity of individuals, and are easiest to communicate, they are used to purchase every other distinction. By this observation we are enabled to judge pretty exactly how far a people has departed from its primitive constitution, and of its progress towards the extreme term of corruption. I could explain how much this universal desire for reputation, honours and advancement, which inflames us all, exercises and holds up to comparison our faculties and powers; how it excites and multiplies our passions, and, by creating universal competition and rivalry, or rather enmity, among men, occasions numberless failures, successes and disturbances of all kinds by making so many aspirants run the same course. I could show that it is to this desire of being talked about, and this unremitting rage of distinguishing ourselves, that we owe the best and the worst things we possess, both our virtues and our vices, our science and our errors, our conquerors and our philosophers; that is to say, a great many bad things, and a very few good ones. In a word, I could prove that, if we have a few rich and powerful men on the pinnacle of fortune and grandeur, while the crowd grovels in want and obscurity, it is because the former prize what they enjoy only in so far as others are destitute of it; and because, without changing their condition, they would cease to be happy the moment the people ceased to be wretched.

These details alone, however, would furnish matter for a considerable work, in which the advantages and disadvantages of every kind of government might be weighed, as they are related to man in the state of nature, and at the same time all the different aspects, under which inequality has up to the present appeared, or may appear in ages yet to come, according to the nature of the several governments, and the alterations which time must unavoidably occasion in

(continued)

Discourse on Inequality   (continued)

them, might be demonstrated. We should then see the multitude oppressed from within, in consequence of the very precautions it had taken to guard against foreign tyranny. We should see oppression continually gain ground without it being possible for the oppressed to know where it would stop, or what legitimate means was left them of checking its progress. We should see the rights of citizens, and the freedom of nations slowly extinguished, and the complaints, protests and appeals of the weak treated as seditious murmurings. We should see the honour of defending the common cause confined by statecraft to a mercenary part of the people. We should see taxes made necessary by such means, and the disheartened husbandman deserting his fields even in the midst of peace, and leaving the plough to gird on the sword. We should see fatal and capricious codes of honour established; and the champions of their country sooner or later becoming its enemies, and for ever holding their daggers to the breasts of their fellow-citizens. The time would come when they would be heard saying to the oppressor of their country—

> Pectore si fratris gladium juguloque parentis
> Condere me jubeas, gravidœque in viscera partu
> Conjugis, invitâ peragam tamen omnia dexirâ.
>
> Lucan. i, 376.

From great inequality of fortunes and conditions, from the vast variety of passions and of talents, of useless and pernicious arts, of vain sciences, *would arise a multitude of prejudices equally contrary to reason, happiness and virtue*. We should see the magistrates fomenting everything that might weaken men united in society, by promoting dissension among them; everything that might sow in it the seeds of actual division, while it *gave society the air of harmony*; everything that might inspire the different ranks of people with mutual hatred and distrust, by setting the rights and interests of one against those of another, and so strengthen the power which comprehended them all.

It is *from the midst of this disorder and these revolutions*, that despotism, gradually raising up its hideous head and devouring everything that remained sound and untainted in any part of the State, would at length trample on both the laws and the people, and establish itself on the ruins of the republic. The times which immediately preceded this last change would be times of trouble and calamity; but at length the monster would swallow up everything, and the people would no longer have either chiefs or laws, but only tyrants. *From this moment there would be no question of virtue or morality*; for despotism *cui ex honesto nulla est spes,* wherever it prevails, admits no other master; it no sooner speaks than probity and duty lose their weight and blind obedience is the only virtue which slaves can still practise.

This is the last term of inequality, the extreme point that closes the circle, and meets that from which we set out. Here all private persons return to their first equality, because they are nothing; and, subjects having no law but the will of their master, and their master no restraint but his passions, all notions of good and all principles of equity again vanish. There is here a complete return to the law of the strongest, and so to a new state of nature, differing from that we set out from; for *the one was a state of nature in its first purity, while this is the consequence of* excessive corruption. There is so little difference between the two states in other respects, and the contract of government is so completely dissolved by despotism, that the despot is master only *so long as he remains* the .strongest; as soon as he can be expelled, he has no right to complain of violence. The popular insurrection that ends in the death or deposition of a Sultan is as lawful an act as those by which he disposed, the day before, of the lives and fortunes of his subjects. *As he was maintained by force alone, it is force alone that overthrows him.* Thus everything takes place according to the natural order; and, whatever may be the result of such frequent and precipitate revolutions, no one man has reason to complain of the injustice of another, but only of his own ill-fortune or indiscretion.

If the reader thus discovers and retraces the lost and forgotten road, by which man must have passed from the state of nature to the state of society; if he carefully restores, along with the *intermediate situations, which I have just described*, those which want of time has compelled me to suppress, or my imagination has failed to suggest, he cannot fail to be struck by the vast distance which separates the two states. It is in tracing this slow succession that he will find the solution of a number of problems of politics and morals, which philosophers cannot settle. He will feel that, men being different in different ages, the reason why Diogenes could not find a man was that he sought among his contemporaries a man of an earlier period. He will see that Cato died with *Rome and* liberty, because he did not fit the age in which he *lived*; the greatest of men served only to astonish a world which he would certainly have ruled, had he lived five hundred years sooner. *In a word*, he will explain how the soul and the passions of men insensibly change their very nature; why our wants and pleasures in the end seek new objects; and why, the original man having vanished by degrees, society offers to us only an assembly of artificial men and factitious passions, which are the work of all these new relations, and without any real foundation in nature. We are taught nothing on this subject, by reflection, that is not entirely confirmed by observation. The savage and the civilised man differ so much in the bottom of their hearts and in their inclinations, that what constitutes the supreme happiness of one would reduce the other to despair. The former breathes only peace and liberty; he desires only to live and be free from labour; even the *ataraxia* of the Stoic falls far short of his profound indifference to every other object. Civilised man, on the other hand, is always *moving, sweating, toiling* and racking his brains to find still more laborious occupations: he goes on in drudgery to his last moment, and even seeks death to put himself in a position to live, or renounces life to acquire immortality. He *pays his* court to men in power, whom he hates, and to the wealthy, whom he despises; he stops at nothing to have the honour of serving them; he is *not ashamed* to value himself on his own meanness and their protection; and, proud of his slavery, he speaks with disdain of those, who have not the honour of sharing it. What a sight would the perplexing and envied labours of a European minister of State present to the eyes of a Caribean! How many cruel deaths would not this indolent savage prefer to the horrors of such a life, which is seldom even sweetened by the pleasure of doing good! But, for him to see into the motives of all this solicitude, the words *power* and *reputation*, would have to bear some meaning in his mind; he would have to know that there are men who set a value on the opinion of the rest of the world; who can be made happy and satisfied with themselves rather on the testimony of other people than on their own. *In reality, the source of all these differences is, that the savage lives within* himself, while *social man lives constantly* outside himself, and only knows how to live in the opinion of others, so that he *seems* to receive the *consciousness* of his own existence merely from the judgment of others concerning him. It is not to my present purpose to insist on the indifference to good and evil which arises from this disposition, in spite of our many fine works on morality, or to show how, everything being reduced to appearances, there is but art and mummery in even honour, friendship, virtue, and often vice itself, of which we at length learn the secret of boasting; to show, in short, how, always asking others what we are, and never daring to ask ourselves, in the midst of so much philosophy, humanity and civilisation, and of such sublime codes of morality, we have nothing to show for ourselves but a frivolous and deceitful appearance, honour without virtue, reason without wisdom, and pleasure without happiness. It is sufficient that I have proved that this is not by any means the original state of man, but that it, is merely the spirit of society, and the inequality which society produces, that thus transform and alter all our natural inclinations.

I have endeavoured to trace the origin and progress of inequality, and the institution and abuse of political societies, as far as these are capable of being deduced from the nature of man merely by the light of reason, and independently of those sacred dogmas which give the sanction of divine right to sovereign authority. It follows from this survey that, as there is hardly any inequality in the state of nature, all the inequality which now prevails owes its strength and growth to the development of our faculties and the advance of the human mind, and becomes at last permanent and legitimate by the establishment of property and laws. Secondly, it follows that moral inequality, authorised by positive right alone, clashes with natural right, whenever it is not proportionate to physical inequality; a distinction which sufficiently determines what we ought to think of that species of inequality which prevails in all civilised countries; since it is plainly contrary to the law of nature, however defined, that children should command old men, fools wise men, and that the privileged few should gorge themselves with superfluities, while the starving multitude are in want of the bare necessities of life.

(continued)

Discourse on Inequality   (continued)

NOTES

1. Ovid, Metamorphoses xi, 127. Both rich and poor, shocked at their new-found ills, Would fly from wealth, and lose what they had sought.
2. Of the Rights of the Most Christian Queen over various States of the Monarchy of Spain, 1667.

A Vindication of the Rights of Woman
Mary Wollstonecraft

Chapter II
The Prevailing Opinion of a Sexual Character Discussed

To account for, and excuse the tyranny of man, many ingenious arguments have been brought forward to prove, that the two sexes, in the acquirement of virtue, ought to aim at attaining a very different character; or, to speak explicitly, women are not allowed to have sufficient strength of mind to acquire what really deserves the name of virtue. Yet it should seem, allowing them to have souls, that there is but one way appointed by Providence to lead *mankind* to either virtue or happiness.

If then women are not a swarm of ephemeron triflers, why should they be kept in ignorance under the specious name of innocence? Men complain, and with reason, of the follies and caprices of our sex, when they do not keenly satirize our headstrong passions and grovelling vices. Behold, I should answer, the natural effect of ignorance! The mind will ever be unstable that has only prejudices to rest on, and the current will run with destructive fury when there are no barriers to break its force. Women are told from their infancy, and taught by the example of their mothers, that a little knowledge of human weakness, justly termed cunning, softness of temper, *outward* obedience, and a scrupulous attention to a puerile kind of propriety, will obtain for them the protection of man; and should they be beautiful, everything else is needless, for, at least, twenty years of their lives.

Thus Milton describes our first frail mother; though when he tells us that women are formed for softness and sweet attractive grace, I cannot comprehend his meaning, unless, in the true Mahometan strain, he meant to deprive us of souls, and insinuate that we were beings only designed by sweet attractive grace, and docile blind obedience, to gratify the senses of man when he can no longer soar on the wing of contemplation.

How grossly do they insult us who thus advise us only to render ourselves gentle, domestic brutes! For instance, the winning softness so warmly, and frequently, recommended, that governs by obeying. What childish expressions, and how insignificant is the being—can it be an immortal one? who will condescend to govern by such sinister methods? "Certainly," says Lord Bacon, "man is of kin to the beasts by his body; and if he be not of kin to God by his spirit, he is a base and ignoble creature!" Men, indeed, appear to me to act in a very unphilosophical manner when they try to secure the good conduct of women by attempting to keep them always in a state of childhood. Rousseau was more consistent when he wished to stop the progress of reason in both sexes, for if men eat of the tree of knowledge, women will come in for a taste; but, from the imperfect cultivation which their understandings now receive, they only attain a knowledge of evil.

Children, I grant, should be innocent; but when the epithet is applied to men, or women, it is but a civil term for weakness. For if it be allowed that women were destined by Providence to acquire human virtues, and by the exercise of their understandings, that stability of character which is the firmest ground to rest our future hopes upon, they must be permitted to turn to the fountain of light, and not forced to shape their course by the twinkling of a mere satellite. Milton, I grant, was of a very different opinion; for he only bends to the indefeasible right of beauty, though it would be difficult to render two passages which I now mean to contrast, consistent. But into similar inconsistencies are great men often led by their senses.

> "To whom thus Eve with *perfect beauty* adorn'd.
> My Author and Disposer, what thou bidst
> *Unargued* I obey; so God ordains;
> God is *thy law, thou mine:* to know no more.
> Is Woman's *happiest* knowledge and her *praise.*"

These are exactly the arguments that I have used to children; but I have added, your reason is now gaining strength, and, till it arrives at some degree of maturity, you must look up to me for advice—then you ought to *think,* and only rely on God.

Yet in the following lines Milton seems to coincide with me; when he makes Adam thus expostulate with his Maker.

> "Hast thou not made me here thy substitute,
> And these inferior far beneath me set?
> Among *unequals what* society
> Can sort, what harmony or true delight?
> Which must be mutual, in proportion due
> Giv'n and receiv'd; but in *disparity*
> The one intense, the other still remiss
> Cannot well suit with either, but soon prove
> Tedious alike: of *fellowship* I speak
> Such as I seek, fit to participate
> All rational delight—"

In treating, therefore, of the manners of women, let us, disregarding sensual arguments, trace what we should endeavour to make them in order to co-operate, if the expression be not too bold, with the supreme Being.

By individual education, I mean, for the sense of the word is not precisely defined, such an attention to a child as will slowly sharpen the senses, form the temper, regulate the passions as they begin to ferment, and set the understanding to work before the body arrives at maturity; so that the man may only have to proceed, not to begin, the important task of learning to think and reason.

To prevent any misconstruction, I must add, that I do not believe that a private education can work the wonders which some sanguine writers have attributed to it. Men and women must be educated, in a great degree, by the opinions and manners of the society they live in. In every age there has been a stream of popular opinion that has carried all before it, and given a family character, as it were, to the century. It may then fairly be inferred, that, till society be differently constituted, much cannot be expected from education. It is, however, sufficient for my present purpose to assert, that, whatever effect circumstances have on the abilities, every being may become virtuous by the exercise of its own reason; for if but one being was created with vicious inclinations, that is positively bad, what can save us from atheism? or if we worship a God, is not that God a devil?

Consequently, the most perfect education, in my opinion, is such an exercise of the understanding as is best calculated to strengthen the body and form the heart. Or, in other words, to enable the individual to attain such habits of virtue as will render it independent. In fact, it is a farce to call any being virtuous whose virtues do not result from the exercise of its own reason. This was Rousseau's opinion respecting men: I extend it to women, and confidently assert that they have been drawn out of their sphere by false refinement, and not by an endeavour to acquire masculine qualities. Still the regal homage which they receive is so intoxicating, that till the manners of the times are changed, and formed on more reasonable principles, it may be impossible to convince them that the illegitimate power, which they obtain, by degrading themselves, is a curse, and that they must return to nature and equality, if they wish to secure the placid satisfaction that unsophisticated affections impart. But for this epoch we must wait—wait, perhaps, till kings and nobles,

(continued)

A Vindication of the Rights of Woman (*continued*)

enlightened by reason, and, preferring the real dignity of man to childish state, throw off their gaudy hereditary trappings: and if then women do not resign the arbitrary power of beauty—they will prove that they have *less* mind than man.

I may be accused of arrogance; still I must declare what I firmly believe, that all the writers who have written on the subject of female education and manners, from Rousseau to Dr. Gregory, have contributed to render women more artificial, weak characters, than they would otherwise have been; and consequently, more useless members of society. I might have expressed this conviction in a lower key; but I am afraid it would have been the whine of affectation, and not the faithful expression of my feelings, of the clear result which experience and reflection have led me to draw. When I come to that division of the subject, I shall advert to the passages that I more particularly disapprove of, in the works of the authors I have just alluded to; but it is first necessary to observe, that my objection extends to the whole purport of those books, which tend, in my opinion, to degrade one half of the human species, and render women pleasing at the expense of every solid virtue.

Though, to reason on Rousseau's ground, if man did attain a degree of perfection of mind when his body arrived at maturity, it might be proper, in order to make a man and his wife *one*, that she should rely entirely on his understanding; and the graceful ivy, clasping the oak that supported it, would form a whole in which strength and beauty would be equally conspicuous. But, alas! husbands, as well as their helpmates, are often only overgrown children; nay, thanks to early debauchery, scarcely men in their outward form—and if the blind lead the blind, one need not come from heaven to tell us the consequence.

Many are the causes that, in the present corrupt state of society, contribute to enslave women by cramping their understandings and sharpening their senses. One, perhaps, that silently does more mischief than all the rest, is their disregard of order.

To do everything in an orderly manner, is a most important precept, which women, who, generally speaking, receive only a disorderly kind of education, seldom attend to with that degree of exactness that men, who from their infancy are broken into method, observe. This negligent kind of guess-work, for what other epithet can be used to point out the random exertions of a sort of instinctive common sense, never brought to the test of reason? prevents their generalizing matters of fact—so they do to-day, what they did yesterday, merely because they did it yesterday.

This contempt of the understanding in early life has more baneful consequences than is commonly supposed; for the little knowledge which women of strong minds attain, is, from various circumstances, of a more desultory kind than the knowledge of men, and it is acquired more by sheer observations on real life, than from comparing what has been individually observed with the results of experience generalized by speculation. Led by their dependent situation and domestic employments more into society, what they learn is rather by snatches; and as learning is with them, in general, only a secondary thing, they do not pursue any one branch with that persevering ardour necessary to give vigour to the faculties, and clearness to the judgment In the present state of society, a little learning is required to support the character of a gentleman; and boys are obliged to submit to a few years of discipline. But in the education of women, the cultivation of the understanding is always subordinate to the acquirement of some corporeal accomplishment; even while enervated by confinement and false notions of modesty, the body is prevented from attaining that grace and beauty which relaxed half-formed limbs never exhibit. Besides, in youth their faculties are not brought forward by emulation; and having no serious scientific study, if they have natural sagacity it is turned too soon on life and manners. They dwell on effects, and modifications, without tracing them back to causes; and complicated rules to adjust behaviour are a weak substitute for simple principles.

As a proof that education gives this appearance of weakness to females, we may instance the example of military men, who are, like them, sent into the world before their minds have been stored with knowledge or fortified by principles. The consequences are similar; soldiers acquire a little superficial knowledge, snatched from the muddy current of conversation, and, from continually mixing with society, they gain, what is termed a knowledge of the world; and this acquaintance with manners and customs has frequently been confounded with a knowledge of the human heart. But can the crude fruit of casual observation, never brought to the test of judgment, formed by comparing speculation and experience, deserve such a distinction? Soldiers, as well as women, practice the minor virtues with punctilious politeness. Where is then the sexual difference, when the education has been the same? All the difference that I can discern, arises from the superior advantage of liberty, which enables the former to see more of life.

It is wandering from my present subject, perhaps, to make a political remark; but, as it was produced naturally by the train of my reflections, I shall not pass it silently over.

Standing armies can never consist of resolute robust men; they may be well disciplined machines, but they will seldom contain men under the influence of strong passions, or with very vigorous faculties. And as for any depth of understanding, I will venture to affirm, that it is as rarely to be found in the army as amongst women; and the cause, I maintain, is the same. It may be further observed, that officers are also particularly attentive to their persons, fond of dancing, crowded rooms, adventures, and ridicule.[1] Like the *fair* sex, the business of their lives is gallantry. They were taught to please, and they only live to please. Yet they do not lose their rank in the distinction of sexes, for they are still reckoned superior to women, though in what their superiority consists, beyond what I have just mentioned, it is difficult to discover.

The great misfortune is this, that they both acquire manners before morals, and a knowledge of life before they have, from reflection, any acquaintance with the grand ideal outline of human nature. The consequence is natural; satisfied with common nature, they become a prey to prejudices, and taking all their opinions on credit, they blindly submit to authority. So that, if they have any sense, it is a kind of instinctive glance, that catches proportions, and decides with respect to manners; but fails when arguments are to be pursued below the surface, or opinions analyzed.

May not the same remark be applied to women? Nay, the argument may be carried still further, for they are both thrown out of a useful station by the unnatural distinctions established in civilized life. Riches and hereditary honours have made cyphers of women to give consequence to the numerical figure; and idleness has produced a mixture of gallantry and despotism into society, which leads the very men who are the slaves of their mistresses to tyrannize over their sisters, wives, and daughters. This is only keeping them in rank and file, it is true. Strengthen the female mind by enlarging it, and there will be an end to blind obedience; but, as blind obedience is ever fought for by power, tyrants and sensualists are in the right when they endeavour to keep women in the dark, because the former only want slaves, and the latter a plaything. The sensualist, indeed, has been the most dangerous of tyrants, and women have been duped by their lovers, as princes by their ministers, whilst dreaming that they reigned over them.

I now principally allude to Rousseau, for his character of Sophia is, undoubtedly, a captivating one, though it appears to me grossly unnatural; however it is not the superstructure, but the foundation of her character, the principles on which her education was built, that I mean to attack; nay, warmly as I admire the genius of that able writer, whose opinions I shall often have occasion to cite, indignation always takes place of admiration, and the rigid frown of insulted virtue effaces the smile of complacency, which his eloquent periods are wont to raise, when I read his voluptuous reveries. Is this the man, who, in his ardour for virtue, would banish all the soft arts of peace, and almost carry us back to Spartan discipline? Is this the man who delights to paint the useful struggles of passion, the triumphs of good dispositions, and the heroic flights which carry the glowing soul out of itself?—How are these mighty sentiments lowered when he describes the pretty foot and enticing airs of his little favourite! But, for the present, I waive the subject, and, instead of severely reprehending the transient effusions of overweening sensibility, I shall only observe, that whoever has cast a benevolent eye on society, must often have been gratified by the sight of humble mutual love, not dignified by sentiment, or strengthened by a union in intellectual pursuits. The domestic trifles of the day have afforded matters for cheerful converse, and innocent caresses have softened toils which did not require great exercise of mind or stretch of thought: yet, has not the sight of this moderate felicity excited more tenderness than respect? An emotion similar to what we feel when children are playing, or animals sporting,[2] whilst the contemplation of the noble struggles of suffering merit has raised admiration, and carried our thoughts to that world where sensation will give place to reason.

(continued)

A Vindication of the Rights of Woman (*continued*)

Women are, therefore, to be considered either as moral beings, or so weak that they must be entirely subjected to the superior faculties of men.

Let us examine this question. Rousseau declares that a woman should never, for a moment, feel herself independent, that she should be governed by fear to exercise her *natural* cunning, and made a coquettish slave in order to render her a more alluring object of desire, a *sweeter* companion to man, whenever he chooses to relax himself. He carries the arguments, which he pretends to draw from the indications of nature, still further, and insinuates that truth and fortitude, the corner stones of all human virtue, should be cultivated with certain restrictions, because, with respect to the female character, obedience is the grand lesson which ought to be impressed with unrelenting rigour.

What nonsense! when will a great man arise with sufficient strength of mind to puff away the fumes which pride and sensuality have thus spread over the subject! If women are by nature inferior to men, their virtues must be the same in quality, if not in degree, or virtue is a relative idea; consequently, their conduct should be founded on the same principles, and have the same aim.

Connected with man as daughters, wives, and mothers, their moral character may be estimated by their manner of fulfilling those simple duties; but the end, the grand end of their exertions should be to unfold their own faculties and acquire the dignity of conscious virtue. They may try to render their road pleasant; but ought never to forget, in common with man, that life yields not the felicity which can satisfy an immortal soul. I do not mean to insinuate that either sex should be so lost in abstract reflections or distant views, as to forget the affections and duties that lie before them, and are, in truth, the means appointed to produce the fruit of life: on the contrary, I would warmly recommend them, even while I assert, that they afford most satisfaction when they are considered in their true, sober light.

Probably the prevailing opinion, that woman was created for man, may have taken its rise from Moses's poetical story; yet, as very few, it is presumed, who have bestowed any serious thought on the subject, ever supposed that Eve was, literally speaking, one of Adam's ribs, the deduction must be allowed to fall to the ground; or, only be so far admitted as it proves that man, from the remotest antiquity, found it convenient to exert his strength to subjugate his companion, and his invention to show that she ought to have her neck bent under the yoke, because the whole creation was only created for his convenience or pleasure.

Let it not be concluded that I wish to invert the order of things; I have already granted, that, from the constitution of their bodies, men seem to be designed by Providence to attain a greater degree of virtue. I speak collectively of the whole sex; but I see not the shadow of a reason to conclude that their virtues should differ in respect to their nature. In fact, how can they, if virtue has only one eternal standard? I must therefore, if I reason consequentially, as strenuously maintain that they have the same simple direction, as that there is a God.

It follows then that cunning should not be opposed to wisdom, little cares to great exertions, or insipid softness, varnished over with the name of gentleness, to that fortitude which grand views alone can inspire.

I shall be told that woman would then lose many of her peculiar graces, and the opinion of a well-known poet might be quoted to refute my unqualified assertion. For Pope has said, in the name of the whole male sex,

> "Yet ne'er so sure our passion to create,
> As when she touch'd the brink of all we hate."

In what light this sally places men and women, I shall leave to the judicious to determine; meanwhile I shall content myself with observing, that I cannot discover why, unless they are mortal, females should always be degraded by being made subservient to love or lust.

To speak disrespectfully of love is, I know, high treason against sentiment and fine feelings; but I wish to speak the simple language of truth, and rather to address the head than the heart. To endeavour to reason love out of the world, would be to out Quixote Cervantes, and equally offend against common sense; but an endeavour to restrain this tumultuous passion, and to prove that it should not be allowed to dethrone superior powers, or to usurp the sceptre which the understanding should ever coolly wield, appears less wild.

Youth is the season for love in both sexes; but in those days of thoughtless enjoyment provision should be made for the more important years of life, when reflection takes place of sensation. But Rousseau, and most of the male writers who have followed his steps, have warmly inculcated that the whole tendency of female education ought to be directed to one point:—to render them pleasing.

Let me reason with the supporters of this opinion who have any knowledge of human nature, do they imagine that marriage can eradicate the habitude of life? The woman who has only been taught to please will soon find that her charms are oblique sunbeams, and that they cannot have much effect on her husband's heart when they are seen every day, when the summer is passed and gone. Will she then have sufficient native energy to look into herself for comfort, and cultivate her dormant faculties? or, is it not more rational to expect that she will try to please other men; and, in the emotions raised by the expectation of new conquests, endeavour to forget the mortification her love or pride has received? When the husband ceases to be a lover—and the time will inevitably come, her desire of pleasing will then grow languid, or become a spring of bitterness; and love, perhaps, the most evanescent of all passions, gives place to jealousy or vanity.

I now speak of women who are restrained by principle or prejudice; such women, though they would shrink from an intrigue with real abhorrence, yet, nevertheless, wish to be convinced by the homage of gallantry that they are cruelly neglected by their husbands; or, days and weeks are spent in dreaming of the happiness enjoyed by congenial souls till their health is undermined and their spirits broken by discontent. How then can the great art of pleasing be such a necessary study? it is only useful to a mistress; the chaste wife, and serious mother, should only consider her power to please as the polish of her virtues, and the affection of her husband as one of the comforts that render her talk less difficult and her life happier. But, whether she be loved or neglected, her first wish should be to make herself respectable, and not to rely for all her happiness on a being subject to like infirmities with herself.

The worthy Dr. Gregory fell into a similar error. I respect his heart; but entirely disapprove of his celebrated Legacy to his Daughters.

He advises them to cultivate a fondness for dress, because a fondness for dress, he asserts, is natural to them. I am unable to comprehend what either he or Rousseau mean, when they frequently use this indefinite term. If they told us that in a pre-existent state the soul was fond of dress, and brought this inclination with it into a new body, I should listen to them with a half smile, as I often do when I hear a rant about innate elegance. But if he only meant to say that the exercise of the faculties will produce this fondness—I deny it. It is not natural; but arises, like false ambition in men, from a love of power.

Dr. Gregory goes much further; he actually recommends dissimulation, and advises an innocent girl to give the lie to her feelings, and not dance with spirit, when gaiety of heart would make her feet eloquent without making her gestures immodest. In the name of truth and common sense, why should not one woman acknowledge that she can take more exercise than another? or, in other words, that she has a sound constitution; and why, to damp innocent vivacity, is she darkly to be told that men will draw conclusions which she little thinks of?—Let the libertine draw what inference be pleases; but, I hope, that no sensible mother will restrain the natural frankness of youth by instilling such indecent cautions. Out of the abundance of the heart the mouth speaketh; and a wiser than Solomon hath said, that the heart should be made clean, and not trivial ceremonies observed, which it is not very difficult to fulfil with scrupulous exactness when vice reigns in the heart.

Women ought to endeavour to purify their heart; but can they do so when their uncultivated understandings make them entirely dependent on their senses for employment and amusement, when no noble pursuit sets them above the little vanities of the day, or enables them to curb the wild emotions that agitate a reed over which every passing breeze has power? To gain the affections of a virtuous man, is affectation necessary? Nature has given woman a weaker frame than man; but, to ensure her husband's affections, must a wife, who by the exercise of her mind and body whilst she was discharging the duties of a daughter, wife, and mother, has allowed her constitution to retain its natural strength, and her nerves a healthy tone, is she, I say, to condescend to use art and feign a sickly delicacy in order to secure her husband's affection? Weakness may excite tenderness, and gratify the arrogant pride of man; but the lordly caresses of a protector will not

(continued)

A Vindication of the Rights of Woman   (*continued*)

gratify a noble mind that pants for, and deserves to be respected. Fondness is a poor substitute for friendship!

In a seraglio, I grant, that all these arts are necessary; the epicure must have his palate tickled, or he will sink into apathy; but have women so little ambition as to be satisfied with such a condition? Can they supinely dream life away in the lap of pleasure, or the languor of weariness, rather than assert their claim to pursue reasonable pleasures and render themselves conspicuous by practising the virtues which dignify mankind? Surely she has not an immortal soul who can loiter life away merely employed to adorn her person, that she may amuse the languid hours, and soften the cares of a fellow-creature who is willing to be enlivened by her smiles and tricks, when the serious business of life is over.

Besides, the woman who strengthens her body and exercises her mind will, by managing her family and practising various virtues, become the friend, and not the humble dependant of her husband; and if she, by possessing such substantial qualities, merit his regard, she will not find it necessary to conceal her affection, nor to pretend to an unnatural coldness of constitution to excite her husband's passions. In fact, if we revert to history, we shall find that the women who have distinguished themselves have neither been the most beautiful nor the most gentle of their sex.

Nature, or, to speak with strict propriety, God, has made all things right; but man has sought him out many inventions to mar the work. I now allude to that part of Dr. Gregory's treatise, where he advises a wife never to let her husband know the extent of her sensibility or affection. Voluptuous precaution, and as ineffectual as absurd. Love, from its very nature, must be transitory. To seek for a secret that would render it constant, would be as wild a search as for the philosopher's stone, or the grand panacea: and the discovery would be equally useless, or rather pernicious, to mankind. The most holy band of society is friendship. It has been well said, by a shrewd satirist, "that rare as true love is, true friendship is still rarer."

This is an obvious truth, and the cause not lying deep, will not elude a slight glance of inquiry.

Love, the common passion, in which chance and sensation take place of choice and reason, is, in some degree, felt by the mass of mankind; for it is not necessary to speak, at present, of the emotions that rise above or sink below love. This passion, naturally increased by suspense and difficulties, draws the mind out of its accustomed state, and exalts the affections; but the security of marriage, allowing the fever of love to subside, a healthy temperature is thought insipid, only by those who have not sufficient intellect to substitute the calm tenderness of friendship, the confidence of respect, instead of blind admiration, and the sensual emotions of fondness.

This is, must be, the course of nature,—friendship or indifference inevitably succeeds love. And this constitution seems perfectly to harmonize with the system of government which prevails in the moral world. Passions are spurs to action, and open the mind; but they sink into mere appetites, become a personal and momentary gratification, when the object is gained, and the satisfied mind rests in enjoyment. The man who had some virtue whilst he was struggling for a crown, often becomes a voluptuous tyrant when it graces his brow; and, when the lover is not lost in the husband, the dotard, a prey to childish caprices, and fond jealousies, neglects the serious duties of life, and the caresses which should excite confidence in his children are lavished on the overgrown child, his wife.

In order to fulfil the duties of life, and to be able to pursue with vigour the various employments which form the moral character, a master and mistress of a family ought not to continue to love each other without passion. I mean to say, that they ought not to indulge those emotions which disturb the order of society, and engross the thoughts that should be otherwise employed. The mind that has never been engrossed by one object wants vigour—if it can long be so, it is weak.

A mistaken education, a narrow, uncultivated mind, and many sexual prejudices, tend to make women more constant than men; but, for the present, I shall not touch on this branch of the subject. I will go still further, and advance, without dreaming of a paradox, that an unhappy marriage is often very advantageous to a family, and that the neglected wife is, in general, the best mother. And this would almost always be the consequence if the female mind were more enlarged: for, it seems to be the common dispensation of Providence, that what we gain in present enjoyment should be deducted from the treasure of life, experience; and that when we are gathering the flowers of the day and revelling in pleasure, the solid fruit of toil and wisdom should not be caught at the same time. The way lies before us, we must turn to the right or left; and he who will pass life away in bounding from one pleasure to another, must not complain if he acquire neither wisdom nor respectability of character.

Supposing, for a moment, that the soul is not immortal, and that man was only created for the present scene,—I think we should have reason to complain that love, infantine fondness, ever grew insipid and palled upon the sense. Let us eat, drink, and love, for to-morrow we die, would be, in fact, the language of reason, the morality of life; and who but a fool would part with a reality for a fleeting shadow? But, if awed by observing the improbable powers of the mind, we disdain to confine our wishes or thoughts to such a comparatively mean field of action; that only appears grand and important, as it is connected with a boundless prospect and sublime hopes, what necessity is there for falsehood in conduct, and why must the sacred majesty of truth be violated to detain a deceitful good that saps the very foundation of virtue? Why must the female mind be tainted by coquettish arts to gratify the sensualist, and prevent love from subsiding into friendship, or compassionate tenderness, when there are not qualities on which friendship can be built? Let the honest heart show itself, and *reason* teach passion to submit to necessity; or, let the dignified pursuit of virtue and knowledge raise the mind above those emotions which rather embitter than sweeten the cup of life, when they are not restrained within due bounds.

I do not mean to allude to the romantic passion, which is the concomitant of genius. Who can clip its wing? But that grand passion not proportioned to the puny enjoyments of life, is only true to the sentiment, and feeds on itself. The passions which have been celebrated for their durability have always been unfortunate. They have acquired strength by absence and constitutional melancholy. The fancy has hovered round a form of beauty dimly seen—but familiarity might have turned admiration into disgust; or, at least, into indifference, and allowed the imagination leisure to start fresh game. With perfect propriety, according to this view of things, does Rousseau make the mistress of his soul, Eloifa, love St. Preux, when life was fading before her; but this is no proof of the immortality of the passion.

Of the same complexion is Dr. Gregory's advice respecting delicacy of sentiment, which he advises a woman not to acquire, if she have determined to marry. This determination, however, perfectly consistent with his former advice, he calls *indelicate,* and earnestly persuades his daughters to conceal it, though it may govern their conduct:—as if it were indelicate to have the common appetites of human nature.

Noble morality! and consistent with the cautious prudence of a little soul that cannot extend its views beyond the present minute division of existence. If all the faculties of woman's mind are only to be cultivated as they respect her dependence on man; if, when a husband be obtained, she have arrived at her goal, and meanly proud rests satisfied with such a paltry crown, let her grovel contentedly, scarcely raised by her employments above the animal kingdom; but, if, struggling for the prize of her high calling, she look beyond the present scene, let her cultivate her understanding without stopping to consider what character the husband may have whom she is destined to marry. Let her only determine, without being too anxious about present happiness, to acquire the qualities that ennoble a rational being, and a rough inelegant husband may shock her taste without destroying her peace of mind. She will not model her soul to suit the frailties of her companion, but to bear with them: his character may be a trial, but not an impediment to virtue.

If Dr. Gregory confined his remark to romantic expectations of constant love and congenial feelings, he should have recollected that experience will banish what advice can never make us cease to wish for, when the imagination is kept alive at the expense of reason.

I own it frequently happens that women who have fostered a romantic unnatural delicacy of feeling, waste their[3] lives in *imagining* how happy they should have been with a husband who could love them with a fervid increasing affection every day, and all day. But they might as well pine married as single—and would not be a jot more unhappy with a bad husband than longing for a good one. That a proper education; or, to speak with more precision, a well stored mind, would enable a woman to support a single life with dignity, I grant; but that she should avoid cultivating her taste, lest her husband should occasionally shock it, is quitting a substance for a shadow. To say the truth, I do not know of what use is an improved taste, if the individual be not

(continued)

A Vindication of the Rights of Woman   (*continued*)

rendered more independent of the casualties of life; if new sources of enjoyment, only dependent on the solitary operations of the mind, are not opened. People of taste, married or single, without distinction, will ever be disgusted by various things that touch not less observing minds. On this conclusion the argument must not be allowed to hinge; but in the whole sum of enjoyment is taste to be denominated a blessing?

The question is, whether it procures most pain or pleasure? The answer will decide the propriety of Dr. Gregory's advice, and show how absurd and tyrannic it is thus to lay down a system of slavery; or to attempt to educate moral beings by any other rules than those deduced from pure reason, which apply to the whole species.

Gentleness of manners, forbearance and long-suffering, are such amiable God-like qualities, that in sublime poetic strains the Deity has been invested with them; and, perhaps, no representation of his goodness so strongly fastens on the human affections as those that represent him abundant in mercy and willing to pardon. Gentleness, considered in this point of view, bears on its front all the characteristics of grandeur, combined with the winning graces of condescension; but what a different aspect it assumes when it is the submissive demeanour of dependence, the support of weakness that loves, because it wants protection; and is forbearing, because it must silently endure injuries; smiling under the lash at which it dare not snarl. Abject as this picture appears, it is the portrait of an accomplished woman, according to the received opinion of female excellence, separated by specious reasoners from human excellence. Or, they[4] kindly restore the rib, and make one moral being of a man and woman; not forgetting to give her all the "submissive charms."

How women are to exist in that state where there is to be neither marrying or giving in marriage, we are not told. For though moralists have agreed that the tenor of life seems to prove that *man* is prepared by various circumstances for a future state, they constantly concur in advising *woman* only to provide for the present. Gentleness, docility, and a spaniel-like affection are, on this ground, consistently recommended as the cardinal virtues of the sex; and, disregarding the arbitrary economy of nature, one writer has declared that it is masculine for a woman to be melancholy. She was created to be the toy of man, his rattle, and it must jingle in his ears whenever, dismissing reason, he chooses to be amused.

To recommend gentleness, indeed, on a broad basis is strictly philosophical. A frail being should labour to be gentle. But when forbearance confounds right and wrong, it ceases to be a virtue; and, however convenient it may be found in a companion—that companion will ever be considered as an inferior, and only inspire a vapid tenderness, which easily degenerates into contempt. Still, if advice could really make a being gentle, whose natural disposition admitted not of such a fine polish, something towards the advancement of order would be attained; but if, as might quickly be demonstrated, only affectation be produced by this indiscriminate counsel, which throws a stumbling-block in the way of gradual improvement, and true melioration of temper, the sex is not much benefited by sacrificing solid virtues to the attainment of superficial graces, though for a few years they may procure the individuals regal sway.

As a philosopher, I read with indignation the plausible epithets which men use to soften their insults; and, as a moralist, I ask what is meant by such heterogeneous associations, as fair defects, amiable weaknesses, & c.? If there be but one criterion of morals, but one archetype for man, women appear to be suspended by destiny, according to the vulgar tale of Mahomet's coffin; they have neither the unerring instinct of brutes, nor are allowed to fix the eye of reason on a perfect model. They were made to be loved, and must not aim at respect, lest they should be hunted out of society as masculine.

But to view the subject in another point of view. Do passive indolent women make the best wives? Confining our discussion to the present moment of existence, let us see how such weak creatures perform their part? Do the women who, by the attainment of a few superficial accomplishments, have strengthened the prevailing prejudice, merely contribute to the happiness of their husbands? Do they display their charms merely to amuse them? And have women, who have early imbibed notions of passive obedience, sufficient character to manage a family or educate children? So far from it, that, after surveying the history of woman, I cannot help, agreeing with the severest satirist, considering the sex as the weakest as well as the most oppressed half of the species. What does history disclose but marks of inferiority, and how few women have emancipated themselves from the galling yoke of sovereign man?—So few, that the exceptions remind me of an ingenious conjecture respecting Newton: that he was probably a being of superior order, accidentally caged in a human body. Following the same train of thinking, I have been led to imagine that the few extraordinary women who have rushed in eccentrical directions out of the orbit prescribed to their sex, were *male* spirits, confined by mistake in female frames. But if it be not philosophical to think of sex when the soul is mentioned, the inferiority must depend on the organs; or the heavenly fire, which is to ferment the clay, is not given in equal portions.

But avoiding, as I have hitherto done, any direct comparison of the two sexes collectively, or frankly acknowledging the inferiority of woman, according to the present appearance of things, I shall only insist that men have increased that inferiority till women are almost sunk below the standard of rational creatures. Let their faculties have room to unfold, and their virtues to gain strength, and then determine where the whole sex must stand in the intellectual scale. Yet let it be remembered, that for a small number of distinguished women I do not ask a place.

It is difficult for us purblind mortals to say to what height human discoveries and improvements may arrive when the gloom of despotism subsides, which makes us stumble at every step; but, when morality shall be settled on a more solid basis, then, without being gifted with a prophetic spirit, I will venture to predict that woman will be either the friend or slave of man. We shall not, as at present, doubt whether she is a moral agent, or the link which unites man with brutes. But, should it then appear, that like the brutes they were principally created for the use of man, he will let them patiently bite the bridle, and not mock them with empty praise; or, should their rationality be proved, he will not impede their improvement merely to gratify his sensual appetites. He will not, with all the graces of rhetoric, advise them to submit implicitly their understanding to the guidance of man. He will not, when he treats of the education of women, assert that they ought never to have the free use of reason, nor would he recommend cunning and dissimulation to beings who are acquiring, in like manner as himself, the virtues of humanity.

Surely there can be but one rule of right, if morality has an eternal foundation, and whoever sacrifices virtue, strictly so called, to present convenience, or whose *duty* it is to act in such a manner, lives only for the passing day, and cannot be an accountable creature.

The poet then should have dropped his sneer when he says,

"If weak women go astray,
The stars are more in fault than they."

For that they are bound by the adamantine chain of destiny is most certain, if it be proved that they are never to exercise their own reason, never to be independent, never to rise above opinion, or to feel the dignity of a rational will that only bows to God, and often forgets that the universe contains any being but itself and the model of perfection to which its ardent gaze is turned, to adore attributes that, softened into virtues, may be imitated in kind, though the degree overwhelms the enraptured mind.

If, I say, for I would not impress by declamation when Reason offers her sober light, if they be really capable of acting like rational creatures, let them not be treated like slaves; or, like the brutes who are dependent on the reason of man, when they associate with him; but cultivate their minds, give them the salutary, sublime curb of principle, and let them attain conscious dignity by feeling themselves only dependent on God. Teach them, in common with man, to submit to necessity, instead of giving, to render them more pleasing, a sex to morals.

Further, should experience prove that they cannot attain the same degree of strength of mind, perseverance, and fortitude, let their virtues be the same in kind, though they may vainly struggle for the same degree; and the superiority of man will be equally clear, if not clearer; and truth, as it is a simple principle, which admits of no modification, would be common to both. Nay, the order of society as it is at present regulated, would not be inverted, for woman would then only have the rank that reason assigned her, and arts could not be practised to bring the balance even, much less to turn it.

These may be termed utopian dreams. Thanks to that Being who impressed them on my soul, and gave me sufficient strength of mind to dare to exert my own reason, till, becoming dependent only on him for the support of my virtue, I view, with indignation, the mistaken notions that enslave my sex.

(continued)

A Vindication of the Rights of Woman Chapter 2 (*continued*)

I love man as my fellow; but his sceptre, real, or usurped, extends not to me, unless the reason of an individual demands my homage; and even then the submission is to reason, and not to man. In fact, the conduct of an accountable being must be regulated by the operations of its own reason; or on what foundation rests the throne of God?

It appears to me necessary to dwell on these obvious truths, because females have been insulated, as it were; and, while they have been stripped of the virtues that should clothe humanity, they have been decked with artificial graces that enable them to exercise a short-lived tyranny. Love, in their bosoms, taking place of every nobler passion, their sole ambition is to be fair, to raise emotion instead of inspiring respect; and this ignoble desire, like the servility in absolute monarchies, destroys all strength of character. Liberty is the mother of virtue, and if women be, by their very constitution, slaves, and not allowed to breathe the sharp invigorating air of freedom, they must ever languish like exotics, and be reckoned beautiful flaws in nature.

As to the argument respecting the subjection in which the sex has ever been held, it retorts on man. The many have always been enthralled by the few; and monsters, who scarcely have shewn any discernment of human excellence, have tyrannized over thousands of their fellow-creatures. Why have men of superior endowments submitted to such degradation ? For, is it not universally acknowledged that kings, viewed collectively, have ever been inferior, in abilities and virtue, to the same number of men taken from the common mass of mankind—yet, have they not, and are they not still treated with a degree of reverence that is an insult to reason? China is not the only country where a living man has been made a God. *Men* have submitted to superior strength to enjoy with impunity the pleasure of the moment—*women* have only done the same, and therefore till it is proved that the courtier, who servilely resigns the birthright of a man, is not a moral agent, it cannot be demonstrated that woman is essentially inferior to man because she has always been subjugated.

Brutal force has hitherto governed the world, and that the science of politics is in its infancy, is evident from philosophers scrupling to give the knowledge most useful to man that determinate distinction.

I shall not pursue this argument any further than to establish an obvious inference, that as sound politics diffuse liberty, mankind, including woman, will become more wise and virtuous.

NOTES

1. Why should women be censured with petulant acrimony, because they seem to have a passion for a scarlet coat? Has not educatioin placed them more on a level with soldiers than any other class of men?
2. Similar feelings has Milton's pleasing picture of paradisaical happiness ever raised in my mind; yet, instead of envying the lovely pair, I have, with conscious dignity, or Satanic pride, turned to hell for sublimer objects. In the same style, when viewing some noble monument of human art, I have traced the emanation of the Deity in the order I admired, till, descending from that giddy height, I have caught myself contemplating the grandest of all human fights;-for fancy quickly placed, in some solitary recess, an outcast of fortune, rising superior to passion and discontent.
3. For example, the herd of Novelists.
4. Vide Rousseau, and Swedenborg.

The Subjection of Women
John Stuart Mill

Chapter I

The object of this Essay is to explain as clearly as I am able grounds of an opinion which I have held from the very earliest period when I had formed any opinions at all on social political matters, and which, instead of being weakened or modified, has been constantly growing stronger by the progress reflection and the experience of life. That the principle which regulates the existing social relations between the two sexes—the legal subordination of one sex to the other—is wrong itself, and now one of the chief hindrances to human improvement; and that it ought to be replaced by a principle of perfect equality, admitting no power or privilege on the one side, nor disability on the other . . .

The generality of a practice is in some cases a strong presumption that it is, or at all events once was, conducive to laudable ends. This is the case, when the practice was first adopted, or afterwards kept up, as a means to such ends, and was grounded on experience of the mode in which they could be most effectually attained. If the authority of men over women, when first established, had been the result of a conscientious comparison between different modes of constituting the government of society; if, after trying various other modes of social organisation—the government of women over men, equality between the two, and such mixed and divided modes of government as might be invented—it had been decided, on the testimony of experience, that the mode in which women are wholly under the rule of men, having no share at all in public concerns, and each in private being under the legal obligation of obedience to the man with whom she has associated her destiny, was the arrangement most conducive to the happiness and well-being of both; its general adoption might then be fairly thought to be some evidence that, at the time when it was adopted, it was the best: though even then the considerations which recommended it may, like so many other primeval social facts of the greatest importance, have subsequently, in the course of ages, ceased to exist. But the state of the case is in every respect the reverse of this. In the first place, the opinion in favour of the present system, which entirely subordinates the weaker sex to the stronger, rests upon theory only; for there never has been trial made of any other: so that experience, in the sense in which it is vulgarly opposed to theory, cannot be pretended to have pronounced any verdict. And in the second place, the adoption of this system of inequality never was the result of deliberation, or forethought, or any social ideas, or any notion whatever of what conduced to the benefit of humanity or the good order of society. It arose simply from the fact that from the very earliest twilight of human society, every woman owing to the value attached to her by men, combined with her inferiority in muscular strength) was found in a state of bondage to some man. Laws and systems of polity always begin by recognising the relations they find already existing between individuals. They convert what was a mere physical fact into a legal right, give it the sanction of society, and principally aim at the substitution of public and organised means of asserting and protecting these rights, instead of the irregular and lawless conflict of physical strength. Those who had already been compelled to obedience became in this manner legally bound to it. Slavery, from be inn a mere affair of force between the master and the slave, became regularised and a matter of compact among the masters, who, binding themselves to one another for common protection, guaranteed by their collective strength the private possessions of each, including his slaves. In early times, the great majority of the male sex were slaves, as well as the whole of the female. And many ages elapsed, some of them ages of high cultivation, before any thinker was bold enough to question the rightfulness, and the absolute social necessity, either of the one slavery or of the other. By degrees such thinkers did arise; and (the general progress of society assisting) the slavery of the male sex has, in all the countries of Christian Europe at least (though, in one of them, only within the last few years) been at length abolished, and that of the female sex has been gradually changed into a milder form of dependence. But this dependence, as it exists at present, is not an original institution, taking a fresh start from considerations of justice and social expediency—it is the primitive state of slavery lasting on, through successive mitigations and modifications occasioned by the same causes which have softened the general manners, and brought all human relations more under the control of justice and the influence of humanity. It has not lost the taint of its brutal origin. No presumption in its favour, therefore, can be drawn from the fact of its existence. The only such presumption which it could be supposed to have, must be grounded on its having lasted till now, when so many other things which came down from the same odious source have been done away with. And this, indeed, is what makes it strange to ordinary ears, to hear it asserted that the inequality of rights between men and women has no other source than the law of the strongest . . .

Some will object, that a comparison cannot fairly be made between the government of the male sex and the forms of unjust power which I have adduced in illustration of it, since these are arbitrary, and the effect of mere usurpation, while it on the contrary is natural. But was there ever any domination which did not appear natural to those who possessed it? There was a time when the division of mankind into two classes, a small one of masters and a numerous one of slaves,

(continued)

The Subjection of Women (*continued*)

appeared, even to the most cultivated minds, to be natural, and the only natural, condition of the human race. No less an intellect, and one which contributed no less to the progress of human thought, than Aristotle, held this opinion without doubt or misgiving; and rested it on the same premises on which the same assertion in regard to the dominion of men over women is usually based, namely that there are different natures among mankind, free natures, and slave natures; that the Greeks were of a free nature, the barbarian races of Thracians and Asiatics of a slave nature. But why need I go back to Aristotle? Did not the slave-owners of the Southern United States maintain the same doctrine, with all the fanaticism with which men cling to the theories that justify their passions and legitimate their personal interests? Did they not call heaven and earth to witness that the dominion of the white man over the black is natural, that the black race is by nature incapable of freedom, and marked out for slavery? some even going so far as to say that the freedom of manual labourers is an unnatural order of things anywhere. Again, the theorists of absolute monarchy have always affirmed it to be the only natural form of government; issuing from the patriarchal, which was the primitive and spontaneous form of society, framed on the model of the paternal, which is anterior to society itself, and, as they contend, the most natural authority of all. Nay, for that matter, the law of force itself, to those who could not plead any other has always seemed the most natural of all grounds for the exercise of authority. Conquering races hold it to be Nature's own dictate that the conquered should obey the conquerors, or as they euphoniously paraphrase it, that the feebler and more unwarlike races should submit to the braver and manlier. The smallest acquaintance with human life in the middle ages, shows how supremely natural the dominion of the feudal nobility over men of low condition appeared to the nobility themselves, and how unnatural the conception seemed, of a person of the inferior class claiming equality with them, or exercising authority over them. It hardly seemed less so to the class held in subjection. The emancipated serfs and burgesses, even in their most vigorous struggles, never made any pretension to a share of authority; they only demanded more or less of limitation to the power of tyrannising over them. So true is it that unnatural generally means only uncustomary, and that everything which is usual appears natural. The subjection of women to men being a universal custom, any departure from it quite naturally appears unnatural. But how entirely, even in this case, the feeling is dependent on custom, appears by ample experience. Nothing so much astonishes the people of distant parts of the world, when they first learn anything about England, as to be told that it is under a queen; the thing seems to them so unnatural as to be almost incredible. To Englishmen this does not seem in the least degree unnatural, because they are used to it; but they do feel it unnatural that women should be soldiers or Members of Parliament. In the feudal ages, on the contrary, war and politics were not thought unnatural to women, because not unusual; it seemed natural that women of the privileged classes should be of manly character, inferior in nothing but bodily strength to their husbands and fathers. The independence of women seemed rather less unnatural to the Greeks than to other ancients, on account of the fabulous Amazons (whom they believed to be historical), and the partial example afforded by the Spartan women; who, though no less subordinate by law than in other Greek states, were more free in fact, and being trained to bodily exercises in the same manner with men, gave ample proof that they were not naturally disqualified for them. There can be little doubt that Spartan experience suggested to Plato, among many other of his doctrines, that of the social and political equality of the two sexes.

But, it will be said, the rule of men over women differs from all these others in not being a rule a rule of force: it is accepted voluntarily; women make no complaint, and are consenting parties to it. In the first place, a great number of women do not accept it. Ever since there have been women able to make their sentiments known by their writings (the only mode of publicity which society permits to them), an increasing number of them have recorded protests against their present social condition: and recently many thousands of them, headed by the most eminent women known to the public, have petitioned Parliament for their admission to the Parliamentary Suffrage The claim of women to be educated as solidly, and in the same branches of knowledge, as men, is urged with growing intensity, and with a great prospect of success; while the demand for their admission into professions and occupations hitherto closed against them, becomes every year more urgent. Though there are not in this country, as there are in the United States, periodical conventions and an organised party to agitate for the Rights of Women, there is a numerous and active society organised and managed by women, for the more limited object of obtaining the political franchise. Nor is it only in our own country and in America that women are beginning to protest, more or less collectively, against the disabilities under which they labour. France, and Italy, and Switzerland, and Russia now afford examples of the same thing. How many more women there are who silently cherish similar aspirations, no one can possibly know; but there are abundant tokens how many would cherish them, were they not so strenuously taught to repress them as contrary to the proprieties of their sex. . . .

All causes, social and natural, combine to make it unlikely that women should be collectively rebellious to the power of men. They are so far in a position different from all other subject classes, that their masters require something more from them than actual service. Men do not want solely the obedience of women, they want their sentiments. All men, except the most brutish, desire to have, in the woman most nearly connected with them, not a forced slave but a willing one, not a slave merely, but a favourite. They have therefore put everything in practice to enslave their minds. The masters of all other slaves rely, for maintaining obedience, on fear; either fear of themselves, or religious fears. The masters of women wanted more than simple obedience, and they turned the whole force of education to effect their purpose. All women are brought up from the very earliest years in the belief that their ideal of character is the very opposite to that of men; not self will, and government by self-control, but submission, and yielding to the control of other. All the moralities tell them that it is the duty of women, and all the current sentimentalities that it is their nature, to live for others; to make complete abnegation of themselves, and to have no life but in their affections. And by their affections are meant the only ones they are allowed to have—those to the men with whom they are connected, or to the children who constitute an additional and indefeasible tie between them and a man. When we put together three things—first, the natural attraction between opposite sexes; secondly, the wife's entire dependence on the husband, every privilege or pleasure she has being either his gift, or depending entirely on his will; and lastly, that the principal object of human pursuit, consideration, and all objects of social ambition, can in general be sought or obtained by her only through him, it would be a miracle if the object of being attractive to men had not become the polar star of feminine education and formation of character. And, this great means of influence over the minds of women having been acquired, an instinct of selfishness made men avail themselves of it to the utmost as a means of holding women in subjection, by representing to them meekness, submissiveness, and resignation of all individual will into the hands of a man, as an essential part of sexual attractiveness. Can it be doubted that any of the other yokes which mankind have succeeded in breaking, would have subsisted till now if the same means had existed, and had been so sedulously used, to bow down their minds to it . . .

The preceding considerations are amply sufficient to show that custom, however universal it may be, affords in this case no presumption, and ought not to create any prejudice, in favour of the arrangements which place women in social and political subjection to men . . .

. . . It will not do, for instance to assert in general terms, that the experience of mankind has pronounced in favour of the existing system. Experience cannot possibly have decided between two courses, so long as there has only been experience of one. If it be said that the doctrine of the equality of the sexes rests only on theory, it must be remembered that the contrary doctrine also has only theory to rest upon. All that is proved in its favour by direct experience, is that mankind have been able to exist under it, and to attain the degree of improvement and prosperity which we now see; but whether that prosperity has been attained sooner, or is now greater, than it would have been under the other system, experience does not say. On the other hand, experience does say, that every step in improvement has been so invariably accompanied by a step made in raising the social position of women, that historians and philosophers have been led to adopt their elevation or debasement as on the whole the surest test and most correct measure of the civilisation of a people or an age. Through all the progressive period of human history, the condition of women has been approaching nearer to equality with men. This does not of itself prove that the assimilation must go on to complete equality; but it assuredly affords some presumption that such is the case.

Neither does it avail anything to say that the nature of the two sexes adapts them to their present functions and position, and renders these appropriate to them. Standing on the ground of common sense and the constitution of the human mind, I deny that anyone knows, or can know, the nature of

(continued)

The Subjection of Women (*continued*)

the two sexes, as long as they have only been seen in their present relation to one another. If men had ever been found in society without women, or women without men, or if there had been a society of men and women in which the women were not under the control of the men, something might have been positively known about the mental and moral differences which may be inherent in the nature of each. What is now called the nature of women is an eminently artificial thing—the result of forced repression in some directions, unnatural stimulation in others. It may be asserted without scruple, that no other class of dependents have had their character so entirely distorted from its natural proportions by their relation with their masters; for, if conquered and slave races have been, in some respects, more forcibly repressed, whatever in them has not been crushed down by an iron heel has generally been let alone, and if left with any liberty of development, it has developed itself according to its own laws; but in the case of women, a hot-house and stove cultivation has always been carried on of some of the capabilities of their nature, for the benefit and pleasure of their masters Then, because certain products of the general vital force sprout luxuriantly and reach a great development in this heated atmosphere and under this active nurture and watering, while other shoots from the same root, which are left outside in the wintry air, with ice purposely heaped all round them, have a stunted growth, and some are burnt off with fire and disappear; men, with that inability to recognise their own work which distinguishes the unanalytic mind, indolently believe that the tree grows of itself in the way they have made it grow, and that it would die if one half of it were not kept in a vapour bath and the other half in the snow . . .

Even the preliminary knowledge, what the differences between the sexes now are, apart from all question as to how they are made what they are, is still in the crudest and most' incomplete state. Medical practitioners and physiologists have ascertained, to some extent, the differences in bodily constitution; and this is an important element to the psychologist: but hardly any medical practitioner is a psychologist. Respecting the mental characteristics of women; their observations are of no more worth than those of common men. It is a subject on which nothing final can be known, so long as those who alone can really know it, women themselves, have given but little testimony, and that little, mostly suborned. It is easy to know stupid women. Stupidity is much the same all the world over. A stupid person's notions and feelings may confidently be inferred from those which prevail in the circle by which the person is surrounded. Not so with those whose opinions and feelings are an emanation from their own nature and faculties. It is only a man here and there who has any tolerable knowledge of the character even of the women of his own family. I do not mean, of their capabilities; these nobody knows, not even themselves, because most of them have never been called out. I mean their actually existing thoughts and feelings. Many a man think he perfectly understands women, because he has had amatory relations with several, perhaps with many of them. If he is a good observer, and his experience extends to quality as well as quantity, he may have learnt something of one narrow department of their nature—an important department, no doubt. But of all the rest of it, few persons are generally more ignorant, because there are few from whom it is so carefully hidden. The most favourable case which a man can generally have for studying the character of a woman, is that of his own wife: for the opportunities are greater, and the cases of complete sympathy not so unspeakably rare. And in fact, this is the source from which any knowledge worth having on the subject has, I believe, generally come. But most men have not had the opportunity of studying in this way more than a single case: accordingly one can, to an almost laughable degree, infer what a man's wife is like, from his opinions about women in general. To make even this one case yield any result, the woman must be worth knowing, and the man not only a competent judge, but of a character so sympathetic in itself, and so well adapted to hers, that he can either read her mind by sympathetic intuition, or has nothing in himself which makes her shy of disclosing it, Hardly anything, I believe, can be more rare than this conjunction. It often happens that there is the most complete unity of feeling and community of interests as to all external things, yet the one has as little admission into the internal life of the other as if they were common acquaintance. Even with true affection, authority on the one side and subordination on the other prevent perfect confidence. Though nothing may be intentionally withheld, much is not shown. In the analogous relation of parent and child, the corresponding phenomenon must have been in the observation of everyone. As between father and son, how many are the cases in which the father, in spite of real affection on both sides, obviously to all the world does not know, nor suspect, parts of the son's character familiar to his companions and equals. The truth is, that the position of looking up to another is extremely unpropitious to complete sincerity and openness with him. The fear of losing ground in his opinion or in his feelings is so strong, that even in an upright character, there is an unconscious tendency to show only the best side, or the side which, though not the best, is that which he most likes to see: and it may be confidently said that thorough knowledge of one another hardly ever exists, but between persons who, besides being intimates, are equals. How much more true, then, must all this be, when the one is not only under the authority of the other, but has it inculcated on her as a duty to reckon everything else subordinate to his comfort and pleasure, and to let him neither see nor feel anything coming from her, except what is agreeable to him. All these difficulties stand in the way of a man's obtaining any thorough knowledge even of the one woman whom alone, in general, he has sufficient opportunity of studying. When we further consider that to understand one woman is not necessarily to understand any other woman; that even if he could study many women of one rank, or of one country, he would not thereby understand women of other ranks or countries; and even if he did, they are still only the women of a single period of history; we may safely assert that the knowledge which men can acquire of women, even as they have been and are, without reference to what they might be, is wretchedly imperfect and superficial, and always will be so, until women themselves have told all that they have to tell . . .

NOTE

1. Title-page of Mme de Stael's Delphine.

Chapter II

It will be well to commence the detailed discussion of the subject by the particular branch of it to which the course of our observations has led us: the conditions which the laws of this and all other countries annex to the marriage contract. Marriage being the destination appointed by society for women, the prospect they are brought up to, and the object which it is intended should be sought by all of them, except those who are too little attractive to be chosen by any man as his companion; one might have supposed that everything would have been done to make this condition as eligible to them as possible, that they might have no cause to regret being denied the option of any other. Society, however, both in this, and, at first, in all other cases, has preferred to attain its object by foul rather than fair means: but this is the only case in which it has substantially persisted in them even to the present day. Originally women were taken by force, or regularly sold by their father to the husband. Until a late period in European history, the father had the power to dispose of his daughter in marriage at his own will and pleasure, without any regard to hers. The Church, indeed, was so far faithful to a better morality as to require a formal "yes" from the woman at the marriage ceremony; but there was nothing to show that the consent was other than compulsory; and it was practically impossible for the girl to refuse compliance if the father persevered, except perhaps when she might obtain the protection of religion by a determined resolution to take monastic vows. After marriage, the man had anciently (but this was anterior to Christianity) the power of life and death over his wife. She could invoke no law against him; he was her sole tribunal and law. For a long time he could repudiate her, but she had no corresponding power in regard to him. By the old laws of England, the husband was called the lord of the wife; he was literally regarded as her sovereign, inasmuch that the murder of a man by his wife was called treason (petty as distinguished from high treason), and was more cruelly avenged than was usually the case with high treason, for the penalty was burning to death. Because these various enormities have fallen into disuse (for most of them were never formally abolished, or not until they had long ceased to be practised) men suppose that all is now as it should be in regard to the marriage contract; and we are continually told that civilisation and Christianity have restored to the woman her just rights. Meanwhile the wife is the actual bond servant of her husband: no less so, as far as legal obligation goes, than slaves commonly so called. She vows a livelong obedience to him at the altar, and is held to it all through her life by law. Casuists may say that the obligation of obedience stops short of participation in crime, but it certainly extends to everything else. She can do no act whatever but by his permission, at least tacit. She can acquire

(continued)

The Subjection of Women (*continued*)

no property but for him; the instant it becomes hers, even if by inheritance, it becomes ipso facto his. In this respect the wife's position under the common law of England is worse than that of slaves in the laws of many countries: by the Roman law, for example, a slave might have his peculium, which to a certain extent the law guaranteed to him for his exclusive use. The higher classes in this country have given an analogous advantage to their women, through special contracts setting aside the law, by conditions of pin-money, etc.: since parental feeling being stronger with fathers than the class feeling of their own sex, a father generally prefers his own daughter to a son-in-law who is a stranger to him. By means of settlements, the rich usually contrive to withdraw the whole or part of the inherited property of the wife from the absolute control of the husband: but they do not succeed in keeping it under her own control; the utmost they can do only prevents the husband from squandering it, at the same time debarring the rightful owner from its use. The property itself is out of the reach of both; and as to the income derived from it, the form of settlement most favourable to the wife (that called "to her separate use") only precludes the husband from receiving it instead of her: it must pass through her hands, but if he takes it from her by personal violence as soon as she receives it, he can neither be punished, nor compelled to restitution. This is the amount of the protection which, under the laws of this country, the most powerful nobleman can give to his own daughter as respects her husband. In the immense majority of cases there is no settlement: and the absorption of all rights, all property, as well as all freedom of action, is complete. The two are called "one person in law," for the purpose of inferring that whatever is hers is his, but the parallel inference is never drawn that whatever is his is hers; the maxim is not applied against the man, except to make him responsible to third parties for her acts, as a master is for the acts of his slaves or of his cattle. I am far from pretending that wives are in general no better treated than slaves; but no slave is a slave to the same lengths, and in so full a sense of the word, as a wife is. Hardly any slave, except one immediately attached to the master's person, is a slave at all hours and all minutes; in general he has, like a soldier, his fixed task, and when it is done, or when he is off duty, he disposes, within certain limits, of his own time, and has a family life into which the master rarely intrudes. "Uncle Tom" under his first master had his own life in his "cabin," almost as much as any man whose work takes him away from home, is able to have in his own family. But it cannot be so with the wife. Above all, a female slave has (in Christian countries) an admitted right, and is considered under a moral obligation, to refuse to her master the last familiarity. Not so the wife: however brutal a tyrant she may unfortunately be chained to—though she may know that he hates her, though it may be his daily pleasure to torture her, and though she may feel it impossible not to loathe him—he can claim from her and enforce the lowest degradation of a human being, that of being made the instrument of an animal function contrary to her inclinations. While she is held in this worst description of slavery as to her own person, what is her position in regard to the children in whom she and her master have a joint interest? They are by law his children. He alone has any legal rights over them. Not one act can she do towards or in relation to them, except by delegation from him. Even after he is dead she is not their legal guardian, unless he by will has made her so. He could even send them away from her, and deprive her of the means of seeing or corresponding with them, until this power was in some degree restricted by Serjeant Talfourd's Act. This is her legal state. And from this state she has no means of withdrawing herself. If she leaves her husband, she can take nothing with her, neither her children nor anything which is rightfully her own. If he chooses, he can compel her to return, by law, or by physical force; or he may content himself with seizing for his own use anything which she may earn, or which may be given to her by her relations. It is only legal separation by a decree of a court of justice, which entitles her to live apart, without being forced back into the custody of an exasperated jailer—or which empowers her to apply any earnings to her own use, without fear that a man whom perhaps she has not seen for twenty years will pounce upon her some day and carry all off. This legal separation, until lately, the courts of justice would only give at an expense which made it inaccessible to anyone out of the higher ranks. Even now it is only given in cases of desertion, or of the extreme of cruelty; and yet complaints are made every day that it is granted too easily. Surely, if a woman is denied any lot in life but that of being the personal body-servant of a despot, and is dependent for everything upon the chance of finding one who may be disposed to make a favourite of her instead of merely a drudge, it is a very cruel aggravation of her fate that she should be allowed to try this chance only once. The natural sequel and corollary from this state of things would be, that since her all in life depends upon obtaining a good master, she should be allowed to change again and again until she finds one. I am not saying that she ought to be allowed this privilege. That is a totally different consideration. The question of divorce, in the sense involving liberty of remarriage, is one into which it is foreign to my purpose to enter. All I now say is, that to those to whom nothing but servitude is allowed, the free choice of servitude is the only, though a most insufficient, alleviation. Its refusal completes the assimilation of the wife to the slave—and the slave under not the mildest form of slavery: for in some slave codes the slave could, under certain circumstances of ill usage, legally compel the master to sell him. But no amount of ill usage, without adultery superadded, will in England free a wife from her tormentor.

I have no desire to exaggerate, nor does the case stand in any need of exaggeration. I have described the wife's legal position, not her actual treatment. The laws of most countries are far worse than the people who execute them, and many of them are only able to remain laws by being seldom or never carried into effect. If married life were all that it might be expected to be, looking to the laws alone, society would be a hell upon earth. Happily there are both feelings and interests which in many men exclude, and in most, greatly temper, the impulses and propensities which lead to tyranny: and of those feelings, the tie which connects a man with his wife affords, in a normal state of things, incomparably the strongest example. The only tie which at all approaches to it, that between him and his children, tends, in all save exceptional cases, to strengthen, instead of conflicting with, the first. Because this is true; because men in general do not inflict, nor women suffer, all the misery which could be inflicted and suffered if the full power of tyranny with which the man is legally invested were acted on; the defenders of the existing form of the institution think that all its iniquity is justified, and that any complaint is merely quarrelling with the evil which is the price paid for every great good . . .

When we consider how vast is the number of men, in any great country, who are little higher than brutes, and that this never prevents them from being able, through the law of marriage, to obtain a victim, the breadth and depth of human misery caused in this shape alone by the abuse of the institution swells to something appalling. Yet these are only the extreme cases. They are the lowest abysses, but there is a sad succession of depth after depth before reaching them. In domestic as in political tyranny, the case of absolute monsters chiefly illustrates the institution by showing that there is scarcely any horror which may not occur under it if the despot pleases, and thus setting in a strong light what must be the terrible frequency of things only a little less atrocious. Absolute fiends are as rare as angels, perhaps rarer: ferocious savages, with occasional touches of humanity, are however very frequent: and in the wide interval which separates these from any worthy representatives of the human species, how many are the forms and gradations of animalism and selfishness, often under an outward varnish of civilisation and even cultivation, living at peace with the law, maintaining a creditable appearance to all who are not under their power, yet sufficient often to make the lives of all who are so, a torment and a burthen to them! . . .

. . . In a family, as in a state, some one person must be the ultimate ruler. Who shall decide when married people differ in opinion? Both cannot have their way, yet a decision one way or the other must be come to.

It is not true that in all voluntary association between two people, one of them must be absolute master: still less that the law must determine which of them it shall be. The most frequent case of voluntary association, next to marriage, is partnership in business: and it is not found or thought necessary to enact that in every partnership, one partner shall have entire control over the concern, and the others shall be bound to obey his orders. No one would enter into partnership on terms which would subject him to the responsibilities of a principal, with only the powers and privileges of a clerk or agent. If the law dealt with other contracts as it does with marriage, it would ordain that one partner should administer the common business as if it was his private concern; that the others should have only delegated powers; and that this one should be designated by some general presumption of law, for example as being the eldest. The law never does this: nor does experience show it to be necessary that any theoretical inequality of power should exist between the partners, or that the partnership should have any other conditions than what they may themselves appoint by their articles of agreement. Yet it might seem that the exclusive power

(continued)

The Subjection of Women (*continued*)

might be conceded with less danger to the rights and interests of the inferior, in the case of partnership than in that of marriage, since he is free to cancel the power by withdrawing from the connexion. The wife has no such power, and even if she had, it is almost always desirable that she should try all measures before resorting to it.

It is quite true that things which have to be decided everyday, and cannot adjust themselves gradually, or wait for a compromise, ought to depend on one will; one person must have their sole control. But it does not follow that this should always be the same person. The natural arrangement is a division of powers between the two; each being absolute in the executive branch of their own department, and any change of system and principle requiring the consent of both. The division neither can nor should be pre-established by the law, since it must depend on individual capacities and suitabilities. If the two persons chose, they might pre-appoint it by the marriage contract, as pecuniary arrangements are now often pre-appointed. There would seldom be any difficulty in deciding such things by mutual consent, unless the marriage was one of those unhappy ones in which all other things, as well as this, become subjects of bickering and dispute. The division of rights would naturally follow the division of duties and functions; and that is already made by consent, or at all events not by law, but by general custom, modified and modifiable at the pleasure of the persons concerned . . .

There are, no doubt, women, as there are men, whom equality of consideration will not satisfy; with whom there is no peace while any will or wish is regarded but their own. Such persons are a proper subject for the law of divorce. They are only fit to live alone, and no human beings ought to be compelled to associate their lives with them. But the legal subordination tends to make such characters among women more, rather than less, frequent. If the man exerts his whole power, the woman is of course crushed: but if she is treated with indulgence, and permitted to assume power, there is no rule to set limits to her encroachments. The law, not determining her rights, but theoretically allowing her none at all, practically declares that the measure of what she has a right to, is what she can contrive to get.

The equality of married persons before the law, is not only the sole mode in which that particular relation can be made consistent with justice to both sides, and conducive to the happiness of both, but it is the only means of rendering the daily life of mankind, in any high sense, a school of moral cultivation. Though the truth may not be felt or generally acknowledged for generations to come, the only school of genuine moral sentiment is society between equals. The moral education of mankind has hitherto emanated chiefly from the law of force, and is adapted almost solely to the relations which force creates. In the less advanced states of society, people hardly recognise any relation with their equals. To be an equal is to be an enemy. Society, from its highest place to its lowest, is one long chain, or rather ladder, where every individual is either above or below his nearest neighbour, and wherever he does not command he must obey. Existing moralities, accordingly, are mainly fitted to a relation of command and obedience. Yet command and obedience are but unfortunate necessities of human life: society in equality is its normal state. Already in modern life, and more and more as it progressively improves, command and obedience become exceptional facts in life, equal association its general rule. The morality of the first ages rested on the obligation to submit to power; that of the ages next following, on the right of the weak to the forbearance and protection of the strong. How much longer is one form of society and life to content itself with the morality made for another? We have had the morality of submission, and the morality of chivalry and generosity; the time is now come for the morality of justice. Whenever, in former ages, any approach has been made to society in equality, Justice has asserted its claims as the foundation of virtue. It was thus in the free republics of antiquity. But even in the best of these, the equals were limited to the free male citizens; slaves, women, and the unenfranchised residents were under the law of force. The joint influence of Roman civilisation and of Christianity obliterated these distinctions, and in theory (if only partially in practice) declared the claims of the human being, as such, to be paramount to those of sex, class, or social position. The barriers which had begun to be levelled were raised again by the northern conquests; and the whole of modern history consists of the slow process by which they have since been wearing away. We are entering into an order of things in which justice will again be the primary virtue; grounded as before on equal, but now also on sympathetic association; having its root no longer in the instinct of equals for self protection, but in a cultivated sympathy between them; and no one being now left out, but an equal measure being extended to all. It is no novelty that mankind do not distinctly foresee their own changes, and that their sentiments are adapted to past, not to coming ages. To see the futurity of the species has always been the privilege of the intellectual elite, or of those who have learnt from them; to have the feelings of that futurity has been the distinction, and usually the martyrdom, of a still rarer elite. Institutions, books, education, society, all go on training human beings for the old, long after the new has come; much more when it is only coming. But the true virtue of human beings is fitness to live together as equals; claiming nothing for themselves but what they as freely concede to everyone else; regarding command of any kind as an exceptional necessity, and in all cases a temporary one; and preferring, whenever possible, the society of those with whom leading and following can be alternate and reciprocal. To these virtues, nothing in life as at present constituted gives cultivation by exercise. The family is a school of despotism, in which the virtues of despotism, but also its vices, are largely nourished. Citizenship, in free countries, is partly a school of society in equality; but citizenship fills only a small place in modern life, and does not come near the daily habits or inmost sentiments. The family, justly constituted, would be the real school of the virtues of freedom. It is sure to be a sufficient one of everything else. It will always be a school of obedience for the children, of command for the parents. What is needed is, that it should be a school of sympathy in equality, of living together in love, without power on one side or obedience on the other. This it ought to be between the parents. It would then be an exercise of those virtues which each requires to fit them for all other association, and a model to the children of the feelings and conduct which their temporary training by means of obedience is designed to render habitual, and therefore natural, to them. The moral training of mankind will never be adapted to the conditions of the life for which all other human progress is a preparation, until they practise in the family the same moral rule which is adapted to the normal constitution of human society. Any sentiment of freedom which can exist in a man whose nearest and dearest intimacies, are with those of whom he is absolute master, is not the genuine or Christian love of freedom, but, what the love of freedom generally was in the ancients and in the middle ages—an intense feeling of the dignity and importance of his own personality; making him disdain a yoke for himself, of which he has no abhorrence whatever in the abstract, but which he is abundantly ready to impose on others for his own interest or glorification.

I readily admit (and it is the very foundation of my hopes) that numbers of married people even under the present law (in the higher classes of England probably a great majority), live in the spirit of a just law of equality. Laws never would be improved, if there were not numerous persons whose moral sentiments are better than the existing laws. Such persons ought to support the principles here advocated; of which the only object is to make all other married couples similar to what these are now. But persons even of considerable moral worth, unless they are also thinkers, are very ready to believe that laws or practices, the evils of which they have not personally experienced, do not produce any evils, but (if seeming to be generally approved of) probably do good, and that it is wrong to object to them. It would, however, be a great mistake in such married people to suppose, because the legal conditions of the tie which unites them do not occur to their thoughts once in a twelve month, and because they live and feel in all respects as if they were legally equals, that the same is the case with all other married couples, wherever the husband is not a notorious ruffian. To suppose this, would be to show equal ignorance of human nature and of fact. The less fit a man is for the possession of power—the less likely to be allowed to exercise it over any person with that person's voluntary consent—the more does he hug himself in the consciousness of the power the law gives him, exact its legal rights to the utmost point which custom (the custom of men like himself) will tolerate, and take pleasure in using the power, merely to enliven the agreeable sense of possessing it. What is more; in the most naturally brutal and morally uneducated part of the lower classes, the legal slavery of the woman, and something in the merely physical subjection to their will as an instrument, causes them to feel a sort of disrespect and contempt towards their own wife which they do not feel towards any other woman, or any other human being, with whom they come in contact; and which makes her seem to them an appropriate subject for any kind of indignity. Let an acute observer of the signs of feeling, who has the requisite opportunities, judge for himself whether this is not the case: and if he finds that it is, let him not wonder at any amount of

(continued)

The Subjection of Women (*continued*)

disgust and indignation that can be felt against institutions which lead naturally to this depraved state of the human mind.

We shall be told, perhaps, that religion imposes the duty of obedience; as every established fact which is too bad to admit of any other defence, is always presented to us as an injunction of religion. The Church, it is very true, enjoins it in her formularies, but it would be difficult to derive any such injunction from Christianity. We are told that St. Paul said, "Wives, obey your husbands": but he also said, "Slaves, obey your masters." It was not St. Paul's business, nor was it consistent with his object, the propagation of Christianity, to incite anyone to rebellion against existing laws. The Apostle's acceptance of all social institutions as he found them, is no more to be construed as a disapproval of attempts to improve them at the proper time, than his declaration, "The powers that be are ordained of God," gives his sanction to military despotism, and to that alone, as the Christian form of political government, or commands passive obedience to it. To pretend that Christianity was intended to stereotype existing forms of government and society, and protect them against change, is to reduce it to the level of Islamism or of Brahminism. It is precisely because Christianity has not done this, that it has been the religion of the progressive portion of mankind, and Islamism, Brahminism, etc. have been those of the stationary portions; or rather (for there is no such thing as a really stationary society) of the declining portions. There have been abundance of people, in all ages of Christianity, who tried to make it something of the same kind; to convert us into a sort of Christian Mussulmans, with the Bible for a Koran, prohibiting all improvement: and great has been their power, and many have had to sacrifice their lives in resisting them. But they have been resisted, and the resistance has made us what we are, and will yet make us what we are to be.

After what has been said respecting the obligation of obedience, it is almost superfluous to say anything concerning the more special point included in the general one—a woman's right to her own property; for I need not hope that this treatise can make any impression upon those who need anything to convince them that a woman's inheritance or gains ought to be as much her own after marriage as before. The rule is simple: whatever would be the husband's or wife's if they were not married, should be under their exclusive control during marriage; which need not interfere with the power to tie up property by settlement, in order to preserve it for children. Some people are sentimentally shocked at the idea of a separate interest in money matters as inconsistent with the ideal fusion of two lives into one. For my own part, I am one of the strongest supporters of community of goods, when resulting from an entire unity of feeling in the owners, which makes all things common between them. But I have no relish for a community of goods resting on the doctrine, that what is mine is yours, but what is yours is not mine; and I should prefer to decline entering into such a compact with anyone, though I were myself the person to profit by it.

This particular injustice and oppression to women, which is, to common apprehensions, more obvious than all the rest, admits of remedy without interfering with any other mischiefs: and there can belittle doubt that it will be one of the earliest remedied. Already, in many of the new and several of the old States of the American Confederation, provisions have been inserted even in the written Constitutions, securing to women equality of rights in this respect: and thereby improving materially the position, in the marriage relation, of those women at least who have property, by leaving them one instrument of power which they have not signed away; and preventing also the scandalous abuse of the marriage institution, which is perpetrated when a man entraps a girl into marrying him without a settlement, for the sole purpose of getting possession of her money. When the support of the family depends, not on property, but on earnings, the common arrangement, by which the man earns the income and the wife superintends the domestic expenditure, seems to me in general the most suitable division of labour between the two persons. If, in addition to the physical suffering of bearing children, and the whole responsibility of their care and education in early years, the wife undertakes the careful and economical application of the husband's earnings to the general comfort of the family; she takes not only her fair share, but usually the larger share, of the bodily and mental exertion required by their joint existence. If she undertakes any additional portion, it seldom relieves her from this, but only prevents her from performing it properly. The care which she is herself disabled from taking of the children and the household, nobody else takes; those of the children who do not die, grow up as they best can, and the management of the household is likely to be so bad, as even in point of economy to be a great drawback from the value of the wife's earnings. In another wise just state of things, it is not, therefore, I think, a desirable custom, that the wife should contribute by her labour to the income of the family. In an unjust state of things, her doing so may be useful to her, by making her of more value in the eyes of the man who is legally her master; but, on the other hand, it enables him still farther to abuse his power, by forcing her to work, and leaving the support of the family to her exertions, while he spends most of his time in drinking and idleness. The power of earning is essential to the dignity of a woman, if she has not independent property. But if marriage were an equal contract, not implying the obligation of obedience; if the connexion were no longer enforced to the oppression of those to whom it is purely a mischief, but a separation, on just terms (I do not now speak of a divorce), could be obtained by any woman who was morally entitled to it; and if she would then find all honourable employments as freely open to her as to men; it would not be necessary for her protection, that during marriage she should make this particular use of her faculties. Like a man when he chooses a profession, so, when a woman marries, it may in general be understood that she makes choice of the management of a household, and the bringing up of a family, as the first call upon her exertions, during as many years of her life as may be required for the purpose; and that she renounces, not all other objects and occupations, but all which are not consistent with the requirements of this. The actual exercise, in a habitual or systematic manner, of outdoor occupations, or such as cannot be carried on at home, would by this principle be practically interdicted to the greater number of married women. But the utmost latitude ought to exist for the adaptation of general rules to individual suitabilities; and there ought to be nothing to prevent faculties exceptionally adapted to any other pursuit, from obeying their vocation notwithstanding marriage: due provision being made for supplying otherwise any falling-short which might become inevitable, in her full performance of the ordinary functions of mistress of a family. These things, if once opinion were rightly directed on the subject, might with perfect safety be left to be regulated by opinion, without any interference of law.

The Second Sex
Simone de Beauvoir

Introduction

Woman as Other

FOR a long time I have hesitated to write a book on woman. The subject is irritating, especially to women; and it is not new. Enough ink has been spilled in quarrelling over feminism, and perhaps we should say no more about it. It is still talked about, however, for the voluminous nonsense uttered during the last century seems to have done little to illuminate the problem. After all, is there a problem? And if so, what is it? Are there women, really? Most assuredly the theory of the eternal feminine still has its adherents who will whisper in your ear: 'Even in Russia women still are women'; and other erudite persons—sometimes the very same—say with a sigh: 'Woman is losing her way, woman is lost.' One wonders if women still exist, if they will always exist, whether or not it is desirable that they should, what place they occupy in this world, what their place should be. 'What has become of women?' was asked recently in an ephemeral magazine.

But first we must ask: what is a woman? 'Tota mulier in utero', says one, 'woman is a womb'. But in speaking of certain women, connoisseurs declare that they are not women, although they are equipped with a uterus like the rest. All agree in recognising the fact that females exist in the human species; today as always they make up about one half of humanity. And yet we are told that femininity is in danger; we are exhorted to be women, remain women, become women. It would appear, then, that every female human being is not necessarily a woman; to be so considered she must share in that mysterious and threatened reality known as femininity. Is this attribute something secreted by the

(continued)

The Second Sex (continued)

ovaries? Or is it a Platonic essence, a product of the philosophic imagination? Is a rustling petticoat enough to bring it down to earth? Although some women try zealously to incarnate this essence, it is hardly patentable. It is frequently described in vague and dazzling terms that seem to have been borrowed from the vocabulary of the seers, and indeed in the times of St Thomas it was considered an essence as certainly defined as the somniferous virtue of the poppy.

But conceptualism has lost ground. The biological and social sciences no longer admit the existence of unchangeably fixed entities that determine given characteristics, such as those ascribed to woman, the Jew, or the Negro. Science regards any characteristic as a reaction dependent in part upon a *situation*. If today femininity no longer exists, then it never existed. But does the word *woman*, then, have no specific content? This is stoutly affirmed by those who hold to the philosophy of the enlightenment, of rationalism, of nominalism; women, to them, are merely the human beings arbitrarily designated by the word *woman*. Many American women particularly are prepared to think that there is no longer any place for woman as such; if a backward individual still takes herself for a woman, her friends advise her to be psychoanalysed and thus get rid of this obsession. In regard to a work, *Modern Woman: The Lost Sex*, which in other respects has its irritating features, Dorothy Parker has written: 'I cannot be just to books which treat of woman as woman . . . My idea is that all of us, men as well as women, should be regarded as human beings.' But nominalism is a rather inadequate doctrine, and the antifeminists have had no trouble in showing that women simply *are* not men. Surely woman is, like man, a human being; but such a declaration is abstract. The fact is that every concrete human being is always a singular, separate individual. To decline to accept such notions as the eternal feminine, the black soul, the Jewish character, is not to deny that Jews, Negroes, women exist today—this denial does not represent a liberation for those concerned, but rather a flight from reality. Some years ago a well-known woman writer refused to permit her portrait to appear in a series of photographs especially devoted to women writers; she wished to be counted among the men. But in order to gain this privilege she made use of her husband's influence! Women who assert that they are men lay claim none the less to masculine consideration and respect. I recall also a young Trotskyite standing on a platform at a boisterous meeting and getting ready to use her fists, in spite of her evident fragility. She was denying her feminine weakness; but it was for love of a militant male whose equal she wished to be. The attitude of defiance of many American women proves that they are haunted by a sense of their femininity. In truth, to go for a walk with one's eyes open is enough to demonstrate that humanity is divided into two classes of individuals whose clothes, faces, bodies, smiles, gaits, interests, and occupations are manifestly different. Perhaps these differences are superficial, perhaps they are destined to disappear. What is certain is that they do most obviously exist.

If her functioning as a female is not enough to define woman, if we decline also to explain her through 'the eternal feminine', and if nevertheless we admit, provisionally, that women do exist, then we must face the question "what is a woman"?

To state the question is, to me, to suggest, at once, a preliminary answer. The fact that I ask it is in itself significant. A man would never set out to write a book on the peculiar situation of the human male. But if I wish to define myself, I must first of all say: 'I am a woman'; on this truth must be based all further discussion. A man never begins by presenting himself as an individual of a certain sex; it goes without saying that he is a man. The terms *masculine* and *feminine* are used symmetrically only as a matter of form, as on legal papers. In actuality the relation of the two sexes is not quite like that of two electrical poles, for man represents both the positive and the neutral, as is indicated by the common use of *man* to designate human beings in general; whereas woman represents only the negative, defined by limiting criteria, without reciprocity. In the midst of an abstract discussion it is vexing to hear a man say: 'You think thus and so because you are a woman'; but I know that my only defence is to reply: 'I think thus and so because it is true,' thereby removing my subjective self from the argument. It would be out of the question to reply: 'And you think the contrary because you are a man', for it is understood that the fact of being a man is no peculiarity. A man is in the right in being a man; it is the woman who is in the wrong. It amounts to this: just as for the ancients there was an absolute vertical with reference to which the oblique was defined, so there is an absolute human type, the masculine. Woman has ovaries, a uterus: these peculiarities imprison her in her subjectivity, circumscribe her within the limits of her own nature. It is often said that she thinks with her glands. Man superbly ignores the fact that his anatomy also includes glands, such as the testicles, and that they secrete hormones. He thinks of his body as a direct and normal connection with the world, which he believes he apprehends objectively, whereas he regards the body of woman as a hindrance, a prison, weighed down by everything peculiar to it. 'The female is a female by virtue of a certain lack of qualities,' said Aristotle; 'we should regard the female nature as afflicted with a natural defectiveness.' And St Thomas for his part pronounced woman to be an 'imperfect man', an 'incidental' being. This is symbolised in Genesis where Eve is depicted as made from what Bossuet called 'a supernumerary bone' of Adam.

Thus humanity is male and man defines woman not in herself but as relative to him; she is not regarded as an autonomous being. Michelet writes: 'Woman, the relative being . . . ' And Benda is most positive in his *Rapport d'Uriel:* 'The body of man makes sense in itself quite apart from that of woman, whereas the latter seems wanting in significance by itself . . . Man can think of himself without woman. She cannot think of herself without man.' And she is simply what man decrees; thus she is called 'the sex', by which is meant that she appears essentially to the male as a sexual being. For him she is sex—absolute sex, no less. She is defined and differentiated with reference to man and not he with reference to her; she is the incidental, the inessential as opposed to the essential. He is the Subject, he is the Absolute—she is the Other.'

The category of the *Other* is as primordial as consciousness itself. In the most primitive societies, in the most ancient mythologies, one finds the expression of a duality—that of the Self and the Other. This duality was not originally attached to the division of the sexes; it was not dependent upon any empirical facts. It is revealed in such works as that of Granet on Chinese thought and those of Dumézil on the East Indies and Rome. The feminine element was at first no more involved in such pairs as Varuna-Mitra, Uranus-Zeus, Sun-Moon, and Day-Night than it was in the contrasts between Good and Evil, lucky and unlucky auspices, right and left, God and Lucifer. Otherness is a fundamental category of human thought.

Thus it is that no group ever sets itself up as the One without at once setting up the Other over against itself. If three travellers chance to occupy the same compartment, that is enough to make vaguely hostile 'others' out of all the rest of the passengers on the train. In small-town eyes all persons not belonging to the village are 'strangers' and suspect; to the native of a country all who inhabit other countries are 'foreigners'; Jews are 'different' for the anti-Semite, Negroes are 'inferior' for American racists, aborigines are 'natives' for colonists, proletarians are the 'lower class' for the privileged.

Lévi-Strauss, at the end of a profound work on the various forms of primitive societies, reaches the following conclusion: 'Passage from the state of Nature to the state of Culture is marked by man's ability to view biological relations as a series of contrasts; duality, alternation, opposition, and symmetry, whether under definite or vague forms, constitute not so much phenomena to be explained as fundamental and immediately given data of social reality.' These phenomena would be incomprehensible if in fact human society were simply a *Mitsein* or fellowship based on solidarity and friendliness. Things become clear, on the contrary, if, following Hegel, we find in consciousness itself a fundamental hostility towards every other consciousness; the subject can be posed only in being opposed—he sets himself up as the essential, as opposed to the other, the inessential, the object.

But the other consciousness, the other ego, sets up a reciprocal claim. The native travelling abroad is shocked to find himself in turn regarded as a 'stranger' by the natives of neighbouring countries. As a matter of fact, wars, festivals, trading, treaties, and contests among tribes, nations, and classes tend to deprive the concept *Other* of its absolute sense and to make manifest its relativity; willy-nilly, individuals and groups are forced to realize the reciprocity of their relations. How is it, then, that this reciprocity has not been recognised between the sexes, that one of the contrasting terms is set up as the sole essential, denying any relativity in regard to its correlative and defining the latter as pure otherness? Why is it that women do not dispute male sovereignty? No subject will readily volunteer to become the object, the inessential; it is not the Other who, in defining himself as the Other, establishes the One. The Other is posed as such by the One in defining himself as the One. But if the Other is not to regain the status of being the One, he must be submissive enough to accept this alien point of view. Whence comes this submission in the case of woman?

(continued)

The Second Sex (*continued*)

There are, to be sure, other cases in which a certain category has been able to dominate another completely for a time. Very often this privilege depends upon inequality of numbers—the majority imposes its rule upon the minority or persecutes it. But women are not a minority, like the American Negroes or the Jews; there are as many women as men on earth. Again, the two groups concerned have often been originally independent; they may have been formerly unaware of each other's existence, or perhaps they recognised each other's autonomy. But a historical event has resulted in the subjugation of the weaker by the stronger. The scattering of the Jews, the introduction of slavery into America, the conquests of imperialism are examples in point. In these cases the oppressed retained at least the memory of former days; they possessed in common a past, a tradition, sometimes a religion or a culture.

The parallel drawn by Bebel between women and the proletariat is valid in that neither ever formed a minority or a separate collective unit of mankind. And instead of a single historical event it is in both cases a historical development that explains their status as a class and accounts for the membership of *particular individuals* in that class. But proletarians have not always existed, whereas there have always been women. They are women in virtue of their anatomy and physiology. Throughout history they have always been subordinated to men, and hence their dependency is not the result of a historical event or a social change—it was not something that *occurred*. The reason why otherness in this case seems to be an absolute is in part that it lacks the contingent or incidental nature of historical facts. A condition brought about at a certain time can be abolished at some other time, as the Negroes of Haiti and others have proved: but it might seem that natural condition is beyond the possibility of change. In truth, however, the nature of things is no more immutably given, once for all, than is historical reality. If woman seems to be the inessential which never becomes the essential, it is because she herself fails to bring about this change. Proletarians say 'We'; Negroes also. Regarding themselves as subjects, they transform the bourgeois, the whites, into 'others'. But women do not say 'We', except at some congress of feminists or similar formal demonstration; men say 'women', and women use the same word in referring to themselves. They do not authentically assume a subjective attitude. The proletarians have accomplished the revolution in Russia, the Negroes in Haiti, the Indo-Chinese are battling for it in Indo-China; but the women's effort has never been anything more than a symbolic agitation. They have gained only what men have been willing to grant; they have taken nothing, they have only received.

The reason for this is that women lack concrete means for organising themselves into a unit which can stand face to face with the correlative unit. They have no past, no history, no religion of their own; and they have no such solidarity of work and interest as that of the proletariat. They are not even promiscuously herded together in the way that creates community feeling among the American Negroes, the ghetto Jews, the workers of Saint-Denis, or the factory hands of Renault. They live dispersed among the males, attached through residence, housework, economic condition, and social standing to certain men—fathers or husbands—more firmly than they are to other women. If they belong to the bourgeoisie, they feel solidarity with men of that class, not with proletarian women; if they are white, their allegiance is to white men, not to Negro women. The proletariat can propose to massacre the ruling class, and a sufficiently fanatical Jew or Negro might dream of getting sole possession of the atomic bomb and making humanity wholly Jewish or black; but woman cannot even dream of exterminating the males. The bond that unites her to her oppressors is not comparable to any other. The division of the sexes is a biological fact, not an event in human history. Male and female stand opposed within a primordial *Mitsein*, and woman has not broken it. The couple is a fundamental unity with its two halves riveted together, and the cleavage of society along the line of sex is impossible. Here is to be found the basic trait of woman: she is the Other in a totality of which the two components are necessary to one another.

One could suppose that this reciprocity might have facilitated the liberation of woman. When Hercules sat at the feet of Omphale and helped with her spinning, his desire for her held him captive; but why did she fail to gain a lasting power? To revenge herself on Jason, Medea killed their children; and this grim legend would seem to suggest that she might have obtained a formidable influence over him through his love for his offspring. In *Lysistrata* Aristophanes gaily depicts a band of women who joined forces to gain social ends through the sexual needs of their men; but this is only a play. In the legend of the Sabine women, the latter soon abandoned their plan of remaining sterile to punish their ravishers. In truth woman has not been socially emancipated through man's need—sexual desire and the desire for offspring—which makes the male dependent for satisfaction upon the female.

Master and slave, also, are united by a reciprocal need, in this case economic, which does not liberate the slave. In the relation of master to slave the master does not make a point of the need that he has for the other; he has in his grasp the power of satisfying this need through his own action; whereas the slave, in his dependent condition, his hope and fear, is quite conscious of the need he has for his master. Even if the need is at bottom equally urgent for both, it always works in favour of the oppressor and against the oppressed. That is why the liberation of the working class, for example, has been slow.

Now, woman has always been man's dependant, if not his slave; the two sexes have never shared the world in equality. And even today woman is heavily handicapped, though her situation is beginning to change. Almost nowhere is her legal status the same as man's, and frequently it is much to her disadvantage. Even when her rights are legally recognised in the abstract, long-standing custom prevents their full expression in the mores. In the economic sphere men and women can almost be said to make up two castes; other things being equal, the former hold the better jobs, get higher wages, and have more opportunity for success than their new competitors. In industry and politics men have a great many more positions and they monopolise the most important posts. In addition to all this, they enjoy a traditional prestige that the education of children tends in every way to support, for the present enshrines the past—and in the past all history has been made by men. At the present time, when women are beginning to take part in the affairs of the world, it is still a world that belongs to men—they have no doubt of it at all and women have scarcely any. To decline to be the Other, to refuse to be a party to the deal—this would be for women to renounce all the advantages conferred upon them by their alliance with the superior caste. Man-the-sovereign will provide woman-the-liege with material protection and will undertake the moral justification of her existence; thus she can evade at once both economic risk and the metaphysical risk of a liberty in which ends and aims must be contrived without assistance. Indeed, along with the ethical urge of each individual to affirm his subjective existence, there is also the temptation to forgo liberty and become a thing. This is an inauspicious road, for he who takes it—passive, lost, ruined—becomes henceforth the creature of another's will, frustrated in his transcendence and deprived of every value. But it is an easy road; on it one avoids the strain involved in undertaking an authentic existence. When man makes of woman the Other, he may, then, expect to manifest deep-seated tendencies towards complicity. Thus, woman may fail to lay claim to the status of subject because she lacks definite resources, because she feels the necessary bond that ties her to man regardless of reciprocity, and because she is often very well pleased with her role as the Other.

But it will be asked at once: how did all this begin? It is easy to see that the duality of the sexes, like any duality, gives rise to conflict. And doubtless the winner will assume the status of absolute. But why should man have won from the start? It seems possible that women could have won the victory; or that the outcome of the conflict might never have been decided. How is it that this world has always belonged to the men and that things have begun to change only recently? Is this change a good thing? Will it bring about an equal sharing of the world between men and women?

These questions are not new, and they have often been answered. But the very fact that woman *is the Other* tends to cast suspicion upon all the justifications that men have ever been able to provide for it. These have all too evidently been dictated by men's interest. A little-known feminist of the seventeenth century, Poulain de la Barre, put it this way: 'All that has been written about women by men should be suspect, for the men are at once judge and party to the lawsuit.'

Chapter 5
Ethics

It is a dark and stormy night. You are tired and hungry and have a massive headache brought about by your professor's insistence upon lecturing for the entire three-hour class. As you move toward the parking lot, you notice a fellow student who seems to be in a state of distress. As you move closer, you see that the student's car has a flat tire and the student seems to be at a loss as to what to do.

Let us assume that there is no conspiracy here to trick you. The student is not trying to lure you close in order to beat you with a tire iron or kidnap you like something from *The Silence of the Lambs*.[1] It is a sincere student with an honest problem.

What would you do? And equally important: *Why* do you do what you do? It is a matter of ethics.

If you simply ignored the student's plight and just went on your merry way, many people would judge you harshly. But they might be basing their judgment solely on *what they see and not what they know*. Perhaps you thought that someone else would help out momentarily or perhaps you do not know how to change a flat tire or perhaps you just did not care. If any of these were the case, you might be said to be acting out of your own self-interest. This is known as "ethical egoism". People who do not assist others might come across as being mean and cold-hearted, but we have to be careful to assess all the facts before we make any conclusions. . . .

Some philosophers argue that the morally right thing to do is to act so as to promote your own self-interest. After all, if you severely injure yourself, no one is going to complain about how "selfish" you are if you seek medical attention. If you decide to help the student in need you may be sacrificing some time and energy but you may feel better about yourself. That is being self-interested. You act to help others because you want to feel good about what you do. So, ethical egoism is not necessarily a bad thing. If you did stop to help because you thought you would be rewarded for your action or if you help because you would want someone to help you if you were in this situation, or if you help out simply because you do not want to feel guilty all night, you are still acting out of self-interest. In all of these cases, you are not helping because of the other person's predicament; you are acting so as to satisfy some personal desire or need. You are still an "egoist."

Let us suppose you do decide to help the student. The reason for your choosing to do so is significant. For although different moral theories can sometimes lead us to the same conclusion (e.g., that you should help), they will offer different justifications. In other circumstances they might come to radically different conclusions. Thus, it is important to understand the reasons as well as the conclusions so that you act consistently in similar situations.

If you just went to help without thinking, you might be an altruist because you are sacrificing your interests for the sake of others. Few people are pure altruists, however, because it would entail that you would sacrifice *all* your desires, needs and wants for others.

If the stranded student says "Thanks—You're a very nice person," they would be in agreement with Aristotle who looked at the character of the person and not merely his or her deeds as the defining element of morality. Aristotle's virtue theory of ethics maintains that a virtuous person is one who habitually does the right thing because it is the right thing to do and subsequently this person will be more likely to achieve personal happiness. Aristotelian virtues include wisdom, fortitude, temperance, and justice. The virtuous person acts in accordance with Aristotle's Golden Mean: "In all things, moderation." Compare for example the person who thinks he can fend off a charging army with a spoon with the person who is afraid being attacked by a child with a butterfly net. We would not call either person "courageous" by any stretch of the imagination. Compare for example the person who goes into a blind rage when cut off by a fellow driver with the person who shrugs her shoulders when someone purposely rams her car. In neither case would these people be considered "temperate," for although you should not get too mad when someone causes you a minor inconvenience you should be upset when someone does something terrible to you. We should, an Aristotelian would argue, maintain a proper balance between these contrasting qualities.

For Aristotle there are right actions and there are virtuous people. I may do the former without being the latter, but not vice versa. Becoming good takes practice. We become virtuous by doing right actions out of habit. A morally vicious person on the other hand does wrong actions out of spite. That is, they know that an act is wrong and yet they still do it. The virtuous person uses wisdom to make the right decision and then acts on it. You cannot be ignorant and just guess as to what is the right thing to do and expect to be considered morally good. If any good comes from your act, it would be due to sheer luck.

---

[1] In *Silence of the Lambs,* the serial killer Jame "Buffalo Bill" Gumb wears a fake cast on his arm and pretends to be having difficulty getting a couch inside the doors of an old van. His victim approaches and offers help. Stepping inside the van with one end of the couch, the victim, Catherine Martin, daughter of a U.S. senator, finds herself trapped.

Sometimes we do the right thing but really do not want to. The morally continent person makes the right decision, acts on it, but has a desire to do otherwise; while the morally incontinent person can make the right decision but suffers from weakness of will and so does not perform the right act. Compare the continent person who wants to do something bad (e.g., cheat on a test) but ultimately does not because he or she knows it is wrong with the incontinent person who knows what is the right thing to do (e.g., helping the stranded student), but purposely does not do it.

Here is another example of virtue ethics at work. The Academy Award–winning film *Gladiator* takes place in Roman times but Aristotle's views are right there in the foreground. The weak and devious Commodus (played by Joaquin Phoenix) complains to his ailing father, the Emperor:

> COMMODUS   You wrote to me once, listing the four chief virtues. Wisdom, Justice, Fortitude and Temperance. As I read the list I knew I had none of them. But I have other virtues, father. Ambition, that can be a virtue when it drives us to excel. Resourcefulness. Courage. Perhaps not on the battlefield but there are many forms of courage. Devotion, to my family, to you. But none of my virtues were on your list. Even then, it was as if you didn't want me for your son.
>
> MARCUS AURELIUS   Oh Commodus, you go too far.
>
> COMMODUS   I searched the faces of the gods for ways to please you, to make you proud. One kind word, one full hug while you pressed me to your chest and held me tight, would've been like the sun on my heart for a thousand years. What is in me that you hate so much?
>
> MARCUS AURELIUS   Shh, Commodus.
>
> COMMODUS   All I've ever wanted was to live up to you. Caesar. Father.

Commodus then places a pillow over his father's face, smothering him to death.

One can understand why then Marcus Aurelius did not see anything virtuous in him. Furthermore, this short scene establishes Commodus general character. We know what he is like, what he thinks, and how he acts. Virtue ethics is important for it tells us that regardless of the situation, if we know the person, we can predict how they will respond. If we know the virtuous person, we can rely on them to attempt to do what is best.

If you decide to help the student because "it's just the right thing to do" or because your parents always told you that you should help others or because you recall that good Samaritans often get rewarded for doing good deeds, then your action might be judged morally right or morally good. According to Immanuel Kant (1724–1804), people can do right things but for the wrong reasons. That I help you because I want you to think "Gee, what a nice guy", is not as commendable as my acting is simply because I know that it is my duty to do so. In the first case, I have an ulterior motive even though I am still doing the right thing by helping out. Being honest, returning what has been borrowed, helping others, etc., may be morally right things to do, but they cannot be judged morally good until we know the motive behind why the person did these things. Is the person doing what he or she has a responsibility to do because he or she is trying to win favor, or is the person doing it because he or she knows that that is what one should be doing? For Aristotle, it is the person's character that matters; for Kant it is the person's motive.

The morally right thing to do according to Kant is to do your duty. Kant is a Deontologist. That is, morality is about obligation, responsibility, and performing your duty. For Kant, your duty is to follow what he calls "the Categorical Imperative." According to the Categorical Imperative morally right if you can at the same time will that it be a universal law. In other words, before you act, consider what would happen if everyone did the same action. But it is not enough just to realize that the world would be a terrible place if everyone decided not to be honest with each other. It would be terrible of course, but that is irrelevant. If you are thinking about lying to someone, even if you are doing it because you want to prevent the person from being hurt (e.g., you do not want to offend a friend by telling him that he looks really ugly in those pants), imagine what would happen to the concept of "honesty." It would cease to make any sense. If honesty simply entailed that we could tell the truth when we want to and lie when we want to, the concept would no longer be meaningful. We have a moral imperative that states, "Do not cause needless harm to others." Now imagine you are about to run a red light, so you create a rule based on the Categorical Imperative: "Do not run red lights unless you are my situation." This rule has to apply to everyone, so now everyone is saying "Do not run red lights unless you are in my situation," but now everyone could be in a different situation applying this rule! Do we want to risk morality being placed in the hands of individuals to make personal judgments about what is right and wrong? If so, we will have a lot of people lying, cheating, stealing, and running red lights because their exception to the rule becomes the rule and we will never know for sure if the person we are talking to is telling the truth, or being honest, and so forth.

So if you go to help the student with the flat tire because you believe it is the right thing to do and that it is your moral duty to help others when you can, then you may be a Kantian. In *The Maltese Falcon*, Sam Spade (played by Humphrey Bogart) has a classic line that is perfectly in keeping with the deontology school of ethics:

> SPADE When a man's partner is killed, he's supposed to do something about it. It doesn't make any difference what you thought of him. He was your partner and you're supposed to do something about it. And it happens we're in the detective business. Well, when one of your organization gets killed, it's—it's bad business to let the killer get away with it, bad all around, bad for every detective everywhere.

On this account, doing the right thing is not about making people happy; it is about doing one's duty.

If you go to help the student with the flat tire because you think to yourself, "I have a headache, but having a flat tire is a lot worse so I'll go help," then you could be adopting a Utilitarian approach. Classic Utilitarians like Jeremy Bentham (1748–1832) and John Stuart Mill (1806–1873) claim that the morally right thing to do is that act which will promote the greatest amount of good for the greatest number of people. For both Bentham and Mill, "pleasure" or "happiness" is considered the ultimate good.

A utilitarian would consider the consequence of his or her action as the determining factor for deciding what to do. Consider our flat tire case again. If you help the student, you will be home a bit later, your headache might be a bit worse, and you might be a bit more tired and hungry. Compare that discomfort and inconvenience with what the student with the flat tire may experience. There is the possibility that the student may be helped by the very next person, or perhaps the student may be beaten up in the dark by a drunk who wants to sleep in the car. Is the amount of pleasure that you would receive by getting home sooner greater than the amount of pain or suffering that the student could receive if you did not help? If you do decide to help, will the amount of pleasure that the student is going to receive outweigh your loss as a result of getting home a bit later? If your answers are "No" and "Yes" to these two questions, then you should indeed help the student.

Utilitarian ethics is often played out in the movies. Consider an obvious reference to this tradition in *Star Trek II: The Wrath of Kahn*. The starship Enterprise is badly damaged by an attacking ship named The Reliant. The Enterprise is adrift in a Nebula and to make matters worse, a planet-making device is about to detonate, destroying everything in the nearby space. Mr. Spock, the science officer, realizes that the only way to save the ship and its crew is to restore its power; but in order to do so he must endure a lethal dose of radiation. If Spock does nothing, they will surely all die whereas if he attempts to save the ship he will die but everyone else will have the chance to outrun the explosion. Spock, a Vulcan who prides himself on his use of logic and reason over emotion and intuition, chooses to save the ship.

Int. Enterprise Engine Room

Spock rushes in. Bones ministers to Scotty, Spock sizes up the situation, starts for the radiation room, Bones intercepts him.

BONES Are you out of your Vulcan mind? No human can tolerate the radiation that's in there!

SPOCK As you are so fond of observing, Doctor, I am not human.

BONES You're not going in there - !

SPOCK Perhaps you're right. What is Mister Scott's condition?

BONES Well, I don't think that he . . .

He gives Bones the Vulcan nerve pinch. Bones goes down. <cut>

REVERSE ANGLE as Spock works inside with radiation, lifts top of radiation container, releasing power as it bursts up into his face.

SCOTTY No! God, don't, Spock!

WITHIN

WE CAN SEE the silent urging of Bones and Scotty. Spock is oblivious. Amid the fire-blue arcs, he moves to the control panel. Between his hands and the controls, power arcs insanely. Spock is an inferno, a radiation hell, fighting now with all his strength to control it. Slowly, the damping rods move out. Spock moves to a manual control, begins to turn it.

With a burst of warp speed, Enterprise accelerates out of the lazy pace and whooshes OUT OF SCENE, leaving Reliant behind.

KIRK (continuing, on intercom) Engine room. Well done, Scotty.

BONES' VOICE (after a beat)

Jim! I think you'd better get down here.

The tone frightens Kirk.

Int. Enterprise Engine Room
Kirk emerges to encounter Scotty and Bones. Their looks tell him. He sees the flashing light over the reactor room. He dashes for the control panel. Bones grabs him.

BONES Don't! You'll flood the whole compartment . . . !

KIRK He'll die - !

SCOTTY (also holds him)

Sir! He's dead already!

Kirk's eyes bulge.

BONES It's too late.

Angle at Reactor Room Glass Door
With stunned understanding, Kirk stumbles to the door, sees Spock on his knees, hands blackened, face cracked with radiation lines and scars.

Spock shakes his head. With a feeble hand he reaches the intercom button: FILTERED communication.

KIRK (mouths word) Spock!

(calls out into intercom)

Spock!

SPOCK Ship—out of danger?

KIRK Yes -

Spock is satisfied; he fights for breath.

SPOCK Do not grieve, Admiral—it is logical: the needs of the many outweigh—

He almost keels over. Kirk has tears steaming down his face.

KIRK . . . the needs of the few . . .

SPOCK Or the one.

He props a hand on the glass to support himself. Kirk's hand reflexively goes to match Spock's on the other side of the glass—

SPOCK (continuing) I never took the Kobayashi Maru test—until now.

What do you think of my solution?

KIRK Spock . . . !

SPOCK I have been—and always will be—your friend . . .

Live. Long. And. Prosper.

Notice how Spock's actions are done with the intent of giving the Enterprise crew a fighting chance. Even if he did save them, there was the very real possibility that the planetary device or the other ship would still be able to destroy the Enterprise. Was sacrificing his own life for a mere chance of saving others worth it? The utilitarian would say that the answer is obviously in the affirmative since one option leads to the death of everyone on board the Enterprise and the other option turns their certain death into a fighting chance for survival. In either case Spock dies, so his death is not the deciding factor.[2]

Here is a different case where the Utilitarian would condemn the actions of a character (as do those in the film) because of the negative consequences. *The Third Man* is a post–World War II film set in Vienna, Austria. Holly Martins, an American writer of pulp fiction, is visiting the city with the intent to see his friend Harry Lime. Unfortunately, Harry is not a very upstanding moral citizen. In fact it appears he has been murdered by one of his own criminal partners. In the following exchange Major Calloway is explaining Harry Lime's crimes to Holly Martins.

CALLOWAY Have you ever heard of penicillin?

MARTINS Well?

CALLOWAY In Vienna there hasn't been enough penicillin to go round. So a nice trade started here. Stealing penicillin from the military hospitals, diluting it to make it go further and selling it to patients. Do you see what that means?

MARTINS Are you too busy chasing a few tubes of penicillin to investigate a murder (of Harry Lime)?

---

[2] It should be pointed out that in *Star Trek VII: Insurrection*, a distinctly anti-Utilitarian theme is developed. This seventh film in the series features the movie debut of the next generation crew of the *Enterprise*. In it, the crew is determined to stop the forced relocation of six hundred people from a planet that holds the key to improving the lives of billions of individuals. Captain Picard asks at one point "How many people does it take (to remove) before it becomes wrong? One thousand? Fifty thousand? A million?"

CALLOWAY   These were murders. Men with gangrene legs, women in childbirth, and there were children, too. They used some of this diluted penicillin against meningitis. The lucky children died. The unlucky ones went off their heads. You can see them now in the mental ward. That is the racket Harry Lime organized.

Here then we have a case where one man is profiting financially off the suffering of others. A Kantian would point to the duty not to kill as the reason for why Harry Lime is evil, but the Utilitarian has a more "practical" response: The harm done to so many victims surely outweigh the money that one man obtains in exchange.

Yet Harry Lime has a reply.

HARRY   Old man, you never should have gone to the police. You know you ought to leave this thing alone.

MARTINS   Have you ever seen any of your victims?

HARRY   You know, I don't ever feel comfortable on these sort of things. Victims? Don't be melodramatic. Look down there. Would you feel any pity if one of those dots stopped moving forever? If I offered you 20,000 pounds for every dot that stopped moving, would you really, old man, tell me to keep my money? Or would you calculate how many dots you could afford to spare? Free of income tax, old man. Free of income tax. It's the only way to save money nowadays.

MARTINS   A lot of good your money will do you in jail.

HARRY   That jail is in another zone. There's no proof against me, besides you.

MARTINS   I should be pretty easy to get rid of.

HARRY   Pretty easy.

MARTINS   I wouldn't be too sure.

HARRY   I carry a gun. I don't think they'd look for a bullet wound after you'd hit that ground.

MARTINS   They have dug up your coffin.

HARRY   And found Harbin? Hmm, pity. Oh, Holly, what fools we are, talking to each other this way. As though I would do anything to you, or you to me. You're just a little mixed up about things in general. Nobody thinks in terms of human beings. Governments don't, so why should we? They talk about the people and the proletariat. I talk about the suckers and the mugs. It's the same thing. They have their five year plans, and so have I.

MARTINS   You used to believe in God.

HARRY   I still do believe in God, old man. I believe in God and Mercy and all that. The dead are happier dead. They don't miss much here, poor devils. What do you believe in? Well, if you ever get Anna out of this mess, be kind to her. You'll find she's worth it. I wish I had asked you to bring me some of these tablets from home. Holly, I would like to cut you in, old man. Nobody left in Vienna I can really trust, and we have always done everything together. When you make up your mind, send me a message. I'll meet you any place, any time. And when we do meet, old man, it's you I want to see, not the police. Remember that, won't you? Don't be so gloomy. After all, it's not that awful. Remember what the fellow said. In Italy, for thirty years under the Borgias they had warfare, terror, murder, bloodshed, but they produced Michelangelo, Leonardo da Vinci and the Renaissance. In Switzerland they had brotherly love. They had five hundred years of democracy and peace, and what did that produce? The cuckoo clock.

Harry's logic is self-serving of course. He seems to be suggesting that by his own utilitarian calculations, he is doing the right thing because the deceased victims are not living in misery. If they were still alive, the city of Vienna (which was heavily damaged during the war) will not have much to offer them. He, on the other hand, is quite happy and so by his reckoning, he is not as bad as people are making him out to be. He is happy and the dead are not suffering and that is better than his being poor (and unhappy) and others living in misery. He is just thinking about the welfare of others, by golly! Some people may argue that a life of constant suffering would be worse than a peaceful death, but part of the problem of Harry's argument is that his dilution of the penicillin is the very cause of the misery that he is talking about relieving!

Many war films and related subjects such as the Holocaust present us with ethical dilemmas, including dilemmas for utilitarianism.

Which would you prefer, a long life with very little happiness, or a short life with some happiness? What is more important to you: quality of life or quantity of life? If we calculated the total amount of happiness in both situations, that is, a long life with very little happiness and a short life but with a great deal of happiness, What if the sums came out to be the equal? How would you choose between them if the sums came out to be equal? For a Utilitarian, this would be a hard decision since the ultimate harm or benefit is apparently the same. This sort of dilemma is but one issue that comes out of the bleak film *The Grey Zone*.

Based on Miklos Nyiszli's biography, *The Grey Zone* tells the tale of a unit of Jewish prisoners (called Sonderkommando) in the Auschwitz death camp who were provided with a better quality of life in exchange for helping exterminate their fellow prisoners.[3] The Sonderkommando would lead victims into the gas chambers, clean up the mess, and put the bodies in the ovens. In return, they received no more than six months of life where they could eat and drink whatever they wanted (many, as you can well imagine, drank alcohol constantly). The film does not make these characters out to be good or bad, but self-serving. What if you could live a better life by helping take the lives of others? Surely we would agree that this is morally reprehensible. But what if these lives would be taken no matter what you did? Either you would have to do it, or someone else would. What would you do?

Part of this complex true story involves the discovery of a young girl who beyond all odds manages to survive the gas chamber. The Sonderkommando risk everything in order to revive this girl. One has to ask whether their actions are morally right. If the girl is found, she will be killed and so will the members of the unit. If the girl is not found, the chances of her survival are unknown. She may live to escape, or she may live and be returned to the horrors of the camp. And even if she does live, the Nazis may decide to kill her saviors in retribution. What complicates this scenario even more is that many prisoners have been planning and working hard to get weapons to attempt an escape and an uprising. Some prisoners have already been tortured and killed in an unsuccessful attempt to find out about this plan. If the Nazi's discover the girl, their interest in the "goings-on" may be piqued and the plans for the uprising will be severely compromised and the chance for another planned escape will be lost. It is only one girl, and many lives are at stake.

It would seem that a Utilitarian would, at first glance, choose not to save the girl. Critics might argue that who we are, and what makes us human, is more complex than just receiving a bit of pleasure. The members of the Sonderkommando may in fact want to risk it all in order to save their own humanity. They may believe that trying to save one life, no matter how pointless, is so essential to restoring faith in themselves that they think it is the right thing to do. Perhaps this action gives them a sense of control in a world where they otherwise have very little. Perhaps saving one life, after participating in taking so many others, shows that there can be glimmer of light in a world of darkness. Might they gain some degree of happiness from this choice even though it means risking everything? Might this amount of happiness outweigh the costs? That there is no clear answer to this question is but one reason the film is aptly named The Grey Zone.[4]

In *Saving Private Ryan*, we have another instance of when it seems that the Utilitarian would reject the actions of the main characters. Yet, perhaps there is a greater good that should be promoted for the greatest number of people, even if the greatest amount of pleasure or happiness is not achieved. This film starts on D-Day, June 6, 1944. Three out of the four Ryan brothers have been killed in various battles and the U.S. government decides that the only remaining brother, James, who is somewhere in France, must be found and sent home to his mother at all costs. In an early scene, General George C. Marshall reads a letter where he attempts to justify this decision.

> MARSHALL   I have here a very old letter, written to a Mrs. Bixby in Boston. "Dear Madam: I have been shown in the files of the War Department a statement of the Adjutant-General of Massachusetts that

---

[3] Miklos Nyiszli, *I was Doctor Mengele's Assistant* (Oswiecim, 2001).

[4] Here is the other reason why it is called The Grey Zone:

> DEAD GIRL: After the revolt, half the ovens remain, and we are carried to them together. I catch fire, quickly. The first part of me rises, in dense smoke that mingles with the smoke of others. Then there are the bones, which settle in ash, and these are swept up to be carried to the river. And last, bits of our dust, that simply float there, in air, around the working of the new group . . . These bits of dust are grey. We settle on their shoes, and on their faces, and in their lungs. And they become so used to us, that soon they don't cough, and they don't brush us away. At this point, they are just moving, breathing and moving, like anyone else, still alive in that place. And this is how the work . . . continues.

you are the mother of five sons who have died gloriously on the field of battle. I feel how weak and fruitless must be any words of mine which should attempt to beguile you from the grief of a loss so overwhelming. But I cannot refrain from tendering to you the consolation that may be found in the thanks of the Republic they died to save. I pray that our heavenly Father may assuage the anguish of your bereavement, and leave you only the cherished memory of the loved and lost, and the solemn pride that must be yours to have laid so costly a sacrifice upon the altar of freedom. Yours very sincerely and respectfully, Abraham Lincoln."

Tom Hanks plays Captain Miller. And we pick up the story right after the Normandy Beach landings.

COLONEL ANDERSON   Where are your men now?

MILLER   Pinned down, a mile east of here, waiting for some help from the navy guns.

COLONEL ANDERSON   I'm sending Simpson to take over for you, the division is going to Caen, you're not coming with us, I have something else for you.

MILLER   Sir?

COLONEL ANDERSON   There's a Private James Ryan who parachuted in with the Hundred-and-First near Ramelle. I want you to take a squad up there. If he's alive, bring him back to the beach for debarkation. Take whoever you need, you've got your pick of the company.

MILLER   A private, sir?

COLONEL ANDERSON   He's the last of four brothers, the other three were killed in action. This is straight from the Chief of Staff.

MILLER   But, sir . . . I . . . I . . .

COLONEL ANDERSON   Spit it out, Captain.

Miller Hesitates, Then:

MILLER   Respectfully, sir, sending men all the way up to Ramelle to save one private doesn't make a fucking, goddamned bit of sense. (beat) Sir.

Miller and his platoon finally catch up to the elusive James Ryan who is oblivious to Miller's orders and to the fate of his own brothers. Yet when he does discover what has happened, he makes a startling decision:

RYAN   I'm not leaving, sir.

Miller starts to boil over.

MILLER   The hell you aren't, you're comin' with me if I have to drag you every inch of the way. You hear me, Private?

RYAN   I hear you sir, but I'm not leaving.

Miller grabs Ryan by the lapels and shakes him. Ryan doesn't resist.

MILLER   Listen you little son-of-a-bitch you're coming with me or I'll . . . I'll . . .

Ryan speaks softly.

RYAN   What are you going to do, sir, shoot me?

Miller considers it. Then REIBEN SPEAKS UP from behind Miller.

REIBEN   (politely)
Uh, excuse me, Captain.

Miller slowly turns and glares.

REIBEN   (continuing)
So, what are a few tanks, sir?

Miller's more amazed than pissed off. Reiben smiles.

REIBEN   (continuing)
He's right, we can't shoot him . . . well, we could but we'd get in an enormous amount of trouble. And he's right about the bridge, it's a hell of a lot more important than he is.

Jackson Steps Forward.

JACKSON   Cap'n . . . ?

Miller turns his glare on Jackson.

JACKSON   (continuing)
Seems to me, we got us a opportunity, here, to kill two birds with one stone. Command seems to think keepin' this boy alive is worth somethin'. If we was to do that and hold this bridge, good chance we'd get us a bucket full of medals. I might even get me one 'a them big, fancy ones like you got, so's I could sass any officer in the whole dang army, you included.

Is it right to send a group of men on a dangerous mission when we can assume some of them will not be returning, just to save one man? How much happiness is gained by the saving of one son, when the risk to the sons of other parents being killed or wounded is quite high? When Miller finally finds Ryan and decides to dig in and fight alongside him to stop the approaching Germans, one could argue that this consequence is good (as Jackson remarks above), but it is not a consequence that could have been foreseen. It is unreasonable (because it is impossible) to weigh into our moral calculations outcomes that may be possible, but are unknown. Captain Miller—who dies in the end—is right to question the reasoning of his seniors. The men who will be killed trying to complete this mission may have gone on to be married, have families of their own, and live long, happy lives. Miller's dying words to Ryan are "Earn this." Whether Ryan could ever be able to meet this demand remains a question for discussion.

It has been argued that one of the main reasons that the Atomic Bombs were dropped over Japan during World War II was that it would prevent the far greater loss of life that would occur if the Americans had to invade the country. But one questions whether sheer numbers are sufficient to look at when considering the moral rightness or wrongness of this action. Is the wartime killing of innocent men, women, and children morally the same as the killing of soldiers in battle? If fewer civilians were killed than soldiers, would the ends justify the means?

This question of appropriate proportionality and maximizing the efficiency of action arises in the last film we are going to consider. Errol Morris's documentary *The Fog of War* looks at the life of Robert McNamara who was the Secretary of Defense for the United States during the Vietnam War. In the following excerpt, he is speaking about the American decision to firebomb Japan during World War II.

> MCNAMARA I was on the island of Guam in his (General LaMay's) command in March of 1945. In that single night, we burned to death 100,000 Japanese civilians in Tokyo: men, women, and children.
>
> MORRIS Were you aware this was going to happen?
>
> MCNAMARA Well, I was part of a mechanism that in a sense recommended it.

I analyzed bombing operations, and how to make them more efficient. i.e., not more efficient in the sense of killing more, but more efficient in weakening the adversary. I wrote one report analyzing the efficiency of the B—29 operations. The B—29 could get above the fighter aircraft and above the air defense, so the loss rate would be much less. The problem was the accuracy was also much less. Now I don't want to suggest that it was my report that led to, I'll call it, the firebombing. It isn't that I'm trying to absolve myself of blame. I don't want to suggest that it was I who put in LeMay's mind that his operations were totally inefficient and had to be drastically changed. But, anyhow, that's what he did. He took the B—29s down to 5,000 feet and he decided to bomb with firebombs.

> MORRIS Why was it necessary to drop the nuclear bomb if LeMay was burning up Japan?
>
> MCNAMARA And he went on from Tokyo to firebomb other cities. 58% of Yokohama. Yokohama is roughly the size of Cleveland. 58% of Cleveland destroyed. Tokyo is roughly the size of New York. 51% percent of New York destroyed. 99% of the equivalent of Chattanooga, which was Toyama. 40% of the equivalent of Los Angeles, which was Nagoya. This was all done before the dropping of the nuclear bomb, which by the way was dropped by LeMay's command. Proportionality should be a guideline in war. Killing 50% to 90% of the people of 67 Japanese cities and then bombing them with two nuclear bombs is not proportional, in the minds of some people, to the objectives we were trying to achieve.
>
> LeMay said, 'If we'd lost the war, we'd all have been prosecuted as war criminals.' And I think he's right. He, and I'd say I, were behaving as war criminals. LeMay recognized that what he was doing would be thought immoral if his side had lost. But what makes it immoral if you lose and not immoral if you win?

Clearly, the continued bombing of Japanese cities that culminated in the almost utter destruction of Hiroshima and Nagasaki raises the question, "Is it moral?" Utilitarianism is concerned about promoting pleasure, but when that is not possible, utilitarianism also seeks to minimize pain. If evil is necessary, then let the least amount of evil be done in order to achieve the best possible outcome. If a reduction of harm is a driving force behind the decision, might not the detonation of an atomic bomb on an uninhabited island achieve the same success (e.g., the surrender of Japan)? If the end result was the same, the Utilitarian would favor the least harmful means to achieve it, namely a display of this horrendous power rather than the real application of it on civilians.

Answers to all of these questions is difficult. Yet, if morality were merely a matter of opinion, then we would hold fast to the rule that any opinion was as valid as any other. However, this position is hard to maintain when one realizes that many in society wish to impress their views on you and ultimately the state will use some moral rules to establish what should be done, what can be done, and what is prohibited. Understanding different views and seeing their positive and negative elements, is the first step that must be taken before you can begin to criticize them and, ultimately begin to shape your own consistent point of view. These are essential steps that we must all take as human beings.

Films Cited

Fog of War: The Eleven Lessons from the Life of Robert S. McNamara. Dir. Errol Morris. Perfs. Robert McNamara. Film. Sony Pictures Classics. 2003.
Gladiator. Dir. Ridley Scott. Perfs. Russell Crowe, Joaquin Phoenix. Film. Dreamworks SKG. 2000.
Grey Zone. The Dir. Tim Blake Nelson. Perfs. David Arquette, Velizar Binev. Film. The Goatsingers. 2001.
Maltese Falcon. The Dir. John Huston. Perfs. Humphrey Bogart, Mary Astor. Film. Warner Bros. Pictures. 1941.
Saving Private Ryan. Dir. Steven Spielberg. Perfs. Tom Hanks, Matt Damon. Film. Amblin Entertainment. 1998.
Silence of the Lambs. Dir. Jonathan Demme. Perfs. Jodie Foster, Anthony Hopkins. Film. Orion Pictures Corporation. 1991.
Star Trek II: Wrath of Kahn. Dir. Nicholas Meyer. Perfs. William Shatner, Leonard Nimoy. Film. Paramount Pictures. 1982.
Third Man. The Dir. Carol Reed. Perfs. Joseph Cotten, Alida Valli. Film. London Film Productions. 1949.

ADDITIONAL MOVIES FOR FURTHER VIEWING

(For a comprehensive listing of movies and themes, please consult the online appendix.)

1. *4 Months, 3 Weeks, 2 Days*—Abortion
2. *Atonement*—Harm to others
3. *Crimes and* Misdemeanors—Trust and promises
4. *Dead Man Walking*—Forgiveness and capital punishment
5. *Quiz Show*—Moral responsibility and cheating
6. *Schindler's List*—Human cruelty and kindness, virtue and egoism
7. *The Corporation*—Capitalism and business ethics
8. *The Insider*—Moral responsibility and whistle-blowing
9. *Unforgiven*—Ethical dilemma and moral blame
10. *Wall Street*—Greed

Nicomachean Ethics

Aristotle

Book I

1

Every art and every inquiry, and similarly every action and pursuit, is thought to aim at some good; and for this reason the good has rightly been declared to be that at which all things aim. But a certain difference is found among ends; some are activities, others are products apart from the activities that produce them. Where there are ends apart from the actions, it is the nature of the products to be better than the activities. Now, as there are many actions, arts, and sciences, their ends also are many; the end of the medical art is health, that of shipbuilding a vessel, that of strategy victory, that of economics wealth. But where such arts fall under a single capacity—as bridle-making and the other arts concerned with the equipment of horses fall under the art of riding, and this and every military action under strategy, in the same way other arts fall under yet others—in all of these the ends of the

(continued)

Nicomachean Ethics (*continued*)

master arts are to be preferred to all the subordinate ends; for it is for the sake of the former that the latter are pursued. It makes no difference whether the activities themselves are the ends of the actions, or something else apart from the activities, as in the case of the sciences just mentioned.

2

If, then, there is some end of the things we do, which we desire for its own sake (everything else being desired for the sake of this), and if we do not choose everything for the sake of something else (for at that rate the process would go on to infinity, so that our desire would be empty and vain), clearly this must be the good and the chief good. Will not the knowledge of it, then, have a great influence on life? Shall we not, like archers who have a mark to aim at, be more likely to hit upon what is right? If so, we must try, in outline at least, to determine what it is, and of which of the sciences or capacities it is the object. It would seem to belong to the most authoritative art and that which is most truly the master art. And politics appears to be of this nature; for it is this that ordains which of the sciences should be studied in a state, and which each class of citizens should learn and up to what point they should learn them; and we see even the most highly esteemed of capacities to fall under this, e.g., strategy, economics, rhetoric; now, since politics uses the rest of the sciences, and since, again, it legislates as to what we are to do and what we are to abstain from, the end of this science must include those of the others, so that this end must be the good for man. For even if the end is the same for a single man and for a state, that of the state seems at all events something greater and more complete whether to attain or to preserve; though it is worth while to attain the end merely for one man, it is finer and more godlike to attain it for a nation or for city-states. These, then, are the ends at which our inquiry aims, since it is political science, in one sense of that term.

3

Our discussion will be adequate if it has as much clearness as the subject-matter admits of, for precision is not to be sought for alike in all discussions, any more than in all the products of the crafts. Now fine and just actions, which political science investigates, admit of much variety and fluctuation of opinion, so that they may be thought to exist only by convention, and not by nature. And goods also give rise to a similar fluctuation because they bring harm to many people; for before now men have been undone by reason of their wealth, and others by reason of their courage. We must be content, then, in speaking of such subjects and with such premises to indicate the truth roughly and in outline, and in speaking about things which are only for the most part true and with premises of the same kind to reach conclusions that are no better. In the same spirit, therefore, should each type of statement be received; for it is the mark of an educated man to look for precision in each class of things just so far as the nature of the subject admits; it is evidently equally foolish to accept probable reasoning from a mathematician and to demand from a rhetorician scientific proofs.

Now each man judges well the things he knows, and of these he is a good judge. And so the man who has been educated in a subject is a good judge of that subject, and the man who has received an all-round education is a good judge in general. Hence a young man is not a proper hearer of lectures on political science; for he is inexperienced in the actions that occur in life, but its discussions start from these and are about these; and, further, since he tends to follow his passions, his study will be vain and unprofitable, because the end aimed at is not knowledge but action. And it makes no difference whether he is young in years or youthful in character; the defect does not depend on time, but on his living, and pursuing each successive object, as passion directs. For to such persons, as to the incontinent, knowledge brings no profit; but to those who desire and act in accordance with a rational principle knowledge about such matters will be of great benefit.

These remarks about the student, the sort of treatment to be expected, and the purpose of the inquiry, may be taken as our preface.

4

Let us resume our inquiry and state, in view of the fact that all knowledge and every pursuit aims at some good, what it is that we say political science aims at and what is the highest of all goods achievable by action. Verbally there is very general agreement; for both the general run of men and people of superior refinement say that it is happiness, and identify living well and doing well with being happy; but with regard to what happiness is they differ, and the many do not give the same account as the wise. For the former think it is some plain and obvious thing, like pleasure, wealth, or honour; they differ, however, from one another and often even the same man identifies it with different things, with health when he is ill, with wealth when he is poor; but, conscious of their ignorance, they admire those who proclaim some great ideal that is above their comprehension. Now some thought that apart from these many goods there is another, which is self-subsistent and causes the goodness of all these as well. To examine all the opinions that have been held were perhaps somewhat fruitless; enough to examine those that are most prevalent or that seem to be arguable.

Let us not fail to notice, however, that there is a difference between arguments from and those to the first principles. For Plato, too, was right in raising this question and asking, as he used to do, 'are we on the way from or to the first principles?' There is a difference, as there is in a race-course between the course from the judges to the turning-point and the way back. For, while we must begin with what is known, things are objects of knowledge in two senses—some to us, some without qualification. Presumably, then, we must begin with things known to us. Hence any one who is to listen intelligently to lectures about what is noble and just, and generally, about the subjects of political science must have been brought up in good habits. For the fact is the starting-point, and if this is sufficiently plain to him, he will not at the start need the reason as well; and the man who has been well brought up has or can easily get startingpoints. And as for him who neither has nor can get them, let him hear the words of Hesiod:

> Far best is he who knows all things himself;
> Good, he that hearkens when men counsel right;
> But he who neither knows, nor lays to heart
> Another's wisdom, is a useless wight.

5

Let us, however, resume our discussion from the point at which we digressed. To judge from the lives that men lead, most men, and men of the most vulgar type, seem (not without some ground) to identify the good, or happiness, with pleasure; which is the reason why they love the life of enjoyment. For there are, we may say, three prominent types of life—that just mentioned, the political, and thirdly the contemplative life. Now the mass of mankind are evidently quite slavish in their tastes, preferring a life suitable to beasts, but they get some ground for their view from the fact that many of those in high places share the tastes of Sardanapallus. A consideration of the prominent types of life shows that people of superior refinement and of active disposition identify happiness with honour; for this is, roughly speaking, the end of the political life. But it seems too superficial to be what we are looking for, since it is thought to depend on those who bestow honour rather than on him who receives it, but the good we divine to be something proper to a man and not easily taken from him. Further, men seem to pursue honour in order that they may be assured of their goodness; at least it is by men of practical wisdom that they seek to be honoured, and among those who know them, and on the ground of their virtue; clearly, then, according to them, at any rate, virtue is better. And perhaps one might even suppose this to be, rather than honour, the end of the political life. But even this appears somewhat incomplete; for possession of virtue seems actually compatible with being asleep, or with lifelong inactivity, and, further, with the greatest sufferings and misfortunes; but a man who was living so no one would call happy, unless he were maintaining a thesis at all costs. But enough of this; for the subject has been sufficiently treated even in the current discussions. Third comes the contemplative life, which we shall consider later.

The life of money-making is one undertaken under compulsion, and wealth is evidently not the good we are seeking; for it is merely useful and for the sake of something else. And so one might rather take the aforenamed objects to be ends; for they are loved for themselves. But it is evident that not even these are ends; yet many arguments have been thrown away in support of them. Let us leave this subject, then.

(continued)

Nicomachean Ethics (*continued*)

6

We had perhaps better consider the universal good and discuss thoroughly what is meant by it, although such an inquiry is made an uphill one by the fact that the Forms have been introduced by friends of our own. Yet it would perhaps be thought to be better, indeed to be our duty, for the sake of maintaining the truth even to destroy what touches us closely, especially as we are philosophers or lovers of wisdom; for, while both are dear, piety requires us to honour truth above our friends.

The men who introduced this doctrine did not posit Ideas of classes within which they recognized priority and posteriority (which is the reason why they did not maintain the existence of an Idea embracing all numbers); but the term 'good' is used both in the category of substance and in that of quality and in that of relation, and that which is per se, i.e., substance, is prior in nature to the relative (for the latter is like an off shoot and accident of being); so that there could not be a common Idea set over all these goods. Further, since 'good' has as many senses as 'being' (for it is predicated both in the category of substance, as of God and of reason, and in quality, i.e., of the virtues, and in quantity, i.e., of that which is moderate, and in relation, i.e., of the useful, and in time, i.e., of the right opportunity, and in place, i.e., of the right locality and the like), clearly it cannot be something universally present in all cases and single; for then it could not have been predicated in all the categories but in one only. Further, since of the things answering to one Idea there is one science, there would have been one science of all the goods; but as it is there are many sciences even of the things that fall under one category, e.g., of opportunity, for opportunity in war is studied by strategies and in disease by medicine, and the moderate in food is studied by medicine and in exercise by the science of gymnastics. And one might ask the question, what in the world they mean by 'a thing itself', is (as is the case) in 'man himself' and in a particular man the account of man is one and the same. For in so far as they are man, they will in no respect differ; and if this is so, neither will 'good itself' and particular goods, in so far as they are good. But again it will not be good any the more for being eternal, since that which lasts long is no whiter than that which perishes in a day. The Pythagoreans seem to give a more plausible account of the good, when they place the one in the column of goods; and it is they that Speusippus seems to have followed.

But let us discuss these matters elsewhere; an objection to what we have said, however, may be discerned in the fact that the Platonists have not been speaking about all goods and that the goods that are pursued and loved for themselves are called good by reference to a single Form, while those which tend to produce or to preserve these somehow or to prevent their contraries are called so by reference to these, and in a secondary sense. Clearly, then, goods must be spoken of in two ways, and some must be good in themselves, the others by reason of these. Let us separate, then, things good in themselves from things useful, and consider whether the former are called good by reference to a single Idea. What sort of goods would one call good in themselves? Is it those that are pursued even when isolated from others, such as intelligence, sight, and certain pleasures and honours? Certainly, if we pursue these also for the sake of something else, yet one would place them among things good in themselves. Or is nothing other than the Idea of good good in itself? In that case the Form will be empty. But if the things we have named are also things good in themselves, the account of the good will have to appear as something identical in them all, as that of whiteness is identical in snow and in white lead. But of honour, wisdom, and pleasure, just in respect of their goodness, the accounts are distinct and diverse. The good, therefore, is not some common element answering to one Idea.

But what then do we mean by the good? It is surely not like the things that only chance to have the same name. Are goods one, then, by being derived from one good or by all contributing to one good, or are they rather one by analogy? Certainly as sight is in the body, so is reason in the soul, and so on in other cases. But perhaps these subjects had better be dismissed for the present; for perfect precision about them would be more appropriate to another branch of philosophy. And similarly with regard to the Idea; even if there is some one good which is universally predicable of goods or is capable of separate and independent existence, clearly it could not be achieved or attained by man; but we are now seeking something attainable. Perhaps, however, some one might think it worth while to recognize this with a view to the goods that are attainable and achievable; for having this as a sort of pattern we shall know better the goods that are good for us, and if we know them shall attain them. This argument has some plausibility, but seems to clash with the procedure of the sciences; for all of these, though they aim at some good and seek to supply the deficiency of it, leave on one side the knowledge of the good. Yet that all the exponents of the arts should be ignorant of, and should not even seek, so great an aid is not probable. It is hard, too, to see how a weaver or a carpenter will be benefited in regard to his own craft by knowing this 'good itself', or how the man who has viewed the Idea itself will be a better doctor or general thereby. For a doctor seems not even to study health in this way, but the health of man, or perhaps rather the health of a particular man; it is individuals that he is healing. But enough of these topics.

7

Let us again return to the good we are seeking, and ask what it can be. It seems different in different actions and arts; it is different in medicine, in strategy, and in the other arts likewise. What then is the good of each? Surely that for whose sake everything else is done. In medicine this is health, in strategy victory, in architecture a house, in any other sphere something else, and in every action and pursuit the end; for it is for the sake of this that all men do whatever else they do. Therefore, if there is an end for all that we do, this will be the good achievable by action, and if there are more than one, these will be the goods achievable by action.

So the argument has by a different course reached the same point; but we must try to state this even more clearly. Since there are evidently more than one end, and we choose some of these (e.g., wealth, flutes, and in general instruments) for the sake of something else, clearly not all ends are final ends; but the chief good is evidently something final. Therefore, if there is only one final end, this will be what we are seeking, and if there are more than one, the most final of these will be what we are seeking. Now we call that which is in itself worthy of pursuit more final than that which is worthy of pursuit for the sake of something else, and that which is never desirable for the sake of something else more final than the things that are desirable both in themselves and for the sake of that other thing, and therefore we call final without qualification that which is always desirable in itself and never for the sake of something else.

Now such a thing happiness, above all else, is held to be; for this we choose always for self and never for the sake of something else, but honour, pleasure, reason, and every virtue we choose indeed for themselves (for if nothing resulted from them we should still choose each of them), but we choose them also for the sake of happiness, judging that by means of them we shall be happy. Happiness, on the other hand, no one chooses for the sake of these, nor, in general, for anything other than itself.

From the point of view of self-sufficiency the same result seems to follow; for the final good is thought to be self-sufficient. Now by self-sufficient we do not mean that which is sufficient for a man by himself, for one who lives a solitary life, but also for parents, children, wife, and in general for his friends and fellow citizens, since man is born for citizenship. But some limit must be set to this; for if we extend our requirement to ancestors and descendants and friends' friends we are in for an infinite series. Let us examine this question, however, on another occasion; the self-sufficient we now define as that which when isolated makes life desirable and lacking in nothing; and such we think happiness to be; and further we think it most desirable of all things, without being counted as one good thing among others—if it were so counted it would clearly be made more desirable by the addition of even the least of goods; for that which is added becomes an excess of goods, and of goods the greater is always more desirable. Happiness, then, is something final and self-sufficient, and is the end of action.

Presumably, however, to say that happiness is the chief good seems a platitude, and a clearer account of what it is still desired. This might perhaps be given, if we could first ascertain the function of man. For just as for a flute-player, a sculptor, or an artist, and, in general, for all things that have a function or activity, the good and the 'well' is thought to reside in the function, so would it seem to be for man, if he has a function. Have the carpenter, then, and the tanner certain functions or activities, and has man none? Is he born without a function? Or as eye, hand, foot, and in general each of the parts evidently has a function, may one lay it down that man similarly has a function apart from all these? What then can this be? Life seems to be common even to plants, but we

(continued)

Nicomachean Ethics (*continued*)

are seeking what is peculiar to man. Let us exclude, therefore, the life of nutrition and growth. Next there would be a life of perception, but it also seems to be common even to the horse, the ox, and every animal. There remains, then, an active life of the element that has a rational principle; of this, one part has such a principle in the sense of being obedient to one, the other in the sense of possessing one and exercising thought. And, as 'life of the rational element' also has two meanings, we must state that life in the sense of activity is what we mean; for this seems to be the more proper sense of the term. Now if the function of man is an activity of soul which follows or implies a rational principle, and if we say 'so-and-so-and 'a good so-and-so' have a function which is the same in kind, e.g., a lyre, and a good lyre-player, and so without qualification in all cases, eminence in respect of goodness being added? to the name of the function (for the function of a lyre-player is to play the lyre, and that of a good lyre-player is to do so well): if this is the case, and we state the function of man to be a certain kind of life, and this to be an activity or actions of the soul implying a rational principle, and the function of a good man to be the good and noble performance of these, and if any action is well performed when it is performed in accordance with the appropriate excellence: if this is the case, human good turns out to be activity of soul in accordance with virtue, and if there are more than one virtue, in accordance with the best and most complete.

But we must add 'in a complete life.' For one swallow does not make a summer, nor does one day; and so too one day, or a short time, does not make a man blessed and happy.

Let this serve as an outline of the good; for we must presumably first sketch it roughly, and then later fill in the details. But it would seem that any one is capable of carrying on and articulating what has once been well outlined, and that time is a good discoverer or partner in such a work; to which facts the advances of the arts are due; for any one can add what is lacking. And we must also remember what has been said before, and not look for precision in all things alike, but in each class of things such precision as accords with the subject-matter, and so much as is appropriate to the inquiry. For a carpenter and a geometer investigate the right angle in different ways; the former does so in so far as the right angle is useful for his work, while the latter inquires what it is or what sort of thing it is; for he is a spectator of the truth. We must act in the same way, then, in all other matters as well, that our main task may not be subordinated to minor questions. Nor must we demand the cause in all matters alike; it is enough in some cases that the fact be well established, as in the case of the first principles; the fact is the primary thing or first principle. Now of first principles we see some by induction, some by perception, some by a certain habituation, and others too in other ways. But each set of principles we must try to investigate in the natural way, and we must take pains to state them definitely, since they have a great influence on what follows. For the beginning is thought to be more than half of the whole, and many of the questions we ask are cleared up by it.

8

We must consider it, however, in the light not only of our conclusion and our premises, but also of what is commonly said about it; for with a true view all the data harmonize, but with a false one the facts soon clash. Now goods have been divided into three classes, and some are described as external, others as relating to soul or to body; we call those that relate to soul most properly and truly goods, and psychical actions and activities we class as relating to soul. Therefore our account must be sound, at least according to this view, which is an old one and agreed on by philosophers. It is correct also in that we identify the end with certain actions and activities; for thus it falls among goods of the soul and not among external goods. Another belief which harmonizes with our account is that the happy man lives well and does well; for we have practically defined happiness as a sort of good life and good action. The characteristics that are looked for in happiness seem also, all of them, to belong to what we have defined happiness as being. For some identify happiness with virtue, some with practical wisdom, others with a kind of philosophic wisdom, others with these, or one of these, accompanied by pleasure or not without pleasure; while others include also external prosperity. Now some of these views have been held by many men and men of old, others by a few eminent persons; and it is not probable that either of these should be entirely mistaken, but rather that they should be right in at least some one respect or even in most respects.

With those who identify happiness with virtue or some one virtue our account is in harmony; for to virtue belongs virtuous activity. But it makes, perhaps, no small difference whether we place the chief good in possession or in use, in state of mind or in activity. For the state of mind may exist without producing any good result, as in a man who is asleep or in some other way quite inactive, but the activity cannot; for one who has the activity will of necessity be acting, and acting well. And as in the Olympic Games it is not the most beautiful and the strongest that are crowned but those who compete (for it is some of these that are victorious), so those who act win, and rightly win, the noble and good things in life.

Their life is also in itself pleasant. For pleasure is a state of soul, and to each man that which he is said to be a lover of is pleasant; e.g., not only is a horse pleasant to the lover of horses, and a spectacle to the lover of sights, but also in the same way just acts are pleasant to the lover of justice and in general virtuous acts to the lover of virtue. Now for most men their pleasures are in conflict with one another because these are not by nature pleasant, but the lovers of what is noble find pleasant the things that are by nature pleasant; and virtuous actions are such, so that these are pleasant for such men as well as in their own nature. Their life, therefore, has no further need of pleasure as a sort of adventitious charm, but has its pleasure in itself. For, besides what we have said, the man who does not rejoice in noble actions is not even good; since no one would call a man just who did not enjoy acting justly, nor any man liberal who did not enjoy liberal actions; and similarly in all other cases. If this is so, virtuous actions must be in themselves pleasant. But they are also good and noble, and have each of these attributes in the highest degree, since the good man judges well about these attributes; his judgement is such as we have described. Happiness then is the best, noblest, and most pleasant thing in the world, and these attributes are not severed as in the inscription at Delos—

Most noble is that which is justest, and best is health;
But pleasantest is it to win what we love.

For all these properties belong to the best activities; and these, or one—the best—of these, we identify with happiness.

Yet evidently, as we said, it needs the external goods as well; for it is impossible, or not easy, to do noble acts without the proper equipment. In many actions we use friends and riches and political power as instruments; and there are some things the lack of which takes the lustre from happiness, as good birth, goodly children, beauty; for the man who is very ugly in appearance or ill-born or solitary and childless is not very likely to be happy, and perhaps a man would be still less likely if he had thoroughly bad children or friends or had lost good children or friends by death. As we said, then, happiness seems to need this sort of prosperity in addition; for which reason some identify happiness with good fortune, though others identify it with virtue.

9

For this reason also the question is asked, whether happiness is to be acquired by learning or by habituation or some other sort of training, or comes in virtue of some divine providence or again by chance. Now if there is any gift of the gods to men, it is reasonable that happiness should be god-given, and most surely god-given of all human things inasmuch as it is the best. But this question would perhaps be more appropriate to another inquiry; happiness seems, however, even if it is not god-sent but comes as a result of virtue and some process of learning or training, to be among the most godlike things; for that which is the prize and end of virtue seems to be the best thing in the world, and something godlike and blessed.

It will also on this view be very generally shared; for all who are not maimed as regards their potentiality for virtue may win it by a certain kind of study and care. But if it is better to be happy thus than by chance, it is reasonable that the facts should be so, since everything that depends on the action of nature is by nature as good as it can be, and similarly everything that depends on art or any rational cause, and especially if it depends on the best of all causes. To entrust to chance what is greatest and most noble would be a very defective arrangement.

The answer to the question we are asking is plain also from the definition of happiness; for it has been said to be a virtuous activity of soul, of a certain kind. Of the remaining goods, some must necessarily pre-exist as conditions of happiness, and others are naturally co-operative and useful as

(continued)

Nicomachean Ethics (*continued*)

instruments. And this will be found to agree with what we said at the outset; for we stated the end of political science to be the best end, and political science spends most of its pains on making the citizens to be of a certain character, viz. good and capable of noble acts.

It is natural, then, that we call neither ox nor horse nor any other of the animals happy; for none of them is capable of sharing in such activity. For this reason also a boy is not happy; for he is not yet capable of such acts, owing to his age; and boys who are called happy are being congratulated by reason of the hopes we have for them. For there is required, as we said, not only complete virtue but also a complete life, since many changes occur in life, and all manner of chances, and the most prosperous may fall into great misfortunes in old age, as is told of Priam in the Trojan Cycle; and one who has experienced such chances and has ended wretchedly no one calls happy.

10

Must no one at all, then, be called happy while he lives; must we, as Solon says, see the end? Even if we are to lay down this doctrine, is it also the case that a man is happy when he is dead? Or is not this quite absurd, especially for us who say that happiness is an activity? But if we do not call the dead man happy, and if Solon does not mean this, but that one can then safely call a man blessed as being at last beyond evils and misfortunes, this also affords matter for discussion; for both evil and good are thought to exist for a dead man, as much as for one who is alive but not aware of them; e.g., honours and dishonours and the good or bad fortunes of children and in general of descendants. And this also presents a problem; for though a man has lived happily up to old age and has had a death worthy of his life, many reverses may befall his descendants—some of them may be good and attain the life they deserve, while with others the opposite may be the case; and clearly too the degrees of relationship between them and their ancestors may vary indefinitely. It would be odd, then, if the dead man were to share in these changes and become at one time happy, at another wretched; while it would also be odd if the fortunes of the descendants did not for some time have some effect on the happiness of their ancestors.

But we must return to our first difficulty; for perhaps by a consideration of it our present problem might be solved. Now if we must see the end and only then call a man happy, not as being happy but as having been so before, surely this is a paradox, that when he is happy the attribute that belongs to him is not to be truly predicated of him because we do not wish to call living men happy, on account of the changes that may befall them, and because we have assumed happiness to be something permanent and by no means easily changed, while a single man may suffer many turns of fortune's wheel. For clearly if we were to keep pace with his fortunes, we should often call the same man happy and again wretched, making the happy man out to be chameleon and insecurely based. Or is this keeping pace with his fortunes quite wrong? Success or failure in life does not depend on these, but human life, as we said, needs these as mere additions, while virtuous activities or their opposites are what constitute happiness or the reverse.

The question we have now discussed confirms our definition. For no function of man has so much permanence as virtuous activities (these are thought to be more durable even than knowledge of the sciences), and of these themselves the most valuable are more durable because those who are happy spend their life most readily and most continuously in these; for this seems to be the reason why we do not forget them. The attribute in question, then, will belong to the happy man, and he will be happy throughout his life; for always, or by preference to everything else, he will be engaged in virtuous action and contemplation, and he will bear the chances of life most nobly and altogether decorously, if he is 'truly good' and 'foursquare beyond reproach.'

Now many events happen by chance, and events differing in importance; small pieces of good fortune or of its opposite clearly do not weigh down the scales of life one way or the other, but a multitude of great events if they turn out well will make life happier (for not only are they themselves such as to add beauty to life, but the way a man deals with them may be noble and good), while if they turn out ill they crush and maim happiness; for they both bring pain with them and hinder many activities. Yet even in these nobility shines through, when a man bears with resignation many great misfortunes, not through insensibility to pain but through nobility and greatness of soul.

If activities are, as we said, what gives life its character, no happy man can become miserable; for he will never do the acts that are hateful and mean. For the man who is truly good and wise, we think, bears all the chances life becomingly and always makes the best of circumstances, as a good general makes the best military use of the army at his command and a good shoemaker makes the best shoes out of the hides that are given him; and so with all other craftsmen. And if this is the case, the happy man can never become miserable; though he will not reach blessedness, if he meet with fortunes like those of Priam.

Nor, again, is he many-coloured and changeable; for neither will he be moved from his happy state easily or by any ordinary misadventures, but only by many great ones, nor, if he has had many great misadventures, will he recover his happiness in a short time, but if at all, only in a long and complete one in which he has attained many splendid successes.

When then should we not say that he is happy who is active in accordance with complete virtue and is sufficiently equipped with external goods, not for some chance period but throughout a complete life? Or must we add 'and who is destined to live thus and die as befits his life'? Certainly the future is obscure to us, while happiness, we claim, is an end and something in every way final. If so, we shall call happy those among living men in whom these conditions are, and are to be, fulfille—but happy men. So much for these questions.

11

That the fortunes of descendants and of all a man's friends should not affect his happiness at all seems a very unfriendly doctrine, and one opposed to the opinions men hold; but since the events that happen are numerous and admit of all sorts of difference, and some come more near to us and others less so, it seems a long—nay, an infinite—task to discuss each in detail; a general outline will perhaps suffice. If, then, as some of a man's own misadventures have a certain weight and influence on life while others are, as it were, lighter, so too there are differences among the misadventures of our friends taken as a whole, and it makes a difference whether the various suffering befall the living or the dead (much more even than whether lawless and terrible deeds are presupposed in a tragedy or done on the stage), this difference also must be taken into account; or rather, perhaps, the fact that doubt is felt whether the dead share in any good or evil. For it seems, from these considerations, that even if anything whether good or evil penetrates to them, it must be something weak and negligible, either in itself or for them, or if not, at least it must be such in degree and kind as not to make happy those who are not happy nor to take away their blessedness from those who are. The good or bad fortunes of friends, then, seem to have some effects on the dead, but effects of such a kind and degree as neither to make the happy unhappy nor to produce any other change of the kind.

12

These questions having been definitely answered, let us consider whether happiness is among the things that are praised or rather among the things that are prized; for clearly it is not to be placed among potentialities. Everything that is praised seems to be praised because it is of a certain kind and is related somehow to something else; for we praise the just or brave man and in general both the good man and virtue itself because of the actions and functions involved, and we praise the strong man, the good runner, and so on, because he is of a certain kind and is related in a certain way to something good and important. This is clear also from the praises of the gods; for it seems absurd that the gods should be referred to our standard, but this is done because praise involves a reference, to something else. But if praise is for things such as we have described, clearly what applies to the best things is not praise, but something greater and better, as is indeed obvious; for what we do to the gods and the most godlike of men is to call them blessed and happy. And so too with good things; no one praises happiness as he does justice, but rather calls it blessed, as being something more divine and better.

Eudoxus also seems to have been right in his method of advocating the supremacy of pleasure; he thought that the fact that, though a good, it is not praised indicated it to be better than the things that are praised, and that this is what God and the good are; for by reference to these all other things are judged. Praise is appropriate to virtue, for as a result of virtue men tend to do noble deeds, but encomia are bestowed on acts, whether of the body or of the soul. But

(continued)

Nicomachean Ethics (*continued*)

perhaps nicety in these matters is more proper to those who have made a study of encomia; to us it is clear from what has been said that happiness is among the things that are prized and perfect. It seems to be so also from the fact that it is a first principle; for it is for the sake of this that we all do all that we do, and the first principle and cause of goods is, we claim, something prized and divine.

13

Since happiness is an activity of soul in accordance with perfect virtue, we must consider the nature of virtue; for perhaps we shall thus see better the nature of happiness. The true student of politics, too, is thought to have studied virtue above all things; for he wishes to make his fellow citizens good and obedient to the laws. As an example of this we have the lawgivers of the Cretans and the Spartans, and any others of the kind that there may have been. And if this inquiry belongs to political science, clearly the pursuit of it will be in accordance with our original plan. But clearly the virtue we must study is human virtue; for the good we were seeking was human good and the happiness human happiness. By human virtue we mean not that of the body but that of the soul; and happiness also we call an activity of soul. But if this is so, clearly the student of politics must know somehow the facts about soul, as the man who is to heal the eyes or the body as a whole must know about the eyes or the body; and all the more since politics is more prized and better than medicine; but even among doctors the best educated spend much labour on acquiring knowledge of the body. The student of politics, then, must study the soul, and must study it with these objects in view, and do so just to the extent which is sufficient for the questions we are discussing; for further precision is perhaps something more laborious than our purposes require.

Some things are said about it, adequately enough, even in the discussions outside our school, and we must use these; e.g., that one element in the soul is irrational and one has a rational principle. Whether these are separated as the parts of the body or of anything divisible are, or are distinct by definition but by nature inseparable, like convex and concave in the circumference of a circle, does not affect the present question.

Of the irrational element one division seems to be widely distributed, and vegetative in its nature, I mean that which causes nutrition and growth; for it is this kind of power of the soul that one must assign to all nurslings and to embryos, and this same power to fullgrown creatures; this is more reasonable than to assign some different power to them. Now the excellence of this seems to be common to all species and not specifically human; for this part or faculty seems to function most in sleep, while goodness and badness are least manifest in sleep (whence comes the saying that the happy are not better off than the wretched for half their lives; and this happens naturally enough, since sleep is an inactivity of the soul in that respect in which it is called good or bad), unless perhaps to a small extent some of the movements actually penetrate to the soul, and in this respect the dreams of good men are better than those of ordinary people. Enough of this subject, however; let us leave the nutritive faculty alone, since it has by its nature no share in human excellence.

There seems to be also another irrational element in the soul—one which in a sense, however, shares in a rational principle. For we praise the rational principle of the continent man and of the incontinent, and the part of their soul that has such a principle, since it urges them aright and towards the best objects; but there is found in them also another element naturally opposed to the rational principle, which fights against and resists that principle. For exactly as paralysed limbs when we intend to move them to the right turn on the contrary to the left, so is it with the soul; the impulses of incontinent people move in contrary directions. But while in the body we see that which moves astray, in the soul we do not. No doubt, however, we must none the less suppose that in the soul too there is something contrary to the rational principle, resisting and opposing it. In what sense it is distinct from the other elements does not concern us. Now even this seems to have a share in a rational principle, as we said; at any rate in the continent man it obeys the rational principle and presumably in the temperate and brave man it is still more obedient; for in him it speaks, on all matters, with the same voice as the rational principle.

Therefore the irrational element also appears to be two-fold. For the vegetative element in no way shares in a rational principle, but the appetitive and in general the desiring element in a sense shares in it, in so far as it listens to and obeys it; this is the sense in which we speak of 'taking account' of one's father or one's friends, not that in which we speak of 'accounting for a mathematical property. That the irrational element is in some sense persuaded by a rational principle is indicated also by the giving of advice and by all reproof and exhortation. And if this element also must be said to have a rational principle, that which has a rational principle (as well as that which has not) will be twofold, one subdivision having it in the strict sense and in itself, and the other having a tendency to obey as one does one's father.

Virtue too is distinguished into kinds in accordance with this difference; for we say that some of the virtues are intellectual and others moral, philosophic wisdom and understanding and practical wisdom being intellectual, liberality and temperance moral. For in speaking about a man's character we do not say that he is wise or has understanding but that he is good-tempered or temperate; yet we praise the wise man also with respect to his state of mind; and of states of mind we call those which merit praise virtues.

Book II

1

Virtue, then, being of two kinds, intellectual and moral, intellectual virtue in the main owes both its birth and its growth to teaching (for which reason it requires experience and time), while moral virtue comes about as a result of habit, whence also its name (ethike) is one that is formed by a slight variation from the word ethos (habit). From this it is also plain that none of the moral virtues arises in us by nature; for nothing that exists by nature can form a habit contrary to its nature. For instance the stone which by nature moves downwards cannot be habituated to move upwards, not even if one tries to train it by throwing it up ten thousand times; nor can fire be habituated to move downwards, nor can anything else that by nature behaves in one way be trained to behave in another. Neither by nature, then, nor contrary to nature do the virtues arise in us; rather we are adapted by nature to receive them, and are made perfect by habit.

Again, of all the things that come to us by nature we first acquire the potentiality and later exhibit the activity (this is plain in the case of the senses; for it was not by often seeing or often hearing that we got these senses, but on the contrary we had them before we used them, and did not come to have them by using them); but the virtues we get by first exercising them, as also happens in the case of the arts as well. For the things we have to learn before we can do them, we learn by doing them, e.g., men become builders by building and lyre players by playing the lyre; so too we become just by doing just acts, temperate by doing temperate acts, brave by doing brave acts.

This is confirmed by what happens in states; for legislators make the citizens good by forming habits in them, and this is the wish of every legislator, and those who do not effect it miss their mark, and it is in this that a good constitution differs from a bad one.

Again, it is from the same causes and by the same means that every virtue is both produced and destroyed, and similarly every art; for it is from playing the lyre that both good and bad lyre-players are produced. And the corresponding statement is true of builders and of all the rest; men will be good or bad builders as a result of building well or badly. For if this were not so, there would have been no need of a teacher, but all men would have been born good or bad at their craft. This, then, is the case with the virtues also; by doing the acts that we do in our transactions with other men we become just or unjust, and by doing the acts that we do in the presence of danger, and being habituated to feel fear or confidence, we become brave or cowardly. The same is true of appetites and feelings of anger; some men become temperate and good-tempered, others self-indulgent and irascible, by behaving in one way or the other in the appropriate circumstances. Thus, in one word, states of character arise out of like activities. This is why the activities we exhibit must be of a certain kind; it is because the states of character correspond to the differences between these. It makes no small difference, then, whether we form habits of one kind or of another from our very youth; it makes a very great difference, or rather all the difference.

(continued)

Nicomachean Ethics (continued)

2

Since, then, the present inquiry does not aim at theoretical knowledge like the others (for we are inquiring not in order to know what virtue is, but in order to become good, since otherwise our inquiry would have been of no use), we must examine the nature of actions, namely how we ought to do them; for these determine also the nature of the states of character that are produced, as we have said. Now, that we must act according to the right rule is a common principle and must be assumed-it will be discussed later, i.e., both what the right rule is, and how it is related to the other virtues. But this must be agreed upon beforehand, that the whole account of matters of conduct must be given in outline and not precisely, as we said at the very beginning that the accounts we demand must be in accordance with the subject-matter; matters concerned with conduct and questions of what is good for us have no fixity, any more than matters of health. The general account being of this nature, the account of particular cases is yet more lacking in exactness; for they do not fall under any art or precept but the agents themselves must in each case consider what is appropriate to the occasion, as happens also in the art of medicine or of navigation.

But though our present account is of this nature we must give what help we can. First, then, let us consider this, that it is the nature of such things to be destroyed by defect and excess, as we see in the case of strength and of health (for to gain light on things imperceptible we must use the evidence of sensible things); both excessive and defective exercise destroys the strength, and similarly drink or food which is above or below a certain amount destroys the health, while that which is proportionate both produces and increases and preserves it. So too is it, then, in the case of temperance and courage and the other virtues. For the man who flies from and fears everything and does not stand his ground against anything becomes a coward, and the man who fears nothing at all but goes to meet every danger becomes rash; and similarly the man who indulges in every pleasure and abstains from none becomes self-indulgent, while the man who shuns every pleasure, as boors do, becomes in a way insensible; temperance and courage, then, are destroyed by excess and defect, and preserved by the mean.

But not only are the sources and causes of their origination and growth the same as those of their destruction, but also the sphere of their actualization will be the same; for this is also true of the things which are more evident to sense, e.g., of strength; it is produced by taking much food and undergoing much exertion, and it is the strong man that will be most able to do these things. So too is it with the virtues; by abstaining from pleasures we become temperate, and it is when we have become so that we are most able to abstain from them; and similarly too in the case of courage; for by being habituated to despise things that are terrible and to stand our ground against them we become brave, and it is when we have become so that we shall be most able to stand our ground against them.

3

We must take as a sign of states of character the pleasure or pain that ensues on acts; for the man who abstains from bodily pleasures and delights in this very fact is temperate, while the man who is annoyed at it is self-indulgent, and he who stands his ground against things that are terrible and delights in this or at least is not pained is brave, while the man who is pained is a coward. For moral excellence is concerned with pleasures and pains; it is on account of the pleasure that we do bad things, and on account of the pain that we abstain from noble ones. Hence we ought to have been brought up in a particular way from our very youth, as Plato says, so as both to delight in and to be pained by the things that we ought; for this is the right education.

Again, if the virtues are concerned with actions and passions, and every passion and every action is accompanied by pleasure and pain, for this reason also virtue will be concerned with pleasures and pains. This is indicated also by the fact that punishment is inflicted by these means; for it is a kind of cure, and it is the nature of cures to be effected by contraries.

Again, as we said but lately, every state of soul has a nature relative to and concerned with the kind of things by which it tends to be made worse or better; but it is by reason of pleasures and pains that men become bad, by pursuing and avoiding these—either the pleasures and pains they ought not or when they ought not or as they ought not, or by going wrong in one of the other similar ways that may be distinguished. Hence men even define the virtues as certain states of impassivity and rest; not well, however, because they speak absolutely, and do not say 'as one ought' and 'as one ought not' and 'when one ought or ought not', and the other things that may be added. We assume, then, that this kind of excellence tends to do what is best with regard to pleasures and pains, and vice does the contrary.

The following facts also may show us that virtue and vice are concerned with these same things. There being three objects of choice and three of avoidance, the noble, the advantageous, the pleasant, and their contraries, the base, the injurious, the painful, about all of these the good man tends to go right and the bad man to go wrong, and especially about pleasure; for this is common to the animals, and also it accompanies all objects of choice; for even the noble and the advantageous appear pleasant.

Again, it has grown up with us all from our infancy; this is why it is difficult to rub off this passion, engrained as it is in our life. And we measure even our actions, some of us more and others less, by the rule of pleasure and pain. For this reason, then, our whole inquiry must be about these; for to feel delight and pain rightly or wrongly has no small effect on our actions.

Again, it is harder to fight with pleasure than with anger, to use Heraclitus' phrase', but both art and virtue are always concerned with what is harder; for even the good is better when it is harder. Therefore for this reason also the whole concern both of virtue and of political science is with pleasures and pains; for the man who uses these well will be good, he who uses them badly bad.

That virtue, then, is concerned with pleasures and pains, and that by the acts from which it arises it is both increased and, if they are done differently, destroyed, and that the acts from which it arose are those in which it actualizes itself—let this be taken as said.

4

The question might be asked, what we mean by saying that we must become just by doing just acts, and temperate by doing temperate acts; for if men do just and temperate acts, they are already just and temperate, exactly as, if they do what is in accordance with the laws of grammar and of music, they are grammarians and musicians.

Or is this not true even of the arts? It is possible to do something that is in accordance with the laws of grammar, either by chance or at the suggestion of another. A man will be a grammarian, then, only when he has both done something grammatical and done it grammatically; and this means doing it in accordance with the grammatical knowledge in himself.

Again, the case of the arts and that of the virtues are not similar; for the products of the arts have their goodness in themselves, so that it is enough that they should have a certain character, but if the acts that are in accordance with the virtues have themselves a certain character it does not follow that they are done justly or temperately. The agent also must be in a certain condition when he does them; in the first place he must have knowledge, secondly he must choose the acts, and choose them for their own sakes, and thirdly his action must proceed from a firm and unchangeable character. These are not reckoned in as conditions of the possession of the arts, except the bare knowledge; but as a condition of the possession of the virtues knowledge has little or no weight, while the other conditions count not for a little but for everything, i.e., the very conditions which result from often doing just and temperate acts.

Actions, then, are called just and temperate when they are such as the just or the temperate man would do; but it is not the man who does these that is just and temperate, but the man who also does them as just and temperate men do them. It is well said, then, that it is by doing just acts that the just man is produced, and by doing temperate acts the temperate man; without doing these no one would have even a prospect of becoming good.

But most people do not do these, but take refuge in theory and think they are being philosophers and will become good in this way, behaving somewhat like patients who listen attentively to their doctors, but do none of the things they are ordered to do. As the latter will not be made well in body by such a course of treatment, the former will not be made well in soul by such a course of philosophy.

(continued)

Nicomachean Ethics (*continued*)

5

Next we must consider what virtue is. Since things that are found in the soul are of three kinds—passions, faculties, states of character, virtue must be one of these. By passions I mean appetite, anger, fear, confidence, envy, joy, friendly feeling, hatred, longing, emulation, pity, and in general the feelings that are accompanied by pleasure or pain; by faculties the things in virtue of which we are said to be capable of feeling these, e.g., of becoming angry or being pained or feeling pity; by states of character the things in virtue of which we stand well or badly with reference to the passions, e.g., with reference to anger we stand badly if we feel it violently or too weakly, and well if we feel it moderately; and similarly with reference to the other passions.

Now neither the virtues nor the vices are passions, because we are not called good or bad on the ground of our passions, but are so called on the ground of our virtues and our vices, and because we are neither praised nor blamed for our passions (for the man who feels fear or anger is not praised, nor is the man who simply feels anger blamed, but the man who feels it in a certain way), but for our virtues and our vices we are praised or blamed.

Again, we feel anger and fear without choice, but the virtues are modes of choice or involve choice. Further, in respect of the passions we are said to be moved, but in respect of the virtues and the vices we are said not to be moved but to be disposed in a particular way.

For these reasons also they are not faculties; for we are neither called good nor bad, nor praised nor blamed, for the simple capacity of feeling the passions; again, we have the faculties by nature, but we are not made good or bad by nature; we have spoken of this before. If, then, the virtues are neither passions nor faculties, all that remains is that they should be states of character.

Thus we have stated what virtue is in respect of its genus.

6

We must, however, not only describe virtue as a state of character, but also say what sort of state it is. We may remark, then, that every virtue or excellence both brings into good condition the thing of which it is the excellence and makes the work of that thing be done well; e.g., the excellence of the eye makes both the eye and its work good; for it is by the excellence of the eye that we see well. Similarly the excellence of the horse makes a horse both good in itself and good at running and at carrying its rider and at awaiting the attack of the enemy. Therefore, if this is true in every case, the virtue of man also will be the state of character which makes a man good and which makes him do his own work well.

How this is to happen we have stated already, but it will be made plain also by the following consideration of the specific nature of virtue. In everything that is continuous and divisible it is possible to take more, less, or an equal amount, and that either in terms of the thing itself or relatively to us; and the equal is an intermediate between excess and defect. By the intermediate in the object I mean that which is equidistant from each of the extremes, which is one and the same for all men; by the intermediate relatively to us that which is neither too much nor too little—and this is not one, nor the same for all. For instance, if ten is many and two is few, six is the intermediate, taken in terms of the object; for it exceeds and is exceeded by an equal amount; this is intermediate according to arithmetical proportion. But the intermediate relatively to us is not to be taken so; if ten pounds are too much for a particular person to eat and two too little, it does not follow that the trainer will order six pounds; for this also is perhaps too much for the person who is to take it, or too little—too little for Milo, too much for the beginner in athletic exercises. The same is true of running and wrestling. Thus a master of any art avoids excess and defect, but seeks the intermediate and chooses this—the intermediate not in the object but relatively to us.

If it is thus, then, that every art does its work well—by looking to the intermediate and judging its works by this standard (so that we often say of good works of art that it is not possible either to take away or to add anything, implying that excess and defect destroy the goodness of works of art, while the mean preserves it; and good artists, as we say, look to this in their work), and if, further, virtue is more exact and better than any art, as nature also is, then virtue must have the quality of aiming at the intermediate. I mean moral virtue; for it is this that is concerned with passions and actions, and in these there is excess, defect, and the intermediate. For instance, both fear and confidence and appetite and anger and pity and in general pleasure and pain may be felt both too much and too little, and in both cases not well; but to feel them at the right times, with reference to the right objects, towards the right people, with the right motive, and in the right way, is what is both intermediate and best, and this is characteristic of virtue. Similarly with regard to actions also there is excess, defect, and the intermediate. Now virtue is concerned with passions and actions, in which excess is a form of failure, and so is defect, while the intermediate is praised and is a form of success; and being praised and being successful are both characteristics of virtue. Therefore virtue is a kind of mean, since, as we have seen, it aims at what is intermediate.

Again, it is possible to fail in many ways (for evil belongs to the class of the unlimited, as the Pythagoreans conjectured, and good to that of the limited), while to succeed is possible only in one way (for which reason also one is easy and the other difficult—to miss the mark easy, to hit it difficult); for these reasons also, then, excess and defect are characteristic of vice, and the mean of virtue; For men are good in but one way, but bad in many.

Virtue, then, is a state of character concerned with choice, lying in a mean, i.e., the mean relative to us, this being determined by a rational principle, and by that principle by which the man of practical wisdom would determine it. Now it is a mean between two vices, that which depends on excess and that which depends on defect; and again it is a mean because the vices respectively fall short of or exceed what is right in both passions and actions, while virtue both finds and chooses that which is intermediate. Hence in respect of its substance and the definition which states its essence virtue is a mean, with regard to what is best and right an extreme.

But not every action nor every passion admits of a mean; for some have names that already imply badness, e.g., spite, shamelessness, envy, and in the case of actions adultery, theft, murder; for all of these and suchlike things imply by their names that they are themselves bad, and not the excesses or deficiencies of them. It is not possible, then, ever to be right with regard to them; one must always be wrong. Nor does goodness or badness with regard to such things depend on committing adultery with the right woman, at the right time, and in the right way, but simply to do any of them is to go wrong. It would be equally absurd, then, to expect that in unjust, cowardly, and voluptuous action there should be a mean, an excess, and a deficiency; for at that rate there would be a mean of excess and of deficiency, an excess of excess, and a deficiency of deficiency. But as there is no excess and deficiency of temperance and courage because what is intermediate is in a sense an extreme, so too of the actions we have mentioned there is no mean nor any excess and deficiency, but however they are done they are wrong; for in general there is neither a mean of excess and deficiency, nor excess and deficiency of a mean.

7

We must, however, not only make this general statement, but also apply it to the individual facts. For among statements about conduct those which are general apply more widely, but those which are particular are more genuine, since conduct has to do with individual cases, and our statements must harmonize with the facts in these cases. We may take these cases from our table. With regard to feelings of fear and confidence courage is the mean; of the people who exceed, he who exceeds in fearlessness has no name (many of the states have no name), while the man who exceeds in confidence is rash, and he who exceeds in fear and falls short in confidence is a coward. With regard to pleasures and pains—not all of them, and not so much with regard to the pains—the mean is temperance, the excess self-indulgence. Persons deficient with regard to the pleasures are not often found; hence such persons also have received no name. But let us call them 'insensible.'

With regard to giving and taking of money the mean is liberality, the excess and the defect prodigality and meanness. In these actions people exceed and fall short in contrary ways; the prodigal exceeds in spending and falls short in taking, while the mean man exceeds in taking and falls short in spending. (At present we are giving a mere outline or summary, and are satisfied with this; later these states will be more exactly determined.) With regard to money there are also other dispositions—a mean, magnificence (for the magnificent man differs from the liberal man; the former deals with large sums, the latter with small ones), an excess, tastelessness and vulgarity, and a deficiency, niggardliness; these differ from the states opposed to liberality, and the mode of their difference will be stated later. With regard to honour and dishonour the mean is proper pride, the excess is known as a sort of 'empty vanity', and the deficiency is undue humility; and as we said liberality was related to magnificence, differing from it by dealing with small sums, so there is a state similarly related to proper pride,

(continued)

Nicomachean Ethics (*continued*)

being concerned with small honours while that is concerned with great. For it is possible to desire honour as one ought, and more than one ought, and less, and the man who exceeds in his desires is called ambitious, the man who falls short unambitious, while the intermediate person has no name. The dispositions also are nameless, except that that of the ambitious man is called ambition. Hence the people who are at the extremes lay claim to the middle place; and we ourselves sometimes call the intermediate person ambitious and sometimes unambitious, and sometimes praise the ambitious man and sometimes the unambitious. The reason of our doing this will be stated in what follows; but now let us speak of the remaining states according to the method which has been indicated.

With regard to anger also there is an excess, a deficiency, and a mean. Although they can scarcely be said to have names, yet since we call the intermediate person good-tempered let us call the mean good temper; of the persons at the extremes let the one who exceeds be called irascible, and his vice irascibility, and the man who falls short an inirascible sort of person, and the deficiency inirascibility.

There are also three other means, which have a certain likeness to one another, but differ from one another: for they are all concerned with intercourse in words and actions, but differ in that one is concerned with truth in this sphere, the other two with pleasantness; and of this one kind is exhibited in giving amusement, the other in all the circumstances of life. We must therefore speak of these too, that we may the better see that in all things the mean is praise-worthy, and the extremes neither praiseworthy nor right, but worthy of blame. Now most of these states also have no names, but we must try, as in the other cases, to invent names ourselves so that we may be clear and easy to follow. With regard to truth, then, the intermediate is a truthful sort of person and the mean may be called truthfulness, while the pretence which exaggerates is boastfulness and the person characterized by it a boaster, and that which understates is mock modesty and the person characterized by it mock-modest. With regard to pleasantness in the giving of amusement the intermediate person is ready-witted and the disposition ready wit, the excess is buffoonery and the person characterized by it a buffoon, while the man who falls short is a sort of boor and his state is boorishness. With regard to the remaining kind of pleasantness, that which is exhibited in life in general, the man who is pleasant in the right way is friendly and the mean is friendliness, while the man who exceeds is an obsequious person if he has no end in view, a flatterer if he is aiming at his own advantage, and the man who falls short and is unpleasant in all circumstances is a quarrelsome and surly sort of person.

There are also means in the passions and concerned with the passions; since shame is not a virtue, and yet praise is extended to the modest man. For even in these matters one man is said to be intermediate, and another to exceed, as for instance the bashful man who is ashamed of everything; while he who falls short or is not ashamed of anything at all is shameless, and the intermediate person is modest. Righteous indignation is a mean between envy and spite, and these states are concerned with the pain and pleasure that are felt at the fortunes of our neighbours; the man who is characterized by righteous indignation is pained at undeserved good fortune, the envious man, going beyond him, is pained at all good fortune, and the spiteful man falls so far short of being pained that he even rejoices. But these states there will be an opportunity of describing elsewhere; with regard to justice, since it has not one simple meaning, we shall, after describing the other states, distinguish its two kinds and say how each of them is a mean; and similarly we shall treat also of the rational virtues.

8

There are three kinds of dispositions, then, two of them vices, involving excess and deficiency respectively, and one a virtue, viz. the mean, and all are in a sense opposed to all; for the extreme states are contrary both to the intermediate state and to each other, and the intermediate to the extremes; as the equal is greater relatively to the less, less relatively to the greater, so the middle states are excessive relatively to the deficiencies, deficient relatively to the excesses, both in passions and in actions. For the brave man appears rash relatively to the coward, and cowardly relatively to the rash man; and similarly the temperate man appears self-indulgent relatively to the insensible man, insensible relatively to the self-indulgent, and the liberal man prodigal relatively to the mean man, mean relatively to the prodigal. Hence also the people at the extremes push the intermediate man each over to the other, and the brave man is called rash by the coward, cowardly by the rash man, and correspondingly in the other cases.

These states being thus opposed to one another, the greatest contrariety is that of the extremes to each other, rather than to the intermediate; for these are further from each other than from the intermediate, as the great is further from the small and the small from the great than both are from the equal. Again, to the intermediate some extremes show a certain likeness, as that of rashness to courage and that of prodigality to liberality; but the extremes show the greatest unlikeness to each other; now contraries are defined as the things that are furthest from each other, so that things that are further apart are more contrary.

To the mean in some cases the deficiency, in some the excess is more opposed; e.g., it is not rashness, which is an excess, but cowardice, which is a deficiency, that is more opposed to courage, and not insensibility, which is a deficiency, but self-indulgence, which is an excess, that is more opposed to temperance. This happens from two reasons, one being drawn from the thing itself; for because one extreme is nearer and liker to the intermediate, we oppose not this but rather its contrary to the intermediate. For example, since rashness is thought liker and nearer to courage, and cowardice more unlike, we oppose rather the latter to courage; for things that are further from the intermediate are thought more contrary to it. This, then, is one cause, drawn from the thing itself; another is drawn from ourselves; for the things to which we ourselves more naturally tend seem more contrary to the intermediate. For instance, we ourselves tend more naturally to pleasures, and hence are more easily carried away towards self-indulgence than towards propriety. We describe as contrary to the mean, then, rather the directions in which we more often go to great lengths; and therefore self-indulgence, which is an excess, is the more contrary to temperance.

9

That moral virtue is a mean, then, and in what sense it is so, and that it is a mean between two vices, the one involving excess, the other deficiency, and that it is such because its character is to aim at what is intermediate in passions and in actions, has been sufficiently stated. Hence also it is no easy task to be good. For in everything it is no easy task to find the middle, e.g., to find the middle of a circle is not for every one but for him who knows; so, too, any one can get angry—that is easy—or give or spend money; but to do this to the right person, to the right extent, at the right time, with the right motive, and in the right way, that is not for every one, nor is it easy; wherefore goodness is both rare and laudable and noble.

Hence he who aims at the intermediate must first depart from what is the more contrary to it, as Calypso advises—

Hold the ship out beyond that surf and spray.

For of the extremes one is more erroneous, one less so; therefore, since to hit the mean is hard in the extreme, we must as a second best, as people say, take the least of the evils; and this will be done best in the way we describe. But we must consider the things towards which we ourselves also are easily carried away; for some of us tend to one thing, some to another; and this will be recognizable from the pleasure and the pain we feel. We must drag ourselves away to the contrary extreme; for we shall get into the intermediate state by drawing well away from error, as people do in straightening sticks that are bent.

Now in everything the pleasant or pleasure is most to be guarded against; for we do not judge it impartially. We ought, then, to feel towards pleasure as the elders of the people felt towards Helen, and in all circumstances repeat their saying; for if we dismiss pleasure thus we are less likely to go astray. It is by doing this, then, (to sum the matter up) that we shall best be able to hit the mean.

But this is no doubt difficult, and especially in individual cases; for or is not easy to determine both how and with whom and on what provocation and how long one should be angry; for we too sometimes praise those who fall short and call them good-tempered, but sometimes we praise those who get angry and call them manly. The man, however, who deviates little from goodness is not blamed, whether he do so in the direction of the more or of the less, but only the man who deviates more widely; for he does not fail to be noticed. But up to what point and to what extent a man must deviate before he becomes blameworthy it is not easy to determine by reasoning, any more than anything else that is perceived by the senses; such things depend on particular facts, and the decision rests with perception. So much, then, is plain, that the intermediate state is in all things to be praised, but that we must incline sometimes towards the excess, sometimes towards the deficiency; for so shall we most easily hit the mean and what is right.

Republic, Book II

Plato

The Individual, the State, and Education

SOCRATES, GLAUCON

WITH these words I was thinking that I had made an end of the discussion; but the end, in truth, proved to be only a beginning. For Glaucon, who is always the most pugnacious of men, was dissatisfied at Thrasymachus's retirement; he wanted to have the battle out. So he said to me: Socrates, do you wish really to persuade us, or only to seem to have persuaded us, that to be just is always better than to be unjust?

I should wish really to persuade you, I replied, if I could.

Then you certainly have not succeeded. Let me ask you now: How would you arrange goods—are there not some which we welcome for their own sakes, and independently of their consequences, as, for example, harmless pleasures and enjoyments, which delight us at the time, although nothing follows from them?

I agree in thinking that there is such a class, I replied.

Is there not also a second class of goods, such as knowledge, sight, health, which are desirable not only in themselves, but also for their results?

Certainly, I said.

And would you not recognize a third class, such as gymnastic, and the care of the sick, and the physician's art; also the various ways of money-making—these do us good but we regard them as disagreeable; and no one would choose them for their own sakes, but only for the sake of some reward or result which flows from them?

There is, I said, this third class also. But why do you ask?

Because I want to know in which of the three classes you would place justice?

In the highest class, I replied—among those goods which he who would be happy desires both for their own sake and for the sake of their results.

Then the many are of another mind; they think that justice is to be reckoned in the troublesome class, among goods which are to be pursued for the sake of rewards and of reputation, but in themselves are disagreeable and rather to be avoided.

I know, I said, that this is their manner of thinking, and that this was the thesis which Thrasymachus was maintaining just now, when he censured justice and praised injustice. But I am too stupid to be convinced by him.

I wish, he said, that you would hear me as well as him, and then I shall see whether you and I agree. For Thrasymachus seems to me, like a snake, to have been charmed by your voice sooner than he ought to have been; but to my mind the nature of justice and injustice has not yet been made clear. Setting aside their rewards and results, I want to know what they are in themselves, and how they inwardly work in the soul. If you please, then, I will revive the argument of Thrasymachus. And first I will speak of the nature and origin of justice according to the common view of them. Secondly, I will show that all men who practise justice do so against their will of necessity, but not as a good. And thirdly, I will argue that there is reason in this view, for the life of the unjust is after all better far than the life of the just—if what they say is true, Socrates, since I myself am not of their opinion. But still I acknowledge that I am perplexed when I hear the voices of Thrasymachus and myriads of others dinning in my ears; and, on the other hand, I have never yet heard the superiority of justice to injustice maintained by anyone in a satisfactory way. I want to hear justice praised in respect of itself; then I shall be satisfied, and you are the person from whom I think that I am most likely to hear this; and therefore I will praise the unjust life to the utmost of my power, and my manner of speaking will indicate the manner in which I desire to hear you too praising justice and censuring injustice. Will you say whether you approve of my proposal?

Indeed I do; nor can I imagine any theme about which a man of sense would oftener wish to converse.

I am delighted, he replied, to hear you say so, and shall begin by speaking, as I proposed, of the nature and origin of justice.

They say that to do injustice is, by nature, good; to suffer injustice, evil; but that the evil is greater than the good. And so when men have both done and suffered injustice and have had experience of both, not being able to avoid the one and obtain the other, they think that they had better agree among themselves to have neither; hence there arise laws and mutual covenants; and that which is ordained by law is termed by them lawful and just. This they affirm to be the origin and nature of justice; it is a mean or compromise, between the best of all, which is to do injustice and not be punished, and the worst of all, which is to suffer injustice without the power of retaliation; and justice, being at a middle point between the two, is tolerated not as a good, but as the lesser evil, and honored by reason of the inability of men to do injustice. For no man who is worthy to be called a man would ever submit to such an agreement if he were able to resist; he would be mad if he did. Such is the received account, Socrates, of the nature and origin of justice.

Now that those who practise justice do so involuntarily and because they have not the power to be unjust will best appear if we imagine something of this kind: having given both to the just and the unjust power to do what they will, let us watch and see whither desire will lead them; then we shall discover in the very act the just and unjust man to be proceeding along the same road, following their interest, which all natures deem to be their good, and are only diverted into the path of justice by the force of law. The liberty which we are supposing may be most completely given to them in the form of such a power as is said to have been possessed by Gyges, the ancestor of Croesus the Lydian.[1] According to the tradition, Gyges was a shepherd in the service of the King of Lydia; there was a great storm, and an earthquake made an opening in the earth at the place where he was feeding his flock. Amazed at the sight, he descended into the opening, where, among other marvels, he beheld a hollow brazen horse, having doors, at which he, stooping and looking in, saw a dead body of stature, as appeared to him, more than human and having nothing on but a gold ring; this he took from the finger of the dead and reascended. Now the shepherds met together, according to custom, that they might send their monthly report about the flocks to the King; into their assembly he came having the ring on his finger, and as he was sitting among them he chanced to turn the collet of the ring inside his hand, when instantly he became invisible to the rest of the company and they began to speak of him as if he were no longer present. He was astonished at this, and again touching the ring he turned the collet outward and reappeared; he made several trials of the ring, and always with the same result—when he turned the collet inward he became invisible, when outward he reappeared. Whereupon he contrived to be chosen one of the messengers who were sent to the court; where as soon as he arrived he seduced the Queen, and with her help conspired against the King and slew him and took the kingdom. Suppose now that there were two such magic rings, and the just put on one of them and the unjust the other; no man can be imagined to be of such an iron nature that he would stand fast in justice. No man would keep his hands off what was not his own when he could safely take what he liked out of the market, or go into houses and lie with anyone at his pleasure, or kill or release from prison whom he would, and in all respects be like a god among men. Then the actions of the just would be as the actions of the unjust; they would both come at last to the same point. And this we may truly affirm to be a great proof that a man is just, not willingly or because he thinks that justice is any good to him individually, but of necessity, for wherever anyone thinks that he can safely be unjust, there he is unjust. For all men believe in their hearts that injustice is far more profitable to the individual than justice, and he who argues as I have been supposing, will say that they are right. If you could imagine anyone obtaining this power of becoming invisible, and never doing any wrong or touching what was another's, he would be thought by the lookers-on to be a most wretched idiot, although they would praise him to one another's faces, and keep up appearances with one another from a fear that they too might suffer injustice. Enough of this.

Now, if we are to form a real judgment of the life of the just and unjust, we must isolate them; there is no other way; and how is the isolation to be effected? I answer: Let the unjust man be entirely unjust, and the just man entirely just; nothing is to be taken away from either of them, and both are to be perfectly furnished for the work of their respective lives. First, let the unjust be like other distinguished masters of craft; like the skilful pilot or physician, who knows intuitively his own

(continued)

Republic, Book II (continued)

powers and keeps within their limits, and who, if he fails at any point, is able to recover himself. So let the unjust make his unjust attempts in the right way, and lie hidden if he means to be great in his injustice (he who is found out is nobody): for the highest reach of injustice is, to be deemed just when you are not. Therefore I say that in the perfectly unjust man we must assume the most perfect injustice; there is to be no deduction, but we must allow him, while doing the most unjust acts, to have acquired the greatest reputation for justice. If he have taken a false step he must be able to recover himself; he must be one who can speak with effect, if any of his deeds come to light, and who can force his way where force is required by his courage and strength, and command of money and friends. And at his side let us place the just man in his nobleness and simplicity, wishing, as Æschylus says, to be and not to seem good. There must be no seeming, for if he seem to be just he will be honored and rewarded, and then we shall not know whether he is just for the sake of justice or for the sake of honor and rewards; therefore, let him be clothed in justice only, and have no other covering; and he must be imagined in a state of life the opposite of the former. Let him be the best of men, and let him be thought the worst; then he will have been put to the proof; and we shall see whether he will be affected by the fear of infamy and its consequences. And let him continue thus to the hour of death; being just and seeming to be unjust. When both have reached the uttermost extreme, the one of justice and the other of injustice, let judgment be given which of them is the happier of the two.

Heavens! my dear Glaucon, I said, how energetically you polish them up for the decision, first one and then the other, as if they were two statues.

I do my best, he said. And now that we know what they are like there is no difficulty in tracing out the sort of life which awaits either of them. This I will proceed to describe; but as you may think the description a little too coarse, I ask you to suppose, Socrates, that the words which follow are not mine. Let me put them into the mouths of the eulogists of injustice: They will tell you that the just man who is thought unjust will be scourged, racked, bound—will have his eyes burnt out; and, at last, after suffering every kind of evil, he will be impaled. Then he will understand that he ought to seem only, and not to be, just; the words of Æschylus may be more truly spoken of the unjust than of the just. For the unjust is pursuing a reality; he does not live with a view to appearances—he wants to be really unjust and not to seem only—

"His mind has a soil deep and fertile,
Out of which spring his prudent counsels."[1]

In the first place, he is thought just, and therefore bears rule in the city; he can marry whom he will, and give in marriage to whom he will; also he can trade and deal where he likes, and always to his own advantage, because he has no misgivings about injustice; and at every contest, whether in public or private, he gets the better of his antagonists, and gains at their expense, and is rich, and out of his gains he can benefit his friends, and harm his enemies; moreover, he can offer sacrifices, and dedicate gifts to the gods abundantly and magnificently, and can honor the gods or any man whom he wants to honor in a far better style than the just, and therefore he is likely to be dearer than they are to the gods. And thus, Socrates, gods and men are said to unite in making the life of the unjust better than the life of the just.

I was going to say something in answer to Glaucon, when Adeimantus, his brother, interposed: Socrates, he said, you do not suppose that there is nothing more to be urged?

Why, what else is there? I answered.

The strongest point of all has not been even mentioned, he replied.

Well, then, according to the proverb, "Let brother help brother"—if he fails in any part, do you assist him; although I must confess that Glaucon has already said quite enough to lay me in the dust, and take from me the power of helping justice.

Nonsense, he replied. But let me add something more: There is another side to Glaucon's argument about the praise and censure of justice and injustice, which is equally required in order to bring out what I believe to be his meaning. Parents and tutors are always telling their sons and their wards that they are to be just; but why? not for the sake of justice, but for the sake of character and reputation; in the hope of obtaining for him who is reputed just some of those offices, marriages, and the like which Glaucon has enumerated among the advantages accruing to the unjust from the reputation of justice. More, however, is made of appearances by this class of persons than by the others; for they throw in the good opinion of the gods, and will tell you of a shower of benefits which the heavens, as they say, rain upon the pious; and this accords with the testimony of the noble Hesiod and Homer, the first of whom says that the gods make the oaks of the just—

> "To bear acorns at their summit, and bees in the middle;
> And the sheep are bowed down with the weight of their fleeces,"[2]

and many other blessings of a like kind are provided for them. And Homer has a very similar strain; for he speaks of one whose fame is

> "As the fame of some blameless king who, like a god,
> Maintains justice; to whom the black earth brings forth
> Wheat and barley, whose trees are bowed with fruit,
> And his sheep never fail to bear, and the sea gives him fish."[3]

Still grander are the gifts of heaven which Musœus and his son[4] vouchsafe to the just; they take them down into the world below, where they have the saints lying on couches at a feast, everlastingly drunk, crowned with garlands; their idea seems to be that an immortality of drunkenness is the highest meed of virtue. Some extend their rewards yet further; the posterity, as they say, of the faithful and just shall survive to the third and fourth generation. This is the style in which they praise justice. But about the wicked there is another strain; they bury them in a slough in Hades, and make them carry water in a sieve; also while they are yet living they bring them to infamy, and inflict upon them the punishments which Glaucon described as the portion of the just who are reputed to be unjust; nothing else does their invention supply. Such is their manner of praising the one and censuring the other.

Once more, Socrates, I will ask you to consider another way of speaking about justice and injustice, which is not confined to the poets, but is found in prose writers. The universal voice of mankind is always declaring that justice and virtue are honorable, but grievous and toilsome; and that the pleasures of vice and injustice are easy of attainment, and are only censured by law and opinion. They say also that honesty is for the most part less profitable than dishonesty; and they are quite ready to call wicked men happy, and to honor them both in public and private when they are rich or in any other way influential, while they despise and overlook those who may be weak and poor, even though acknowledging them to be better than the others. But most extraordinary of all is their mode of speaking about virtue and the gods: they say that the gods apportion calamity and misery to many good men, and good and happiness to the wicked. And mendicant prophets go to rich men's doors and persuade them that they have a power committed to them by the gods of making an atonement for a man's own or his ancestor's sins by sacrifices or charms, with rejoicings and feasts; and they promise to harm an enemy, whether just or unjust, at a small cost; with magic arts and incantations binding heaven, as they say, to execute their will. And the poets are the authorities to whom they appeal, now smoothing the path of vice with the words of Hesiod:

> "Vice may be had in abundance without trouble; the way is smooth and her dwelling-place is near. But before virtue the gods have set toil,"[5]

and a tedious and uphill road: then citing Homer as a witness that the gods may be influenced by men; for he also says:

> "The gods, too, may be turned from their purpose; and men pray to them and avert their wrath by sacrifices and soothing entreaties, and by libations and the odor of fat, when they have sinned and trangressed."[6]

And they produce a host of books written by Musæus and Orpheus, who were children of the Moon and the muses—that is what they say—according to which they perform their ritual, and

(continued)

Republic, Book II (continued)

persuade not only individuals, but whole cities, that expiations and atonements for sin may be made by sacrifices and amusements which fill a vacant hour, and are equally at the service of the living and the dead; the latter sort they call mysteries, and they redeem us from the pains of hell, but if we neglect them no one knows what awaits us.

He proceeded: And now when the young hear all this said about virtue and vice, and the way in which gods and men regard them, how are their minds likely to be affected, my dear Socrates—those of them, I mean, who are quick-witted, and, like bees on the wing, light on every flower, and from all that they hear are prone to draw conclusions as to what manner of persons they should be and in what way they should walk if they would make the best of life? Probably the youth will say to himself in the words of Pindar:

> "Can I by justice or by crooked ways of deceit ascend a loftier tower which may be a fortress to me all my days?"

For what men say is that, if I am really just and am not also thought just, profit there is none, but the pain and loss on the other hand are unmistakable. But if, though unjust, I acquire the reputation of justice, a heavenly life is promised to me. Since then, as philosophers prove, appearance tyrannizes over truth and is lord of happiness, to appearance I must devote myself. I will describe around me a picture and shadow of virtue to be the vestibule and exterior of my house; behind I will trail the subtle and crafty fox, as Archilochus, greatest of sages, recommends. But I hear someone exclaiming that the concealment of wickedness is often difficult; to which I answer, Nothing great is easy. Nevertheless, the argument indicates this, if we would be happy, to be the path along which we should proceed. With a view to concealment we will establish secret brotherhoods and political clubs. And there are professors of rhetoric who teach the art of persuading courts and assemblies; and so, partly by persuasion and partly by force, I shall make unlawful gains and not be punished. Still I hear a voice saying that the gods cannot be deceived, neither can they be compelled. But what if there are no gods? or, suppose them to have no care of human things—why in either case should we mind about concealment? And even if there are gods, and they do care about us, yet we know of them only from tradition and the genealogies of the poets; and these are the very persons who say that they may be influenced and turned by "sacrifices and soothing entreaties and by offerings." Let us be consistent, then, and believe both or neither. If the poets speak truly, why, then, we had better be unjust, and offer of the fruits of injustice; for if we are just, although we may escape the vengeance of heaven, we shall lose the gains of injustice; but, if we are unjust, we shall keep the gains, and by our sinning and praying, and praying and sinning, the gods will be propitiated, and we shall not be punished. "But there is a world below in which either we or our posterity will suffer for our unjust deeds." Yes, my friend, will be the reflection, but there are mysteries and atoning deities, and these have great power. That is what mighty cities declare; and the children of the gods, who were their poets and prophets, bear a like testimony.

On what principle, then, shall we any longer choose justice rather than the worst injustice? when, if we only unite the latter with a deceitful regard to appearances, we shall fare to our mind both with gods and men, in life and after death, as the most numerous and the highest authorities tell us. Knowing all this, Socrates, how can a man who has any superiority of mind or person or rank or wealth, be willing to honor justice; or indeed to refrain from laughing when he hears justice praised? And even if there should be someone who is able to disprove the truth of my words, and who is satisfied that justice is best, still he is not angry with the unjust, but is very ready to forgive them, because he also knows that men are not just of their own free will; unless, peradventure, there be someone whom the divinity within him may have inspired with a hatred of injustice, or who has attained knowledge of the truth—but no other man. He only blames injustice, who, owing to cowardice or age or some weakness, has not the power of being unjust. And this is proved by the fact that when he obtains the power, he immediately becomes unjust as far as he can be.

The cause of all this, Socrates, was indicated by us at the beginning of the argument, when my brother and I told you how astonished we were to find that of all the professing panegyrists of justice—beginning with the ancient heroes of whom any memorial has been preserved to us, and ending with the men of our own time—no one has ever blamed injustice or praised justice except with a view to the glories, honors, and benefits which flow from them. No one has ever adequately described either in verse or prose the true essential nature of either of them abiding in the soul, and invisible to any human or divine eye; or shown that of all the things of a man's soul which he has within him, justice is the greatest good, and injustice the greatest evil. Had this been the universal strain, had you sought to persuade us of this from our youth upward, we should not have been on the watch to keep one another from doing wrong, but everyone would have been his own watchman, because afraid, if he did wrong, of harboring in himself the greatest of evils. I dare say that Thrasymachus and others would seriously hold the language which I have been merely repeating, and words even stronger than these about justice and injustice, grossly, as I conceive, perverting their true nature. But I speak in this vehement manner, as I must frankly confess to you, because I want to hear from you the opposite side; and I would ask you to show not only the superiority which justice has over injustice, but what effect they have on the possessor of them which makes the one to be a good and the other an evil to him. And please, as Glaucon requested of you, to exclude reputations; for unless you take away from each of them his true reputation and add on the false, we shall say that you do not praise justice, but the appearance of it; we shall think that you are only exhorting us to keep injustice dark, and that you really agree with Thrasymachus in thinking that justice is another's good and the interest of the stronger, and that injustice is a man's own profit and interest, though injurious to the weaker. Now as you have admitted that justice is one of that highest class of goods which are desired, indeed, for their results, but in a far greater degree for their own sakes—like sight or hearing or knowledge or health, or any other real and natural and not merely conventional good—I would ask you in your praise of justice to regard one point only: I mean the essential good and evil which justice and injustice work in the possessors of them. Let others praise justice and censure injustice, magnifying the rewards and honors of the one and abusing the other; that is a manner of arguing which, coming from them, I am ready to tolerate, but from you who have spent your whole life in the consideration of this question, unless I hear the contrary from your own lips, I expect something better. And therefore, I say, not only prove to us that justice is better than injustice, but show what they either of them do to the possessor of them, which makes the one to be a good and the other an evil, whether seen or unseen by gods and men.

I had always admired the genius of Glaucon and Adeimantus, but on hearing these words I was quite delighted, and said: Sons of an illustrious father, that was not a bad beginning of the elegiac verses which the admirer of Glaucon made in honor of you after you had distinguished yourselves at the battle of Megara:

"Sons of Ariston," he sang, "divine offspring of an illustrious hero."

The epithet is very appropriate, for there is something truly divine in being able to argue as you have done for the superiority of injustice, and remaining unconvinced by your own arguments. And I do believe that you are not convinced—this I infer from your general character, for had I judged only from your speeches I should have mistrusted you. But now, the greater my confidence in you, the greater is my difficulty in knowing what to say. For I am in a strait between two; on the one hand I feel that I am unequal to the task; and my inability is brought home to me by the fact that you were not satisfied with the answer which I made to Thrasymachus, proving, as I thought, the superiority which justice has over injustice. And yet I cannot refuse to help, while breath and speech remain to me; I am afraid that there would be an impiety in being present when justice is evil spoken of and not lifting up a hand in her defence. And therefore I had best give such help as I can.

Glaucon and the rest entreated me by all means not to let the question drop, but to proceed in the investigation. They wanted to arrive at the truth, first, about the nature of justice and injustice, and secondly, about their relative advantages. I told them, what I really thought, that the inquiry would be of a serious nature, and would require very good eyes. Seeing then, I said, that we are no great wits, I think that we had better adopt a method which I may illustrate thus; suppose that a short-sighted person had been asked by someone to read small letters from a distance; and it occurred to someone else that

(continued)

Republic, Book II (*continued*)

they might be found in another place which was larger and in which the letters were larger—if they were the same and he could read the larger letters first, and then proceed to the lesser—this would have been thought a rare piece of good-fortune.

Very true, said Adeimantus; but how does the illustration apply to our inquiry?

I will tell you, I replied; justice, which is the subject of our inquiry, is, as you know, sometimes spoken of as the virtue of an individual, and sometimes as the virtue of a State.

True, he replied.

And is not a State larger than an individual?

It is.

Then in the larger the quantity of justice is likely to be larger and more easily discernible. I propose therefore that we inquire into the nature of justice and injustice, first as they appear in the State, and secondly in the individual, proceeding from the greater to the lesser and comparing them.

That, he said, is an excellent proposal.

And if we imagine the State in process of creation, we shall see the justice and injustice of the State in process of creation also.

I dare say.

When the State is completed there may be a hope that the object of our search will be more easily discovered.

Yes, far more easily.

But ought we to attempt to construct one? I said; for to do so, as I am inclined to think, will be a very serious task. Reflect therefore.

I have reflected, said Adeimantus, and am anxious that you should proceed.

A State, I said, arises, as I conceive, out of the needs of man kind; no one is self-sufficing, but all of us have many wants. Can any other origin of a State be imagined?

There can be no other.

Then, as we have many wants, and many persons are needed to supply them, one takes a helper for one purpose and another for another; and when these partners and helpers are gathered together in one habitation the body of inhabitants is termed a State.

True, he said.

And they exchange with one another, and one gives, and another receives, under the idea that the exchange will be for their good.

Very true.

Then, I said, let us begin and create in idea a State; and yet the true creator is necessity, who is the mother of our invention.

Of course, he replied.

Now the first and greatest of necessities is food, which is the condition of life and existence.

Certainly.

The second is a dwelling, and the third clothing and the like.

True.

And now let us see how our city will be able to supply this great demand: We may suppose that one man is a husbandman, another a builder, someone else a weaver—shall we add to them a shoemaker, or perhaps some other purveyor to our bodily wants?

Quite right.

The barest notion of a State must include four or five men.

Clearly.

And how will they proceed? Will each bring the result of his labors into a common stock?—the individual husbandman, for example, producing for four, and laboring four times as long and as much as he need in the provision of food with which he supplies others as well as himself; or will he have nothing to do with others and not be at the trouble of producing for them, but provide for himself alone a fourth of the food in a fourth of the time, and in the remaining three-fourths of his time be employed in making a house or a coat or a pair of shoes, having no partnership with others, but supplying himself all his own wants?

Adeimantus thought that he should aim at producing food only and not at producing everything.

Probably, I replied, that would be the better way; and when I hear you say this, I am myself reminded that we are not all alike; there are diversities of natures among us which are adapted to different occupations.

Very true.

And will you have a work better done when the workman has many occupations, or when he has only one?

When he has only one.

Further, there can be no doubt that a work is spoilt when not done at the right time?

No doubt.

For business is not disposed to wait until the doer of the business is at leisure; but the doer must follow up what he is doing, and make the business his first object.

He must.

And if so, we must infer that all things are produced more plentifully and easily and of a better quality when one man does one thing which is natural to him and does it at the right time, and leaves other things.

Undoubtedly.

Then more than four citizens will be required; for the husbandman will not make his own plough or mattock, or other implements of agriculture, if they are to be good for anything. Neither will the builder make his tools—and he, too, needs many; and in like manner the weaver and shoemaker.

True.

Then carpenters and smiths and many other artisans will be sharers in our little State, which is already beginning to grow?

True.

Yet even if we add neatherds, shepherds, and other herdsmen, in order that our husbandmen may have oxen to plough with, and builders as well as husbandmen may have draught cattle, and curriers and weavers fleeces and hides—still our State will not be very large.

That is true; yet neither will it be a very small State which contains all these.

Then, again, there is the situation of the city—to find a place where nothing need be imported is well-nigh impossible.

Impossible.

Then there must be another class of citizens who will bring the required supply from another city?

There must.

But if the trader goes empty-handed, having nothing which they require who would supply his need, he will come back empty-handed.

That is certain.

And therefore what they produce at home must be not only enough for themselves, but such both in quantity and quality as to accommodate those from whom their wants are supplied.

Very true.

Then more husbandmen and more artisans will be required?

They will.

Not to mention the importers and exporters, who are called merchants?

Yes.

Then we shall want merchants?

We shall.

And if merchandise is to be carried over the sea, skilful sailors will also be needed, and in considerable numbers?

Yes, in considerable numbers.

Then, again, within the city, how will they exchange their productions? To secure such an exchange was, as you will remember, one of our principal objects when we formed them into a society and constituted a State.

Clearly they will buy and sell.

Then they will need a market-place, and a money-token for purposes of exchange.

Certainly.

(continued)

Republic, Book II (*continued*)

Suppose now that a husbandman or an artisan brings some production to market, and he comes at a time when there is no one to exchange with him—is he to leave his calling and sit idle in the market-place?

Not at all; he will find people there who, seeing the want, undertake the office of salesmen. In well-ordered States they are commonly those who are the weakest in bodily strength, and therefore of little use for any other purpose; their duty is to be in the market, and to give money in exchange for goods to those who desire to sell, and to take money from those who desire to buy.

This want, then, creates a class of retail-traders in our State. Is not "retailer" the term which is applied to those who sit in the market-place engaged in buying and selling, while those who wander from one city to another are called merchants?

Yes, he said.

And there is another class of servants, who are intellectually hardly on the level of companionship; still they have plenty of bodily strength for labor; which accordingly they sell, and are called, if I do not mistake, hirelings, "hire" being the name which is given to the price of their labor.

True.

Then hirelings will help to make up our population?

Yes.

And now, Adeimantus, is our State matured and perfected?

I think so.

Where, then, is justice, and where is injustice, and in what part of the State did they spring up?

Probably in the dealings of these citizens with one another. I cannot imagine that they are more likely to be found anywhere else.

I dare say that you are right in your suggestion, I said; we had better think the matter out, and not shrink from the inquiry.

Let us then consider, first of all, what will be their way of life, now that we have thus established them. Will they not produce corn and wine and clothes and shoes, and build houses for themselves? And when they are housed, they will work, in summer, commonly, stripped and barefoot, but in winter substantially clothed and shod. They will feed on barley-meal and flour of wheat, baking and kneading them, making noble cakes and loaves; these they will serve up on a mat of reeds or on clean leaves, themselves reclining the while upon beds strewn with yew or myrtle. And they and their children will feast, drinking of the wine which they have made, wearing garlands on their heads, and hymning the praises of the gods, in happy converse with one another. And they will take care that their families do not exceed their means; having an eye to poverty or war.

But, said Glaucon, interposing, you have not given them a relish to their meal.

True, I replied, I had forgotten; of course they must have a relish—salt and olives and cheese—and they will boil roots and herbs such as country people prepare; for a dessert we shall give them figs and peas and beans; and they will roast myrtle-berries and acorns at the fire, drinking in moderation. And with such a diet they may be expected to live in peace and health to a good old age, and bequeath a similar life to their children after them.

Yes, Socrates, he said, and if you were providing for a city of pigs, how else would you feed the beasts?

But what would you have, Glaucon? I replied.

Why, he said, you should give them the ordinary conveniences of life. People who are to be comfortable are accustomed to lie on sofas, and dine off tables, and they should have sauces and sweets in the modern style.

Yes, I said, now I understand: the question which you would have me consider is, not only how a State, but how a luxurious State is created; and possibly there is no harm in this, for in such a State we shall be more likely to see how justice and injustice originate. In my opinion the true and healthy constitution of the State is the one which I have described. But if you wish also to see a State at fever-heat, I have no objection. For I suspect that many will not be satisfied with the simpler way of life. They will be for adding sofas and tables and other furniture; also dainties and perfumes and incense and courtesans and cakes, all these not of one sort only, but in every variety. We must go beyond the necessaries of which I was at first speaking, such as houses and clothes and shoes; the arts of the painter and the embroiderer will have to be set in motion, and gold and ivory and all sorts of materials must be procured.

True, he said.

Then we must enlarge our borders; for the original healthy State is no longer sufficient. Now will the city have to fill and swell with a multitude of callings which are not required by any natural want; such as the whole tribe of hunters and actors, of whom one large class have to do with forms and colors; another will be the votaries of music—poets and their attendant train of rhapsodists, players, dancers, contractors; also makers of divers kinds of articles, including women's dresses. And we shall want more servants. Will not tutors be also in request, and nurses wet and dry, tirewomen and barbers, as well as confectioners and cooks; and swineherds, too, who were not needed and therefore had no place in the former edition of our State, but are needed now? They must not be forgotten: and there will be animals of many other kinds, if people eat them.

Certainly.

And living in this way we shall have much greater need of physicians than before?

Much greater.

And the country which was enough to support the original inhabitants will be too small now, and not enough?

Quite true.

Then a slice of our neighbors' land will be wanted by us for pasture and tillage, and they will want a slice of ours, if, like ourselves, they exceed the limit of necessity, and give themselves up to the unlimited accumulation of wealth?

That, Socrates, will be inevitable.

And so we shall go to war, Glaucon. Shall we not?

Most certainly, he replied.

Then, without determining as yet whether war does good or harm, thus much we may affirm, that now we have discovered war to be derived from causes which are also the causes of almost all the evils in States, private as well as public.

Undoubtedly.

And our State must once more enlarge; and this time the enlargement will be nothing short of a whole army, which will have to go out and fight with the invaders for all that we have, as well as for the things and persons whom we were describing above.

Why? he said; are they not capable of defending themselves?

No, I said; not if we were right in the principle which was acknowledged by all of us when we were framing the State. The principle, as you will remember, was that one man cannot practise many arts with success.

Very true, he said.

But is not war an art?

Certainly.

And an art requiring as much attention as shoemaking?

Quite true.

And the shoemaker was not allowed by us to be a husbandman, or a weaver, or a builder—in order that we might have our shoes well made; but to him and to every other worker was assigned one work for which he was by nature fitted, and at that he was to continue working all his life long and at no other; he was not to let opportunities slip, and then he would become a good workman. Now nothing can be more important than that the work of a soldier should be well done. But is war an art so easily acquired that a man may be a warrior who is also a husbandman, or shoemaker, or other artisan; although no one in the world would be a good dice or draught player who merely took up the game as a recreation, and had not from his earliest years devoted himself to this and nothing else? No tools will make a man a skilled workman or master of defence, nor be of any use to him who has not learned how to handle them, and has never bestowed any attention upon them. How, then, will he who takes up a shield or other implement of war become a good fighter all in a day, whether with heavy-armed or any other kind of troops?

Yes, he said, the tools which would teach men their own use would be beyond price.

(continued)

Republic, Book II (continued)

And the higher the duties of the guardian, I said, the more time and skill and art and application will be needed by him?

No doubt, he replied.

Will he not also require natural aptitude for his calling?

Certainly.

Then it will be our duty to select, if we can, natures which are fitted for the task of guarding the city?

It will.

And the selection will be no easy matter, I said; but we must be brave and do our best.

We must.

Is not the noble youth very like a well-bred dog in respect of guarding and watching?

What do you mean?

I mean that both of them ought to be quick to see, and swift to overtake the enemy when they see him; and strong too if, when they have caught him, they have to fight with him.

All these qualities, he replied, will certainly be required by them.

Well, and your guardian must be brave if he is to fight well?

Certainly.

And is he likely to be brave who has no spirit, whether horse or dog or any other animal? Have you never observed how invincible and unconquerable is spirit and how the presence of it makes the soul of any creature to be absolutely fearless and indomitable?

I have.

Then now we have a clear notion of the bodily qualities which are required in the guardian.

True.

And also of the mental ones; his soul is to be full of spirit?

Yes.

But are not these spirited natures apt to be savage with one another, and with everybody else?

A difficulty by no means easy to overcome, he replied.

Whereas, I said, they ought to be dangerous to their enemies, and gentle to their friends; if not, they will destroy themselves without waiting for their enemies to destroy them.

True, he said.

What is to be done, then? I said; how shall we find a gentle nature which has also a great spirit, for the one is the contradiction of the other?

True.

He will not be a good guardian who is wanting in either of these two qualities; and yet the combination of them appears to be impossible; and hence we must infer that to be a good guardian is impossible.

I am afraid that what you say is true, he replied.

Here feeling perplexed I began to think over what had preceded. My friend, I said, no wonder that we are in a perplexity; for we have lost sight of the image which we had before us.

What do you mean? he said.

I mean to say that there do exist natures gifted with those opposite qualities.

And where do you find them?

Many animals, I replied, furnish examples of them; our friend the dog is a very good one: you know that well-bred dogs are perfectly gentle to their familiars and acquaintances, and the reverse to strangers.

Yes, I know.

Then there is nothing impossible or out of the order of nature in our finding a guardian who has a similar combination of qualities?

Certainly not.

Would not he who is fitted to be a guardian, besides the spirited nature, need to have the qualities of a philosopher?

I do not apprehend your meaning.

The trait of which I am speaking, I replied, may be also seen in the dog, and is remarkable in the animal.

What trait?

Why, a dog, whenever he sees a stranger, is angry; when an acquaintance, he welcomes him, although the one has never done him any harm, nor the other any good. Did this never strike you as curious?

The matter never struck me before; but I quite recognize the truth of your remark.

And surely this instinct of the dog is very charming; your dog is a true philosopher.

Why?

Why, because he distinguishes the face of a friend and of an enemy only by the criterion of knowing and not knowing. And must not an animal be a lover of learning who determines what he likes and dislikes by the test of knowledge and ignorance?

Most assuredly.

And is not the love of learning the love of wisdom, which is philosophy?

They are the same, he replied.

And may we not say confidently of man also, that he who is likely to be gentle to his friends and acquaintances, must by nature be a lover of wisdom and knowledge?

That we may safely affirm.

Then he who is to be a really good and noble guardian of the State will require to unite in himself philosophy and spirit and swiftness and strength?

Undoubtedly.

Then we have found the desired natures; and now that we have found them, how are they to be reared and educated? Is not this an inquiry which may be expected to throw light on the greater inquiry which is our final end—How do justice and injustice grow up in States? for we do not want either to omit what is to the point or to draw out the argument to an inconvenient length.

Adeimantus thought that the inquiry would be of great service to us.

Then, I said, my dear friend, the task must not be given up, even if somewhat long.

Certainly not.

Come then, and let us pass a leisure hour in story-telling, and our story shall be the education of our heroes.

By all means.

And what shall be their education? Can we find a better than the traditional sort?—and this has two divisions, gymnastics for the body, and music for the soul.

True.

Shall we begin education with music, and go on to gymnastics afterward?

By all means.

And when you speak of music, do you include literature or not?

I do.

And literature may be either true or false?

Yes.

And the young should be trained in both kinds, and we begin with the false?

I do not understand your meaning, he said.

You know, I said, that we begin by telling children stories which, though not wholly destitute of truth, are in the main fictitious; and these stories are told them when they are not of an age to learn gymnastics.

Very true.

That was my meaning when I said that we must teach music before gymnastics.

Quite right, he said.

You know also that the beginning is the most important part of any work, especially in the case of a young and tender thing; for that is the time at which the character is being formed and the desired impression is more readily taken.

Quite true.

And shall we just carelessly allow children to hear any casual tales which may be devised by casual persons, and to receive into their minds ideas for the most part the very opposite of those which we should wish them to have when they are grown up?

We cannot.

(continued)

Republic, Book II (continued)

Then the first thing will be to establish a censorship of the writers of fiction, and let the censors receive any tale of fiction which is good, and reject the bad; and we will desire mothers and nurses to tell their children the authorized ones only. Let them fashion the mind with such tales, even more fondly than they mould the body with their hands; but most of those which are now in use must be discarded.

Of what tales are you speaking? he said.

You may find a model of the lesser in the greater, I said; for they are necessarily of the same type, and there is the same spirit in both of them.

Very likely, he replied; but I do not as yet know what you would term the greater.

Those, I said, which are narrated by Homer and Hesiod, and the rest of the poets, who have ever been the great storytellers of mankind.

But which stories do you mean, he said; and what fault do you find with them?

A fault which is most serious, I said; the fault of telling a lie, and, what is more, a bad lie.

But when is this fault committed?

Whenever an erroneous representation is made of the nature of gods and heroes—as when a painter paints a portrait not having the shadow of a likeness to the original.

Yes, he said, that sort of thing is certainly very blamable; but what are the stories which you mean?

First of all, I said, there was that greatest of all lies in high places, which the poet told about Uranus, and which was a bad lie too—I mean what Hesiod says that Uranus did, and how Cronus retaliated on him.[7] The doings of Cronus, and the sufferings which in turn his son inflicted upon him, even if they were true, ought certainly not to be lightly told to young and thoughtless persons; if possible, they had better be buried in silence. But if there is an absolute necessity for their mention, a chosen few might hear them in a mystery, and they should sacrifice not a common [Eleusinian] pig, but some huge and unprocurable victim; and then the number of the hearers will be very few indeed.

Why, yes, said he, those stories are extremely objectionable.

Yes, Adeimantus, they are stories not to be repeated in our State; the young man should not be told that in committing the worst of crimes he is far from doing anything outrageous; and that even if he chastises his father when he does wrong, in whatever manner, he will only be following the example of the first and greatest among the gods.

I entirely agree with you, he said; in my opinion those stories are quite unfit to be repeated.

Neither, if we mean our future guardians to regard the habit of quarrelling among themselves as of all things the basest, should any word be said to them of the wars in heaven, and of the plots and fightings of the gods against one another, for they are not true. No, we shall never mention the battles of the giants, or let them be embroidered on garments; and we shall be silent about the innumerable other quarrels of gods and heroes with their friends and relatives. If they would only believe us we would tell them that quarrelling is unholy, and that never up to this time has there been any quarrel between citizens; this is what old men and old women should begin by telling children; and when they grow up, the poets also should be told to compose them in a similar spirit. But the narrative of Hephæstus binding Here his mother, or how on another occasion Zeus sent him flying for taking her part when she was being beaten, and all the battles of the gods in Homer—these tales must not be admitted into our State, whether they are supposed to have an allegorical meaning or not. For a young person cannot judge what is allegorical and what is literal; anything that he receives into his mind at that age is likely to become indelible and unalterable; and therefore it is most important that the tales which the young first hear should be models of virtuous thoughts.

There you are right, he replied; but if anyone asks where are such models to be found and of what tales are you speaking—how shall we answer him?

I said to him, You and I, Adeimantus, at this moment are not poets, but founders of a State: now the founders of a State ought to know the general forms in which poets should cast their tales, and the limits which must be observed by them, but to make the tales is not their business.

Very true, he said; but what are these forms of theology which you mean?

Something of this kind, I replied: God is always to be represented as he truly is, whatever be the sort of poetry, epic, lyric, or tragic, in which the representation is given.

Right.

And is he not truly good? and must he not be represented as such?

Certainly.

And no good thing is hurtful?

No, indeed.

And that which is not hurtful hurts not?

Certainly not.

And that which hurts not does no evil?

No.

And can that which does no evil be a cause of evil?

Impossible.

And the good is advantageous?

Yes.

And therefore the cause of well-being?

Yes.

It follows, therefore, that the good is not the cause of all things, but of the good only?

Assuredly.

Then God, if he be good, is not the author of all things, as the many assert, but he is the cause of a few things only, and not of most things that occur to men. For few are the goods of human life, and many are the evils, and the good is to be attributed to God alone; of the evils the causes are to be sought elsewhere, and not in him.

That appears to me to be most true, he said.

Then we must not listen to Homer or to any other poet who is guilty of the folly of saying that two casks

"Lie at the threshold of Zeus, full of lots, one of good, the other of evil lots,"[8]

and that he to whom Zeus gives a mixture of the two

"Sometimes meets with evil fortune, at other times with good;"

but that he to whom is given the cup of unmingled ill,

"Him wild hunger drives o'er the beauteous earth."

And again—

"Zeus, who is the dispenser of good and evil to us."

And if anyone asserts that the violation of oaths and treaties, which was really the work of Pandarus,[9] was brought about by Athene and Zeus, or that the strife and contention of the gods were instigated by Themis and Zeus,[10] he shall not have our approval; neither will we allow our young men to hear the words of Æschylus, that

"God plants guilt among men when he desires utterly to destroy a house."

And if a poet writes of the sufferings of Niobe—the subject of the tragedy in which these iambic verses occur—or of the house of Pelops, or of the Trojan War or on any similar theme, either we must not permit him to say that these are the works of God, or if they are of God, he must devise some explanation of them such as we are seeking: he must say that God did what was just and right, and they were the better for being punished; but that those who are punished are

(continued)

Republic, Book II (continued)

miserable, and that God is the author of their misery—the poet is not to be permitted to say; though he may say that the wicked are miserable because they require to be punished, and are benefited by receiving punishment from God; but that God being good is the author of evil to anyone is to be strenuously denied, and not to be said or sung or heard in verse or prose by anyone whether old or young in any well-ordered commonwealth. Such a fiction is suicidal, ruinous, impious.

I agree with you, he replied, and am ready to give my assent to the law.

Let this then be one of our rules and principles concerning the gods, to which our poets and reciters will be expected to conform—that God is not the author of all things, but of good only.

That will do, he said.

And what do you think of a second principle? Shall I ask you whether God is a magician, and of a nature to appear insidiously now in one shape, and now in another—sometimes himself changing and passing into many forms, sometimes deceiving us with the semblance of such transformations; or is he one and the same immutably fixed in his own proper image?

I cannot answer you, he said, without more thought.

Well, I said; but if we suppose a change in anything, that change must be effected either by the thing itself or by some other thing?

Most certainly.

And things which are at their best are also least liable to be altered or discomposed; for example, when healthiest and strongest, the human frame is least liable to be affected by meats and drinks, and the plant which is in the fullest vigor also suffers least from winds or the heat of the sun or any similar causes.

Of course.

And will not the bravest and wisest soul be least confused or deranged by any external influence?

True.

And the same principle, as I should suppose, applies to all composite things—furniture, houses, garments: when good and well made, they are least altered by time and circumstances.

Very true.

Then everything which is good, whether made by art or nature, or both, is least liable to suffer change from without?

True.

But surely God and the things of God are in every way perfect?

Of course they are.

Then he can hardly be compelled by external influence to take many shapes?

He cannot.

But may he not change and transform himself?

Clearly, he said, that must be the case if he is changed at all.

And will he then change himself for the better and fairer, or for the worse and more unsightly?

If he change at all he can only change for the worse, for we cannot suppose him to be deficient either in virtue or beauty.

Very true, Adeimantus; but then, would anyone, whether God or man, desire to make himself worse?

Impossible.

Then it is impossible that God should ever be willing to change; being, as is supposed, the fairest and best that is conceivable, every God remains absolutely and forever in his own form.

That necessarily follows, he said, in my judgment.

Then, I said, my dear friend, let none of the poets tell us that

"The gods, taking the disguise of strangers from other lands, walk up and down cities in all sorts of forms;"[11] and let no one slander Proteus and Thetis, neither let anyone, either in tragedy or in any other kind of poetry, introduce Here disguised in the likeness of a priestess asking an alms

"For the life-giving daughters of Inachus the river of Argos;"

—let us have no more lies of that sort. Neither must we have mothers under the influence of the poets scaring their children with a bad version of these myths—telling how certain gods, as they say, "Go about by night in the likeness of so many strangers and in divers forms;" but let them take heed lest they make cowards of their children, and at the same time speak blasphemy against the gods.

Heaven forbid, he said.

But although the gods are themselves unchangeable, still by witchcraft and deception they may make us think that they appear in various forms?

Perhaps, he replied.

Well, but can you imagine that God will be willing to lie, whether in word or deed, or to put forth a phantom of himself?

I cannot say, he replied.

Do you not know, I said, that the true lie, if such an expression may be allowed, is hated of gods and men?

What do you mean? he said.

I mean that no one is willingly deceived in that which is the truest and highest part of himself, or about the truest and highest matters; there, above all, he is most afraid of a lie having possession of him.

Still, he said, I do not comprehend you.

The reason is, I replied, that you attribute some profound meaning to my words; but I am only saying that deception, or being deceived or uninformed about the highest realities in the highest part of themselves, which is the soul, and in that part of them to have and to hold the lie, is what mankind least like;—that, I say, is what they utterly detest.

There is nothing more hateful to them.

And, as I was just now remarking, this ignorance in the soul of him who is deceived may be called the true lie; for the lie in words is only a kind of imitation and shadowy image of a previous affection of the soul, not pure unadulterated falsehood. Am I not right?

Perfectly right.

The true lie is hated not only by the gods, but also by men?

Yes.

Whereas the lie in words is in certain cases useful and not hateful; in dealing with enemies—that would be an instance; or again, when those whom we call our friends in a fit of madness or illusion are going to do some harm, then it is useful and is a sort of medicine or preventive; also in the tales of mythology, of which we were just now speaking—because we do not know the truth about ancient times, we make falsehood as much like truth as we can, and so turn it to account.

Very true, he said.

But can any of these reasons apply to God? Can we suppose that he is ignorant of antiquity, and therefore has recourse to invention?

That would be ridiculous, he said.

Then the lying poet has no place in our idea of God?

I should say not.

Or perhaps he may tell a lie because he is afraid of enemies?

That is inconceivable.

But he may have friends who are senseless or mad?

But no mad or senseless person can be a friend of God.

Then no motive can be imagined why God should lie?

None whatever.

Then the superhuman, and divine, is absolutely incapable of falsehood?

Yes.

Then is God perfectly simple and true both in word and deed; he changes not; he deceives not, either by sign or word, by dream or waking vision.

Your thoughts, he said, are the reflection of my own.

(continued)

Republic, Book II (continued)

You agree with me then, I said, that this is the second type or form in which we should write and speak about divine things. The gods are not magicians who transform themselves, neither do they deceive mankind in any way.

I grant that.

Then, although we are admirers of Homer, we do not admire the lying dream which Zeus sends to Agamemnon; neither will we praise the verses of Æschylus in which Thetis says that Apollo at her nuptials

"was celebrating in song her fair progeny whose days were to be long, and to know no sickness. And when he had spoken of my lot as in all things blessed of heaven, he raised a note of triumph and cheered my soul. And I thought that the word of Phœbus, being divine and full of prophecy, would not fail. And now he himself who uttered the strain, he who was present at the banquet, and who said this—he it is who has slain my son."[12]

These are the kind of sentiments about the gods which will arouse our anger; and he who utters them shall be refused a chorus; neither shall we allow teachers to make use of them in the instruction of the young, meaning, as we do, that our guardians, as far as men can be, should be true worshippers of the gods and like them.

I entirely agree, he said, in these principles, and promise to make them my laws.

NOTES

1. "Seven against Thebes," 574.
2. Hesiod, "Work" and Days," 230.
3. Homer, "Odyssey," xix. 109.
4. Eumolpus
5. Hesiod, "Works and Days," 287.
6. Homer, "Iliad," lx. 493.
7. Hesiod, "Theogony," 154, 459.
8. "Iliad," xxiv. 527.
9. "Iliad," ii. 69.
10. "Iliad," xx.
11. Hom, "Odyssey," xvii. 485.
12. From a lost play.

An Introduction to the Principles of Morals and Legislation

Jeremy Bentham

Chapter I
Of the Principle of Utility

Mankind governed by pain and pleasure.

I. Nature has placed mankind under the governance of two sovereign masters, *pain* and *pleasure*. It is for them alone to point out what we ought to do, as well as to determine what we shall do. On the one hand the standard of right and wrong, on the other the chain of causes and effects, are fastened to their throne. They govern us in all we do, in all we say, in all we think; every effort we can make to throw off our subjection, will serve but to demonstrate and confirm it. In words a man may pretend to abjure their empire: but in reality he will remain subject to it all the while. The *principle of utility*[1] recognizes the subjection, and assumes it for the foundation of that system, the object of which is to rear the fabric of felicity by the hands of reason and of law. Systems which attempt to question it, deal in sounds instead of sense, in caprice instead of reason, in darkness instead of light.

But enough of metaphor and declamation: it is not by such means that moral science is to be improved.

Principle of utility, what.

II. The principle of utility is the foundation of the present work; it will be proper therefore at the outset to give an explicit and determinate account of what is meant by it. By the principle[2] of utility is meant that principle which approves or disapproves of every action whatsoever, according to the tendency which it appears to have to augment or diminish the happiness of the party whose interest is in question; or, what is the same thing in other words, to promote or to oppose that happiness. I say of every action whatsoever; and therefore not only of every action of a private individual, but of every measure of government.

Utility, what.

III. By utility is meant that property in any object, whereby it tends to produce benefit, advantage, pleasure, good, or happiness, (all this in the present case comes to the same thing) or (what comes again to the same thing) to prevent the happening of mischief, pain, evil, or unhappiness to the party whose interest is considered: if that party be the community in general, then the happiness of the community: if a particular individual, then the happiness of that individual.

Interest of the community, what.

IV. The interest of the community is one of the most general expressions that can occur in the phraseology of morals: no wonder that the meaning of it is often lost. When it has a meaning, it is this. The community is a fictitious *body*, composed of the individual persons who are considered as constituting as it were its *members*. The interest of the community then is, what?–the sum of the interests of the several members who compose it.

V. It is in vain to talk of the interest of the community, without understanding what is the interest of the individual.[3] A thing is said to promote the interest, or to be *for* the interest, of an individual, when it tends to add to the sum total of his pleasures: or, what comes to the same thing, to diminish the sum total of his pains.

An action comformable to the principle of utility, what.

VI. An action then may be said to be conformable to the principle of utility, or, for shortness' sake, to utility, (meaning with respect to the community at large) when the tendency it has to augment the happiness of the community is greater than any it has to diminish it.

A measure of government conformable to the principle of utility, what.

VII. A measure of government (which is but a particular kind of action, performed by a particular person or persons) may be said to be conformable to or dictated by the principle of utility, when in like manner the tendency which it has to augment the happiness of the community is greater than any which it has to diminish it.

Laws or dictates of utility, what.

VIII. When as action, or in particular a measure of government, is supposed by a man to be conformable to the principle of utility, it may be convenient, for the purposes of discourse, to imagine a kind of law or dictate, called a law or dictate of utility: and to speak of the action in question, as being conformable to such law or dictate.

A partizan of the principle of utility, who.

IX. A man may be said to be a partizan of the principle of utility, when the approbation or disapprobation he annexes to any action, or to any measure, is determined by and proportioned to the tendency which he conceives it to have to augment or to diminish the happiness of the community: or in other words, to its conformity or unconformity to the laws or dictates of utility.

(continued)

An Introduction to the Principles of Morals and Legislation (*continued*)

Ought, ought not, right and wrong, &c., how to be understood.

X. Of an action that is conformable to the principle of utility, one may always say either that it is one that ought to be done, or at least that it is not one that ought not to be done. One may say also, that it is right it should be done; at least that it is not wrong it should be done: that it is a right action; at least that it is not a wrong action. When thus interpreted, the words *ought*, and *right* and *wrong*, and others of that stamp, have a meaning: when otherwise, they have none.

To prove the rectitude of this principle is at once unnecessary and impossible.

XI. Has the rectitude of this principle been ever formally contested? It should seem that it had, by those who have not known what they have been meaning. Is it susceptible of any direct proof? It should seem not, for that which is used to prove everything else, cannot itself be proved; a chain of proofs must have their commencement somewhere. To give such proof is as impossible as it is needless.

It has seldom, however, as yet been consistently pursued.

XII. Not that there is or ever has been that human creature breathing, however stupid or perverse, who has not on many, perhaps on most occasions of his life, deferred to it. By the natural constitution of the human frame, on most occasions of their lives men in general embrace this principle, without thinking of it; if not for the ordering of their own actions, yet for the trying of their own actions, as well as of those of other men. There have been, at the same time, not many, perhaps, even of the most intelligent, who have been disposed to embrace it purely and without reserve. There are even few who have not taken some occasion or other to quarrel with it, either on account of their not understanding always how to apply it, or on account of some prejudice or other which they were afraid to examine into, or could not bear to part with. For such is the stuff that man is made of: in principle and in practice, in a right track and in a wrong one, the rarest of all human qualities is consistency.

It can never be consistently combated.

XIII. When a man attempts to combat the principle of utility, it is with reason drawn, without his being aware of it, from that very principle itself.[4] His arguments, if they prove anything, prove not that the principle is *wrong*, but that, according to the applications he supposes to be made of it, it is *misapplied*. Is it possible for a man to move the earth? Yes; but he must first find our another earth to stand upon.

Courses to be taken for surmounting prejudices that may have been entertained against it.

XIV. To disapprove the propriety of it by arguments is impossible; but, from the causes that have been mentioned, or form some confused or partial view of it, a man may happen to be disposed not to relish it. Where this is the case, if he thinks the settling of his opinions on such a subject worth the trouble, let him take the following steps, and at length, perhaps, he may come to reconcile himself to it.

1. Let him settle with himself, whether he would wish to discard this principle altogether; if so, let him consider what it is that all his reasonings (in matters of politics especially) can amount to?
2. If he would, let him settle with himself, whether he would judge and act without any principle, or whether there is any other he would judge and act by?
3. If there be, let him examine and satisfy himself whether the principle he thinks he has found *is* really any separate intelligible principle; or whether it be not a mere principle in words, a kind of phrase, which at bottom expresses neither more nor less than the mere averment of his own unfounded sentiments; that *is*, what in another person he might be apt to call caprice?
4. If he is inclined to think that his own approbation or disapprobation, annexed to the idea of an act, without any regard to its consequences, is a sufficient foundation for him to judge and act upon, let him ask himself whether his sentiment is to be a standard of right and wrong, with respect to every other man, or whether every man's sentiment has the same privilege of being a standard to itself?

5. In the first case, let him ask himself whether his principle is not despotical, and hostile to all the rest of the human race?
6. In the second case, whether it is not anarchical, and whether at this rate there are not as many different standards of right and wrong as there are men? and whether even to the same man, the same thing, which is right today, may not (without the least change in its nature) be wrong tomorrow? and whether the same thing is not right and wrong in the same place at the same time? and in either case, whether all argument is not at an end? and whether, when two men have said, "I like this," and "I don't-like it," they can (upon such principle) have anything more to say?
7. If he should have said to himself. No: for that the sentiment which he proposes as a standard must be grounded on reflection, let him say on what particulars the reflection is to turn? if on particulars having relation to the utility of the act, then let him say whether this is not deserting his own principle, and borrowing assistance from that very one in opposition to which he sets it up: or if not on those particulars, on what other particulars?
8. If he should be for compounding the matter, and adopting his own principle in part, and the principle of utility in part, let him say how far he will adopt it?
9. When he has settled with himself where he will stop, then let him ask himself how he justifies to himself the adopting it so far? and why he will not adopt it any farther?
10. Admitting any other principle than the principle of utility to be a right principle, a principle that it is right for a man to pursue; admitting (what is not true) that the word *right* can have a meaning without reference to utility, let him say whether there is any such thing as a *motive* that a man can have to pursue the dictates of it: if there is, let him say what that motive is, and how it is to be distinguished from those which enforce the dictates of utility: if not, then lastly let him say what it is other principle can be good for?

Chapter IV Value of a Lot of Pleasure or Pain, How to Be Measured

Use of this chapter.

Circumstances to be taken into account in estimating the value of a pleasure or pain considered with reference to a single person, and by itself.

—considered as connected with other pleasures or pains.

I. Pleasures then, and the avoidance of pains, are the *ends* which the legislator has in view; it behoves him therefore to understand their *value*. Pleasures and pains are the *instruments* he has to work with: it behoves his therefore to understand their force, which is again, in other words, their value.

II. To a person considered *by himself,* the value of a pleasure or pain considered *by itself,* will be greater or less, according to the four following circumstances.[5]

1. Its *intensity*.
2. Its *duration*.
3. Its *certainty* or *uncertainty*.
4. Its *propinquity* or *remoteness*.

III. These are the circumstances which are to be considered in estimating a pleasure or a pain considered each of them by itself. But when the value of any pleasure or pain is considered for the purpose of estimating the tendency of any *act* by which it is produced, there are two other circumstances to be taken into the account; these are.

5. Its *fecundity,* or the chance it has of being followed by sensations of the *same* kind: that is, pleasures, if it be a pleasure: pains, if it be a pain.
6. Its *purity,* or the chance it has of *not* being followed by sensations of the *opposite* kind: that is, pains, if it be a pleasure: pleasures, if it be a pain.

These two last, however, are in strictness scarcely to be deemed properties of the pleasures or the pain itself; they are not, therefore, in strictness to be taken into the account of the value of that pleasure or that pain. They are in strictness to

(continued)

An Introduction to the Principles of Morals and Legislation (*continued*)

be deemed properties only of the act, or other event, by which such pleasure or pain has been produced; and accordingly are only to be taken into the account of the tendency of such act or such event.

—considered with reference to a number of persons.

IV. To a *number* of persons, with reference to each of whom the value of a pleasure or a pain is considered, it will be greater or less, according to seven circumstances: to wit, the six preceding ones; *viz.*

1. Its intensity.
2. Its *propinquity or remoteness.*
3. Its *duration*.
4. Its *propinquity* or
5. Its *certainty or uncertainty.*
6. Its *purity.*

And one other; to wit:

7. Its *extent;* that is, the number of persons to whom it *extends;* or (in other words) who are affected by it.

Process for estimating the tendency of any act or event.

V. To take an exact account then of the general tendency of any act, by which the interests of a community are affected, proceed as follows. Begin with any one person of those whose interests seem most immediately to be affected by it: and take an account,

1. Of the value of each distinguishable *pleasure* which appears to be produced by it in the *first* instance.
2. Of the value of each *pain* which appears to be produced by it in the *first* instance.
3. Of the value of each pleasure which appears to be produced by it *after* the first. This constitutes the *fecundity* of the first *pleasure* and the *impurity* of the first *pain*.
4. Of the value of each *pain* which appears to be produced by it after the first. This constitutes the *fecundity* of the first *pain*, and the *impurity* of the first pleasure.
5. Sum up all the values of all the *pleasures* on the one side, and those of all the pains on the other. The balance, if it be on the side of pleasure, will give the *good* tendency of the act upon the whole, with respect to the interests of that *individual* person; if on the side of pain, the *bad* tendency of it upon the whole.
6. Take an account of the *number* of persons whose interests appear to be concerned; and repeat the above process with respect to each. *Sum up* the numbers expressive of the degrees of *good* tendency, which the act has, with respect to each individual, in regard to whom the tendency of it is *good* upon the whole: do this again with respect to each individual, in regard to whom the tendency of it is *bad* upon the whole. Take the *balance;* which, if on the side of *pleasure,* will give the general *good tendency* of the act, with respect to the total number of community of individuals concerned; if on the side of pain the general *evil tendency,* with respect to the same community.

Use of the foregoing process.

VI. It is not to be expected that this process should be strictly pursued previously to every moral judgment, or to every legislative or judicial operation. It may, however, be always kept in view: and as near as the process actually pursued on these occasions approaches to it, so near will such process approach to the character of an exact one.

The same process applicable to good and evil, profit and mischief, and all other modifications of pleasure and pain.

VII. The same process is alike applicable to pleasure and pain in whatever shape they appear: and by whatever denomination they are distinguished: to pleasure, whether it be called *good* (which is properly the cause or instrument of pleasure), or *profit* (which is distant pleasure, or the cause or instrument of distant pleasure), or *convenience,* or *advantage, benefit, emolument, happiness,* and so forth: to pain, whether it be called *evil* (which corresponds to *good*), or *mischief,* or *inconvenience,* or *disadvantage,* or *loss,* or *unhappiness,* and so forth.

Conformity of men's practice to this theory.

VIII. Nor is this a novel and unwarranted, any more than it is a useless theory. In all this there is nothing but what the practice of mankind, wheresoever they have a clear view of their own interest, is perfectly conformable to. An article of property, an estate in land, for instance, is valuable, on what account? On account of the pleasures of all kinds which it enables a man to produce, and what comes to the same thing, the pains of all kinds which it enables him to avert. But the value of such an article of property is universally understood to rise or fall according to the length or shortness of the time which a man has in it: the certainty or uncertainty of its coming into possession: and the nearness or remoteness of the time at which, if at all, it is to come into possession. As to the *intensity* of the pleasures which a man may derive from it, this is never thought of, because it depends upon the use which each particular person may com to make of it; which cannot be estimated till the particular pleasures he may come to derive from it, or the particular pains he may come to exclude by means of it, are brought to view. For the same reason, neither does he think of the *fecundity* or *purity* of those pleasures.

Chapter X Motives § 2. No Motives Either Constantly Good, or Constantly Bad

Nothing can act of itself as a motive but the ideas of pleasure or pain.

IX. In all this chain of motives, the principle or original link seems to be the last internal motive in prospect; it is to this that all the other motives in prospect owe their materiality; and the immediately acting motive its existence. This motive in prospect, we see, is always some pleasure, or some pain; some pleasure, which the act in question is expected to be a means of continuing or producing: some pain which it is expected to be a means of discontinuing or preventing. A motive is substantially nothing more than pleasure or pain, operating in a certain manner.

No sort of motive is in itself a bad one.

X. Now, pleasure is in *itself* a good: nay, even setting aside immunity from pain, the only good: pain is in itself an evil; and, indeed, without exception, the only evil; or else the words good and evil have no meaning. And this is alike true of every sort of pain, and of every sort of pleasure. It follows, therefore, immediately and incontestably, that *there is no such thing as any sort of motive that is in itself a bad one.*[6]

Inaccuracy of expressions in which *good* or *bad* are applied to motives.

XI. It is common, however, to speak of actions as proceeding from *good* or *bad* motives: in which case the motives meant are such as are internal. The expression is far from being an accurate one; and as it is apt to occur in the consideration of almost every kind of offence, it will be requisite to settle the precise meaning of it, and observe how far it quadrates with the truth of things.

Any sort of motive may give birth to any sort of act.

XII. With respect to goodness and badness, as it is with everything else that is not itself either pain or pleasure, so is it with motives. If they are good or bad, it is only on account of their effects: good, on account of their tendency to produce pleasure, or avert pain: bad, on account of their tendency to produce pain, or avert pleasure. Now the case is, that from one and the same motive, and from every kind of motive, may proceed actions that are good, others that are bad, and others that are indifferent. This we shall proceed to show with respect to all the different kinds of motives, as determined by the various kinds of pleasures and pains.

Difficulties which stand in the way of an analysis of this sort.

XIII. Such an analysis, useful as it is, will be found to be a matter of no small difficulty; owing, in great measure, to a certain perversity of structure which prevails more or less throughout all languages. To speak of motives, as of anything else, one must call them by their names. But the misfortune is that it is rare to meet with a motive of which the name expresses that and nothing more. Commonly along with the very name of the motive, is tacitly involved a proposition imputing to it a certain quality; a quality which, in many cases, will appear to include that very goodness or badness, concerning which we are here inquiring whether, properly speaking, it be or be not imputable to motives. To use the common phrase, in most cases, the name of the motive is a word which is employed either only in a *good sense*, or else only in a *bad sense*. Now, when a word is spoken of as being used in a good sense, all that is necessarily meant is

(continued)

An Introduction to the Principles of Morals and Legislation   (*continued*)

this: that in conjunction with the idea of the object it is put to signify, it conveys an idea of *approbation:* that is, of a pleasure or satisfaction, entertained by the person who employs the term at the thoughts of such object. In like manner, when a word is spoken of as being used in a bad sense, all that is necessarily meant is this: that, in conjunction with the idea of the object it is put to signify, it conveys an idea of *disapprobation:* that is, of a displeasure entertained by the person who employs the term at the thoughts of such object. Now, the circumstance on which such approbation is grounded, will, as naturally as any other, be the opinion of the *goodness* of the object in question, as above explained: such, at least, it must be, upon the principle of utility: so, on the other hand, the circumstance on which any such disapprobation is grounded, will, as naturally as any other, be the opinion of the *badness* of the object: such, at least, it must be, in as far as the principle of utility is taken for the standard.

Now there are certain motives which, unless in a few particular cases, have scarcely any other name to be expressed by but such a word as is used only in a good sense. This is the case, for example, with the motives of piety and honour. The consequence of this is, that if, in speaking of such a motive, a man should have occasion to apply the epithet bad to any actions which he mentions as apt to result from it, he must appear to be guilty of a contradiction in terms. But the names of motives which have scarcely any other name to be expressed by, but such a word as is used only in a bad sense, are many more.[7] This is the case, for example, with the motives of lust and avarice. And, accordingly, if in speaking of any such motive, a man should have occasion to apply the epithets good or indifferent to any actions which he mentions as apt to result from it, he must here also appear to be guilty of a similar contradiction.[8]

NOTES

1. Note by the Author, July, 1812.
   To this denomination has of late been added, or substituted, the *greatest happiness or greatest felicity* principle: this for shortness, instead of saying at length *that principle* which states the greatest happiness of all those whose interest is in question, as being the right and proper, and only right and proper and universally desirable, end of human action: of human action in every situation, and in particular in that of a functionary or set of functionaries exercising the powers of government. The word *utility* does not so clearly point to the ideas of *pleasure* and *pain* as the words *happiness* and *felicity* do: nor does it lead us to the consideration of the number, of the interests affected; to the *number*, as being the circumstance, which contributes, in the largest proportion, to the formation of the standard here in question; the *standard of right and wrong*, by which alone the propriety of human conduct, in every situation, can with propriety be tried. This want of a sufficiently manifest connexion between the ideas of *happiness* and *pleasure* on the one hand, and the idea of *utility* on the other, I have every now and then found operating, and with but too much efficiency, as a bar to the acceptance, that might otherwise have been given, to this principle.
2. The word principle is derived from the Latin principium: which seems to be compounded of the two words *primus*, first, or chief, and *cipium*, a termination which seems to be derived from *capio*, to take, as in *mancipium, municipium;* to which are analogous, *auceps, forceps*, and others. It is a term of very vague and very extensive signification: it is applied to any thing which is conceived to serve as a foundation or beginning to any series of operations: in some cases, of physical operations; but of mental operations in the present case.
   The principle here in question may be taken for an act of the mind; a sentiment; a sentiment of approbations; a sentiment which, when applied to an action, approves of its utility, as that quality of it by which the measure of approbation or disapprobation bestowed upon it ought to be governed.
3. Interest is one of those words, which not having any superior *genus*, cannot in the ordinary way be defined.
4. 'The principle of utility, (I have heard it said) is a dangerous principle: it is dangerous on certain occasions to consult it.' This is as much as to say, what? that it is not consonant to utility, to consult utility: in short, that it is *not* consulting it, to consult it.

Addition by the Author, July 1822.

Not long after the publication of the Fragment on Government, anno 1776, in which, in the character of an all-comprehensive and all-commanding principle, the principle of utility was brought to view, one person by whom observation to the above effect was made was *Alexander Wedderburn*, at that time Attorney or Solicitor General, afterwards successively Chief Justice of the Common Pleas, and Chancellor of England, under the successive titles of Lord Loughborough and Earl of Rosslyn. It was made-not indeed in my hearing, but in the hearing of a person by whom it was almost immediately communicated to me. So far from being self-contradictory, it was a shrewd and perfectly true one. By that distinguished functionary, the state of the Government was thoroughly understood: by the obscure individual, at that time not so much as supposed to be so: his disquisitions had not been as yet applied, with any thing like a comprehensive view, to the field of Constitutional Law, nor therefore to those features of the English Government, by which the greatest happiness of the ruling *one* with or without that of a favoured few, are now so plainly seen to be the only ends to which the course of it has at any time been directed. The *principle of utility* was an appellative, at that time employed-employed by me, as it had been by others, to designate that which, in a more perspicuous and instructive manner, may, as above, be designated by the name of the greatest happiness principle. 'This principle (said Wedderburn) is a dangerous one.' Saying so, he said that which, to a certain extent, is strictly true: a principle, which lays down, as the only *right* and justifiable end of Government, the greatest happiness of the greatest number-how can it be denied to be a dangerous one? dangerous it unquestionably is, to every government which has for its *actual* end or object, the greatest happiness of a certain *one*, with or without the addition of some comparatively small number of others, whom it is matter of pleasure or accommodation to him to admit, each of them, to a share in the concern, on the footing of so many junior partners. *Dangerous* it therefore really was, to the interest-the sinister interest-of all those functionaries, himself included, whose interest it was, to maximize delay, vexation, and expense, in judicial and other modes of procedure, for the sake of the profit, extractible out of the expense. In a Government which had for its end in view the greatest happiness of the greatest number, Alexander Wedderburn might have been Attorney General and then Chancellor: but he would not have been Attorney General with £15,000 a year, nor Chancellor, with a peerage with a veto upon all justice, with £25,000 a year, and with 500 sinecures at his disposal, under the name of Ecclesiastical Benefices, besides *et caeteras*.

5. These circumstances have since been denominated *elements* or *dimensions* of *value* in a pleasure or a pain.

Not long after the publication of the first edition, the following memoriter verses were framed, in the view of lodging more effectually, in the memory, these points, on which the whole fabric of morals and legislation may be seen to rest:

Intense, long, certain, speedy, fruitful, pure—
Such marks in *pleasures* and in *pains* endure.
Such pleasures seek, if *private* be thy end:
If it be *public*, wide let them *extend*.
Such *pains* avoid, whichever be thy view:
If pains *must* come, let them *extend* to few.

6. Let a man's motive be ill-will; call it even malice, envy, cruelty; it is still a kind of pleasure that is his motive: the pleasure he takes at the thought of the pain which he sees, or expects to see, his adversary undergo. Now even this wretched pleasure, taken by itself, is good: it may be faint; it may be short: it must at any rate be impure: yet while it lasts, and before any bad consequences arrive, it is good as any other that is not more intense. See ch. iv. (Value).

7. For the reason, see chap. Xi. (Dispositions), par. Xvii. note.

8. To this imperfection of language, and nothing more, are to be attributed, in great measure, the violent clamours that have from time to time been raised against those ingenious moralists, who, travelling out of the beaten tract of speculation, have found more or less difficulty in disentangling themselves from the shackles of ordinary language: such as Rochefoucault, Mandeville and Helvetius. To the unsoundness of their opinions, and, with still greater injustice, to the corruption of their hearts, was often imputed, what was most commonly owing either to a want of skill, in matters of language on the part of the author, or a want of discernment, possibly now and then in some instances a want of probity, on the part of the commentator.

Utilitarianism
John Stuart Mill

1. General Remarks

THERE ARE A FEW CIRCUMSTANCES, among those which make up the present condition of human knowledge, more unlike what might have been expected, or more significant of the backward state in which speculation on the most important subjects still lingers, than the little progress which has been made in the decision of the controversy respecting the criterion of right and wrong. From the dawn of philosophy, the question concerning the *summum bonum* or, what is the same thing, concerning the foundation of morality, has been accounted the main problem in speculative thought, has occupied the most gifted intellects and divided them into sects and schools, carrying on a vigorous warfare against one another. And, after more than two thousand years, the same discussions continue, philosophers are still ranged under the same contending banners, and neither thinkers nor mankind at large seem nearer to being unanimous on the subject than when the youth Socrates listened to the old Protagoras, and asserted (if Plato's dialogue be grounded on a real conversation) the theory of utilitarianism against the popular morality of the so-called Sophist.

It is true that similar confusion and uncertainty, and in some cases similar discordance, exist respecting the first principles of all the sciences, not excepting that which is deemed the most certain of them—mathematics—without much impairing, generally indeed without impairing at all, the trustworthiness of the conclusions of those sciences. An apparent anomaly, the explanation of which is that the detailed doctrines of a science are not usually deduced from, nor depend for their evidence upon, what are called its first principles. Were it not so, there would be no science more precarious, or whose conclusions were more insufficiently made out, than algebra, which derives none of its certainty from what are commonly taught to learners as its elements, since these, as laid down by some of its most eminent teachers, are as full of fictions as English law, and of mysteries as theology. The truths which are ultimately accepted as the first principles of a science are really the last results of metaphysical analysis practiced on the elementary notions with which the science is conversant, and their relation to the science is not that of foundations to an edifice, but of roots to a tree, which may perform their office equally well though they be never dug down to and exposed to light. But though, in science the particular truths precede the general theory, the contrary might be expected to be the case with a practical art, such as morals or legislation. All action is for the sake of some end; and rules of action, it seems natural to suppose, must take their whole character and color from the end to which they are subservient. When we engage in a pursuit, a clear and precise conception of what we are pursuing would seem to be the first thing we need, instead of the last we are to look forward to. A test of right and wrong must be the means, one would think, of ascertaining what is right or wrong, and not a consequence of having already ascertained it.

The difficulty is not avoided by having recourse to the popular theory of a natural faculty, a sense or instinct, informing us of right and wrong. For, besides that the existence of such a moral instinct is itself one of the matters in dispute, those believers in it who have any pretensions to philosophy have been obliged to abandon the idea that it discerns what is right or wrong in the particular case in hand, as our other senses discern the sight or sound actually present. Our moral faculty, according to all those of its interpreters who are entitled to the name of thinkers, supplies us only with the general principles of moral judgments; it is a branch of our reason, not of our sensitive faculty, and must be looked to for the abstract doctrines of morality, not for perception of it in the concrete. The intuitive, no less than what may be termed the inductive, school of ethics, insists on the necessity of general laws. They both agree that the morality of an individual action is not a question of direct perception, but of the application of a law to an individual case. They recognize also, to a great extent, the same moral laws, but differ as to their evidence, and the source from which they derive their authority. According to the one opinion, the principles of morals are evident *a priori*, requiring nothing to command assent, except that the meaning of the terms be understood. According to the other doctrine, right and wrong, as well as truth and falsehood, are questions of observation and experience. But both hold equally that morality must be deduced from principles, and the intuitive school affirm, as strongly as the inductive, that there is a science of morals. Yet they seldom attempt to make out a list of the *a priori* principles which are to serve as the premises of the science; still more rarely do they make any effort to reduce those various principles to one first principle, or common ground of obligation. They either assume the ordinary precepts of morals as of *a priori* authority, or they lay down as the common groundwork of those maxims some generality much less obviously authoritative than the maxims themselves, and which has never succeeded in gaining popular acceptance. Yet, to support their pretensions, there ought either to be some one fundamental principle or law at the root of all morality, or, if there be several, there should be a determinate order of precedence among them, and the one principle, or the rule for deciding between the various principles when they conflict, ought to be self-evident.

To inquire how far the bad effects of this deficiency have been mitigated in practice, or to what extent the moral beliefs of mankind have been vitiated or made uncertain by the absence of any distinct recognition of an ultimate standard, would imply a complete survey and criticism of past and present ethical doctrine. It would, however, be easy to show that whatever steadiness or consistency these moral beliefs have attained has been mainly due to the tacit influence of a standard not recognized. Although the nonexistence of an acknowledged first principle has made ethics not so much a guide as a consecration of men's actual sentiments, still, as men's sentiments, both of favor and of aversion, are greatly influenced by what they suppose to be the effects of things upon their happiness, the principle of utility, or, as Bentham latterly called it, the greatest-happiness principle, has had a large share in forming the moral doctrines even of those who most scornfully reject its authority. Nor is there any school of thought which refuses to admit that the influence of actions on happiness is a most material and even predominant consideration in many of the details of morals, however unwilling to acknowledge it as the fundamental principle of morality and the source of moral obligation. I might go much further, and say that, to all those *a priori* moralists who deem it necessary in argue at all, utilitarian arguments are indispensable. It is not my present purpose to criticize these thinkers, but I cannot help referring, for illustration, to a systematic treatise by one of the most illustrious of them—the *Metaphysics of Ethics,* by Kant. This remarkable man, whose system of thought will long remain one of the landmarks in the history of philosophical speculation, does, in the treatise in question, lay down a universal first principle as the origin and ground of moral obligation. It is this: "So act, that the rule on which thou actest would admit of being adopted as a law by all rational beings." But when he begins to deduce from this precept any of the actual duties of morality, he fails, almost grotesquely, to show that there would be any contradiction, any logical (not to say physical) impossibility, in the adoption by all rational beings of the most outrageously immoral rules of conduct. All he shows is that the *consequences* of their universal adoption would be such as no one would choose to incur.

On the present occasion, I shall, without further discussion of the other theories, attempt to contribute something towards the understanding and appreciation of the Utilitarian or Happiness theory and towards such proof as it is susceptible of. It is evident that this cannot be proof in the ordinary and popular meaning of the term. Questions of ultimate ends are not amenable to direct proof. Whatever can be proved to be good, must be so by being shown to be a means to something admitted to be good without proof. The medical art is proved to be good by its conducing to health, but how is it possible to prove that health is good? The art of music is good, for the reason, among others, that it produces pleasure, but what proof is it possible to give that pleasure is good? If, then, it is asserted that there is a comprehensive formula, including all things which are in themselves good, and that whatever else is good is not so as an end, but as a mean, the formula may be accepted or rejected, but is not a subject of what is commonly understood by proof. We are not, however, to infer that its acceptance or rejection must depend on blind impulse or arbitrary choice. There is a larger meaning of the word "proof," in which this question is as amenable to it as any other of the disputed questions of philosophy. The subject is within the cognizance of the rational faculty, and neither does that faculty deal with it solely in the way of intuition. Considerations may be presented capable of determining the intellect either to give or with-hold its assent to the doctrine, and this is equivalent to proof.

We shall examine presently of what nature are these considerations, in what manner they apply to the case, and what rational grounds, therefore, can be given for accepting or rejecting the

(continued)

Utilitarianism (continued)

utilitarian formula. But it is a preliminary condition of rational acceptance or rejection that the formula should be correctly understood. I believe that the very imperfect notion ordinarily formed of its meaning is the chief obstacle which impedes its reception, and that, could it be cleared even from only the grosser misconceptions, the question would be greatly simplified, and a large proportion of its difficulties removed. Before, therefore, I attempt to enter into the philosophical grounds which can be given for assenting to the utilitarian standard, I shall offer some illustrations of the doctrine itself, with the view of showing more clearly what it is, distinguishing it from what it is not, and disposing of such of the practical objections to it as either originate in, or are closely connected with, mistaken interpretations of its meaning. Having thus prepared the ground, I shall afterwards endeavor to throw such light as I can upon the question, considered as one of philosophical theory.

2. What Utilitarianism Is

A passing remark is all that needs be given to the ignorant blunder of supposing that those who stand up for utility, as the test of right and wrong, use the term in that restricted and merely colloquial sense in which utility is opposed to pleasure. An apology is due to the philosophical opponents of utilitarianism for even the momentary appearance of confounding them with any one capable of so absurd a misconception, which is the more extraordinary, in as much as the contrary accusation, of referring every thing to pleasure, and that, too, in its grossest form, is another of the common charges against utilitarianism, and, as has been pointedly remarked by an able writer, the same sort of persons, and often the very same persons, denounce the theory "as impracticably dry when the word 'utility' precedes the word 'pleasure,' and as too practically voluptuous when the word 'pleasure' precedes the word 'utility.'" Those who know any thing about the matter are aware that every writer from Epicurus to Bentham who maintained the theory of utility meant by it, not something to be contradistinguished from pleasure, but pleasure itself, together with exemption from pain, and, instead of opposing the useful to the agreeable or the ornamental, have always declared that the useful means these, among other things. Yet the common herd, including the herd of writers, not only in newspapers and periodicals, but in books of weight and pretension, are perpetually falling into this shallow mistake. Having caught up the word "utilitarian," while knowing nothing whatever about it but its sound, they habitually express by it the rejection or the neglect of pleasure in some of its forms, of beauty, of ornament, or of amusement. Nor is the term thus ignorantly misapplied solely in disparagement, but occasionally in compliment, as though it implied superiority to frivolity and the mere pleasures of the moment. And this perverted use is the only one in which the word is popularly known, and the one from which the new generation are acquiring their sole notion of its meaning. Those who introduced the word, but who had for many years discontinued it as a distinctive appellation, may well feel themselves called upon to resume it, if by doing so they can hope to contribute any thing towards rescuing it from this utter degradation.

The creed which accepts as the foundation of morals Utility, or the Greatest-happiness Principle, holds that actions are right in proportion as they tend to promote happiness, wrong as they tend to produce the reverse of happiness. By happiness is intended pleasure and the absence of pain, by un-happiness, pain and the privation of pleasure. To give a clear view of the moral standard set up by the theory, much more requires to be said, in particular, what things it includes in the ideas of pain and pleasure, and to what extent this is left an open question. But these supplementary explanations do not affect the theory of life on which this theory of morality is grounded—namely, that pleasure and freedom from pain are the only things desirable as ends, and that all desirable things (which are as numerous in the utilitarian as in any other scheme) are desirable either for the pleasure inherent in themselves, or as means to the promotion of pleasure and the prevention of pain.

Now, such a theory of life excites in many minds, and among them in some of the most estimable in feeling and purpose, inveterate dislike. To suppose that life has (as they express it) no higher end than pleasure—no better and nobler object of desire and pursuit—they designate as utterly mean and groveling, as a doctrine worthy only of swine, to whom the followers of Epicurus were, at a very early period, contemptuously likened; and modern holders of the doctrine are occasionally made the subject of equally polite comparisons by its German, French, and English assailants.

When thus attacked, the Epicureans have always answered, that it is not they, but their accusers, who represent human nature in a degrading light, since the accusation supposes human beings to be capable of no pleasures except those of which swine are capable. If this supposition were true, the charge could not be gainsaid but would then be no longer an imputation; for, if the sources of pleasure were precisely the same to human beings and to swine, the rule of life which is good enough for the one would be good enough for the other. The comparison of the Epicurean life to that of beasts is felt as degrading, precisely because a beast's pleasures do not satisfy a human being's conceptions of happiness. Human beings have faculties more elevated than the animal appetites, and, when once made conscious of them, do not regard any thing as happiness which does not include their gratification. I do not, indeed, consider the Epicureans to have been by any means faultless in drawing out their scheme of consequences from the utilitarian principle. To do this in any sufficient manner, many Stoic as well as Christian elements require to be included. But there is no known Epicurean theory of life which does not assign to the pleasures of the intellect, of the feelings and imagination, and of the moral sentiments, a much higher value as pleasures than to those of mere sensation. It must be admitted, however, that utilitarian writers in general have placed the superiority of mental over bodily pleasures chiefly in the greater permanency, safety, uncostliness, etc., of the former—that is, in their circumstantial advantages rather than in their intrinsic nature. And, on all these points, utilitarians have fully proved their case, but they might have taken the other, and, as it may be called, higher ground, with entire consistency. It is quite compatible with the principle of utility to recognize the fact that some *kinds* of pleasure are more desirable and more valuable than others. It would be absurd that while, in estimating all other things, quality is considered as well as quantity, the estimation of pleasures should be supposed to depend on quantity alone.

If I am asked what I mean by difference of quality in pleasures, or what makes one pleasure more valuable than another, merely as a pleasure, except its being greater in amount, there is but one possible answer. Of two pleasures, if there be one to which all or almost all who have experience of both give a decided preference, irrespective of any feeling of moral obligation to prefer it, that is the more desirable pleasure. If one of the two is, by those who are competently acquainted with both, placed so far above the other that they prefer it, even though knowing it to be attended with a greater amount of discontent, and would not resign it for any quantity of the other pleasure which their nature is capable of, we an justified in ascribing to the preferred enjoyment a superiority in quality so far outweighing quantity, as to render it, in comparison, of small account.

Now, it is an unquestionable fact, that those who are equally acquainted with and equally capable of appreciating and enjoying both do give a most marked preference to the manner of existence which employs their higher faculties. Few human creatures would consent to be changed into any of the lower animals for a promise of the fullest allowance of a beast's pleasures; no intelligent human being would consent to be a fool, no instructed person would be an ignoramus, no person of feeling and conscience would be selfish and base, even though they should be persuaded that the fool, the dunce, or the *rascal* is better satisfied with his lot than they are with theirs. They would not resign what they possess more than he for the most complete satisfaction of all the desires which they have in common with him. If they ever fancy they would, it is only in cases of unhappiness so extreme that, to escape from it, they would exchange their lot for almost any other, however undesirable in their own eyes. A being of higher faculties requires more to make him happy, is capable probably of more acute suffering, and certainly accessible to it at more points, than one of an inferior type, but, in spite of these liabilities, he can never really wish to sink into what he feels to be a lower grade of existence. We may give what explanation we please of this unwillingness: we may attribute it to pride, a name which is given indiscriminately to some of the most and to some of the least estimable feelings of which mankind are capable; we may refer it to the love of liberty and personal independence—an appeal to which was with the Stoics one of the most effective means for the inculcation of it; to the love of power, or to the love of excitement, both of which do really enter into and contribute to it; but its most appropriate appellation is a sense of dignity, which all human beings possess in one form or other, and in some, though by no means in exact, proportion to their higher faculties, and which is so essential a part of the happiness of those in whom it is strong, that nothing which conflicts with it could be, otherwise than momentarily, an object of desire to them. Whoever supposes that this preference takes place at a sacrifice of happiness, that the superior

(continued)

Utilitarianism (continued)

being, in any thing like equal circumstances, is not happier than the inferior—confounds the two very different ideas of happiness and content. It is indisputable that the being whose capacities of enjoyment are low has the greatest chance of having them fully satisfied, and a highly endowed being will always feel that any happiness which he can look for, as the world is constituted, is imperfect. But he can learn to bear its imperfections, if they are at all bearable, and they will not make him envy the being who is indeed unconscious of the imperfections, but only because he feels not at all the good which those imperfections qualify. It is better to be a human being dissatisfied than a pig satisfied, better to be Socrates dissatisfied than a fool satisfied. And if the fool or the pig are of a different opinion, it is because they only know their own side of the question. The other party to the comparison knows both sides.

It may be objected that many who are capable of the higher pleasures occasionally, under the influence of temptation, postpone them to the lower. But this is quite compatible with a full appreciation of the intrinsic superiority of the higher. Men often, from infirmity of character, make their election for the nearer good, though they know it to be the less valuable, and this no less when the choice is between two bodily pleasures than when it is between bodily and mental. They pursue sensual indulgences to the injury of health, though perfectly aware that health is the greater good. It may be further objected, that many who begin with youthful enthusiasm for everything noble, as they advance in years sink into indolence and selfishness. But I do not believe that those who undergo this very common change voluntarily choose the lower description of pleasures in preference to the higher. I believe that, before they devote themselves exclusively to the one, they have already become incapable of the other. Capacity for the nobler feelings is in most natures a very tender plant, easily killed, not only by hostile influences but by mere want of sustenance, and, in the majority of young persons, it speedily dies away if the occupations to which their position in life has devoted them, and the society into which it has thrown them, are not favorable to keeping that higher capacity in exercise. Men lose their high aspirations as they lose their intellectual tastes, because they have not time or opportunity for indulging them, and they addict themselves to inferior pleasures, not because they deliberately prefer them, but because they are either the only ones to which they have access or the only ones which they are any longer capable of enjoying. It may be questioned whether any one who has remained equally susceptible to both classes of pleasures ever knowingly and calmly preferred the lower, though many in all ages have broken down in an ineffectual attempt to combine both.

From this verdict of the only competent judges, I apprehend there can be no appeal. On a question which is the best worth having of two pleasures, or which of two modes of existence is the most grateful to the feelings, apart from its moral attributes and from its consequences, the judgment of those who are qualified by knowledge of both, or, if they differ, that of the majority among them, must be admitted as final. And there needs be the less hesitation to accept this judgment respecting the quality of pleasures, since there is no other tribunal to be referred to even on the question of quantity. What means are there of determining which is the acutest of two pains, or the intensest of two pleasurable sensations, except the general suffrage of those who are familiar with both? Neither pains nor pleasures are homogeneous, and pain is always heterogeneous with pleasure. What is there to decide whether a particular pleasure is worth purchasing at the cost of a particular pain, except the feelings and judgment of the experienced? When, therefore, those feelings and judgment declare the pleasures derived from the higher faculties to be preferable *in kind*, apart from the question of intensity, to those of which the animal nature disjoined from the higher faculties is susceptible, they are entitled on this subject to the same regard.

I have dwelt on this point, as being a necessary part of a perfectly just conception of Utility or Happiness, considered as the directive rule of human conduct. But it is by no means an indispensable condition to the acceptance of the utilitarian standard, for that standard is not the agent's own greatest happiness, but the greatest amount of happiness altogether; and if it may possibly be doubted whether a noble character is always the happier for its nobleness, there can be no doubt that it makes other people happier, and that the world in general is immensely a gainer by it. Utilitarianism, therefore, could only attain its end by the general cultivation of nobleness of character, even if each individual were only benefited by the nobleness of others, and his own, so far as happiness is concerned, were a sheer deduction from the benefit. But the bare enunciation of such an absurdity as this last renders refutation superfluous.

According to the Greatest-happiness Principle, as above explained, the ultimate end with reference to and for the sake of which all other things are desirable (whether we are considering our own good or that of other people) is an existence exempt as far as possible from pain, and as rich as possible in enjoyments, both in point of quantity and quality; the test of quality, and the rule for measuring it against quantity, being the preference felt by those who in their opportunities of experience, to which must be added their habits of self-consciousness and self-observation, are best furnished with the means of comparison. This being, according to the utilitarian opinion, the end of human action is necessarily also the standard of morality; which may accordingly be defined, the rules and precepts for human conduct by the observance of which an existence such as has been described might be, to the greatest extent possible, secured to all mankind, and not to them only but, so far as the nature of things admits, to the whole sentient creation.

Against this doctrine, however, arises another class of objectors who say that happiness, in any form, cannot be the rational purpose of human life and action, because, in the first place, it is unattainable; and they contemptuously ask, What right hast thou to be happy? a question which Mr. Carlyle clinches by the addition, What right, a short time ago, hadst thou even *to be*? Next they say that men can do *without* happiness, that all noble human beings have felt this, and could not have become noble but by learning the lesson of *Entsagen* or renunciation, which lesson, thoroughly learned and submitted to, they affirm to be the beginning and necessary condition of all virtue.

The first of these objections would go to the root of the matter, were it well founded; for, if no happiness is to be had at all by human beings, the attainment of it cannot be the end of morality, or of any rational conduct. Though, even in that case, something might still be said for the utilitarian theory, since utility includes not solely the pursuit of happiness, but the prevention or mitigation of unhappiness; and, if the former aim be chimerical, there will be all the greater scope and more imperative need for the latter, so long at least as mankind think fit to live, and do not take refuge in the simultaneous act of suicide recommended under certain conditions by Novalis. When, however, it is thus positively asserted to be impossible that human life should be happy, the assertion, if not something like a verbal quibble, is at least an exaggeration. If by happiness be meant a continuity of highly pleasurable excitement, it is evident enough that this is impossible. A state of exalted pleasure lasts only moments, or in some cases, and with some intermissions, hours or days, and is the occasional brilliant flash of enjoyment, not its permanent and steady flame. Of this the philosophers who have taught that happiness is the end of life were as fully aware as those who taunt them. The happiness which they meant was not a life of rapture, but moments of such, in an existence made up of few and transitory pains, many and various pleasures, with a decided predominance of the active over the passive, and having, as the foundation of the whole, not to expect more from life than it is capable of bestowing. A life thus composed, to those who have been fortunate enough to obtain it, has always appeared worthy of the name of "happiness." And such an existence is even now the lot of many, during some considerable portion of their lives. The present wretched education and wretched social arrangements are the only real hindrance to its being attainable by almost all.

The objectors, perhaps, may doubt whether human beings, if taught to consider happiness as the end of life, would be satisfied with such a moderate share of it. But great numbers of mankind have been satisfied with much less. The main constituents of a satisfied life appear to be two, either of which by itself is often found sufficient for the purpose—tranquillity and excitement. With much tranquillity, many find that they can be content with very little pleasure; with much excitement, many can reconcile themselves to a considerable quantity of pain. There is assuredly no inherent impossibility in enabling even the mass of mankind to unite both, since the two are so far from being incompatible, that they are in natural alliance, the prolongation of either being a preparation for, and exciting a wish for, the other. It is only those in whom indolence amounts to a vice that do not desire excitement after an interval of repose; it is only those in whom the need of excitement is a disease, that feel the tranquillity which follows excitement dull and insipid, instead of pleasurable in direct proportion to the excitement which preceded it. When people who are tolerably fortunate

(continued)

Utilitarianism (continued)

in their outward lot do not find in life sufficient enjoyment to make it valuable to them, the cause generally is caring for nobody but themselves. To those who have neither public nor private affections, the excitements of life are much curtailed and, in any case, dwindle in value as the time approaches when all selfish interests must be terminated by death; while those who leave after them objects of personal affection, and especially those who have also cultivated a fellow feeling with the collective interests of mankind, retain as lively an interest in life on the eve of death as in the vigor of youth and health. Next to selfishness, the principal cause which makes life unsatisfactory is want of mental cultivation. A cultivated mind—I do not mean that of a philosopher, but any mind to which the fountains of knowledge have been opened, and which has been taught, in any tolerable degree, to exercise its faculties—finds sources of inexhaustible interest in all that surrounds it, in the objects of nature, the achievements of art, the imaginations of poetry, the incidents of history, the ways of mankind past and present, and their prospects in the future. It is possible, indeed, to become indifferent to all this, and that, too, without having exhausted a thousandth part of it, but only when one has had from the beginning no moral or human interest in these things, and has sought in them only the gratification of curiosity.

Now, there is absolutely no reason in the nature of things why an amount of mental culture sufficient to give an intelligent interest in these objects of contemplation should not be the inheritance of every one born in a civilized country. As little is there an inherent necessity that any human being should be a selfish egotist, devoid of every feeling or care but those which center in his own miserable individuality. Something far superior to this is sufficiently common even now to give ample earnest of what the human species may be made. Genuine private affections and a sincere interest in the public good are possible, though in unequal degrees, to every rightly brought up human being. In a world in which there is so much to interest, so much to enjoy, and so much also to correct and improve, every one who has this moderate amount of moral and intellectual requisites is capable of an existence which may be called enviable; and unless such a person, through bad laws or subjection to the will of others, is denied the liberty to use the sources of happiness within his reach, he will not fail to find this enviable existence, if he escape the positive evils of life, the great sources of physical and mental suffering—such as indigence, disease, and the unkindness, worthlessness, or premature loss, of objects of affection. The main stress of the problem lies, therefore, in the contest with these calamities, from which it is a rare good fortune entirely to escape, which, as things now are, cannot be obviated, and often cannot be in any material degree mitigated. Yet no one whose opinion deserves a moment's consideration can doubt that most of the great positive evils of the world are in themselves removable, and will, if human affairs continue to improve, be in the end reduced within narrow limits. Poverty, in any sense implying suffering, may be completely extinguished by the wisdom of society, combined with the good sense and providence of individuals. Even that most intractable of enemies, disease, may be indefinitely reduced in dimensions by good physical and moral education, and proper control of noxious influence, while the progress of science holds out a promise for the future of still more direct conquests over this detestable foe. And every advance in that direction relieves us from some, not only of the chances which cut short our own lives but, what concerns us still more, which deprive us of those in whom our happiness is wrapped up. As for vicissitudes of fortune and other disappointments connected with worldly circumstances, these are principally the effect either of gross imprudence, of ill-regulated desires, or of bad or imperfect social institutions. All the grand sources, in short, of human suffering are in a great degree, many of them almost entirely, conquerable by human care and effort; and though their removal is grievously slow, though a long succession of generations will perish in the breach before the conquest is completed, and this world becomes all that, if will and knowledge were not wanting, it might easily be made—yet every mind sufficiently intelligent and generous to bear a part, however small and unconspicuous, in the endeavor will draw a noble enjoyment from the contest itself, which he would not, for any bribe in the form of selfish indulgence, consent to be without.

And this leads to the true estimation of what is said by the objectors concerning the possibility and the obligation of learning to do without happiness. Unquestionably, it is possible to do without happiness; it is done involuntarily by nineteen-twentieths of mankind, even in those parts of our present world which are least deep in barbarism, and it often has to be done voluntarily by the hero or the martyr, for the sake of something which he prizes more than his individual happiness. But this something—what is it, unless the happiness of others, or some of the requisites of happiness? It is noble to be capable of resigning entirely one's own portion of happiness, or chances of it; but, after all, this self-sacrifice must be for some end; it is not its own end, and if we are told that its end is not happiness but virtue, which is better than happiness, I ask, Would the sacrifice be made if the hero or martyr did not believe that it would earn for others immunity from similar sacrifices? Would it be made if he thought that his renunciation of happiness for himself would produce no fruit for any of his fellow-creatures but to make their lot like his, and place them also in the condition of persons who have renounced happiness? All honor to those who can abnegate for themselves the personal enjoyment of life, when by such renunciation they contribute worthily to increase the amount of happiness in the world, but he who does it, or professes to do it, for any other purpose is no more deserving of admiration than the ascetic mounted on his pillar. He may be an inspiriting proof of what men *can* do, but assuredly not an example of what they *should*.

Though it is only in a very imperfect state of the world's arrangements that any one can best serve the happiness of others by the absolute sacrifice of his own, yet, so long as the world as in that imperfect state, I fully acknowledge that the readiness to make such a sacrifice is the highest virtue which can be found in man. I will add that in this condition of the world, paradoxical as the assertion may be, the conscious ability to do without happiness gives the best prospect of realizing such happiness as is attainable. For nothing except that consciousness can raise a person above the chances of life, by making him feel that, let fate and fortune do their worst, they have not power to subdue him; which, once felt, frees him from excess of anxiety concerning the evils of life, and enables him, like many a Stoic in the worst times of the Roman Empire, to cultivate in tranquillity the sources of satisfaction accessible to him, without concerning himself about the uncertainty of their duration, any more than about their inevitable end.

Meanwhile, let utilitarians never cease to claim the morality of self-devotion as a possession which belongs by as good a right to them as either to the Stoic or to the Transcendentalist. The utilitarian morality does recognize in human beings the power of sacrificing their own greatest good for the good of others. It only refuses to admit that the sacrifice is itself a good. A sacrifice which does not increase, or tend to increase, the sum total of happiness, it considers as wasted. The only self-renunciation which it applauds is devotion to the happiness, or to some of the means of happiness, of others, either of mankind collectively, or of individuals within the limits imposed by the collective interests of mankind.

I must again repeat what the assailants of utilitarianism seldom have the justice to acknowledge, that the happiness which forms the utilitarian standard of what is right in conduct is not the agent's own happiness but that of all concerned. As between his own happiness and that of others, utilitarianism requires him to be as strictly impartial as a disinterested and benevolent spectator. In the golden rule of Jesus of Nazareth, we read the complete spirit of the ethics of utility. To do as you would be done by, and to love you neighbor as yourself, constitute the ideal perfection of utilitarian morality. As the means of making the nearest approach to this ideal, utility would enjoin, first, that laws and social arrangements should place the happiness or (as, speaking practically, it may be called) the interest of every individual as nearly as possible in harmony with the interest of the whole; and secondly, that education and opinion, which have so vast a power over human character, should so use that power as to establish in the mind of every individual an indissoluble association between his own happiness and the good of the whole—especially between his own happiness, and the practice of such modes of conduct, negative and positive, as regard for the universal happiness prescribes—so that not only he may be unable to conceive the possibility of happiness to himself consistently with conduct opposed to the general good, but also that a direct impulse to promote the general good may be in every individual one of the habitual motives of action, and the sentiments connected therewith may fill a large and prominent place in every human being's sentient existence. If the impugners of the utilitarian morality represented it to their own minds in this its true character, I know not what recommendation possessed by any other morality they could possibly affirm to be wanting to it, what more

(continued)

Utilitarianism (*continued*)

beautiful or more exalted developments of human nature any other ethical system can be supposed to foster, or what springs of action, not accessible to the utilitarian, such systems rely on for giving effect to their mandates.

The objectors to utilitarianism cannot always be charged with representing it in a discreditable light. On the contrary, those among them who entertain any thing like a just idea of its disinterested character sometimes find fault with its standard as being too high for humanity. They say it is exacting too much to require that people shall always act from the inducement of promoting the general interests of society. But this is to mistake the very meaning of a standard of morals, and confound the rule of action with the motive of it. It is the business of ethics to tell us what are our duties or by what test we may know them, but no system of ethics requires that the sole motive of all we do shall be a feeling of duty; on the contrary, ninety-nine hundredths of all our actions are done from other motives, and rightly so done, if the rule of duty does not condemn them. It is the more unjust to utilitarianism that this particular misapprehension should be made a ground of objection to it, inasmuch as utilitarian moralists have gone beyond almost all others in affirming that the motive has nothing to do with the morality of the action though much with the worth of the agent. He who saves a fellow creature from drowning does what is morally right, whether his motive be duty or the hope of being paid for his trouble; he who betrays the friend that trusts him is guilty of a crime, even if his object be to serve another friend to whom he is under greater obligations.[2] But to speak only of actions done from the motive of duty, and in direct obedience to principle: it is a misapprehension of the utilitarian mode of thought to conceive it as implying that people should fix their minds upon so wide a generality as the world or society at large. The great majority of good actions are intended, not for the benefit of the world but for that of individuals, of which the good of the world is made up; and the thoughts of the most virtuous man need not on these occasions travel beyond the particular persons concerned, except so far as is necessary to assure himself that, in benefiting them, he is not violating the rights—that is, the legitimate and authorized expectations—of any one else. The multiplication of happiness is, according to the utilitarian ethics, the object of virtue; the occasions on which any person (except one in a thousand) has it in his power to do this on an extended scale—in other words, to be a public benefactor—are but exceptional, and on these occasions alone is he called on to consider public utility; in every other case, private utility, the interest or happiness of some few persons, is all he has to attend to. Those alone, the influence of whose actions extends to society in general, need concern themselves habitually about so large an object. In the case of abstinences indeed—of things which people forbear to do from moral considerations, though the consequences in the particular case might be beneficial—it would be unworthy of an intelligent agent not to be consciously aware that the action is of a class which, if practised generally, would be generally injurious, and that this is the ground of the obligation to abstain from it. The amount of regard for the public interest implied in this recognition is no greater than is demanded by every system of morals, for they all enjoin to abstain from whatever is manifestly pernicious to society.

The same considerations dispose of another reproach against the doctrine of utility, founded on a still grosser misconception of the purpose of a standard of morality, and of the very meaning of the words "right" and "wrong." It is often affirmed that utilitarianism renders men cold and unsympathizing, that it chills their moral feelings towards individuals, that it makes them regard only the dry and hard consideration of the consequences of actions, not taking into their moral estimate the qualities from which those actions emanate. If the assertion means that they do not allow their judgment respecting the rightness or wrongness of an action to be influenced by their opinion of the qualities of the person who does it, this is a complaint, not against utilitarianism but against having any standard of morality at all; for certainly no known ethical standard decides an action to be good or bad because it is done by a good or bad man, still less because done by a amiable, a brave, or a benevolent man, or the contrary. These considerations are relevant, not to the estimation of actions, but of persons, and there is nothing in the utilitarian theory inconsistent with the fact that there are other things which interest us in persons besides the rightness and wrongness of their actions. The Stoics indeed, with the paradoxical misuse of language which was part of their system and by which they strove to raise themselves above all concern about any thing but virtue, were fond of saying that he who has that has everything, that he, and one he, is rich, is beautiful, is a king. But no claim of this description is made for the virtuous man by the utilitarian doctrine. Utilitarians are quite aware that there are other desirable possessions and qualities besides virtue, and are perfectly willing to allow to all of them their full worth. They are also aware that a right action does not necessarily indicate a virtuous character, and that actions which are blamable often proceed from qualities entitled to praise. When this is apparent in any particular case, it modifies their estimation, not certainly of the act but of the agent. I grant that they are notwithstanding of opinion that, in the long run, the best proof of a good character is good actions, and resolutely refuse to consider any mental disposition as good, of which the predominant tendency is to produce bad conduct. This makes them unpopular with many people; but it is unpopularity which they must share with every one who regards the distinction between right and wrong in a serious light, and the reproach is not one which a conscientious utilitarian need be anxious to repel.

If no more be meant by the objection than that many utilitarians look on the morality of actions, as measured by the utilitarian standards, with too exclusive a regard, and do not lay sufficient stress upon the other beauties of character which go towards making a human being lovable or admirable, this may be admitted. Utilitarians who have cultivated their moral feelings but not their sympathies nor their artistic perceptions, do fall into this mistake, and so do all other moralists under the same conditions. What can be said in excuse for other moralists is equally available for them, namely that, if there is to be any error, it is better that it should be on that side. As a matter of fact, we may affirm that among utilitarians, as among adherents of other systems, there is every imaginable degree of rigidity and of laxity in the application of their standard; some are even puritanically rigorous, while others are as indulgent as can possibly be desired by sinner or by sentimentalist. But on the whole, a doctrine which brings prominently forward the interest that mankind have in the repression and prevention of conduct which violates the moral law, is likely to be inferior to no other in turning the sanctions of opinion against such violations. It is true, the question, What does violate the moral law? Is one on which those who recognize different standards of morality are likely now and then to differ. But difference of opinion on moral questions was not first introduced into the world by utilitarianism, while that doctrine does supply, if not always an easy, at all events a tangible and intelligible mode of deciding such differences.

It may not be superfluous to notice a few more of the common misapprehensions of utilitarian ethics, even those which are so obvious and gross that it might appear impossible for any person of candor and intelligence to fall into them, since persons even of considerable mental endowments often give themselves so little trouble to understand the bearings of any opinion against which they entertain a prejudice, and men are in general so little conscious of this voluntary ignorance as a defect, that the vulgarest misunderstandings of ethical doctrines are continually met with the deliberate writings of persons of the greatest pretensions both to high principle and to philosophy. We not uncommonly hear the doctrine of utility inveighed against as a *godless* doctrine. If it be necessary to say any thing at all against so mere an assumption, we may say that the question depends upon what idea we have formed of the moral character of the Deity. If it be a true belief that God desires, above all things, the happiness of his creatures, and that this was his purpose in their creation, utility is not only not a godless doctrine but more profoundly religious than any other. If it be meant that utilitarianism does not recognize the revealed will of God as the supreme law of morals, I answer that an utilitarian, who believes in the perfect goodness and wisdom of God, necessarily believes that whatever God has thought fit to reveal on the subject of morals must fulfil the requirements of utility in a supreme degree. But others besides utilitarians have been of opinion that the Christian revelation was intended, and is fitted, to inform the hearts and minds of mankind with a spirit which should enable them to find for themselves what is right and incline them to do it when found, rather than to tell them, except in a very general way, what it is, and that we need a doctrine of ethics, carefully followed out, to *interpret* to us the will of God. Whether this opinion is correct or not, it is superfluous here to discuss, since whatever aid religion, either natural or revealed, can afford to ethical investigation, is as open to the utilitarian moralist as to any other. He can use it as the testimony of God to the usefulness or hurtfulness of any given course of action, by as good a

(continued)

Utilitarianism (*continued*)

right as others can use it for the indication of a transcendental law, having no connection with usefulness or with happiness.

Again: Utility is often summarily stigmatized as an immoral doctrine by giving it the name of Expediency and, taking advantage of the popular use of that term, to contrast it with Principle. But the Expedient, in the sense in which it is opposed to the Right, generally means that which is expedient for the particular interest of the agent himself, as when a minister sacrifices the interests of his country to keep himself in place. When it means any thing better than this, it means that which is expedient for some immediate object, some temporary purpose, but which violates a rule whose observance is expedient in a much higher degree. The Expedient, in this sense, instead of being the same thing with the useful, is a branch of the hurtful. Thus it would often be expedient, for the purpose of getting over some momentary embarrassment or attaining some object immediately useful to ourselves or others, to tell a lie. But inasmuch as the cultivation in ourselves of a sensitive feeling on the subject of veracity is one of the most useful, and the enfeeblement of that feeling one of those most hurtful, things to which our conduct can be instrumental, and inasmuch as any, even unintentional, deviation from truth does that much towards weakening the trustworthiness of human assertion, which is not only the principal support of all present social well-being, but the insufficiency of which does more than any one thing that can be named to keep back civilization, virtue, every thing on which human happiness on the largest scale depends—we feel that the violation, for a present advantage, of a rule of such transcendent expediency is not expedient, and that he who, for the sake of a convenience to himself or to some other individual, does what depends on him to deprive mankind of the good, and inflict upon them the evil, involved in the greater or less reliance which they can place in each other's word, acts the part of one of their worst enemies. Yet that even this rule, sacred as it is, admits of possible exceptions is acknowledged by all moralists, the chief of which is, when the withholding of some fact (as of information from a malefactor, or of bad news from a person dangerously ill) would save an individual (especially an individual other than one's self) from great and unmerited evil and when the withholding can only be effected by denial. But in order that the exception may not extend itself beyond the need and may have the least possible effect in weakening reliance on veracity, it ought to be recognized and, if possible, its limits defined, and, if the principle of utility is good for any thing, it must be good for weighing these conflicting utilities against one another, and marking out the region within which one or the other preponderates.

Again: defenders of utility often find themselves called upon to reply to such objections as this—that there is not time, previous to action, for calculating and weighing the effects of any line of conduct on the general happiness. This is exactly as if any one were to say that it is impossible to guide our conduct by Christianity, because there is not time, on every occasion on which any thing has to be done, to read through the Old and New Testaments. The answer to the objection is that there has been ample time, namely, the whole past duration of the human species. During all that time, mankind have been learning by experience the tendencies of actions, on which experience all the prudence as well as all the morality of life are dependent. People talk as if the commencement of this course of experience had hitherto been put off and as if, at the moment when some man feels tempted to meddle with the property of life of another, he had to begin considering for the first time whether murder and theft are injurious to human happiness. Even then, I do not think that he would find the question very puzzling, but at all events the matter is now done to his hand. It is truly a whimsical supposition that, if mankind were agreed in considering utility to be the test of morality, they would remain without any agreement as to what *is* useful, and would take no measures for having their notions on the subject taught to the young and enforced by law and opinion. There is no difficulty in proving any ethical standard whatever to work ill, if we suppose universal idiocy to be conjoined with it; but on any hypothesis short of that, mankind must by this time have acquired positive beliefs as to the effects of some actions on their happiness, and the beliefs which have thus come down are the rules of morality for the multitude, and for the philosopher, until he has succeeded in finding better. That philosophers might easily do this, even now, on many subjects, that the received code of ethics is by no means of divine right, and that mankind have still much to learn as to the effects of actions on the general happiness—I admit or, rather, earnestly maintain. The corollaries from the principle of utility, like the precepts of every practical art, admit of indefinite improvement and, in a progressive state of the human mind, their improvement is perpetually going on. But to consider the rules of morality as improvable is one thing; to pass over the intermediate generalizations entirely, and endeavor to test each individual action directly by the first principle, is another. It is a strange notion, that the acknowledgment of a first principle is inconsistent with the admission of secondary ones. To inform a traveler respecting the place of his ultimate destination is not to forbid the use of landmarks and direction posts on the way. The proposition that happiness is the end and aim of morality does not mean that no road ought to be laid down to that goal, or that persons going thither should not be advised to take one direction rather than another. Men really ought to leave off talking a kind of nonsense on this subject which they would neither talk nor listen to on other matters of practical concernment. Nobody argues that the art of navigation is not founded on astronomy, because sailors cannot wait to calculate the "Nautical Almanac." Being rational creatures, they go to sea with it ready calculated, and all rational creatures go out upon the sea of life with their minds made up on the common questions of right and wrong, as well as on many of the far more difficult questions of wise and foolish. And this, as long as foresight is a human quality, it is to be presumed they will continue to do. Whatever we adopt as the fundamental principle of morality, we require subordinate principles to apply it by; the impossibility of doing without them, being common to all systems, can afford no argument against any one in particular; but gravely to argue as if no such secondary principles could be had, and as if mankind had remained till now and always must remain without drawing any general conclusions from the experience of human life, is as high a pitch, I think, as absurdity has ever reached in philosophical controversy.

The remainder of the stock arguments against utilitarianism mostly consist in laying to its charge the common infirmities of human nature, and the general difficulties which embarrass conscientious persons in shaping their course through life. We are told that an utilitarian will be apt to make his own particular case an exception to moral rules and, when under temptation, will see an utility in the breach of a rule greater than he will see in its observance. But is utility the only creed which is able to furnish us with excuses for evil-doing, and means of cheating our own conscience? They are afforded in abundance by all doctrines which recognize as a fact in morals the existence of conflicting considerations, which all doctrines do that have been believed by sane persons. It is not the fault of any creed, but of the complicated nature of human affairs, that rules of conduct cannot be so framed as to require no exceptions, and that hardly any kind of action can safely be laid down as either always obligatory or always condemnable. There is no ethical creed which does not temper the rigidity of its laws by giving a certain latitude, under the moral responsibility of the agent, for accommodation to peculiarities of circumstances and, under every creed, at the opening thus made, self-deception and dishonest casuistry get in. There exists no moral system under which there do not arise unequivocal cases of conflicting obligation. These are the real difficulties, the knotty points both in the theory of ethics and in the conscientious guidance of personal conduct. They are overcome practically with greater or with less success according to the intellect and virtue of the individual, but it can hardly be pretended that any one will be the less qualified for dealing with them, from possessing an ultimate standard to which conflicting rights and duties can be referred. If utility is the ultimate source of moral obligations, utility may be invoked to decide between them when their demands are incompatible. Though the application of the standard may be difficult, it is better than none at all; while in other systems, the moral laws all claiming independent authority, there is no common umpire entitled to interfere between them, their claims to precedence one over another rest on little better than sophistry, and unless determined, as they generally are, by the unacknowledged influence of considerations of utility, afford a free scope for the action of personal desires and partialities. We must remember that only in these cases of conflict between secondary principles is it requisite that first principles should be appealed to. There is no case of moral obligation in which some secondary principle is not involved and, if only one, there can seldom be any real doubt which one it is, in the mind of any person by whom the principle itself is recognized.

The Challenge of Cultural Relativism

James Rachels

How Different Cultures Have Different Moral Codes

DARIUS, A KING OF ANCIENT PERSIA, was intrigued by the variety of cultures he encountered in his travels. He had found, for example, that the Callatians (a tribe of Indians) customarily ate the bodies of their dead fathers. The Greeks, of course, did not do that–the Greeks practiced cremation and regarded the funeral pyre as the natural and fitting way to dispose of the dead. Darius thought that a sophisticated understanding of the world must include an appreciation of such differences between cultures. One day, to teach this lesson, he summoned some Greeks who happened to be present at his court and asked them what they would take to eat the bodies of their dead fathers. They were shocked, as Darius knew they would be, and replied that no amount of money could persuade them to do such a thing. Then Darius called in some Callatians, and while the Greeks listened asked them what they would take to burn their dead fathers' bodies. The Callatians were horrified and told Darius not even to mention such a dreadful thing.

This story, recounted by Herodotus in his *History*, illustrates a recurring theme in the literature of social science: different cultures have different moral codes.[1] What is thought right within one group may be utterly abhorrent to the members of another group, and vice versa. Should we eat the bodies of the dead or burn them? If you were a Greek, one answer would seem obviously correct; but if you were a Callatian, the opposite would seem equally certain.

It is easy to give additional examples of the same kind. Consider the Eskimos. They are a remote and inaccessible people. Numbering only about 25,000, they live in small, isolated settlements scattered mostly along the northern fringes of North America and Greenland. Until the beginning of this century, the outside world knew little about them. Then explorers began to bring back strange tales.

Eskimo customs turned out to be very different from our own. The men often had more than one wife, and they would share their wives with guests, lending them for the night as a sign of hospitality. Moreover, within a community, a dominant male might demand—and get—regular sexual access to other men's wives. The women, however, were free to break these arrangements simply by leaving their husbands and taking up with new partners—free, that is, so long as their former husbands chose not to make trouble. All in all, the Eskimo practice was a volatile scheme that bore little resemblance to what we call marriage.

But it was not only their marriage and sexual practices that were different. The Eskimos also seemed to have less regard for human life. Infanticide, for example, was common. Knud Rasmussen, one of the most famous early explorers, reported that he met one woman who had borne twenty children but had killed ten of them at birth. Female babies, he found, were especially liable to be destroyed, and this was permitted simply at the parents' discretion, with no social stigma attached to it. Old people also, when they became too feeble to contribute to the family, were left out in the snow to die. So there seemed to be, in this society, remarkably little respect for life.[2]

To the general public, these were disturbing revelations. Our own way of living seems so natural and right that for many of us it is hard to conceive of others living so differently. And when we do hear of such things, we tend immediately to categorize those other peoples as "backward" or "primitive." But to anthropologists and sociologists, there was nothing particularly surprising about the Eskimos. Since the time of Herodotus, enlightened observers have been accustomed to the idea that conceptions of right and wrong differ from culture to culture. If we assume that *our* ideas of right and wrong will be shared by all peoples at all times, we are merely naive.

Cultural Relativism

To many thinkers, this observation—"Different cultures have different moral codes"—has seemed to be the key to understanding morality. The idea of universal truth in ethics, they say, is a myth. The customs of different societies are all that exist. These customs cannot be said to be "correct" or "incorrect," for that implies we have an independent standard of right and wrong by which they may be judged. But there is no such independent standard; every standard is culture-bound. The great pioneering sociologist William Graham Sumner, writing in 1906, put the point like this:

> The "right" way is the way which the ancestors used and which has been handed down. The tradition is its own warrant. It is not held subject to verification by experience. The notion of right is in the folkways. It is not outside of them, of independent origin, and brought to test them. In the folkways, whatever is, is right. This is because they are traditional, and therefore contain in themselves the authority of the ancestral ghosts. When we come to the folkways we are at the end of our analysis.[3]

This line of thought has probably persuaded more people to be skeptical about ethics than any other single thins. *Cultural Relativism*, as it has been called, challenges our ordinary belief in the objectivity and universality of moral truth. It says, in effect, that there is no such thing as universal truth in ethics; there are only the various cultural codes, and nothing more. Moreover, our own code has no special status; it is merely one among many.

As we shall see, this basic idea is really a compound of several different thoughts. It is important to separate the various elements of the theory because, on analysis, some parts of the theory turn out to be correct, whereas others seem to be mistaken. As a beginning, we may distinguish the following claims, all of which have been made by cultural relativists:

1. Different societies have different moral codes.
2. There is no objective standard that can be used to judge on societal code better than another.
3. The moral code of our own society has no special status; it is merely one among many.
4. There is no "universal truth" in ethics—that is, there are no moral truths that hold for all peoples at all times.
5. The moral code of a society determines what is right within that society; that is, if the moral code of a society says that a certain action is right, then that action *is* right, at least within that society.
6. It is mere arrogance for us to try to judge the conduct of other peoples. We should adopt an attitude of tolerance toward the practices of other cultures.

Although it may seem that these six propositions go naturally together, they are independent of one another, in the sense that some of them might be true even if others are false. In what follows, we will try to identify what is correct in Cultural Relativism, but we will also be concerned to expose what is mistaken about it.

The Cultural Differences Argument

Cultural Relativism is a theory about the nature of morality. At first blush it seems quite plausible. However, like all such theories, it may be evaluated by subjecting it to rational analysis; and when we analyze Cultural Relativism we find that it is not so plausible as it first appears to be.

The first thing we need to notice is that at the heart of Cultural Relativism there is a certain *form of argument*. The strategy used by cultural relativists is to argue from facts about the differences between cultural outlooks to a conclusion about the status of morality. Thus we are invited to accept this reasoning:

1. The Greeks believed it was wrong to eat the dead, whereas the Callatians believed it was right to eat the dead.
2. Therefore, eating the dead is neither objectively right nor objectively wrong. It is merely a matter of opinion, which varies from culture to culture.

Or, alternatively:

1. The Eskimos see nothing wrong with infanticide, whereas Americans believe infanticide is immoral.
2. Therefore, infanticide is neither objectively right nor objectively wrong. It is merely a matter of opinion, which varies from culture to culture.

(continued)

The Challenge of Cultural Relativism (*continued*)

Clearly, these arguments are variations of one fundamental idea. They are both special cases of a more general argument, which says:

1. Different cultures have different moral codes.
2. Therefore, there is no objective "truth" in morality. Right and wrong are only matters of opinion, and opinions vary from culture to culture.

We may call this the *Cultural Differences Argument*. To many people, it is very persuasive. But from a logical point of view, is it a *sound* argument?

It is not sound. The trouble is that the conclusion does not really follow from the premise—that is, even if the premise is true, the conclusion still might be false. The premise concerns what people *believe:* in some societies, people believe one thing; in other societies, people believe differently. The conclusion, however, concerns *what really is the case.* The trouble is that this sort of conclusion does not follow logically from this sort of premise.

Consider again the example of the Greeks and Callatians. The Greeks believed it was wrong to eat the dead; the Callatians believed it was right. Does it follow, *from the mere fact that they disagreed,* that there is no objective truth in the matter? No, it does not follow; for it *could* be that the practice was objectively right (or wrong) and that one or the other of them was simply mistaken.

To make the point clearer, consider a very different matter. In some societies, people believe the earth is flat. In other societies, such as our own, people believe the earth is (roughly) spherical. Does it follow, *from the mere fact that they disagree,* that there is no "objective truth" in geography? Of course not; we would never draw such a conclusion because we realize that, in their beliefs about the world, the members of some societies might simply be wrong. There is no reason to think that if the world is round everyone must know it. Similarly, there is no reason to think that if there is moral truth everyone must know it. The fundamental mistake in the Cultural Differences Argument is that it attempts to derive a substantive conclusion about a subject (morality) from the mere fact that people disagree about it.

It is important to understand the nature of the point that is being made here. We are *not* saying (not yet, anyway) that the conclusion of the argument is false. Insofar as anything being said here is concerned, it is still an open question whether the conclusion is true. We *are* making a purely logical point and saying that the conclusion does not *follow from* the premise. This is important, because in order to determine whether the conclusion is true, we need arguments in its support. Cultural Relativism proposes this argument, but unfortunately the argument turns out to be fallacious. So it proves nothing.

The Consequences of Taking Cultural Relativism Seriously

Even if the Cultural Differences Argument is invalid, Cultural Relativism might still be true. What would it be like if it were true?

In the passage quoted above, William Graham Sumner summarizes the essence of Cultural Relativism. He says that there is no measure of right and wrong other than the standards of one's society: "The notion of right is in the folkways. It is not outside of them, of independent origin, and brought to test them. In the folkways, whatever is, is right."

Suppose we took this seriously. What would be some of the consequences?

1. *We could no longer say that the customs of other societies are morally inferior to our own.* This, of course, is one of the main points stressed by Cultural Relativism. We would have to stop condemning other societies merely because they are "different." So long as we concentrate on certain examples, such as the funerary practices of the Greeks and Callatians, this may seem to be a sophisticated, enlightened attitude.

However, we would also be stopped from criticizing other, less benign practices. Suppose a society waged war on its neighbors for the purpose of taking slaves. Or suppose a society was violently anti-Semitic, and its leaders set out to destroy the Jews. Cultural Relativism would preclude us from saying that either of these practices was wrong. We would not even be able to say that a society tolerant of Jews is *better* than the anti-Semitic society, for that would imply some sort of transcultural standard of comparison. The failure to condemn *these* practices does not seem "enlightened"; on the contrary, slavery and anti-Semitism seem wrong *wherever* they occur. Nevertheless, if we took Cultural Relativism seriously, we would have to admit that these social practices also are immune from criticism.

2. *We could decide whether actions are right or wrong just by consulting the standards of our society.* Cultural Relativism suggests a simple test for determining what is right and what is wrong; all one has to do is ask whether the action is in accordance with the code of one's society. Suppose a resident of South Africa is wondering whether his country's policy of *apartheid*—rigid racial segregation-is morally correct. All he has to do is ask whether this policy conforms to his society's moral code. If it does, there is nothing to worry about, at least from a moral point of view.

This implication of Cultural Relativism is disturbing because few of us think that our society's code is perfect—we can think of ways it might be improved. Yet Cultural Relativism would not only forbid us from criticizing the codes of *other* societies; it would stop us from criticizing our *own*. After all, if right and wrong are relative to culture, this must be true for our own culture just as much as for others.

3. *The idea of moral progress is called into doubt*. Usually, we think that at least some changes in our society have been for the better. (Some, of course, may have been changes for the worse.) Consider this example: Throughout most of Western history the place of women in society was very narrowly circumscribed. They could not own property; they could not vote or hold political office; with a few exceptions, they were not permitted to have paying jobs; and generally they were under the almost absolute control of their husbands. Recently much of this has changed, and most people think of it as progress.

If Cultural Relativism is correct, can we legitimately think of this as progress? Progress means replacing a way of doing things with a *better* way. But by what standard do we judge the new ways as better? If the old ways were in accordance with the social standards of their time, then Cultural Relativism would say it is a mistake to judge them by the standards of a different time. Eighteenth-century society was, in effect, a different society from the one we have now. To say that we have made progress implies a judgment that present-day society is better, and that is just the sort of transcultural judgment that, according to Cultural Relativism, is impermissible.

Our idea of social *reform* will also have to be reconsidered. A reformer such as Martin Luther King, Jr., seeks to change his society for the better. Within the constraints imposed by Cultural Relativism, there is one way this might be done. If a society is not living up to its own ideals, the reformer may be regarded as acting for the best: the ideals of the society are the standard by which we judge his or her proposals as worthwhile. But the "reformer" may not challenge the ideals themselves, for those ideals are by definition correct. According to Cultural Relativism, then, the idea of social reform makes sense only in this very limited way.

These three consequences of Cultural Relativism have led many thinkers to reject it as implausible on its face. It does make sense, they say, to condemn some practices, such as slavery and anti-Semitism, wherever they occur. It makes sense to think that our own society has made some moral progress, while admitting that it is still imperfect and in need of reform. Because Cultural Relativism says that these judgments make no sense, the argument goes, it cannot be right.

Why there is Less Disagreement than it Seems

The original impetus for Cultural Relativism comes from the observation that cultures differ dramatically in their views of right and wrong. But just how much do they differ? It is true that there are differences. However, it is easy to overestimate the extent of those differences. Often, when we examine what *seems* to be a dramatic difference, we find that the cultures do not differ nearly as much as it appears.

Consider a culture in which people believe it is wrong to eat cows. This may even be a poor culture, in which there is not enough food; still, the cows are not to be touched. Such a society would *appear* to have values very different from our own. But does it? We have not yet asked why these people will not eat cows. Suppose it is because they believe that after death the souls of humans inhabit the bodies of animals, especially cows, so that a cow may be someone's grandmother. Now do we want to say that their values are different from ours? No, the difference lies

(continued)

The Challenge of Cultural Relativism (*continued*)

elsewhere. The difference is in our belief systems, not in our values. We agree that we shouldn't eat Grandma; we simply disagree about whether the cow *is* (or could be) Grandma.

The general point is this. Many factors work together to produce the customs of a society. The society's values are only one of them. Other matters such as the religious and factual beliefs held by its members and the physical circumstances in which they must live, are also important. We cannot conclude, then, merely because customs differ, that there is a disagreement about *values*. The difference in customs may be attributable to some other aspect of social life. Thus there may be less disagreement about values than there appears to be.

Consider the Eskimos again. They often kill perfectly normal infants, especially girls. We do not approve of this at all; a parent who did this in our society would be locked up. Thus there appears to be a great difference in the values of our two cultures. But suppose we ask *why* the Eskimos do this. The explanation is not that they have less affection for their children or less respect for human life. An Eskimo family will always protect its babies if conditions permit. But they live in a harsh environment, where food is often in short supply. A fundamental postulate of Eskimo thought is: "life is hard, and the margin of safety small." A family may want to nourish its babies but be unable to do so.

As in many "primitive" societies, Eskimo mothers will nurse their infants over a much longer period of time than mothers in our culture. The child will take nourishment from its mother's breast for four years, perhaps even longer. So even in the best of times there are limits to the number of infants that one mother can sustain. Moreover, the Eskimos are a nomadic people—unable to farm, they must move about in search of food. Infants must be carried, and a mother can carry only one baby in her parka as she travels and goes about her outdoor work. Other family members can help, but this is not always possible.

Infant girls are more readily disposed of because, first, in this society the males are the primary food providers—they are the hunters, according to the traditional division of labor—and it is obviously important to maintain a sufficient number of food gatherers. But there is an important second reason as well. Because the hunters suffer a high casualty rate, the adult men who die prematurely far outnumber the women who die early. Thus if male and female infants survived in equal numbers, the female adult population would greatly outnumber the male adult population. Examining the available statistics, one writer concluded that "were it not for female infanticide . . . there would be approximately one-and-a-half times as many females in the average Eskimo local group as there are food-producing males."[4]

So among the Eskimos, infanticide does not signal a fundamentally different attitude toward children. Instead, it is a recognition that drastic measures are sometimes needed to ensure the family's survival. Even then, however, killing the baby is not the first option considered. Adoption is common; childless couples are especially happy to take a more fertile couple's "surplus." Killing is only the last resort. I emphasize this in order to show that the raw data of the anthropologists can be misleading; it can make the differences in values between cultures appear greater than they are. The Eskimos' values are not all that different from our values. It is only that life forces upon them choices that we do not have to make.

How All Cultures Have Some Values in Common

It should not be surprising that, despite appearances, the Eskimos are protective of their children. How could it be otherwise? How could a group survive that did *not* value its young? This suggests a certain argument, one which shows that all cultural groups must be protective of their infants:

1. Human infants are helpless and cannot survive if they are not given extensive care for a period of years.
2. Therefore, if a group did not care for its young, the young would not survive, and the older members of the group would not be replaced. After a while the group would die out.
3. Therefore, any cultural group that continues to exist must care for its young. Infants that are *not* cared for must be the exception rather than the rule.

Similar reasoning shows that other values must be more or less universal. Imagine what it would be like for a society to place no value at all on truth telling. When one person spoke to another, there would be no presumption at all that he was telling the truth—for he could just as easily be speaking falsely. Within that society, there would be no reason to pay attention to what anyone says. (I ask you what time it is, and you say "four o'clock." But there is no presumption that you are speaking truly; you could just as easily have said the first thing that came into your head. So I have no reason to pay attention to your answer—in fact, there was no point in my asking you in the first place!) Communication would then be extremely difficult, if not impossible. And because complex societies cannot exist without regular communication among their members, society would become impossible. It follows that in any complex society there *must* be a presumption in favor of truthfulness. There may of course be exceptions to this rule: there may be situations in which it is thought to be permissible to lie. Nevertheless, these will be exceptions to a rule that *is* in force in the society.

Let me give one further example of the same type. Could a society exist in which there was no prohibition on murder? What would this be like? Suppose people were free to kill other people at will, and no one thought there was anything wrong with it. In such a "society," no one could feel secure. Everyone would have to be constantly on guard. People who wanted to survive would have to avoid other people as much as possible. This would inevitably result in individuals trying to become as self-sufficient as possible—after all, associating with others would be dangerous. Society on any large scale would collapse. Of course, people might band together in smaller groups with others that they *could* trust not to harm them. But notice what this means: they would be forming smaller societies that *did* acknowledge a rule against murder. The prohibition of murder, then, is a necessary feature of all societies.

There is a general theoretical point here, namely that *there are some moral rules that all societies will have in common, because those rules are necessary for society to exist.* The rules against lying and murder are two examples. And in fact, we do find these rules in force in all viable cultures. Cultures may differ in what they regard as legitimate exceptions to the rules, but this disagreement exists against a background of agreement on the larger issues. Therefore, it is a mistake to overestimate the amount of difference between cultures. Not *every* moral rule can vary from society to society.

What Can be Learned from Cultural Relativism

At the outset, I said that we were going to identify both what is right and what is wrong in Cultural Relativism. Thus far I have mentioned only its mistakes: I have said that it rests on an invalid argument, that it has consequences that make it implausible on its face, and that the extent of cultural disagreement is far less than it implies. This all adds up to a pretty thorough repudiation of the theory. Nevertheless, it is still a very appealing idea, and the reader may have the feeling that all this is a little unfair. The theory *must* have something going for it, or else why has it been so influential? In fact, I think there *is* something right about Cultural Relativism, and now I want to say what that is. There are two lessons we should learn from the theory, even if we ultimately reject it.

1. Cultural Relativism warns us, quite rightly, about the danger of assuming that all our preferences are based on some absolute rational standard. They are not. Many (but not all) of our practices are merely peculiar to our society, and it is easy to lose sight of that fact. In reminding us of it, the theory does a service.

Funerary practices are one example. The Callatians, according to Herodotus, were "men who ate their fathers"—a shocking idea, to us at least. But eating the flesh of the dead could be understood as a sign of respect. It could be taken as a symbolic act that says: We wish this person's spirit to dwell within us. Perhaps this was the understanding of the Callatians. On such a way of thinking, burying the dead could be seen as an act of rejection, and burning the corpse as positively scornful. If this is hard to imagine, then we may need to have our imaginations stretched. Of course we may feel a visceral repugnance at the idea of eating human flesh in any circumstances. But what of it? This repugnance may be, as the relativists say, only a matter of what is customary in our particular society.

There are many other matters that we tend to think of in terms of objective right and wrong, but that are really nothing more than social conventions. Should women cover their breasts? A publicly exposed breast is scandalous in our society, whereas in other cultures it is unremarkable. Objectively speaking, it is neither right nor wrong—there is no objective reason why either custom is better. Cultural Relativism begins with the valuable insight that many of our practices are like this—they are only cultural products. Then it goes wrong by concluding that, because *some* practices are like this, *all* must be.

(continued)

The Challenge of Cultural Relativism   (*continued*)

2. The second lesson has to do with keeping an open mind. In the course of growing up, each of us has acquired some strong feelings: we have learned to think of some types of conduct as acceptable, and others we have learned to regard as simply unacceptable. Occasionally, we may find those feelings challenged. We may encounter someone who claims that our feelings are mistaken. For example, we may have been taught that homosexuality is immoral, and we may feel quite uncomfortable around gay people and see them as alien and "different." Now someone suggests that this may be a mere prejudice; that there is nothing evil about homosexuality; that gay people are just people, like anyone else, who happen, through no choice of their own, to be attracted to others of the same sex. But because we feel so strongly about the matter, we may find it hard to take this seriously. Even after we listen to the arguments, we may still have the unshakable feeling that homosexuals *must*, somehow, be an unsavory lot.

Cultural Relativism, by stressing that our moral views can reflect the prejudices of our society, provides an antidote for this kind of dogmatism. When he tells the story of the Greeks and Callatians, Herodotus adds:

> For if anyone, no matter who, were given the opportunity of choosing from amongst all the nations of the world the set of beliefs which he thought best, he would inevitably, after careful consideration of their relative merits, choose that of his own country. Everyone without exception believes his own native customs, and the religion he was brought up in, to be the best.[5]

Realizing this can result in our having more open minds. We can come to understand that our feelings are not necessarily perceptions of the truth—they may be nothing more than the result of cultural conditioning. Thus when we hear it suggested that some element of our social code is *not* really the best, and we find ourselves instinctively resisting the suggestion, we might stop and remember this. Then we may be more open to discovering the truth, whatever that might be.

We can understand the appeal of Cultural Relativism, then, even though the theory has serious shortcomings. It is an attractive theory because it is based on a genuine insight—that many of the practices and attitudes we think so natural are really only cultural products. Moreover, keeping this insight firmly in view is important if we want to avoid arrogance and have open minds. These are important points, not to be taken lightly. But we can accept these points without going on to accept the whole theory.

NOTES

1. Herodotus, *The Histories,* translated by Aubrey de Selincourt, revised by A. R. Burn (Harmondsworth, Middlesex: Penguin Books, 1972), pp. 219–220.
2. Information about the Eskimos was taken from Peter Freuchen, *Book of the Eskimos* (New York: Fawcett, 1961); and E. Adamson Hoebel, *The Law of Primitive Man* (Cambridge: Harvard University Press, 1954), Chapter 5.
3. William Graham Sumner, *Folkways* (Boston: Ginn and Company, 1906), p. 28.
4. Hoebel, *The Law of Primitive Man*.
5. Herodotus, *The Histories*.

Foundations of the Metaphysics of Morals
Immanuel Kant

Everything in nature works according to laws. Rational beings alone have the faculty of acting according to the conception of laws, that is according to principles, i.e., have a will. Since the deduction of actions from principles requires reason, the will is nothing but practical reason. If reason infallibly determines the will, then the actions of such a being which are recognised as objectively necessary are subjectively necessary also, i.e., the will is a faculty to choose that only which reason independent of inclination recognises as practically necessary, i.e., as good. But if reason of itself does not sufficiently determine the will, if the latter is subject also to subjective conditions (particular impulses) which do not always coincide with the objective conditions; in a word, if the will does not in itself completely accord with reason (which is actually the case with men), then the actions which objectively are recognised as necessary are subjectively contingent, and the determination of such a will according to objective laws is obligation, that is to say, the relation of the objective laws to a will that is not thoroughly good is conceived as the determination of the will of a rational being by principles of reason, but which the will from its nature does not of necessity follow.

The conception of an objective principle, in so far as it is obligatory for a will, is called a command (of reason), and the formula of the command is called an imperative.

All imperatives are expressed by the word ought [or shall], and thereby indicate the relation of an objective law of reason to a will, which from its subjective constitution is not necessarily determined by it (an obligation). They say that something would be good to do or to forbear, but they say it to a will which does not always do a thing because it is conceived to be good to do it. That is practically good, however, which determines the will by means of the conceptions of reason, and consequently not from subjective causes, but objectively, that is on principles which are valid for every rational being as such. It is distinguished from the pleasant, as that which influences the will only by means of sensation from merely subjective causes, valid only for the sense of this or that one, and not as a principle of reason, which holds for every one.[1]

A perfectly good will would therefore be equally subject to objective laws (viz., laws of good), but could not be conceived as obliged thereby to act lawfully, because of itself from its subjective constitution it can only be determined by the conception of good. Therefore no imperatives hold for the Divine will, or in general for a holy will; ought is here out of place, because the volition is already of itself necessarily in unison with the law. Therefore imperatives are only formulae to express the relation of objective laws of all volition to the subjective imperfection of the will of this or that rational being, e.g., the human will.

Now all imperatives command either hypothetically or categorically. The former represent the practical necessity of a possible action as means to something else that is willed (or at least which one might possibly will). The categorical imperative would be that which represented an action as necessary of itself without reference to another end, i.e., as objectively necessary.

Since every practical law represents a possible action as good and, on this account, for a subject who is practically determinable by reason, necessary, all imperatives are formulae determining an action which is necessary according to the principle of a will good in some respects. If now the action is good only as a means to something else, then the imperative is hypothetical; if it is conceived as good in itself and consequently as being necessarily the principle of a will which of itself conforms to reason, then it is categorical.

Thus the imperative declares what action possible by me would be good and presents the practical rule in relation to a will which does not forthwith perform an action simply because it is good, whether because the subject does not always know that it is good, or because, even if it know this, yet its maxims might be opposed to the objective principles of practical reason.

Accordingly the hypothetical imperative only says that the action is good for some purpose, possible or actual. In the first case it is a problematical, in the second an assertorial practical principle. The categorical imperative which declares an action to be objectively necessary in itself without reference to any purpose, i.e., without any other end, is valid as an apodeictic (practical) principle.

Whatever is possible only by the power of some rational being may also be conceived as a possible purpose of some will; and therefore the principles of action as regards the means necessary to attain some possible purpose are in fact infinitely numerous. All sciences have a practical part, consisting of problems expressing that some end is possible for us and of imperatives directing how it may be attained. These may, therefore, be called in general imperatives of skill. Here there is no question whether the end is rational and good, but only what one must do in order to attain it. The precepts for the physician to make his patient thoroughly healthy, and for a poisoner to ensure certain death, are of equal value in this respect, that each serves to effect its purpose perfectly. Since in early youth it cannot be known what ends are likely to occur to us in the course of life, parents seek to have their children taught a great many things, and provide for their skill in the use of means for all

(continued)

Foundations of the Metaphysics of Morals   (*continued*)

sorts of arbitrary ends, of none of which can they determine whether it may not perhaps hereafter be an object to their pupil, but which it is at all events possible that he might aim at; and this anxiety is so great that they commonly neglect to form and correct their judgement on the value of the things which may be chosen as ends.

There is one end, however, which may be assumed to be actually such to all rational beings (so far as imperatives apply to them, viz., as dependent beings), and, therefore, one purpose which they not merely may have, but which we may with certainty assume that they all actually have by a natural necessity, and this is happiness. The hypothetical imperative which expresses the practical necessity of an action as means to the advancement of happiness is assertorial. We are not to present it as necessary for an uncertain and merely possible purpose, but for a purpose which we may presuppose with certainty and a priori in every man, because it belongs to his being. Now skill in the choice of means to his own greatest well-being may be called prudence,[2] in the narrowest sense. And thus the imperative which refers to the choice of means to one's own happiness, i.e., the precept of prudence, is still always hypothetical; the action is not commanded absolutely, but only as means to another purpose.

Finally, there is an imperative which commands a certain conduct immediately, without having as its condition any other purpose to be attained by it. This imperative is categorical. It concerns not the matter of the action, or its intended result, but its form and the principle of which it is itself a result; and what is essentially good in it consists in the mental disposition, let the consequence be what it may. This imperative may be called that of morality.

There is a marked distinction also between the volitions on these three sorts of principles in the dissimilarity of the obligation of the will. In order to mark this difference more clearly, I think they would be most suitably named in their order if we said they are either rules of skill, or counsels of prudence, or commands (laws) of morality. For it is law only that involves the conception of an unconditional and objective necessity, which is consequently universally valid; and commands are laws which must be obeyed, that is, must be followed, even in opposition to inclination. Counsels, indeed, involve necessity, but one which can only hold under a contingent subjective condition, viz., they depend on whether this or that man reckons this or that as part of his happiness; the categorical imperative, on the contrary, is not limited by any condition, and as being absolutely, although practically, necessary, may be quite properly called a command. We might also call the first kind of imperatives technical (belonging to art), the second pragmatic[3] (to welfare), the third moral (belonging to free conduct generally, that is, to morals).

Now arises the question, how are all these imperatives possible? This question does not seek to know how we can conceive the accomplishment of the action which the imperative ordains, but merely how we can conceive the obligation of the will which the imperative expresses. No special explanation is needed to show how an imperative of skill is possible. Whoever wills the end, wills also (so far as reason decides his conduct) the means in his power which are indispensably necessary thereto. This proposition is, as regards the volition, analytical; for, in willing an object as my effect, there is already thought the causality of myself as an acting cause, that is to say, the use of the means; and the imperative educes from the conception of volition of an end the conception of actions necessary to this end. Synthetical propositions must no doubt be employed in defining the means to a proposed end; but they do not concern the principle, the act of the will, but the object and its realization. For example, that in order to bisect a line on an unerring principle I must draw from its extremities two intersecting arcs; this no doubt is taught by mathematics only in synthetical propositions; but if I know that it is only by this process that the intended operation can be performed, then to say that, if I fully will the operation, I also will the action required for it, is an analytical proposition; for it is one and the same thing to conceive something as an effect which I can produce in a certain way, and to conceive myself as acting in this way.

If it were only equally easy to give a definite conception of happiness, the imperatives of prudence would correspond exactly with those of skill, and would likewise be analytical. For in this case as in that, it could be said: "Whoever wills the end, wills also (according to the dictate of reason necessarily) the indispensable means thereto which are in his power." But, unfortunately, the notion of happiness is so indefinite that although every man wishes to at it, yet he never can say definitely and consistently what it is that he really wishes and wills. The reason of this is that all the elements which belong to the notion of happiness are altogether empirical, i.e., they must be borrowed from experience, and nevertheless the idea of happiness requires an absolute whole, a maximum of welfare in my present and all future circumstances. Now it is impossible that the most clear-sighted and at the same time most powerful being (supposed finite) should frame to himself a definite conception of what he really wills in this. Does he will riches, how much anxiety, envy, and snares might he not thereby draw upon his shoulders? Does he will knowledge and discernment, perhaps it might prove to be only an eye so much the sharper to show him so much the more fearfully the evils that are now concealed from him, and that cannot be avoided, or to impose more wants on his desires, which already give him concern enough. Would he have long life? who guarantees to him that it would not be a long misery? would he at least have health? how often has uneasiness of the body restrained from excesses into which perfect health would have allowed one to fall? and so on. In short, he is unable, on any principle, to determine with certainty what would make him truly happy; because to do so he would need to be omniscient. We cannot therefore act on any definite principles to secure happiness, but only on empirical counsels, e.g., of regimen, frugality, courtesy, reserve, etc., which experience teaches do, on the average, most promote well-being. Hence it follows that the imperatives of prudence do not, strictly speaking, command at all, that is, they cannot present actions objectively as practically necessary; that they are rather to be regarded as counsels (consilia) than precepts of reason, that the problem to determine certainly and universally what action would promote the happiness of a rational being is completely insoluble, and consequently no imperative respecting it is possible which should, in the strict sense, command to do what makes happy; because happiness is not an ideal of reason but of imagination, resting solely on empirical grounds, and it is vain to expect that these should define an action by which one could attain the totality of a series of consequences which is really endless. This imperative of prudence would however be an analytical proposition if we assume that the means to happiness could be certainly assigned; for it is distinguished from the imperative of skill only by this, that in the latter the end is merely possible, in the former it is given; as however both only ordain the means to that which we suppose to be willed as an end, it follows that the imperative which ordains the willing of the means to him who wills the end is in both cases analytical. Thus there is no difficulty in regard to the possibility of an imperative of this kind either.

On the other hand, the question how the imperative of morality is possible, is undoubtedly one, the only one, demanding a solution, as this is not at all hypothetical, and the objective necessity which it presents cannot rest on any hypothesis, as is the case with the hypothetical imperatives. Only here we must never leave out of consideration that we cannot make out by any example, in other words empirically, whether there is such an imperative at all, but it is rather to be feared that all those which seem to be categorical may yet be at bottom hypothetical. For instance, when the precept is: "Thou shalt not promise deceitfully"; and it is assumed that the necessity of this is not a mere counsel to avoid some other evil, so that it should mean: "Thou shalt not make a lying promise, lest if it become known thou shouldst destroy thy credit," but that an action of this kind must be regarded as evil in itself, so that the imperative of the prohibition is categorical; then we cannot show with certainty in any example that the will was determined merely by the law, without any other spring of action, although it may appear to be so. For it is always possible that fear of disgrace, perhaps also obscure dread of other dangers, may have a secret influence on the will. Who can prove by experience the non-existence of a cause when all that experience tells us is that we do not perceive it? But in such a case the so-called moral imperative, which as such appears to be categorical and unconditional, would in reality be only a pragmatic precept, drawing our attention to our own interests and merely teaching us to take these into consideration.

We shall therefore have to investigate a priori the possibility of a categorical imperative, as we have not in this case the advantage of its reality being given in experience, so that [the elucidation of] its possibility should be requisite only for its explanation, not for its establishment. In the meantime it may be discerned beforehand that the categorical imperative alone has the purport of a practical law; all the rest may indeed be called principles of the will but not laws, since whatever is only necessary for the attainment of some arbitrary purpose may be considered as in itself contingent, and we can at any time be free from the precept if we give up the purpose; on

(continued)

Foundations of the Metaphysics of Morals (continued)

the contrary, the unconditional command leaves the will no liberty to choose the opposite; consequently it alone carries with it that necessity which we require in a law.

Secondly, in the case of this categorical imperative or law of morality, the difficulty (of discerning its possibility) is a very profound one. It is an a priori synthetical practical proposition;[4] and as there is so much difficulty in discerning the possibility of speculative propositions of this kind, it may readily be supposed that the difficulty will be no less with the practical.

In this problem we will first inquire whether the mere conception of a categorical imperative may not perhaps supply us also with the formula of it, containing the proposition which alone can be a categorical imperative; for even if we know the tenor of such an absolute command, yet how it is possible will require further special and laborious study, which we postpone to the last section.

When I conceive a hypothetical imperative, in general I do not know beforehand what it will contain until I am given the condition. But when I conceive a categorical imperative, I know at once what it contains. For as the imperative contains besides the law only the necessity that the maxims[5] shall conform to this law, while the law contains no conditions restricting it, there remains nothing but the general statement that the maxim of the action should conform to a universal law, and it is this conformity alone that the imperative properly represents as necessary.

There is therefore but one categorical imperative, namely, this: Act only on that maxim whereby thou canst at the same time will that it should become a universal law.

Now if all imperatives of duty can be deduced from this one imperative as from their principle, then, although it should remain undecided what is called duty is not merely a vain notion, yet at least we shall be able to show what we understand by it and what this notion means.

Since the universality of the law according to which effects are produced constitutes what is properly called nature in the most general sense (as to form), that is the existence of things so far as it is determined by general laws, the imperative of duty may be expressed thus: Act as if the maxim of thy action were to become by thy will a universal law of nature.

We will now enumerate a few duties, adopting the usual division of them into duties to ourselves and ourselves and to others, and into perfect and imperfect duties.[6]

1. A man reduced to despair by a series of misfortunes feels wearied of life, but is still so far in possession of his reason that he can ask himself whether it would not be contrary to his duty to himself to take his own life. Now he inquires whether the maxim of his action could become a universal law of nature. His maxim is: "From self-love I adopt it as a principle to shorten my life when its longer duration is likely to bring more evil than satisfaction." It is asked then simply whether this principle founded on self-love can become a universal law of nature. Now we see at once that a system of nature of which it should be a law to destroy life by means of the very feeling whose special nature it is to impel to the improvement of life would contradict itself and, therefore, could not exist as a system of nature; hence that maxim cannot possibly exist as a universal law of nature and, consequently, would be wholly inconsistent with the supreme principle of all duty.

2. Another finds himself forced by necessity to borrow money. He knows that he will not be able to repay it, but sees also that nothing will be lent to him unless he promises stoutly to repay it in a definite time. He desires to make this promise, but he has still so much conscience as to ask himself: "Is it not unlawful and inconsistent with duty to get out of a difficulty in this way?" Suppose however that he resolves to do so: then the maxim of his action would be expressed thus: "When I think myself in want of money, I will borrow money and promise to repay it, although I know that I never can do so." Now this principle of self-love or of one's own advantage may perhaps be consistent with my whole future welfare; but the question now is, "Is it right?" I change then the suggestion of self-love into a universal law, and state the question thus: "How would it be if my maxim were a universal law?" Then I see at once that it could never hold as a universal law of nature, but would necessarily contradict itself. For supposing it to be a universal law that everyone when he thinks himself in a difficulty should be able to promise whatever he pleases, with the purpose of not keeping his promise, the promise itself would become impossible, as well as the end that one might have in view in it, since no one would consider that anything was promised to him, but would ridicule all such statements as vain pretences.

3. A third finds in himself a talent which with the help of some culture might make him a useful man in many respects. But he finds himself in comfortable circumstances and prefers to indulge in pleasure rather than to take pains in enlarging and improving his happy natural capacities. He asks, however, whether his maxim of neglect of his natural gifts, besides agreeing with his inclination to indulgence, agrees also with what is called duty. He sees then that a system of nature could indeed subsist with such a universal law although men (like the South Sea islanders) should let their talents rest and resolve to devote their lives merely to idleness, amusement, and propagation of their species—in a word, to enjoyment; but he cannot possibly will that this should be a universal law of nature, or be implanted in us as such by a natural instinct. For, as a rational being, he necessarily wills that his faculties be developed, since they serve him and have been given him, for all sorts of possible purposes.
4. A fourth, who is in prosperity, while he sees that others have to contend with great wretchedness and that he could help them, thinks: "What concern is it of mine? Let everyone be as happy as Heaven pleases, or as be can make himself; I will take nothing from him nor even envy him, only I do not wish to contribute anything to his welfare or to his assistance in distress!" Now no doubt if such a mode of thinking were a universal law, the human race might very well subsist and doubtless even better than in a state in which everyone talks of sympathy and goodwill, or even takes care occasionally to put it into practice, but, on the other side, also cheats when he can, betrays the rights of men, or otherwise violates them. But although it is possible that a universal law of nature might exist in accordance with that maxim, it is impossible to will that such a principle should have the universal validity of a law of nature. For a will which resolved this would contradict itself, inasmuch as many cases might occur in which one would have need of the love and sympathy of others, and in which, by such a law of nature, sprung from his own will, he would deprive himself of all hope of the aid he desires.

These are a few of the many actual duties, or at least what we regard as such, which obviously fall into two classes on the one principle that we have laid down. We must be able to will that a maxim of our action should be a universal law. This is the canon of the moral appreciation of the action generally. Some actions are of such a character that their maxim cannot without contradiction be even conceived as a universal law of nature, far from it being possible that we should will that it should be so. In others this intrinsic impossibility is not found, but still it is impossible to will that their maxim should be raised to the universality of a law of nature, since such a will would contradict itself. It is easily seen that the former violate strict or rigorous (inflexible) duty; the latter only laxer (meritorious) duty. Thus it has been completely shown how all duties depend as regards the nature of the obligation (not the object of the action) on the same principle.

If now we attend to ourselves on occasion of any transgression of duty, we shall find that we in fact do not will that our maxim should be a universal law, for that is impossible for us; on the contrary, we will that the opposite should remain a universal law, only we assume the liberty of making an exception in our own favour or (just for this time only) in favour of our inclination. Consequently if we considered all cases from one and the same point of view, namely, that of reason, we should find a contradiction in our own will, namely, that a certain principle should be objectively necessary as a universal law, and yet subjectively should not be universal, but admit of exceptions. As however we at one moment regard our action from the point of view of a will wholly conformed to reason, and then again look at the same action from the point of view of a will affected by inclination, there is not really any contradiction, but an antagonism of inclination to the precept of reason, whereby the universality of the principle is changed into a mere generality, so that the practical principle of reason shall meet the maxim half way. Now, although this cannot be justified in our own impartial judgement, yet it proves that we do really recognise the validity of the categorical imperative and (with all respect for it) only allow ourselves a few exceptions, which we think unimportant and forced from us.

We have thus established at least this much, that if duty is a conception which is to have any import and real legislative authority for our actions, it can only be expressed in categorical and not at all in hypothetical imperatives. We have also, which is of great importance, exhibited clearly and definitely for every practical application the content of the categorical imperative, which must contain the principle of all duty if there is such a thing at all. We have not yet, however, advanced so far

(continued)

Foundations of the Metaphysics of Morals (*continued*)

as to prove a priori that there actually is such an imperative, that there is a practical law which commands absolutely of itself and without any other impulse, and that the following of this law is duty.

With the view of attaining to this, it is of extreme importance to remember that we must not allow ourselves to think of deducing the reality of this principle from the particular attributes of human nature. For duty is to be a practical, unconditional necessity of action; it must therefore hold for all rational beings (to whom an imperative can apply at all), and for this reason only be also a law for all human wills. On the contrary, whatever is deduced from the particular natural characteristics of humanity, from certain feelings and propensions, nay, even, if possible, from any particular tendency proper to human reason, and which need not necessarily hold for the will of every rational being; this may indeed supply us with a maxim, but not with a law; with a subjective principle on which we may have a propension and inclination to act, but not with an objective principle on which we should be enjoined to act, even though all our propensions, inclinations, and natural dispositions were opposed to it. In fact, the sublimity and intrinsic dignity of the command in duty are so much the more evident, the less the subjective impulses favour it and the more they oppose it, without being able in the slightest degree to weaken the obligation of the law or to diminish its validity.

Here then we see philosophy brought to a critical position, since it has to be firmly fixed, notwithstanding that it has nothing to support it in heaven or earth. Here it must show its purity as absolute director of its own laws, not the herald of those which are whispered to it by an implanted sense or who knows what tutelary nature. Although these may be better than nothing, yet they can never afford principles dictated by reason, which must have their source wholly a priori and thence their commanding authority, expecting everything from the supremacy of the law and the due respect for it, nothing from inclination, or else condemning the man to self-contempt and inward abhorrence.

Thus every empirical element is not only quite incapable of being an aid to the principle of morality, but is even highly prejudicial to the purity of morals, for the proper and inestimable worth of an absolutely good will consists just in this, that the principle of action is free from all influence of contingent grounds, which alone experience can furnish. We cannot too much or too often repeat our warning against this lax and even mean habit of thought which seeks for its principle amongst empirical motives and laws; for human reason in its weariness is glad to rest on this pillow, and in a dream of sweet illusions (in which, instead of Juno, it embraces a cloud) it substitutes for morality a bastard patched up from limbs of various derivation, which looks like anything one chooses to see in it, only not like virtue to one who has once beheld her in her true form.[7]

The question then is this: "Is it a necessary law for all rational beings that they should always judge of their actions by maxims of which they can themselves will that they should serve as universal laws?" If it is so, then it must be connected (altogether a priori) with the very conception of the will of a rational being generally. But in order to discover this connexion we must, however reluctantly, take a step into metaphysic, although into a domain of it which is distinct from speculative philosophy, namely, the metaphysic of morals. In a practical philosophy, where it is not the reasons of what happens that we have to ascertain, but the laws of what ought to happen, even although it never does, i.e., objective practical laws, there it is not necessary to inquire into the reasons why anything pleases or displeases, how the pleasure of mere sensation differs from taste, and whether the latter is distinct from a general satisfaction of reason; on what the feeling of pleasure or pain rests, and how from it desires and inclinations arise, and from these again maxims by the co-operation of reason: for all this belongs to an empirical psychology, which would constitute the second part of physics, if we regard physics as the philosophy of nature, so far as it is based on empirical laws. But here we are concerned with objective practical laws and, consequently, with the relation of the will to itself so far as it is determined by reason alone, in which case whatever has reference to anything empirical is necessarily excluded; since if reason of itself alone determines the conduct (and it is the possibility of this that we are now investigating), it must necessarily do so a priori.

The will is conceived as a faculty of determining oneself to action in accordance with the conception of certain laws. And such a faculty can be found only in rational beings. Now that which serves the will as the objective ground of its self-determination is the end, and, if this is assigned by reason alone, it must hold for all rational beings. On the other hand, that which merely contains the ground of possibility of the action of which the effect is the end, this is called the means. The subjective ground of the desire is the spring, the objective ground of the volition is the motive; hence the distinction between subjective ends which rest on springs, and objective ends which depend on motives valid for every rational being. Practical principles are formal when they abstract from all subjective ends; they are material when they assume these, and therefore particular springs of action. The ends which a rational being proposes to himself at pleasure as effects of his actions (material ends) are all only relative, for it is only their relation to the particular desires of the subject that gives them their worth, which therefore cannot furnish principles universal and necessary for all rational beings and for every volition, that is to say practical laws. Hence all these relative ends can give rise only to hypothetical imperatives.

Supposing, however, that there were something whose existence has in itself an absolute worth, something which, being an end in itself, could be a source of definite laws; then in this and this alone would lie the source of a possible categorical imperative, i.e., a practical law.

Now I say: man and generally any rational being exists as an end in himself, not merely as a means to be arbitrarily used by this or that will, but in all his actions, whether they concern himself or other rational beings must be always regarded at the same time as an end. All objects of the inclinations have a conditional worth, for if the inclinations and the wants founded on them did not exist, then their object would be without value. But the inclinations, themselves being sources of want, are so far from having an absolute worth for which they should be desired that on the contrary it must be the universal wish of every rational being to be wholly free from them. Thus, the worth of any object which is to be acquired by our action is always conditional. Beings whose existence depends not on our will but on nature's, have nevertheless, if they are irrational beings, only a relative value as means, and are therefore called things; rational beings, on the contrary, are called persons, because their very nature points them our as ends in themselves, that is as something which must not be used merely as means, and so far therefore restricts freedom of action (and is an object of respect). These, therefore, are not merely subjective ends whose existence has a worth for us as an effect of our action, but objective ends, that is, things whose existence is an end in itself; an end moreover for which no other can be substituted, which they should subserve merely as means, for otherwise nothing whatever would possess absolute worth; but if all worth were conditioned and therefore contingent, then there would be no supreme practical principle of reason whatever.

If then there is a supreme practical principle or, in respect of the human will, a categorical imperative, it must be one which, being drawn from the conception of that which is necessarily an end for everyone because it is an end in itself, constitutes an objective principle of will, and can therefore serve as a universal practical law. The foundation of this principle is: rational nature exists as an end in itself. Man necessarily conceives his own existence as being so; so far then this is a subjective principle of human actions. But every other rational being regards its existence similarly, just on the same rational principle that holds for me:[8] so that it is at the same time an objective principle, from which as a supreme practical law all laws of the will must be capable of being deduced. Accordingly the practical imperative will be as follows: So act as to treat humanity, whether in thine own person or in that of any other, in every case as an end withal, never as means only. We will now inquire whether this can be practically carried out.

To abide by the previous examples:

Firstly, under the head of necessary duty to oneself: He who contemplates suicide should ask himself whether his action can be consistent with the idea of humanity as an end in itself. If he destroys himself in order to escape from painful circumstances, he uses a person merely as a mean to maintain a tolerable condition up to the end of life. But a man is not a thing, that is to say, something which can be used merely as means, but must in all his actions be always considered as an end in himself. I cannot, therefore, dispose in any way of a man in my own person so as to mutilate him, to damage or kill him. (It belongs to ethics proper to define this principle more precisely, so as to avoid all misunderstanding, e.g., as to the amputation of the limbs in order to preserve myself, as to exposing my life to danger with a view to preserve it, etc. This question is therefore omitted here.)

Secondly, as regards necessary duties, or those of strict obligation, towards others: He who is thinking of making a lying promise to others will see at once that he would be using another man merely as a mean, without the latter containing at the same time the end in himself, For he whom I propose by such premise to use for my own purposes cannot possibly assent to my mode of acting towards him and, therefore, cannot himself contain the end of this action. This violation of the

(continued)

Foundations of the Metaphysics of Morals (*continued*)

principle of humanity in other men is more obvious if we take in examples of attacks on the freedom and property of others. For then it is clear that he who transgresses the rights of men intends to use the person of others merely as a means, without considering that as rational beings they ought always to be esteemed also as ends, that is, as beings who must be capable of containing in themselves the end of the very same action.[9]

Thirdly, as regards contingent (meritorious) duties to oneself: It is not enough that the action does not violate humanity in our own person as an end in itself, it must also harmonize with it. Now there are in humanity capacities of greater perfection, which belong to the end that nature has in view in regard to humanity in ourselves as the subject: to neglect these might perhaps be consistent with the maintenance of humanity as an end in itself, but not with the advancement of this end.

Fourthly, as regards meritorious duties towards others: The natural end which all men have is their own happiness. Now humanity might indeed subsist, although no one should contribute anything to the happiness of others, provided he did not intentionally withdraw anything from it; but after all this would only harmonize negatively not positively with humanity as an end in itself, if every one does not also endeavour, as far as in him lies, to forward the ends of others. For the ends of any subject which is an end in himself ought as far as possible to be my ends also, if that conception is to have its full effect with me.

This principle, that humanity and generally every rational nature is an end in itself (which is the supreme limiting condition of every man's freedom of action), is not borrowed from experience, firstly, because it is universal, applying as it does to all rational beings whatever, and experience is not capable of determining anything about them; secondly, because it does not present humanity as an end to men (subjectively), that is as an object which men do of themselves actually adopt as an end; but as an objective end, which must as a law constitute the supreme limiting condition of all our subjective ends, let them be what we will; it must therefore spring from pure reason. In fact the objective principle of all practical legislation lies (according to the first principle) in the rule and its form of universality which makes it capable of being a law (say, e.g., a law of nature); but the subjective principle is in the end; now by the second principle the subject of all ends is each rational being, inasmuch as it is an end in itself. Hence follows the third practical principle of the will, which is the ultimate condition of its harmony with universal practical reason, viz: the idea of the will of every rational being as a universally legislative will.

On this principle all maxims are rejected which are inconsistent with the will being itself universal legislator. Thus the will is not subject simply to the law, but so subject that it must be regarded as itself giving the law and, on this ground only, subject to the law (of which it can regard itself as the author)

In the previous imperatives, namely, that based on the conception of the conformity of actions to general laws, as in a physical system of nature, and that based on the universal prerogative of rational beings as ends in themselves—these imperatives, just because they were conceived as categorical, excluded from any share in their authority all admixture of any interest as a spring of action; they were, however, only assumed to be categorical, because such an assumption was necessary to explain the conception of duty. But we could not prove independently that there are practical propositions which command categorically, nor can it be proved in this section; one thing, however, could be done, namely, to indicate in the imperative itself, by some determinate expression, that in the case of volition from duty all interest as renounced, which is the specific criterion of categorical as distinguished from hypothetical imperatives. This is done in the present (third) formula of the principle, namely, in the idea of the will of every rational being as a universally legislating will.

For although a will which is subject to laws may be attached to this law by means of an interest, yet a will which is itself a supreme lawgiver so far as it is such cannot possibly depend on any interest, since a would so dependent would itself still need another law restricting the interest of us self-love by the condition that it should be valid as universal law.

Thus the principle that every human will is a will which in all its maxims gives universal laws,[10] provided it be otherwise justified, would be very well adapted to be the categorical imperative, in this respect, namely, that just because of the idea of universal legislation it is not based on interest, and therefore it alone among all possible imperatives can be unconditional. Or still better, converting the proposition, if there is a categorical imperative (i.e., a law for the will of every rational being), it can only command that everything be done from maxims of one's will regarded as a will which could at the same time will that it should itself give universal laws, for in that case only the practical principle and the imperative which it obeys are unconditional, since they cannot be based on any interest.

NOTES

1. The dependence of the desires on sensations is called inclination, and this accordingly always indicates a want. The dependence of a contingently determinable will on principles of reason is called an interest. This therefore, is found only in the case of a dependent will which does not always of itself conform to reason; in the Divine will we cannot conceive any interest. But the human will can also take an interest in a thing without therefore acting from interest. The former signifies the practical interest in the action, the latter the pathological in the object of the action. The former indicates only dependence of the will on principles of reason in themselves; the second, dependence on principles of reason for the sake of inclination, reason supplying only the practical rules how the requirement of the inclination may be satisfied. In the first case the action interests me; in the second the object of the action (because it is pleasant to me). We have seen in the first section that in an action done from duty we must look not to the interest in the object, but only to that in the action itself, and in its rational principle (viz., the law).
2. The word prudence is taken in two senses: in the one it may bear the name of knowledge of the world, in the other that of private prudence. The former is a man's ability to influence others so as to use them for his own purposes. The latter is the sagacity to combine all these purposes for his own lasting benefit. This latter is properly that to which the value even of the former is reduced, and when a man is prudent in the former sense, but not in the latter, we might better say of him that he is clever and cunning, but, on the whole, imprudent.
3. It seems to me that the proper signification of the word pragmatic may be most accurately defined in this way. For sanctions are called pragmatic which flow properly not from the law of the states as necessary enactments, but from precaution for the general welfare. A history is composed pragmatically when it teaches prudence, i.e., instructs the world how it can provide for its interests better, or at least as well as, the men of former time.
4. I connect the act with the will without presupposing any condition resulting from any inclination, but a priori, and therefore necessarily (though only objectively, i.e., assuming the idea of a reason possessing full power over all subjective motives). This is accordingly a practical proposition which does not deduce the willing of an action by mere analysis from another already presupposed (for we have not such a perfect will), but connects it immediately with the conception of the will of a rational being, as something not contained in it.
5. A maxim is a subjective principle of action, and must be distinguished from the objective principle, namely, practical law. The former contains the practical rule set by reason according to the conditions of the subject (often its ignorance or its inclinations), so that it is the principle on which the subject acts; but the law is the objective principle valid for every rational being, and is the principle on which it ought to act that is an imperative.
6. It must be noted here that I reserve the division of duties for a future metaphysic of morals; so that I give it here only as an arbitrary one (in order to arrange my examples). For the rest, I understand by a perfect duty one that admits no exception in favour of inclination and then I have not merely external but also internal perfect duties. This is contrary to the use of the word adopted in the schools; but I do not intend to justify there, as it is all one for my purpose whether it is admitted or not.
7. To behold virtue in her proper form is nothing else but to contemplate morality stripped of all admixture of sensible things and of every spurious ornament of reward or self-love. How much she then eclipses everything else that appears charming to the affections, every one may readily perceive with the least exertion of his reason, if it be not wholly spoiled for abstraction.
8. This proposition is here stated as a postulate. The ground of it will found in the concluding section.
9. Let it not be thought that the common "quod tibia non vis fieri, etc." could serve here as the rule or principle. For it is only a deduction from the former, though with several limitations; it cannot be a universal law, for it does not contain the principle of duties to oneself, nor of the duties of benevolence to others (for many a one would gladly consent that others should not benefit him, provided only that he might be excused from showing benevolence to them), nor finally that of duties of strict obligation to one another, for on this principle the criminal might argue against the judge who punishes him, and so on.
10. http://www.grtbooks.com/exitfram.asp?idx=2&yr=1724&caa=SA&at=I&ref=kant&URL= http://www.constitution.org/kant/metamora.htm

An Enquiry Concerning the Principles of Morals
David Hume

Section I. Of the General Principles of Morals

Disputes with men, pertinaciously obstinate in their principles, are, of all others, the most irksome; except, perhaps, those with persons entirely disingenuous, who really do not believe the opinions they defend, but engage in the controversy, from affectation, from a spirit of opposition, or from a desire of showing wit and ingenuity, superior to the rest of mankind. The same blind adherence to their own arguments is to be expected in both; the same contempt of their antagonists; and the same passionate vehemence, in inforcing sophistry and falsehood. And as reasoning is not the source, whence either disputant derives his tenets; it is in vain to expect, that any logic, which speaks not to the affections, will ever engage him to embrace sounder principles.

Those who have denied the reality of moral distinctions, may be ranked among the disingenuous disputants; nor is it conceivable, that any human creature could ever seriously believe, that all characters and actions were alike entitled to the affection and regard of every one. The difference, which nature has placed between one man and another, is so wide, and this difference is still so much farther widened, by education, example, and habit, that, where the opposite extremes come at once under our apprehension, there is no scepticism so scrupulous, and scarce any assurance so determined, as absolutely to deny all distinction between them. Let a man's insensibility be ever so great, he must often be touched with the images of RIGHT and WRONG; and let his prejudices be ever so obstinate, he must observe, that others are susceptible of like impressions. The only way, therefore, of converting an antagonist of this kind, is to leave him to himself. For, finding that no body keeps up the controversy with him, it is probable he will, at last, of himself, from mere weariness, come over to the side of common sense and reason.

There has been a controversy started of late, much better worth examination, concerning the general foundation of MORALS; whether they be derived from REASON, or from SENTIMENT; whether we attain the knowledge of them by a chain of argument and induction, or by an immediate feeling and finer internal sense; whether, like all sound judgment of truth and falsehood, they should be the same to every rational intelligent being; or whether, like the perception of beauty and deformity, they be founded entirely on the particular fabric and constitution of the human species.

The ancient philosophers, though they often affirm, that virtue is nothing but conformity to reason, yet, in general, seem to consider morals as deriving their existence from taste and sentiment. On the other hand, our modern enquirers, though they also talk much of the beauty of virtue, and deformity of vice, yet have commonly endeavoured to account for these distinctions by metaphysical reasonings, and by deductions from the most abstract principles of the understanding. Such confusion reigned in these subjects, that an opposition of the greatest consequence could prevail between one system and another, and even in the parts of almost each individual system; and yet no body, till very lately, was ever sensible of it. The elegant Lord SHAFTESBURY, who first gave occasion to remark this distinction, and who, in general, adhered to the principles of the ancients, is not, himself, entirely free from the same confusion.

It must be acknowledged, that both sides of the question are susceptible of specious arguments. Moral distinctions, it may be said, are discernible by pure *reason:* Else, whence the many disputes that reign in common life, as well as in philosophy, with regard to this subject: The long chain of proofs often produced on both sides; the examples cited, the authorities appealed to, the analogies employed, the fallacies detected, the inferences drawn, and the several conclusions adjusted to their proper principles. Truth is disputable; not taste: What exists in the nature of things is the standard of our judgment; what each man feels within himself is the standard of sentiment. Propositions in geometry may be proved, systems in physics may be controverted; but the harmony of verse, the tenderness of passion, the brilliancy of wit, must give immediate pleasure. No man reasons concerning another's beauty; but frequently concerning the justice or injustice of his actions. In every criminal trial the first object of the prisoner is to disprove the facts alleged, and deny the actions imputed to him: The second to prove, that, even if these actions were real, they might be justified, as innocent and lawful. It is confessedly by deductions of the understanding, that the first point is ascertained: How can we suppose that a different faculty of the mind is employed in fixing the other?

On the other hand, those who would resolve all moral determinations into *sentiment*, may endeavour to show, that it is impossible for reason ever to draw conclusions of this nature. To virtue, say they, it belongs to be *amiable*, and vice *odious*. This forms their very nature or essence. But can reason or argumentation distribute these different epithets to any subjects, and pronounce before-hand, that this must produce love, and that hatred? Or what other reason can we ever assign for these affections, but the original fabric and formation of the human mind, which is naturally adapted to receive them?

The end of all moral speculations is to teach us our duty; and, by proper representations of the deformity of vice and beauty of virtue, beget correspondent habits, and engage us to avoid the one, and embrace the other. But is this ever to be expected from inferences and conclusions of the understanding, which of themselves have no hold of the affections, or set in motion the active powers of men? They discover truths: But where the truths which they discover are indifferent, and beget no desire or aversion, they can have no influence on conduct and behaviour. What is honourable, what is fair, what is becoming, what is noble, what is generous, takes possession of the heart, and animates us to embrace and maintain it. What is intelligible, what is evident, what is probable, what is true, procures only the cool assent of the understanding; and gratifying a speculative curiosity, puts an end to our researches.

Extinguish all the warm feelings and prepossessions in favour of virtue, and all disgust or aversion to vice: Render men totally indifferent towards these distinctions; and morality is no longer a practical study, nor has any tendency to regulate our lives and actions.

These arguments on each side (and many more might be produced) are so plausible, that I am apt to suspect, they may, the one as well as the other, be solid and satisfactory, and that *reason* and *sentiment* concur in almost all moral determinations and conclusions. The final sentence, it is probable, which pronounces characters and actions amiable or odious, praise-worthy or blameable; that which stamps on them the mark of honour or infamy, approbation or censure; that which renders morality an active principle, and constitutes virtue our happiness, and vice our misery: It is probable, I say, that this final sentence depends on some internal sense or feeling, which nature has made universal in the whole species. For what else can have an influence of this nature? But in order to pave the way for such a sentiment, and give a proper discernment of its object, it is often necessary, we find, that much reasoning should precede, that nice distinctions be made, just conclusions drawn, distant comparisons formed, complicated relations examined, and general facts fixed and ascertained. Some species of beauty, especially the natural kinds, on their first appearance, command our affection and approbation; and where they fail of this effect, it is impossible for any reasoning to redress their influence, or adapt them better to our taste and sentiment. But in many orders of beauty, particularly those of the finer arts, it is requisite to employ much reasoning, in order to feel the proper sentiment; and a false relish may frequently be corrected by argument and reflection. There are just grounds to conclude, that moral beauty partakes much of this latter species, and demands the assistance of our intellectual faculties, in order to give it a suitable influence on the human mind.

But though this question, concerning the general principles of morals, be curious and important, it is needless for us, at present, to employ farther care in our researches concerning it. For if we can be so happy, in the course of this enquiry, as to discover the true origin of morals, it will then easily appear how far either sentiment or reason enters into all determinations of this nature.[1] In order to attain this purpose, we shall endeavour to follow a very simple method: We shall analyse that complication of mental qualities, which form what, in common life, we call PERSONAL MERIT: We shall consider every attribute of the mind, which renders a man an object either of esteem and affection, or of hatred and contempt; every habit or sentiment or faculty, which, if ascribed to any person, implies either praise or blame, and may enter into any panegyric or satire of his character and manners. The quick sensibility, which, on this head, is so universal among mankind, gives a philosopher sufficient assurance, that he can never be considerably mistaken in framing the catalogue, or incur any danger of misplacing the objects of his contemplation: He needs only enter into his own breast for a moment, and consider whether or not he should desire to have this or that quality ascribed to him, and whether such or such an imputation would proceed from a friend or an enemy. The very nature of language guides us almost infallibly in forming a judgment of this nature; and as every tongue possesses one set of words which are taken in a good sense, and another in

(continued)

An Enquiry Concerning the Principles of Morals   (continued)

the opposite, the least acquaintance with the idiom suffices, without any reasoning, to direct us in collecting and arranging the estimable or blameable qualities of men. The only object of reasoning is to discover the circumstances on both sides, which are common to these qualities; to observe that particular in which the estimable qualities agree on the one hand, and the blameable on the other; and thence to reach the foundation of ethics, and find those universal principles, from which all censure or approbation is ultimately derived. As this is a question of fact, not of abstract science, we can only expect success, by following the experimental method, and deducing general maxims from a comparison of particular instances. The other scientific method, where a general abstract principle is first established, and is afterwards branched out into a variety of inferences and conclusions, may be more perfect in itself, but suits less the imperfection of human nature, and is a common source of illusion and mistake in this as well as in other subjects. Men are now cured of their passion for hypotheses and systems in natural philosophy, and will hearken to no arguments but those which are derived from experience. It is full time they should attempt a like reformation in all moral disquisitions; and reject every system of ethics, however subtle or ingenious, which is not founded on fact and observation.

We shall begin our enquiry on this head by the consideration of social virtues, benevolence and justice: The explication of them will probably give us an opening by which others may be accounted for.

Section II. Of Benevolence

Part I

It may be esteemed, perhaps, a superfluous task to prove, that the benevolent or softer affections are ESTIMABLE; and wherever they appear, engage the approbation, and good-will of mankind. The epithets *sociable, good-natured, humane, merciful, grateful, friendly, generous, beneficent*, or their equivalents, are known in all languages, and universally express the highest merit, which *human nature* is capable of attaining. Where these amiable qualities are attended with birth and power and eminent abilities, and display themselves in the good government or useful instruction of mankind, they seem even to raise the possessors of them above the rank of *human nature*, and make them approach in some measure to the divine. Exalted capacity, undaunted courage, prosperous success; these may only expose a hero or politician to the envy or ill-will of the public: But as soon as the praises are added of humane and beneficent; when instances are displayed of lenity, tenderness, or friendship: envy itself is silent, or joins the general voice of approbation and applause.

Part II

We may observe, that, in displaying the praises of any humane, beneficent man, there is one circumstance which never fails to be amply insisted on, namely, the happiness and satisfaction, derived to society from his intercourse and good offices. To his parents, we are apt to say, he endears himself by his pious attachment and duteous care, still more than by the connexions of nature. His children never feel his authority, but when employed for their advantage. With him, the ties of love are consolidated by beneficence and friendship. The ties of friendship approach, in a fond observance of each obliging office, to those of love and inclination. His domestics and dependants have in him a sure resource; and no longer dread the power of fortune, but so far as she exercises it over him. From him the hungry receive food, the naked cloathing, the ignorant and slothful skill and industry. Like the sun, an inferior minister of providence, he cheers, invigorates, and sustains the surrounding world.

If confined to private life, the sphere of his activity is narrower; but his influence is all benign and gentle. If exalted into a higher station, mankind and posterity reap the fruit of his labours.

As these topics of praise never fail to be employed, and with success, where we would inspire esteem for any one; may it not thence be concluded, that the UTILITY, resulting from the social virtues, forms, at least, a *part* of their merit, and is one source of that approbation and regard so universally paid to them?

In all determinations of morality, this circumstance of public utility is ever principally in view; and wherever disputes arise, either in philosophy or common life, concerning the bounds of duty, the question cannot, by any means, be decided with greater certainty, than by ascertaining, on any side, the true interests of mankind. If any false opinion, embraced from appearances, has been found to prevail; as soon as farther experience and sounder reasoning have given us juster notions of human affairs; we retract our first sentiment, and adjust anew the boundaries of moral good and evil.

Giving alms to common beggars is naturally praised; because it seems to carry relief to the distressed and indigent: But when we observe the encouragement thence arising to idleness and debauchery, we regard that species of charity rather as a weakness than a virtue.

Tyrannicide, or the assassination of usurpers and oppressive princes, was highly extolled in ancient times; because it both freed mankind from many of these monsters, and seemed to keep the others in awe, whom the sword or poinard could not reach. But history and experience having since convinced us, that this practice encreases the jealousy and cruelty of princes, a Timoleon and a Brutus, though treated with indulgence on account of the prejudices of their times, are now considered as very improper models for imitation.

Liberality in princes is regarded as a mark of beneficence: But when it occurs, that the homely bread of the honest and industrious is often thereby converted into delicious cates for the idle and the prodigal, we soon retract our heedless praises. The regrets of a prince, for having lost a day, were noble and generous: But had he intended to have spent it in acts of generosity to his greedy courtiers, it was better lost than misemployed after that manner.

Luxury, or a refinement on the pleasures and conveniencies of life, had long been supposed the source of every corruption in government, and the immediate cause of faction, sedition, civil wars, and the total loss of liberty. It was, therefore, universally regarded as a vice, and was an object of declamation to all satyrists, and severe moralists. Those, who prove, or attempt to prove, that such refinements rather tend to the increase of industry, civility, and arts, regulate anew our *moral* as well as *political* sentiments, and represent, as laudable or innocent, what had formerly been regarded as pernicious and blameable.

Upon the whole, then, it seems undeniable, *that* nothing can bestow more merit on any human creature than the sentiment of benevolence in an eminent degree; and *that* a *part*, at least, of its merit arises from its tendency to promote the interests of our species, and bestow happiness on human society. We carry our view into the salutary consequences of such a character and disposition; and whatever has so benign an influence, and forwards so desirable an end, is beheld with complacency and pleasure. The social virtues are never regarded without their beneficial tendencies, nor viewed as barren and unfruitful. The happiness of mankind, the order of society, the harmony of families, the mutual support of friends, are always considered as the result of their gentle dominion over the breasts of men.

How considerable a *part* of their merit we ought to ascribe to their utility, will better appear from future disquisitions;[8] as well as the reason, why this circumstance has such a command over our esteem and approbation.[9]

Section III. Of Justice

Part I

That Justice is useful to society, and consequently that *part* of its merit, at least, must arise from that consideration, it would be a superfluous undertaking to prove. That public utility is the *sole* origin of justice, and that reflections on the beneficial consequences of this virtue are the *sole* foundation of its merit; this proposition, being more curious and important, will better deserve our examination and enquiry.

Let us suppose, that nature has bestowed on the human race such profuse *abundance* of all *external* conveniences, that, without any uncertainty in the event, without any care or industry on our part, every individual finds himself fully provided with whatever his most voracious appetites can want, or luxurious imagination wish or desire. His natural beauty, we shall suppose, surpasses all acquired ornaments: The perpetual clemency of the seasons renders useless all cloaths or covering: The raw herbage affords him the most delicious fare; the clear fountain, the richest beverage. No laborious occupation required: No tillage: No navigation. Music, poetry, and contemplation, form his sole business: Conversation, mirth, and friendship his sole amusement.

(continued)

An Enquiry Concerning the Principles of Morals   (continued)

It seems evident, that, in such a happy state, every other social virtue would flourish, and receive tenfold encrease; but the cautious, jealous virtue of justice would never once have been dreamed of. For what purpose make a partition of goods, where every one has already more than enough? Why give rise to property, where there cannot possibly be any injury? Why call this object *mine*, when, upon the seizing of it by another, I need but stretch out my hand to possess myself of what is equally valuable? Justice, in that case, being totally USELESS, would be an idle ceremonial, and could never possibly have place in the catalogue of virtues.

We see, even in the present necessitous condition of mankind, that, wherever any benefit is bestowed by nature in an unlimited abundance, we leave it always in common among the whole human race, and make no subdivisions of right and property. Water and air, though the most necessary of all objects, are not challenged as the property of individuals; nor can any man commit injustice by the most lavish use and enjoyment of these blessings. In fertile extensive countries, with few inhabitants, land is regarded on the same footing. And no topic is so much insisted on by those, who defend the liberty of the seas, as the unexhausted use of them in navigation. Were the advantages, procured by navigation, as inexhaustible, these reasoners had never had any adversaries to refute; nor had any claims ever been advanced of a separate, exclusive dominion over the ocean.

It may happen, in some countries, at some periods, that there be established a property in water, none in land; if the latter be in greater abundance than can be used by the inhabitants, and the former be found, with difficulty, and in very small quantities.

Again; suppose, that, though the necessities of human race continue the same as at present, yet the mind is so enlarged, and so replete with friendship and generosity, that every man has the utmost tenderness for every man, and feels no more concern for his own interest than for that of his fellows: It seems evident, that the USE of justice would, in this case, be suspended by such an extensive benevolence, nor would the divisions and barriers of property and obligation have ever been thought of. Why should I bind another, by a deed or promise, to do me any good office, when I know that he is already prompted, by the strongest inclination, to seek my happiness, and would, of himself, perform the desired service; except the hurt, he thereby receives, be greater than the benefit accruing to me? in which case, he knows, that, from my innate humanity and friendship, I should be the first to oppose myself to his imprudent generosity. Why raise land-marks between my neighbour's field and mine, when my heart has made no division between our interests; but shares all his joys and sorrows with the same force and vivacity as if originally my own? Every man, upon this supposition, being a second self to another, would trust all his interests to the discretion of every man; without jealousy, without partition, without distinction. And the whole human race would form only one family; where all would lie in common, and be used freely, without regard to property; but cautiously too, with as entire regard to the necessities of each individual, as if our own interests were most intimately concerned.

In the present disposition of the human heart, it would, perhaps, be difficult to find compleat instances of such enlarged affections; but still we may observe, that the case of families approaches towards it; and the stronger the mutual benevolence is among the individuals, the nearer it approaches; till all distinction of property be, in a great measure, lost and confounded among them. Between married persons, the cement of friendship is by the laws supposed so strong as to abolish all division of possessions: and has often, in reality, the force ascribed to it. And it is observable, that, during the ardour of new enthusiasms, when every principle is inflamed into extravagance, the community of goods has frequently been attempted: and nothing but experience of its inconveniencies, from the returning or disguised selfishness of men, could make the imprudent fanatics adopt anew the ideas of justice and of separate property. So true is it, that this virtue derives its existence entirely from its necessary *use* to the intercourse and social state of mankind.

To make this truth more evident, let us reverse the foregoing suppositions; and carrying every thing to the opposite extreme, consider what would be the effect of these new situations. Suppose a society to fall into such want of all common necessaries, that the utmost frugality and industry cannot preserve the greater number from perishing, and the whole from extreme misery: It will readily, I believe, be admitted, that the strict laws of justice are suspended, in such a pressing emergence, and give place to the stronger motives of necessity and self-preservation. Is it any crime, after a shipwreck, to seize whatever means or instrument of safety one can lay hold of, without regard to former limitations of property? Or if a city besieged were perishing with hunger; can we imagine, that men will see any means of preservation before them, and lose their lives, from a scrupulous regard to what, in other situations, would be the rules of equity and justice? The USE and TENDENCY of that virtue is to procure happiness and security, by preserving order in society: But where the society is ready to perish from extreme necessity, no greater evil can be dreaded from violence and injustice; and every man may now provide for himself by all the means, which prudence can dictate, or humanity permit. The public, even in less urgent necessities, opens granaries, without the consent of proprietors; as justly supposing, that the authority of magistracy may, consistent with equity, extend so far: But were any number of men to assemble, without the tye of laws or civil jurisdiction; would an equal partition of bread in a famine, though effected by power and even violence, be regarded as criminal or injurious?

Suppose likewise, that it should be a virtuous man's fate to fall into the society of ruffians, remote from the protection of laws and government; what conduct must he embrace in that melancholy situation? He sees such a desperate rapaciousness prevail; such a disregard to equity, such contempt of order, such stupid blindness to future consequences, as must immediately have the most tragical conclusion, and must terminate in destruction to the greater number, and in a total dissolution of society to the rest. He, mean while, can have no other expedient than to arm himself, to whomever the sword he seizes, or the buckler, may belong: To make provision of all means of defence and security: And his particular regard to justice being no longer of USE to his own safety or that of others, he must consult the dictates of self-preservation alone, without concern for those who no longer merit his care and attention.

When any man, even in political society, renders himself, by his crimes, obnoxious to the public, he is punished by the laws in his goods and person; that is, the ordinary rules of justice are, with regard to him, suspended for a moment, and it becomes equitable to inflict on him, for the *benefit* of society, what, otherwise, he could not suffer without wrong or injury.

The rage and violence of public war; what is it but a suspension of justice among the warring parties, who perceive, that this virtue is now no longer of any *use* or advantage to them? The laws of war, which then succeed to those of equity and justice, are rules calculated for the *advantage* and *utility* of that particular state, in which men are now placed. And were a civilized nation engaged with barbarians, who observed no rules even of war; the former must also suspend their observance of them, where they no longer serve to any purpose; and must render every action or rencounter as bloody and pernicious as possible to the first aggressors.

Thus, the rules of equity or justice depend entirely on the particular state and condition, in which men are placed, and owe their origin and existence to that UTILITY, which results to the public from their strict and regular observance. Reverse, in any considerable circumstance, the condition of men: Produce extreme abundance or extreme necessity: Implant in the human breast perfect moderation and humanity, or perfect rapaciousness and malice: By rendering justice totally *useless*, you thereby totally destroy its essence, and suspend its obligation upon mankind.

The common situation of society is a medium amidst all these extremes. We are naturally partial to ourselves, and to our friends; but are capable of learning the advantage resulting from a more equitable conduct. Few enjoyments are given us from the open and liberal hand of nature; but by art, labour, and industry, we can extract them in great abundance. Hence the ideas of property become necessary in all civil society: Hence justice derives its usefulness to the public: And hence alone arises its merit and moral obligation.

These conclusions are so natural and obvious, that they have not escaped even the poets, in their descriptions of the felicity, attending the golden age or the reign of SATURN. The seasons, in that first period of nature, were so temperate, if we credit these agreeable fictions, that there was no necessity for men to provide themselves with cloaths and houses, as a security against the violence of heat and cold: The rivers flowed with wine and milk: The oaks yielded honey; and nature spontaneously produced her greatest delicacies. Nor were these the chief advantages of that happy age. Tempests were not alone removed from nature; but those more furious tempests were unknown to human breasts, which now cause such uproar, and engender such confusion. Avarice, ambition, cruelty, selfishness, were never heard of: Cordial affection, compassion, sympathy, were the only movements with which the mind was yet acquainted. Even the punctilious distinction of

(continued)

An Enquiry Concerning the Principles of Morals   (*continued*)

mine and *thine* was banished from among that happy race of mortals, and carried with it the very notion of property and obligation, justice and injustice.

This *poetical* fiction of the *golden age* is, in some respects, of a piece with the *philosophical* fiction of the *state of nature*; only that the former is represented as the most charming and most peaceable condition, which can possibly be imagined; whereas the latter is painted out as a state of mutual war and violence, attended with the most extreme necessity. On the first origin of mankind, we are told, their ignorance and savage nature were so prevalent, that they could give no mutual trust, but must each depend upon himself, and his own force or cunning for protection and security. No law was heard of: No rule of justice known: No distinction of property regarded: Power was the only measure of right; and a perpetual war of all against all was the result of men's untamed selfishness and barbarity.[11]

Whether such a condition of human nature could ever exist, or if it did, could continue so long as to merit the appellation of a *state*, may justly be doubted. Men are necessarily born in a family-society, at least; and are trained up by their parents to some rule of conduct and behaviour. But this must be admitted, that, if such a state of mutual war and violence was ever real, the suspension of all laws of justice, from their absolute inutility, is a necessary and infallible consequence.

The more we vary our views of human life, and the newer and more unusual the lights are, in which we survey it, the more shall we be convinced, that the origin here assigned for the virtue of justice is real and satisfactory.

Were there a species of creatures, intermingled with men, which, though rational, were possessed of such inferior strength, both of body and mind, that they were incapable of all resistance, and could never, upon the highest provocation, make us feel the effects of their resentment; the necessary consequence, I think, is, that we should be bound, by the laws of humanity, to give gentle usage to these creatures, but should not, properly speaking, lie under any restraint of justice with regard to them, nor could they possess any right or property, exclusive of such arbitrary lords. Our intercourse with them could not be called society, which supposes a degree of equality; but absolute command on the one side, and servile obedience on the other. Whatever we covet, they must instantly resign: Our permission is the only tenure, by which they hold their possessions: Our compassion and kindness the only check, by which they curb our lawless will: And as no inconvenience ever results from the exercise of a power, so firmly established in nature, the restraints of justice and property, being totally *useless*, would never have place in so unequal a confederacy.

This is plainly the situation of men, with regard to animals; and how far these may be said to possess reason, I leave it to others to determine. The great superiority of civilized EUROPEANS above barbarous INDIANS, tempted us to imagine ourselves on the same footing with regard to them, and made us throw off all restraints of justice, and even of humanity, in our treatment of them. In many nations, the female sex are reduced to like slavery, and are rendered incapable of all property, in opposition to their lordly masters. But though the males, when united, have, in all countries, bodily force sufficient to maintain this severe tyranny, yet such are the insinuation, address, and charms of their fair companions, that women are commonly able to break the confederacy, and share with the other sex in all the rights and privileges of society.

Were the human species so framed by nature as that each individual possessed within himself every faculty, requisite both for his own preservation and for the propagation of his kind: Were all society and intercourse cut off between man and man, by the primary intention of the supreme Creator: It seems evident, that so solitary a being would be as much incapable of justice, as of social discourse and conversation. Where mutual regards and forbearance serve to no manner of purpose, they would never direct the conduct of any reasonable man. The headlong course of the passions would be checked by no reflection on future consequences. And as each man is here supposed to love himself alone, and to depend only on himself and his own activity for safety and happiness, he would, on every occasion to the utmost of his power, challenge the preference above every other being, to none of which he is bound by any ties, either of nature or of interest.

But suppose the conjunction of the sexes to be established in nature, a family immediately arises; and particular rules being found requisite for its subsistence, these are immediately embraced; though without comprehending the rest of mankind within their prescriptions. Suppose, that several families unite together into one society, which is totally disjoined from all others, the rules, which preserve peace and order, enlarge themselves to the utmost extent of that society; but becoming then entirely useless, lose their force when carried one step farther. But again suppose, that several distinct societies maintain a kind of intercourse for mutual convenience and advantage, the boundaries of justice still grow larger, in proportion to the largeness of men's views, and the force of their mutual connexions. History, experience, reason sufficiently instruct us in this natural progress of human sentiments, and in the gradual enlargement of our regards to justice, in proportion as we become acquainted with the extensive utility of that virtue.

Appendix I
Concerning Moral Sentiment

IF the foregoing hypothesis be received, it will now be easy for us to determine the question first started,[58] concerning the general principles of morals; and though we postponed the decision of that question, lest it should then involve us in intricate speculations, which are unfit for moral discourses, we may resume it at present, and examine how far either *reason* or *sentiment* enters into all decisions of praise or censure.

One principal foundation of moral praise being supposed to lie in the usefulness of any quality or action; it is evident, that *reason* must enter for a considerable share in all decisions of this kind; since nothing but that faculty can instruct us in the tendency of qualities and actions, and point out their beneficial consequences to society and to their possessor. In many cases, this is an affair liable to great controversy: Doubts may arise; opposite interests may occur; and a preference must be given to one side, from very nice views, and a small overbalance of utility. This is particularly remarkable in questions with regard to justice; as is, indeed, natural to suppose, from that species of utility, which attends this virtue.[59] Were every single instance of justice, like that of benevolence, useful to society; this would be a more simple state of the case, and seldom liable to great controversy. But as single instances of justice are often pernicious in their first and immediate tendency, and as the advantage to society results only from the observance of the general rule, and from the concurrence and combination of several persons in the same equitable conduct; the case here becomes more intricate and involved. The various circumstances of society; the various consequences of any practice; the various interests, which may be proposed: These, on many occasions, are doubtful, and subject to great discussion and enquiry. The object of municipal laws is to fix all the questions with regard to justice: The debates of civilians; the reflections of politicians; the precedents of history and public records, are all directed to the same purpose. And a very accurate *reason* or *judgment* is often requisite, to give the true determination, amidst such intricate doubts arising from obscure or opposite utilities.

But though reason, when fully assisted and improved, be sufficient to instruct us in the pernicious or useful tendency of qualities and actions; it is not alone sufficient to produce any moral blame or approbation. Utility is only a tendency to a certain end; and were the end totally indifferent to us, we should feel the same indifference towards the means. It is requisite a *sentiment* should here display itself, in order to give a preference to the useful above the pernicious tendencies. This sentiment can be no other than a feeling for the happiness of mankind, and a resentment of their misery; since these are the different ends which virtue and vice have a tendency to promote. Here, therefore, *reason* instructs us in the several tendencies of actions, and *humanity* makes a distinction in favour to those which are useful and beneficial.

This partition between the faculties of understanding and sentiment, in all moral decisions, seems clear from the preceding hypothesis. But I shall suppose that hypothesis false: It will then be requisite to look out for some other theory, that may be satisfactory; and I dare venture to affirm, that none such will ever be found, so long as we suppose reason to be the sole source of morals. To prove this, it will be proper to weigh the five following considerations.

I. It is easy for a false hypothesis to maintain some appearance of truth, while it keeps wholly in generals, makes use of undefined terms, and employs comparisons, instead of instances. This is particularly remarkable in that philosophy, which ascribes the discernment of all moral distinctions to reason alone, without the concurrence of sentiment. It is impossible that, in any particular instance, this hypothesis can so much as be rendered intelligible; whatever specious figure it may make in general

(continued)

An Enquiry Concerning the Principles of Morals (*continued*)

declamations and discourses. Examine the crime of *ingratitude*, for instance; which has place, wherever we observe good-will, expressed and known, together with good-offices performed, on the one side, and a return of ill-will or indifference, with ill-offices or neglect on the other: Anatomize all these circumstances, and examine, by your reason alone, in what consists the demerit or blame: You never will come to any issue or conclusion.

Reason judges either of *matter of fact* or of *relations*. Enquire then, *first*, where is that matter of fact, which we here call *crime*; point it out; determine the time of its existence; describe its essence or nature; explain the sense or faculty, to which it discovers itself. It resides in the mind of the person who is ungrateful. He must, therefore, feel it, and be conscious of it. But nothing is there, except the passion of ill-will or absolute indifference. You cannot say, that these, of themselves, always, and in all circumstances, are crimes. No: They are only crimes, when directed towards persons, who have before expressed and displayed good-will towards us. Consequently, we may infer, that the crime of ingratitude is not any particular individual *fact*; but arises from a complication of circumstances, which, being presented to the spectator, excites the *sentiment* of blame, by the particular structure and fabric of his mind.

This representation, you say, is false. Crime, indeed, consists not in a particular *fact*, of whose reality we are assured by *reason*: But it consists in certain *moral relations*, discovered by reason, in the same manner as we discover, by reason, the truths of geometry or algebra. But what are the relations, I ask, of which you here talk? In the case stated above, I see first good-will and good-offices in one person; then ill-will and ill-offices in the other. Between these, there is the relation of contrariety. Does the crime consist in that relation? But suppose a person bore me ill-will or did me ill-offices; and I, in return, were indifferent towards him, or did him good-offices: Here is the same relation of contrariety; and yet my conduct is often highly laudable. Twist and turn this matter as much as you will, you can never rest the morality on relation; but must have recourse to the decisions of sentiment.

When it is affirmed, that two and three are equal to the half of ten; this relation of equality, I understand perfectly. I conceive, that if ten be divided into two parts, of which one has as many units as the other; and if any of these parts be compared to two added to three, it will contain as many units as that compound number. But when you draw thence a comparison to moral relations, I own that I am altogether at a loss to understand you. A moral action, a crime, such as ingratitude, is a complicated object. Does morality consist in the relation of its parts to each other? How? After what manner? Specify the relation: Be more particular and explicit in your propositions; and you will easily see their falsehood.

No, say you, the morality consists in the relation of actions to the rule of right; and they are denominated good or ill, according as they agree or disagree with it. What then is this rule of right? In what does it consist? How is it determined? By reason, you say, which examines the moral relations of actions. So that moral relations are determined by the comparison of actions to a rule. And that rule is determined by considering the moral relations of objects. Is not this fine reasoning?

All this is metaphysics, you cry: That is enough: There needs nothing more to give a strong presumption of falsehood. Yes, reply I: Here are metaphysics, surely: But they are all on your side, who advance an abstruse hypothesis, which can never be made intelligible, nor quadrate with any particular instance or illustration. The hypothesis which we embrace is plain. It maintains, that morality is determined by sentiment. It defines virtue to be *whatever mental action or quality gives to a spectator the pleasing sentiment of approbation*; and vice the contrary. We then proceed to examine a plain matter of fact, to wit, what actions have this influence: We consider all the circumstances, in which these actions agree: And thence endeavour to extract some general observations with regard to these sentiments. If you call this metaphysics, and find any thing abstruse here, you need only conclude, that your turn of mind is not suited to the moral sciences.

II. When a man, at any time, deliberates concerning his own conduct (as, whether he had better, in a particular emergence, assist a brother or a benefactor), he must consider these separate relations, with all the circumstances and situations of the persons, in order to determine the superior duty and obligation: And in order to determine the proportion of lines in any triangle, it is necessary to examine the nature of that figure, and the relations which its several parts bear to each other. But notwithstanding this appearing similarity in the two cases, there is, at bottom, an extreme difference between them.

A speculative reasoner concerning triangles or circles considers the several known and given relations of the parts of these figures; and thence infers some unknown relation, which is dependent on the former. But in moral deliberations, we must be acquainted, before-hand, with all the objects, and all their relations to each other; and from a comparison of the whole, fix our choice or approbation. No new fact to be ascertained: No new relation to be discovered. All the circumstances of the case are supposed to be laid before us, ere we can fix any sentence of blame or approbation. If any material circumstance be yet unknown or doubtful, we must first employ our enquiry or intellectual faculties to assure us of it; and must suspend for a time all moral decision or sentiment. While we are ignorant, whether a man were aggressor or not, how can we determine whether the person who killed him, be criminal or innocent? But after every circumstance, every relation is known, the understanding has no farther room to operate, nor any object on which it could employ itself. The approbation or blame, which then ensues, cannot be the work of the judgment, but of the heart; and is not a speculative proposition or affirmation, but an active feeling or sentiment. In the disquisitions of the understanding, from known circumstances and relations, we infer some new and unknown. In moral decisions, all the circumstances and relations must be previously known; and the mind, from the contemplation of the whole, feels some new impression of affection or disgust, esteem or contempt, approbation or blame.

Hence the great difference between a mistake of *fact* and one of *right*; and hence the reason why the one is commonly criminal and not the other. When OEDIPUS killed LAIUS, he was ignorant of the relation, and from circumstances, innocent and involuntary, formed erroneous opinions concerning the action which he committed. But when NERO killed AGRIPPINA, all the relations between himself and the person, and all the circumstances of the fact, were previously known to him: But the motive of revenge, or fear, or interest, prevailed in his savage heart over the sentiments of duty and humanity. And when we express that detestation against him, to which he, himself, in a little time, became insensible; it is not, that we see any relations, of which he was ignorant; but that, from the rectitude of our disposition, we feel sentiments, against which he was hardened, from flattery and a long perseverance in the most enormous crimes. In these sentiments, then, not in a discovery of relations of any kind, do all moral determinations consist. Before we can pretend to form any decision of this kind, every thing must be known and ascertained on the side of the object or action. Nothing remains but to feel, on our part, some sentiment of blame or approbation; whence we pronounce the action criminal or virtuous.

III. This doctrine will become still more evident, if we compare moral beauty with natural, to which, in many particulars, it bears so near a resemblance. It is on the proportion, relation, and position of parts, that all natural beauty depends; but it would be absurd thence to infer, that the perception of beauty, like that of truth in geometrical problems, consists wholly in the perception of relations, and was performed entirely by the understanding or intellectual faculties. In all the sciences, our mind, from the known relations, investigates the unknown: But in all decisions of taste or external beauty, all the relations are before-hand obvious to the eye; and we thence proceed to feel a sentiment of complacency or disgust, according to the nature of the object, and disposition of our organs.

EUCLID has fully explained all the qualities of the circle; but has not, in any proposition, said a word of its beauty. The reason is evident. The beauty is not a quality of the circle. It lies not in any part of the line, whose parts are equally distant from a common center. It is only the effect, which that figure produces upon the mind, whose peculiar fabric or structure renders it susceptible of such sentiments. In vain would you look for it in the circle, or seek it, either by your senses or by mathematical reasonings, in all the properties of that figure.

Attend to PALLADIO and PERRAULT, while they explain all the parts and proportions of a pillar: They talk of the cornice and frieze and base and entablature and shaft and architrave; and give the description and position of each of these members. But should you ask the description and position of its beauty, they would readily reply, that the beauty is not in any of the parts or members of a pillar, but results from the whole, when that complicated figure is presented to an intelligent mind, susceptible to those finer sensations. 'Till such a spectator appear, there is nothing but a figure of such particular dimensions and proportions: From his sentiments alone arise its elegance and beauty.

Again; attend to CICERO, while he paints the crimes of a VERRES or a CATILINE; you must acknowledge that the moral turpitude results, in the same manner, from the contemplation of the whole, when presented to a being, whose organs have such a particular structure and formation. The orator may paint

(continued)

An Enquiry Concerning the Principles of Morals   (*continued*)

rage, insolence, barbarity on the one side: Meekness, suffering, sorrow, innocence on the other: But if you feel no indignation or compassion arise in you from this complication of circumstances, you would in vain ask him, in what consists the crime or villainy, which he so vehemently exclaims against: At what time, or on what subject it first began to exist: And what has a few months afterwards become of it, when every disposition and thought of all the actors is totally altered, or annihilated. No satisfactory answer can be given to any of these questions, upon the abstract hypothesis of morals; and we must at last acknowledge, that the crime or immorality is no particular fact or relation, which can be the object of the understanding: But arises entirely from the sentiment of disapprobation, which, by the structure of human nature, we unavoidably feel on the apprehension of barbarity or treachery.

IV. Inanimate objects may bear to each other all the same relations, which we observe in moral agents; though the former can never be the object of love or hatred, nor are consequently susceptible of merit or iniquity. A young tree, which over-tops and destroys its parent, stands in all the same relations with Nero, when he murdered Agrippina; and if morality consisted merely in relations, would, no doubt, be equally criminal.

V. It appears evident, that the ultimate ends of human actions can never, in any case, be accounted for by *reason*, but recommend themselves entirely to the sentiments and affections of mankind, without any dependance on the intellectual faculties. Ask a man, *why he uses exercise*; he will answer, *because he desires to keep his health*. If you then enquire, why he *desires health,* he will readily reply, *because sickness is painful*. If you push your enquiries farther, and desire a reason, why he hates pain, it is impossible he can ever give any. This is an ultimate end, and is never referred to any other object.

Perhaps, to your second question, *why he desires health*, he may also reply, that it *is necessary for the exercise of his calling*. If you ask, *why he is anxious on that head*, he will answer, *because he desires to get money*. If you demand, *Why*? *It is the instrument of pleasure*, says he. And beyond this it is an absurdity to ask for a reason. It is impossible there can be a progress in infinitum; and that one thing can always be a reason, why another is desired. Something must be desirable on its own account, and because of its immediate accord or agreement with human sentiment and affection.

Now as virtue is an end, and is desirable on its own account, without fee or reward, merely, for the immediate satisfaction which it conveys; it is requisite that there should be some sentiment, which it touches; some internal taste or feeling, or whatever you please to call it, which distinguishes moral good and evil, and which embraces the one and rejects the other.

Thus the distinct boundaries and offices of *reason* and of *taste* are easily ascertained. The former conveys the knowledge of truth and falsehood: The latter gives the sentiment of beauty and deformity, vice and virtue. The one discovers objects, as they really stand in nature, without addition or diminution: The other has a productive faculty, and gilding or staining all natural objects with the colours, borrowed from internal sentiment, raises, in a manner, a new creation. Reason, being cool and disengaged, is no motive to action, and directs only the impulse received from appetite or inclination, by showing us the means of attaining happiness or avoiding misery: Taste, as it gives pleasure or pain, and thereby constitutes happiness or misery, becomes a motive to action, and is the first spring or impulse to desire and volition. From circumstances and relations, known or supposed, the former leads us to the discovery of the concealed and unknown: After all circumstances and relations are laid before us, the latter makes us feel from the whole a new sentiment of blame or approbation. The standard of the one, being founded on the nature of things, is eternal and inflexible, even by the will of the Supreme Being: The standard of the other, arising from the internal frame and constitution of animals, is ultimately derived from that Supreme Will, which bestowed on each being its peculiar nature, and arranged the several classes and orders of existence.

Appendix II
Of Self-Love

There is a principle, supposed to prevail among many, which is utterly incompatible with all virtue or moral sentiment; and as it can proceed from nothing but the most depraved disposition, so in its turn it tends still further to encourage that depravity. This principle is, that all *benevolence* is mere hypocrisy, friendship a cheat, public spirit a farce, fidelity a snare to procure trust and confidence; and that, while all of us, at bottom, pursue only our private interest, we wear these fair disguises, in order to put others off their guard, and expose them the more to our wiles and machinations. What heart one must be possessed of who professes such principles, and who feels no internal sentiment that belies so pernicious a theory, it is easy to imagine: And also, what degree of affection and benevolence he can bear to a species, whom he represents under such odious colours, and supposes so little susceptible of gratitude or any return of affection. Or if we should not ascribe these principles wholly to a corrupted heart, we must, at least, account for them from the most careless and precipitate examination. Superficial reasoners, indeed, observing many false pretences, among mankind, and feeling, perhaps, no very strong restraint in their own disposition, might draw a general and a hasty conclusion, that all is equally corrupted, and that men, different from all other animals, and indeed from all other species of existences, admit of no degrees of good or bad, but are, in every instance, the same creatures under different disguises and appearances.

There is another principle, somewhat resembling the former; which has been much insisted on by philosophers, and has been the foundation of many a system; that, whatever affection one may feel, or imagine he feels for others, no passion is, or can be disinterested; that the most generous friendship, however sincere, is a modification of self-love; and that, even unknown to ourselves, we seek only our own gratification, while we appear the most deeply engaged in schemes for the liberty and happiness of mankind. By a turn of imagination, by a refinement of reflection, by an enthusiasm of passion, we seem to take part in the interests of others, and imagine ourselves divested of all selfish considerations: But, at bottom, the most generous patriot and most niggardly miser, the bravest hero and most abject coward, have, in every action, an equal regard to their own happiness and welfare.

Whoever concludes from the seeming tendency of this opinion, that those, who make profession of it, cannot possibly feel the true sentiments of benevolence, or have any regard for genuine virtue, will often find himself, in practice, very much mistaken. Probity and honour were no strangers to EPICURUS and his sect. ATTICUS and HORACE seem to have enjoyed from nature, and cultivated by reflection, as generous and friendly dispositions as any disciple of the austerer schools. And among the moderns, HOBBES and LOCKE, who maintained the selfish system of morals, lived irreproachable lives; though the former lay not under any restraint of religion, which might supply the defects of his philosophy.

An EPICUREAN or a HOBBIST readily allows, that there is such a thing as friendship in the world, without hypocrisy or disguise; though he may attempt, by a philosophical chemistry to resolve the elements of this passion, if I may so speak, into those of another, and explain every affection to be self-love, twisted and moulded, by a particular turn of imagination, into a variety of appearances. But as the same turn of imagination prevails not in every man, nor gives the same direction to the original passion; this is sufficient, even according to the selfish system, to make the widest difference in human characters, and denominate one man virtuous and humane, another vicious and meanly interested. I esteem the man, whose self-love, by whatever means, is so directed as to give him a concern for others, and render him serviceable to society: As I hate or despise him, who has no regard to any thing beyond his own gratifications and enjoyments. In vain would you suggest, that these characters, though seemingly opposite, are, at bottom, the same, and that a very inconsiderable turn of thought forms the whole difference between them. Each character, notwithstanding these inconsiderable differences, appears to me, in practice, pretty durable and untransmutable. And I find not in this more than in other subjects, that the natural sentiments, arising from the general appearances of things, are easily destroyed by subtile reflections concerning the minute origin of these appearances. Does not the lively, chearful colour of a countenance inspire me with complacency and pleasure; even though I learn from philosophy, that all difference of complexion arises from the most minute differences of thickness, in the most minute parts of the skin; by means of which a superficies is qualified to reflect one of the original colours of light, and absorb the others?

But though the question, concerning the universal or partial selfishness of man be not so material, as is usually imagined, to morality and practice, it is certainly of consequence in the speculative science of human nature, and is a proper object of curiosity and enquiry. It may not, therefore, be unsuitable, in this place, to bestow a few reflections upon it.

The most obvious objection to the selfish hypothesis, is, that, as it is contrary to common feeling and our most unprejudiced notions, there is required the highest stretch of philosophy to establish so extraordinary a paradox. To the most careless observer, there appear to be such dispositions

(continued)

An Enquiry Concerning the Principles of Morals   (*continued*)

as benevolence and generosity; such affections as love, friendship, compassion, gratitude. These sentiments have their causes, effects, objects, and operations, marked by common language and observation, and plainly distinguished from those of the selfish passions. And as this is the obvious appearance of things, it must be admitted; till some hypothesis be discovered, which, by penetrating deeper into human nature, may prove the former affections to be nothing but modifications of the latter. All attempts of this kind have hitherto proved fruitless, and seem to have proceeded entirely, from that love of *simplicity*, which has been the source of much false reasoning in philosophy. I shall not here enter into any detail on the present subject. Many able philosophers have shown the insufficiency of these systems. And I shall take for granted what, I believe, the smallest reflection will make evident to every impartial enquirer.

But the nature of the subject furnishes the strongest presumption, that no better system will ever, for the future, be invented, in order to account for the origin of the benevolent from the selfish affections, and reduce all the various emotions of the human mind to a perfect simplicity. The case is not the same in this species of philosophy as in physics. Many an hypothesis in nature, contrary to first appearances, has been found, on more accurate scrutiny, solid and satisfactory. Instances of this kind are so frequent, that a judicious, as well as witty philosopher, has ventured to affirm, if there be more than one way, in which any phenomenon may be produced, that there is a general presumption for its arising from the causes, which are the least obvious and familiar. But the presumption always lies on the other side, in all enquiries concerning the origin of our passions, and of the internal operations of the human mind. The simplest and most obvious cause, which can there be assigned for any phenomenon, is probably the true one. When a philosopher, in the explication of his system, is obliged to have recourse to some very intricate and refined reflections, and to suppose them essential to the production of any passion or emotion, we have reason to be extremely on our guard against so fallacious an hypothesis. The affections are not susceptible of any impression from the refinements of reason or imagination; and it is always found, that a vigorous exertion of the latter faculties, necessarily, from the narrow capacity of the human mind, destroys all activity in the former. Our predominant motive or intention is, indeed, frequently concealed from ourselves, when it is mingled and confounded with other motives, which the mind, from vanity or self-conceit, is desirous of supposing more prevalent: But there is no instance, that a concealment of this nature has ever arisen from the abstruseness and intricacy of the motive. A man, that has lost a friend and patron, may flatter himself, that all his grief arises from generous sentiments, without any mixture of narrow or interested considerations: But a man, that grieves for a valuable friend, who needed his patronage and protection; how can we suppose, that his passionate tenderness arises from some metaphysical regards to a self-interest, which has no foundation or reality? We may as well imagine, that minute wheels and springs, like those of a watch, give motion to a loaded wagon, as account for the origin of passion from such abstruse reflections.

Animals are found susceptible of kindness, both to their own species and to ours; nor is there, in this case, the least suspicion of disguise or artifice. Shall we account for all *their* sentiments, too, from refined deductions of self-interest? Or if we admit a disinterested benevolence in the inferior species, by what rule of analogy can we refuse it in the superior?

Love between the sexes begets a complacency and good-will, very distinct from the gratification of an appetite. Tenderness to their offspring, in all sensible beings, is commonly able alone to counter-balance the strongest motives of self-love, and has no manner of dependance on that affection. What interest can a fond mother have in view, who loses her health by assiduous attendance on her sick child, and afterwards languishes and dies of grief, when freed, by its death, from the slavery of that attendance?

Is gratitude no affection of the human breast, or is that a word merely, without any meaning or reality? Have we no satisfaction in one man's company above another's, and no desire of the welfare of our friend, even though absence or death should prevent us from all participation it it? Or what is it commonly, that gives us any participation in it, even while alive and present, but our affection and regard to him?

These and a thousand other instances are marks of a general benevolence in human nature, where no *real* interest binds us to the object. And how an *imaginary* interest, known and avowed for such, can be the origin of any passion or emotion, seems difficult to explain. No satisfactory hypothesis of this kind has yet been discovered; nor is there the smallest probability, that the future industry of men will ever be attended with more favourable success.

But farther, if we consider rightly of the matter, we shall find, that the hypothesis, which allows of a disinterested benevolence, distinct from self-love, has really more *simplicity* in it, and is more conformable to the analogy of nature, than that which pretends to resolve all friendship and humanity into this latter principle. There are bodily wants or appetites, acknowledged by every one, which necessarily precede all sensual enjoyment, and carry us directly to seek possession of the object. Thus, hunger and thirst have eating and drinking for their end; and from the gratification of these primary appetites arises a pleasure, which may become the object of another species of desire or inclination, that is secondary and interested. In the same manner, there are mental passions, by which we are impelled immediately to seek particular objects, such as fame, or power, or vengeance, without any regard to interest; and when these objects are attained, a pleasing enjoyment ensues, as the consequence of our indulged affections. Nature must, by the internal frame and constitution of the mind, give an original propensity to fame, ere we can reap any pleasure from that acquisition, or pursue it from motives of self-love, and a desire of happiness. If I have no vanity, I take no delight in praise: If I be void of ambition, power gives me no enjoyment: If I be not angry, the punishment of an adversary is totally indifferent to me. In all these cases, there is a passion, which points immediately to the object, and constitutes it our good or happiness; as there are other secondary passions, which afterwards arise, and pursue it as a part of our happiness, when once it is constituted such by our original affections. Were there no appetite of any kind antecedent to self-love, that propensity could scarcely ever exert itself; because we should, in that case, have felt few and slender pains or pleasures, and have little misery or happiness to avoid or to pursue.

Now, where is the difficulty in conceiving, that this may likewise be the case with benevolence and friendship and that, from the original frame of our temper, we may feel a desire of another's happiness or good, which, by means of that affection, becomes our own good, and is afterwards pursued, from the combined motives of benevolence and self-enjoyment? Who sees not that vengeance, from the force alone of passion, may be so eagerly pursued, as to make us knowingly neglect every consideration of ease, interest, or safety; and, like some vindictive animals, infuse our very souls into the wounds we give an enemy? And what a malignant philosophy must it be, that will not allow, to humanity and friendship, the same privileges, which are undisputably granted to the darker passions of enmity and resentment? Such a philosophy is more like a satyr than a true delineation or description of human nature; and may be a good foundation for paradoxical wit and raillery, but is a very bad one for any serious argument or reasoning.

Chapter 6
Science

How does science work? How does it differ from other areas of inquiry? In a succinct article, Michael Ruse (1940–) presents us with the essential characteristics of science. He does so by contrasting it with creation-science. Ruse points out that creation-science fails on all grounds of being a science as science involves the use of evidence and theory. Creation-scientists are religious fundamentalists who reject claims of evolution. Furthermore, they adhere to the belief that the Christian Bible is the literal truth. Of course such a claim has difficulties even within the sphere of religion. Other Christians accept many scientific tenets including evolution, while followers of other religions are perturbed by the Creationist claim that the Bible accurately describes the origins of the universe as opposed to their own holy teachings.

In the fourteenth century, William of Ockham proposed that we ought not to "multiply the existence of things unnecessarily." If two theories predict the same thing but one theory is more complex than the other, then using Ockham's Razor we adopt the simpler theory. Consider:

a. The planets revolve around the Sun in a predictable manner because of certain forces.
b. The planets revolve around the Sun in a predictable manner because of certain forces and God ensures that forces are consistent.

Ockham's Razor would reject b. in favor of a. In other words, if we can explain something without use of extraneous things, then we ought not to. In twenty-first-century parlance, this means we should "Keep it simple, stupid!" If we include talk of God, then we have to explain God's existence and all the complexities that that creates. Yet there may in fact be a God and the world may be more complicated than we think, so we should not dogmatically state that since science says such and such is so, that it is so. Besides, when we think about simple scientific theories, we find that they can become complex fast. They posit that there is something called "air" and air is composed of hydrogen and oxygen and these molecules break down further into smaller parts and these parts break down into even smaller parts and so on. Even though simplicity does not guarantee that the theory is correct, it is a general assumption that scientists make. This is one reason why they all seek a unifying account of science: one grand theory to explain it all.

Science also looks for order. If something happens that does not fit into what scientists predict, then their theory is partly or wholly false and needs to be modified or rejected. When scientists do not find order when order is expected then they become anxious but not nervous. They have simply shown that the previously adopted theory is problematic. In doing so, they have gained greater insight into the way things really are by showing one way that they are *not*. Any explanation or theory has a useful role to play in science even if it is just to point to its own internal inconsistencies. But this does not mean any explanation or theory is workable. Here too we can see the contrast with religion. Religion does not seem to be bothered by events that are unexpected and out of order. For although theists may claim that God brought order to chaos when He created the universe, when some singularly chaotic event or anomaly happens that Believers would call a "miracle" this does not seem to alter the theist's explanation. If the sun rotated in the opposite direction it is God's doing. That it does not rotate in the opposite direction is also God's doing. That a man rises from the dead or does not, the explanation is always the same: God. Nothing, in other words, would or could falsify God's role.[1] In science, however, such unique events would call for a reinvestigation of our observations, our methods, our hypotheses, our theories, and our predictions, and our claims of knowledge.

Science also makes predictions. It is testable. We can confirm things by predicting outcomes, and we can use these outcomes to caste doubt or falsify our scientific claims. Science is tentative. Its theories are open to criticism and to outright rejection if there are counter-examples that cannot be accounted for. For religion, however, counter-examples are just as good as examples in reaffirming one's belief. One can always fall back on the religiously useful but ultimately empty explanation that God works in mysterious ways. With this explanation, fundamentalists do not need to challenge or reassess any of their beliefs. Unlike the scientist who when confronted with apparent inconsistencies is open to changing his or her beliefs, the fundamentalist would never conclude that some other religion (that is, some other religion-based worldview) might be the right one instead.

---

[1] People sometimes use the term 'miracle' when some medical ailment they suffer from suddenly disappears. Some people find prayer healing and it may be; but perhaps only because it gives a person a sense of control or a positive outlook—both of which might affect one's overall well being. Yet diseases are known to go into remission, and not everything about every disease has been discovered or learned yet. Perhaps it was merely a very unfortunate misdiagnosis. Either that or God selected this one person out of all the millions of virtuous but ill people to save. Although tumors might shrink and cancers disappear, one never hears about severed limbs growing back . . .

Creationists[2] have a response to those who point to how apparently successful science has been so far in explaining things. They argue that in creation, "God used processes which are not now operating anywhere in the natural universe"[3] and that "It is thus quite plain that the processes used by God in the creation were utterly different from the processes which now operate in the universe!"[4] In other words, in explaining things Creationists can fall back on science for everything *but* the origins of the universe. The reason for this is that the fundamentalists do not have a system themselves to explain anything successfully without falling back on ambiguity, dogma, and religious conjecture. Creationists do not run tests and make predictions; these would be unproductive since what God did does not apply anymore. Although as Ruse points out, fundamentalists still assert that God has stepped in at various times throughout Earth's history to intercede and affect human outcomes (e.g., the destruction of Sodom and Gomorrah, and even 9/11[5] perhaps?) God's stepping in and out of our history is the reason for miracles. But then much work has to be done on justifying why he does so rarely. Again, this concern is drawn in part from the application of Ockham's Razor.

A scientific theory also must be verifiable. Astrology is an example of a pseudo-science that does not permit verification. Let us say that the following is your horoscope for today.

> Today you will learn something new that will possibly affect your personal life. Money will be important for your future plans. Consider saving more or cutting down on any excesses. You will find that some people are more receptive to your ideas than others. Express yourself well today and you may be surprised. Thinking ahead will help you avoid potential problems. You enjoy the company of close friends. You set goals that are not always achievable or realistic. You pride yourself on being an independent thinker and are not easily persuaded to act without justification. Be careful to think twice before acting impulsively today because you may unknowingly lose an opportunity to discover a potential romantic partner.

Are any of these claims verifiable? They all seem to be, but that should not be surprising because we would like them all to be true. The Amazing Randi, a noted debunker of the paranormal, conducted a well-known demonstration with horoscopes. In a classroom full of students, he announced that he had an astrologer do personal horoscopes for each one of them based on the personal data that each student had provided to him earlier. He read out their names and handed them a sealed envelope. After reading the contents, Randi asked the students to rate the accuracy of the reading on a scale of 1 to 5 with 5 being extremely accurate. Almost all of the students gave their readings a score of 5 (the others gave it a 4). Randi then announced that a mistake had been made and that he accidentally gave each student's horoscope to the person behind him or her. The students switch readings and discover that all the sheets of paper had the exact same horoscope on it.[6]

The Amazing Randi's point is that people will read what they want to read into almost anything they are given.[7] We all want to be well liked. We all have

---

[2]Ruse points out that we should not call them creation-scientists since they do not use the methods of science.
[3]Duane T. Gish quoted in Ruse.
[4]John Whitcomb, Jr., and Henry M. Morris quoted in Ruse.
[5]Reverend Jerry Falwell once blamed the terror attacks on the World Trade Center on the moral evil of gays, lesbians, and other "miscreants." He later apologized.

> JERRY FALWELL: And I agree totally with you that the Lord has protected us so wonderfully these 225 years. And since 1812, this is the first time that we've been attacked on our soil and by far the worst results. And I fear, as Donald Rumsfeld, the Secretary of Defense, said yesterday, that this is only the beginning. And with biological warfare available to these monsters—the Husseins, the Bin Ladens, the Arafats—what we saw on Tuesday, as terrible as it is, could be miniscule if, in fact—if, in fact—God continues to lift the curtain and allow the enemies of America to give us probably what we deserve.
> PAT ROBERTSON: Jerry, that's my feeling. I think we've just seen the antechamber to terror. We haven't even begun to see what they can do to the major population.
> JERRY FALWELL: The ACLU's got to take a lot of blame for this.
> PAT ROBERTSON: Well yes.
> JERRY FALWELL: And, I know that I'll hear from them for this. But, throwing God out successfully with the help of the federal court system, throwing God out of the public square, out of the schools. The abortionists have got to bear some burden for this because God will not be mocked. And when we destroy 40 million little innocent babies, we make God mad. I really believe that the pagans, and the abortionists, and the feminists, and the gays and the lesbians who are actively trying to make that an alternative lifestyle, the ACLU, People For the American Way—all of them who have tried to secularize America—I point the finger in their face and say "you helped this happen."

Partial transcript of comments from the September 13, 2001, telecast of the 700 Club.
If this were God's doing and for the reasons Falwell gives, one wonders why He would not strike the offending individuals directly rather than taking it out on so many "innocents" who were "upstanding" citizens.

[6]For similar stories about pseudo-science, see James Randi *Flim Flam!* (Amherst, NY: Prometheus Books, 1982).
[7]For a discussion of the significance of this experiment, see: http://www.bobmarksastrologer.com/skeptics.htm. (visited Feb. 2008).

some degree of insecurity. Money is always an issue, whether you have it or not. Affirmation statements such as "You are an independent thinker" are things people will not reject even if false. General statements are put forward in such a way that they sound like specific traits or helpful tips. You are told to think carefully today, as if today is somehow different from other days. And surely if you did not enjoy the company of your close friends, they would not be your friends! Terms like "may," "might," and "could" are also vague and impossible to deny. How would you falsify the claim that you MAY have a great idea today?[8]

The twentieth-century Austrian philosopher Karl Popper (1902–1994) added a highly influential element to the analysis of science. From the empirical observation that the crow outside your window is black, you might offer the generalized statement: "All crows are black." In order to verify this claim empirically, you would have to scrutinize *every* crow. This is an impossible task since you would have to examine all crows now, all crows in the future, and all crows in the past. Every black crow you see simply reaffirms the veracity of the statement. The more crows you examine, the stronger your claim becomes but at the same time you run the greater risk of finding a non-black crow. So although "All crows are black" is non-verifiable, it is falsifiable. For Popper, that a theory is falsifiable is what makes it scientific as opposed to non-scientific.

Scientists are like detectives: They search for clues and draw conclusions based on them. How can we determine when the next earthquake will be? How does cancer alter healthy body cells? In *The Andromeda Strain*, science plays a much larger role than it usually does in such films. Here scientists have to solve a murder mystery.

In this film, the U.S. government attempts to retrieve one of its satellites that has crashed in a small Nevada town. When the recovery team arrives, it discovers that every person has been stopped dead in their tracks. Clearly the satellite brought back something lethal. An emergency team of scientists is brought in to determine what caused the death of the townsfolk. They are sequestered in a secret underground government facility designed just for the purpose of isolating such biological threats. If by chance the virulent gets out, the facility has a self-destruct capability. As the scientists race to figure out what they are dealing with, the president is advised to drop a nuclear bomb on the town to stop whatever it is from spreading around the earth. It is a recommendation that turns out to be exactly the wrong thing to do.

Two of the four scientists tour the crash site. The town is littered with bodies of humans and livestock. The scientists' exchange mimics empirical observation and analysis that is common in science.

STONE   Hall? Take a look at this.

[gestures to dead man with peaceful facial expression]

Are you sure this isn't coronary?

HALL   No, coronary is painful. They should grimace.

STONE   If it was fast, they wouldn't have time.

HALL   Fast? These people were cut down in mid-stride!

Each line of dialogue corresponds to a sequence of scientific steps:

- Observation (of the deceased)
- Hypothesis of causality (a coronary?)
- Counter analysis (if he had a heart attack, he would be grimacing; he isn't grimacing, so he didn't have a heart attack)
- Rebuttal (hypothesizing additional factors: if the heart attack was fast, the deceased might not have time to grimace)
- Integration of additional factors supporting counter analysis (it cannot be a heart attack because the person died immediately in 'mid stride')

And then there would be:

- Verification (by autopsy) that would confirm or disconfirm the explanation.

Director Robert Wise allows the various scientific discussions to unfold naturally within the pressing deadline. Time and care are taken to explain the various steps and methods that are used to uncover the truth. For some viewers this might seem like a very slow action film, but it is the science and not the fiction that makes it a riveting tale. Let us walk through some of the main examples where we can see scientific method and critical thinking in practice.

On entering the facility, the chief scientist speaks with the communications officer.

STONE   Any messages for me from the White House?

SERGEANT   Not a thing Dr. STONE or you'd have it

---

[8] And if you come up with a way to falsify this claim, they you have just proven it since you have come up with a great idea!

LEAVITT   No personal messages?

SERGEANT   No Ma'am.

STONE   Nothing from Dr. Robertson?

SERGEANT   Dr. Stone sir, I have one thing to do—just one. Everything else is fully automatic, computerized, and self-regulated. I listen for a little bell in here (referring to the teletext machine) "ding-a-ling"! That means there's a message coming in from the Wildfire team.

STONE   Precisely, a MCN communication. I'm expecting one.

SERGEANT   Yes, sir. Top priority. 'Ding-a-ling'! I push a button and all five control centers are notified at the same time you are. The bell hasn't rung sir.

This plot device plays an important role later in the film but more importantly the Sergeant's logic is faulty. He puts forward the following argument

Premise   If the bell rings, then there will be a message.

Premise   The bell has not rung.

Conclusion   So there are no messages.

This is known as the Fallacy of Denying the Antecedent. Compare the Sergeant's argument with similarly formulated ones:

Premise   If the person is a mother, then the person is female.

Premise   The person is not a mother.

Conclusion   So the person is not female.

—But clearly there are women who are not mothers.

Premise   If I have a billion dollars, then I am rich.

Premise   I do not have a billion dollars.

Conclusion   So I am not rich.

—But clearly millionaires are also considered rich.

Unfortunately, this fallacy is a common mistake to make. One has incorrectly switched the proper denial of the consequence (the part of the sentence that comes after the "then") with the antecedent (the part of the sentence that comes immediately after the "if"). It is an important fallacy to recognize because one has to draw the right conclusion so that one can know the proper cause of events. Consider the following faulty medical diagnosis.

Premise   If he has the flu, then he will have a high fever.

Premise   He does not have the flu.

Conclusion   So he will not have a high fever.

—But high fevers can be caused by other things such as infections.

The correct conclusion that one may draw from the initial premise would be: "He does not have a high fever, so he does not have the flu," or "He has the flu, so he has a high fever." Either one of these would work because the flu causes the fever; the fever does not cause the flu.

Likewise, one has to be careful not to argue the following:

Premise   If he has the flu, then he will have a high fever.

Premise   He has a high fever.

Conclusion   So he has the flu.

This is also an inappropriate conclusion since the patient may have a high fever because of some other ailment. Just because one piece of evidence has been confirmed and is linked to another piece of evidence it does not entail that you can draw any connection (e.g., one of cause and effect) whatsoever between the two.

In *The Andromeda Strain*, unbeknown to the sergeant, the communication bell has not rung, but it was because a tiny slip of paper has fallen between the bell mechanism and the clapper, not because there are no messages. In fact urgent messages have been sent, but the bell is not making any sound.

In another key scene, a fictional scientific hypothesis is[9] introduced to justify a certain decision. Because the facility is equipped with a self-destruct capability, Dr. Stone gives Dr. Hall a key that will deactivate it. Hall is told he was selected to have this power because he is the "Odd Man."

HALL   Look, I'm the new boy here, why me?

STONE   Because you're single.

LEAVITT   You should have done your homework sport. Page 255, Robbie's Odd Man Hypothesis, (she reads from the manual)

---

[9] A hypothetical hypothetical, if you please.

"Results of testing confirm the Odd Man Hypothesis that an unmarried male should carry out command decisions involving thermal nuclear destruct contexts."

(We see the document which she is reading from):

Summary of the Robertson Odd Man Hypothesis

Group Index of Effectiveness

Married Males .343

Married Females .399

Single Females .402

Single Males .824

According to this fictional hypothesis, an unmarried man is more likely (i.e., his effectiveness is closest to 1.0) to act as is necessary because there is a lesser degree of probability that there will be outside factors working against him. That is, he does not have to consider his wife or children and possibly hesitate in doing what needs to be done. This does not mean that he is guaranteed to do what is necessary as there are other possible factors such as religious beliefs, family upbringing, worldviews, etc. Carl Hempel (1905–1997) refers to this kind of explanation that does not have a guarantee of certainty as having a probabilistic-statistical form. Here, it is the assertion that if certain specified conditions are realized (e.g., male, single), then an occurrence of such-and-such a kind (e.g., the person will use the key) will come about with such-and-such a statistical probability (e.g., 0.824).

Much of our knowledge is based on empirical generalizations. The sun will rise tomorrow and the next day because it has done so in the past, but one day it will not rise, although probably not in our lifetimes. Global climate change will result in some changes to our environment, but we can only estimate what they might be. As we gain more information and create better computer models, our estimates may become more accurate but no climatologist would offer her predictions as certainties.[10]

Fortunately we can be reassured that the laws of nature are not matters of statistical probability. So we do not need to worry that gravity is in effect only 99.9 times out of 100.

The Andromeda Strain's presentation of the aim and methods that are used by Dr. Stone echoes those expressed by Hempel. Hempel writes that science is motivated in large part by a human desire to predict and control. This desire is the practical or instrumental value of science. Secondly, there is a human desire to learn, know, explain, and therefore understand the world around us. This is the inherent value of science.

STONE   I planned our work in three stages.

One, detection. Confirm that an organism is present.

Two, characterization. How's it structured, how does it work?

And three, control. How to contain and exterminate it.

[The satellite is placed in a sealed room and a cage with a rat is introduced into the environment. The rat dies almost immediately.]

STONE   Whatever killed them in Piedmont is still there and as potent as ever.

Stone's conclusion is pretty strong but there could be the slight possibility that the death of the rat was a coincidence.

LEAVITT   If potent's the word. Let's try a rhesus.

They repeat the test with the rhesus monkey and death is almost immediate. Therefore, it is safe for them to conclude that when exposed to the satellite the animals died as a result of something in their new environment. But what? Stone's stage one—detection has been confirmed. As we have noted, scientific results must be verified. One dead rat and one dead monkey aren't enough to give conclusive evidence of the cause.

[A tube is hooked up to the airtight rat cage that contains the dead rat and this tube is then connected to another cage with another live rat. The second rat dies.]

DUTTON   Transmitted by air just as we thought. Now we have to figure out its size. Could be a gas or a virus. We'll use a 100 angstrom filter to begin. About the size of a small virus.

[They put a filter between the infected cage and another live specimen.

---

[10] Indeed, it's an old joke that weather forecasters are the only ones who can put forward claims with 50% failure rate and still keep their jobs.

430 Chapter 6 • Science

Air hisses and nothing happens. The live rat is not affected.]

DUTTON Whatever it is, it's larger than a virus. We'll try a one-micron filter.

ASSISTANT Hang in there baby.

[The filter size is increased. We hear the hissing of air . . .]

ASSISTANT Must be pretty big. I'm gonna get me a flyswatter.

DUTTON You do that. Here goes with two microns.

[The filter size is increased again.

This time the rat staggers and shakes violently and dies.]

DUTTON Nasty. At least we'll be able to get a good look at it.

[He turns to the intercom]

Dutton to Stone. We just found out its size about two microns.

STONE Big enough to be a cell. Interesting.

These tests illustrate that getting a satisfactory answer begins with getting repeated verification.

[Stone and Leavitt are at the computer control desk. Scanning satellite interior with remote cameras, they watch their monitors. Stone and Leavitt see a shadow on the mesh.]

STONE Hold it. At the edge of that shadow. I think there's . . .

LEAVITT Me too.

STONE It's an indentation.

LEAVITT About the size of a pencil point.

STONE Go to [magnification] 40.

[We see the indentation better.]

Go to 60.

LEAVITT Do you thing maybe . . .

[We see an extremely small stone].

STONE Maybe its just a grain of sand.

Go to 80

[We see now that there are flecks of luminescent green in the tiny stone.]

LEAVITT What about the bits of green?

STONE Paint.

LEAVITT For God's sake!

STONE Pistachio ice cream! Don't assume anything yet!

LEAVITT You're too good a scientist not to be thinking the same thing I am. If this is really something new, some brand-new form of life . . .

STONE Our best hope is to be grindingly thorough, using computer number one

[He taps Leavitt on the head signifying her brain]

Ok? Now let's get on with it.

Stone's point is that scientists must be objective and open to any and all possibilities no matter how remote. Is it more likely that the rock is a new type of life form or something more normal, Earth-based, but when seen out of context appears bizarre and mysterious? Maybe the particle was always there in the satellite as the result of shoddy construction. Maybe the person who put the lid on the satellite had a bit of green pistachio ice cream on his suit and it fell off. These are not outrageous possibilities. The scientists' close examination of the satellite continues.

[As Stone gets up to look at the monitor, Leavitt sees the green "paint" pulsate. She stares in disbelief.]

LEAVITT Jeremy

STONE What?

LEAVITT Nothing.

[She shakes her head and rubs her eyes.]

STONE You okay?

LEAVITT Just my eyes getting tired.

Leavitt is thinking critically here. What is more likely to be the case: that she perceives something strange because she is overly tired, or that the rock-like object actually pulsated?

Moments later Stone sees the object pulsate as well. Now Leavitt is able to use her reasoning skills to draw a different conclusion. What is the likelihood that two people would perceive the same thing happening as a result of both being tired? Therefore, what they saw is more probably the result of something else.

Later the entire scientific team runs a chemical analysis of the green "paint". The results are displayed on a computer screen.

LEAVITT   No amino acids!

DUTTON   No proteins, no enzymes, no nucleic acid. Impossible. No organism can maintain life without them.

HALL   You mean no earth organism. It must have evolved in a totally different way.

LEAVITT   You got it. It can't be from here.

Here we have an example of what Hempel refers to as a deductive-nomological explanation. The object cannot be from Earth because it violates the universally valid law that anything that is an Earth organism must have properties X, Y, and Z. This particular green object has none of these properties (i.e., no acids, proteins, etc.), so it cannot be from Earth. Nevertheless, one might argue that the team should have concluded that either the object is an organism that is not from Earth *or* it is not an organism at all. However, they have already deduced that the object is an organism based on seeing it grow. Any object that spontaneously grows is a living thing; this object grows, so it too must be a living thing.[11] Still, their thinking is not perfect.

The team's conclusions are influenced by their acceptance of the law that a living organism must fall within certain already established parameters. But what if that law is wrong? We have good reason to believe that there are thousands of as yet unidentified species of plants and insects in the tropical rain forests. What if, odds against odds, we discover one that looks alive, acts as if it were alive (e.g., moves, grows, reproduces, etc.), and yet has a biological make-up exactly the same as the Andromeda organism? There are two options for us. We either reject what our observations tell us, namely, we deny that this thing is alive, or we modify our foundational assumption: we change the law. This fictional case and the consequential conundrum it creates places us in what Thomas Kuhn (1922–1996) refers to as a scientific crisis. Simple testing of our observations would not be possible because we are working within an old world view that this thing cannot be alive. Yet it sure seems to meet the criteria! Therefore, we need to rethink what we thought was true. Such a discovery of an Andromeda-like organism would result not merely in the evolution of our existing theory but in a complete revolution. We could not merely "expand" our view of what is life since this discovery would send ripples of change throughout the biological sciences. We cannot just add this to what we already know because what we previously knew explicitly ruled out exactly this sort of new information. This crisis results as two competing worldviews collide, as Kuhn argues. The end result is what he calls a "Paradigm Shift."

Consider the following lighthearted example of competing paradigms. In the quirky film *The Gods Must Be Crazy!* an African nomad is hunting. Out of nowhere he is hit on the head by a Coke bottle. He has never seen one of these. He knows nothing of modern society or its consumer goods. He looks at the bottle and is puzzled at what he sees and what it means. He concludes that the gods must be crazy, for why else would they drop such a thing on him? In actuality the bottle fell from an airplane that flew high overhead. If this tribesman were to meet the person who dropped it, would he laugh at his own foolishness? No. He would simply see the person as one of the gods. After all, this individual is the one who dropped it and only gods can drop such things from the heavens. In other words, this tribesman has a worldview that includes gods but not airplanes. Any new information, observations, or experiences will be interpreted within the confines of his worldview which includes the existence of gods. This worldview is a paradigm. The moviegoers have a different paradigm. A passenger from a small plane dropped a coke bottle. End of story. No magic or mystery involved.

But the mystery remains for there are now two interpretations of the same event and neither one is going to fit into the other worldview. Thus we have a scientific crisis regarding the true nature of the cause of the pop bottle hitting the man. The resolution of this crisis will be a revolution since one person cannot just absorb the other's version into their own. One of the competing worldviews (presumably the nomad's) has to be rejected. Scientific revolutions are incredibly significant since they entail that we see the world in a new way. Kuhn argues that history is replete with example after example of such revolutions; a Ptolemaic cosmology to a Copernican one, a Newtonian physics and Einsteinian one, Creationist biology to evolution, psychoanalysis to neurochemistry . . .

So will we ever know what there really is out there? Perhaps all we can say of those beliefs we claim to be true is that they work reasonably well for now. Are we (to wax poetically) sailing ever closer toward the final answer, or are we just changing ships unaware of our destination?

---

[11]One might think that this would therefore include icicles, but icicles only grow because of the *addition* of frozen water.

Films Cited

Andromeda Strain, The. Dir. Robert Wise. Perfs. Arthur Hill, David Wayne. Film. Universal Pictures. 1971.

Gods Must Be Crazy! The. Dir. Jamie Uys. Perfs. Marius Weyers, Sandra Prinsloo. Film. CAT Films. 1980.

ADDITIONAL MOVIES FOR FURTHER VIEWING

(For a comprehensive listing of movies and themes, please consult the online appendix.)

1. *A Beautiful Mind*—The scientific mind
2. *A Brief History of Time*—Scientific theory and explanation
3. *An Inconvenient Truth*—Scientific knowledge and its impact; environmental science
4. *Contact*—Science and religion, explanation and doubt
5. *Experiment, Das*—Dangers of scientific experimentation
6. *Gattaca*—Cloning science well presented
7. *Jurassic Park*—The dangers of scientific intervention in nature
8. *Kinsey*—Science versus social norms
9. *Rosenkrantz and Guildernstern are Dead*—Scientific discovery
10. *What the #$*! Do We (K)now!?*—Pseudo-science

Creation Science Is Not Science
Michael Ruse

In December 1981, I appeared as an expert witness for the plaintiffs and the American Civil Liberties Union (ACLU) in their successful challenge of Arkansas Act 590, which demanded that teachers give "balanced treatment" to "creation-science" and evolutionary ideas.[1] My presence occasioned some surprise, for I am an historian and philosopher of science. In this essay, I do not intend to apologize for either my existence or my calling, nor do I intend to relive past victories;[2] rather, I want to explain why a philosopher and historian of science finds the teaching of "creation-science" in science classrooms offensive.

Obviously, the crux of the issue—the center of the plaintiffs' case—is the status of creation-science. Its advocates claim that it is genuine science and may, therefore, be legitimately and properly taught in the public schools. Its detractors claim that it is not genuine science but a form of religion—dogmatic Biblical literalism by another name. Which is it, and who is to decide?

It is somewhat easier to describe who should participate in decisions on this issue. On the one hand, one naturally appeals to the authority of religious people and theologians. Does creation-science fit the accepted definitions of a religion? (In Arkansas, the ACLU produced theologians who said that indeed it did.) One also appeals to the authority of scientists. Does creation-science fit current definitions of science? (In Arkansas, the ACLU produced scientists who said that indeed it did not.)[3]

Having, as it were, appealed to the practitioners—theologians and scientists—a link still seems to be missing. Someone is needed to talk at a more theoretical level about the nature of science—any science—and then show that creation-science simply does not fit the part. As a philosopher and an historian, it is my job to look at science, and to ask precisely those questions about defining characteristics.

What Is Science?

It is simply not possible to give a neat definition—specifying necessary and sufficient characteristics—which separates all and only those things that have ever been called "science." The concept "science" is not as easily definable as, for example, the concept "triangle." Science is a phenomenon that has developed through the ages—dragging itself apart from religion, philosophy, superstition, and other bodies of human opinion and belief.[4]

What we call "science" today is a reasonably striking and distinctive set of claims, which have a number of characteristic features. As with most things in life, some items fall on the borderline between science and nonscience (e.g., perhaps Freudian psychoanalytic theory). But it is possible to state positively that, for example, physics and chemistry are sciences, and Plato's Theory of Forms and Swedenborgian theology are not.[5]

In looking for defining features, the obvious place to start is with science's most striking aspect—it is an empirical enterprise about the real world of sensation. This is not to say that science refers only to observable entities. Every mature science contains unobservables, like electrons and genes, but ultimately, they refer to the world around us. Science attempts to understand this empirical world. What is the basis for this understanding? Surveying science and the history of science today, one thing stands out: science involves a search for order. More specifically, science looks for unbroken, blind, natural regularities (*laws*). Things in the world do not happen in just any old way. They follow set paths, and science tries to capture this fact. Bodies of science, therefore, known variously as "theories" or "paradigms" or "sets of models," are collections of laws.[6]

Thus, in Newtonian physics we find Newton's three laws of motion, the law of gravitational attraction, Kepler's laws of planetary motion, and so forth. Similarly, for instance, in population genetics we find the Hardy-Weinberg law. However, when we turn to something like philosophy, we do not find the same appeal to empirical law. Plato's Theory of Forms only indirectly refers to this world. Analogously, religion does not insist on unbroken law. Indeed, religious beliefs frequently allow or suppose events outside law or else events that violate law (miracles). Jesus feeding the 5,000 with the loaves and fishes was one such event. This is not to say that religion is false, but it does say that religion is not science. When the loaves and fishes multiplied to a sufficiency to feed so many people, things happened that did not obey natural law, and hence the feeding of the 5,000 is an event beyond the ken of science.[7]

A major part of the scientific enterprise involves the use of law to effect *explanation*. One tries to show why things are as they are—and how they fall beneath or follow from law (together perhaps with certain specified initial conditions). Why, for example, does a cannon ball go in a parabola and not in a circle? Because of the constraints of Newton's laws. Why do two blue-eyed parents always have blue-eyed children? Because this trait obeys Mendel's first law, given the particular way in which the genes control eye-color. A scientific explanation must appeal to law and must show that what is being explained had to occur. The explanation excludes those things that did not happen.[8]

The other side of explanation is *prediction*. The laws indicate what is going to happen: that the ball will go in a parabola, that the child will be blue-eyed. In science, as well as in futurology, one can also, as it were, predict backwards. Using laws, one infers that a particular, hitherto-unknown phenomenon or event took place in the past. Thus, for instance, one might use the laws of physics to infer back to some eclipse of the sun reported in ancient writings.

Closely connected with the twin notions of explanation and prediction comes *testability*. A genuine scientific theory lays itself open to check against the real world: the scientist can see if the inferences made in explanation and prediction actually obtain in nature. Does the chemical reaction proceed as suspected? In Young's double slit experiment, does one find the bands of light and dark predicted by the wave theory? Do the continents show the expected after-effects of drift?

Testability is a two-way process. The researcher looks for some positive evidence, for *confirmation*. No one will take seriously a scientific theory that has no empirical support (although obviously a younger theory is liable to be less well-supported than an older theory). Conversely, a theory must be open to possible refutation. If the facts speak against a theory, then it must go. A body of science must be *falsifiable*. For example, Kepler's laws could have been false: if a planet were discovered going in squares, then the laws would have been shown to be incorrect. However, in distinguishing science from nonscience, no amount of empirical evidence can disprove, for example, the Kantian philosophical claim that one ought to treat people as ends rather than means. Similarly, Catholic religious claims about transubstantiation (the changing of the bread and wine into the body and blood of Christ) are unfalsifiable.[9]

Science is *tentative*. Ultimately, a scientist must be prepared to reject his theory. Unfortunately, not all scientists are prepared to do in practice what they promise to do in theory; but the weaknesses of individuals are counterbalanced by the fact that, as a group, scientists do give up theories that fail to answer to new or reconsidered evidence. In the last 30 years, for example, geologists have reversed their strong convictions that the continents never move.

Scientists do not, of course, immediately throw their theories away as soon as any counter-evidence arrives. If a theory is powerful and successful, then some problems will be tolerated, but scientists must be prepared to change their minds in the face of the empirical evidence. In this regard, the scientists

(continued)

Creation Science Is Not Science (*continued*)

differ from both the philosophers and the theologians. Nothing in the real world would make the Kantian change his mind, and the Catholic is equally dogmatic, despite any empirical evidence about the stability of bread and wine. Such evidence is simply considered irrelevant.[10]

Some other features of science should also be mentioned, for instance, the urge for simplicity and unification; however, I have now listed the major characteristics. Good science—like good philosophy and good religion—presupposes an attitude that one might describe as professional *integrity*. A scientist should not cheat or falsify data or quote out of context or do any other thing that is intellectually dishonest. Of course, as always, some individuals fail; but science as a whole disapproves of such actions. Indeed, when transgressors are detected, they are usually expelled from the community. Science depends on honesty in the realm of ideas. One may cheat on one's taxes; one may not fiddle the data.[11]

Creation-Science Considered

How does creation-science fit the criteria of science listed in the previous section? By "creation-science" in this context, I refer not just to the definition given in Act 590, but to the whole body of literature which goes by that name. The doctrine includes the claims that the universe is very young (6,000 to 20,000 years), that everything started instantaneously, that human beings had ancestry separate from apes, and that a monstrous flood once engulfed the entire earth.[12]

Laws—Natural Regularities

Science is about unbroken, natural regularity. It does not admit miracles. It is clear, therefore, that again and again, creation science invokes happenings and causes outside of law. For instance, the only reasonable inference from Act 590 (certainly the inference that was accepted in the Arkansas court) is that for creation-science the origin of the universe and life in it is not bound by law. Whereas the definition of creation-science includes the unqualified phrase "sudden creation of the universe, energy and life from nothing," the definition of evolution specifically includes the qualification that its view of origins is "naturalistic." Because "naturalistic" means "subject to empirical law," the deliberate omission of such a term in the characterization of creation-science means that no laws were involved.

In confirmation of this inference, we can find identical claims in the writings of creation scientists: for instance, the following passage from Duane T. Gish's popular work *Evolution—The Fossils Say No!*

> CREATION. By creation we mean the bringing into being of the basic kinds of plants and animals by the process of sudden, or fiat, creation described in the first two chapters of Genesis. Here we find the creation by God of the plants and animals, each commanded to reproduce after its own kind using processes which were essentially instantaneous.
>
> We do not know how God created, what processes He used, *for God used processes which are not now operating anywhere in the natural universe*. This is why we refer to divine creation as special creation. We cannot discover by scientific investigations anything about the creative processes used by God.[13]

By Gish's own admission, we are not dealing with science. Similar sentiments can be found in *The Genesis Flood* by John Whitcomb, Jr., and Henry M. Morris:

> But during the period of Creation, God was introducing order and organization and energization into the universe in a very high degree, even to life itself! *It is thus quite plain that the processes used by God in creation were utterly different from the processes which now operate in the universe!* The Creation was a unique period, entirely incommensurate with this present world. This is plainly emphasized and reemphasized in the divine revelation which God has given us concerning Creation, which concludes with these words: 'And the heavens and the earth were *finished,* and *all* the host of them. And on the seventh day God *finished* His work which He had made; and He *rested* on the seventh day from *all His work* which He had made. And God blessed the seventh day, and hallowed it; because that in it He *rested* from *all* his work which God had created and made.' In view of these strong and

repeated assertions, is it not the height of presumption for man to attempt to study Creation in terms of present processes?[14]

Creation scientists generally acknowledge this work to be *the* seminal contribution that led to the growth of the creation-science movement. Morris, in particular, is the father figure of creation-science and Gish his chief lieutenant.

Creation scientists also break with law in many other instances. The creationists believe that the Flood, for example, could not have just occurred through blind regularities. As Whitcomb and Morris make very clear, certain supernatural interventions were necessary to bring about the Flood.[15] Similarly, in order to ensure the survival of at least some organisms, God had to busy himself and break through law.

Explanation and Prediction

Given the crucial role that law plays for the scientist in these processes, neither explanation nor prediction is possible where no law exists. Thus, explanation and prediction simply cannot even be attempted when one deals with creation-science accounts either of origins or of the Flood.

Even against the broader vistas of biology, creation-science is inadequate. Scientific explanation/prediction must lead to the thing being explained/predicted, showing why that thing obtains and not other things. Why does the ball go in a parabola? Why does it not describe a circle? Take an important and pervasive biological phenomenon, namely, "homologies," the isomorphisms between the bones of different animals. These similarities were recognized as pervasive facets of nature even before Darwin published *The Origin of Species*. Why are the bones in the forelimbs of men, horses, whales, and birds all so similar, even though the functions are quite different? Evolutionists explain homologies naturally and easily, as a result of common descent. Creationists can give no explanation, and make no predictions. All they can offer is the disingenuous comment that homology signifies nothing, because classification is all man-made and arbitrary anyway. Is it arbitrary that man is not classified with the birds?[16] Why are Darwin's finches distributed in the way that we find on the Galapagos? Why are there 14 separate species of this little bird, scattered over a small group of islands in the Pacific on the equator? On those rare occasions when Darwin's finches do fly into the pages of creation-science, it is claimed either that they are all the same species (false), or that they are a case of degeneration from one "kind" created back at the beginning of life.[17] Apart from the fact that "kind" is a term of classification to be found only in Genesis, this is no explanation. How could such a division of the finches have occurred, given the short span that the creationists allow since the Creation? And, in any case, Darwin's finches are anything but degenerates. Different species of finch have entirely different sorts of beaks, adapted for different foodstuffs—evolution of the most sophisticated type.[18]

Testability, Confirmation, and Falsifiability

Testability, confirmation, and falsifiability are no better treated by creation-science. A scientific theory must provide more than just after-the-fact explanations of things that one already knows. One must push out into the frontiers of new knowledge, trying to predict new facts, and risking the theory against the discovery of possible falsifying information. One cannot simply work at a secondary level, constantly protecting one's views against threat: forever inventing *ad hoc* hypotheses to save one's core assumptions.

Creation scientists do little or nothing by way of genuine test. Indeed, the most striking thing about the whole body of creation-science literature is the virtual absence of *any* experimental or observational work by creation scientists. Almost invariably, the creationists work exclusively with the discoveries and claims of evolutionists, twisting the conclusions to their own ends. Argument proceeds by showing evolution (specifically Darwinism) wrong, rather than by showing Creationism right.

However, this way of proceeding—what the creationists refer to as the "two model approach"—is simply a fallacious form of argument. The views of people like Fred Hoyle and N.C. Wickramasinghe, who believes that life comes from outer space, are neither creationist nor truly evolutionist.[19] Denying evolution in no way proves Creationism. And, even if a more straightforward either/or between evolution and Creationism existed, the perpetually negative approach is just not

(continued)

Creation Science Is Not Science (*continued*)

the way that science proceeds. One must find one's own evidence in favor of one's position, just as physicists, chemists, and biologists do.

Do creation scientists ever actually expose their theories and ideas to test? Even if they do, when new counter-empirical evidence is discovered, creation scientists appear to pull back, refusing to allow their position to be falsified.

Consider, for instance, the classic case of the "missing link"—namely, that between man and his ancestors. The creationists say that there are no plausible bridging organisms whatsoever. Thus, this super-gap between man and all other animals (alive or dead) supposedly underlines the creationists' contention that man and apes have separate ancestry. But what about the australopithecines, organisms that paleontologists have, for most of this century, claimed are plausible human ancestors? With respect, argue the creationists, australopithecines are not links, because they had ape-like brains, they *walked* like apes, and they used their knuckles for support, just like gorillas. Hence, the gap remains.[20]

However, such a conclusion can be maintained only by blatant disregard of the empirical evidence. *Australopithecus afarensis* was a creature with a brain the size of that of an ape which walked upright.[21] Yet the creationists do not concede defeat. They then argue that the *Australopithecus afarensis* is like an orangutan.[22] In short, nothing apparently makes the creationists change their minds, or allow their views to be tested, lest they be falsified.

Tentativeness

Creation-science is not science because there is absolutely no way in which creationists will budge from their position. Indeed, the leading organization of creation-science, The Creation Research Society (with 500 full members, all of whom must have an advanced degree in a scientific/technological area), demands that its members sign a statement affirming that they take the Bible as literally true.[23] Unfortunately, an organization cannot require such a condition of membership, and then claim to be a scientific organization. Science must be open to change, however confident one may feel at present. Fanatical dogmatism is just not acceptable.

Integrity

Creation scientists use any fallacy in the logic books to achieve their ends. Most particularly, apart from grossly distorting evolutionists' positions, the creation scientists frequently use inappropriate or incomplete quotations. They take the words of some eminent evolutionist, and attempt to make him or her say exactly the opposite to that intended. For instance, in *Creation: The Facts of Life*, author Gary E. Parker constantly refers to "noted Harvard geneticist" Richard Lewontin as claiming that the hand and the eye are the best evidence of God's design.[24] Can this reference really be true? Has the author of *The Genetic Basis of Evolutionary Change*[25] really foresworn Darwin for Moses? In fact, when one looks at Lewontin's writings, one finds that he says that *before Darwin*, people believed the hand and the eye to be the effect of direct design. Today, scientists believe that such features were produced by the natural process of evolution through natural selection; but, a reader learns nothing of this from Parker's book.

What are the essential features of science? Does creation-science have any, all, or none of these features? My answer to this is none. By every mark of what constitutes science, creation-science fails. And, although it has not been my direct purpose to show its true nature, it is surely there for all to see. Miracles brought about by an intervening supervising force speak of only one thing. Creation "science" is actually dogmatic religious Fundamentalism. To regard it as otherwise is an insult to the scientist, as well as to the believer who sees creation-science as a blasphemous distortion of God-given reason. I believe that creation-science should not be taught in the public schools because creation-science is not science.

NOTES

1. In fact, Act 590 demanded that *if* one teach evolution, *then* one must also teach creation science. Presumably a teacher could have stayed away from origins entirely—albeit with large gaps in some courses. [See Act 590, Acts of Arkansas, reprinted elsewhere in this issue.]

2. For a brief personal account of my experiences, see Michael Ruse, "A Philosopher at the Monkey Trial," *New Scientist* (1982): 317–319.
3. Judge William Overton's ruling on the constitutionality (or, rather, unconstitutionality) of Act 590 gives a fair and full account of the various claims made by theologians (including historians and sociologists of religion) and scientists. [See the Opinion in *McLean v. Arkansas*, reprinted elsewhere in this issue.]
4. In my book, *The Darwinian Revolution: Science Red in Tooth and Claw* (Chicago, IL: University of Chicago Press, 1979), I look at the way science was breaking apart from religion in the 19th century.
5. What follows is drawn from a number of basic books in the philosophy of science, including R. B. Braithwaite, *Scientific Explanation* (Cambridge, England: Cambridge University Press, 1953); Karl R. Popper, *The Logic of Scientific Discovery* (London: Hutchinson, 1959); E. Nagel, *The Structure of Science* (London: Routledge and Kegan Paul, 1961); Thomas S. Kuhn, *The Structure of Scientific Revolutions* (Chicago, IL: University of Chicago Press, 1962); and C. G. Hempel, *The Philosophy of Natural Science* (Englewood Cliffs, NJ: Prentice-Hall, 1966). The discussion is the same as what I provided for the plaintiffs in a number of position papers. It also formed the basis of my testimony in court, and, as can be seen from Judge Overton's ruling, was accepted by the court virtually verbatim.
6. One sometimes sees a distinction drawn between "theory" and "model." At the level of this discussion, it is not necessary to discuss specific details. I consider various uses of these terms in my book, *Darwinism Defended: A Guide to the Evolution Controversies* (Reading, MA: Addison-Wesley, 1982).
7. For more on science and miracles, especially with respect to evolutionary questions, see my *Darwinian Revolution, op. cit.*
8. The exact relationship between laws and what they explain has been a matter of much debate. Today, I think most would agree that the connection must be fairly tight—the thing being explained should follow. For more on explanation in biology see Michael Ruse, *The Philosophy of Biology* (London: Hutchinson, 1973); and David L. Hull, *The Philosophy of Biological Science* (Englewood Cliffs, NJ: Prentice-Hall, 1974). A popular thesis is that explanation of laws involves deduction from other laws. A theory is a body of laws bound in this way: a so-called "hypothetico-deductive" system.
9. Falsifiability today has a high profile in the philosophical and scientific literature. Many scientists, especially, agree with Karl Popper, who has argued that falsifiability is *the* criterion demarcating science from non-science (see especially his *Logic of Scientific Discovery*). My position is that falsifiability is an important part, but only one part, of a spectrum of features required to demarcate science from non-science. For more on this point, see my *Is Science Sexist! And Other Problems in the Biomedical Sciences* (Dordrecht, Holland: D. Reidel Publishing Company, 1981).
10. At the Arkansas trial, in talking of the tentativeness of science, I drew an analogy in testimony between science and the law. In a criminal trial, one tries to establish guilt "beyond a reasonable doubt." If this can be done, then the criminal is convicted. But, if new evidence is ever discovered that might prove the convicted person innocent, cases can always be reopened. In science, too, scientists make decisions less formally but just as strongly—and get on with business, but cases (theories) can be reopened.
11. Of course, the scientist as citizen may run into problems here!
12. The key definitions in Arkansas Act 590, requiring "balanced treatment" in the public schools, are found in Section 4. [See the Act reprinted on pp. 11–13.] Section 4(a)(b) does not specify exactly how old the earth is supposed to be, but in court a span of 6,000 to 20,000 years emerged in testimony.

    The fullest account of the creation-science position is given in Henry M. Morris, ed., *Scientific Creationism* (San Diego, CA: Creation-Life Publishers, 1974).
13. Duane T. Gish, *Evolution—The Fossils Say No!* (San Diego, CA: Creation-Life Publishers, 1973), pp. 22–25, his italics.
14. John Whitcomb, Jr., and Henry M. Morris, *The Genesis Flood* (Philadelphia, PA: Presbyterian and Reformed Publishing Company, 1961), pp. 223–224, their italics.
15. *Ibid*, p. 76.
16. See Morris, *op. cit.*, pp. 71–72, and my discussion in *Darwinism Defended, op. cit.*
17. For instance, in John N. Moore and H. S. Slusher, *Biology/A Search for Order in Complexity* (Grand Rapids, MI: Zondervan, 1977).
18. D. Lack, *Darwin's Finches* (Cambridge, England: Cambridge University Press, 1947).
19. Fred Hoyle and N. C. Wickramasinghe, *Evolution from Space* (London: Dent, 1981).
20. Morris, *op. cit.*, p. 173.
21. Donald Johanson and M. Edey, *Lucy: The Beginnings of Humankind* (New York, NY: Simon and Schuster, 1981).
22. Gary E. Parker, *Creation: The Facts of Life* (San Diego, CA: Creation-Life Publishers, 1979), p. 113.
23. For details of these statements, see reference 7 in Judge Overton's ruling (footnote number 7).

(continued)

Creation Science Is Not Science   (continued)

24. Parker, *op. cit.* See, for instance, pp. 55 and 144. The latter passage is worth quoting in full:

    Then there's 'the marvelous fit of organisms to the environment,' the special adaptations of cleaner fish, woodpeckers, bombardier beetles, etc., —what Darwin called 'Difficulties with the Theory,' and what Harvard's Lewontin (1978) called 'the chief evidence of a Supreme Designer.' Because of their 'perfection of structure,' he says, organisms 'appear to have been carefully and artfully designed.'

    The pertinent article by Richard Lewontin is "Adaptation," *Scientific American* (September 1978).
25. Richard C. Lewontin, *The Genetic Basis of Evolutionary Change* (New York, NY: Columbia University Press, 1974).

Science, Conjecture and Refutation
Karl Popper

Mr. Turnbull had presided evil consequences. . . . and was now doing the best in his power to bring about the verification of his own prophecies.

Anthony Trollope

I

WHEN I received the list of participants in this course and realized that I had been asked to speak to philosophical colleagues I thought, after some hesitation and consultation, that you would probably prefer me to speak about those problems which interest me most, and about those developments with which I am most intimately acquainted. I therefore decided to do what I have never done before: to give you a report on my own work in the philosophy of science, since the autumn of 1919 when I first began to grapple with the problem, *'When should a theory be ranked as scientific?'* or *'is there a criterion for she scientific character or status of a theory?"*

The problem which troubled me at the time was neither, 'When is a theory true?' nor, 'When is a theory acceptable?' My problem was different. I *wished to distinguish between science and pseudo-science;* knowing very well that science often errs, and that pseudo-science may happen to stumble on the truth.

I knew, of course, the most widely accepted answer to my problem: that science is distinguished from pseudo-science—or from 'metaphysics'—by its *empirical method,* which is essentially *inductive,* proceeding from observation or experiment. But this did not satisfy me. On the contrary, I often formulated my problem as one of distinguishing between a genuinely empirical method and a. non-empirical or even a pseudo-empirical method—that is to say, a method which, although it appeals to observation and experiment, nevertheless does not come up to scientific standards. The latter method may be exemplified by astrology, with its stupendous mass of empirical evidence based on observation—on horoscopes and on biographies.

But as it was not the example of astrology which led me to my problem I should perhaps briefly describe the atmosphere in which my problem arose and the examples by which it was stimulated. After the collapse of the Austrian Empire there had been a revolution in Austria: the air was full of revolutionary slogans and ideas, and new and often wild theories. Among the theories which interested me Einstein's theory of relativity was no doubt by far the most important. Three others were Marx's theory of history, Freud's psycho-analysis, and Alfred Adler's so-called 'individual psychology.'

There was a lot of popular nonsense talked about these theories, and especially about relativity (as still happens even today), but I was fortunate in those who introduced me to the study of this theory. We all—the small circle of students to which I belonged—were thrilled with the result of Eddington's eclipse observations which in 1919 brought the first important confirmation of

Einstein's theory of gravitation. It was a great experience for us, and one which had a lasting influence on my intellectual development.

The three other theories I have mentioned were also widely discussed among students at that time. I myself happened to come into personal contact with Alfred Adler, and even to co-operate with him in his social work among the children and young people in the working-class districts of Vienna where he had established social guidance clinics.

It was during the summer of 1919 that I began to feel more and more dissatisfied with these three theories—the Marxist theory of history, psychoanalysis, and individual psychology; and I began to feel dubious about their claims to scientific status. My problem perhaps first took the simple form, 'What is wrong with Marxism, psycho-analysis, and individual psychology? Why are they so different from physical theories, from Newton's theory, and especially from the theory of relativity?'

To make this contrast clear I should explain that few of us at the time would have said that we believed in the *truth* of Einstein's theory of gravitation. This shows that it was not my doubting the *truth* of those other three theories which bothered me, but something else. Yet neither was it that I merely felt mathematical physics to be more *exact* than the sociological or psychological type of theory. Thus what worried me was neither the problem of truth, at that stage at least, nor the problem of exactness or measurability. It was rather that I felt that these other three theories, though posing as sciences, had in fact more in common with primitive myths than with science; that they resembled astrology rather than astronomy.

I found that those of my friends who were admirers of Marx, Freud, and Adler, were impressed by a number of points common to these theories, and especially by their apparent *explanatory power*. These theories appeared to be able to explain practically everything that happened within the fields to which they referred. The study of any of them seemed to have the effect of an intellectual conversion or revelation, opening your eyes to a new truth hidden from those not yet initiated. Once your eyes were thus opened you saw confirming instances everywhere: the world was full of *verifications* of the theory. Whatever happened always confirmed it. Thus its truth appeared manifest; and unbelievers were clearly people who did not want to see the manifest truth; who refused to see it, either because it was against their class interest, or because of their repressions which were still 'un-analysed' and crying aloud for treatment.

The most characteristic element in this situation seemed to me the incessant stream of confirmations, of observations which 'verified' the theories in question; and this point was constantly emphasized by their adherents. A Marxist could not open a newspaper without finding on every page confirming evidence for his interpretation of history; not only in the news, but also in its presentation—which revealed the class bias of the paper—and especially of course in what the paper did *not* say. The Freudian analysts emphasized that their theories were constantly verified by their 'clinical observations'. As for Adler, I was much impressed by a personal experience. Once, in 1919, I reported to him a case which to me did not seem particularly Adlerian, but which he found no difficulty in analysing in terms of his theory of inferiority feelings, although he had not even seen the child. Slightly shocked, I asked him how he could be so sure. 'Because of my thousandfold experience,' he replied; whereupon I could not help saying: 'And with this new case, I suppose, your experience has become thousand-and-one-fold.'

What I had in mind was that his previous observations may not have been much sounder than this new one; that each in its turn had been interpreted in the light of 'previous experience', and at the same time counted as additional confirmation. What, I asked myself, did it confirm? No more than that a case could be interpreted in the light of the theory. But this meant very little, I reflected, since every conceivable case could be interpreted in the light of Adler's theory, or equally or Freud's. I may illustrate this by two very different examples of human behaviour: that of a man who pushes a child into the water with the intention of drowning it; and that of a man who sacrifices his life in an attempt to save the child. Each of these two cases can be explained with equal ease in Freudian and in Adlerian terms. According to Freud the first man suffered from repression (say, of some component of his Oedipus complex), while the second man had achieved sublimation. According to Adler the first man suffered from feelings of inferiority (producing perhaps the need to prove to himself that he dared to commit some crime), and so did the second man (whose need was to prove to himself that

(continued)

Science, Conjecture and Refutation (*continued*)

he dared to rescue the child). I could not think of any human behaviour which could not be interpreted in terms of either theory. It was precisely this fact—that they always fitted, that they were always confirmed—which in the eyes of their admirers constituted the strongest argument in favour of these theories. It began to dawn on me that this apparent strength was in fact their weakness.

With Einstein's theory the situation was strikingly different. Take one typical instance—Einstein's prediction, just then confirmed by the findings of Eddington's expedition. Einstein's gravitational theory had led to the result that light must be attracted by heavy bodies (such as the sun), precisely as material bodies were attracted. As a consequence it could be calculated that light from a distant fixed star whose apparent position was close to the sun would reach the earth from such a direction that the star would seem to be slightly shifted away from the sun; or, in other words, that stars close to the sun would look as if they had moved a little away from the sun, and from one another. This is a thing which cannot normally be observed since such stars are rendered invisible in daytime by the sun's overwhelming brightness; but during an eclipse it is possible to take photographs of them. If the same constellation is photographed at night one can measure the distances on the two photographs, and check the predicted effect.

Now the impressive thing about this case is the *risk* involved in a prediction of this kind. If observation shows that the predicted effect is definitely absent, then the theory is simply refuted. The theory is *incompatible with certain possible results of observation*—in fact with results which everybody before Einstein would have expected.[1] This is quite different from the situation I have previously described, when it turned out that the theories in question were compatible with the most divergent human behaviour, so that it was practically impossible to describe any human behaviour that might not be claimed to be a verification of these theories.

These considerations led me in the winter of 1919–20 to conclusions which I may now reformulate as follows.

1. It is easy to obtain confirmations, or verifications, for nearly every theory—if we look for confirmations.
2. Confirmations should count only if they are the result of *risky predictions;* that is to say, if, unenlightened by the theory in question, we should have expected an event which was incompatible with the theory—an event which would have refuted the theory.
3. Every 'good' scientific theory is a prohibition: it forbids certain things to happen. The more a theory forbids, the better it is.
4. A theory which is not refutable by any conceivable event is non-scientific. Irrefutability is not a virtue of a theory (as people often think) but a vice.
5. Every genuine *test* of a theory is an attempt to falsify it, or to refute it. Testability is falsifiability; but there are degrees of testability: some theories are more testable, more exposed to refutation, than others; they take, as it were, greater risks.
6. Confirming evidence should not count *except when it is the result of a genuine test of the theory;* and this means that it can be presented as a serious but unsuccessful attempt to falsify the theory. (I now speak in such cases of 'corroborating evidence.')
7. Some genuinely testable theories, when found to be false, are still up-held by their admirers—for example by introducing *ad* hoc some auxiliary assumption, or by re-interpreting the theory *ad hoc* in such a way that it escapes refutation. Such a procedure is always possible, but it rescues the theory from refutation only at the price of destroying, or at least lowering, its scientific status. (I later described such a rescuing operation as a *'conventionalist twist'* or a *'conventionalist stratagem.'*)

One can sum up all this by saying that *the criterion of the scientific status of theory is its falsifiability,* or *refutability,* or *testability.*

II

I may perhaps exemplify this with the help of the various theories so far mentioned. Einstein's theory of gravitation clearly satisfied the criterion of falsifiability. Even if our measuring instruments at the time did not allow us to pronounce on the results of the tests with complete assurance, there was clearly a possibility of refuting the theory.

Astrology did not pass the test. Astrologers were greatly impressed, and misled, by what they believed, to be confirming evidence—so much that they were quite unimpressed by any unfavourable evidence. Moreover, by making their interpretations and prophecies sufficiently vague they were able to explain away anything that might have been a refutation of the theory had the theory and the prophecies been more precise. In order to escape falsification they destroyed the testability of their theory. It is a typical soothsayer's trick to predict things so vaguely that the predictions can hardly fail: that they become irrefutable.

The Marxist theory of history, in spite of the serious efforts of some of its founders and followers, ultimately adopted this soothsaying practice. In some of its earlier formulations (for example in Marx's analysis of the character of the 'coming social revolution') their predictions were testable, and in fact falsified.[2] Yet instead of accepting the refutations the followers of Marx re-interpreted both the theory and the evidence in order to make them agree. In this way they rescued the theory from refutation; but they did so at the price of adopting a device which made it irrefutable. They thus gave a 'conventionalist twist' to the theory; and by this stratagem they destroyed its much advertised claim to scientific status.

The two psycho-analytic theories were in a different class. They were simply non-testable, irrefutable. There was no conceivable human behaviour which could contradict them. This does not mean that Freud and Adler were not seeing certain things correctly: I personally do not doubt that much of what they say is of considerable importance, and may well play its part one day in a psychological science which is testable. But it does mean that those 'clinical observations' which analysts naively believe confirm their theory cannot do this any more than the daily confirmations which astrologers find in their practice.[3] And as for Freud's epic of the Ego, the Super-ego, and the Id, no substantially stronger claim to scientific status can be made for it than for Homer's collected stories from Olympus. These theories describe some facts, but in the manner of myths. They contain most interesting psychological suggestions, but not in a testable form.

At the same time I realized that such myths may be developed, and become testable; that historically speaking all—or very nearly all—scientific theories originate from myths, and that a myth may contain important anticipations of scientific theories. Examples are Empedocles' theory of evolution by trial and error, or Parmenides' myth of the unchanging block universe in which nothing ever happens and which, if we add another dimension, becomes Einstein's block universe (in which, too, nothing ever happens, since everything is, four-dimensionally speaking, determined and laid down from the beginning). I thus felt that if a theory is found to be non-scientific, or 'metaphysical' (as we might say), it is not thereby found to be unimportant, or insignificant, or 'meaningless', or 'nonsensical'.[4] But it cannot claim to be backed by empirical evidence in the scientific sense—although it may easily be, in some genetic sense, the 'result of observation'.

(There were a great many other theories of this pre-scientific or pseudo-scientific character, some of them, unfortunately, as influential as the Marxist interpretation of history; for example, the racialist interpretation of history—another of those impressive and all-explanatory theories which act upon weak minds like revelations.)

Thus the problem which I tried to solve by proposing the criterion of falsifiability was neither a problem of meaningfulness or significance, nor a problem of truth or acceptability. It was the problem of drawing a line (as well as this can be done) between the statements, or systems of statements, of the empirical sciences, and all other statements—whether they are of a religious or of metaphysical character, or simply pseudo-scientific. Years later—it must have been in 1928 or 1929—I called this first problem of mine the *'problem demarcation'*. The criterion of falsifiability is a solution to this problem of demarcation, for it says that statements or systems of statements, in order to be ranked as scientific, must be capable of conflicting with possible, or conceivable, observations. . . .

IV

I have discussed the problem of demarcation in some detail because I believe that its solution is the key to most of the fundamental problems of the philosophy of science. I am going to give you later a list of some of these other problems, but only one of them—the *problem of induction*—can be discussed here at any length.

(continued)

Science, Conjecture and Refutation (*continued*)

I had become interested in the problem of induction in 1923. Although this problem is very closely connected with the problem of demarcation, I did not fully appreciate the connection for about five years.

I approached the problem of induction through Hume. Hume, I felt, was perfectly right in pointing out that induction cannot be logically justified. He held that there can be no valid logical[5] arguments allowing us to establish *'that instances, of which we have had no experience, resemble those, of which we have had experience'*. Consequently *'even after the observation of the frequent or constant conjunction of objects, we have no reason to draw any inference concerning any object beyond those of which we have had experience'*. For 'shou'd it be said that we have experience'[6]—experience teaching us that objects constantly conjoined with certain other objects continue to be so conjoined—then, Hume says, 'I wou'd renew my question, *why from this experience we form any conclusion beyond those past instances, of which we have had experience'*. In other words, an attempt to justify the practice of induction by an appeal to experience must lead to an *infinite regress*. As a result we can say that theories can never be inferred from observation statements, or rationally justified by them.

I found Hume's refutation of inductive inference clear and conclusive. But I felt completely dissatisfied with his psychological explanation of induction in terms of custom or habit.

It has often been noticed that this explanation of Hume's is philosophically not very satisfactory. It is, however, without doubt intended as *a psychological* rather than a philosophical theory; for it tries to give a causal explanation of a psychological fact—*the fact that we believe in laws*, in statements asserting regularities or constantly conjoined kinds of events—by asserting that this fact is due to (i.e., constantly conjoined with) custom or habit. But even this reformulation of Hume's theory is still unsatisfactory; for what I have just called a 'psychological fact' may itself be described as a custom or habit—the custom or habit of believing in laws or regularities; and it is neither very surprising not very enlightening to hear that such a custom or habit mast be explained as due to, or conjoined with, a custom or habit (even though a different one). Only when we remember that the words 'custom' and 'habit' are used by Hume, as they are in ordinary language, not merely to *describe* regular behaviour, but rather to *theorize about its origin* (ascribed to frequent repetition), can we reformulate his psychological theory in a more satisfactory way. We can then say that, like other habits, *our habit of believing in laws is the product of frequent repetition*—of the repeated observation that things of a certain kind are constantly conjoined with things of another kind. . . .

VIII

Let us now turn from our logical criticism of the *psychology of experience* to our real problem—the problem of *the logic of science*. Although some of the things I have said may help us here, in so far as they may have eliminated certain psychological prejudices in favour of induction, my treatment of the *logical problem of induction* is completely independent of this criticism, and of all psychological considerations. Provided you do not dogmatically believe in the alleged psychological fact that we make inductions, you may now forget my whole story with the exception of two logical points: my logical remarks on testability or falsifiability as the criterion of demarcation; and Hume's logical criticism of induction.

From what I have said it is obvious that there was a close link between the two problems which interested me at that time: demarcation, and induction or scientific method. It was easy to see that the method of science is criticism, i.e., attempted falsifications. Yet it took me a few years to notice that the two problems—of demarcation and of induction—were in a sense one.

Why, I asked, do so many scientists believe in induction? I found they did so because they believed natural science to be characterized by the inductive method—by a method starting from, and relying upon, long sequences of observations and experiments. They believed that the difference between genuine science and metaphysical or pseudo-scientific speculation depended solely upon whether or not the inductive method was employed. They believed (to put it in my own terminology) that only the inductive method could provide a satisfactory *criterion of demarcation*.

I recently came across an interesting formulation of this belief in a remarkable philosophical book by a great physicist—Max Born's *Natural Philosophy of Cause and Chance*.[7] He writes: 'Induction allows us to generalize a number of observations into a general rule: that night follows day and day follows night . . . But while everyday life has no definite criterion, for the validity of an induction, . . . science has worked out a code, or rule of craft, for its application.' Born nowhere reveals the contents of this inductive code (which, as his wording shows, contains a 'definite criterion for the validity of an induction'); but he stresses that 'there is no logical argument' for its acceptance: 'it is a question of faith'; and he is therefore 'willing to call induction a metaphysical principle'. But why does he believe that such a code of valid inductive rules must exist? This becomes clear when he speaks of the 'vast communities of people ignorant of, or rejecting, the rule of science, among them the members of anti-vaccination societies and believers in astrology. It is useless to argue with them; I cannot compel them to accept the same criteria of valid induction in which I believe: the code of scientific rules.' This makes it quite clear that *'valid induction' was here meant to serve as a criterion of demarcation between science and pseudo-science.*

But it is obvious that this rule or craft of 'valid induction' is not even metaphysical: it simply does not exist. No rule can ever guarantee that a generalization inferred from true observations, however often repeated, is true. (Born himself does not believe in the truth of Newtonian physics, in spite of its success, although he believes that it is based on induction.) And the success of science is not based upon rules of induction, but depends upon luck, ingenuity, and the purely deductive rules of critical argument.

I may summarize some of my conclusions as follows:

1. Induction, i.e., inference based on many observations, is a myth. It is neither a psychological fact, nor a fact of ordinary life, nor one of scientific procedure.
2. The actual procedure of science is to operate with conjectures: to jump to conclusions—often after one single observation (as noticed for example by Hume arid Born).
3. Repealed observations and experiments function in science as *tests* of our conjectures or hypotheses, i.e., as attempted refutations.
4. The mistaken belief in induction is fortified by the need for a criterion of demarcation which, it is traditionally but wrongly believed, only the inductive method can provide.
5. The conception of such an inductive method, like the criterion of verifiability, implies a faulty demarcation.
6. None of this is altered in the least if we say that induction makes theories only probable rather than certain. (See especially chapter 10, below.)

IX

If, as I have suggested, the problem of induction is only an instance or facet of the problem of demarcation, then the solution to the problem of demarcation must provide us with a solution to the problem of induction. This is indeed the case, I believe, although it is perhaps not immediately obvious.

For a brief formulation of the problem of induction we can turn again to Born, who writes: '. . . no observation or experiment, however extended, can give more than a finite number of repetitions'; therefore, 'the statement of a law—B depends on A—always transcends experience. Yet this kind of statement is made everywhere and all the time, and sometimes from scanty material.'[8]

In other words, the logical problem of induction arises from *(a)* Hume's discovery (so well expressed by Born) that it is impossible to justify a law by observation or experiment, since it 'transcends experience'; *(b)* the fact that science proposes and uses laws 'everywhere and all the time'. (Like Hume, Born is struck by the 'scanty material', i.e., the few observed instances upon which the law may be based.) To this we have to add *(c) the principle of empiricism* which asserts that in science, only observation and experiment may decide upon the *acceptance or rejection* of scientific statements, including laws and theories.

These three principles, *(a)*, *(b)*, and *(c)*, appear at first sight to clash; and this apparent clash constitutes the *logical problem of induction*.

Faced with this clash, Born gives up (c), the principle of empiricism (as Kant and many others, including Bertrand Russell, have done before him), in favour of what he calls a 'metaphysical principle';

(continued)

Science, Conjecture and Refutation (*continued*)

a metaphysical principle which he does not even attempt to formulate; which he vaguely describes as a 'code or rule of craft'; and of which I have never seen any formulation which even looked promising and was not clearly untenable.

But in fact the principles *(a)* to *(c)* do not clash. We can see this the moment we realize that the acceptance by science of a law or of a theory is *tentative only;* which is to say that all laws and theories are conjectures, or tentative *hypotheses* (a position which I have sometimes called 'hypotheticism'); and that we may reject a law or theory on the basis of new evidence, without necessarily discarding the old evidence which originally led us to accept it.[9]

The principle of empiricism *(c)* can be fully preserved, since the fate of a theory, its acceptance or rejection, is decided by observation and experiment—by the result of tests. So long as a theory stands up to the severest tests we can design, it is accepted; if it does not, it is rejected. But it is never inferred, in any sense, from the empirical evidence. There is neither a psychological nor a logical induction. *Only the falsity of the theory can be inferred from empirical evidence, and this inference is a purely deductive one.*

Hume showed that it is not possible to infer a theory from observation statements; but this does not affect the possibility of refuting a theory by observation statements. The full appreciation of this possibility makes the relation between theories and observations perfectly clear.

This solves the problem of the alleged clash between the principles *(a)*, *(b)*, and *(c)*, and with it Hume's problem of induction.

X

Thus the problem of induction is solved. But nothing seems less wanted than a simple solution to an age-old philosophical problem. Wittgenstein and his school hold that genuine philosophical problems do not exist;[10] from which it clearly follows that they cannot be solved. Others among my contemporaries do believe that there are philosophical problems, and respect them; but they seem to respect them too much; they seem to believe that they are insoluble, if not taboo; and they are shocked and horrified by the claim that there is a simple, neat, and lucid, solution to any of them. If there is a solution it must be deep, they feel, or at least complicated.

However this may be, I am still waiting for a simple, neat and lucid criticism of the solution which I published first in 1933 in my letter to the Editor of *Erkenntnis*,[11] and later in *The Logic of Scientific Discovery*.

Of course, one can invent new problems of induction, different from the one I have formulated and solved. (Its formulation was half its solution.) But I have yet to see any reformulation of the problem whole solution cannot be easily obtained from my old solution. I am now going to discuss some of these re-formulations.

One question which may be asked is this: how do we really jump from an observation statement to a theory?

Although this question appears to be psychological rather than philosophical, one can say something positive about it without invoking psychology. One can say first that the jump is not from an observation statement, but from a problem-situation, and that the theory must allow us *to explain* the observations, which created the problem (that is, *to deduce* them from the theory strengthened by other accepted theories and by other observation statements, the so-called initial conditions). This leaves, of course, an immense number of possible theories, good and bad; and it thus appears that our question has not been answered.

But this makes it fairly clear that when we asked our question we had more in mind than, 'How do we jump from an observation statement to a theory?' The question we had in mind was, it now appears, 'How do we jump from an observation statement to a *good* theory?' But to this the answer is: by jumping first to *any* theory and then testing it, to find whether it is good or not; i.e., by repeatedly applying the critical method, eliminating many bad theories, and inventing many new ones. Not everybody is able to do this; but there is no other way.

Other questions have sometimes been asked. The original problem of induction, it was said, is the problem of *justifying* induction, i.e., of justifying inductive inference. If you answer this problem by saying that what is called an 'inductive inference' is always invalid and therefore clearly not justifiable, the following new problem must arise: how do you justify your method of trial and error? Reply: the method of trial and error is a *method of eliminating false theories* by observation statements; and the justification for this is the purely logical relationship of deducibility which allows us to assert the falsity of universal statements if we accept the truth of singular ones.

Another question sometimes asked is this: why is it reasonable to prefer non-falsified statements to falsified ones? To this question some involved answers have been produced, for example pragmatic answers. But from a pragmatic point of view the question does not arise, since false theories often serve well enough: most formulae used in engineering or navigation are known to be false, although they may be excellent approximations and easy to handle; and they are used with confidence by people who know them to be false.

The only correct answer is the straightforward one: because we search for truth (even though we can never be sure we have found it), and because the falsified theories are known or believed to be false, while the non-falsified theories may still be true. Besides, we do not prefer *every* non-falsified theory—only one which, in the light of criticism, appears to be better than its competitors: which solves our problems, which is well tested, and of which we think, or rather conjecture or hope (considering other provisionally accepted theories), that it will stand up to further tests.

It has also been said that the problem of induction is, 'Why is it *reasonable* to believe that the future will be like the past?', and that a satisfactory answer to this question should make it plain that such a belief is, in fact, reasonable. My reply is that it is reasonable to believe that the future will be very different from the past in many vitally important respects. Admittedly it is perfectly reasonable to *act* on the assumption that it will, in many respects, be like the past, and that well-tested laws will continue to hold (since we can have no better assumption to act upon); but it is also reasonable to believe that such a course of action will lead us at times into severe trouble, since some of the laws upon which we now heavily rely may easily prove unreliable. (Remember the midnight sun!) One might even say that to judge from past experience, and from our general scientific knowledge, the future will *not* be like the past, in perhaps most of the ways which those have in mind who say that it will. Water will sometimes not quench thirst, and air will choke those who breathe it. An apparent way out is to say that the future will be like the past *in the sense that the laws of nature will not change,* but this is begging the question. We speak of a 'law of nature' only if we think that we have before us a regularity which does not change; and if we find that it changes then we shall not continue to call it a 'law of nature'. Of course our search for natural laws indicates that we hope to find them, and that we believe that there are natural laws; but our belief in any particular natural law cannot have a safer basis than our unsuccessful critical attempts to refute it.

I think that those who put the problem of induction in terms of the *reasonableness* of our beliefs are perfectly right if they are dissatisfied with a Humean, or post-Humean, sceptical despair of reason. We must indeed reject the view that a belief in science is as irrational as a belief in primitive magical practices—that both are a matter of accepting a 'total ideology', a convention of a tradition based on faith. But we must be cautions if we formulate our problem, with Hume, as one of the reasonableness of our *beliefs*. We should split this problem into three—our old problem of demarcation, or of how to *distinguish* between science and primitive magic; the problem of the rationality of the scientific or critical *procedure*, and of the role of observation within it; and lastly the problem of the rationality of our *acceptance* of theories for scientific and for practical purposes. To all these three problems solutions have been offered here.

One should also be careful not to confuse the problem of the reasonableness of the scientific procedure and the (tentative) acceptance of the results of this procedure—i.e., the scientific theories—with the problem of the rationality or otherwise *of the belief that this procedure will succeed*. In practice, in practical scientific research, this belief is no doubt unavoidable and reasonable, there being no better alternative. But the belief is certainly unjustifiable in a theoretical sense, as I have argued (in section v). Moreover, if we could show, on general logical grounds, that the scientific quest is likely to succeed, one could not understand why anything like success has been so rare in the long history of human endeavours to know more about our world.

(continued)

Science, Conjecture and Refutation (*continued*)

Yet another way of putting the problem of induction is in terms of probability. Let t be the theory and e the evidence: we can ask for $P(t,e)$, that is to say, the probability of t, given e. The problem of induction, it is often believed, can then be put thus: construct a *calculus of probability* which allows us to work out for any theory t what its probability is, relative to any given empirical evidence e; and show that $P(t,e)$ increases with the accumulation of supporting evidence, and reaches high values—at any rate values greater than 1/2.

In *The Logic of Scientific Discovery* I explained why I think that this approach to the problem is fundamentally mistaken.[12] To make this clear, I introduced there the distinction between *probability* and *degree of corroboration or confirmation*. (The term 'confirmation' has lately been so much used and misused that I have decided to surrender it to the verificationists and to use for my own purposes 'corroboration' only. The term 'probability' is best used in some of the many senses which satisfy the well-known calculus of probability, axiomatized, for example, by Keynes, Jeffreys, and myself; but nothing of course depends on the choice of words, as long as we do not *assume*, uncritically, that degree of corroboration must also be a probability—that is to say, that it must satisfy the calculus of probability.)

I explained in my book why we are interested in theories with a *high degree of corroboration*. And I explained why it is a mistake to conclude from this that we are interested in *highly probable* theories. I pointed out that the probability of a statement (or set of statements) is always the greater the less the statement says: it is inverse to the content or the deductive power of the statement, and thus to its explanatory power. Accordingly every interesting and powerful statement must have a low probability; and *vice versa*: a statement with a high probability will be scientifically uninteresting, because it says little and has no explanatory power. Although we seek theories with a high degree of corroboration, *as scientists we do not seek highly probable theories but explanations; that is to say, powerful and improbable theories*.[13] The opposite view—that science aims at high probability—is a characteristic development of verificationism: if you find that you cannot verify a theory, or make it certain by induction, you may turn to probability as a kind of '*Ersatz*' for certainty, in the hope that induction may yield at least that much.

I have discussed the two problems of demarcation and induction at some length. Yet since I set out to give you in this lecture a kind of report on the work I have done in this field I shall have to add, in the form of an Appendix, a few words about some other problems on which I have been working, between 1934 and 1953. I was led to most of these problems by trying to think out the consequences of the solutions to the two problems of demarcation and induction. But time does not allow me to continue my narrative, and to tell you how my new problems arose out of my old ones. Since I cannot even start a discussion of these further problems now, I shall have to confine myself to giving you a bare list of them, with a few explanatory words here and there. But even a bare list may be useful, I think. It may serve to give an idea of the fertility of the approach. It may help to illustrate what our problems look like; and it may show how many there are, and so convince you that there is no need whatever to worry over the question whether philosophical problems exist, or what philosophy is really about. So this list contains, by implication, an apology for my unwillingness to break with the old tradition of trying to solve problems with the help of rational argument, and thus for my unwillingness to participate wholeheartedly in the developments, trends, and drifts, of contemporary philosophy.

NOTES

1. This is a slight oversimplification, for about half of the Einstein effect may be derived from the classical theory, provided we assume a ballistic theory of light.
2. See, for example, my *Open Society and Its Enemies*, ch. 15, section iii, and notes 13–14.
3. 'Clinical observations', like all other observations, are *interpretations in the light of theories* (see below, sections iv ff.); and for this reason alone they are apt to seem to support those theories in the light of which they were interpreted. But real support can be obtained only from observations undertaken as

tests (by 'attempted refutations'); and for this purpose *criteria of refutation* have to be laid down beforehand: it must be agreed which observable situations, if actually observed, mean that the theory is refuted. But what kind of clinical responses would refute to the satisfaction of the analyst not merely a particular analytic diagnosis but psycho-analysis itself? And have such criteria ever been discussed or agreed upon by analysts? Is there not, on the contrary, a whole family of analytic concepts, such as 'ambivalence' (I do not suggest that there is no such thing as ambivalence), which would make it difficult, if not impossible, to agree upon such criteria? Moreover, how much headway has been made in investigating the question of the extent to which the (conscious or unconscious) expectations and theories held by the analyst influence the 'clinical responses' of the patient? (To say nothing about the conscious attempts to influence the patient by proposing interpretations to him, etc.) Years ago I introduced the term '*Oedipus effect*' to describe the influence of a theory or expectation or prediction *upon the event which it predicts* or describes: it will be remembered that the causal chain leading to Oedipus' parricide was started by the oracle's prediction of this event. This is a characteristic and recurrent theme of such myths, but one which seems to have failed to attract the interest of the analysts, perhaps not accidentally. (The problem of confirmatory dreams suggested by the analyst is discussed by Freud, for example in *Gesammelte Schriften*, III, 1925, where he says on p. 314: 'If anybody asserts that most of the dreams which can be utilized in an analysis . . . owe their origin to [the analyst's] suggestion, then no objection can be made from the point of view of analytic theory. Yet there is nothing in this fact', he surprisingly adds, 'which would detract from the reliability of our results.')

4. The case of astrology, nowadays a typical pseudo-science, may illustrate this point. It was attacked, by Aristotelians and other rationalists, down to Newton's day, for the wrong reason—for its now accepted assertion that the planets had an 'influence' upon terrestrial ('sublunar') events. In fact Newton's theory of gravity, and especially the lunar theory of the tides, was historically speaking an offspring of astrological lore. Newton, it seems, was most reluctant to adopt a theory which came from the same stable as for example the theory that 'influenza' epidemics are due to an astral 'influence'. And Galileo, no doubt for the same reason, actually rejected the lunar theory of the tides; and his misgivings about Kepler may easily be explained by his misgivings about astrology.
5. Hume does not say 'logical' but 'demonstrative', a terminology which, I think, is a little misleading. The following two quotations are from the *Treatise of Human Nature*, Book I, Part III, sections vi and xii. (The italics are all Hume's.)
6. This and the next quotation are from *loc. cit.*, section vi. See also Hume's *Enquiry Concerning Human Understanding*, section IV, Part II, and his *Abstract*, edited 1938 by J. M. Keynes and P. Sraffa, p. 15, and quoted in *L.Sc.D.*, new appendix *VII, text to note 6.
7. Max Born, *Natural Philosophy of Cause and Chance*, Oxford, 1949, p. 7.
8. *Natural Philosophy of Cause and Chance*, p. 6.
9. I do not doubt that Born and many others would agree that theories are accepted only tentatively. But the widespread belief in induction shows that the far-reaching implications of this view are rarely seen.
10. Wittgentein still held this belief in 1946; see note 8 to ch. 2. below.
11. See note 5 above.
12. *L.Sc.D.* (see note 5 above), ch. x, especially sections 80 to 83, also section 34 ff. See also my note 'A Set of Independent Axioms for Probability', *Mind* N.S. 47, 1938, p. 275. (This note has since been reprinted, with corrections, in the new appendix *ii of *L.Sc.D.* See also the next note but one to the present chapter.)
13. A definition, in terms of probabilities (see the next note), of $C(t,e)$, i.e., of the degree of corroboration (of a theory t relative to the evidence e) satisfying the demands indicated in my *L.Sc.D.*, sections 82 to 83, is the following:

$$C(t, e) = E(t,e)(1 + P(t)P(t,e)),$$

where $E(t,e) = (P(e,t) - P(e))/(P(e,t) + P(e))$ is a (non-additive) measure of the explanatory power of t with respect to e. Note that $C(t,e)$ is not a probability: it may have values between -1 (refutation of t by e) and $C(t,t) \leq +1$. Statements t which are lawlike and thus non-verifiable cannot even reach $C(t,e) = C(t,t)$ upon empirical evidence e. $C(t,t)$ is the *degree of corroborability* of t, and is equal to the *degree of testability* of t, or to the *content* of t. Because of the demands implied in point (6) at the end of section I above, I do not think, however, that it is possible to give a complete formalization of the idea of corroboration (or, as I previously used to say, of confirmation).

(Added 1955 to the first proofs of this paper:)
See also my note 'Degree of Confirmation', *British Journal for the Philosophy of Science*, 5, 1954, pp. 143 ff. (See also 5, pp. 334.) I have since simplified this definition as follows (*B.J.P.S.*, 1955, 5, p. 359:)

$$C(t,e) = (P(e,t) - P(e))/(P(e,t) - P(et) + P(e))$$

For a further improvement, see *B.J.P.S.* 6, 1955, p. 56.

The Structure of Scientific Revolutions
Thomas Kuhn

IX. The Nature and Necessity of Scientific Revolutions

These remarks permit us at last to consider the problems that provide this essay with its title. What are scientific revolutions, and what is their function in scientific development? Much of the answer to these questions has been anticipated in earlier sections. In particular, the preceding discussion has indicated that scientific revolutions are here taken to be those non-cumulative developmental episodes in which an older paradigm is replaced in whole or in part by an incompatible new one. There is more to be said, however, and an essential part of it can be introduced by asking one further question. Why should a change of paradigm be called a revolution? In the face of the vast and essential differences between political and scientific development, what parallelism can justify the metaphor that finds revolutions in both?

One aspect of the parallelism must already be apparent. Political revolutions are inaugurated by a growing sense, often restricted to a segment of the political community, that existing institutions have ceased adequately to meet the problems posed by an environment that they have in part created. In much the same way, scientific revolutions are inaugurated by a growing sense, again often restricted to a narrow subdivision of the scientific community, that an existing paradigm has ceased to function adequately in the exploration of an aspect of nature to which that paradigm itself had previously led the way. In both political and scientific development the sense of malfunction that can lead to crisis is prerequisite to revolution. Furthermore, though it admittedly strains the metaphor, that parallelism holds not only for the major paradigm changes, like those attributable to Copernicus and Lavoisier, but also for the far smaller ones associated with the assimilation of a new sort of phenomenon, like oxygen or X-rays. Scientific revolutions, as we noted at the end of Section V, need seem revolutionary only to those whose paradigms are affected by them. To outsiders they may, like the Balkan revolutions of the early twentieth century, seem normal parts of the developmental process. Astronomers, far example, could accept X-rays as a mere addition to knowledge, for their paradigms were unaffected by the existence of the new radiation. But for men like Kelvin, Crookes, and Roentgen, whose research dealt with radiation theory or with cathode ray tubes, the emergence of X-rays necessarily violated one paradigm as it created another. That is why these rays could be discovered only through something's first going wrong with normal research.

This genetic aspect of the parallel between political and scientific development should no longer be open to doubt. The parallel has, however, a second and more profound aspect upon which the significance of the first depends. Political revolutions aim to change political institutions in ways that those institutions themselves prohibit. Their success therefore necessitates the partial relinquishment of one set of institutions in favor of another, and in the interim, society is not fully governed by institutions at all. Initially it is crisis alone that attenuates the role of political institutions as we have already seen it attenuate the role of paradigms. In increasing numbers individuals become increasingly estranged from political life and behave more and more eccentrically within it. Then, as the crisis deepens, many of these individuals commit themselves to some concrete proposal for the reconstruction of society in a new institutional framework. At that point the society is divided into competing or comps parties, one seeking to defend the old institutional constellation, the others seeking to institute some new one. And, once that polarization has occurred, *political recourse fails*. Because they differ about the institutional matrix within which political change is to be achieved and evaluated, because they acknowledge no supra-institutional framework for the adjudication of revolutionary difference, the parties to a revolutionary conflict must finally resort to the techniques of mass persuasion, often including force. Though revolutions have had a vital role in the evolution of political institutions, that role depends upon their being partially extrapolitical or extrainstitutional events.

The remainder of this essay aims to demonstrate that the historical study of paradigm change reveals very similar characteristics in the evolution of the sciences. Like the choice between competing political institutions, that between competing paradigms proves to be a choice between incompatible modes of community life. Because it has that character, the choice is not and cannot be determined merely by the evaluative procedures characteristic of normal science, for these depend in part upon a particular paradigm, and that paradigm is at issue. When paradigms enter, as they must, into a debate about paradigm choice, their role is necessarily circular. Each group uses its own paradigm to argue in that paradigm's defense.

The resulting circularity does not, of course, make the arguments wrong or even ineffectual. The man who premises a paradigm when arguing in its defense can nonetheless provide a clear exhibit of what scientific practice will be like for those who adopt the new view of nature. That exhibit can be immensely persuasive, often compellingly so. Yet, whatever its force, the status of the circular argument is only that of persuasion. It cannot be made logically or even probabilistically compelling for those who refuse to step into the circle. The premises and values shared by the two parties to a debate over paradigms are not sufficiently extensive for that. As in political revolutions, so in paradigm choice—there is no standard higher than the assent of the relevant community. To discover how scientific revolutions are effected, we shall therefore have to examine not only the impact of nature and of logic, but also the techniques of persuasive argumentation effective within the quite special groups that constitute the community of scientists.

To discover why this issue of paradigm choice can never be unequivocally settled by logic and experiment alone, we must shortly examine the nature of the differences that separate the proponents of a traditional paradigm from their revolutionary successors. That examination is the principal object of this section and the next. We have, however, already noted numerous examples of such differences, and no one will doubt that history can supply many others. What is more likely to be doubted than their existence—and what must therefore be considered first—is that such examples provide essential information about the nature of science. Granting that paradigm rejection has been a historic fact, does it illuminate more than human credulity and confusion? Are there intrinsic reasons why the assimilation of either a new sort of phenomenon or a new scientific theory must demand the rejection of an older paradigm?

First notice that if there are such reasons, they do not derive from the logical structure of scientific knowledge. In principle, a new phenomenon might emerge without reflecting destructively upon any part of past scientific practice. Though discovering life on the moon would today be destructive of existing paradigms (these tell us things about the moon that seem incompatible with life's existence there), discovering life in some less well-known part of the galaxy would not. By the same token, a new theory does not have to conflict with any of its predecessors. It might deal exclusively with phenomena not previously known, as the quantum theory deals (but, significantly, not exclusively) with subatomic phenomena unknown before the twentieth century. Or again, the new theory might be simply a higher level theory than those known before, one that linked together a whole group of lower level theories without substantially changing any. Today, the theory of energy conservation provides just such links between dynamics, chemistry, electricity, optics, thermal theory, and so on. Still other compatible relationships between old and new theories can be conceived. Any and all of them might be exemplified by the historical process through which science has developed. If they were, scientific development would be genuinely cumulative. New sorts of phenomena would simply disclose order in an aspect of nature where none had been seen before. In the evolution of science new knowledge would replace ignorance rather than replace knowledge of another and incompatible sort.

Of course, science (or some other enterprise perhaps less effective) might have developed in that fully cumulative manner. Many people have believed that it did so, and most still seem to suppose that cumulation is at least the ideal that historical development would display if only it had not so often been distorted by human idiosyncrasy. There are important reasons for that belief. In Section X, we shall discover how closely the view of science-as-cumulation is entangled with a dominant epistemology that takes knowledge to be a construction placed directly upon raw sense data by the mind. And in Section XI we shall examine the strong support provided to the same historiographic schema by the techniques of effective science pedagogy. Nevertheless, despite the immense plausibility of that ideal image, there is increasing reason to wonder whether it can possibly be an image of *science*. After the pre-paradigm period the assimilation of all new theories and of almost all new sorts of phenomena has in fact demanded the destruction of a prior paradigm and a consequent conflict between competing schools of scientific thought. Cumulative acquisition of unanticipated novelties proves to be an almost non-existent exception to the rule of scientific development. The man who takes historic fact seriously must suspect that science does not tend toward the ideal that our image of its cumulativeness has suggested. Perhaps it is another sort of enterprise.

(continued)

The Structure of Scientific Revolutions   (continued)

If, however, resistant facts can carry us that far, then a second look at the ground we have already covered may suggest that cumulative acquisition of novelty is not only rare in fact but improbable in principle. Normal research, which *is* cumulative, owes its success to the ability of scientists regularly to select problems that can be solved with conceptual and instrumental techniques close to those already in existence. (That is why an excessive concern with useful problems, regardless of their relation to existing knowledge and technique, can so easily inhibit scientific development.) The man who is striving to solve a problem defined by existing knowledge and technique is not, however, just looking around. He knows what he wants to achieve, and he designs his instruments and directs his thoughts accordingly. Unanticipated novelty, the new discovery, can emerge only to the extent that his anticipations about nature and his instruments prove wrong. Often the importance of the resulting discovery will itself be proportional to the extent and stubbornness of the anomaly that foreshadowed it. Obviously, then, there must be a conflict between the paradigm that discloses anomaly and the one that later renders the anomaly law-like. The examples of discovery through paradigm destruction examined in Section VI did not confront us with mere historical accident. There is no other effective way in which discoveries might be generated.

The same argument applies even more clearly to the invention of new theories. There are, in principle, only three types of phenomena about which a new theory might be developed. The first consists of phenomena already well explained by existing paradigms, and these seldom provide either motive or point of departure for theory construction. When they do, as with the three famous anticipations discussed at the end of Section VII, the theories that result are seldom accepted, because nature provides no ground for discrimination. A second class of phenomena consists of those whose nature is indicated by existing paradigms but whose details can be understood only through further theory articulation. These are the phenomena to which scientists direct their research much of the time, but that research aims at the articulation of existing paradigms rather than at the invention of new ones. Only when these attempts at articulation fail do scientists encounter the third type of phenomena, the recognized anomalies whose characteristic feature is their stubborn refusal to be assimilated to existing paradigms. This type alone gives rise to new theories. Paradigms provide all phenomena except anomalies with a theory-determined place in the scientist's field of vision.

But if new theories are called forth to resolve anomalies in the relation of an existing theory to nature, then the successful new theory must somewhere permit predictions that are different from those derived from its predecessor. That difference could not occur if the two were logically compatible. In the process of being assimilated, the second must displace the first. Even a theory like energy conservation, which today seems a logical superstructure that relates to nature only through independently established theories, did not develop historically without paradigm destruction. Instead, it emerged from a crisis in which an essential ingredient was the incompatibility between Newtonian dynamics and some recently formulated consequences of the caloric theory of heat. Only after the caloric theory had been rejected could energy conservation become part of science.[1] And only after it had been part of science for some time could it come to seem a theory of a logically higher type, one not in conflict with its predecessors. It is hard to see how new theories could arise without these destructive changes in beliefs about nature. Though logical inclusiveness remains a permissible view of the relation between successive scientific theories, it is a historical implausibility.

A century ago it would, I think, have been possible to let the case for the necessity of revolutions rest at this point. But today, unfortunately, that cannot be done because the view of the subject developed above cannot be maintained if the most prevalent contemporary interpretation of the nature and function of scientific theory is accepted. That interpretation, closely associated with early logical positivism and not categorically rejected by its successors, would restrict the range and meaning of an accepted theory so that it could not possibly conflict with any later theory that made predictions about some of the same natural phenomena. The best-known and the strongest case for this restricted conception of a scientific theory emerges in discussions of the relation between contemporary Einsteinian dynamics and the older dynamical equations that descend from Newton's *Principia*. From the viewpoint of this essay these two theories are fundamentally incompatible in the sense illustrated by the relation of Copernican to Ptolemaic astronomy: Einstein's theory can be accepted only with the recognition that Newton's was wrong. Today this remains a minority view.[2] We must therefore examine the most prevalent objections to it.

The gist of these objections can be developed as follows. Relativistic dynamics cannot have shown Newtonian dynamics to be wrong, for Newtonian dynamics is still used with great success by most engineers and, in selected applications, by many physicists. Furthermore, the propriety of this use of the older theory can be proved from the very theory that has, in other applications, replaced it. Einstein's theory can he used to show that predictions from Newton's equations will be as good as our measuring instruments in all applications that satisfy a small number of restrictive conditions. For example, if Newtonian theory is to provide a good approximate solution, the relative velocities of the bodies considered in must be small compared with the velocity of light. Subject to this condition and a few others, Newtonian theory seems to be derivable from Einsteinian, of which it is therefore a special case.

But, the objection continues, no theory can possibly conflict with one of its special cases. If Einsteinian science seems to make Newtonian dynamics wrong, that is only because some Newtonians were so incautious as to claim that Newtonian theory yielded entirely precise results or that it was valid at very high relative velocities. Since they could not have had any evidence for such claims, they betrayed the standards of science when they made them. In so far as Newtonian theory was ever a truly scientific theory supported by valid evidence, it still is. Only extravagant claims for the theory—claims that were never properly parts of science—can have been shown by Einstein to be wrong. Purged of these merely human extravagances, Newtonian theory has never been challenged and cannot be.

Some variant of this argument is quite sufficient to make any theory ever used by a significant group of competent scientists immune to attack. The much-maligned phlogiston theory, for example, gave order to a large number of physical and chemical phenomena. It explained why bodies burned—they were rich in phlogiston—and why metals had so many more properties in common than did their ores. The metals were all compounded from different elementary earths combined with phlogiston, and the latter, common to all metals, produced common properties. In addition, the phlogiston theory accounted for a number of reactions in which acids were formed by the combustion of substances like carbon and sulphur. Also, it explained the decrease of volume when combustion occurs in a confined volume of air—the phlogiston released by combustion "spoils" the elasticity of the air that absorbed it, just as fire "spoils" the elasticity of a steel spring.[3] If these were the only phenomena that the phlogiston theorists had claimed for their theory, that theory could never have been challenged. A similar argument will suffice for any theory that has ever been successfully applied to any range of phenomena at all.

But to save theories in this way, their range of application must be restricted to those phenomena and to that precision of observation with which the experimental evidence in hand already deals.[4] Carried just a step further (and the step can scarcely be avoided once the first is taken), such a limitation prohibits the scientist from claiming to speak "scientifically" about any phenomenon not already observed. Even in its present form the restriction forbids the scientist to rely upon a theory in his own research whenever that research enters an area or seeks a degree of precision for which past practice with the theory offers no precedent. These prohibitions are logically unexceptionable. But the result of accepting them would be the end of the research through which science may develop further.

By now that point too is virtually a tautology. Without commitment to a paradigm there could be no normal science. Furthermore, that commitment must extend to areas and to degrees of precision for which there is no full precedent. If it did not, the paradigm could provide no puzzles that had not already been solved. Besides, it is not only normal science that depends upon commitment to a paradigm. If existing theory binds the scientist only with respect to existing applications, then there can be no surprises, anomalies, or crises. But these are just the signposts that point the way to extraordinary science. If positivistic restrictions on the range of a theory's legitimate applicability are taken literally, the mechanism that tells the scientific community what problems may lead to fundamental change must cease to function. And when that occurs, the community will inevitably return to something much like its pre-paradigm state, a condition in which all members practice science but in which their gross product scarcely resembles science at all. Is it really any wonder that the price of significant scientific advance is a commitment that runs the risk of being wrong?

More important, there is a revealing logical lacuna in the positivist's argument, one that will reintroduce us immediately to the nature of revolutionary change. Can Newtonian dynamics really be

(continued)

The Structure of Scientific Revolutions   (continued)

derived from relativistic dynamics? What would such a derivation look like? Imagine a set of statements, $E_1 E_2, \ldots E_n$, which together embody the laws of relativity theory. These statements contain variables and parameters representing spatial position, time, rest mass, etc. From them, together with the apparatus of logic and mathematics, is deducible a whole set of further statements including some that can be checked by observation. To prove the adequacy of Newtonian dynamics as a special case, we must add to the E_1s additional statements, like $(v/c)^2 \ll 1$, restricting the range of the parameters and variables, This enlarged set of statements is then manipulated to yield a new set, $N_1 N_2, \ldots, N_m$, which is identical in form with Newton's laws of motion, the law of gravity, and so on. Apparently Newtonian dynamics has been derived from Einsteinian, subject to a few limiting conditions.

Yet the derivation is spurious, at least to this point. Though the N_1's are a special case of the laws of relativistic mechanics, they are not Newton's Laws. Or at least they are not unless those laws are reinterpreted in a way that would have been impossible until after Einstein's work. The variables and parameters that in the Einsteinian E_1,'s represented spatial position, time, mass, etc., still occur in the N_1,'s; and they there still represent Einsteinian space, time, and mass. But the physical referents of these Einsteinian concepts are by no means identical with those of the Newtonian concepts that bear the same name. (Newtonian mass is conserved; Einsteinian is convertible with energy. Only at low relative velocities may the two be measured in the same way, and even then they must not be conceived to be the same.) Unless we change the definitions of the variables in the N_i's, the statements we have derived are not Newtonian. If we do change them, we cannot properly be said to have *derived* Newton's Laws, at least not in any sense of "derive" now generally recognized. Our argument has, of course, explained why Newton's Laws ever seemed to work. In doing so it has justified, say, an automobile driver in acting as though he lived in a Newtonian universe. An argument of the same type is used to justify teaching earth-centered astronomy to surveyors. But the argument has still not done what it purported to do. It has not, that is, shown Newton's Laws to be a limiting case of Einstein's. For in the passage to the limit it is not only the forms of the laws that have changed. Simultaneously we have had to alter the fundamental structural elements of which the universe to which they apply is composed.

This need to change the meaning of established and familiar concepts is central to the revolutionary impact of Einstein's theory. Though subtler than the changes from geocentrism to heliocentrism, from phlogiston to oxygen, or from corpuscles to waves, the resulting conceptual transformation is no less decisively destructive of a previously established paradigm. We may even come to see it as a prototype for revolutionary reorientations in the sciences. Just because it did not involve the introduction of additional objects or concepts, the transition from Newtonian to Einsteinian mechanics illustrates with particular clarity the scientific revolution as a displacement of the conceptual network through which scientists view the world.

These remarks should suffice to show what might, in another philosophical climate, have been taken for granted. At least for scientists, most of the apparent differences between a discarded scientific theory and its successor are real. Though an out-of-date theory can always be viewed as a special case of its up-to-date successor, it must be transformed for the purpose. And the transformation is one that can be undertaken only with the advantages of hindsight, the explicit guidance of the more recent theory. Furthermore, even if that transformation were a legitimate device to employ in interpreting the older theory, the result of its application would be a theory so restricted that it could only restate what was already known. Because of its economy, that restatement would have utility, but it could not suffice for the guidance of research.

Let us, therefore, now take it for granted that the differences between successive paradigms are both necessary and irreconcilable. Can we then say more explicitly what sorts of differences these are? The most apparent type has already been illustrated repeatedly. Successive paradigms tell us different things about the population of the universe and about that population's behavior. They differ, that is, about such questions as the existence of subatomic particles, the materiality of light, and the conservation of heat or of energy. These are the substantive differences between successive paradigms, and they require no further illustration. But paradigms differ in more than substance, for they are directed not only to nature but also back upon the science that produced them. They are the source of the methods, problem-field, and standards of solution accepted by any mature scientific community at any given time. As a result, the reception of a new paradigm often necessitates a redefinition of the corresponding science. Some old problems may be relegated to another science or declared entirely "unscientific." Others that were previously non-existent or trivial may, with a new paradigm, become the very archetypes of significant scientific achievement. And as the problems change, so, often, does the standard that distinguishes a real scientific solution from a mere metaphysical speculation, word game, or mathematical play. The normal-scientific tradition that emerges from a scientific revolution is not only incompatible but often actually incommensurable with that which has gone before.

The impact of Newton's work upon the normal seventeenth- century tradition of scientific practice provides a striking example of these subtler effects of paradigm shift. Before Newton was born the "new science" of the century had at last succeeded in rejecting Aristotelian and scholastic explanations expressed in terms of the essences of material bodies. To say that a stone fell because its "nature" drove it toward the center of the universe had been made to look a mere tautological word-play, something it had not previously been. Henceforth the entire flux of sensory appearances, including color, taste, and even weight, was to be explained in terms of the size, shape, position, and motion of the elementary corpuscles of base matter. The attribution of other qualities to the elementary atoms was a resort to the occult and therefore out of bounds for science. Molière caught the new spirit precisely when he ridiculed the doctor who explained opium's efficacy as a soporific by attributing to it a dormitive potency. During the last half of the seventeenth century many scientists preferred to say that the round shape of the opium particles enabled them to sooth the nerves about which they moved.[5]

In an earlier period explanations in terms of occult qualities had been an integral part of productive scientific work. Nevertheless, the seventeenth century's new commitment to mechanico-corpuscular explanation proved immensely fruitful for a number of sciences, ridding them of problems that had defied generally accepted solution and suggesting others to replace them. In dynamics, for example, Newton's three laws of motion are less a product of novel experiments than of the attempt to reinterpret well-known observations in terms of the motions and interactions of primary neutral corpuscles. Consider just one concrete illustration. Since neutral corpuscles could act on each other only by contact, the mechanico-corpuscular view of nature directed scientific attention to a brand-new subject of study, the alteration of particulate motions by collisions. Descartes announced the problem and provided its first putative solution. Huyghens, Wren, and Wallis carried it still further, partly by experimenting with colliding pendulum bobs, but mostly by applying previously well-known characteristics of motion to the new problem. And Newton embedded their results in his laws of motion. The equal "action" and "reaction" of the third law are the changes in quantity of motion experienced by the two parties to a collision. The same change of motion supplies the definition of dynamical force implicit in the second law. In this case, as in many others during the seventeenth century, the corpuscular paradigm bred both a new problem and a large part of that problem's solution.[6]

Yet, though much of Newton's work was directed to problems and embodied standards derived from the mechanico-corpuscular world view, the effect of the paradigm that resulted from his work was a further and partially destructive change in the problems and standards legitimate for science. Gravity, interpreted as an innate attraction between every pair of particles or matter, was an occult quality in the same sense as the scholastics' "tendency to fall" had been. Therefore, while the standards of corpuscularism remained in effect, the search for a mechanical explanation of gravity was one of the most challenging problems for those who accepted the *Principia* as paradigm. Newton devoted much attention to it and so did many of his eighteenth-century successors. The only apparent option was to reject Newton's theory for its failure to explain gravity, and that alternative, too, was widely adopted. Yet neither of these views ultimately triumphed. Unable either to practice science without the *Principia* or to make that work conform to the corpuscular standards of the seventeenth century, scientists gradually accepted the view that gravity was indeed innate. By the mid-eighteenth century that interpretation had been almost universally accepted, and the result was a genuine reversion (which is not the same as a retrogression) to

(continued)

The Structure of Scientific Revolutions   (continued)

a scholastic standard. Innate attractions and repulsions joined size, shape, position, and motion as physically irreducible primary properties of matter.[7]

The resulting change in the standards and problem-field of physical science was once again consequential. By the 1740's, for example, electricians could speak of the attractive "virtue" of the electric fluid without thereby inviting the ridicule that had greeted Molière's doctor a century before. As they did so, electrical phenomena increasingly displayed an order different from the one they had shown when viewed as the effects of a mechanical effluvium that could act only by contact. In particular, when electrical action-at-a-distance became a subject for study in its own right, the phenomenon we now call charging by induction could be recognized as one of its effects. Previously, when seen at all, it had been attributed to the direct action of electrical "atmospheres" or to the leakages inevitable in any electrical laboratory. The new view of inductive effects was, in turn, the key to Franklin's analysis of the Leyden jar and thus to the emergence of a new and Newtonian paradigm for electricity. Nor were dynamics and electricity the only scientific fields affected by the legitimization of the search for forces innate to matter. The large body of eighteenth-century literature on chemical affinities and replacement series also derives from this supramechanical aspect of Newtonianism. Chemists who believed in these differential attractions between the various chemical species set up previously unimagined experiments and searched for new sorts of reactions. Without the data and the chemical concepts developed in that process, the later work of Lavoisier and, more particularly, of Dalton would be incomprehensible.[8] Changes in the standards governing permissible problems, concepts, and explanations can transform a science. In the next section I shall even suggest a sense in which they transform the world.

Other examples of these nonsubstantive differences between successive paradigms can be retrieved from the history of any science in almost any period of its development. For the moment let us be content with just two other and far briefer illustrations. Before the chemical revolution, one of the acknowledged tasks of chemistry was to account for the qualities of chemical substances and for the changes these qualities underwent during chemical reactions. With the aid of a small number of elementary "principles"—of which phlogiston was one—the chemist was to explain why some substances are acidic, others metalline, combustible, and so forth. Some success in this direction had been achieved. We have already noted that phlogiston explained why the metals were so much alike, and we could have developed a similar argument for the acids, Lavoisier's reform, however, ultimately did away with chemical "principles," and thus ended by depriving chemistry of some actual and much potential explanatory power. To compensate for this loss, a change in standards was required. During much of the nineteenth century failure to explain the qualities of compounds was no indictment of a chemical theory.[9]

Or again, Clerk Maxwell shared with other nineteenth-century proponents of the wave theory of light the conviction that light waves must be propagated through a material ether. Designing a mechanical medium to support such waves was a standard problem for many of his ablest contemporaries. His own theory, however, the electromagnetic theory of light, gave no account at all of a medium able to support light waves, and it clearly made such an account harder to provide than it had seemed before. Initially, Maxwell's theory was widely rejected for those reasons. But, like Newton's theory, Maxwell's proved difficult to dispense with, and as it achieved the status of a paradigm, the community's attitude toward it changed. In the early decades of the twentieth century Maxwell's insistence upon the existence of a mechanical ether looked more and more like lip service, which it emphatically had not been, and the attempts to design such an ethereal medium were abandoned. Scientists no longer thought it unscientific to speak of an electrical "displacement" without specifying what was being displaced. The result, again, was a new set of problems and standards, one which, in the event, had much to do with the emergence of relativity theory.[10]

These characteristic shifts in the scientific community's conception of its legitimate problems and standards would have less significance to this essay's thesis if one could suppose that they always occurred from some methodologically lower to some higher type. In that case their effects, too, would seem cumulative. No wonder that some historians have argued that the history of science records a continuing increase in the maturity and refinement of man's conception of the nature of science.[11] Yet the case for cumulative development of science's problems and standards is even harder to make than the case for cumulation of theories. The attempt to explain gravity, though fruitfully abandoned by most eighteenth-century scientists, was not directed to an intrinsically illegitimate problem; the objections to innate forces were neither inherently unscientific nor metaphysical in some pejorative sense. There are no external standards to permit a judgment of that sort. What occurred was neither a decline nor a raising of standards, but simply a change demanded by the adoption of a new paradigm. Furthermore, that change has since been reversed and could be again. In the twentieth century Einstein succeeded in explaining gravitational attractions, and that explanation has returned science to a set of canons and problems that are, in this particular respect, more like those of Newton's predecessors than of his successors. Or again, the development of quantum mechanics has reversed the methodological prohibition that originated in the chemical revolution. Chemists now attempt, and with great success, to explain the color, state of aggregation, and other qualities of the substances used and produced in their laboratories. A similar reversal may even he underway in electromagnetic theory. Space, in contemporary physics, is not the inert and homogenous substratum employed in both Newton's and Maxwell's theories; some of its new properties are not unlike those once attributed to the ether; we may someday come to know what an electric displacement is.

By shifting emphasis from the cognitive to the normative functions of paradigms, the preceding examples enlarge our understanding of the ways in which paradigms give form to the scientific life. Previously, we had principally examined the paradigm's role as a vehicle for scientific theory. In that role it functions by telling the scientist about the entities that nature does and does not contain and about the ways in which those entities behave. That information provides a map whose details are elucidated by mature scientific research. And since nature is too complex and varied to be explored at random, that map is as essential as observation and experiment to science's continuing development. Through the theories they embody, paradigms prove to be constitutive of the research activity. They are also, however, constitutive of science in other respects, and that is now the point. In particular, our most recent examples show that paradigms provide scientists not only with a map but also with some of the directions essential for map-making. In learning a paradigm the scientist acquires theory, methods, and standards together, usually in an inextricable mixture. Therefore, when paradigms change, there are usually significant shifts in the criteria determining the legitimacy both of problems and of proposed solutions.

That observation returns us to the point from which this section began, for it provides our first explicit indication of why the choice between competing paradigms regularly raises questions that cannot be resolved by the criteria of normal science. To the extent, as significant as it is incomplete, that two scientific schools disagree about what is a problem and what a solution, they will inevitably talk through each other when debating the relative merits of their respective paradigms. In the partially circular arguments that regularly result, each paradigm will be shown to satisfy more or less the criteria that it dictates for itself and to fall short of a few of those dictated by its opponent. There are other reasons, too, for the incompleteness of logical contact that consistently characterizes paradigm debates. For example, since no paradigm ever solves all the problems it defines and since no two paradigms leave all the same problems unsolved, paradigm debates always involve the question: Which problems is it more significant to have solved? Like the issue of competing standards, that question of values can be answered only in terms of criteria that lie outside of normal science altogether, and it is that recourse to external criteria that most obviously makes paradigm debates revolutionary. Something even more fundamental than standards and values is, however, also at stake. I have so far argued only that paradigms are constitutive of science. Now I wish to display a sense in which they are constitutive of nature as well.

NOTES

1. Silvanus P. Thompson, *Life of William Thomson Baron Kelvin of Largs* (London, 1910), I, 266–281.
2. See, for example, the remarks by P. P. Wiener in *Philosophy of Science,* XXV (1958), 298.

(continued)

The Structure of Scientific Revolutions (*continued*)

3. James B. Conant, *Overthrow of the Phlogiston Theory* (Cambridge, 1950), pp. 13–16; and J. R. Partington, *A Short History of Chemistry* (2d ed.; London, 1951), pp. 85–88. The fullest and most sympathetic account of the phlogiston theory's achievements is by H. Metzger, *Newton, Stahl, Boerhaave et la doctrine chimique* (Paris, 1930), Part II.
4. Compare the conclusions reached through a very different sort of analysis by R. B. Braithwaite, *Scientific Explanation* (Cambridge, 1953), pp. 50–87, esp. p. 76.
5. For corpuscularism in general, see Marie Boas, "The Establishment of the Mechanical Philosophy," *Osiris*, X (1952), 412–541. For the effect of particle-shape on taste, see *ibid.*, p. 483.
6. R. Dugas, *La mécanique au XVIIe siècle* (Neuchatel, 1954), pp. 177–85, 284–98, 345–56.
7. I. B. Cohen, *Franklin and Newton: An Inquiry into Speculative Newtonian Experimental Science and Franklin's Work in Electricity as an Example There of* (Philadelphia, 1956), chaps. vi–vii.
8. For electricity, see *ibid*, chaps. viii–ix. For chemistry, see Metzger. *op. cit.*, Part I.
9. E. Meyerson, *Identity and Reality* (New York, 1930), chap. x.
10. E. T. Whittaker, *A History of the Theories of Aether and Electricity,* II (London, 1953), pp. 28–30.
11. For a brilliant and entirely up-to-date attempt to fit scientific development into this Procrustean bed, see C. C. Gillispie, *The Edge of Objectivity: An Essay in the History of Scientific Ideas* (Princeton, 1960).

How To Defend Society Against Science
Paul K. Feyerabend

Fairytales

I want to defend society and its inhabitants from all ideologies, science included. All ideologies must be seen in perspective. One must not take them too seriously. One must read them like fairy-tales which have lots of interesting things to say but which also contain wicked lies, or like ethical prescriptions which may be useful rules of thumb but which are deadly when followed to the letter.

Now, is this not a strange and ridiculous attitude? Science, surely, was always in the forefront of the fight against authoritarianism and superstition. It is to science that we owe our increased intellectual freedom vis-a-vis religious beliefs; it is to science that we owe the liberation of mankind from ancient and rigid forms of thought. Today these forms of thought are nothing but bad dreams—and this we learned from science. Science and enlightenment are one and the same thing—even the most radical critics of society believe this. Kropotkin wants to overthrow all traditional institutions and forms of belief, with the exception of science. Ibsen criticises the most intimate ramifications of nineteenth-century bourgeois ideology, but he leaves science untouched. Levi-Strauss has made us realise that Western Thought is not the lonely peak of human achievement it was once believed to be, but he excludes science from his relativization of ideologies. Marx and Engels were convinced that science would aid the workers in their quest for mental and social liberation. Are all these people deceived? Are they all mistaken about the role of science? Are they all the victims of a chimaera?

To these questions my answer is a firm *Yes and No*.

Now, let me explain my answer.

My explanation consists of two parts, one more general, one more specific.

The general explanation is simple. Any ideology that breaks the hold a comprehensive system of thought has on the minds of men contributes to the liberation of man. Any ideology that makes man question inherited beliefs is an aid to enlightenment. A truth that reigns without checks and balances is a tyrant who must be overthrown, and any falsehood that can aid us in the over throw of this tyrant is to be welcomed. It follows that seventeenth- and eighteenth-century science indeed *was* an instrument of liberation and enlightenment. It does not follow that science is bound to *remain* such an instrument. There is nothing inherent in science or in any other ideology that makes it *essentially* liberating. Ideologies can deteriorate and become stupid religions. Look at Marxism. And that the science of today is very different from the science of 1650 is evident at the most superficial glance.

For example, consider the role science now plays in education. Scientific "facts" are taught at a very early age and in the very same manner in which religious "facts" were taught only a century ago. There is no attempt to waken the critical abilities of the pupil so that he may be able to see things in perspective. At the universities the situation is even worse, for indoctrination is here carried out in a much more systematic manner. Criticism is not entirely absent. Society, for example, and its institutions, are criticized most severely and often most unfairly and this already at the elementary school level. But science is excepted from the criticism. In society at large the judgement of the scientist is received with the same reverence as the judgement of bishops and cardinals was accepted not too long ago. The move towards "demythologization," for example, is largely motivated by the wish to avoid any clash between Christianity and scientific ideas. If such a clash occurs, then science is certainly right and Christianity wrong. Pursue this investigation further and you will see that science has now become as oppressive as the ideologies it had once to fight. Do not be misled by the fact that today hardly anyone gets killed for joining a scientific heresy. This has nothing to do with science. It has something to do with the general quality of our civilization. Heretics in science are still made to suffer from the *most severe* sanctions this relatively tolerant civilization has to offer.

But—is this description not utterly unfair? Have I not presented the matter in a very distorted light by using tendentious and distorting terminology? Must we not describe the situation in a very different way? I have said that science has become *rigid*, that it has ceased to be an instrument of *change* and *liberation*, without adding that it has found the *truth*, or a large part thereof. Considering this additional fact we realise, so the objection goes, that the rigidity of science is not due to human wilfulness. It lies in the nature of things. For once we have discovered the truth—what else can we do but follow it?

This trite reply is anything but original. It is used whenever an ideology wants to reinforce the faith of its followers. "Truth" is such a nicely neutral word. Nobody would deny that it is commendable to speak the truth and wicked to tell lies. Nobody would deny that—and yet nobody knows what such an attitude amounts to. So it is easy to twist matters and to change allegiance to truth in one's everyday affairs into allegiance to the Truth of an ideology which is nothing but the dogmatic defense of that ideology. And it is of course *not* true that we *have* to follow the truth. Human life is guided by many ideas. Truth is one of them. Freedom and mental independence are others. If Truth, as conceived by some ideologists, conflicts with freedom, then we have a choice. We may abandon freedom. But we may also abandon Truth. (Alternatively, we may adopt a more sophisticated idea of truth that no longer contradicts freedom; that was Hegel's solution.) My criticism of modern science is that it inhibits freedom of thought. If the reason is that it has found the truth and now follows it, then I would say that there are better things than first finding, and then following such a monster.

This finishes the general part of my explanation.

There exists a more specific argument to defend the exceptional position science has in society today. Put in a nutshell the argument says (1) that science has finally found the correct method for achieving results and (2) that there are many results to prove the excellence of the method. The argument is mistaken—but most attempts to show this lead into a dead end. Methodology has by now become so crowded with empty sophistication that it is extremely difficult to perceive the simple errors at the basis. It is like fighting the hydra—cut off one ugly head, and eight formalizations take its place. In this situation the only answer is superficiality: when sophistication loses content then the only way of keeping in touch with reality is to be crude and superficial. This is what I intend to be.

Against Method

There is a method, says part (1) of the argument. What is it? How does it work? One answer which is no longer as popular as it used to be is that science works by collecting facts and inferring theories from them. The answer is unsatisfactory as theories never follow from facts in the strict logical sense. To say that they may yet be supported from facts assumes a notion of support that (a) does not show this defect and (b) is sufficiently sophisticated to permit us to say to what extent, say, the theory of relativity is supported by the facts. No such notion exists today, nor is it likely that it will ever be found (one of the problems is that we need a notion of support in which grey ravens can

(continued)

How To Defend Society Against Science (continued)

be said to support "all ravens are black"). This was realised by conventionalists and transcendental idealists who pointed out that theories shape and order facts and can therefore be retained come what may. They can be retained because the human mind either consciously or unconsciously carries out its ordering function. The trouble with these views is that they assume for the mind what they want to explain for the world, viz., that it works in a regular fashion. There is only one view which overcomes all these difficulties. It was invented twice in the nineteenth century, by Mill, in his immortal essay *On Liberty,* and by some Darwinists who extended Darwinism to the battle of ideas. This view takes the bull by the horns: theories cannot be justified and their excellence cannot be shown without reference to other theories. We may explain the *success* of a theory by reference to a more comprehensive theory (we may explain the success of Newton's theory by using the general theory of relativity); and we may explain our preference for it by comparing it with other theories.

Such a comparison does not establish the intrinsic excellence of the theory we have chosen. As a matter of fact, the theory we have chosen may be pretty lousy. It may contain contradictions, it may conflict with well-known facts, it may be cumbersome, unclear, *ad hoc* in decisive places, and so on. But it may still be better than any other theory that is available at the time. It may in fact be the best lousy theory there is. Nor are the standards of judgement chosen in an absolute manner. Our sophistication increases with every choice we make, and so do our standards. Standards compete just as theories compete and we choose the standards most appropriate to the historical situation in which the choice occurs. The rejected alternatives (theories; standards; "facts") are not eliminated. They serve as correctives (after all, we may have made the wrong choice) and they also explain the content of the preferred views (we understand relativity better when we understand the structure of its competitors; we know the full meaning of freedom only when we have an idea of life in a totalitarian state, of its advantages—and there are many advantages—as well as of its disadvantages). Knowledge so conceived is an ocean of alternatives channelled and subdivided by an ocean of standards. It forces our mind to make imaginative choices and thus makes it grow. It makes our mind capable of choosing, imagining, criticising.

Today this view is often connected with the name of Karl Popper. But there are some very decisive differences between Popper and Mill. To start with, Popper developed his view to solve a special problem of epistemology—he wanted to solve "Hume's problem." Mill, on the other hand, is interested in conditions favourable to human growth. His epistemology is the result of a certain theory of man, and not the other way around. Also Popper, being influenced by the Vienna Circle, improves on the logical form of a theory before discussing it, while Mill uses every theory in the form in which it occurs in science. Thirdly, Popper's standards of comparison are rigid and fixed, while Mill's standards are permitted to change with the historical situation. Finally, Popper's standards eliminate competitors once and for all: theories that are either not falsifiable or falsifiable and falsified have no place in science. Popper's criteria are clear, unambiguous, precisely formulated; Mill's criteria are not. This would be an advantage if science itself were clear, unambiguous, and precisely formulated. Fortunately, it is not.

To start with, no new and revolutionary scientific theory is ever formulated in a manner that permits us to say under what circumstances we must regard it as endangered: many revolutionary theories are unfalsifiable. Falsifiable versions do exist, but they are hardly ever in agreement with accepted basic statements: every moderately interesting theory is falsified. Moreover, theories have formal flaws, many of them contain contradictious, *ad hoc* adjustments, and so on and so forth. Applied resolutely, Popperian criteria would eliminate science without replacing it by anything comparable. They are useless as an aid to science. In the past decade this has been realised by various thinkers, Kuhn and Lakatos among them. Kuhn's ideas are interesting but, alas, they are much too vague to give rise to anything but lots of hot air. If you don't believe me, look at the literature. Never before has the literature on the philosophy of science been invaded by so many creeps and incompetents. Kuhn encourages people who have no idea why a stone falls to the ground to talk with assurance about scientific method. Now I have no objection to incompetence but I do object when incompetence is accompanied by boredom and self-righteousness. And this is exactly what happens. We do not get interesting false ideas, we get boring ideas or words connected with no ideas at all. Secondly, wherever one tries to make Kuhn's ideas more definite one finds that they are *false*.

Was there ever a period of normal science in the history of thought? No—and I challenge anyone to prove the contrary.

Lakatos is immeasurably more sophisticated than Kuhn. Instead of theories he considers research programmes which are sequences of theories connected by methods of modification, so-called heuristics. Each theory in the sequence may be full of faults. It may be beset by anomalies, contradictions, ambiguities. What counts is not the shape of the single theories, but the tendency exhibited by the sequence. We judge historical developments and achievements over a period of time, rather than the situation at a particular time. History and methodology are combined into a single enterprise. A research programme is said to progress if the sequence of theories leads to novel predictions. It is said to degenerate if it is reduced to absorbing facts that have been discovered without its help. A decisive feature of Lakatos' methodology is that such evaluations are no longer tied to methodological rules which tell the scientist either to retain or to abandon a research programme. Scientists may stick to a degenerating programme; they may even succeed in making the programme overtake its rivals and they therefore proceed rationally whatever they are doing (provided they continue calling degenerating programmes degenerating and progressive programmes progressive). This means that Lakatos offers *words* which *sound* like the elements of a methodology; he does not offer a methodology. There is no method according to the most advanced and sophisticated methodology in existence today. This finishes my reply to part (1) of the specific argument.

Against Results

According to part (2), science deserves a special position because it has produced *results*. This is an argument only if it can be taken for granted that nothing else has ever produced results. Now it may be admitted that almost everyone who discusses the matter makes such an assumption. It may also be admitted that it is not easy to show that the assumption is false. Forms of life different from science either have disappeared or have degenerated to an extent that makes a fair comparison impossible. Still, the situation is not as hopeless as it was only a decade ago. We have become acquainted with methods of medical diagnosis and therapy which are effective (and perhaps even more effective than the corresponding parts of Western medicine) and which are yet based on an ideology that is radically different from the ideology of Western science. We have learned that there are phenomena such as telepathy and telekinesis which are obliterated by a scientific approach and which could be used to do research in an entirely novel way (earlier thinkers such as Agrippa of Nettesheim, John Dee, and even Bacon were aware of these phenomena). And then—is it not the case that the Church saved souls while science often does the very opposite? Or course, nobody now believes in the ontology that underlies this judgement. Why? Because of ideological pressures identical with those which today make us listen to science to the exclusion of everything else. It is also true that phenomena such as telekinesis and acupuncture may eventually be absorbed into the body of science and may therefore be called "scientific." But note that this happens only after a long period of resistance during which a science *not yet* containing the phenomena wants to get the upper hand over forms of life that contain them. And this leads to a further objection against part (2) of the specific argument. The fact that science has results counts in its favour only if these results were achieved by science alone, and without any outside help. A look at history shows that science hardly ever gets its results in this way. When Copernicus introduced a new view of the universe, he did not consult *scientific* predecessors, he consulted a crazy Pythagorean such as Philolaos. He adopted his ideas and he maintained them in the face of all sound rules of scientific method. Mechanics and optics owe a lot to artisans, medicine to midwives and witches. And in *our* own day we have seen how the interference of the state can advance science: when the Chinese communists refused to be intimidated by the judgement of experts and ordered traditional medicine back into universities and hospitals there was an outcry all over the world that science would now be ruined in China. The very opposite occurred: Chinese science advanced and Western science learned from it. Wherever we look we see that great scientific advances are due to outside interference which is made to prevail in the face of the most basic and most "rational" methodological rules. The lesson is plain: there does not exist a single argument that could be used to support the exceptional role which science today plays in society. Science has done many things, but so have other ideologies. Science often

(continued)

How To Defend Society Against Science   (continued)

proceeds systematically, but so do other ideologies (just consult the records of the many doctrinal debates that took place in the Church) and, besides, there are no overriding rules which are adhered to under any circumstances; there is no "scientific methodology" that can be used to separate science from the rest. *Science is just one of the many ideologies that propel society and it should be treated as such* (this statement applies even to the most progressive and most dialectical sections of science). What consequences can we draw from this result?

The most important consequence is that there must be a *formal separation between state and science* just as there is now a formal separation between state and church. Science may influence society but only to the extent to which any political or other pressure group is permitted to influence society. Scientists may be consulted on important projects but the final judgement must be left to the democratically elected consulting bodies. These bodies will consist mainly of laymen. Will the laymen be able to come to a correct judgement? Most certainly, for the competence, the complications and the successes of science are vastly exaggerated. One of the most exhilarating experiences is to see how a lawyer, who is a layman, can find holes in the testimony, the technical testimony, of the most advanced expert and thus prepare the jury for its verdict. Science is not a closed book that is understood only after years of training. It is an intellectual discipline that can be examined and criticised by anyone who is interested and that looks difficult and profound only because of a systematic campaign of obfuscation carried out by many scientists (though, I am happy to say, not by all). Organs of the state should never hesitate to reject the judgement of scientists when they have reason for doing so. Such rejection will educate the general public, will make it more confident, and it may even lead to improvement. Considering the sizeable chauvinism of the scientific establishment we can say: the more Lysenko affairs, the better (it is not the *interference* of the state that is objectionable in the case of Lysenko, but the *totalitarian* interference which kills the opponent rather than just neglecting his advice). Three cheers to the fundamentalists in California who succeeded in having a dogmatic formulation of the theory of evolution removed from the textbooks and an account of Genesis included. (But I know that they would become as chauvinistic and totalitarian as scientists are today when given the chance to run society all by themselves. Ideologies are marvellous when used in the companies of other ideologies. They become boring and doctrinaire as soon as their merits lead to the removal of their opponents.) The most important change, however, will have to occur in the field of education.

Education and Myth

The purpose of education, so one would think, is to introduce the young into life, and that means: into the *society* where they are born and into the *physical universe* that surrounds the society. The method of education often consists in the teaching of some *basic myth*. The myth is available in various versions. More advanced versions may be taught by initiation rites which firmly implant them into the mind. Knowing the myth, the grown-up can explain almost everything (or else he can turn to experts for more detailed information). He is the master of Nature and of Society. He understands them both and he knows how to interact with them. However, *he is not the master of the myth that guides his understanding.*

Such further mastery was aimed at, and was partly achieved, by the Presocratics. The Presocratics not only tried to understand the *world*. They also tried to understand, and thus to become the masters of, the *means of understanding the world*. Instead of being content with a single myth they developed many and so diminished the power which a well-told story has over the minds of men. The sophists introduced still further methods for reducing the debilitating effect of interesting, coherent, "empirically adequate" etc., tales. The achievements of these thinkers were not appreciated and they certainly are not understood today. When teaching a myth we want to increase the chance that it will be understood (i.e., no puzzlement about any feature of the myth), believed, *and accepted*. This does not do any harm when the myth is counterbalanced by other myths: even the most dedicated (i.e., totalitarian) instructor in a certain version of Christianity cannot prevent his pupils from getting in touch with Buddhists, Jews and other disreputable people. It is very different in the case of science, or of rationalism where the field is almost completely dominated by the believers. In this case it is of paramount importance to strengthen the minds of the young, and "strengthening the minds of the young" means strengthening them *against* any easy acceptance of comprehensive views. What we need here is an education that makes people *contrary, counter-suggestive,* without making them incapable of devoting themselves to the elaboration of any single view. How can this aim be achieved?

It can be achieved by protecting the tremendous imagination which children possess and by developing to the full the spirit of contradiction that exists in them. On the whole children are much more intelligent than their teachers. They succumb, and give up their intelligence because they are bullied, or because their teachers get the better of them by emotional means. Children can learn, understand, and keep separate two to three different languages ("children" and by this I mean three to five year-olds, *not* eight year-olds who were experimented upon quite recently and did not come out too well; why? because they were already loused up by incompetent teaching at an earlier age). Of course, the languages must be introduced in a more interesting way than is usually done. There are marvellous writers in all languages who have told marvellous stories—let us begin our language teaching with *them* and not with "der Hund hat einen Schwanz" and similar inanities. Using stories we may of course also introduce "scientific" accounts, say, of the origin of the world and thus make the children acquainted with science as well. But science must not be given any special position except for pointing out that there are lots of people who believe in it. Later on the stories which have been told will be supplemented with "reasons", where by reasons I mean further accounts of the kind found in the tradition to which the story belongs. And, of course, there will also be contrary reasons. Both reasons and contrary reasons will be told by the experts in the fields and so the young generation becomes acquainted with all kinds of sermons and all types of wayfarers. It becomes acquainted with them, it becomes acquainted with their stories, and every individual can make up his mind which way to go. By now everyone knows that you can earn a lot of money and respect and perhaps even a Nobel Prize by becoming a scientist, so many will become scientists. They will *become* scientists *without having been taken in by the ideology of science*, they will *be* scientists *because they have made a free choice.* But has not much time been wasted on unscientific subjects and will this not detract from their competence once they have become scientists? Not at all! The progress of science, of good science depends on novel ideas and on intellectual freedom: science has very often been advanced by outsiders (remember that Bohr and Einstein regarded themselves as outsiders). Will not many people make the wrong choice and end up in a deadend? Well, that depends on what you mean by a "dead end." Most scientists today are devoid of ideas, full of fear, intent on producing some paltry result so that they can add to the flood of inane papers that now constitutes "scientific progress" in many areas. And, besides, what is more important? To lead a life which one has chosen with open eyes, or to spend one's time in the nervous attempt of avoiding what some not so intelligent people call "dead ends"? Will not the number of scientists decrease so that in the end there is nobody to run our precious laboratories? I do not think so. Given a choice many people may choose science, for a science that is run by free agents looks much more attractive than the science of today which is run by slaves, slaves of institutions and slaves of "reason". And if there is a temporary shortage of scientists the situation may always be remedied by various kinds of incentives. Of course, scientists will not play any predominant role in the society I envisage. They will be more than balanced by magicians, or priests, or astrologers. Such a situation is unbearable for many people, old and young, right and left. Almost all of you have the firm belief that at least *some* kind of truth has been found, that it must be preserved, and that the method of teaching I advocate and the form of society I defend will dilute it and make it finally disappear. You have this firm belief; many of you may even have reasons. *But what you have to consider is that the absence of good contrary reasons is due to a historical accident;* it does *not* lie in the nature of things. Build up the kind of society I recommend and the views you now despise (without knowing them, to be sure) will return in such splendour that you will have to work hard to maintain your own position and will perhaps be entirely unable to do so. You do not believe me? Then look at history. Scientific astronomy was firmly founded on Ptolemy and Aristotle, two of the greatest minds in the history of Western Thought. Who upset their well-argued, empirically adequate and precisely formulated system? Philolaos the mad and antediluvian Pythagorean. How was it that Philolaos could stage such a comeback? Because he found an able defender: Copernicus. Of course, you may follow your intuitions as I am following mine. But remember that your intuitions are the result of your "scientific" training where by science I also

(continued)

How To Defend Society Against Science   (*continued*)

mean the science of Karl Marx. My training, or, rather, my non-training, is that of a journalist who is interested in strange and bizarre events. Finally, is it not utterly irresponsible, in the present world situation, with millions of people starving, others enslaved, downtrodden, in abject misery of body and mind, to think luxurious thoughts such as these? Is not freedom of choice a luxury under such circumstances? Is not the flippancy and the humour I want to see combined with the freedom of choice a luxury under such circumstances? Must we not give up all self-indulgence and *act*? Join together, and *act*? This is the most important objection which today is raised against an approach such as the one recommended by me. It has tremendous appeal, it has the appeal of unselfish dedication. Unselfish dedication—to what? Let us see!

We are supposed to give up our selfish inclinations and dedicate ourselves to the liberation of the oppressed. And selfish inclinations are what? They are our wish for maximum liberty of thought in the society in which we live *now*, maximum liberty not only of an abstract kind, but expressed in appropriate institutions and methods of teaching. This wish for concrete intellectual and physical liberty in our own surroundings is to be put aside, for the time being. This assumes, first, that we do not need this liberty for our task. It assumes that we can carry out our task with a mind that is firmly closed to some alternatives. It assumes that the correct way of liberating others *has always been found* and that all that is needed is to carry it out. I am sorry, I cannot accept such doctrinaire self-assurance in such extremely important matters. Does this mean that we cannot act at all? It does not. But it means that *while acting we have to try to realise as much of the freedom I have recommended so that our actions may be corrected in the light of the ideas we get while increasing our freedom*. This will slow us down, no doubt, but are we supposed to charge ahead simply because some people tell us that they have found an explanation for all the misery and an excellent way out of it? Also we want to liberate people not to make them succumb to a new kind of slavery, *but to make them realise their own wishes,* however different these wishes may be from our own. Self-righteous and narrow-minded liberators cannot do this. As a rule they soon impose a slavery that is worse, because more systematic, than the very sloppy slavery they have removed. And as regards humour and flippancy the answer should be obvious. Why would anyone want to liberate anyone else? Surely not because of some *abstract* advantage of liberty but because liberty is the best way to free development *and thus to happiness*. We want to liberate people so that *they can smile*. Shall we be able to do this if we ourselves have forgotten how to smile and are frowning on those who still remember? Shall we then not spread another disease, comparable to the one we want to remove, the disease of puritanical self-righteousness? Do not object that dedication and humour do not go together—Socrates is an excellent example to the contrary. *The hardest task needs the lightest hand or else its completion will not lead to freedom but to a tyranny much worse than the one it replaces.*

Chapter 7
Aesthetics

Aesthetics is the philosophical study of the nature of beauty. Specifically, it is concerned with such topics as the definition of art, the social purpose of art, and the relevance of artistic intent. Aesthetics also examines the role of personal taste, artistic meaning, and the objectivity of artistic value.

Plato did not put much value on the arts, arguing instead that the artist does not contribute to society because he or she is not engaged in creating something worthy. Yet if a movie provides a few hours of entertainment does that diminish its value or importance? The Oliver Stone film *JFK* concerning the assassination of John F. Kennedy was attacked by many people as twisting the facts to fit Stone's agenda. But the film was not meant as a documentary, and there have been hundreds of films based on or inspired by real events and persons—should they all be dismissed as trifle irrelevancies or even dangerous? Director Mel Gibson had his actors speak in the historically accurate languages for *The Passion of the Christ* and *Apocalpyto,* should we also insist that movies about Nazis be more truthful and in German? Should the Spartans in *300* have spoken ancient Greek, which even modern Greek moviegoers do not speak and should the film be deemed valueless because it was historically inaccurate?

While Plato might not like art, what *is* art? Imagine you are in the Canadian Artic and come across a pile of rocks that seem to take the form of a human figure. Is this art? Would it make a difference if you knew how it came to be? Natural artifacts can be beautiful, but while they may inspire us to make art they are not themselves works of art. Only if one also argued that there was a divine artist could this be so. Furthermore, just because someone intended to put a bunch of rocks together it does not mean that they have created a work of art. It may just be a pile of rocks moved out of the way or it may be intended to function as a windbreak or some other device. Northern Canadian rock formation in the shape of human is called an Inusuk; it is intended to be a marker to show Inuit hunters the way home and yet it can also be seen as a thing of beauty.[1] When does something that is done with intentionality become a work of art? If I disposed of a used wad of bubble gum by smearing it on the wall, people would admonish me for being disgusting. But if I put a frame around it is it now a work of art? Why is it when a child deliberately throws paint on the floor she deserves scolding but when Jackson Pollack did it, he deserved millions of dollars? Is it what goes on the canvas that matters or what goes on inside the head of the artist? Or maybe it is both as the film *Pollack* suggests:

What's this?
I see the head . . .
the body—
This isn't cubism, Jackson . . .
because you're not really breaking down the figure . . .
into multiple views.
You're just showing us one side.
What is this? Free association? Automatism?
I'm just painting, Lee.
But what you're doing, Jackson—
Don't tell me you don't know what you're doing.
Are you experimenting with surrealism?
Is this a dream?
Even if it's a dream, it's still what you see.
It's life.
You're not just randomly putting paint on the canvas.
You're painting something.
You can't abstract from nothing.
You can only abstract from life— from nature.
I am nature.

Some may argue that just because a creative object is highly popular does not entail that it is "art"—in fact in some cases it almost seems that there is an inverse relationship![2] For decades films were not regarded as art but as mindless entertainment. This view has since been corrected with almost every large university offering courses in film studies. In North America comic books were seen as trifle amusements for children, but this view is starting to be readdressed.[3] Open up comic books today and you will see a degree of artistic expression and ability that is unquestionably excellent. The suggestion that because something merely entertains consequently excludes it from being high art is a misunderstanding of the history of various classical masterpieces. The works of the Old Masters when they were alive were often seen as popular or "low art"—after all, they often did their work on commission. Michelangelo painted ceilings and Shakespeare wrote for the masses and Strauss

---

[1] The Inusuk was also used as the logo for the 2010 Vancouver Olympic games.

[2] Compare for example the box office grosses of a summer block bluster movie with a typical Oscar-winning picture.
[3] Comics aimed at adults are now called "Graphic Novels" to give them a greater sense of acceptability, but they are still pages drawn by cartoonists and the content of these "novels" is not always fiction.

wrote the equivalent of Top 40 pop tunes. This does not mean that what is considered pure pop is going to be with us forever. Instead it means that we need to be more appreciative and open-minded regarding the different creative outlets of humans. We cannot deny the simple fact that if a work of creativity brings pleasure to a person then it has some value, no matter how minimal or brief that pleasure lasts.

We might argue that determining what is high or low, or good or bad art is just a matter of personal taste. We all like and dislike different things, so we should be willing to accept artistic variety into our lives since it gives us choice. When we go to the large movie houses we are presented with a selection of half a dozen different films of different genres. Within each genre we will refine our tastes even further, choosing to see a movie with this actor instead of that one or this director instead of that one. Is it possible to use our own personal preferences as a measure of the aesthetic value of a work of art? David Hume discusses personal taste in his aptly named selection included in this chapter.

Differences in taste may be benign as in the case of liking one movie genre over another, but they can also be more socially significant; what is enjoyable to one person may be objectionable and offensive to the other.

While it is easy to find examples of things that people find offensive because it seems that most people can be offended about anything, here is a famous scene from Monty Python's *The Meaning of Life*, which intentionally pushes the boundaries of good taste. Given what occurs in it, there is no reason for the writers to claim that it is not intended as anything less than an affront to the viewer's senses.

MAITRE D   Ah good afternoon, sir, and how are we today?

MR. CREOSOTE   Better . . .

MAITRE D   Better?

MR. CREOSOTE   Better get a bucket, I'm going to throw up.

MAITRE D   Gaston! A bucket for monsieur!

[They seat him at his usual table. A gleaming silver bucket is placed beside him and he leans over and throws up into it.]

MAITRE D   Merci Gaston.

[He claps his hands and the bucket is whisked away.]

MR. CREOSOTE   I haven't finished!

MAITRE D   Oh! Pardon! Gaston! . . . A thousand pardons monsieur. [Puts the bucket back.]

[The Maitre D produces the menu as Mr. Creosote continues spewing.]

MAITRE D   Now this afternoon we monsieur's favorite—the jugged hare. The hare is *very* high, and the sauce is very rich with truffles, anchovies, Grand Marnier, bacon and cream.

[Mr. Creosote pauses. The Maitre D claps his hands and signs to Gaston, who whisks away the bucket.]

MAITRE D   Thank you, Gaston.

MR. CREOSOTE   There's still more.

[Gaston rapidly replaces the bucket.]

MAITRE D   Allow me! A new bucket for monsieur.

[The Maitre D picks the bucket up and hands it over to Gaston. Mr. Creosote leans over and throws up onto the floor.]

And the cleaning woman.

[Gaston hurries off. The Maitre D takes care to avoid the vomit and places the menu in front of Mr Creosote.]

And maintenant, would monsieur care for an aperitif?

[Creosote vomits over the menu. It is covered.]

Or would you prefer to order straight away? Today for appetizers . . . er . . . excuse me . . .

This scene continues until everyone in the restaurant is vomiting until . . .

MAITRE D   And finally, monsieur, a wafer-thin mint.

MR. CREOSOTE   No.

MAITRE D   Oh sir! It's only a tiny little thin one.

MR. CREOSOTE   No. F*ck off—I'm full . . . [Belches]

MAITRE D   Oh sir . . . it's only *wafer* thin.

MR. CREOSOTE   Look—I couldn't eat another thing. I'm absolutely stuffed. Bugger off.

MAITRE D   Oh sir, just . . . just *one* . . .

MR. CREOSOTE   Oh all right. Just one.

MAITRE D Just the one, sir . . . voila . . . bon appetite . . .

[Mr. Creosote somehow manages to stuff the wafer-thin mint into his mouth and then swallows. The Maitre D takes a flying leap and cowers behind some potted plants. There is an ominous splitting sound. Mr. Creosote looks rather helpless and then he explodes, covering waiters, diners, and technicians in a truly horrendous mix of half digested food, entrails and parts of his body. People start vomiting.]

MAITRE D [returns to Mr. Creosote's table] Thank you, sir, and now the check.

Given the above scene, movie patrons may want to be forewarned about the nature of this film (and others) before choosing to see it. Personal choice and preferences based upon taste can only be exercised when one has knowledge. The Motion Picture Association of America (MPAA) provides an important service by letting people know what is in the movie, but some critics are concerned that they are doing much more. Here is an example of the MPAA rating system:

> A G-rated motion picture contains nothing in theme—language, nudity, sex, violence or other matters—that, in the view of the rating board, would offend parents whose younger children view the motion picture. The G rating is not a "certificate of approval," nor does it signify a "children's" motion picture. Some snippets of language may go beyond polite conversation, but they are common everyday expressions. No stronger words are present in G-rated motion pictures. Depictions of violence are minimal. No nudity, sex scenes, or drug use are present in the motion picture.
>
> An R-rated motion picture, in the view of the rating board, contains some adult material. An R-rated motion picture may include adult themes, adult activity, hard language, intense or persistent violence, sexually oriented nudity, drug abuse, or other elements, so parents are counseled to take this rating very seriously. Children under seventeen are not allowed to attend R-rated motion pictures unaccompanied by a parent or adult guardian. Parents are strongly urged to find out more about R-rated motion pictures in determining their suitability for their children. Generally, it is not appropriate for parents to bring their young children with them to R-rated motion pictures.[4]

The MPAA is not merely being descriptive (i.e., telling people that there is violence or sex in the films) but it is also being prescriptive. It is telling people that the violence is such that, for example, people under the age of eighteen are not permitted or should not be permitted to view it. Some argue that these restrictions remove the parents' ability to determine what they personally would permit their children to see. Furthermore, critics charge that the MPAA is acting as a censor board because it knows that a movie that is given an R rating will get fewer ticket buyers and so the director will be pressured to make cuts and alter his or her initial vision. Likewise a movie given an NC-17 rating will almost kill its box office potential because the rating effectively compares the film to pornography.

In Canada, there are ratings boards for each province and there are slight variations among their guidelines.[5] Some make restrictions on the basis that the film *may* contain violence and/or sexuality; others state that there *will likely* be violence and/or sexuality; still others state that there *definitely will be* violence and/or sexuality. Thus some provinces make their decisions based on mere "possibility"; others on "probability"; and others on definitive presence of violence and/or sexuality. The Ontario board goes so far as to explain what psychological effects viewers may experience from the film[6]. Are these differing standards

---

[4] See Motion Picture Association of America http://www.mpaa.org/FlmRat_Ratings.asp (visited Feb. 2008).
[5] See Media Awareness Network http://www.media-awareness.ca/english/resources/ratings_classification_systems/film_classification/canada_film_classification.cfm (visited Feb. 2008).
[6] For example, they state: **Restricted (R)** Restricted to persons 18 years of age or over.

Language: No restriction.
Violence: Visually explicit portrayals of violence, which may be characterized by extreme brutality, extreme bloodletting and extreme tissue damage. May include torture, horror, sexual violence.
Nudity: Full frontal nudity in a sexual situation.
Sexual Activity: Simulated sexual activity; limited instances of brief, non-violent explicit sexual activity.
Horror: Horrific themes, incidents and images will have a more prolonged or graphic focus and greater frequency.
Psychological Impact: Scenes and situations may cause extreme adverse psychological impact. Could involve intense and compelling terror, acts of degradation, threats of violence, and continuous acts of non-extreme violence. Such situations could be accompanied by coarse, abusive, and degrading dialogue. See Media Awareness Network http://www.media-awareness.ca/english/resources/ratings_classification_systems/film_classification/ont_film_classification.cfm (visited Feb. 2008).

suggesting that people have different tolerance levels solely based on where they live in the country? Perhaps this is true, for you will find different countries tolerate different things. For example, it is often pointed out that full frontal nudity (especially male) in U.S. films is not tolerated whereas extreme violence is considered acceptable. European audiences seem to be more tolerant of nudity than violence, yet a film like *300*, which consists almost entirely of extreme albeit comic-book style violence, received a restricted rating in the United States[7] while in France twelve-year-olds were allowed in.[8]

One reason why people have different preferences or levels of tolerance is that they get different messages from the work of art. One person sees the artist as saying something positive, while their neighbor looking at the same piece sees it as saying something negative. Can art have different meanings? Can we determine what an artwork means? Is it enough to ask or know what the creator intended to express in order to know that that is what is meant? Surely it is *prima facie* odd to say to an artist: "You tell me that this work was intended to mean X, but you are wrong, it actually means Y." How bizarre it must be for an author to hear "You are wrong about the meaning of your own work." And yet, how are we to assess it? E. D. Hirsh, Jr. (1928–) tells us that a work of art means what the artist intended it to mean and nothing more or less, while William Kurtz Wimsatt (1907–1975) and Monroe Beardsley (1915–1985) claim that we do not need to ask what the creator meant by his or her art to know what it means.

Think about writing an essay for your instructor. When you get it back, he or she has given you a low grade. You protest when they point out numerous instances of vagueness and retort, "But what I really meant was . . . " Unfortunately, what you really meant is inaccessible to the professor because what you wrote is all that he or she has by which to judge your intentions. If the purpose of your work is to convince another person that your view is correct, then it must be unambiguous and clear. But with art it is not so apparent that there is an argument or message being put forward. A black strip across a red canvas means what? A live performance with ten dancing figures dressed as cows means what? A three hour recital piece of repetitive atonal music is intended to tell the listener what? Would it help us understand if these works had titles?

The conclusion of Wimsatt and Beardsley's argument in 'The Intentional Fallacy" is that that "critical inquiries are not settled by consulting the Oracle" (i.e., the author), while Hirsh argues that the author's intent must be acknowledged and discovered for "a vague or ambiguous text is just as determinate as a logical proposition, it means what it means and nothing else." In an argumentative essay the writer's intent is presented in black and white. You will often find at the very beginning of the paper a statement of purpose. Art should not be like that. A novelist should not have a need to state in the preface, "This is a book about jealously." If the writer has to explain using words outside what he or she already provided, then the writer has failed. Moreover, if the writer or painter wants to consciously push the message, then the reader or observer is left with nothing to do. Art should be an activity. It should be a shared experience where writer and artist, and reader and observer bring something of themselves to the piece. Is it possible that a creator may not know what he or she has in mind when putting the piece together? Can there be another reading or another interpretation that even the creator will accept?

Determining artistic intent is made more complicated when the work has more than one creator, as is the case with many films. The screenwriter, director, actors, editors, cinematographers, production designers, *et al.,* all contribute something to the end product. What filmmakers intend the viewer to get out of it is known as the "dominant film reading." So for a film that is offered as pure entertainment, a movie is just a movie. You pay your money, you have some fun for one hundred minutes or so, and hopefully you go away happy. If by chance you read something into it that is not up there on the screen (but perhaps is inside you) this only gives you more value for your money.

For example, is there some deeper meaning in having an obscenely obese man eat until he explodes, as in the scene from *The Meaning of Life?* Is it a commentary on American consumerism? Maybe the filmmakers are suggesting that military superpowers that attempt to interfere in every political crisis (i.e., eat everything that is put on the table in front of them) will discover that their own social conflicts will cause them to "explode" from the inside out? Just how far can one go in pushing the meaning, any meaning, of a work of art? What if the filmmakers put

---

[7] See The Classification and Rating Administration http://www.film-ratings.com (visited Feb. 2008).
[8] See Centre national de la cinematographie http://www.cnc.fr/Site/Teniplate/A2.aspx?SELECTID=20&lD=21i&cnc=2007293216&visa=117322&pageSelected=2&t=l (visited Feb. 2008).

468 Chapter 7 • Aesthetics

out a press release stating that one of the previous examples was their true intent? Would they be right that Mr. Creosote is about consumerism? Would we actually believe them?

Philip Pullman, author of *His Dark Materials*[9] trilogy of which the first book *The Golden Compass* was released as a film in late 2007, offered these informal comments about his creative intentions:

> My intention was to write a story, and there it is. [There is a] very interesting discussion [going on], between those writers [of children's literature] who think it's the readers' job to discover the writer's true intentions and interpret them accurately—those who think in other words, that there is a 'correct' reading of a book; and those other writers such as myself who believe that once a book is out there in the world, it has to argue its own case, make itself understood as well as it can, and that readers have every right to make whatever meaning they care to from the words on the page. The catch as far as eccentric or paradoxical readings are concerned is that if that reader wants to persuade others of the merits of their reading, they have to do all the things that traditional literary criticism does: find evidence in the text, quote accurately and relevantly, marshal their arguments logically, and so on.
>
> What that amounts to is that I'm with [Sam Goldwyn—the 'G' in MGM] who said: "If you want to send a message, use Western Union."[10] If my novel persuades you that it's a fine thing to live in a world without God, well and good; if you find that it contains a secret code giving the true location of the Holy Grail, bully for you; if you come to the conclusion that *despite appearances* I am a devout Christian and *His Dark Materials* a work of the most orthodox piety, then again—hoorah. All you have to do is demonstrate why.[11]

In a similar vein, Danny Fingeroth, longtime Marvel Comics writer and editor and now non-fiction author,[12] states:

> To most civilian viewers of a work, the creators' intention is irrelevant. They go to be entertained on Saturday night, even if they're going to an 'art' movie or whatever.
>
> As a creator of stories, I like to have it both (or many) ways. I want to entertain people, and I want to believe they will only take positive messages away from what I write or edit. That is to say, if every Spider-Man story is ultimately about 'Power brings Responsibility,' then I want people to take that idea away from any Spidey story I'm involved with. If the story involves Venom [ed. note: a villain who made his film debut in Spider-Man III], then I want people to come away with the feeling that his abuse of power is wrong. But I'm fully aware that many people may take the opposite away instead or in addition: that it's cool to (as Venom does) have a living costume to carry out your every whim and give you giant muscles and make people fear and obey you. At a certain point you just have to tell the story you need to tell, otherwise, you become creatively paralyzed.[13]

Film critics and the public may find that they not only get the intended message from the film but find other meanings as well, which is what we call "negotiated readings." For example, we can look back in time and read more into the films from different periods. In the 1930s, screwball comedies were all the rage. Slight, innocent, and frivolous, films like *Flying Down to Rio* or *My Man Godfrey* were in direct contrast to the reality of the times.[14] The United States and Canada were in the midst of a horrible depression with little work or hope for the people. Moviegoers turned to the cinema to flee their dreary lives, and Hollywood was eager to oblige them with all sorts of tales that would allow them to escape for a

---

[9] Book One of *His Dark Materials* was published in 1996 by Scholastic Point.
[10] Although most commonly attributed to Sam Goldwyn (which is why I inserted it into Pullman's quote), this saying has also been attributed to his partner at MGM Louis B. Mayer.
[11] An e-mail to the editor, dated August 20, 2007.
[12] Fingeroth, Danny, *Superman on the Couch: What Superheroes Really Tell Us About Ourselves and Our Society* (New York: Continuum International Publishing Group, 2004).
[13] From an e-mail to the editor, October 10, 2007.
[14] Other notable 1930s films about the adventures of the rich include *Dodson, The Thin Man, Topper, The Awful Truth, You Can't Take it With You,* and *The Footloose Heiress*.

short while. Thus one can imagine that moviegoers walked out thinking that life can and will get better. In the late 1940s, film noir (literally "black film") created the anti-hero and the femme fatale. Movies such as *The Big Sleep* or *Double Indemnity* were like their genre's namesake—dark in appearance and story.[15] These were just another sign of the post war times that would seem out of place now unless the particular film (such as *L.A. Confidential*) was an intentional homage to that period. In the 1950s, giant bug and monster movies like *Tarantula*, *Deadly Mantis*, *Them!* and of course *Godzilla* came into popularity just as the atomic age was gaining hold.[16] As well, the Red Scare over communism (which replaced fears of Nazism) was reflected in such drive-in classics as *Flying Saucer*, *War of the Worlds*, *It Came from Outer Space!* and the not so subtly titled *Red Planet Mars*.[17] Nor could we trust our friends and neighbors to help us for aliens might replace their bodies by exact duplicates, which happened in such films as *The Body Snatchers* or *The Thing from Another World*. They ("they" being the Communists) may look like us, but they are plotting our destruction, seeking to destroy our way of life.[18]

By looking at the times and the context of the films' release we can negotiate new meanings into them. During the second U.S.–Iraq war, the film *300* took on new meaning. Even though it was based on a graphic novel written in 1999 (four years before the American offensive) some viewers argued that the film, which depicts the heroic yet doomed last stand of Sparta against Persia, really was about the "invading hordes of Islam on Western democracies." At the time of the film's release, American President Bush was (or so the argument goes) defending freedom against individuals and ideologies like those in the film. Such claims were based on snippets of film dialogue like these:

a. SPARTAN KING LEONIDAS The world will know that freemen stood against a tyrant, that few stood against many, and that before this battle is done, that even a god king can bleed.

b. XERXES Yours is a fascinating tribe . . . defiant even in the face of annihilation. There is much our cultures could share.

SPARTAN KING LEONIDAS Perhaps you haven't noticed, but we've been sharing our culture with you all morning.

c. DILIOS [It is] An army of slaves vast beyond imagination ready to devour tiny Greece, ready to snuff out the world's one hope for reason and justice. A beast approaches.

d. SPARTAN KING LEONIDAS Then what must a king do to save his world when the very laws he has sworn to protect force him to do nothing?

e. QUEEN GORGO Freedom isn't free at all. It comes with the highest costs—the cost of blood.

f. QUEEN GORGO I am not here to represent Leonidas; his actions speak louder than my words ever could. I am here for all those voices which cannot be heard: mothers, daughters, fathers, sons—three hundred families that bleed for our rights, and for the very principles this room was built upon. We are at war, gentlemen. We must send the entire Spartan army to aid our king in the preservation of not just ourselves, but of our children. Send the army for the preservation of liberty. Send it for justice. Send it for law and order. Send it for reason. But most importantly, send our army for hope—hope that a king and his men have not been wasted to the pages of history—that their courage bonds us together, that we are made stronger by their actions, and that your choices today reflect their bravery.

Given the context of the U.S.–Iraq war and a preoccupation with terrorism, *The Lord of the Rings* seems to take on a new meaning as well. It is as if the hobbit Samwise Gamgee is speaking directly to American citizens sitting in the theater when he tells Frodo not to give up on their quest even though it seems hopeless and the enemy seems everywhere about them:

> *[Back to Osgiliath, Frodo walks out into the open.]*
>
> SAM What are you doing? Where are you going?
>
> *(The Ringwraith riding the Fell Beast approaches. Frodo is about to put on the Ring when Sam runs up and tackles him.*

---

[15] Such films also had great titles, such as *Murder, My Sweet*, *Shadow of Suspicion*, *Phantom Lady*, and *D.O.A.*
[16] See also *The Black Scorpion*, *The Beast from 20,000 Fathoms*, *The Thing from Another World*, *Monster from Green Hell*, and *Earth versus The Spider*.
[17] Other classics of the time period include *Rocket Ship X-M*, *The Day the Earth Stood Still*, *Invaders from Mars*, *Earth vs. the Flying Saucers*, *Forbidden Planet*, *Destination Moon*, *This Island Earth*, and *Not of this Earth*.
[18] Interestingly, aliens always seemed to land in the United States, but this only made sense since (we are told by some protagonist in the movie) whatever threatens the United States is a *de facto* threat to the entire world.

Faramir shoots the Ringwraith's steed with his bow. The hobbits roll down the stairs, Sam landing on Frodo who rolls over and draws his sword preparing to kill Sam.)

It's me. It's your Sam. Don't you know your Sam?

(Frodo comes to his senses and drops Sting.)

FRODO   I can't do this, Sam.

SAM   I know. It's all wrong. By rights we shouldn't even be here. But we are. It's like in the great stories, Mr. Frodo. The ones that really mattered. Full of darkness and danger they were. And sometimes you didn't want to know the end. Because how could the end be happy? How could the world go back to the way it was when so much bad had happened. But in the end, it's only a passing thing, this shadow. Even darkness must pass. A new day will come. And when the sun shines it will shine out the clearer. Those were the stories that stayed with you. That meant something. Even if you were too small to understand why. But I think, Mr. Frodo, I do understand. I know now. Folk in those stories had lots of chances of turning back only they didn't. They kept going. Because they were holding on to something.

FRODO   What are we holding on to, Sam?

SAM   *(He helps Frodo up and says:)*

That there's some good in this world, Mr. Frodo. And it's worth fighting for.

The historical period that the art was created in and the period in which the art is ultimately viewed (which can be a separation of decades or hundreds of years) must not be discounted. A work that was once ignored or discounted may gain new significance and vice versa because viewers bring the times with them. Sam's comforting words to Frodo may have reassured a few moviegoers in ways that the screenwriters did not originally intend.

Negotiated or Oppositional readings—where the viewer comes to a contrary or contradictory conclusion about the intent of the artwork from that of the artist—depend as much on the individual viewer as does the actual artwork. Race, class, gender, ethnicity, religion, culture, and political beliefs are all elements that can feed into formations about how one perceives the work.

If I am a devout Christian, I might see certain films like *The Life of Brian* as not only potentially offensive (which it is) but also as blasphemous. I might also react to more heartfelt works about religion such as *The Last Temptation of Christ* in the same way depending on my own level of tolerance. Influential film critic Roger Ebert when asked about artistic intentionality replied that "It is possible to identify and observe the director's intention, and also note if the film in fact argues a point he didn't intend. Notice the divergence between how Scorsese intended *The Last Temptation of Christ* and how fundamentalists took it."[19,20]

---

[19] E-mail to editor, August 20, 2007.
[20] Here is a summary of the reaction as described by PBS.

> Before *The Last Temptation of Christ* is completed, Christian groups worldwide condemn it as blasphemous, although Christian theology teaches that Jesus is both fully human and fully divine, and that to say otherwise is heresy. Preproduction begins at Universal Studios in 1983, and until the film's release in 1988, groups affiliated with the Christian right demonstrate against *The Last Temptation of Christ* through petitions, phone campaigns, radio broadcasts, and street protests.
>
> Aware of mounting organized pressure against the film, in 1987, Universal hires a liaison with the Christian community, a born-again Christian himself, and arranges a private advance screening for agitated groups, including Reverend Donald Wildmon's American Family Association and Bill Bright's Campus Crusade for Christ. The audience is especially disgusted by a closing image: Christ on the cross is tempted by Satan with visions of a "normal" life with the prostitute Mary Magdalene, replete with sex, marriage, and children. Some 1,200 Christian radio stations in California denounce the film, and Mastermedia International urges a boycott against parent company MCA. Bill Bright offers to reimburse Universal for its investment in *The Last Temptation of Christ* in exchange for all existing prints, which he vows to destroy. Universal responds with an open letter in newspapers across the country, saying that acquiescence to these forces would infringe on the First Amendment rights of all Americans. On the day the letter appears, more than 600 protesters, sponsored by a Christian radio station in Los Angeles, picket MCA headquarters.
>
> The protests are effective. Edwards Theaters, with 150 theaters nationwide, refuses to screen the film, as do United Artists and General Cinemas, with 3,500 theaters between them. In August 1988, Universal opens *The Last Temptation of Christ* in nine major cities in the United States and Canada. The day before its premiere, Citizens for a Universal Appeal, a coalition of religious groups from Orange County, CA, stages a protest in front of Universal's L.A. headquarters that attracts some 25,000 participants. By the time *The Last Temptation of Christ* goes into wide release in September, the national controversy has waned, but now individual cities and towns seek bans. Among them, Savannah, GA, New Orleans, Oklahoma City, and Santa Ana, CA, succeed.
>
> In 1989, Blockbuster Video declines to carry the film in its stores. The policy remains, though it is available for purchase on the chain's Web site. In the mid-90s, *The Last Temptation of Christ* reignites protests in Canada and Russia when it airs on national television. Although critics give the movie mixed reviews on aesthetic grounds, the film earns Martin Scorsese an Academy Award nomination for Best Director. http://www.pbs.org/wqbh/cultureshock/flashpoints/theater/lasttemptation.html (visited Feb. 2008)

The Last Temptation of Christ is a deeply religious film by Martin Scorsese and screenwriter Paul Schrader. They give us a Jesus who is both a man and a messiah. The film is challenging and is not preaching to the already converted but is telling a story about a man who is also God. In it we are presented with a man who is fully human and thus possesses all the traits of humans—both good and bad. In doing so, the filmmakers allow the audience to identify more with a personal Jesus than Jesus as an icon. That in itself is controversial but more so is the sort of man Jesus is revealed to be.

In the beginning of the film, Jesus is portrayed as a troubled man tormented by temptation and doubt. We hear him talk to his God through voiceovers. We are allowed into his mind to hear of his fears and doubts and decisions. When first we meet Jesus it is as a carpenter. He builds the very crosses that are used to crucify thieves and prophets.

> JUDAS Romans can't find carpenters to make crosses. Except for you. You throw yourself into it like a madman. Everybody thinks you're crazy. But not me. I can see through this act of yours. Fainting, hearing voices, having visions. Everyone thinks you're a madman. But I know what you are. You're an enemy. You're worse than the Romans. You're a Jew who's killing Jews. And you're not ashamed. You don't even have any pride.
>
> JESUS No, I don't have any pride. I don't go to Synagogue. I disobey the Commandments. I work on the Sabbath. Your Messiahs? You find them, I'll crucify them.
>
> *Judas hits Jesus across the mouth.*

Jesus is also a man who hears voices. These voices are not presented as divine communications but more akin to someone who is suffering from schizophrenia.

> **Int. House—Night**
>
> JESUS Speak softer! I can't understand! Softer!
>
> *(Silence).*
>
> JESUS I still can't . . . stop . . . Are you trying to make me understand, or do you just want to hurt me?
>
> *(pause; then, as if answering)*
>
> Well, if I don't belong here, with men, where do I belong? Tell me! Or do you just want to punish me?
>
> *(Still silence).*
>
> Now we see the whole room, which is a small area just off the kitchen. Jesus is alone. His Mother enters. Jesus looks over.
>
> MARY (MOTHER OF JESUS) What are you hearing?
>
> *(She sits near him and puts her hand over his).*
>
> JESUS They want to know if I'm afraid. Afraid! Of course I'm afraid!
>
> *(looking up)*
>
> Hear that? I am afraid. Is that what you want? Alright.
>
> MARY (MOTHER OF JESUS) What do they want?
>
> JESUS They want me to speak. To go out and speak!
>
> MARY (MOTHER OF JESUS) Speak about what?
>
> JESUS About the Kingdom of Heaven. But I don't care about the Kingdom of Heaven. I like earth. I like to eat, sleep, see a woman without my head being torn in half.
>
> MARY (MOTHER OF JESUS) But you can have that right now.
>
> JESUS No! Because anytime I try to get what everybody else has, the pain starts. And the voices.
>
> MARY (MOTHER OF JESUS) And so you make crosses!
>
> JESUS Yes, I make crosses! To keep him quiet. To make God hate me! To make him find somebody else.

Jesus is also portrayed as a man with a violent temper:

> JESUS God can save your soul.
>
> MAGDALENE I don't want him. He's already broken my heart. Say the truth.
>
> *(Mary is half in darkness. As she speaks her legs partially open and one hand slips between them. Her other hand covers her breasts).*
>
> MAGDALENE You want to save my soul? This is where you'll find it. You're the same as the others only you can't admit it. You lie about it. You're pitiful. I hate you. Here's my body. Kiss it. Save it.

(Jesus, angry, lunges for her and hits her hand away very hard. She pulls back on the couch and they stare at each other).

Most contentious of all was the fact that the film-makers have Jesus hallucinating about the life he may have had if he did not make his supreme sacrifice. We see him growing old and living a normal life, with love, marriage, sex, and children. Scorsese offers a deeply personal and thoughtful imagining of Christ with whom believers and non-believers can identify with as a complex, sometimes confused human being. Was this film any more offensive and outrageous than Monty Python's take on Jesus in *The Life of Brian?*

Three camels are silhouetted against the bright stars of the moonless sky, moving slowly along the horizon. A star leads them towards Bethlehem. The Wise Men enter the gates of the sleeping town and make their way through the deserted streets. A dog snarls at them. They approach a stable, out of which streams a beam of light. They dismount and enter to find a typical manger scene, with a baby in a rough crib of straw and patient animals standing around. The mother nods by the side of the child. Suddenly she wakes from her lightish doze, sees them, shrieks and falls backwards off her straw. She's up again in a flash, looking guardedly at them. She is a ratbag.

MANDY   Who are you?

WISE MAN 1   We are three wise men.

WISE MAN 2   We are astrologers. We have come from the East.

MANDY   Is this some kind of joke?

WISE MAN 1   We wish to praise the infant.

WISE MAN 2   We must pay homage to him.

MANDY   Homage!! You're all drunk you are. It's disgusting. Out, out!

WISE MAN 3   No, no.

MANDY   Coming bursting in here first thing in the morning with some tale about Oriental fortune tellers . . . get out!

WISE MAN 1   No. No we must see him.

MANDY   Go and praise someone else's brat, go on.

WISE MAN 2   We were led by a star.

MANDY   Led by a bottle, more like. Get out!

WISE MAN 2   We must see him. We have brought presents.

MANDY   Out!

WISE MAN 1   Gold, frankincense, myrrh.

(her attitude changes immediately)

MANDY   Well, why didn't you say so? He's over here . . . Sorry this place is a bit of a mess. What is myrrh, anyway?

WISE MAN 3   It is a valuable balm.

MANDY   A balm, what are you giving him a balm for? It might bite him.

WISE MAN 3   What?

MANDY   It's a dangerous animal. Quick, throw it in the trough.

WISE MAN 3   No it isn't.

MANDY   Yes it is.

WISE MAN 3   No, no, it is an ointment.

MANDY   An ointment?

WISE MAN 3   Look.

MANDY

(sampling the ointment with a grubby finger)

Oh. There is an animal called a balm or did I dream it? You astrologers, eh? Well, what's he then?

WISE MAN 2   H'm?

MANDY   What star sign is he?

WISE MAN 2   Capricorn.

MANDY   Capricorn, eh, what are they like?

WISE MAN 2   He is the son of God, our Messiah.

WISE MAN 1   King of the Jews.

MANDY   And that's Capricorn, is it?

WISE MAN 3   No, no, that's just him.

MANDY   Oh, I was going to say, otherwise there'd be a lot of them.

Objectors to the Monty Python film might argue that it is less offensive than *The Last Temptation of Christ* because it is clearly meant as a comedy where as Scorsese's work is meant as a serious portrayal of their messiah. In otherwords, they might criticize the lack of reverence in *The Life of Brian* and thus dismiss it as unworthy of further comment while Scorsese's work challenges fundamental church doctrine. On the otherhand, by making people laugh, satirists can subtly reduce the power that the subject matter originally held over the viewers.

Returning to Pullman's comments on meaning and interpretation we note that his challenge to an oppositional reading is telling. "If you come to the conclusion that *despite appearances* (italics added) I am a devout Christian and *His Dark Materials* a work of the most orthodox piety, then again—hoorah. *All you have to do is demonstrate why.*" (italics added)

His challenge is insightful. You cannot simply offer any interpretation of art that you want; you must support it with evidence. One such oppositional reading of his work is by Donna Freitas and Jason King, who argue that *His Dark Materials* trilogy, unlike what Pullman himself claims, is actually a Christian classic. The authors contend that the god that Pullman kills off in the third book is not the Christian God but an imposter.[21] Pullman's god is a weak, decrepit, violent senile character. He is a pathetic creature that deceived and lied to the angels. Freitas and King contend that since Pullman portrays God as someone who is so feeble-minded as to not know what is going on around him and who uses force to get his way, then this god does not match their conception of the Christian God. Since it does not match their conception, it must not be the Christian God. This argument is seriously flawed. It is as if someone insults your friend by calling them ugly and you respond that since you believe your friend is attractive, it must not be your friend whom they are talking about!

So despite appearances and verbal admissions, we have critics claiming that Pullman does not know what he is up to in his books. Although Hirsh would reject this line of reasoning, we must admit that we cannot always rely on the stated intent of the writer. Artists can become aware of things in their own creations that did not seem to be there originally. Screenwriter and Professor of Film Studies George Toles[22] writes:

> I'm very concerned with identifying other artists' intentions (to my own satisfaction) when I teach literature and film and write critical essays. I regard imaginative empathy as one of the great, necessary pleasures . . . and maybe the essential starting point for any writing on art that matters to me. But I am under no illusion about intention being a sharply focused thing. I tell my screenwriting students not to over-plan or over-conceptualize before they begin the day's writing. Yes, structure is crucially important but even structure needs to be elastic and able to breathe as it comes into being. It has to be an attractive meeting ground for contingency and fate. I suppose I have some sort of intention in mind as I write sentences, but it seems to grow dim and be almost unrecoverable once a writing session is over. The sentences, like dramatic scenes, to a very real extent, write themselves after a certain point. For a while your mind is pushing logically or at least rationally in a certain direction, and then (if you're lucky) intuition and daydream take over.
>
> It is important that one not know too well or too much about the effect or meaning you're trying to produce. Something unforeseen and maybe inexplicable needs to get into the mix if a script or performance is to take wing: a mystery element, but of an authentic sort. Not cooked up symbolic obscurity, which is another way of controlling (unduly) and over-thinking the process. A film project I have recently been working on, entitled *Spoiled*, has an important scene close to the end where a sister who has been abandoned without explanation by the brother she is in love with calls him back to her by winding up the musical spigot that was their magical shared plaything as children. He does return to her shortly afterward and they talk at cross-purposes. He rejects her coldly and tosses the spigot into the pond which they are facing. Shortly after his departure, she drowns herself.
>
> Though I talked about this scene on and off for months with my fellow-writers and the film's director, it was not until I watched the final cut in post-production that it became clear to me—blindingly clear—that the brother hadn't really returned at all. The sister had only imagined that he had. This "reading", which is now the only one which makes sense to me, was not part of anyone's intention in the writing, acting, or shooting process. And yet it accords perfectly with the inner logic of the narrative as

---

[21] Donna Freitas and Jason King, *Killing the Imposter God: Philip Pullman's Spiritual Imagination in His Dark Materials* (San Francisco: Jossey-Bass, 2007).
[22] Writer of such films as *Archangel* (1990), *The Saddest Music in the World* (2003), and *Edison and Leo* (2008).

a whole. I would bet that many viewers would understand the scene as hallucinatory without any special prompting. Strange that it should elude the entire team of collaborators throughout the long production process. I am very much in the "Trust the tale, not the teller" school, but as I began by saying, I think one should do one's best to get inside the creator's intention when thinking about art—because it is necessary to reach out to the art as something OTHER than you in order to have it show you things. All of this is extremely paradoxical, and all the more precious (to the non-philosopher at least) for being so.[23]

Director Guy Maddin,[24] who is often a partner in the filmmaking process with Toles, adds:

[The] anecdote about the evolving awareness of intention in [Toles's] own writing, specifically about the brother's return [is wonderful]. I have been thrilled a few times by finding things I have either accidentally or subconsciously embedded in writing. In order to congratulate myself, I rationalize that this brilliant eventuality came about as a result of the courageous honesty I've deployed in the name of getting some of my own soul on the screen. But I'm aware that the best results are sometimes the effects of unknown or mixed causes, some of them primal urges fighting for expression, some of them mere coincidences—film flam after-the-fact justifications of heedless gestures.[25]

The artistic process and aesthetic appreciation is embedded within the myriad of contexts and influences and perceptions of all those involved. The artist, the observer, the society, and the historical period all have something significant to contribute to the entirety of the meaning and the role of art in human experience. This complexity justifies the need for continued discussion and evaluation such as you will find in the readings in this chapter. Such complexity also reaffirms the importance of philosophy in understanding the world and our place within it.[26]

---

[23] E-mail to editor, August 31 2007.
[24] Director of such films as *Tales from the Gimli Hospital* (1988), *Archangel* (1990), *Dracula: Pages from a Virgin's Diary* (2000), *The Saddest Music in the World* (2003), *Brand Upon the Brain!* (2006), and *My Winnipeg* (2007).
[25] E-mail response to Tole's comments, August 31, 2007.
[26] This is one of my favorite lessons I learned from Gene Walz (University of Manitoba) who gave me this offhanded remark one day within the context of seeing a favorite film over and over again.

Films Cited

300. Dir. Zack Snyder. Perfs. Gerard Butler, Lena Headey. Film. Warner Bros. Pictures. 2006.

Apocalypto. Dir. Mel Gibson. Perfs. Rudy Youngblood, Dalia Hernández. Film. Icon Entertainment International. 2006.

Archangel. Dir. Guy Maddin. Perfs. Michael Gottli, David Falkenburg. Film. Cinephile. 1990.

Awful Truth, The. Dir. Leo McCarey. Perfs. Irene Dunne, Cary Grant. Film. Columbia Pictures Corporation. 1937.

Beast from 20,000 Fathoms, The. Dir. Eugene Lourié. Perfs. Paul Hubschmid, Paula Raymond. Film. Jack Dietz Productions. 1953.

Big Sleep, The. Dir. Howard Hawks. Perfs. Humphrey Bogart, Lauren Bacall. Film. Warner Bros. Pictures. 1946.

Black Scorpion, The. Dir. Edward Ludwig. Perfs. Richard Denning, Mara Corday. Film. Amex Productions. 1957.

Body Snatchers, The. Dir. Robert Wise. Perfs. Boris Karloff, Bela Lugosi. Film. RKO Radio Pictures. 1945.

Brand Upon the Brain! Dir. Guy Maddin. Perfs. Gretchen Krich, Sullivan Brown. Film. The Film Company. 2006.

D.O.A. Dir. Annabel Jankel, Rocky Morton. Perfs. Dennis Quaid, Meg Ryan. Film. Bigelow Pictures. 1988.

Day the Earth Stood Still, The. Dir. Robert Wise. Perfs. Michael Rennie, Patricia Neal. Film. Twentieth Century–Fox Film Corporation. 1951.

Deadly Mantis. Dir. Nathan Juran. Perfs. Craig Stevens, William Hopper. Film. Universal International Pictures (UI). 1957.

Destination Moon. Dir. Irving Pichel. Perfs. John Archer, Warner Anderson. Film. George Pal Productions. 1950.

Double Indemnity. Dir. Billy Wilder. Perfs. Fred MacMurray, Barbara Stanwyck. Film. Paramount Pictures. 1944.

Dracula: Pages from a Virgin's Diary. Dir. Guy Maddin. Perfs. Wei-Qiang Zhang, Tara Birtwhistle. Film. Canadian Broadcasting Corporation. 2002.

Earth versus The Spider. Dir. Bert I. Gordon. Perfs. Ed Kemmer, June Kenney. Film. Santa Rosa Productions. 1958.

Earth vs. the Flying Saucers. Dir. Fred F. Sears. Perfs. Hugh Marlowe, Joan Taylor. Film. Clover Productions. 1956.
Edison and Leo. Dir. Jesse Rosensweet. Perfs. Gregory Smith, Carly Pope. Film. Perfect Circle Productions. 2008.
Flying Down to Rio. Dir. Thorton Freeland. Perfs. Dolores del Rio, Gene Raymond. Film. RKO Radio Pictures. 1933.
Flying Saucer. Dir. Mikel Conrad. Perfs. Mikel Conrad, Pat Garrison. Film. Colonial Productions. 1950.
Footloose Heiress, The. Dir. William Clemens. Perfs. Craig Reynolds, Ann Sheridan. Film. Warner Bros. Pictures. 1937.
Godzilla. Dir. Roland Emmerich. Perfs. Matthew Broderick, Jean Reno. Film. Centropolis Film Productions. 1998.
Golden Compass, The. Dir. Chris Weitz. Perfs. Nicole Kidman, Daniel Craig. Film. New Line Cinema. 2007.
Invaders from Mars. Dir. William Cameron Menzies. Perfs. Helena Carter, Arthur Franz. Film. National Pictures Corporation. 1953.
It Came from Outer Space! Dir. Jack Arnold. Perfs. Richard Carlson, Barbara Rush. Film. Universal International Pictures. 1953.
JFK. Dir. Oliver Stone. Perfs. Kevin Costner, Tommy Lee Jones. Film. Alcor Films. 1991.
L.A. Confidential. Dir. Curtis Hanson. Perfs. Kevin Spacey, Russell Crowe. Film. Monarchy Enterprises B.V. 1997.
Last Temptation of Christ, The. Dir. Martin Scorsese. Perfs. Willem Dafoe, Harvey Keitel. Film. Cineplex-Odeon Films. 1988.
Life of Brian, The. Dir. Terry Jones, Perfs. Graham Chapman, John Cleese. Film. HandMade Films. 1979.
Lord of the Rings, The. Dir. Peter Jackson. Perfs. Ian McKellen, Elijah Wood, Viggo Mortensen, Squire. Film. New Line Cinema. 2001.
Meaning of Life, The. Dir. Terry Jones & Terry Gilliam. Perfs. Graham Chapman, John Cleese. Film. Celandine Films. 1983.
Monster from Green Hell. Dir. Kenneth G. Crane. Perfs. Jim Davis, Robert Griffin. Film. Gross-Krasne Productions. 1958.
Murder, My Sweet. Dir. Edward Dmytryk. Perfs. Dick Powell, Claire Trevor. Film. RKO Radio Pictures. 1944.
My Man Godfrey. Dir. Gregory La Cava. Perfs. William Powell, Carole Lombard. Film. Universal Pictures. 1936.
My Winnipeg. Dir. Guy Maddin. Perfs. Darcy Fehr, Ann Savage. Film. Buffalo Gal Pictures. 2007.
Not of this Earth. Dir. Jim Wynorski. Perfs. Traci Lords, Arthur Roberts. Film. Miracle Pictures. 1988.
Passion of the Christ, The. Dir. Mel Gibson. Perfs. James Caviezel, Maia Morgenstern. Film. Icon Productions. 2004.

Phantom Lady. Dir. Robert Siodmak. Perfs. Franchot Tone, Ella Raines. Film. Universal Pictures (UI). 1944.
Pollock. Dir. Ed Harris. Perfs. Ed Harris, Marcia Gay Harden. Film. Brant-Allen. 2000.
Red Planet Mars. Dir. Harry Horner. Perfs. Peter Graves, Andrea King. Film. Melaby Pictures Corp. 1952.
Rocket Ship X-M. Dir. Kurt Neumann. Perfs. Lloyd Bridges, Osa Massen. Film. Lippert Pictures. 1950.
Saddest Music in the World, The. Dir. Guy Maddin. Perfs. Mark McKinney, Isabella Rossellini. Film. Buffalo Gal Pictures. 2003.
Shadow of Suspicion. Dir. William Beaudine. Perfs. Marjorie Weaver, Peter Cookson. Film. Monogram Pictures Corporation. 1944.
Tales from the Gimli Hospital. Dir. Guy Maddin. Perfs. Kyle McCulloch, Michael Gottli. Film. Extra Large Productions. 1988.
Tarantula. Dir. Jack Arnold. Perfs. John Agar, Mara Corday. Film. Universal International Pictures. 1955.
Them! Dir. Gordon Douglas. Perfs. James Whitmore, Edmund Gwenn. Film. Warner Bros. Pictures. 1954.
Thin Man, The. Dir. W. S. Van Dyke. Perfs. William Powell, Myrna Loy. Film. Cosmopolitan Productions. 1934.
Thing from Another World, The. Dir. Christian Nyby. Perfs. Margaret Sheridan, Kenneth Tobey. Film. Winchester Pictures Corporation. 1951.
This Island Earth. Dir. Joseph M. Newman. Perfs. Jeff Morrow, Faith Domergue. Film. Universal International Pictures (UI). 1955.
Topper. Dir. Norman Z. McLeod. Perfs. Constance Bennett, Cary Grant. Film. Hal Roach Studios Inc. 1937.
War of the Worlds. Dir. Steven Spielberg. Perfs. Tom Cruise, Dakota Fanning. Film. Paramount Pictures. 2005.
You Can't Take it With You. Dir. Frank Capra. Perfs. Jean Arthur, Lionel Barrymore. Film. Columbia Pictures Corporation. 1938.

ADDITIONAL MOVIES FOR FURTHER VIEWING

(For a comprehensive listing of movies and themes, please consult the online appendix.)

1. *Adaptation*—Nature of the art and the artist process
2. *Art School Confidential*—Introduction to art
3. *Crumb*—Nature of the art and the artist
4. *Finding Neverland*—Sources for artistic inspiration
5. *Frida*—Nature of art and the artist
6. *Girl with a Pearl Earring*—The artistic process
7. *I Shot Andy Warhol*—Avant garde art
8. *I'm Not There*—Nature of the artist
9. *Quills*—Art, obscenity and art
10. *Topsy-Turvy*—The nature of art and the artists

Of the Standard of Taste

David Hume

THE great variety of Taste, as well as of opinion, which prevails in the world, is too obvious not to have fallen under every one's observation. Men of the most confined knowledge are able to remark a difference of taste in the narrow circle of their acquaintance, even where the persons have been educated under the same government, and have early imbibed the same prejudices. But those who can enlarge their view to contemplate distant nations and remote ages are still more surprised at the great inconsistence and contrariety. We are apt to call *barbarous* whatever departs widely from our own taste and apprehension; but soon find the epithet of reproach retorted on us. And the highest arrogance and self-conceit is at last startled, on observing an equal assurance on all sides, and scruples, amidst such a contest of sentiment, to pronounce positively in its own favour.

As this variety of taste is obvious to the most careless inquirer, so will it be found, on examination, to be still greater in reality than in appearance. The sentiments of men often differ with regard to beauty and deformity of all kinds, even while their general discourse is the same. There are certain terms in every language which import blame, and others praise; and all men who use the same tongue must agree in their application of them. Every voice is united in applauding elegance, propriety, simplicity, spirit in writing; and in blaming fustian, affectation, coldness, and a false brilliancy. But when critics come to particulars, this seeming unanimity vanishes; and it is found, that they had affixed a very different meaning to their expressions. In all matters of opinion and science, the case is opposite; the difference among men is there oftener found to lie in generals than in particulars, and to be less in reality than in appearance. An explanation of the terms commonly ends the controversy: and the disputants are surprised to find that they had been quarrelling, while at bottom they agreed in their judgment.

Those who found morality on sentiment, more than on reason, are inclined to comprehend ethics under the former observation, and to maintain, that, in all questions which regard conduct and manners, the difference among men is really greater than at first sight it appears. It is indeed obvious, that writers of all nations and all ages concur in applauding justice, humanity, magnanimity, prudence, veracity; and in blaming the opposite qualities. Even poets and other authors, whose compositions are chiefly calculated to please the imagination, are yet found, from Homer down to Fenelon, to inculcate the same moral precepts, and to bestow their applause and blame on the same virtues and vices. This great unanimity is usually ascribed to the influence of plain reason, which, in all these cases, maintains similar sentiments in all men, and prevents those controversies to which the abstract sciences are so much exposed. So far as the unanimity is real, this account may be admitted as satisfactory. But we must also allow, that some part of the seeming harmony in morals may be accounted for from the very nature of language. The word *virtue*, with its equivalent in every tongue, implies praise, as that of *vice* does blame; and no one, without the most obvious and grossest impropriety, could affix reproach to a term, which in general acceptation is understood in a good sense: or bestow applause, where the idiom requires disapprobation. Homer's general precepts, where he delivers any such, will never be controverted; but it is obvious, that, when he draws particular pictures of manners, and represents heroism in Achilles, and prudence in Ulysses, he intermixes a much greater degree of ferocity in the former, and of cunning and fraud in the latter, than Fenelon would admit of. The sage Ulysses, in the Greek poet, seems to delight in lies and fictions, and often employs them without any necessity, or even advantage. But his more scrupulous son, in the French epic writer, exposes himself to the most imminent perils, rather than depart from the most exact line of truth and veracity.

The admirers and followers of the Alcoran insist on the excellent moral precepts interspersed throughout that wild and absurd performance. But it is to be supposed, that the Arabic words, which correspond to the English, equity, justice, temperance, meekness, charity, were such as, from the constant use of that tongue, must always be taken in a good sense: and it would have argued the greatest ignorance, not of morals, but of language, to have mentioned them with any epithets, besides those of applause and approbation. But would we know, whether the pretended prophet had really attained a just sentiment of morals, let us attend to his narration, and we shall soon find, that he bestows praise on such instances of treachery, inhumanity, cruelty, revenge, bigotry, as are utterly incompatible with civilized society. No steady rule of right seems there to be attended to; and every action is blamed or praised, so far only as it is beneficial or hurtful to the true believers.

The merit of delivering true general precepts in ethics is indeed very small. Whoever recommends any moral virtues, really does no more than is implied in the terms themselves. That people who invented the word *charity*, and used it in a good sense, inculcated more clearly, and much more efficaciously, the precept, *Be charitable,* than any pretended legislator or prophet, who should insert such a *maxim* in his writings. Of all expressions, those which, together with their other meaning, imply a degree either of blame, or approbation, are the least liable to be perverted or mistaken.

It is natural for us to seek a *Standard of Taste;* a rule by which the various sentiments of men may be reconciled; at least a decision afforded confirming one sentiment, and condemning another.

There is a species of philosophy, which cuts off all hopes of success in such an attempt, and represents the impossibility of ever attaining any standard of taste. The difference, it is said, is very wide between judgment and sentiment. All sentiment is right; because sentiment has a reference to nothing beyond itself, and is always real, wherever a man is conscious of it. But all determinations of the understanding are not right; because they have a reference to something beyond themselves, to wit, real matter of fact; and are not always conformable to that standard. Among a thousand different opinions which different men may entertain of the same subject, there is one, and but one, that is just and true: and the only difficulty is to fix and ascertain it. On the contrary, a thousand different sentiments, excited by the same object, are all right; because no sentiment represents what is really in the object. It only marks a .certain conformity or relation between the object and the organs or faculties of the mind; and if that conformity did not really exist, the sentiment could never possibly have being. Beauty is no quality in things themselves: It exists merely in the mind which contemplates them; and each mind perceives a different beauty. One person may even perceive deformity, where another is sensible of beauty; and every individual ought to acquiesce in his own sentiment, without pretending to regulate those of others. To seek the real beauty, or real deformity, is as fruitless an inquiry, as to pretend to ascertain the real sweet or real bitter. According to the disposition of the organs, the same object may be both sweet and bitter; and the proverb has justly determined it to be fruitless to dispute concerning tastes. It is very natural, and even quite necessary, to extend this axiom to mental, as well as bodily taste; and thus common sense, which is so often at variance with philosophy, especially with the sceptical kind, is found, in one instance at least, to agree in pronouncing the same decision.

But though this axiom, by passing into a proverb, seems to have attained the sanction of common sense; there is certainly a species of common sense, which opposes it, at least serves to modify and restrain it. Whoever would assert an equality of genius and elegance between Ogilby and Milton, or Bunyan and Addison, would be thought to defend no less an extravagance, than if he had maintained a mole-hill to be as high as Teneriffe, or a pond as extensive as the ocean. Though there may be found persons, who give the preference to the former authors; no one pays attention to such a taste; and we pronounce, without scruple, the sentiment of these pretended critics to be absurd and ridiculous. The principle of the natural equality of tastes is then totally forgot, and while we admit it on some occasions, where the objects seem near an equality, it appears an extravagant paradox, or rather a palpable absurdity, where objects so disproportioned are compared together.

It is evident that none of the rules of composition are fixed by reasonings *a priori,* or can be esteemed abstract conclusions of the understanding, from comparing those habitudes and relations of ideas, which are eternal and immutable. Their foundation is the same with that of all the practical sciences, experience; nor are they any thing but general observations, concerning what has been universally found to please in all countries and in all ages. Many of the beauties of poetry, and even of eloquence, are founded on falsehood and fiction, on hyperboles, metaphors, and an abuse or perversion of terms from their natural meaning. To check the sallies of the imagination, and to reduce every expression to geometrical truth and exactness, would be the most contrary to the laws of criticism; because it would produce a work, which, by universal experience, has been found the most insipid and disagreeable. But though poetry can never submit to exact truth, it must be confined by rules of art, discovered to the author either by genius or observation. If some negligent or irregular writers have pleased, they have not pleased by their transgressions of rule or order, but in spite of these transgressions: They have possessed other beauties, which were conformable to just criticism; and the force of these beauties has been able to overpower censure,

(continued)

Of the Standard of Taste   (continued)

and give the mind a satisfaction superior to the disgust arising from the blemishes. Ariosto pleases; but not by his monstrous and improbable fictions, by his bizarre mixture of the serious and comic styles, by the want of coherence in his stories, or by the continual interruptions of his narration. He charms by the force and clearness of his expression, by the readiness and variety of his inventions, and by his natural pictures of the passions, especially those of the gay and amorous kind: And, however his faults may diminish our satisfaction, they are not able entirely to destroy it. Did our pleasure really arise from those parts of his poem, which we denominate faults, this would be no objection to criticism in general: It would only be an objection to those particular rules of criticism, which would establish such circumstances to be faults, and would represent them as universally blameable. If they are found to please, they cannot be faults, let the pleasure which they produce be ever so unexpected and unaccountable.

But though all the general rules of art are founded only on experience, and on the observation of the common sentiments of human nature, we must not imagine that, on every occasion, the feelings of men will be conformable to these rules. Those finer emotions of the mind are of a very tender and delicate nature, and require the concurrence of many favourable circumstances to make them play with facility and exactness, according to their general and established principles. The least exterior hinderance to such small springs, or the least internal disorder, disturbs their motion, and confounds the operation of the whole machine. When we would make an experiment of this nature, and would try the force of any beauty or deformity, we must choose, with care a proper time and place, and bring the fancy to a suitable situation and disposition. A perfect serenity of mind, a recollection of thought, a due attention to the object; if any of these circumstances be wanting, our experiment will be fallacious, and we shall be unable to judge of the catholic and universal beauty. The relation, which nature has placed between the form and the sentiment, will at least be more obscure; and it will require greater accuracy to trace and discern it. We shall be able to ascertain its influence, not so much from the operation of each particular beauty, as from the durable admiration which attends those works that have survived all the caprices of mode and fashion, all the mistakes of ignorance and envy.

The same Homer who pleased at Athens and Rome two thousand years ago, is still admired at Paris and at London. All the changes of climate, government, religion, and language, have not been able to obscure his glory. Authority or prejudice may give a temporary vogue to a bad poet or orator; but his reputation will never be durable or general. When his compositions are examined by posterity or by foreigners, the enchantment is dissipated, and his faults appear in their true colours. On the contrary, a real genius, the longer his works endure, and the more wide they are spread, the more sincere is the admiration which he meets with. Envy and jealousy have too much place in a narrow circle; and even familiar acquaintance with his person may diminish the applause due to his performances: But when these obstructions are removed, the beauties, which are naturally fitted to excite agreeable sentiments, immediately display their energy; and while the world endures, they maintain their authority over the minds of men.

It appears, then, that amidst all the variety and caprice of taste, there are certain general principles of approbation or blame, whose influence a careful eye may trace in all operations of the mind. Some particular forms or qualities, from the original structure of the internal fabric, are calculated to please, and others to displease; and if they fail of their effect in any particular instance, it is from some apparent defect or imperfection in the organ. A man in a fever would not insist on his palate as able to decide concerning flavours; nor would one affected with the jaundice pretend to give a verdict with regard to colours. In each creature there is a sound and a defective state; and the former alone can be supposed to afford us a true standard of taste and sentiment. If, in the sound state of the organ, there be an entire or a considerable uniformity of sentiment among men, we may thence derive an idea of the perfect beauty; in like manner as the appearance of objects in daylight, to the eye of a man in health, is denominated their true and real colour, even while colour is allowed to be merely a phantasm of the senses.

Many and frequent are the defects in the internal organs, which prevent or weaken the influence of those general principles, on which depends our sentiment of beauty or deformity. Though some objects, by the structure of the mind, be naturally calculated to give pleasure, it is not to be expected that in every individual the pleasure will be equally felt. Particular incidents and situations occur, which either throw a false light on the objects, or hinder the true from conveying to the imagination the proper sentiment and perception.

One obvious cause why many feel not the proper sentiment of beauty, is the want of that *delicacy* of imagination which is requisite to convey a sensibility of those finer emotions. This delicacy every one pretends to: Every one talks of it; and would reduce every kind of taste or sentiment to its standard. But as our intention in this Essay is to mingle some light of the understanding with the feelings of sentiment, it will be proper to give a more accurate definition of delicacy than has hitherto been attempted. And not to draw our philosophy from too profound a source, we shall have recourse to a noted story in Don Quixote.

It is with good reason, says Sancho to the squire with the great nose, that I pretend to have a judgment in wine: This is a quality hereditary in our family. Two of my kinsmen were once called to give their opinion of a hogshead, which was supposed to be excellent, being old and of a good vintage. One of them tastes it, considers it; and, after mature reflection, pronounces the wine to be good, were it not for a small taste of leather which he perceived in it. The other, after using the same precautions, gives also his verdict in favour of the wine; but with the reserve of a taste of iron, which he could easily distinguish. You cannot imagine how much they were both ridiculed for their judgment. But who laughed in the end? On emptying the hogshead, there was found at the bottom an old key with a leathern thong tied to it.

The great resemblance between mental and bodily taste will easily teach us to apply this story. Though it be certain that beauty and deformity, more than sweet and bitter, are not qualities in objects, but belong entirely to the sentiment, internal or external, it must be allowed, that there are certain qualities in objects which are fitted by nature to produce those particular feelings. Now, as these qualities may be found in a small degree, or may be mixed and confounded with each other, it often happens that the taste is not affected with such minute qualities, or is not able to distinguish all the particular flavours, amidst the disorder in which they are presented. Where the organs are so fine as to allow nothing to escape them, and at the same time so exact as to perceive every ingredient in the composition this we call delicacy of taste, whether we employ these terms in the literal or metaphorical sense. Here then the general rules of beauty are of use, being drawn from established models, and from the observation of what pleases or displeases, when presented singly and in a high degree; and if the same qualities, in a continued composition, and in a smaller degree, affect not the organs with a sensible delight or uneasiness, we exclude the person from all pretensions to this delicacy. To produce these general rules or avowed patterns of composition, is like finding the key with the leathern thong, which justified the verdict of Sancho's kinsmen, and confounded those pretended judges who had condemned them. Though the hogshead had never been emptied, the taste of the one was still equally delicate, and that of the other equally dull and languid; but it would have been more difficult to have proved the superiority of the former, to the conviction of every bystander. In like manner, though the beauties of writing had never been methodized, or reduced to general principles; though no excellent models had ever been acknowledged, the different degrees of taste would still have subsisted, and the judgment of one man been preferable to that of another; but it would not have been so easy to silence the bad critic, who might always insist upon his particular sentiment, and refuse to submit to his antagonist. But when we show him an avowed principle of art; when we illustrate this principle by examples, whose operation, from his own particular taste, he acknowledges to be conformable to the principle; when we prove that the same principle may be applied to the present case, where he did not perceive or feel its influence: he must conclude, upon the whole, that the fault lies in himself, and that he wants the delicacy which is requisite to make him sensible of every beauty and every blemish in any composition or discourse.

It is acknowledged to be the perfection of every sense or faculty, to perceive with exactness its most minute objects, and allow nothing to escape its notice and observation. The smaller the objects are which become sensible to the eye, the finer is that organ, and the more elaborate its make and composition. A good palate is not tried by strong flavours, but by a mixture of small ingredients, where we are still sensible of each part, notwithstanding its minuteness and its confusion with the rest. In like manner, a quick and acute perception of beauty and deformity must be the perfection of our mental taste; nor can a man be satisfied with himself while he suspects that

(continued)

Of the Standard of Taste   (continued)

any excellence or blemish in a discourse has passed him unobserved. In this case, the perfection of the man, and the perfection of the sense of feeling, are found to be united. A very delicate palate, on many occasions, may be a great inconvenience both to a man himself and to his friends. But a delicate taste of wit or beauty must always be a desirable quality, because it is the source of all the finest and most innocent enjoyments of which human nature is susceptible. In this decision the sentiments of all mankind are agreed. Wherever you can ascertain a delicacy of taste, it is sure to meet with approbation; and the best way of ascertaining it is, to appeal to those models and principles which have been established by the uniform consent and experience of nations and ages.

But though there be naturally a wide difference, in point of delicacy, between one person and another, nothing tends further to increase and improve this talent, than *practice* in a particular art, and the frequent survey or contemplation of a particular species of beauty. When objects of any kind are first presented to the eye or imagination, the sentiment which attends them is obscure and confused; and the mind is, in a great measure, incapable of pronouncing concerning their merits or defects. The taste cannot perceive the several excellences of the performance, much less distinguish the particular character of each excellency, and ascertain its quality and degree. If it pronounce the whole in general to be beautiful or deformed, it is the utmost that can be expected; and even this judgment, a person so unpractised will be apt to deliver with great hesitation and reserve. But allow him to acquire experience in those objects, his feeling becomes more exact and nice: He not only perceives the beauties and defects of each part, but marks the distinguishing species of each quality, and assigns it suitable praise or blame. A clear and distinct sentiment attends him through the whole survey of the objects; and he discerns that very degree and kind of approbation or displeasure which each part is naturally fitted to produce. The mist dissipates which seemed formerly to hang over the object; the organ acquires greater perfection in its operations, and can pronounce, without danger of mistake, concerning the merits of every performance. In a word, the same address and dexterity which practice gives to the execution of any work, is also acquired by the same means in the judging of it.

So advantageous is practice to the discernment of beauty, that, before we can give judgment on any work of importance, it will even be requisite that that very individual performance be more than once perused by us, and be surveyed in different lights with attention and deliberation. There is a flutter or hurry of thought which attends the first perusal of any piece, and which confounds the genuine sentiment of beauty. The relation of the parts is not discerned: The true characters of style are little distinguished. The several perfections and defects seem wrapped up in a species of confusion, and present themselves indistinctly to the imagination. Not to mention, that there is a species of beauty, which, as it is florid and superficial, pleases at first; but being found incompatible with a just expression either of reason or passion, soon palls upon the taste, and is then rejected with disdain, at least rated at a much lower value.

It is impossible to continue in the practice of contemplating any order of beauty, without being frequently obliged to form *comparisons* between the several species and degrees of excellence, and estimating their proportion to each other. A man who has had no opportunity of comparing the different kinds of beauty, is indeed totally unqualified to pronounce an opinion with regard to any object presented to him. By comparison alone we fix the epithets of praise or blame, and learn how to assign the due degree of each. The coarsest daubing contains a certain lustre of colours and exactness of imitation, which are so far beauties, and would affect the mind of a peasant or Indian with the highest admiration. The most vulgar ballads are not entirely destitute of harmony or nature; and none but a person familiarized to superior beauties would pronounce their numbers harsh, or narration uninteresting. A great inferiority of beauty gives pain to a person conversant in the highest excellence of the kind, and is for that reason pronounced a deformity; as the most finished object with which we are acquainted is naturally supposed to have reached the pinnacle of perfection, and to be entitled to the highest applause. One accustomed to see, and examine, and weigh the several performances, admired in different ages and nations, can alone rate the merits of a work exhibited to his view, and assign its proper rank among the productions of genius.

But to enable a critic the more fully to execute this undertaking, he must preserve his mind free from all *prejudice,* and allow nothing to enter into his consideration, but the very object which is submitted to his examination. We may observe, that every work of art, in order to produce its due effect on the mind, must be surveyed in a certain point of view, and cannot be fully relished by persons whose situation, real or imaginary, is not conformable to that which is required by the performance. An orator addresses himself to a particular audience, and must have a regard to their particular genius, interests, opinions, passions, and prejudices; otherwise he hopes in vain to govern their resolutions, and inflame their affections. Should they even have entertained some prepossessions against him, however unreasonable, he must not overlook this disadvantage; but, before he enters upon the subject, must endeavour to conciliate their affection, and acquire their good graces. A critic of a different age or nation, who should peruse this discourse, must have all these circumstances in his eye, and must place himself in the same situation as the audience, in order to form a true judgment of the oration. In like manner, when any work is addressed to the public, though I should have a friendship or enmity with the author, I must depart from this situation, and, considering myself as a man in general, forget, if possible, my individual being, and my peculiar circumstances. A person influenced by prejudice complies not with this condition, but obstinately maintains his natural position, without placing himself in that point of view which the performance supposes. If the work be addressed to persons of a different age or nation, he makes no allowance for their peculiar views and prejudices; but, full of the manners of his own age and country, rashly condemns what seemed admirable in the eyes of those for whom alone the discourse was calculated. If the work be executed for the public, he never sufficiently enlarges his comprehension, or forgets his interest as a friend or enemy, as a rival or commentator. By this means his sentiments are perverted; nor have the same beauties and blemishes the same influence upon him, as if he had imposed a proper violence on his imagination, and had forgotten himself for a moment. So far his taste evidently departs from the true standard, and of consequence loses all credit and authority.

It is well known, that, in all questions submitted to the understanding, prejudice is destructive of sound judgment, and perverts all operations of the intellectual faculties: It is no less contrary to good taste; nor has it less influence to corrupt our sentiment of beauty. It belongs to *good sense* to check its influence in both cases; and in this respect, as well as in many others, reason, if not an essential part of taste, is at least requisite to the operations of this latter faculty. In all the nobler productions of genius, there is a mutual relation and correspondence of parts; nor can either the beauties or blemishes be perceived by him whose thought is not capacious enough to comprehend all those parts, and compare them with each other, in order to perceive the consistence and uniformity of the whole. Every work of art has also a certain end or purpose for which it is calculated; and is to be deemed more or less perfect, as it is more or less fitted to attain this end. The object of eloquence is to persuade, of history to instruct, of poetry to please, by means of the passions and the imagination. These ends we must carry constantly in our view when we peruse any performance; and we must be able to judge how far the means employed are adapted to their respective purposes. Besides, every kind of composition, even the most poetical, is nothing but a chain of propositions and reasonings; not always, indeed, the justest and most exact, but still plausible and specious, however disguised by the colouring of the imagination. The persons introduced in tragedy and epic poetry must be represented as reasoning, and thinking, and concluding, and acting, suitably to their character and circumstances; and without judgment, as well as taste and invention, a poet can never hope to succeed in so delicate an undertaking. Not to mention, that the same excellence of faculties which contributes to the improvement of reason, the same clearness of conception, the same exactness of distinction, the same vivacity of apprehension, are essential to the operations of true taste, and are its infallible concomitants. It seldom or never happens, that a man of sense, who has experience in any art, cannot judge of its beauty; and it is no less rare to meet with a man who has a just taste without a sound understanding.

Thus, though the principles of taste be universal, and nearly, if not entirely, the same in all men; yet few are qualified to give judgment on any work of art, or establish their own sentiment as the standard of beauty. The organs of internal sensation are seldom so perfect as to allow the general principles their full play, and produce a feeling correspondent to those principles. They either labour under some defect, or are vitiated by some disorder; and by that means excite a sentiment, which may be pronounced erroneous. When the critic has no delicacy, he judges without any distinction, and is only affected by the grosser and more palpable qualities of the object: The finer touches pass unnoticed and disregarded. Where he is not aided by practice, his verdict is attended with confusion

(continued)

Of the Standard of Taste (*continued*)

and hesitation. Where no comparison has been employed, the most frivolous beauties, such as rather merit the name of defects, are the object of his admiration. Where he lies under the influence of prejudice, all his natural sentiments are perverted. Where good sense is wanting, he is not qualified to discern the beauties of design and reasoning, which are the highest and most excellent. Under some or other of these imperfections, the generality of men labour; and hence a true judge in the finer arts is observed, even during the most polished ages, to be so rare a character: Strong sense, united to delicate sentiment, improved by practice, perfected by comparison, and cleared of all prejudice, can alone entitle critics to this valuable character; and the joint verdict of such, wherever they are to be found, is the true standard of taste and beauty.

But where are such critics to be found? By what marks are they to be known? How distinguish them from pretenders? These questions are embarrassing; and seem to throw us back into the same uncertainty from which, during the course of this Essay, we have endeavoured to extricate ourselves.

But if we consider the matter aright, these are questions of fact, not of sentiment. Whether any particular person be endowed with good sense and a delicate imagination, free from prejudice, may often be the subject of dispute, and be liable to great discussion and inquiry: But that such a character is valuable and estimable, will be agreed in by all mankind. Where these doubts occur, men can do no more than in other disputable questions which are submitted to the understanding: They must produce the best "arguments that their invention suggests to them; they must acknowledge a true and decisive standard to exist somewhere, to wit, real existence and matter of fact; and they must have indulgence to such as differ from them in their appeals to this standard. It is sufficient for our present purpose, if we have proved, that the taste of all .individuals is not upon an equal footing, and that some men in general, however difficult to be particularly pitched upon, will be acknowledged by universal sentiment to have a preference above others.

But, in reality, the difficulty of finding, even in particulars, the standard of taste, is not so great as it is represented. Though in speculation we may readily avow a certain criterion in science, and deny it in sentiment, the matter is found in practice to be much more hard to ascertain in the former case than in the latter. Theories of abstract philosophy, systems of profound theology, have prevailed during one age: in a successive period these have been universally exploded: Their absurdity has been detected: Other theories and systems have supplied their place, which again gave place to their successors: And nothing has been experienced more liable to the resolutions of chance and fashion than these pretended decisions of science. The case is not the same with the beauties of eloquence and poetry. Just expressions of passion and nature are sure, after a little time, to gain public applause, which they maintain for ever. Aristotle, and Plato, and Epicurus, and Descartes, may successively yield to each other: But Terence and Virgil maintain an universal, undisputed empire over the minds of men. The abstract philosophy of Cicero has lost its credit: The vehemence of his oratory is still the object of our admiration.

Though men of delicate taste be rare, they are easily to be distinguished in society by the soundness of their understanding, and the superiority of their faculties above the rest of mankind. The ascendant, which they acquire, gives a prevalence to that lively approbation with which they receive any productions of genius, and renders it generally predominant. Many men, when left to themselves, have but a faint and dubious perception of beauty, who yet are capable of relishing any fine stroke which is pointed out to them. Every convert to the admiration of the real poet or orator, is the cause of some new conversion. And though prejudices may prevail for a time, they never unite in celebrating any rival to the true genius, but yield at last to the force of nature and just sentiment. Thus, though a civilized nation may easily be mistaken in the choice of their admired philosopher, they never have been found long to err, in their affection for a favourite epic or tragic author.

But notwithstanding all our endeavours to fix a standard of taste, and reconcile the discordant apprehensions of men, there still remain two sources of variation, which are not sufficient indeed to confound all the boundaries of beauty and deformity, but will often serve to produce a difference in the degrees of our approbation or blame. The one is the different humours of particular men; the other, the particular manners and opinions of our age and country. The general principles of taste are uniform in human nature: Where men vary in their judgments, some defect or perversion in the faculties may commonly be remarked; proceeding either from prejudice, from want of practice, or want of delicacy:

and there is just reason for approving one taste, and condemning another. But where there is such a diversity in the internal frame or external situation as is entirely blameless on both sides, and leaves no room to give one the preference above the other; in that case a certain degree of diversity in judgment is unavoidable, and we seek in vain for a standard, by which we can reconcile the contrary sentiments.

A young man, whose passions are warm, will be more sensibly touched with amorous and tender images, than a man more advanced in years, who takes pleasure in wise, philosophical reflections, concerning the conduct of life, and moderation of the passions. At twenty, Ovid may be the favourite author, Horace at forty, and perhaps Tacitus at fifty. Vainly would we, in such cases, endeavour to enter into the sentiments of others, and divest ourselves of those propensities which are natural to us. We choose our favourite author as we do our friend, from a conformity of humour and disposition. Mirth or passion, sentiment or reflection; whichever these most predominates in our temper, it gives us a peculiar sympathy with the writer who resembles us.

One person is more pleased with the sublime, another with the tender, a third with raillery. One has a strong sensibility to blemishes, and is extremely studious of correctness; another has a more lively feeling of beauties, and pardons twenty absurdities and defects for one elevated or pathetic stroke. The ear of this man is entirely turned towards conciseness and energy; that man is delighted with a copious, rich, and harmonious expression. Simplicity is affected by one; ornament by another. Comedy, tragedy, satire, odes, have each its partisans, who prefer that particular species of writing to all others. It is plainly an error in a critic, to confine his approbation to one species or style of writing, and condemn all the rest. But it is almost impossible not to feel a predilection for that which suits our particular turn and disposition. Such preferences are innocent and unavoidable and can never reasonably be the object of dispute, because there is no standard by which they can be decided.

For a like reason, we are more pleased, in the course of our reading, with pictures and characters that resemble objects which are found in our own age or country, than with those which describe a different set of customs. It is not without some effort that we reconcile ourselves to the simplicity of ancient manners, and behold princesses carrying water from the spring, and kings and heroes dressing their own victuals. We may allow in general, that the representation of such manners is no fault in the author, nor deformity in the piece; but we are not so sensibly touched with them. For this reason, comedy is not easily transferred from one age or nation to another. A Frenchman or Englishman is not pleased with the *Andria* of Terence, or *Clitia* of Machiavel; where the fine lady, upon whom all the play turns, never once appears to the spectators, but is always kept behind the scenes, suitably to the reserved humour of the ancient Greeks and modern Italians. A man of learning and reflection can make allowance for these peculiarities of manners; but a common audience can never divest themselves so far of their usual ideas and sentiments, as to relish pictures which nowise resemble them.

But here there occurs a reflection, which may, perhaps, be useful in examining the celebrated controversy concerning ancient and modern learning; where we often find the one side excusing any seeming absurdity in the ancients from the manners of the age, and the other refusing to admit this excuse, or at least admitting it only as an apology for the author, not for the performance. In my opinion, the proper boundaries in this subject have seldom been fixed between the contending parties. Where any innocent peculiarities of manners are represented, such as those above mentioned, they ought certainly to be admitted; and a man who is shocked with them, gives an evident proof of false delicacy and refinement. The poet's *monument more durable than brass,* must fall to the ground like common brick or clay, were men to make no allowance for the continual revolutions of manners and customs, and would admit of nothing but what was suitable to the prevailing fashion. Must we throw aside the pictures of our ancestors, because of their ruffs and farthingales? But where the ideas of morality and decency alter from one age to another, and where vicious manners are described, without being marked with the proper characters of blame and disapprobation, this must be allowed to disfigure the poem, and to be a real deformity. I cannot, nor is it proper I should, enter into such sentiments; and however I may excuse the poet, on account of the manners of his age, I can never relish the composition. The want of humanity and of decency, so conspicuous in the characters drawn by several of the ancient poets, even sometimes by Homer and the Greek tragedians, diminishes considerably the merit of their noble performances, and gives modern

(continued)

Of the Standard of Taste   (continued)

authors an advantage over them. We are not interested in the fortunes and sentiments of such rough heroes; we are displeased to find the limits of vice and virtue so much confounded; and whatever indulgence we may give to the writer on account of his prejudices, we cannot prevail on ourselves to enter into his sentiments, or bear an affection to characters which we plainly discover to be blameable.

The case is not the same with moral principles as with speculative opinions of any kind. These are in continual flux and revolution. The son embraces a different system from the father. Nay, there scarcely is any man, who can boast of great constancy and uniformity in this particular. Whatever speculative errors may be found in the polite writings of any age or country, they detract but little from the value of those compositions. There needs but a certain turn of thought or imagination to make us enter into all the opinions which then prevailed, and relish the sentiments or conclusions derived from them. But a very violent effort is requisite to change our judgment of manners, and excite sentiments of approbation or blame, love or hatred, different from those to which the mind, from long custom, has been familiarized. And where a man is confident of the rectitude of that moral standard by which he judges, he is justly jealous of it, and will not pervert the sentiments of his heart for a moment, in complaisance to any writer whatsoever.

Of all speculative errors, those which regard religion are the most excusable in compositions of genius: nor is it ever permitted to judge of the civility or wisdom of any people, or even of single persons, by the grossness or refinement of their theological principles. The same good sense that directs men in the ordinary occurrences of life, is not hearkened to in religious matters, which are supposed to be placed altogether above the cognizance of human reason. On this account, all the absurdities of the Pagan system of theology must be overlooked by every critic, who would pretend to form a just notion of ancient poetry; and our posterity, in their turn, must have the same indulgence to their forefathers. No religious principles can ever be imputed as a fault to any poet, while they remain merely principles, and take not such strong possession of his heart as to lay him under the imputation of *bigotry or superstition*. Where that happens, they confound the sentiments of morality, and alter the natural boundaries of vice and virtue. They are therefore eternal blemishes, according to the principle above mentioned; nor are the prejudices and false opinions of the age sufficient to justify them.

It is essential to the Roman Catholic religion to inspire a violent hatred of every other worship, and to represent all Pagans, Mahometans, and heretics, as the objects of divine wrath and vengeance. Such sentiments, though they are in reality very blameable, are considered as virtues by the zealots of that communion, and are represented in their tragedies and epic poems as a kind of divine heroism. This bigotry has disfigured two very fine tragedies of the French theatre, POLIEUCTE and ATHALIA; where an intemperate zeal for particular modes of worship is set off with all the pomp imaginable, and forms the predominant character of the heroes. 'What is this,' says the sublime Joad to Josabet, finding her in discourse with Mathan the priest of Baal, 'Does the daughter of David speak to this traitor? Are you not afraid lest the earth should open, and pour forth flames to devour you both? Or lest these holy walls should fall and crush you together? What is his purpose? Why comes that enemy of God hither to poison the air, which we breathe, with his horrid presence?' Such sentiments are received with great applause on the theatre of Paris; but at London the spectators would be full as much pleased to hear Achilles tell Agamemnon, that he was a dog in his forehead, and a deer in his heart; or Jupiter threaten Juno with a sound drubbing, if she will not be quiet.

Religious principles are also a blemish in any polite composition, when they rise up to superstition, and intrude themselves into every sentiment, however remote from any connection with religion. It is no excuse for the poet, that the customs of his country had burdened life with so many religious ceremonies and observances, that no part of it was exempt from that yoke. It must for ever be ridiculous in Petrarch to compare his mistress, Laura, to Jesus Christ. Nor is it less ridiculous in that agreeable libertine, Boccace, very seriously to give thanks to God Almighty and the ladies, for their assistance in defending him against his enemies.

Republic, Book X
Plato

SOCRATES, GLAUCON

Of the many excellences which I perceive in the order of our State, there is none which upon reflection pleases me better than the rule about poetry.

To what do you refer?

To the rejection of imitative poetry, which certainly ought not to be received; as I see far more clearly now that the parts of the soul have been distinguished.

What do you mean?

Speaking in confidence, for I should not like to have my words repeated to the tragedians and the rest of the imitative tribe—but I do not mind saying to you, that all poetical imitations are ruinous to the understanding of the hearers, and that the knowledge of their true nature is the only antidote to them.

Explain the purport of your remark.

Well, I will tell you, although I have always from my earliest youth had an awe and love of Homer, which even now makes the words falter on my lips, for he is the great captain and teacher of the whole of that charming tragic company; but a man is not to be reverenced more than the truth, and therefore I will speak out.

Very good, he said.

Listen to me, then, or, rather, answer me.

Put your question.

Can you tell me what imitation is? for I really do not know.

A likely thing, then, that I should know.

Why not? for the duller eye may often see a thing sooner than the keener.

Very true, he said; but in your presence, even if I had any faint notion, I could not muster courage to utter it. Will you inquire yourself?

Well, then, shall we begin the inquiry in our usual manner: Whenever a number of individuals have a common name, we assume them to have also a corresponding idea or form; do you understand me?

I do.

Let us take any common instance; there are beds and tables in the world—plenty of them, are there not?

Yes.

But there are only two ideas or forms of them—one the idea of a bed, the other of a table.

True.

And the maker of either of them makes a bed or he makes a table for our use, in accordance with the idea—that is our way of speaking in this and similar instances—but no artificer makes the ideas themselves: how could he?

Impossible.

And there is another artist—I should like to know what you would say of him.

Who is he?

One who is the maker of all the works of all other workmen.

What an extraordinary man!

Wait a little, and there will be more reason for your saying so. For this is he who is able to make not only vessels of every kind, but plants and animals, himself and all other things—the earth and heaven, and the things which are in heaven or under the earth; he makes the gods also.

He must be a wizard and no mistake.

Oh! you are incredulous, are you? Do you mean that there is no such maker or creator, or that in one sense there might be a maker of all these things, but in another not? Do you see that there is a way in which you could make them all yourself?

What way?

(continued)

Republic, Book X (*continued*)

An easy way enough; or rather, there are many ways in which the feat might be quickly and easily accomplished, none quicker than that of turning a mirror round and round—you would soon enough make the sun and the heavens, and the earth and yourself, and other animals and plants, and all the other things of which we were just now speaking, in the mirror.

Yes, he said; but they would be appearances only.

Very good, I said, you are coming to the point now. And the painter, too, is, as I conceive, just such another—a creator of appearances, is he not?

Of course.

But then I suppose you will say that what he creates is untrue. And yet there is a sense in which the painter also creates a bed?

Yes, he said, but not a real bed.

And what of the maker of the bed? were you not saying that he too makes, not the idea which, according to our view, is the essence of the bed, but only a particular bed?

Yes, I did.

Then if he does not make that which exists he cannot make true existence, but only some semblance of existence; and if anyone were to say that the work of the maker of the bed, or of any other workman, has real existence, he could hardly be supposed to be speaking the truth.

At any rate, he replied, philosophers would say that he was not speaking the truth.

No wonder, then, that his work, too, is an indistinct expression of truth.

No wonder.

Suppose now that by the light of the examples just offered we inquire who this imitator is?

If you please.

Well, then, here are three beds: one existing in nature, which is made by God, as I think that we may say—for no one else can be the maker?

No.

There is another which is the work of the carpenter?

Yes.

And the work of the painter is a third?

Yes.

Beds, then, are of three kinds, and there are three artists who superintend them: God, the maker of the bed, and the painter?

Yes, there are three of them.

God, whether from choice or from necessity, made one bed in nature and one only; two or more such ideal beds neither ever have been nor ever will be made by God.

Why is that?

Because even if He had made but two, a third would still appear behind them which both of them would have for their idea, and that would be the ideal bed and not the two others.

Very true, he said.

God knew this, and he desired to be the real maker of a real bed, not a particular maker of a particular bed, and therefore he created a bed which is essentially and by nature one only.

So we believe.

Shall we, then, speak of him as the natural author or maker of the bed?

Yes, he replied; inasmuch as by the natural process of creation he is the author of this and of all other things.

And what shall we say of the carpenter—is not he also the maker of the bed?

Yes.

But would you call the painter a creator and maker?

Certainly not.

Yet if he is not the maker, what is he in relation to the bed?

I think, he said, that we may fairly designate him as the imitator of that which the others make.

Good, I said; then you call him who is third in the descent from nature an imitator?

Certainly, he said.

And the tragic poet is an imitator, and, therefore, like all other imitators, he is thrice removed from the king and from the truth?

That appears to be so.

Then about the imitator we are agreed. And what about the painter? I would like to know whether he may be thought to imitate that which originally exists in nature, or only the creations of artists?

The latter.

As they are or as they appear? you have still to determine this.

What do you mean?

I mean, that you may look at a bed from different points of view, obliquely or directly or from any other point of view, and the bed will appear different, but there is no difference in reality. And the same of all things.

Yes, he said, the difference is only apparent

Now let me ask you another question: Which is the art of painting designed to be—an imitation of things as they are, or as they appear—of appearance or of reality?

Of appearance.

Then the imitator, I said, is a long way off the truth, and can do all things because he lightly touches on a small part of them, and that part an image. For example: A painter will paint a cobbler, carpenter, or any other artist, though he knows nothing of their arts; and, if he is a good artist, he may deceive children or simple persons, when he shows them his picture of a carpenter from a distance, and they will fancy that they are looking at a real carpenter.

Certainly.

And whenever anyone informs us that he has found a man who knows all the arts, and all things else that anybody knows, and every single thing with a higher degree of accuracy than any other man—whoever tells us this, I think that we can only imagine him to be a simple creature who is likely to have been deceived by some wizard or actor whom he met, and whom he thought all-knowing, because he himself was unable to analyze the nature of knowledge and ignorance and imitation.

Most true.

And so, when we hear persons saying that the tragedians, and Homer, who is at their head, know all the arts and all things human, virtue as well as vice, and divine things too, for that the good poet cannot compose well unless he knows his subject, and that he who has not this knowledge can never be a poet, we ought to consider whether here also there may not be a similar illusion. Perhaps they may have come across imitators and been deceived by them; they may not have remembered when they saw their works that these were but imitations thrice removed from the truth, and could easily be made with- out any knowledge of the truth, because they are appearances only and not realities? Or, after all, they may be in the right, and poets do really know the things about which they seem to the many to speak so well?

The question, he said, should by all means be considered.

Now do you suppose that if a person were able to make the original as well as the image, he would seriously devote himself to the image-making branch? Would he allow imitation to be the ruling principle of his life, as if he had nothing higher in him?

I should say not.

The real artist, who knew what he was imitating, would be interested in realities and not in imitations; and would desire to leave as memorials of himself works many and fair; and, instead of being the author of encomiums, he would prefer to be the theme of them.

Yes, he said, that would be to him a source of much greater honor and profit.

Then, I said, we must put a question to Homer; not about medicine, or any of the arts to which his poems only incidentally refer: we are not going to ask him, or any other poet, whether he has cured patients like Asclepius, or left behind him a school of medicine such as the Asclepiads were, or whether he only talks about medicine and other arts at second-hand; but we have a right to know respecting military tactics, politics, education, which are the chiefest and noblest subjects of his poems, and we may fairly ask him about them. "Friend Homer," then we say to him, "if you are only in the second remove from truth in what you say of virtue, and not in the third—not an image maker or imitator—and if you are able to discern what pursuits make men better or worse in private or public life, tell us

(continued)

Republic, Book X (continued)

what State was ever better governed by your help? The good order of Lacedæmon is due to Lycurgus, and many other cities, great and small, have been similarly benefited by others; but who says that you have been a good legislator to them and have done them any good? Italy and Sicily boast of Charondas, and there is Solon who is renowned among us; but what city has anything to say about you?" Is there any city which he might name?

I think not, said Glaucon; not even the Homerids themselves pretend that he was a legislator.

Well, but is there any war on record which was carried on successfully by him, or aided by his counsels, when he was alive?

There is not.

Or is there any invention of his, applicable to the arts or to human life, such as Thales the Milesian or Anacharsis the Scythian, and other ingenious men have conceived, which is attributed to him?

There is absolutely nothing of the kind.

But, if Homer never did any public service, was he privately a guide or teacher of any? Had he in his lifetime friends who loved to associate with him, and who handed down to posterity a Homeric way of life, such as was established by Pythagoras, who was so greatly beloved for his wisdom, and whose followers are to this day quite celebrated for the order which was named after him?

Nothing of the kind is recorded of him. For, surely, Socrates, Creophylus, the companion of Homer, that child of flesh, whose name always makes us laugh, might be more justly ridiculed for his stupidity, if, as is said, Homer was greatly neglected by him and others in his own day when he was alive?

Yes, I replied, that is the tradition. But can you imagine, Glaucon, that if Homer had really been able to educate and improve mankind—if he had possessed knowledge, and not been a mere imitator—can you imagine, I say, that he would not have had many followers, and been honored and loved by them? Protagoras of Abdera and Prodicus of Ceos and a host of others have only to whisper to their contemporaries: "You will never be able to manage either your own house or your own State until you appoint us to be your ministers of education"—and this ingenious device of theirs has such an effect in making men love them that their companions all but carry them about on their shoulders. And is it conceivable that the contemporaries of Homer, or again of Hesiod, would have allowed either of them to go about as rhapsodists, if they had really been able to make mankind virtuous? Would they not have been as unwilling to part with them as with gold, and have compelled them to stay at home with them? Or, if the master would not stay, then the disciples would have followed him about everywhere, until they had got education enough?

Yes, Socrates, that, I think, is quite true.

Then must we not infer that all these poetical individuals, beginning with Homer, are only imitators; they copy images of virtue and the like, but the truth they never reach? The poet is like a painter who, as we have already observed, will make a likeness of a cobbler though he understands nothing of cobbling; and his picture is good enough for those who know no more than he does, and judge only by colors and figures.

Quite so.

In like manner the poet with his words and phrases[1] may be said to lay on the colors of the several arts, himself understanding their nature only enough to imitate them; and other people, who are as ignorant as he is, and judge only from his words, imagine that if he speaks of cobbling, or of military tactics, or of anything else, in metre and harmony and rhythm, he speaks very well—such is the sweet influence which melody and rhythm by nature have. And I think that you must have observed again and again what a poor appearance the tales of poets make when stripped of the colors which music puts upon them, and recited in simple prose.

Yes, he said.

They are like faces which were never really beautiful, but only blooming; and now the bloom of youth has passed away from them?

Exactly.

Here is another point: The imitator or maker of the image knows nothing of true existence; he knows appearances only. Am I not right?

Yes.

Then let us have a clear understanding, and not be satisfied with half an explanation.

Proceed.

Of the painter we say that he will paint reins, and he will paint a bit?

Yes.

And the worker in leather and brass will make them?

Certainly.

But does the painter know the right form of the bit and reins? Nay, hardly even the workers in brass and leather who make them; only the horseman who knows how to use them—he knows their right form.

Most true.

And may we not say the same of all things?

What?

That there are three arts which are concerned with all things: one which uses, another which makes, a third which imitates them?

Yes.

And the excellence or beauty or truth of every structure, animate or inanimate, and of every action of man, is relative to the use for which nature or the artist has intended them.

True.

Then the user of them must have the greatest experience of them, and he must indicate to the maker the good or bad qualities which develop themselves in use; for example, the flute-player will tell the flute-maker which of his flutes is satisfactory to the performer; he will tell him how he ought to make them, and the other will attend to his instructions?

Of course.

The one knows and therefore speaks with authority about the goodness and badness of flutes, while the other, confiding in him, will do what he is told by him?

True.

The instrument is the same, but about the excellence or badness of it the maker will only attain to a correct belief; and this he will gain from him who knows, by talking to him and being compelled to hear what he has to say, whereas the user will have knowledge?

True.

But will the imitator have either? Will he know from use whether or no his drawing is correct or beautiful? or will he have right opinion from being compelled to associate with another who knows and gives him instructions about what he should draw?

Neither.

Then he will no more have true opinion than he will have knowledge about the goodness or badness of his imitations?

I suppose not.

The imitative artist will be in a brilliant state of intelligence about his own creations?

Nay, very much the reverse.

And still he will go on imitating without knowing what makes a thing good or bad, and may be expected therefore to imitate only that which appears to be good to the ignorant multitude?

Just so.

Thus far, then, we are pretty well agreed that the imitator has no knowledge worth mentioning of what he imitates. Imitation is only a kind of play or sport, and the tragic poets, whether they write in iambic or in heroic verse, are imitators in the highest degree?

Very true.

And now tell me, I conjure you, has not imitation been shown by us to be concerned with that which is thrice removed from the truth?

Certainly.

And what is the faculty in man to which imitation is addressed?

What do you mean?

(continued)

Republic, Book X (continued)

I will explain: The body which is large when seen near, appears small when seen at a distance?
True.
And the same objects appear straight when looked at out of the water, and crooked when in the water; and the concave becomes convex, owing to the illusion about colors to which the sight is liable. Thus every sort of confusion is revealed within us; and this is that weakness of the human mind on which the art of conjuring and of deceiving by light and shadow and other ingenious devices imposes, having an effect upon us like magic.
True.
And the arts of measuring and numbering and weighing come to the rescue of the human understanding—there is the beauty of them—and the apparent greater or less, or more or heavier, no longer have the mastery over us, but give way before calculation and measure and weight?
Most true.
And this, surely, must be the work of the calculating and rational principle in the soul?
To be sure.
And when this principle measures and certifies that some things are equal, or that some are greater or less than others, there occurs an apparent contradiction?
True.
But were we not saying that such a contradiction is impossible—the same faculty cannot have contrary opinions at the same time about the same thing?
Very true.
Then that part of the soul which has an opinion contrary to measure is not the same with that which has an opinion in accordance with measure?
True.
And the better part of the soul is likely to be that which trusts to measure and calculation?
Certainly.
And that which is opposed to them is one of the inferior principles of the soul?
No doubt.
This was the conclusion at which I was seeking to arrive when I said that painting or drawing, and imitation in general, when doing their own proper work, are far removed from truth, and the companions and friends and associates of a principle within us which is equally removed from reason, and that they have no true or healthy aim.
Exactly.
The imitative art is an inferior who marries an inferior, and has inferior offspring.
Very true.
And is this confined to the sight only, or does it extend to the hearing also, relating in fact to what we term poetry?
Probably the same would be true of poetry.
Do not rely, I said, on a probability derived from the analogy of painting; but let us examine further and see whether the faculty with which poetical imitation is concerned is good or bad.
By all means.
We may state the question thus: Imitation imitates the actions of men, whether voluntary or involuntary, on which, as they imagine, a good or bad result has ensued, and they rejoice or sorrow accordingly. Is there anything more?
No, there is nothing else.
But in all this variety of circumstances is the man at unity with himself—or, rather, as in the instance of sight there were confusion and opposition in his opinions about the same things, so here also are there not strife and inconsistency in his life? though I need hardly raise the question again, for I remember that all this has been already admitted; and the soul has been acknowledged by us to be full of these and ten thousand similar oppositions occurring at the same moment?
And we were right, he said.
Yes, I said, thus far we were right; but there was an omission which must now be supplied.
What was the omission?
Were we not saying that a good man, who has the misfortune to lose his son or anything else which is most dear to him, will bear the loss with more equanimity than another?

Yes.

But will he have no sorrow, or shall we say that although he cannot help sorrowing, he will moderate his sorrow?

The latter, he said, is the truer statement.

Tell me: will he be more likely to struggle and hold out against his sorrow when he is seen by his equals, or when he is alone?

It will make a great difference whether he is seen or not.

When he is by himself he will not mind saying or doing many things which he would be ashamed of anyone hearing or seeing him do?

True.

There is a principle of law and reason in him which bids him resist, as well as a feeling of his misfortune which is forcing him to indulge his sorrow?

True.

But when a man is drawn in two opposite directions, to and from the same object, this, as we affirm, necessarily implies two distinct principles in him?

Certainly.

One of them is ready to follow the guidance of the law?

How do you mean?

The law would say that to be patient under suffering is best, and that we should not give way to impatience, as there is no knowing whether such things are good or evil; and nothing is gained by impatience; also, because no human thing is of serious importance, and grief stands in the way of that which at the moment is most required.

What is most required? he asked.

That we should take counsel about what has happened, and when the dice have been thrown order our affairs in the way which reason deems best; not, like children who have had a fall, keeping hold of the part struck and wasting time in setting up a howl, but always accustoming the soul forthwith to apply a remedy, raising up that which is sickly and fallen, banishing the cry of sorrow by the healing art.

Yes, he said, that is the true way of meeting the attacks of fortune.

Yes, I said; and the higher principle is ready to follow this suggestion of reason?

Clearly.

And the other principle, which inclines us to recollection of our troubles and to lamentation, and can never have enough of them, we may call irrational, useless, and cowardly?

Indeed, we may.

And does not the latter—I mean the rebellious principle—furnish a great variety of materials for imitation? Whereas the wise and calm temperament, being always nearly equable, is not easy to imitate or to appreciate when imitated, especially at a public festival when a promiscuous crowd is assembled in a theatre. For the feeling represented is one to which they are strangers.

Certainly.

Then the imitative poet who aims at being popular is not by nature made, nor is his art intended, to please or to affect the rational principle in the soul; but he will prefer the passionate and fitful temper, which is easily imitated?

Clearly.

And now we may fairly take him and place him by the side of the painter, for he is like him in two ways: first, inasmuch as his creations have an inferior degree of truth—in this, I say, he is like him; and he is also like him in being concerned with an inferior part of the soul; and therefore we shall be right in refusing to admit him into a well-ordered State, because he awakens and nourishes and strengthens the feelings and impairs the reason. As in a city when the evil are permitted to have authority and the good are put out of the way, so in the soul of man, as we maintain, the imitative poet implants an evil constitution, for he indulges the irrational nature which has no discernment of greater and less, but thinks the same thing at one time great and at another small—he is a manufacturer of images and is very far removed from the truth.[2]

Exactly.

(continued)

Republic, Book X (continued)

But we have not yet brought forward the heaviest count in our accusation: the power which poetry has of harming even the good (and there are very few who are not harmed), is surely an awful thing?

Yes, certainly, if the effect is what you say.

Hear and judge: The best of us, as I conceive, when we listen to a passage of Homer or one of the tragedians, in which he represents some pitiful hero who is drawling out his sorrows in a long oration, or weeping, and smiting his breast—the best of us, you know, delight in giving way to sympathy, and are in raptures at the excellence of the poet who stirs our feelings most.

Yes, of course, I know.

But when any sorrow of our own happens to us, then you may observe that we pride ourselves on the opposite quality—we would fain be quiet and patient; this is the manly part, and the other which delighted us in the recitation is now deemed to be the part of a woman.

Very true, he said.

Now can we be right in praising and admiring another who is doing that which any one of us would abominate and be ashamed of in his own person?

No, he said, that is certainly not reasonable.

Nay, I said, quite reasonable from one point of view.

What point of view?

If you consider, I said, that when in misfortune we feel a natural hunger and desire to relieve our sorrow by weeping and lamentation, and that this feeling which is kept under control in our own calamities is satisfied and delighted by the poets; the better nature in each of us, not having been sufficiently trained by reason or habit, allows the sympathetic element to break loose because the sorrow is another's; and the spectator fancies that there can be no disgrace to himself in praising and pitying anyone who comes telling him what a good man he is, and making a fuss about his troubles; he thinks that the pleasure is a gain, and why should he be supercilious and lose this and the poem too? Few persons ever reflect, as I should imagine, that from the evil of other men something of evil is communicated to themselves. And so the feeling of sorrow which has gathered strength at the sight of the misfortunes of others is with difficulty repressed in our own.

How very true!

And does not the same hold also of the ridiculous? There are jests which you would be ashamed to make yourself, and yet on the comic stage, or indeed in private, when you hear them, you are greatly amused by them, and are not at all disgusted at their unseemliness; the case of pity is repeated; there is a principle in human nature which is disposed to raise a laugh, and this which you once restrained by reason, because you were afraid of being thought a buffoon, is now let out again; and having stimulated the risible faculty at the theatre, you are betrayed unconsciously to yourself into playing the comic poet at home.

Quite true, he said.

And the same may be said of lust and anger and all the other affections, of desire, and pain, and pleasure, which are held to be inseparable from every action—in all of them poetry feeds and waters the passions instead of drying them up; she lets them rule, although they ought to be controlled, if mankind are ever to increase in happiness and virtue.

I cannot deny it.

Therefore, Glaucon, I said, whenever you meet with any of the eulogists of Homer declaring that he has been the educator of Hellas, and that he is profitable for education and for the ordering of human things, and that you should take him up again and again and get to know him and regulate your whole life according to him, we may love and honor those who say these things—they are excellent people, as far as their lights extend; and we are ready to acknowledge that Homer is the greatest of poets and first of tragedy writers; but we must remain firm in our conviction that hymns to the gods and praises of famous men are the only poetry which ought to be admitted into our State. For if you go beyond this and allow the honeyed muse to enter, either in epic or lyric verse, not law and the reason of mankind, which by common consent have ever been deemed best, but pleasure and pain will be the rulers in our State.

That is most true, he said.

And now since we have reverted to the subject of poetry, let this our defence serve to show the reasonableness of our former judgment in sending away out of our State an art having the tendencies which we have described; for reason constrained us. But that she may not impute to us any harshness or want of politeness, let us tell her that there is an ancient quarrel between philosophy and poetry; of which there are many proofs, such as the saying of "the yelping hound howling at her lord," or of one "mighty in the vain talk of fools," and "the mob of sages circumventing Zeus," and the "subtle thinkers who are beggars after all"; and there are innumerable other signs of ancient enmity between them. Notwithstanding this, let us assure our sweet friend and the sister art of imitation, that if she will only prove her title to exist in a well-ordered State we shall be delighted to receive her—we are very conscious of her charms; but we may not on that account betray the truth. I dare say, Glaucon, that you are as much charmed by her as I am, especially when she appears in Homer?

Yes, indeed, I am greatly charmed.

Shall I propose, then, that she be allowed to return from exile, but upon this condition only—that she make a defence of herself in lyrical or some other metre?

Certainly.

And we may further grant to those of her defenders who are lovers of poetry and yet not poets the permission to speak in prose on her behalf: let them show not only that she is pleasant, but also useful to States and to human life, and we will listen in a kindly spirit; for if this can be proved we shall surely be the gainers—I mean, if there is a use in poetry as well as a delight?

Certainly, he said, we shall be the gainers.

If her defence fails, then, my dear friend, like other persons who are enamoured of something, but put a restraint upon themselves when they think their desires are opposed to their interests, so, too, must we after the manner of lovers give her up, though not without a struggle. We, too, are inspired by that love of poetry which the education of noble States has implanted in us, and therefore we would have her appear at her best and truest; but so long as she is unable to make good her defence, this argument of ours shall be a charm to us, which we will repeat to ourselves while we listen to her strains; that we may not fall away into the childish love of her which captivates the many. At all events we are well aware that poetry being such as we have described is not to be regarded seriously as attaining to the truth; and he who listens to her, fearing for the safety of the city which is within him, should be on his guard against her seductions and make our words his law.

Yes, he said, I quite agree with you.

Yes, I said, my dear Glaucon, for great is the issue at stake, greater than appears, whether a man is to be good or bad. And what will anyone be profited if under the influence of honor or money or power, aye, or under the excitement of poetry, he neglect justice and virtue?

Yes, he said; I have been convinced by the argument, as I believe that anyone else would have been.

And yet no mention has been made of the greatest prizes and rewards which await virtue.

What, are there any greater still? If there are, they must be of an inconceivable greatness.

Why, I said, what was ever great in a short time? The whole period of threescore years and ten is surely but a little thing in comparison with eternity?

Say rather 'nothing' he replied.

And should an immortal being seriously think of this little space rather than of the whole?

Of the whole, certainly. But why do you ask?

Are you not aware, I said, that the soul of man is immortal and imperishable?

He looked at me in astonishment, and said: No, by heaven: And are you really prepared to maintain this?

Yes, I said, I ought to be, and you too—there is no difficulty in proving it.

I see a great difficulty; but I should like to hear you state this argument of which you make so light.

Listen, then.

I am attending.

There is a thing which you call good and another which you call evil?

(continued)

Republic, Book X *(continued)*

Yes, he replied.

Would you agree with me in thinking that the corrupting and destroying element is the evil, and the saving and improving element the good?

Yes.

And you admit that everything has a good and also an evil; as ophthalmia is the evil of the eyes and disease of the whole body; as mildew is of corn, and rot of timber, or rust of copper and iron: in everything, or in almost everything, there is an inherent evil and disease?

Yes, he said.

NOTES

1. Or, "with his nouns and verbs."
2. Reading

Poetics

Aristotle

VI

Of the poetry which imitates in hexameter verse, and of Comedy, we will speak hereafter. Let us now discuss Tragedy, resuming its formal definition, as resulting from what has been already said.

Tragedy, then, is an imitation of an action that is serious, complete, and of a certain magnitude; in language embellished with each kind of artistic ornament, the several kinds being found in separate parts of the play; in the form of action, not of narrative; through pity and fear effecting the proper purgation of these emotions. By 'language embellished,' I mean language into which rhythm, 'harmony,' and song enter. By 'the several kinds in separate parts,' I mean, that some parts are rendered through the medium of verse alone, others again with the aid of song.

Now as tragic imitation implies persons acting, it necessarily follows, in the first place, that Spectacular equipment will be a part of Tragedy. Next, Song and Diction, for these are the medium of imitation. By 'Diction' I mean the mere metrical arrangement of the words: as for 'Song,' it is a term whose sense every one understands.

Again, Tragedy is the imitation of an action; and an action implies personal agents, who necessarily possess certain distinctive qualities both of character and thought; for it is by these that we qualify actions themselves, and these—thought and character—are the two natural causes from which actions spring, and on actions again all success or failure depends. Hence, the Plot is the imitation of the action:—for by plot I here mean the arrangement of the incidents. By Character I mean that in virtue of which we ascribe certain qualities to the agents. Thought is required wherever a statement is proved, or, it may be, a general truth enunciated. Every Tragedy, therefore, must have six parts, which parts determine its quality—namely, Plot, Character, Diction, Thought, Spectacle, Song. Two of the parts constitute the medium of imitation, one the manner, and three the objects of imitation. And these complete the list. These elements have been employed, we may say, by the poets to a man; in fact, every play contains Spectacular elements as well as Character, Plot, Diction, Song, and Thought.

But most important of all is the structure of the incidents. For Tragedy is an imitation, not of men, but of an action and of life, and life consists in action, and its end is a mode of action, not a quality. Now character determines men's qualities, but it is by their actions that they are happy or the reverse. Dramatic action, therefore, is not with a view to the representation of character: character comes in as subsidiary to the actions. Hence the incidents and the plot are the end of a tragedy; and the end is the chief thing of all. Again, without action there cannot be a tragedy; there may be without character. The tragedies of most of our modern poets fail in the rendering of character; and of poets in general this is often true. It is the same in painting; and here lies the difference between Zeuxis and Polygnotus. Polygnotus delineates character well: the style of Zeuxis is devoid of ethical quality. Again, if you string together a set of speeches expressive of character, and well finished in point of diction and thought, you will not produce the essential tragic effect nearly so well as with a play which, however deficient in these respects, yet has a plot and artistically constructed incidents. Besides which, the most powerful elements of emotional interest in Tragedy—Peripeteia or Reversal of the Situation, and Recognition scenes—are parts of the plot. A further proof is, that novices in the art attain to finish of diction and precision of portraiture before they can construct the plot. It is the same with almost all the early poets.

The Plot, then, is the first principle, and, as it were, the soul of a tragedy: Character holds the second place. A similar fact is seen in painting. The most beautiful colours, laid on confusedly, will not give as much pleasure as the chalk outline of a portrait. Thus Tragedy is the imitation of an action, and of the agents mainly with a view to the action.

Third in order is Thought,—that is, the faculty of saying what is possible and pertinent in given circumstances. In the case of oratory, this is the function of the political art and of the art of rhetoric: and so indeed the older poets make their characters speak the language of civic life; the poets of our time, the language of the rhetoricians. Character is that which reveals moral purpose, showing what kind of things a man chooses or avoids. Speeches, therefore, which do not make this manifest, or in which the speaker does not choose or avoid anything whatever, are not expressive of character. Thought, on the other hand, is found where something is proved to be or not to be, or a general maxim is enunciated.

Fourth among the elements enumerated comes Diction; by which I mean, as has been already said, the expression of the meaning in words; and its essence is the same both in verse and prose.

Of the remaining elements Song holds the chief place among the embellishments.

The Spectacle has, indeed, an emotional attraction of its own, but, of all the parts, it is the least artistic, and connected least with the art of poetry. For the power of Tragedy, we may be sure, is felt even apart from representation and actors. Besides, the production of spectacular effects depends more on the art of the stage machinist than on that of the poet.

VII

These principles being established, let us now discuss the proper structure of the Plot, since this is the first and most important part of Tragedy.

Now, according to our definition, Tragedy is an imitation of an action that is complete, and whole, and of a certain magnitude; for there may be a whole that is wanting in magnitude. A whole is that which has a beginning, a middle, and an end. A beginning is that which does not itself follow anything by causal necessity, but after which something naturally is or comes to be. An end, on the contrary, is that which itself naturally follows some other thing, either by necessity, or as a rule, but has nothing following it. A middle is that which follows something as some other thing follows it. A well constructed plot, therefore, must neither begin nor end at haphazard, but conform to these principles.

Again, a beautiful object, whether it be a living organism or any whole composed of parts, must not only have an orderly arrangement of parts, but must also be of a certain magnitude; for beauty depends on magnitude and order. Hence a very small animal organism cannot be beautiful; for the view of it is confused, the object being seen in an almost imperceptible moment of time. Nor, again, can one of vast size be beautiful; for as the eye cannot take it all in at once, the unity and sense of the whole is lost for the spectator; as for instance if there were one a thousand miles long. As, therefore, in the case of animate bodies and organisms a certain magnitude is necessary, and a magnitude which may be easily embraced in one view; so in the plot, a certain length is necessary, and a length which can be easily embraced by the memory. The limit of length in relation

(continued)

Poetics (continued)

to dramatic competition and sensuous presentment, is no part of artistic theory. For had it been the rule for a hundred tragedies to compete together, the performance would have been regulated by the water-clock,—as indeed we are told was formerly done. But the limit as fixed by the nature of the drama itself is this:—the greater the length, the more beautiful will the piece be by reason of its size, provided that the whole be perspicuous. And to define the matter roughly, we may say that the proper magnitude is comprised within such limits, that the sequence of events, according to the law of probability or necessity, will admit of a change from bad fortune to good, or from good fortune to bad.

VIII

Unity of plot does not, as some persons think, consist in the unity of the hero. For infinitely various are the incidents in one man's life which cannot be reduced to unity; and so, too, there are many actions of one man out of which we cannot make one action. Hence the error, as it appears, of all poets who have composed a Heracleid, a Theseid, or other poems of the kind. They imagine that as Heracles was one man, the story of Heracles must also be a unity. But Homer, as in all else he is of surpassing merit, here too—whether from art or natural genius—seems to have happily discerned the truth. In composing the Odyssey he did not include all the adventures of Odysseus—such as his wound on Parnassus, or his feigned madness at the mustering of the host—incidents between which there was no necessary or probable connexion: but he made the Odyssey, and likewise the Iliad, to centre round an action that in our sense of the word is one. As therefore, in the other imitative arts, the imitation is one when the object imitated is one, so the plot, being an imitation of an action, must imitate one action and that a whole, the structural union of the parts being such that, if any one of them is displaced or removed, the whole will be disjointed and disturbed. For a thing whose presence or absence makes no visible difference, is not an organic part of the whole.

IX

It is, moreover, evident from what has been said, that it is not the function of the poet to relate what has happened, but what may happen,—what is possible according to the law of probability or necessity. The poet and the historian differ not by writing in verse or in prose. The work of Herodotus might be put into verse, and it would still be a species of history, with metre no less than without it. The true difference is that one relates what has happened, the other what may happen. Poetry, therefore, is a more philosophical and a higher thing than history: for poetry tends to express the universal, history the particular. By the universal I mean how a person of a certain type will on occasion speak or act, according to the law of probability or necessity; and it is this universality at which poetry aims in the names she attaches to the personages. The particular is—for example—what Alcibiades did or suffered. In Comedy this is already apparent: for here the poet first constructs the plot on the lines of probability, and then inserts characteristic names;—unlike the lampooners who write about particular individuals. But tragedians still keep to real names, the reason being that what is possible is credible: what has not happened we do not at once feel sure to be possible: but what has happened is manifestly possible: otherwise it would not have happened. Still there are some tragedies in which there are only one or two well known names, the rest being fictitious. In others, none are well known,—as in Agathon's Antheus, where incidents and names alike are fictitious, and yet they give none the less pleasure. We must not, therefore, at all costs keep to the received legends, which are the usual subjects of Tragedy. Indeed, it would be absurd to attempt it; for even subjects that are known are known only to a few, and yet give pleasure to all. It clearly follows that the poet or 'maker' should be the maker of plots rather than of verses; since he is a poet because he imitates, and what he imitates are actions. And even if he chances to take an historical subject, he is none the less a poet; for there is no reason why some events that have actually happened should not conform to the law of the probable and possible, and in virtue of that quality in them he is their poet or maker.

Of all plots and actions the epeisodic are the worst. I call a plot 'epeisodic' in which the episodes or acts succeed one another without probable or necessary sequence. Bad poets compose such pieces by their own fault, good poets, to please the players; for, as they write show pieces for competition, they stretch the plot beyond its capacity, and are often forced to break the natural continuity.

But again, Tragedy is an imitation not only of a complete action, but of events terrible and pitiful. Such an effect is best produced when the events come on us by surprise; and the effect is heightened when, at the same time, they follow as cause and effect. The tragic wonder will then be greater than if they happened of themselves or by accident; for even coincidences are most striking when they have an air of design. We may instance the statue of Mitys at Argos, which fell upon his murderer while he was a spectator at a festival, and killed him. Such events seem not to be due to mere chance. Plots, therefore, constructed on these principles are necessarily the best. . . .

XIII

As the sequel to what has already been said, we must proceed to consider what the poet should aim at, and what he should avoid, in constructing his plots; and by what means the specific effect of Tragedy will be produced.

A perfect tragedy should, as we have seen, be arranged not on the simple but on the complex plan. It should, moreover, imitate actions which excite pity and fear, this being the distinctive mark of tragic imitation. It follows plainly, in the first place, that the change of fortune presented must not be the spectacle of virtuous men brought from prosperity to adversity: for this moves neither pity nor fear; it merely shocks us. Nor, again, that of a bad man passing from adversity to prosperity: for nothing can be more alien to the spirit of Tragedy; it possesses no single tragic quality; it neither satisfies the moral sense nor calls forth pity or fear. Nor, again, should the downfall of the utter villain be exhibited. A plot of this kind would, doubtless, satisfy the moral sense, but it would inspire neither pity nor fear; for pity is aroused by unmerited misfortune, fear by the misfortune of a man like ourselves. Such an event, therefore, will be neither pitiful nor terrible. There remains, then, the character between these two extremes,—that of a man who is not eminently good and just, yet whose misfortune is brought about not by vice or depravity, but by some error or frailty. He must be one who is highly renowned and prosperous,—a personage like Oedipus, Thyestes, or other illustrious men of such families.

A well constructed plot should, therefore, be single in its issue, rather than double as some maintain. The change of fortune should be not from bad to good, but, reversely, from good to bad. It should come about as the result not of vice, but of some great error or frailty, in a character either such as we have described, or better rather than worse. The practice of the stage bears out our view. At first the poets recounted any legend that came in their way. Now, the best tragedies are founded on the story of a few houses,—on the fortunes of Alcmaeon, Oedipus, Orestes, Meleager, Thyestes, Telephus, and those others who have done or suffered something terrible. A tragedy, then, to be perfect according to the rules of art should be of this construction. Hence they are in error who censure Euripides just because he follows this principle in his plays, many of which end unhappily. It is, as we have said, the right ending. The best proof is that on the stage and in dramatic competition, such plays, if well worked out, are the most tragic in effect; and Euripides, faulty though he may be in the general management of his subject, yet is felt to be the most tragic of the poets.

In the second rank comes the kind of tragedy which some place first. Like the Odyssey, it has a double thread of plot, and also an opposite catastrophe for the good and for the bad. It is accounted the best because of the weakness of the spectators; for the poet is guided in what he writes by the wishes of his audience. The pleasure, however, thence derived is not the true tragic pleasure. It is proper rather to Comedy, where those who, in the piece, are the deadliest enemies—like Orestes and Aegisthus—quit the stage as friends at the close, and no one slays or is slain.

XIV

Fear and pity may be aroused by spectacular means; but they may also result from the inner structure of the piece, which is the better way, and indicates a superior poet. For the plot ought to be so constructed that, even without the aid of the eye, he who hears the tale told will thrill with horror and melt to pity at what takes place. This is the impression we should receive from hearing the story of the Oedipus. But to produce this effect by the mere spectacle is a less artistic method, and dependent on extraneous aids. Those who employ spectacular means to create a sense not of the terrible but only of the monstrous, are strangers to the purpose of Tragedy; for we must not demand of Tragedy any and every kind of pleasure, but only that which is proper to it. And since the

(continued)

Poetics (continued)

pleasure which the poet should afford is that which comes from pity and fear through imitation, it is evident that this quality must be impressed upon the incidents.

Let us then determine what are the circumstances which strike us as terrible or pitiful.

Actions capable of this effect must happen between persons who are either friends or enemies or indifferent to one another. If an enemy kills an enemy, there is nothing to excite pity either in the act or the intention,—except so far as the suffering in itself is pitiful. So again with indifferent persons. But when the tragic incident occurs between those who are near or dear to one another [sic]—if, for example, a brother kills, or intends to kill, a brother, a son his father, a mother her son, a son his mother, or any other deed of the kind is done—these are the situations to be looked for by the poet. He may not indeed destroy the framework of the received legends—the fact, for instance, that Clytemnestra was slain by Orestes and Eriphyle by Alcmaeon—but he ought to show invention of his own, and skilfully handle the traditional material. Let us explain more clearly what is meant by skilful handling.

The action may be done consciously and with knowledge of the persons, in the manner of the older poets. It is thus too that Euripides makes Medea slay her children. Or, again, the deed of horror may be done, but done in ignorance, and the tie of kinship or friendship be discovered afterwards. The Oedipus of Sophocles is an example. Here, indeed, the incident is outside the drama proper; but cases occur where it falls within the action of the play: one may cite the Alcmaeon of Astydamas, or Telegonus in the Wounded Odysseus. Again, there is a third case,—<to be about to act with knowledge of the persons and then not to act. The fourth case is > when some one is about to do an irreparable deed through ignorance, and makes the discovery before it is done. These are the only possible ways. For the deed must either be done or not done,—and that wittingly or unwittingly. But of all these ways, to be about to act knowing the persons, and then not to act, is the worst. It is shocking without being tragic, for no disaster follows. It is, therefore, never, or very rarely, found in poetry. One instance, however, is in the Antigone, where Haemon threatens to kill Creon. The next and better way is that the deed should be perpetrated. Still better, that it should be perpetrated in ignorance, and the discovery made afterwards. There is then nothing to shock us, while the discovery produces a startling effect. The last case is the best, as when in the Cresphontes Merope is about to slay her son, but, recognising who he is, spares his life. So in the Iphigenia, the sister recognises the brother just in time. Again in the Helle, the son recognises the mother when on the point of giving her up. This, then, is why a few families only, as has been already observed, furnish the subjects of tragedy. It was not art, but happy chance, that led poets to look for such situations and so impress the tragic quality upon their plots. They are compelled, therefore, to have recourse to those houses whose history contains moving incidents like these.

Enough has now been said concerning the structure of the incidents and the proper constitution of the plot.

XV

In respect of Character there are four things to be aimed at. First, and most important, it must be good. Now any speech or action that manifests moral purpose of any kind will be expressive of character: the character will be good if the purpose is good. This rule is relative to each class. Even a woman may be good, and also a slave; though the woman may be said to be an inferior being, and the slave quite worthless. The second thing to aim at is propriety. There is a type of manly valour; but valour in a woman, or unscrupulous cleverness, is inappropriate. Thirdly, character must be true to life: for this is a distinct thing from goodness and propriety, as here described. The fourth point is *consistency*: for though the subject of the imitation, who suggested the type, be inconsistent, still he must be consistently inconsistent. As an example of motiveless degradation of character, we have Menelaus in the Orestes: of character indecorous and inappropriate, the lament of Odysseus in the Scylla, and the speech of Melanippe: of inconsistency, the Iphigenia at Aulis,—for Iphigenia the suppliant in no way resembles her later self.

As in the structure of the plot, so too in the portraiture of character, the poet should always aim either at the necessary or the probable. Thus a person of a given character should speak or act in a given way, by the rule either of necessity or of probability; just as this event should follow that by necessary or probable sequence. It is therefore evident that the unravelling of the plot, no less than the complication, must arise out of the plot itself, it must not be brought about by the *Deus ex Machina*—as in the Medea, or in the Return of the Greeks in the Iliad. The *Deus ex Machina* should be employed only for events external to the drama,—for antecedent or subsequent events, which lie beyond the range of human knowledge, and which require to be reported or foretold; for to the gods we ascribe the power of seeing all things. Within the action there must be nothing irrational. If the irrational cannot be excluded, it should be outside the scope of the tragedy. Such is the irrational element in the Oedipus of Sophocles.

Again, since Tragedy is an imitation of persons who are above the common level, the example of good portrait-painters should be followed. They, while reproducing the distinctive form of the original, make a likeness which is true to life and yet more beautiful. So too the poet, in representing men who are irascible or indolent, or have other defects of character, should preserve the type and yet ennoble it. In this way Achilles is portrayed by Agathon and Homer.

These then are rules the poet should observe. Nor should he neglect those appeals to the senses, which, though not among the essentials, are the concomitants of poetry; for here too there is much room for error. But of this enough has been said in the published treatises.

The Intentional Fallacy
W. K. Wimsatt, Jr., and M. C. Beardsley

He owns with toil he wrote the following scenes;
But, if they're naught, ne'er spare him for his pains:
Damn him the more; have no commiseration
For dullness on mature deliberation.

William Congreve, Prologue to *The Way of the World*

The claim of the author's "intention" upon the critic's judgment has been challenged in a number of recent discussions, notably in the debate entitled *The Personal Heresy,* between Professors Lewis and Tillyard, and at least implicitly in periodical essays like those in the "Symposiums" of 1940 in the *Southern* and *Kenyon Reviews*.[1] But it seems doubtful if this claim and most of its romantic corollaries are as yet subject to any widespread questioning. The present writers, in a short article entitled "Intention" for a *Dictionary*[2] of literary criticism, raised the issue but were unable to pursue its implications at any length. We argued that the design or intention of the author is neither available nor desirable as a standard for judging the success of a work of literary art, and it seems to us that this is a principle which goes deep into some differences in the history of critical attitudes. It is a principle which accepted or rejected points to the polar opposites of classical "imitation" and romantic expression. It entails many specific, truths about inspiration, authenticity, biography, literary history and scholarship, and about some trends of contemporary poetry, especially its allusiveness. There is hardly a problem of literary criticism in which the critic's approach will not be qualified by his view of "intention."

"Intention," as we shall use the term, corresponds to *what he intended* in a formula which more or less explicitly has had wide acceptance. "In order to judge the poet's performance, we must know *what he intended.*" Intention is design or plan in the author's mind. Intention has obvious affinities for the author's attitude toward his work, the way he felt, what made him write.

We begin our discussion with a series of propositions summarized and abstracted to a degree where they seem to us axiomatic, if not truistic.

1. A poem does not come into existence by accident. The words of a poem, as Professor Stoll has remarked, come out of a head, not out of a hat. Yet to insist on the designing intellect as a *cause* of a poem is not to grant the design or intention as a *standard*.

2. One must ask how a critic expects to get an answer to the question about intention. How is he to find out what the poet tried to do? If the poet succeeded in doing it, then the poem itself

(continued)

The Intentional Fallacy (continued)

shows what he was trying to do. And if the poet did not succeed, then the poem is not adequate evidence, and the critic must go outside the poem—for evidence of an intention that did not become effective in the poem. "Only one *caveat* must be borne in mind," says an eminent intentionalist[3] in a moment when his theory repudiates itself; "the poet's aim must be judged at the moment of the creative act, that is to say, by the art of the poem itself."

3. Judging a poem is like judging a pudding or a machine. One demands that it work. It is only because an artifact works that we infer the intention of an artificer. "A poem should not mean but be." A poem can *be* only through its *meaning*—since its medium is words—yet it *is*, simply *is*, in the sense that we have no excuse for inquiring what part is intended or meant.[4] Poetry is a feat of style by which a complex of meaning is handled all at once. Poetry succeeds because all or most of what is said or implied is relevant; what is irrelevant has been excluded, like lumps from pudding and "bugs" from machinery. In this respect poetry differs from practical messages, which are successful if and only if we correctly infer the intention. They are more abstract than poetry.

4. The meaning of a poem may certainly be a personal one, in the sense that a poem expresses a personality or state of soul rather than a physical object like an apple. But even a short lyric poem is dramatic, the response of a speaker (no matter how abstractly conceived) to a situation (no matter how universalized). We ought to impute the thoughts and attitudes of the poem immediately to the dramatic *speaker*, and if to the author at all, only by a biographical act of inference.

5. If there is any sense in which an author, by revision, has better achieved his original intention, it is only the very abstract, tautological, sense that he intended to write a better work and now has done it. (In this sense every author's intention is the same.) His former specific intention was not his intention. "He's the man we were in search of, that's true"; says Hardy's rustic constable, "and yet he's not the man we were in search of. For the man we were in search of was not the man we wanted."[5]

"Is not a critic," asks Professor Stoll, ". . . a judge, who does not explore his own consciousness, but determines the author's meaning or intention, as if the poem were a will, a contract, or the constitution? The poem is not the critic's own."[6] He has diagnosed very accurately two forms of irresponsibility, one of which he prefers. Our view is yet different. The poem is not the critic's own and not the author's (it is detached from the author at birth and goes about the world beyond his power to intend about it or control it). The poem belongs to the public. It is embodied in language, the peculiar possession of the public, and it is about the human being, an object of public knowledge. What is said about the poem is subject to the same scrutiny as any statement in linguistics or in the general science of psychology or morals. Mr. Richards has aptly called the poem a *class*—"a class of experiences which do not differ in any character more than a certain amount . . . from a standard experience."

And he adds, "We may take as this standard experience the relevant experience of the poet when contemplating the completed composition." Professor Wellek in a fine essay on the problem has preferred to call the poem "a system of norms," "extracted from every individual experience," and he objects to Mr. Richards' deference to the poet as reader. We side with Professor Wellek in not wishing to make the poet (outside the poem) an authority.

A critic of our *Dictionary* article, Mr. Ananda K. Coomaraswamy, has argued[7] that there are two kinds of enquiry about a work of art: (1) whether the artist achieved his intentions; (2) whether the work of art "ought ever to have been undertaken at all" and so "whether it is worth preserving." Number (2), Mr. Coomaraswamy maintains, is not "criticism of any work of art *qua* work of art," but is rather moral criticism; number (1) is artistic criticism. But we maintain that (2) need not be moral criticism: that there is another way of deciding whether works of art are worth preserving and whether, in a sense, they "ought" to have been undertaken, and this is the way of objective criticism of works of art as such, the way which enables us to distinguish between a skilful murder and a skilful poem. A skilful murder is an example which Mr. Coomaraswamy uses, and in his system the difference between the murder and the poem is simply a "moral" one, not an "artistic" one, since each if carried out according to plan is "artistically" successful. We maintain that (2) is an enquiry of more worth than (1), and since (2), and not (1) is capable of distinguishing poetry from murder, the name "artistic criticism" is properly given to (2).

II

It is not so much an empirical as an analytic judgment, not a historical statement, but a definition, to say that the intentional fallacy is a romantic one. When a rhetorician, presumably of the first century A.D., writes: "Sublimity is the echo of a great soul," or tells us that "Homer enters into the sublime actions of his heroes" and "shares the full inspiration of the combat," we shall not be surprised to find this rhetorician considered as a distant harbinger of romanticism and greeted in the warmest terms by so romantic a critic as Saintsbury. One may wish to argue whether Longinus should be called romantic,[8] but there can hardly be a doubt that in one important way he is.

Goethe's three questions for "constructive criticism" are "What did the author set out to do? Was his plan reasonable and sensible, and how far did he succeed in carrying it out?" If one leaves out the middle question, one has in effect the system of Croce—the culmination and crowning philosophic expression of romanticism. The beautiful is the successful intuition—expression, and the ugly is the unsuccessful; the intuition or private part of art is *the* aesthetic fact, and the medium or public part is not the subject of aesthetic at all. Yet aesthetic reproduction takes place only "if all the other conditions remain equal."

> Oil-paintings grow dark, frescoes fade, statues lose noses . . . the text of a poem is corrupted by bad copyists or bad printing.
>
> The Madonna of Cimabue is still in the Church of Santa Maria Novella; but does she speak to the visitor of today as to the Florentines of the thirteenth century?
>
> *Historical interpretation* labours . . . to reintegrate in us the psychological conditions which have changed in the course of history. It . . . enables us to see a work of art (a physical object) as its *author saw it* in the moment of production.[9]

The first italics are Croce's, the second ours. The upshot of Croce's system is an ambiguous emphasis on history. With such passages as a point of departure a critic may write a close analysis of the meaning or "spirit" of a play of Shakespeare or Corneille—a process that involves close historical study but remains aesthetic criticism—or he may write sociology, biography, or other kinds of non-aesthetic history. The Crocean system seems to have given more of a boost to the latter way of writing.

"What has the poet tried to do," asks Spingarn in his 1910 Columbia Lecture from which we have already quoted, "and how has he fulfilled his intention?" The place to look for "insuperable" ugliness, says Bosanquet, in his third *Lecture* of 1914, is the "region of insincere and affected art." The seepage of the theory into a non-philosophic place may be seen in such a book as Marguerite Wilkinson's inspirational *New Voices,* about the poetry of 1919 to 1931—where symbols "as old as the ages . . . retain their strength and freshness" through "Realization." We close this section with two examples from quarters where one might least expect a taint of the Crocean. Mr. I. A. Richards' fourfold distinction of meaning into "sense," "feeling," "tone," "intention" has been probably the most influential statement of intentionalism in the past fifteen years, though it contains a hint of self-repudiation: "This function [intention]," says Mr. Richards, "is not on all fours with the others." In an essay on "Three Types of Poetry" Mr. Allen Tate writes as follows:

> We must understand that the lines
>
> Life like a dome of many-colored glass
> Stains the white radiance of eternity

are not poetry; they express the *frustrated will* trying to compete with science. The *will* asserts a rhetorical proposition about the whole of life, but the *imagination* has not seized upon the materials of the poem and made them into a whole. Shelley's simile is imposed upon the material from above; it does not grow out of the material.

The last sentence contains a promise of objective analysis which is not fulfilled. The reason why the essay relies so heavily throughout on the terms "will" and "imagination" is that Mr. Tate is accusing the romantic poets of a kind of insincerity (romanticism in reverse) and at the same time is trying to

(continued)

The Intentional Fallacy (*continued*)

describe something mysterious and perhaps indescribable, an "imaginative whole of life," a "wholeness of vision at a particular moment of experience," something which "yields us the quality of the experience." If a poet had a toothache at the moment of conceiving a poem, that would be part of the experience, but Mr. Tate of course does not mean anything like that. He is thinking about some kind of "whole" which in this essay at least he does not describe, but which doubtless it is the prime need of criticism to describe—in terms that may be publicly tested.

III

I went to the poets; tragic, dithyrambic, and all sorts. . . . I took them some of the most elaborate passages in their own writings, and asked what was the meaning of them. . . . Will you believe me? . . . there is hardly a person present who would not have talked better about their poetry than they did themselves. Then I knew that not by wisdom do poets write poetry, but by a sort of genius and inspiration.

That reiterated mistrust of the poets which we hear from Socrates may have been part of a rigorously ascetic view in which we hardly wish to participate, yet Plato's Socrates saw a truth about the poetic mind which the world no longer commonly sees—so much criticism, and that the most inspirational and most affectionately remembered, has proceeded from the poets themselves.

Certainly the poets have had something to say that the analyst and professor could not say; their message has been more exciting: that poetry should come as naturally as leaves to a tree, that poetry is the lava of the imagination, or that it is emotion recollected in tranquillity. But it is necessary that we realize the character and authority of such testimony. There is only a fine shade between those romantic expressions and a kind of earnest advice that authors often give. Thus Edward Young, Carlyle, Walter Pater:

> I know two golden rules from *ethics*, which are no less golden in *Composition*, than in life.
> 1. *Know thyself*; 2dly, *Reverence thyself*.

This is the grand secret for finding readers and retaining them: let him who would move and convince others, be first moved and convinced himself. Horace's rule, *Si vis me flere*,[10] is applicable in a wider sense than the literal one. To every poet, to every writer, we might say: Be true, if you would be believed. Truth! there can be no merit, no craft at all, without that. And further, all beauty is in the long run only *fineness* of truth, or what we call expression, the finer accommodation of speech to that vision within.

And Housman's little handbook to the poetic mind yields the following illustration:

> Having drunk a pint of beer at luncheon—beer is a sedative to the brain, and my afternoons are the least intellectual portion of my life—I would go out for a walk of two or three hours. As I went along, thinking of nothing in particular, only looking at things around me and following the progress of the seasons, there would flow into my mind, with sudden and unaccountable emotion, sometimes a line or two of verse, sometimes a whole stanza at once. . . .

This is the logical terminus of the series already quoted. Here is a confession of how poems were written which would do as a definition of poetry just as well as "emotion recollected in tranquillity"—and which the young poet might equally well take to heart as a practical rule. Drink a pint of beer, relax, go walking, think on nothing in particular, look at things, surrender yourself to yourself, search for the truth in your own soul, listen to the sound of your own inside voice, discover and express the *vraie vérité*.[11]

It is probably true that all this is excellent advice for poets. The young imagination fired by Wordsworth and Carlyle is probably closer to the verge of producing a poem than the mind of the student who has been sobered by Aristotle or Richards. The art of inspiring poets, or at least of inciting something like poetry in young persons, has probably gone further in our day than ever before. Books of creative writing such as those issued from the Lincoln School are interesting evidence of what a child can do if taught how to manage himself honestly.[12] All this, however, would appear to belong to an art separate from criticism, or to a discipline which one might call the psychology of composition, valid and useful, an individual and private culture, yoga, or system of self-development which the young poet would do well to notice, but different from the public science of evaluating poems.

Coleridge and Arnold were better critics than most poets have been, and if the critical tendency dried up the poetry in Arnold and perhaps in Coleridge, it is not inconsistent with our argument, which is that judgment of poems is different from the art of producing them. Coleridge has given us the classic "anodyne" story, and tells what he can about the genesis of a poem, which he calls a "psychological curiosity," but his definitions of poetry and of the poetic quality "imagination" are to be found elsewhere and in quite other terms.

The day may arrive when the psychology of composition is unified with the science of objective evaluation, but so far they are separate. It would be convenient if the passwords of the intentional school, "sincerity," "fidelity," "spontaneity," "authenticity," "genuineness," "originality," could be equated with terms of analysis such as "integrity," "relevance," "unity," "function"; with "maturity," "subtlety," and "adequacy," and other more precise axiological terms—in short, if "expression" always meant aesthetic communication. But this is not so.

"Aesthetic" art, says Professor Curt Ducasse, an ingenious theorist of expression, is the conscious objectification of feelings, in which an intrinsic part is the critical moment. The artist corrects the objectification when it is not adequate, but this may mean that the earlier attempt was not successful in objectifying the self, or "it may also mean that it was a successful objectification of a self which, when it confronted us clearly, we disowned and repudiated in favor of another."[13] What is the standard by which we disown or accept the self? Professor Ducasse does not say. Whatever it may be, however, this standard is an element in the definition of art which will not reduce to terms of objectification. The evaluation of the work of art remains public; the work is measured against something outside the author.

IV

There is criticism of poetry and there is, as we have seen, author psychology, which when applied to the present or future takes the form of inspirational promotion; but author psychology can be historical too, and then we have literary biography, a legitimate and attractive study in itself, one approach, as Mr. Tillyard would argue, to personality, the poem being only a parallel approach. Certainly it need not be with a derogatory purpose that one points out personal studies, as distinct from poetic studies, in the realm of literary scholarship. Yet there is danger of confusing personal and poetic studies; and there is the fault of writing the personal as if it were poetic.

There is a difference between internal and external evidence for the meaning of a poem. And the paradox is only verbal and superficial that what is (1) internal is also public: it is discovered through the semantics and syntax of a poem, through our habitual knowledge of the language, through grammars, dictionaries, and all the literature which is the source of dictionaries, in general through all that makes a language and culture; while what is (2) external is private or idiosyncratic; not a part of the work as a linguistic fact: it consists of revelations (in journals, for example, or letters or reported conversations) about how or why the poet wrote the poem—to what lady, while sitting on what lawn, or at the death of what friend or brother. There is (3) an intermediate kind of evidence about the character of the author or about private or semi-private meanings attached to words or topics by an author or by a coterie of which he is a member. The meaning of words is the history of words, and the biography of an author, his use of a word, and the associations which the word had for *him,* are part of the word's history and meaning.[14] But the three types of evidence, especially (2) and (3), shade into one another so subtly that it is not always easy to draw a line between examples, and hence arises the difficulty for criticism. The use of biographical evidence need not involve intentionalism, because while it may be evidence of what the author intended, it may also be evidence of the meaning of his words and the dramatic character of his utterance. On the other hand, it may not be all this. And a critic who is concerned with evidence of type (1) and moderately with that of type (3) will in the long run produce a different sort of comment from that of the critic who is concerned with type (2) and with (3) where it shades into (2).

(continued)

The Intentional Fallacy   (*continued*)

The whole glittering parade of Professor Lowes' *Road to Xanadu,* for instance, runs along the border between types (2) and (3) or boldly traverses the romantic region of (2). "'Kubla Khan,'" says Professor Lowes, "is the fabric of a vision, but every image that rose up in its weaving had passed that way before. And it would seem that there is nothing haphazard or fortuitous in their return." This is not quite clear—not even when Professor Lowes explains that there were clusters of associations, like hooked atoms, which were drawn into complex relation with other clusters in the deep well of Coleridge's memory, and which then coalesced and issued forth as poems. If there was nothing "haphazard or fortuitous" in the way the images returned to the surface, that may mean (1) that Coleridge could not produce what he did not have, that he was limited in his creation by what he had read or otherwise experienced, or (2) that having received certain clusters of associations, he was bound to return them in just the way he did, and that the value of the poem may be described in terms of the experiences on which he had to draw. The latter pair of propositions (a sort of Hartleyan associationism which Coleridge himself repudiated in the *Biographia*) may not be assented to. There were certainly other combinations, other poems, worse or better, that might have been written by men who had read Bartram and Purchas and Bruce and Milton. And this will be true no matter how many times we are able to add to the brilliant complex of Coleridge's reading. In certain flourishes (such as the sentence we have quoted) and in chapter headings like "The Shaping Spirit," "The Magical Synthesis," "Imagination Creatrix," it may be that Professor Lowes pretends to say more about the actual poems than he does. There is a certain deceptive variation in these fancy chapter titles; one expects to pass on to a new stage in the argument, and one finds—more and more sources, more about "the streamy nature of association."[15]

"Wohin der Weg?"[16] quotes Professor Lowes for the motto of his book. "Kein Weg! Ins Unbetrctene."[17] Precisely because the way is *unbetreten,* we should say, it leads away from the poem. Bartram's *Travels* contains a good deal of the history of certain words and romantic Floridan conceptions that appear in "Kubla Khan." And a good deal of that history has passed and was then passing into the very stuff of our language. Perhaps a person who has read Bartram appreciates the poem more than one who has not. Or, by looking up the vocabulary of "Kubla Khan" in the *Oxford English Dictionary,* or by reading some of the other books there quoted, a person may know the poem better. But it would seem to pertain little to the poem to know that *Coleridge* has read Bartram. There is a gross body of life, of sensory and mental experience, which lies behind and in some sense causes every poem, but can never be and need not be known in the verbal and hence intellectual composition which is the poem. For all the objects of our manifold experience, especially for the intellectual objects, for every unity, there is an action of the mind which cuts off roots, melts away context—or indeed we should never have objects or ideas or anything to talk about.

It is probable that there is nothing in Professor Lowes' vast book which could detract from anyone's appreciation of either *The Ancient Mariner* or *Kubla Khan*. We next present a case where preoccupation with evidence of type (3) has gone so far as to distort a critic's view of a poem (yet a case not so obvious as those that abound in our critical journals).

In a well-known poem by John Donne appears the following quatrain:

Moving of th' earth brings harmes and feares,
Men reckon what it did and meant,
But trepidation of the spheares,
Though greater farre, is innocent.

A recent critic in an elaborate treatment of Donne's learning has written of this quatrain as follows:

. . . he touches the emotional pulse of the situation by a skillful allusion to the new and the old astronomy. . . . Of the new astronomy, the "moving of the earth" is the most radical principle; of the old, the "trepidation of the spheres" is the motion of the greatest complexity. . . . As the poem is a valediction for-bidding mourning, the poet must exhort his love to quietness and calm upon his departure; and for this purpose the figure based upon the latter motion (trepidation), long absorbed into the traditional astronomy, fittingly suggests the tension of the moment without arousing the "harmes and feares" implicit in the figure of the moving earth.[18]

The argument is plausible and rests on a well-substantiated thesis that Donne was deeply interested in the new astronomy and its repercussions in the theological realm. In various works Donne shows his familiarity with Kepler's *De Stella Nova*, with Galileo's *Siderius Nuncius*, with William Gilbert's *De Magnete*, and with Clavius's commentary on the *De Sphaera* of Sacrobosco. He refers to the new science in his Sermon at Paul's Cross and in a letter to Sir Henry Goodyer. In *The First Anniversary* he says the "new philosophy calls all in doubt." In the *Elegy on Prince Henry* he says that the "least moving of the center" makes "the world to shake."

It is difficult to answer argument like this, and impossible to answer it with evidence of like nature. There is no reason why Donne might not have written a stanza in which the two kinds of celestial motion stood for two sorts of emotion at parting. And if we become full of astronomical ideas and see Donne only against the background of the new science, we may believe that he did. But the text itself remains to be dealt with, the analyzable vehicle of a complicated metaphor. And one may observe: (1) that the movement of the earth according to the Copernican theory is a celestial motion, smooth and regular, and while it might cause religious or philosophic fears, it could not be associated with the crudity and earthiness of the kind of commotion which the speaker in the poem wishes to discourage; (2) that there is another moving of the earth, an earthquake, which has just these qualities and is to be associated with the tear-floods and sigh-tempests of the second stanza of the poem; (3) that "trepidation" is an appropriate opposite of earthquake, because each is a shaking or vibratory motion; and "trepidation of the spheres" is "greater far" than an earth-quake, but not much greater (if two such motions can be compared as to greatness) than the annual motion of the earth; (4) that reckoning what it "did and meant" shows that the event has passed, like an earthquake, not like the incessant celestial movement of the earth. Perhaps a knowledge of Donne's interest in the new science may add another shade of meaning, an overtone to the stanza in question, though to say even this runs against the words. To make the geo-centric and helio-centric antithesis the core of the metaphor is to disregard the English language, to prefer private evidence to public, external to internal.

V

If the distinction between kinds of evidence has implications for the historical critic, it has them no less for the contemporary poet and his critic. Or, since every rule for a poet is but another side of a judgment by a critic, and since the past is the realm of the scholar and critic, and the future and present that of the poet and the critical leaders of taste, we may say that the problems arising in literary scholarship from the intentional fallacy are matched by others which arise in the world of progressive experiment.

The question of "allusiveness," for example, as acutely posed by the poetry of Eliot, is certainly one where a false judgment is likely to involve the intentional fallacy. The frequency and depth of literary allusion in the poetry of Eliot and others has driven so many in pursuit of full meanings to the *Golden Bough* and the Elizabethan drama that it has become a kind of commonplace to suppose that we do not know what a poet means unless we have traced him in his reading—a supposition redolent with intentional implications. The stand taken by Mr. F. O. Matthiessen is a sound one and partially forestalls the difficulty.

> If one reads these lines with an attentive ear and is sensitive to their sudden shifts in movement, the contrast between the actual Thames and the idealized vision of it during an age before it flowed through a megalopolis is sharply conveyed by that movement itself, whether or not one recognizes the refrain to be from Spenser.

Eliot's allusions work when we know them—and to a great extent even when we do not know them, through their suggestive power.

But sometimes we find allusions supported by notes, and it is a very nice question whether the notes function more as guides to send us where we may be educated, or more as indications in

(continued)

The Intentional Fallacy (*continued*)

themselves about the character of the allusions. "Nearly everything of importance . . . that is apposite to an appreciation of 'The Waste Land,'" writes Mr. Matthiessen of Miss Weston's book, "has been incorporated into the structure of the poem itself, or into Eliot's Notes." And with such an admission it may begin to appear that it would not much matter if Eliot invented his sources (as Sir Walter Scott invented chapter epigraphs from "old plays" and "anonymous" authors, or as Coleridge wrote marginal glosses for *The Ancient Mariner*). Allusions to Dante, Webster, Marvell, or Baudelaire, doubtless gain something because these writers existed, but it is doubtful whether the same can be said for an allusion to an obscure Elizabethan:

> The sound of horns and motors, which shall bring
> Sweeney to Mrs. Porter in the spring.

"Cf. Day, *Parliament of Bees*": says Eliot,

> When of a sudden, listening, you shall hear,
> A noise of horns and hunting, which shall bring
> Actaeon to Diana in the spring,
> Where all shall see her naked skin. . . .

The irony is completed by the quotation itself; had Eliot, as is quite, conceivable, composed these lines to furnish his own background, there would be no loss of validity. The conviction may grow as one reads Eliot's next note: "I do not know the origin of the ballad from which these lines are taken: it was reported to me from Sydney, Australia." The important word in this note—on Mrs. Porter and her daughter who washed their feet in soda water—is "ballad." And if one should feel from the lines themselves their "ballad" quality, there would be little need for the note. Ultimately, the inquiry must focus on the integrity of such notes as parts of the poem, for where they constitute special information about the meaning of phrases in the poem, they ought to be subject to the same scrutiny as any of the other words in which it is written. Mr. Matthiessen believes the notes were the price Eliot "had to pay in order to avoid what he would have considered muffling the energy of his poem by extended connecting links in the text itself." But it may be questioned whether the notes and the need for them are not equally muffling. The omission from poems of the explanatory stratum on which is built the dramatic or poetic stuff is a dangerous responsibility. Mr. F. W. Bateson has plausibly argued that Tennyson's "The Sailor Boy" would be better if half the stanzas were omitted, and the best versions of ballads like "Sir Patrick Spens" owe their power to the very audacity with which the minstrel has taken for granted the story upon which he comments. What then if a poet finds he cannot take so much for granted in a more recondite context and rather than write informatively, supplies notes? It can be said in favor of this plan that at least the notes do not pretend to be dramatic, as they would if written in verse. On the other hand, the notes may look like unassimilated material lying loose beside the poem, necessary for the meaning of the verbal symbol, but not integrated, so that the symbol stands incomplete.

We mean to suggest by the above analysis that whereas notes tend to seem to justify themselves as external indexes to the author's *intention,* yet they ought to be judged like any other parts of a composition (verbal arrangement special to a particular context), and when so judged their reality as parts of the poem, or their imaginative integration with the rest of the poem, may come into question. Mr. Matthiessen, for instance, sees that Eliot's titles for poems and his epigraphs are informative apparatus, like the notes. But while he is worried by some of the notes and thinks that Eliot "appears to be mocking himself for writing the note at the same time that he wants to convey something by it," Mr. Matthiessen believes that the "device" of epigraphs "is not at all open to the objection of not being sufficiently structural." "The *intention,*" he says, "is to enable the poet to secure a condensed expression in the poem itself." "In each case the epigraph is *designed* to form an integral part of the effect of the poem." And Eliot himself, in his notes, has justified his poetic practice in terms of intention.

> The Hanged Man, a member of the traditional pack, fits my purpose in two ways: because he is associated in my mind with the Hanged God of Frazer, and because I associate

him with the hooded figure in the passage of the disciples to Emmaus in Part V. . . . The man with Three Staves (an authentic member of the Tarot pack) I associate, quite arbitrarily, with the Fisher King himself.

And perhaps he is to be taken more seriously here, when off guard in a note, than when in his Norton Lectures he comments on the difficulty of saying what a poem means and adds playfully that he thinks of prefixing to a second edition of *Ash Wednesday* some lines from *Don Juan:*

> I don't pretend that I quite understand
> My own meaning when I would be *very* fine;
> But the fact is that I have nothing planned
> Unless it were to be a moment merry.

If Eliot and other contemporary poets have any characteristic fault, it may be in *planning* too much.[19]

Allusiveness in poetry is one of several critical issues by which we have illustrated the more abstract issue of intentionalism, but it may be for today the most important illustration. As a poetic practice allusiveness would appear to be in some recent poems an extreme corollary of the romantic intentionalist assumption, and as a critical issue it challenges and brings to light in a special way the basic premise of intentionalism. The following instance from the poetry of Eliot may serve to epitomize the practical implications of what we have been saying. In Eliot's "Love Song of J. Alfred Prufrock," towards the end, occurs the line: "I have heard the mermaids singing, each to each," and this bears a certain resemblance to a line in a Song by John Donne, "Teach me to heare Mermaides singing," so that for the reader acquainted to a certain degree with Donne's poetry, the critical question arises: Is Eliot's line an allusion to Donne's? Is Prufrock thinking about Donne? Is Eliot thinking about Donne? We suggest that there are two radically different ways of looking for an answer to this question. There is (1) the way of poetic analysis and exegesis, which inquires whether it makes any sense if Eliot-Prufrock *is* thinking about Donne. In an earlier part of the poem, when Prufrock asks, "Would it have been worth while, . . . To have squeezed the universe into a ball," his words take half their sadness and irony from certain energetic and passionate lines of Marvell "To His Coy Mistress." But the exegetical inquirer may wonder whether mermaids considered as "strange sights" (To hear them is in Donne's poem analogous to getting with child a mandrake root) have much to do with Prufrock's mermaids, which seem to be symbols of romance and dynamism, and which incidentally have literary authentication, if they need it, in a line of a sonnet by Gérard de Nerval. This method of inquiry may lead to the conclusion that the given resemblance between Eliot and Donne is without significance and is better not thought of, or the method may have the disadvantage of providing no certain conclusion. Nevertheless, we submit that this is the true and objective way of criticism, as contrasted to what the very uncertainty of exegesis might tempt a second kind of critic to undertake: (2) the way of biographical or genetic inquiry, in which, taking advantage of the fact that Eliot is still alive, and in the spirit of a man who would settle a bet, the critic writes to Eliot and asks what he meant, or if he had Donne in mind. We shall not here weigh the probabilities—whether Eliot would answer that he meant nothing at all, had nothing at all in mind—a sufficiently good answer to such a question—or in an unguarded moment might furnish a clear and, within its limit, irrefutable answer. Our point is that such an answer to such an inquiry would have nothing to do with the poem "Prufrock"; it would not be a critical inquiry. Critical inquiries, unlike bets, are not settled in this way. Critical inquiries are not settled by consulting the oracle.

NOTES

1. Cf. Louis Teeter, "Scholarship, and the Art of Criticism," *ELH,* V (Sept. 1938), pp. 173–94; René Wellek, review of Geoffrey Tillotson's *Essays in Criticism and Research, Modern Philology,* XLI (May, 1944), p. 262; G. Wilson Knight, *Shakespeare and Tolstoy,* English Association Pamphlet No. 88 (April 1934), p. 10; Bernard C. Heyl, *New Bearings in Esthetics and Art Criticism* (New Haven, 1943), pp. 66, 113, 149.
2. *Dictionary of World Literature,* ed. Joseph T. Shipley (New York, 1942), pp. 326–339.

(continued)

The Intentional Fallacy (*continued*)

(Oct. 1943). Authors often judge their own works in the same way. See *This is My Best*, ed. Whit Burnett (New York, 1942), for example, pp. 539–540.

3. J. E. Spingarn, "The New Criticism," in *Criticism and America* (New York, 1924), pp. 24–25.
4. As critics and teachers constantly do. "We have here a deliberate blurring. . . ." "Should this be regarded as ironic or as unplanned?" ". . . is the literal meaning intended . . .?" ". . . a paradox of religious faith which is intended to exult. . . ." "It seems to me that Herbert intends. . . ." These examples are chosen from three pages of an issue of *The Explicator* (Fredericksburg, Va.) vol. II, no. 1
5. A close relative of the intentional fallacy is that of talking about "means" and "end" in poetry instead of "part" and "whole." We have treated this relation concisely in our dictionary article.
6. F. E. Stoll, "The Tempest," *PMLA*, XLIV (Sept. 1932), p. 703.
7. Ananda K. Coomaraswamy, "Intention," *The American Bookman*, I (Winter, 1944), pp. 41–48.
8. For the relation of Longinus to modern romanticism, see R. S. Crane, review of Samuel Monk's *The Sublime*, *Philological Quarterly*, XV (April, 1936), pp. 165–66.
9. It is true that Croce himself in his *Ariosto, Shakespeare and Corneille*, trans. Douglas Ainslie (London, 1920) Chapter VII, "The Practical Personality and the Poetical Personality," and in his *Defence of Poetry*, trans. E. F. Carritt (Oxford, 1933), p. 24, has delivered a telling attack on intentionalism, but the prevailing drift of such passages in the *Aesthetic* as we quote is in the opposite direction.
10. [If you wish me to weep.—HORACE *De Arte Poetica*.]
11. [Absolute truth.]
12. See Hughes Mearns, *Creative Youth* (Garden City, 1925) esp. pp. 10, 27–29. The technique of inspiring poems keeps pace today with a parallel analysis of the process of inspiration in successful artists. See Rosamond E. M. Harding, *An Anatomy of Inspiration*, Cambridge, 1940; Julius Portnoy, *A Psychology of Art Creation*, Philadelphia, 1942.
13. Curt Ducasse, *The Philosophy of Art* (New York, 1929), p. 116.
14. And the history of words after a poem is written may contribute meanings which if relevant to the original pattern should not be ruled out by a scruple about intention. Cf. C. S. Lewis and E. M. W. Tillyard, *The Personal Heresy* (Oxford, 1939), p. 16; Teeter, *loc. cit.*, pp. 183, 192; review of Tillotson's *Essays*, TLS, XLI (April, 1942), 174.
15. Chapters VIII, "The Pattern," and XVI, "The Known and Familiar Landscape," will be found of most help to the student of the poem.
    For an extreme example of intentionalistic criticism, see Kenneth Burke's analysis of *The Ancient Mariner* in *The Philosophy of Literary Form* (Louisiana State University Press, 1941), pp. 22–23, 93–102. Mr. Burke must be credited "with realizing very clearly what he is up to.
16. [Where does the path go?.]
17. [No path into the unknown (untrod).]
18. Charles M. Coffin, *John Donne and the New Philosophy* (New York, 1927), pp. 97–98.
19. In his critical writings Eliot has expressed the right view of author psychology (See *The Use of Poetry and the Use of Criticism*, Cambridge, 1933, p. 139 and "Tradition and the Individual Talent" in *Selected Essays*, New York, 1932), though his record is not entirely consistent (See *A Choice of Kipling's Verse*, London, 1941, pp. 10–11, 20–21).

In Defense of the Author

E. D. Hirsch, Jr.

I

IT IS A TASK FOR the historian of culture to explain why there has been in the past four decades a heavy and largely victorious assault on the sensible belief that a text means what its author meant. In the earliest and most decisive wave of the attack (launched by Eliot, Pound, and their associates) the battleground was literary: the proposition that textual meaning is independent of the author's control was associated with the literary doctrine that the best poetry is impersonal, objective, and autonomous; that it leads an afterlife of its own, totally cut off from the life of its author.[1] This programmatic notion of what poetry should be became subtly identified with a notion of what all poetry and indeed all forms of literature necessarily must be. It was not simply desirable that literature should detach itself from the subjective realm of the author's personal thoughts and feelings; it was, rather, an indubitable fact that all written language remains independent of that subjective realm. At a slightly later period, and for different reasons, this same notion of semantic autonomy was advanced by Heidegger and his followers.[2] The idea also has been advocated by writers who believe with Jung that individual expressions may quite unwittingly express archetypal, communal meanings. In some branches of linguistics, particularly in so-called information theory, the semantic autonomy of language has been a working assumption. The theory has found another home in the work of non-Jungians who have interested themselves (as Eliot did earlier) in symbolism, though Cassirer, whose name is sometimes invoked by such writers, did not believe in the semantic autonomy of language.[3] As I said, it is the job of the cultural historian to explain why this doctrine should have gained currency in recent times, but it is the theorist's job to determine how far the theory of semantic autonomy deserves acceptance.

Literary scholars have often contended that the theory of authorial irrelevance was entirely beneficial to literary criticism and scholarship because it shifted the focus of discussion from the author to his work. Made confident by the theory, the modern critic has faithfully and closely examined the text to ferret out its independent meaning instead of its supposed significance to the author's life. That this shift toward exegesis has been desirable most critics would agree, whether or not they adhere to the theory of semantic autonomy. But the theory accompanied the exegetical movement for historical not logical reasons, since no logical necessity compels a critic to banish an author in order to analyze his text. Nevertheless, through its historical association with close exegesis, the theory has liberated much subtlety and intelligence. Unfortunately, it has also frequently encouraged willful arbitrariness and extravagance in academic criticism and has been one very important cause of the prevailing skepticism which calls into doubt the possibility of objectively valid interpretation. These disadvantages would be tolerable, of course, if the theory were true. In intellectual affairs skepticism is preferable to illusion.

The disadvantages of the theory could not have been easily predicted in the exciting days when the old order of academic criticism was being overthrown. At that time such naivetés as the positivistic biases of literary history, the casting about for influences and other causal patterns, and the post-romantic fascination with the habits, feelings, and experiences surrounding the act of composition were very justly brought under attack. It became increasingly obvious that the theoretical foundations of the old criticism were weak and inadequate. It cannot be said, therefore, that the theory of authorial irrelevance was inferior to the theories or quasi-theories it replaced, nor can it be doubted that the immediate effect of banishing the author was wholly-beneficial and invigorating. Now, at a distance of several decades, the difficulties that attend the theory of semantic autonomy have clearly emerged and are responsible for that uneasiness which persists in the academies, although the theory has long been victorious.

That this state of academic skepticism and disarray results largely from the theory of authorial irrelevance is, I think, a fact of our recent intellectual history. For, once the author had been ruthlessly banished as the determiner of his text's meaning, it very gradually appeared that no adequate principle existed for judging the validity of an interpretation. By an inner necessity the study of "what a text says" became the study of what it says to an individual critic. It became fashionable to talk about a critic's "reading" of a text, and this word began to appear in the titles of scholarly works. The word seemed to imply that if the author had been banished, the critic still remained, and his new, original, urbane, ingenious, or relevant "reading" carried its own interest.

What had not been noticed in the earliest enthusiasm for going back to "what the text says" was that the text had to represent *somebody's* meaning—if not the author's, then the critic's. It is true that a theory was erected under which the meaning of the text was equated with everything it could plausibly be taken to mean. (I have described in Appendix I the fallacies of this and other descriptions of meaning that were contrived to escape the difficulties of authorial irrelevance.)[4] The theory of semantic autonomy forced itself into such unsatisfactory, ad hoc formulations because in its zeal to banish the author it ignored the fact that meaning is an affair of consciousness not of words. Almost any word sequence can, under the conventions of language, legitimately represent more than one complex of meaning.[5] A word sequence means nothing in particular until somebody

(continued)

In Defense of the Author (*continued*)

either means something by it or understands something from it. There is no magic land of meanings outside human consciousness. Whenever meaning is connected to words, a person is making the connection, and the particular meanings he lends to them are never the only legitimate ones under the norms and conventions of his language.

One proof that the conventions of language can sponsor different meanings from the same sequence of words resides in the fact that interpreters can and do disagree. When these disagreements occur, how are they to be resolved? Under the theory of semantic autonomy they cannot be resolved, since the meaning is not what the author meant, but "what the poem means to different sensitive reader."[6] One interpretation is as valid as another, so long as it is "sensitive" or "plausible" Yet the teacher of literature who adheres to Eliot's theory is also by profession the preserver of a heritage and the conveyor of knowledge. On what ground does he claim that his "reading" is more valid than that of any pupil? On no very firm ground. This impasse is a principle cause of the loss of bearings sometimes felt though not often confessed by academic critics.

One ad hoc theory that has been advanced to circumvent this chaotic democracy of "readings" deserves special mention here because it involves the problem of value, a problem that preoccupies some modern literary theorists. The most valid reading of a text is the "best" reading.[7] But even if we assumed that a critic did have access to the divine criteria by which he could determine the best reading, he would still be left with two equally compelling normative ideals—the best meaning and the author's meaning. Moreover, if the best meaning were not the author's, then it would have to be the critic's—in which case the critic would be the author of the best meaning. Whenever meaning is attached to a sequence of words it is impossible to escape an author.

Thus, when critics deliberately banished the original author, they themselves usurped his place, and this led unerringly to some of our present-day theoretical confusions. Where before there had been but one author, there now arose a multiplicity of them, each carrying as much authority as the next. To banish the original author as the determiner of meaning was to reject the only compelling normative principle that could lend validity to an interpretation. On the other hand, it might be the case that there does not really exist a viable normative ideal that governs the interpretation of texts. This would follow if any of the various arguments brought against the author were to hold. For if the meaning of a text is not the author's, then no interpretation can possibly correspond to *the* meaning of the text, since the text can have no determinate or determinable meaning. My demonstration of this point will be found [in the following section].

II

Reproducibility is a quality of verbal meaning that makes interpretation possible: if meaning were not reproducible, it could not be actualized by someone else and therefore could not be understood or interpreted. Determinacy, on the other hand, is a quality of meaning required in order that there *be* something to reproduce. Determinacy is a necessary attribute of any sharable meaning, since an indeterminacy cannot be shared: if a meaning were indeterminate, it would have no boundaries, no self-identity, and therefore could have no identity with a meaning entertained by someone else. But determinacy does not mean definiteness or precision. Undoubtedly, most verbal meanings are imprecise and ambiguous, and to call them such is to acknowledge their determinacy: they are what they are—namely, ambiguous and imprecise—and they are not univocal and precise. This is another way of saying that an ambiguous meaning has a boundary like any other verbal meaning, and that one of the frontiers on this boundary is that between ambiguity and univocality. Some parts of the boundary might, of course, be thick; that is, there might at some points be a good many submeanings that belonged equally to the meaning and not to it—borderline meanings. However, such ambiguities would, on another level, simply serve to define the character of the meaning so that any overly imprecise construing of it would constitute a misunderstanding. Determinacy, then, first of all means self-identity. This is the minimum requirement for sharability. Without it neither communication nor validity in interpretation would be possible.

But by determinacy I also mean something more. Verbal meaning would be determinate in one sense even if it were merely a locus of possibilities—as some theorists have considered it. However, this is a kind of determinacy that cannot be shared in any act of understanding or interpretation. An array of *possible* meanings is no doubt a determinate entity in the sense that it is not an array of *actual* meanings; thus it too has a boundary. But the human mind cannot entertain a possible meaning; as soon as the meaning is entertained it is actual. "In that case, then," the proponent of such a view might argue, "let us consider the text to represent and array of different, *actual* meanings, corresponding to different actual interpretations." But this escape from the frying pan leads right into the amorphous fire of indeterminacy. Such a conception really denies the self-identity of verbal meaning by suggesting that the meaning of the text can be one thing and also another, different thing, and also another; and this conception (which has nothing to do with the ambiguity of meaning) is simply a denial that the text means anything in particular. I have already shown that such an indeterminate meaning is not sharable. Whatever it may be, it is not verbal meaning nor anything that could be validly interpreted.

"Then," says the advocate of rich variousness, "let us be more precise. What I really mean is that verbal meaning is historical or temporal. It is something in particular for a span of time, but it is something different in a different period of time." Certainly the proponent of such a view cannot be reproached with the accusation that he makes verbal meaning indeterminate. On the contrary, he insists on the self-identity of meaning at any moment of time. But this remarkable, quantum-leap theory of meaning has no foundation in the nature of linguistic acts not does it provide any criterion of validity in interpretation. If a meaning can change its identity and in fact does, then we have no norm for judging whether we are encountering the real meaning in a changed form or some spurious meaning that is pretending to be the one we seek. Once it is admitted that a meaning can change its characteristics, then there is no way of finding the true Cinderella among all the contenders. There is no dependable glass slipper we can use as a test, since the old slipper will no longer fit the new Cinderella. To the interpreter this lack of a stable normative principle is equivalent to the indeterminacy of meaning. As far as his interests go, the meaning could have been defined as indeterminate from the start, and his predicament would have been precisely the same.

When, therefore, I say that a verbal meaning is determinate, I mean that it is an entity which is self-identical. Furthermore, I also mean that it is an entity which always remains the same from one moment to the next—that it is changeless. Indeed, these criteria were already implied in the requirement that verbal meaning be reproducible, that it be always the same in different acts of construing. Verbal meaning, then, is what it is and not something else, and it is always the same. That is what I mean by determinacy.

A determinate verbal meaning requires a determining will. Meaning is not made determinate simply by virtue of its being represented by a determinate sequence of words. Obviously, any brief word sequence could represent quite different complexes of verbal meaning, and the same is true of long word sequences, though it is less obvious. If that were not so, competent and intelligent speakers of a language would not disagree as they do about the meaning of texts. But if a determinate word sequence does not in itself necessarily represent one, particular, self-identical, unchanging complex of meaning, then the determinacy of its verbal meaning must be accounted for by some other discriminating force which causes the meaning to be *this* instead of *that* or *that* or *that*, all of which it could be. That discriminating force must involve an act of will, since unless one particular complex of *meaning* is willed (no matter how "rich" and "various" it might be), there would be no distinction between what an author does mean by a word sequence and what he could mean by it. Determinacy of verbal meaning requires an act of will.

It is sometimes said that "meaning is determined by context," but this is a very loose way of speaking. It is true that the surrounding text or the situation in which a problematical word sequence is found tends to narrow the meaning probabilities for that particular word sequence; otherwise, interpretation would be hopeless. And it is a measure of stylistic excellence in an author that he should have managed to formulate a decisive context for any particular word sequence within his text. But this is certainly not to say that context determines verbal meaning. At best a context determines the guess of an interpreter (though his construction of the context may be wrong, and his guess correspondingly so). To speak of context as a determinant is to confuse an exigency of interpretation with an author's determining acts. An author's verbal meaning is limited

(continued)

In Defense of the Author (continued)

by linguistic possibilities but is determined by his actualizing and specifying some of those possibilities. Correspondingly, the verbal meaning that an interpreter construes is determined by *his* act of will, limited by those same possibilities. The fact that a particular context has led the interpreter to a particular choice does not change the fact that the determination is a choice, even when it is unthinking and automatic. Furthermore, a context is something that has itself been determined—first by an author and then, through a construction, by an interpreter. It is not something that is simply there without anybody having to make any determinations . . .

III

I [have] defined textual meaning as the verbal intention of the author, and this argues implicitly that hermeneutics must stress a reconstruction of the author's aims and attitudes in order to evolve guides and norms for constructing the meaning of his text. It is frequently argued, however, that textual meaning has nothing to do with the author's mind but only with his verbal achievement, that the object of interpretation is not the author but his text. This plausible argument assumes, of course, that the text automatically has a meaning simply because it represents an unalterable sequence of words. It assumes that the meaning of a word sequence is directly imposed by the public norms of language, that the text as a "piece of language" is a public object whose character is defined by public norms.[8] This view is in one respect sound, since textual meaning must conform to public norms if it is in any sense to be verbal (i.e., sharable) meaning; on no account may the interpreter permit his probing into the author's mind to raise private associations (experience) to the level of public implications (content).

However, this basically sound argument remains one-sided, for even though verbal meaning must confirm to public linguistic norms (these are highly tolerant, of course), no mere sequence of words can represent an actual verbal meaning with reference to public norms alone. Referred to these alone, the text's meaning remains indeterminate. This is true even of the simplest declarative sentence like "My car ran out of gas" (did my Pullman dash from a cloud of Argon?). The fact that no one would radically misinterpret such a sentence simply indicates that its frequency is high enough to give its usual meaning the apparent status of an immediate given. But this apparent immediacy obscures a complex process of adjudications among meaning possibilities. Under the public norms of language alone no such adjudications can occur, since the array of possibilities presents a face of blank indifference. The array of possibilities only begins to become a more selective system of *probabilities* when, instead of confronting merely a word sequence, we also posit a speaker who very likely means something. Then and only then does the most usual sense of the word sequence become the most probable or "obvious" sense. The point holds true a fortiori, of course, when we confront less obvious word sequences like those found in poetry. A careful exposition of this point may be found in the first volume of *Cassirer's Philosophy of Symbolic Forms*, which is largely devoted to a demonstration that verbal meaning arises from the "reciprocal determination" of public linguistic possibilities and subjective specifications of those possibilities.[9] Just as language constitutes and colors subjectivity, so does subjectivity color language. The author's or speaker's subjective act is formally necessary to verbal meaning, and any theory which tries to dispense with the author as specifier of meaning by asserting that textual meaning is purely objectively determined finds itself chasing will-o'-the-wisps. The burden of this section is, then, an attack on the view that a text is a "piece of language" and a defense of the notion that a text represents the determinate verbal meaning of an author.

One of the consequences arising from the view that a text is a piece of language—a purely public object—is the impossibility of defining in principle the nature of a correct interpretation. This is the same impasse which results from the theory that a text leads a life of its own, and, indeed, the two notions are corollaries, since any "piece of language" must have a changing meaning when the changing public norms of language are viewed as the only ones which determine the sense of the text. It is therefore not surprising to find that Wellek subscribes implicitly to the text-as-language theory. The text is viewed as representing not a determinate meaning, but rather a system of meaning potentials specified not by a meaner but by the vital potency of language itself. Wellek acutely perceives the danger of the view:

Thus the system of norms is growing and changing and will remain, in some sense, always incompletely and imperfectly realized. But this dynamic conception does not mean mere subjectivism and relativism. All the different points of view are by no means equally right. It will always be possible to determine which point of view grasps the subject most thoroughly and deeply. A hierarchy of viewpoints, a criticism of the grasp of norms, is implied in the concept of the adequacy of interpretation.[10]

The danger of the view is, of course, precisely that it opens the door to subjectivism and relativism, since linguistic norms may be invoked to support any verbally possible meaning. Furthermore, it is not clear how one may criticize a grasp of norms which will not stand still.

Wellek's brief comment on the problem involved in defining and testing correctness in interpretation is representative of a widespread conviction among literary critics that the most correct interpretation is the most "inclusive" one. Indeed, the view is so widely accepted that Wellek did not need to defend his version of it (which he calls "Perspectivism") at length. The notion behind the theory is reflected by such phrases as "always incompletely and imperfectly realized" and "grasps the subject most thoroughly." This notion is simply that no single interpretation can exhaust the rich system of meaning potentialities represented by the text. Hence, every plausible reading which remains within public linguistic norms is a correct reading so far as it goes, but each reading is inevitably partial since it cannot realize all the potentialities of the text. The guiding principle in criticism, therefore, is that of the inclusive interpretation. The most "adequate" construction is the one which gives the fullest coherent account of all the text's potential meanings."

Inclusivism is desirable as a position which induces a readiness to consider the results of others, but, aside from promoting an estimable tolerance, it has little theoretical value. Although its aim is to reconcile different plausible readings in an ideal, comprehensive interpretation, it cannot, in fact, either reconcile different readings or choose between them. As a normative ideal, or principle of correctness, it is useless. This point any be illustrated by citing two expert readings of a well-known poem by Wordsworth. I shall first quote the poem and then quote excerpts from two published exegeses to demonstrate the kind of impasses which inclusivism always provokes when it attempts to reconcile interpretations and, incidentally, to demonstrate the very kind of interpretive problem which calls for a guiding principle.[11]

> A slumber did my spirit seal;
> I had no human fears.
> She seemed a thing that could not feel
>   The touch of earthly years.
> No motion has she now, no force;
>   She neither hears nor sees,
> Rolled round in earth's diurnal course
> With rocks, and stones, and trees.

Here are excerpts from two commentaries on the final lines of the poem; the first is by Cleanth Brooks, the second by F. W. Bateson.

> [The poet] attempts to suggest something of the lover's agonized shock at the loved one's present lack of motion—of his response to her utter and horrible inertness. . . . Part of the effect, of course, resides in the fact that a dead lifelessness is suggested more sharply by an object's being whirled about by something else than by an image of the object in repose. But there are other matters which are at work here: the sense of the girl's falling back into the clutter of things, companioned by things chained like a tree to one particular spot, or by things completely inanimate like rocks and stones. . . . [She] is caught up helplessly into the empty whirl of the earth which measures and makes time. She is touched by and held by earthly time in its most powerful and horrible image.
>
> The final impression the poem leaves is not of two contrasting moods, but of a single mood mounting to a climax in the pantheistic magnificence of the last two lines. . . . The vague living-Lucy of this poem is opposed to the grander dead-Lucy who has become

(continued)

In Defense of the Author   (continued)

involved in the sublime processes of nature. We put the poem down satisfied, because its last two lines succeed in effecting a reconciliation between the two philosophies or social attitudes. Lucy is actually more alive now that she is dead, because she is now a part of the life of Nature and not just a human "thing."[12]

If we grant, as I think we must, that both the cited interpretations are permitted by the text, the problem for the inclusivist is to reconcile the two readings.

Three modes of reconciliation are available to the inclusivist:

1. Brooks's reading includes Bateson's; it shows that any affirmative suggestions in the poem are negated by the bitterly ironical portrayal of the inert girl being whirled around by what Bateson calls the "sublime processes of Nature."
2. Bateson's reading includes Brooks's; the ironic contrast between the active, seemingly immortal girl and the passive, inert, dead girl is overcome by a final unqualified affirmation of immortality.
3. Each of the readings is partially right, but they must be fused to supplement one another.

The very fact that the critics differ suggests that the meaning is essentially ambiguous. The emotion expressed is ambivalent and comprises both bitter regret and affirmation. The third mode of reconciliation is the one most often employed and is probably, in this case, the most satisfactory. A fourth type of resolution, which would insist that Brooks is right and Bateson wrong (or vice versa), is not available to the inclusivist, since the text, as language, renders both readings plausible.

Close examination, however, reveals that none of the three modes of argument manages to reconcile or fuse the two different readings. Mode I, for example, insists that Brooks's reading comprehends Bateson's, but although it is conceivable that Brooks implies all the meanings which Bateson has perceived, Brooks also implies a pattern of emphasis which cannot be reconciled with Bateson's reading. While Bateson construes a primary emphasis on life and affirmation, Brooks emphasizes deadness and inertness. No amount of manipulation can reconcile these divergent emphases, since one pattern of emphasis irrevocably excludes other patterns, and, since emphasis is always crucial to meaning, die two constructions of meaning rigorously exclude one another. Precisely the same strictures hold, of course, for the argument that Bateson's reading comprehends that of Brooks. I escape with impunity. Although it seems to preserve a stress both on negation and on affirmation, thereby coalescing the two readings, it actually excludes both readings and labels them not simply partial, but wrong. For if the poem gives equal stress to bitter irony and to affirmation, then any construction which places a primary stress on either meaning is simply incorrect.

The general principle implied by my analysis is very simple. The submeanings of a text are not blocks which can be brought together additively. Since verbal (and any other) meaning is a *structure* of component meanings, interpretation has not done its job when it simply enumerates what the component meanings are. The interpreter must also determine their probable structure and particularly their structure of emphases. Relative emphasis is not only crucial to meaning (perhaps it is the most crucial and problematical element of all), it is also highly restrictive; it excludes alternatives. It may be asserted as a general rule that whenever a reader confronts two interpretations which impose different emphases on similar meaning components, at least one of the interpretations must be wrong. They cannot be reconciled.

By insisting that verbal meaning always exhibits a determinate structure of emphases, I do not, however, imply that a poem or any other text must be unambiguous. It is perfectly possible, for example, that Wordsworth's poem ambiguously implies both bitter irony and positive affirmation. Such complex emotions are commonly expressed in poetry, but if that is the kind of meaning the text represents, Brooks and Bateson would be wrong to emphasize one emotion at the expense of the other. Ambiguity or, for that matter, vagueness is not the same as indeterminateness. This is the crux of the issue. To say that verbal meaning is determinate is not to exclude complexities of meaning but only to insist that a text's meaning is what it is and not a hundred other things. Taken in this sense, a vague or ambiguous text is just as determinate as a logical proposition; it means what it means and nothing else. This is true even if one argues that a text could display shifting emphases like those magic squares which first seem to jut out and then to jut in. With texts of this character (if any exist), one need only say that the emphases shift and must not, therefore, be construed statically. Any static construction would simply be wrong. The fundamental flaw in the "theory of the most inclusive interpretation" is that it overlooks the problem of emphasis. Since different patterns of emphasis exclude one another, inclusivism is neither a genuine norm nor an adequate guiding principle for establishing an interpretation.

NOTES

1. The classic statement is in T.S. Eliot, "Tradition and the Individual Talent," Selected *Essays* (New York: Harcourt, Brace, 1932).
2. See, for example, Martin Heidegger, *Unterwegs zur Sprache* (Pfullingen: Neske, 1959).
3. See Ernst Cassirer, *The Philosophy of Symbolic Forms*; vol. 1, *Language*, trans. Ralph Manheim (New Haven: Yale University Press, 1953), particularly pp. 69, 178. 213, 249–50, and passim.
4. [Part of this appendix is included as the final section of this chapter—Ed.]
5. The random example that I use later in the book is the sentence "I am going to town today." Different sense can be lent to the sentence by the simple device of placing a strong emphasis on any of the six different words.
6. The phrase is from T.S. Eliot, *On Poetry and Poets* (New York: Farrar, Strauss and Cudahy, 1957), p. 126.
7. It would be invidious to name any individual critic as the begetter of this widespread and imprecise notion. By the "best" reading, of course, some critics mean the most valid reading, but the idea of bestness is widely used to embrace indiscriminately both the idea of validity and of such aesthetic values as richness, inclusiveness, tension, or complexity—as though validity and aesthetic excellence must somehow be identical.
8. The phrase "piece of language" comes from the first paragraph of William Empson's *Seven Types of Ambiguity* (New York: Meridian, 1955). It is typical of the critical school Empson founded.
9. Cassirer, *Philosophy of Symbolic Forms*, vol. I, Language. It is ironic that Cassirer's work should be used to support the notion that a text speaks for itself. The realm of language is autonomous for Cassirer only in the sense that it follows an independent development which is reciprocally determined by objective and subjective factors. See pp. 69, 178, 213, 249–50, and passim.
10. Rene Wellek and Austin Warren, *Theory of Literature* (New York: Harcourt, Brace, 1956). p. 144.
11. Every interpretation is necessarily incomplete in the sense that it fails to explicate all a text's implications. But this kind of incomplete interpretation may still carry in absolutely correct system of emphases and an accurate sense of the whole meaning. This kind of incompleteness is radically different from that postulated by the inclusivists, for whom a sense of the whole means a grasp of the various possible meanings on which a text can plausibly represent.
12. Cleanth Brooks, "Irony as a Principle of Structure," in *Literary Opinion in America*, ed. M. D. Zabel, 2d ed (New York: Harper, 1951), p. 736; F. W. Pateson, *English Poetry A Critical Introduction* (London: Longmans, Green 1950). PP. 33, 80, 8.

Art and Authenticity

Nelson Goodman

. . . the most tantalizing question of all: If a fake is so expert that even after the most thorough and trustworthy examination its authenticity is still open to doubt, is it or is it not as satisfactory a work of art as if it were unequivocally genuine?

Aline B. Saarinen

1. The Perfect Fake

Forgeries of works of art present a nasty practical problem to the collector, the curator, and the art historian, who must often expend taxing amounts of time and energy in determining whether or not particular objects are genuine. But the theoretical problem raised is even more acute. The hard-headed question why there is any aesthetic difference between a deceptive forgery and an original work challenges a basic premiss on which the very functions of collector, museum, and art historian depend. A philosopher of art caught without an answer to this question is at least as badly off as a curator of paintings caught taking a Van Meegeren for a Vermeer.

(continued)

Art and Authenticity *(continued)*

The question is most strikingly illustrated by the case of a given work and a forgery or copy or reproduction of it. Suppose we have before us, on the left, Rembrandt's original painting *Lucretia* and, on the right, a superlative imitation of it. We know from a fully documented history that the painting on the left is the original; and we know from X-ray photographs and microscopic examination and chemical analysis that the painting on the right is a recent fake. Although there are many differences between the two—e.g., in authorship, age, physical and chemical characteristics, and market value—we cannot see any difference between them; and if they are moved while we sleep, we cannot then tell which is which by merely looking at them. Now we are pressed with the question whether there can be any aesthetic difference between the two pictures; and the questioner's tone often intimates that the answer is plainly *no,* that the only differences here are aesthetically irrelevant.

We must begin by inquiring whether the distinction between what can and what cannot be seen in the pictures by 'merely looking at them' is entirely clear. We are looking at the pictures, but presumably not 'merely looking' at them, when we examine them under a microscope or fluoroscope. Does merely looking, then, mean looking without the use of any instrument? This seems a little unfair to the man who needs glasses to tell a painting from a hippopotamus. But if glasses are permitted at all, how strong may they be, and can we consistently exclude the magnifying glass and the microscope? Again, if incandescent light is permitted, can violet-ray light be ruled out? And even with incandescent light, must it be of medium intensity and from a normal angle, or is a strong raking light permitted? All these cases might be covered by saying that 'merely looking' is looking at the pictures without any use of instruments other than those customarily used in looking at things in general. This will cause trouble when we turn, say, to certain miniature illuminations or Assyrian cylinder seals that we can hardly distinguish from the crudest copies without using a strong glass. Furthermore, even in our case of the two pictures, subtle differences of drawing or painting discoverable only with a magnifying glass may still, quite obviously, be aesthetic differences between the pictures. If a powerful microscope is used instead, this is no longer the case; but just how much magnification is permitted? To specify what is meant by merely looking at the pictures is thus far from easy; but for the sake of argummt,[1] let us suppose that all these difficulties have been resolved and the notion of 'merely looking' made clear enough.

Then we must ask who is assumed to be doing the looking. Our questioner does not, I take it, mean to suggest that there is no aesthetic difference between two pictures if at least one person, say a cross-eyed wrestler, can see no difference. The more pertinent question is whether there can be any aesthetic difference if nobody, not even the most skilled expert, can ever tell the pictures apart by merely looking at them. But notice now that no one can ever *ascertain by merely looking at the pictures that no one ever has been or will be able to tell them apart by merely looking at them.* In other words, the question in its present form concedes that no one can ascertain by merely looking at the pictures that there is no aesthetic difference between them. This seems repugnant to our questioner's whole motivation. For if merely looking can never establish that two pictures are aesthetically the same, something that is beyond the reach of any given looking is admitted as constituting an aesthetic difference. And in that case, the reason for not admitting documents and the results of scientific tests becomes very obscure.

The real issue may be more accurately formulated as the question whether there is any aesthetic difference between the two pictures *for me* (or for x) if I (or x) cannot tell them apart by merely looking at them. But this is not quite right either. For I can never ascertain merely by looking at the pictures that even I shall never be able to see any difference between them. And to concede that something beyond any given looking at the pictures by me may constitute an aesthetic difference between them *for me* is, again, quite at odds with the tacit conviction or suspicion that activates the questioner.

Thus the critical question amounts finally to this: is there any aesthetic difference between the two pictures for *x* at *t*, where *t* is a suitable period of time, if *x* cannot tell them apart by merely looking at them at *t*? Or in other words, can anything that *x* does not discern by merely looking at the pictures at *t* constitute an aesthetic difference between them for *x* at *t*?

2. The Answer

In setting out to answer this question, we must bear clearly in mind that what one can distinguish at any given moment by merely looking depends not only upon native visual acuity but upon practice end training.[2] Americans look pretty much alike to a Chinese who has never looked at many of them. Twins may be indistinguishable to all but their closest relatives and acquaintances. Moreover, only through looking at them when someone has named them for us can we learn to tell Joe from Jim upon merely looking at them. Looking at people or things attentively, with the knowledge of certain presently invisible respects in which they differ, increases our ability to discriminate between them—and between other things or other people—upon merely looking at them. Thus pictures that look just alike to the newsboy come to look quite unlike to him by the time he has become a museum director.

Although I see no difference now between the two pictures in question, I may learn to see a difference between them. I cannot determine now by merely looking at them, or in any other way, that I *shall* be able to learn. But the information that they are very different, that the one is the original and the other the forgery, argues against any inference to the conclusion that I *shall not* be able to learn. And the fact that I may later be able to make a perceptual distinction between the pictures that I cannot make now constitutes an aesthetic difference between them that is important to me now.

Furthermore, to look at the pictures now with the knowledge that the left one is the original and the other the forgery may help develop the ability to tell which is which later by merely looking at them. Thus, with information not derived from the present or any past looking at the pictures, the present looking may have a quite different bearing upon future lookings from what it would otherwise have. The way the pictures in fact differ constitutes an aesthetic difference between them for me now because my knowledge of the way they differ bears upon the role of the present looking in training my perceptions to discriminate between these pictures, and between others.

But that is not all. My knowledge of the difference between the two pictures, just because it affects the relationship of the present to future lookings, informs the very character of my present looking. This knowledge instructs me to look at the two pictures differently now, even if what I see is the same. Beyond testifying that I may learn to see a difference, it also indicates to some extent the kind of scrutiny to be applied now, the comparisons and contrasts to be made in imagination, and the relevant associations to be brought to bear. It thereby guides the selection, from my past experience, of items and aspects for use in my present looking. Thus not only later but right now, the unperceived difference between the two pictures is a consideration pertinent to my visual experience with them.

In short, although I cannot tell the pictures apart merely by looking at them now, the fact that the left-hand one is the original and the right-hand one a forge my constitutes an aesthetic difference between them for me now because knowledge of this fact (1) stands as evidence that there may be a difference between them that I can learn to perceive, (2) assigns the present looking a role as training toward such a perceptual discrimination, and (3) makes consequent demands that modify and differentiate my present experience in looking at the two pictures.[3]

Nothing depends here upon my ever actually perceiving or being able to perceive a difference between the two pictures. What informs the nature and use of my present visual experience is not the fact or the assurance that such a perceptual discrimination is within my reach, but evidence that it may be; and such evidence is provided by the known factual differences between the pictures. Thus the pictures differ aesthetically for me now even if no one will ever be able to tell them apart merely by looking at them.

But suppose it could be *proved* that no one ever will be able to see any difference? This is about as reasonable as asking whether, if it can be proved that the market value and yield of a given U.S. bond and one of a certain nearly bankrupt company will always be the same, there is any financial difference between the two bonds. For what sort of proof could be given? One might suppose that if nobody—not even the most skilled expert—has ever been able to see any difference between the pictures, then the conclusion that I shall never be able to is quite safe; but, as in the case of the Van Meegeren forgeries[4] (of which, more later), distinctions not visible to the expert up to a given time may later become manifest even to the observant layman. Or one might think of

(continued)

Art and Authenticity (continued)

some delicate scanning device that compares the color of two pictures at every point and registers the slightest discrepancy. What, though, is meant here by "at every point"? At no mathematical point, of course, is there any color at all; and even some physical particles are too small to have color. The scanning device must thus cover at each instant a region big enough to have color but at least as small as any perceptible region. Just how to manage this is puzzling since "perceptible" in the present content means "discernible by merely looking", and thus the line between perceptible and nonperceptible regions seems to depend on the arbitrary line between a magnifying glass and a microscope. If some such line is drawn, we can never be sure that the delicacy of our instruments is superior to the maximal attainable acuity of unaided perception. Indeed, some experimental psychologists are inclined to conclude that every measurable difference in light can sometimes be detected by the naked eye.[5] And there is a further difficulty. Our scanning device will examine color—that is, reflected light. Since reflected light depends partly upon incident light, illumination of every quality, of every intensity, and from every direction must be tried. And for each case, especially since the paintings do not have a plane surface, a complete scanning must be made from every angle. But of course we cannot cover every variation, or even determine a single absolute correspondence, in even one respect. Thus the search for a proof that I shall never be able to see any difference between the two pictures is futile for more than technological reasons.

Yet suppose we are nevertheless pressed with the question whether, if proof *were* given, there would then be any aesthetic difference for me between the pictures. And suppose we answer this farfetched question in the negative. This will still give our questioner no comfort. For the net result would be that if no difference between the pictures can in fact be perceived, then the existence of an aesthetic difference between them will rest entirely upon what is or is not proved by means other than merely looking at them. This hardly supports the contention that there can be no aesthetic difference without a perceptual difference.

Returning from the realm of the ultra-hypothetical, we may be faced with the protest that the vast aesthetic difference thought to obtain between the Rembrandt and the forgery cannot be accounted for in terms of the search for, or even the discovery of, perceptual differences so slight that they can be made out, if at all, only after much experience and long practice. This objection can be dismissed at once; for minute perceptual differences can bear enormous weight. The clues that tell me whether I have caught the eye of someone across the room are almost indiscernible. The actual differences in sound that distinguish a fine from a mediocre performance can be picked out only by the well-trained ear. Extremely subtle changes can alter the whole design, feeling, or expression of a painting. Indeed, the slightest perceptual differences sometimes matter the most aesthetically; gross physical damage to a fresco may be less consequential than slight but smug retouching.

All I have attempted to show, of course, is that the two pictures can differ aesthetically, not that the original is better than the forgery. In our example, the original probably is much the better picture, since Rembrandt paintings are in general much better than copies by unknown painters. But a copy of a Lastman by Rembrandt may well be better than the original. We are not called upon here to make such particular comparative judgments or to formulate canons of aesthetic evaluation. We have fully met the demands of our problem by showing that the fact that we cannot tell our two pictures apart merely by looking at them does not imply that they are aesthetically the same—and thus does not force us to conclude that the forgery is as good as the original.

The example we have been using throughout illustrates a special case of a more general question concerning the aesthetic significance of authenticity. Quite aside from the occurrence of forged duplication, does it matter whether an original work is the product of one or another artist or school or period? Suppose that I can easily tell two pictures apart but cannot tell who painted either except by using some device like X-ray photography. Does the fact that the picture is or is not by Rembrandt make any aesthetic difference? What is involved here is the discrimination not of one picture from another but of the class of Rembrandt paintings from the class of other paintings. My chance of learning to make this discrimination correctly—of discovering projectible characteristics that differentiate Rembrandts in general from non-Rembrandts—depends heavily upon the set of examples available as a basis. Thus the fact that the given picture belongs to the one class or the other is important for me to know in learning how to tell Rembrandt paintings from others. In other words, my present (or future) inability to determine the authorship of the given picture without use of scientific apparatus does not imply that the authorship makes no aesthetic difference to me; for knowledge of the authorship, no matter how obtained, can contribute materially toward developing my ability to determine without such apparatus whether or not any picture, including this one on another occasion, is by Rembrandt.

Incidentally, one rather striking puzzle is readily solved in these terms. When Van Meegeren sold his pictures as Vermeers, he deceived most of the best-qualified experts; and only by his confession was the fraud revealed.[6] Nowadays even the fairly knowing layman is astonished that any competent judge could have taken a Van Meegeren for a Vermeer, so obvious are the differences. What has happened? The general level of aesthetic sensibility has hardly risen so fast that the layman of today sees more acutely than the expert of twenty years ago. Rather, the better information now at hand makes the discrimination easier. Presented with a single unfamiliar picture at a time, the expert had to decide whether it was enough like known Vermeers to be by the same artist. And every time a Van Meegeren was added to the corpus of pictures accepted as Vermeers, the criteria for acceptance were modified thereby; and the mistaking of further Van Meegerens for Vermeers became inevitable. Now, however, not only have the Van Meegerens been subtracted from the precedent-classes for Vermeer, but also a precedent-class for Van Meegeren has been established. With these two precedent-classes before us, the characteristic differences become so conspicuous that telling other Van Meegerens from Vermeers offers little difficulty. Yesterday's expert might well have avoided his errors if he had had a few known Van Meegerens handy for comparison. And today's layman who so cleverly spots a Van Meegeren may well be caught taking some quite inferior school-piece for a Vermeer.

In answering the questions raised above, I have not attempted the formidable task of defining "aesthetic" in general,[7] but have simply argued that since the exercise, training, and development of our powers of discriminating among works of art are plainly aesthetic activities, the aesthetic properties of a picture include not only those found by looking at it but also those that determine how it is to be looked at. This rather obvious fact would hardly have needed underlining but for the prevalence of the time-honored Tingle-Immersion theory,[8] which tells us that the proper behavior on encountering a work of art is to strip ourselves of all the vestments of knowledge and experience (since they might blunt the immediacy of our enjoyment), then submerge ourselves completely and gauge the aesthetic potency of the work by the intensity and duration of the resulting tingle. The theory is absurd on the face of it and useless for dealing with any of the important problems of aesthetics; but it has become part of the fabric of our common nonsense.

3. The Unfakable

A second problem concerning authenticity is raised by the rather curious fact that in music, unlike painting, there is no such thing as a forgery of a known work. There are, indeed, compositions falsely purporting to be by Haydn as there are paintings falsely purporting to be by Rembrandt; but of the *London Symphony,* unlike the *Lucretia,* there can be no forgeries. Haydn's manuscript is no more genuine an instance of the score than is a printed copy off the press this morning, and last night's performance no less genuine than the premiere. Copies of the score may vary in accuracy, but all accurate copies, even if forgeries of Haydn's manuscript, are equally genuine instances of the score. Performances may vary in correctness and quality and even in 'authenticity' of a more esoteric kind; but all correct performances are equally genuine instances of the work.[9] In contrast, even the most exact copies of the Rembrandt painting are simply imitations or forgeries, not new instances, of the work. Why this difference between the two arts?

Let us speak of a work of art as *autographic* if and only if the distinction between original and forgery of it is significant; or better, if and only if even the most exact duplication of it does not thereby count as genuine.[10] If a work of art is autographic, we may also call that art autographic. Thus painting is autographic, music nonautographic, or *allographic.* These terms are introduced purely for convenience; nothing is implied concerning the relative individuality of expression demanded by or attainable in these arts. Now the problem before us is to account for the fact that some arts but not others are autographic.

One notable difference between painting and music is that the composer's work is done when he has written the score, even though the performances are the end-products, while the painter has to finish the picture. No matter how many studies or revisions are made in either case, painting is in this sense

(continued)

Art and Authenticity (*continued*)

a one-stage and music a two-stage art. Is an art autographic, then, if and only if it is one-stage? Counterexamples come readily to mind. In the first place, literature is not autographic though it is one-stage. There is no such thing as a forgery of Gray's *Elegy*. Any accurate copy of the text of a poem or novel is as much the original work as any other. Yet what the writer produces is ultimate; the text is not merely a means to oral readings as a score is a means to performances in music. An unrecited poem is not so forlorn as an unsung song; and most literary works are never read aloud at all. We might try to make literature into a two-stage art by considering the silent readings to be the end-products, or the instances of a work; but then the lookings at a picture and the listenings to a performance would qualify equally as end-products or instances, so that painting as well as literature would be two-stage and music three-stage. In the second place, printmaking is two-stage and yet autographic. The etcher, for example, makes a plate from which impressions are then taken on paper. These prints are the end-products; and although they may differ appreciably from one another, all are instances of the original work. But even the most exact copy produced otherwise than by printing from that plate counts not as an original but as an imitation or forgery.

So for, our results are negative: not all one-stage arts are autographic and not all autographic arts are one-stage. Furthermore, the example of printmaking refutes the unwary assumption that in every autographic art a particular work exists only as a unique object. The line between an autographic and an allographic art does not coincide with that between a singular and a multiple art. About the only positive conclusion we can draw here is that the autographic arts are those that are singular in the earliest stage; etching is singular in its first stage—the plate is unique—and painting in its only stage. But this hardly helps; for the problem of explaining why some arts are singular is much like the problem of explaining why they are autographic.

4. The Reason

Why, then, can I no more make a forgery of Haydn's symphony or of Gray's poem than I can make an original of Rembrandt's painting or of his etching *Tobit Blind?* Let us suppose that there are various handwritten copies and many editions of a given literary work. Differences between them in style and size of script or type, in color of ink, in kind of paper, in number and layout of pages, in condition, etc., do not matter. All that matters is what may be called *sameness of spelling*: exact correspondence as sequences of letters, spaces, and punctuation marks. Any sequence—even a forgery of the author's manuscript or of a given edition—that so corresponds to a correct copy is itself correct, and nothing is more the original work than is such a correct copy. And since whatever is not an original of the work must fail to meet such an explicit standard of correctness, there can be no deceptive imitation, no forgery, of that work. To verify the spelling or to spell correctly is all that is required to identify an instance of the work or to produce a new instance. In effect, the fact that a literary work is in a definite notation, consisting of certain signs or characters that are to be combined by concatenation, provides the means for distinguishing the properties constitutive of the work from all contingent properties—that is, for fixing the required features and the limits of permissible variation in each. Merely by determining that the copy before us is spelled correctly we can determine that it meets all requirements for the work in question. In painting, on the contrary, with no such alphabet of characters, none of the pictorial properties—none of the properties the picture has as such—is distinguished as constitutive; no such feature can be dismissed as contingent, and no deviation as insignificant. The only way of ascertaining that the *Lucretia* before us is genuine is thus to establish the historical fact that it is the actual object made by Rembrandt. Accordingly, physical identification of the product of the artist's hand, and consequently the conception of forgery of a particular work, assume a significance in painting that they do not have in literature.[11]

What has been said of literary texts obviously applies also to musical scores. The alphabet is different; and the characters in a score, rather than being strung one after the other as in a text, are disposed in a more complex array. Nevertheless, we have a limited set of characters and of positions for them; and correct spelling, in only a slightly expanded sense, is still the sole requirement for a genuine instance of a work. Any false copy is wrongly spelled—has somewhere in place of the right character either another character or an illegible mark that is not a character of the notation in question at all.

But what of performances of music? Music is not autographic in this second stage either, yet a performance by no means consists of characters from an alphabet. Rather, the constitutive properties demanded of a performance of the symphony are those *prescribed in* the score; and performances that comply with the score may differ appreciably in such musical features as tempo, timbre, phrasing and expressiveness. To determine compliance requires, indeed, something more than merely knowing the alphabet; it requires the ability to correlate appropriate sounds with the visible signs in the score—to recognize, so to speak, correct pronunciation though without necessarily understanding what is pronounced. The competence required to identify or produce sounds called for by a score increases with the complexity of the composition, but there is nevertheless a theoretically decisive test for compliance; and a performance, whatever its interpretative fidelity and independent merit, has or has not all the constitutive properties of a given work, and is or is not strictly a performance of that work, according as it does or does not pass this test. No historical information concerning the production of the performance can affect the result. Hence deception as to the facts of production is irrelevant, and the notion of a performance that is a forgery of the work is quite empty.

Yet there are forgeries of performances as there are of manuscripts and editions. What makes a performance an instance of a given work is not the same as what makes a performance a premiere, or played by a certain musician or upon a Stradivarius violin. Whether a performance has these latter properties is a matter of historical fact; and a performance falsely purporting to have any such property counts as a forgery, not of the musical composition but of a given performance or class of performances.

The comparison between printmaking and music is especially telling. We have already noted that etching, for example, is like music in having two stages and in being multiple in its second stage; but that whereas music is autographic in neither stage, printmaking is autographic in both. Now the situation with respect to the etched plate is clearly the same as with respect to a painting: assurance of genuineness can come only from identification of the actual object produced by the artist. But since the several prints from this plate are all genuine instances of the work, however much they differ in color and amount of ink, quality of impression, kind of paper, etc., one might expect here a full parallel between prints and musical performances. Yet there can be prints that are forgeries of the *Tobit Blind* but not performances that are forgeries of the *London Symphony.* The difference is that in the absence of a notation, not only is there no test of correctness of spelling for a plate but there is no test of compliance with a plate for a print. Comparison of a print with a plate, as of two plates, is no more conclusive than is comparison of two pictures. Minute discrepancies may always go unnoticed; and there is no basis for ruling out any of them as inessential. The only way of ascertaining whether a print is genuine is by finding out whether it was taken from a certain plate.[12] A print falsely purporting to have been so produced is in the full sense a forgery of the work.

Here, as earlier, we must be careful not to confuse genuineness with aesthetic merit. That the distinction between original and forgery is aesthetically important does not, we have seen, imply that the original is superior to the forgery. An original painting may be less rewarding than an inspired copy; a damaged original may have lost most of its former merit; an impression from a badly worn plate may be aesthetically much further removed from an early impression than is a good photographic reproduction. Likewise, an incorrect performance, though therefore not strictly an instance of a given quartet at all, may nevertheless—either because the changes improve what the composer wrote or because of sensitive interpretation—be better than a correct performance.[13] Again, several correct performances of about equal merit may exhibit very different specific aesthetic qualifies—power, delicacy, tautness, stodginess, incoherence, etc. Thus even where the constitutive properties of a work are clearly distinguished by means of a notation, they cannot be identified with the aesthetic properties.

Among other arts, sculpture is autographic; cast sculpture is comparable to printmaking while carved sculpture is comparable to painting. Architecture and the drama, on the other hand, are more nearly comparable to music. Any building that conforms to the plans and specifications, any performance of the text of a play in accordance with the stage directions, is as original an instance of the work as any other. But architecture seems to differ from music in that testing for compliance of a building with the specifications requires not that these be pronounced, or transcribed into sound, but that their application be understood. This is true also for the stage directions, as contrasted with the dialogue, of a play. Does this make architecture and the drama less purely allographic arts? Again, an architect's plans seem a good deal like a painter's sketches; and painting is an autographic art. On what grounds can we say that in the one case but not the other a veritable notation is involved? Such questions cannot be answered until we have carried through some rather painstaking analysis.

(continued)

Art and Authenticity   (*continued*)

Since an art seems to be allographic just insofar as it is amenable to notation, the case of the dance is especially interesting. Here we have an art without a traditional notation; and an art where the ways, and even the possibility, of developing an adequate notation are still matters of controversy. Is the search for a notation reasonable in the case of the dance but not in the case of painting? Or, more generally, why is the use of notation appropriate in some arts but not in others? Very briefly and roughly, the answer may be somewhat as follows. Initially, perhaps, all arts are autographic. Where the works are transitory, as in sinking and reciting, or require many persons for their production, as in architecture and symphonic music, a notation may be devised in order to transcend the limitations of time and the individual. This involves establishing a distinction between the constitutive and the contingent properties of a work (and in the case of literature, texts have even supplanted oral performances as the primary aesthetic objects). Of course, the notation does not dictate the distinction arbitrarily, but must fallow generally—even though it may amend—lines antecedently drawn by the informal classification of performances into works and by practical decisions as to what is prescribed and what is optional. Amenability to notation depends upon a precedent practice that develops only if works of the art in question are commonly either ephemeral or not producible by one person. The dance, like the drama and symphonic and choral music, qualifies on both scores, while painting qualifies on neither.

The general answer to our somewhat slippery second problem of authenticity can be summarized in a few words. A forgery of a work of art is an object falsely purporting to have the history of production requisite for the (or an) original of the work. Where there is a theoretically decisive test for determining that an object has all the constitutive properties of the work in question without determining how or by whom the object was produced, there is no requisite history of production and hence no forgery of any given work. Such a test is provided by a suitable notational system with an articulate set of characters and of relative positions for them. For texts, scores, and perhaps plans, the test is correctness of spelling in this notation; for buildings and performances, the test is compliance with what is correctly spelled. Authority for a notation must be found in an antecedent classification of objects or events into works that cuts across, or admits of a legitimate projection that cuts across, classification by history of production; but definitive identification of works, fully freed from history of production, is achieved only when a notation is established. The allographic art has won its emancipation not by proclamation but by notation.

5. A Task

The two problems of authenticity I have been discussing are rather special and peripheral questions of aesthetics. Answers to them do not amount to an aesthetic theory or even the beginning of one. But failure to answer them can well be the end of one; and their exploration points the way to more basic problems and principles in the general theory of symbols.

Many matters touched upon here need much more careful study. So far, I have only vaguely described, rather than defined, the relations of compliance and of sameness of spelling. I have not examined the features that distinguish notations or notational languages from other languages and from nonlanguages. And I have not discussed the subtle differences between a score, a script, and a sketch. What is wanted now is a fundamental and thoroughgoing inquiry into the nature and function of notation in the arts. This will be undertaken in the next two chapters.

NOTES

1. And only for the sake of argument—only in order not to obscure the central issue. All talk of mere looking in what follows is to be understood as occurring within the scope of this temporary concession, not as indicating any acceptance of the notion on my part.
2. Germans learning English often cannot, without repeated effort and concentrated attention, hear any difference at all between the vowel sounds in "cup" and "cop". Like effort may sometimes be needed by the native speaker of a language to discern differences in color, etc., that are not marked by his elementary vocabulary. Whether language affects actual sensory discrimination has long been debated among psychologists, anthropologists, and linguists; see the survey of experimentation and controversy in Segall, Campbell, and Herskovits, *The Influence of Culture on Visual Perception* (Indianapolis and New York,

The Bobbs-Merrill Co., Inc., 1966), pp. 34–48. The issue is unlikely to be resolved without greater clarity in the use of "sensory", "perceptual", and "cognitive", and more care in distinguishing between what a person can do at a given time and what he can learn to do.
3. In saying that a difference *between the pictures* that is thus relevant to my present experience in looking at them constitutes an aesthetic difference between them, I am of course not saying that everything (e.g., drunkenness, snow blindness, twilight) that may cause my experiences of them to differ constitutes such an aesthetic difference. Not every difference in or arising from how the pictures happen to be they are to looked at counts; only differences in or arising from how they are to be looked at. Concerning the aesthetic, more will be said later in this section and in VI, pp. 3–6.
4. For a detailed and fully illustrated account, see P. B. Coremans, *Van Meegeren's Faked Vermeers and De Hooghs,* trans. A. Hardy and C. Hutt (Amsterdam, J. M. Meulenhoff, 1949). The story is outlined in Sepp Schüller, *Forgers, Dealers, Experts,* trans. J. Cleugh (New York, G. P. Putnam's Sons, 1960), pp. 95–105.
5. Not surprisingly, since a single quantum of light may excite a retinal receptor. See M.H. Pirenne and F. H. C. Marriott, "The Quantum Theory of Light and the Psycho-Physiology of Vision", in *Psychology,* ed. S. Koch (New York and London, McGraw-Hill Co., Inc., 1959), vol. I, p. 290; also Theodore C. Ruch, "Vision", in *Medical Psychology and Biophysics* (Philadelphia, W. B. Saunders Co., 1960), p. 426.
6. That the forgeries purported to have been painted during a period from which no Vermeers were known made detection more difficult but does not essentially alter the case. Some art historians, on the defensive for their profession, claim that the most perceptive critics suspected the forgeries very early; but actually some of the foremost recognized authorities were completely taken in and for some time even refused to believe Van Meegeren's confession. The reader has a more recent example now before him in the revelation that the famous bronze horse, long exhibited in the Metropolitan Museum and proclaimed as a masterpiece of classical Greek sculpture, is a modern forgery. An official of the museum noticed a seam that apparently neither he nor anyone else had ever seen before, and scientific testing followed. No expert has come forward to claim earlier doubts on aesthetic grounds.
7. I shall come to that question much later, in Chapter VI.
8. Attributed to Immanuel Tingle and Joseph Immersion (ca. 1800).
9. There may indeed be forgeries of performances. Such forgeries are performances that purport to be by a certain musician, etc; but these, if in accordance with the score, are nevertheless genuine instances of the work. And what concerns me here is a distinction among the arts that depends upon whether there can be forgeries of works, not upon whether there can be forgeries of instances of works. See further what is said in section 4 below concerning forgeries of editions of literary works and of musical performances.
10. This is to be taken as a preliminary version of a difference we must seek to formulate more precisely. Much of what follows in this chapter has likewise the character of an exploratory introduction to matters calling for fuller and more detailed inquiry in later chapters.
11. Such identification does not guarantee that the object possesses the pictorial properties it had originally. Rather, reliance on physical or historical identification is transcended only where we have means of ascertaining that the requisite properties are present.
12. To be original a print must be from a certain plate but need not be printed by the artist. Furthermore, in the case of a woodcut, the artist sometimes only draws upon the block, leaving the cutting to someone else—Holbein's blocks, for example, were usually cut by Lützelberger. Authenticity in an autographic art always depends upon the object's having the requisite, sometimes rather complicated, history of production; but that history does not always include ultimate execution by the original artist.
13. Of course, I am not saying that a correct (ly spelled) performance is correct in any of a number of other usual senses. Nevertheless, the composer or musician is likely to protest indignantly at refusal to accept a performance with a few wrong notes as an instance of a work; and he surely has ordinary usage on his side. But ordinary usage here points the way to disaster for theory (see V, 2).

APPENDIX

Films for Further Philosophical Consideration

Title	Year	Director	Plot	Theme	Chapter, Topic
11th Hour, The	2007	Leila Conners, and Nadia Conners	Documentary concerning the global environmental crisis.	Environmental ethics	Ethics
12:08 East of Bucharest	2006	Corneliu Porumboiu	16 years after the revolution in Romania people still ask if delivered what it promised.	Revolution, Social realities	Socio-political
1408	2007	Mikael Hafstrom	A man who debunks paranormal events checks into mysterious hotel room.	Appearance-Reality	Epistemology
17 Again	2009	Burr Steers	A man is able to revisit his life and attempts to rewrite it.	Cause-effect, Determinism	Metaphysics
21	2008	Robert Luketic	Six MIT students count cards and win millions in Las Vegas.	Cheating	Ethics
24 City	2008	Jia Zhangke	Life in a Chinese factory.	Worker life	Socio-political
27 Dresses	2008	Anne Fletcher	A long-time bridesmaid considers whether to reveal that she loves her sister's soon- to-be husband.	Portrayal of women	Socio-political, Ethics
28 Weeks Later	2007	Juan Carlos Fresnadillo	Months after a deadly virus has been contained, NATO is ready to repopulate the city of London.	Military actions, Personal Identity, Mind-body problem	Socio-political, Metaphysics
300	2007	Zack Snyder	A Greek king is vastly outnumbered by invading army but stands his ground and does battle.	Just war, Gender roles in society	Socio-political
4 Months, 3 Weeks, 2 Days	2007	Cristian Mungiu	A woman assists her friend to arrange for an illegal abortion in 1980s Romania.	Abortion	Ethics
49 Up	2006	Michael Apted	Documentary follow-up on previous interviewees and how their lives have been affected by the documentary.	Privacy, Media influences	Ethics
9th Company	2006	Fyodor Bondarchuk	The Afghanistan war from the perspective of young Soviet soldiers.	War, Sacrifice	Socio-political
A Christmas Tale	2008	Arnaud Desplechin	Family members return for the holidays and bring with them emotional baggage.	Meaning of life	Metaphysics
A Man's Fear of God	2006	Özer Kiziltan	The financial organizer of a Muslim group struggles with his morality.	Islam, Fundamentalism, Moral crises	Religion, Ethics

Title	Year	Director	Plot	Theme	Chapter, Topic
A Prophet	2009	Jacques Audiard	An Arabian becomes a kingpin inside a French prison.	Prison life, Cultural clashes	Socio-political
A Serious Man	2009	Ethan Coen, Joel Coen	A physics professor whose wife leaves him reaches out to three Rabbis for advice.	Religion and faith	Religion
A Ton of Luck	2006	Rodrigo Triana	The true story of Colombian soldiers who find an illegal fortune and decide to spend it.	War, Effects of money	Socio-political
After the Wedding	2006	Susanne Bier	A social worker in India goes home to Denmark as a man may fund his projects and he makes a shocking discovery.	Moral dilemmas	Ethics
Ahimsa: Stop to Run	2006	Kittikorn Liasirikun	A man is told that he should have died at birth.	Karma, Determinism	Religion, Metaphysics
Akeelah and the Bee	2006	Doug Atchison	A black girl in LA suppresses her intelligence but then is entered into a spelling contest.	Race and gender roles	Socio-political
Alpha Dog	2007	Nick Cassavetes	A young drug dealer gets involved in the kidnapping and murder of a 15-year-old boy.	Immoral behavior Responsibility	Ethics
Amazing Grace	2006	Michael Apted	An Abolitionist fights to have 18th-century Britain end the slave trade.	Rights, Respect, Racism, Justice	Socio-political, Ethics
Amazing Journey: The Story of The Who	2007	Paul Crowder, Murray Lerner	Documentary concerning the band The Who.	Art and artistry	Aesthetics
Amelia	2009	Mira Nair	The life and times of pilot Amelia Earhart.	Women in society	Socio-political
American Zeitgeist	2006	Rob McGann	Documentary concerning the American response to terrorism since 2001.	Terrorism	Socio-political
An Education	2009	Lone Scherfig	A young girl falls in love with an older man and learns about love.	Nature of love, relationships	Socio-political, Ethics
Angels and Demons	2009	Ron Howard	A symbologist is called in to thwart the destruction of the Vatican by the Illuminati	Religion and conspiracy	Religion, Epistemology
Antichrist	2009	Lars von Trier	A grieving couple's troubled marriage turns to sex and violence.	Sex and violence, Censorship	Socio-political, Aesthetics
Anvil: The Story of Anvil	2009	Sacha Gervasi	The story of an influential but ultimately unsuccessful heavy metal band.	Art and artistry	Aesthetics

(continued)

Title	Year	Director	Plot	Theme	Chapter, Topic
Apocalypto	2006	Mel Gibson	A 16th century Mayan tribe captures individuals from another tribe to sacrifice to the gods.	Ethical Relativism	Ethics
Appaloosa	2008	Ed Harris	Two men are hired to protect a small town that is under the control of a rancher.	Power	Socio-political
Art School Confidential	2006	Terry Zwigoff	No one takes a freshman's art seriously while others get away with producing trash.	Standards of taste, Values, Introduction to art	Aesthetics
Atonement	2007	Joe Wright.	A young girl seeks to make amends for falsely accusing a man of sexual assault.	Responsibility, Harm to others, War, Perception	Socio-political, Ethics Epistemology
Avatar	2009	James Cameron	A Marine infiltrates an alien race by taking control of an alien body and succumbs to the beauty of the aliens' planet.	Environmental concerns, pantheism	Religion, Ethics
Baader Meinhof Complex, The	2008	Uli Edel	An examination of the German Red Army Faction terrorist group.	Terrorism, Means to an end	Socio-political, Ethics
Babel	2006	Alejandro González Iñárritu	Tragedy strikes a couple travelling in Morocco, which sets off a series of interrelated events involving seemingly unrelated people.	Cause and effect	Metaphysics
Bad Lieutenant: Port of Call New Orleans	2009	Werner Herzog	A drug and gambling addicted detective investigates the murder of five people.	Nihilism	Ethics
Beaches of Agnès, The	2008	Agnès Varda	Autobiography of director Varda.	Art and artistry	Aesthetics
Becoming Jane	2007	Julian Jarrold	For the sake of her family, Jane Austen ends her one romance and instead puts her life into her writings.	Feminism, Gender roles in society	Socio-political
Belle Toujours	2006	Manoel de Oliveira	A man follows woman he hasn't seen in 40 years to tell her a secret.	Desire, Nature of aging	Socio-political, Ethics
Ben X	2007	Nic Balthazar	An autistic boy escapes into the world of online games.	Mistreatment, escapism, Personal identity	Ethics, Metaphysics
Beyond the Gates	2006	Michael Caton-Jones	A look at white pacifists during Rwandan genocide against Tutus in 1994.	Duty, Genocide, Pacifism	Socio-political

Title	Year	Director	Plot	Theme	Chapter, Topic
Black Book	2006	Paul Verhoeven	A Jewish singer infiltrates the Gestapo.	Sacrifice, understanding the enemy	Socio-political
Black Snake Moan	2007	Craig Brewer	A deeply religious farmer tries to help a young nymphomaniac recover from a beating and heal her from her sinful ways	Sin, Redemption	Religion
Blind Side, The	2009	John Lee Hancock	A poorly educated teen is molded into a college football player.	Racism, social realities	Socio-political
Blood Diamond	2006	Edward Zwick	A mercenary teams up with displaced black fisherman who is searching for his family.	Racism, Corruption, Greed, Political Unrest	Socio-political
Borat: Cultural Learnings of America for Make Benefit Glorious Nation of Kazakhstan	2006	Larry Charles	A naïve reporter visits America to learn about the country and its peoples.	Cultural relativism	Ethics
Bosta	2006	Philippe Aractingi	A Lebanese man wants to reform a dance band.	National identity, War and its consequences	Socio-political
Box, The	2009	Richard Kelly	Contestants can win a million dollars in a game but a stranger has to die.	Utilitarianism	Ethics
Boy in the Striped Pajamas, The	2008	Mark Herman	A German boy unknowingly befriends a boy in a Concentration camp.	War, Holocaust	Socio-political, Ethics
Brand Upon the Brain!	2006	Guy Maddin	A man with messed up childhood returns home to restore the old lighthouse.	Surrealism	Epistemology, Aesthetics
Brave One, The	2007	Neil Jordan	Unhappy with the police response to her and her fiancé's assault, a woman seeks out those responsible.	Feminism, Justice	Socio-political
Breach	2007	Billy Ray	A new FBI agent is assigned to monitor a senior agent who is suspected of spying for the Soviet Union.	Duty	Ethics
Bright Star	2009	Jane Campion	The love story between 19th-century poet John Keats and Fanny Brawne.	Art and artistry	Aesthetics
Brüno	2009	Larry Charles	A gay fashion reporter visits the USA in order to reestablish his career.	Gay portrayals, Stereotypes	Socio-political

(continued)

Title	Year	Director	Plot	Theme	Chapter, Topic
Capitalism: A Love Story	2009	Michael Moore	A critical examination of capitalism in America	Capitalism, Greed	Socio-political
Caramel	2007	Nadine Labaki	The lives of five different women in Lebanon are followed.	World religions, Cultural differences	Religion, Socio-political
Catch a Fire	2006	Phillip Noyce	Wrongly accused of terrorism, a South African joins the freedom fighters.	Honor, Misuse of power, Racism	Socio-political
Catch and Release	2007	Susannah Grant	After the death of her fiancé, a young woman finds out that he had a secret life.	Appearance-Reality	Epistemology
Cave of the Yellow Dog, The	2006	Byambasuren Davaa	The simple life of a girl in the Mongolian valley.	State of Nature,	Socio-political
Changeling	2008	Clint Eastwood	A mother fights the LAPD when it tries to convince her that they have found her missing child.	Faith, Hope, Love, Challenging Authority,	Religion, Ethics, Socio-political
Chariton's Choir	2006	Grigoris Karantinakis	A school master spreads his love of life through his school's choir.	Hedonism	Ethics
Charlie Wilson's War	2007	Mike Nichols	A Congressman and rogue CIA operative launch an operation to help the Afghan Mujahedeen during the Soviet war in Afghanistan	Political war	Socio-political
Children of Men	2006	Alfonso Cuarón	In the year 2027 women are sterile except for one and she must be protected at all cost.	Role of Women in society, State of Nature, Utopia, Fascism	Socio-political
Class, The	2008	Ilmar Raag	A teacher is frustrated that the traditional school plan doesn't excite the working class students.	Communicating Knowledge	Epistemology
Coco Before Chanel	2009	AnneFontaine	The rise of Coco Chanel to the top of the fashion world.	Art and artistry	Aesthetics
Coeurs	2006	Alain Renais	Parisians look for love.	Appearance-Reality, The Human Condition	Epistemology, Metaphysics
Cold Souls	2009	Sophia Barthes	An actor has his soul removed so that he can manage the content of the Anton Chekhov play he is preparing for.	Philosophy of Mind, Materialism, Art and artistry	Metaphysics, Aesthetics
Condemned, The	2007	Scott Wiper	Ten condemned criminals are offered the opportunity to win back their freedom by fighting to the death.	Retribution, Survival of the fittest, Censorship	Socio-political

Title	Year	Director	Plot	Theme	Chapter, Topic
Coraline	2009	Henry Selick	A young girl finds another world that is very similar to the real one, with a few nasty surprises.	Appearance-reality, Nature of Truth	Metaphysics, Epistemology
Cove, The	2009	Louie Psihoyos	Documentary concerning the Japanese mass killing of dolphins.	Animal rights	Ethics, Cultural Relativism
Curious Case of Benjamin Button, The	2008	David Fincher	A man ages backwards.	Time,	Metaphysics
Curse of the Golden Flower	2006	Zhang Yimou	The Tang dynasty emperor gains control over China	Power	Socio-political
Da Vinci Code, The	2006	Ron Howard	A man follows clues around Europe that reveal secret knowledge that would harm the Roman Catholic Church.	Faith and religious truth	Religion
Dark Knight, The	2008	Christopher Nolan	Batman must deal with the anarchistic terrorist Joker.	Sacrifice, Utilitarianism Nature of Justice	Ethics Socio-political
Das Leben der Anderen	2006	Florian Henckel von Donnersmarck	In Communist East Berlin a man secretly listens to the lives of a writer and his lover.	Communism	Socio-political
Day Night Day Night	2006	Julia Loktev	A 19-year-old girl prepares to become a suicide bomber in Times Square.	Fanaticism	Religion
Days of Darkness	2007	Denys Arcand	A bureaucrat escapes his life by fantasizing himself as a hero.	Bureaucracy, Appearance-reality	Socio-political, Metaphysics
Death of a President	2006	Gabriel Range	Make belief story about the assassination of President G.W. Bush.	Political exploitation	Socio-political
Death Proof	2007	Quentin Tarantino	A psychopathic man targets young women, murdering them with his "death proof" stunt car.	Gender roles in society	Socio-political
Defenders of Riga	2008	Aigars Grauba	The battle for Latvian independence on November 11, 1919.	War and sacrifice	Socio-political
Déjà Vu	2006	Tony Scott	An FBI agent enters the past to investigate and stop a murder.	Determinism and fate, Time-travel, Cause and effect	Metaphysics
Deliver us from Evil	2006	Amy Berg	Documentary about the Catholic church's ignoring child abuse.	Organized religion and moral hypocrisy	Religion, Ethics
Devil Wears Prada	2006	David Frankel	A college student becomes the personal assistant of a tought fashion magazine editor.	Feminism	Socio-political

(continued)

Title	Year	Director	Plot	Theme	Chapter, Topic
District 9	2009	Neill Blomkamp	Aliens are forced to live in poverty and are valued only for their advanced technologies.	Racism, Respect, Kantianism	Socio-political, Ethics
Disturbia	2007	J. D. Caruso	A teenager on house arrest begins to suspect something sinister is going on with one of his neighbors	Appearance-Reality, Skepticism	Epistemology
Dog Eat Dog	2008	Carlos Moreno	Two Colombian criminals violate the code of ethics.	Code of ethics	Ethics
Downloading Nancy	2009	Johan Renck	A desperately depressed woman seeks a man to kill her husband.	Nature of love and marriage	Socio-political
Dream Weavers	2008	Yu Gun	Five stories related to the 2008 Summer Olympics.	Sport in society	Socio-political
Duchess, The	2008	Saul Dibb	The life, loves and politics of a duchess.	Political Power, Class	Socio-political
Duchess of Langeais, The	2008	Jacques Rivette	Two members of high society drive each other mad as they play the game of love.	Men-women relationships	Socio-political
Eagle Eye	2008	D.J. Caruso	Two strangers are forced to engage in dangerous situations by an unknown person who tracks their every movement.	Big Brother	Socio-political
Eduart	2007	Angeliki Antoniou	A reckless youth is imprisoned for murder and learns to feel guilt.	Self-sacrifice, Human condition, Justice	Ethics
El Benny	2006	Jorge Luis Sánchez	Biography of Cuban singer Benny More.	Art and the artist	Aesthetics
Eldorado	2008	Bouli Lanners	Instead of calling the police a man gives a young burglar a ride home and they discover truths about themselves.	Sympathy	Ethics
Elizabeth: The Golden Age	2007	Shekhar Kapur	While Spain prepares for attack, Queen Elizabeth is being pressured into marriage so that the throne will not pass to her cousin.	War, Monarchy, Feminism	Socio-political
En la cama	2006	Matías Bize	Partners engaged in casual sex take it to the next level of intimacy.	Nature of Sex and love, Hedonism	Ethics
Evan Almighty	2007	Tom Shadyac	A family man is told by God to build a modern day Ark.	Religious belief	Religion
Everlasting Moments	2008	Jan Troell	A poor Swedish woman wins a camera and it changes her life.	Reality and perception	Metaphysics

Appendix 531

Title	Year	Director	Plot	Theme	Chapter, Topic
Fast Food Nation	2006	Richard Linklater	Documentary concerning the life of the immigrant working in a meat-packing plant serving the needs of the American public.	Animal Ethics, Consumerism	Socio-political
Flags of our Fathers	2006	Clint Eastwood	The flag raisers on Iwo Jima become fund raisers as they tour the United States.	War, Using people	Socio-political, Ethics
Food, Inc.	2009	Robert Kenner	A critical examination of the corporate-controlled food industry in United States.	Animal and environmental issues, Capitalism	Socio-political, Ethics
For Your Consideration	2006	Christopher Guest	Actors start believing the hype surrounding their chances of winning an Oscar for their performances.	Value judgments concerning entertainment	Socio-political, Aesthetics
Fountain, The	2006	Daren Aronofsky	Man exists in three different times and he seeks to understand the nature of existence in all of them.	Meaning of life	Metaphysics
Freedom Writers	2007	Richard LaGravenese	A teacher uses journal writing to educate her tough street students about racism and respect.	Social awareness	Socio-political
Frost/Nixon	2008	Ron Howard	The retelling of post-Watergate interviews with Richard Nixon conducted by David Frost.	Politics and power, Journalistic integrity, Truth	Socio-political, Epistemology
George A. Romero's Diary of the Dead	2008	George A. Romero	Students try to film what really happened when the dead came alive.	Criticism of media and government	Socio-political
Ghost Rider	2007	Mark Steven Johnson	Mephistopheles promises to give a man his soul back if he defeats his son and the fallen angels.	Good versus Evil	Ethics
Golden Door, The	2006	Emanuele Crialese	Poor Sicilians travel to the new world and a new life in America.	Social realities, Utopia	Socio-political
Gomorra	2008	Matteo Garrone	Different individuals make contracts with an Italian mob family.	Crime	Socio-political
Gone with the Woman	2007	Petter Naess	A woman starts running a man's life and he falls in love with her.	Male/female relationships	Socio-political
Good German, The	2006	Steven Soderbergh	Berlin after the war is in physical and moral ruin as Germans do what they can to survive.	Immorality and choices	Ethics
Goya's Ghosts	2007	Miloš Forman	The Spanish Inquisition is disturbed by the evil portrayed in artist Francisco Goya's life.	Religion and art	Religion

(continued)

Title	Year	Director	Plot	Theme	Chapter, Topic
Gracie	2007	Davis Guggenheim	A girl overcomes the loss of her brother playing varsity soccer on an all-boys team.	Feminism	Socio-political
Gran Torino	2008	Clint Eastwood	An angry Vietnam vet tries to reform his young immigrant neighbor.	Racism	Socio-political
Grbavica: Land of My Dreams	2006	Jasmila Žbanić	A woman and her child struggle after the Balkan war.	War and its aftermath	Socio-political
Great New Wonderful, The	2006	Danny Leiner	People try to make sense out of the terror attack on U.S. soil on Sept. 11, 2001.	Existentialism	Socio-political
Grindhouse	2007	Robert Rodriguez, Quentin Tarantino	Two stories: Life as a zombie; and man terrorizes women with his car.	Zombies and materialism, Treatment of women	Metaphysics, Socio-political
Ground Truth, The	2006	Patricia Foulkrod	Documentary on the impact of the Iraq war on youthful soldiers who are sent over to fight.	Insanity of war, Government deception	Socio-political
Grow Your Own	2007	Richard Laxton	A group of community gardeners react angrily when a group of refugees are given plots at the site	Cultural differences, Tolerance	Socio-political
Hancock	2008	Peter Berg	A superhero falls out of favor with his public.	Personal responsibility, Sacrifice	Ethics
Hannibal Rising	2007	Peter Webber	A young boy who will grow up to be an infamous cannibal witnesses the death of his family by Russian soldiers	Cause and effect, Free will, Responsibility	Metaphysics, Ethics
Happening, The	2008	M. Night Shyamalan	A pandemic strikes the USA.	Environmentalism, Medical issues	Ethics
Hard Candy	2006	David Slade	A young girl turns the tables on her would-be Internet attacker.	Justice	Ethics
Harry Potter and the Order of the Phoenix	2007	David Yates	Young wizards band together to stop autocratic rule of their school.	Authoritarianism	Socio-political
Haunting in Connecticut, The	2009	Peter Cornwell	A family's home is a former mortuary.	Supernatural	Metaphysics
Headless Woman, The	2008	Lucrecia Martel	A woman thinks she has run over someone and is overcome by guilt.	Rich and poor	Socio-political
He's Just Not that Into You	2009	Ken Kwapis	Young adults struggle to try to figure out the opposite sex.	Relationships, Honesty	Socio-political, Ethics

Title	Year	Director	Plot	Theme	Chapter, Topic
Hunger	2009	Steve McQueen	The last six weeks of Irish republican Bobby Sands's hunger strike.	Politics, Personal sacrifice, Protest	Socio-political, Ethics
I Am Legend	2007	Francis Lawrence	A virologist works to create a cure while living in a city inhabited by mutant victims of the plague.	State of nature	Socio-political, Metaphysics
I Just Didn't Do It	2007	Masayuki Suo	A man is accused of assaulting a girl and goes through numerous trials while pleading his innocence.	Crime and punishment, Judicial system	Socio-political, Ethics
I Love You, Man	2009	John Hamburg	A man seeks male friendship since he never has had a "buddy."	Friendship, Relationships	Ethics
I Served the King of England	2007	Jiri Menzel	The daily life of a man who works in a posh Czech hotel is contrasted with the guests.	Class issues	Socio-political
Ice Cream, I Scream	2006	Yüksel Aksu	A Turkish ice cream salesman fights against the larger brands.	Capitalism, Socialism	Socio-political
Idiocracy	2006	Mike Judge	Stupid people have more children than smart so they take over society in a Darwinian reversal.	Social darwinism	Socio-political
Illusionist, The	2006	Neil Burger	A magician is seen as a romantic rival to Vienna's Crown Prince Leopold.	Appearance–Reality	Epistemology
I'm Not There	2007	Todd Haynes	Singer-songwriter Bob Dylan is seen in seven distinct stages of his life.	Art and artistry, Personal Identity	Aesthetics, Metaphysics
In the Land of Women	2007	Jon Kasdan	After being rejected by his girlfriend, a young man takes care of his sick grandmother and bonds with her female neighbors.	Women in society	Socio-political
In the Loop	2009	Armando Iannucci	The U.S. president and UK prime minister want to make war but not everyone agrees.	War and politics	Socio-political
Inconvenient Truth, An	2006	Davis Guggenheim	Documentary on the cause and effect of global climate change.	Scientific knowledge and its impact, Environmental Ethics	Science, Ethics
'Informant!, The	2009	Steven Soderbergh	The vice-president of a large company turns informant on its price-fixing schemes.	Capitalism	Socio-political, Ethics

(continued)

Title	Year	Director	Plot	Theme	Chapter, Topic
Inglourious Basterds	2009	Quentin Tarantino	A group of Jewish soldiers hunt down Nazis.	War, revisionist history, Appearance-reality	Socio-political, Metaphysics
Inland Empire	2006	David Lynch	The same actress plays many different roles or perhaps it is the same role?	Perception of reality, Personal Identity	Metaphysics, Aesthetics
International, The	2009	Tom Tykwer	An Interpol agent tries to uncover the secrets of the world wide control held by a financial institution.	Economics, Conspiracy	Socio-political, Ethics
Invention of Lying, The	2009	Ricky Gervais, Matthew Robinson	In a world where everyone tells the truth, a writer discovers that he has the ability to lie.	Knowledge, religious belief, Trust	Epistemology, Religion
Invisible, The	2007	David S. Goyer	A high school senior is severely beaten and he is trapped somewhere between life and death.	Death	Metaphysics
Iraq in Fragments	2006	James Longley	Documentary on the effect of war and religion on Iraq.	Impact of war, Exclusive religious belief	Socio-political, Religion
Iron Man	2008	Jon Favreau	A wealthy industrialist faces mortality and decides to fight back against his own weapons.	Sacrifice	Ethics
Island, The	2008	Sherif Arafa	A Russian monk's bizarre behavior may be a gift of faith.	Faith	Religion
It's Hard to be Nice	2007	Srdan Vuletic	The postwar Bosnia is populated with people who have been beaten down by their experiences.	War and its consequences	Socio-political
Jerusalema	2008	Ralph Ziman	A South African gangster rises to power.	Crime and fatalism	Socio-political
Jesus Camp	2006	Heidi Ewing, Rachel Grady	Documentary about the evangelistic indoctrination of children.	Faith, Dogma	Religion
Jindabyne	2006	Ray Lawrence	Since there is nothing that they can do, three friends leave a dead woman in the river and continue fishing.	Non-action, Mysticism	Religion, Ethics
Julie & Julia	2009	Nora Ephron	The start of Julia Child's cooking career.	Art and artistry	Aesthetics
Jumper	2008	Doug Liman	A man discovers he can teleport himself anywhere and finds himself in the middle of a war.	Cause-Effect	Metaphysics, Science
Juno	2007	Jason Reitman	A young girl is intent on carrying her pregnancy to term and to give the infant up for adoption.	Abortion, Sacrifice, Happiness	Ethics

Title	Year	Director	Plot	Theme	Chapter, Topic
Karamazovs, The	2008	Petr Zelenka	Czech actors performing a theatrical adaptation of a Dostoyevsky novel step in and out of their roles.	Life imitating art	Aesthetics
Katyń	2007	Andrzej Wajda	Thousands of Poles are executed by the Soviets in 1940.	War crimes	Socio-political, Ethics
Knocked Up	2007	Judd Apatow	Loser gets nice girl pregnant and they decide to keep the baby.	Gender roles in society, Duty, Abortion	Socio-political, Ethics
Knowing	2009	Alex Proyas	A mathematician deciphers a complex formula that reveals the future.	Cause and effect, Predetermination	Metaphysics
La Danse: The Paris Opera Ballet	2009	Frederick Wiseman	Seven ballets are produced and performed by the company.	Art and artistry	Aesthetics
La Vie En Rose	2007	Olivier Dahan	The life of singer Edith Piaf.	Art and artistry	Aesthetics
Lake House, The	2006	Alejandro Agresti	A man develops pen pal with someone who lives in a different time than he does.	Time, Determinism	Metaphysics
Last House on the Left, The	2009	Dennis Iliadis	A prison escapee finds himself in the home of the parents of one of his victims.	Revenge	Ethics
Last King of Scotland, The	2006	Kevin Macdonald	A doctor aids Ugandan dictator and faces moral choices.	State of Nature, Brutality, Dictatorship, Responsibility	Socio-political, Ethics
Last Mimzy, The	2007	Bob Shaye	Two children find special toys sent from the future.	Time-travel, Environmental issues	Metaphysics, Ethics
Last Station, The	2009	Michael Hoffman	Author Leo Tolstoy is challenged by his success and his desire to live a simple life.	Art and artistry, Values	Aesthetics, Socio-political, Ethics
Last Stop 174	2008	Bruno Barreto	The story of a bus hijacking in Rio.	Determinism and fate	Metaphysics
Letters From Iwo Jima	2006	Clint Eastwood	WW2 Japanese soldiers write letters home knowing they will not survive the upcoming battle.	War and its consequences, Humanism	Socio-political
Lion's Den	2008	Pablo Trapero	A pregnant woman is sent to jail to await trial.	Crime and punishment	Ethics
Looking for Comedy in the Muslim World	2006	Albert Brooks	A man is hired by U.S. government to find out what is funny in Muslim world.	Cultural relativism, Relativism of humor	Socio-political, Aesthetics
Lost City, The	2006	Andy Garcia	Father and sons become part of the 1950s Cuban revolution.	Social revolution	Socio-political

(continued)

Title	Year	Director	Plot	Theme	Chapter, Topic
Love for Share	2006	Nia di Nata	Three Malay women discuss polygamy.	Polygamy, cultural relativity	Socio-political, Ethics
Lust, Caution	2007	Ang Lee	A group of patriotic Chinese students use a young woman to entice and then kill a member of the Japanese collaborationist government of Wang Jingwei.	Sexuality, Political unrest, Just killing	Socio-political
Maid, The	2009	Sebastián Silva	A maid lives with her employers and faces the reality of not really being one of the family.	Class struggle	Socio-political
Marie Antoinette	2006	Sofia Coppola	The young Austrian is married off to French Louis XIV and spends her days being bored.	Women in society	Socio-political
Me and Orson Welles	2009	Richard Linklater	A young man is cast in a play directed by a young Orson Welles.	Art and artistry	Aesthetics
Mermaid	2008	Anna Melikyan	A young Russian girl believes she can make dreams come true.	Magical realism, Cause and effect	Metaphysics
Messenger, The	2009	Oren Moverman	A soldier is assigned the job of informing loved ones of the death of their sons and daughters.	Impact of war, Sacrifice	Socio-political, Ethics
Michael Clayton	2007	Tony Gilroy	An attorney seeks to find the reasons for a colleague's apparent mental breakdown and the corruption within his law firm.	Justice	Socio-political
Mighty Heart	2007	Michael Winterbottom	A woman searches for Wall Street Journal reporter Daniel Pearl who was kidnapped and murdered.	War, Courage, Journalism ethics	Socio-political, Ethics
Milk	2008	Gus Van Sant	The story of openly gay Alderman who was assassinated	Gay Rights	Socio-political
Miss Pettigrew Lives for a Day	2008	Bharat Nalluri	A governess finds herself in high society.	Class issues	Socio-political
Miss Potter	2006	Chris Noonan	Beatrix Potter and her stories about rabbits.	Art and artistry, Feminism	Aesthetics, Socio-political
Mongol	2007	Sergei Bodrov	The early life of Genghis Khan.	Power	Socio-political
More than a Game	2009	Kristopher Belman	An examination of a high school basketball team that includes a future NBA star.	Sports, Men in society	Socio-political
Mr. Brooks	2007	Bruce A. Evans	A family man is actually a serial killer decides to stage another killing in order to protect his daughter.	Appearance-Reality	Epistemology

Title	Year	Director	Plot	Theme	Chapter, Topic
Music and Lyrics	2007	Marc Lawrence	A washed up Pop star and English literature major try to write a hit song for a singer in just 3 days.	Art and artistry	Aesthetics
My Winnipeg	2007	Guy Maddin	Documentary concerning director's home town and the pull it continues to have on him.	Nature of community and the self	Socio-political
Namesake, The	2007	Mira Nair	A couple has an arranged marriage and move to NYC where their son has mixed emotions about his heritage.	Cultural differences and relativism	Socio-political
Nativity Story, The	2006	Catherine Hardwicke	Story of Mary, Joseph, and Jesus.	Religion and humanity	Religion
Nefes: Vatan sagolsun	2009	Levent Semerci	A group of Turkish soldiers struggle to survive during the climax of the war.	War, Sacrifice	Socio-political
Necessities of Life, The	2008	Benoît Pilon	An Inuit with TB must recuperate in a sanatorium in Quebec City.	Necessities of life, Alienation	Metaphysics, socio-political
Next	2007	Lee Tamahori	A clairvoyant is able to see two minutes into his own future is sought after by the FBI to prevent a terrorist attack.	Determinism	Metaphysics
No Country for Old Men	2007	Joel and Ethan Coen	A drug deal goes very wrong and three men cross each other's paths West Texas with violent consequences.	Fate, Justice	Metaphysics, Ethics
No One's Son	2008	Arsen Anton Ostojić	A family is condemned to a bleak future after the Bosnian war.	War and its consequences	Socio-political
No Reservations	2007	Scott Hicks	A master chef in New York City runs her life like she does her work but must change after becoming guardian to her niece.	Women in society	Socio-political
Notorious Bettie Page, The	2006	Mary Harron	A naïve girl becomes famous pin up model.	Women in society	Socio-political
Number 23, The	2007	Joel Schumacher	After reading a book a man becomes obsessed with an esoteric belief that all incidents and events are directly connected to the number 23.	False beliefs	Epistemology
Of Time and the City	2009	Terence Davies	The transformation of the city of Liverpool through history.	Social realities	Socio-political
Offside	2006	Jafar Panahi	Iranian girls are arrested for trying to pretend to be men in order to see a soccer match.	Women in society	Socio-political

(continued)

Title	Year	Director	Plot	Theme	Chapter, Topic
On the Wings of Dreams	2007	Golam Rabbany Biplob	An Indian family tries to raise itself out of poverty.	Social realities	Socio-political
One Night with the King	2006	Michael O. Sajbel	An orphan must rediscover her Jewish heritage since she is chosen to be Xerxes's queen.	Religion and identity	Religion
Other Boleyn Girl, The	2008	Justin Chadwick	Anne and Mary Boleyn compete for King Henry VIII's affections	Struggle for power	Socio-political
Pan's Labyrinth	2006	Guillermo del Toro	A girl escapes brutal fascist stepfather by entering a fantasy world.	Fascism	Socio-political
Paranormal Activity	2007	Oren Peli	A young couple become subject to supernatural disturbances.	Supernatural elements	Epistemology, Metaphysics, Religion
Persepolis	2007	Vincent Paronnaud, Marjane Satrapi	An outspoken girl grows up in Iran.	Women in society	Socio-political
Pope's Toilet, The	2007	Cesar Charlone, Enrique Fernandez	A poor South American town prepares for the Pope's visit.	Poverty, Social realities, Church attitudes	Socio-political, Religion
Precious: Based on the Novel "Push" by Sapphire	2009	Lee Daniels	A poor, pregnant, overweight, and illiterate teen hopes to find a new direction with her life.	Life issues	Socio-political
Premonition	2007	Mennan Yapo	A woman lives the days of a week out of chronological order.	Cause and effect	Metaphysics
Princess and the Frog, The	2009	Ron Clements, John Musker	A Princess meets a frog prince who wants to be human again.	Inter-racial relationships	Socio-political
Purple Rose of Cairo, The	2006	Woody Allen	A movie fan's life is thrown into turmoil when her favorite star literally walks off the screen and into her life.	Appearance-Reality	Metaphysics
Quantum of Solace	2008	Marc Forster	A secret agent does battle against a man who seeks to privatize a country's water supply.	Environmental issues, Privatization and public goods	Socio-political, Ethics
					Socio-political
Reader, The	2008	Stephen Daldry	A boy falls in love with an illiterate woman who was a concentration camp guard and keeps her secret.	Secrets, Personal responsibility, War	Socio-political, Ethics
Reaping, The	2007	Stephen Hopkins	A woman who lost her faith investigates claims of miracles and supernatural plagues.	Miracles, Faith	Religion

Title	Year	Director	Plot	Theme	Chapter, Topic
Religulous	2008	Larry Charles	An examination of the rationality of various religious beliefs.	Faith and belief	Religion
Renaissance	2006	Christian Volckman	In the future, a geneticist who has found the formula for immortality is kidnapped.	Scientific theories	Science
Rendition	2007	Gavin Hood	When a terrorist suspect disappears on a flight to Washington, D.C., his American wife tries to learn the reason for his disappearance.	Justice, Terrorism, Utilitarianism	Socio-political, Ethics
Resident Evil: Extinction	2007	Russell Mulcahy	The corporation responsible for turning the world's creatures into zombies creates clones of a superior human to do battle against them.	Bad science, Corporate ethics	Science, Ethics
Rest is Silence, The	2008	Nae Caranfil	The making of the first Romanian film in 1911 serves as a backdrop to depicting life at the beginning of the century.	Film-making	Aesthetics
Retrieval	2006	Slawomir Fabicki	A hardworking but poor man gets a taste of the rich, but criminal life.	Personal integrity, capitalism	Socio-political, Ethics
Revanche	2008	Götz Spielmann	A criminal's girlfriend is shot by a policeman and revenge is in order.	Revenge	Ethics
Righteous Kill	2008	Jon Avnet	Police try to solve a series of revenge executions.	Revenge	Ethics
Road to Guantanamo, The	2006	Michael Winterbottom	While touring their homeland, four young men are mistaken for Taliban members and wind up in a notorious U.S. prison camp.	War, Injustice	Socio-political
Road, The	2009	John Hillcoat	A father and son try to survive a postapocalyptic world.	Familial Responsibilities, Dystopia	Socio-political, Ethics
Satanás	2007	Andi Baiz	Three lives will intertwine in the build up to a mass murder.	Moral corruption	Ethics
Savages, The	2007	Tamara Jenkins	Siblings have to look after ailing father.	Role responsibility	Ethics
Saw VI	2009	Kevin Geutert	A healthcare policy insurer must choose which lives to save in a gruesome game.	Healthcare Ethics	Ethics
Scanner Darkly, A	2006	Richard Linklater	Three men live in a house but one is actually a narcotics officer who is trying to track down drug dealers.	Utopia & dystopia	Socio-political

(continued)

Title	Year	Director	Plot	Theme	Chapter, Topic
Science of Sleep, The	2006	Michel Gondry	A man's inability to tell the dream world from the real world is made even more complicated when he falls in love.	Appearance-Reality	Epistemology
September Dawn	2007	Cristopher Cain	A Mormon boy, Christian girl fall in love in Utah 1857.	Religious differences	Religion
Seven Pounds	2008	Gabriele Muccino	An IRS agent with a secret changes the lives of strangers.	Sacrifice, Redemption	Ethics
Sex and the City	2008	Michael Patrick King	The exploits of four female best friends in New York.	Portrayal of women, Sexuality	Socio-political
Shortcut to Happiness	2007	Alec Baldwin	A down-on-his-luck writer agrees to exchange his soul for success but then must enlist the help of a famous orator to help him get out of the deal.	Greed	Ethics
Sicko	2007	Michael Moore	Documentary concerning the American health care system, focusing on its for-profit health insurance and pharmaceutical industry.	Healthcare ethics	Ethics
Sin Nombre	2009	Cary Fukunaga	A Honduran girl who dreams of living in America crosses paths with a Mexican gang member who also seeks to cross the border.	Social realities, Immigration	Socio-political
Sivaji	2007	S. Shankar	A man blackmails individuals who possess substantial quantities of illegal money and uses their "donations" to support his own non-profit education foundation.	Utilitarianism	Ethics
Sketches of Frank Gehry	2006	Sydney Pollack	Documentary concerning noted architect.	Art and artistry	Aesthetics
Slumdog Millionaire	2008	Danny Boyle, Loveleen Tandan	A boy from the slums of India is a contestant on a popular game show and is suspected of cheating.	Poverty, Cultural issues	Socio-political
Soloist, The	2009	Joe Wright	A reporter befriends a homeless violin player and witnesses life on the street for the mentally ill.	Treatment of the mentally ill	Socio-political
Snow	2008	Aida Begic	The remaining villagers try to survive after the Bosnian war.	War and its consequences	Socio-political
Still Walking	2009	Hirokazu Kore-eda	A family reunites to remember the anniversary of the death of the eldest son.	Meaning of life, Familial relationships	Metaphysics, Socio-political, Ethics

Title	Year	Director	Plot	Theme	Chapter, Topic
Street Kings	2008	David Ayer	A police officer is implicated in the murder of a fellow cop and he realizes he cannot trust anyone.	Culture of authority	Socio-political
Sugar	2009	Anna Boden, Ryan Fleck	Baseball players in the Dominican Republic face cultural challenges while attempting to make it in the U.S. Major Leagues.	Sports, cultural differences, Meaning of life	Socio-political, Metaphysics
Sukkar banat	2007	Nadine Labaki	The lives and loves of five Lebanese women living in Beirut.	Women in society	Socio-political
Summer Hours	2009	Olivier Assayas	Children of a dying woman confront her wish to get rid of her "things," which are to them their "memories."	Identity, memories, Meaning of life	Metaphysics
Sunshine	2007	Danny Boyle	In the year 2057, the Sun is failing, and the Icarus project has been formed with the intent of travelling to the sun and detonating a massive thermonuclear payload to reignite it.	Utilitarianism, Bad Science	Ethics, Science
Superman Returns	2006	Bryan Singer	Superman returns to earth after a long disappearance.	Faith and resurrection	Religion
Surrogates	2009	Jonathan Mostow	Humans remain safe while living their lives vicariously through surrogate robots.	Artificial Intelligence, Using people	Metaphysics, Ethics
Syndromes and a Century	2006	Apichatpong Weerasethakul	A director reminiscences about growing up with doctors as parents.	Medical ethics	Ethics
Synecdoche, New York	2008	Charlie Kaufman	A director attempts to reproduce New York life size in a warehouse.	Appearance-Reality, Nature of family	Metaphysics, Socio-political
Taxidermia	2007	György Pálfi	Three generations of men engage in bizarre sexual and violent activities.	Violence and sex, Censorship	Ethics
Teeth	2007	Mitchell Lichtenstein.	A young woman discovers that she has an extra set of teeth located in a most awkward spot for her boyfriends.	Sexual morality, Gender roles in society	Socio-political, Ethics
Ten Canoes	2006	Rolf de Heer	A fable concerning an ancient aboriginal society and one man's desire for his brother's wife.	State of nature	Socio-political
Terminator Salvation	2009	McG	A small group of rebels fight against machines who have taken over the earth.	Technology, Dystopia	Metaphysics, Socio-political

(continued)

Title	Year	Director	Plot	Theme	Chapter, Topic
Thank You for Smoking	2006	Jason Reitman	The spokesman for Tobacco industry argues his case to the American public.	Healthcare and industry, Liberty, Harm to self	Socio-political, Ethics
Thieves and Liars	2006	Ricardo Méndez Matta	Drugs and corruption in Puerto Rico.	Social realities	Socio-political
This Film Is Not Yet Rated	2006	Kirby Dick	Documentary concerning the American movie ratings board.	Censorship	Socio-political
This is It!	2009	Kenny Ortega	Michael Jackson prepares for what will be his last concert.	Art and artisry	Aesthetics
Time Traveler's Wife, The	2009	Robert Schwentke	A man time travels at unexpected moments, causing various complications in his life.	Cause-effect, Determinism	Metaphysics
Tony Manero	2008	Pablo Larraín	In Pinochet's Chile, a serial killer is obsessed with the film Saturday Night Fever.	Totalitarianism, Dystopia	Socio-political
Trade	2007	Marco Kreuzpaintner	Mexican Kidnappers sell their young victims as sex slaves.	Using persons, Immoral behavior	Ethics
Transit Café	2006	Kambuzia Partovi	A widow takes over her husband's truck stop restaurant in Tehran.	Women in society	Socio-political
Tropic Thunder	2008	Ben Stiller	Actors playing soldiers become real soldiers in a real battle.	Appearance-Reality, Racial portrayals	Metaphysics, Socio-political
Trouble the Water	2008	Carl Deal Tia Lessin	Documentary concerning the struggles of the poor in New Orleans in the aftermath of the Katrina hurricane.	Social realities, Injustice	Socio-political
Tour, The	2008	Goran Marković	A group of Serbian actors find themselves on the front line of the war.	War, savagery	Socio-political
Trap, The	2007	Srdan Golubović	A Serbian must choose between life and the death of his own child.	Existentialism, Social realities	Socio-political, Ethics
Under the Bombs	2008	Philippe Aractingi	A woman looks for her missing son during the Israeli/Lebanon war of 2006.	War and its consequences	Socio-political
United 93	2006	Paul Greengrass	The Sept 11, 2001, flight is hijacked by terrorists, and the passengers attempt to do something about it.	Sacrifice	Ethics
Unreasonable Man, An	2007	Henriette Mantel	Documentary concerning social activist Ralph Nader.	Social activism	Socio-political

Title	Year	Director	Plot	Theme	Chapter, Topic
Untraceable	2008	Gregory Hoblit	A computer expert tortures people live on the Internet.	Internet culture	Socio-political, Metaphysics, Ethics
Up	2009	Pete Doctor, Bob Peterson	An old man ties balloons to his house so that he can float around the world and see it before he dies.	Friendship, Ageism, Meaning of life	Socio-political, Ethics Metaphysics
Up in the Air	2009	Jason Reitman	A man's job is to travel around and fire his company's employees.	Worker relations	Socio-Politics
V for Vendetta	2006	James McTeigue	A man seeks to restore liberty in fascist London by destroying Parliament.	Liberty, Violence as a solution, Authoritarianism	Socio-political
Valkyrie	2008	Bryan Singer	The true story of the attempted assassination of Adolf Hitler.	Authoritarianism, Self-sacrifice	Socio-political, Ethics
Vicky Cristina Barcelona	2008	Woody Allen	Two girlfriends in Spain fight over a man and then his ex-wife shows up.	Portrayal of women, Relationships	Socio-political
Volver	2006	Pedro Almodóvar	A woman who tries hard to fulfill her various roles has odd family members to deal with.	Women in society	Socio-political
W.	2008	Oliver Stone	Profile of President George W. Bush.	Politics and power	Socio-political
Wall-E	2008	Andrew Stanton	A lonely robot on a devastated earth embarks on a mission that could save mankind.	Artificial Intelligence, Environmental Issues	Metaphysics, Ethics
Waltz with Bashir	2008	Ari Folman	A man and his friends struggle to remember details of the Lebanon war that they were involved in.	War and its consequences, Memory and truth	Socio-political, Epistemology
Watchmen	2009	Zack Snyder	Superheroes are being murdered in a world where they are also banned.	Utilitarianism, Friendship	Ethics
Way I Spent the End of the World, The	2006	Catalin Mitulescu	Communism falls in Romania.	Communism, Nationalism	Socio-political
Wedding Chest, The	2006	Nurbek Egen	A Parisian woman struggles against the prejudices of her Kyrgyzstanian fiancé's relatives.	Tradition and modernism	Socio-political
When the Levees Broke	2006	Spike Lee	The role of the U.S. government in responding to Hurricane Katrina.	Governmental responsibility	Socio-political

(continued)

Title	Year	Director	Plot	Theme	Chapter, Topic
Which Way Home	2009	Rebecca Cammisa	Children leave home because they cannot obtain the basic necessities of life.	Social realities, Poverty	Socio-political
White Palms	2006	Szabolcs Hajdu	A boy trains to be a gymnast in a communist world and then becomes a coach in a Western democracy.	Communism, Sports	Socio-political
Who Killed the Electric Car?	2006	Chris Paine	Documentary concerning the possible conspiracy to halt the creation of an electric car.	Conspiracy, science, Environmental ethics	Epistemology, Science, Ethics
Why We Fight	2006	Eugene Jarecki	Documentary concerning the industrial complex involvement in American wars.	Capitalism and war	Socio-political
White Silk Dress, The	2007	Luu Huynh	A Vietnam family faces difficulties in surviving during the 1950s.	Sacrifice, Social realities	Socio-political, Ethics
Women, The	2008	Diane English	A woman bonds with other high society women at a resort.	Portrayal of women, Relationships	Socio-political
Wrestler, The	2008	Darren Aronofsky	An aged wrestler seeks redemption.	Meaning of life, Personal transformation	Metaphysics
Yacoubian Building, The	2006	Marwan Hamed	Taboo issues are dealt with in Cairo.	Prostitution, Homosexuality, Corruption, Religious fundamentalism	Socio-political, Religion, Ethics
Year My Parents Went On Vacation, The	2007	Cao Hamburger	A boy is left alone while Brazil faces dictatorship and football.	Dictatorship	Socio-political
Young Victoria, The	2009	Jean-Marc Vallee	Queen Victoria's first few years on the throne are difficult.	Expectations of royalty, Personal sacrifice	Socio-political
Wind That Shakes the Barley, The	2006	Kenneth Loach	An Irish doctor transforms into member of the IRA.	Social and political activism	Socio-political
World Trade Center	2006	Oliver Stone	Plight of firefighters in WTC on Sept 11, 2001.	Duty, Sacrifice	Ethics
Worlds Apart	2008	Niels Arden Oplev	The daughter of a Jehovah Witness must decide between religion and love.	Faith and inner conflict	Religion
Wristcutters: A Love Story	2007	Goran Dukic	In the afterworld, people who commit suicide waste their death in the same ways as they wasted their lives.	Meaning of life, Existentialism	Metaphysics

Title	Year	Director	Plot	Theme	Chapter, Topic
X-Men: The Last Stand	2006	Brett Ratner	Superhero mutants are reviled by humans and do battle among themselves.	Intolerance	Socio-political
XXY	2007	Lucia Puenzo	An intersexed teenager and her family cope as best as they can with her condition.	Gender, Sex roles	Socio-political
You Bet Your Life	2006	Antonin Svoboda	A gambler risks it all with fate.	Fate, Personal responsibility	Metaphysics, Ethics
Zack and Miri Make a Porno	2008	Kevin Smith	A couple decides to make money by making a pornographic movie.	Pornography	Socio-political, Ethics
Zodiac	2007	David Fincher	Hunt for serial killer becomes obsession for one man.	Seeking justice	Socio-political
Zombieland	2009	Ruben Fleischer	Two strangers are able to survive in a world of zombies.	Mind-body, Life after death	Metaphysics

CREDITS

Introduction

Page 2: The Value of Philosophy by Bertrand Russell, *The Problems of Philosophy*, 2e; Oxford University Press; A Galaxy Book; pp. 89–94 (1967). Page 4: The Apology of Socrates by Plato, *The Apology of Socrates from The Works of Plato: A New and Literal Version* Vol. I. Trans. By Henry Cary. Published by G. Bell & Sons, London (1881); pp. 3–29.

Chapter 1

Page 27: Pyrrhonic Sketches, Book I, Chapters I–XVI, XVIII–XXVII by Sextus Empiricus, from *Sextus Empiricus and Greek Scepticism*. Trans. By Mary Mills Patrick. Published by George Bell & Sons, London (1899); pp. 101–152. Page 35: Mediations I & II by René Descartes, *Mediations,* trans. John Veitch (1901). Page 42: An Essay Concerning Human Understanding, Book 1, Chapter II by John Locke, *An Essay Concerning Human Understanding,* 29e; Published by Printed for Thomas Tegg, London (1841); pp. 8–19. Page 49: Critique of Pure Reason by Immanuel Kant, *Critique of Pure Reason, Revised Edition*. Trans. By J. M. D. Meiklejohn. The Colonial Press, New York (1899); pp. 1–18. Page 58: An Argument against Skepticism by John Hospers, *An Introduction to Philosophical Analysis, 2e*; Prentice Hall (1967), pp. 180–188. Page 64: Truth and Falsehood from Problems of Philosophy by Russell Bertrand, *The Problems of Philosophy*, 2e; Oxford University Press; *A Galaxy Book;* pp. 69–75 (1967). Page 68: Pragmatism by William James, Longman, Green, and Co; New York (1907); *Excerpts from Lectures II and VI.* Page 73: An Enquiry Concerning Human Understanding (1777 edition) by David Hume, *An Enquiry Concerning Human Understanding;* (London: 1777). Page 79: Science and the Physical World by W.T. Stace, *Science and the Physical World* (from Man Against Science University of Pittsburgh, 1967).

Chapter 2

Page 94: The Nature of Metaphysics by Peter van Inwagen, Stephen Laurence and Cynthia Macdonald (eds.), *Contemporary Readings in the Foundations of Metaphysics,* Wiley-Blackwell (1998). Page 101: Allegory of the Cave by Plato, trans. *Republic* (1930), Harvard University Press, Cambridge, Mass.Book VII, pp. 514a–520a. Page 105: Parmenides by Plato, F.M. Cornford, trans. *Parmenides* (1939), Routledge and Kegan Paul, London, pp. 126–135d. Page 110: Categories by Aristotle, Trans G.S Bowe. Page 114: De Interpretatione by Aristotle, *Chapter Nine of De Interpretatione for 28* Blaise Pascal—Pensées (book title) section 233 (1910, Trotter translation. Page 119, of Liberty and Necessity, David Hume, *An Enquiry Concerning Human Understanding;* Vol. XXXVII, Part 3. The Harvard Classics. New York: P.F. Collier & Son, 1909–14. Page 126: Freedom and Determinism by Richard Taylor, *Metaphysics*, 4e; Prentice-Hall (1992). Page 138: Minds, Brains, and Programs by John R. Searle, from *The Behavioral and Brain Sciences*, Vol 3.,Cambridge University Press, (1980). Page 150: Reductive and Eliminative Materialism by Paul Churchland, *Matter and Consciousness: a Contemporary Introduction to the Philosophy of Mind MIT Press* (1984). Page 156: What is it like to be a Bat? By Thomas Nagel, from *Philosophical Review* 83, pp. 435–450, Duke University Press (1974). Page 163: Other Minds are Known by Analogy from One's Own Case by Bertrand Russell, *Human Knowledge: Its Scope and Limits,* pp. 482–486, George Allen and Unwin, (1948).

Chapter 3

Page 175: Ontological argument, by St. Anselm, from *Proslogium*. Translated by Sidney Norton Deane; Open Court Publishing Company, Chicago (1903); pp. 52–57. Page 177: The Five Ways by Aquinas, The Summa Theologica of St. Thomas Aquinas. Literally translated by Fathers of the English Dominican Province; Second and Revised Edition; Burns, Oates & Washbourne Ltd., London (1920). Page 178: The Watch and the Watchmaker by William Paley, *Natural Theology* (1800). Page 183: Of the Necessity of the Wager Pascal by Blaise Pascal—*Of the Necessity of the Wager from Thoughts*. Trans by W.F. Trotter; Published by P.F. Collier & son, New York (1910); pp. 83–87, 99, 160–161, 174, 176, 200, 201. Page 187: Some Major Strands of Theodicy by Richard Swinburne, from *The Evidential Argument from Evil,* Daniel Howard-Snyder ed., Indiana University Press (1996), pp. 30–48. Page 200: Section X of Miracles by David Hume, *Of Miracles from Enquiries Concerning the Human Understanding, and Concerning the Principles of Morals,* 2nd Edition. Reprinted from the Posthumous Edition of 1777; ed. L.A. Selby-Biggie. Late Fellow of University College, Oxford (1902). Page 209: Religious Belief Without Evidence by Alvin Plantinga, from *Religious Experience and Religious Belief: Essays in Epistemology* ed. Joseph Runzo and Craig Ihara, University Press of America (1986). Page 218: The Will to Believe and other Essays in Popular Philosophy by William James, *The Will to Believe and Other Essays in Popular Philosophy,* Henry Holt & Co. (1892). Page 229: Fear and Trembling: A Dialectical Lyric by Soren Kierkegaard, *Fear and Trembling: A Dialectical Lyric,* (1843). Page 233: Problems of Religious Pluralism by John Hick, *"A Philosophy of Pluralism" Problems of Religious Pluralism,* St. Martin's Press, 28–46 (1985).

Chapter 4

Page 247: Leviathan by Thomas Hobbes, *Leviathan* (1651). Page 259: Second Treatise of Government by John Locke, *Two Treatises of Government,* (1680–1690). Page 277: A Theory of Justice by John Rawls, *A Theory of Justice,* Harvard University Press, pp. 3–5, 11–13, 60–65 (1971). Page 281: Anarchy, State, and Utopia by R. Nozick, Anarchy, State and Utopia (excerpts from Anarchy, *State and Utopia,* Basic Books NY 1974), pp. ix, 30–32, 149–164, 167–174. Page 291: Discourse on Inequality by Jean-Jacques Rousseau, *Discourse on the Origin of Inequality, the Second Part from The Social Contract and Discourses.* Trans.by G. D. H. Cole. Published by J. M. Dent & Sons, Ltd., London & E. P. Dutton & Co., New York (1920); pp. 207–238. Page 306: A Vindication of the Rights of Woman by Mary Wollstonecraft, from *A Vindication of the Rights of Woman with Strictures on Political and Moral Subjects.* Published by T. Fisher Unwin, London (1891); pp. 49–73. Page 316: The Subjection of Women by John Stuart Mill, *The Subjection of Women* (1869). Page 327: The Second Sex by Simone de Beauvoir, *The Second Sex,* trans. HM Parshley, Alfred A Knopf (1980).

Chapter 5

Page 341: Nicomachean Ethics by Aristotle, *Nicomachean Ethics,* trans. W.D. Ross, Clarendon Press (1905). Page 358: Republic, Book II by Plato, from *The Republic of Plato: An Ideal Commonwealth.* Trans. by Benjamin Jowett; The Colonial Press, New York (1901); pp. 35–65. Page 374: An Introduction to the Principles of Morals and Legislation by Jeremy Bentham, *An Introduction to the Principles of Morals and Legislation,* (1823). Page 382: Utilitarianism by John Stuart Mill, *Utilitarianism,* (1863). Page 394: The Challenge of Cultural Relativism by James Rachels, *The Elements of Moral Philosophy* 5e, McGraw Hill, 2007, pp 16–31. Page 400: Foundations of the Metaphysics of Morals by Immanuel Kant, *Foundations of the Metaphysics of Morals,* trans. Lewis White Beck, Liberal Arts Press, division of The Bobbs-Merrill Company (1959), 29–51, 54–56. Page 410: An Enquiry Concerning the Principles of Morals by David Hume, *An Enquiry Concerning the Principles of Morals* (1777).

Chapter 6

Page 432: Creation Science Is Not Science by Michael Ruse, *Creation Science Is Not Science, Science, Technology & Human Values,* Jul 1982; vol. 7: pp. 72–78. Page 438: Science, Conjecture and Refutation by Karl Popper, *Science, Conjecture and Refutation: The Growth of Scientific Knowledge,* Harper Torchbooks, pp. 33–39,42,43,52–58 (1962). Page 448: The Structure of Scientific Revolutions by Thomas Kuhn, *The Structure of Scientific Revolutions,* 2e, University of Chicago Press, pp. 92–110 (1970). Page 456: How To Defend Society Against Science by Paul K. Feyerabend, *Radical Philosophy* 2 Summer 1975 pp. 4–8.

Chapter 7

Page 476: Of the Standard of Taste by David Hume, *Of The Standard Of Taste from The Philosophical Works* of David Hume in Four Volumes, Vol. III (Essays Moral, Political, And Literary). Published by Printed for A. Black and W. Tait, London (1826); pp. 256–282. Page 485: Republic, Book X by Plato, *Republic Book X from The Republic of Plato: An Ideal Commonwealth.* Trans. by Benjamin Jowett; The Colonial Press, New York (1901); pp. 299–316. Page 494: Poetics by Aristotle, Poetics from *The Poetics of Aristotle,* Fourth Edition. Ed. S. H. Butcher, Macmillan (1907); pp. 23–39, 45–57. Page 499: The Intentional Fallacy by W. K. Wimsatt, JR., and M. C. Beardsley, *The Sewanee Review* Vol. 54, pp. 468–488 (1946). Page 508: In Defense of the Author by E. D. Hirsch, JR., *In Defense of the Author* (from Validity in Interpretation New Haven Yale University Press pp. 1–6, 44–48, 1967). Page 515: Art and Authenticity by Nelson Goodman, *Art and Authenticity* (from Languages of Art: An Approach to a Theory of Symbols Hackett Publ. 1976).

INDEX

Note: Page numbers followed by an *n* refer to notes. Page numbers followed by a *ph* refer to photographs.

A

Abraham, 230, 232
Absolute, 72–73
Absolute ideas, 108–109
Absolute monarchy, 265–266, 318
Absolutist, 222, 228
Abstract (Hume, David), 447*n*.4
Abstract thought, 107–108
Academic criticism, 509
Academic philosophy, 27
The Accused, 242
(ACLU) American Civil Liberties Union, 432
Acquisition of holdings, 283
Action, 55n, 71, 121–126, 132–137, 381, 397, 494–497
Adaptation (Lewontin, Richard C.), 438*n*.24
Adeimantus, 360, 363–364, 366, 369–370, 372
Adler, Alfred, 439, 441
Adonai, 238
Advantage, 380
Æschylus, 360, 374
Aesthetic criticism, 501–502
Aesthetics, 464, 516–523
Affirmation, 114–118
Agathon, 499
    Works: *Antheus*, 496
Agency/agents, 136–138, 494–495
Agriculture, 296–297
AI (artificial intelligence), 138–143
Alcibiades, 496
Alexander, 204
Algebra, 382
Alienation of labour, 271–272, 275–276
Aliens, 242
Aliens, 469*n*.18
All Dogs go to Heaven, 90*n*.7
Allah, 238
Allegory of the Cave (Plato), 85, 101–104
Allographic, 520–521, 523
Allusiveness, 506, 508
Alston, William, 101*n*.8
Altruist, 333
The Amazing Randi, 426
Ambition, 356
American Civil Liberties Union (ACLU), 432
American Family Association, 470*n*.20
Analogy, 163–164
Analytical *à priori* knowledge, 57
Analytical judgements, 52–53, 501
Analytical propositions, 54, 403
Anarchism From Theory to Practice (Guerin, Daniel), 291*n*.5
The Anarchists (Mackay, Henry), 291*n*.5
Anarchy, 288
Anarchy, State, and Utopia (Nozick), 281–291
Anaxagoras, 30
The Ancient Mariner (Coleridge), 505
Andria (Terence), 483
The Andromeda Strain, 424*ph*, 427–431

Animals, 422
Anselm, Saint, *Ontological Argument*, 167, 175–176
Antheus (Agathon), 496
Anti-metaphysics, 97
Antiphon, 105–110
Anti-realism, 97
Antonioni, Michael, 25–26
Apelles, 30
Aphasia, 33–34
Apocalypto, 464
Apodeictic principle, 401
The Apology of Socrates (Plato), 4–18, 502
Appearance, 94, 100
Approbation, 381
Aquinas, Saint, *The Five Ways*, 167, 177–178
Arbitrary lots, 258
Arbitrary power, 268, 303
Arbitrator, 258
Architecture, 523
An Argument against Skepticism (Hospers, John), 58–64
The Argument from Design, 167
Arguments, 75, 78–79
Ariosto, 478
Ariosto, Shakespeare and Corneille (Croce), 501*n*.9
Aristocracy, 303
Aristophanes, *Lysistrata*, 330
Aristoteles. *See* Aristotle
Aristotle, 105–110, 333–334, 461, 482
    Works: *Categories*, 110–113; *De Interpretatione*, 114–118; *Nicomachean Ethics*, 341–357, 440–441; *Physics*, 85; *Poetics*, 494–499; *Politics*, 257
Aristotle's Golden Mean, 333
Arithmetic (Segner), 54
Arkansas Act 590, 432, 434, 436*n*.1, 437*n*.3, 437*n*.10, 437*n*.12
Arnold, 503
Art, 23, 464, 464–474, 515–523
Art and Authenticity (Goodman, Nelson), 515–523
Artificial intelligence, 138–149
Artist, 485–489
Artistic criticism, 501
Artistic process, 473–474, 503
Astrology/astrologers, 426, 440, 447*n*.4
Astronomy, 451
Ataraxia, 27–30, 35
Athalia, 484
Atheist/atheism, 182, 209
Atom, 80, 82
Augmentative judgements, 52
Auschwitz, 338
Austen, Jane, *Sense and Sensibility*, 240*ph*, 244–245
Authenticity, 515–523
Author psychology, 504
Authorial irrelevance, 509
Autographic, 520–522
Ayers, A. J., *Language, Truth and Logic*, 217

B

Back to the Future, 84*ph*, 87–88
Badlands, 169*n*.1
Badness, 381
Baillie, Donald, *God Was in Christ*, 235
Baillie, John, *The Place of Jesus Christ in Modern Christianity*, 235
Barbarism, 389
Barbeyrac, 301
Bartram, *Travels*, 505
Basicality, 216–218
Bateson, F. W., 507, 513–514
Bats, 157–163
Baudelaire, 506
Beardsley, Monroe, 499–508
    Works: *The Intentional Fallacy*, 467
Beauty, 464, 477–482, 495–496
Beauvoir, Simone de, *The Second Sex*, 327–331
Beetlejuice, 90*n*.6
Behavior, 127–137, 146–149, 163–165, 241
Behavioral and Brain Sciences (Searle, John R.), 138–149
Behaviorism, 151
Belief(s)
    determinism, 130–131
    eliminative materialism, 155
    existence of properties, 99
    and fact, 65–66
    false, 189
    in God, 174, 183–184
    good, in the way of, 72
    justified, 20–21, 25, 36–40
    in miracles, 203
    religious, 209–218, 228, 233–244, 255
Benda, *Rapport d'Uriel*, 329
Benefits, 241–242, 250, 277, 279–280, 380
Benevolence, 412–413, 422–423
Bentham, Jeremy, 335
    Works: *An Introduction to the Principles of Morals and Legislation*, 374–376, 381*n*.15, 378, 380–381
Bertrand, Russell, *Truth and Falsehood from Problems of Philosophy*, 64–68
Bible, 261, 392, 425, 436
    Acts 20:35, 195
    Psalms xiv. 1, 175–176
Biblical literalism, 432, 436
The Big Sleep, 469
Bigotry, 484
Biographia (Coleridge), 504–505
Blanshard, Brand, *Reason and Belief*, 211
Blind men, elephant (allegory), 236
Block, Ned, 149*n*.3
Blockbuster Video, 470*n*.20
Blow Up (Antonioni, Michael), 25–26
Body, 38–42, 89–93, 104, 125
Body Snatchers, 469
Bogart, Humphrey, 335
Book ll from Republic (Plato), 358–374
Born, Max, *Natural Philosophy of Cause and Chance*, 443
Bosanquet, *Lecture*, 502

548

The Boston Strangler, 169n.1
A Boy and His Dog, 241n.3
Brain damage, 154
Brain simulator reply, 144
Braisidas, 300
Braithwaite, R. B., *Scientific Explanation*, 437n.5
Bright, Bill, 470n.20
British Journal for the Philosophy of Science, 447n.13
British Philosophy, 438
Brooks, Cleanth, 513–514
Burdens, 241–242
Burke, Kenneth, *Philosophy of Literary Form*, 508n.15
"Butcher of Riga", 169

C

Calamities, 388
Calculus of probability, 446
Caloric, 152–153
Calvin, John, 215
Campus Crusade for Christ, 470n.20
Capitalist, 275
Carritt, E. F., *Defence of Poetry*, 508n.9
Cartesian dualism, 149
Cassirer, Ernst, 509, 515n.9
Cassirer's Philosophy of Symbolic Forms (Cassirer, Ernst), 512, 515n.9
Cast Away, 167
Categorical imperative, 334, 401–402, 404, 406, 408
Categories (Aristotle), 110–113
Catholic religion, 484
Causal necessity, 131
Causal properties, 144–147, 149, 165
Causal relations, 151
Causal responsibility, 86
Causation, 79–80, 125, 137
Cause, 50–51, 55
Cause and effect, 74–80, 82, 86, 88, 120–128, 177, 197
The Cell, 89–90
Certainty, 122
Chalcedonian Definition, 235
The Challenge of Cultural Relativism (Rachels, James), 394–400
Chamberlain, Wilt, 286–287
Change, 50
Chaplin, Charlie, 245–246
Character, 494–495, 497–498
Chemical principles, 454
Chemical revolution, 454–455
Chemistry/chemist, 449, 454–455
Children, 263, 306, 347, 370, 398, 461
Chinese science, 459
Chisholm, Roderick, 217
    Works: *Theory of Knowledge*, 212
Choice, 198, 461–462
Christian exclusivism, 235
Christianity/Christian, 391–392, 425, 457, 460, 470–473
Christology, 235–236
Churchland, Paul
    Works: *Matter and Consciousness*, 150–155; *Reductive and Eliminative Materialism*, 150–155
Cicero, 482
Cinderella (Disney), 242
Circulus in probando, 31–32

Citizens for a Universal Appeal, 470n.20
Citizenship, 345
Civil distinctions, 303
Civil estate, 252
Classical foundationalism, 213–214, 217
Classifications, movie, 466–467
Clavius, *De Sphaera of Sacrobosco*, 505
Clifford, W. K., 209, 221
Clitia (Machiavel), 483
Cognition, 50–52, 56–58, 108, 141–144, 146–148, 152
Coherence, 65
Coke, Sir Edward
    Works: *Commentary on Littleton*, 254; *Institution*, 259n.5
In Cold Blood, 169n.1
Coleridge, 503
    Works: *The Ancient Mariner*, 505; *Biographia*, 504–505; *Kubla Kahn*, 505
Combination, 114
Combination reply, 145
Comedy, 494, 497
Comic books, 464
Command of reason, 401
Commentary on Littleton (Coke, Sir Edward), 254
Commercials, 20
Commodification, 246
Common-sense, 150–151, 477
Commonwealth, 254, 265, 267
Communication, 399
Community, 266–267, 269–270, 375–376
Comparison, 480
Compensation, 198
Competing paradigms, 431, 448, 456
Competition, 247, 270
Complaisance, 256
Complex unity, 68
Comprehension, 32
Computers, 138–149
Conception, 51–55, 150, 154, 157–163, 176–177
Concretisation, 238
Confirmation, 433, 435, 439
Conformity, 255
Congreve, William, *The Way of the World*, 499
Conjugal society, 263–264
Conjunctions, 115, 120, 122–125, 130, 142
Conscious experience, 156–157
Consciousness, 156–157
Consequences, 251
Consistency, 126, 498
Constant conjunction, 124–125
Constituents of the judgement, 67
Constraint, 132–134
Contact, 166ph, 170, 172
Context, 94–96
Contract, 250–251, 303
Contradiction, 31, 54–56, 59, 115–116, 118
Contraries, 113, 116
Contrivance, 179–182
Convenience, 380
The Conversation (Coppola, Francis Ford), 25–26
Coomaraswamy, Ananda K., 501
Copernicus, 459
Coppola, Francis Ford, 25–26
Corneille, 502
Corpuscular paradigm, 453

Corpuscularism, 454
Correspondence with fact, 66
Cosmos (Sagan, Carl), 95
Courage, 355
Covenant, 250–255
Creation, 434–435
Creation Research Society, 436
Creation Science is not Science (Ruse, Michael), 432–438
Creationism/creationist, 425–426, 435
Creation-science, 425, 432, 434–436, 437n.12
Creativity, 464–474
Creator, 182–183, 485–486
Creophylus, 488
Crime/criminal, 418–420
Criterion of demarcation, 443–444
Criterion of skepticism, 29
Criticism, 123, 457, 476–484, 499–514
Critique of Pure Reason (Kant, Immanuel), 49–58
Croce, 501–502
    Works: *Ariosto, Shakespeare and Corneille*, 508n.9
Crocean system, 502
Cultural differences, 395, 398
Cultural Differences Argument, 395–396
Cultural feminism, 243
Cultural relativism, 394–400
Culture, moral codes of, 394, 398, 400
Cumulative acquisition, 449–450
Curtius, Quintus, 121
Customary transition, 124

D

Dance, 523
Dante, 506
Darius (King of Persia), 394
Darwin, Charles, *The Origin of Species*, 435
Darwinism, 458
Davidson, Donald, 162
Dawn of the Dead, 92
The Day After Tomorrow, 169n.2
Day of the Dead, 91–92
Deadly Mantis, 469
Death, 88–90, 199n.8, 255, 348–349
Debates, 210
Deception, 36–40
Deductive-nomological explanation, 431
Deep Impact, 169n.2
Defence of Poetry (Carritt, E. F.), 508n.9
In Defense of the Author (Hirsch, E. D. Jr.), 508–515
Deities, 238
Deliberation, 129–131, 138
Delicacy of imagination, 479–482
Delusions, 204, 206
Demarcation, 442–444, 446–447
Democracy, 303
Demon hypothesis, 23, 37
Demonstrative reasoning, 77
Demythologization, 457
Denial, 114–118
Deontologist, 334
Descartes, René, 20, 453, 482
    Works: *Meditations*, 20, 22–25, 89; *Meditations on First Philosophy*, 35–42; *Second Meditation*, 25
Design, 167, 179–182, 507
Desires, 189–192, 195, 199n.7

Despotism, 304–305, 324
Determinate verbal meaning, 510–512
Determinism, 86–88, 90, 127–137
Deus ex Machina, 499
Devaluation, 271
Dharmakaya, 237
Dick, Philip K., *Total Recall*, 21–22
Diction, 494–495
Differentiae, 111–113
Diffidence, 247
Diogenes, 305
Direct introspection, 90
Discourse on the Origin of Inequality, the Second Part (Rousseau, Jean-Jacques), 291–306, 309–310
Dissent, 287
Dissolution of government, 269
Distinctions, 411
Distribution, 242
Distributive justice, 256–257, 282–283, 286, 288–290
Divine impersona, 239
Divine persona, 239
Divine will, 401
Division, 56
Doctrine of the elements, 58
Doctrine of the method of pure reason, 58
Dogmatic/Dogmatist, 27–29, 31–35
Dominant film reading, 467
Don Quixote, 479
Donne, John, 505–506, 508
    Works: *Elegy on Prince Henry*, 506; *The First Anniversary*, 506
Double Indemnity, 469
Doubt, 171, 229
Doubting School, 27
Drama, 523
Dreams, 23, 36–40
Dreyfus, Hubert, 149n.3
Dualism, 89–90, 93, 149
Ducasse, Curt, 503–504
Duties, 405, 408
Dynamics, 453
Dynamis, 27

E

Ebert, Roger, 470
Ecclesiastical Benefices, 381n.14
Eclipse observations, 438
Economic and Philosophical Manuscripts of 1844 Estranged Labour (Marx, Karl), 270–277
Economics, 342
Economist, political, 270–271
Eddington, 410
Education, 104, 460
Edwards Theaters, 470n.20
Einstein, Albert, 81, 442
Einsteinian dynamics, 450–452
Einstein's theory of gravitation, 439
Einstein's theory of relativity, 438, 442
Elegy, (Gray), 520
Elegy on Prince Henry (Donne, John), 506
Eliminative materialism, 152–155
Eliot, T. S., 506–507, 509–510
    Works: *Ash Wednesday*, 507; *Love Song of J. Alfred Prufrock*, 508
Emancipation of workers, 276
Empirical cognition, 50

Empirical conception, 51
Empirical generalizations, 429
Empirical judgement, 50
Empirical physical science, 55n
Empirical universality, 50–51
Empirically adequate, 460
Empiricist, 222, 224, 228
Empiricus, Sextus, *Pyrrhonic Sketches*, 27–35
Energy, 82
Engaging in metaphysics, 94
An Enquiry Concerning Human Understanding (Hume, David), 73–79, 119–126, 200, 447n.4
An Enquiry Concerning the Principles of Morals (Hume, David), 410, 412–423
Entertainment, 464–470, 473
Entitlement, rules of, 241
Entitlement Theory, 281, 283
Entsagen, 387
Epicurean, 384–385, 421
Epicurus, 482
Epiphenomenology, 90
Epistemic probability, 199n.15
Epistemology, 20–42, 69
Epoche, 27–28, 31–34
Equality, 247, 259, 262–263, 266, 296, 382
Equity, rules of, 415
Erkenntnis, 445
Essays in Popular Philosophy (James), 218
Essential being, 273
Estranged/alienated labour, 272–276
Ethical dilemmas, 338
Ethical doctrine, 383
Ethical egoism, 333
Ethics, 333–338, 341–342, 344–345, 390, 395, 476
Euclid, 72–73, 419
Eudoxus, 349
Euripides, 497–498
European Renaissance, 233
Evidence, 201
Evidentialist, 210, 213–214
Evil, 168–169, 185–191, 194–197, 359, 493–494
Evolution, theory of, 425, 432, 434–435, 460
Evolution-The Fossils Say No! (Gish, Duane T.), 434
Existence, 39–42, 78, 82, 105–106, 126, 175–177, 486–490
Existential quantifier, 101n.6
Expedient, 392
Experience
    cause and effect, 74–80
    conscious, 156–163
    creativity and, 501–502, 504
    infallible, 200–202
    judgements of, 53–54
    and knowledge, 49–52
    mental, 114
    metaphysics, 90, 97
    pragmatism, 70
    visual, 517–520
Experiment, 78, 444
Explanation, 81, 435
Explicative judgements, 52
Expressions, 119, 381
External conveniences, 413
External labour, 272

External sanctions, 241
Extrinsic properties, 68
Exultet, 194, 199n.13

F

Fact, 65, 68, 126, 159
Faith, 169, 208, 229–230, 233–234, 250
Faith, knight of, 231–232
Fallacy of Denying the Antecedent, 428
Falsehood, 64–71, 74, 85–86, 96, 114, 117
Falsifiability, 435, 437n.9, 442
Falwell, Jerry, 426n.5
Family, 264–265, 293–294, 312–313, 315, 322–327, 417
Fanaticism, 303
Fatal Attraction, 242
Fatalism, 138
Fear and Trembling, Dialectical Lyric (Kierkegaard), 229
Fecundity, 379–380
Feelings, human, 392
Felicity, 247, 255, 300, 309–310, 375, 415
Feminism, 243
Feyerabend, Paul K., *How to Defend Society Against Science*, 456–462
Field, Sally, 245
Fingeroth, Danny, 468
The First Anniversary (Donne, John), 506
First cause, 181
First Meditation (Descartes, René), 23
First seizure, 258
The Five Ways (Aquinas), 167, 177–178
Flew, Antony, 209–210
Flintstones, 20n
Flying Down to Rio, 468
Flying Saucer, 469
The Fog of War: Eleven Lessons From the Life of Robert McNamara, 340
Folk psychology, 152–155
Food, 366
Forbidden Planet, 92n.15
Force, 132
Forced labour, 272, 289–290
Ford, Harrison, 20n.1
Forgeries, 515–522
Forms, 343–344
Fortitude, 333
Fortune, 348
Fossey, Dian, 243
Foster, Jodie, 166ph, 242
The Foundation of the Metaphysics of Morals (Kant, Immanuel), 281n.1, 383, 400–409
Fragment on Government (anno 1776), 377n.5
Free will, 193, 199n.10
Freedom, 51, 132–136, 462
Freedom and Determination (Taylor, Richard), 126–138
Freitas, Donna, 473
Freud, Sigmund, *Gesammelte Schriften*, 446n.3–447n.3
Friday the 13th, 169n.1
Friendship/friends, 349, 414
The Frighteners, 91
From Hell, Summer of Sam, 169n.1
Fugitive (Ford, Harrison), 20n.1
Functionalism, 149, 151–152
Functionally isomorphic, 151
Fundamentalists, 425–426, 460

G

Galileo, 447*n*.4
   Works: *Siderius Nuncius*, 505
The Game, 23–24
Gedanken experiment, 139–143
Genera, 111
General assent, 42, 46–49
General Cinema, 470*n*.20
Generosity, 422
The Genesis Flood (Whitcomb, John Jr. and Morris, Henry M.), 434
Genus, 112–113
Geocentrism, 452
Gesammelte Schriften (Freud, Sigmund), 447*n*.3–447*n*.3
Ghosts, 90–91
Gibson, Mel, 241, 464
Gilbert, William, *De Magnete*, 505
Gish, Duane T., *Evolution-The Fossils Say No!*, 434
Gladiator, 334
Glaucon, 103, 105, 485–494
Glory, 247
God. *See also* Gods, mythological
   absolute ideas, 109–110
   covenant with, 252
   and creation, 261–262, 391, 434, 485–486
   creationists and, 426
   evolution and, 434
   existence of, 175–178
   fear of, 253–254
   lie, willing to, 373–374
   man and, 260, 306
   promises of, 251
   pure reason, 51
   represented as, 371
   and science, 425
   search for, 73
   theodicy and, 187, 193
   works of, 372
God as Spirit (Lampe), 235
God Was in Christ (Baillie), 235
The Godfather (Coppola, Francis Ford), 25*n*.9
Gods, mythological, 261, 274, 361–362, 370–371, 373–374
The Gods Must Be Crazy!, 431
Godzilla, 469
Goethe, 501
Golden age, 416
Golden Bough, 506
The Golden Compass (Pullman, Philip), 468
The Golden Rule, 174
Goldwyn, Sam, 468
Good, 72, 345, 381, 493–494
Goodman, Nelson, *Art and Authenticity*, 515–523
Goodness, 185–188, 190–195, 197
The Goonies, 172
Gorillas in the Mist, 243
Governance, 178
Government, 268–269, 299, 301–305, 375–376, 380*n*.5–381*n*.5
Grace, 256
Gradation, 178
Graphic novels, 464*n*.3
Gratitude, 256, 422
Gravitation, 81
Gray, *Elegy*, 520
Greatest-Happiness Principle, 384, 387

The Grey Zone, 338
The Grounds of Moral Judgment, (Grice, G. R.), 281*n*.1
Guarantee, 22
Guerin, Daniel, *Anarchism From Theory to Practice*, 291*n*.5

H

Habit, 71, 351
Habituation, 102–103
Halloween, 169*n*.1
Hanks, Tom, 339
Happiness, 190, 338, 343–350, 376, 383–392, 402–403, 414, 423
Hardy-Weinberg law, 433
Harris, Ed, *Pollock*, 463*ph*, 464
Harry Potter and the Order of the Phoenix, 169*n*.3
Haugeland, John, 149*n*.3
The Haunting, 91
Haydn, *London Symphony*, 520–522
Heaven Can Wait, 90*n*.5
Heidegger, Martin, 509
Heliocentrism, 452
Hellas, 492
Helter Skelter, 169*n*.1
Helvetius, 381*n*.18
Hempel, C. G., 429, 431
   Works: *Philosophy of Natural Science, The*, 437*n*.5
Henry: Portrait of a Serial Killer, 169*n*.1
Heracleid, 496
Here Comes Mr. Jordan, 90*n*.5
Herodotus, 496
   Works: *History*, 394
Hesoid, 488
Heuristics, 459
Hick, John, *Problems of Religious Pluralism*, 233
Hirsh, E. D. Jr., 467
   Works: *In Defense of the Author*, 508–515
To His Coy Mistress (Marvell), 508
His Dark Materials (Pullman, Philip), 468, 473
Historical interpretation, 501
History, 123
History (Herodotus), 394
History of European Morals from Augustus to Charlemagne (Lecky), 200*n*.18
Hobbes, Thomas, *Leviathan*, 241, 247–259
Hobbist, 421
Hoi tropoi tes epoches, 27
Holbein, 522*n*.12
Homer, 476, 478, 485, 487–488, 492–493, 499
   Works: *Iliad*, 496; *Odyssey*, 496–497
Homonymous, 110
Homosexuality, 400
Honesty, 334
Honor, 343
Horace, 503
   Works: *Odes*, 200*n*.18
Hospers, John, *An Argument against Skepticism*, 58–64
Housman, 503
How to Defend Society Against Science (Feyerabend, Paul K.), 456–462
Hoyle, Fred, 435

Hull, David L., *The Philosophy of Biological Science*, 437*n*.8
Human
   behavior, 127–134, 136–137, 152
   intellect, 50
   knowledge, 51, 58
   mind, 38–42, 67
   nature, 78, 120–126, 128–130, 412, 416
   reason, 56, 73
   rights, 241–242
   species, 416
   understanding, 139–143
Humanity, 417
The Humanity and Divinity of Christ (Knox), 235
Hume, David, 25, 55, 172, 442–443, 445, 465
   Works: *Abstract*, 447*n*.6; *An Enquiry Concerning Human Understanding*, 73–79; *An Enquiry Concerning Human Understanding*, 200; *Enquiry Concerning the Principle of Morals*, 442*n*.4; *An Enquiry Concerning the Principles of Morals*, 410–423; *Of Liberty and Necessity*, 119–126; *Sceptical Doubts Concerning the Operations of the Understanding*, 73–79; *Of the Standard of Taste*, 476–484; *Treatise of Human Nature*, 447*n*.5
"Hume's problem", 458
Huyghens, 453
Hypothesis, 31–32, 66, 80, 219
Hypothetical imperative, 401–404, 406, 409
Hypothetico-deductive system, 437*n*.8

I

Idea, 56, 69–70
Identity theory, 150–152
Idiocracy, 241*n*.2
Iliad (Homer), 496
Imagination, 40–42, 75, 82, 162*n*.8, 163*n*.11, 163, 479
Imitation, 485–492, 494, 498–499
Immorality, 420
Immortality, 51
Impediment, 132
Imperative of duty, 404
Imperative of morality, 403
Imperatives, 401–404
Imperfection, 182
Impossibility, 131
Impressions, 50
Impurity, 379
Incarnation, doctrine of, 235
Inclusivism, 234–235, 513–515
Inconformity, 255
Indeterminism, 34, 134–137
Individual, 116, 376, 413
The Individual, the State, and Education (Socrates and Glaucon), 358–374
Induction, 442–445, 447
Inequality, 291–292, 294, 303–306
Inference, 120, 123–126, 163–165
Inferential reasoning, 80
Infinity, 183
The Influence of Culture on Visual Perception (Segall, Campbell, and Herskovits), 522*n*.2
Information processing, 147

Ingratitude, 418
Injustice, 250, 254–255, 268, 359–361, 363–364, 366–367
Inspiration, 503
Institution (Coke, Sir Edward), 259*n*.5
Integrity, 436
Intellect, 31–32, 50, 154
Intellectual virtue, 351
Intellectualist, 68–69
Intelligence, 178
Intended reference, 95
Intention, 499–508
The Intentional Fallacy (Wimsatt and Beardsley), 466–467, 499–508
Intentionality, 90, 149*n*.2, 145–149, 155
Intentions, 501
Interactionist Substance Dualist theory of mind, 89–93
Interpretation, 95, 101*n*.6, 510–515
De Interpretatione (Aristotle), 114–118
Intertheoretic reduction, 150–153
An Introduction to the Principles of Morals and Legislation, (Bentham, Jeremy), 374–376, 377*n*.5, 378, 380–381
Intuition, 52–54
Inusuk, 464
Investigation, 63
Irrational element, 351
Is Science Sexist! And Other Problems in the Biomedical Sciences (Ruse, Michael), 437*n*.9
The Island, 246
Isostheneia ton logon, 27
It Came from Outer Space!, 469
"It is up to me", 130–131

J

James, William, 25–26, 174
  Works: *Essays in Popular Philosophy,* 218; *Pragmatism,* 68–73
Jehovah. *See* Yahweh
Jesuits, 206
Jesus, 389, 470–472
JFK (Stone, Oliver), 464
Judgement, 52–53, 66–68, 203, 410, 417
Jung, 509
Justice
  acquisitions in, 283–284
  of actions, 255–256
  Aristotelian virtue of, 333
  censured, 358, 361
  commutative, 256
  current time slice, principles of, 284
  definition of, 254
  distributive, 256–257, 282–283, 286, 288–290
  end-result principle of, 284–285, 290
  end-state principle of, 290–291
  as fairness, 277–280
  historical principles of, 284–285, 290
  as lesser evil, 359
  principles of, 278–279, 281, 284–285, 291
  side constraints of, 291
  social, 277
  society, useful to, 413
  superiority over injustice, 363
  theory of, 278, 284
  time-slice principles of, 284–285
  virtue of, 277, 414
  and war, 248

K

Kant, Immanuel, 237, 334
  Works: *Critique of Pure Reason,* 49–58; *Foundations of the Metaphysics of Morals,* 281*n*.1, 400–409; *Metaphysics of Ethics,* 383; *Political Writings,* 281*n*.2
Kant; The Philosophy of Right (Murphy, J.G.), 281*n*.2
Kantian principle, 282
Kepler, *De Stella Nova,* 505
Kidman, Nicole, 25*n*.7
Kierkegaard, Søren, 169
  Works: *Fear and Trembling, Dialectical Lyric,* 229
King, Jason, 473
King, Martin Luther Jr., 397
Knowledge. *See also* epistemology
  à posteriori, 50
  à priori, 50–58, 74–78, 127
  absolute, 109–110
  certainty, 63–64
  defined, 25
  doubt, 63–64
  dualism, 64–65
  eliminative materialism, 155
  empirical, 49–52, 54
  error, 64–65
  evidence, 60, 62
  good and evil, 188
  human, 51
  metaphysics and, 104
  objective requirement, 59
  philosophy and, 2–4
  pure, 50, 52
  requirements for, 58
  strong sense, 61–63
  subjective requirement, 59
  transcendental, 57
  weak sense, 61–62
Knox, John, *The Humanity and Divinity of Christ,* 235
Krimmerman, *Patterns of Anarchy,* 291*n*.5
Kripke, Saul, 162*n*.1
Kubla Kahn (Coleridge), 505
Kuhn, Thomas, 431, 458
  Works: *The Structure of Scientific Revolutions,* 437*n*.5, 448–452, 454–456

L

L.A. Confidential, 469
Labor, 242
Lakatos, 458–459
Lampe, Geoffrey, *God as Spirit,* 235
Language, 508–512, 522*n*.2
Language, Truth and Logic (Ayers), 217
The Last Temptation of Christ, 470–472
Lavosiers reform, 454
Law(s)
  civil rights, 298
  external sanctions, 241
  gospel, of the, 249, 261–263, 326, 391, 434
  of government, 269
  morality, 402, 404
  natural regularities of, 434
  of nature, 249, 253–266, 268–269, 405–406, 433, 447
  objective, 401, 407
  of political economy, 272
  of reason, 263
  universal, 409
Learning, 154
Lecky, W. E. H., *History of European Morals From Augustus to Charlemagne,* 169*n*.2, 200*n*.18
Lecture (Bosanquet), 502
Legislative power, 268–269
Legislators, 351
Leviathan (Hobbes, Thomas), 241, 247–259
Lévi-Strauss, Claude, 329, 456
Lewontin, Richard, 438*n*.24
  Works: *Adaptation,* 438*n*.24
Liberal feminism, 243–244
Liberality, 413
Liberty, 119, 125–126, 249, 259–260, 279–280, 286, 301–305, 413, 462
On Liberty (Mill, John Stuart), 458
Of Liberty and Necessity (Hume, David), 119–126
Life (Stephen), 218
The Life of Brian, 470, 472
Likeness, 105–106, 108
Literary biography, 504
Literary criticism, 499
Literature, 476–484
Locke, John
  Works: *No Innate Principles in the Mind,* 42–49; *Second Treatise of Government,* 260–270, 281*n*.1, 301
The Logic of Scientific Discovery (Popper, Karl), 437*n*.5, 437*n*.9, 445, 447
Logical necessity, 131
Logical positivist, 97
Logoi, 31
London Symphony (Haydn), 520–522
Longinus, 501
The Lord of the Rings, 469–470
Lost in Space, 92*n*.15
Lots, 258
Louis XIV (France), 300
Love, 191, 422
Love Song of J. Alfred Prufrock (Eliot, T. S.), 508
Lowe, *Road to Xanadu,* 504–505
Lucian, 204–205
Lucretia (Rembrandt), 516, 519–521
Luther, 169
Luther, Martin, 169
Lützelberger, 523*n*.12
Luxury, 413
Lying/lies, 373
Lyne, Adrian, 242
Lysistrata (Aristophanes), 330

M

Machiavel, *Clitia,* 483
Mackay, Henry, *The Anarchists,* 291*n*.5
Mad Max II: The Road Runner, 241
Mad Max III: Beyond Thunderdome, 241*n*.3
Maddin, Guy, 474
Madonna of Cimabue, 501
Magistrate, 303
De Magnete (Gilbert, William), 505
Mahdi, 220
Mahometans, 484
The Maltese Falcon, 335
Man
  civilized, 305

essential being of, 273
estrangement of, 274–275
function of, 346
judgment of, 342–343
justness of, 359
nature of, 368
needs of, 273, 364
origins of, 261, 271, 292–294
physical need of, 274
qualities of, 412
self-preservation of, 292
social, 305
as species-being, 273–274
universality of, 273
Mandeville, 381n.18
Mankind, natural condition of, 247–249, 253, 255, 261, 292–296, 345, 376, 415
Manner, 494
Many, 105–108
Many mansions reply, 146–148
The Marathon Man, 169n.3
Market, 366
Marriage, 264–265, 311–313, 320–327, 394, 414
Marshall, George C., 338
Martyr, Justin, 211
Marvell, 506
    Works: *To His Coy Mistress*, 508
Marx, Karl, 241
    Works: *Economic and Philosophical Manuscripts of 1844 Estranged Labour*, 270–277
Marxism, 456
Marxist theory of history, 438–439
Master craftsman, 360
Materialist/materialism, 91–93, 98
Mathematical formula, 82
Mathematical judgements, 53–54
Mathematical science, 55
Mathematics, 51–52, 81
The Matrix, 85
Matter and Consciousness (Churchland, Paul), 150–155
Matters of fact, 73–74
Matthiessen, F. O., 506–507
Maxim, 409n.5, 405–406
Maxwell, Clerk, 455
McConaughey, Matthew, 166ph
McNamara, Robert, 340
Mean, 356–357
The Meaning of Life (Python, Monty), 465–467
Mechanico-corpuscular explanation, 453–454
Meditation (Descartes, René), 20, 22–25, 89
Meditations on First Philosophy (Descartes, René), 35–42
Melitus, 5–6, 8–16
Memento, 20–21
Memory, 20–21, 154
Mental dysfunction, 153
Mental illness, 154
Mental phenomenon, 156–157
Merit, 242, 251, 412–413
Metallurgy and agriculture, 295–296
Metaphysical principle, 444
Metaphysical statements, 94–97
Metaphysician, 99
Metaphysics, 51, 55–56, 85–101, 418
Metaphysics (Taylor, Richard), 126–138
Metaphysics of Ethics (Kant, Immanuel), 383

Method, 457
Methodologically autonomy, 152
Michelangelo, 464
Microchiroptera, 157–163
Mill, John Stuart
    Works: *On Liberty*, 458; *The Subjection of Women*, 316–327, 335; *Utilitarianism*, 382–393
Milton, 306–307, 316n.2
Mind, 89–93
Mind-body problem, 156, 159
Minds, Brains, and Programs (Searle, John R.), 138–149
Miracles, 202–203, 208, 425n.1
Misery, 247, 297–298, 349
"Missing link", 436
Mission to Mars, 167
Modern Times, 245–246
Modern Woman: The Last Sex (Parker, Dorothy), 328
Modesty, 356
Moliére, 453–454
Monarchy, 303
Money, 343, 355
Monopoly, doctrine of, 270
Monster, 169n.1
Monthly Review, 287
Morality, 58, 284, 295, 333, 341, 382–383, 387–393, 399–402, 410
Moral(s)
    in beauty, 419
    codes, 394–396
    determinism and, 128–130
    distinctions of, 410
    ethics, 340, 476
    evidence, 123
    excellence in, 352
    imperative, 334–335
    natural, 123
    praise, 417
    progress, 397
    question, 226
    reasoning, 77
    relations, 418
    responsibility, 86, 132
    science, 375
    sentiment, 417
    speculation, 411
    virtue, 351
Morris, Errol, 340
Motion, 177
Motion, laws of, 433
Motion Picture Association of America (MPAA), 466
Motives, 380–381, 422
Movies, 466–470, 473–474
Music, 520–521
My Man Godfrey, 468
Myth, 460
The Myth of God Incarnate, 235

N

Nagel, E., *The Structure of Science*, 437n.5
Nagel, Thomas, 88–89
The Name of the Rose, 170
Natural
    ascendancy, 303
    causes, 199n.17
    evidence, 123
    lots, 258

philosophy, 54–55
powers, 77
probability, 199n.15
science, 29, 55
theology, 210
Natural Philosophy of Cause and Chance (Born, Max), 443
Nature, 186, 259–260
The Nature of Metaphysics (Van Inwagen, Peter), 94–101, 261
Necessity, 50–51, 53–54, 119–120, 125–126, 177–178
Needs, 241–242, 272–274, 289–290, 293–296, 330, 364–366
Negotiated readings, 470
Nerval, Gérard de, 508
New Voices (Wilkinson, Marguerite), 502
Newton, Sir Isaac, 80–81, 433, 447n.4, 452–453
    Works: *Principia*, 450, 454
Newtonian dynamics, 451–453
Newtonian physics, 433
Newtonianism, 454
Nicomachean Ethics (Aristotle), 341–357, 439–441
The Nightmare Before Christmas, 90n.8
Nirguna Brahman, 237
Nirmanakaya, 237
No Innate Principles in the Mind (Locke, John), 42–49
Nominalist, 99–101
Nonautographic, 520
Norma Rae, 245
Normative contention, 211
Not-Self, 3–4
Noun, 114
Nozick, R., *Anarchy, State, and Utopia*, 281–291
Nuclear physics, 59
Nudity, 466–467

O

Oaths, 253
Object of labour, 275
Objectification, 271
Objective
    conditions, 401
    evidence, 222–223
    principle, 401, 408–409
    requirement, 157, 160–162
    world, 273
Object-relation, 68
Objects, 67–69, 75, 78–79, 101
Object-terms, 68
Obligations, 211–213
Observable behavior, 164–165
"Observables", 153
Observation, 75, 439, 444, 456
Obstacle, 132
Ockham's Razor, 425–426
Odes (Horace), 200n.18
The Odessa File, 168
Odyssey (Homer), 496–497
Oedipus, 497
"Oedipus effect", 446n.3–447n.3
Omnipotence, 188, 198
One person law, 322
Ontological Argument (St. Anselm), 167, 175–176
Ontological commitment, 99n.6, 101

Ontology, 97–98, 101n.8, 152–153
Operationalism, 148–149
Opinion, 476–484
Oppositional readings, 470
Oppression, 304
Options, 219
Oratory, 495
Order, 67–68, 179
Origin of Species (Darwin, Charles), 435
Other Minds Are Known by Analogy form One's Own Case (Russell, Bertrand), 163–165
Other minds reply, 146
The Others, 25n.7
Overton, William, 437n.3

P

Pagans, 484
Pain, 194, 352, 374, 378–380, 420
Painter/painting, 485–489, 495
Paley, William
 Works: *Teleological Argument*, 167; *The Watch and the Watchmaker*, 178–183
Paphlagonia, 204
Papini, 73
Paradigm, 431, 433, 448–450, 453, 455–456
Paradigm Shift, 431, 453
Paradox of grace, 235
Parallelism, 90, 448
Paramatma, 238
Paraphrase, 98, 100, 101n.9
Parental authority, 300–301
Paris, Abb, 206
Parker, Dorothy, *Modern Woman: The Last Sex*, 300, 328
Parliament, 318
Parmenides (Plato), 105–110
Paronymous, 110
Pascal, Blaise, *Pascal's Wager*, 174, 183–187, 220
Pascal's Wager (Pascal), 174, 183–187, 220
Passion, 352, 354–356
The Passion of the Christ, 464
Paternal authority, 262
Patterns of Anarchy (Krimmerman, Leonard, and Perry, Lewis), 291n.5
Pentateuch, 208
Perception, 40–42, 80, 82
Perceptual discrimination, 517–520
Perceptual imagination, 162n.11–163n.11
Performance, 125n
Peripeteia, 495
Person, 137
The Personal Heresy (Lewis and Tillyard), 499
Personal merit, 411
Personal studies, 504
Perspectivism, 513
Pet Semetary, 90n.8
Phasis, 33
Phenomena, 29–30
Phenomenology, 163
Philolaos, 459, 461
Philosophic contemplation, 3–4
Philosophic wisdom, 346, 351
Philosophy, Science, and Method, 289n.6
Philosophy, value of, 1–18
The Philosophy of Biology (Ruse, Michael), 437n.8
Philosophy of Literary Form (Burke, Kenneth), 508n.15

The Philosophy of Natural Science (Hempel, C. G.), 437n.5
Philosophy of Science: a Personal Report, 438
Phlogiston theory, 153, 451–452, 454
Phoenix, Joaquin, 334
Physical necessity, 124
Physical probability, 199n.15
Physical science, 454
Physical universe, 460
Physicalist theory, 157, 161–162
Physics, 54
Physics (Aristotle), 85
Pittenger, Norman, *The Word Incarnate*, 235
The Place of Jesus Christ in Modern Christianity (Baillie), 235
Planet of the Apes, 241n.3
Plantinga, Alvin, *Religious Belief Without Evidence*, 209
Plato, 52, 343, 464, 482
 Works: *Allegory of the Cave*, 85, 101–104; *The Apology of Socrates*, 4–18, 502; *Book ll from Republic*, 358–374; *Parmenides*, 105–110; *Republic*, 485–494
Platonists, 99–101, 344
Plato's Theory of Forms, 432–433
Pleasure, 189, 347–349, 352–353, 374–375, 378–381, 384–387, 420
Plot, 494–497
Pluralism, 235–237, 239
Poetic studies, 504
Poetical imitations, 485–487, 490–492
Poetics (Aristotle), 494–499
Poetry, 477–478, 481–483, 485–487, 490–502, 508–515
Polieucte, 484
Political
 development, 448
 distinctions, 303
 economy, 270–272, 275–276
 philosophy, 281–282
 revolutions, 448–449
 science, 342–343, 347–348, 350, 353
 societies, 265–267, 299, 305
Politicians, 300
Politics, 123. See also Political; Politicians
Politics (Aristotle), 257
Pollock (Harris, Ed), 463pb, 464
Poltergeist, 25n.7
Polygnotus, 495
Poor, 299
Popper, Karl, 427, 458
 Works: *The Logic of Scientific Discovery*, 437n.5, 437n.9, 445, 447; *Science, Conjecture and Refutation*, 438, 442, 444, 446
Population genetics, 433
The Poseidon Adventure, 169n.2
Positivists, 216
Possibility, 51, 131, 177–178
Posteriority, 344
Poulain de la Barre, François, 331
Poverty, 388
Power over children, 263
Practice, 480
Pragmatic, 409n.3*
Pragmatism, 68–73
Pragmatism (James, William), 68–73
Predicate, 116
Prediction, 80–81, 97, 425, 433, 435

Prejudice, 304, 377, 480–482
Presocratics, 460
Presumed Innocent (Ford, Harrison), 20n
Pretty Woman, 242
Primary Philosophy (Scriven), 211
Primary substances, 111–113
Primogeniture, 258
Principia (Newton, Sir Isaac), 450, 454
Principle
 of contradiction, 54
 of empiricism, 444–445
 of justice, 274, 279–281, 283–284, 382
 of morality, 393, 407, 411
 of reason, 401
 of utility, 281, 374–378, 383
Principles, 42–49, 51, 77
Priori authority, 383
Priori principles, 383
Priority, 344
Private experiences, 90
Private property, 270, 275–276, 288
Probability, 201
Problems of Philosophy (Russell, Bertrand), 2–4
Problems of Religious Pluralism (Hick), 233
Prodicus of Ceos, 488
Product of labour, 271, 273–276
Production/product, 271–277
Profit, 270, 276, 380
Proletarians, 330
Properties, 98–101
Property, 260–262, 270, 275–276, 297, 301, 380, 414
Prophecies, 208
Propositions, 54–55, 85, 114–118
Protagoras, 382
Protagoras of Abdera, 488
Proudhon, 276
Prudence, 409n.3*
Pseudo-science, 426, 438, 442
Psycho, 169n.1, 242
Psychophysical reduction, 160
Psychosis, 153
Ptolemy, 461
Puffendorf, 301
Pullman, Philip
 Works: *The Golden Compass*, 468; *His Dark Materials*, 468, 473
Pure cognition, 50
Pure conception, 52
Pure mathematics, 54
Pure reason, 54–57
Purity, 379
Purpose, 167–168
Pyrrhonean School, 27–28
Pyrrhonic Sketches (Empiricus, Sextus), 27–35
Pythagoras, 488
Pythagoreans, 344, 355
Python, Monty, *The Meaning of Life*, 465–467

Q

Quarrel, 247–248
Quine, W. V. O., 98–99, 101

R

Rachels, James, *The Challenge of Cultural Relativism*, 394–400
Radical feminism, 243

Rage, 333
Ransom, 252
Rapport d'Uriel (Benda), 329
Ratings, movie, 466–467
Rational principle, 351, 409*n*.1*
Rationalism, 73
Rawls, John, *A Theory of Justice*, 242, 277–278
Reaction, 58*n*.2
Real presence, 200
Realist, 101*n*.5
Reality, 68–69, 85, 94–102, 117, 126–127, 175–176, 487
Reality-centeredness, 233
Realization, 502
Reason, 44–47, 49–62, 76–80, 123, 192, 410–411, 417–418, 477
Reason and Belief (Blanshard), 211
Recognition scenes, 495
Red Planet Mars, 469
Redistribution, 288
Reductive and Eliminative Materialism (Churchland, Paul), 150–155
Reductive materialism, 150–151, 156–157
Refinement, superior, 343
Reflection, 125*n*
Regressus in infinitum, 31–32
Relation, 31, 66–67
Relations of ideas, 73
Relativism, 513
Relativistic dynamics, 451–452
Relativity, theory of, 81, 438
Religion, 73, 207, 227, 233, 432–433, 484
Religionist, 203
Religious Belief Without Evidence (Plantinga), 209
Religious beliefs, 3, 37–38, 90–91
Religious pluralism, 174
Religious traditions, 233–234
Rembrandt
  Works: *Lucretia*, 516, 519–521; *Tobit Blind*, 521–522
Reproducibility, 510
Reproductions, 515–522
Republic (Plato), 485–494
Research, 450
Resident Evil, 90*n*.8
Resignation, act of, 232
Responsibility, 86, 193
Retz, Jean François Paul de Gondi de, 205
Revealer (Qur'an), 238
Reversal of the situation, 495
Revisionary materialism, 155
Revolutions, 448, 450
Rhetoric, 342, 495
Richards, I. A., 502
Rich/wealthy, 297–298
Right, 382, 395, 410
Right of Nature, 249
Rights
  civil, 298
  contract of, 250
  distribution of, 281
  entitlement theory of, 281
  human, 241–242
  individual, 281, 294
  oppression of, 304
  property, 288
  renouncing, 250
  side constraints of, 282
  transferring of, 250, 252
Road to Xanadu (Lowe), 504–505
Roberts, Julia, 242
Robertson, Pat, 426*n*.5
Robot reply, 143–144
Rochefoucault, 381*n*.18
Roger and Me, 246
Roman Catholics, 484
Roschmann, Eduard, 169
Rousseau, Jean-Jacques, 307–308
  Works: *Discourse on the Origin of Inequality, the Second Part*, 291–306, 309–310; *The Social Contract*, 281*n*.1
Rumsfeld, Donald, 426*n*.5
Run Lola Run, 85
Ruse, Michael, 425, 437*n*.2
  Works: *Creation Science is not Science*, 432–438; *Darwinism Defended: A Guide to the Evolution Controversies*, 437*n*.6; *Is Science Sexist! And Other Problems in the Biomedical Sciences*, 437*n*.9; *Philosophy of Biology, The*, 437*n*.8
Russell, Bertrand, 25, 209
  Works: *Other Minds Are Known by Analogy form One's Own Case*, 163–165; *Problems of Philosophy*, 2–4

S

Saarinen, Aline B., 515
Sagan, Carl, *Cosmos*, 95
Saguna Brahman, 237
The Sailor Boy (Tennyson), 507
Saintsbury, 501
Sambhogakaya, 237
Saragossa, 205
Saving Private Ryan, 332*ph*, 338–340
Sceptical Doubts Concerning the Operations of the Understanding (Hume, David), 73–79
Sceptical formula, 33–35
Sceptic/Scepticism, 27–35, 79
Schank, Roger, 139–143, 149*n*.3
Schematisation, 238
Schrader, Paul, 471
Schwarzenegger, Arnold, 19*ph*, 21–22, 86–87
Science
  analysis of, 427
  anomalies, 450
  astrology and, 426
  biblical literalism and, 432
  characteristics of, 425
  and children, 461
  Chinese, 459
  and confirmation, 433, 435
  corroboration, degree of, 447
  and creation, 435
  creationists and, 426
  as cumulation, 449
  definition of, 432
  demarcation, criterion of, 443
  doctrines of, 382
  in education, 457
  empirical method, 438
  empirical observation of, 427, 434
  evolution and, 425, 432
  experiment, 444
  explanation and, 435
  falsifiability and, 427, 435
  features of, 433
  and God, 425
  history of, 455
  homologies and, 435
  inductive method, 443–444
  metaphysics, 438
  natural laws, 433
  natural regularities of, 434
  and observation, 444–445
  and Ockham's Razor, 426
  paradigms of, 433, 448–449, 455
  phenomena, 450
  phlogiston theory, 451–452, 454
  positivists in, 452
  predictions of, 425, 433, 435
  principle of empiricism, 444
  probability and, 447
  professional integrity of, 434
  progress of, 388
  and religion, 432–433
  results and, 459
  revolutions of, 431, 448
  rigidity of, 457
  simplicity of, 434
  society, defence against, 456
  as tentative, 433
  and testability, 433, 435
  and theory, 433, 438, 446, 450
  unification of, 434
Science, Conjecture and Refutation (Popper, Karl), 438, 442, 444, 446
Science and the Physical World (Stace, W. T.), 79–82
Scientific
  arguments, 459
  astronomy, 461
  character, 438
  development, 448
  methodology, 460
  procedure, 446
  revolutions, 448, 453
  theory, 450
Scientific American, 437*n*.24–438*n*.24
Scientific Creationism (Morris, Henry M.), 437*n*.12
Scientific Explanation (Braithwaite, R. B.), 437*n*.5
Scientists, 427, 432–433, 436, 439, 443, 450–454, 459–461
Scores, 520–522
Scorsese, Martin, 470*n*.20, 471–472
Scott, Walter, 506
Scriven, Michael, *Primary Philosophy*, 211
Sculpture, 523
Searle, John R.
  Works: *Behavioral and Brain Sciences*, 138–149; *Minds, Brains, and Programs*, 138–149
Second Meditation (Descartes, René), 25
The Second Sex (Beauvoir, Simone de), 327–331
Second Treatise of Government (Locke, John), 259–270, 281*n*.1
Secondary substances, 111–112
Secret powers, 78
Seeking School, 27
Self, 3–4, 137
Self interest, 333
Self-consciousness, 387
Self-contempt, 407

Self-estrangement, 275
Self-existent ideas, 108–109
Self-identity, 510–511
Self-indulgence, 352, 357
Self-interest, 422
Self-love, 420–421, 423
Self-observation, 387
Self-referentially incoherent, 97
Self-righteous, 462
Self-sacrifice, 389
Self-serving, 338
Self-sufficiency, 345
Semantic autonomy, 509–510
Sensations, 82
Sense, 58, 68
Sense and Sensibility (Austen, Jane), 240*ph*, 244–245
Sensibility, 31–32
Sensible qualities, 78–79
Sensory appearances, 453
Sentence, 114–115
Sentiment, 410–411, 419, 422, 477–480, 483–484
Serjeant Talfourd's Act, 322
The Serpent and the Rainbow, 91*n*.11
Servitude, 276
Sexual activity, 466–467
Shaftesbury, Lord, 410
Shakespeare, 464, 502
Shiva, 238
Siderius Nuncius (Galileo), 505
Signs, 251
The Silence of the Lambs, 169*n*.1, 333
Simple indeterminism, 134–136
Simplicity, 422–423
Simulation, 139–149
Sir Patrick Spens (Tennyson), 507
Sixth Sense, 25*n*.7
Skepticism, 509
Slavery, 300, 303
Sleep, 154
Sliding Doors, 85–86
Smith, Wilfred Cantwell, 233
Sociable, 256
Social
  contract, 278
  feminism, 243–244
  institutions, 277
  justice, 277
  organism, 226
  science, 394
  values, 280
  virtues, 412
Society
  capitalist, 244
  civil, 263, 266
  complex, 399
  conjugal, 263–265, 293
  customs of, 396
  and family, 293
  ideologies of, 460
  individuals in, 270
  justice in, 279, 289
  law, 298–299
  moral codes of, 394–396, 398
  needs of, 241–242
  political, 263, 266, 299, 415
  and the poor, 298
  position in, 242
  post-apocalyptic, 242
  power of, 270
  primitive, 398
  principles of, 279
  property ownership in, 295
  rules of, 399
  science in, 457
  and scientists, 461
  sexuality and, 400
  state of, 365
  theory of, 280
  values of, 280
  women in, 317
Socio-political mottos, 241–242
Socrates, 4–18, 105–110, 382, 462, 485–494
  Works: *The Individual the State, and Education*, 358–374
Soft determinism, 132–134
Solipsism, 162*n*.11–163*n*.11
Some Major Strands of Theodicy (Swinburne), 187
Sonderkommando, 338
Song, 494–495
Sophist, 382
Sophistication, 170
Soul, 104
Southern and Kenyon Reviews, 499
Sovereignty, 255
Soylent Green, 246
Species, 112
Species-being, 273–274
Species-life, 273–274
Species-power, 274
Spectacle, 494
Spider-Man (Fingeroth, Danny), 468
Spoiled (Toles, George), 473–474
Spoken word, 114
Springarn, 502
Stace, W. T., *Science and the Physical World*, 79–82
Standard, 500, 503–504
Standard of taste, 477
Of the Standard of Taste (Hume, David), 476–484
Standards, 458
Star Trek, 92*n*.13
Star Trek: First Contact, 23
Star Trek II: The Wrath of Kahn, 335–336
Star Trek VII: Insurrection, 336*n*.2
State, 366–367, 371
State of Nature
  commonwealth, 266–267
  community, 267
  executioner of, 268
  fiction of, 416
  freedom, 267
  God, 261
  indifferent judge of, 268
  law, 268
  liberty, 259–260
  peace and preservation of all, 260
  political power, 259–260
  power, 268
  property, 260, 262
  society, 266–268
Statement, metaphysical, 94–97
Statement, sufficiently general, 95–96
De Stella Nova (Kepler), 505
Stephen, Fitz James, 229
Stephen, Leslie, *Life*, 218
Stoics, 305, 385
Stone, Oliver, *JFK*, 464
Strategy, 342
Strauss, 464–465
Strength, 241–242, 255, 299, 352
Strict universality, 50–51
Structure of meaning, 514
The Structure of Science, (Nagel, E.), 437*n*.5
The Structure of Scientific Revolutions (Kuhn, Thomas S.), 437*n*.5, 448–452, 454–456
Subject, 110–111, 116–117
Subjection of Women (Mill, John Stuart), 316–327
Subjective conditions, 401
Subjective requirement, 157, 159–162, 165
Subjectivism, 513
Subordination, 318
Substance, 111–113
Successive paradigm, 453–454
Suffering, 197, 199*n*.17
Sufficient justification, 22
Sufficiently general statement, 95–96
Summum bonum, 382
Sumner, William Graham, 395–396
Superior refinement, 343
Superiority, 416
Superstition, 484
Supreme practical principle, 408
Suspending School, 27
Swinburne, Richard, *Some Major Strands of Theodicy*, 187
Symbol manipulation, 141–147
Sympathetic imagination, 162*n*.11–163*n*.11
Symposiums, 499
Synonymous, 110
Synthetical *à priori* knowledge, 57–58
Synthetical judgements, 52–53, 55
Synthetical proposition, 54–55, 403
Systems reply, 141–143

T

Tales/stories, 370
Tarantula, 469
Taste, 476–484
Tate, Allen, *Three Types of Poetry*, 502
Taxation, 289
Taylor, Richard
  Works: *Freedom and Determination*, 126–138; *Metaphysics*, 126–138
Teleological Argument (Paley), 167
Temperance, 333, 351–352, 357
Tennyson
  Works: *The Sailor Boy*, 507; *Sir Patrick Spens*, 507
Tentativeness, 436
Terence, 482–483
Terminator, 19*ph*, 86–88
Terminator II, 242
Terminology, 119
Testability, 433, 435
Testimony, 201–203, 207
Texas Chain Saw Massacre, 169*n*.1
Text-as-language theory, 512
Textual meaning, 500, 504, 508–512
Thelma and Louise, 242
Them!, 469
Theodicy, 168, 187–189, 193
Theology, 371, 484
Theoretical sciences, 53
Theory

Adlerian, 439–440
calculus of probability in, 446
classic stages of, 68
clinical observations of, 446n.3–447n.3
confirmation of, 439
Einstein's dynamics, 451
electromagnetic of light, 455
of energy, 449
energy conservation, 450
of evolution, 425, 432, 434–436, 460
explanatory power of, 439
and fact, 457–458
false, 445–446
false, elimination of, 447
falsifiability and, 442, 458
of forms, 432
Freudian, 439–440
genuine test of, 439
of gravitation, 439
heuristics and, 459
of history, 438, 440
improbable, 447
of justice, 278
Marxist, 439–440
new, 450
Newtonian dynamics, 451, 454
non-scientific, 442
"Oedipus effect" on, 446n.3–447n.3
philosophical, 443
phlogiston, 451
predictions in, 439
prohibition in, 439
psycho-analytic, 440
refutation of, 446n.3–447n.3
of relativity, 439, 452, 458
as scientific, 438, 449
of utility, 384
verification of, 439
wave of light, 455
Theory of agency, 136–138
A Theory of Justice (Rawls, John), 242, 277–278
Theory of Knowledge (Chisholm), 212
Theseid, 496
The Thing from Another World, 469
The Third Man, 336–337
Thought, 494–495
Thrasymachus, 358, 363
Three hundred 300, 464, 467, 469
Three Types of Poetry (Tate, Allen), 502
Tillyard, 504
Time-travel, 86–88
Tingle-Immersion theory, 520
Tobit Blind (Rembrandt), 521–522
Toles, George, 473–474
Tootsie, 243
Total Recall (Dick, Philip K.), 21–22
Totalitarianism, 460
The Towering Inferno, 169n.2
Tradition, 207
Traditional interpretation, 155
Tragedians, 487, 492, 496
Tragedy, 494–499
Transcendental philosophy, 57–58
Transfer of holdings, 283
Travels (Bartram), 505
Treatise of Human Nature (Hume), 447n.5
Treatise of Tenure (de Littleton, Sir Thomas), 259n.5

Trinity, 185, 235
Trollope, Anthony, 438
Tropes, 31–32
Tropoi, 31
Truth, 42–48, 59–74, 85–86, 95–96, 109, 114–117, 410–411, 457, 507
Truth and Falsehood from Problems of Philosophy (Bertrand, Russell), 64–68
Turing test, 149
Twister, 169n.2
Two thousand one 2001: A Space Odyssey, 92n.14
Tyrannicide, 413
Tyranny, 462

U

Ultimate Reality, 237–239
Unanimity, 476
Uncertainty, 122
Understanding, 58, 126, 139–145, 175–176, 477
Uniformity of action, 121–123
United Artists, 470n.20
Universal
consent, 43–49
good, 344
law, 405, 409
practical reason, 409
truth, 395
voice of mankind, 361
Universal Studios, 470n.20
Universality, 50–51, 53, 55, 496
Universals, 97–98, 101, 116–118
Universe, 426
Unlikeness, 105–106
Utilitarian ethics, 390–391
Utilitarianism, 211, 338, 340–341, 382–384, 386–387, 389–393
Utilitarianism (Mill, John Stuart), 382–393
Utility, 392–393, 412, 415, 417

V

Validation, 69
Values of society, 280
Van Inwagen, Peter, 94–101
Van Meegeren, 517–520
Vegetative element, 351
Veitch, John, 35–42
Verb, 114–115
Verbal manipulation, 64
Verification, 69–71, 225, 439
Vermeer, 519–520
Vespasian, 205
Vice, 353, 361, 411, 476
Vienna Circle, 458
Vietnam, 340
A Vindication of the Rights of Women (Wollstonecraft, Mary), 306–316
Violence, 466–467
Virgil, 482
Virtue
character, as a state of, 354–355
defined, 476
desirable, 420
equity, 415
ethics theory of, 333
goodness, 350, 352
as habit, 351
happiness as a, 347–350, 392
honorable, 361

human, 350
intellectual, 351
of justice, 414–415
as a mean, 355
as modes of choice, 353
moral, 351, 357
proper form of, 409n.7*
social, 414
Vishnu, 238
Vlachos, Georges, *La Pensée politique de Kant*, 281n.5
Volcano, 169n.2
Vraie vérité, 503

W

Wages/ labor, 242, 270, 275–276, 289–291, 331
Wallis, 453
Walz, Gene, 474n.26
Wants, 242, 290, 367, 369
War and peace, 248–249, 340, 415
War of the Worlds, 469
The Waste Land (Weston), 506
Watch, 178–179
The Watch and the Watchmaker (Paley), 178–183
Waterworld, 241n.3
Wax, 40–42
The Way of the World (Congreve, William), 499
Weakness, 241–242, 298–299, 334
Wealth, 242, 279, 297, 300, 305, 343
Weaver, Sigourney, 243
Webster, 506
Wellek, Rene, 501, 512–513
Western science, 459
Weston, *The Waste Land*, 506
What is it Like to Be a Bat? (Nagel, Thomas), 156–163
Wickramasinghe, N.C., 435
Wildmon, Donald, 470n.20
Wilensky, Robert, 149n.3
Wilkinson, Marguerite, *New Voices*, 502
Will, 126
William of Ockham, 425
Willing nature, 221–222
Willis, Bruce, 25n.7
Wimsatt, William Kurtz, 499–508
Works: *The Intentional Fallacy*, 467
Winograd, Terry, 149n.3
Wisdom, 333
Wise, Robert, 427
Wittgenstein, 445
Wizard of Oz, 25
Wollstonecraft, Mary, *A Vindication of the Rights of Woman*, 306–316
Women
childbearing, 326
and Christianity, 324, 326
and church, 321
and divorce, 323
Dr. Gregory's advice to, 311–314
education of, 307–310
and family, 288, 293, 312–313, 315, 322–323, 325–327
femininity in, 327–328
gentleness in, 314–315
laws and, 322
and love, 311–312
and marriage, 311–313, 320–327

Women (*continued*)
   Milton's description of, 306–307
   nature of, 320
   and one person law, 322
   as the Other, 329, 331
   Parliament and, 318
   political subjection of, 319
   qualities of, 314–316
   religion and, 326
   Rights of, 319
   role models for, 242–243, 318
   rule of men over, 317–319, 331
   Serjeant Talfourd's Act, 322
   as sexual characters, 306, 329, 331
   sexual discrimination, 243, 330
   slavery of, 416
   subjection of, 316, 318, 321–322
   submission of, 319
   subordination of, 317–318, 330
   suffrage, 318
   and tyranny of man, 306
   wealth and, 322
   as a womb, 327
The Word Incarnate (Pittenger), 235
Wordsworth, 513–514
Workers/laborer, 271–274, 367
World, 126–127
World War ll, 340
Wormholes, 172
Wren, 453
Wristwatch, 179
Wrong, 382, 395, 410

Y
Yahweh, 238. *See also* God

Z
Zeno, 105–110
Zeuxis, 495
Zodiac, 169*n*.1
Zombie, 91, 93